Theresienstadt 1941–1945
The Face of a Coerced Community

First published in German in 1955, with a revised edition appearing five years later, H. G. Adler's *Theresienstadt 1941–1945* is a foundational work in the field of Holocaust studies. As the first scholarly monograph to describe the particulars of a single camp – the Jewish ghetto in the Czech town of Terezín – it is the single most detailed and comprehensive account of any concentration camp. Adler, a survivor of the camp, organized the book into three sections: a history of the ghetto, a detailed institutional and social logical analysis of the camp, and an attempt to understand the psychology of the perpetrators and the victims. A collaborative effort between the United States Holocaust Memorial Museum and the Terezín Publishing Project makes this authoritative text on Holocaust history available for the first time in English, with a new afterword by the author's son, Jeremy Adler.

Poet, novelist, and scholar H. G. Adler (1910–88) was deported with his family to the Theresienstadt Ghetto in 1942. From there, they were transported to Auschwitz. He was then dispatched to two outlying camps of Buchenwald. Eighteen members of his family, including his first wife, Gertrud Klepetar, perished in the camps. He returned to his birthplace of Prague in 1945 and then, in 1947, went into voluntary exile in the United Kingdom, where he wrote a total of twenty-seven books, including the celebrated Holocaust trilogy *Panorama*, *The Journey*, and *The Wall*. He received several awards for his work, including the Leo Baeck Prize for *Theresienstadt 1941–1945*.

Belinda Cooper is a senior fellow at the World Policy Institute in New York and an adjunct professor at NYU's Center for Global Affairs and Columbia University's Institute for the Study of Human Rights. She has written for a wide variety of publications in German and English and has translated German scholarly books and articles for twenty-five years.

Amy Loewenhaar-Blauweiss is founding director of the Terezín Publishing Project. She is Language and Thinking faculty at Bard College and is curator of the Music in the Holocaust, Jewish Identity and Cosmopolitanism series for Bard's Hannah Arendt Center for Politics and the Humanities. She is author of the forthcoming book *Songs in the Wilderness: Music in the Holocaust and Betrayal of "Bildung."*

Jeremy Adler is Emeritus Professor of German and Senior Research Fellow in the Department of German at King's College London. The author or editor of numerous books, he is a member of the German Academy of Language and Literature.

Theresienstadt 1941–1945

The Face of a Coerced Community

H. G. ADLER

Translated by
BELINDA COOPER

General Editor
AMY LOEWENHAAR-BLAUWEISS
The Terezín Publishing Project

With an afterword by
JEREMY ADLER
King's College London

Published in association with the

and

CAMBRIDGE
UNIVERSITY PRESS

University Printing House, Cambridge CB2 0BS, United Kingdom

One Liberty Plaza, 20th Floor, New York, NY 10006, USA

477 Williamstown Road, Port Melbourne, VIC 3207, Australia

314-321, 3rd Floor, Plot 3, Splendor Forum, Jasola District Centre, New Delhi - 110025, India

103 Penang Road, #05-06/07, Visioncrest Commercial, Singapore 238467

Cambridge University Press is part of the University of Cambridge.

It furthers the University's mission by disseminating knowledge in the pursuit of
education, learning and research at the highest international levels of excellence.

www.cambridge.org
Information on this title: www.cambridge.org/9781108728683
DOI: 10.1017/9781139017053

First and second German-language editions © Verlag J.C.B. Mohr 1955, 1960
English-language edition © the Estate of H. G. Adler 2017
English-language edition translation © Belinda Cooper 2017
English-language edition © Amy Loewenhaar-Blauweiss 2017
Afterword © Jeremy Adler 2004 and 2017

This publication is in copyright. Subject to statutory exception
and to the provisions of relevant collective licensing agreements,
no reproduction of any part may take place without the written
permission of Cambridge University Press.

First published in German 1955
Revised German-language edition published 1960
First published in English 2017
First paperback edition 2022

A catalogue record for this publication is available from the British Library

Library of Congress Cataloging in Publication data
Adler, H. G., author.
[Theresienstadt, 1941–1945. English]
Theresienstadt, 1941–1945: the face of a coerced community / H.G. Adler, Belinda Cooper,
Amy Loewenhaar-Blauweiss, Jeremy Adler ; afterword by Jeremy Adler.
pages cm
ISBN 978-0-521-88146-3 (Hardback)
1. Theresienstadt (Concentration camp) 2. World War, 1939–1945 – Concentration camps.
I. Cooper, Belinda, author. II. Loewenhaar-Blauweiss, Amy, author. III. Adler, Jeremy D., author.
IV. Title.
D805.C9A713 2015
940.53´1853716–dc23
2014037665

ISBN 978-0-521-88146-3 Hardback
ISBN 978-1-108-72868-3 Paperback

The assertions, arguments, and conclusions herein are those of the author or other contributors. They do
not necessarily reflect the opinions of the United States Holocaust Memorial Museum.

This book is published with the support of the Jack, Joseph and Morton Mandel Center for Advanced
Holocaust Studies, United States Holocaust Memorial Museum.

Cambridge University Press has no responsibility for the persistence or
accuracy of URLs for external or third-party internet websites referred to in
this publication, and does not guarantee that any content on such websites is,
or will remain, accurate or appropriate.

FOR GERALDINE, AS A MEMORIAL.
GERALDINE, DR. GERTRUD ADLER-KLEPETAR, BORN ON
DECEMBER 9, 1905, IN PRAGUE, MURDERED BY GASSING AND
INCINERATED ON OCTOBER 14, 1944, IN AUSCHWITZ-BIRKENAU,
ALONG WITH HER MOTHER.

FOR THIRTY-TWO MONTHS AND AT THE LIMITS OF HER
ENORMOUS STRENGTH, SHE GAVE HER ALL IN
THERESIENSTADT FOR HER FAMILY, FOR MANY FRIENDS,
AND FOR COUNTLESS AFFLICTED.

TIRELESSLY, SHE SACRIFICED HERSELF. IT IS FOR HER
MOTHER THAT SHE WENT TO HER DEATH.

IN HER, HUMAN DIGNITY DAILY CELEBRATED THE VICTORY
OF HUMILITY OVER THE THREATS FROM IGNOMINY.

Just because God may grant forgiveness, it does not mean that he renders the forgiven sin harmless. This is an act of man.

If God forgives a sin, this does not mean that the effects of this sin are no longer being felt. The entire world suffers as a consequence of sins, those that are forgiven as well as those that are not forgiven. In this sense there is no difference between those sins that are forgiven and those that are not forgiven. Nevertheless, we must make an effort to seek forgiveness for our sins. This is an act of man.

Can this act of man succeed? It is the same as with every other human act: before it is completed, there is always the possibility that God will intervene. Without falling into heathen optimism, we can easily say that it is not necessary for human acts to fail. On the contrary. When speaking of an act of man – as opposed to an act of nature – we are referring to the latent possibility of Divine intervention.

It is therefore possible that any sin may be forgiven. And so it is possible that *all* sins will be forgiven!

Can this act of man, that which makes sins harmless, succeed? We merely know that to believe that something must fail is a superstition. What, then, constitutes the possibility for success?

So long as HE has not forgiven *all* sins, *we* too cannot render a *single one* harmless. We use a strange term to describe rendering a human sin harmless: doing good.

Given that until now the do-gooders have achieved nothing, absolutely nothing, we may conclude that the totality of humanity's sins has still not been forgiven. And given that new do-gooders are still being born and tormenting themselves, we may conclude that God remains prepared to forgive our sins.

Franz Baermann Steiner, "Essays and Discoveries"

London, August 1943

Contents

Acknowledgments by Amy Loewenhaar-Blauweiss	*page* ix
Foreword by Leo Baeck	xi
Preface to the Second Edition by H. G. Adler	xiii
Preface to the First Edition by H. G. Adler	xxiii

I. HISTORY — 1

1	The Jews in the "Protectorate," 1939–1941	3
2	Theresienstadt: History and Establishment	13
3	Deportations to and from Theresienstadt	31
	Overview of the Deportations to Theresienstadt	32
	Overview of the Victims and Deportations from Theresienstadt	38
	The Technical Aspects of the Transports to Theresienstadt	51
	Remarks Preliminary to Chapters 4–7	61
4	The Closed Camp, November 1941–July 1942	63
5	The "Ghetto," July 1942–Summer 1943	86
6	The "Jewish Settlement Area," Summer 1943–September 1944	123
7	Decline and Dissolution, September 1944–May 1945	150

II. SOCIOLOGY — 179

8	Administration	181
	Overview of the Administrative Structure	182
	Description and Discussion	204
9	The Transports	225
	Incoming Transports	227
	Outgoing Transports	240
	The Sinister Nature of the Transports	248
10	Population	252
11	Housing	272

viii   *Contents*

12 Nutrition   294
- Food Rations   294
- Bread and Allocation of Unprepared Foodstuffs   307
- The Kitchens   308
- Individual Meals (*Speisen*)   309
- Actual Amounts versus Recorded Amounts   314
- "Supplemental Fare" and "Food Bonuses"   315
- The Hopeless Fight for Fair Distribution of Food   319
- The Method of Distribution   322
- Nutrition as the Main Problem   323

13 Labor   325
- Labor Deployment Statistics I   330
- Characterization of Administrative Work   347
- Documents Pertaining to the Work of the Central Labor Office   349
- Labor Deployment Statistics II   357
- Working Conditions and Overall Production   370

14 Economy   373
- External Economy   374
- Internal Economy   390
- Petty Economy   396

15 Legal Conditions   400

16 Health Conditions   437
- Typical Diseases   454
- Births   465
- Mortality and Death   466
- Public Health Care, Medical Research, and Medical Education   472

17 Welfare   474
- Welfare for the Elderly and Infirm   474
- Youth Welfare   486

18 Contact with the Outside World   509

19 Cultural Life   517

III. PSYCHOLOGY   555

20 The Psychological Face of the Coerced Community   557
- Experimentation and Destiny in History   557
- Theresienstadt as an Episode in Simultaneous History   559
- Theresienstadt as an Episode in Jewish History   571
- The Typology of Individual Behavior   578
- On "Reality"   585
- The Practical Psychology of the Camp   587
- Conclusion   599

Chronological Summary   603
Sources and Literature   621
Afterword by Jeremy Adler   803
Index   829

Acknowledgments

A project of this size, scope, and complexity involves too many people to thank here individually, so I must confine myself to those whose involvement and participation proved essential in bringing this volume to completion.

At Mohr-Siebeck, thanks are due to a tremendously supportive Jill Sopper, without whom this project would have been impossible.

In London, thanks are due to Jeremy and Eva Adler, for their remarkable patience across many years of struggle, and to Jeremy for his meticulous review of the manuscript.

I also thank the extraordinary Belinda Cooper, for her unwavering intelligence and care, her generosity, and her belief in the importance of this book, as well as the group of scholars who worked with her on parts of the translation: Talia Bloch, Gabrielle Friedman, Laura Jokusch, Sheryl Oring, Jeremiah Riemer, Julia Steinmetz, Imogen von Tannenberg, Taryn Toro, Katja Vehlow, and John Zindar.

Frank Mecklenburg at the Leo Baeck Institute in New York not only provided expertise but also helped smooth the way at critical junctures. Thanks are also due to Atina Grossman, Angelique Graux, the Low Wood Foundation, the Memorial Foundation for Jewish Culture, Inter Nationes, the generosity of the Larchmont Temple Brotherhood, Dr. Robert Sadowsky, Robert Rothman, and Jill Sarkozi.

Thanks are due, also, to Jonathan Schorsch, Istvan and Gloria Deak, and the late Stan Blevis. Geoffrey Hartman's initial efforts to help secure a publisher, as well as his wisdom, insight, kindness, and friendship, were invaluable in every way.

In London, Germany, and elsewhere, I would like to thank the many friends of H. G. Adler who were willing to share memories: Yehuda Bacon, Thomas Mandl, Ruth Rix and Helga Michie, Derek Bolton, and Friedrich Danielis. In Prague, I owe a debt of gratitude to William McEnchroe, whose Aislaby Press was the precursor to the Terezín Publishing Project and who first suggested Adler's masterwork on Theresienstadt as *the* project we ought to take on. Many thanks are due, too, to Stephen Blauweiss and to Henry Shapiro, who first approached Jeremy Adler on our behalf.

In New York, I thank Tali Makell, Thomas Coote, Greta Flaum and her extensive network of Viennese refugees, Nancy McNaughton, and the many generous people who ensured that our fundraising effort was successful, along with Marcus DeLoach; the Andy Statman trio (Andy Statman, Larry Eagle, and Jim Whitney); Herman at

ix

Acknowledgments

Darech Amuno; Helen Kamins; Dolly Shivers; Beth Palazzo; Jim Korn; Eddie Cooper; and, finally, the late, great David Rakoff, whose talent and sensitivity made extremely difficult material remarkably alive and accessible.

At Bard, I owe a debt of gratitude to my various colleagues, most particularly my friend Peter Filkins and the inveterate Roger Berkowitz at the Hannah Arendt Center for Politics and the Humanities. And, for the most valuable kind of encouragement, I thank Edie Meidav and Stan Stroh. As always, I am particularly indebted to Mikhail Rudolfovich Shkolnikov, who offered unflagging assistance over many years and made so much of this publication directly possible. I would also like to thank most warmly all those supporters of this project who wish to remain anonymous but have helped this translation come into being. A debt of particular gratitude is owed, as well, to Benton Arnovitz, my opposite number at the Jack, Joseph and Morton Mandel Center for Advanced Holocaust Studies of the United States Holocaust Memorial Museum, whose persistence and "Sitzfleisch" may well be unmatched in the annals of publishing, for bringing the Museum and the Terezín Publishing Project to a collaborative position; to Eric Crahan, formerly of Cambridge University Press, for his willingness to go to bat for us in so many ways; and to the lovely Deborah Gershenowitz, our editor at Cambridge, under whose pragmatic wings this project ultimately took shelter, and to her assistant, Dana Bricken. Our copy editor, Laura Wilmot, deserves particular mention for her dedicated implementation of the seemingly endless editorial decisions on this project.

Thanks, finally, to my daughter Elischka, for keeping me mindful of what my priorities are, and to Jonathan Nedbor, for providing, in ways too numerous to list here, a safe haven for the final stretch.

Amy Loewenhaar-Blauweiss

Foreword

Many of the acts perpetrated during those dark days could be titled "evil as an experiment." In a very particular way, the concentration camp of Theresienstadt – Terezín, occasionally called the ghetto of Theresienstadt for the outside world – which was dedicated exclusively to the Jews, was such an experiment in the will to evil.

Minimal chances of remaining healthy in the camp were coupled with a great likelihood of becoming ill; the realm of life was replaced by the realm of death. This was one aspect of it.

More and more people were crammed into a small, ever-shrinking space, so that each person was constantly bumping into and rubbing up against everyone else; as intended, all manner of selfishness and greed blossomed, and all decency withered away. This was the second aspect of it.

And, finally, the third aspect was that crowded together into these confines were Jews from many parts of Europe – people, in other words, who for generations had been distinct from one another geographically, culturally, and linguistically; inevitably, so it seemed, every little jealousy and sense of superiority was unleashed and any sense of a collective identity decayed.

Any undertaking to depict all of this will be fraught with difficulties, but it is of significance in understanding human psychology and moral psychology in general, as well as the psychology of Jews in particular. Dr. H. G. Adler has taken on this task, and he has, it may be said, done it admirable justice. His book on Theresienstadt combines the human gift for remaining close to one's subject, empathizing and sympathizing with it, with the mental ability to step back and maintain the detachment necessary to become aware of the dominant features shaping the whole.

A scientific rigor that does not overlook any fact and is always in search of new data is united with an artistic sensibility that is able to understand or intuit the underlying causes.

Anyone who is prepared to recognize that which occurred, and therefore anyone, wherever he may be, who has been granted new life, will remain deeply indebted to Dr. Adler for his work.

Leo Baeck

Preface to the Second Edition

It fills me with gratitude and satisfaction that in 1958, three years after the publication of this book, it became necessary to print a second edition, which was delayed due neither to any fault of my own nor to that of the publisher. This book's success testifies to a salutary sympathy for the latest unfathomable calamity to befall the Jewish people. Its success was supported by insightful and detailed reviews in Germany and in many other countries. I am therefore now able to present a carefully revised, in many ways improved and partly expanded, text, which also benefited from the unintended delay in publication. I was able to expand the "Sources and Literature" section from 261 items to 634, some of which are extensively annotated so that this section will hopefully provide a useful list of resources for future research, especially because it includes previously unknown works or little-known publications. I recognize, however, that despite all this, this section, as well as the entire book, still contains errors and may be further improved on. I can only repeat my request that readers continue to provide me with corrections, lend me source materials, and keep me in mind when it comes to useful information and tips of any kind, all of which I or future researchers shall gratefully make use of. The account of business transactions and the background behind them remains particularly sketchy. Certainly there is much that could be added here. Nevertheless, it was possible to clarify or more thoroughly shed light on some essential matters, such as the nature of the deportees – of which it is always difficult to get a clear picture – the interventions by the International Red Cross, the major propaganda film of 1944, and the events of the last days and weeks prior to liberation and immediately thereafter.

Many corrections in the documentation occurred because of additional information I received in response to the bibliographic "Sources and Literature" section; this information, which I did not have access to when I originally wrote this book, usually served to confirm facts I had presented or views I had expressed. Furthermore, whereas previously I often had to rely on document copies, I have, in the interim, been able to compare some of these with their originals; this too gave rise to emendations, even if not terribly radical ones. Above all, however, the book's warm reception made it possible for me – with help from the New York–based Conference on Jewish Material Claims against Germany and with the cooperation of my always sympathetic and supportive publisher, Mr. Hans G. Siebeck, both of whom I would hereby like to thank – to fulfill one of the wishes I expressed in the first edition: to put together and publish a book of documentary material from Theresienstadt, *Die Verheimlichte Wahrheit (The Hidden Truth*, 1958), with which I was able to round out and conclude my research on the topic. The two books complement each other; they presuppose each other; and only the two together can provide a sense of the scope of the issues addressed. The second book fills in gaps left by the first book and brings more detailed factual evidence to bear, thereby demonstrating clearly that, within the greater context of Nazi Germany's and the Reich Security Main Office's policy toward the Jews, this camp played a unique role as the first and most important camp for executing the so-called Final Solution to the Jewish Question. The true nature of this privileged camp thereby becomes just as transparent as the propagandistic purposes for which it was only too successfully maintained.

If, by adding the second book, I have succeeded in making this book somewhat more comprehensive factually, I must nevertheless confess that after careful deliberation, I stand by the first book's structure and development, its central tenets, and the in-depth manner in which it explores and interprets the issues it takes up. In these respects, nothing of consequence has been added, with the exception of a reevaluation of the Zionist youth's position in the camp (a word on that later); nothing whatsoever has been changed. This is why I would like to take the time here to respond to the diverse objections that have been raised by my well-meaning critics.

Various readers, many of them former inmates of Theresienstadt, wished I had gone into greater detail on one or the other point, something that may have been particularly advisable in depicting the camp's latter days. Yet, given that this book is already of considerable length – in its first edition alone it is the longest work ever published about a coerced community to date – and that it has just grown some more, it was impossible to comply with such requests. Despite one's best efforts, not everything that occurred in Theresienstadt can be covered. One has to set limits somewhere and abide by them. Nevertheless, the extensive additions made to the bibliography as well as *The Hidden Truth* should satisfy many of these requests. In 1957, through Zeev Shek, I discovered that valuable source materials on Theresienstadt have been preserved in Israel, but that they are not yet available to researchers. Apparently, they primarily consist of yearly and monthly reports prepared by the Jewish leaders for the German camp commanders. The hope is that these documents will be processed and published, at least in excerpts, in the coming years. It will then be possible to depict the camp's internal history much more comprehensively and in near microscopic detail, even if the language and the already familiar bias of such official reports only reveal a particular and narrowly defined aspect of the total picture. I have also been told that there is quite a bit of material among these unexplored documents in Israel that sheds light on the activities of the "Youth Welfare Office" and the illegal Zionist youth movement at the camp, as well as on the artistic work of numerous artists and laypeople.

Where some wished for greater detail, others were critical of the plethora of citations or of my having gone so far as to interpolate entire documents into the text, and they took issue with the numerous references I make to the "Sources and Literature" section, which, this opinion holds, slow down and exhaust the reader. Others saw merits in this approach. I side with the latter opinion, because I believe that it was in this way that I was able to connect the material presented with an intellectual analysis that unifies the whole. Naturally, not everyone appreciates

Preface to the Second Edition xv

statistics or other details, but it is easy to skip over interpolations, whereas, on the other hand, the expanded index allows one to pick out the relevant passages on most of the topics covered. Maybe one day there will be an opportunity to publish a simplified, popular edition.

Some suggested that, instead of prefacing the history of the camp with a brief overview of the persecution of the Jews in the then "Protectorate," it would have been better to report on the circumstances in Germany, where Jews were being persecuted starting some six years prior. This point is well taken, but it overlooks what is established at the start of the first chapter; the current structure is therefore justified.

A few critics, none of whom were former camp inmates, doubted my claim that most people in Theresienstadt were not aware of the fate awaiting those deported to the East, particularly in Auschwitz. But this was the case. In the first edition I corroborated this by examining the psychology of the prisoners and by presenting several bibliographic references; now there is much more evidence for this lack of knowledge (e.g., 272) provided throughout the "Sources and Literature" section.

Some readers wished I had covered the SS functionaries in Theresienstadt in greater detail, particularly their fate after the war. I consciously chose not to do so and discussed these men only insofar as it seemed relevant to an understanding of the camp's history. So much has already been written about this group that it is not necessary to also do so here; examining the sociology of the SS, the Reich Security Main Office, the Gestapo, the Eichmann Group, and the camp staff remains a task unto itself. Theresienstadt does not lend itself to this, because, to date, not a single document has surfaced regarding the private or official activities of the SS staff there. Describing what happened to some of these men in the aftermath – whose fate could only be successfully discovered by studying judicial case files, most of which cannot be obtained from Czechoslovakia – would do absolutely nothing to shed light on our own problems.

Sources in Holland made me aware of errors, which have since been corrected, particularly with respect to the Barneveld and Westerbork camps; moreover, I was chided for how I sized up the Dutch Jews in Theresienstadt. In doing so, my critics failed to consider that the Jews from Holland only started arriving in Theresienstadt in significant numbers in January 1944, and almost half of them only started coming in September of that year, so they did not have much of an impact on events prior to the camp's final stages. What I have learned in the meantime, especially also regarding Westerbork, only seems to confirm my views and supports my overall assessment, made in the first edition, that they played a limited role. To the best of my abilities, I made every effort to accurately portray the role and particular ways of each of the groups in Theresienstadt. It was inherent to the history of this camp that the Bohemian-Moravian Jews and the German and Viennese Jews, who left their indelible mark beginning in the fall of 1941 and the summer of 1942, respectively, played the most prominent roles.

Some suggested that I draw parallels between the conditions in Theresienstadt and those in the Jewish camps in the East, such as in Łódź, Vilna, and Warsaw, whereby I was asked to compare such common traits as corruption and the internal camp bureaucrats responsible for it. I think this is a subject for a later study and is beyond the scope of this almost all-encompassing monograph; nevertheless, I have taken steps to satisfy this request this way: in defending my depiction of the Jewish

xvi   *Preface to the Second Edition*

"self-administration" in charge of Theresienstadt, I draw on basic theses set forth by
a venerated scholar in his examination of the Warsaw Jewish Council. When
depicting the coerced community in which the SS imprisoned the Jews, it is essential
to present a balanced picture. Such an assessment must foreground the leaders in
charge in the Jewish administration and examine them much more closely than it
does other eminent personalities who may have lived in the camps and may have
distinguished themselves in myriad ways through their humane behavior. It is
because of this that, in the case of Theresienstadt, figures such as Robert Stricker,
Franz Kahn, and even the most admired among them all, Leo Baeck, are covered in a
relatively cursory fashion. The history of a community cannot turn into biography;
otherwise it would go on ad infinitum, especially given that residing in this small
town over the long and short term were so many outstanding women and men who
had achieved prominence prior to coming to the camp, either in the Jewish world and
or in the general community, and who often certainly also stood out in the camp.
Only studies dedicated to these particular individuals could depict their impact;
regrettably, this cannot be undertaken here.

Those familiar with the circumstances at the camp will also allow that it was with
good reason that I portrayed the "outsider" Karl Loewenstein in greater depth than
I did many of the others. Even if some may find it disagreeable, it remains a fact that,
for a year, Loewenstein – with his great virtues and obvious faults – was a decisive
force in shaping the camp's history. To ignore this would be a gross distortion of the
truth; because Loewenstein has been treated quite unfairly in the past, there is all the
more reason to emphasize his historical significance here and so try to strip away
some of this injustice. Within the overall tragedy that was Theresienstadt it was a
particular catastrophe that, of all things, those at the helm of the Jewish administration did not understand this man and were so myopically suspicious of him that
they caused his downfall in a manner that struck at the foundations of this coerced
community, while, for his part, Loewenstein was not able to adequately recognize
and deal flexibly with the social fabric of this community into which he was so
bizarrely forced. Admittedly, it remains unlikely whether, even then, he could have
ultimately prevailed in his uncompromising fight against corruption. It is unfortunate
that, from the start and for better or for worse, the Jewish camp administrators,
although mainly Zionists, allied themselves with Karl Schliesser, a devotee of Czech
assimilationism and the head of the Jewish Economics Department, which, under his
direction, became the center of corruption in the camp and where primarily those
who shared Schliesser's ideology were employed in a business that was both lucrative
and easily exploited. The internal administration almost consistently covered up for
these employees, even when they were compromised by grave mismanagement.

I am grateful for how rarely and with how much restraint I was criticized by those
in Israel and from within Zionist circles more generally for my assessment of the
internal administration in Theresienstadt, which was led for the most part by well-
known, often established Zionists. Such care was taken to protect me that when there
was disagreement, the objections often reached me privately, and if they were raised
in public it was done in muted tones. My critics were usually individuals who had
known the Jewish camp administrators prior to the war. Often they had been close to
them; in much rarer cases they knew them from the camps. This restraint is all the
more noble given that in my treatment of various figures I seem to question an ideal
that is held dear by many. Admittedly, I did not wish to target this ideal or any ideal,

Preface to the Second Edition   xvii

but, rather, I only wanted to get at its ideological and therefore far from ideal guise. Above all, I wanted to examine human behavior, which during the course of events – that is, history as we wish to nail it down in retrospect – supersedes every ideal. Ideals may determine history; patterns of behavior – ethos in the broadest sense – create the history that we experience and judge. This ethos, as one reader correctly asserts, is not a "character trait" but rather a strength that one has. One either possesses it or one doesn't. The way things turn out, the way things could have been, all these are acts of man, which we judge, as soon as we – who are also not free of human weakness – are driven to speak out in accordance with our own conscience. Then we give voice to an authority that is greater than ourselves. This is a moral calling that one can either heed or ignore. One cannot dismiss this obligation by saying, "You, who were just a lowly inmate and were not burdened with such grave responsibilities, how would you have acted had you been in these men's shoes?" The issues, which I raise in all seriousness, are not meant to incriminate or exonerate anyone; they are only intended to deepen our insight into the tragedy that befell those who were in charge – a tragedy for which they remain blameless – and our understanding of their failures, for which they may be blamed. By the time the first inmates arrived in Theresienstadt it was clear that this tragedy was already unfolding and could no longer be averted; it was inescapable. I never, however, assailed our martyred heroes – who were robbed of almost any free will – for their doomed fate. I only critiqued those at the head of this inmate community for acts that exceeded the orders they were forced to carry out; there was much they could have done or could have refrained from doing, which, especially given the circumstances, was also their duty. That's what counts. Just because those I have attacked were Zionists, but I myself was not a Zionist, does not mean that I am attacking Zionism. What's being attacked are individuals who actively participated in these events and who opened themselves up to attack for ideals that they dragged down with them into ossification and decay, even though they may have originally had a pure belief in their ideals and even though they believed they still represented these ideals – ideals that they no longer could represent, and that, in the affliction that was the camp, could no longer even be represented. Above all, it is this thesis that this book carefully explores.

One thing should be stated clearly, and I am doing so here: everything related to this issue in this book should be read as I describe it previously; particularly in such instances, I have not made the slightest change to the text. There is one thing, however, that I had overlooked, and I am grateful that it was kindly brought to my attention: the status of Zionist or Zionist-educated youth and their caretakers – who still were but adolescents themselves – in the camp. They all filled their young lives – spent in this most miserable of circumstances, in which there was no mercy and no way out – with values that provided comfort and a way to endure and beautify the present and to imbue the future with promise and meaning; for these young people, who, like all youth, were impressionable and credulous, the leaders of the "self-administration" represented venerable role models and a source of support. I have recognized and previously already stated that the youth were not at fault if they were misled in the process; what I say does not apply to those who were children at the time or to those among their caretakers who were still adolescents themselves. Many of them were terribly persecuted and humiliated while they were still living in apparent freedom, and so they only experienced a certain sense of freedom – that was theirs alone – once they were imprisoned in the camp and in the relatively

Preface to the Second Edition

sheltered community of the "youth homes" created by the other inmates. I have written a new ending to Chapter 17 in order to do justice to the point of view of these youths, who led an isolated, privileged existence in the camp that was uncharacteristic of the general circumstances. One of the youth leaders, to whom I owe valuable insights into this issue, confessed to me how much fulfillment he found in everything symbolized by the figure of the first Jewish Elder, Jakob Edelstein – later called "Illusion Theresienstadt" by the few out of this group who survived – but how all of this crumbled when he was confronted with the reality of Auschwitz in the fall of 1944. Then the illusion became clear; those who were responsible for it lost esteem, accordingly. My source is beyond all reproach, for he remained true to his ideals and is now serving in the government of Israel.

Some readers and critics could not reconcile themselves to how I present Edelstein's work and that of his successor, Paul Eppstein. My critics cited many of their own memories to argue against my portrayal. Readers pointed to these men's past, their intentions, and their terrible demise at the hands of murderers. In responding to these objections, which are obvious on humane grounds, I do not wish to go much beyond what has already been conclusively chronicled in the documents on many pages of this book. An examination of such passages, which may be found throughout most of this book's chapters – and which are supported by accounts in Chapters 12 and 14 as well as by witnesses featured in the "Sources and Literature" section – refutes practically every charge made by my critics. Some wished, and rightfully so, that I had mentioned the fact that Edelstein and Eppstein, as well as Otto Zucker and, incidentally, also Leo Baeck, could have emigrated prior to the war or even, in part, during the first years of the war and could have saved themselves. Instead, they remained with the besieged. But what was so beneficial in Baeck's case was not a blessing in the case of the others. Even if this affects how harshly they are judged, it does not justify their later acts. The words of Franz Kafka that I used as an epigraph for Part 1 apply here: "Betrayed! Betrayed! Once one responds to a false alarm on the night bell, there's no making it right – not ever."

Edelstein led his wife and even his child to their doom; by, at first, voluntarily cooperating with Hans Günther, Eichmann's representative in Prague – against the advice of Franz Kahn and other Zionists – he started down a path that, despite the best of intentions, could only lead into the abyss. Although he warned the Zionist youth who were prepared to resist against doing so, when he traveled to Amsterdam with Günther in 1941 – in order to assist in setting up a "Jewish council" and to arrange for its cooperation with the Dutch "Central Bureau," that is, Eichmann's office – Edelstein himself already understood how far he had gone when he said he would probably be turned into the messenger of such terrible tidings for the Jews that his own people would despise and scorn him. No, this man does not deserve our hatred and scorn, but when we look back at the impact he had, he also does not merit being turned into a role model or hero. The fact that he did not avoid the unavoidable only fits into the larger picture, but the fact that he also did not shy away from what was avoidable tarnishes his memory. There is no need to recount here what could have been avoided; the pages that follow disclose this. They also report on Edelstein's last days as an inmate in Auschwitz, where, in the cathartic last few months of his life, he lifted himself out of the abyss of his years in Theresienstadt, so that a fellow inmate from this time, a Jew from Poland who had never been in Theresienstadt, stated that he was "like a saint." Yet, because we are writing about the history and people of

Preface to the Second Edition xix

Theresienstadt, we must restrict ourselves to what occurred in this camp. There we see Edelstein stoop to new lows, which is also confirmed by documents presented in *The Hidden Truth*. His martyrdom will remain in our memories.

Among Eppstein's apologists were Professor Ernst Simon – whose arguments unfortunately are not based in fact (see 243c) – and Dr. Berthold Simonsohn, to whom I cede the floor in the annotated bibliography (243e). Perhaps I may reveal in this connection that, prior to the publication of the first edition of this book, I discussed one question repeatedly and at length with the late Leo Baeck: how to portray various individuals in relaying the history of Theresienstadt. I did not write anything about anyone in this book without first discussing it with Baeck. I may be the responsible party, because I shaped the sentences, but Baeck approved them and endorsed them with his preface. There was a lot more on Baeck's mind concerning Eppstein that he confided in me than is included here. Because Eppstein has been publicly defended in reviews that were published in 1959 in response to *The Hidden Truth*, I have found it necessary to allow other camp inmates to speak out about this man, at least in the "Sources and Literature" section (see 55b, 78a, 93, 243a). Eppstein went down a fateful path, in which he took the disaster that was already unfolding by the time he arrived at the camp and deepened it. He pushed people onto transports to the East only because they, Zionists like himself, dared to speak the truth. In this connection, I would like to mention the case of Vladimír Weiss, a Zionist from Prague, who was deported to Auschwitz in September 1943, with his wife and child, because he sent Eppstein a memo on corruption, reprinted here in Chapter 12. This was not an instance in which Eppstein succumbed to tragic circumstances; these were actions that he deliberated over and undertook out of his own free will. Something like this cannot be whitewashed by pointing to the man's merits; it overshadows his merits. We may only hope that this score was settled by the cruel fate that Eppstein met in the "Small Fortress" – the final judgment is not ours to make.

There were those who spoke out for others in the administration, particularly for Otto Zucker, Edelstein's deputy and the third person in the triumvirate – consisting of Eppstein, Benjamin Murmelstein, and Zucker – that took on the responsibility of leading the internal administration in the period following Edelstein's arrest and deportation to Auschwitz. His "acerbic wit and plucky pessimism" were cited. Although this may have been true of him, I cannot change my opinion of this clearly talented and unusual man. He too was so deeply enmeshed in the complicated, collective game of the Jewish administration that he must also be held accountable for not avoiding the avoidable. The observations Michel Mazor makes concerning the "Jewish Council" – to date the most insightful ones on the topic – in passages throughout *The Vanished City*, his book about the Warsaw Ghetto, apply to Zucker, just as they do to the other men who first acquiesced to and then became addicted to this game. Although the following sentences were written about the Warsaw Ghetto, which Mazor experienced, with minor modifications they may also be applied to Theresienstadt:

"It seems to me that as soon as any Jew became a member of a 'Jewish Council,' he was called upon to account for the role he was asked to play and for his culpability." "Certainly, there can be no doubt that some members of the Jewish Council were sincerely convinced that, given the prevailing circumstances and the persecutions, only these institutions could alleviate the suffering of the Jews. To the extent that they did not interfere in internal Jewish affairs this may, to some extent have been the case. But this cannot be allowed to distract from the fact that under orders from the Germans these individuals became 'Jewish Fuhrers,' who, despite their good intentions, inevitably came to pursue a disastrous path that rendered them pliant tools in the hands of the Germans." "Nevertheless, the 'Jewish Councils' cannot be viewed as agents of collaboration. The term 'collaboration', as we came to define it during the previous war, assumes that the Germans granted the persons concerned, as well as those around them who were drawn into voluntary cooperation (collaboration), a certain, even if slim amount, of freedom. This was not the case with the 'Jewish Councils.'" "The community's circumstances were extremely difficult and there were no good solutions to the problems that arose in this city of death. Nevertheless, it may be argued that no efforts were made to capitalize on those opportunities, however few and far between, that did present themselves to alleviate the suffering of the most miserable sectors of the population." "As soon as they locked the Jews up in the ghetto, the Germans took little interest ... in them and interfered relatively little in their lives or in their internal affairs.... . It was the 'Jewish Councils' who were vested with the power of authority over this. Within the limits of what was possible ... the 'Jewish Council' could organize and direct the lives of the Jews. This is why history will hold the 'Jewish Council' completely accountable for its actions and its impotence in this area. It is responsible ... for the corruption that permeated all of its institutions and for many other things besides. But, above all, the 'Jewish Council' of Warsaw may be accused of having been completely indifferent to the terrible suffering of the masses and for not taking measures that were within its powers to alleviate the misery of the most needy strata of ghetto society."

If I have gone so far as to pass judgment on these topics as well as on a host of other matters, then it remains, I confess, a risk I have taken, as I have already stated in my closing remarks to Chapter 20, but I thought that I should not avoid doing so, and I answer for it with my own conscience. I will applaud and be grateful to whosoever seeks to provide factual evidence to correct my daring assertions. I have not written to favor anyone nor to harm anyone; I tried, to the best of my ability, to advocate for Judaism as a particular expression of humaneness, to the extent that I understood what humaneness is. What brings me into conflict with other opinions, among them ones espoused by old campmates, is my conception of Judaism. There have been complaints that I openly call a spade a spade, that I do not disguise anything, that in depicting the abysmal catastrophe that befell us I have chosen to illuminate certain matters while keeping others in the dark, and that I also direct my accusations against my Jewish brothers. I cannot and could not have done otherwise. The more deeply I profess my allegiance to Judaism, to my people, and to the members of the coerced community of Theresienstadt – among whom I, as the least of them, never and nowhere exclude myself from its existing and possible circle of guilt – the more I must strive to reveal the truth and saturate the memory of the generations to come with this, as painful and as bitter as it may be.

No nation in history has dared to go to such lengths to blame itself as has the Jewish people; from Moses onward, its great teachers and admonishers have never done otherwise. Keeping guilt hidden exacerbates it and has a corroding effect, but revealing and investigating guilt has a cleansing effect and promotes the inscrutable mysterious workings of grace, which stir up the healing powers of the conscience and which cleanse the conscience of guilt unto the end of days, when the great promises made to humanity will be fulfilled and "though all the peoples walk each in the name

Preface to the Second Edition

of its gods, we will walk in the name of the Lord, our God, forever and ever" (Micah 4:5). In answer to questions from several critics, I hereby state that the concept of goodness in the name of the Eternal that we have been taught about ourselves – most forcefully through the commandment to love one's neighbor as oneself – and a view of the Everlasting determined my understanding of Judaism and are, as I am describing them here, the spiritual underpinnings for the opinions expressed in this book and for the standards applied when passing judgment.

This is also how one is to understand what I mean when I discuss Judaism and describe its role in Theresienstadt in the final chapter of the book. In that passage, I write,

> One's own guilt, the guilt that, as a Jew, one has to account for through Judaism, was not taken as a starting point to develop a creative principle. People did not realize that those who suffer the most are those who always blame others and believe themselves to be blameless. In the relatively bearable conditions of Theresienstadt people failed to realize that persecution presented an opportunity for a human catharsis and for the rediscovery of a Judaism that most knew only superficially. Hardly anyone found his way back to Judaism as a result of being in Theresienstadt, nor did being there cause those who already were followers of a "Jewish" ideology to find their way to a freer and deeper approach.

I stand by this statement, but I have softened it a bit, because I put it too unconditionally originally; I have thus replaced "most" with "very many" and "hardly anyone" with "few."

Dr. Benjamin Murmelstein took issue with how I worded the last sentence on p. 190 of the first edition; the sentence begins, "Following the departure from camp of the final transport, which Rahm and Möhs put together alone, and only with Murmelstein's assistance . . ." Dr. Murmelstein read the word "assistance" to mean that he was being accused of actively collaborating with the Gestapo in assembling the final transport. This was not at all my intention and is also not implied by the context; with these words I intended neither to accuse him of active participation nor to implicate him in the least. But because Dr. Murmelstein felt my wording was unclear and others too could misunderstand it, I have omitted the words "and only with Murmelstein's assistance."

Finally, I wish to conclude my observations with a number of acknowledgments for which previously I did not find a place. First of all, I would like to thank ministerial counselor Dr. Richard Korherr for how generously he forgave me for causing damage to his reputation with a passage (p. 53) in the first edition that, as it turns out now, contains factually unfounded information, but for whose contents I cannot be held responsible. This passage has been omitted, and everything relevant to this matter can be found under number 156 in the bibliography. Because Dr. Korherr never belonged to the SS and because he has been rehabilitated on account of his behavior during the years of National Socialist rule, I have also emphatically decided that it was wrong to list Dr. Korherr as an "SS statistician" in the index of names.

My special thanks, once again, goes to the Wiener Library in London and its friendly staff, and especially to Dr. Alfred Wiener. I would also like to express my heartfelt thanks once again to this institution's research director, Dr. Eva G. Reichmann. Over the course of the past few years, she always took an active

Preface to the Second Edition

interest in my work and supported my efforts with her wise counsel. For their generous support I would also like to thank the Centre de Documentation Juive Contemporaine in Paris (specifically Dr. Michel Mazor), the Institute of Contemporary History in Munich (specifically Dr. Helmut Krausnick), Yad Vashem in Jerusalem, the Jewish Historical Institute in Warsaw (specifically Professor Dr. B. Mark), and the Rijksinstituut voor Oorlogsdocumentatie in Amsterdam (specifically Dr. L. de Jong), which was particularly forthcoming in its assistance. I am also much obliged to Dr. Gerhart Riegner who, via a very unusual cooperation, permitted me access to the important Archive of the World Jewish Congress in Geneva. In addition, I would like to extend a great thanks to all those who have helped me with documentation, eyewitness testimony, information, advice, critiques, and more. Of particular note for their assistance were the late Professor Philip Friedman and Klara Caro, Eva Manes, Dora Philippson, Grete Salus, Dr. Selma Segall, and Getty Spies, as well as Jehuda Bacon, Professor David Cohen, Dr. M. Dvorjetski, Maurits Frankenhuis, Dr. Alexander Gutfeld, Sender Israels, Friedrich Klein, Bernhard Kolb, Ota Kraus, Erich Kulka, Dr. Karl Loewenstein, Thomas Mandl, Sven Mayer, Oskar Perschke, Mozes Meijer Poppers, Karl Georg Roessler, Morten Ruge (MA), Zeev Shek, Dr. Berthold Simonsohn, Kazimierz Smolén (MA), and the assistant professor Dr. Aron Vedder.

In conclusion, I would like to point out that although several details in the preface to the first edition are now outdated, it is nevertheless being reprinted here unchanged.

H. G. Adler
London
July 1960

Preface to the First Edition

Although I made an effort to write this book using an untainted German, because of the topic involved – an SS camp set up for Jewish inmates – the text came to reflect and was often subject to the general deterioration of language in the age of mechanical materialism, as well as, in particular, the amorphous, coerced language of the National Socialists and the colloquialisms and written language of Theresienstadt. But the demon that created this camp and left it to vegetate must, certainly, also be conquered linguistically. To show that a sound mind seeks to distance itself from amorphous words and phrases, which have been emptied of meaning, have been perverted to mean their opposite, or are simply wrong, I most often put such terms into quotation marks, even if I make frequent use of them. I purposely placed the glossary – which helps explain the nature of this "ghetto" and also demonstrates what components went into creating the camp's language – at the beginning and not the end. The glossary makes no claims to being complete.*

To the best of my knowledge, this book is the first comprehensive monograph to attempt so extensively to depict not only the history of a purely Jewish coerced camp of the SS, but also its societal makeup; moreover, no one has, as of yet, so exhaustively portrayed even a regular concentration camp under any regime whatsoever. I do not mean hereby to detract from the value of previous books and studies. On the contrary, without these previous studies – among them, the work by Zdeněk Lederer, until now the most important on Theresienstadt – it would have been difficult to realize this one; it is indebted to all of its predecessors. Naturally, I sought to present things accurately and properly, but I recognize that such a book will always contain errors. Mistakes and oversights creep in. Amendments will be necessary. Much has been left in the dark that remains to be illuminated. I may have missed some previously published works. And, above all, there remains unpublished material that I am unaware of, as well as eyewitnesses who could emend what is portrayed here in various ways. I am always grateful for any pertinent information that could be of use to a new edition of this book or for other projects.

---

* The glossary, which appears in the German edition, has not been translated.

xxiv *Preface to the First Edition*

The syntax, spelling, and punctuation of citations have been left basically unchanged, no matter how much they may violate the rules; however, when they could have led to misunderstandings in the text, obvious errors were quietly corrected. One should bear in mind that many documents, such as some of the "orders of the day" and activity reports, were written either by native Czech speakers who could write German only poorly or by authors who were stylistically untrained and awkward. Furthermore, many documents had to be drafted in the greatest of haste. All of this, along with the psychological pressure weighing on their authors, contributed to the odd language found in most, if not all, of the documents – which I had to present just as they were without changing a whit, because only their faithful rendering could accurately reflect the nature of the coerced community in Theresienstadt. Usually, when possible, Czech texts were faithfully translated into the German commonly used in the camps; that is, they were not improved in the German translation, as would have been possible. Other foreign-language citations were also translated, with the exception of the French report written by the International Red Cross delegate in Theresienstadt. Numbers listed following citations correspond to numbers in the "Sources and Literature" section. When such numbers are missing, the citations come from documents, which may be found under number 307 and under numbers 176, 218, 219, 310, and 311, as well as in the preface to "Sources and Literature." Even when I use information from Lederer's book (166) and Prochnik's survey (216), I do not always make explicit reference to them. For abridged citations or where additions or explanations were necessary, I used square brackets [-], whereas any text in parentheses (-) appeared as such in the original. Where text was omitted from a citation, two dots (. .) usually indicate that no more than three words were omitted, three dots indicate that part of a sentence or a short sentence were omitted, and four or more dots indicate that a longer passage was omitted.

Numbers within the body of the text likewise correspond to numbers in the "Sources and Literature" section, which also replaces the footnotes that I have avoided, although even when I do not refer to this bibliography there are many instances in which my book has benefited from these sources in the way of knowledge, inspiration, or corroboration. Furthermore, this annotated bibliography seeks to offer more than would a regular bibliography; many sources are briefly assessed, important information is cited or briefly described, and for the first time the outlines of the larger set of issues that this book attempts to address clearly emerge. This is why I would recommend that the reader devote a good deal of his attention to this bibliography, which mentions many matters not found in other parts of the book.

My greatest thanks go to Dr. Leo Baeck, without whose active assistance, encouragement, and never-flagging advice this book would not have been completed. I thank the Jewish Museum in Prague and its employees from 1945 to 1947 for their support, which enabled me to acquire most of the documents for my work. For his help in diverse and equally important ways, I would like to thank Dr. Alfred Wiener, as well as Dr. Eva G. Reichmann, Ilse Wolff, and all the other employees of his Wiener Library in London, whose treasure trove of books and other collections was generously put at my disposal. Professor Philip Friedman at YIVO in New York gave me bibliographic data for which I was grateful. Mr. A. Opitz of the International Tracing Service in Arolsen kindly made materials from his institute available to me. I would like to thank my late friend Dr. Franz Baermann Steiner, as well as Mrs. Else Dormitzer, Miss Grete Fischer, and Mr. Jehuda Bacon, Dr. Franz Bass, Dr. Elias

Preface to the First Edition

Canetti, His Excellency Frants Hvass, Captain Josef Klaber, Friedrich Klein, Zdeněk Lederer, Dr. Karl Loewenstein, Thomas Mandl, Gerald Reitlinger, Dr. Werner Rosenstock, and Professor Emil Utitz for providing materials, advice, and other assistance. For their moral support, which paved the way for the publication of this book, I am also much obliged to Professor Theodor W. Adorno, Dr. Franz Calvelli-Adorno, Professor Hanns W. Eppelsheimer, Dr. Fritz Hodeige, and Willi Sternfeld. For including this book in the Civitas Gentium series I thank Professor Max Graf zu Solms, Dr. Fritz Hodeige, and Dr. Karl Heinz Pähler, who also offered his critique. The publication of this book was substantially eased and supported by the Federal Office for Educational Materials in Bonn, whose director, Dr. Paul Franken, and his colleague Dr. Wilhelm von Hahn I would like particularly to thank. I am no less obliged to my publisher, Mr. Hans Siebeck, who generously took on my book and who met all of my material needs. I thank Dr. Konrad F. Hirsch for his assistance in reading the edited version and his countless valuable suggestions. And finally, my sincere thanks go to my wife, who faithfully stood by my side and offered her wise counsel throughout the many years that I was working on this book.

H. G. Adler
London
July 1955

PART I

HISTORY

Betrayed! Betrayed! Once one responds to a false alarm on the night bell, there's no making it right – not ever.

Franz Kafka, "A Country Doctor"

I

The Jews in the "Protectorate," 1939–1941

The fate of the Jews in the "Protectorate of Bohemia and Moravia" from 1939 to 1941 provided a foretaste of the tragedies that would take place in the Theresienstadt "ghetto" from 1941 to 1945. Therefore, I provide a brief overview of the situation in the "Protectorate," keeping in mind the following:

1. Theresienstadt, in Bohemia, was politically part of the "Protectorate."
2. The preliminary history and establishment and, to a significant degree, the further development of the Theresienstadt camp were largely determined by German and Jewish officials in Prague.
3. Theresienstadt first served as a collection camp for Jews in the "Protectorate," most of whom spent some time there.
4. Jews from Bohemia and Moravia lent the camp its character, at first exclusively and later in great measure.
5. Although the details of the persecution of Jews under Hitler differed in the countries from which prisoners came to Theresienstadt, the basic characteristics of the policies followed were generally similar to those of the "Protectorate."

In the years before the Munich agreement, and before a "protectorate" over the remaining parts of Bohemia and Moravia was forced on the Czechs on March 14 and 15, 1939, thus splitting Czechoslovakia, Jews in these countries had already seen warning signs. German Jews from the Reich had found refuge here for longer or shorter periods, and they were joined in 1939 by Austrian Jews; the number of these refugees has been estimated at 15,000 by mid-March 1939. At the same time, roughly 25,000 refugees from the ceded "Sudetengau," where 1,534 Jews still remained in May 1939, lived in the "Protectorate." Altogether, a total of 118,310 Jews lived there; these included 14,350 people who, according to Nazi definitions under the Nuremberg Laws, were "racial" Jews or were Jews legally (*Geltungsjuden*) rather than "by faith" (*Glaubensjuden*). Because 121,512 people of the Jewish faith were resident in the same region on December 31, 1938, it is clear that emigration had begun before the German occupation, although only to a relatively minor extent.

In the few months following the Munich dictat and before the creation of the "Protectorate," various organizations, including the Refugee-Welfare Institute of the

Czechoslovak Ministry of Social Welfare, promoted the emigration of foreign Jews and those from the Sudeten area, but they were working with insufficient financial and other resources. There was no systematic action; only individuals were enabled to emigrate in this way. It was extremely difficult, costly, and time-consuming to obtain emigration papers and permission to take possessions out of the country, and far too little support was forthcoming from abroad. Some refugees and many native Jews lacked real foresight. Responsible Jewish officials and irresponsible private persons (who unscrupulously organized illegal, generally unsuccessful transports) provided little assistance with emigration. Abroad, international and Jewish willingness to help was largely absent. There was distressingly little understanding, foresight, willingness to sacrifice, or even goodwill; this was typical of a period in which cumbersome state bureaucracies, as well as public and private institutions, no longer dealt with actual people but treated individuals merely as inventoried items represented by file cards. Therefore, the significance of notable exceptions should not be underestimated (see 185a).

Confusion increased after March 15, 1939. The Czechs were powerless, and besides, they were too busy with their own problems to promote Jewish emigration effectively; but officials were more helpful than in previous months. The borders were closed for a short time; emigration then became possible for a few weeks, with Gestapo permission. In this way, at least, a considerable number managed to go abroad. But this relatively easy method was soon blocked, and complicated formalities had to be completed in order to emigrate. Until the beginning of the war, many people chose to escape illegally through Poland or Slovakia, but even thereafter, some succeeded in fleeing across the Slovakian border. Jewish offices – of which the Palestine Office, led by Jakob Edelstein, the first "Jewish Elder" of Theresienstadt, was probably the most active – helped with legal emigration. By the end of July 1939, 9,186 people had made it abroad in various ways, 888 of them through the Palestine Office. Altogether, by the end of the year, 19,016 people had escaped the "Protectorate."

On July 22, 1939, the official Prague daily newspaper, *Der neue Tag*, announced the establishment of the "Central Office for Jewish Emigration in Bohemia and Moravia" on the orders of Reichsprotektor Konstantin von Neurath. Oberführer Franz Stahlecker was appointed its head, as the Sicherheitsdienst (Security Service [SD]) leader and commander in Bohemia and Moravia. SS-Sturmbannführer Hans Günther would serve as department head until the end of the war; he has been identified incorrectly as the son of Hans Friedrich Karl Günther, the so-called race researcher. This office, often called the "Central Office" (Zentralamt), was set up by SS-Hauptsturmführer Adolf Eichmann along the lines of the "Reich Central Office for Jewish Emigration," which had been established on January 24, 1939, at Hermann Göring's behest. Reinhard Heydrich – who was of Jewish origin, as Hitler and Himmler were aware (see 79b, 95d, 139) – was appointed to head it; he may be considered the main instrument of the Jewish policies of Hitler's Germany. Heydrich and Ernst Kaltenbrunner, his successor, along with their superior, Heinrich Himmler, led the "Central Office" only by virtue of their functions in the hierarchy, whereas Eichmann became the head in practice and remained so until the war's end. Göring had issued his order to the Reich minister of the interior, Dr. Hans Frick, which might give the impression that the "Central Office" was a department of the Ministry of the Interior. This, however, was merely a fiction that was dispensed with in

September 1939, when the SD joined with the Sicherheitspolizei (Security Police [Sipo]) under the title Reichssicherheitshauptamt (Reich Security Main Office [RSHA]) and was placed under the command of SS-Obergruppenführer Reinhard Heydrich and, after his death, of Dr. Kaltenbrunner. The Gestapo was integrated into the RSHA under SS-Gruppenführer Heinrich Müller as "Department [*Amt*] IV," entitled "Investigating and Combating Opponents." Department IV was divided into six groups (1943); Group IV B, which had four subgroups, dealt with churches, sects, freemasons, and Jews. Subgroup IV B 4, always headed by Eichmann, was assigned the following areas of responsibility: "Jewish matters, evacuation matters, confiscation of public and anti-state property, deprivation of Reich German citizenship." This listing itself – even if this formulation originated only later, perhaps in 1943 – makes transparent the essential stages of the extermination campaign against the Jews, of which Subgroup IV B 4 would become the essential executive organ. The administrative scheme alone still fails to make it entirely clear what an enormous role Eichmann played, but it is known how broad and barely limited his authority was within the entire party system, indeed even within the RSHA itself. Eichmann acted in collaboration with Müller and often received his orders directly from Himmler, Heydrich, and Kaltenbrunner. The "Central Office" was identical to RSHA IV B 4, perhaps not theoretically but certainly practically; this also makes clear the scope and hierarchy of authority that applied to the Prague "Central Office." It was answerable through the RSHA to the SS, the most powerful group in the state – that is, Himmler, Heydrich, Müller, and Eichmann – as well as to the "commander of the Sipo and SD" in Prague and was thus centrally dependent on the Reich authorities and regionally dependent on the Protectorate authorities of the same SS apparatus. It acquired powers that rapidly made it the unrestricted, and soon almost the exclusive, ruler over all Jews in the "Protectorate" – later it was assigned the Theresienstadt "ghetto." At first, the "Central Office" did actually help with emigration, at least to some extent. The change of name to "Central Office for the Regulation of the Jewish Question in Bohemia and Moravia" simply tracked the circumstances created by the Wannsee conference (see Chapter 2); this occurred when it was no longer possible to speak of "emigration" but only of "regulation," in the SS sense. The scope of authority of the "Central Office" originally encompassed only Prague and its surroundings but was extended on February 16, 1940, to the entire "Protectorate" (see 352a).

For the sake of a rounded presentation, the following paragraphs describe the further process of emigration, which officially ceased in the entire area of the Reich on October 1, 1941; however, some emigration took place after this date. The beginning of the war diminished the few existing opportunities for emigration. For Czech Jews alone, fifteen hundred permits to emigrate to the British Empire became invalid. Prospects for emigrating to the United States were unfavorable, in part because of the low quota (the U.S. quota for all of Czechoslovakia was 2,700, as opposed to 27,000 for Germany, excluding Austria) and in part because the Prague consulate, which closed down on October 15, 1940, was not very forthcoming. Other foreign countries' consulates that had closed even earlier occasionally behaved improperly; in any case, they did nothing to snatch the Jews from certain destruction. These countries' constantly changing immigration requirements contributed to the difficulties, in conjunction with Germany's arbitrary and equally changeable emigration rules (see 39). Unlimited patience, strong nerves, a great deal of luck, and, above all, significant resources were necessary for a successful escape. Mention should be made of a settlement project for "farmers" in Santo Domingo (Dominican Republic) in 1940. The group was about to depart, after receiving Italian transit visas, when Italy blocked transit and the transport had to be rerouted from the Italian border to the "Protectorate." The occupation of Holland and Belgium closed off a further escape route abroad. Italy's entry into the war prevented travel to Shanghai, for which some people had only recently received permits. In August 1940, a way opened up to Japan via Russia, but only for a few, especially as Japan blocked transit visas in February 1941. The U.S. Consulate General in Vienna, which was in charge of emigration at that time, closed in June 1941. Emigration was then planned to Cuba by way of Lisbon. But it was already too late. Despite everything, even after the general prohibition of emigration – at a time when deportations already had begun everywhere but before the beginning of the war with America – 584 people were brought out of the Reich through Sweden and Spain in cooperation with the "Reich Association of Jews in Germany"; however, very few of those individuals were from the "Protectorate" (see also 217). After that, by March 1943, only 93 Jews had left the Reich legally to go abroad, usually as a result of exchanges, including some with Palestine. Once the war began, legal emigration to Palestine became impossible. Certificates were available only after long residence in neutral foreign countries. The last illegal transport to Palestine – of 652 people from the "Protectorate" – departed on September 2, 1940.

The Palestine Office was liquidated on May 10, 1941, after having to carry out a special task. Applications for emigration, which had to be submitted in a "portfolio" (*Mappe*), also required a high fee that the official Jewish Community (hereinafter JKG [Jüdische Kultusgemeinde]) in Prague had to pay for those without funds. Now the "Central Office" ordered all Jews to submit "portfolios." This kept the Jews, the Palestine Office, and the JKG busy for a long time. Shanghai had to be given as the destination. This was a farce, as the SS knew that no one could "emigrate." The number of people classified as Jews shrank from 118,310 on March 15, 1939, to 97,961 on December 31, 1939, 90,041 on December 31, 1940, and 88,686 on June 30, 1941; these numbers included refugees from Germany, Austria, and the Sudeten region who were still living in the country. This reduction in the Jewish population can be traced mainly to emigration. According to the figures for July 15, 1943, after March 15, 1939, roughly 26,100 people emigrated from the "Protectorate." As their destination, 1,482 gave North America, 671 Central America, 4,673 South America, 176 Australia, 167 Africa, 2,117 Palestine, 4,042 the rest of Asia, and 12,765 European countries. The distribution of the figures is inexact, in part because it is not known whether the emigrants reached their destinations and in part because illegal travelers to Palestine, as well as others emigrating illegally, listed on their applications countries for which they had obtained entry visas (see 217).

Once the "Protectorate" was created, the Jews were caught in a trap from which escape was difficult and soon all but impossible. Nevertheless, the worst of the panic receded surprisingly rapidly, especially because, in the context of their hostile country, the Germans had other things to worry about besides the Jews who had failed to escape them. Life resumed its "normal course." How important was it, after all, that some rich Jews were fleeced and that Jewish socialists, or others who fell out of favor, were arrested and deported? Or that, on March 16, 1939, even before any German decree, all Jewish lawyers were forced to give up their offices immediately? Or that

Jews were thrown out of government positions and other posts? Such measures had been expected, and people were glad nothing worse had happened. Soon they nurtured the hope that somehow things would go on, that they simply had to "see it through." There developed an understandable but fatal type of behavior that would also characterize Theresienstadt – lives lived with a mixture of fear and numbness, as though after a blow, but at the same time in a euphoric, optimistic state in which people refused to see, or denied, the existing dangers. As an example, in Theresienstadt, a man with an objective mind opined to an intelligent person that it would be an optimistic estimate if 20–30% of those shipped to the East survived the war; the horrified addressee thereupon turned away, with hostile, abusive words, while smiling at the assumption.

It was not long before harsh measures were introduced; these measures would increase in number and intrusiveness, wearing down the Jews' internal resistance (see 79, 109, 218, 254, 324). Many people were in poor psychological, and in some cases physical, condition by the time they were deported. Prohibitions and decrees were issued; those issued in Berlin applied to the entire Reich, whereas in the "Protectorate" they came from the following offices: Reich German ministries and the Berlin "Central Office" (Zentralamt), the "Reichsprotecktor," the Gestapo and the "Central Office" (Zentralstelle), local German authorities, the government and police of the "Protectorate," various autonomous bodies, and, last but not least, the JKG, which was more and more becoming an executive arm of the "Central Office."

Starting in June 1939, all possessions were secured or their unrestricted use prohibited, and sales and purchases were forbidden. "Trustees" were soon appointed, especially for profitable businesses. Once again, all property had to be declared, and valuable objects and securities deposited. Gradually, all Jewish businesses were expropriated or closed, a process completed on March 31, 1941. The "Emigration Fund for Bohemia and Moravia," created in early 1940, functioned as the receiver; later, it had to pay the subsidies required for the Theresienstadt camp. Its statute tersely provided that "it is released from all taxes." One of Heydrich's decrees preparatory to financial evaluation of the deportations, on October 12, 1941, provided that "the Central Office ... can undertake to liquidate the property of emigrating Jews if this is applied for in writing to the authorized administrator" (218). The "emigrants" *had to* apply as soon as they arrived at the collection point for deportation. Using "referral orders" (*Einweisungsbescheid*), the "Central Office" passed on to the "emigration fund" the property extorted in this way; "all rights of the former owner" were thereby transferred to the fund. The following decree from the Central Office, published by *Der neue Tag* on November 2, 1941, was issued in connection with the start of the deportations: "Jews are without exception prohibited from disposing of any property (such as furniture and articles of everyday use, accounts [*Forderungen*], etc.) without an individual official permit. Violations will lead to the most serious police measures against both the Jew and the purchaser" (218). This style was typical of all decrees from SS offices. All sales even had to be reported retroactively back to October 10, 1940. Any payments to Jews, such as rent, had to be made to a blocked account. On October 23, 1940, 1,500 kronen (or 150 Reichsmark) was declared the maximum amount that could be withdrawn from blocked accounts per family per week. Starting in 1941, a single person could withdraw K 2,000 per month, and married couples could withdraw K 3,000. An additional

K 500 could be withdrawn for each additional Jewish member of the household. Pensions were similarly limited to an annual maximum of K 50,000 per family.

Jews were, by and large, excluded from all professions, especially the more elite ones. They could be treated by only their own doctors. Harshly restrictive labor laws applied to Jews throughout the Reich; at the same time, they were obligated to take on any work assigned to them by the labor offices. Beginning in late 1941, non-Jewish employers could request Jewish workers for only a limited period, and permission could be revoked at any time.

Shortly after the war began, Jews were forbidden to leave their homes after 8 P.M., pursuant to a Gestapo order given orally to the JKG; but it took months before word of this unwritten decree got around, following raids in restaurants and on the streets. Jews no longer could ride in taxis and soon were forbidden to ride in railway sleeping and dining cars. In February 1940 they were forbidden to attend movie houses and theaters, although this already had been prohibited or was at least a risky undertaking. In July 1940, they were forbidden to ride in riverboats and to attend sporting events. A particularly drastic prohibition, originally decreed only for Prague on October 25, 1940, forbade Jews "any change in their permanent residence" or even "temporary absence" from the city. There followed prohibitions on setting foot in certain streets; for example, in Prague Jews were not allowed in the vicinity of the commodities market during trading sessions. As early as August 1939, Jews were excluded from all public swimming pools in Prague, and on May 17, 1940, they were denied entry to all Prague parks; as a result, the only place left for Jews to "relax" was in their cemeteries. This prohibition later was interpreted so meticulously that even walking on the sidewalk next to a park was dangerous. In summer 1941, Jews were forbidden to enter city forests or to walk on the banks of the Vltava. In June 1942, they were even prohibited from using Prague's main streets, and other convenient streets, between 3 P.M. on Saturday and 8 A.M. on Monday. Similar prohibitions were announced in other cities. In September 1940, the use of Prague streetcars was made more difficult. Starting in November 1941, Jews were unable to ride buses or trolleys without special permission. Later, the use of public transportation in Prague became all but impossible, and in other cities it was unconditionally prohibited.

The harshest measure was Heydrich's "Police Decree on the Identification of the Jews," which went into force throughout the Reich on September 19, 1941, and established the yellow star and the general prohibition on leaving one's neighborhood. Although it still was possible to take the train with a special permit or official summons, after October 14, 1941, Jews could ride only in the last cars in third-class railroad carriages: "In cases of overcrowding, Jews are to be excluded from transit entirely" (218). This regulation was made even stricter later on, so that only the last compartment of the last car could be used. If Prague streetcars were too crowded, Jews were forced to get off.

Starting on April 19, 1940, all changes of residence had to be reported to the JKG. There were more and more evictions without notice, especially in better apartment buildings. Owners of houses or villas were forced to abandon their property. Starting on September 13, 1940, Jews in Prague could no longer rent apartments but instead had to sublet from other Jews through the JKG. Only the "Central Office," not the building owner, could rent out housing that became vacant. In early 1941, Jews had to give up their telephones, with the exception only of administrative offices and physicians. A year or so later, all households in which Jews lived had their telephones removed. Jews were forbidden from using telephone booths, and even telephoning at all.

Starting on August 28, 1939, Jews were forbidden from entering a variety of restaurants, and Jewish sections had to be set up in those that remained, unless the establishment declared itself purely "Jewish" or "Aryan." At the same time, all Jewish-owned businesses and factories were identified as Jewish. The separation of Jews and non-Jews proceeded systematically and was implemented with increasing harshness. In August 1940, restaurants had to decide whether to continue to operate as "Aryan" or "Jewish," and the special Jewish sections had to be closed. Fewer and fewer establishments were accessible to Jews, and, in the course of 1941, Jews were forbidden to enter almost all of them.

In August 1940, special shopping hours for Jews – 11 A.M.–1 P.M. and 3 P.M.–4:30 P.M. – were introduced in non-Jewish stores. In February 1941, these hours were limited to 3–5 P.M., and shopping was totally forbidden in many stores. During 1941, the hours when Jews could visit administrative offices were limited; even going to the police was impossible except during a few hours in the morning. In every city, after September 29, 1941, Jews could use only one post office, and only in the afternoon. This was especially burdensome in Prague, where one small post office served 40,000 Jews from 12 to 5 P.M. (later only 2:30–5 P.M.), and most had to make the long trip by foot. Most offices were open to Jews for only a few hours each morning, and sometimes only once or twice a week, unless an individual was officially summoned. Banks and insurance companies kept the same hours, which were later reduced to only one hour in the afternoon. Hairdressers were open to Jews only between 8 and 10 A.M., and soon not at all. In early 1942, Jews were forbidden to use laundries, dyeing works, and cleaning agencies. The prohibition on using libraries hit especially hard. Only in urgent cases was it possible to go to a pharmacy outside regular shopping hours, which were the same as for stores. In hospitals, clinics, mental hospitals, and so on, Jews were carefully isolated or not admitted at all. They were forced to establish their own modest health service in the JKG. Ambulances refused to transport even seriously ill Jews or those involved in serious accidents on the street; they failed to come at all or went away empty. Treatment by "Aryan" doctors was later expressly forbidden, except in the interests of public hygiene.

Soon, too, the availability of goods was greatly restricted, not a difficult task in a controlled economy in which soon almost nothing would be available for purchase on the open market. Jews received no clothing cards; only in urgent cases could they later obtain a special permit for work clothes. Jews were denied special allotments, for example, of fruit or sugar, to which the public was entitled. Starting on October 1, 1941, they were forbidden to buy tobacco; smoking on the street became danger-ous. The strict prohibition on smoking in Theresienstadt, a measure generally unknown in other camps, followed the regulations in the "Protectorate."

On October 23, 1941, the minister for agriculture announced, "Any provision, with or without compensation, of fruit of any sort, fresh, dried, or otherwise preserved, including dried fruits and nuts, also marmalade, jam, cheese, sweets, fish and fish products, poultry and game of any sort to Jews is forbidden. This prohibition applies equally to growers, producers, processors, dealers and consumers" (218). This prohibition was later extended to include "wine and spirits of any sort," onions, garlic, and pork, and still later all vegetables, mushrooms, syrups, and yeast. The purchase of potatoes was made very difficult. Starting in October 1941, Jews received no shaving lotion; rations of additional soap for small children were reduced. Jews' personal identification documents and ration cards were marked with a *J*. Surprisingly, the forced addition of the names "Israel" and "Sara" required in the Reich never occurred here.

Starting with the 1939–40 school year, all Jewish children were excluded from German-language public and private schools; in 1940–41, this was also the case for all Czech schools. Finally, on July 24, 1942, the "Central Office" decreed: "All Jewish schools are to be closed, with immediate effect. All schooling of Jewish children, including in private, is forbidden. Violations will be dealt with by the police. First degree Jewish *Mischlinge* are to be excluded from public schools" (218). In March 1941, all private "retraining courses" had to end; later, the JKG was also prohibited from holding them. In the same year, public religious services were forbidden. Curiously, it should be mentioned that Jewish music – orchestrions and barrel organs were not forgotten – was not forbidden until September 1941. Even months after the occupation, the Czech national theater performed *Tales of Hoffmann*. In January 1942, the sale of Czech, and soon after German, newspapers to Jews was forbidden. Neither "*Mischlinge*" nor even their "Aryan" sublettors could subscribe to newspapers.

Soon after the creation of the "Central Office," the JKG became its executive body. Even the personally unobjectionable views of some of its members could not prevent its being seen by the Jews as an office of the German police, and feared nearly as much. This is illustrated by a "joke" making the rounds at the time: "In the middle of the night, the bell begins to peal at the Kohns: 'Gestapo, open up immediately!' The occupants breathe a sigh of relief and say, 'Thank God, we thought it was the Community!'" This was, of course, exaggerated, but it characterized the situation. Soon the JKG had to get involved in everything; every step a Jew took had to go through the JKG, for better or worse. On March 15, 1940, all "non-Mosaic" Jews were required to register with the JKG. Provincial communities were now answerable to it; this was effected by means of a "decision-making authority" (*Weisungsrecht*) issued by the "Central Office": "On the basis of this authority, we call attention to the fact that all decrees and instructions issued by the Jewish Community in Prague for the individual communities are to be followed by all members of the communities as soon as they have been announced by the responsible community (218)." On March 27, 1942, after the deportations had begun, the provincial communities were dissolved and continued operating, where necessary, as "branch offices" of the Prague JKG. Their property was "transferred to the emigration fund."

The ouster of Jews from public life and the difficult work of liquidation that arose from this process were largely transferred to the JKG by the "Central Office," and the JKG soon became a massive operation. Many Jews believed a position in the JKG offered "security," which led to especially unfortunate results once the deportations began. The JKG housing office and, before long, its labor office in particular were feared and hated. Jewish laborers were grouped together and sent to factories or assigned to carry out earthworks – for example, road building, railroad construction, coal mining, and clay works. The men were examined for fitness for physical labor and were divided into categories, which would retain their importance later in Theresienstadt. In 1940, the "Linden Retraining Camp" (Lipa) was opened on a confiscated Jewish estate in southeastern Bohemia. Young Jews had to work there for

The Jews in the "Protectorate," 1939–1941

several months, at first under tolerable conditions. Later, the length of the stay became unlimited, and the camp did not much differ from a concentration camp. In 1943 and 1945, the inmates were deported to Theresienstadt.

The threat of the Gestapo explicitly stood behind every single request the JKG made of a Jew. The JKG had to carry out a series of "special operations." On Yom Kippur 1939, all radios had to be surrendered within a few hours (see 233a). Toward the end of 1941, a series of forcible confiscations ensued: furs, woolens (except for the most urgently needed garments), musical instruments, gramophones, records, optical instruments, measuring instruments, film and photographic equipment, type-writers and sewing machines, bicycles, skis, and so on, and later even pets (dogs, cats, and canaries) were taken away.

Life became more and more difficult. House-to-house searches could happen every hour, and Jews feared the loss of apartments, raids, and conscious or unconscious violations of the thicket of prohibitions and regulations, which could lead to black-mail and reports to the police. There was hardly a Jew who did not violate a rule here or there – it was impossible not to. Individual behavior differed depending on character and situation, including careful efforts to obey all the rules, foolish or carefully considered breaches, intelligence, cleverness, and also foolhardiness. Things generally went badly for those who were caught; often it meant death in a concen-tration camp. People were arrested on the most flimsy pretexts. This was much worse in Brünn [Brno]* and the provinces than in Prague. In Pilsen, for example, respected Jews were arrested as hostages at the outbreak of the war and were sent to Buchenwald. A concentration camp was set up in Svatobořice in 1942 for relatives of Czechs and Czech Jews who were active among political émigrés or fighting in military organizations. Jews were relieved to be sent from there to Theresienstadt. During the snowy winters of the first two years of the war, Jews were assigned snow-clearing tasks; in Prague this went off without serious consequences, but it was worse in the provinces. In some towns, local German authorities or Czech fascists made Jews' lives hell; examples include Roudnice and Klattau, where they were not allowed on the sidewalks. Attacks were rare and were carried out only by the Hitler Youth (in Brünn [Brno] and Ostrau [Ostrava]) or the Czech Nazi group "Vlajka," without the support of the population. Thus they did not succeed in mobilizing Czech "popular wrath," although in newspapers, books, and a servile press that promoted the most vile hatred of Jews, traitors displayed a level of rabble-rousing propaganda that outdid even the *Stürmer* in offensiveness and stupidity. In some places, synagogues and cemeteries were damaged or destroyed.

The situation became unbearable once Heydrich took office as deputy "Reichsprotektor." He imposed martial law, and soon many Jews, along with Czechs, were being executed for minor infractions. In Brünn [Brno], executions became almost a public spectacle. Even youngsters were killed for not wearing the yellow star. This was the period of "registration" of all Jews, in direct preparation for the deportations. Soon after, following the first deportations, "property declar-ations" were also required; these went into almost unbelievable detail.

---

* H. G. Adler is not always consistent in his use of Czech or German for place names. In the interests of clarity, we have kept the German names and added the Czech names in square brackets. Translator's note.

Jewish adaptability proved extraordinary. It is true that some people's morale and attitude suffered or were even destroyed, but many people constantly displayed humor, even if it was gallows humor, and indulged in optimistic dreams. At the same time, they attempted to meet their supposed needs by learning various skills. Very few expected a long war, and almost all believed Germany would be defeated. This mood was nourished by the Czechs' boundless optimism. Few were skeptical or even pessimistic, and suicides were rare. Many exploited the narrow limits of the freedom that remained, as far as this was still possible, and were not afraid to violate the law. Czech and German friends often remained loyal until the last moment and maintained this loyalty until liberation or even after the destruction of the Jews, as evidenced by the fact that many safeguarded Jews' property, provided support in the form of packages, and welcomed returnees. But disloyalty and misdeeds also spread; bad experiences unfortunately outweighed good ones. Christian friends seldom displayed great courage, and almost none dared to hide Jews until the end of the war. A total of 424 Jews are believed to have survived "underground" in Bohemia and Moravia until the liberation. In none of the countries occupied by Hitler, not even in Germany itself, were "illegal" rescues of Jews as rare as in the territory of the "Protectorate." And often the help of so-called friends came at a very high price.

Many Jews became pleasure-seeking and played cards all day, for example, for lack of any other enjoyment or occupation. Others turned to serious study, read avidly, and achieved a level of mental concentration that they could not have mustered in normal times. Many were in great need and were forced to sell illegally what little they had. No public cultural life, on the order of the "Jewish Cultural Association" (*Jüdischer Kulturbund*) in Germany, was permitted. People kept a low profile and came together in small groups, in which they often played music. Some worked illegally in order to earn at least a little money. The deportations, about which one heard from Germany and Vienna, drew ever more threateningly near. Little information trickled through about what was happening to the Jews in Poland or other conquered countries. Many people were preoccupied with thoughts of relatives and friends in other countries. A dull weight lay on each day and the feared morrow. Everyone felt that things could not go on like this; people suspected what was coming: the transport. With a bleak sense of expectancy, they felt themselves at the mercy of its horrors.

2

Theresienstadt

History and Establishment

For the National Socialists, the "solution to the Jewish question" meant the systematic extermination of the Jewish people. This "solution" could be carried out, despite all external and internal obstacles, only as a result of the outbreak of war. It became an ever more important – and, ultimately, at least in Hitler's practical sense, almost the exclusive – goal of the war; through Hitler's testament, it even became a pseudo-eschatological task for all time. This was why the extermination was also called "the Final Solution." Before the war, the "legal" groundwork for this solution was first laid by the Reich Citizenship Law and its ten supplemental decrees, and Hitler's Germany had to be satisfied, as the *Völkischer Beobachter* opined on July 7, 1939, with seeing the "main issue" as "that we will soon be rid of them, soon and completely." By September 1, 1939, Hitler was already using much clearer language in the Reichstag, and he repeated his threat on January 30, 1941. The Jews, he said, "may still be laughing today, just as they used to laugh at my prophecies. The coming months and years will prove that my prophecies were correct here too" (103, vol. II, p. 222). The fact that they did not entirely succeed in accomplishing this goal was due to their fear of world opinion, a fear that never faded, and to the extremism of this "solution," which encountered resistance even in Germany, as the events of November 1938 had shown (see also 125). Further reasons included disagreement among officials, such that implementation of the radical plans was delayed and only gradually accepted, and, finally, the tactics and the corruption of the SS, which made possible the rescue of some Jewish prisoners toward the end of the war. The Theresienstadt "Ghetto" and its history were determined by the special interests of the SS.

The confinement and deportation of Jews began in all the occupied countries following the defeat of Poland. An order by Himmler on October 8, 1939, indicates that the Jews in the "Protectorate" were to be deported to the area between the Bug and the Vistula, but at first what happened did not follow any unified plan. Nevertheless, in the same month, the first confused measures to create a Jewish "settlement district" in the Lublin area were already being taken. Male Jews between the ages of sixteen and seventy from the Moravian districts of Ostrau [Ostrava] and Frdek-Mistek [Frýdek-Místek] were registered, and a total of 1,291 people who were unable to save themselves through skill or patronage were sent "voluntarily" on October 17 and 26 to the "reeducation camp" at Nisko on the San, where they joined

Jews from Vienna, Bielitz [Bielsko], and Katowice. Furthermore, transports from Vienna had to be conducted to other places in the "settlement area," at the expense of the JKG. The future Jewish Elders Jakob Edelstein and Benjamin Murmelstein were among those who spent some time in Nisko. The camp did not exist for long; many people died or escaped across the San to Russia, and 123 of the escapees returned to Czechoslovakia with the Red Army. In April 1940, the camp was closed down, and the survivors, including 460 people from Moravia, were sent home (see 77a, 78a, 94, 175b, 194, 350). Remarkably, the miserable hovels in Nisko were later used as a collection camp for Volhynian Germans being brought into the Reich. At this point a period of calm began in the "Protectorate," apart from expulsions from some rural communities, generally to Prague (starting in August 1939). The reason for this was a surprising order, by Göring on March 23, 1940, that stopped all deportations from the Reich territory. Shortly before this, approximately another 1,000 Jews from Stettin (see 1, 185a) and Western Pomerania (February 22) and 160 from Schneidemühl had been deported to Poland.

Before the systematic expulsion of the Jews began, there were another two deportations from Central Europe. On October 22, 1940, the "Bürckel Operation" was carried out, involving 6,504 Jews from Baden and the Palatinate and some 1,000 from Alsace-Lorraine. It is striking and unique that these transports were taken across the western border of the Reich to the camps at Les Milles, Gurs, and Rivesaltes in unoccupied France. Few people were able to save themselves, and many died; the survivors ended up in Auschwitz by November 1942 (see 339). After February 1941, five transports from Vienna, with 5,000 victims, were sent randomly to the Polish "settlement area" (see 175b). Due to the resistance of the local civil authorities, only one of these transports reached its original planned destination. It was already becoming clear that the "settlement district" was an illusion, something of which "Generalgouvernour" Frank made sure by constantly resisting taking in Jews from the West, although not out of human kindness.

The outbreak of war with Russia brought the long-nourished plans out of their quasi-experimental preparatory period to fruition, and when the United States entered the war, almost all inhibitions disappeared. As early as March 1941, Hitler is believed to have ordered that, in case of war with Russia, Jews, Gypsies, Soviet commissars, and "asocials" were to be exterminated. The following instruction from Göring to Heydrich was contained in a letter dated July 31, 1941:

> Amending the assignment conferred upon you by the decree of 24 January 1939, of finding as convenient a solution as possible to the Jewish question, given the time constraints, in the form of emigration or evacuation, I hereby authorize you to take all necessary preparatory measures, from an organizational, concrete and material point of view, for a total solution of the Jewish question in the German sphere of influence in Europe.
>
> Where this would affect the jurisdiction of other central offices, they are to participate.
> (123, 710-PS)

Only then could transports begin from the entire territory of the Reich, including the "Protectorate," followed in 1942 by transports from France and the other occupied countries. This process was initiated in the Reich territory in September 1941 by marking people with the "Jewish star" (the Western countries followed suit in 1942; the practice had already been generally introduced in Poland on November 23, 1939).

The commander of the Order Constabulary, Kurt Daluege, signed the first general deportation order on October 14, 1941; another followed ten days later (see 46ax). The first order was supposed to refer to a destination across the Polish border, but because the Wehrmacht caused difficulties, this group was routed only to Łódź, to which 19,837 Jews were deported between October 16 and November 4 from Prague, Vienna, Berlin, Cologne, Frankfurt, Hamburg, Düsseldorf, and Luxembourg (see 24). The second order was supposed to involve 50,000 victims, whose destinations were to be Minsk, Riga, and Kovno, but only around 30,000 went this route in the period between mid-November 1941 and the end of January 1942; of these, 6,000–7,000 – rather than 25,000, as planned – went to Minsk. At the same time, the extermination camps, meant for mass murder, were already nearing completion; of these, Chelmno [Chełmno] (see 14) was the first to go into operation, on December 8, 1941, and a month later, it had already consumed Jews from Central Europe. Such camps – which were sometimes connected with work camps, for which a small fraction of the arrivals were chosen – were the main destination of Jewish transports from the West after July 1942. But first, there was a pause in the deportations around mid-January 1942, and afterward, from March to June 1942, many thousands followed the fateful path to extermination one last time through Poland's overcrowded ghettos and transit camps, especially in the Lublin region.

For the sake of an overview, the preceding discussion moved ahead in the time line; we now turn again to the situation in the Bohemian lands. In late summer 1941, everyone felt that the situation was hopeless, and all were seized by panic. Desperate cries for help in letters from Viennese Jews in Poland reached relatives in Bohemia. From then on, "transport" remained the most terrifying word for every Jew. The majority clung to the blind hope that the "Protectorate" would be spared because it was "technically impossible to deport everyone." Thus, many people in Pilsen, the first provincial city to be "cleansed" of Jews, believed that the city's turn would not come so soon, even as its fate was already determined and deportations from Prague and Brünn [Brno] were already going ahead at full speed. The JKG was aware of the impending measures in summer 1941, yet it was silenced not only by a strict injunction but also apparently by the desire to keep this a secret, for it feared panic and illconsidered acts by individuals and worried about catastrophic consequences for its functionaries if they divulged it.

It is not known who first came up with the idea of building a Jewish camp in the "Protectorate." What is certain is that the JKG did everything to promote the idea to Günther, the head of the "Central Office," and his staff. It was suggested to them that they might become superfluous if all Jews were deported, whereas they would still maintain authority if there were camps in the country. At the behest of the SS, various locations – for example, a particularly bad quarter of the city of Tabor – were visited to find a suitable place to concentrate the Czech Jews. The men of the JKG told themselves that anything was better than deportation to Poland, and, like the "Reich Association" in Berlin, they hoped at least to delay the deportations. The course of events would disappoint these hopes.

From the beginning, there were only two possibilities: (1) They might have decided in March 1939, even at the cost of their lives, to dissolve all Jewish communities and institutions and destroy all records and documents. (2) They would have to follow policies aimed at delaying the worst and cleverly negotiating and easing the situation. This second path was followed to the bitter end, with ever more terrible

16 *History*

entanglements, and it led to failure (see 25). The men responsible should not be blindly condemned for this. Many displayed goodwill and self-sacrifice, but almost all of them had many weaknesses, such that they were often in an inferior position to the SS, even in areas in which correct assessment of the enemy, intelligence, greater prudence and foresight, and sometimes also greater courage could have achieved more, at least for the moment. The tragic dilemma that prevailed here was recognized by Reszö Kasztner, who was granted an unusual role in the Jewish resistance to the SS:

> If it [the Jewish Council] functions, if it is compliant, it may accelerate the process of liquidation. If it refuses obedience, it provokes sanctions against the community, without the certainty of having thus stopped the liquidation process....
>
> Almost everywhere in Europe, the Jewish Councils took the same path. They were gradually made compliant. At first, harmless things were demanded of them. Assets, property, housing: replaceable goods. Later this was followed by people's personal freedom, and finally, naked existence itself, for which it was up to the Jewish Council to determine the order: who goes sooner, who later? ... It was a slippery slope that almost inevitably led into the abyss. Everywhere, the Jewish Councils faced the same problem: Should I ... be the traitor, in order to be able to be the helper or even rescuer here and there, or should I abandon the community and deliver it into the hands of others? Is flight from responsibility not also something like betrayal? And if I take it on, where is the line at which I must stop? In order, at the cost of self-destruction, suicide or execution ... to finally be rid of an unbearable responsibility? The line ... between self-sacrifice and betrayal is almost impossible to draw with human faculties. To judge the Jewish Councils in retrospect ... exceeds in difficulty pretty much anything that earthly justice has ever had to accomplish.
>
> The dilemma of the Jewish Councils is ... not merely a typically Jewish phenomenon. In the moral decay of the years of war and occupation, the European nations offered even worse examples of self-forgetfulness. Few remained firm at moments when the psychological pressures exceeded the tension that people can normally bear. Yet a comparison between the Jewish Councils and the usual Quislings ... would be completely out of place. No other community had to bear the nightmare of *total physical annihilation*.... If anything about it can be considered specifically Jewish, it was precisely the high expectations that the Jewish community believed it could place on every one of its sons, even in moments of greatest danger and the most desperate decisions. (135, p. 67 et seq.)

Standing firm was, however, very difficult in Prague, as the case of the head of the JKG "Transport Department," Dr. Hanuš Bonn, and his colleague Dr. Emil Kafka attests. In the early days of the deportations, both declared, "It won't go so quickly"; Günther's deputy Karl Rahm had them arrested for "sabotage" and sent to Mauthausen, where they died within two weeks. Then it did, in fact, go quickly. We also cannot ignore the fact that bad people offer themselves up for bad things. If they are not originally bad, they become bad as a result of circumstances. Therefore, most of the functionaries of the "Transport Department," and some others in the JKG, were a disreputable lot who wished to profit from the misfortunes of their neighbors; while they clung to their posts as "indispensable" people, they helped to deport all other Jews (see 78a, 214, 215). The SS sought everywhere to use such individuals as a base, and Heydrich – the "non-Aryan" – is considered the inventor of this method of exterminating Jews through their community leaders. The majority of the better representatives of the JKG who were involved in establishing the Theresienstadt camp went there willingly.

Theresienstadt: History and Establishment

In the midst of preparations for a Jewish camp in the territory came the order to send five transports, each consisting of 1,000 people, from Prague to Łódź (see 53, 175) and one from Brünn [Brno] to Minsk. They left at intervals of a few days starting on October 16, 1941. Of the Łódź group, many died on the spot; a considerable number were killed in Chelmno [Chełmno] in 1942; some languished until October 1943 in the work camp established in Posen [Poznan] (see 242); and others remained in Łódź until the ghetto was dissolved in late summer 1944, when they were sent to Auschwitz. Two hundred and fifty-three survivors came forward after the war. Eleven people returned from Minsk – where the ghetto was dissolved on May 8, 1943 – after perilous adventures.

In summer 1941, a Department G (for Ghetto) was established in the JKG; it engaged itself with planning a Jewish camp in the territory and thus soon devised the plan for Theresienstadt. The background of the establishment of this "ghetto" was, at first, and also later, largely hidden from the Jews involved. Edelstein, as he himself expressed it there, wished to justify and retain Theresienstadt as a refuge for 20,000 younger Jews from within the country. Heydrich's plans, however, were very different, as we now know from the document "Notes from the October 10, 1941, Meeting on the Solution of Jewish Questions." Because this document is important in equal measure for the history of Theresienstadt and for the "solution of the Jewish question" within the entire Reich territory, we are publishing the entire text for the first time in the Sources and Literature section (see 46b). Theresienstadt was selected to be a collection point, at first for Bohemian and later also for Moravian Jews, but at the same time a transit point "to the Eastern Territories," which Edelstein did not know about. He was certainly not told that, because of high-level intervention on behalf of certain Jews immediately after the start of the deportations from Germany, Theresienstadt was being used to achieve very different aims, which over time were adapted to many practical exigencies. As we will soon discover from the infamous protocols of the Wannsee Conference, Theresienstadt offered the opportunity – in Eichmann's words – to "save face towards the outside world" (see 3b, document [doc.] 1). The highest-level party functionaries thus had special, if oft-changing, plans for Theresienstadt from the very beginning. The unique role of this camp continued to have an effect even in the defense of Joachim von Ribbentrop by his lawyer, Dr. Martin Horn, before the Nuremberg Tribunal and is also reflected in Himmler's negotiations on April 20, 1945, with Norbert Masur of Stockholm, certainly the only discussion between the Reichsführer-SS and a free Jew:

> Himmler emphasized that Theresienstadt was not a camp in the actual sense of the word, but a city peopled by Jews, that it was administered by them and that they did all the work there. "This type of camp was created by me and my friend Heydrich," he said, "and we would have liked all camps to be like this."

External reasons for this choice of location included the presence of the fortress, which made it easy to guard; its geographically central location and favorable transport connections; and, finally, the fact that little consideration needed to be taken of the Czech residents when evacuating the city. The internal reasons become clear if one keeps in mind that a location was needed to which one could bring Jews with far-flung connections or an international name, where they would not immediately "disappear," at least at first, but would remain reachable and, if necessary, could also be produced. Because this involved people who were not suited to "Jewish

History

work deployment" as the SS imagined it, they could make Edelstein and the Bohemian Jews believe that they had "their" own camp, while gaining indispensable labor, and everyone else could be sent to the East just as easily from there as from their homes.

Hitler was the driving demon behind the extermination of the Jews; he repeatedly ordered it – on November 11, 1941, for example – for Himmler knew on that day that there would be "much suffering among the Jews." Himmler and his colleagues saw to its implementation. After repeated postponements, Heydrich called a meeting in a villa on the Wannsee on January 20, 1942, on the "Final Solution to the Jewish Question." Among the sixteen participants were Müller and Eichmann (see 106d, 106e). According to the protocol, Heydrich declared:

> In the meantime the Reichsführer-SS ... had prohibited emigration of Jews due to the dangers of an emigration in wartime and due to the possibilities of the East.
>
> Another possible solution of the problem has now taken the place of emigration, i.e., the evacuation of the Jews to the East, provided that the Führer gives the appropriate approval in advance.
>
> These actions are, however, only to be considered provisional, but practical experience is already being collected which is of the greatest importance in relation to the future Final Solution of the Jewish Question.
>
> Approximately 11 million Jews will be involved in the Final Solution of the European Jewish Question. [There follows a list of the Jews of *all* European countries!]
>
> ... Under proper guidance, in the course of the Final Solution the Jews are to be allocated for appropriate labor in the East. Able-bodied Jews, separated according to sex, will be taken in large work columns to these areas for work on roads, in the course of which action doubtless a large portion will be eliminated by natural causes.
>
> The possible final remnant will, since it will undoubtedly consist of the most resistant portion, have to be treated accordingly, because it is the product of natural selection and would, if released, act as a the seed of a new Jewish revival (see the experience of history.)
>
> In the course of the practical execution of the Final Solution, Europe will be combed through from west to east. Germany proper, including the Protectorate of Bohemia and Moravia, will have to be handled first due to the housing problem and additional social and political necessities.
>
> The evacuated Jews will first be sent, group by group, to so-called transit ghettos, from which they will be transported to the East....
>
> ... It is not intended to evacuate Jews over 65 years old, but to send them to an old-age ghetto – Theresienstadt is being considered for this purpose.
>
> In addition to these age groups – of the approximately 280,000 Jews in Germany proper and Austria on 31 October 1941, approximately 30% are over 65 years old – severely wounded veterans and Jews with war decorations (Iron Cross, First Class) will be accepted in the old-age ghettos. With this expedient solution, in one fell swoop many interventions will be prevented.
>
> ... [Persons of mixed blood of the first degree would be sterilized or evacuated; they are to be treated like Jews, while people of mixed blood of the second degree are to be treated essentially as Aryans. For Jewish-German mixed marriages, it must be decided whether the Jew is to be evacuated or] whether, with regard to the effects of such a step on the German relatives, [this mixed marriage] should be sent to an old-age ghetto. [This essentially applied also to childless marriages between people of mixed blood of the first degree and Germans, and also to such marriages with children, if the people of mixed blood and their children counted as Jews. Partners in marriages between people of

mixed blood and Jews or between people of mixed blood of the first or second degree were to be evacuated or sent to an old-age ghetto.] ...

[Heydrich indicated that Jews in work deployment who had not yet been replaced] would not be evacuated according to the rules [he] had approved for carrying out the evacuations then underway.

... In conclusion, the different types of possible solutions were discussed, during which discussion both Gauleiter Dr. [Alfred] Meyer and State Secretary Dr. [Josef] Bühler took the position that certain preparatory activities for the Final Solution should be carried out immediately in the territories in question, in which process alarming the populace must be avoided. (117, 213a)

This protocol is the key to understanding official policy on the Jews, from autumn 1941 until well into 1944 (see 125, 188) and, in the case of some measures, even into the final months of the war; for this reason, we must briefly consider this document in comparison with the situation that was created.

Emigration was prohibited for Jews within Hitler's immediate sphere of power, but it was also almost impossible, practically speaking. All reachable areas were "evacuated," systematically and to the broadest possible extent, from 1941 until the final weeks of the war. The use of the phrase "provisional measures" for the measures being initiated expresses the fact that the daily achievements of the execution machinery, including burying or destroying the corpses in the extermination camps, which were generally not yet established, lagged in comparison with the extent and tempo of the deportations. The Jews were therefore "sent to transit ghettos"; this stopped in June 1942, once the extermination camps began to satisfy the demands of mass murder. That was the meaning of the note at the end of the protocol that encouraged "certain preparatory activities for the Final Solution ... in the territories in question." What is said about the surviving "remnant" of Jewish workers shows the desire for absolute annihilation and also explains their pitiless treatment in the concentration camps. Jews in the armaments industry mainly worked in Berlin. In response to requests, Heydrich had at first to agree to spare them; thus they remained until February 27, 1943, when they, too, were deported: the majority went to Auschwitz, and the rest to Theresienstadt (see 190a). The urgent implementation of the deportations from the Reich territory brings to the fore the motive of pure theft for the sake of German beneficiaries, in sociopolitical disguise. The motive for preferring deportation to Theresienstadt, aside from which no other "old-age ghetto" was established, ultimately revealed itself with shameless clarity. Time spent in this camp was not called "evacuation" (see 3b, doc. 5), which indicates that Heydrich already saw this expression to mean gradual physical extermination; in contrast, the word "transfer" (*Überstellung*) – a typical Nazi word – was chosen for the "old-age ghetto," which suggested a permanent arrest-like imprisonment, without forcibly expedited extermination. It is noteworthy that almost another five months passed from the day of the conference until the start of the deportations of the intended groups from Germany and Austria. The reason for this delay, however, is devoid of human emotion, for nothing was done in Theresienstadt, in the meantime, for the reception of old people and cripples; however, the expatriation of the Czechs from the city was completed only in late 1942. Nevertheless, the preferred groups listed in the protocol were ultimately brought to Theresienstadt (see Chapter 3), but in the case of the "mixed marriages" and "persons of mixed blood," greater difficulties seemed to arise than had been expected, such that very few of the latter were sent, and, of the former, the Jewish partners were generally not sent until January 1943.

Theresienstadt's role, developed at Wannsee on January 20, 1942 (see 3b, 124, 160), probably was definitively determined days earlier, when Eichmann visited the "ghetto," which had then existed for only eight weeks. This is not a daring conjecture if one considers the first three points on the "orders of the day" for prisoners on January 19, 1942:

1) Inspection
On the morning of 19 January 1942, the ghetto was inspected by SS-Obersturmbannführer Eichmann, accompanied by SS-Sturmbannführer Stingel, camp commandant Obersturmbannführer Dr. Seidl, and camp inspector SS-Untersturmführer Bergel. During the inspection, there was no cause for complaint.

2) Bedsteads
SS-Obersturmbannführer Eichmann viewed the rooms with bunk beds in the Sudeten Kaserne [barracks] and approved the type with bunk beds in groups of four, which were ready to be installed in rooms 68, 69, 70a, 70b, and 70c. To effectuate an acceleration of the building of bunk beds, double-shift work will begin as quickly as possible according to orders.

3) Postal service
At the request of the Jewish Elder, SS-Obersturmbannführer Eichmann permitted the submission of a petition asking for an easing of the mail ban. The camp commandant will inform the Council of Elders when and to what extent an easing of the mail ban will occur. (301)

Edelstein unsuspectingly worked to ensure a tolerable refuge for the Bohemian and Moravian Jews and sought to influence the lords and masters in this direction, but their plans had long since thwarted and transcended the well-meaning intentions of the powerless Jew (see 111). It is only this realization that makes clear the full tragedy reflected by the previous autumn's efforts, which is described in the following paragraphs.

We now consider the "file notes" or petitions from the JKG to the "Central Office" in the period from October to early December 1941 on the history of the "ghetto" in Theresienstadt. There already prevailed a practice that could be observed continually in Theresienstadt until the end of the war: the SS, as the Jews' sole German negotiating partner, never gave an order or piece of news in writing but instead ordered the Jewish offices, or left it to them, to put each transaction into written form. The significance and consequences of this would become clear later, when everything that occurred in Theresienstadt was to appear to be an autonomous act of "self-administration." The "Memo on Proper Quartering ... in Barracks," from October 9, 1941, stated:

For the roughly 88,000 Jews living in the Protectorate, there are neither completed settlement possibilities nor other adaptable facilities that would be able to take in such a number of people. However, if there were instructions to implement this task, we would face the resolution of the following alternatives:

a)   a collection camp for all Jews, or
b)   several barracks for 10,000 to 15,000 Jews each. (310)

Later on in this document's text, it points out the costs and difficulties and – in a small attempt to preserve something – states:

> Recently, it has become possible [through forced labor] to use a relatively large amount of Jewish labor in economically profitable fashion....
>
> In regard to sanitation, rapidly-built barracks camps are inferior even to primitive accommodations in towns. The danger that epidemics could emerge and quickly spread is especially great in such camps.

The plan for such a camp was made. It was decided to use one or more locations. An undated "memo" titled "Jewish City" is noteworthy:

> The concentration of all Jews in the Protectorate ... in one city has proven unfeasible if only one location with a population of 5,000 to 6,000 is considered. Four or five centers must be created in order to be able to solve the entire problem practically. Such Jewish cities must be located near towns in which greater labor possibilities are available. [A commission should be set up to study this problem.] In the Jewish city mentioned, there will probably not be enough opportunities for work and income, so that workplaces will have to be sought outside the Jewish city as well. Therefore, provisions will have to be made to permit the Jews to leave the Jewish city for purposes of taking up work. (310)

The SS could not comply with this, as a similar development phase in Poland had shown. They wished to strictly isolate the Jews as the preliminary phase of extermination. The "memo" continued: "It will be most important to maintain contact offices of the Jewish communities in the cities of Prague and Brünn [Brno], in order ... especially to receive the instructions of superior authorities; these contact offices would also be important in acquiring material, etc." A "contact office" – "Department G," really – was maintained in Prague; it was possible to communicate with it from Theresienstadt only through the SS. Only once were two high-level functionaries, Karl Schliesser and the engineer Max Sever, allowed to go to Prague to make purchases, accompanied by gendarmes; there they accidentally encountered Dr. František Weidmann, the head of the JKG, at the "Central Office." A conversation was immediately prevented, and a strict order was given that no one else could go to Prague. The "memo" cited suggested that the Jews be concentrated in one suburb of Prague, one of Brünn [Brno], and another of Ostrau [Ostrava]: "This procedure would be much simpler, because a range of technical and economic problems would be eliminated; the transport problem especially would be simplified ... also the deployment of Jewish labor ... would be easier to implement." This was not an option for the SS.

At this point the plans concentrated on small cities. A request by Günther is found in a "confidential memorandum" of October 11, 1941:

> It will be determined whether there is a place in Moravia occupied by a disproportionate number of Jews.
>
> A report should be drawn up on the possibility of combining Jews in one or more cities in Bohemia and Moravia. Places to be considered are those with a population of 5,000 to 6,000. All legal issues, internal matters, organizational questions, etc., shall be very carefully examined. Such a settlement would be divided into a supply and a work division. The completed products would be exchanged for goods. Of course, areas with buildings with first-class residential decor are not to be considered. (310)

The JKG then submitted the following elaboration: "It was first and foremost necessary to find a suitable location. Only statistical manuals with outdated figures were available, geography textbooks, firm indexes, telephone books and other incomplete tools. Considering that questions were impossible and information could not be obtained, the report cannot be complete" (310). A number of Bohemian sites were described as unsuitable, with brief explanations – for example, "Tschaslau [Čáslav]: too large, too pretty." Only three Bohemian and two Moravian sites were suggested; these did not include Theresienstadt, which was not mentioned at all.

The attached "organizational plan" provided for the following departments: administration (the Council of Elders), internal administration (which included the "internal administrative" [*innere Administrative*], population, administration of justice [including "local police"], and transport administration [including post] divisions), finance administration, economy, technical management, social welfare (including old-age homes, homes for the infirm and children, soup kitchens, and clothing storage), schools (kindergartens, trade courses, etc.), and "health services." The later-implemented structure of the administration can be seen even in the naming, which is only understandable in light of its Prague history (see especially Chapter 8, but also Chapters 4 and 7).

The "implementation plan" required relatively careful preparation and was summarized in five main points: "Determination of the site of settlement by the authorities, on-site viewing and examination to determine local conditions, technical planning, obtaining materials, and gradual evacuation and settlement of the site." Solid preparation was the last thing with which an SS establishment would have been blessed. There was only one kind of preparation: precipitously sending people to a place and then having them build a camp with the most meager of materials, if any.

There are three versions of JKG information on Theresienstadt for the "Central Office." Versions 1 and 2 are almost entirely in agreement; version 3 is from October 19, 1941. At the time, the SS had already made its choice. There is no doubt – and this is reflected in the text of the Jewish documents – that the SS had chosen Theresienstadt, as there could not have been a site better suited to its intentions. The dilettantish information on the city and the planning of the camp came from JKG functionaries. According to version 2,

Theresienstadt:
 According to the 1930 census, 7,181 people lived in Theresienstadt, 673 of them German, in 219 buildings, on an area of 411 hectares.

The number of buildings is very small, as is the area. As evidence, for example, the village of Soubenitz [Souběnice] in the same district has 327 residents, on a land-use area of 449 hectares.

 The city of Leitmeritz [Litoměřice], in the immediate neighborhood, has 1,465 buildings on 1,456 hectares with a population of 18,500. Thus in Leitmeritz [Litoměřice] there are 12.6 residents per building ... while in Theresienstadt there are 32.5 residents per building. The notably small number of buildings ... can be explained by the fact that a large number of the residents were soldiers who were quartered in a small number of large buildings. The population density of such military quarters cannot be increased in the same way as in normal buildings, as the living space appears already to be heavily utilized.

 If one were to begin settling only 50,000 people in the built-up part of the center of the city, one would arrive at ... an average of 250 people per building....

 It should additionally be pointed out that in the surrounding area ... there is no possibility of usefully employing large masses of Jews. The need for artisans is also extremely limited. (310)

The conditions of the area were especially unsuited to dealing with an artificially forced problem – enough reason for the SS to choose just this site; their convenience was served by the fact that the city was so easy to shut off from the outside world. The possibility of sensible design did not interest the SS. The SS had very little interest in the productive exploitation of the Jews, on which the Jewish functionaries, misunderstanding the mentality, had always based their hopes.

A good description of the site is provided in version 3:

> Only a few Jewish women, married to Aryans, still live in Theresienstadt. Thus it was not possible to investigate on-site [the JKG was supposed to conduct inquiries, but they could only question Jews and not "Aryans"]. In order to preserve the confidentiality of the matter, only a few specifics could be determined in Raudnitz [Roudnice nad Labem]; they are repeated in the following, with corresponding reservations:
>
> Theresienstadt is not directly accessible by train; the Bauschowitz [Bohušovice] train station, on the Prague-Aussig [Ústí nad Laben] line, is some 3 kilometers from the city. On the Prague-Tetschen [Děčín] line, the nearest place is the city of Leitmeritz [Litoměřice], which is already located outside the Protectorate area.
>
> The city itself it situated near where the Ohře flows into the Elbe. Part of the front of the fortress lies within the flood plain of the Ohře River (the straightening of the Ohře River has not yet been completed), namely the so-called Small Fortress.
>
> The Leitmeritz [Litoměřice]-Prague road leads directly past the city. [It goes through it. Other than a road to Bohušovice (Bauschowitz) and two secondary roads that join with the main road mentioned, it is the only connection between the fortress, surrounded by ramparts and moats, and the outside world.]
>
> Only the area surrounded by the former fortress ramparts belongs to the city, along with a part of the glacis between the city and the road from Leitmeritz [Litoměřice] to [Bohušovice]. On this part there is a military hospital ["reserve hospital"] and a former gymnasium. The city also has an electrical plant [actually a transfer station from the Türmitz (Trmice) transmission center near Aussig (Ústí nad Laben)] and a water main, but both are probably relatively small. There is not yet a gas facility.
>
> Within the fortress ramparts, three rows of housing blocks are grouped around a central main square. The small number of 219 houses mentioned in the 1935 statistics is probably correct. On the main square are a hotel, the city bank, a post office, the church, a barracks and private houses [as well as the city hall and two buildings used by the military command]. The buildings are all older and apparently often consist of former military buildings that have been adapted for private purposes.
>
> A considerable portion of the rooms found in the city still serve military purposes. Aside from some large barracks, there are also military justice buildings, command posts, storehouses, etc.
>
> Under the fortress ramparts are mainly casemates, arched elongated shelters with walls several meters thick, incompletely illuminated and ventilated only by hatches cut into the thick walls. They are partly used today for commercial purposes. They apparently have not been used as military quarters for decades.
>
> Northeast of the city, or of the fortress itself, is the so-called Small Fortress on the Eger; this is an outer work whose ditches are constantly under water and cannot be kept dry, because they are in the flood plain. In the casemates of this outer work, which reach to the ground water and are thus always very damp, there once were prisons that were still known as particularly unhealthy in the time of the Austro-Hungarian state. Barracks are still apparently located in the area of the Small Fortress. (310)

They did not dare to say in this report, although the JKG as well as the "Central Office" knew it, that the "Small Fortress" was, by then, a concentration camp. It had been called a "police prison" since June 14, 1940, but it was definitely used by the SS as a concentration camp until the end of the war, although it was never connected with the "ghetto" either administratively or practically (see 40, 97, 162, 188, 232, 321a, 333). The report ends as follows:

> It should be noted that the groundwater table in the area of the fortress probably is relatively high. It cannot be determined whether the building within the fortress has a cellar or not. If that should be the case, the cellar probably will be damp and unable to be made deeper.
> In the area around Theresienstadt there is as good as no industry. The area is agriculturally cultivated, and there is some vegetable cultivation. A sugar factory is located in Bauschowitz [Bohušovice]. (310)

In order better to introduce the city, the following paragraphs add detail to this grim and daunting picture. Theresienstadt lies somewhat more than sixty kilometers north of Prague on a fertile and quite warm plain. The entire level area of the city and its closest surroundings are rather insalubrious. The landscape is replete with many fields, interspersed with meadows, gardens, fruit trees, and here and there forests of conifers. Some attractive elements include picturesque patches of trees and the many high poplars along the Elbe, which flows between the city and the "Small Fortress," and farther along the banks of the Elbe. To the north and northwest rise the volcanic domes of the Bohemian uplands, some of them only a few kilometers distant, right behind Leitmeritz [Litoměřice] on the other side of the Elbe and the Protectorate border at the time; one can walk to Leitmeritz [Litoměřice] from Theresienstadt in half an hour.

Theresienstadt was founded in the second half of the eighteenth century by Joseph II. He chose the name in honor of his mother, Maria Theresa; this monarch herself left bleak memories in the history of the Bohemian Jews. That the Prague Jews were too friendly to Friedrich II during the Second Silesian War served as an excuse for her expulsion order against the Bohemian Jews on December 18, 1744. Most of the fortress was finished in the year of the empress's death, 1780; two years later, it was declared a royal free city, and on September 22, 1784, it was declared a closed city. The fortress was never besieged, and after being ignored by the Prussians in 1866 (see 321a), it was abandoned in 1882, but Theresienstadt remained a small military city. Only around the end of 1941 and beginning of 1942 was the garrison slowly withdrawn in order to make room for the Jewish camp.

The star-shaped, twelve-pointed fortress (1,200 x 920 m in size) with six gates was erected by the hard labor of the population of the surrounding area, under the direction of Italian master builders, using the most modern ideas of the time. The small area designated for the city within the fortress was 700 m long and 500 m wide. Only a few newer buildings – the water tower, the gymnasium, the military hospital, and some civilian houses – most of which were not included in the camp, lie westward, outside the inner fortress rampart in the so-called Kreta as well as on the other bank of the Eger, near the "Small Fortress." The city is integrated into the area to such an extent that, either from nearby or from the mountains near Leitmeritz [Litoměřice], one cannot see more than the church tower, the water tower, and the chimneys of a small brewery, the only industrial facility in the town. As extended arched casemates, some barracks are attached to the inner fortress rampart, which is 8–12 m high and is planted with lawns and trees. These barracks, massive red brick

Theresienstadt: History and Establishment

structures, are hardly suitable as quarters, due to their darkness and cold damp. Only one (E 1) was remodeled and made livable after World War I. The other, equally primitive, generally two-story barracks were also built in the eighteenth century; they are handsome buildings in a late baroque style typical of Austrian military buildings, with open arcades and broad courtyards on the inside. Another barracks from an earlier period (E VI) is laid out differently, with an attractive front garden; it served as the division hospital. This is where Gavrilo Princip, the murderer of the heir to the throne, who was serving his sentence in the "Small Fortress," died of tuberculosis. Additional military buildings included an officers' casino (G II); two attractive Empire buildings on either side of the church, in which the division command and the military court were housed (E Vb and E Va); the armory (parts of H IV); the field bakery (A IV); military workshops in the "building yard" (H II); and storerooms. The private houses were generally uncomfortable and were more than 100 years old; most were one-story buildings, but some had two stories. They typically lacked any modern sanitary facilities. Attached to the houses were small or large badly kept yards, outbuildings, sheds, and occasionally a modest garden. Many houses had terraces and open galleries on the yard; especially during the camp period, their colorfulness evoked a poor Italian town.

The garrison provided the population with its main source of income. Aside from numerous inns, there were three larger hotels (Q 403, Q 416, and L 324). The best hotel, a modern structure (L 324), was furnished by the Jews during the camp period with every imaginable luxury; it served as an "SS *Kameradschafts* hostel," and as the residence of the camp leader and his closest staff members. Two cinemas (the gymnasium and L 514) provided entertainment. There were numerous stores, but crafts, agriculture, garden cultivation, and a small amount of grain trade also provided the city with a livelihood. Two buildings were schools (L 124 and L 417), and one was a poorhouse. Of the slightly more than 3,000 civilians, the average person lived in modest circumstances. The town's poverty persisted in the camp that was forced into this meager city. The streets, which crossed each other at right angles, were wide enough but were badly paved or merely rolled; thus dust swirled on dry days, and after rainfalls everything turned into a quagmire. Two large and two small parks, as well as several green spaces with groups of trees on the edges of town, provided a pleasant contrast. The large, angular city square (110 x 70 m in size), with its pretty rows of trees along all sides, certainly had a magnificent effect during military parades. On the opposite bank of the Eger lay the "sluice mill," a complex in which the camp laundry operated, and a swimming facility.

On November 6, 1941, the JKG submitted to the "Central Office" a memorandum on the "ghettoization of the Jews in the Protectorate," with a draft description of the "ghetto administration": "As its own function, it is to carry out the internal organization . . . in particular to build up the public facilities . . . in its assigned sphere, it must fulfill the tasks assigned it by the authorities" (310). The following departments were proposed as "organs of the Jewish settlement": "administration" (including an administrator and a deputy), the Council of Elders (which had seven members), and the "Liaison Office in Prague." The various departments that would later be created, including the police and courts, were hinted at. Extensive connections with the outside world were still provided for, as shown by the proposals for, in addition to the "Liaison Office," a "legal assistance service for courts and authorities outside the settlement" and "a Post and Telegraph Service and a Transit Office" (!).

Again and again, Jewish concerns focused on the value of labor. It was expected that 40% of the men and women would be fully capable of working: "[At first, the workers] shall be used almost exclusively for building tasks.... One group... will be productively employed in the area around the Jewish settlement in construction, agriculture, etc." The majority were to work within the "settlement" in industries "that are economically necessary and offer market opportunities." Some would work for the "settlement's" own needs. For example, the leadership suggested the creation of a carpentry shop, a metalworking shop, a toolmaking shop, a brush bindery, and a book bindery. Other proposed industries included electromechanics; manufacturing cardboard containers; fabricating optical articles in bulk; making tablets for the pharmaceutical industry; sewing clothes, underclothes, caps, and gloves; machine knitting; making knitted bags – "for this purpose, the sewing machines already in the Jewish households can be put to use" – handweaving; and constructing wooden toys, wire-paper notions, and simple wooden goods. A good number of these proposals were later implemented (see Chapters 13 and 14).

The authors of this draft were aware of difficulties with the electricity and water supply, sewers, and sanitary conditions:

> All persons who are to come to the ghetto as settlers shall first be kept segregated for 3–5 days. In this period, the newcomers will be examined by a doctor; infectious diseases in particular should be ruled out.... Adults should be vaccinated against typhus, children against diphtheria. [Disinfection of clothing and "household goods" is also provided for.] The segregation period for newcomers will end with a bath in a central shower area yet to be created. [A "central laundry" and a crematorium are also mentioned.] The hospital should be of such dimensions that there are ten beds for every 1,000 persons.

During the course of November, the "Central Office" submitted a range of cost estimates and plans for primitive bed frames, other simple furnishings, and tools. Precise registries were prepared for a "Construction Kommando" that would be dispatched to prepare the camp. Most of the discussions took place between Edelstein and the intended camp commandant, Dr. Siegfried Seidl. The "Construction Kommando" was made up of specialists in the areas of administration, economy, finance, technology, medicine, and crafts, as well as construction workers and unskilled workers.

A "memorandum" on November 10, 1941, determined that

> the Central Office is in charge of regulating the issue of transport from the railway station to the settlement point.
>
> SS-Obersturmführer Dr. Seidl informed us that the functionaries would be quartered separately and that additional suggestions can be submitted in regard to this as well.
>
> SS-Obersturmführer Dr. Seidl underscored that families were not to be torn apart and that, therefore, family members remaining in Prague should be excluded from transports.
>
> The functionaries' journey from the settlement area to Prague will be authorized based on need by the city command.
>
> Food is to be brought along for only the first few days. After that, the Central Office ... will ensure constant provisioning. (310)

Appearances had to be upheld so that it looked as though the departure of the "Construction Kommando" was not a deportation, because people distinguished it from "transports," that is, deportation to the East, from which the families in the group were to be spared (a promise that was not always kept). This already hints at the preferential accommodation of Jewish functionaries, which would cause a great deal of mischief later on. As the first Jewish Elder, Jakob Edelstein was the key Jewish personality in regard to the history and early stages of the camp. Now he was expected to choose his closest colleagues; in the process, he often demonstrated bad judgment or was badly advised, because his choices – admittedly forced at a precipitous tempo – soon would have disastrous consequences. As his deputy, he appointed the highly talented engineer Otto Zucker, who had until then headed the JKG in Brünn [Brno].

The camp's initial hours were specified in a "memo" on November 19, 1941: "SS-Obersturmführer Dr. Seidl ordered that the Construction Kommando be ready in Theresienstadt on Monday, 24 November 1941, 12 o'clock noon.... The Jewish Community shall take the necessary measures to ensure its dispatch" (310). Edelstein and Zucker were to remain in Prague for the time being. On November 20, Seidl was informed that the *kommando* had been formed; the intended director of the "Department of Internal Administration," Dr. Egon Popper, was appointed its head. Seidl decreed:

> In regard to the participants' equipment ... we have been informed that hand luggage, such as a backpack with three blankets and eating utensils, etc., as well as other luggage, can be taken along.... The Construction Kommando will go on foot ... from the train station; the equipment and other baggage will be conveyed by horse cart. (310)

Until November 20, 1941, the Theresienstadt project was a secret, unknown to the country's Jews: "It is noted that through formation of the Construction Kommando and additional preparatory work, it will no longer be possible to observe the imperative of silence. SS-Obersturmführer Dr. Seidl takes note of the actual report." Edelstein's request to go with the "Construction Kommando" was denied. A "memo" from November 25 stated that Seidl had informed him "that next week 1,000 people, mainly workers, probably would be allowed to go [and] that in any case there would be a period of several days between an evacuation transport and the transport to Theresienstadt" (310). This promise was promptly broken. It also is apparent from this that the Jewish leadership itself was not yet aware that all transports, without distinction, now would go to Theresienstadt. The SS technique was always the same: unclear information, deception, and lies. The victims, however, interpreted everything according to their temperament, let themselves be fooled, and over and over were willing to believe. The SS was already planning railroad and street building, as Seidl asked belatedly if an expert had accompanied the kommando.

Important orders were contained in a "file note" on December 1, 1941:

> SS-Sturmbannführer Günther orders Edelstein to appear in Theresienstadt with a staff of employees on Thursday, 4 December 1941. Edelstein and his deputy will determine the basic direction of the work and will assign technical tasks to the proper personnel for completion. [Günther] decrees that contact between the ghetto ... and the Jewish Community in Prague should at first occur only in writing. All communications are to be made via the city commandant's office. (310)

This remained so, not only "at first." The promised free postal link was also dispensed with, because "for the next 4 weeks, postal correspondence between inmates of the Jewish ghetto and their relatives is to cease. During this period, no

28 *History*

letters or packages may enter the Jewish ghetto." It was promised that, later on, they would be given permission to write twice a month, but this promise was never fulfilled. It was duplicitously stated that "travel is not desired for the time being. In especially urgent cases, the commandant's office will make a decision. [Günther decrees] that a ghetto guard is to be appointed. The guard will consist of a commander, two deputies, and twenty men. [It is decreed that in the camp], every Jew [will] wear two stars." This adjustment, which was implemented in Poland, did not happen.

Finally, a "statute" and a "draft structure of the ghetto administration" were submitted to the SS in Prague:

> The ghetto is a self-contained Jewish settlement built according to instructions from the Central Office ... and led by a Jewish administration. The Jewish administration is subject to ... the German bodies installed for the ghetto. (City Command). The ghetto administration is a managerial body led by a leader.... Ghetto residents are persons who ... are considered Jews and are chosen ... by the Central Office ... for settlement.... The ghetto administration will ensure systematic work in all areas of activity that ... affect the interests of the ghetto as a unit. In particular, it is responsible for:
>
> Administration of justice and adjudication
> Ensuring public order, security and peace
> Financial and economic guidance
> Labor deployment
> Health and social welfare
> Space management (310)

The intended administrative organs included leaders, with deputies, department heads, and a "professional assembly" that was never implemented. Leaders and deputies were appointed and removed by the "Central Office," the Council of Elders, and department heads with the approval of the leader. He was responsible for representing the ghetto and its residents vis-à-vis the authorities.

The "Professional Assembly" was intended as a democratic institution that would put forward the public's suggestions for improvement and its wishes: "Ghetto dwellers are equal in the ghetto. Ghetto dwellers have the right to be in the area of the ghetto. Every ghetto dweller is allowed to move freely in the area of the ghetto. They may leave the ghetto temporarily to carry out ... their work .. on the basis of a valid pass." The "Draft Structure of the Ghetto Administration," written by Edelstein and his colleagues, formed the basis for the development of the camp. Some things were not carried out or were done differently, but much began with it. A comparison with the 1944 "organizational plan" (see Chapter 8) shows to what extent the development of the "ghetto" was already provided for in Prague.

Six departments were planned:

1. The administration and the Council of Elders, with the Central Secretariat.
2. The "Administrative" Department (implemented as the "Internal Administration" Department), which was subdivided into the President's Office (including the secretariat, the Central Personnel Office, the Central Statistics Office, a division responsible for newspapers and posters, the Office of Legislative Work, the Organization Office, the Central Registry and Archive, the "Central Auditing" Department,

and the Prague Contact Office), the Justice Administration (i.e., the Office of Courts, with arbitral tribunals, civil and criminal courts, a public prosecutor, and an office of legal representation), the Police and Legal Executive Department (i.e., the Order Constabulary and detectives, those charged with the "execution of administration," and the prisons), the Public Registry (including the Registration Office, Public Index, Registry Office, and the division charged with recording population statistics), and the Transport and Communications Administration (the post, with telephone and telegraph services, a postal bank, shipping and vehicles services, and the "Central Arrivals Office and Express Messenger Service").

3. The Economics Department, which included the secretariat and departments responsible for economic planning and oversight, "work deployment" (a registry of those able to work, with aptitude tests, an index of workers and statistics, and information related to labor exchange and workers' welfare), the "procurement system" (the purchase of goods), the camp system (food and kitchen equipment, raw materials and commercial equipment, cleaning and heating materials, medications and remedies, and office supplies and furnishings), production (workshops and home work and food industries such as kitchens, a butcher smokehouse, a nursery, poultry and cattle raising, a dairy, and agriculture), cleaning operations (laundry, "painting," and pest extermination), distribution (ration cards and coupons, wholesale and retail trade, and restaurants), and "space management" (an office of space planning, building management, and real estate management).

4. The Finance Department, including the Cash Department and Central Auditing Department; the drafters' thought processes still were so civilized that they did not even forget a "revenue administration," with a tax office and offices of monopolies and various types of income.

5. The Technical Department, including subdepartments responsible for technical planning and oversight (projects, building permits and oversight, a drawing room, and technical statistics), public supply operation (water and filtration plants, a power plant, garbage collection and incineration, street cleaning, sewers and sewage treatment, firefighting, and air raid protection), and construction, with offices for structural and civil engineering, excavations, sewer systems, and hydraulics.

6. The Department of "Health and Social Welfare," including subdepartments charged with health oversight and registry (district physician, a screening office, and an index of health statistics), health services (quarantines, a bathing facility, a delousing site, disinfection, and an inoculation site), medical facilities (an outpatient clinic, hospitals, a pulmonary clinic, and homes for the feebleminded), social welfare (including nursing homes and youth homes), and burial facilities and crematoria.

The structure was set, and the history of the "ghetto" began. Its establishment was given legal expression in the "Order by the Reichsprotektor in Bohemia and Moravia

Regarding Measures to Accommodate the Jews in Closed Settlements of 16 February 1942," published in the Reichsprotektor's legal bulletin on February 28, 1942: "[The] dissolution of the city of Theresienstadt [is ordered]. Its rights and obligations will be discharged by the state authorities in Prague" (218). Community employees were to be relocated to other communities. The registry offices were to be shut down by May 1, 1942, and their files were to be transferred to Roudnice.

> The property entered in the title registries and land tables ... will be expropriated with suitable compensation ... and after 31 May 1942 will become the property of the emigration fund for Bohemia and Moravia. [Exceptions are made for real estate and furniture belonging to the Reich or the Protectorate and] property that directly serves the practice of religion. [Compensation will be made] for expropriated property and businesses, for resettlement costs, and for unavoidable loss of income connected with the resettlement. The compensation will be paid in cash if not otherwise agreed.

The money was paid by the "emigration fund," from expropriated Jewish property (we should add here that state buildings were leased for the duration of the war). One important section of the order, section 14, gave the "Reichsprotektor" or the empowered organs the "legal basis" for any sort of arbitrary action:

> The orders necessary to carry out, implement and supplement this order are to be issued by the Reichsprotektor.... The commander of the Security Police for the Reichsprotektor ... will take the measures necessary to construct the Jewish settlement, through administrative channels. He can issue orders that deviate from the laws of the Protectorate of Bohemia and Moravia.

This is the only document by which the public was made officially aware of the Jewish camp in Theresienstadt.

3

Deportations to and from Theresienstadt

In the "Protectorate," Jews usually were deported in group transports (*Sammeltransporte*). Following the Reich German model, the "Protectorate" was divided into fifteen administrative districts, headed by senior district administrators (*Oberlandräte*). Their offices were the respective assembly points for deportations from their districts. Only a few smaller groups came directly from other camps, specifically from the Lipa "retraining camp" and from Panenské Březany, an estate near Prague belonging to Heydrich and later to his widow, who kept a number of Jewish slave laborers (see 202b). At its point of departure, each transport was assigned a letter code. The preparation and execution of the transports were largely the task of the Prague JKG (Jüdische Kultusgemeinde) and its "Transport Department." Those concerned were notified by messenger and received a "transport number" (*Transportnummer*). For the duration of their term in Theresienstadt, this number essentially became a part of their name and had to be included in official communications. A person could, for instance, have the "transport number" W 982 or AAl 475 or Cv 13. This meant that the person had come to Theresienstadt with transport W or AAl or Cv and was listed in the respective "transport list" as number 982 or 475 or 13. The "transport lists" were compiled by the JKG at the behest of the "Central Office"; several copies were made, and they were given to the commander of the German escort to Theresienstadt. Once they reached Theresienstadt, the "Central Secretariat" and the "Central Registry," that is, the Jewish offices, each received a copy. Usually, a transport numbered 1,000 persons; larger or smaller transports also occasionally occurred. After the large-scale deportations in the "Protectorate" had been completed in the spring of 1943, small and very small transports were put together. Larger transports only began again with the deportation of Jews in "mixed marriages" at the beginning of 1945.

Transports to Theresienstadt from other countries usually were accompanied by lists, but they were not given the designations that would be adopted in the camp. Sometimes the deportees had not received a number, or at least did not have it with them. On occasion, neither the names nor the number of people on the lists was correct. The "Transport Department" and the "Central Registry" in Theresienstadt thus compiled final lists; the transports were named, and deportees were given their own "transport numbers." Roman numerals – from I to XXVI – formed the basis, with each numeral standing for a specific place of origin, which usually corresponded to a specific Gestapo district. Thus "I" denoted Berlin; "IV," Vienna; and "XXIV," the Netherlands. Each transport also received an Arabic numeral; for example, I/90 was the ninetieth transport from Berlin. The deportees were assigned "transport numbers" in consecutive order, so that individual numbers, for example, under Roman numeral I, were not repeated. In the cases of cities such as Berlin or Vienna, the personal numbers could run into the thousands. To every long-term resident of Theresienstadt, each prisoner's number was an indication of his origin and the duration of his term in the camp. Transports from most of Germany usually brought fewer than 1,000 people; from Berlin and Munich, the transports generally brought no more than 50 to 100 people, although the first thirteen transports from Vienna and several from Germany numbered 1,000 victims.

Furthermore, "individual travelers" came to Theresienstadt under police escort; these were people who had been deported for "punitive" or all sorts of other reasons. "Individual travelers" from the "Protectorate" were labeled EZ (*Einzelzuwachs*, or "individual additions") and received consecutive numbers. If an "individual traveler" came from another country, he usually was added to the last transport that had come from his place of origin.

Transports from Theresienstadt were given the same designations as transports from the "Protectorate" to Theresienstadt, but their letter combinations were never repeated. The numbers of all deportees corresponded to the "transport lists" compiled by the "Central Registry." This list was given to the commander of the German escort by the SS.

OVERVIEW OF THE DEPORTATIONS TO THERESIENSTADT

In the period from November 24, 1941, to April 15, 1945, the following transports arrived in Theresienstadt:

> 1 transport of more than 2,000 people (from Westerbork)
> 72 transports (45 from the "Protectorate") of 1,000–1,999 people, although
> 1,000-person transports were most common
> 49 transports (33 from the "Protectorate") of 500–999 people
> 118 transports (8 from the "Protectorate") of 100–499 people
> 103 transports (12 from the "Protectorate") of 50–99 people

There were also a large number of even smaller transports and "individual travelers."

It probably never will be possible to arrive at the exact number of those deported to Theresienstadt, because no papers from the SS "office" (*Dienststelle*) have survived, and all written material from the "self-administration," especially with regard to the period before 1945, was destroyed on order of the SS. The records for 1945 also suffered; they still were kept pedantically during the final weeks but no longer were entirely reliable. Still, much material survived, some illegally, by being copied or by chance, and so it is possible to gain a sufficient overview of the period leading up to the final phase, as well as of the final phase itself. A "transport overview" (306b) compiled in the camp serves as a starting point for our breakdown; I have not yet come across a more precise or detailed list, but unfortunately it ends on October 12, 1944. Another basis is a list (307a) of all transports that reached Theresienstadt between January 1 and April 10, 1945. For the period between October 13 and December 31, 1944, another transport record from Theresienstadt (307b) had to be consulted, which was almost identical to the lists in the official postwar Czech publication *Terezín Ghetto* (302, pp. xvi–xxii) and tables IV and V in Lederer (166, pp. 252–62). During these eleven weeks, few people – probably not more than 678 – arrived in the camp. Further, the lists by Prochnik (216), compiled in Theresienstadt in July 1945, and Lesný (168), as well as any other accessible materials, were consulted. Extensive comparisons and the elimination of some mistakes make it possible to compile an overview of all those who arrived on "normal" transports or as individuals up to April 20, 1944, after which date evacuated prisoners arrived. Our list cannot be free of mistakes, but it comes very close to the truth and should be regarded as final pending the discovery of other possibly surviving original materials. Anyone interested in further information on this issue is referred to bibliographic notes 22a, 48, 83, 95c, 97b, 99, 106a, 114, 156a, 166b, 168, 175b, 178, 216, 264b, 286, 299c, 302, 306b, 307a, 307b, 309, and 321a, as well as Lederer's book (166). Twelve hundred and sixty Jewish children from Poland are missing from all surviving lists, because their information was kept separately and never was entered into the records of the "Central Registry." They have been included here.

In the period between November 24, 1941, and April 20, 1945, after which date no further "normal" prisoners were sent, the following numbers of people were deported to Theresienstadt:

1941	Protectorate (5,365 from Prague; 2,000 from Brünn)	7,365
1942	Protectorate	54,272
	Sudetengau (starting November 13)	355
	Czechoslovakia	54,627
	Old Reich (starting June 2)	32,878
	Danzig (starting December 11)	110
	Germany	32,988
	Austria (starting June 21; almost all were from Vienna)	13,922
	Luxembourg (starting July 30)	213
	by Gestapo	11
	- -	
	TOTAL	101,761
1943	Protectorate	7,877
	Sudetengau	17
	Czechoslovakia	7,894
	Old Reich	5,281
	Danzig	4
	Germany	5,285
	Austria	1,096
	Luxembourg	96
	Holland (April 22; Amsterdam, immigrants)	297
	Poland (August 24; Bialystok [Białystok] children)	1,260
	Denmark	456
	by Gestapo	5
	- -	
	TOTAL	16,388
1944	Protectorate	420
	Sudetengau	81
	Slovakia (starting December 23; Sered)	416
	Czechoslovakia	917
	Old Reich (2 children from Lublin)	1,669

	Danzig	3
	Germany	1,672
	Austria	228
	Luxembourg	1
	Holland (from January 20;, Westerbork, Bergen-Belsen)	4,597
	Denmark (Ravensbrück, Oranienburg near Berlin)	20
	France (to Bergen-Belsen with the Dutch)	3
	by Gestapo	1
	TOTAL	7,439
1945	Protectorate	3,669
	Sudetengau	158
	Slovakia	1,031
	Czechoslovakia	4,858
	Germany (no one from Danzig)	1,954
	Austria	22
	Hungary (starting March 8;, through Vienna, Amstetten)	1,150
	TOTAL	7,984
1941–45	Protectorate	73,603
	Sudetengau	611
	Slovakia	1,447
	Czechoslovakia	75,661
	Old Reich	41,782
	Danzig	117
	Germany	41,900
	Austria	15,267
	Luxembourg	310
	Holland	4,894
	Poland	1,260
	Denmark	476
	France	3
	Hungary	1,150
	by Gestapo	17
	TOTAL	140,937

The following deportees should be added to those born in Theresienstadt:

	Protectorate	Germany	Austria	Total
1942	68	10		78
1943	66	17	3	86
1944	20	8		28
1945	13			13
TOTAL	167	35	3	205

There were an additional twenty births in the camp (see 302), which have been taken into account in the final list of those deported and born between 1941 and 1945:

Czechoslovakia	75,828	
Germany	41,935	
Austria	15,269	
Luxembourg	310	
Holland	4,894	
Poland	1,260	
Denmark	476	
France	3	
Hungary	1,150	
Undetermined	37	
- - - - - - - - - - - - - - - - -		
TOTAL	141,162	

For the period before October 1, 1944 – during which, aside from the children from Bialystok [Białystok], 130,955 prisoners arrived (another 8,722 people came later) – we can provide a gender and age breakdown that was typical of the social structure of the camp except during the last four months prior to liberation; this

		All ages	Ages 0–14	Ages 15–45	Ages 46–60	Ages 60+
1941						
Men	Czechoslovakia	4,075	261	2,520	1,058	236
Women	Czechoslovakia	3,290	255	1,767	1,047	221
Total	Czechoslovakia	7,365	516	4,287	2,105	457
1942						
Men	Czechoslovakia	22,776	2,147	8,255	5,940	6,434
	Germany	11,137	207	386	1,165	9,379
	Austria	4,832	125	409	663	3,635
	Unknown	6		2	3	1
	Total	38,751	2,479	9,052	7,771	19,449
Women	Czechoslovakia	31,851	2,142	10,990	8,922	9,797
	Germany	22,064	206	903	2,538	18,417
	Austria	9,090	128	927	1,265	6,770
	Unknown	2		1	1	
	Total	63,007	2,476	12,821	12,726	34,984
Total	Czechoslovakia	54,627	4,289	19,245	14,862	16,231
	Germany	33,201	413	1,289	3,703	27,796
	Austria	13,922	253	1,336	1,928	10,405
	Unknown	8		3	4	1
	Total	101,758	4,955	21,873	20,497	54,433
	Origin, sex, and age unknown	3				
1943						
Men	Czechoslovakia	3,818	414	1,843	946	615
	Germany	2,159	165	368	710	916
	Austria	445	39	147	142	117
	Holland	168	15	19	99	35
	Denmark	241	25	118	48	50

(continued)

History

(continued)

		All ages	Ages 0–14	Ages 15–45	Ages 46–60	Ages 60+
	Unknown	8		4	2	2
	Total	6,839	658	2,499	1,947	1,735
Women	Czechoslovakia	4,070	332	1,905	978	855
	Germany	3,222	160	729	763	1,570
	Austria	651	26	193	180	252
	Holland	129	11	35	64	19
	Denmark	215	15	91	54	55
	Unknown	3			1	2
	Total	8,290	544	2,040	2,040	2,753
Total	Czechoslovakia	7,888	746	3,748	1,924	1,470
	Germany	5,381	325	1,097	1,473	2,486
	Austria	1,096	65	340	322	369
	Holland	297	26	54	163	54
	Denmark	456	40	209	102	105
	Unknown	11		4	3	4
	Total	15,129	1,202	5,452	3,987	4,488

1944 (until September 30)

		All ages	Ages 0–14	Ages 15–45	Ages 46–60	Ages 60+
Men	Czechoslovakia	147	23	40	49	35
	Germany	474	35	68	134	237
	Austria	98	2	17	42	37
	Holland	2,135	324	939	555	317
	Denmark	4	3		1	
	Unknown	5		2	1	2
	Total	2,863	387	1,066	782	628
Women	Czechoslovakia	304	21	120	90	73
	Germany	984	16	120	381	467
	Austria	123	8	19	34	62
	Holland	2,410	301	1,185	531	393
	Denmark	7	1	5	1	
	Unknown	9		3	4	2
	Total	3,837	347	1,452	1,041	997
Total	Czechoslovakia	451	44	160	139	108
	Germany	1,458	51	188	515	704
	Austria	221	10	36	76	99
	Holland	4,545	625	2,124	1,086	710
	Denmark	11	4	5	2	
	Unknown	14		5	5	4
	Total	6,700	734	2,518	1,823	1,625

November 24, 1941–September 30, 1944

		All ages	Ages 0–14	Ages 15–45	Ages 46–60	Ages 60+
Men	Czechoslovakia	30,816	2,845	12,658	7,993	7,320
	Germany	13,770	407	822	2,009	10,532
	Austria	5,375	166	573	847	3,789
	Holland	2,303	339	958	654	352
	Denmark	245	28	118	49	50
	Unknown	19		8	6	5
	Total	52,528	3,785	15,137	11,558	22,048
Women	Czechoslovakia	39,515	2,750	14,782	11,037	10,946

		All ages	Ages 0–14	Ages 15–45	Ages 46–60	Ages 60+
	Germany	26,270	382	1,752	3,682	20,454
	Austria	9,864	162	1,139	1,479	7,084
	Holland	2,539	312	1,220	595	412
	Denmark	222	16	96	55	55
	Unknown	14		4	6	4
	Total	78,424	3,622	18,993	16,854	38,955
Total	Czechoslovakia	70,331	5,595	27,440	19,030	18,266
	Germany	40,040	789	2,574	5,691	30,986
	Austria	15,239	828	1,712	2,326	10,873
	Holland	4,842	651	2,178	1,249	764
	Denmark	467	44	214	104	105
	Unknown	33		12	12	9
	Total	130,952	7,407	34,130	28,412	61,003
	No information	3				
	Grand total	130,955				

social structure gave it its unique character. The data are listed according to the following countries: Czechoslovakia (no Slovakia as yet), Germany (including people from Danzig and Luxembourg and some Danes), Austria, the Netherlands (including three Frenchmen), Denmark, and unidentified.

The majority of the Theresienstadt prisoners came from five cities; the following list presents the approximate numbers:

Prague: 40,000
Vienna: 15,000
Berlin: 13,500
Brünn (Brno): 9,000
Frankfurt: 4,000

From April 20 until the end of the war, and even afterward, evacuation transports from concentration camps and their satellite camps arrived at Theresienstadt or in its vicinity, often after many weeks of travel and marches, and were taken into the camp. Among these were an indeterminate number of people – approximately 500 – who had previously been deported from there to the East. One transport from Bergen-Belsen was explicitly destined for Theresienstadt; the other transports were brought there in fulfillment of an agreement between the International Red Cross (IRC) and Minister K. H. Frank. After wandering about helplessly once they entered Bohemia, these transports were directed toward Theresienstadt. It should be emphasized that this fortunate measure can be credited to Paul Dunant, the IRC delegate for Theresienstadt. The concentration camp prisoners came from Bergen-Belsen, Buchenwald and its satellite camp Flößberg, Gleina-Rehmsdorf, Meuselwitz, Raguhn, Schlieben and Tröglitz, the Flossenbürg satellite camp Gröditz, Helmbrechts, Leitmeritz, Öderan, Penig, Scharfenstein, Wilischtal, Zschopau, Zwickau and Zwodau, and the Sachsenhausen satellite camp Schwarzheide, and probably also from other places. More than 8,500 arrived in the first two days – April 20 and 21 – and at least another 4,200 by May 1. Later, fewer arrived, but an overview of the first third of May has been lost (62a, 172a, 228). On May 6, approximately 2,000 prisoners, men and young people, as well as 600 prisoners of war, were received. Efforts were made to register the new arrivals properly, but it seems that the two latter groups were omitted from all records. We will also leave them out of consideration, because they reached the camp only after the SS had left. The overall number was 12,854, according to Haber (see 95c) (among these were 77 who arrived dead); Dunant reports 12,863 (228, p. 132; see also 294c); and the council of the Jewish communities of Bohemia and Moravia estimated 14,000. Prochnik probably came closest to the truth when he calculated 13,500 and found that another 1,500 lost their way at the end of the war and were never counted by camp officials. These prisoners, among whom were a small number of non-Jews, came from the following countries:

Czechoslovakia	690
Germany	13
Austria	106
Holland	115
Poland	4,200
Hungary	5,376
Belgium	50
France	450
Greece	80
Great Britain	20
Italy	70
Yugoslavia	450
Luxembourg	30
Romania	1,000
United States	10
USSR	800
Other	40
TOTAL	13,500

The Czech repatriation office lists 12,451 people by name. According to this, the following inmates were in Theresienstadt:

People who arrived before the final phase or were born there	141,162
People who came from concentration camps at the end of the war	13,500
Of the above, people who, had been in Theresienstadt twice (approximate figure)	500
People who were in the camp at one time or another (approximate figure)	154,200

OVERVIEW OF THE VICTIMS AND DEPORTATIONS FROM THERESIENSTADT

The council of the Jewish communities in Bohemia and Moravia registered 33,521 people who died from "exhaustion and illness" in Theresienstadt (Prochnik gives the same number) and 86,934 who were deported from there. Lederer gives a figure of 33,419 for the deceased among the actual inmates of Theresienstadt by May 5, 1945. All sources agree with regard to the number of deportees from the camp; only Prochnik, for reasons that are not apparent, lists 87,063 deportees. For the period up to October 12, 1944, we follow the same "transport overview" (306b) as before, which cites 80,183 deportees, to which Lederer (166, table III, p. 250f.; see also 302, p. XXVf.) adds five additional transports with 6,753 victims, a total of 86,936 people. We add another

1,260 Polish children and arrive at a total of 88,196 deportees. Our "transport overview" has the advantage of also giving information about those delivered into the hands of the Gestapo, individual deportees, refugees, and those who were released. Here, too, all available sources were compared. The deportations break down by year as follows:

	Number of people	Number of transports
1942 (first half)	16,001	16
1942 (second half)	27,870	19
1942 (total)	43,871	35
1943	18,328	10
1944	25,997	18
TOTAL, 1942–44	88,196	63

Only Prochnik's list allows an overview of the countries of origin of the deportees and those taken out of the camp in other ways. However, here, as in all other lists, the countries of origin only identify the original point of departure and are not necessarily the same as the deportees' nationality:

Protectorate	60,382
Germany (including Luxemburg, Sudetengau, and Danzig)	16,098
Austria	7,572
Holland	3,010
Poland	1,260
Denmark	1
- -	
TOTAL	88,323

Up to October 12, 1944, the gender and age of the deportees are as follows:

	All ages	Ages 0–14	Ages 15–45	Ages 46–60	Ages 61+
Men					
1942	16,807	1,045	4,968	4,309	6,485
1943	7,520	669	3,638	2,227	986
1944	9,129	855	4,261	2,831	1,182
Total	33,456	2,569	12,867	9,367	8,653
Women					
1942	27,064	1,049	6,843	6,666	12,506
1943	9,548	628	3,895	3,426	1,599
1944	10,115	760	3,589	2,811	2,955
Total	46,727	2,437	14,327	12,903	17,060
TOTAL					
1942	43,871	2,094	11,811	10,975	18,991
1943	17,068	1,297	7,533	5,653	2,585
1944	19,244	2,615	7,850	5,642	4,137
TOTAL	80,183	5,006	27,194	22,270	25,713
After October 12, 1944	6,753				
1943 (Polish children)	1,260				
TOTAL	88,196				

40 History

Another 1,200 people left for Switzerland on February 5, 1945; they are included in the documents as "transport." They can be classified as follows (see also 296):

Protectorate 91
Germany 523
Austria 153
Holland 433
- - - - - - - - - - - - - -
TOTAL 1,200

On April 15, 1945, 423 people were sent to Sweden. The number of deceased in Theresienstadt by April 20, 1945, is as follows:

Protectorate	6,152
Germany (including Luxemburg, Sudetengau, and Danzig)	20,848
Austria	6,228
Holland	169
Denmark	52
Slovakia	37
Hungary	35
TOTAL	33,521
Deaths as of May 10, 1945	430
Total	33,951
Deaths as of June 30, 1945	1,137
TOTAL	35,088

Apart from those included in group transports, an additional six persons were individually deported from Theresienstadt. Two hundred and thirty-nine people were handed over to the Gestapo before October 12, 1944. These unlucky ones usually disappeared into the "Small Fortress" and generally were not seen again:

1941 1
1942 16
1943 113
1944 109
- - - - - - - - - -
TOTAL 239

A further 37 people were taken away by the Gestapo on February 20, 1945. At least 276 persons left Theresienstadt in this manner.

Thirty-one lucky ones were, as far as is known, released or, as it was called, "deghettoized" (*entghettoisiert*). The following fled or were returned to the camp:

	Number of people who fled	Number of people who were brought back
1941	3	
1942	11	5
1943	14	6
1944	9	1
TOTAL	37	12

It is unlikely that all 25 who did not return to Theresienstadt were able to save themselves. They included 2 women (aged 15–45 years) and 23 men (one was 0–14 years old, nineteen were 15–45, two were 46–60, and one was more than 61). Among the 12 who were unsuccessful were 11 men (one was 0–14 years old, nine were 15–45, and one was more than 61) and 1 woman (aged 15–45). In April 1945, 5 young men fled the camp, and from May 1 to May 4, 87 persons left the camp by their own unauthorized action. From May 5, when the SS handed over the camp management, until final liberation on May 8, 547 people escaped. Altogether, 764 of those who left can be considered escapees.

To the extent that numbers can substitute for a vivid picture, the following overview suggests the fate of the original Theresienstadt prisoners, not including concentration camp prisoners, on May 9, 1945, the first day of freedom. A total of 141,162 prisoners came to Theresienstadt. The following table shows the number of departures:

Prisoners who died before May 9, 1945	33,456
Prisoners who were deported on transports	88,196
Prisoners who were separately deported	6
Prisoners who were transferred to the Gestapo	276
Prisoners who were released into neutral countries	1,623
Prisoners who were released separately	31
Escapees	764
Total number of departures	124,352

If we deduct the number of departures from the number of prisoners (141,162 − 124,352), we find that there were 16,810 persons in the camp on May 9, 1945. On May 9, 1945, 16,832 prisoners were registered at Theresienstadt.

We have thus succeeded in proving the correctness, with only minor errors, of our statistics concerning the number of Theresienstadt prisoners. It makes little sense to incorporate into the overview the number of inmates who did not arrive until the end of the war, and whose number can only be estimated. However, it should be mentioned that on May 10, 1945, 29,284 people had been identified as being in the camp, and 911 as already repatriated – a total of 30,195 persons – which allows an estimate of around 13,500 concentration camp prisoners in Theresienstadt. As only 11,077 people remained in the camp following the departure of the last deportation transport, it becomes clear from our overview how few people were able to remain in Theresienstadt without being deported, even if we include those released to Switzerland and Sweden.

Deportations from Theresienstadt were carried out in the period from January 9, 1942, to October 28, 1944. Until September 1942, each group numbered 1,000 victims. The so-called transports of the elderly (*Alterstransporte*) in fall 1942 each involved approximately 2,000 persons. Later on, transports of around 1,000, 1,500, 2,000, or 2,500 people were assembled. In 1944, four small transports of 10 to 45 persons, one of which contained mentally ill prisoners, left for Bergen-Belsen. The SS avoided this name and instead spoke of Celle, which was located near Bergen-Belsen. Officially, and correctly, the destination was given as Riga only for the first two transports, in January 1942. After that, it was given only as "East." However, for the "transports of the elderly," the SS took care to spread rumors that Ostrowo [Ostrow Wielkopolski] in Posen [Poznan] was the destination, although there was never a camp in a place with this name (see 3b, doc. 77). In September and December 1943, as well as May 1944, transports for "work deployment" were announced, both to mislead about the real destination and to avoid naming the feared Poland. Birkenau in "Upper Silesia" was given as a destination, presented as a family and labor camp, and any association of the name with Auschwitz was avoided. For the transports of January 1943, the SS had already notified the Jewish leadership that the destination was the Birkenau "labor camp," but most prisoners had not yet learned of this. The transports in fall 1944 were supposed to go to the "Reich territory," and Riesa and other places in Saxony were hinted at as destinations. In fact, these transports also went to Birkenau (Auschwitz II). Among those left behind, only rumors prevailed about the fate of the deportees and, from the Riga transports to the mythically concealed Birkenau in fall 1943, about the destinations. The only thing known for sure was that many went to Poland, to the district of Lublin. Izbica (see 114b, 192d) and Piaski (see 205a) were mentioned by name. It became known that people lived there in poverty and hunger, and one heard tell of pogroms. In contrast, some claimed on occasion to have received positive news. Only after September 1943 were deportees allowed to write to Theresienstadt "from Birkenau"; this practice was continued until October of the following year. This was a transparent ploy, but the prisoners did not see through it often enough. Only a small number of these stereotypic cards, which only came from recent deportees, were distributed in Theresienstadt, and at least once, in June 1944, reply postcards outside the usual allowance were permitted. These cards, however, never reached their addressees, few of whom were still alive. At about the same time, the reliable news spread that individual deportees – who, however, had not left Theresienstadt before December 1943 – were working in various places in Germany. That sounded reassuring, as hardly anyone knew under what conditions these people had left Auschwitz and how they labored now. Little exact knowledge about the fate of the deportees was disseminated before December 1944, and many people were so blind that they comprehended the almost unmistakable truth only when faced with the wretched figures who arrived late in April 1945 (see 69).

The exact destinations of some transports are unknown to this day, and with regard to others only justified estimates exist; however, there is clarity about the majority, thanks to the studies by Zdeněk Lederer. Additional material can be found in document collections and accounts of the Jewish tragedy in the East. The deportations from Theresienstadt mirror each stage of the general deportation and annihilation policy toward the Jews.

Of the 2,000 deportees to Riga, 117 survivors are recorded. Only the first Riga transport, on January 9, 1942, arrived, after a four-day journey, in the ghetto quarter in Riga; this ghetto had been designated for Central European Jews, whose fate the transportees would share. The second Riga transport, on January 15, 1942, did not go to the ghetto. Strong young people were directed toward work camps, whereas the overwhelming majority were shot beside open mass graves (see 136, 223c, 348).

The next group of deportees, who left Theresienstadt in fourteen transports of 14,001 people between March 11 and June 13, 1942, faced, if possible, an even grimmer fate. We know of only 50 survivors. With the exception of 1,000 men who came to the Warsaw Ghetto (8 survivors) and soon followed the deadly trail to Treblinka, most seem to have reached the district of Lublin. However, the destination of three transports is not certain; one is unknown, and none of their 4,000 victims ever returned. This group was first brought to the overflowing old ghettos and the improvised transit camps in this region, where Jews were subjected to the horrible "operations" (*Aktionen*) that took place between March and October 1942. Those not immediately massacred ended up in the gas chambers of the Bełżec extermination camp or in Sobibór. Izbica, Trawniki, and Zamość, the destination of six of these transports, are known to have been transit camps for Bełżec, and in Sobibór, where one of these transports is thought to have gone via the Ossow camp, documents issued in Prague were seen among the luggage of the victims. The fate of those transports shows, both as an example and in documentary form, the implementation of the technique for mass murder of Jews that was agreed on at Wannsee. In a "memorandum" from Lublin on March 17, 1942, a functionary named Reuter writes what Hauptsturmführer Höfle, the founder of Bełżec, had told him days previously:

1. It would be expedient to separate the Jewish transports arriving in the Lublin district into Jews capable of labor deployment at the departure station. If this separation is not possible at the departure station, we must perhaps consider separating the transport in Lublin from the abovementioned point of view.
2. Jews not capable of labor deployment will all be sent to Bełżec, the farthest border station in the Zamość district.
3. Hauptsturmführer Höfle is building a large camp in which Jews capable of working will be registered in batches according to their occupations and can be requested from there. [This definitely refers to Majdanek.]
4. Piaski will be freed of Polish Jews and will become a collection point for Jews coming from the Reich.
5. Travniki will not be occupied by Jews for now.
6. H[öfle] has asked whether 60,000 Jews may be unloaded on the Lublin-Travniki line. Now oriented regarding the outgoing Jewish transports from us, H. explained that, of the 500 Jews arrived in Susiec, those not capable of work can be separated out and sent to Bełżec. According to a telegram from the government [the Generalgouvernement in Cracow] on 4 March 1942, a Jewish transport is to be sent from the Protectorate, destined for Travniki. [This was probably a typing or copying error; the date cited had to be the 14th, and the comment can only refer to the transport that left Theresienstadt on March 11]. These Jews were not unloaded in Travniki, but were brought to Isbica. [The survivors also say that this was the destination of the above-mentioned transport.] An inquiry from the District Captain of Zamość about enlisting 2,000 Jews from there for labor was approved by H[öfle]. Finally, he explained that he could take on 4–5 transports a day of 1,000 Jews each with Bełżec as the destination. These Jews come across the border and will never return to the Generalgouvernement. (138, p. 32 et seq.; 222, p. 30)

On the same day this "memorandum" was written, the mass murders began in Bełżec (see 222). Initially, Travniki seems not to have been "occupied by Jews," and the transport that left Theresienstadt on June 12, 1942, probably was the first with that destination. What was done with the possessions of the deportees is revealed in another document from that period:

Regarding: JSS [Jewish *Samopomoc Spoleczna* (Self-Help)] Reowitz Delegation.
    The delegation informed me that on 17 April 1942, 2 transports of settlers from Slovakia and the Protectorate arrived. The settlers' luggage remained in Lublin and the delegation requests the release of the luggage, which contains mainly bed linens ... [Here, too, the date is incorrect. This must refer to the transport of April 18, 1942, from Theresienstadt to Rejowiece (Reowitz).] (138, p. 49)

From April 1942 onward, foreign Jews fit to work, first from Slovakia and then from the "Protectorate," were deported from transit camps in the Lublin region to Majdanek, which officially bore the name KL (concentration camp) Lublin. Nevertheless, this concentration camp, which also devoured innumerable victims, was never purely an extermination camp. It functioned as an extermination camp through abuses and inhuman working and living conditions, faithful to the principles of the murderous clique that had assembled in Wannsee. From summer 1942, a surviving list of the deceased and a list of pocket watches confiscated from the prisoners in Majdanek, as well as some personal documents of the victims, prove the sojourn and ruin of many inmates from Theresienstadt in one of the most horrific concentration camps under the governance of the SS (see 211). Only some of the strongest had limited chances of survival, as did the few lucky ones who succeeded in fleeing. Teenagers up to eighteen years of age, people over forty, and those not entirely healthy perished without exception.

In June 1942, the practice of sending Jews at least temporarily for "sorting" purposes to ghetto-like camps in the long-since illusory Lublin "settlement district" seems to have been abandoned; there, even elderly people sometimes were left alive for several months after their arrival (for the conditions in Poland, see also 7, 26, 118, 138, 211, 212, 237, 241). Outright extermination camps, or the reception (*Auffang*) and transit camps mainly designated for Jewish transports and prisoners from Theresienstadt, soon constituted their most important – and then their sole – destination. Initially, Belorussia seems to have been the most frequent destination – in particular, Trostinetz near Minsk [Maly Trostenets] (see 314), which was the definite destination of five of the next thirteen transports in the period from July 14 to September 29, 1942; the most likely destination of another five; and the probable destination of two. There were thus twelve transports of 17,004 victims, including five "transports of the elderly" containing 10,004 elderly people from Germany and Austria. If they were old, these unfortunates ended up in the machinery of extermination immediately or, with rare exceptions, very soon thereafter. Those who arrived in the Minsk region at the time usually perished in the gas trucks, or *Duschegubky* – "devourers of souls" – as they were so sadly called in Russian. We know of only ten survivors from these transports, probably all escapees who found their way to the partisans. Nobody survived the "transports of the elderly." It is possible that one or another of the three transports in this group with an unknown destination ended up at Sobibór or Treblinka. One transport from this period, from August 1, 1942, was directed to Raasika in Estonia (see 189), where even the young men soon perished, whereas a group of forty-five young girls survived the war.

The next five transports, two "normal" and three "transports of the elderly" (6,000 victims), left Theresienstadt for Treblinka between October 5 and October 22, 1942, with 8,000 people (see 92, 345). In any case, the only two survivors of this group, who survived as "Aryan civilian workers" in Mannheim after a daring escape, saw the luggage of the murdered from these transports in Treblinka.

In the period preceding the subsequent deportations to Auschwitz, thirty-four transports were sent to the East. Of these, we are aware of 223 survivors of eighteen transports, through whom we also know the destination. Of the remaining sixteen transports – 20,004 people! – we know of only one survivor, who saved himself by jumping from the moving train near Dresden; in four cases, we are not sure of the

Deportations to and from Theresienstadt 45

destination and can only guess at the region in which it ended, and in twelve cases, we rely on trustworthy witnesses and other indicators.

	Number of Deportees	Number of Survivors
Latvia	2,000	117
Poland	22,001	52
Izbica (near Lublin)	3,001	10
Lublin	1,000	1
Piaski (near Lublin)	2,000	5
Rejowiece (near Lublin)	1,000	2
Warsaw	1,000	8
Zamość (near Lublin)	2,000	24
Treblinka	8,000	2
Other places (near Lublin)	4,000	0
Estonia (Raasika)	1,000	45
USSR (Minsk area)	17,004	10
TOTAL (January 9–October 22, 1942)	42,005	224

Apart from the 10,004 victims of the five "transports of the elderly," of whom roughly two-thirds consisted of Reich Germans and one-third of Austrians, the deportees of this period originated in the "Protectorate," for which Theresienstadt in particular served as a transit camp. Otherwise, only individual non-Czech Jews were deported before May 1944. In the period from October 26, 1942, to October 28, 1944, twenty-five transports consisting of 46,101 persons left for Auschwitz, and four small transports of 90 people went to Bergen-Belsen, a total of 46,191. After the war, 2,747 returnees, mostly young people, registered in Czechoslovakia, but none were less than fourteen and only a few were more than forty years old. As the age and health of the deportees from the Netherlands, and especially those from Germany and Austria, were rarely favorable, the assumption that there were an additional 500 survivors seems optimistic. According to this, the total number of survivors from the sixty-three transports (a total of 88,196 victims) was at most 3,500 people, among them 2,971 Czech Jews, which is hardly 4% of the total number. Of the deportees before the Auschwitz transports alone, fewer than 0.6% survived.

So much informative material is available on the possible fates a Jew could suffer in Auschwitz, if he survived his arrival in Birkenau, that nothing general needs to be said here (see also 10b, 10c, 10d, 11a, 30, 75, 76, 78, 106d, 106e, 160a, 164, 167, 174, 196, 210, 220, 239a, 243, 252, 257). However, we will consider those transports that were destined for special treatment. The first Auschwitz transport from Theresienstadt, on October 26, 1942, was also the last "transport of the elderly" and contained 1,866 Czech Jews. The relatively high number of survivors can be explained by the fact that many young people went voluntarily or involuntarily with their parents, and by the fact that Birkenau, in contrast to Bełżec, Chełmno (Kulmhof), Sobibór, and Treblinka, may have been the largest camp but was never exclusively an extermination camp. Even in 1942–43, some particularly resilient people, at least on some transports from the West, blessed by lucky circumstances, had a chance of surviving. The difference from Treblinka becomes particularly obvious if we compare the twenty-eight survivors of the last "transport of the elderly" to the two known surviving escapees from the two transports of October 5 and October 8, 1942, to Treblinka, which had a "normal" age structure and included 2,000 victims (see 106).

The next Auschwitz group left at the beginning of 1943 and consisted of the following transports:

	Number of Deportees	Number of Survivors
January 20	2,000	2
January 23	2,000	3
January 26	1,000	39
January 29	1,000	23
January 1	1,001	29
TOTAL	7,001	96

Nothing proves the evil extermination policy more clearly than these numbers, because, on average, they represent people fit to work, all less than 65 years old. In addition, the authorities had earmarked them as workers, and so the terrible human attrition is particularly obvious, even when no immediate murder was intended. On December 16, 1942, Müller wrote to Himmler that 45,000 Jews were to be brought to Auschwitz in the period from January 11 to January 31, 1943, among them

> 10,000 Jews from the Theresienstadt ghetto, 5,000 of them Jews capable of working, who had so far been used for smaller jobs required in the ghetto, and 5,000 Jews generally capable of working, including those over 60 years of age, in order to use this opportunity to somewhat reduce the camp stock [*Lagerbestand*] of 48,000, which is too high, in the interest of building up the ghetto. I ask for issuance of a special permit for this. As always, only Jews who have no special relationships and connections or important decorations will be included in the deportation.... [The total of 45,000] includes the annex of those incapable of working (old Jews and children). If an appropriate standard is set, at least 10,000 to 15,000 workers will accrue at the mustering of the arriving Jews in Auschwitz. (123, 1472-PS)

The intention was to gain slave laborers and to "sort out" (*ausmustern*) the unfit, that is, to exterminate them immediately. But Müller had made it clear that the Theresienstadters had to be mainly workers, and they were chosen with this principle in mind, even in the camp, apart from a relatively high proportion of children. Why only 7,000 were sent instead of the 10,000 that had been announced in the "orders of the day" for January 10, 1943, in Theresienstadt is unknown. Here, as is the case for so many other documented intended deportations, implementation lagged behind intent, in terms of numbers as well as, frequently, schedule. On January 27, 1943, when 5,000 people were deported, SS-Obergruppenführer Oswald Pohl, the head of the Economics and Administration Main Office (*Wirtschafts-* and *Verwaltungshauptamtes*) (D II), whose seat was in Oranienburg, made the following request of the Auschwitz commandant:

> According to a telegram we have received from the Reich Security Main Office IV B 4, on the 20th, 23rd and 26th a total of 5,000 Jews from the Theresienstadt Ghetto were delivered to the Auschwitz concentration camp. I request that the prisoners transferred on this transport be carefully recorded and that I be given a list of these Jewish prisoners

by age. The prisoners are to be used in the Auschwitz construction management office and the Buna plant. (26, p. 115)

Apparently he received no reply, and the request was repeated on February 16, 1943, without mentioning the additional 2,001 victims: "I request news by telegram regarding the state and the usefulness of the 5,000 Jews transferred from Theresienstadt. The Jews were delivered to Auschwitz only for purposes of labor" (26, p. 116). To this he received a response that likewise failed to make note of the new arrivals:

> Total number of arrivals on [January 21, 1943], 2,000 Jews, 418 of them chosen for labor deployment – 254 men and 164 women – 20.9%; on [January 24, 1943], 2,029 Jews, 228 of them chosen for labor deployment – 148 men and 80 women – 11.2%; on [January 27, 1943], 43,993 Jews, 284 of them chosen for labor deployment – 212 men and 72 women – 11.2%. Accommodated separately on [January 21, 1943] were 1,582 – 602 men and 980 women and children, on [January 27, 1943], 709 – 197 men and 512 women and children. The men were housed separately due to great frailty, the women because most of them were children [!].
>
> All men were assigned to construction after completion of quarantine on [February 15, 1943].
>
> Age of the men: 18–40 years
> Age of the women: 18–33 years
>
> Sig. Schwarz
Obersturmführer (26, p. 117)

First of all, it is striking that the Auschwitz commandant's office counted twenty-two more arrivals than can be found in the figures from Theresienstadt and the Reich Security Main Office (RSHA). This discrepancy remains unresolved and shows that it never will be possible to arrive at exact figures for this "model camp," let alone for other camps. Their exaggerated pedantry, together with their profound contempt for humankind, could yield no other result. Besides, the administrators at Auschwitz were lazy and were not interested in doing anything about the outdated numbers. The expectations of Pohl, the bureaucrat, were disappointed, as he obviously had reckoned on a high percentage of workers, and it now became clear that only 930, or some 18.6%, had survived the first selection. Yet only forty-four – 0.88% of the total number, or 3.8% of the chosen workers – registered after the war as returnees (*Heimkehrer*)!

The following table illustrates the tragedy:

	All ages	Ages 0–14	Ages 15–45	Ages 46–60	Ages 61+
Men	3,076	287	1,445	1,341	3
Women	3,925	254	1,727	1,937	7
TOTAL	7,001	541	3,172	3,278	10

Apart from this, it turned out that not even Kaltenbrunner knew of the deportation of 7,000 rather than 5,000 people (see 256a, published in 3b, doc. 216). This was how the SS economy looked; it was an economy that far outdid all other modern slaveholders in its consumption of human beings.

48 *History*

A particularly tragic fate overtook the double transport of 5,007 men to Auschwitz on September 6, 1943, which had been announced as "labor deployment," about which more is told in Chapter 5. Here we include an account provided by a Slovak Jew after his successful flight abroad (explanatory and supplementary additions are provided in square brackets):

> In the week after 3 September [1943], [2] family transports ... arrived from Theresienstadt. We could not understand at all why these transports enjoyed an unheard-of status. The families were not separated, not a single one went to the gassing that was so normal to us; their hair was not even cut, and they were housed as they had come, men, women and children together, in a separate section of the camp [B IIb], and could even keep their luggage. The men did not have to go to work [!], and for the children, a school was opened under the direction of Fredy Hirsch, Maccabi Prague. They even had permission to write freely. They were merely bullied by their camp elder, a Reich German professional criminal named Arno Böhm ... one of the biggest bandits in the camp, in outrageous fashion. Our amazement only grew when, after a while, we got to see the official name of this transport; its inscription read "SB [*Sonderbehandlung* (special treatment), the code word for secret execution (see 244b)] – Transport of Czech Jews with six-month quarantine." ... But the closer the end of this ... period came, the more we became convinced that the fate of these Jews would also end in the gas chamber. We sought an opportunity to make contact with the leaders of this group. We made clear to them ... what they could expect. Some of them, especially Fredy Hirsch, who apparently had the most ... trust, let us know that, if our fears should prove true, they would organize resistance. The people of the Sonderkommando [in the gassing facilities] promised us that they would join in if the Czech Jews fought back. Some hoped in this way to organize a general revolt in the camp. On 6 March 1944, we learned that the crematoria were being prepared to receive the Czech Jews. I hurried to Fredy Hirsch ... and urged him to act immediately, since they had nothing more to lose. He answered that he knew his duty. In the evening, I once again slipped into the Czech camp. Here I learned that Fredy Hirsch was dying. He had poisoned himself with Veronal. The next day, on 7 March he was taken unconscious, with his 3,791 fellows, by truck to the crematoria and gassed. The young people rode singing to their deaths. To our great disappointment, there was no resistance. The men of the Sonderkommando, who had determined to join them, had waited in vain. Five hundred older people [actually some 1,170] had already died during the quarantine period; only eleven twins [and a number of doctors and nurses] were ... kept alive. Various medical experiments were carried out on these children in Auschwitz. A week before the gassing, on 1 March 1944, all the camp inmates had to write to their relatives abroad [and domestically] about their welfare. They were told to ask their relatives abroad for packages. (243, p. 104 et seq.)

Most of those who were spared this mass murder, a total of thirty-seven people, survived the war (see also 10b, 11a, 237).

No less gruesome was the destiny of the next transport of 1,260 children, from Bialystok [Białystok], who left the camp on October 5, 1943, together with an escort consisting of 53 old Theresienstadt inmates. How these children arrived in Theresienstadt and how they lived there is described in Chapter 6 (see also 124). Here, we shall explain why these Polish-Jewish children had been brought from the East to Central Europe, in an incident unique in the history of the Jewish deportations by the SS. On February 30 [sic], 1943, the Office for Jewish Affairs in the Foreign Office demanded 30,000 Jews from Allied countries, including the USSR, for purposes of an exchange. Kaltenbrunner authorized the security commander in the East to choose suitable Jews in the ghettos. On April 5, 1943, the representative of the Foreign Office in Riga, Adolf Windecker, pointed out that it, if they used Jews for exchanges, it might be difficult to prevent the news of their execution from being used politically against Germany. On May 10, Windecker was advised that the Foreign Office was aware of this difficulty. In any case, in April 1943, in Bergen-Belsen, a "convalescent, transit and exchange camp" (*Erholungs-, Durchgangs- und Austauschlager*) was set up; it was supposed to serve such special purposes. A group of Dutch Jews spent some time there in 1944 before coming to Theresienstadt, and ninety people were sent there from Theresienstadt in the same year. Two transports consisting of 1,686 persons – Hungarian Jews – were in fact sent from Bergen-Belsen to Switzerland in August and December 1944, whereas in April 1945, even just before the liberation of Bergen-Belsen, another transport was sent to Theresienstadt from there and, in fact, reached it after an ordeal of several weeks (see 160c, 341a).

Our discussion has jumped ahead in the time line; let us return to the period under consideration. At the end of May 1943, the Swiss ambassador in Berlin notified the Foreign Office official in charge of Jewish affairs, Eberhard von Thadden, of an offer by the British government to accept 5,000 Jews, 85% of whom were children, from Poland, Latvia, and Lithuania. Eichmann insisted on exchanging them for 20,000 Germans fit for military duty. This had to happen soon, however, as, because of German measures, the time was fast approaching when the emigration of 5,000 Jewish children would be impossible. The ghetto of Bialystok [Białystok] was dissolved in the period between August 21 and September 15, 1943, and, at the beginning of this operation, the children, among whom officially none were allowed to be more than fourteen years old, were brought to Theresienstadt (see 40a). In the meantime, the "South Barracks" (Südbaracken) had been constructed there; this complex was intended as a children's camp. At this point, news trickled down from the SS that this transfer was related to an exchange; the care given to the children confirmed this information. But Eichmann was correct: for unknown reasons, the children did not go abroad with their escort but instead went to Auschwitz, and no one survived the transport. Concerns of the sort brought forth by Windecker sadly carried the day and involved the criminals in new crimes. Meanwhile, this attractive project continued to be discussed abroad, and the British offer was still declared to be in force on May 2, 1944! Von Thadden then had Eichmann let it be known that Łódź was the only place where 5,000 Jewish children could be found; however, they were to go not to Palestine but to England, in order to spread antisemitism. Four months later, Auschwitz had also devoured the children from Łódź.

The next two transports, containing 5,007 people, left Theresienstadt in mid-December 1943, destined for the same fate as the unhappy double transport of September 1943: "SB [special treatment] with six months quarantine." In Auschwitz, the arrivals were also housed in section B IIb, called the "family camp," and received the same privileges. The newcomers were isolated from the horror that had devoured the September group. At the beginning of May 1944, just before the arrival of the next group, more than 3,000 people from Theresienstadt are thought to have been in the "family camp." At this time, a change occurred, probably not in Hitler's but in Himmler's Jewish policy, which would in part influence the semiofficial negotiations with Jewish officials in the West but would especially aid in a somewhat more economical use of the workforce. Whereas, in 1942, all concentration camps in Germany had been almost emptied of Jews, beginning in May 1944, large numbers were again conveyed from Auschwitz, especially to the newly erected work camps that were under the administrative control of the large, older camps. Thus, a few weeks after the end of the six months, a sizeable number still were killed by gas, but a considerable number were left alive. This explains why 705 members of this group (approximately 13%) are known to have survived; to these, some who did not originate in the "Protectorate" might be added.

In May 1944, three transports brought 7,503 people to Birkenau; they were likewise sent to the "family camp" and told to write postcards. In the first week of July, the "family camp" was dissolved; the strongest were assigned to work, and the majority were exterminated by gas on July 7. Of this group, which included many elderly and sick people (3,391 people more than 61 years of age), only 385 returnees registered in Czechoslovakia, but we may also assume that there were a small number of survivors from the Netherlands, Germany, and Austria.

The last group left Theresienstadt from September 28 to October 28, 1944. A total of 18,404 people were deported in eleven transports; they were condemned to death or slavery immediately on their arrival. Fourteen hundred and ninety-six survivors from Czechoslovakia were registered, but 400–500 people from the Netherlands, Austria, and Germany should be added to this number.

The following table provides an overview of the numbers, rounded down:

People who came to Theresienstadt before the dissolution phase	141,000
People who died in the camp	33,500
People who were sent out of the camp	88,000
People sent out who then died	84,500
People sent out who survived	3,500
People who died (total)	118,000
People who were saved (total)	23,000
People who came to the camp after November 1, 1944	9,000
People who were released (Switzerland and Sweden)	1,600
People who came to the camp before November 1, 1944, and stayed	10,500

One-seventh of those deported to Theresienstadt before April 20, 1945, were saved, but only slightly more than a tenth of those deported before November 1, 1944, survived. The largest number of arrivals and departures were in 1942, whereas the "quietest" year in relative terms was 1943.

Following the deportations to Theresienstadt, only one "punishment transport" went from the "Protectorate" directly to Poland, after the elimination of Heydrich; this transport moved 1,000 people from Prague to Ujazdow, near Lublin, and one returnee has been reported. As it happens, this transport received the designation AAh, which was read as an abbreviation of "assassination of Heydrich."

The following table reports the number of "racial Jews" living in the "Protectorate":

June 30, 1941 (before the deportations)	88,686
March 31, 1943	11,267 (6,137 of whom were Mosaic)
May 5, 1945 (at liberation)	2,803 (820 of whom were Mosaic)

Most of the deported Czech Jews were at least temporarily in Theresienstadt. At the end of 1946, somewhat more than 19,000 Jews lived in the Czech lands of

Deportations to and from Theresienstadt

Czechoslovakia; of these, slightly more than half had not lived there before the war. Added to this were an additional 5,000 people who were persecuted as "racial Jews" (*Rassejuden*) during the occupation. At least half of the Jews emigrated in the course of the next few years from Czechoslovakia to Israel and the West (185, 317, 321a).

THE TECHNICAL ASPECTS OF THE TRANSPORTS TO THERESIENSTADT

Of the documents from the Nuremberg trial, Protocol 2376-PS, written by Dr. Rudolf Mildner, provides information on the origins of all Jewish group transports:

> The orders to send them ... to work and concentration camps were issued by R. F. SS Himmler. The orders carried his signature. They passed through Chief of the Security Police and SD, Dr. Kaltenbrunner, previously Heydrich, as "secret Reich matters" to the Office Head IV, RHSA Gruppenführer Müller. Gruppenführer Müller discussed their implementation orally with the head of Department IV A [B] 4, SS Obersturmbann-führer Eichmann.... .
>
> The orders also passed directly from R.F. SS Himmler to the locally responsible Higher SS and Police Leader, and for informational purposes to the chief of the SIPO and SD, Dr. Kaltenbrunner.... .
>
> The above-cited orders dealt only with transfer of the Jews to the concentration or work camps.... .
>
> Orders from R.F. SS Himmler regarding the type of labor deployment of the prisoners or the extermination of the Jews ... went directly through Obergruppenführer Pohl, Gruppenführer Glücks ... to the commandant of the concentration camp as "secret Reich matters." (122)

This shows the bureaucratic scheme that was also standard for the Theresienstadt transports and that determined the role of Eichmann and his staff, as well as the local offices in the respective countries, especially the Prague "Central Office," whose head, Günther, was also the head of the SS "office" in Theresienstadt.

Obtaining railroad trains for the deportations was an important task, which also was left to Eichmann to solve. His transport officer, Hauptsturmführer Franz Nowak, had to contact a specific office of the Railroad Ministry, the head of which then submitted the request to the regional transport command of the Wehrmacht. They could veto it; this was probably effective only while the army was advancing but hardly was effective in the desperate situation in 1944. Many SS documents and actions make it clear that, for the inner circle of the party and the RSHA, the deportation and extermination of the Jews was a more important war aim for Hitler's Germany than victory at the front (see also 9, 312d).

In Germany, the Jewish offices, that is, the authorized JKG (which, in Berlin, was called the Jüdische Kultusvereinigung), summoned the victims to collection camps or collected them in furniture vans, unless the SS or other organs of the police paid them more or less surprise visits at home, or sometimes at work; ordered them to pack immediately; and escorted them to a collection camp (see 46c, 52b, 190a). A standing question among Jewish friends characterizes the mood in Berlin: "Do you want to take your life or take it with you when they evacuate you?" Nursing homes, synagogues, schools, and so on, served as collection camps, and the sojourn rarely lasted more than a few days (see also 95, 341). The treatment and food in Berlin were simple, and the accommodations sometimes were bearable, as long as this was left to the JKG. Luggage was more or less strictly searched, body searches were common, and money and jewelry in particular were confiscated. However, in some towns and some transports, things were much worse. In Berlin, on the day of deportation, people were woken at 2 A.M.; they received some breakfast at 3 A.M., and at 4 A.M. they had to assemble in the street with their hand luggage and were brought to Anhalter Railway Station by streetcar, which they otherwise no longer were permitted to use. Many Berlin and Munich transports were small, consisting of 100 or 50 people, and they were loaded into passenger cars that were coupled to scheduled trains. The first Berlin transports were allowed to receive a hot meal from the Jewish community as they passed through Dresden. Otherwise, the German as well as the Viennese transports were crammed into cattle cars, usually with meager luggage. Sometimes people had brought along some provisions; sometimes they had received some rations. Little provision, or none at all, was made for cleanliness, sanitary facilities, or even the most primitive medical assistance. Conditions often were no better in passenger trains. In all countries, German police served as the escort; in the best case, they did not bother with the prisoners, but often they sadly distinguished themselves through harshness and abuse. Water and other small privileges were rare or not at all available, although the journey could take a long time, as much as two days and nights. From Dresden and the "Sudetengau," people also came by bus. Smaller groups from all countries were transported with escorts in special compartments of regular trains.

The term "deportation" was nowhere permitted; officially, in Germany, it was called "migration" or "evacuation," or, for Theresienstadt, "change of residence." Who was chosen to go to Theresienstadt depended essentially upon the principles agreed at the Wannsee Conference (see Chapter 2). People over age sixty-five, who generally were not deported before June 1942, usually came to Theresienstadt after that date. Younger Jews continued to be sent to the East, except for some categories of wounded and decorated war veterans, with their wives and (sometimes) minor children. "Half" Jews, known as *Geltungsjuden*; Jewish parents of *Mischlinge*; and various privileged people, among them prominent personalities and selected members of the "Reich Association of Jews in Germany" – as well as some dubious characters – went to Theresienstadt. Often those who had been driven together in a collection camp did not know where they would be taken. Before the deportation of Reich Germans to Theresienstadt began, the "Special Account H" was established for the "Reich Association," on the orders of the "Supervisory Authority" (Aufsichtsbehörde). Most of those deported from Berlin to Theresienstadt after 1942 had to transfer their moveable assets, specifically securities, bank accounts, and mortgages, to this account, which was with the banking house Heinz Tecklenburg & Co. in Berlin and was accessible by the RSHA. This was done in the form of a "home purchase agreement" (*Heimeinkaufvertrag*), which had to be concluded with the "Reich Association" (see 3b, 22a, 151a, 183, 243b, 274a, 343). The assets transferred in this way had to be sold, and the proceeds transferred to the account of the "Emigration Fund for Bohemia and Moravia" at the Böhmische Unionbank in Prague. The people forced into these contracts either wrongly took them to be some kind of "old-age pension" until death or did not understand them at all. How this awful swindle affected the poor people is shown in Chapter 5.

In Austria – which was basically synonymous with Vienna – the assembly of the transports was left to the Israelitische Kultusgemeinde (IKG) (see 243f). As some of those targeted did not appear in the collection camp, the authorities soon switched to brutal methods: SS men or a group of thugs – in the form of the Jewish police, or "Jupo," who hardly lagged behind the Gestapo in inhuman harshness – dragged people out of their houses. The victims were set upon unprepared; they had to hastily pack a few possessions and were brought to the collection camp, which was full of lice and where scandalous conditions prevailed. A stay here could last up to several weeks. For the deportation to Theresienstadt or the East, the same principles were in force as in Germany, but there were no "home purchase agreements." The confiscation of people's entire fortunes was carried out according to almost the same guidelines as in the "Protectorate" (see 175b). When the Vienna IKG was liquidated toward the end of 1942, its assets were transferred to the Prague "emigration fund," which also had to pay for the support of the Viennese Jews in Theresienstadt.

The first transport from the Netherlands came from Amsterdam and was composed almost exclusively of emigrants who were privileged as decorated war veterans or otherwise (see 49); all others came from the Westerbork camp, in some cases after an interim stay in Bergen-Belsen, and all were members of privileged groups or were privileged in their own right (see Chapter 6 and 3b, docs. 12–14; 17; 52a; 69; 69a; 99; 106; 106a; 160c; 229; 292; 344).

Hardly a tenth of the Jews of Denmark, whose fate would have a special influence on the history of Theresienstadt (see Chapter 6), fell into the hands of the SS. It is to the credit of a German, [Georg Ferdinand] Duckwitz, a naval attaché to the Reich plenipotentiary in Copenhagen (see 18a, 42, 42a, 50b, 234), that most were able to escape to Sweden in time. He thus proved that, even in Hitler's Germany, personal courage and decisiveness could save Jews from destruction. Duckwitz warned the Danish authorities, via the resistance movement, of the impending operation against the Jews, who then were actively helped by the Danish police and other authorities. Thus the only ones caught were those whose attempt to escape failed, often on the open sea, or those who lived in the western part of the country. Those who were arrested were sent to Theresienstadt (see also 2, 3b, 44, 73, 184b, 199).

At a time when transports to the East were no longer possible, Slovak Jews were sent to Theresienstadt (see 193c). A transport of Hungarian Jews survived a long trek to Austria and then forced labor before being loaded onto a train in Vienna. It should also be mentioned that small groups arrived directly or indirectly from concentration or work camps, as well as from prisons, mental hospitals, and so on (Svatobořice [see 91a], Lípa and Bergen-Belsen [160c, 272], and Ravensbrück [184b], among others). No transports from other countries were planned. Three prominent Frenchmen came with the Dutch from Bergen-Belsen. In Saloniki, privileged Jews were promised a transport to the "free ghetto" of Theresienstadt in May 1943, but like the "non-privileged," they traveled to Auschwitz (see 184a, 188b, cf. 30a).

As a typical example, we will describe a Prague transport in detail. Once the Jews learned that there would be a transport, they first were overcome with fear for everyone who could be affected; they also feared the Jewish functionaries who were involved in implementing it. This fear was paralyzing, and it led to both sensible and senseless preparations. Fear was the driving force in all conversations and actions, even for courageous people. Courage and firmness were only heroic reactions to overwhelming fear. Useful things were purchased: suitable clothing, provisions, and equipment. Property was given away, hidden, or sold to obtain money for purchases. Everything was done in fear, because it was illegal. Most of the purchases were prohibited. Luggage was organized, hoarded, or made at home; practical bedding

54 *History*

was prepared, sheets were dyed, suitable eating utensils were found, clothing and shoes were readied. It was important that these things not be too "nice" or stand out. Forbidden items such as money and jewelry were sewn into clothing or hidden in other ways to prevent discovery. Many believed they had correct information on what to do and how. Others, especially those who were elderly and alone, did nothing at all and let things take their course. Some hoped blindly, or by putting their trust in all kinds of reasons, that they would be "safe"; they were "indispensable," relied on good connections, or thought they would try to bribe Jewish officials or the SS.

The mood is illustrated by a letter from a young man from Pilsen [Plsen], who wrote to a friend in Prague on December 26, 1941, just before the transports from this town:

> My mother is visibly better since I have been home, but understandably has enough worries [his father had been held hostage in Buchenwald since the start of the war]. According to everything I am hearing, I am no longer worried about my 75-year-old grandmother, whose property has been confiscated. I do not know how things are with all the other relatives, but I fear for all of them, especially for my 65-year-old diabetic aunt. My mother *might* be the most likely to be able to stay here, because of my father and her mother, whom she has to take care of. But I cannot find out anything for sure; people tell me that *wives* of prisoners in protective custody will not be included in transports, but I don't know of any concrete positive or negative cases. [Everyone, without exception, went on the transports, though rumors raised hopes.] The transport is a fact here; the K. G. officers from Prague have already been chosen. When and how is still unknown. Only now are people here beginning to accept the idea. We are pretty prepared, but we lack the experience that people already have in Prague. We have down quilts in the form that you indicate, but sleeping stockings are completely new to us. Unfortunately we don't have a list from someone with practical experience. I know there is nothing official, but people have had some experience. In regard to food, for example, we have no idea how and what.

Fear led to strange ideas. In 1946, a collection tin at the grave of the venerable Rabbi Loew at the old Jewish cemetery in Prague was opened and a piece of paper was found, covered in a young girl's handwriting:

> My dear good *Wunderrebbe*,
>   Please please help me, so that mommy can come home this week and doesn't go on the transport.
>
> Thank you.
Yours
Dita

Chapter 1 mentioned the "registration" of all Jews in the "Protectorate," carried out in the period between the transports to Poland and the first transports to Theresienstadt. Using the card index compiled then, the "Central Office" selected an ample number of names, which enabled the JKG to put together "transport lists" (see 78a). Where no "instructions" were given, the JKG had a measure of liberty in its selection, unless all the Jews in the area of the specific district administrator had to leave within a short period of time. This limited freedom existed only in Prague and, for a short period, also in Brünn [Brno]. The prepared "transport lists" were discussed in an internal JKG procedure, and select individuals, together with their closest relatives, sometimes were taken off the list.

The lists always also contained a "reserve" of twenty names, in order to reach the prescribed number of people in case of last-minute shortfalls. Very few Jewish functionaries were able to see the lists, the compilation of which was often accompanied by shady machinations, as was the acceptance of objections. The completed lists were given to the "Central Office," whose headquarters, a confiscated Jewish villa, also housed a branch of the JKG.

The "call up" for a transport and for the "reserve" was often delivered by an employee of the JKG, very often at night. Usually – but by no means in every case – an entire family was affected. On pain of unnamed "measures," they were ordered to arrive at the JKG headquarters at a given time to receive new orders. It was possible to volunteer, but this did not have to be accepted. Appeals were possible and, in the early months, were even treated with a certain sympathy; later they became almost futile. The only possible reasons were illness and, later, explicitly, "inability to be transported" due to illness. The final decision depended on the JKG's head physician and on confirmation by the "Central Office." For those taken off the list, substitutes were called in, often at the last minute. The period between notification and departure lasted an average of a week, sometimes more. The JKG was burdened with a pile of printed material and forms in German and Czech (in conformity with the regulations in the "Protectorate," the JKG had to officiate in German and Czech, whereas only German was permitted as the official language in Theresienstadt).

As soon as someone's lot had come up, feverish activity began, even if he had long been prepared for this moment. It took a great deal of time just to study all the instructions and fill out the required forms. The attachment to the "official summons," slightly shortened, permits the best overview:

Explanation of the official summons

1. Who is to appear.
   The official summons must be obeyed by all summoned persons without exception. The sick also are obliged to appear and will have the opportunity to be examined at the place of summons by an officially provided physician. Anyone who fails to obey the official summons will be brought in by the police.
2. Where and when the summoned are to appear.
   The summoned are to appear on the day named in the official summons at the time named in the official summons at the named place. Late appearance will result in harsh measures.
3. What the summoned should have prepared.
   a) Up to fifty kg. of luggage may accompany each person. Blankets and food for five days are included in the weight of the luggage. If the luggage exceeds the permitted weight, it must be left behind. The choice of items to bring and the packaging must therefore be carefully prepared. Only items of practical use are to be taken along....
   b) The main luggage (accompanying luggage) will be loaded in its own rail car. It cannot be expected that owners will access to this luggage. Before arrival at the destination, blankets and provisions for five days, as well as the most necessary items for several days' subsistence, must therefore be placed in manageable bags (hand luggage) (large handbags, haversacks, small knapsacks, or small suitcases). The main luggage is to be packed in larger suitcases or knapsacks.... Pieces of luggage that are too large will be left behind....

c) All pieces of luggage are to be marked indelibly with the name, transport designation, and the simultaneously issued number, or with the same number made by the summoned. Distribution of items will occur according to these numbers.... In addition, at the top of every piece of luggage, a piece of paper with the same number, first name, last name and date of birth ... must be placed, so that the owner can be found should the number notation affixed to the outside be lost....

d) The Jewish *Kultusgemeinde* has set up a collection service that will bring the luggage to the loading site. The luggage will be picked up at the time indicated on the accompanying yellow slip. The collection service must not be delayed, as otherwise it will not be possible to pick up luggage everywhere. Therefore, it is absoutely essential that all items to be taken be ready at the given time and that someone who can hand over the items to be collected be in the apartment the entire day. If the collection service finds no one at home, or if the luggage is not fully packed when they arrive, the persons involved must themselves be responsible for getting their luggage to the summons site on time.... If, therefore, the luggage cannot be picked up in the course of the day, the summoned person must nevertheless appear with luggage on time at the summons site....

It is strictly forbidden to make knapsacks or bags out of Persian rugs, coats, valuable cloth remnants, etc.

e) Collect the items that you are to bring under Point 4 to the summons site.

f) Fill out the attached form, "Property Declaration." We point out that all information on individual assets, especially, for example, accounts at financial institutions, securities, insurance policies, etc., must be precise and complete. It is therefore, for example, necessary to name the financial or insurance company. Those not obeying this order will be harshly punished. The attachment "Home Furnishings and House-hold Items" ... must be attached to the property declaration in every case. In this attachment are to be listed only those items that the transport participant is not taking along. Further, the "Annex to Property Declaration" must be attached, with information on genuine rugs, valuable collections, etc.

Allowing third parties to see these forms is forbidden.

g) Owners as well as co-owners of real estate or houses that ... are located in the Protectorate must in addition to the "Property Declaration" also fill out the form for the emigration fund, for houses the "questionnaire" and "list," for real estate only the "questionnaire" in duplicate. They must be filled out with ink in legible writing.

All forms must be completed.... The forms will be provided at the Jewish *Kultusgemeinde* during issuance of the summons and the additional forms....

The completed forms including evidence are to be submitted at the summons site along with the Property Declaration.

h) Attach the number distributed to you, on hard cardboard, to the article of clothing you will wear on top. Also, mark the key to your apartment or your room or your closet with the same number, if you must surrender it under Point 4, no. 1.

4. What is to be brought to the summons site
Aside from the luggage already mentioned, which is to be sent ahead of time to the summons site, and the small hand luggage ... those summoned must bring:

a) all personal documents (passports, citizen's ID [*Bürgerlegitimation*], police registration form, etc.).

The transport participants need not cancel their police registration;

b) all of their cash;

c) securities, bank books, jewelry ... to the extent these items are not deposited;

d) insurance policies of all kinds;

e) military ration cards ...

f) all remaining ration cards, potato-, egg- and soap-cards. The only parts of the ration cards and soap cards that may be used must correspond to the period until the day of entry into the assembly site. ...

The submitted cards will be carefully checked and each transport participant risks the danger of prosecution if he surrenders fewer ration cards ... ;

g) a cancellation confirmation from the fat-supplier, the provisions-supplier, precisely filled out and confirmed. The transport participants need not cancel their registration with the municipality;

h) the report of fuel acceptance ... ;

i) the precisely filled out Property Declaration under Point 3);

k) for owners of houses and real estate, the precisely filled out "questionnaire" under Point 3 g) ... ;

l) the apartment key, closet or room key, if the summoned person is a tenant or subtenant.

The above-mentioned documents and items are not to be placed in luggage, but brought separately to the summons site. It is specifically emphasized that it is forbidden to bring couch cushions ... and parts of furnishings ...

5. Prohibition of disposition of property

Selling, giving away, or lending items currently found in your possession is forbidden. Failure to follow this order will be punished.

6. Behaviorial measures for the day of summons

The summons occurs by hour. It is absolutely essential to appear on time. All summoned persons must visibly wear the numbers given them. Similarly, all items must be marked ... with the same number. The entire process is built upon this number. Sleeping sites, train seats and food will be allotted according to this number. ... . Smoking is forbidden at the summons site. Thus matches, lighters and smoking materials may not be taken along. The orders of official organs are to be obeyed to the letter. The summoned must expect that they will no longer be able to leave the site of summons once they have entered. They must therefore make their arrangements in a timely fashion.

7. Aid service

a) Old, sick persons and invalids who cannot alone collect and pack the items to be brought will be helped by the women's or youth aid service. ... People who take advantage of the aid service must register ... on their own.

b) Persons who remain completely without care after the departure of a transport participant to whose care they were entrusted should register with the Jewish *Kultusgemeinde* social counseling. (219)

The "property declaration" was a long form consisting of eight pages and had to be filled out separately for each family member: "Every question must be

58   *History*

answered!" After general personal information, the following points had to be dealt with:

A.   Active
      I.   Liquid assets
            1.   cash
            2.   deposits in financial institutions at home and abroad
            3.   securities
            4.   valuables
            5.   safe deposit boxes
     II.   Real estate
    III.   Claims
            1.   claims secured in the land registry
            2.   other claims (bills of exchange)
            3.   life insurance
            4.   Did you or do you have pension insurance, social security?
            5.   Do you receive a pension?
            6.   security deposits?
            7.   inheritance or legacy?
            8.   rights of *usufruct* or reserved use?
            9.   claims from licensing agreements, patents, trademarks and copyrights?
           10.   alimony claims?
           11.   future interests?
     IV.   Commercial property
      V.   Art objects
     VI.   Are items belonging to you in the custody of others?
    VII.   Other property
   VIII.   Are property restrictions in place?
B.   Passive
      I.   Taxes owed, insurance companies, social security, etc.
     II.   Alimony
    III.   Possible trials and compensation claims
     IV.   Executions in process
      V.   Obligations of various kinds
     VI.   Other passives (219)

People were particularly upset by the attachment "apartment furnishings and household items," which, for unclear reasons – perhaps merely out of greedy pedantry or even as mockery – demanded a meticulous listing of everything left behind in the apartment, including its estimated value in crowns. To take just a few examples, there were questions about irons, preserved food, potatoes, fuel, tailcoats, jackets, umbrellas, and handbags; even items such as automobiles that long since had been surrendered or confiscated were not forgotten. Once this was taken care of, one might turn to the next form:

Instructions for the Assembly of Equipment
(to be treated only as guidelines, not as regulations)

    1.   Hand luggage ...
         Blanket or sleeping bag, food for five days, provision bowl or pot, eating utensils, canteen, drinking cup (metal), pocket knife, flashlight and batteries, 1 teeth-cleaning implement, washing items.... 1 shaving implement, toilet paper, necessary laundry for a week, seat cushion or air pillow.

2. Accompanying luggage ...

Clothing; warm suit – dress, light suit – dress, knee socks – skirt, winter coat, raincoat, warm head covering.

Linens: warm shirts, light shirts, undershirts, warm underwear (long), light underwear (short), wool stockings ... , stockings ... , flannel pajamas, pajamas, handkerchiefs, towels, dishtowels, corsets, bed linens.

Shoes: solid laced shoes, light shoes, warm slippers.

Supplementary: track suit, pullover ... with long sleeves, blankets, warm gloves (mittens), wool shawl, ear muffs.

Basic articles: tools, clothing brush, dirt brush ... shoe cleaning materials, belt ... small leather belt, shoelaces, garters, shoe polish, complete sewing equipment ... writing paper, spirit or petroleum cooker, ½-liter pot, washing sand, candles.

Appliances: The transport participants are to bring the following items, if they own them:

1 small oven, pickax, shovel, hatchet, hand saw, frame saw, carpenter's ax, hammer ... , all kinds of tongs.

These items ... are not included in the permitted 50 kg. of weight.

Of the items listed here, the following were confiscated from the new arrivals in Theresienstadt: flashlights and batteries, toothpaste, shaving equipment, toilet paper, air pillows, writing paper, cookers of all kinds, and candles.

For a long time, the assembly point in Prague was situated on the grounds of the trade fair hall in a wooden exhibition shack that was unsuitable spatially and otherwise. It was not waterproof, was unheatable and thus bitterly cold in winter, and was neglected and dark, as there was only a small skylight. This miserable place had the euphemistic name "exhibition palace" (*Messepalast*). The entry was guarded by Czech police. On arrival, the heavily loaded victims, wearing cards marked with their "transport numbers" on strings around their necks, had to identify themselves at the entrance. Then they passed through the reception office of the "transport department" of the JKG and – after endless lines and many procedures, without the slightest consideration for the elderly, the sick, or children – they arrived at their assigned place to sleep, where they had to spend all their time. The room, which was dim day and night, was dismal, and the air was sticky and, depending on the weather, icy, damp, or oppressively hot. Their stay until departure usually lasted three to four days. The commander of the area was Hauptscharführer Johannes Fidler (a.k.a. Hans Fiedler) of the "Central Office," who was feared for his brutality, as were his helpers.

All the formalities cited previously had to be carried out to the letter. Those who were not smart or courageous enough cleverly to smuggle forbidden items and to keep silent about them were left with nothing. The transfer of property was often nasty, as Fidler was not satisfied with the process, and he tried especially hard to find money, valuables, and tobacco. The "Transport Department" was responsible for "smooth execution"; its infamous leader, Robert Mandler, along with his assistants, was a true Jewish scoundrel. Even the Czech police trembled before Mandler, with whom the SS could be satisfied; he forced the police by threats to address him only in German. With his riding boots and his leather jacket, Mandler even looked like an SS man.

People were diligently robbed of their money; if it had not already been surrendered, they had to bring their silver and turn it in. All documents were confiscated; only the citizen's ID was returned, after being stamped "evacuated" or "ghettoized." By signing a declaration, a person "voluntarily" gave all his property to the "emigration fund." The slightest transgressions were punished and were taken out on the community by withholding rations and by blackouts. The relatively good food, which was better than any of the provisions in Theresienstadt, was delivered from a community kitchen. Men's hair was to be cut off, or at least cut short, but this order was not strictly followed, particularly later on. Head coverings could not be worn. Although prohibited, letters and parcels could be smuggled into the assembly site.

Most people's mood was depressed. Many lost their bearings; nervous breakdowns and hysterical fits were common, and the more level-headed had difficulty bringing order to the chaos. Days and nights passed in noisy hustle and bustle. The functionaries of the "Transport Department" wore white armbands with the inscription "J.K.G." A "transport leader" was chosen from among the victims, as well as several "stewards," who were responsible for quiet and order during roll calls, the loading, and the journey. These people usually received yellow armbands, which also were handed out to others on the transport and read, for example, "Jewish physician" or "Jewish nurse." The clinic at the assembly point was in miserable condition, and the doctors could offer little more than consolation.

Then, in the early hours of the morning, they marched, escorted by German and Czech police, to a nearby suburban train station. Before that, they were forced to spend many hours standing in the courtyard of the property of the trade fair, in all weather, with no consideration for age or illness. Those who collapsed were laid on stretchers, along with those who could not walk or were recognized as "seriously ill." During the march, they were subject to harassment by the SS and their Jewish lackeys. Abuse was a constant accompaniment to all deportations in Hitler's Reich. The equipment and private "additional luggage" accompanying the transport was loaded onto separate freight cars. Fifty to sixty people, always sorted according to "transport numbers," were loaded into each passenger or freight car, along with their "hand luggage." A transport of 1,000 people took not quite four hours to load. After the escort of German policeman had boarded, the train departed. In two to three hours it arrived at the train station of Theresienstadt, in Bohušovice.

Remarks Preliminary to Chapters 4–7

Preparations for the camp were well advanced, but none of the Jews involved had foreseen the confusing abundance of events that would ultimately determine its real conditions. Only after long development did the procedure achieve a certain monotony in many respects. This impression is relative, however, as the everyday life of the camp unfolded before ever-new prisoners. Compared with a normal society, these new arrivals were the equivalent of new generations who generally know only imprecise bits and pieces about the similar fates of their "ancestors."

Four clearly distinguishable phases of the history of the camp suggest themselves almost naturally. As in the history of all communities, these phases are not disconnected segments. They have multiple connections and transitions. Old institutions continue to exist, and the seeds of later conditions are sown. Every community is conditioned by circumstances that combine inner developments and external influences. This interaction was not suspended in the camp but was pathologically influenced and altered. Undisguised concentration camps generally featured only the structures prescribed by a higher power. In Theresienstadt, the Jews and the SS waged a complicated struggle for a self-administration that was real, or simulated but pretending to be real. From afar, the makeup of the prisoners allows comparison with a "normal" populace; such a composition was never seen in the actual concentration camps. Both sexes and all ages were represented, but, in contrast to the old ghettos in the East – ghettos that had been turned into forced labor camps – here there were *only* deportees. Theresienstadt shared one characteristic with all camps founded by the SS: a constant coming and going of people, of whom only a small percentage stayed in the camp for a longer time. Very few people experienced Theresienstadt from beginning to end.

Life in the "ghetto" was not limited by the natural course of life in the order of normal societies – in which all phases, from childhood to old age, unfold in a natural process. An abrupt act suddenly would bring a number of people unwillingly into this community, which no one wished to join voluntarily, and about which no one had previously received sufficient information. If an individual did not die, he was then again deported in an abrupt act, and his destination was unknown to him or to those left behind. Thus entry to and exit from this community occurred not through birth and death but, rather, through unforeseeable, if expected, events. To the newcomer, arrival in the camp signified birth, whereas deportation resembled death. Human beings cry at their physical birth. It is not wrong to understand that the same is true of the new arrival to the camp. If he is unbroken and viable, he will experience his camp childhood with many parallels to the experience and destiny of actual childhood. Similarly, the later steps in natural and camp life also exhibit analogous characteristics. As a human being generally employs his vital energies in the service of his struggle against death, so here he fights against his deportation and fears the transport.

Thus we describe the pathology of this history and uncover the deepest methods for understanding it. The goals of this history are simpler than is ever the case in normal communities. There was only one goal, resolved in one word: end. If the goal of this history was its end, for the individual, the goal was to survive imprisonment in Theresienstadt – there, if possible, and not in another, unknown camp. Everybody hoping for personal survival was conscious of this goal. Everybody knew that the goal coincided with the end of the war and of National Socialism. The relationship to this goal was subject to changes in connection with conditions in the camp, conditions that roughly correspond to the phases of this history.

At the beginning, level-headed people believed that it was possible that the war would last a long time. This was consistent with the necessity of construction and of establishing a system in which it was possible to live, in whatever way. This was the period of the "closed camp" and also of the "ghetto." The gradual, feigned pacification and consolidation of conditions during the phases of the "ghetto" and the "settlement area" added preservationist intentions to the constructing tendencies that still were at work. This was the "maturing phase" of the camp. Anyone who thus far had been allowed to stay made his arrangements and hoped to hold out until the end. The simple initial structure became more and more complicated. There developed a communal life that was faintly reminiscent of normal society. During the "settlement area" period, the signs of National Socialism's approaching demise began to multiply. The meaning and order of the camp seemed fulfilled when, beginning in fall 1944, sudden deportations – resembling liquidations – initiated the phase of decay. Those left behind saw how the camp became paralyzed and began to disintegrate, as in the late stages of other communities. The following chapters will illustrate the progress of these four phases.

4

The Closed Camp, November 1941–July 1942

Our discussion of Theresienstadt's early history showed how the first Jewish Elder, Edelstein, strove to keep in the camp as many Jews from the "Protectorate" as possible and, in this way, to save them, through productive labor for the SS. Until 1943, many measures taken by the Jewish leadership originated in this intention. The leadership's repeated failures explain why the prisoners failed to understand their endeavors. Edelstein's policies may have delayed the extermination work of the SS, but surely only for a short time, and even this is not very likely. There is no doubt that Edelstein had the best of intentions at first, but it is equally clear that these became increasingly obscured by the growing corruption of many of the leading functionaries around Edelstein – both with and without his knowledge. It is also extremely difficult to draw a line between feigned servility toward the SS in order to save lives and spineless collaboration. When SS tactics showed that Edelstein's plans had failed, choosing a different policy had long since become impossible, and the camp developed in ways that no longer could be changed by anyone.

The following report demonstrates Edelstein's behavior in the camp's early period:

[Following Edelstein's arrival] we knew right away that this was supposed to be more of a prison than a Jewish city.... When [Sturmbannführer] Günther installed himself in Theresienstadt in the early days, and Edelstein accused him of deception, Günther answered, "Now, when you're sitting in garbage, Jews, show what you can do!" [Sentiment against Edelstein:] The initial hatred of him and his colleagues abated, and he even gained sympathy.... Everyone trusted that he spoke the truth, that our interests were also his, and that he could represent our interests to the Germans as could no one else. [Edelstein often said:] They [the SS] want to offer us [the Jewish leaders] all possible and impossible privileges so that we forget that we represent the Jews and feel more of an affiliation with them, and above all, they want to breed the hatred of the masses against us. [As an example, the suggestion of creating a special kitchen, with reference to military provisioning of officers and soldiers, was mentioned.] Edelstein refused this, and the answer [from the SS] was: "Communist methods!" [Edelstein clung to his theory of rescue through work, even after the first deportations from Theresienstadt:] To break out of the intended concentration of the Jews, we must send workers to places outside Theresienstadt and get orders from Aryan firms. (201)

64   *History*

Edelstein therefore endeavored to build up productive factories in the "ghetto" and tried to place his work groups outside the camp. He also believed it was important to keep the SS constantly busy, which explains the countless, lavishly supplied reports full of statistics and illustrations, which exceeded even the already absurd amount of information that the SS demanded and kept the administrative apparatus in constant suspense. The "Central Office" already had been swamped by such concoctions by the JKG in Prague. Like spoiled children, the SS wanted more and more, even the most ludicrous lists that wasted time and effort, and the Jews offered them more and more. The way in which Edelstein organized his reports may not demonstrate clear vision but does show a sense of responsibility and sometimes unusual courage. He continually pointed out the lack of workers or described health risks. Edelstein hardly suspected the degree to which his honest efforts provided only worthless enjoyment to the SS. His highest goal was to prevent transports and gain time. His labor was only rarely rewarded with fruitful results, which were soon destroyed. This best side of Edelstein's activities must be recognized, in all its tragedy.

On November 24, 1941, 340 young men, the first "Construction Kommando" (*Aufbaukommando* [AK I]), arrived in the early hours of the morning and were imprisoned in E I. Neither Edelstein nor SS Camp Commander Dr. Siegfried Seidl was in Theresienstadt. In Prague, the men had been told that they would do various types of construction work but were otherwise free and could visit their families on weekends. The *Aufbaukommando* thus did not realize that, with their departure, they already had been deported. The men discovered a nearly empty, disorderly *Kaserne*, the walls of which, as well as those of the remaining barracks, were covered with heroic or supposedly funny inscriptions and frescoes drawn by the German soldiers who had lived there previously. The "orders of the day" for February 11, 1942, finally ordered the whitewashing of the walls. The only furniture in the dirty barracks consisted of a few damaged beds, tables, and benches. On the ground floor were empty storerooms, horse stables, insufficient and primitive toilets, and a large washroom that, together with a smaller one on the first floor, later would have to suffice for more than 5,000 people. Finally, there were two unequipped, dark kitchens. The first floor housed troop quarters: long and dimly lit vaults. Here the first prisoners lived; here the first primitive offices were set up in small rooms, along with the first poorly equipped outpatient clinic and the first miserable infirmary. On the second floor were seven large rooms with concrete floors; these had served as storehouses and never as accommodations. Workshops were supposed to be established here, but they were turned into living quarters. More than four hundred men were crowded into one room; each room resembled a small camp in its own right. Even after a few small iron stoves had been set up, the fuel they scavenged did not suffice to warm these rooms. The quite spacious courtyard facing the town had been planted with some trees. There was a water faucet and a well that was out of order. The courtyard was bordered by a high wall with two gates, crowned by barbed wire. One of them usually was closed; the second was guarded by Czech gendarmes and soon also by the Ghetto Guard (Ghettowache [GW]) and the Order Constabulary (Ordnungsdienst [OD]). The rear of the barracks hugged the ramparts of the fortification and left room for only two small, long courtyards that, together with the attached entrenchment, remained off limits for a long time.

The gendarmerie, usually 120 to 150 men, formally followed the orders of the Czech authorities, but, in practice, it obeyed the SS and mainly performed the following tasks: guarding the Jews and isolating them from the outside world, escorting transports and work columns outside the barracks (later only outside the "ghetto"), searching the luggage of new arrivals, and guarding cells holding camp inmates who had violated camp rules. The guard room in E I – and, later, in all other barracks – was situated next to the entrance, where the GW was also given a room as a duty room. Approaching the open gate in the daytime or lingering in the courtyards past 8 P.M. was strictly forbidden.

The *Aufbaukommando* could hardly leave the barracks and could not attend to the necessary tasks, but up until December 4, 1941, an additional 3,000 people arrived in three transports from Prague and Brünn [Brno]. One of these transports was the second *Aufbaukommando* (AK II), composed of 1,000 young men who, together with AK I, were supposed to form the core group for building up the camp. The AK was to be headed by the "staff" – Edelstein and his chosen colleagues, nineteen men and four women – who also arrived on December 4. For a long time, the "staff" and the AK transports were regarded as elite and enjoyed allocated and acquired privileges, which were gradually rescinded or simply faded away. AK II consisted of engineers, physicians, technical and administrative experts, craftsmen, and workers: "The task of the Staff [*Stab*] and these two Construction Kommandos was to make the organizational and technical preparations for the reception of a population of an estimated fifty-thousand Jews" (354). After its arrival, the leadership made the following proclamation:

Notice from the Leadership, on 5 December 1941
The leadership is not able to make any promises to its fellow residents in advance. It can only declare that it wishes to devote its best efforts, and [that it] will seek to fulfill the tasks assigned to it honestly and justly.

The work that faces the new leadership is extremely difficult and can only be made somewhat tolerable, in the interests of all residents, if peace, order, and cleanliness, trust and the active cooperation of all is certain. It is necessary to structure the institutions such that discipline, work and life will be possible. The new leadership will use all its efforts to present the wishes and needs of the residents to the offices in charge, and will do everything possible to adapt the internal organization to the requirements.

The new leadership will, however, take steps against any employee and any resident who offends against the orders issued. (289)

The chaos was obvious. On the very first day, a member of the "staff" was called out and arrested. Later, people learned of his execution as a Communist. Nobody knew where to put people when they were allocated the first rooms and halls, in which no preparations had been made. Everything was lacking. Finally, people received some wood shavings and boards, and here and there some sacks of straw, so that women and children did not have to sleep on bare boards in damp rooms. It was fortunate that the initial transports were not robbed of their carefully prepared luggage, with its blankets and warm clothes. People lived almost exclusively from the provisions they had brought with them, but this was not enough to prevent famine during the early weeks. AK I had erected a makeshift kitchen, in which only one pot, with a capacity of 300 L, was usable. This pot then had to be used to cook for thousands of people, and despite unceasing work, this was, of course, insufficient. To receive their meager meals, people had to stand in line for an endless period in the bitter cold and sometimes received nothing. Many did not even receive the bad, unsweetened ersatz coffee. "Lunch" was rarely finished before late afternoon and usually consisted of a handful of low-quality beets, disgustingly mixed with badly peeled potatoes. In time, everyone received his food without long queuing, and meals were available earlier, but the food was also ever more repulsive, because the potatoes and root vegetables were poorly stored and therefore froze or rotted. Every second day, 500 g of bread was distributed; this amount was increased to 700 g from December 17, 1941, on. Margarine hardly found its way into the food; it was occasionally distributed in 20 g slices but often was not given out for weeks. From time to time, prisoners could obtain a small slice of watery sausage, a spoonful of diluted root jam, or, very rarely, a spoonful of sugar.

In the early days, it was almost impossible to leave the barracks; leaving was forbidden without the escort of a gendarme. After the provisional commander, Sturmbannführer Richard Skarabis (see 243f), had handed over the Camp Commandant's Office to Obersturmführer (later Hauptsturmführer) Dr. Seidl and his deputy, Untersturmführer (later Obersturmführer) Karl Bergel, "transit passes" (*Durchlaßscheine*) were introduced in early December; they were valid only in connection with a civilian identity card, and Bergel was to hand them out at Edelstein's suggestion. They were issued in the name of the bearer alone, or with a certain number of unnamed companions, or to a working group with a specific number of people. But, even then, working groups could leave the barracks only if escorted by a gendarme. The destination – such as the barracks, factories, or train station – as well as the time of day and the expiration date of permitted excursions was meticulously noted. Transit passes to the women's barracks were the most coveted. Women received far fewer transit passes than did men. It was difficult and time-consuming to move with these pieces of paper. One first had to report to the GW and then the gendarmerie, both of which had to note the time of exit. On entering barracks not one's own, the arrival and then departure time had to be recorded in a similar manner. The return had to be registered with the gendarmerie and also with the GW. Grave consequences followed if one forgot to do so. One would be called to the gate, and punishments and a box on the ears ensued. The manipulations for large exiting work groups were extremely prolonged; the group members often had to stand for hours until they could pass, after repeated head counts. GW men, as well as one or two gendarmes, would go with them. Singing, and often even speaking, was strictly forbidden. People with "individual transit passes" were unaccompanied. Sidewalks were not to be walked on. Using main streets was likewise forbidden, although, in contradiction to this, the prisoners were required to choose the shortest route possible. The intimidated civilian population was not to come into contact with anyone and was to look away. Transit passes were issued to members of the Council of Elders, which was established after Edelstein's arrival; high functionaries; the GW; physicians; craftsmen; cooks; and transport and shipping workers.

After his arrival, Edelstein and his deputy, the engineer Zucker, were called to the Camp Commandant's Office. Until the end of August 1942, the office was located in L 414, the former division command. All women and children up to the age of twelve had to move to H V on December 6, while the men and the older boys stayed in E I. Especially among the women, this order inspired panic and almost a revolt. Edelstein and his co-workers, who officiated from suitcases in a tiny room, were inundated and overwhelmed. The gendarmes warned the unruly masses that a visit from the SS at this moment could have dire consequences:

The Closed Camp, November 1941–July 1942

The GW takes action for the first time. The ... women are lined up in rows and a three-man delegation is to negotiate with the Jewish Elder. It is already dark. The excitement is ... somewhat moderated by the promised intervention. The delegation demands from the Jewish Elder an immediate end to separation of families. Edelstein [who knew the aforementioned camp in Nisko] ... explained to the women the consequences of not carrying out SS orders immediately. "You must go to the Commandant's Office today!" was the demand.... Edelstein knew that a change or end to the order was ... impossible. "I will go to the Commandant's Office now and will present your wishes and requests." In half an hour, Edelstein returned, saying the camp commandant would not receive him today. In reality, he had not left the barracks, since he could not ... leave the barracks without instructions. (145)

The order was not altered. The move had to be carried out at the prescribed time.

Loaded with knapsacks, columns formed, guarded by the gendarmes and GW, to bring the helpless women's necessities to their barracks and to help them. [Only thirty to fifty men could go to the women's barracks in the morning and afternoon to work. The gendarmes benevolently allowed a larger number.] The attempt was made to introduce a rotation, so that everyone could have a turn in the Dresden Kaserne as quickly as possible.... But the joy of reunion was clouded. It was possible to speak to women and children for only a few minutes, and at constant risk, for an SS man could appear at any moment. The sexes had to remain separate, that was the order. Any meeting in the courtyard or even in a room was punishable. Already a man who has just taken leave of his wife and child has been spotted by an SS man. It ends in several blows to the face and arrest. (145)

It was much rarer for women to get into the men's barracks than vice versa. There were always men in the women's barracks, because only they, then as well as later, held high administrative posts. Cooks and other men were always legally in the women's barracks; some even lived there. The separation of men and woman was a surprising step that had not been foreseen in Prague. "This measure helped to determine the camp-like character of the ghetto in the development period" (354). This is how it was put in the official camp history.

In addition to E I and H V, in 1941 the following barracks were taken over: B V, I IV, E VI, and H IV. The takeover of C III and E VII followed, at the beginning of 1942; a little later, A IV (the bakery) was occupied. Only shortly before the city was taken over, the camp was expanded into B IV; the "armory" (*Zeughaus*), part of H IV; A II; and E IIIa (where the gendarmerie had been housed until then). The men's barracks included E I; at times, E VII and H IV; most of B V; and, after takeover, B IV. The women's barracks included H V; C III; and, at times, H IV. The Magdeburg Kaserne (B V) soon became the residence of almost all high functionaries, with the Jewish Elder at the head. Their wives and children moved into this barracks beginning in March 1942. The GW also lived there for a long time. However, the barracks mainly served as the seat of the central Jewish authorities. E VI was enlarged starting in early 1942 and was used as the central hospital (previously, the division infirmary was located there). The orders of the day for January 20, 1942, announced the consent of the commandant's office to housing old men and women together in E VI. Thus the first "home for the infirm" (*Siechenheim*) came into being there, with separate rooms for both sexes. E VI was connected to E VII (Kavalier Kaserne) by a courtyard with old chestnut trees. For decades, there had been only storerooms there; the dreary casemates had not been lived in for a long time. At this point E VII became a housing barracks and remained one of the worst quarters; it was almost without a place to wash and other creature comforts. For many months, almost all arriving transports came there, to the *Schleuse* (funnel). Then this miserable building was labeled a "home for the elderly and infirm" and was filled with unfortunates of both sexes. I IV was only at times occupied, except for being used occasionally as the Schleuse. The "Central Camp Office" was housed there, but it had to move to the similarly constructed A IV in late June 1942, while the "clothing warehouse" controlled by the SS was set up in I IV. Starting in March 1943, I IV lay outside the camp and could only be visited with a transit pass. A IV housed the bakery and soon also the "Central Camp" and "Central Provisions" Offices. This barracks, too, housed only a few people, but A IV was also used as the Schleuse, as were almost all barracks at times, as well as other buildings. The building always remained within the camp but also could be entered only with a transit pass. E III became a "home for the infirm" and a hospital in summer 1943. It was a site of unspeakable misery, with its stuffy rooms packed with tuberculosis patients and helpless old people. A II was a desolate, small, dark barracks that served for a time as the Schleuse before becoming a quarantine for "people with lice [and those] who were unable to walk" – a place of horror, hunger, and death. In summer 1943, A II became a men's barracks.

> Persons over 60 years of age were housed without being separated by sex in the Kavalier Kaserne [E VII], and later also in the Bodenbach Kaserne [H IV]. Very soon, the necessity of establishing a central hospital became clear; it was created in January 1942 in the Hohenelber Kaserne [E VI], though part of this barracks still had to serve as a home for the infirm. The very crowded housing, the elimination of family life, and the combination of men and women by rooms into living groups, as well as the necessity of organizing all the details of life, in accordance with the available primitive means, in barracks-like fashion, compelled a rigid camp-like leadership of the ghetto.... It became clear that the leadership's original intention of establishing the settlement as a ghetto and not as a camp was infeasible under the existing conditions. The intention was not abandoned, but for the time being postponed.... The smallest organizational unit was the room, which was led by a room elder who was responsible for quiet, order, cleanliness, and registration, as well as for ensuring that his inmates went to work, and was also to supervise the distribution of food to them. (354)

In the beginning, the room inmates, led by their elders, were supposed to pick up their meals from the kitchen hatches according to a specific schedule. This order, like so many others, could not be implemented and was soon disregarded. "The rooms were aggregated in groups and led by group elders who acted as assistance organs to the building elders.... The building elders received their orders from Central Building Management. The administration's announcements were, and still are [at the end of 1943], made public in the form of orders of the day and musters [*Appelle*]" (354). The first "children's home" was established in E I. Others followed only after a scarlet fever ward had been opened in the hospital.

> Each barracks was a self-contained whole in which each department of the Council of Elders had a branch office. It had its Building Management, its Provisions and kitchens, its outpatient clinics and infirmaries, its Work Deployment, its Technical Building Management, its Cleaning and Order Services. Because food and necessities were distributed, in the early months, to all inmates equally without distinction ... a communal lifestyle of a special sort ... developed. Not only was it difficult to house people without beds, without any furnishings, not even with mattresses or palliasses; providing meals caused

extraordinary difficulty, because the available cooking pots were far too small and there was no kitchen equipment. At the beginning ... since the pots were insufficient ... cooking had to be done and food distributed all day, and it happened every day that hundreds of people ... received nothing to eat. Then ration cards were introduced.... In the early months there were no nails or ... other places to ... hang up a coat, the electric lights from the too-weak facility constantly failed, the administrative work had to be completed almost without desks, without lockable cabinets, just with a wholly insufficient number of chairs and seats, and at the beginning ... there were only two typewriters in the ghetto. The first outpatient clinic ... was equipped most primitively, like the first infirmary.... After a few days, a provisional operating room was set up in the Dresden Kaserne, in which some difficult operations were carried out using the most primitive means. At first, only a few private trucks and tractors were available ... as means of transportation, later a few horses. But this was hardly enough to obtain the necessary transport of food, materials and luggage from the Bauschowitz [Bohušovice] train station. All other transport without exception had to be performed by porter crews. Despite these extremely primitive conditions, an administration began to be created immediately upon the Staff's arrival, according to the principles established in Prague.... The Jewish Elder and his deputy formed the leadership. They are supported by the Central Secretariat and its personnel office. The administration is divided into five main departments.

I.   Department of Internal Administration

    It includes Building Management, with the Rationing Service, Cleaning and Order Services, the Central Registry with Family Registry and Statistics, the Birth and Death Lists and Funeral Services, the Legal Department ... , Transport Management ... , Space Management and the Post Office, as well as Central Labor, which ... was later directly subordinated to the Administration.

II.   Economics Department

    It is responsible for obtaining and storing all the materials and provisions, for general feeding, via Central Provisioning, by the kitchens and by direct distribution ... Shipping Department ... Agriculture. A particularly important department is "Production," which has to work not only for internal use, but also for delivery outside the ghetto.

III.   Finance Department

    Essentially its task is only economic statistics, as purchase and payment of suppliers to the ghetto is done by the Camp Commandant's Office.

IV.   Technical Department

    It includes engineering, waterworks, electricity, rail and street work, installation and heating technology, building police, garbage disposal, technical administration and maintenance of buildings.

V.   Health Services ...

    The Ghetto Guard [GW] was created on 6 December 1941, and wore an officially approved uniform cap and a duty belt. (354)

Initially, the GW consisted of 35 men. After it had been restructured several times, it reached a high point in February 1943 with 420 men, in addition to reserves, but was soon changed again and reduced to 150 men.

It was responsible for overseeing the post, lockup and other security services in the manner of a disciplined police squad. To strengthen communal discipline, starting on 28 December 1941, with the approval of the camp commandant's office, comradeship evenings were organized, from which special events for Recreation [*Freizeitgestaltung*] developed.... The first kitchen in the Sudeten Kaserne [E I] consisted of a dark room with a half-broken oven.... The tiles for rebuilding the stove had to be broken off the redoubts. On 26 November 1941, the first warm meal was … handed out. Kitchen equipment and places to keep cooking pots were a constant problem for the ghetto administration, which is still **not** [at the end of 1943!] completely solved. For a normal mass kitchen operation, one needs a kitchen space sufficient to provide for 1.2 liters per person. Although all … available military kitchens were restored as fast as possible, the kitchen space was never enough. On 1 January 1942, people had over .78 liters per head; on 30 January 1942, it was only over .66…. Modern cooking pots were successfully obtained, but there were no workers for installation. Otherwise, the kitchens lacked other necessary equipment as well. People had no scales or weights, no containers, no scoop to distribute food. The cooking pots, constantly sitting over the fire, were damaged; every moment, another one failed. Again and again, the regular and timely distribution of food was affected by technical disruptions. The lack of water was another source of difficulties for cooking….

Until … the end of 1941, provisioning was done almost exclusively with the food that the transports brought with them. On 15 December … it was announced what ration could be used per person and day…. It was around 1,640 calories. [This was an illusory figure; see Chapter 12.] (354)

Efforts at "production" already were being made during the initial weeks:

[On December 15, 1941, the "Agriculture Department" took over the first gardens. Beginning in January 1942, this involved horses, and then other animals; beginning in late April 1942, fields, meadows, and forests were put to use. In April, 150 people worked in agriculture. The yield was delivered to the SS.] Until around March 1942, the aim of Production … was to concentrate on setting up the most important enterprises for [the ghetto's] own needs. In the area of outside production, … the planning work begun in Prague was carried on…. In January 1942, the workshops from the Sudeten Kaserne were transferred to the *Bauhof* [garrison workshop] … despite all the difficulties, in January 1942 a small locksmith's shop was already in operation, as well as a workshop for sewing machine repair, a carpentry shop with two foremen and 39 workers, which [brought about] above all the production of the bunk beds that were so important … with the dense crowding, a glazier's, a room paint shop, a tailor shop with 2 masters and 33 skilled workers, a shoemaker's with one master and 13 skilled workers, a bag-maker, a small paper container workshop…. Shortly after the end of the first quarter year, some 900 sewing machines … were available; these were intended to be used for making clothing. [That never happened, and most of the machines rusted away.] The Central Laundry and the Central Bath were also taken over during this period. The Laundry and the Collection Service started up … in modest fashion, while the Central Bath could only later … be used. (354)

As soon as a barracks had been taken over, outpatient clinics and infirmaries were established. There was a particular lack of nurses.

A sudden outbreak of a scarlet fever epidemic compelled the establishment of an Infectious Disease Ward on 10 January 1942…. The principle that has been applied to this day: decentrally-led health units, corresponding to the separate housing units, which at the time were strictly separated; however, central administration, supported by a precise registration service. Daily status reports in the evening gave those in charge a full picture of the state of health at any time. In the early period, the Health Service was also responsible for funeral services…. Within the framework of the Health Service, the first barber shops were created, and the sub-department "Delousing" was established…. Lice infestations were minimal….. (354)

In the beginning, the camp was run very strictly and differed little from a "normal" concentration camp. The arrivals on the first transports did not feel "arrested," as they had come "freely." The reception in the camp brought hardship,

The Closed Camp, November 1941–July 1942

but, at least initially, these hardships were milder than they would be later and always remained far more benign than in a strict camp. In the beginning, the inmates made efforts to ease the acclimatization of the new arrivals, so they were better able to assimilate than was the case later on. Many a new arrival who had dreaded the deportation even breathed a sigh of relief in the early days, succumbing to the illusion that the uncertainty, the constant upheaval, and the worst were over. In the chaos of life in the camp, newcomers in that period were even less able to recognize a structured plan and a pattern than they were later. The SS vigorously countered this seemingly loose structure, in order to intimidate prisoners who obviously lacked the awareness that they were in a camp and at the mercy of the SS. The SS came into much closer contact with such prisoners than would be the norm later on in Theresienstadt, when they remained more in the background, from whence they did not seem to get close to individual prisoners, except during transports.

But, initially, the SS intervened repeatedly and abruptly. At the beginning of December, a roll call of all men was held in E I by Camp Inspector Karl Bergel, during which he spoke of his "hard and soft heart." Which one he would show, he said, depended on the behavior of the Jews. In the future, he often displayed his "hard" heart, and for a long time, because of his brutality, he was the most feared member of the SS. After the roll call, Bergel had all the men, including the Jewish leadership, do physical exercises and jogging.

These roll calls soon ceased, but internal roll calls were maintained; they were only gradually given up on the arrival of many infirm people. The most dangerous man besides Bergel throughout his stay was the commander of the gendarmerie, Oberleutnant Theodor Janeček, an unscrupulous Czech collaborator. He spoke only German on principle and was a cruel man who reported every trifling matter to the SS. The gendarmes, too, feared him; usually they were not bad fellows and did not care about the Jews, and some were even friendly. Bergel, Janeček, and some other SS men were constantly looking for "culprits" during the early months, especially in the women's barracks, where they hoped to catch "black" (illegal) visitors or smokers. Bags were searched for forbidden goods and letters. The victims were beaten and usually locked in cells, where more maltreatment followed, or, even worse, they were sent to the SS; some were beaten to death there – cause of death: "heart attack" – whereas others disappeared forever into a concentration camp. In the best case, one might be released, which happened more frequently later on. But this was often misleading luck, because these persons usually left "on orders" with the next transport. Before deportations, Edelstein made efforts to free prisoners and usually was successful. It was easy for the SS to make this humane gesture, as the fate of the deportees was no secret to them.

Apart from the separate incarceration of men and women, the strict prohibition of mail to the outside world was most keenly felt. Sometimes even mail deliveries from barracks to barracks were forbidden. Many promises made to the AK transports were quickly rescinded. Driven by hunger, fear, and recognition of their situation, some attempted to flee – they rarely succeeded – or to help themselves by making forbidden purchases in the town's shops, making illegal contact with gendarmes and civilians, sending "black" mail deliveries, or obtaining money. The consequences were stricter controls and surveillance. Once or twice daily, complicated head counts were carried out in all quarters.

From December 15, 1941, onward, the leadership issued almost daily "orders of the day" to publicize SS orders and its own announcements. Later on, these did not occur on Saturdays and became rarer. To the displeasure of those involved, these orders replaced the "newspaper" for which plans had been made in Prague. In addition to this, the barracks administrations gave out their own orders of the day under the heading "Memorandum [*Rundschreiben*] from the building elder." Both were posted, and room elders had to read them aloud to the prisoners.

In order to prevent flight, prisoners were ordered to have their hair cut short; men's hair was to be 3 mm long, and women were to be given "men's cuts." The Council of Elders and the "staff" were exempt from these requirements. Apart from some early attempts, this order was not implemented. A "duty to salute" was instituted, most emphatically expressed in the orders of the day for December 21, 1941: "By order of the authorities, all camp inmates must salute members of the camp commandant's office, the SS, the government gendarmerie, and any uniform wearer. Violations of this order will be punished in future with 10 lashes. Marching groups of workers are to take off their caps without command" (301). Men had to take off their head coverings, and women had to bow. Later, when many elderly people arrived, they did not comprehend these and similar orders. Some were made aware of their "duty to salute" in a painful manner, even though they did not understand the reason. As German was the official language of the camp, orders during this militaristic phase had to be belted out in German. Never again was so much shouting and shrill noisemaking with whistles heard as in these first months. The "Jewish Star" had to be worn, of course, even inside the barracks. When, during the warm season, men worked without shirts, the orders of the day for June 16, 1942, ordered that a star be affixed to their pants; the star was "to be immediately removed [from the pants] once the upper body was covered."

To foster discipline, it was ordered that all transgressions discovered or punished by the GW be immediately reported to the SS. Luckily, the GW was sensible and tolerant, preventing much damage in those evil days. Still, many tragic events occurred.

> It was announced by the authorities: [six names follow]. All of those listed left the work column on the 17th of this month without permission and had contact with women. They are guilty of violating the camp rules and are sentenced to 25 lashes, which punishment will be carried out by the Ghetto Guard.
>
> Dr. Georg König, born [September 18, 1901], Sudeten Kaserne.
>
> The above-named left his work column without permission and made contact with his wife and daughter. Asked about this, he denied the fact; only after a longer investigation was he convicted of the act and admitted to it. He will be punished for misleading the authorities and violating the prohibition on visiting the women's barracks with one month's imprisonment and 25 lashes. The imprisonment will end on [January 19, 1942] at 5 P.M. (orders of the day, December 21, 1941)

Bergel frequently came into the cells of E I with a stick. He would choose two strong GW men and sentence detainees to 25 strokes with the stick. If Bergel was dissatisfied with the way in which these were carried out, the GW men themselves received a beating of 25 or even more strokes and were removed from the GW.

On the street, inspections for letters and parcels increased, and every transgressor received the usual punishments. Some spent many months in the custody of the gendarmerie in the prisons of E I and H V. Later, the SS ordered the Jews to build a dungeon, the "bunker," in the cold room of a former hotel (Q 416). There, victims were kept incarcerated in the dark, without heating or sanitary facilities, and were always at the mercy of the SS. But nothing could break the prisoners' will to

The Closed Camp, November 1941–July 1942

transgress the "prohibitions and orders in force"; they only tried to be more careful. In the second half of December, Seidl and Bergel ordered a roll call for the men of E I. Seidl announced that letters had been sent through some civilians who had already been arrested. Anyone who had sent forbidden letters was called on to turn himself in, with the assurance that he would not be punished; otherwise, the "ghetto" should expect severe punishment. Seidl gave them two minutes. Two men answered. They were immediately arrested and hanged on January 10, 1942. From then on, escape attempts and illegal mail contacts were expressly punishable with the death penalty.

[On January 9, 1942, the Council of Elders was summoned by the SS.] Sworn to silence upon threat of death, they are informed that the next day a number of prisoners will ... be executed by hanging. A double gallows is to be erected in the ditch of the Aussiger barracks [I IV] and 25 coffins are to be prepared. Everything must be ready by 9 A.M.... The Council of Elders ... confers.... The head of the GW is summoned by the Jewish Elder. He is given ... the assignment of preparing rope to tie hands and feet and two ropes for strangulation. The commander of the GW with 10 GW men will take part in the execution. This assignment may be announced only tomorrow morning. The head of the technical department must prepare ... the gallows, coffins, and a mass grave right near the gallows. A work group digs the grave through the night in the frozen ground, supervised by the SS. Another erects the gallows. In the office of the GW head, the ropes for hands and feet are made out of short hemp, for there is nothing else available..... Thus a sleepless night is spent by those in the know. At 6 in the morning, the GW assembles.... The head of the GW announces the assignment of having to provide 11 men for the execution, and asks for volunteers.... Not a word is heard from the ranks. The commander explains that it has to happen.... The execution commando is assembled from volunteers and receives instructions to report at 9 A.M.... to SS-USTF [SS-Untersturmführer] Bergel. At 6:30 A.M., Bergel appears, completely drunk ... and calls for the Jewish Elder. A short consultation ... the head of the GW is summoned by the Jewish Elder.... "You have until 9:30 A.M. to summon two 'people of the worst repute' to be executioners. That is the order I just received from Bergel...." "Whom should I designate the one with the worst reputation and expect such a task?" ... The time passes, and it is almost 9 o'clock. "If you don't go soon and provide the executioner, Bergel will give you the task of executioner or shoot you," says Edelstein.... Meanwhile, the building elders assemble as ordered ... in front of the Jewish Elder's room, for the Council of Elders must ... also be present. Both the civilian population and the ... ghetto inmates were already forbidden to use the streets or courtyards at night, or to stand at windows. All streets have been occupied by the gendarmerie.... The head of the GW asks the building elder of the Sudeten Kaserne ... to accompany him.... Fog, empty streets and windows. Only the patrolling gendarmes. Icy cold – it is well under 20 degrees [Celsius]. "Do you know what I'm thinking of? We will assemble all the butchers and ask for two ... volunteers; they are best suited to take on this assignment and not torment the victims." ... 15 gendarmes are assembled, aside from the normal guard, in the guard room. They sense what is coming. But those condemned to death still don't know! The GW's guardroom is cleared, while the building elder alerts the butchers. In a few minutes, 8 men appear.... "How old are you?" "17!" "And you?" "18!" "And you?" "60!" "You three can leave!" ... "I have sad news for you, but also an urgent request. Some of our comrades have been condemned to death by hanging. The sentence will be executed at 10 o'clock, and two of you must carry it out. I am supposed to designate the two individuals of the most evil repute in the ghetto for this, that's the assignment.... I cannot carry out this order. But I ask you to volunteer to take on this terrible assignment." All turn pale. "I have diabetes and have two children." "I was in the World War, have many decorations, was a gendarmerie officer, but I cannot take this assignment!" So nothing remains to be done but a lottery.... At this moment, a small, broad-shouldered, almost crooked man enters, "I was supposed to report here, what's it about?" ... "I'll do it. What type of hanging are we talking about?" ... "I worked at an anatomical and pathological institute and later assisted the Prague executioner." Now he asks a 22-year-old man to do the work with him. He says he doesn't need to do much, as he will take care ... of the most important things. After some hesitation and convincing, the young man decides.... On the way, the executioner requests that Bergel be asked for a bottle of rum and chewing tobacco after the execution, because he needs that afterwards to calm himself..... Right on time, the group arrives at the gallows. "Herr Untersturmführer, I bring two volunteers." ... "Bravo!" is the answer from the still half-drunk Bergel.... Now 9 condemned men, escorted by 15 gendarmes, march and are stood in the redoubt ditch. In the next minutes, a group of SS, among them Sturmbannführer Günther from Prague, ... Dr. Seidl, the district administrator of Kladno. Seidl waves to the Council of Elders ... to follow him. Both groups approach the 9 victims, at which the camp commandant reads the following: "By order of the commander of the security service of Bohemia and Moravia, the following Jews are condemned to death by hanging for defaming the German Reich." ... The condemned are stripped to their undershirts and underpants in the terrible cold and tied together in pairs by their hands. They received the sentence without collapsing, but with firm courage. One says, "I only wrote to my grandmother," at which all the others cry, "Be quiet and don't violate your honor!" One asks, "Take my wedding ring and remember me to my wife!" The faces of the guarding gendarmes are pale, one sees the tears in their eyes, they want to speak but are not allowed to. As the victims come near the Council of Elders, one hears from the midst of the kommando, "Eyes right, honor to you and the executed!" One sings the battle song *Když nás půjdou....*" In front of the gallows, one says, "They won't win their war this way!" A second, to whom an SS man says, "Now, you cowardly dog, come here!" answers, "I'm not as cowardly as you, but innocent!" and puts the noose around his neck himself. "We are not afraid, but you won't win the war" and similar remarks are ... heard.... With the first victim, the rope breaks, the man falls to the ground. The executioners report, "Herr Lagerkommandant, the sentence is carried out according to law." An upward movement of the riding crop is the answer.... It takes almost two hours before the last man, half-frozen, is pulled onto the gallows.... When the Ghetto Guard had nearly completed the burial of the nine victims, the SS and the Council of Elders leave. The gendarmerie hurries over and joins the ranks of the GW. "Present arms!" sounds the command of the gendarmerie staff sergeant.... What was the defamation of the German Reich? One sent greetings to his grandmother and asked for some food, another wanted to buy gingerbread in a store and took off his Jewish star, which was called an escape attempt.... One had waited for a group of workers in the barracks courtyard without noticing an SS man behind him, who suddenly called him. He turned around and, apparently unintentionally, touched the SS man with his elbow, which was qualified as physical resistance. (145)

After the execution, *kaddish*, the mourner's prayer, was secretly recited at the Jewish Elder's and in most of the other quarters. Bergel held roll calls with Edelstein for the room elders. The latter announced the executions, while the former threatened and warned.

Roll Call of Room Elders:

On Saturday ... a roll call took place for room elders, in the presence of the official representatives. On this occasion, a report was made on the execution of the death sentence against 9 persons. The room elders were reminded of their duties and tasks and

The Closed Camp, November 1941–July 1942

called upon to see to it with all their energy and stamina that all rules be obeyed unconditionally. They were especially enjoined to make clear to the camp inmates the seriousness of offenses such as smuggling letters and escape attempts, in order to avoid further tragic consequences. (orders of the day, January 10, 1942)

On February 26, 1942, another seven young men were hanged for the same reasons and in a similar manner (see 250). A plea to the room elders read:

> The superior authorities requested that I inform you that 7 inmates of the ghetto were condemned today to death by hanging for violating the rules. . . . .
>
> We are all deeply distressed that another 7 ghetto inmates must go to their deaths.
>
> I appeal to all of you to do everything possible to protect the ghetto from a repetition of such a misfortune.
>
> You as room elders are asked to make clear to every single ghetto inmate that only extreme internal discipline and order can protect us from repeating such unfortunate hours.

Later, executions ceased. Edelstein's courage may have contributed to this, as he refused to witness the executions. He is said to have expressed this in the following words: "I will not watch this!" For this reason, he offered his resignation, which was not accepted. But by that point the policy had become more moderate.

Despite the harsh life, a good mood and, unfortunately, often exaggerated optimism prevailed in the early weeks, before the first executions. People treated one another with great camaraderie, which did not occur so generally later on. No great social differences were yet visible. Initially, the transfer of the Jewish Elder and his "staff" from E I to B V, announced shortly before Christmas, did not change this. Edelstein did not claim a room of his own, and the members of the Council of Elders lived together in modestly furnished rooms. Still, this isolation was the beginning of all evil – the SS had planned well. The "staff" was supposed to be completely isolated, but Edelstein knew how to circumvent this. He explained: "I want to disappear with the others into the chaos; otherwise the SS will always snoop around our own building." A noticeable change for the worse occurred with the arrival of the wives and families of the high functionaries, from March 1942 onward. The women brought much luggage, and their husbands accompanied them in an almost triumphal manner to the accommodation that had been prepared for them in B V; thus they never experienced the dreadfulness of the Schleuse and of the camp generally. The important gentlemen took up a family-oriented life in their own rooms. A "better" society evolved, setting a bad example; in this way, the distance between the elite and the simple prisoners began. The disastrous seeds of the camp's moral disintegration began to grow inexorably.

On December 23, 1941, the orders of the day stated: "Ghetto inmates of the Christian faith are informed that visiting a church is not permitted by the authorities, but that there are no objections to holding services within the buildings." The orders of the day on December 28, 1941, permitted "comradeship evenings." The "Central Secretariat" had to be notified of the program in advance, and the building elders were accountable. An example of the exaggerated optimism of this period was a man who consumed or gave away all his provisions, because he was sure that he would be home by New Year's 1942, after the happy end of the war. New Year's Eve was celebrated enthusiastically. With the acquiescence of sympathetic gendarmes, provisions, alcoholic beverages, and even some musical instruments were smuggled into the barracks. The possession of musical instruments and of many other things was strictly prohibited at the time; various exceptions applied only to the Council of Elders, the "staff," and the GW.

Soon after New Year's 1942, the gravity of the situation became clear. At the end of 1941, 4,045 men, 3,294 women, and 11 children under two years old lived in the barracks. On January 5, 1942, the orders of the day announced the first "transport to the East" on January 9. One thousand men and women had to go. The hope of being in a safe camp was shattered forever.

> After the directive is given, the transport is assembled at night and the people assigned to it notified that they are to make themselves ready early on the 9th in the courtyard of the barracks in which they are housed. From midnight on there was no sleep; the barracks inmates are awake. It is 23 degrees below zero [Celsius]. From 3 o'clock in the morning on, the transport participants ... are gathered in the courtyards and divided into groups of 50–80 persons. Half-frozen and in darkness, the groups begin to move at 6 A.M., escorted by gendarmes and GW, toward the Bohušovice train station. A sad picture, the people wading in snow and holding small children's hands, with knapsacks and all sorts of luggage, who can be seen for not quite 3 km. on the street. The walk takes 1½ to 2 hours. Within a few hours, they have been loaded into unheated cattle cars, each with 50–70 persons. The cars are sealed. After many hours of waiting, the train begins moving ... towards Dresden. (145)

From then until February 1943, the arrival and departure of transports became the norm and created unceasing restlessness. The camp could never achieve a stage of undisturbed work or consolidate itself. At the beginning of March 1942, the reasons for an appeal against "inclusion" (*Einreihung*) were formulated, and the terrible word *Familienzerreißung* (tearing apart of families) was first mentioned. Recognized reasons for appeal included *Familienzerreißung*, being more than sixty-five years of age, holding important war decorations, having a war-related disability of at least 60%, being involved in a current "Aryan mixed marriage," and holding foreign citizenship – in most existing countries except Poland, Luxembourg, the USSR, and later also Slovakia, Croatia, Rumania, and Hungary, although the USSR sometimes afforded temporary protection. Soon afterward, it was announced that the family members of the AK would be protected from being transported (this policy was more favorable for AK I than for AK II); this remained effective for a long time. Finally, the "inability to be transported" (*Transportunfähigkeit*), if attested by a physician, could serve as protection. Contact between family members who had been dispersed over several barracks and who had received their "call-up" was very difficult and added to the desperation. Some attempted, through additional mail services, to help those affected.

On January 4, 1942, the previously prohibited mail service between the individual barracks was restored. The unsealed letters had to be written in German. Small parcels, too, could be transported. Bowls or pots with some potatoes, wrapped in a towel, often wandered to the men's barracks and returned empty to the women's barracks. On January 23, 1942, limited mail contact with the "Protectorate" was permitted – one postcard with thirty words, written in print, per month. This permission was only on paper, however; the messages never reached their destinations. On May 14, 1942, the SS rescinded this illusory favor.

Funerals, and later cremations, always appeared miserable, but the most miserable were the events accompanying the first fatalities. The corpses were transferred to a barracks shack with the inscription "mortuary." From it a pungent smell of lime escaped, intermingling disgustingly with the stench of the nearby toilets. The dead were placed in unplaned, raw boxes. Short memorial services were held in the middle

The Closed Camp, November 1941–July 1942   77

of the staircase of E I. During the singing, life continued all around without any consideration. There was no silence, nor the least amount of respect for the dead. Fellows passed by with their food bowls, rattling their spoons. They did so not intentionally but out of dull indifference. The casket was loaded onto a cart or a horse carriage in the courtyard. The few mourners – hardly anyone was allowed to come from other barracks; those were treated as far-away worlds, even if they were only a few minutes away – followed the carriage to the gate. They were not allowed to continue. Gravediggers, two GW men, and a gendarme went out to the graveyard, which was situated next to a cemetery, between Theresienstadt and Bohušovice, for Russian prisoners of war from World War I. Later, the crematorium was built there. It was difficult to dig the graves in the cold winter weather. The high groundwater level made it difficult to reach much deeper than 60 cm into the frozen soil.

In spite of the continuing deportations, the number of prisoners grew steadily, and a dearth of space threatened. Interior "transfers" became necessary, to house specific groups together or to win space for factories and offices. In order not to lose track of the number of inmates in this chaos, "head counts" were ordered and were always accompanied by unpleasantness. The first census was carried out on December 25, 1941, during "barracks curfew."

The order of the day for December 25, 1941, announced that "squadrons" (*Hundertschaften*) should be set up. In the first month, the squadrons served as the core units for all jobs, as there were initially hardly any professional divisions – almost everyone worked everywhere and in whatever work was deemed necessary at the moment. This contributed to the camaraderie among the younger prisoners.

A building elder was responsible for every *Kaserne*, assisted by the group elder, who was subordinate to him. The building elder coordinated the activity of the "branches" of the individual central offices in his barracks, for example, the "Deployment Office," the "Central Labor Office," and the departments responsible for "space management," "transport management," "registry," "building maintenance," and "provisions." The building elder was responsible for "quiet, order and cleanliness," as well as the daily "status reports." His additional obligations included organization of proper blackouts, supervision of curfew from 10 P.M. to 6 A.M., enforcement of lights-out in the living quarters at 10 P.M. (at first, in E I, "night watches" helped enforce lights-out, at least in the halls, and, in addition, men from the OD patrolled the corridors and halls – at that time, the OD served as a police force inside the barracks, whereas the GW operated outside the barracks), oversight of the "water service" (older people with white armbands supervised the economical use of water in the washrooms and at all faucets), supervision of electricity usage (on February 25, 1941, extremely sparing use of electricity was ordered and electric cooking prohibited; beginning in March, the electricity was switched off for one or more hours, even in the evenings, and only one weak light bulb was permitted to be lit in every room – how often were similar orders issued over the years!), supervision of heating (to the extent it was still permitted, or if fuel was available, rooms with concrete floors could be heated to twelve degrees Celsius – in reality, the temperature rarely exceeded the freezing point!), and the collection of garbage (called "scrap"; precious raw materials were wasted in all concentration camps, but, at the same time, their miserable garbage had to help finance the war!). Orders concerning daily life changed constantly; they were generally prohibitions or restrictions. For example, closing times for the insufficient washrooms were instituted on December 19, 1941. The strain on the insufficient water pipes and the insufficient electricity supply also had a negative effect. Almost every day, there occurred short circuits that often took hours to fix; additionally, in the evening, electricity worked only at half power, so the lamps gave only a dim light.

On December 23, 1941, the orders of the day reported the beginning of bed production. On February 5, 1942, it was announced that 1,089 people had beds, and on February 22, 1942, 2,185 "beds" had been set up in 58 rooms.

There were constant comings and goings in the camp. Some families had only just arrived when they already had to leave. Some stayed for several months or weeks, and others only for days or even hours. In many cases, they never even left the Schleuse, where they were immediately informed of their further deportation. On February 1, 1942, 9,903 people were counted, among them 5,027 men, 4,863 women, and 13 children under two years of age; on April 1, 1942, there were 15,372 people; and on May 1, 1942, 12,896 people, among them 5,819 men, 5,657 women, and 57 toddlers. On the date last mentioned, 1,354 people were outside the camp doing "outside work," among them 997 women working in the woods in Křivoklát and 297 and 100 men working in coal mines near Kladno and Oslavany, respectively; 60 men were doing road construction in Budweis. On July 1, 1942, the number of prisoners had grown to 21,269.

The realization that only holding an important job could assure a stay in the "ghetto" caused the prisoners to deluge all Jewish offices with requests. The "Economics Department" announced in the orders of the day for January 20, 1942, that 2,500 job applications had been submitted. For this reason, the orders of the day for January 28, 1942, made it known that a " central reception office" had been opened at the "Central Secretariat," to which all inquiries should be directed. Requests for a "work assignment" had to contain a "curriculum vitae," including one's name, date of birth, transport number, camp address, education, experience, and references. However, this path did not usually lead to a job if it had not been paved by connections, which were already all-powerful. Starting on May 8, 1942, everyone "capable of working" had to carry a "work pass" (see Chapter 13). The orders of the day for June 28, 1942, announced the official working hours: in production enterprises, if work was not divided into three shifts, it lasted from 8 A.M. to 12 P.M. and from 2 P.M. to 6 P.M. – fifty-two hours a week in total – with free afternoons on Saturday, and in offices, prisoners worked from 7 A.M. to 11:45 A.M. and from 1 P.M. to 5:45 P.M. – fifty-seven working hours in total – with free Saturdays. This order existed only on paper, however, and the working hours were often substantially exceeded, because of the many special orders or during transport periods, and the free days were frequently dropped.

Until the end of May 1942, around 29,000 persons arrived and some 14,000 were sent on. The deportations in April put the camp's continued existence into question and almost completely terminated the construction of the camp, which was always endangered (see Chapter 9). Edelstein's intention of saving young people in work groups outside the camp succeeded only for a short while. The 1,000 women in Křivoklát got the best of it. Receiving sufficient provisions and tolerant supervision by the gendarmes and far-reaching support from Czech peasants, they worked in the forest from April to June and returned well rested. The small groups of men who had to work in coal mines or in road construction from February 1942 onward had to work hard but were likewise supported by the populace. Later, their situation deteriorated, such that in summer 1943, the last of them were glad to be back in the "ghetto." "Free" Jews, that is, men in "mixed marriages," had to take over their

The Closed Camp, November 1941–July 1942

positions. The absentees were permitted to stay in mail contact with their families in Theresienstadt via the Camp Commandant's Office (see 60b, 306b).

> [For allocation to transports to the East], certain norms were prescribed ... therefore, ... in assembling them ... it was always necessary to resort to those capable of working, or parts of the population important because of their specialized knowledge. Persons who had only recently been integrated into the organization of the ghetto were once again torn out.... The apparatus was constantly shaken by these subtractions ... and had to be expanded and filled ... with newly arrived ... staff, though these newly-engaged people frequently ... again left for the East. Despite all efforts to ... retain the necessary people, the ghetto lost a large number of the most valuable workers, and the administrative apparatus repeatedly faced collapse. After the ghetto had existed for five months, in many areas it had to begin again from the beginning. Through the transports, the age stratification had ... been considerably altered.... Those aged 65 and over, who in January ... had made up only 6%, increased in February to nearly 10%, and in May to 27%.... The constantly increasing aging of the population ... allows one to assume that the goal of the development was a ghetto for the elderly, but this was contradicted by official orders to exclude skilled works from the transports to the East as far as possible ... and so to justify the criteria of a work ghetto. The increase in available people able to work, [an increase] that came with the growth in population, did not correspond with the much more heavily increasing [growth] in demands. From January 1942, Work Deployment was ... organized in ... squadrons..... While the number of people engaged in constant work in the same place made up only 14% of the entire deployment in January, this portion was already 79% in June 1942. [In contrast, the number of those involved in "mobile deployment" decreased]. In January, 77% of all ... men were capable of working; in June, in contrast, it was only 51%.... In June, 42% more people had to be deployed than there were people capable of working, which was possible only by putting old people and youngsters to work at jobs to which they could not be completely equal. (354)

There was a particular shortage of craftsmen. The orders of the day on December 23, 1941, announced the establishment of a shoe repair shop and a tailor shop where only minor repairs were possible.

> Thus at the end of May 1942, one hundred fifty shoemakers were necessary, while only fifty trained shoemakers were available in the ghetto.... In February, the daily average of workers was already 2,875 men and 1,875 women, in March it was 3,527 men and 2,692 women, in April 4,030 men and 3,450 women, and in May, 3,812 men and 3,584 women ... altogether 7,396 persons, while at the time, there were available only 6,830 people who were fully capable of work. This difference could be made up only by putting to work persons over 60 years of age and youngsters under 16 years. The difficulties ... worsened in June.... [Of those] between 16 and 60 years of age, the 3,393 men capable of work faced a .. deployment of 4,816 men..... Because in May and June ... the demands ... increased further, a provisional solution was found in the form of Administrative Squadrons.... Suitable administrative staffers from the Administration were temporarily deployed for difficult and intermediate work. (354)

There were attempts to improve the food: "The Economics Department intends, as soon as technical difficulties in certain barracks are overcome, to offer soup with a side dish for lunch" (orders of the day, December 22, 1941). For a long time, only a meager meal was cooked at lunch. An attempt was made to distribute three deciliters of a rather worthless watery soup before the previously described main course. Initially, the food was unequal in the various barracks and was particularly scanty in the E I men's barracks. Later, the same food – in roughly the same amounts and of the same quality – was prepared everywhere. After the rotten roots had been used up in May 1942, the food became a little better. The orders of the day for January 1, 1942, promised milk distribution; each person received a quarter liter of skim milk once a week, or even less frequently. A three-person "rationing commission" was instituted in each kitchen, to protect the recipients of food from being cheated too badly (see Chapter 12). Irregular deliveries caused food shortages, and therefore the provisions that had been approved could not be distributed. Thus, for example, the orders of the day for May 26, 1942, announced the distribution of 30 g of margarine for everyone as a replacement for the period in which none had been available. The orders of the day for April 15, 1942, determined that food left over in the kitchens should be handed out as "replenishment" (*Nachschub*) based on "Central Labor Office" lists. In May 1942, at Edelstein's instigation, the bread rations for nonworkers were cut back, and the rations for those performing heavy labor were increased. The rations, now handed out every three days, amounted to 500, 375, or 333 g per day, depending on the "bread category" to which one was entitled.

> An improvement in the provisioning of those doing the hardest work, at the expense of non-workers, proved essential. In the month of May, it was decided that the distribution of food would be readjusted.... Those performing heavy and normal labor received, at the expense of non-workers, a weekly meat supplement in the form of canned goods. [This included approximately 62.5 g of liverwurst or black pudding, 30 g of sugar, and approximately 40 g of margarine per week]. At the same time, special kitchens were introduced for children and the sick.... Starting on 25 June, the distinctions ... were also extended to cooked food. On that day, the first hundred and fifty of those performing heavy labor received supplemental provisions.... The number had to be gradually increased and reached ... up to 2,000 portions. [The portion size was originally double – later only one and a half times – the normal portion size.] ... The work of building the camp became possible at all ... only as a result of that decision. (354)

Even if this had been true, the reduction constituted an extraordinary hardship, in particular for the elderly, that could hardly be justified (see Chapter 12). At that time, the Jewish administration took over the municipal food-provisioning establishments; in June, they took over the butcher shop, and, in May, the army bakery:

> When it was taken over, there were only nine bakers, some of them fully trained, some of them retrained. Starting on 1 May 1942, one shift could already bake 1,200 loaves of bread daily; beginning in 4 May, it was two shifts and 2,400 loaves of bread, and starting on 26 May, 3,700 loaves. [Later much more was baked.] (354)

In the first six months of the camp's existence, the public facilities and workshops of the city and the army were transferred to the Jewish administration. The power station kept its civilian German director, under whom the Jews had to work. By early 1942 the garrison's army workshops, the so-called *Bauhof* (H II), already had been handed over to the camp.

The waterworks were taken over in March. For a long time, the water supply did not meet the demand. Only a few houses besides the larger barracks were connected to the waterworks. Otherwise, there were polluted wells whose water could not be drunk and a defective river-water pipe that had been shut down. The waterworks had only one deep well, which was insufficient; the primitive facility was neglected, the water pressure was too low, and the pipes leaked. To ensure minimum amounts of

The Closed Camp, November 1941–July 1942

water for cooking and washing, the supply was cut down daily for many hours. Although the average daily per capita consumption is calculated to have been at least 60 L of water (see 354), initially only 26 L was available. The ration was increased to 32 L after the repair of some damage, but in May, due to the increase in population, it dropped again, to 23 L. After a temporary improvement, the average for 58,000 people even sank as low as 19.5 L in mid-September 1942.

The sewer system was sufficient for even the most dense crowding. On the other hand, it was necessary to provide for sterilization of the sewage by building a water-purification plant and a pumping station to the Eger River. After the cold winter of 1941–1942, the flooding of the Eger necessitated the establishment of a special team, a "flood readiness unit," to break the ice and take care of other safety measures.

The equipment of the municipal volunteer fire department was taken over in the spring. The pumper was the only motorized vehicle operated by camp inmates themselves. Bergel was particularly amused by the fire department, which, over time, took on more and more responsibilities. He displayed a childish interest, supervised the exercises, and loved to trigger false alarms.

On May 4, 1942, the erection of a crematorium in the Bohušovice hollow, next to the former cemetery, was begun. A report to the SS once found that this was the most efficient crematorium in Europe. The unsuspecting Edelstein did not know yet of the "efficiency" of the ovens in Auschwitz and other sacrificial altars in Eastern Europe! A pathology department, too, was established in the crematorium.

A series of production plants were opened, dedicated to industries such as metal processing; crafts, notions, and glove manufacture; and the production of wooden soles and cowhide galoshes. The latter two factories worked for the army; the others, for private businesses. At the end of June 1942, 1,022 workers and 117 technical and administrative workers were occupied in the "Production Department." The construction of wooden barracks for the "Production Department" was begun on both sides of block B V (the Magdeburg Kaserne).

The "Health Services Department" made slow progress, as there were shortages of everything, and it is surprising that a halfway orderly and fairly successful health service could develop at all. The hygienic conditions were extremely unfavorable. There was barely enough water for washing, and on January 4, 1942, the newly opened bath and showers had to be closed again. At the beginning of February, an order of the day reported that, after six weeks in the camp, everybody was entitled to a piece of soap, but the order of the day on May 2, 1942, revealed that a piece would be given out every seven instead of every six weeks. And this was bad, ersatz soap; it did not foam and barely removed dirt. "The director of the Health Services calls upon the inmates of the ghetto to provide fever thermometers.... To provide an illustration, in the infectious disease ward, only one thermometer was available for 58 patients (orders of the day for February 16, 1942)." The Health Services Department also instituted immunizations against scarlet fever and typhus. The orders of the day for May 18, 1942, announced the opening of a "central bath" in E VI. Before using the shower, one had to undergo a medical examination. For a long time, the bath had little practical significance. A bathing schedule was introduced, but it could take two months before one's turn came.

In June 1942, the Health Services had eight health units with 34 infirmaries and outpatient clinics ... and one hospital (with interns, infectious disease ward, a surgery and other facilities). In addition, it had set up a Home for the Infirm in the Hohenelber Kaserne [E VI], as well as rooms for the infirm in various housing units. A psychiatric ward was housed in the Kavalier Kaserne [E VIII]. The number of active doctors came to some two hundred, and the nursing personnel was approximately a thousand. (354)

Slowly, the strict policies of the camp administration ameliorated, or, more accurately, more neutral methods were chosen. Collective punishments became more frequent, whereas individuals were penalized in a less demonstrative fashion, although not more gently, with deportation. Executions as "deterrent examples" were abandoned. The suffering with which people were afflicted no longer originated in visible personal intrusions but arose from administrative measures. The individual was nothing more than an arbitrary, sometimes "registered" quantum of "mass," dealt with through "directives." No administrative organ addressed the individual or even thought about him. The idea of habeas corpus or human rights was not only practically but even theoretically eliminated. The "mass" was "dealt with" by a distanced and increasingly less visible office, the Camp Commandant's Office, which represented "absolute power," in the shadow of which the Jewish self-administration emerged ever more noticeably. Initially, these conditions were not so marked, but they slowly formed themselves and became ever more visible the more invisible the SS became. One example illustrates this. Whereas during the early months the SS had concerned itself with adherence to all orders, after this period Jewish authorities were increasingly obligated to supervise adherence to the "orders and prohibitions." To be sure, the Jewish leadership did so reluctantly and under duress, but they did it with an arrogance of power that grew as they took themselves more seriously, even if they ridiculed their role with irony or cynicism. The following letter shows the self-administration at the beginning of this road, in a way that well suited the SS:

> Theresienstadt, [May 21, 1942]
> Health Services
> Dr. Bass 3 Su III

> The Central Secretariat requests from us a report on whether you in fact entered the Hamburg Kaserne [C III] on Sunday, the 17th of this month, for official purposes and what official assignment you were carrying out there. Because entering the women's barracks is permitted only in fulfillment of an official task, the Central Secretariat calls attention to the fact that in all such cases in which no proof can be shown of the official necessity of entering the women's barracks, the Transit Pass will be confiscated.
> We expect an immediate response.
>
> > The Director of the Health Services
> > Dr. Erich Munk

At the end of the period under discussion here, the process of the "civilizing" (*Zivilisierung*) of the "ghetto" began to be perceptible; it was always in effect but was promoted for different reasons by the SS *and* the Jews. Efforts in this direction took rather convoluted paths and suffered serious setbacks, especially during the ensuing months. It would take a long time for the endeavor to degenerate into "beautification" (*Verschönerung*), but it was the "civilization" that finally gave this "ghetto" its characteristic image; it dissolved into nothing only during the catastrophes accompanying the days of the camp's collapse. Two early signs of this effort can be singled out:

1. The order of the day for February 16, 1942, announced that from then on – during this period the barracks were strictly sealed off – children

The Closed Camp, November 1941–July 1942

should visit their parents for two hours on Sundays. It was a distressing sight to watch the children approach the men's barracks in closed ranks, accompanied by gendarmes and the GW, after which they dispersed throughout the building and later were collected and departed.

2. The order of the day for June 26, 1942, declared that people were allowed to remain in the courtyards until 9.30 P.M. Until then, they had had to crowd into the rooms in the evenings.

Because almost nothing was permitted, the forbidden became the hidden basis of life in every concentration camp. The SS knew that its victims always acted "illegally." This was partly tolerated and even silently encouraged, as it could, at any moment, serve as an excuse for intervention and punishment. In December 1941, an "obligation to surrender" forbidden items, so-called "contraband," was announced. This included mainly money, postage stamps, and valuables that the gendarmes had confiscated from the luggage of arriving transports in the Schleuse, the possession of which was illegal in Theresienstadt. The SS knew perfectly well that there was always "contraband" – a complete listing can be found in Chapter 9 – to be found in the camp, and that it was constantly brought in by smuggling and arriving transports. Therefore, they constantly sought forbidden objects, traced connections to the outside world, or tracked down smokers. Theresienstadt was one of the few camps in which smoking was always prohibited. To my knowledge, there was no other camp in which smokers were persecuted with such an unrelenting harshness; indeed smokers were all but threatened with the death penalty, at least in the practical consequences. Warnings, renewed prohibitions, and calls to surrender forbidden objects were often repeated, especially during the early months. The order of the day for January 18, 1942, for example, gave everyone stern warning, as spot checks had discovered money in prisoners' luggage, and some had been caught gambling. In April 1942, access to the private luggage that many had stored in warehouses for lack of space and fear of theft was closed off for many days in order to track down forbidden objects. Confiscation and punishment followed. From the end of April onward, SS searches increased.

On May 2, 1942, a "special order of the day" was published, which read as follows:

Final, urgent warning.

In recent days, some ghetto inmates have once again given reason for harsh measures by the superior authorities. The persons involved are guilty of infractions of existing regulations. They attempted to make contact with the non-Jewish surroundings, etc. The Council of Elders makes all ghetto inmates aware, at the express orders of the Camp Commandant's Office, that the slightest repetition of such infractions will lead to the harshest consequences, both for those involved and for the entire community.

The Council of Elders notes with pleasure the successful efforts to free a large number of prisoners and protect them from serious consequences.

The Council of Elders does not intend to have this success undermined by irresponsible behavior by individual persons. The Council of Elders will therefore act with harsh severity against any person, no matter what his function, who is guilty of disobeying the existing regulations. The Ghetto Guard is instructed to watch with the greatest care and to report to the Council of Elders every single ghetto inmate who violates an order.

A ghetto guard who himself commits an infraction is doubly and triply guilty, as he abuses the trust placed in him, and must, because of his recklessness, expect the harshest punishment. The camp commandant's office has placed particular emphasis on prosecution of infractions by the Ghetto Guard.

The tasks entrusted to the Council of Elders are becoming increasingly difficult, the conditions of our work more complicated, and thus every disruption and every setback represents an irreparable shock to the entire organization, and the entire communal life of the ghetto.

The Council of Elders thus in this way exhorts all ghetto inmates without exception to exercise the most strict discipline, and warns every single person of the terrible consequences of ignoring this final and most urgent warning.

For the Council of Elders
Dr. Janowitz m.p.

P.S. We take this opportunity to refer again to order of the day no. 9 for 24 December 1941, and call on all ghetto inmates immediately to surrender to the building elders all items subject to surrender that remain in [inmates'] possession.

Soon afterward, "black" or "illegal" letters and other forbidden objects were once more discovered, some among members of the GW. This resulted in revocation of the illusory permission to use the mail service as well as other punishments. The order of the day on May 15, 1942, concerned itself with these events and announced an "additional grace period" for punishment-free surrender of all forbidden objects, which were to be handed in anonymously to the building elder.

Herr Camp Commandant ... informs all ghetto inmates, by way of the Council of Elders, ... that after the expiration of this period every ghetto inmate can expect the harshest measures if even the smallest of the forbidden items is found on him. A half cigarette or 50 Hellers are enough to punish most severely both the one guilty of the infraction and all additional persons who knew about it. Herr Camp Commandant ... also makes it known that not only the guilty will be called to account, the entire ghetto will be most seriously affected by measures of the most drastic sort, such as prohibition of the care of young people, etc.

At the same time, in a roll call before Seidl, the GW was informed of its dissolution. In its place, and from its ranks, fifty men were appointed as the "Order Guard" (Ordnerwache [OW]). They received only some of the GW's privileges. The OW was charged with maintaining peace and order in the barracks, providing service as ordered for the senior Jewish Elder, and escorting work columns and transports. The members of the OW were deprived of their operetta-like equipment, including a cap and belt; only their yellow armbands distinguished them as guards. As the squad was not sufficient for the amount of work that the transports required, the "Transport Guard," whose members wore green armbands, was added. Gradually, the OW regained the same tasks, equipment, and original number of men as the GW. Finally, they were given back their old name, and in October 1942, the members were awarded brass badges with the letters "GW" and a number.

Until the end of the "grace period," all "orders of the day" repeatedly requested voluntary surrender of forbidden objects, accompanied by threats in case of non-compliance. The room elders had to exert great pressure on all inmates to hand over "contraband" – in particular, money – and, after much persuasion and arguing, the prisoners were convinced of the necessity of sacrificing at least a few crowns, so that too miserable a result would not provoke the SS to new "measures." Much was collected in this manner, but it was only a fraction of the illegal property.

The downfall of Heydrich, a main participant in the special destiny of the Theresienstadt camp, was mirrored in the "ghetto," as was the tragedy of Lidice, which was triggered by it. News of the assassination attempt quickly spread in the camp. When the SS brought its flags to half-mast – one always flew in the "ghetto," at the commandant's building – the prisoners knew of Heydrich's end. Officially, however, they were not supposed to know anything. This made even more grotesque and ghostly the comedy to which the "unsuspecting" prisoners were subjected. Everywhere in the "Protectorate," posters were put up, complete with a depiction of the objects that the assassins had left behind at the scene of the crime. The orders of the day for June 16, 1942, read:

> Search operation. On Tuesday, 16 June, all inmates of the ... barracks assembled to give their signatures. The assembly took place by room; the operation lasted from 6 A.M. to 9:30 A.M. In all buildings, the status was correct, so that there were no complaints. The signature operation in the Sudeten Kaserne [E I] will take place ... tomorrow.

What was going on? The Jews marched in rows past a group of gendarmes in the courtyards of the barracks. A table, with lists, had been set up there. Next to the table were affixed posters with depictions of a briefcase, a coat, and other objects. After briefly viewing them, people were asked, often with a smile, if they recognized any of the objects. They said no and signed the list. Nothing could have allowed one to guess what all this meant. It was enough that the questioning happened, and the administration could properly report that no trace of the perpetrators had been found in the "ghetto."

The murderous burning of Lidice led to a tragic connection with the Jews of Theresienstadt:

> On 10 June, Seidl ordered 30 young men to equip themselves with shovels, pickaxes and the like at once and make themselves ready. In the afternoon, a truck drives up with Seidl and two gendarmes, loads the 30 men and drives off with them. No one knows where or for what. After around a day and a half, the group returns, exhausted and with bloody hands and welts. Apathetically answering no questions addressed to them, they go ... to sleep. At Seidl's orders, they are not allowed to tell where they were and what they experienced. This secret cannot be kept for long.... After a few hours' drive, the boys came to a burning village surrounded by the SS. The 2 gendarmes were not allowed to go any farther. Seidl took the lead, with some SS men. And now the work that had been ordered began. Under Seidl's lash, a mass grave was dug. Without pause, without food, with constant threats and lashes, they worked for 36 hours. Bonfires were built of furniture, doors etc. for illumination at night. In the 4-meter-deep grave, the proportions of which were 12 x 9 meters, the bodies were first stacked next to each other, but later just thrown in. Shoes and clothes were taken off the victims, as well as the contents of their pockets. Money disappeared into the SS's pockets. Now lime was poured in, and finally two shot dogs were thrown in by the drunken SS and Gestapo people, who had made a banquet with provisions they had found. Sheep, goats, geese, and other animals were driven to the Theresienstadt Ghetto from Lidice. (145; see also 148 and 173)

5

The "Ghetto," July 1942–Summer 1943

At the same time as the evacuation order was issued to the civilian population of Theresienstadt, a commission began to meet in E IIIa. Consisting of representatives of Czech ministries and the municipality, its purpose was to advise the inhabitants, undertake the sale of private property, and direct the "resettlement." Jews from the "ghetto" also worked there. The Theresienstadters were informed and threatened by placards on the street. Initially, the evacuation was supposed to be carried out by the end of April, but it did not begin until nearly May and lasted until nearly the end of June.

> On 27 June 1942, the city, which had now been completely cleared of its Aryan population, was in its entirety, given over to the ghetto administration. Only the market place, with the Commandant's Office, the former hotel "Victoria" [now the SS *Kameradschafts* home], together with the former officers' casino [now the gendarmes' barracks], and the Fountain [Brunnen] Park between them and the not-yet-laid road connecting Leitmeritz [Litoměřice] and Prague, formed within the city a contiguous zone that was not accessible to the Jewish population.

On July 1, the military names of the *Kaserne*, as well as the civilian street names, were eliminated and replaced by combinations of letters and numbers. In June, the first civilian houses were handed over to the "ghetto." The transition from "closed camp" to "open ghetto" was marked by many directives.

> The Camp Commandant's Office has issued the following orders for regulation of the security services in the ghetto:
>
> a) The Gendarmerie will be withdrawn from the barracks today, 6 July 1942.
> b) The Order Guards will take responsibility for maintaining order in the ghetto.
> c) Transit passes no longer will be given to the Camp Commandant's Office for signature. The senior Jewish Elder ... receives the authority to sign passes himself.... Separate accommodation ... of men and women will be maintained, however the prohibition on mutual visitation is ended. Escort of work groups within the city is eliminated.... Persons who cross the city boundary [still only with a transit pass from the SS] are to leave their identification in the gendarmerie guardhouse at the city boundary and pick

The police sentries at the gates of the barracks will be removed and posted at the city's sally ports in the fortress ramparts. The barracks gates will be opened, and the Jewish population can now move freely within the city. The Administration has made all preparations to do justice to the new situation.

it up again upon return.... Leaving the barracks will be regulated as follows:

1. Old people unfit for work can leave the housing units throughout the entire day until 6 o'clock in groups, under the responsibility of an escort person....
2. The same rules apply to children....
3. Persons of working age are permitted to leave the housing units only until 6 o'clock, with a pass.... All persons who comply with their work duties can leave the housing units from 6 P.M. to 9 P.M. without a pass. Those who still have official work to perform after 9 P.M. must identify themselves with a pass after 9 P.M. Lingering in the courtyard is ... permitted until 10 P.M. Curfew is at 10 P.M.
4. Entering other housing units is permitted only to those persons who can identify themselves with a pass. Between 6 P.M. and 9 P.M., free entry is ... permitted.
5. Entering the workplaces, such as the workshop and the Central Bakery, and the Schleuse, continues to be permitted only with a transit pass, in which the name of the workplace is explicitly ... cited.

(orders of the day for September 4, 1942)

The police sentries at the gates of the barracks will be removed and posted at the city's sally ports in the fortress ramparts. The barracks gates will be opened, and the Jewish population can now move freely within the city. The Administration has made all preparations to do justice to the new situation.

(354)

The existing system for issuing passes will be changed. In the future ... passes will be issued that are valid only until 9 P.M. Issuance of passes for other times of day will cease.

(orders of the day, September 4, 1942)

On October 4, the curfew was moved to 8 P.M. Although prior to the "opening of the city" all streets could be used (with passes), from October 4 on, ever-stricter orders were in force, making it difficult to move freely within the town and requiring long detours. The city square was off limits (except for the sidewalks along the three inhabited rows of houses), as were the Prague-Leitmeritz [Litoměřice] road (called the "Aryan Street"), all parks, and the ramparts of the fortress. Once the commandant's office had moved to the other side of the square, into one of the best houses – Q 414 (the former bank) – and the adjoining house Q 416 (a former hotel) at the end of August 1942, and after completion of the "bypass road" on March 18, 1943, which redirected passing traffic to the outskirts of town, the restrictions remained relatively consistent for a long time. Before completion of the "bypass road," street Q 7, which served long-distance traffic, could be crossed at only two places, sometimes only at one (L 4 and L 5), under the supervision of the gendarmerie and the Ghetto Guard (Ghettowache [GW]). The various barriers were cumbersome and forced long detours, as a look at the map makes clear. If, for example, one wanted to get from a building in block F III to a building in block G IV, which was almost across from it, one had to go to lane Q 3 and walk along street L 4, and sometimes even L 5, in order to reach one's destination via Q 8 – a walk of at least ten minutes; in contrast, the direct route would have taken one minute at most for healthy pedestrians! The square and all forbidden zones were surrounded by wooden fences as tall as a man. Gates were supposed to form the few outlets, but because construction material was lacking, wooden barriers, operated by a GW man, had to suffice. Double guards were posted in front of the barriers. The town exits were also blocked with barriers, guarded by gendarmes and the GW. Freedom of movement was limited by a further order: "On instructions from the Camp Commandant's Office, during incoming and outgoing transports the streets through which the transports will travel are not to be used. Windows and doors are to be closed" (orders of the day, July 27, 1942). For the deportees, especially for the new arrivals, the strictly cordoned-off streets deepened the camp's sinister impression. It seemed as if they had arrived in a place devoid of life, and they were thus even more confused and unsuspecting when they reached the Schleuse.

The abandonment of transit passes within the town merely legalized a situation that already existed in practice. In a camp, one asked few questions about the validity of prohibitions that could be transgressed easily and with relatively little danger. To prisoners who had been in Theresienstadt longer – and, especially at first, it did not take very long for people to feel that they had been in the camp for a "long time," as days and weeks seemed like months and years – this "freedom," announced overnight, was an unforgettable event. People streamed from the barracks, astonished at this easing of conditions. They did not immediately dare to use the sidewalks, and a mention in an "order of the day" was necessary to make people aware of this "right." Given this giddy atmosphere, it was at first reasonable and even necessary to partially limit freedom of movement. Especially in the first few days, it was a strange feeling to meander in the evening through the overflowing streets, which contrasted eerily with the recently evacuated, deserted houses, with their dirty, uncurtained windows. The as-yet uninhabited houses were locked. After they were all too rapidly overfilled, "house guards" were positioned before the gates, sometimes in specially constructed sentry booths. With ridiculous strictness, these guards tried to prevent anyone from entering or exiting outside visiting hours. Usually, the house guards were elderly people, who were often accustomed to "Prussian order," and they fulfilled their duties with tragicomic pedantry. Soon after permission had been granted to move about freely during the day, the house guards disappeared.

For long-time residents, the freedom to meet without punishment was a great event. What must it have meant for them to be permitted to do something for which they had been threatened with abuse, transport, or death only yesterday! Now one could talk to one's wife, mother, or children and sit in their rooms. Insecure and cautious, they entered the rooms in which their relatives lived. Brief exchanges of words gave way to intimate conversation. It took some time before this seemed normal again. But people soon realized that this relief did not rectify the terrible general situation, as the overwhelming majority were denied the right to really live together. For newcomers, however, the problem was very different. They had not suffered the earlier conditions, were mostly elderly, and were placed not in men's or women's barracks but in joint barracks or former civilian houses – the "blocks." They were indeed housed separately by sex, but they never lost sight of one another and could spend almost the whole day together, help one another, and share one another's fate.

The makeup of the camp inmate population changed approximately at the same time as the "opening of the city." Together, both events form the starkest disruption in the history of the camp. Until then, all prisoners had come from the "Protectorate"; the majority spoke Czech, which almost all understood; and, despite their individual differences, in comparison with the newcomers they constituted a relatively uniform community.

> Transports from the Old Reich [Altreich] and the East Mark [Ostmark, or pre-Anschluss Austria] brought mainly persons from a well-off, established milieu, from well-run old-age homes with strong religious ties. There arose the task of bringing together the two groups in the ghetto, shaping their mutual relationship as well as possible, and smoothing out possible antagonisms as they appeared, to the extent possible.... The coming period of settlement of the entire city ... with its heretofore unimaginable number of arriving and departing transports, deep changes in population structure, and social and economic organization, presented tasks of a magnitude that could not have been imagined in the building phase, which itself certainly was not lacking in difficulties.
>
> (354)

In June 1942, the first transports arrived from Berlin, Munich, Cologne, and Vienna. In the course of the following weeks and months, more and more transports from all regions of Germany – as well as numerous transports from the "Protectorate," mainly from Prague – deluged the camp. Immense chaos, a hardly controllable anarchic turmoil, was the result. Those who came from the "Protectorate" were at least less filled with illusions; they knew a little about the situation from hearsay and generally were assisted by relatives and friends, but how different it was for those from Germany and Vienna!

Often, they were barely prepared, were naïve in every regard, and knew no one. Although communication was not impossible, many of the words and phrases of the language spoken here were incomprehensible to them. Long-time residents, however, could not and did not wish to understand the new arrivals. The mood of many young Czech Jews in regard to the elderly people from Germany is unfortunately only too well expressed in the following:

> We had convinced ourselves that when we arrived in Czechoslovakia, we would be arriving in a friendly country, united with us in our hatred for Hitler and his henchmen. But what a disappointment for us! The Czechs hated us just as we hated Hitler, and they held us partly responsible for the misfortune they had met with. They did not see in us fellow sufferers, but only Germans whom they hated.
>
> (55, see also 30b)

With few exceptions, the new arrivals were elderly, tired, and usually frail or even mortally ill people. They came from nursing homes or from strongly assimilated environments and often had not directly experienced any terrible persecutions. Most of their children or younger relatives had escaped abroad; a smaller number had been sent to factories, labor camps, or the nameless misery in the East. They rarely were able to pack their bags properly, and often were physically incapable of doing so. Nobody could or would help them. They had been brought to collection camps, where they waited, sometimes for weeks, in the most miserable conditions; there – especially in the camps in Vienna – they descended into physical and mental wretchedness, for which other Jews were partially to blame. Thus they were already neglected, dirty, and often half-starved before they were loaded onto cattle cars. The journey completed their misery, bringing them to the edge of living decay. Although from some places the journey took days, nothing had been prepared in the trains for these poor people's sanitary needs. No water was distributed to these unfortunates, and often they did not even have food for the trip. Medical help was not available. One must imagine that these travelers were usually seventy or eighty years old, and there were even ninety-year-olds among them! And so, devastated in body and spirit, they arrived, no longer capable of making decisions, no longer in control of their senses or limbs. German officials had shamelessly promised these people an impending good and carefree future, consciously misleading them so that their preparations would be as useless and senseless as possible. These Jews, among them thousands of war-wounded and decorated veterans, had been raised in and were accustomed to a fixed order. Ultimately frozen in a blind trust in this order, they did not notice that it had long since been debased and corroded by lies and evil. Thus it was easy to fool these unfortunates in almost unbelievably stupid ways. They harbored no suspicions, despite all the lies they were told, but readily trusted again and again. This can be seen in the contents of their luggage, to the extent that the victims were given a choice in this. Because they had been told all sorts of stories about the comfortable and cozy conditions in the "Reich old-age home" in "Theresienbad" and in the "Theresienstadt spa," with its friendly villas, pensions, and pleasant nursing homes, they brought curtains, vases, and family memorabilia and cherished items that were pointless in a camp, but with which they hoped to make their new environment more comfortable. The clothes they chose were suitable for a summer vacation. In the bags they carried with them, they had brought a few cigars, or perhaps a bottle of good wine. But what the camp required, what they could have used, was often completely absent. They lacked blankets and other warm, practical items. Some had been forbidden to bring knives and other indispensable objects. Others had no spoons – the universal instrument in all camps – and they had no containers for receiving food. They lacked items for washing and towels. Those things, they assumed, would be plentifully available in the comfort they had been promised and that they expected.

Finally they arrived at the train station, exhausted and destroyed – with the SS, gendarmes, and other Jews yelling at them – with confused expressions, uncomprehending desperate looks, and anxious gestures. Perhaps a picture might convey an idea of the state of some western German, let alone Viennese, transports, but language hardly can. These debilitated people were then expected to begin the arduous march to the camp, unrefreshed and burdened with their miserable possessions; often they were no longer able to go on. In that case, they were loaded onto trucks or tractor trailers like cattle, packed together so tightly that they could neither lie down nor sit. Therefore, they had to stand – ill, exhausted, thirsty, apathetic or screaming, women with tangled hair, invalids on crutches, blind people with trembling limbs – to be driven into town. Once, one of the drivers, a young SS novice known as "SS Children's Home," catapulted twenty-seven people from the wagon while recklessly taking a curve. Ten died on the spot; the others died in the hospital or were crippled.

The arrivals sometimes asked, as soon as they had reached the train station or in the Schleuse, whether one or two rooms had been reserved for them or requested the south side and a balcony. They presented confirmations of large sums of money, sometimes more than 500,000 Reichsmark, with which they had bought themselves a lifetime stay in Theresienstadt, including room and board. In exchange, they had "voluntarily" handed over their fortune to the Reichsvereinigung, that is, the SS. Now they squatted or lay on the floor of one of the many stinking Schleusen in stuffy, damp casemates or dusty attics, mercilessly exposed to the dull summer heat, in yellowish half-darkness, with the remnants of their luggage. Not even goodwill could have helped to cope with this disaster or even eased it much, but generally this, too, was lacking. When some who later also got to know Auschwitz claimed, after the war, how "good" Theresienstadt had been, one should have reminded them of this misery, which was no less inhumane and wretched to those involved than the tragedy survived by those with stronger natures in what were surely much harsher camps. What was endured by these elderly people in Theresienstadt brooks no intensification, as long as there still is life left in a body, for the intensification of suffering is not death but the degree of degradation and indignity inflicted on a living human being. Edelstein reported the deception that had been perpetrated on the German Jews in the form of "home purchase agreements" (*Heimeinkaufverträge*; see Chapter 3) to the Camp Commandant's Office. Seidl replied: "I will report to Berlin and let you know." Finally, they promised to pay out five Reichsmark a month per person from the extorted money – and a promise it remained.

If, with some justification, summer 1942 appeared to the long-term inmates to be an easier period, for most of the population it was the darkest and most confusing epoch of the camp. Many arrivals from Vienna and Cologne were afflicted with clothing lice and head lice. No provisions had been made for effective disinfection. The civilian houses, which had stood empty for a few days, became living quarters on July 7 and soon were overcrowded as never before. These buildings looked anything but welcoming – most of them had not been in the best condition even when occupied by their earlier inhabitants! The owners had taken everything that was not nailed down, and often even more. Stoves were lacking, lighting wiring had been torn out with the sockets, the toilets usually did not flush and were useless, and the walls, doors, and windows – everything – were miserable and decrepit! Mountains of garbage lay in the rooms and in the courtyards. Rats and vermin had made their homes there, creating problems that could not be remedied in days or weeks. There were no hospitals or infirmaries. The sick were placed onto the bare floor; often they remained uncovered, as did the people in the other rooms. People died without peace, untended, without a word of comfort or a friendly glance. This misery in no way differed from perishing in the "hospital" (*Revier*) of any other concentration camp – it was an anonymous death. There was no one to bury the dead. On hot days, up to 500 corpses lay in the casemate called the "Central Mortuary," by the exit gate of the street leading to Bohušovice. The dead, poorly covered by a cloth, were wheeled on handcarts across town. From there, the caskets, around thirty at a time, were brought to the burial site in an open horse cart. How often did transports encounter this wagon on their march into the camp! Some realized that this would be the only available egress from Theresienstadt. In those days, arrivals were often unloaded as corpses, others died in the Schleuse, and sometimes no one could say who they were; thus their obituaries read "unknown man" or "unknown woman." Until then, the orders of the day had published each death, citing the deceased's name, "transport number," and year of birth. This ceased on September 19, 1942, and the dead were announced with notices put up in several places. At night, after work, men had to be conscripted to dig mass graves.

The situation of the arrivals became harder after July 10, 1942, through the general confiscation of their "accompanying luggage" (*Mitgepäck*). If they received anything, it was their small "hand luggage."

92   *History*

> Considering the rapid succession of transports arriving in the ghetto in the month of July, not all hand luggage such as blankets, knapsacks, etc. could yet be delivered to the ghetto inmates from the last transports.

> The transport administration is making efforts to find the missing pieces of hand luggage and continues to deliver them to the owners. Requests for preferential delivery ... cannot, however, be considered. Accompanying luggage can be delivered only after successful processing [*Durchschleusung*]. The exact time will be announced.
>
> > (orders of the day, August 3, 1942)

This "exact time" never occurred, because the confiscated "additional luggage" was stored and finally brought to the "clothing warehouse," meaning it was earmarked for SS purposes. The foreign new arrivals, in particular, were hard hit by this development, whereas it actually helped some people from the "Protectorate," who could expect help if friends succeeded in boldly saving their luggage before it was confiscated. Unfortunately, these conditions caused Edelstein to make a baffling – to put it mildly – decision. He permitted, or at least countenanced, employees of the "transport administration" and the "Transport Squadron" feasting on food from the "lost" luggage and tolerated the theft of the luggage of arriving prisoners.

The large number of elderly people inundated the town but could not get their bearings. They forgot almost everything in distressing confusion, or suppressed the unbearable present through amnesia, and could not recall which quarters were theirs, and often even their own names.

> The OW [GW] has set up an Orientation Service in B V; its task is to bring home persons who have gotten lost or are encountered on the street and do not know where they live. These persons are taken to the OW guardhouse and from there brought to their quarters.... Missing persons reports from inmates are to be ... addressed to ... these orientation points.
>
> > (orders of the day, August 10, 1942)

> Old and infirm people lose their personal documents, forget their names and residences, and wander helplessly through the streets.... The streets are constantly patrolled, and not infrequently 40–50 lost persons each day are brought to their homes after hours of searching. The Orientation Service's guardhouse refreshes and shelters such needy people even at night.
>
> > (144, see also 178c)

People who had gotten themselves lost also lost their paltry possessions. Lost-and-found offices were established in eight barracks; these offices were answerable to the "Central Lost Property Office." One office operated in the Schleuse for arriving transports. On the arrival of one transport in the summer of 1942, 2,000–6,000 items were collected. The "Central Lost Property Office" registered about 1,000 visitors daily.

The average age of those in the AK transports had been thirty-one, and the remaining transports from the "Protectorate" averaged forty-six years of age; but, on average, the arrivals from Berlin and Munich were sixty-nine; from Cologne, seventy; and from Vienna, as high as seventy-three years of age. Out of the 4,213 people who had arrived in June from Germany and Vienna, only 242 were of an age fit to work, and only 178 (4.23%) were really able to work.

> A ... commission ... was formed to consolidate and direct the most varied, interconnected work.... Its first job was to prepare a settlement plan that would distribute the

The "*Ghetto*," *July 1942–Summer 1943*

population to various areas of the city ... according to a consistent plan. Taking into account the extraordinarily dense settlement that was to be expected ... the separation of the sexes in accommodations was maintained, as assigning individual quarters to families ... was possible in only very special, exceptional cases.... The principle of separately accommodating those capable and incapable of work was also established.... Young people between 10 and 16 years of age were in large part also quartered together, in special units. For the very large number of bedridden sick people ... suitable sickness centers, as well as correctly distributed health units, were planned, as well as special homes for accommodation of the physically handicapped and the blind.

(354)

Today, some 8,000 persons still are quartered in attics that were thrown together and, taking account of the lack of wood that arose during the month of the report, in some cases not even adapted; before the cold weather begins, they must be resettled into existing housing, since the makeshift quarters involved are unheatable and in some cases not even rain-resistant....

The building of beds and serial production suffered greatly from the lack of wood; the labor program was thus limited to the production of bedding pads [*Betteneinlage*] which, laid onto the floor, made it possible to create provisional sleeping places, as well as the production of coffins, in particular a new type of coffin for the crematorium. In consequence of the high death rate, the demand for coffin production was especially high....

Welfare activities. (1) Care of the infirm. More than 4,000 of the infirm ... are subject to group care. Accommodating these together is completely impossible at this time. (2) Care of the blind. The Blind Care Service is looking after approximately 1,000 blind people, some of whom will be moved together into one house in the next few days. (3) Care of war-wounded. The welfare office is making efforts to concentrate war invalids, who have common complaints and wishes, in one house and ease their fate through various privileges.

Mortality. The daily number of deaths totaled 130 to 150. The most frequent cause of death was enteritis, which led to two-thirds or more of all deaths on some days. In the month of the report [September 1942], 1,395 men and 2,546 women died. The average age was 76 years.

Delousing ... Sanitary disinfection was carried out in 187 cases. Vermin (bedbugs, fleas, flies, wasps, head lice, and clothing lice) were exterminated in 2,259 cases. Fourteen hundred sixty-six garbage deposit sites were chlorinated, rats and mice exterminated in 2,328 cases, and in more than 100 rooms, periodic disinfections were carried out.

(276)

A II became the quarantine for the lice-ridden only later in the fall, when most elderly people were already suffering from lice. The orders of the day for November 5, 1942, announced strict isolation rules for these barracks. The conditions of this quarantine surpassed almost everything else in the "ghetto" in terms of horror. Care was miserable; the inmates were mercilessly cheated of their food and were literally eaten alive by vermin.

Despite the deportation of some 18,000 elderly persons in September and October, the problem of accommodation remained unresolved for many months. The orders of the day for November 30, 1942, addressed the prisoners as follows: "A large number of persons are still located in attics, where they cannot remain any longer because of the impending winter.... The Council of Elders therefore requests sympathetic cooperation from the staff of Space Management ... in increasing the occupancy of houses and buildings."

94   *History*

The orders of the day for October 20, 1942, reported that winter clothes, if they had not yet been delivered to the "clothing warehouse," could be requested from the Camp Commandant's Office. Otherwise, the requests were to address the Distribution Office. The misery was unending. People walked around in rags. Anything that had not been confiscated disappeared during disinfection of personal effects; other things were stolen or lost. On December 19, 1942, the orders of the day contained the following appeal:

> Persons who were deloused in the months of October and November, and who are missing the luggage brought with them to their delousing, are requested immediately to submit a lost item report to the Central Lost Property Office. The lost item report must contain: name, transport, house and room number of the petitioner, time of delousing, exact description of missing items.
>
> Space ... also had to be planned for the workshops and storehouses, as well as for the administration.... The working men's center is the ... Sudeten Kaserne (E 1), with an occupancy of around 4,000 persons, as well as ... the Hanover Kaserne (B IV); the working women's center was to be the Hamburg Kaserne (C III), with some attached blocks.
>
> (354)

Several workshops were set up, especially in the riding school (Q 320) and in the barracks on both sides of B V. A IV and part of I IV were designated the Economics Building and storehouse. A II, along with L 506 (the brewery), was reserved for quarantine and disinfection facilities. The "settlement plan" never could be carried out as intended. Hardly had something been decided when SS orders or internal measures forced all plans to be abandoned, changed, or postponed.

"This settlement plan for the first time provided for separate and preferential accommodation of so-called "notables" [*Prominente*] in a single house, later in a single block. This was a new category of ghetto inmates, Jews who had gained recognition in their previous lives and who had been specially identified to the ghetto administration by the authorities" (354). The separation of the prisoners into privileged and ordinary inmates had a great impact on camp life (on the "notables," see Chapter 10). Taken out of anonymous squalor, some were destined for a better existence, although this existence was much more meager than the comforts that some obtained by virtue of their position or by dishonesty. Just as the introduction of the group of "notables" set a pernicious example for competition among the overly diligent, both groups awakened the jealousy of the ordinary prisoners, and almost all comradely solidarity disappeared.

> The city was divided into four districts, in which the residents of a district were supposed to be uniform. Thus the first and second districts were inhabited largely by working people, the fourth district contained the great majority of ... the Health Service. The districts were headed by district elders, who now were assigned the deployment offices, registry offices, and a separate, limited administrative apparatus. Also, each district had separate outpatient facilities and infirmaries. For the newly-acquired civilian houses, house elders were appointed; these, however, did not have the same position as the building elders in the barracks ... they were not answerable directly to the district elders, as were the building elders, but through their group elders.
>
> (354)

The camp's population statistics illustrate the difficulties of these months. In July 1942, fifty-eight transports with 25,111 people arrived, and 2,000 people were deported. In that month, the number of inhabitants rose from 21,304 to 43,403. In August, 13,469 persons arrived in thirty-six transports, whereas 3,000 had to leave. In September, thirty-eight transports came, with 18,647 people, and 13,005 people were deported on eight transports. On September 8 alone, four transports carrying 1,995 people arrived, and 1,000 people left on one transport. In the same month, 3,941 deaths were registered. This was the most eventful and perhaps the most difficult month. Then the number of arrivals slowly sank. On September 30, 53,264 people were counted. In October, 5,004 people were admitted, 9,866 were deported on six transports, and 3,096 died. On November 1, 45,312 were counted, but on December 24, there were again 50,006 people. If, however, the total numbers at the beginning of November are compared to those at the end of this phase, the number remains unchanged, as 45,635 prisoners were counted on September 1, 1943.

By the end of September, the worst turbulence of those wild months was over, but what does the word "worst" mean in view of the misery concealed behind the numbers for November 1942 through September 1943! How many people came to Theresienstadt within these ten months! And how many fates were sealed in a cruel death! In this period, 7,000 people were shipped to the East, and almost all of them perished. The unfathomable extermination figures in the enormous death factories have deadened the hearts and minds not only of the murderers but also of the entire world toward the meaning of a single human life destroyed in an SS camp. In being overwhelmed by the unimaginable statistics of millions of lives lost, the world has lost its sense of the sea of guilt that caused the violent extinction of each individual heart.

To the Jews in the "ghetto," even the short halt to the deportations, which lasted for three months between the end of October 1942 and the end of January 1943, must have seemed a relief – and even more so the seven-month break from early February to early September 1943! In November, "only" 4,579 people arrived, and in December, 4,127. On February 1, 1943, 44,672 people were counted, although another 4,821 prisoners had been admitted in January. One should compare this sum to the 50,006 people from the end of 1942, in order always to keep at bay the insensitivity to which figures can lead, in a world of "masses" and mechanical quantities.

Starting in fall 1942, a number of younger people came from Vienna, and, starting in spring 1943, from Berlin as well: "[They] consisted of staff of the Israelite Community in Vienna, or the Reich Association of Jews in Germany, Berlin, as well as people who for important reasons had been kept behind for work until the final transports" (274). From August 1942, the number of Czechoslovakians was exceeded by the number of Germans and Austrians. Their predominance was most pronounced in October and November. By January 1943, the balance had been restored by the high mortality rate of the elderly German Jews and by new Czech transports. As long as labor and administration were almost exclusively in the hands of Czech Jews, the social changes in the "ghetto" had only a limited effect. The helpless German and Viennese Jews felt – rightly and wrongly – disadvantaged and therefore demanded fair representation in the self-administration. When younger German and Austrian Jews finally arrived, they soon occupied various positions. There were splendid people among them, but also a number of sinister figures, with bad reputations, who had acted in unfortunate ways in the Jewish offices in Berlin, and especially in Vienna; these included, for example, the infamous Viennese "Jupo" (*Judenpolizei*, or Jewish police), accomplices of the SS who had participated in the arrest of Jews and their inhumane treatment in the collection camps or who were pathetic spies. Some were received accordingly by their compatriots in Theresienstadt and were given a proper beating; they were afforded no protection from the SS. Nevertheless, these creatures received comfortable positions, apparently by order of the SS.

From Berlin, orders came to grant the German and Austrian Jews representation in the administration. The representatives consisted at first of worthy former functionaries in the Viennese or Reich German communities, and later of energetic younger men who had worked their way up to influential positions only in recent years. Some had failed to exhibit anything like irreproachably humane behavior or had been unable to maintain it unwaveringly.

The orders of the day for October 3, 1942, announced a reform of the Council of Elders. It remained a body consisting of twelve members, but six Czech Jews withdrew and four Reich German and two Viennese Jews took their place. Heinrich Stahl, the former head of the Berlin community, became Edelstein's deputy, but he passed away on November 4, 1942. On November 24, 1942, the former head of the Viennese community, Dr. Desider Friedmann, was appointed, and an additional German Jew was added to the Council of Elders in order to complete the number once more. The reshuffling of the leadership, announced in the orders of the day for January 31, 1943, would be far more drastic. Dr. Paul Eppstein, a member of the board of the "Reich Association," had arrived from Berlin and, from Vienna, Rabbi Dr. Benjamin Murmelstein, Deputy Senior Jewish Elder there. A bevy of personal assistants attached themselves to these two men. Eppstein became the senior Jewish Elder, Edelstein his first deputy, and Murmelstein his second deputy. Internally, the three men were considered equals, or "coordinated," but Eppstein was responsible to the SS as sole spokesman. Leadership of the camp was divided into "departments" (*Dezernate*), which were distributed among the members of the triumvirate; it was a hostile, divided triumvirate.

Edelstein felt – not without reason, yet unwisely – that he had been edged out. Constantly taxed to the end of his strength, he was exhausted. He was now expected to deliver his roughly completed work into the hands of the quite differently natured Eppstein. Edelstein would have preferred to withdraw, as a "simple" worker, as he put it, but, pressured by his supporters, he took over the function of second-in-command, and his energy markedly waned. He curtly rejected Murmelstein. It is not easy to do Edelstein justice. He was descended from a pious Galician family, and for many years had been a Zionist-socialist functionary of Poale Zion in Prague. He was religious and took care to observe the Sabbath and the holidays even in Theresienstadt. His demeanor was simple and modest but lacked openness. He was of average intelligence, which a degree of artfulness could not hide. Although his opinions lacked depth and sufficient perspective, they were subjectively honest but dogmatically rigid, almost prejudiced. He had a good sense of humor and was always courageous, and sometimes quite clever, in his negotiations with SS men in Prague as well as in Theresienstadt; however, he was far more inferior to his German associates than he realized. The longer he had to associate with them, the more obvious it became that he was no match for them, and he did not comprehend soon enough the game they were playing with him. As is often the case with lower-level political functionaries, his appearances before the camp as spokesman were not without demagoguery. His ideas of Judaism were blurred by a not-very-clear Zionist lens. Unfortunately, he was unable to put it aside when dealing with matters other than personal, if entirely upright, ideas. Edelstein was broken by his task, broken by Theresienstadt, but he must be given credit for manliness. His tragic downfall ennobles him, and he tried his best, even if he not only was bound to fail on a terrible path but also sometimes foundered due to his own weaknesses (see 3b, 11a, 33, 52a, 78a, 146b, 201, 202, 238, 312c).

Eppstein chose a different tactic. He did not have his own strategy and did not continue Edelstein's courageous and even audacious policy. Although Edelstein may not have been a great man, in his dealings with the SS he was man enough always to be mindful of Jewish interests and never to consider the well-being of his own person. Eppstein was ambitious, but courage was not his strong point. Edelstein was well attuned to Commandant Seidl, but Eppstein did not get along with him, and sad jokes circulated in the camp about this. He was a show-off, theatrical, soft, and vain. His expression was one of timid anxiety and sorrow. He was almost always somewhat hunched over, like a man who feels he can barely cope with the tasks weighing on him. One had the impression that he advocated Jewish interests to the SS weakly and with little resistance; he accepted their orders and carried them out. He certainly was not a monster – his gloomy character argued against that – but it cannot be said that he was warm or kind.

Repulsive womanizing by a leading functionary in a camp always has a disastrous effect on the community, and Eppstein, this broken man whom the SS already had reduced to a tool in Berlin through threats and imprisonment, was entangled in just such an unrestrained lifestyle. Despairing of himself and his calling, he lacked Edelstein's temperament, in which optimism repeatedly prevailed, as is so often the case with Eastern European Jews. Eppstein was a committed Zionist socialist, but he was always an admirer of power, even in National Socialist form. He came from Mannheim and had studied economics and sociology; he was educated, interested in many fine things, sensitive, and originally surely had been what one might call an idealist. In the camp, he seemed a weakling, always fleeing a present that was terrible to him, and whose corrupting violence had worn him down. He therefore attempted to numb himself and long since had left the path of a strictly righteous person (see 3b, 36, 55b, 78a, 93, 115a, 243a, 243c, 243e).

After Eppstein, Murmelstein, the last Jewish Elder, had a different and certainly far stronger personality than his two colleagues and predecessors. No good reputation had preceded him from Vienna. Murmelstein, who came from Galicia, had studied philosophy and had become a rabbi. A Falstaff in his outward appearance, he was smart, clear, superior, cynical, sly, and far superior to his colleagues in intelligence, and especially in cunning. His demeanor was ice cold and self-assured. His small, deep-set eyes seemed empty; his character was inscrutable, unmoved, and calculating. He was nevertheless subject to strong emotions, and even though no one in the camp but his closest associates could attribute a good word or deed to him, he had his rare soft moments. Unfortunately, this talented man did not often indulge this character trait; he was feared no less than he was hated. He seemed indifferent to the Jews for whom he was responsible. He carried out SS orders precisely and promptly, and it is little excuse that he may have believed that only intelligent obedience could save what there was to save. He did not heed prisoners' pleas but rejected them coldly or cynically or in choleric fits, whereas Edelstein and Eppstein at least offered words of consolation when no help was possible. Murmelstein seemed well armed against compassion. Whenever, toward the end of the war, he dared to put in a word on behalf of the camp, he did so under considerable pressure and when the risk to this cunning negotiator had already been diminished. Murmelstein's personal opinions were not known in Theresienstadt (see 3b, 193c, 243f, 294b).

These three men would now represent the fate of the community, as it seems hardly possible to speak of leadership, given their lack of power. It was unfortunate that no cooperation occurred. They had their personal followers, who eyed one another suspiciously; none of them put his own interests last, and each was engaged in intrigues both large and small. These men certainly failed drastically in their function as supreme leaders, and, just as certainly, the SS desired and exploited these internal conflicts. This made it much easier to control the camp than would have been the case if the camp representatives had confronted the SS with a united will, which Edelstein had at least attempted to create. He and Eppstein in particular did not get along, plotting against each other until Edelstein was finally defeated. Eppstein knew how to slowly neutralize his predecessor, whom he soon stopped taking along to his morning reports to the camp commandant. Eppstein was warned that it would be hard to prove later on what he had or had not been ordered to do by the SS if he talked to the camp commandant without witnesses. To this, the senior Jewish Elder replied contemptuously that he wanted nothing to do with Edelstein, whom he called "that trade union secretary."

We turn again to conditions in the camp:

Housing these masses, who arrived in close succession, was an almost insoluble task. The barracks were already fully occupied by July [1942] and the houses completely settled by August, though the mainly old and infirm people could not use the bunk beds prepared for the dense occupation. In August, each ghetto inhabitant already had an average of 1.6 square meters of living space on which he had not only to sleep, but also to keep his possessions. Nothing remained but to occupy rooms that had until now been considered uninhabitable. The attics were now occupied, though they were not prepared in any way, had no insulation against cold and heat, no lighting fixtures, no toilets and no water pipes. In the summer heat, temperatures prevailed that made staying there extraordinarily difficult, in addition to which many infirm and sick people were unable to use the stairs to leave their attic quarters during the heat of the day. More than 6,000 people were housed in attics. Because, at around the same time, a broad securing of accompanying luggage took place (that is, the aforementioned confiscation), the arrivals at first brought to the quarters only possessions that they themselves could carry. They were housed in the recently-acquired, only provisionally cleaned, unfurnished rooms or attics, largely without mattresses, straw palliasses, or blankets, without the facilities necessary for bodily cleanliness or laundry, and without eating utensils. Because some of this transport of the elderly ... came with lice, and because, in this initial difficult period, no cleanliness or delousing ... was possible, the lice problem increased considerably. Illnesses also raged, especially in the old people's quarters.... While in the months of May and June 1942, the number of deaths rarely exceeded ten per day, mortality ... began to rise sharply. In July, there already were days with more than 50 deaths. In August ... up to 113 ... , while September 1942 ... brought days with up to 156 deaths....

Great difficulties in provisioning also had to be overcome. The cooking pots were increasingly insufficient. By the month of August, there was only .34 liters of cooking

The "Ghetto," July 1942–Summer 1943

pot content per person. Lunch had to be cooked and distributed in several shifts. There were not enough means of transport to bring the food to the old people in the houses. The majority had to pick up their food in the large kitchens. Only some of the blocks could be supplied by transport crews. The food had generally become cold before it reached the hands of the block inmates. Some 52% of the portions could be distributed to the inmates of the barracks themselves, only 11% ... could be brought to ... the block inmates ... 37% ... of mainly old people from the small housing units had to pick up the food themselves, though most of these people did not even possess eating utensils.

(354)

The difficulties had already become much greater towards the end of the month [September 1942], as the weather, because of the season, is not suited to distribution of food outdoors. There already has arisen the necessity of setting up new distribution points for the residents of the blocks or houses, for it is not acceptable for them to spend 2 to 3 hours in the open each day to pick up meals. In the month of the report, distribution was as follows:

544,021 portions to inmates in *Kaserne*,
943,687 portions to inmates in the blocks in *Kaserne*,
152,218 portions were delivered to the blocks.

(276)

The age distribution toward mid-September became less and less favorable for the working conditions; for every one hundred people, four to five were under sixteen years old, nineteen were between sixteen and forty-five years old, twenty-one were between forty-five and sixty-five years old, and fifty-five to fifty-six were more than sixty-five years old. On July 1, the proportion of elderly people already had reached 36%; one month later, it reached 50%; and in August, 56%. The high mortality rate and the deportation of 18,000 of these unfortunates at first created tolerable conditions for the continued existence of the "ghetto," but the conditions became increasingly difficult. Those fit to work were kept extraordinarily busy. A complicated system of bonuses was introduced for them. It never really did justice to their needs; it provided for small food distributions to be made weekly, which later was extended to every ten days. "During this period, on average, for transport and kitchen work 80 to 110 hours a week were necessary, including night work; for nursing, 75 to 85 hours and 20 hours of night work ... for craftsmen, 65 to 75 hours per week and 10 nighttime hours; for administrative staff, 78 hours per week and 16 nighttime hours" (354). On average, 12,615 people worked in August and 15,396 in September, of whom 7,648 were men and 7,748 women.

Conditions were similar to the previous month [August], such that 40 to 60% more people were deployed than were fit for work, so that the difference had to be made up by the overaged, youngsters, and those less able-bodied. These figures ... do not take account of the so-called "house duties." This must be understood as the deployment of some 4,000 persons (approximately 2,300 women and 1,700 men) in the houses where some 30,000 old, sick and infirm people live. This house duty, carried out almost entirely by the very aged, was responsible for cleaning the houses and meeting the needs of those who could not walk, providing the gate-, water-, and other guards, carrying out house administration, etc.... A particularly critical question in the first ten months was that of male workers. By recruiting the administrative squadron each day in particularly large numbers, through temporary use of work groups for additional work, and through

removal of quickly-assigned workers from their sections, the special tasks and requirements that arose could be carried out.

(276)

"Labor monitoring" (*Arbeitskontrolle*) was introduced to supervise performance and
speed and to track down shirkers.

The Identity Card Control carried out a total of 2,000 checks and 15 large-scale
inspections. [Through one check of the sick,] a strict and complete registration of all
the sick was possible, [so that] any sort of abuse was precluded. [During this month,
1,800 people received heavy-laborer rations and 4,000 received S-bread (*Schwer*, or
heavy-laborer rations).] Both measures were carried out as part of the overall
distribution and through cost savings among the aged.... Provisioning plans had
to be submitted daily, sometimes even twice in one day, since for lunch and the
evening meal, arriving and departing transports could change the numbers or the
housing units.

(276)

In late September, the number of persons over 65 years of age had sunk to 45% and
diminished ... by the end of December 1942 to 33%, a proportion that remained more
or less the same from then on. The proportion of persons from 45 to 65 years of age rose
in late September to 26%, towards the end of the year to 31%, while ... the number
from 16 to 45 years of age again came to 23% at the end of September and had risen by
the end of the year to nearly 29%.

(354)

In all areas of public welfare, overpopulation caused extreme difficulties. The
construction of four deep wells was supposed to alleviate the water shortage, in
order to reach an average daily amount of 80 L per person. Drilling began at the
beginning of July 1942. By the end of the year, fifty houses had been newly connected
to the network. Unsanitary wells were blocked off. The water supply did not improve
significantly until 1943, when all houses had been connected to the water pipes that
finally carried sufficient water, except that water still often had to be carried to the
upper floors. The crematorium was opened on September 7, 1942, and by the
beginning of October, all four ovens, with a daily capacity of 180 corpses, were up
and working (see 146b). Starting on July 19, 1942, the dead were buried in mass
graves – initially, twenty-four of the dead were buried in caskets, whereas, later on,
up to sixty corpses would be interred without caskets. The last mass grave was dug
on October 6, 1942. At the end of October, the construction of a chlorination facility
for the sewer system began.

The newly acquired houses had to be examined, the necessary repairs determined and
carried out, specifically involving sewers, installation, toilet facilities.... This necessary
work had to be carried out on 160 houses in approximately 6 weeks. Meanwhile, the
ghetto had only ... some 27 masons.... The civilian residential houses, arranged in
blocks, had angular, narrow courtyards, in some places with completely uninhabitable
old sheds, stalls. In order to be able to combine these blocks into functioning units and to
improve sanitary conditions in the courtyards, generous refurbishing was planned; it
mainly consisted of tearing down the dividing courtyard walls and the uninhabitable,
sometimes dirty sheds and stalls that blocked the ventilation. So far, this work could
only be partially completed, but already [late 1943!] it has made possible significantly
better operation of the houses. In order to supplement the insufficient toilet facilities ...

The "Ghetto," July 1942–Summer 1943 101

in the ... courtyards, concrete, flushable latrines and washing sheds were constructed; these were connected to the sewer system.

(354)

Existing kitchen facilities were also improved and new ones built: "By the end ... of 1942, the available cooking pot volume was brought to 20,560 liters" (354). In order to protect from the elements those who spent hours waiting for their food, wooden protective roofs were erected at the kitchen distribution hatches. People worked busily to make the attics more habitable, which later was done mainly through private initiative. New bedsteads were built, among them a particularly uncomfortable variety called "chamber beds" (*Schlauchbett*), which were bedsteads for many people in which one slept as if in a casket. "In order not to depend on trained carpenters, nailed, standardized interchangeable construction modules were produced. These were used for meal distribution points, sheds, and latrines. The completion of the attics was aided by roofing paper and lightweight insulation" (354).

The beginning of consolidation in the camp was unsettled by the "transports of the elderly" in September and October 1942. Unfit to work, the elderly were an unbearable burden on camp construction, but rather than at least temporarily delaying the heedless arrival of more and more transports to Theresienstadt, the SS decided on a "solution" that they much preferred: deportation "to another maintenance ghetto [*Versorgungsghetto*]," as they were officially called – that is, to mass murder in the extermination camps. The SS took care to spread a rumor that the destination was Ostrowo [Ostrow Wielkopolski] in Posen [Poznan], a camp "with conditions as good as in Theresienstadt," and the victims as well as the families they left behind believed this fairy tale (see 3b, doc. 77). There was great agitation and desperation, but the truth was not known or sensed. Thus far, people older than sixty-five had been spared deportation. After some initial problems, many of the elderly had adjusted surprisingly well to the difficult conditions, and their children and grandchildren were relieved to find their loved ones protected and in relative security. This protection was no longer available, as the transports were specifically meant for people over age sixty-five. Younger prisoners were not selected, but they could volunteer to accompany their relatives. In September, approximately 10,000 elderly people from Germany and Vienna left, and a matching number of people from the "Protectorate" were supposed to follow in October, but, thanks to Edelstein's intervention, and because there were not enough elderly Bohemian Jews, the SS did not insist on this number and was satisfied with 8,000 victims. The 18,000 people left in nine transports, each containing approximately 2,000 people.

A cruel comedy preceded the deportation in the form of an agonizing procedure. All prisoners over sixty-five, and, if they were married, their younger spouses as well, were brought in long lines to a complicated "registration" process, which was divided into two stages. First, Jewish officials had to fill out long forms with the elderly in the courtyard and in the offices of B V. In small groups, they were then brought to the commandant's office, where the SS asked questions and beside every name on their lists noted "T" or "O," which meant "Theresienstadt" or "*Osten* (East)." Although the SS made the decisions in this case, it seems that their decisions were not strictly binding on the Jewish leadership when it came to the composition of the transports. At least some of those who had been classified as "O" could be saved from deportation. Among the crucial reasons for mercy or deportation were the following: having suffered from severe war wounds, having been decorated at least at the level of the Iron Cross First Class, holding certain foreign citizenship, having half-Jewish children, and so on. Anyone who could stand on his own feet had to go to the registration area personally; others were sought out. Because they had to stand in rank and file for many hours, many collapsed. During the departure of the transports, terrible incidents occurred, unique even in the history of the deportations, over-abundant as they were in barbarity.

Next it was the turn of the German Jews. These helpless, abandoned people did not know where to begin and were not able to prepare for disaster. Many were lying in so-called infirmaries and "homes for the sick," in so-called rooms, and in attics, incapable of making decisions or acting. Many were in bad shape, ill, lice-ridden, half-starved, and no longer in control of their senses; many were marked by death, which certainly would have overtaken them right there within a few days. But now they had to leave – anyone with the least spark of compassion would have let them die there. They were mercilessly driven, collected, dragged to the trains, and loaded onto carts like garbage. With their ragged bundles and in all weathers, they were hauled on wretched, absurd hearses, which had been brought to Theresienstadt, months before from all Jewish communities in Bohemia and Moravia as a means of transportation, and this living freight was shoved to the collection point in the Schleuse. No one was there to provide comfort or encouragement, time was pressing, and the so-called transport help, like the "transport administration," was concerned only that the correct number of victims arrived on time. They did not even think to send back the half-dead, agonized shadows of human beings because of "unfitness for transport." Apparently everyone was well enough to be loaded onto a cattle truck or passenger train, crowded fifteen or twenty to a compartment. There was no son, no daughter, no friend to care for those robbed of their dignity or to provide a little compassion. No one even had the opportunity to check on them, because each was surrounded by so much misfortune in his own family. It was hard enough merely for someone to strive to stand by his own mother and get her a spoonful of soup, when, at the end of the day, he himself was weary after working almost constantly day and night, devoured what little food he had, and, exhausted, sought to sleep for a few hours.

Nothing should be palliated here, though those who *could not* offer sufficient help should not be judged too harshly; but there can be no pardon for vile meanness: there was shameless gloating, which hardened in the face of this immense suffering and led people to comment nastily that these transports did not concern the Czech Jews because now "the Germans" would finally see what a transport was, and so on, and similarly depraved remarks. Such crudeness certainly was not universal, but that it appeared at all must be noted. The behavior of some of the prisoners employed at the transports was also shameful. They increased the cruelty of the transports beyond measure through their own cruelty, treating the most unfortunate like soulless rubbish (because even cattle are treated better); rushing, driving, chasing, and hounding the confused people; helping themselves to the sad debris of their remaining belongings; and even laying hands on the victims themselves. These were exceptions, to be sure, but they did occur. Those who still were able to do so had to drag themselves to the distant train station. The others were loaded onto trucks at the Schleuse, with up to sixty persons to a truck. At the train station, they were abused and crowded onto the train, where the SS robbed many of their remaining luggage. Blows rained upon these lost ones – remember that they were old people over eighty years of age! – before they were finally driven to their deaths.

The deportation of the elderly from the "Protectorate" was similar, if not quite as bad. This time the German Jews displayed gratification. But otherwise this was very different, as the victims usually had children or friends in the camp. People who had been unconcerned only a month before became desperate and attempted to rescue their loved ones through connections, but few could be saved in this way. Thus these unfortunates, too, met their inevitable fate. Again, the departure was brutal, alleviated only slightly by offers of help as well as by the grief and compassion of those left behind. Few decided to share their parents' fate, especially as the parents usually refused this sacrifice.

At the end of October, the "ghetto," as overcrowded as it still was, resembled a city hit by a natural disaster. "Psychologically, the so-called 'transports of the elderly' were a great burden on the ghetto. Under the existing living conditions, family relationships had gained increased significance. Thus the effect of families being torn apart was especially unfortunate" (354). Various reforms introduced from September 1942 onward contrasted with these tragic events. The reforms were intended to create a superficial normalization and, as they progressively developed, lent the camp the appearance that would fully unfold in summer 1944.

In September 1942, the future "money economy" was announced. January 1, 1943, was designated for the distribution of "ghetto crowns" (GK), an internal currency, but the notes did not go into circulation until May 1943. A preliminary design, featuring Jewish symbols, was produced in the camp by the illustrators Heilbron and Peter Kien. But in the end the notes, probably printed in Berlin, showed Moses with the tablets, disfigured by a crooked nose, sidelocks, and other crude attributes, along with Jakob Edelstein's signature. Notes were printed in various sizes and colors, with values of one, two, five, ten, twenty, fifty, and one hundred crowns (see 3b, doc. 109). "To introduce a money economy, wage payments to laborers were to take place according to a wage scale to be developed. For those being cared for, too [nonworkers], specific monthly payments were planned" (354). In connection with this, a fictitious "bank of the Jewish self-administration" was established in the former city hall (Q 619); it was adorned with a lovely sign and was quite luxuriously furnished. In August 1944, it traded places with the "SS office," as the Camp Commandant's Office was now called. In November 1942, a "wage system" was formally introduced (see Chapters 13 and 14).

The final changeover ... to a money economy occurred in May 1943. Thereby there arose the need to express all economic transactions, especially work performance, in money. Thus every ghetto inmate had to be assigned an income that covered the costs of his upkeep and that allowed the purchase of additional goods. The ghetto crown was introduced as a monetary unit ... which had purchasing power only within the Jewish settlement area and had no exchange value with official currencies. A six-tiered wage scale, differing for men and women, was introduced; it also provided for payments to non-workers at the lowest rate level. The rate combined cash payments and non-cash vouchers to a blocked bank account. ... In this way, the ghetto inmate each month was to receive a sum of money that corresponded to his work performance, and with which he ... made cash purchases and could thus satisfy his additional needs. The cost of basic necessities such as housing, food, medical care, and tax contributions was covered without cash through wage deductions cleared through the bank. The residual amounts left after these deductions and the cash payments were made were credited to the ghetto inmates' obligatory savings accounts, for which each ghetto inmate was issued a savings card. On 21 April 1943, the bank ... was transferred some 53 million crowns of ghetto money. On 12 May, the first payments were made by the bank, which assumed full operation on that day. Its main attention was to be ... focused on making sure the issuance of notes corresponded to a corresponding return flow, in order ... to prevent hoarding of currency. Because of a lack of goods in the stores, however, sufficient return flow of notes could not be achieved. A note distribution of some five million ghetto crowns per month was met by a return flow of only some two million.... In order to remedy this deficiency, fees ... were first of all imposed for recreation and for packages. In addition, the relationship between cash payments and vouchers was ... controlled such that cash payments were reduced while vouchers were increased accordingly. [Not until October 1943 did the outflows more or less equal the returns. Administrative reforms were necessary. Monthly "wage lists" had to be kept in all the workplaces, and by the house elders in the case of nonworkers. The workplaces had to set up "money income statements."]

With the introduction of the money economy, the activities of the distribution office, which until then had been authorized to distribute clothing and basic items even without vouchers or points in cases of need, were suspended. To match the purchasing opportunities of the various income levels, three types of goods were introduced, according to quality and price range ... and three types of voucher coupons, red, green, and blue, were issued. ... The number of stores was increased from ten to fourteen. The purchase of expensive items ... whole suits, shoes ... made ... the use of special voucher coupons necessary, for which, in case of insufficient amounts of cash on the part of the purchaser, solutions were prepared for granting credit.

(354)

In order to portray the development of the "money economy" in context, we have gotten ahead of ourselves. The introduction of the fake money was preceded by the establishment of "sales points" on short notice, in the midst of the chaos of the "transports of the elderly." Housed in former stores, they simulated actual shops, with window displays and signs. In the hasty overcrowding of the town, all the shops had been converted into mass housing. Now some of these buildings had to be quickly evacuated. "Personnel" were hurriedly employed. The SS had no problems obtaining merchandise. Low-quality items from confiscated luggage and items from the storehouses already in the camp and the long-existing "Distribution Office," whose supplies were sustained mainly by the possessions of the deceased, were allotted to the stores as "merchandise." They were replenished from time to time, depending on the amount of confiscated possessions available. Initially, eight shops were opened. Soon their number increased to fourteen, including shops selling items such as groceries, men's wear, ladies' wear, lingerie, shoes, household items (hardware, dishes, etc.), notions and perfumery (also stationery), and suitcases. The very listing of the different types of business – as well as the accompanying propaganda – illustrates the SS's grotesque mockery of the prisoners as well as their propaganda and the SS's play instinct. No additional branches were launched, but some of the existing types were divided into two stores that were supposed to offer merchandise of differing quality. Other things also changed in these shops, which were not spared the resettlement sickness so typical of Theresienstadt. The differences in quality depending on level of income existed only on paper, and the price differences were unimportant, as "ghetto money" never had any value and was easily obtainable, should the need arise. The "money economy" and the stores were not to be taken seriously. The prisoners made fun of them, and their derision was perhaps sometimes mixed with anger, but they were extraordinarily burdensome on the internal administrative apparatus.

The displays always had to be filled with good merchandise that could not, however, be purchased. Some stores were not without a certain tragicomedy. For instance, among the "household objects" were vases, knickknacks, and other junk, useless here, from the luggage of German Jews who had come to the "Theresienstadt spa" in good faith. The "notions store," with its brooches, chains, and colorful bangles, contained mainly the worthless remains of theft that apparently were of no use anymore and thus found their way back to the "ghetto." That is how most things looked in the stores, and some people even used their "vouchers" (*Bezugsscheine*) (see 3b, doc. 113) to "buy" back their own property with "ghetto money." The "suitcase store" was the most exciting. Wardrobes and other furniture did not exist, and thus suitcases were needed for people's meager belongings. Thus this store actually would have made sense if one could have bought anything useful there. But there were only dented and damaged pieces bearing the names and "transport numbers" of the former owners. It is impossible to imagine the stories behind each and every suitcase – thus this was the cemetery of all property in the camp. The "food store" (see Chapter 12) stocked no stolen goods, nor, for the most part, did the stores for "household goods" – dishes and spoons – or the perfumes, notions, and stationery stores. Often, however, they offered unsellable items that were either occasionally distributed, such as the usual camp soap, or that were destined only for the house management, such as cleaning supplies or nails. The "shoe store" sometimes offered the wooden shoes manufactured in the camp, as well as wooden sandals. Finding a new pair of overalls in the "clothing store" was like winning the jackpot.

On September 13, 1942, the orders of the day announced the establishment of the stores and the distribution of "vouchers," which initially were uniform for everyone. Goods were available for purchase on rotation; the length of the rotation differed for the different types of articles. To make the camp seem even more like a normal town, other businesses, too, were turned into stores. The "butcher shop" was tantalizing, with its large sign and shop window filled with pieces of meat and large sausages. Unfortunately, access was forbidden, and the entrance from the street was locked. The butcher shop was supposed to meet the needs of the entire camp, and it delivered the approved amounts only to the kitchens. But even the smallest rations for a camp of this size appeared abundant when displayed in a single store. The pharmacy, located in the old city pharmacy, also was inaccessible; it supplied only the hospitals, outpatient clinics, and special distribution offices, where drugs were obtained by prescription. Furthermore, most of the barbershops became hair salons; the same was done with some of the workshops: watchmaking, fountain pen repair, bandage manufacture, and repair of optical equipment. Originally, a "book shop" had been planned, too, but the idea was abandoned and instead a library was established (see Chapter 19). "During these months, the ghetto lost much of its camp-like character" (354).

Perhaps the most important step on the road to the normalization of conditions was the introduction, finally, of a mail service. Although it remained limited, it seemed like a great blessing. Unfortunately, it also led to disastrous social differences, as contrasts were made between those who received parcels and those who received only a few or none at all. The revocation of the ban on mail was made public in the orders of the day on September 16, 1942. Starting on September 20, messages to the "Greater German Reich" were permitted; the prisoners took turns according to transport group, and the messages were restricted to thirty words written in print,

106   *History*

including the greeting and signature, plus the address and return address. This changed with the orders of the day for September 24, 1942; after that point, one postcard per month was allowed, with writing on one side and an unlimited number of words. Letters required a special permit. Short letters to friendly or neutral countries and Red Cross forms to enemy countries were to be introduced. In reality, however, domestic or international communication was rarely possible for the prisoners. Nor did monthly postcard-writing ever happen. Receiving postcards was also now permitted, in accordance with specific rules, and packages could be received from the area of the "Greater German Reich," with the exception of the General-gouvernement; this could be mentioned in the correspondence. Later, packages from other countries were also allowed.

On May 24, 1943, the orders of the day announced new postal regulations, effective June 1. After that point, only one postcard was allowed every three months. Only then did posted mail regularly reach its addressees. The orders of the day for October 16, 1942, permitted deportees to issue predeportation "mail authorizations" (*Postvollmacht*) (see 3b, doc. 157) for arriving postcards and packages to others who had stayed behind. After the mass deportations of fall 1944, these powers of attorneys were declared invalid. Only months after they were permitted did packages reach the prisoners in noticeable numbers. This was due partly to the impossibility of asking explicitly for packages, partly to the small amount of mail that was actually transported, but above all to the criminal mismanagement of the Jewish post office. This office was staffed with scoundrels who delayed the distribution of mail prior to transports and appropriated many packages, whether they were going to deportees or to prisoners in the camp. The booty went to a small circle that wallowed in luxury.

Finally, on the eve of the new year, 1943, this group had no qualms about inviting a number of people to a banquet. They also invited artists, who contributed to the success of the scandalous feast with a variety show. Each guest received a package with 2 kg of food as a present. This outrageous revelry caused a serious scandal, although it was largely hushed up. The orders of the day for February 16, 1943, announced the arrest of some post office staff, among them the deputy manager. The manager and many other functionaries were dismissed, and new staff were appointed. The main culprits were convicted, but the penalties imposed by the "ghetto court" – prison sentences of up to three months – seemed ridiculously light. From then on, the situation at the post office improved.

During this period, the final step toward "normalization" was the opening of a "coffeehouse." A former pub on the town square (Q 418), until then used as mass lodgings, was evacuated, renovated, and connected to the burgeoning "Recreation Office" (Freizeitgestaltung). The orders of the day for December 6, 1942, announced its opening on December 8 and its business hours, from 10 A.M. to 7.30 P.M. (see 3b, doc. 173).

> Allocations [*Answeisungen*] will be provided for visiting the coffeehouse; these will be issued for a particular day and will be valid for two hours.... They will be issued by turns according to the number available. Separately from this rotation, a preferential series is planned for the war-wounded, decorated veterans, and prominent persons.... Because there is room for only 100 persons for now, 500 people will be able to visit the coffeehouse each day. In a short while, the coffeehouse will be expanded with rooms on the second floor. Newspapers will be available in the coffeehouse; in the afternoon, beginning at 2 P.M., an orchestra will play.
>
> (orders of the day, December 6, 1942)

Music, thus far forbidden, now was permitted. A small orchestra was created, as were musical ensembles. Instruments arrived, taken from confiscated Jewish property in Prague, as in the case of so many other acquisitions. These reforms alleviated the situation somewhat, but they lent the "ghetto" an increasingly eerie character. Newspapers, incidentally, did not enter this strange "coffeehouse," but toward the end of 1942, the Prague newspaper *Der Neue Tag* was posted here and there. However, a few weeks later, after the Stalingrad catastrophe, which no longer could be concealed, the SS decided that a daily newspaper was not fit reading material for Jews, and *Der Neue Tag* disappeared.

The cessation of transports, from early February until early September 1943, had a favorable impact on the situation. But every improvement in the difficult living conditions at the same time contributed to the prisoners' deception and self-deception. Furthermore, the longer one stayed in the camp, the more the dangerous power of habit grew. Many became dull and slack; it was a seductive danger. These symptoms overshadowed and all too often suffocated the motivation to remain keenly alert. Thus the seeds of decay were sown; this decay at first grew in a stealthy and barely noticeable fashion, but its symptoms already were taking effect.

When the deportations were announced in early 1943, protection of the AK transports was no longer mentioned, although it was still allowed to remain in force. The camp no longer absolutely needed these men, and so the SS dropped them, as the phase of building finally was over. The new internal leadership did not feel connected to this old guard, and there emerged a new dominant class that, however, absorbed a large number of the AK people. In September 1943, the AK transports still were protected by the self-administration, but the SS culled some who appeared too well dressed and were not marked as "workers" by calluses or other characteristics.

In April 1943, the first Dutch transport arrived from Amsterdam. The 300 new arrivals were mainly privileged German emigrants, war-wounded veterans, and so on; there also were a few Dutch Jews (see 49).

After the long break in the deportations, at the end of August 1943, rumors leaked out about impending transports. Because they were specifically supposed to involve people fit to work, everyone strove to save himself from deportation through "indispensable" work, meaning physical labor. A few newly formed groups – "K-production" and "barracks construction" – supplied that opportunity. Finally, a double transport of 5,000 people was announced for September 6, 1943, as a "work transport." It was the largest number of people that had ever left the camp on a single day. The things that were believed to protect one from transport were no more or less helpful than in the past. Particularly hard hit were the recently dismissed GW men, who had until then enjoyed the most reliable protection. As always, the transport was filled with elderly and sick people up to age sixty-five who were unable to work, as well as young people.

This was also the first transport to take away one of the most influential men in the leadership: the director of the Central Secretariat, Dr. Leo Janowitz, one of Edelstein's closest associates. The background of his case has never been explained. Prior to the departure of the transport, his living quarters were searched, and the SS found written material related to the "transport list" that was to be compiled. This was not unusual, but the SS could interpret this however it chose, and Janowitz was immediately arrested. It is unclear if this was one of the usual terror measures, or if the new German commandant, Anton Burger, sought a reason to destroy an unpopular man and friend of Edelstein, whom he hated.

108   *History*

This transport had a unique role, as emerges from the report presented in Chapter 3. German officials wanted to counter the reports that were spreading abroad about the not-quite-believed and unbelievable horrors of Auschwitz and other extermination camps. To that end, they wished to document the "harmlessness" of Germany's Jewish policy. The double transport arrived at Auschwitz II (Birkenau) in two trains on September 8, 1943. Some 1,140 people died there in the following months, until, exactly six months after their arrival, with some exceptions, the survivors were killed in the gas chambers during the night of March 8, 1944. According to the Jewish religious calendar, this day coincided with the festival of Purim.

For what purpose had these people been spared for such a long time? They were placed into a camp that had been established especially for them and, relative to conditions in Auschwitz, were housed well, with their families. Children were placed into children's homes. They were allowed a degree of self-administration, and no labor was required beyond fulfillment of individual needs. They were even given some of their luggage, were allowed to wear their own clothes, and in many cases did not even have their hair cut. For Auschwitz, this was unheard of. They had to write harmless postcards to Bohemia and Moravia, as well as to Theresienstadt, in which they reported that they were well, asked for news, and gave Birkenau as their place of residence. In Theresienstadt and elsewhere in the "Protectorate" it was not known that Auschwitz was identical to the harmless-sounding Birkenau. People in Theresienstadt were permitted to respond outside the usual correspondence schedule. Letters also were sent from the "Protectorate," as were packages, the arrival of which was duly noted and confirmed. Almost immediately prior to the mass murder, on March 5, the unsuspecting people were again told to write, using the dates March 25–27. The postcards reached their destinations weeks after the ashes of the asphyxiated victims had been scattered. At least in Theresienstadt, the deception was successful. People felt that Birkenau could not be so terrible and that it probably resembled conditions in Theresienstadt. Perhaps things were not "quite that good," but surely it was the "second-best" camp, where life was more tolerable, and it was easier to survive the war there than in a concentration camp or a Polish "ghetto." In this manner, the future victims were lulled into a false sense of security. Poland had to be bad, as unquestioned news of pogroms had leaked out, but not Birkenau ... And since the unmistakable change of fortunes in the war, the Germans had to be more careful; in the outside world, people had become aware of the Jews in the camps and in Theresienstadt, and a general improvement in conditions, a more humane and benign policy seemed clear. Almost everyone in Theresienstadt thought this, or something similar.

If we defined the goal of the history of the "ghetto" as its end, it becomes clear that the duration of camp was fraught with battles against difficulties that were only created and constantly promoted through its inhumane establishment and its continuing criminality. In Theresienstadt, the prisoners were presented with the impossible – although the SS never admitted as much – task of creating a functioning community. This challenge was set before them not only by their instinct for self-preservation but also by the SS, which required them to overcome the irresolvable. Therefore, apart from a fate shared by all individuals as well as the community as a whole, in Theresienstadt events happened through countless acts that united a constantly constrained and yet still independent collective. The inmates of this "ghetto" therefore shaped their own history to a much greater degree than could be said for all the other concentration camps, which had been established by the SS

The "Ghetto," July 1942–Summer 1943

and had not emerged out of existing settlements such as the conventional ghettoes in the East.

Thus the establishment of the camp was supposed to contribute to the development of societal institutions that could be considered normal, or at least approximated to such norms. In the phase described here, much was ordered that was wrong, in this sense, and much that was right was permitted. Welfare institutions and production sites were created and expanded. All the barracks rooms were furnished with bedsteads. Single beds were nailed together with shelves at their heads, and these bed frames were used to establish infirmaries (*Krankenstuben*), "homes for invalids" (siechenheime), and rooms for the "notables" and higher functionaries. The collection sites for laundry and the repair workshops were opened or enlarged. The "Central Clothes Mending Workshop" was established, and soon 800 workers labored there in two shifts to meet the needs of the prisoners and the "stores." "In the clothes-mending workshops, people began, as a result of the shortage of material, to produce useable work clothes and shoes from old scraps of material" (354). Additionally, "the most urgent need for mending in the various houses is to be satisfied by auxiliary workshops. In each of the houses, a sewing machine will be set up, at which aged women will do the most urgent minor mending" (276).

By 1943 the water problems had been largely overcome. The productivity of the waterworks reached 13,400 m^3 in November 1941 and 29,000 m^3 by April 1, 1943. But in the course of the same year, it rose to 87,000 m^3, the equivalent of 65 L per person per day.

"The growing plague of vermin made the building of an ... efficient delousing station necessary. This was begun immediately" (354). Many months were spent trying to alleviate this malady, without achieving halfway satisfactory results. Again and again, new transports brought more lice-ridden people who hardly could be isolated. Only healthy younger people who lived in better accommodations almost always knew how to protect themselves from contagion. Those with lice could not be bathed or properly washed, and effective disinfectants were lacking. Thus began the laborious process of setting up a disinfection facility in the former brewery (L 506–L 605).

A small steam disinfection boiler that worked day and night proved insufficient. The brewery's malt drying room was called into service. It was built for lower temperatures and, when the heat had to be kept at 110 degrees for a longer period, it caught fire.

(354)

On Thursday, 20 August 1942, a fire broke out in the Central Disinfection Station. At 2:25 P.M., the ghetto fire fighters arrived at the scene of the fire. The fire was extinguished in 45 minutes, and a report on the localization of the fire could be made to Camp Inspector SS-Untersturmführer Bergel, who was present. The Council of Elders expressed its appreciation to the fire fighters.

(orders of the day, August 21, 1942)

Once again, people were helpless. Only the procurement of hydrogen cyanide made it possible to take up the fight against lice in makeshift gas chambers. The shower had to be closed to the non-lice-ridden, and for months ... only people with lice could bathe.

(354)

Anyone who could still go to the delousing area by himself was lucky. It has already been described how the frail and lice-ridden lived. Once bathed and freed from vermin, their weakened bodies often no longer were able to recover. Therefore, many strove to escape the infamous quarantine and to conceal their lice. Children prevented their parents from being sent and, at great sacrifice, sought to rid them of the malady in other ways, which sometimes saved their lives. Those who left the quarantine alive often found their psychological resistance affected. Even if they had returned lice-free from quarantine, the elderly were again exposed to lice once they returned to their quarters. In the course of 1943 this evil was suppressed, but it was never entirely eliminated. In April, the boilers in the brewery were repaired, and an effective disinfection unit was established with a bath and gas chambers for clothes and luggage (see 356).

In the brewery, a heating plant was constructed and connected to three large-scale kitchens, as well as to the "Central Bath" for the healthy inmates (it also had its own boiler room); the former riding school (Q 321), with its mechanical workshops for woodworking; and several smaller operations. Two new kitchens were built, and the others were renovated and their productivity decidedly enhanced. Several special kitchens were opened, among them a "central children's kitchen" and later a "dietary kitchen" for the hospital in E VI. Cooking could now take place on a regular basis, and the food could be prepared more carefully and made more palatable. Distribution hours were regulated, and waiting periods were shortened to become more tolerable. A pastry bakery supplied the kitchens with baked goods. The "Central Bakery," which prepared bread almost exclusively, received new, more efficient machines, so that its productivity could be increased considerably with the same number of workers. The "Central Laundry," located on the opposite bank of the Eger, was improved through annexes and reorganization, but its productivity always lagged far behind demand.

Construction of a rail line from the Bohušovice train station to the camp became important. Construction began on August 24, 1942. Two tracks that ended far down L 2 street became the transshipment point for all arriving and departing transports. Another track turned off to the left and continued alongside barracks A II, where a loading ramp was built, and thus the camp had its own "freight depot." Lingering near the tracks was forbidden, but this prohibition was enforced only during transports. The track arrival point along the main street leading out of Bohušovice was blocked off by a fence-like wooden gate, guarded and operated by a GW man.

> On 1 June 1943, traffic began on the connecting track from the Bauschowitz [Bohušovice] train station to the ghetto, with a mixed passenger and freight train. The project for this 2.5 kilometer line was developed in late 1941.... In 245 work days, approximately 300 people dug up, moved and dumped onto embankments 19,000 cubic meters of soil, carted away 1,500 cubic meters of brickwork from the fortifications, unloaded and laid 2,800 cubic meters of gravel, and installed 2,600 meters of track and three switches.
>
> (orders of the day, June 8, 1943)

It was typical for an SS camp to have the prisoners, if possible, build tracks from the nearest train station, better to isolate the camp from its surroundings. This construction was not for the comfort of the prisoners or to ease workloads. However, the prisoners also gained an advantage from the train in that they did not have to drag their luggage the entire long distance from the camp to the train station during transports. But this connection to "traffic" also brought new mental anguish; now that the tracks were visible, the sinister sense of unknown deportation destinations seemed clearer and served as a warning, if foolishness and optimism led one to forget the constant danger.

The construction of shacks to house production facilities, begun in spring 1942, was completed in the summer. Export factories began to operate, producing goods such as women's clothing, wooden and educational games, and "rabbit-fur shearing scissors," and engaging in operations such as mica splitting.

> In the manufacture of women's clothing, some 1,000 dresses and aprons were produced in the month of the report [September 1942]. [Four thousand pairs of calf-leather galoshes were shipped, and 1,500 were prepared for shipping]. The notions and crafts workshops had very stable work. The production of bookmarks, watercolors, parchment items, oil paintings, [reproductions of] maxims, puzzles, jewelry, educational games, envelopes, and other notions had reached a considerable high point. The quality of the products is so good that complaints do not occur. [In mica production, because of a materials shortage], it was necessary to resort to [using what otherwise would have been] rejects.
>
> (276)

It did not bother the SS that Jewish hands produced Nazi propaganda pictures and bookmarks. Only later was production of such articles stopped.

Work was to become more efficient. Workers were submitted to mass screening to establish their degree of aptitude for physical labor, so that they could be moved from administration and less important factories to where they were needed to fulfill numerous special orders. Production facilities were converted increasingly to factories that "were important for the war." A "uniform repair workshop" replaced clothing manufacture. Production of crafts was greatly reduced after the owner of the Prague German firm Lautsch, which owned workshops in the camp, was reported to the police for smuggling tobacco, food, and money (see 349b). In the *Bauhof*, a new factory was established for cardboard packaging; it produced powder dispensers and boxes for detonators. In the western area in front of the fortress, opposite the gymnasium, five spacious wooden barracks were erected, later named the "West Barracks"; they were empty at first and later housed the children from Bialystok [Białystok], before housing 1,150 people (see Chapter 6). Soon afterward, construction of some twenty barracks was begun in the Bohušovicer Kessel, close to the street and the connecting train. These "south shacks," which were not completed until the early winter of 1943, were at first intended to house a large Jewish children's camp, the purpose of which emerged from the planned exchange described in Chapter 3. But, even before the end of construction, everything that had been installed for housing purposes had to be torn out and the bed frames removed. After that, the barracks were constructed such that factories could be housed there, of which the "mica splitting plant" soon would be the most important.

Somewhat earlier, at the end of May 1943, "box [*Kisten*] production," or "K-production," for short, was ordered; aside from mica-splitting requests, it was the largest army order that the "ghetto" had to fulfill. It kept more than 1,000 people occupied for nearly six months, until November 19, 1943. Three tall tents, much like circus tents, each about 100 meters long, were hastily erected on the fenced-off and so far unused town square. Here, standard boxes were continuously produced from special boards supplied by the Łódź Ghetto (see 98b). They held devices to prevent truck engines from freezing. The contract was for 120,000 boxes and was to be completed in three months. The pace of work suffered, however, from a shortage of materials, because the equipment was not delivered on time. The factory was inspected by several German authorities, for whom a show was performed. As no new goods were available, already-packed boxes were unpacked before the visitors arrived, to be repacked in front of the inspectors, who could then admire the wonderfully functioning factory and the useful work of the Jews under the competent leadership of the SS.

In September 1942, the number of nonworkers reached a peak, at 38,912 people. By that point there was a surplus of women among the workers, and among the prisoners in general. They numbered some 10,000 on August 1, 1942, and 12,000 in October 1942. The average number of workers rose constantly from January 1943 on; they totaled 20,543 in January and 24,746 in February and reached 29,603 persons in August 1943.

The evacuation of barracks E I and H IV, with the "armory," and of two civilian houses (Q 802 and 804) had a drastic impact. This evacuation had been rumored for some time, and a sudden order arrived at the end of July 1943. The first four transports had been quartered in E 1, and many had been living there since November 1941; this was where the early history of the camp had unfolded. It was and remained, soon along with B V, the heart of the camp: there one could find the camp's head, the leadership, as well as its hands, the workers for the self-administration. These barracks, with more than 5,000 inmates, had evolved into a town in itself, with its own ways of life that did not exist elsewhere in similar form. There existed a certain camaraderie that already was crumbling but still perceptible. Such close bonds did not develop in other quarters or among the women. With great diligence, and without great individual differences, a modest comfort had been achieved in the rooms and sleeping areas. People were more united than in the general chaos of the rest of the camp and showed more self-restraint. All of this was destroyed in a single stroke. The evacuation was also disadvantageous to the Jewish leadership. They always had had here a core group of able and willing young men who could be called upon day or night to manage the frequent special tasks, such as transport work to be completed within a few hours, the transfer of the "Central Camp Office" in one night, and so on.

The evacuation order came from Berlin, where the "Reich Security Main Office" no longer felt safe from air raids. Under the code name "Iltis," Theresienstadt was chosen as "temporary quarters" for the archives of Department IV A 6a (concentration camp papers); there they would enjoy protection through the presence of those very Jews to whom the same authority brought only death and destruction. Thus E 1 became the "Berlin Office" (Dienststelle); the remaining emptied buildings served as living quarters for the civil servants who were brought in.

The evacuation had to take place within twenty-four hours. The chaos is hard to imagine; it pervaded the town like a whirlwind, streaming in waves from E 1 and its courtyard. Innumerable primitive vehicles, loaded with all possible and impossible household goods, mattresses, palliasses, luggage, furnishings, bedding, bundles, knapsacks, sacks, and parcels, in addition to the furnishings from the offices and factories and from the outpatient clinics and infirmaries (a "disinfection hut" that had been erected in the courtyard had to be dismantled) and kitchen equipment – in short, everything from the large building, with its 5,400 inmates – poured out into the town, together with the remaining refugees. It resembled a startled rag market, overflowing in colorful and shrill ways and dissolving in hounded haste and resounding tumult. The lice-ridden frames that had served as beds were torn apart, divided up, hacked to pieces, and taken away. Suitcases and equipment blocked corridors and staircases. Everyone surged forth with his belongings, and each strove to find

The "Ghetto," July 1942–Summer 1943 113

halfway suitable quarters, so as not to have to depend on the miserable attics that the "Space Management Office" had assigned to them in "transfer papers." These assignments were often not complied with, and order was only gradually restored. The "Space Management Office" was lenient and legalized many unauthorized quarters. After the evacuation, the empty buildings had to be thoroughly restored, as the "Berlin Office," which included 220 people, planned to move in soon (see 3b, doc. 195). Report 354 mentions the clearing of the buildings, "which were separate from the ghetto and allocated for official purposes. This meant the sudden resettlement of 5,692 persons, who, to the extent they were workers, had to be housed in part in ... [A II], and otherwise had to be housed by consolidation of the paneling and through rapid extension of attic rooms."

The "Berlin Office" permanently employed some prisoners for cleanup, maintenance of the heating system, and minor services. The gates of E 1 were shut and guarded by GW men. As there was no entrance that would have avoided the camp area, the wall of the courtyard was altered and expanded to include a corridor to a wooden bridge protected by high stone walls, which crossed street L 1 in front of the entrance to the *Bauhof*. Had this not been the only entrance to the workshop center, the "ghetto" would have been made smaller for the convenience of the important gentlemen. As it was, however, they came up with this grotesque solution, which contributed significantly to the frenetically altered image of this once-simple town. Beyond the bridge, the road led into the "nonghetto" area in the forbidden neighborhoods near the "Brunnenpark."

Since the inundation of the camp with elderly persons, the "health services" were faced with major tasks. In August 1942, 176,538 medical interventions were carried out. There was hardly an elderly arrival who was not in need of a physician; at the time there was one "block doctor" for every 1,500 or 1,600 people. There were no beds, mattresses, or palliasses for the sick, and few nurses or medications. Transports from Germany brought the fixtures of old-age homes, and some physicians were allowed to bring their equipment to the camp. After many difficulties had been overcome, equipment, medication, and vaccines were approved and acquired. Three additional hospitals were built, along with a large "home for the infirm." But whatever was done was much less than was needed. Typhus, scarlet fever, measles, and especially enteritis raged. In August 1942, 400 scarlet fever patients were hospitalized.

> In comparison with the first half of 1942, in the second half of the year the number of bedridden patients had increased tenfold, and of ambulatory patients, thirteen-fold.... In the second half of 1942 there were 896 cases of scarlet fever, 831 measles cases, 600 cases of jaundice, 536 cases of typhus, 4,500 of eye diseases, and some 35,000 cases of enteritis...That fact that we succeeded in overcoming all these dangers made the further existence of the ghetto at all possible.... The plague of vermin [bedbugs and fleas] that emerged with particular virulence in the summer of 1943 in the quarters, which in some buildings led to complete suspension of lights-out for the residents, was effectively combated with large-scale disinfestation [*sic*] of entire buildings; in June, the disinfestation of the larger housing units and the houses was undertaken.
>
> (354)

This was a major exaggeration, as the flea and bug plague was never overcome. Many houses were never, or never seriously, disinfected, and time and again new vermin were imported into the cleaned quarters. In spring 1943 the camp experienced a severe typhus epidemic. Special hospitals were established for the typhus patients, and, by vaccinating the prisoners, the epidemic could be contained.

It was in this phase of the history that the development and premature collapse of the only institution that ever heralded the consolidation of internal power occurred. This was the "Security Service," whose history is tied to its director, Dr. Karl Loewenstein. Of half-Jewish descent, Loewenstein had been a naval officer in imperial Germany and had been close to the German crown prince for many years. After the war, he participated in the fighting in Upper Silesia and then became a banker in Berlin. As a member of the Confessing Church, he came into conflict with the Gestapo; he was arrested in November 1941 and deported to the Minsk "Ghetto." After six months in this camp of unspeakable horrors, he was sent to Vienna in May 1942, after General Commissar Wilhelm Kube intervened on his behalf at the highest levels. A few days later, he was sent to Theresienstadt. Because of the terrible abuse he had suffered in Minsk, Loewenstein arrived in bad health. He was immediately taken into custody and guarded by Czech gendarmes. The camp command apparently did not know what to do with him, feared his knowledge of the events in Minsk, and waited for orders from Berlin. In the meantime, he was well accommodated in prison and was provided with better food. On September 23, 1942, he was taken from prison by the camp commandant and was named head of the "Security Service." In this position, newly created and then eliminated after his downfall, Loewenstein became, alongside the senior Jewish Elder, the most powerful man in the self-administration. His rule was toppled on August 16, 1943, after the change in the German camp leadership, when Seidl was replaced by Obersturmführer Anton Burger on July 3, 1943.

The new department combined the "Ghetto Guard," the fire department, the "Detective Department," and the "Economic Control Office." Loewenstein directed these groups with a firm hand and, after initial hesitation, gained the trust of most of his subordinates. But he soon made enemies in his own ranks and, especially, in other departments and in the leadership, where his every move was observed with suspicion and who soon fought him using questionable methods. Initially, his relationship with Edelstein was good, but it became increasingly difficult, and his relations with Eppstein were unbearable. Loewenstein had free access to the camp commandant, who was impressed with his fearless and easy demeanor. For this reason, the [Jewish] leadership and high functionaries liked to use him for difficult interventions. Corporal punishment and many other hardships were abolished; Loewenstein achieved much for the camp by intervention with the SS. He did for his subordinates whatever was in his power. His directives were brief, to the point, and given with military precision. He hoped in this way to achieve the discipline he deemed necessary to establish and maintain order. He hated injustice and crooked ways. He was not afraid harshly to attack abuses, particularly theft and corruption. Unfortunately, he acted undiplomatically and waged an ever more complicated struggle against almost all departments; thus he made more enemies than necessary. Had his demeanor been as firm in principle but more conciliatory and cautious in form, much good would have been achieved for the camp – more slowly, it is true, but it would have been much more lasting. As it was, he was always a gentleman, in the best sense of the word, without fear or censure but unable to avoid errors due to a lack of discretion and understanding of human nature. Overly trusting, he tolerated around him people who not only did harm to his intentions but also contributed to his downfall. As he ever more relentlessly uncovered abuses within the administration, he finally became so unpopular that a well-prepared attack was launched against him, toppling him

The "Ghetto," July 1942–Summer 1943

through disgusting intrigues, in a "trial" before the "ghetto court" that was rife with perversions of justice. He was sentenced to four months in prison, like a common criminal. Burger would have spared him this humiliation, but no SS man was able to move Loewenstein to speak. He preferred to be humiliated by this punishment and determinedly refused all the positions that were offered him despite everything. Loewenstein remained in Theresienstadt until the end of the war and outlived most of his adversaries.

Loewenstein's achievements brought many boons to the camp, and his downfall brought only misfortune. It was difficult to comprehend and fairly judge his activities in the stifling atmosphere of the camp. The circumstances of his arrival in the "ghetto," his German origin, his past as an officer (although there were other elderly high officers of the German and Austrian armies in the camp), and his obviously privileged position with the SS seemed mysterious and aroused suspicion. People looked less at the man and his activities than at these circumstances and the silence about his recent past, a silence that Loewenstein had to impose, like it or not. Particularly for the sick and the frail, his measures to ensure fair distribution of goods was significant. He knew how to obtain precious medications. He enforced proper rationing of food and meals. Everything had to be preweighed or given out already packaged. When the director of the Central Provisions Office claimed that no measuring cups could be obtained and no lead for the filling of weights could be found, Loewenstein procured measuring cups and lead. Kitchens and provisioning centers were strictly monitored. This was popular with many prisoners but displeased those who were doing well. Suddenly, all the rations became larger, without the overall allotment having grown. He took vigorous action in the "homes for the infirm" and in the living quarters of the neediest. For many years after the war, Loewenstein was accused of having not entirely sincere motivations; it was said that he cared only to gain popularity and to satisfy his hunger for power. This is not true, and it is only fair to examine his views in his own words:

> I will never forget how horrified I was when I saw the starved people lying on trucks in the twilight, marching from the Dresden Kaserne [H V] with a small burial kommando, and at the same time the kitchen personnel were preparing themselves an extra meal. I stopped this the same day, and made sure that the kitchen staff received the same food as all other inmates. Mr. Schliesser [the head of the Economics Department] intervened with me without success, claiming that more would be stolen.
>
> (personal communication)

After the food had been handed out, there sometimes remained leftovers of the low-quality "extract soups," which were nevertheless coveted by the starving. Loewenstein had this food distributed by turns to the elderly. From the SS, he was able to obtain the release of confiscated goods, most of which he passed on to the hospitals. Many of Loewenstein's achievements were undone after his downfall, but a somewhat more just distribution of food was maintained even afterward.

Like Edelstein, Loewenstein intervened successfully with the SS to attain the release of prisoners, and he also was often able to alleviate their conditions when under arrest. A dangerous situation for the camp developed when 120 people failed to appear in the Schleuse before the last "old people's transport" and went into hiding. After the departure of the transport, Seidl imprisoned those who had not appeared; the men were placed in the headquarters, and the women in the prison in H V. Loewenstein brought these unfortunates to his prison and housed them in B V in a hastily emptied storeroom that they could leave during the day. He soon achieved their release, and even the assurance that they would not be automatically deported with the next transport. He also succeeded in transferring the prison in E 1, and soon afterward also the prison in H V, from the authority of the gendarmes to that of the GW, and thus of the camp. He had the prison in E 1 furnished with beds, and walls were broken through to give the prisoners light and more space.

The "Security Service," and especially the GW, a semimilitary unit now housed in building L 313, formed a significant group, even from the point of view of sheer numbers. The GW was trained on the job, and on New Year's 1942, in a parade before the senior Jewish Elder, who gave a speech, they took an oath to him. It is not clear if these formalities helped or harmed the camp, but, certainly, parades with a "standing army" in a "ghetto" should expect to meet with opposition, especially as this particular army was unarmed, except for a brief interlude when they were equipped with wooden clubs; the members of this army did not have to salute the SS but were required to remove their caps before even the most junior SS man, without being acknowledged in response. The prisoners could not take such a group seriously. It was not suitable for any kind of public display but instead served, with ridiculous vanity, to satisfy the play instinct of some of its members. This resulted in the grotesque spectacle of a body asserting itself as an authority that it was not and could not be. Undoubtedly these pretend soldiers made a certain impression on Seidl and other SS men, who, comfortably and without any danger, could act out their pathological military complexes in the face of Jewish troops; after all, most members of the SS were childish, cruelly playful fellows. But, at the higher levels, the SS obviously did not regard the 420 strong young GW men as quite so harmless, especially after the Warsaw Ghetto uprising; thus, a few weeks before his fall, the already weakened Loewenstein had to watch his formation broken up and replaced with 150 new men, who were at least forty-five years of age – which, until then, was the maximum age for joining the GW. In any case, Loewenstein's army, with which he had wanted to do so much good, shared the grotesquely eerie character that could not be avoided by any institution in the camp that acted as an authority.

Unfortunately, Eppstein and Edelstein bear considerable blame for the destruction of the Security Service and the GW. In their blind fear of Loewenstein, they did not even have any qualms about informing on him; they told Hauptsturmführer Ernst Möhs, Eichmann's deputy, that the GW was unreliable. Thus it was Möhs who ordered the transformation and the practical dissolution of the GW, even against the wishes of Seidl and later Burger. Considering that most of the dismissed guards and their families were deported "on orders" in September 1943 – they were told that they would again be guards at their destination – the Jewish leadership made a fateful contribution to these people's demise.

The "Security Service," which was subordinated to the senior Jewish Elder but was in reality nearly independent, was hypertrophied and was useful only as long as it was led by Loewenstein. On the day of his dismissal by Burger for his refusal to act as a spy, the "Security Service" would have collapsed, even if it had not been dissolved and separated into its individual parts. The majority of Loewenstein's subordinates were not as optimistically brave as he was; they played at being officers and became intoxicated with their supposed power, without accepting their leader's idealistic tasks or sharing his sense of responsibility.

The *"Ghetto," July 1942–Summer 1943*

If the "manners" of the SS had alleviated somewhat over time, terrible abuses still occurred. On the crowded streets, young SS men tore the caps off passersby who did not see them and salute quickly enough. They abused frail old men who, in their helpless clumsiness, could not avoid them in time. Once, an old man was shot in the street by an infuriated SS man. The feared Scharführer Rudolf Haindl (or Heindl) had been assigned to the camp from Vienna to take over Bergel's control responsibilities. Any time of the day or night, Haindl could appear where he was least expected. He rode his bicycle into every corner of the town. Informers whom he knew from Vienna told him who possessed illegal items, and at the first opportunity he almost always came upon people in whose pockets he found money or cigarettes. Beatings and imprisonment usually were the consequence. Obersturmführer Otto, from Łódź, spent time in Theresienstadt as a "visitor." He was an evil man who was especially interested in women. Some he took from the street to the "Central Bath," where they had to bathe naked in front of him; he flogged women who were made to undress in the prison.

The *Beruschky* were another feared group; these were German women, responsible to the SS, who raided living quarters in search of forbidden contraband. They came with gendarmes and GW men. When they searched a room, the inmates were required to leave, after which these females began to wreak havoc; they took not only forbidden items but also watches, lingerie, food, and other items that caught their fancy. They also made malicious mischief in the rooms, throwing soap powder on food and causing such chaos that it took days to clean up after their visits. They turned in only some of the "contraband" and appropriated the rest. They denounced or did not denounce owners of forbidden items, as they saw fit. Loewenstein was able to have these women dismissed after proving their thefts. Later, other German women were appointed; under their supervision, GW men had to carry out these room inspections, but at least the malicious abuses ceased. When the camp was to be turned into a model settlement, these visits stopped.

The language of the SS was sometimes still quite clear. The orders of the day of August 28, 1942, read, "According to information from the Camp Commandant's Office, corn has been stolen from the cornfields. . . . The Farm Guards [*Flurenwärter*] are instructed to use their weapons in case of trespass." The orders of the day of August 29, 1942, also mentioned that "Herr Camp Inspector, SS Untersturmführer Bergel, complains strongly that ghetto inmates can be found on the street at night. . . . Herr Camp Inspector Untersturmführer Bergel expressly calls attention to the fact that he will use his firearm against persons found on the streets after midnight without obvious reason."

On September 22, 1942, an announcement was made regarding who was permitted to wear "armbands," which had become a fashion in the camp, along with the general outfit of belts from which a cup hung: the GW received yellow armbands (plus the usual equipment and identification number); the OD, blue (and later also identification numbers); the "orientation service" of the GW, black, marked with the label "Information" in white; the fire department, red; "transport assistance," white, marked with the label "H.D." (*Hilfsdienst*); and the blind and infirm, yellow with black dots (a symbol commonly used in Germany). The original plan was to give armbands to all functionaries, beginning with the senior Jewish Elder, in conformity with the practice in the concentration camps. The semimilitary image of a penitentiary that was prevalent in these camps was blurred in Theresienstadt, partly due to the way in which it had developed and partly due to the imposition of a more civilian character, which meant that prisoners were ever less aware of the social basis on which this coerced community was built – and if they were, their awareness was unclear. The camp's elements were never significantly different from those of a concentration camp, but the self-administration and all its functions had been made so integral to the coerced community that the original circumstances were – or at least seemed to be – camouflaged, and new forms that really changed the social foundation were created.

On October 3, 1942, the SS ordered the sealing of all permitted electrical devices, in particular the cookers, which could be used only at specified times. Jewish and German security organs intervened immediately when these rules were violated. The use of unsealed devices was punishable.

The orders of the day for October 9, 1942, contained a "prohibition. Attention is emphatically called to the fact that singing and whistling in the marching columns on the streets is to cease." Happiness was prohibited in this house of death, unless the SS issued a specific order to laugh and sing.

The entire camp had to make amends when 120 people absented themselves from the last "old people's transport."

> Punitive measures by the Camp Commandant's Office. Because a number of persons did not obey the order to appear for transport, Herr Camp Commandant Obersturmführer Dr. Seidl has ordered the following punitive measures:
>
> 1. Confinement to quarters (confinement to barracks) is moved back to 6 P.M. Confinement to barracks on Saturdays and Sundays.
> 2. Lights will be turned off everywhere at 6 P.M. An exception is made for offices in which work is being performed and facilities in the departments of the Health Services.
> 3. All lecture evenings, comradeship evenings, etc. are forbidden with immediate effect.
>
> (orders of the day, October 27, 1942)

On the following day, the orders of the day announced a "census" in order to determine the now-unclear "camp tally." Everyone who had been counted received the stub of a "census slip," which had to be affixed to his identity card. The census took place from 6 P.M., October 28, until noon on October 29. A strict curfew was in force during this time, from which only workers in essential factories were exempt. The collective punishments were lifted on November 2.

Seidl was obsessed with "order and cleanliness" in his own pedantic manner, but he latched onto this idea without consideration for actual hygienic requirements. "Spitting" and "discarding paper scraps" were repeatedly prohibited. Without prompting, everyone was obliged to remove traces of such misdeeds.

> Warning. Despite repeated admonitions to the ghetto inmates, recently scraps of paper and spitting in the street have been observed.... Anyone found spitting in the courtyards, in halls or in the street must expect immediate, severe punishment. All ghetto inmates are alerted that the Camp Commandant's Office, in addition to harshly punishing the guilty, will take severe measures against the entire ghetto. There will be no further warning.
>
> (orders of the day, February 16, 1943)

Punishments had to be imposed: "The ghetto inmates [names follow] were, by sentence of the head of the Security Service, Department of Crime Control ... sentenced to 48 hours each of imprisonment ... for defiling the public streets ... by spitting" (orders of the day, February 17, 1943).

The orders of the day for February 26, 1943, recalled the ban on smoking and emphasized that the smoking of "teas and herbs of all kinds" was likewise forbidden. "By order of the Camp Commandant's Office, Dr. Desider Israel Friedmann has resigned from the Council of Elders, as he tolerated smoking in his presence" (orders of the day, April 5, 1943). Friedmann was later reinstalled. Some SS men profited well from the ban on smoking, as they were the main suppliers of the illegal cigarette trade and knew its channels. Smoking was no longer immediately life threatening; as stiff as the penalty still could be, it did not inevitably result in deportation. For a while, the SS tolerated the business. However, they intervened and "discovered" the headquarters of the trade whenever the "wholesaler" felt too secure or when cigarette prices fell. Then the game repeated itself. Sometimes even high functionaries were demonstratively punished.

> *Klaber* Josef AK/391, deputy to the head of the security services, was sentenced by Herr Camp Commandant SS Hauptsturmführer Dr. Seidl to six months imprisonment, as well as the loss of all privileges, and is removed from the security services.
> Klaber has admitted that he smoked, borrowed money, and gave it to a woman to buy food. He thus committed an offense against the camp regulations. As an aggravating factor, as deputy to the head of the security services, he also committed a gross breach of trust.
> (orders of the day, June 19, 1943)

Nevertheless, Klaber was not deported and remained in Theresienstadt until the end (he was, however, an old active officer and holder of the highest war decorations, although this did not help others who had not "transgressed" and were sent to their deaths).

Seidl took especially harsh measures after several escape attempts, which in all camps was considered the most severe transgression, and the death penalty usually was the consequence. At this time executions were avoided in Theresienstadt, so the escapees were sent to a concentration camp on "special orders" or were deported on the next normal transport. However, the orders of the day for April 9, 1943, made the following announcement to the "ghetto":

Punitive measures by Camp Commandant's Office
Because of the recent detection of 6 escaping ghetto inmates, of which 3 were caught after escaping, Herr Camp Commandant SS Obersturmführer Dr. Seidl has ordered the following general punitive measures, which will enter into force with immediate effect until further notice.

a) Confinement to quarters
   With immediate effect, a general confinement to quarters is ordered. Only persons who must move around for work or to fulfill official obligations, or for the purpose of picking up food, are permitted to be on the streets.
b) Lights-out
   With immediate effect, a lights-out is ordered. Exceptions are offices, work sites and Health Service facilities. [Flashlights and candles also could not be used.]
c) Cessation of recreational activities
   All events by Recreation must be cancelled.
d) Housing Registry
   Every ghetto inmate must sleep in the sleeping area assigned to him. Anyone found in any other place must expect the severest punishment.

The most severe collective punishment ever imposed on the "ghetto" paralyzed life in the camp for weeks, and the regulations were very strictly monitored. At first, because staircases, washrooms, and toilets could not be lit, there was general disorder, excitement, terrible filth, and even accidents. Fortunately, Loewenstein made it possible for those places to be lit. Only after an entire month had passed – on May 10, 1943 – did the orders of the day announce the lifting of the punishments, except for the ban on lighting, which was no longer strictly enforced but was not expressly cancelled until the orders of the day for May 22, 1943: "Herr Camp Commandant Hauptsturmführer Dr. Seidl has rescinded the lights-out with immediate effect. However, should there be the most minor complaint for a lack of darkening or should paper or spit be encountered in the street, it must be expected that lights out and confinement to quarters will again be imposed."

The orders of the day for June 9, 1943, again announced a fourteen-day deadline for penalty-free surrender of all prohibited devices, including electric cookers.

As already mentioned, there was a change in the German leadership at the beginning of July 1943. Probably at the initiative of Hauptsturmführer Möhs, Seidl lost his post. This intelligent and elegant man, one of Eichmann's main adjutants, was utilized by his boss in many ways and must have been one of the most influential men in his position. He repeatedly, and often decisively, intervened in the history of Theresienstadt. Möhs appeared in the camp from time to time but was hardly personally concerned with the prisoners. However, he emphatically determined the deportation policies and the transformation of the GW in the summer of 1943 into an innocuous group that would offer no embarrassing surprises in case of a disturbance, as had the Warsaw heroes. It is possible – we cannot know for sure, but it seems likely – that Seidl was suspected of having an understanding with Edelstein. This certainly did not exist, but, after two years, these men were more attuned to each other than Berlin desired. It was also said in the camp that Seidl had been slapped by an underling at an SS banquet, and that this loss of respect had undermined his position as camp leader. For the prisoners, this change was not favorable, as it was even more difficult to negotiate with the grim and brutal Burger, who, as a staunch National Socialist, took the official Jewish policy very seriously, more so than had Seidl, who, although not less evil, was at least more intelligent and accessible.

Burger was the only camp leader who never received the senior Jewish Elder without the presence of Bergel or another SS man. As soon as Theresienstadt was to be presented as a model settlement, it became clear that Burger was not really a suitable commander, even in his superiors' eyes. Several signs of the change to come have already been described. Among these was the introduction, in July 1943, of civilian street names, which were obligatory from then onward. "Wallstraße" and "Turngasse" or even "Seestraße," where most of the "notables" lived, looked better as return addresses than "L" and "Q." Similarly, there were no longer any barracks; instead, for example, C III became Langestraße 5. High SS functionaries had already toured Theresienstadt under Seidl, and in May 1943, German press representatives were shown the town. They visited two of the SS's favorite showpieces, the "bank" and the "ghetto court," where a specially selected trial was always presented to visitors from outside. In addition to this, a number of Jewish functionaries were summoned to the commandant's office for an "interview" with the press people. At the insistence of the IRC, the German Red Cross had succeeded in obtaining permission to visit Theresienstadt. Together with Eberhard von Thadden – the Foreign Office's secretary for Jewish affairs who had been delegated by Eichmann – his

The "Ghetto," July 1942–Summer 1943 121

deputies Walter Hartmann and Heinrich Niehaus spent two days in the camp at the end of June 1943. The gentlemen from the Red Cross were horrified by Theresienstadt and made a confidential report on it to a representative of the IRC (see 3b, 228).

The following order by Burger contrasted with the otherwise sought "normalization": "Pregnant Women's Duty to Report. At the request of the Public Health Officer, all pregnant women are immediately to report to the gynecologist during office hours at the proper Health Unit" (orders of the day, July 7, 1943). From then on, abortions were enforced under threat of the most severe punishment (see Chapter 16).

On May 12, 1943, an "order to ensure work discipline" and "regulations for administrative workers" were issued; a "labor court," too, was established. From June 1, 1943, onward, a "juvenile court" with "juvenile court regulations" took effect. The "ghetto court" had been in existence since December 17, 1941; however, its "rules of procedure" were not determined until January 1942, and it was initially almost without significance. The "rules of procedure" "were revised in August 1943, rescinding the types of punishments of a camp-like character, and since then have formed the basis for the cases decided by the ghetto court" (354).

Thus the development of the camp was completed in the summer of 1943. From then on, its operation was artificially continued and exaggerated. At the same time, the beginnings of decay already were evident; the first clear sign of decay was the demise of the "Security Service."

On September 11, 1942, the Jewish leadership addressed two proclamations to the prisoners:

> To all ghetto inmates. For the first time in the existence of the Theresienstadt Ghetto, we are celebrating the [Jewish] New Year.
> On this occasion, the Council of Elders wishes all ghetto inmates the best and expresses the hope that it will again be possible in the coming year to work with success and ensure comradely cooperation.
> As the year ends, the Council of Elders thanks all workers in the workshops, factories, and other work sites, the caretakers and nurses, and all office staff members for their self-sacrificing work, and at the same time calls on all ghetto inmates to continue to maintain iron discipline and employ all their energies toward a tolerable organization of the existence of the community.
>
> (orders of the day, September 11, 1942)

Immediately after these grand words, one reads with a shudder the sober news that transport "Bk with 1,000 persons from the ghetto had left for the East." Only 4 people from this transport, which included 111 children, returned home after the war.

1 Year Theresienstadt Ghetto

Today it has been twelve months since the first Construction Kommando began work … in the ghetto. In the past year, we all faced extraordinary tasks, which had to be dealt with according to the guidelines and instructions of the superior authorities.

In the past months, we have experienced difficulties; it was necessary to bring together thousands of Jews from various social circles, who introduced various worldviews and were used to completely different manners and customs [*sic*], for only in that way was it possible to bring forth the creative forces, totally dedicate them, and overcome difficulties.

The Council of Elders … addresses to all ghetto inmates the admonition to continue to persevere in discipline and loyalty. Branches of our work can point to successes, …

thus the assumption is permissible that ... cooperation would ensure the further success ... of our work.

(order of the day, November 24, 1942)

These clumsy words were influenced by Nazi language and are frightening. To speak of "completely different manners and customs" when contrasting life in freedom and in Theresienstadt; of "total dedication" (*restlosem Einsatz*), this terrible Nazi term; or of a "permissible assumption" that is to ensure "further success" is horrifying in a message from the Jewish leadership, given the conditions we have described.

The aim of this chapter has been to provide highlights of the agonizing and confused reality in the months of life granted to the prisoners from July 1942 to summer 1943. The sad abundance would have been enough bitterness for the long lifetimes of innumerable people in a free community. Words cannot suffice to portray this improbable and dreamlike chaos, in which all standards were confused and distorted. The will to self-assertion, attempts to build, and catastrophes tragically combined, abruptly replaced one another, were muddled together into an inextricable knot, and swirled inexorably ahead into stupefying events that never permitted the collectivity to come to its senses; individuals were able to make sense of things only briefly and rarely. Nevertheless, this was the period of greatest vitality in the camp. Later on, the camp's inhabitants would no longer demonstrate this tough will that tried methodically to preserve the community and that did not think only of personal survival. The transports in September 1943 accelerated rather than interrupted the camp's external development, but, internally, they impacted the camp at its roots. The "society" in the camp had been formed. In the next phase, it further diversified and achieved questionable maturity yet it was already hypertrophied and could barely conceal its decay. After the camp, admittedly surprisingly, overcame the very difficult initial period and many crises, it achieved a degree of normalization of conditions that the "ghetto" was able to bear without collapsing into itself and so avoided blind – and thus internally consistent – acceptance of the grotesque existence intended for it by the SS.

Until this point, creative and understandable goals had applied. This was now over. Forms of coexistence in which collective work was at least attempted would be barely perceptible in the future. People no longer strove to incorporate the tasks of the individual meaningfully into the overall picture. In the next phase, almost all collective striving died out. More and more palpably, in the latter period of all historical communities, the individual rises above his surroundings if he does not soullessly, as it were, to use a modern term, become part of a "mass." This happened in Theresienstadt as well. That is why, in this sense, the history of the camp came to an end in the late summer of 1943. What followed often seemed to be prepared and hinted at by the past, although many "historical" events, even new ones, took place.

6

The "Jewish Settlement Area," Summer 1943–September 1944

"Work Deployment. The Work Deployment Transport, with 5,000 people, left the ghetto on the 6th of this month" (orders of the day, September 8, 1943). This apparently innocent piece of news referred to the double transport, the horrible end of which we recalled in Chapters 3 and 4. Eichmann, who directed the deportations of the Jews in almost all European countries, had explained a few weeks earlier in the presence of the SS camp leadership and leading Jewish functionaries that this camp was to be spared further arrivals and departures. But later many young people were sent away, including many who had participated in the "construction" [*Aufbau*] of the ghetto. Once again, the SS spread the news among the prisoners that, finally, there would be no more transports. Nevertheless, afterward, in December 1943 and May 1944, similar "work deployment transports" consisting of a total of 12,500 people departed. It would not do for the city to seem too crowded, as it had been decided, under heavy pressure, to show Theresienstadt to certain foreigners as proof of how well Hitler's Germany treated Jews. Theresienstadt would no longer be a "ghetto"; instead it would be a "Jewish settlement" in which the Jews lived separately but happily under their own administration, an idyll in the midst of the horrors of a war in which the German civilian population, to say nothing of the fighting troops, fared much worse than the Jews under the special protection of Adolf Hitler, who apparently had made it his task to rescue and protect them from the justified fury of the German people.

After the September transports, the prisoners numbered 40,000, of whom 25,366 were workers. As a consequence of the December transports, the inmate population fell to 34,655 on January 1, 1944, of whom 21,144 were able to work. Forty percent were fully able to work; 30% were less capable of working; and 30% were elderly or young people. After the May transports, only around 28,000 prisoners remained. Theresienstadt became civilized. The appearance of bliss was spread over the suffering of the creatures still intended for extermination. The words that Seidl had once addressed to Edelstein became reality: "You don't know how good you're going to have it; we will make Theresienstadt a paradise ghetto." To create these paradisiacal conditions, 17,500 people first had to vanish into Auschwitz. Simultaneous with the easing of conditions, partly to the benefit of a minority, partly to the benefit of all who remained, they were produced by a will that was responsible for the gas

chambers. That will wore the undeserved and barely camouflaged mask of a benefactor. In this way, developments in Theresienstadt grew into the most gruesome
ghost dance in the history of Hitler's persecution of the Jews.

The Jewish leadership lacked any trace of a plan of its own. Edelstein was
embittered and soon was shut out. At the top were weak men who obeyed orders
and showed no initiative. Disunity and intrigue paralyzed their work, perhaps even
more so than their weak behavior toward the SS. The "bank" and "money
economy," the post office, "businesses," and a "coffeehouse" represented the first
attempts at a new, delusional order. Aside from this, the problems present in most
communities played a role even there, in a coerced community, as soon as even
tightly restricted freedom was permitted.

At first, some progress was reported: "At present [the end of 1943] 1,050 toilets
are available in the ghetto, 60% of them water-closets; 2,000 taps and 650 meters of
wash troughs in the washrooms. Sixty percent of the houses in the block received
their own washrooms, some of them even with warm showers. The delousing
bath ... is also being prepared" (354). The sixteen "south shacks" in the Bohušovic
Kessel were completed and dedicated to production operations. Thus the barracks on
both sides of B V were freed up for living purposes; the "West Barracks," across from
the gymnasium, would not become living quarters.

"From the bank, some 2.6 million is now paid out per month ... and some five
million is credited to blocked accounts. Money circulation amounts to around 14.8
million at present" (354). The absurdity of the "money economy" is obvious.
Divided among 30,000 prisoners, this amounts to less than 500 "ghetto crowns"
(GK) per person, the equivalent of RM 5 at the normal exchange rate in the camp.
The money was not really in circulation and was almost never used by inmates as a
means of payment, except when playing cards. Starting on August 1, 1943, the small
amount of money flowing back to the "bank" forced a deduction of GK 50 from the
monthly payments for "recreation." In addition, incoming packages were taxed up to
GK 50, depending on their size. Some package recipients thus found themselves in
"money difficulties," but they could easily acquire the necessary sums. In the "coffeehouse," a cup of ersatz coffee or ersatz tea and two lumps of sugar cost GK 2.
Because *one* cup of one drink or the other was all one was allowed to enjoy on any
one visit, the bill was affordable (see 151a). Finally, the "recreation office" charged
GK 5 for tickets to popular events. Much later, bathing tickets also were sold, for
GK 2. As of October 1, pay was reduced. Male workers, depending on their
"category," received GK 65–160 (previously GK 105–295); female workers received
GK 60–120 (previously GK 95–205); and "short-time workers" (*Kurzarbeiter*),
"prisoners incapable of work" (*Betreute*), war-wounded prisoners, and "notables"
received GK 50, 40, 60, and 65, respectively (previously GK 80, 70, 105, and 145).
During deportations, people were supposed to surrender their "cash assets," but they
preferred to give them away, like so many other things they had to leave behind.

"[Through the release of the barracks for housing purposes, the progressive
depopulation, and] the further expansion of attics, a noticeable relaxation of living
conditions was achieved" (354). The attics were divided up with insulation sheets
that were hastily plastered and whitewashed; attic skylights were enlarged into small
windows, electric lights were wired, and small stoves were set up. The "Technical
Department" took care of this renovation, or it was carried out, more or less
semilegally, by private persons who, with energy as well as often questionable

proficiency, built tolerable, sometimes even livable quarters for a small number of people or for their own families. Furniture and other fittings were brought in from evacuated Jewish apartments in Prague (see also 214, 215). Generally, these items were inferior junk and were used to furnish the accommodations of the "notables," in particular. The best pieces were distributed through patronage or stolen. For a long time, the furniture was stored, badly guarded, in the courtyards of the barracks. It had all been carelessly stored in Prague and daubed with the "transport numbers" of the expelled owners; the furniture was carelessly shipped and just as carelessly unloaded here. These furnishings clearly reflected the disintegration of a world. There were good, even antique, pieces among them that, with a little restoration, could have stood in any bourgeois home, but most were worthless. Much of it found its way into the offices, which now looked halfway decent. In the camp, too, furniture was built to order or with the tacit tolerance of the Jewish authorities. Generally, this was functional, mass-produced furniture, especially simple bed frames rather than the "bunk beds" that had previously been the norm. The order was given to remove "chamber beds" (*Schlauchbetten*) and "three-story bunk beds" – the top section was sawn off, leaving "two-story bunk beds." Some things that were not at all bad looking were produced for "notables," those with preference, and offices. Protégées obtained wardrobes, tables, chairs, cabinets, shelves, and pull-out couches.

Such measures were, by this point, desired by the SS, even if they were not always entirely legal. Those attempting to better their conditions were actually acting in accordance with the SS's wishes and serving its interests, even if involuntarily. In this way, camp life took on an ever more improbable character; all laws were called into question and ultimately almost abandoned, which deeply shook the social structure. In reality, nothing was allowed, but it seemed that anything was tolerated. All sense of solidarity was lost. Whereas anarchy had theretofore prevailed in the overall circumstances, now a more individual anarchy reigned. Depending on their level of energy, people asserted a law of force that could no longer be curbed by the complicated order that existed on paper. Behind the façade of order and rules, absolutely arbitrary behavior became increasingly common and was only occasionally affected by the terrifying intervention of the SS. Until then, only the SS had made the camp's continued existence questionable, but during this period the camp called itself into question, for its internal order no longer applied to the influential and well-to-do; it applied only to the many defenseless inmates, who now suffered just as much, and perhaps more, than before. It was a covert struggle of all against all, moderated only by fear, in which the morality of a weak minority found itself in a difficult position. The persecutors' evil spirit also gripped many of the prisoners; they allowed this evil spirit, which they still believed was the enemy, to come alive within them and were not even aware of it. This is the tragic heart of the decay that National Socialism brought down upon its supporters *and* its opponents. It was not a political problem but a general human one, beyond any ideology.

> Towards the end of . . . 1943, the Settlement Area had a cooking pot capacity of 26,870 liters, which is 0.77 liters per person per day. . . . At present there are five hospitals with 2,200 beds, five health units . . . additionally five large out-patient centers. . . . Some five thousand people are treated daily in the ambulatory patient centers. In the hospitals and infirmaries . . . there are always 2,500 bedridden patients, and outside the infirmaries an additional 2,500 bedridden patients are treated in the living units. A number of auxiliary

stations of the health service have been set up: the Central Medication Storehouse, the Central Pharmacy, a large center for Dental Technology, orthopedic and optical workshops.

(354)

The "Health Services Department" became a gigantic operation, but none of its progress could eliminate the bad state of health and the misery and suffering of the old and the sick. The "Welfare Department" expanded to become the largest sub-department of the "Health Services Department." Despite some success, everything was in terrible shape. The wretched "homes for the infirm" in barracks E IIIa and E VII and in the neglected house L 504 were not enough. Some of the infirm were brought together; they had thus far been housed wretchedly in certain rooms in the "blockhouses," which were hardly better than "infirm block" G V, and in some other houses. There were not enough care and assistance personnel, and the condition of the attendants themselves made them seem hardly suited for welfare work, unless they were capable of almost superhuman self-denial. At the end of 1943 there were 2,600 "beds for the infirm," which was 600 fewer than were necessary; these additional beds were later made available. Six hundred blind people and approximately 2,000 war wounded, cripples, deaf-mutes, and small children had to be cared for. Mortality decreased, less because of the somewhat improved conditions than because of the significantly reduced number of elderly people. Those who were more robust also held out better once they had settled in. In addition, along with noticeably improved quarters came vaccinations against typhus, scarlet fever, and diphtheria and screenings for tuberculosis, which had a positive effect. The danger of lice was also overcome, although it was never possible to eliminate the plague of fleas and bedbugs. The number of monthly deaths went down from 3,941 in September 1942 to 427 in November 1943. Of nearly 28,000 prisoners, there were some 8 deaths daily in summer 1944.

On August 24, 1943, a transport of 1,260 neglected children arrived. They were shy and seemed mute; many were barefoot; and all wore pitiful rags and were half-starved. In their hands they clutched small packets or prayer books, if they had any "luggage" at all. They were not added to the camp tally and were kept strictly separate from the rest of the prisoners. The children were housed in the "West Barracks," which were ringed with barbed wire. Gendarmes guarded the children's camp, and no one was allowed to approach. An attendant and a doctor were chosen from the "ghetto"; they, too, were not allowed to rejoin the rest of the inmates. Soon after their arrival, the children, who had already experienced all the Jewish suffering in the East in their home, Bialystok [Białystok], were taken in groups to the disinfection bath, where frightening scenes occurred. The children knew about the gas chambers and did not want to enter the bath chambers; they screamed desperately, "No, no! Gas!"

> The children did not want to follow the SS men.... Finally they were shoved in violently by the Germans. The children crowded together despairingly, cried and hugged one another, wailing. We did not understand this agitation, but were not allowed to ask. We had been forbidden to speak with them, on pain of death, since the arrival of the transport.
>
> SS organs were in the courtyard and in all the chambers of the bath, and they made sure that the prohibition on speaking was complied with. But the confusion of the rooms ... and the mass commotion that day made furtive communication possible, if only here and there. A disinfector pulled an older boy from a corner and assured him

The "Jewish Settlement Area," Summer 1943–September 1944   127

that the children would only be deloused and given clean clothes. The boy was suspicious at first. Only when the man showed him the entire facility and the boy saw that one could leave the bath on the other side did he begin to gain trust. He was then the first one to go into the bath and gave the other children courage. Following the delousing and while they were dressing, he began to explain that all the children came from Bialystok [Białystok]. The eldest, at least according to what they told the Germans, were 14 years old, though in reality there were children among them who were several years older. They purposely recently had given a lower age in order to escape death. Before their departure from Bialystok [Białystok] they had been brought to a square with their parents and divided into three groups: men, women, and children up to age 14. Their fathers, mothers, and older siblings were shot before their eyes.

(207, p. 151 et seq.)

Although this incident in the disinfection bath did not remain entirely unknown, no one understood its meaning, for, even afterward, no one ever spoke of the dangers of the gas chambers. They remained a secret. None of the Germans in the hinterland nor the rest of the world believed it, even though trustworthy people who had seen the evil themselves brought the awful news, and the Jews in Theresienstadt, who had been warned, did not want to and could not believe it (see 30). Those who did know the unvarnished truth – of whom there were only a few – kept silent, out of fear or conscience. The first truthful information about Auschwitz appears to have reached the leadership in February 1943. It is possible to definitely identify three sources, through which a small group among the leadership was correctly informed in the course of the same year. In Birkenau, the former central secretary, Janowitz, wrote an illegal letter that reached the leadership (see 284). A certain man by the name of Lederer, who had worked in the fire department at Theresienstadt, was able to escape from Birkenau. He was a member of the Czech underground movement, and, with the help of gendarmes, he repeatedly visited the camp, where he told the Jewish Elders and many of his comrades in the fire department about the gassings. Finally, a Mrs. Frey, a guard in the Jewish camp prison, received clearly comprehensible information in a coded letter; she gave it to the Jewish Elders. In addition, as early as 1941, Dr. Leo Baeck received from a refugee definite news of the gas vans of Chelmno [Chełmno], and in the same month that the Polish children arrived in Theresienstadt he learned more. He was sought out by a Czech Jew who wanted to tell him something but made Baeck promise to keep silent. After the war, he reported as follows the information that had been confided to him:

That night, I was awakened by my best friend, whom I had not seen in a long time. I knew that he had not been sent to Theresienstadt, and therefore I asked him how he had come there. He cut me off and told me to listen carefully. He had something to say to me. I had to know. But first I had to promise to tell no one. He was a half-Jew and had been sent to the East. He came to the large camp in Auschwitz. Like everyone else, he was subjected to a selection and chosen for slave labor. The others were taken away and killed with gas. He knew this for certain, everyone in Auschwitz knew it. He was sent to a work camp, where he escaped and made his way back to Prague. How did he get to Theresienstadt? A Czech gendarme outside took a bribe. We spoke for a short time and then he left. He was very agitated and wanted to warn and rescue me.

(28)

Baeck struggled with himself about whether to get this man to repeat his report at a meeting of the Council of Elders. Finally, Baeck decided not to do so, and he kept the confession to himself, because he did not believe that he could help anyone in the camp by passing on this information. This may be true and, in any case, cannot be refuted; however, it is certain that general ignorance of the probable fate of all who were deported from Theresienstadt to the East led most of those in the camp into a thoughtlessness and self-deception that often bordered on an alteration of consciousness (*Bewusstseinstrübung*) (see 146b, 272).

No one could completely hide the fact that the Polish children must have experienced terrible things, but no one knew what was behind it, and the SS had made sure of this in advance. They ordered that the bedraggled children receive double meals, and they were given decent shoes, underwear, and clothing. At first, hardly a sound emerged from the special camp. Later the children became more lively, and one could hear them talking and even singing. As already described in Chapter 3, in which the reasons for this transport are explained, word got around that the children were being prepared for an exchange operation; Palestine or Switzerland was supposed to be the destination. This sounded even more plausible when, after six weeks, the departure of the visibly recovered children was arranged, and the fifty-three attendants had to confirm in writing that they would not spread horror propaganda abroad. People wished the adults – including Franz Kafka's favorite sister, Ottilie – and the children good luck and thought that the hour of liberation was about to strike for them. The transport left on October 5, 1943 – for Auschwitz and the gas chambers. A number of children who were sick with scarlet fever or other infections were segregated in a cellar in the gymnasium, which served as an infectious disease ward; one night they were taken by SS men, brought to the "Small Fortress," and murdered. Other children were left behind, dead, in the gymnasium.

A few days earlier, in the orders of the day for September 29, 1943, the leadership had commemorated the Jewish New Year:

> The leadership and Council of Elders expresses its best wishes for the New Year to the Jewish community in Theresienstadt. The Jews in Theresienstadt have proven their worth in carrying out their duties. They have shown discipline and community spirit. On the occasion of the New Year, the Council of Elders thanks everyone for the work accomplished in the past year and expects that in the future everyone will remain aware of their responsibility for the community.

The orders of the day for November 24, 1943, read:

> **Two Years of Theresienstadt**
> Today is the second anniversary of the day that the building of the Theresienstadt Ghetto began.
>
> In everything we have experienced in these two years, we have constantly kept in mind how each of us is responsible for our community and is most deeply obligated to it. The first year was marked by construction and assembly; the second year was marked by construction and consolidation. During this year we experienced some difficulty together; we also did our best to adapt and shape our lives in the space allotted to us.

The appeal continues in this vein – after Edelstein's arrest, and after the deportation of nearly 56,000 people! The words sound like empty noise. Even in this world, people twisted language into formulations of the kind that might have served a normal community, but here the words did not mean anything real; they did not express an actual reality. What did "construction" and "consolidation" mean here? Husks and shells of a former reality led a shadowy existence, like the external forms that had asserted themselves or been artificially restored; they wandered like ghosts in this real world of brittle stammering. How could one speak of construction and consolidation where there was nothing but patchwork and decay behind masks? They were no longer even masks, but masks upon masks, creating a distorted reflection – the camp was ripe for the "beautification" that would soon follow.

Only someone able to empathize a bit with this improbable world can grasp the events to come and understand the extent to which this "ghetto" was more uncanny than any of the other camps. Mass murder – a machinery set in motion to devour thousands daily and hundreds and millions of people in the course of two years – is certainly far more terrible than "harmless," "civil" Theresienstadt, but such murder is in part incomprehensible, and in part stripped of its uncanny appearance. Naked brutality acts uniformly and monotonously; any "motives" fall away, and the undisguised beast does the slaughtering, while all other human emotions, for good or for evil, simply exist and express themselves in succinct form. In Theresienstadt, however, the game functioned in an endlessly varied, individual form; everything private and personal contributed to the game, in a ghastly carnival of which almost no one was entirely conscious. In Auschwitz there was only pure despair or an inexorable awareness of the game. Even if a spark of indestructible vitality remained, even if the soul fled, through some transformative magic, into sweeter self-deception (*holder Trug*), still reality had to be seen; no one could really fool themselves. It was different in Theresienstadt, where illusion proliferated and hope, only slightly subdued by feelings of fear, outshone everything else, which was concealed beneath an impenetrable fog. In no other camp had the true face of the times retreated to such a remote distance from the inmates as in Theresienstadt; this condition was even more pronounced than in the Jewish transit camps in Western Europe, especially once "normalization" blinded the prisoners with "city beautification." The truth only occasionally arose out of the darkness, touched people, and then, after a moment of terror, allowed them to fall back into their masked existence.

The unforgettable "census" of November 11, 1943, was one such illuminating lightning moment of truth. Due to the chaos that prevailed through the departure of transports, errors already had slipped into the "status record" (*Standführung*) in 1942. It happened that fewer people were deported than prescribed by and reported to the SS, and thus the "Central Registry" probably listed in its "status report" a number of prisoners that was too low by about fifty people. It has been claimed that Seidl knew about and tolerated these irregularities, in tacit agreement with Edelstein. Burger did not like Edelstein and became aware of the erroneous reports through unexplained channels, possibly through a Jewish traitor. According to Murmelstein, the situation was a little different: "In November [1943], Burger … discovered that included in the submitted status report there were some 55 persons who should have left on a transport before the year was up, but who had not been removed from the list. Edelstein was accused of falsification" (192). Loewenstein gave yet another account: in Prague, he said, Jews who had escaped from Theresienstadt had been arrested. Edelstein had not been betrayed by spies in the camp and had never

> falsified lists in order to free people from the transports, but rather, falsified lists had to be submitted because some 55 people had escaped from Theresienstadt, and he was afraid of reporting such a large number of escapes.

Möhs, Burger and Bergel talked to me about this, because they assumed that I must have known about the escapes, or at least the Ghetto Guard did. I made clear to them that I and the Ghetto Guard could know only what was reported to me and to the Ghetto Guard. (personal communication)

Be that as it may, the whole truth will never be determined. In any case, we do know that in the case of three transports to Auschwitz in January 1943, twenty-two more arrivals were reported than the documents from Theresienstadt indicate were deported. In the confusion of the deportations, during which machinations occurred, the statistical record could have suffered. Suffice it to say, Edelstein was arrested on November 9, 1943, together with the head and two other officers of the "Central Registry." The four men and their families were deported to Auschwitz on the December transport in 1943 and were shot several months later. Eyewitnesses tell of Edelstein's manly behavior at his execution (see 11a, 238). As Edelstein's successor, Zucker was appointed deputy Jewish Elder on January 16, 1944.

Nothing interested the SS in the camp more than precise reporting of the number of prisoners. On the day after Edelstein's arrest, the orders of the day for November 10, 1943, contained an order for a "census," with many instructions. It was not Burger's wish to do this simply and rationally, as in previous censuses. He ordered a census in the living quarters during the night of November 10 and a second one outdoors, in the Bohušovic Kessel, on November 11. That night, an especially strict curfew was imposed from 11 P.M. to 5 A.M.; only the census takers and several specifically named functionaries were excepted. During the census, lights could be lit in the houses. The prisoners were required to fill out complicated questionnaires, whose instructions and explanations filled many pages. Not many prisoners slept during that restless night, especially as most looked forward with trepidation to the next morning.

Both young and old had to assemble for the outdoor count. Kitchens and bakeries had to cease operations. The only exceptions were the essential personnel for boiler rooms, waterworks, power plants, and so on, and the seriously ill; if the ill were not in hospital or "homes," they had to be brought there, where a reduced staff of doctors and nurses was maintained. According to the detailed plan, everyone was to assemble in the courtyards between 5:30 and 9:30 A.M.; they were to march out half an hour later. Because of the nervousness of the house elders and other functionaries, however, assembly happened earlier, which contributed significantly to the agony of that difficult day. Each person received some bread, margarine, liver paste, and sugar as his daily ration, as cooking was not allowed. Concerns were raised: older people, in particular, did not believe they would return, and it looked as though the camp was being dissolved. Some equipped themselves with odds and ends, blankets, eating utensils, and underwear. Old people were so loaded down that they could hardly move, and it was difficult to calm them down a little and persuade them not to take so much along, because they would be back in their rooms that evening. They did not believe this, and the day almost seemed to confirm their fears. After hours of waiting, people were marched off. Members of the various security organs were assigned to keep order during the march and during the lineup in the damp fields on the other side of the fortress walls, under the command of the infamous Robert Mandler, who once again, as during the deportations from the "Protectorate," distinguished himself ingloriously. His people could be identified by their tall white paper turbans, which, amusingly enough, made them look like cooks. On the way they repeatedly counted the rows of people streaming by and positioned them in the field, where places marked on numbered wooden boards were supposed to make group counting easier. No one was allowed to leave his place. A group of at least a hundred portable stretchers was lined up on the side. The field was surrounded by gendarmes, who were under orders to hold their weapons at the ready against the crowds of people.

It was an inclement November day, cool, damp, and foggy. After many hours, SS men finally arrived on motorcycles and went down the rows, counting and miscounting, and beginning again – they certainly did not count the correct "tally" (*Stand*). It was not like a "roll call" in a concentration camp, in which each group itself reported the number, which was then verified. In this case only the annoyed SS men did the counting. If the people did not stand in orderly rows, they were punished with a box on the ears. Some were made to box themselves on the ears. After about two hours, around 5 P.M., the SS left, but no orders followed, and permission to return home was not given. People remained standing and could not leave the line to relieve themselves. It grew colder and began to rain; old people and children froze and became soaked to the bone. It soon grew dark, and more hours passed. The crowd became more and more agitated and was gripped by terrible fear. Many could not take it and collapsed. There was no help, except from person to person. After they had been standing for some fifteen hours, they broke up around 8:30 P.M., but no one knew whether they could actually return home, for nothing had been said, and Mandler and his companions were gone. No one led the return; people panicked and pushed in desperate confusion toward the one exit from this enclosure. The returning flood of more than 30,000 people lasted several hours and was only slightly controlled by some sensible GW men at the exit point, which was completely blocked in order to prevent a worse disaster. Not until around 11 P.M. was the return to the city more or less over, but many elderly and sick people had remained behind because they could not walk. In the darkness, they slipped into the half-finished "south barracks," where they lay helplessly and fell asleep. All night long, they had to be retrieved; the men with the stretchers, who had had to watch passively the whole day and evening, had much to do. Thus ended the only excursion from the "ghetto," which for tens of thousands of people remained the only time they would leave the fortress in all their years in the camp.

Severe colds, pneumonia, and other illnesses were the result of that evil day. Many died right away or shortly after the census. The camp was in confusion for several days; people were exhausted, operations were disrupted, the kitchens functioned badly, and bread distribution was not fully restored for many days. The amounts of food to which the recipients were entitled were replaced in installments. But the census had not succeeded. Another one, which would proceed alphabetically, was arranged for the period between November 19 and November 24, 1943. The bedridden were sought out; the rest had to assemble and were led, after a wait of some two hours, to the counter of the "bank," which had to interrupt its usual operations. Counting was carried out by Jewish functionaries and SS men, by checking identity cards. After this census, on November 30, 1943, the number of prisoners was calculated as 40,145.

But did the prisoners need such unusually horrible days as November 11 to become aware of the ruin that was their lot? Was not the terror that shook the camp at each new wave of deportations enough? It is astonishing how relatively little the surface of daily life in Theresienstadt was affected by the terrible bloodlettings of December 1943 and May 1944, although, in December, more than an eighth – and the next time considerably more than a fifth – of the prisoners were dragged into the maelstrom. But the beguiling illusion of the "beautification" left those who had, this time, been spared so dazed that they soon almost forgot the catastrophe and submerged themselves in the pitiful pleasures offered by the hand of evil and the dubious hope of an imminent, liberating tomorrow. Yet the last May transport produced a spectacle more horrifying than any Theresienstadt had yet seen. Barracks C III was serving as the Schleuse; from its back gate, one could reach the deportation trains directly. The building was filled with 2,500 "participants," including the "reserves." In the late afternoon before the day of departure, Burger's successor, Karl Rahm, appeared with several men from the SS "office" and with members of the Council of Elders who had been summoned. The "participants" assembled in the barracks courtyard. Rahm had them file past him repeatedly and, in a procedure lasting many hours, first by daylight and then in the glare of reflectors, removed 600 mainly strong young people from the transport. This selection, which resembled a solemn march of ghosts and was assisted by Jewish functionaries, was viewed from the open balconies of the first and second floors by many prisoners, including relatives and friends of those involved. At 11 P.M., Zucker dared to point out to Rahm that, with so many people freed, the number demanded could not be reached, which infuriated Rahm, who would brook no disagreement. He shouted, threatened shootings, and wanted to beat Zucker and Eppstein, but he restrained himself and ultimately was brought to reason. At this point spotlights were trained on those selected, who were gathered in a corner of the courtyard, and they were screened yet again. This trade in souls lasted until half an hour past midnight, by which point only 150 people were removed. But the vicious activity did not end once Rahm left the barracks with the SS and Jewish functionaries. It continued the next day, and loading the train took from morning until late afternoon. Once again, Rahm intervened and freed those he happened to like. Many hid, and around 5 P.M. it became apparent that approximately 120 victims were lacking. Then old German Jews from the "transport reserve" were dragged onto the train for "work deployment." When, a few hours later, the number still was not reached, Rahm himself went on the hunt and drove several unfortunates onto the train, which soon left the "paradise ghetto" with the required freight. Some 1,200 tuberculosis patients were ordered to be sent on the May transport, as they did not fit in with the "beautification" (see 284).

In October 1943, more than 450 Jews from Denmark – fewer than 10% of the Jews living in that country – came in three transports. They remained the smallest group in the camp; however, their arrival changed the internal and external development of Theresienstadt to a degree that can hardly be overestimated, through the mere circumstances of their deportation. The Danish Jews influenced the face of the coerced community in this phase as much as the Czechs had influenced the first phase and the German and Austrian Jews the second. Thanks to the active, courageous behavior of the Danish authorities, starting with the king, the prisoners were effectively supported from home, and they were much better off than anyone else once the initial difficulties had been overcome. But more important than the many advantages they would soon enjoy was the Danish government representatives' intervention with German authorities in Copenhagen and Berlin. They fought energetically for a

The *"Jewish Settlement Area," Summer 1943–September 1944*   133

tolerable lot for the deportees and, by October and November 1943, had asked for a visit to Theresienstadt by a delegation of the Danish Red Cross (RC) (see 41 and 227). Thus the fears of Foreign Office state undersecretary Martin Luther during the meeting at Wannsee (see Chapter 2) came to pass – namely, that "difficulties will arise if this problem is dealt with thoroughly and that it will therefore be advisable to defer actions in these countries. Besides, in view of the small numbers of Jews affected, this deferral will not cause any substantial limitation" (117). Now, with the deportation of the Danish Jews, they had put themselves into an embarrassing position and could not, understandably, comply with the request for a visit to Theresienstadt under the prevailing conditions. However, this situation provided the impetus for further "normalization" and "beautification" of the camp, in order to make it superficially presentable to foreigners. For Eichmann and his exterminators of Jews, this was not a simple task, and thus the visit, which certainly had to overcome a great deal of resistance, had to be postponed repeatedly. Finally, in April 1944, Dr. Rudolf Mildner, who had been commander of the Sipo and the SD in Denmark in 1943, convinced Gestapo chief Heinrich Müller to allow a Danish commission into Theresienstadt (see 42a), and they were permitted to come in June.

At first the Danish Jews were held in the "West Barracks," in which the unfortunate Polish children had lived until barely ten days before. The first group was initially received in I IV by Burger, Haindl, and other SS men. The arrivals were greeted cordially by Eppstein, on the SS's orders, and were "entertained" at properly laid tables with dishes prepared especially for them. The SS behaved graciously and did not stop the Danes from smoking. They were then asked to write to Denmark about their positive reception. Then the SS took its leave, and only then were the newcomers robbed of their money and valuables and provided with "Jewish Stars." After a few days they were quartered in the city. At first they found camp life particularly onerous, because they had been taken all of a sudden, without prior persecution, from normal and generally well-off circumstances to the misery of the "ghetto." They could not readily accustom themselves to the food, which was always disgusting for newcomers at the beginning. They had brought little equipment, but it was soon sent from home in large quantities. The Danish authorities kept the keys to their dwellings, which were never plundered, and clothing was taken from those homes and sent to the owners. They soon lived in Theresienstadt as "notables," even if only a few of them were expressly declared to be such, but all were better off than most of the other "notables." They were allowed to write and receive letters frequently, and it is astonishing what was able to pass the SS censors; starting in mid-March 1944, they were regularly provided with generous parcels from the Danish RC and from Sweden. All were protected from deportations to the East, even if they were not Danish citizens but refugees from Germany or other foreigners, who also enjoyed the advantages granted the Danes.

The Dutch, who came between February and September 1944 and numbered 4,600, were a very different element. These Jews already had had camp experience in Westerbork, where, as in Theresienstadt, a typical society had formed (see 17, 69a, 99, 106, 106a, 160c, 344). The names of those who would be more or less protected from deportations – they were called "blocked" (*gesperrt*) prisoners – were recorded on ten "protection lists." Some of the "blocked" prisoners were similar to the "notables"; others were functionaries and therefore temporarily "indispensable." According to trustworthy descriptions, circumstances in Westerbork seem to have been even more depraved than in Theresienstadt. The corruption, the redemption from transports by the payment of "ransom" money, happened much more openly there. People paid, even "legally," up to 40,000 florins to the SS to be "blocked." A very different level of wealth prevailed in the camp than in Theresienstadt, and it seemed to be tacitly tolerated. Westerbork was operated more like a camp than was Theresienstadt, but things seemed more civil in the former than in the latter. There too, sickness, work in "production," positions, and especially patronage provided protection from deportations, but ultimately almost everyone was taken to Auschwitz and Sobibór, and only the privileged ended up in Bergen-Belsen or Theresienstadt. In Westerbork, only 918 people, most of them German Jews, held out until liberation. They occupied the highest positions, a result of the history of the camp, which had been established by the Dutch government near the Reich border in early 1939 as a reception camp for Jewish refugees; it later served the SS as a collection camp for Dutch Jews.

Before the arrival of the Dutch transport, the women's barracks, C III, had to be cleared, and, once again, as half a year before with E I, this had to happen rapidly, although not quite as precipitously as in the previous case. Through this evacuation, the last collective housing for younger people was disrupted. The women were divided among many houses, and those who enjoyed patronage or were clever obtained good quarters or set up an adapted attic with friends or family. Aside from helpless older people or the "incapable" (*untüchtig*), few remained in mass quarters. This important step toward attaining private lives for all prisoners, which the "beautification" campaign sought to achieve, was thus accomplished through Jewish initiative. People generally continued to live in mass accommodations, but they behaved as though, in this makeshift arrangement, they had a right to live as civilly and as well as possible. C III was speedily refurbished; the "double-decker bunk beds," from which people shortly before had sawed off the third tier, disappeared, and rooms were set up for a smaller number of people. Thus C III became the "Dutch" barracks. The newcomers from Westerbork generally did not integrate well, and they constituted the most distinct group to come to Theresienstadt. Although they were considered privileged, more than half of them were deported to Auschwitz from there.

Toward the end of 1943, at the urging of the Foreign Office and the German RC, the SS ordered "city beautification,"

> in the course of which not only are the streets and houses to be overhauled and put in order, but rather the action extends to making the quarters more livable. Three-story bunk beds, a sign of overcrowding during the development period, have largely disappeared, the rooms have received tables, benches and clothes racks. The apartments of notables have also been renovated as part of this operation.

(354)

In late 1943, the prisoners barely knew the phrase "city beautification," but by early 1944 it was on everybody's lips. Burger, the former schoolteacher who was an antagonist of Günther, was not well suited for this game, for which reason he was replaced on February 8, 1944, by a friend of Günther and his erstwhile deputy in the "Central Office"; as a result, the "Central Office's" influence greatly increased in Theresienstadt. The new man was Obersturmführer Karl Rahm, and he remained in this position until the end of the war. Rahm, a trained mechanic, was clever with his

The "Jewish Settlement Area," Summer 1943–September 1944   135

hands and not entirely without organizational skill, with a feel for practical issues, but he was no better than Seidl, Burger, or Bergel, although he exceeded them in ability and intelligence. He was therefore more dangerous than those who had never donned the mask of friendship with the Jews. Basically no less brutal, and terrible in his fury, Rahm understood hypocrisy well and played the part of "kindly Uncle Rahm," as he was jokingly but unfortunately called. He could act as benefactor and supporter; he could even be personally approached, and he ensured "justice." Perhaps for these reasons, Murmelstein called him "otherwise, however, hardly heartless" in his report. Yet during deportations and even in other circumstances, Rahm acted just as barbarously as the other SS officers. He was the right man for the dictated farce, as he knew how to give the "beautification" verve, tempo, and ideas, just as, afterward, he cleverly knew how to play the supposedly better Nazi and helper of Jews.

What was "beautification" supposed to mean? In the early days of 1944, one saw in the city posters with a picture of a morose man and the text, "Herr Cvok: Why City Beautification? I'm going on the transport in any case." This strange, highly unnecessary poster, unfortunately designed by Peter Kien, was supposed to imply that only a fool would oppose the "beautification" and not toil away for it, whatever might happen. In reality, the poster unintentionally hit at the truth – what was the point of city beautification, when one afterward had to go to the transport, to the gas chamber? The purpose of city beautification was to give the Nazis an alibi, so that they could fool the world and continue to commit their crimes unhindered, which, as Rosenberg put it before his execution, had become "notorious."

The "beautification," for which Murmelstein was appointed the main responsible Jewish organizer, consisted of many measures to bring about positive change in the look of the town, or at least in the portions of the camp that were to be shown to a commission. No effort – no money, no labor, and no inducement or reward – was spared to complete this work. All the streets were fixed up, rolled, and cleaned. Until then, the town square had been locked and fenced off from the prisoners; until December 1943, the tents for "K-production" were located there. Now the fence was removed, the ground was tilled, a luxurious lawn with paths was laid out, and 1,200 rose bushes were planted. Across from the "coffeehouse," a wooden music pavilion was erected, reminiscent of a spa. Concrete benches with wooden seats and backs were installed on the square, in the other park areas, and in other places, including the bastion behind A II, which until then only children and some privileged people had been permitted to enter, as well as in the previously inaccessible roof garden of E VII. The ugly fences in various parts of the city were removed; only a few remained along the civilian transit road. Nevertheless, it was no easier to escape, for the few exits from the fortress were well guarded. In a small park area near E VI and E VII a playground was set up for children, and a pavilion was built of wood and glass – an unattainable treasure anywhere in Germany at the time – as a nursery for small children. This "children's pavilion" was decorated on the outside with pictures of animals and was equipped with a kitchen, showers, couchettes, and other brandnew appliances. Behind the pavilion was a merry amusement park with a sandbox, wading pool, carousel, and other nice things. In the gymnasium of the old school building, L 417, a nursery was set up, with new furniture, toys, and a slide. Painted wooden signposts with flowerpots and cheerful carved pictorial representations of the destination were put up in the streets. The inscriptions pointed to the bank, post office, library, fire station, coffeehouse, baths, park, playground, and so on (see 146b). Almost all the buildings looked shabby, with their damaged plasterwork and faded paint; thus everything had to be repaired and painted. This work was also carried out in the neglected courtyards. During the "renovation" (*Assanierung*) in 1942, some of the walls between the courtyards of the civilian buildings had disappeared, or crude passages had been hacked out with pickaxes; as a result, the courtyards looked pitiable. Now this crude work had to be smoothed over, large open spaces were created, and walls were torn down or rebuilt and properly plastered. Every block had its turn. A barracks next to B V was set up as a "dining hall," where one was supposed to get food served properly on plates. The kitchen distribution points were improved. In short, no corner could be overlooked.

Nor was an overhaul of the interior furnishings of all the houses neglected, at least to the extent they were intended for viewing – that is, in particular, the quarters of the "notables," the leading functionaries, the Danes, and the Dutch – and no effort was spared in improving, in particular, the E VI hospital and L 504, the "home for the infirm." There was a certain comic quality to the fact that rooms at ground level were spruced up even in houses that were not supposed to be visited, but that the commission would pass by. Halls and rooms were painted or whitewashed simply but tastefully. Simple furniture that was nevertheless pleasing to the eye was installed, and real living space for families was created. A new type of bed was not enough; cupboards, chests, shelves, tables, and armchairs were added. Beds had so far been nailed together out of unplaned slats, but now everything had to be proper carpentry work. Pictures, mainly stolen from the apartments of Prague Jews, were hung on the walls; on the tables were vases of flowers although, only a year before, picking flowers had been strictly forbidden and punished; brightly painted lampshades were installed, curtains were placed in the windows, and windowsills were decorated with flowerpots. Until then, clothes had hung on nails or simple makeshift contrivances; now everything had to vanish from windows, walls, and doors, either into suitcases or behind curtains.

Many commissions viewed the progress and ordered further improvements or changes. In the past, no one had cared where people were quartered and how their most primitive needs were looked after. Now they were assailed, so to speak, with thoroughly dishonest solicitude. Many people were moved. The deportation in May 1944 was only for the purpose of making the place more attractive and livable. Nevertheless, Mildner, who inspected the camp around June 13, at Müller's orders, found it "overcrowded" but capable of inspection. The residents of many houses were exchanged, and families were quartered individually or in pairs in one room. Interior walls of wood and insulation panels were erected, in order to give the illusion of individual living areas. The "bank" was outfitted with ridiculous luxury; a large desk and a set of leather club chairs were provided for the "director." All "offices" were refurbished, and the window displays were cleaned and decorated, which gave the artists imprisoned in Theresienstadt an opportunity to use their imagination on a larger scale. Company names were brightly painted. The post office in L 414 was outfitted with particular care, so the package distribution point could appear impressive in the performance of its function. "Youth homes" were flawlessly redecorated so that everything looked friendly. A villa at the beginning of "South Street" (the street that led to the mortuary, the "Südbaracken," the crematorium, and then on to Bohušovice), which was still within the fortress and until then occupied by the

The "Jewish Settlement Area," Summer 1943–September 1944 137

German head of "agriculture," was opened as a convalescent home for children with tuberculosis; it looked immaculate.

The offices of the leadership in B V were furnished with attractive furniture built in the camp. A public competition was held to find names for some locations that had only the old military names or none at all. The jury was not satisfied with the results published on April 9, 1944, but, as intended, they nevertheless awarded three prizes and five consolation prizes. The roof of E VIII was now called "Eger Square," and the bastion behind A II, loftily, "Southern Mountain" (Südberg), and sports fields and hiking paths were laid out on it. Operations in the "Central Bath" were unproblematically regulated, and a barracks originally built for package distribution was equipped as a dressing room. The library moved from tight quarters in L 304 to the building of the former "Orel" Theater, L 514, where it gained ample space. The dim movie hall had until then been used a hovel for elderly people. There the old chandelier still hung, the white screen stared down, dark-blue paintings of oversized figures loomed, and the relics of numbered rows of benches remained. Now a theater and concert hall were created there, serving mainly "youth welfare." Thus another representative site was created in addition to the large city hall auditorium, which had already been used for concerts the previous year.

But all this was not enough for this model settlement; thus the gymnasium, across from the "West Barracks," was turned, at considerable expense, into a quite presentable "community house." In the "ghetto," this friendly, modern building set within a garden had quickly fallen into a pitiable state and had long served as a typhus infirmary and "home for the infirm," although the infirm could not even be visited by friends from the camp because the building was, at the time, on the wrong side of the camp border and could not be entered without a special "entry pass" (Durchlaßschein). This building also contained a movie hall, where people lay in semidarkness, without daylight. Now the gendarmerie posts were moved to incorporate the gymnasium into the "Jewish settlement"; this aim could be accomplished by moving the posts only several meters. The movie theater was converted into a hall for theater performances, concerts, and lectures; the other rooms were also nicely refurbished, the gymnasium was transformed into a prayer hall (until then, services had been only tacitly tolerated), and tables with umbrellas and chairs were placed on the terraces to give the illusion of the social activities of a spa. A smaller hall, a "public reading room," was equipped with a reference library where people could devote themselves to the best books, comfortably and without interruption.

The SS did not even forget the dead. The ceremonial rooms at the mortuary now looked decent, painted with Hebrew inscriptions and with a black-draped podium for the prayer leader. Until late 1943, these rooms had been undignified. One no longer needed a special permit to take part in funerals, because this short road at the edge of town was now also freely accessible. The coffins no longer were brought to the crematorium in open coaches, as an actual – although misshapen – hearse was built, and it could carry a large number of coffins. An urn site was laid out across from the mortuary.

During this period, the "Jewish Rescue Committee" in Budapest succeeded in making contact with Theresienstadt through Eichmann and his assistant, Obersturmbannführer Hermann Krumey, although only a single exchange of letters was permitted. It was in Eichmann's interests in May 1944, as the "beautification" neared its height, to make full use of this opportunity for both propaganda and financial

138   *History*

purposes. Ten thousand dollars to support the Theresienstadters, addressed to Dr. Franz Friedmann, the senior Jewish Elder in Prague, and a letter to the Theresienstadt "Jewish Council" were accepted for forwarding. Friedmann and, as a group, six Zionists in Theresienstadt were "allowed" to answer and to send sugarcoated or thoroughly dishonest, or at least misleading, news of the comfortable life in the "Jewish city." Friedmann's letter is dated May 24, 1944:

> I was extremely pleased to get your letter, and it will bring the same joy to our friends in Theresienstadt. We are in constant contact with all of them [!], and so I can tell you that all of them, including their families, are well and satisfied.
>
> All are working in their professions and have made excellent progress in their fields: Erich Munk is head of the health service ... , Erich Österreicher heads the Labor Office there, Kahn is active in Recreation. Schuster devotes himself mainly to his little daughter [!]. The rest are active mainly in Youth Welfare, which is exemplary in Theresienstadt and has achieved outstanding results. They have created a rich Jewish life and are proud of their extremely comprehensive library, large theater with opera performances, daily open-air concerts, coffeehouse, city orchestra, and daily lectures on a very high level. You are surely aware that the area is extremely lovely, and one must add that particularly tasteful parks have been set up.
>
> I am happy to be able to take this opportunity to express my thanks that you thought of our *chaverim* [comrades] with the $10,000, and I can confirm that your help will be fully utilized for packages to the same.
>
> Our friends, as well as we, receive packages, as well as letters from inside and outside the country, without any trouble [!]. Every delivery gives our friends, especially, joy as a sign that people are thinking of them.
>
> (135, appendix)

Friedmann did not know Theresienstadt at all and could only write what Günther instructed or permitted.

The letter from Theresienstadt was decorated at the top with a quaintly lithographed picture of the city (created by Joe Spier), which also was used elsewhere for beautification propaganda, and it was signed by well-known Zionists in the camp, including Eppstein, Zucker, Munk, Österreicher, and Kahn.

THERESIENSTADT
23 May 1944
Dear *Chaver*,

> We confirm your letter of the 8th of this month with sincere thanks. With great joy, we take this opportunity to answer you and to ask you to send greetings to all our friends and thank them for attending to our needs. We may assume, as you make reference to it in your letter, that the many deliveries from Lisbon and Istanbul are the work of our friends. Our friends from Vienna who live with us here have also received deliveries from the above named places. Although our provisioning is quite well regulated and gives no cause for concern, we are always happy about these deliveries, because we see them as a sign of your friendship.
>
> A real Jewish town has arisen in Theresienstadt, in which all work is done by Jews, from street cleaning to a modern health system, with hospitals and a fully organized medical care service with a large staff of nursing personnel; from all technical work to catering in the common kitchens; from our own police and firemen to special court, post office and traffic services [!]; from a bank with its own settlement money and stores for groceries, clothing and household items, to a recreation office, as part of

The *"Jewish Settlement Area," Summer 1943–September 1944*   139

which regular lectures, theater performances and concerts take place. The children, for whom there is particular concern, are quartered in Children's and Youth Homes; people too old to work, in Old-Age Homes and Homes for the Infirm, under the care of doctors and nurses. Those able to work are employed mainly in internal service. Distinguished professionals have come together from all fields. This not only benefits the expert work that needs to be done in technical, hygienic and administrative areas; during leisure time as well, it has also allowed a rich cultural life to develop in Jewish and general areas. A library with nearly 50,000 volumes and several reading rooms and a coffeehouse with constant musical offerings serve as distractions, especially for older people. A Central Bath and Central Laundry ensure general hygiene, upon which of course particular emphasis is laid. Thus one can feel quite comfortable here if one has managed to achieve an external and internal adjustment and integration. [A week earlier, 7,500 people had gone to Auschwitz.] You can see a view of the town on the letterhead.

The health situation may be seen as quite good [!], which can be attributed, in addition to Theresienstadt's climatic situation [!], primarily to the devoted, undaunted work of our doctors and the satisfactory provision of food [!] and medicines. Contributions that we receive are available to us as part of the Jewish self-administration and can be used for supplementary purposes [!]. Thus we have received notice of your contribution and thank you and your friends sincerely for it.

We would also be glad of more frequent opportunities to receive news from you.... Our thoughts often gravitate toward the possibility of *aliyah* [emigration to Palestine].

We thank you for your friendly thoughts and are glad that we can be certain of your solidarity. We hope to hear from you again soon.

(135, appendix)

No one who signed this letter would live to see the last of October of that year.

The "beautification" proceeded at a feverish pace. Thousands were actively affected by it, and almost all prisoners were passively affected. The name "ghetto" was eliminated and replaced by "Jewish settlement area," but the foreign authorities interested in the camp continued to use the word "ghetto." The "Ghetto Guard" (Ghettowache) became the "Community Guard" (Gemeindewache) (both abbreviated "GW"). "Transport numbers" were not eliminated, but now they were innocently called "identification numbers." The prisoners were no longer to be called "workforce" (*Belegschaft*) and instead were called "residents" or "complement of Jews" (*Bestand an Juden*), although one must ask oneself how this terminology sounded better than "workforce." The phrase "orders of the day" was replaced by "announcements from the self-administration" (*Mitteilungen der Selbstverwaltung* [MdS]); a number of lithographed vignettes were supposed to give these documents the appearance of a news sheet (see also 264). The Jewish Elder was introduced to the outside world as mayor. Statistical material can be revealing, and thus "Office Heads ... were called upon to take care not to post statistics publicly any more and until further notice" (memorandum from the Central Secretariat, June 5, 1944). In some cases, however, certain things were not changed in time, and thus the "term for money in the Settlement Area" was only remembered a few weeks after the foreigners visited: "The term 'ghetto money' or 'ghetto kronen' is no longer to be used, with immediate effect. It will be replaced by the name 'Theresienstadt crowns,' abbreviated 'Th-Kr'" (memorandum from the Central Secretariat, July 9, 1944).

The remaining measures brought relief to camp life. The orders of the day for March 6, 1944, announced the end of the "duty to salute" that was so often forcefully announced. As the prisoners had become used to the salute, new instructions were necessary on June 18, 1944, shortly before the arrival of the foreign visitors:

> It must be pointed out again that there is no duty to salute and report. Therefore, everyone must refrain from announcing "attention" and reporting, as well as standing up. In workplaces, only the head ... and in buildings, only the building elder ... must remain available to give information if necessary. All other residents can continue their work, or may act without particular concern for possible visitors. It is understood that the usual civilian conventions are to be observed in case one is addressed.

Whereas, under Burger, permission to go out until 9 P.M. existed for only a short time in summer 1943, the curfew was now extended until 10 P.M. during the summer. Parks and redoubts were freely accessible, and thousands visited them in the evenings. "Recreation," (*Freizeitgestaltung*), which had theretofore only been tolerated and had experienced many setbacks, was officially encouraged. Every day there were numerous events: lectures, concerts, theater performances, cabaret shows, sporting events – all with the blessing of the SS, who now accepted anything that belonged in a place of leisure. Once or twice daily the city orchestra played on the square as if in a spa, and concerts were also given in the coffeehouse. Some of the new buildings – including the children's playground and its facilities – however, could not be used. Some things were completed only shortly before the deadline. Thus the MdS for July 1, 1944, revealed that the "community house" became generally accessible only after the foreign visitors had left.

Before the commission arrived on June 23, 1944, tension rose to fever pitch. Because the visit concerned the well-being of the Danish deportees in particular, they had to be as well treated and well prepared as possible, to prevent any mistakes (see 184b). Rahm and Möhs visited them in their quarters and inquired personally into their well-being. The ludicrousness of the final preparations could hardly be exaggerated. For many days the Jewish leadership worked out a detailed inspection plan that was frequently revised and overturned (see 275). The farce was prepared down to the last detail, to avert any embarrassing blunders. Jewish commissions repeatedly paced out all the paths and rooms to be inspected, and, even at the last moment, new instructions still were being issued and improvements ordered. People worked day and night, as if the happiness of the world were at stake. There still were things to build and beautify. The pavements were washed with soap and polished like parquet. No one was permitted to walk on them. Supply office staff who distributed bread received white gloves. Major concerts, theater performances, lectures, sporting events, and activities in the "children's pavilion" were rehearsed. Old and poorly dressed people were told not to show themselves insofar as possible; everyone was to wear his or her best clothes. War-wounded veterans and cripples were emphatically told not to show themselves on the streets (see 272). The menus and rations for the week in which the visits took place were improved extraordinarily and were raised to at least double portions. The inspection program was charted on the city map, and the amount of time spent in each place was planned to the minute. A number of high Nazi dignitaries, including Minister of State Karl Hermann Frank, the all-powerful man in the "Protectorate," and the Czech traitor Minister Emanuel Moravec visited the camp.

Finally the long-awaited visitors arrived, on a day on which the weather was good. The commission consisted of two Danes and one Swiss – Dr. Maurice Rossel, an IRC functionary, who had had no contact with the Danes before this visit. From Denmark came Frants Hvass, chief of the Foreign Ministry's political department, and physician Juel Henningsen, from the health office of the Ministry of the Interior, as representative of the Danish RC. SS participants included Standartenführer Dr. Rudolf Weinmann, the commander of the Sipo and SD in the "Protectorate"; Günther from Prague and his brother, Sturmbannführer Rolf Günther; Möhs; Kriminalrat Renner from the Sipo in Copenhagen (this SS officer spoke Danish and always stayed near Hvass); Hans Günther's deputy Gerhard Günel; Rahm; and Bergel. Except for Rahm, who was in uniform, all the SS men wore civilian clothes. The Foreign Office (see 312b) was represented by Legationsrat Eberhard von Thadden; the German RC was represented by Dr. Heidenkampf, who behaved passively. Eppstein was the only Jew to accompany them; only he was allowed to speak with the guests, but always in the presence of their German escorts. But the foreigners were not prevented from asking questions of the prisoners from Denmark or the Jewish functionaries, although the camp inmates had been forbidden to speak with the visitors. Words were exchanged with some Danish Jews, who succeeded in hinting at some things to their countrymen, but the prisoners were intimidated and inhibited; thus they simply agreed that conditions had improved in the course of the past half year. The truth about Theresienstadt was not revealed in this way. It is thus no surprise that the guests noted "psychological pressure" on the inmates but otherwise could see little that was bleak. Greetings from the Danish king and the bishop of Copenhagen were conveyed to the Copenhagen chief rabbi, Dr. Max Friediger, on behalf of his countrymen. The lessons Eppstein had to recite and the inspection plan were so cleverly and effectively arranged that even canny observers would have been surprised and confused. The guests were driven back and forth through the town and then taken a little farther, so that they lost any sense of the size of the place.

The Jewish Elder had a few days previously received from the "hardly heartless" Rahm a blow that had left a bruise on his eye. That day he was elegant in a morning coat and derby, like a real mayor. A car stood at the ready, driven by an SS man in civilian clothes; he respectfully doffed his cap to Mr. Mayor. The SS had cleverly realized that it would be much more impressive if they held back and allowed Eppstein to present most of the information. This had a solid, convincing appearance, and the hapless Jewish Elder played his role, both pitiful and desperate, as ordered. Before the visit to the city, the SS made do with a short address by Weinmann. He gave a general historical overview of the camp and explained that fifteen "German Aryans" – he did not say "SS men" – maintained contact with the outside world and served as camp supervisors, while otherwise self-administration prevailed, with Dr. Eppstein, the senior Jewish Elder, at its head. Weinmann thus understated the number of SS personnel by at least ten.

Following this address, the visitors and the Germans, divided among three cars, drove to the "house of the Jewish self-administration," where Eppstein welcomed them in his office, decorated with carpets and flowers, and gave a talk about the institutions in Theresienstadt.

Eppstein did not give the true figure of some 28,000 inmates but instead said that there were 37,000–40,000, of whom 94% were from Germany and the

"Protectorate," 5% from Holland, and 1% from Denmark. These ratios were more or less correct, and the figure of 296 Danes and some 150 migrants from Denmark in the camp was accurate. He also stated correctly that he had two deputies, and incorrectly that there was a "council" with sixty-six members – in fact, the total number of persons at the level of the Council of Elders never exceeded twenty-three at one time. This lie was intended to make the claimed self-administration seem more important. The administration, he said, was divided into ten departments, which also was untrue; Eppstein mentioned security, health, provisioning, construction, and finance systems. In the self-administration, he said, 1,200 – an arbitrarily chosen figure – people were employed as civil servants and functionaries. The average age was insignificantly exaggerated as forty-eight. He claimed that there were 14,600 people over sixty years old, some 6,000 between forty-five and fifty-nine, 12,500 between fifteen and forty-four, 2,000–2,300 between six and fourteen, and 800 under six years old. Eppstein had to falsify the data so that the number of persons below sixty years of age was more or less accurate, or only slightly higher, whereas he added 7,000–8,000 to the older ages, in order to reach the fake residency figures. The large number of elderly people was supposed to indicate the camp's good conditions, as well as the circumstance, known abroad, that Theresienstadt was primarily a camp for the care of the elderly. Eppstein approached the truth when he reported that 59% of the inmates were female; however, he raised the average age at death, which had been below sixty-nine years since the previous month, to seventy-two years.

He claimed that food rations were of the same quantity as in the "Protectorate," except for a lack of eggs and cheese; there was also a lack of butter, he said, but margarine was used instead – the camp documents would have shown the same. He said the daily number of calories was approximately 2,400. This was a fairy tale, as the official average daily figure in 1944 was 1,955 calories; moreover, because of unequal distribution, non-workers received no more – and in reality generally far fewer – than 1,487 calories (see Chapter 12 and 284).

He stated that 24,000 people were employed – here Eppstein had to exaggerate by 7,500 – and that the average working day lasted eight hours. Everyone belonged to one of four labor categories: fully able to work, previously ill but now able to work, conditionally able to work, and unable to work. If Eppstein could have stuck to the truth, he would have described the categories differently: capable of heavy physical labor, capable of medium physical labor, capable of light physical labor, and incapable of physical labor. The Jewish Elder then explained that untrained newcomers joined squadrons, where they were employed in all necessary work, such as cleaning, excavation, and so on. People remained in the squadrons for approximately two weeks, he said, partly in order to learn discipline and a sense of community and partly so that the leaders could decide the sort of work for which the newcomers were suited. Younger people were employed mainly in agriculture and the nursery, and women were employed in caregiving institutions, including hospitals and children's homes, or in the cleaning service. It was considered important that everyone – as far as possible – work at least a few hours, and work was performed both in and outside the town. Agriculture (the fact that its yield was not intended for the camp had to be kept quiet) was devoted to grain and beetroot cultivation, in addition to cultivation of mulberry trees and silkworm breeding. Eppstein could not say that the silkworm breeding – a continuing but always unsuccessful game on which the SS insisted – was

The "Jewish Settlement Area," Summer 1943–September 1944   143

a puny operation that never showed any meaningful yield of cocoons. Instead, he reported that the silk was supplied to the Reich and was indeed the only thing produced in Theresienstadt for export; in return, scrip was made available, with which articles needed in Theresienstadt could be obtained.

He explained that housing and food were free, and there were stores in which one could buy clothing, linens, shoes, and even, in small quantities, food with one's earnings. Piecework had been introduced, and a quick and industrious worker could receive a wage bonus that consisted of either money or meat allocations. The city had its own money and banking system. Monthly, non-workers also received 100 "Theresienstadt kronen," valued at around 10 Reichsmark, of which half was taken out in taxes and contributions.

> According to Dr. Eppstein's account, two types of people were found in the town. The vegetative type, who lived from day to day and thought of the past the entire time, and the other type, who had an inner relationship with life in the town, took part in it and sought to encourage it. To a great extent it had been possible to reeducate people of the vegetative type to become active participants in communal work, and it had to be said, according to Dr. Eppstein, that life in the town was normal and the population as a whole possessed great vitality.
>
> (108)

Thus did Eppstein end his talk.

After this, the tour began with the inspection of some offices in the building, not doing without a presentation of a trial for theft, this before the Jewish court. The SS gave some information on the administration of justice in the camps and was able to refrain generally from formal lies but lied brazenly in claiming that the Council of Elders had a right of pardon. The significance of the self-administration was emphasized with the claim that the Jewish police ensured strict discipline. Eppstein's remark that marriages were possible was, legally speaking, incorrect. After leaving B V, the guests could observe that people moved about freely in town and that they attentively followed the visit. Also viewed were the "laundry collection point," which was well organized in a barracks next to B V, and the steam laundry. The visitors were made to believe that everyone could wash 4 kg of laundry once every two or three weeks, although this usually was not possible more than once every three or four months. They proceeded to the "dining hall," where they could admire white-clothed tables and waitresses with white aprons. Eppstein was supposed to convince the visitors that the "residents" either got groceries to prepare at home or that the kitchens supplied them with prepared meals that they could eat in dining barracks. This was followed by a glance into a housing barracks next to B V; there seventy to eighty workers were quartered. Afterward, they were shown the bakery and then the excellently equipped "children's recreation home."

On the "South Mountain," soccer was being played, and the sports enthusiasts in the audience cheered the teams on with loud shouts. The small allotment garden in the dry moat also caught their eye; it had been given two months ago to internally favored prisoners for cultivation, and their diligence could now prove to the commission what benefits the Jews enjoyed in Theresienstadt. Then they drove to the "community house"; viewed its barely completed, magnificent appointments; and spent a moment attending the performance of a children's opera that was just being presented there. As they departed, the guests were afforded, as though by chance, a

144 *History*

charming pastoral scene: tanned girls marched by with their rakes, singing and laughing. The bread distributors, too, at work in their white gloves, could be noted, in passing, by the visitors, just as they might have noticed the civilian school building, L 124, which had served until the previous month as a hospital but now bore the new inscription "school" – unfortunately it was closed for "vacation." In his report, Henningsen emphasized that he had not seen any actual schools, but only one kindergarten. Then some Danes and "notables" were visited in their apartments near the corner of L 1 and Q 6 streets. Despite all the "beautification," the buildings were found to be overcrowded though clean and impressive in their personal neatness. It was found that there were even house aides (*Hausgehilfen*). Next came the "white bakery" (L 217) and the "children's homes" in block F III. The guests were told the lie that 300–400 children had so far been born in Theresienstadt (in reality, the number was about 230 by the end of the war); that there were birthing facilities, though unfortunately "there was no opportunity to view" them; and that birth control was available (if it was found, it was confiscated). The "apothecary" (Q 412) was then visited, where the visitors, who had themselves brought medicines with them, asked embarrassing questions about medications sent from Switzerland. But everything turned out well. Eppstein explained that enjoyment of tobacco and alcohol was forbidden but, contrary to camp rumor, did not justify this further. He called 10 P.M. the curfew hour but said it was possible for him to give individual permission to go out after this time.

A pause for lunch followed at the office, where the guests were served food but not given any more information on the camp. Eppstein was not brought along. After lunch, they visited the "bank" (Q 619); the post office (L 414), where many parcels and sardine packages were just being distributed; the "boys' home," which lay in the same building; and a "store" and the "butcher" (both in L 415). The fire station in L 502, Bergel's showpiece, seemed old-fashioned to the guests. Then came some pleasant rooms in the formerly infamous "home for the infirm," L 504. As Henningsen noted, they found it "barracks-like" and "completely full," and "many faces were marked by despair." Hvass pointed this out to Eppstein, who agreed with him. "Fifteen hundred beds for the blind, war-wounded, etc.," were also mentioned – a figure that was much too low – but not shown. If one reads the monthly report from the "Welfare Department" in Chapter 17 for the month of the visit, June 1944, it becomes clear why this was so. Following a detour to the carpentry workshop workshop in the old riding school (Q 321), they continued to the "Central Bath" in complex E VI, and this was followed by an inspection of the surgical facilities and some other departments of this building. The head of surgery, Dr. Springer, provided the guests with information on public health issues and also answered questions. Correctly for the time, he spoke of ten to fifteen deaths a day. He gave 2,150 as the number of sickbeds – although it was unclear whether he was talking only of hospital sickbeds; of these, he claimed that 1,700 were occupied – a number that was certainly too low. The Psychiatric Department had fourteen beds available, he said, and cases of psychosis were rare. Springer was not allowed to say that a transport of forty-five persons had been sent from the Psychiatric Department on March 20, its destination being Bergen-Belsen. Then the steam kitchen in E VII was visited; it was found to be orderly but limited in size. Finally, they were brought to the "children's pavilion" to marvel at its delights; it had been created especially for the visit, but not for the children, who were permitted to enjoy it for only twenty-four hours (see 93). This

The "Jewish Settlement Area," Summer 1943–September 1944

ended the tour, which, not counting the lunch break, had lasted five hours and forty minutes; their entire stay in Theresienstadt lasted from 11 A.M. to 7 P.M., that is, eight hours. Dr. Rossel took photographs in the camp – his pictures show only the "beautification" in its gleaming perfection.

Later, Weinmann explained that a range of difficulties had been faced in the establishment of the town, but that the self-administration had largely succeeded. It is understandable that, notwithstanding all due skepticism, the Danish gentlemen, who were quite well informed about conditions in the concentration camps and the tragedy of the Jews in the East, let themselves be fooled and could not quite see through the broad deception, especially given Eppstein's partly false, partly bogus statements. They probably had expected and even recognized that much had been prepared especially for the visit, but they also saw this as an advantage, as they believed that the improvements would be maintained and that they would benefit the prisoners. The reports by Hvass (108) and Henningsen (98) are careful and full of sympathy for the Jews, but they – necessarily – reflect only what had been seen, which offered little cause for justified complaint, and what had been heard, which they could neither judge nor check, and which they also had little cause to doubt. The contents of the Danish reports became known in Copenhagen, but little of this information reached the free world (see 288a). Soon after the visit, the Danish envoy in Berlin, Mohr, thanked State Secretary Steengracht von Moyland in the Foreign Office, in the name of his country. Rossel's report (see 225a) was never published; his judgment was far too favorable and thus harmed the IRC in Geneva (see 2a, 3b, 230a). The international Jewish organizations found out about the dispatch through Dr. Gerhart Riegner (see 301a), a member of the "World Jewish Congress" in Vienna; they recognized that it was too optimistic, and they protested. They demanded the accreditation of another IRC commission. But Theresienstadt had to wait until April 6, 1945, for another visit from Geneva.

In the camp, no one knew who the guests were, but it was known that Danes, and perhaps also a Swiss or a Swede, were involved in the commission, which was thought to be an IRC delegation.

Even if the deception was not entirely successful, it succeeded to the satisfaction of the SS (see 254b). There was general relief; Rahm could be particularly satisfied with its unproblematic implementation, and the prisoners were rewarded for the successful farce: "The Council of Elders thanks all residents for the work they achieved in the past weeks in the service of City Beautification. To honor these achievements there will be a general holiday on 24 June 1944, from 1 P.M., and on June 25" (MdS, June 24, 1944). This was in any case joyfully welcomed, as were the improved food and the many bonuses distributed for special achievements. The majority of prisoners were seized with a euphoric mood, which few were able to evade. The crowd was careless and played along with the farce only too rashly and cynically. On the other hand, the long period of privation makes it understandable that any improvement in the pitiful standard of living was gratefully accepted.

This SS policy unintentionally but considerably accommodated that of the victims to their captors. Frivolity and thoughtlessness were greatly encouraged by the "beautification." The bitter sequel shortly afterward had a correspondingly bad effect. It is difficult to distinguish between enforced participation in a wicked game and the positive face that one puts on it. How easily people soon voluntarily played along and crossed the line between what still seemed to be permitted and what would become a deadly matter. Almost all the prisoners perceived the improbability of this farce; they smiled and scoffed, but how many of them allowed themselves to be unthinkingly swept along by the stream and threw themselves into the lust for pleasure, greedy for the smallest of sensations, which could only have a negative influence. The SS looked on; "kindly Uncle" Rahm tolerated it and must have secretly rejoiced at the blindness of his Jews, who helped themselves to the abundance of evil on offer! Did not misery live close enough to them, hardly separated by soundproof walls? Were not starvation and horror still palpably spread all around the carefree high spirits? Had not relatives and friends traveled to a nameless fate? It had been a long time since mail had come from Birkenau, mail that might have told of the lives of the deportees. Had the Theresienstadters not culpably withdrawn themselves from a threatening reality? Could they really believe that they were no longer under the power of the murderous SS?

People denied their real situation, and it is from this attitude that one must judge the wealth of cultural events and other more entertaining forms of amusement. Often it was neither a desire for education nor a search for solace, as in more difficult times, that led people to crowd the halls, but an intoxication, an empty complacency.

South Mountain [*Südberg*] Competition.
Saturday, 15 May 1944:

3:30 P.M.	handball game	Holland-Protectorate
4:30 P.M.	soccer game	Bohemia-Moravia
6:30 P.M.	"	Prague-Vienna (MdS, May 13, 1944)

Herzl Sporting Event
On the 16th of this month, a Herzl sporting event will take place on the South Mountain at 3 P.M., during which:
   Active games, dancing, a relay race through Theresienstadt, youth soccer games and a bicycle race are planned.

(MdS, July 11, 1944)

Certainly this celebration had been ordered, because it was needed to continue the farce. How else could the prisoners have gotten bicycles, if the SS had not lent them some! But should they have – was it necessary for them to have – added the name "Herzl"? Should an ideal have been invoked here, one that could only have been mocked by this business? How could one lightly, and even with enthusiasm, crowd to take part in or watch such events? Had the responsible leaders and the young Zionists of the "Youth Welfare Office" lost all sense of decency and dignity, that they could let Jewish children march in formation like the League of German Girls, in white blouses, and like the "little scamps" of the Hitler Youth? Did imprisoned Jews, as the victims of Nazism, especially those who should have displayed the most loyalist sense of decency, have to resemble the Nazi Germans in clothing and manners in assimilationist fashion? The environment had such a strong influence that it even communicated itself to those who thought themselves immune to it on principle.

No lessons were learned from the fact that, in the midst of the insanity of beautification, 7,500 people went to Auschwitz. In tragic hope, many of these people had devoted their energy to this very "beautification." "Herr Cvok. . . . I'm just going on the transport anyway" . . . ? Had not their work earned them a permanent stay in the "paradise ghetto"? On March 2, 1944, a group of 200 strong young men were sent to Zossen in Brandenburg, southeast of Berlin, under apparently favorable conditions, to build barracks for the SS. These people were well equipped and left in passenger trains, just like those now used for transports to Birkenau. This was clearly a more "mild" policy! At first, things were bearable for the group in Zossen, but the situation worsened later on (see 74 and 86). They remained in the camp "tally" and, like earlier groups on "outside work," could correspond with their relatives in Theresienstadt. That was taken as a good sign. Transports now were all for "work deployment," so the Germans needed the Jews! The bad times had long passed, and Poland was almost entirely occupied by the Russians. How could a transport still be dangerous? News found its way in that former camp inmates were working in Hamburg and in other German cities, where they were doing well, and that they received packages from home. What was there still to be afraid of? Admittedly, these people's circumstances – as starving slave laborers after their days in Auschwitz – were of course not known.

Two examples show how little the SS terror had changed, and how it had merely moved into the background. The orders of the day for February 15, 1944, stated: "Warning against escape attempts. In the interests of every individual and of the community, it is pointed out that ghetto inmates who allow themselves to be induced to attempt to escape must expect the harshest police measures." In addition, the MdS of August 31, 1944, noted: "Transfers. Eleven persons were transferred to a concentration camp with their family members on the 29th and 30th of this month for repeated smuggling of money and letters and prohibited contact with government gendarmes."

If only people had been more careful! It's not so bad anymore in Theresienstadt; it's the best camp! It's the promised "paradise ghetto"! During the months of illusion, small transports left for Bergen-Belsen, and individuals were sent to the "Small Fortress," where the victims generally came to a bad end. But it was as though all this had become invisible. The prisoners succumbed to the magic and the bewitchment; they listened to spa music while their downfall was already prepared.

Amazingly, the "beautification" continued after a short pause. An additional visit had been announced for September, although it did not happen, and for propaganda reasons the farce was also to be filmed, which was accomplished on a grand scale. A film had already been made in the camp's most eventful period, in September 1942, supposedly for Himmler's private use. It was directed by Peter Kien, who approached the task energetically and realistically; little was posed. The film begins in Prague. It shows first the city, then the Jewish city hall, and then the offices of the JKG with its leading officers. Next we see the "Transport Department" putting together a transport, after which the transport is "carried out." A Jewish family is "called up," and we see how quietly they respond; they pack. Then they "move out." Footage of the journey to Theresienstadt follows, including views of the city, the arrival of the transport, and goings-on in the Schleuse. Various scenes from the "ghetto" follow, showing a cross section of camp life: the crowded halls of E 1, with their three-story bed frames, hung with rags and loaded and obstructed with a mass of bundles and gadgets, with knots of people crowding the halls; street life, with its hopelessly confused drifting and its senseless chaos; groups of people in crowds, sick people, the elderly, workers, and children; various production sites; and activities in the hospital and the laboratories. All this was recorded and also filmed according to Kien's concept. I do not know what became of this film.

The new film of the "beautification" was to look different and was to portray an exalted vision of Theresienstadt with such exaggeration that it would be clear how good the Jews had it – that they had no cares and were still the familiar "parasites" with no thought of anything but folly, coffeehouses, and a life of pleasure and luxury, while the upright "Aryans" bled or at least worked themselves to death. A short film had already been made at the beginning of the year; it showed the friendly reception of an arriving Dutch transport on "Bahnhof Strasse" (L 2) and in the barracks at C III. The charitable SS also took part. Burger gallantly helped elderly ladies from the train, and Haindl played with children. Eppstein had to hold a welcoming address, and then the arrivals were served a meal (see 336a). This time, though, the film was to be a purely Jewish matter; it was so exclusively Jewish that all the work on the film was assigned and left to the Jews, except that the footage, supposedly totaling 15,000 m, was shot by cameramen from the Prague Czech weekly newsreel *Aktualita*. Several drafts of the script were rejected by the SS as too realistic. Finally, the main responsibility was assigned to three men with whose product the SS could be satisfied. These included the Berlin cabaret artist Kurt Gerron; the talented but pliant Dutch illustrator Joe Spier; and the Prague stage designer František Zelenka, who conceptualized the film and directed its production, with the help of others. The prisoners' cooperation, to the extent it did not occur voluntarily, was unceremoniously enforced. Workers were given time off for rehearsals and shootings, and they were sent summonses from the "Recreation Office" to appear at such-and-such a time at the "coffeehouse," in the "community house," or in other places. To the prisoners' credit, it must be said that there was strong opposition to the film, but anyone who did not come willingly received warnings openly threatening that he would be summoned and punished if he did not appear. Almost nothing of the real Theresienstadt was shown. The film was pure fable, representing Jews as the stupidest Jew-hater might like to imagine them to be. One saw very little work being done: there were views of railroad building, a few workshops, "agriculture," and the "garden allotments," which were not typical of the camp. There was no need or misery, but laudable medical and sanitary achievements were shown, along with touching concern for the cheerful youth. One saw all the good living and festivities a masked "paradise ghetto" had to offer. Obvious "Jewish types" were chosen, and everyone was bursting with health. Street life was portrayed as useless strolling, and the city orchestra played in the "music pavilion" for the pleasure of the Jews. Good quarters were shown, with comfortable family life and well-nourished citizens. They had the Council of Elders hold a meeting, at which they had to listen to a speech by Eppstein, but this scene was cut out. The "coffeehouse" could not be left out, with its fancy-dress balls and pleasure-seeking activities. The theater was depicted at length, and rehearsals of three plays –*Tales of Hoffmann*, the children's opera *Brundibár*, and a Yiddish play, *In mitt'n Weg* – were filmed. An orchestra and solo concerts were not forgotten. In the "community house," Professor Emil Utitz was required to hold a lecture, to which the "notables" were ordered to go; any who were sick were taken there. On the terrace of the "community house" sat worthy old ministers and generals, who spoke animatedly. Sporting events also had to be included. But the craziest trick was footage of an open-air pool on the river (to which one was not allowed to go before or later) and an open-air cabaret on the other side of the fortress walls, which many people were ordered to visit (the gendarmes on guard were not shown). A letter has survived from the "Central Labor Office" to its "deployment office" in the men's barracks at A II in connection with this event:

Re.: Film shoot

Tomorrow, the 19th of this month, 1,800 people will be filmed as the audience at a cabaret performance in the Drabschitzer Kessel.

For this purpose, 600 persons will report to the H V barracks at noon. They will leave at 12:45.

In order to ease the processing, we request that four leaders of groups of a hundred or so make themselves available to the HV building elder tomorrow, the 19th of the month, at noon.

(344, p. 404).

Not only was the film itself contrived, but even the voluntary or coerced actors were thoroughly prepared and made up as required for a film. They had to behave "casually" and to loudly applaud all performances. It was as if Theresienstadt had become a distorted kind of Hollywood of the SS victims. The film closed with a comfortable evening meal, with grandparents, parents, and children gathered around a set table. In mid-September 1944, this work of organized insanity finally ended. The most deserving participants were generously rewarded by the SS with presents and perks and, a few weeks later, with the exception of Spier, were sent to the gas chambers. In March 1945 the film was even dubbed with Jewish music; by this point the majority of the participants were already dead, and the rest were scattered among wretched camps throughout Germany or in the disintegrating remains of Theresienstadt.

The "beautification" had served its purpose – the end of the tragedy was still to come. The film must have survived; the screenplay and other materials are available (see 3b/228–237, 81c). This sorry concoction was shown to foreign visitors in early 1945. An excerpt was shown in a German weekly newsreel in autumn 1944. One saw a coffeehouse scene and heard subdued music, and then the picture changed, showing shooting, armed attacks, dirty soldiers, and the explosion of grenades; meanwhile, the announcer could be heard saying, more or less, "While the Jews sit in Theresienstadt with coffee and cake and dance, our soldiers bear all the burdens of a terrible war, want and deprivation, to defend the homeland." In Prague, several excerpts and illegal films by Czech cameramen survived; they probably showed their filmstrips but did not want to give them up. Large portions ended up in Israel.

7

Decline and Dissolution, September 1944–May 1945

In the course of our discussion of the camp's development, thus far the prisoners themselves, although they might not have determined their history, nevertheless essentially shaped it. This was also true, perhaps especially so, when they became mere tools of the will that both determined the special fate of this camp and was itself actually that fate, and that was also primarily responsible for the life and death of the Theresienstadters. After September 1944, this changed, because, for the first time since this history began, interventions from outside did more than just mark the face of the coerced community with special characteristics, sometimes harshly and sometimes cautiously, as had so far been the case in this ongoing game. After this point they harmed the coerced community in a way that all but spelled its destruction, from which the paralyzed remnant could no longer recover, though it might still rally, although only slowly and despite continued interference. The vital right to life asserts itself again and again, and, as long as the germ of the old society and order exists, it can never entirely abandon the forms in which a social community has developed, even if the society is as constrained and almost crushed as the camp at Theresienstadt.

The essential developmental trend of this camp, like the SS's Jewish policy in general since the beginning of the war with Russia, since the Wannsee Conference to the beginning of the year 1942 had been more or less permanently established; thus deviations, temporal delays, and various tactical tricks represented mere insignificant details that could not change the overall plan. Yet during 1944, deviations did occur, and, in the final months of the war, the task of maintaining the camp was carried out with great reluctance. However, this change did not come about directly but was influenced by the goals of several opposing forces that did not themselves progress coherently or uniformly and found themselves in mutual conflict. The opposing sides can be described roughly as Hitler, who remained unswervingly radical on the Jewish question to the end, and, on the other side, some of those surrounding Himmler, such as his personal secretary Rudolf Brandt, Walter Schellenberg, and Kurt Becher of the Waffen-SS's economics staff, which was directly subordinate to Himmler. This was a group that hardly can be suspected of loving the Jews, but they were willing to be influenced by practical considerations, in the broadest sense. The fact that those who remained in Theresienstadt until the end, as well as a significant number of imprisoned Jews in general, survived the war may essentially be attributed to this

Decline and Dissolution, September 1944–May 1945

"moderate" group. But this more rational or realistic, and on occasion even more humanely minded, wing of the SS – to which, after repeated vacillation, Himmler was ever more frequently and perceptibly drawn toward the end of the war – had always to reckon with opposing forces, forces that, although they did not remain entirely true to their principles in all cases, were still defined mainly by their intention to exterminate the Jews. Among these men were Kaltenbrunner, Pohl, Glücks, Müller, and Eichmann and, among the more minor figures, certainly Günther and Möhs. As the military situation increasingly deteriorated, the SS group that was more willing to compromise favored concessions, which would be dearly bought by foreign organizations on the most favorable possible terms. These foreign organizations included the world Jewish organizations, the IRC, and the Swedish RC, as well as covert forces such as Himmler's Baltic doctor, Felix Kersten, and the illegal "Jewish Rescue Committee" in Budapest, which played a unique role as mediator between neutral or hostile foreign countries and the representatives of the SS, especially Becher and Eichmann.

The first breach of the unconditional extermination policy came in March 1944, but, apart from minor partial successes, only in the final weeks of the war did it bring perceptible benefits here and there to those who still survived. After April and May 1944, the lives of Jews no longer seemed absolutely worthy of extermination, and Jewish slave laborers flowed in increasing numbers from Auschwitz, and later from Stutthof and other places, to the German camps. But it still took until November 2, 1944, before Himmler suspended the gassings at Auschwitz, just too late for the new Theresienstadt victims, and moreover ordered that the lives of Jews be respected. This, however, in addition to some other essentially illusory concessions, remained a seldom-followed order down to the final days of the war, for the heads of the SS would have been the last to force their subordinates to obey this of all instructions. Meanwhile, Eichmann continued heedlessly to pursue his deportation policies, encountering effective resistance only when the course of the war, rather than orders, forced him to abandon his goals. Only a fairly small number of specifically Jewish camps and "autonomous ghettos" under the SS's direct authority survived the year 1942, and the next year – aside from transit camps such as Westerbork, Drancy, and so on – all were dissolved except for Łódź and Theresienstadt. While the filmic farce flickered in Theresienstadt, from August 21 to September 15, 1944, the last 60,000 Jews in the Łódź Ghetto were sent on their way to Auschwitz. Some of them, they would claim, had learned that the turn of the people in Theresienstadt would come next. They were right.

It has not hitherto been explained why the "model camp" was so harshly affected. The general overview that we have attempted provides only a few clues regarding the trends prevailing there. There are also some additional indicators:

1. *Fear of the former military officers who had been gathered at Theresienstadt.* It seems that Rahm reported to his superiors in summer 1944 that officers of the various nationalities in the camp had joined together in groups. One day, all officers were registered; most of them, including "notables" and holders of major war decorations, were in fact dispatched with the subsequent transports.
2. *Fear of healthy young men who could organize a rebellion, work with the Czechs in the resistance movement, and become dangerous,*

especially at a critical stage in the war. It is noteworthy that the SS, which expected possible resistance during the early transports, never concentrated so many Czech gendarmes around the camp as in that period.

3. *Interest in a labor force for the armaments industry*. However, one must not overestimate this motive, because it is unlikely that more than 3,000 of the more than 18,000 deportees were allowed to remain alive upon their arrival in Auschwitz. Some highly qualified technicians already had been collected in midsummer for "special labor," supposedly in Reich German factories. They were taken to the Gross-Rosen concentration camp, where their expertise was not even used.

4. *Fear of incriminating witnesses*. Too many people in Theresienstadt knew too much. If this reason were in fact seen as credible, it would have required that the SS dissolve the camp entirely. The intention surely existed, although it was to happen in stages. Statements by Eichmann leave little doubt of this.

But none of the reasons mentioned are sufficient on their own to explain the extensive liquidation of the camp, and certainly the "beautification" effort remains a serious counter-indication; this contradiction can be resolved only through psychology, not logic. The "beautification" served mainly propaganda purposes, certainly; but Eichmann could derive satisfaction from the spoils. The SS's malicious play instinct, which I consider a characteristic of most SS men and that is far too little appreciated, had been amply fulfilled. Their toy, which had become unnecessary, was simultaneously the preferred object of hate and the object of the projected self-hatred of these holders of confused values; now the toy could be discarded and destroyed. One can hardly go wrong if one recognizes, in all the reasons listed and the basic tendencies suggested, the impulses that conjured up a catastrophe in Theresienstadt in the late summer and early autumn of 1944.

Certainly the blow had been planned for some time, and from early September onward it was rumored more and more among the easily frightened prisoners, while the macabre film carnival still was in full swing. The depressing news can be traced to an SS man's indiscretion in speaking of the deportation of 5,000–7,000 prisoners. Inquiries by distraught Jews to members of the leadership were met with energetic denials; but, strangely enough, although the camp always buzzed with the most outrageous rumors, which often contained not even a kernel of truth, when impending transports were spoken of, the rumors were always true. On September 23, 1944, Eppstein announced the transports in an address in the courtyard of the "Dutch" barracks, C III. He began with the words, "I have very bad news." What preceded this speech? The answer is found in the leadership's "file notice" (*Aktenvermerk*) of the same day:

STBF Günther, HSTF Möhs and OSTF Rahm make the following announcement:

As it is necessary to make a large number of Theresienstadt inmates available for total war deployment, and as the inspections performed yesterday showed that this is not possible in Theresienstadt itself due to lack of space, 5,000 suitable workers must be deployed externally for this purpose, of whom 2,500 will depart on Tuesday morning [September 27], and another 2,500 on Wednesday morning [September 28].

Engineer Zucker is charged with building the new labor camp. Only light baggage should be taken, especially clothing, etc., and provisions for 24 hours. Travel will be toward Dresden.

This involves labor deployment similar to that in Zossen. The participants in the deployment will be guaranteed good treatment of their family, children and wives who remain behind. Luggage that may remain behind belonging to single persons will be stored separately and is to be preserved for them; for those who are married or people with other family or relatives here, this luggage can be taken into storage.

Only people completely fit for work and aged up to 50 years old can be employed; Engineer Zucker has the right to choose the individuals. He is instructed to put together a staff that will make it possible for him to set up an administration there; in addition, technicians, craftspeople of all sorts, guards (preferably former community guards) and an adequate number of doctors with medical equipment (bandages, medications), a pharmacist, etc., should go along.

Not to be included in the transport are:

1. persons whose relatives were sent to build barracks [Zossen] (in order to keep the promise made to these people)
2. Danes
3. the Dutch transport from the Barneveld list [see 106a, 114a] and the Protestants
4. notables
5. foreigners
6. war wounded – 50% or more
7. those in protective custody
8. asocial elements should also be excluded.

Selection should proceed such that, as far as possible, of all occupational groups an aliquot should remain here; deployment important to the war effort should be preserved, meaning mica splitting, uniform spraying, uniform tailoring, Rabl & Grün, etc. In contrast, agricultural personnel can be included.

OSTF Rahm declares that the selection should be made such that a certain number of craftspeople from each group should remain here in the most essential quantity.

A report regarding the more detailed composition of the labor deployment transport shall be submitted by tomorrow morning.

Dr. Eppstein is authorized to announce the precise circumstances himself today and to hold a roll call for that reason. Attention is called to the fact that absolute calm must be preserved, for which Dr. Eppstein is especially responsible.

Emphasis is once again laid on the fact that only people fully fit to work may be dispatched. There is a possibility that mail, as in Zossen, can be delivered every 8 or 14 days; however, the destination must not be stated.

According to information from Dr. Eppstein, OSTF Rahm has informed him by telephone that marriage to an Aryan or *Mischling* status does not prevent inclusion and that the age limit of 16 to 55 years can be extended.

(192)

Two days later, it was ordered that, along with Zucker – the erstwhile deputy Jewish Elder and head of the Central Secretariat – Schliesser, the head of the Economics Department and one of the most influential men in the self-administration, would also have to go. The SS justified the order by explaining that, in addition to an experienced engineer (Zucker was an excellent construction engineer), an economics expert of stature would be needed in the new camp. The transports had to be postponed by one day because the trains did not arrive on time. The blow fell with full force and was calculated cunningly and perfidiously. At a time when some 7,700 men were employed in "work deployment," of whom barely 7,000 were less than fifty-five years old, sending 5,000 men away cut off the camp's lifeblood; and now the SS could be certain that its plans for extermination would face little resistance, especially as they continued to proceed with great caution. Meanwhile, the gentlemen from the SS "office" were generous with reassurances that, to replace threatened areas in Upper Silesia, a new center would be created in Saxony for the armaments industry, and locations such as Riesa, Königstein, and other places in the Saxon Erz Mountains were suggested as destinations for the transport. Thus the optimists were able to believe that it would not be so terrible; the explanation provided in the "file" sounded plausible. Although news of the transport engendered some horror, even in a camp in which people already were prepared for the impending and relatively certain end of the war, very few suspected that their doom would be inevitable. The fact that Zucker and Schliesser, who were considered indispensable in Theresienstadt, had been chosen to lead the "new" camp almost instilled confidence, and thus many old functionaries from all the departments reported more or less voluntarily for the new "construction corp.," especially as the protection of the AK transports had finally ended. One could almost see in some people the reawakening of the old pioneer spirit that had kept them going during the initial period in the "ghetto." This time, as with the subsequent transports, the SS was already distributing "directives," through which many leading personalities and people who theretofore had been protected by the leadership were deported. It is noteworthy that the SS no longer followed the Wannsee guidelines, for, aside from the transport of people with war decorations, *Mischlinge* (people of "mixed blood") and *Versippte* (Jews in mixed marriages) too were sacrificed, although the practice proved somewhat more lenient there than the instructions required. Never before had transports consistently affected the working camp elite not only nominally but also practically. Elderly people really were protected; until the end of this transport, except for some people singled out through "directives," no one over sixty-five was removed. It is especially surprising that people with criminal records and the mentally retarded were at first exempted; only the healthy were considered. Thus for this and the next two transports, illness was recognized as a mitigation under the theretofore normal rules. Later this no longer helped.

Half of Kaserne C III had to be cleared immediately in order to serve as the Schleuse. Some transports were deported in passenger trains, which was intended to make it seem that the deportees would receive humane treatment. High function-aries, whose deportation was ordered by means of "directives," entered the better train compartments of the escort team. They were able to travel with a great deal of luggage, while the others could take very little. The prisoners in the camp did not know that Zucker and Schliesser were handcuffed as soon as the first train left Theresienstadt. During the trip, even before Dresden, the men were told to write postcards to their wives. They were to report that they had arrived safely at their destination, that food and accommodation were good, and that the work was not too arduous. The men were told to ask the women to follow them as soon as possible. The first two transports took 4,000 younger men; the last 1,000 people, who were selected on September 23, went with the third transport.

On September 27, the senior Jewish Elder, Eppstein, was suddenly arrested, brought to the "office," and never seen again. Food and warm clothes brought for

Decline and Dissolution, September 1944–May 1945 155

him were accepted. Nothing was learned about Eppstein's fate, and later it was assumed that he was transported to Auschwitz. Not until long after the war did it become known that he was taken to the "Small Fortress" on the day of his arrest and shot (see 162, 284, 321a). The reasons for his end remain unclear. The following incident provided the immediate excuse for his arrest: Rahm ordered Eppstein to take away and surrender a certain type of knapsack from the men traveling with the first transport. Eppstein did not want to do this, as he wanted to avoid creating a disturbance, and explained that such knapsacks were found in the "clothing warehouse" (I IV), which was on the other side of the "bypass road." He went there, accompanied by a GW man. Both were arrested for leaving the camp without a "pass," which the SS could at any time interpret as an escape attempt. It is improbable, however, that this trivial excuse sufficed as a reason to arrest and execute Eppstein, especially as, later on, passes for the "clothing warehouse" were issued by the Jewish leadership and not by the SS. The true reasons must be found in the disfavor into which Eppstein had fallen. It is certain that he committed a gross error when, after the successful invasion in the West, he attempted to counter the boisterous mood in the camp. He hoped to keep the prisoners under firm control, in part to protect them from imprudence, in part to raise his standing, and maybe also to feed his vanity. He therefore prepared a speech, "New Year's Thoughts 7505," in which he first praised and then gave thanks for the work achieved hitherto. He then addressed the current situation, saying, more or less, that

> Theresienstadt can ensure its existence only through scrupulously disciplined labor. We must not talk, but work. One should not speculate about possibilities. We are, so to speak, on a ship that waits before a harbor, but cannot enter it, because its entry is prevented by a thick mine field. Only the ship's leadership knows the narrow path leading to the safety of the shore. They must ignore the deceptive signs and signals coming from the shore. The ship must hold back and wait for instructions. One must trust that the leadership is doing everything in its power to ensure the security of our existence. Thus we will stride seriously and confidently into the new year, with the firm will to persevere and fulfill our duties.
>
> (see also 93, 243e)

He showed the draft to Leo Baeck, who urgently warned Eppstein against recklessness. But he could not be convinced and submitted the text to Rahm, who had no objections. Eppstein gave his speech at the celebration of the Jewish New Year on September 19, before an audience of 1,200. Perhaps the SS, which had long distrusted him, wished to set a trap for him.

After this point Murmelstein was the sole Jewish Elder and remained so until May 5, 1945, although he was officially appointed only later. Thus the leadership fell to a man whom the prisoners distrusted, as they did his aide, Robert Prochnik, who took up the business of the secretariat after Zucker. In any case, the prisoners had not the slightest support from these two.

Although the SS had until that point declared that wives and mothers of the deported would be protected, they suddenly made known, as the third transport – the remaining 1,000 men – was being prepared, that 500 wives of men who already had been dispatched would be allowed to go along. This was presented as a unique opportunity for married couples to reunite. The rumor was spread that the fare would be better than in Theresienstadt and that community life would be possible in the "new" camp. The women had to report within 18 hours, but because not enough people volunteered, the shortfall was forcibly supplemented by the "Transport Department." The wife of Zucker, the engineer, went, bringing eight suitcases (see 146b). Before departure, Rahm told the German transport leader, "This is Mrs. Zucker. You will guarantee for me that Mrs. Zucker will lie in her husband's arms this very day." Zucker's body had already been burned at Auschwitz. Mrs. Zucker also went to her death.

The full flower of the camp was gone by the time Rahm declared to Murmelstein on October 2 that no additional transports would take place; agreed to release the Schleuse, C III, for housing purposes; and even approved the text submitted for an MdS issue in which the end of the transports was to be reported and the prisoners called on to increase their labor output. But now the transports really began in earnest. Hardly had Murmelstein left the SS "office" when Möhs, who at the time was constantly in the camp, ordered new transports. This indicates that Möhs was a representative of the forces around Eichmann, who clung to an absolute extermination policy. However, the above-mentioned indiscrete remark by an SS man leads us to conclude that other circles were interested only in preventing possible resistance in the camp through the deportation of no more than 7,000 people. The overall plan continued to be concealed from the prisoners; it could only be guessed at from the precipitous daily "directives."

Those who still were alive had to leave as soon as they were summoned. Due to the number of transports and the deportation of hitherto leading men, the internal defense completely collapsed. The work of producing "transport lists" for the next six transports of 9,150 people was still in the hands of the "Transport Department," although the number of "directives" grew from one transport to the next. Even before one transport had left, the victims were already summoned for the next one. Few groups were exempt, aside from the elderly; this exception probably was put in place so as not entirely to abandon the illusion that transports were meant for "labor deployment." The SS was devious enough to continue its deception after the conclusion of the deportations and into November; food and fuel for 30,000 people continued to be ordered, as before the start of the transports, and the "registry" had to produce a daily "camp tally" in which the deportees, in the fashion of the Zossen group, were to be listed as "furloughed external labor groups." This included the sick, women, and small children. Indeed, this was necessary, for soon even the sick, along with their doctors and nurses, no longer would be protected, because, it was said, their accommodation, as well as that of small children, was assured in the "new" camp. Some *Mischlinge* could save themselves, whereas *Versippte* generally could not; those with war decorations were barely considered, whereas people with war wounds were "checked" by Möhs and in many cases deported (see 20). In the general chaos, Rahm often played the strict but just man who could answer a plea at the last moment and free some people, even with their families. Generally, however, he hardened himself and beat the victims mercilessly. Ultimately, they no longer knew whom to deport and whom to retain. All departments were depopulated; leaders and indispensable experts, persons privy to dangerous secrets, and even worthless helpers of the SS were sacrificed.

The ninth transport left on October 19. The camp seemed to be dissolving, and few believed SS assurances, on October 20, that around 12,000 people, mostly elderly and women, would be allowed to remain in Theresienstadt. The selection for the last two transports, which left the camp on October 23 and 28 with 3,753

Decline and Dissolution, September 1944–May 1945   157

victims, was made by Möhs and Rahm personally. Because they could not agree in all cases, they once even called in Günther from Prague. Two selections were carried out in front of the "office," one according to "departments" and one alphabetically; each individual case, if it did not involve a member of a generally protected group, was dealt with separately and noted on a list. Each person had to step forward and state his name and workplace. The condemned were noted in red and the spared in blue, after which Murmelstein received the list of decisions. In this way, everyone was deported except the elderly, the Danes, some "notables," the Barnevelder group, Dutch Jews who had been baptized as Protestants, a number of women and children, most of the women from the "mica-splitting" shop, and a core group of craftsmen and officials. No one under sixty-five years of age was kept behind in Theresienstadt as a member of a special group, or personally by the SS. The day after the departure of the penultimate transport, more than thirty people who had eluded deportation were arrested. Nevertheless, it cannot entirely be ruled out that a few people may have successfully avoided deportation (see 240b).

Following the departure from camp of the final transport, which Rahm and Möhs put together alone, twenty young men were taken from the train at the Bohušovice station. They were used to dig up and destroy the remains of the men who had been executed and buried in early 1942 in the courtyard of I IV, as well as for some other "clearing up operations." After completing these tasks, these unfortunates were driven into the "Small Fortress" and mowed down. Here it should also be noted that, in summer 1944, on the orders of the "otherwise hardly heartless" Rahm, a transport from Cologne consisting of sixty women and an unknown number of men was diverted to the "Small Fortress" instead of to the "model settlement," for "rapid liquidation." Among these unfortunates, who quickly perished, was a ninety-two-year-old woman (see 10a, 162).

After these transports, Theresienstadt resembled a shattered city. Life was paralyzed, the camp's institutions were destroyed, and the "beautification" was ended. The streets were thick with dirt. Many buildings were empty; the rooms, furnished so laboriously with so much hard work, were dilapidated; piles of ownerless luggage, including valuable objects, were abandoned and scattered about. "Lights on in many rooms, in the corridors water flowed from the faucets.... In the hospitals, patients fell from their beds and lay on the floor for many nights because of the lack of nursing personnel" (192).

On September 28, 1944, there were 29,481 people in Theresienstadt, a number that was certainly far too high for normal circumstances. But the space was just enough to accommodate these people, after a fashion, and to allow them to lead a more or less tolerable life. On October 28, 1944, there were only 11,077 prisoners, and on October 31, 11,068, including 819 children, 4,543 women, 1,642 men, and 4,064 elderly people (2,816 women and 1,248 men). The number of doctors had fallen from 720 to 76. In reality, there were around 250 fewer men, because that was the number of young men who were in Zossen at the time.

On November 9, 1944, the leadership pulled itself together to offer a weary message that nevertheless retained its old tone in the MdS, which was again being published:

> In the last few weeks, the Jews of Theresienstadt have proven anew their sense of order, discipline and communal responsibility. We must especially underscore the achievements

158   *History*

> of those colleagues who have had to perform their previous tasks many times over and have unfailingly fulfilled their duties.
>
> The reform of the Council of Elders and the recreation of the Jewish self-administration are in progress. In the meantime, it is necessary to ensure that the vital needs of the Jewish settlement area ... continue to be satisfied to the fullest extent, and that all work be continued without hindrance.

The same day, a seventy-hour workweek with free days was announced; all children from the age of ten on were required to work. On February 9, 1945, the working week was reduced to sixty-five hours, and a free afternoon was granted. A new order was laboriously established; the departments were reduced in size, centralized, and once again saddled with a disproportionately large bureaucracy. Most of the work had to be done by women and old men; after a few weeks, they managed to get the most important activities running well enough for bearable conditions to be established. Surprisingly, some things even got better than they had ever been. The food situation, in particular, improved, because the corrupt people in the kitchens and in all the provisioning services, who had formed an impenetrable ring, had been deported, and the prisoners received full portions. In addition, the mail authorizations left by deportees to those who remained behind – euphemistically called "legacies" (*Erben*) – were largely declared invalid; thus the packets accrued to the benefit of the community, especially those groups who previously had been the most disadvantaged. Donations from abroad also became more noticeable (see 229a, 276), but rations were reduced considerably at the end of February 1945; the "supplementary rations" (*Zusatzkost*) for heavy laborers were also greatly reduced. Increased living space for each individual was a sad benefit. Few were happy about all these things; the lethargy was not overcome.

The rest of the history was soon decided only by world events, which were ever more frequently reflected in what was happening in the camp. What came to pass in the camp corresponded to late epochs in every form of community. A process of this kind unfolds as if everything that happened before the final conclusion of the history were being repeated. Institutions, once established, continued and were reanimated. New people, large numbers of whom were brought in especially between the end of January and the middle of March, experienced the same things that many tens of thousands before them had experienced, but the impending end of the war prevented the new arrivals from feeling that they were part of Theresienstadt and from merging with the community of old-timers. This was true in particular of the Jewish spouses from the "Protectorate," who were generally openly hostile to the Theresienstadters and even sabotaged the work that was actually necessary. These people had been transported mainly under the catchphrase "labor deployment" and had been promised freedom of movement and control of any money they brought along. Naturally, all this was immediately taken from them in the Schleuse, and they thus formed a dissatisfied element that was even less integrated into the camp than were the Dutch from Westerbork. They also had so little understanding of the signs of the times that they absolutely did not wish to be counted as Jews. To make these people somewhat more willing to work, the SS gave them preferential rights to write to their relatives. During this period, a total of around 8,600 people were deported to Theresienstadt; aside from the roughly 5,200 "mixed-marriage" partners, who comprised the largest proportion, more than 1,400 prisoners came from Sered in Slovakia, where a labor and transit camp had existed since 1942 (see 193c). This group for the first time brought more detailed news of the fate of those deported to the East, but even then many in Theresienstadt did not believe it. Finally, 1,150 Hungarian Jews arrived from Austria. After endless marches from Budapest, they had endured several months of forced labor near Vienna, and their capacity for physical and psychological resistance had been considerably weakened. Until April 19, 1945, small and very small transports came from many parts of Germany that were not yet occupied, where there apparently was nothing more with which to concern oneself than to quickly flush out and deport a few more Jews. For all these people, who were generally embittered and often demoralized, the camp was new, and the story of arrival, Schleuse, billeting, internal "resettlement," and arranged building evacuations repeated itself. Almost everything that earlier inmates already had experienced repeated itself, without their actually being affected by it. People no longer even felt the semblance that something was being built up, although some SS orders tried to create this impression. Shortly before the end, even the "beautification" campaign had to be repeated. But the whole business was grinding to a halt. The history of the camp was disintegrating. Through the liberation, the few who had held out until then experienced the destination of that history – they experienced the *end*.

We must now relate the most important events and single them out from the sameness of the everyday incidents previously described. Seen from the prisoners' perspective, they were more like occurrences that simply happened than intentional acts. They no longer even seem like history; hardly any objective can be discerned. Frankenhuis's diary provides characteristic glimpses of life during this final phase (see 69).

The MdS of December 13, 1944, announced the "reorganization of the Jewish self-administration":

> Preliminary efforts to rebuild the Jewish self-administration have progressed far enough so that superior authorities can appoint a senior Jewish Elder and the members of the Council of Elders.
>
> As the senior Jewish Elder, Dr. Benjamin Israel Murmelstein will be responsible for leading the Jewish self-administration and representing it to the outside world....
>
> The Jewish Elder, the Council of Elders, and with them, the leading staff ... assume their duties with the sincere desire to serve the community.

The Council of Elders consisted of one representative of each of the five countries of origin: Germany, the "Protectorate," Austria, Holland, and Denmark. The chairman and deputy Jewish Elder was Leo Baeck. The self-administration was divided into the Secretariat, under Prochnik, to which the Accounting Office (Verrechnungsstelle), the "Investigation Group" (Erhebungsgruppe) (Security Service), the Department of Cultural Affairs, and the "Recreation Office" were attached. The old departments were replaced by "subject areas" (*Sachgebiete*). These areas included population matters, building management, space management, economics, labor deployment, technology, workplaces (formerly "production"), agriculture, health services, welfare (directed by Leo Baeck), and legal matters. In addition, there were the "public institutions" of the Community Guard (Gemeindewache [GW]), fire department, post office, and "bank." Thus nothing new was introduced; existing elements were simplified. Only the Department of Cultural Affairs was new. It seems strange that "recreation" was not forgotten. It again led a shadowy existence, although most of the artists were gone. The MdS of December 13, 1944, stated:

Recreation. Coffeehouse. Program daily at 6 P.M.

For workers, Tuesday, Wednesday, Thursday at 7:45 P.M. Community Center.
Westgasse 3, Sunday the 17th of December 1944 7:30 P.M. Main auditorium.
 Evening of light entertainment.
Tuesday 19th of December 1944 7:15 P.M. Terrace Hall, Mozart Evening.

This indicates that the old curfew of 8 P.M., which in the past always had been in force except in summer, was abolished for all practical purposes. Various other "commands and prohibitions" were also forgotten. Some were recalled one last time by a final collective punishment imposed on the camp:

> Some inhabitants of Theresienstadt have violated present rules by importing forbidden goods into the Settlement Area, especially tobacco products, and dealing in them through barter. Investigations have revealed no satisfactory explanation for the origins of the forbidden items.
>
> Since, in addition, the necessarily sparing use of materials, electricity and fuel has also given rise to repeated complaint, it is ordered:
>
> 1. Until the completion of the investigation in progress, the entire operation of recreational activities and of the coffeehouse is suspended.
> 2. Granting of bonus rations from undeliverable packets is suspended until clarification.
> 3. All electric cookers and heating appliances are to be surrendered immediately, on pain of strict punishment....
> 4. A curfew will be introduced with immediate effect from 8 P.M. Unjustified presence on the street after this time will be punished.

(MdS, January 15, 1945)

In the course of the autumn and winter, various pointless construction projects were carried out, in part to serve the SS's unquenchable desire for pleasure and in part apparently as a result of its negotiations with foreign representatives so that Theresienstadt could take in more people as a custody-and-exchange camp. Thus a group of wooden barracks (*Barackenlager*), into which no one moved, was erected hastily on the bastion, along with a new, large kitchen that was never used. The SS had the former city hall (L 318) and the former school (L 417), which had served for so long as a youth home, completely refurbished and equipped, and in H IV, luxurious ceremonial and meeting spaces were created for the "Berlin Office."

The past was to be completely erased. In early November 1944, the order was given to remove the ashes of the dead. Women and children were recruited for this, and they received sardines as a bonus. Macabre scenes played out during this job, which lasted four days. Paper sacks of ash marked with the names of the dead had been stored in a narrow tunnel in the mine; to remove them, prisoners had to pass them along a chain of 200 people, who made jokes such as, "Watch out, that's my uncle!" The ashes were then taken away by truck. The prisoners were told that the ashes had been buried in six mass graves in a Prague Jewish cemetery; they even had to make urns to decorate this cemetery. In fact, the ashes were most likely thrown into the Eger. After December 8, it was ordered that all official records connected with transports and registries be turned over to the SS. The history of the camp before January 1, 1945, was to be covered up. In the second half of April, everything within reach, and ultimately even material regarding the most recent past, was confiscated

Decline and Dissolution, September 1944–May 1945

and burned, along with the SS archives. Thus many documents that could today have systematically illuminated the camp's history were destroyed.

Whatever escaped destruction was preserved illegally or by chance. These documents are merely an inconsiderable remnant of the many tons of paper on which information was recorded with complete pedantry. Did the SS not realize the ludicrousness of their game of hide-and-seek, now that heavily incriminating material had fallen into enemy hands at Majdanek, Auschwitz, and Łódź? It is doubtful whether anything from the SS "office" survived, especially as the chance was missed, following liberation, to salvage any surviving papers. The extensive holdings of the RSHA in E 1 also were burned on April 17, in tall piles, after which the city was wreathed in clouds of smoke and covered with paper ash, as after a volcanic eruption.

The fear of "atrocity documents" led to an inspection of pictures on March 28, 1945. Large pictures were appraised on the spot, whereas smaller ones had to be brought to the secretariat. At the time, many of the remaining pictures were hidden; many others already had been hidden in July 1944, when five painters were arrested for producing "atrocity pictures" and were taken with their families to the "Small Fortress." Prisoners were also forbidden to keep in their quarters pictures of deported relatives.

In January 1945 the efforts of international organizations regarding the prisoners in SS camps increased. During this period, this may have involved around 700,000 people (see 209a), including some 200,000 Jews. The IRC had been negotiating with the SS since the end of January, and the Swedish RC had been negotiating since February 17, 1945, on behalf of the prisoners from the Scandinavian countries. Jewish organizations also were more active but unfortunately did not collaborate sufficiently. On February 3, the inmates heard about the first surprising result of these efforts for Theresienstadt: a transport of 1,200 people to Sweden was announced for February 5, 1945. This event fulfilled an agreement between the former Swiss president Jean-Marie Musy and Himmler on January 12, 1945, and had a long history (see 2a, 3b, 192b–c, 235a–b). In August 1944, some Swiss already had attempted, through the good offices of Himmler's doctor, Kersten, to approach the Reichsführer in order to achieve the release of a large number of Jewish prisoners. Following initially unsuccessful negotiations, Kersten finally persuaded Himmler to make a partial concession on December 8; this doctor, who made ceaseless interventions, committed this to writing in a letter on December 21:

> Finally, I would like to remind you, most honored Mr. Reichsführer, of our discussion about the Jews. I asked you to release 20,000 Jews to Switzerland from Theresienstadt. But you unfortunately told me that you could not do this under any circumstances, but that you would be willing initially to release 2–3,000 Jews on a transport to Switzerland. Should the world press not interpret this as a weakness on Germany's part, you would negotiate further with me in good faith.
>
> (139, p. 277ff.)

The happy news was scarcely believed in the camp, as confidence in SS statements finally had been generally undermined. But some were enthusiastic and strove to be included. Those who were requested to present themselves, "who received an invitation ... for examination of their suitability," had to submit "all official documents." "Persons who do not wish to take part in the transport must also go to the

162   *History*

Community House to sign a waiver" (memorandum from the secretariat on February 3, 1945). There were enough applicants, and Günther and Rahm decided who could go. It was a cause for concern that the same groups who were not transported in autumn 1944 were excluded. In addition, no one whose closest relatives had been deported to the East could go along, and no intellectuals or persons of high status were permitted. On the day of departure, the skeptics began to quiet down.

> 1,200 persons were dispatched to Switzerland in Pullman passenger cars. Only suitcases could be brought along, no knapsacks or bedrolls. We do not believe it. And then the next day, Pullman cars were standing in the station, and 1,200 people, always entire families, in the most civilian of clothes ... with numbered cards (1–1,200) proudly in hand, who had been in quarantine in the barracks across the way all night.
>
> (256)

The people were given cake, cookies, marmalade, vitamin tablets, and so on, as provisions. Rahm told those who were departing, "You will have it good where you are going. But you must never forget that you had it good here too." During the trip, they had to remove their "Jewish stars" (see 85a, 100, 114a, 159, 197, 204, 296a, 296). On February 6, the transport arrived safely in Switzerland, and the next day the national press reported who was responsible for the initiative leading to this rescue operation: "On behalf of the Agudah and the Union of Orthodox Rabbis in the United States and Canada, former Federal Councillor (Bundesrat) Musy was able to have the Jews released from concentration camps and brought to Switzerland" (135, p. 160). A few days after the departure of the Swiss transport, on February 10, the Zossen outside group returned to Theresienstadt in a pathetic condition, following an eight-day round trip.

As a result of the occupation of Hungary, the Budapest Rescue Committee had been dissolved, but its member Dr. Kasztner did not cease his activities and remained in contact with Standartenführer Kurt Becher and other SS representatives. Although his efforts in the case of Theresienstadt were not blessed with the same success that he achieved with two transports from Bergen-Belsen to Switzerland, he constantly worked to prevent extermination plans. On February 24, Hauptsturmführer Dieter Wisliceny in Vienna, admittedly a boastful and not very credible man, informed him:

> I have now been appointed Inspector of Theresienstadt. I happened to be in Berlin when Hunsche [Eichmann's representative] telegraphed from Prague to ask Eichmann what was to happen to Theresienstadt in case of a Russian advance. Eichmann naturally immediately declared that the Jews had to be completely exterminated.
>
> I told him I agreed, but I wanted to know if he believed that all traces of such a mass murder could be erased? ... He answered immediately: No, no! I've had enough! He accepted my suggestion that in case of a Russian advance, the Jews in Theresienstadt be left where they are. They will be guarded by Czech police, and our people will be ordered to retreat to the mountains. There will be no battle for the camp.
>
> ... In Vienna, many Hungarian Jews have now become unemployed due to the destruction of factories. I will redirect a transport of 1,500 from here ... to Theresienstadt. [In reality, 1,150 Hungarian Jews came to Theresienstadt.]
>
> As regards Theresienstadt, Eichmann's order to the commandant has been put in writing.
>
> (135, p. 161 et seq.)

Eichmann's intentions were, however, still to be feared, as two work contracts from the SS to Jewish offices in February demonstrate. The SS ordered the construction of gas-tight rooms with unusual ventilation equipment (to be located between Ravelin XVIII and the Leitmeritz [Litoměřice] Gate), as well as the fencing in of a plateau (in Ravelin XV) that would have made a suitable execution site for the mass shooting of all the prisoners. The prisoners finally had stopped being so trusting, and they suspected the worst. They went directly to Rahm. "What are you thinking, we are not building any gas chambers in Theresienstadt!" the commandant assured them. Murmelstein was besieged, and people pointed out the obvious reason for the construction. He went to Rahm, who explained that these were bomb-proof food storehouses and a theft-proof chicken farm. But it is not clear why high functionaries from Berlin twice came to inspect the "chicken farm." Within a few days, however, Eichmann really did change the building plans to this effect – Wisliceny's explanation to Kasztner is thus probable. Eichmann had suffered a setback, and he had to adjust his evil game and set it onto a different course. But neither he nor, even more so, Günther, would honestly give up until the final days of the war, when all the prisoners, including those in the "Small Fortress," were to be driven into a moat so as to be mowed down from the ramparts with flamethrowers, machine guns and rocket launchers (see 321a).

For the time being, however, Eichmann gave in, and he would no longer get the chance later on. On March 3, he visited the camp and stated, "Anyone would like Theresienstadt as it is." Hardly had he left when orders arrived that made it doubtful whether foreign guests would agree with his assessment of Theresienstadt. Himmler had hinted in talks with Folke Bernadotte, who was technically supposed to implement a large-scale rescue operation, initiated by Dr. Kersten, that all Jews imprisoned in Germany could be handed over to the Allies. However, on March 5, Kaltenbrunner refused to cooperate with the Swede and withdrew all concessions. Then exactly a week later, he received Professor Carl Burckhardt from Switzerland and agreed that a representative of the IRC could reside in every concentration camp until the end of hostilities and could head an on-site relief operation; in addition, he agreed that Jewish children and old people, as well as all inmates of Theresienstadt, could be repatriated. In this period, too, 7,500 Jews were to be brought to Theresienstadt and Landsberg for exchange purposes, but this was made impossible by a typhus epidemic in the concentration camps. The admittance of IRC representatives into the camps was constantly postponed. On March 21, Himmler's secretary, Standartenführer Brandt, wrote to Dr. Kersten: "There is an interesting film about Theresienstadt.... You will further be interested to hear that, on the orders of the Reichsführer-SS, the International Red Cross has been given the opportunity to gain insight into conditions in Theresienstadt" (139, p. 357). On March 23, Gestapo chief Müller finally explained to an IRC delegate that camp visits were not possible, due to a lack of suitable inspectors; only Theresienstadt could be shown in the next few days, "in order to put an end to the enemy's propaganda lies."

Thus Eichmann's orders regarding a "second beautification" of Theresienstadt are understandable; people there soon found out that international visitors were coming. Eichmann ordered that the dead would no longer be burned but instead would be buried; only this method corresponded to Jewish religious ritual, as foreign representatives had pointed out. However, in April, the cremations began again. The urns of those who had died since January 1, 1945, were placed on racks in the crematorium. The graves had to be laid out where burials had stopped in 1942. The mass graves had already been broken up into small hills, to look like individual graves. This time, again, the "beautification" required a substantial effort, although it could not be compared with the previous year's farce. Thus this time there were almost no new facades, but all existing facilities were cleaned. An infants' home with a kindergarten was newly established in Q 403. The former city bank (Q 414) had to serve as the meeting place for the Council of Elders, and it was provided with luxurious offices with telephones and Persian rugs. Before the arrival of the visitors – and this was all they were for the time being, not permanent residents – Günther and Möhs viewed the quarters that were to be displayed "on a trial basis." Friendly questions to elderly people about the health of their relatives were, to the horror of the SS men, answered with complaints and tearful counterquestions about what had happened to the deported children. It was therefore ordered that the visitors should be shown empty quarters. Once again, amusements were rehearsed, as if the SS and the Jews had nothing on their minds at the time but music and theater. At great cost, a Czech children's play, *Fireflies (Broučci)*, based on a well-known children's book, was rehearsed. Thus the Czech language was suddenly permitted again, after having been forbidden during such events by the "Recreation Department" since July 1944. Beautiful programs for this play were lithographed and hand colored.

On April 6, 1945, the IRC delegate in Berlin, Dr. Otto Lehner, arrived with the delegate Paul Dunant, who had been especially appointed in Geneva for Theresienstadt, accompanied by Eichmann, Dr. Weinmann, the Prague representative of the Foreign Office, ambassadors Erich von Luckwald and von Thadden, and the Swiss diplomat Werner Buchmüller. Günther led the commission's tour of the camp, because Rahm had taken ill. Only Weinmann was allowed to answer questions about deportation figures. He spoke of a total of 18,000 deportees, of whom 10,000 had been deported the previous autumn. What was shown to Dunant must have seemed insane. Empty rooms and concerts and theater performances in the middle of the day – that was all a bit too much. Nevertheless, the deception made a strong impression on Lehner (see 3b).

In his report, Lehner wrote:

On April 6, we went to visit the Ghetto of Theresienstadt, where we had plans to discuss rather important matters with Dr. Weinmann ... and also with Oberführer Eichmann, Specialist for all Jewish Questions ... as he had let me know that he was the direct representative for all Jewish questions.... What I was interested in ... was not so much the conditions of lodging or the installations of the Ghetto of Theresienstadt, but to learn whether this was a ghetto or transit camp for the Jews and in what proportion the deportations had been directed to the East (Auschwitz). Indeed, as I was able to discover, the Senior Elder of the Jews, Dr. Eppstein, a trusted man in the camp, had also been deported to Auschwitz at the same time as many others.... Dr. Weinmann confirmed that the last transport had been around six months earlier. It consisted of 10,000 Jews, who had been employed to expand the Auschwitz camp, and most of them had been serving in the administration. Several thousand had been employed to dig trenches.

During that evening, Eichmann elaborated his theories on the Jewish problem. To his mind, the Jews of Theresienstadt were much better favored in terms of food and medical care than were many Germans. He reiterated that Theresienstadt was the creation of Reichsführer-SS Himmler, who had wanted to enable the Jews to organize a community within the ghetto in this camp, with almost complete autonomy; the goal was to awaken a sense of racial community. The Jews of Theresienstadt would then be moved to some regions where they would live, totally separated from the rest of the German population. [See Himmler's similar statement on Theresienstadt in Chapter 2].

Decline and Dissolution, September 1944–May 1945   165

I convinced Dr. Weinmann of the need to establish a delegation of the International Committee of the Red Cross in Prague. The delegate of that town should be permitted to visit the camp of Theresienstadt at any time he chose. It was with the firm commitment by Oberführer Eichmann and the word of honor of Dr. Weinmann that no other Jew would be deported from the camp of Theresienstadt that I left them.

(228 p. 99 et seq., see also 166a, 235c)

On April 13, it was announced in the camp that the Danish Jews had been freed. This was a successful outcome to the operation initiated by Dr. Kersten. The Swedish RC took the group and on April 15 drove them in its own buses to Sweden, where they arrived three days later. Rahm had at first forbidden the Danes to bid farewell to the other prisoners, but he changed his mind and permitted them to do so and, in fact, even ordered the "city orchestra" to play at their departure. On the same day, the smoking ban that had cost so many people in Theresienstadt their lives was lifted, and cigarettes were distributed (see 184b).

Dunant stayed in Prague, where on April 12 he learned that the list of residents of Theresienstadt had been destroyed. He considered this a possible sign of mass executions and therefore traveled to Berlin, where he was assured again by Müller that Theresienstadt's safety would be guaranteed. A few days previously, Himmler had appointed Becher, the liaison to Kasztner, to be Reich special commissar for all the concentration camps. The organized mass murder was to cease. After Becher, accompanied by Krumey and Kasztner, visited the Bergen-Belsen and Neuengamme camps, Kasztner was supposed to visit Theresienstadt on April 16, accompanied by Krumey and Eichmann's deputy, Hauptsturmführer Hunsche. Perhaps on that morning, but probably already on April 12, Musy's son Benoit had visited the camp to effect the release of certain prisoners (see 85a, 192b). Kasztner arrived at three in the afternoon, the first free Jew allowed to see the "settlement area"; he also informed the prisoners that he was a Jew.

After the meal, Rabbi Murmelstein, the "Senior Jewish Elder" of Theresienstadt, awaited us in front of the building housing the commandant's office. He showed us the ghetto. Krumey, Hunsche and the commandant [Rahm] came along. The review began with the beauty salon. This was followed by the coffeehouse, which is still empty. The orchestra played only after 5 P.M. In the building of the Jewish Council, before the gates of which a Jewish policeman stood at attention and greeted us, Murmelstein showed us the courtroom, where the autonomous Jewish Court arraigns violations of the law. Everywhere an oppressive order and cleanliness prevailed. The Chairman of the Court [Dr. Klang], a former member of the Judicial Council from Vienna, gave a frightened greeting when the "Commission" appeared.

In his office, Murmelstein described the origins and development of Theresienstadt in an apathetic voice. He claimed that 20,500 Jews are in the ghetto at the moment [there were actually 17,543]. 350 [actually 423] Danish Jews were freed the day before through an intervention by the Swedish RC and were taken away in Swedish vehicles.

"Can I speak with Dr. Paul Eppstein?" I interrupted him. "No, you can no longer speak with him."

"Is Dr. Franz Kahn here?"

Murmelstein grew nervous.

"Which of the signatories of your letter to Budapest [see Chapter 6] is still here," I asked finally. "Dr. Leo Baeck!" [Baeck was not one of the signatories.] "Have him come here." "I can't do that." "The commandant can't have any objection to that."

"Well, you know," the commandant took over, "I don't want to interfere in this question."

We made the circuit. One after another, the kitchen, the food storehouse, the bakery, the baths, the hospital, the children's and old people's homes were shown. Everything clean. The bread, the cake, excellent. In the food storehouse, thousands of packets from the International and Swedish Red Cross, most to addressees who have meanwhile ceased to exist. Murmelstein assured us that these packets were not confiscated by the Germans but placed at the disposal of the community.

The appearance of the commission caused a great stir. Hundreds of Jews gathered around us at a respectful distance....

Dr. Leo Baeck awaited us on one corner. In between the words of greeting, I told him that all of them will be liberated in a short time and have no reason to fear the final hours. I asked him to let the rest of the camp inmates know this.

In front of the main railroad station, a 3-kilometer-long track has been directed to the middle of the ghetto. The commandant remarked that this is Jewish work. Having its own train line greatly eased things for the German administration. The ... people who were deported to Auschwitz from time to time could be loaded directly in the ghetto.

Near the fire station, Murmelstein acted out an alarm. The Jewish firemen are ready to go in 45 seconds. Wonderful how the Jews in Theresienstadt are protected from the danger of fire.

The library with its 50,000 volumes is impressive. The commandant says that there is "notably little" reading. People prefer to "hang around" on the street.

Along the way, Sturmbannführer Günther joined us.... Mr. Günther was polite. It was 16 April 1945. Still, he didn't give me his hand, just as his boss [Eichmann] never did.

A theater performance was given. On the expressionist stage, boys and girls in Czech national costume sang motifs from "The Bartered Bride" ... a wonderful baritone and a somewhat tired alto supplemented the performances.... The auditorium was full, and there was much applause.

We reached the final item on the agenda of our visit. [Kasztner, Krumey, Hunsche, and Günther are shown the Theresienstadt film from 1944, but Kasztner knows that most of the performers are no longer alive.]

Dinner was served in the hall. Günther was also there and attempted to emphasize his achievements in organizing this model ghetto. Hunsche claimed to have organized Theresienstadt's finances.

Finally Krumey delivered Himmler's order regarding the surrender [of the camp without a fight] and asked who has been charged with implementing the capitulation of Theresienstadt. Günther explained that he will do this alone and will therefore remain in Theresienstadt until the arrival of the Allies. I suggested that Red Cross delegates be involved. Krumey was also in favor of this solution.

[Kasztner demanded that Günther bring an acquaintance and told her privately] that the order to surrender the camp without a fight was delivered to the commandant today and was acknowledged by him. She should pass this news to the other camp inmates.

(135, p. 176 et seq.)

But Günther and probably Rahm as well were not by any means disposed to obey Himmler's order or keep the promises given to Dunant. They were encouraged in this by Eichmann's intransigence and Himmler's indecisive attitude. After the fall of Buchenwald, Himmler already had issued his infamous order that, because of supposed atrocities committed by former prisoners against residents of Weimar, no camps were to be surrendered; instead, the prisoners were to be evacuated or killed. Himmler was even more annoyed following the surrender of Bergen-Belsen without a

Decline and Dissolution, September 1944–May 1945

fight, and in conversation with Masur on April 20, referring to the "incidents" in these two camps, he declared that there could be no more talk of peacefully handing them over. Nevertheless, Himmler was prepared to compromise, and he promised to "release a large number of mainly Dutch Jews in Theresienstadt, listed by name, if the Red Cross can collect them." Himmler gave the number of prisoners held there at the time as 25,000; this number was too high by approximately 7,000–8,000. It is obvious that his concession was not sincere, and thus Günther might have believed he had free rein, even though on April 19, without – improbable as it seems – an express order, he announced a "second transport to Switzerland" (see also 284). In particular, this time, all the prominent figures and those who knew too much, including Murmelstein, would "take a trip" (*verreisen*). Among those chosen there was great joy. Because mail had arrived in the camp from those who had gone, it was known that the first transports had arrived safely in Switzerland. The rumor was spread that the new transport would be taken over by the Red Cross. The only cause for concern was that no waivers of participation were permitted for this transport, as had been permitted before. Suspicion grew when it was discovered that Murmelstein was not going after all; when confronted, he claimed that he could not leave the camp now and had to hold out there until the end. After this, some also declared that they did not want to go; if Murmelstein was going to hold out, they wanted to do the same. They were given to understand that this was not an option, as those who were chosen had to go. Many decided to stay in the camp and hide if necessary. Due to the rush of events, this "transport" never took place; it most likely would have ended quickly and miserably in the "Small Fortress" or in an open field. It is also claimed that these people were to be brought to a "secure location" in Tyrol as hostages. That the SS had evil intentions is evident from the fact that nothing could be said about this transport in front of Dunant during his next visit. But he had found out about it and had gotten K. H. Frank's word of honor in Prague that no transport of this or any other sort would take place.

On April 25, four days after Dunant's second visit, a "barracks construction group" was to leave the camp, supposedly for Bavaria, maybe to the Flossenbürg camp. Murmelstein objected, invoking Dunant's promise that no one else would be removed from Theresienstadt. An SS man was careless enough to reveal that the group was meant to do construction work for an interim camp at which a transport of notables was to be received prior to departure for Switzerland. Then protests were made to Rahm against both the transport to Switzerland and the "barracks construction group." He, however, forced workers to be brought before him to be chosen for this purpose. The SS ultimately planned, in case of retreat, to bring some 1,800 prisoners along to another camp; a number of freight cars arrived for this purpose on April 26. The still-empty cars were not removed until May 6. Ultimately, all these plans and orders were revoked at the end of April by Eichmann, who appeared in Theresienstadt for the last time. The SS finally had played itself out.

The camp continued to function in its normal manner in the second half of April; it continued to function for many weeks after that, but the prisoners' fear of the SS, their obedience, began to dwindle greatly. The mechanisms of the coerced community, embodied in the institutions of the "self-administration," served as a centripetal force that could be weakened, but never destroyed, by catastrophe. The people in the coerced community, through their interests and even their vital drives, functioned as a centrifugal force. The tension between these forces increased during this period and led to the camp's disintegration even before it was dismantled and could dismantle itself. Only when it was free could the conserving elements once again gain the upper hand and complete the final tasks in an orderly fashion, because, through liberation, the end of this story was achieved, and the aims of the dissolving centrifugal force were satisfied. However, before these goals were achieved, they would be anticipated in the chaotic turbulence of those days and put the camp in serious danger. During the night of April 17, a rumor suddenly spread like wildfire, and most of the prisoners believed it: "The war is over, we're free!" People were seized by wild rapture, and anyone who was able ran out onto the street, where there was great excitement. The incident ultimately ended safely with an address by Rahm, in which he cautiously chose a middle way between reassuring and intimidating words, and everyone escaped without punishment.

On April 21, Dunant came to Theresienstadt for a second time and behaved with painstaking correctness and distance toward Germans and Jews equally. His report shows how he allowed himself, even at this time, to be led astray and believed that Theresienstadt had not been specially prepared for outside guests.

On the afternoon of April 21, I revisited Theresienstadt. In getting in touch with the camp commandant, I asked that the Council of Elders be assembled to hear my declaration and be ready to answer diverse questions that I needed to raise.

I shall report, as faithfully as possible, how this phase of my short stay in the ghetto went.

I made the following declaration:

The International Committee of the Red Cross has assigned me to your interests. I have literally consecrated all my time since April 6 to the execution of this mission. The government of the Protectorate has assured me that unless there is a strategic necessity, no one will be deported from the camp until its liquidation. The latter will be entrusted into the care of the International Committee in collaboration with Jewish institutions.

I appeal to you to help me in my work by continuing to handle the administration and the order of this town during this period of transition, as you have done in the past, and kept on doing under the German authority. You probably will have to welcome at Theresienstadt other compatriots from the other camps, civil prisoners, war prisoners and wounded. You should remember that, whatever the conditions of life seen here, you will find more comfort and less risk than on the evacuation paths.

At the end of this meeting, that had been held in the presence of the camp commandant and his lieutenant [Bergel] as well as an inspector of the Police Safety Commission of Prague, I informed the camp commandant that while awaiting the written confirmation I intended to visit Theresienstadt. For two hours, and without any objections from the officers and German civilians, I was able to inspect everything that had aroused my curiosity during my initial visit on April 6. From this totally uncensored view of the town buildings and annexed barracks, I can report that, as I also believed on April 6, no special staging had been prepared to receive us [sic]. The inhabitants of Theresienstadt are living there the way we had to acknowledge, all three times that we came. At this time, all Jewish contingents from other camps are directed towards Theresienstadt. Of course, they are arriving in pitiful shape....

During a previous meeting, Minister of State Frank had given his assurances that all evacuated Jews who would pass the vicinity of the Protectorate would be directed to Theresienstadt; on the same day. I was able to verify the execution of this order in Aussig, where I had gone upon leaving Theresienstadt.

(222, p. 130 et seq.)

Decline and Dissolution, September 1944–May 1945

The MdS of April 22 mentioned only one point regarding Dunant's visit:

Mr. Dunant, a member of the International Red Cross commission that visited the Jewish settlement area Theresienstadt on 6 April, arrived here again yesterday, on 21 April 1945, and at a meeting of the Council of Elders presented a statement to the senior Jewish Elder and the members of the Council of Elders.

The statement said that the Jewish Settlement Area Theresienstadt could continue to be certain of the support of the International Red Cross in every way. Mr. Dunant is charged with the constant and direct handling of all issues connected with relief to Theresienstadt.

This statement is brought to the attention of the residents of the Jewish Settlement Area Theresienstadt with the specific expectation that each one will do his best, in awareness of his responsibility for the community, to ensure the continuation and the success of the work in progress and will cooperate in upholding calm and order.

A confidential report by a Jewish SS-informer conveys noteworthy insights into the events of the last days and the prevailing mood. The report – the only surviving document of its type – which is also surprising in style, deserves note and is reproduced here, in slightly shortened form:

With the departure of the Danes, the excitement began for the Theresienstadt Ghetto.

When the news was spread that, through the medium of the Geneva Convention, the Swedish Red Cross had taken on the home transport of the Danish Jews, the mood in the ghetto was such that one might believe the liquidation of the ghetto was a question of hours. The over-optimistic in all camps packed their bags, and even among the ranks of Protectorate nationals, a great nervousness became apparent....

For the inmates of the ghetto it was a sensation that, through negotiations, the German Reich government was releasing Jews from the ghetto. The transport with the automobiles on Sunday was a sight in itself, and here it should be especially noted that the population unanimously acknowledged the generosity of the chief of the office in that he permitted those remaining behind to betake themselves to the cars. He himself was several times observed going along the column and making no objections, while the senior Jewish Elder could not do enough to consider it unseemly, which however made little impression on the population. A further special topic of talk that day was the fact that SS Obersturmführer Rahm did not punish the Jew Minich, who had been recruited for barracks construction but had failed to report for his work, and instead turned him over to the ghetto judge for trial. The Protectorate members were very surprised at this, and many moods were subdued because of it; people there would have liked it if the office was not so "generous," and it would have been an opportunity to bad-mouth the "Germans." Here it should be mentioned that certain Czech circles, as a result of the situation, cannot do enough to create an additional antagonism between themselves and members of the Reich. One hears more and more the phrase "after the war, the whole lot of you Germans will be thrown right out of the Czech lands."

The passage of the motorized formations of the German army also caused enormous commotion.... There were "rendezvous" at the children's playground.... At times one could see there personalities who would not otherwise associate with the common people. The contact counted a rotation of people up to 200 Jews per hour.

The biggest affair, however, was the "nighttime fanfare" that the ghetto had been transferred into the hands of the Red Cross....

Special Report and Contact Report
On the evening of that particular night, a great disturbance could be noted, and the street traffic was heavier than usual. Rumors about commissions, office changes, etc. sped

from group to group and from one house to another. It was barely possible to follow everything. Around ten o'clock, abrupt calm suddenly ensued when, around midnight or 1 o'clock, the cry rang out: "The ghetto is free, the commission has taken it over, we are protected by the Geneva Convention," This was, of course, something that resembled wildfire. In the Dresden Kaserne ... women appeared in some rooms with supposed copies of the protocol they claimed to have gotten from the Office of the senior Jewish Elder through an indiscretion. In all cases, it was women ... and the instances were fabricated the same way in the Hanover and Hamburger [Barracks] as in the Dresdener. Now it began. Women brought the sensational news to their husbands and vice versa. To find out how much of this was true, people tried to reach Dr. Murmelstein, who also had been informed of the events at this time. He strongly denied that any negotiations were taking place with the "Red Cross," let alone that any changes or relief were to be expected (?!!!!?). At this time ... Rahm was already on his way to the barracks on Hauptstrasse [L 4], where the situation would reach a dramatic climax.

Contacts who live there freely declared that no one at first gave themselves or the Jews even the slightest chance. Only when the chief of the Office had people form a square and began his address with "Gentlemen" was the spell broken, and today, as immediately at the time, it was said, "The Chief of the Office was terrific; in contrast to the Jewish representatives, he reassured us and people are (literally) grateful for the way the situation was resolved." It is however to be noted that the people who live in the barracks are mainly from the most recent Reich and Prague transports and are mainly married to Aryans. To conclude the matter, it should be noted: "SS-Obersturmführer Rahm is the man of the ghetto, and it will be very regrettable if there is a change in command." ...

And now to turn everything on its head, two days after the "restless night," there appeared a Council of Elders announcement on the personal negotiations with Mr. Dunant of the Red Cross. It is simply indescribable what has been happening here since that time, "what the Red Cross is going to do." ... He has unlimited authority from the Swiss Red Cross and he is partly in charge of determining the situation of the ghetto population. Theresienstadt has apparently been declared "extraterritorial" and ... in an accord between the neutral powers and the German Reich government Rahm has been appointed to uphold order, etc. and at the same time representative (diplomatic) to the rank of a General Consul for the German Reich government. It is an established fact that people are fully protected, even if the pessimists state that the reduction in the bread ration is not a good introduction to care by the Swiss Red Cross. (!!) [The rations were reduced to 700 g for four days; 220 g of potatoes were provided per meal.] The 600 departures to Switzerland that were supposed to take place interested mainly those affected, through the general situation created....

The individuals who were on the list, especially the notables, strove to appear reassuring in all cases and especially [the Czech member of the Council of Elders] Mr. [Alfred] Meissner always called only for calm and order.

As a consequence of the newly arrived transports, general unrest overcame the ghetto like a wave. Now a new "homo species" of Polish Jews appeared in the ghetto. Frankly speaking, no one was happy about their arrival, for the introduction was not good and great fear prevailed, especially among the older people, if the "KZ"-ers should come out of quarantine. Sturdy walking sticks are very much in demand. People are also afraid that rations will be reduced again. There have been enough examples that the people are not very pleasant, and the call for security is becoming louder, for some people have already succeeded in escaping from quarantine and hang around the kitchens begging, until they are detained.

The smokers are glad that the prohibition on smoking has ended. The prices of cigarettes have fallen rapidly as a result of the fact that, with the Hungary transports,

Decline and Dissolution, September 1944–May 1945

amounts up to 50 could be taken along. The spot price is 10 cigarettes for an S bread [1,500 g], which is 20 Marks; while until now, three would be traded for a "K" bread [1,000 g].

The latest news that just (Friday [April 27]) rushed through the ghetto: "Through the agency and at the behest of the Geneva Convention, the office head is to remain until the complete liquidation of the ghetto, for security reasons." ...

In general, people here expect an end to the war very soon and await what is to come any hour.

(285)

Nothing can convey a clearer picture of the general breakdown in the final weeks than this primitive and crude report. The SS's uncertainty, the typical feeling of doom, the wildly overheated and in some cases all but ludicrous rumors, the difficult situation of the weak Jewish leadership, the great anxiety, and the extreme unkindness could hardly be more harshly illuminated. The seriousness and devotion of the forces for good – whose effectiveness was more hidden, but of which there was no lack – is not expressed here and could not be expected to be. The informer's report mentions the pitiable evacuees – 13,500 to 15,000 abased souls – who, lost at the lowest level of humanity, arrived in Theresienstadt on April 20 after endless journeys and starvation marches (see Chapter 3). Creatures came from almost all the countries of Europe, and there were also non-Jews among them. Among them there were a few dozen criminals who had been locked in the camps with the other victims, generally to menace the other prisoners and as helpers to the SS. Here and there were some who had once been deported from there to Auschwitz. Now they were deformed strangers; mothers no longer recognized their sons.

It is not necessary to depict these people; they have often, I think all too often, been described, through the horror of their outward appearance. Doing so grips only once but soon instills only disgust and loathing, and then one ignores what is essential and what will continue to be a moral problem for humanity in the future. Thus the world knows, in words and images, how these abased people were ravaged, and at this point the Jews of Theresienstadt also had to know of it. The illusion of the "ghetto" had come to an end.

There was a desire to isolate the new arrivals; in fact this had to be done, for they were a health risk to the inmates. In a few hours, barracks C III and H V were emptied. But soon this was not enough; no one knew what to do with the unfortunates. For many reasons – not hardheartedness – proper quarters were lacking, for these lice-ridden people could not be left in the existing accommodations. Certainly, the Theresienstadters should have immediately voluntarily cleared their rooms and moved in together, but we must not forget how many old, frail people lived there, and in addition, people were so stunned and paralyzed that much was neglected. The best nourishment that Theresienstadt could offer held dangers for the starving people and could not have been enough in amount or quality. Even honest efforts to help were not enough; there was a lack of means and quantity. Thus these weak and submissive people were left to camp in the open. They were to be brought to mine tunnels, but they shudderingly refused. As they knew the whole truth, after their experiences, they did not want to die from poison gas a few hours before liberation. Only with an effort was it possible to convince them of the "harmlessness" of the tunnels and the "harmlessness" of the camp. It was equally difficult to get them to enter the bath and the disinfection facility. Baths were murder to them – they refused, and cried "Gas!" (see 209b).

On April 24, typhoid fever was found for the first time among the newcomers. Soon a hundred cases were diagnosed; the number ultimately grew to well over two thousand, and the natives were not spared. The transports of misery had already brought 400 dead to the camp, where death from exhaustion and disease continued, above all from typhoid fever, although it was possible to keep the death rate from this infection under 25%. Many volunteer helpers were infected, and some could not be saved (see Chapter 16).

No regime mattered now, not even a camp regime; these degraded ones were no longer willing to accept it. How must the "paradise ghetto" have seemed to them? When a human being stands at an end that surrounds him like an implacable abyss – where empty despair is coupled now with apathy, now with furious aggressiveness – who would still conjure there a minimum of discipline and order, even if only to an extent that would have served the good of the unfortunates? How childish and futile must this endeavor have seemed! These people no longer believed; they believed nothing and no one. They no longer believed in themselves. Everything was obliterated, everything devalued. For them there were no more friends, not a breath of human warmth. It was the end, but it was an end different from the illusion of Theresienstadt in which the gullible and trusting had been led to believe. It was the end: the end as doom, as Armageddon – as *nothing*. And there was no more substance. If one did not experience this annihilation oneself, one cannot know, will never know, what it was like. One must be silent. One must listen and examine one's role for oneself and as a human being in the world. But anyone who went through this final despair, this night of nights, this nameless doom – who survived it and attained new life, who once again *is* and has regained his name, which was stolen from him – he should raise his voice and say what it was really like. He should proclaim the reality, beyond the aura of genuine but offended (and therefore not entirely genuine) heroism, beyond the sharp antagonism between the white innocence of the victims and the black guilt of the persecutor, and beyond all the theatrical horror of living decay and dead mountains of bones, which reveal none of the inner truth, for they are merely stigmas, not the truth itself. No, it is necessary to name the reality that a living soul can put up with in such a probing eradication (*Zernichtung*) – separated from any loneliness and any community – the reality of *nothingness*, which is neither imaginable nor comprehensible, for not thinking and not feeling is nothingness. That which has not been created will suffer in the final guilt of the world, where plain *nothingness* figures as the meaning of life in the deepest dungeon of consciousness, in which all form, as the writer of Ecclesiastes understood, becomes a mere conceit. He, the crushed one (*Zerstossene*), has contemplated this reality, the reality of vanity, in which no value, no being still exists, in which nevertheless an unknown, mysterious force continues to act deep in the unconscious stream of life and tries to assert itself, although it is still capable only of acquiescence, which seeks to wrest the substance of Something from the improbable Nothing.

What must happen so that this end, which was Nothing, can still be followed by a beginning that would be Something? Only a few of the survivors, and even fewer of their contemporaries, have answered this. However, as long as this riddle is not satisfactorily solved, this essential question continues to exist for us and all posterity.

How the lost ones in Theresienstadt were seen in those desolate days is made clear by the words of an eyewitness:

In the course of the night two more transports arrive. Yes, evacuees from harsh concentration camps. They are no longer people, they are wild animals. Animals who have not had anything to eat for weeks. Animals into which the German commandant shoots, in vain. His pistol has only 8 bullets. These starving animals know this. [There was no shooting; the report is characterizing a psychological state.] Fear claws at my heart; there is no room, so much food cannot be cooked at one time. These animals knock each other down over a cube of sugar. Sugar? Really sugar? For three years they have known only gas chambers, flaming chimneys, shooting, whipping. Many collapse from exhaustion. We segregated a transport. Typhoid fever. We try in vain to maintain a chain – clean little girls from the Dutch youth cadre with their white kerchiefs – against this wild horde. They race around them, they trample over them. Some of these beasts sit stolidly on the ground. They react only to food. One cannot recognize their features under the dirt and neglect. These greedy features of dull human animals. It is too horrible, one cannot describe it. And one cannot help. We hold the chain. It is impossible to maintain any organization, any type of order.... New transports. People who have been traveling for four weeks. We hold the chain. Our hands shake and we clench them tightly together. We hold together. We hold the chain. We take handcarts and bring those who have collapsed to the labyrinth. We house the people in old mine tunnels. It starts to rain, miserable, unmistakable. Then it's back to foraging [*stöbern*]. A transport in open cars. Traveling for 17 days. Two raw potatoes, a thin slice of bread. Rapacious animals. Ragged, starving, sick. For seven days and nights we are outside almost without pause; new transports arrive constantly. We can't keep up with the accommodations. We stand on the South Mountain and try to kindle an open fire, to roast potatoes. We go home by turns for an hour or two. Go back again. Carry the dying to the hospital on stretchers. And can't keep up.... These nights kill me. I signed up for night shift at the bath. The wild animals are slowly becoming human again; a few days of suitable fare in a heated room and with medical attention. At the bath they receive clothing. And we get ten dekas [100 g] of bread and ten dekas of sausage.... I wrapped these doddering creatures in old clothes. I stand in smoke and steam in nauseating air.

(256)

An American press officer who visited Theresienstadt around May 10 conveys an impression of how the segregated newcomers found their situation and how they felt mistreated by the residents:

> When I went through the dim overcrowded little rooms, some of the survivors who were still clear enough to realize that an American was there threw themselves at me and cried, "Look what they've done with us! Our own Jews! They treat us worse than the Germans in Buchenwald!"

(172, p. 271)

Such generalized judgments certainly missed the truth and must, in their harshness, be refuted, which does not in the least excuse the failure of many Theresienstadters. The fact that such harsh judgments could be made is enough to recognize the entanglement and the confusion into which friend and foe alike sank. Only when we fully recognize this distress, in which the face of the coerced community revealed itself, do we learn to grasp the wisdom lying in the sentence that everything can be understood and everything forgiven (see also 20a, 40b, 69, 181a, 219a, 224c, 234a, 349c).

After Dunant's second visit, anxious days followed in Theresienstadt, but by May 2, when the man from Switzerland arrived again, after a short interim visit, there was at least no more danger to the camp from the creatures of the RSHA. Dunant reported:

After having spent the entire day of April 30 at Theresienstadt, I installed myself there on the 2nd of May. On May 10, I left, having completed my mission.

Despite the decision of the government of the Protectorate to place Theresienstadt ... under the sole authority of the CICR, on May 5th, it had, in fact, already been done on May 2nd. The commandants of the two jails turned all their authority over to me.

Contrary to my fears ... no one had run away from Theresienstadt.

On the other hand, the transfer of 300 persons (notables within the ghetto) into more secure housing, as intended by the authority of the Reich, did not occur. Frank had kept his word. It is also on his instructions, and complying with his commitments, that 12,863 Jews from other concentration camps were sent to Theresienstadt during the month of April.

With the exception of the gardener used by the Germans, who was killed by a German gun, and a Jewish inmate [*interne*], killed in his bed by a Russian bullet, no one died a violent death at Theresienstadt.

(228, p. 132)

Dunant had thus taken over the protection of the "ghetto" and the "Small Fortress" (see 294b). Although the SS still killed prisoners in the "Small Fortress" after Dunant's arrival, Rahm and his subordinates abided by the agreement. On May 3, the SS turned over barracks E 1, to which, from the next day on, the prisoners from the "Small Fortress" were transferred. On May 4, functionaries from the Czech Red Cross and a group of Czech doctors were admitted; they cared mainly for the prisoners from the "Small Fortress," but toward the Jews, especially if they were not Czechoslovaks, they behaved in anything but a friendly manner, and sometimes not even decently.

On May 5, the SS withdrew from Theresienstadt. Rahm was the last to leave his post, in the evening, after calling Murmelstein in for a talk. On that day, too, Murmelstein ended his role as senior Jewish Elder. Rahm was seen in the camp, unarmed, on the morning of May 6, before he fled. The internal leadership fell to the members of what had been the Council of Elders. Leo Baeck was at its head. On May 6, they issued an appeal that, for the first time, was published in two languages, German and Czech:

Men and Women of Theresienstadt!

The International Committee of the Red Cross has taken over the protection of Theresienstadt. The representative of this Committee, Mr. Dunant, has the right to lead Theresienstadt. He has charged the undersigned members of the former Council of Elders with the leadership of the self-administration.

You are safe in Theresienstadt! The war is not yet over! Anyone who leaves Theresienstadt exposes himself to all the risks of war.

Theresienstadt has taken on the care of the martyrs in the Small Fortress. This requires increased work, which is necessary to prepare the transport back. Work must continue.

Mail is now permitted in any language without censorship or other restrictions. To initiate this mail service, each inhabitant of Theresienstadt who so wishes will receive a stamped postcard, as soon as a sufficient number becomes available.

Newspapers will be obtained and publicly posted. The serious illnesses that currently prevail here make necessary strict adherence to the quarantine rules. Therefore, please adhere to them to the letter!

When the war ends, return transports will begin as quickly as possible and will be carried out according to regulations to be issued by the government.

Maintain calm and order! Help us with the work that will make your return journeys possible! Carry out the work assigned to each one at your workplace!

Dr. Leo Baeck, Dr. Alfred Meissner, Dr. Heinrich Klang, Dr. Eduard Meijers

Theresienstadt, 6 May 1945

In the overall chaos, people behaved in very contradictory ways. Some, with the acquiescence of the Czech gendarmerie, took off during the first days of May, at night or even in broad daylight. The SS limited itself to threats, but after May 3 took no action against escapees. Even before the SS withdrew from the camp, Christians came to the camp to pick up their Jewish relatives. Others, who were aware of their duties or did not know where to go, remained, particularly old people and foreigners. The daily routine of camp life, in addition, was so rigid that it continued almost automatically, even months after liberation. Even in freedom, many people still had to reaccustom themselves to a form of society healthier than that of the "ghetto." Many announcements from the months of May through August differ neither in content nor in style from the conventions and expressions of the long years of the camp. Only the "Jewish star" immediately disappeared.

The final days before ultimate liberation were eventful and agitated. On May 5, a Czechoslovak flag had already been hoisted on the building of the camp post office (L 414). It had to be removed; Dunant wisely ordered this, but it was misunderstood and resented by the Czech Jews. By May 6, the SS flag no longer flew over the city hall, the seat of the SS "office"; instead, it had been replaced by the flag of the Red Cross. At least some of the SS personnel seem to have remained in the town, although they stayed outside the camp area in the park in front of the "*Kameradschafts* house"; the camp now was run exclusively by the internal administration, under Dunant's direction. Power over the health sector was largely transferred to the Czech doctors' commission, which, however, was led, before and after liberation, by Dr. Aron Vedder, the Jewish specialist on spotted fever (*Fleckfieber*) (see 330c). On May 6, too, for the last time, a large number of prisoners were taken in; they were in particularly pitiable condition. Dunant had discovered these 1,800 men and 180 young people in three trains at train stations in the area. Finally, another 600 prisoners of war, citizens of Western nations, were housed in Theresienstadt. They were healthy people who imposed no additional burden on the camp. On May 7, from the balcony of the city hall, in French and German, Dunant proclaimed Germany's unconditional surrender.

On May 8, Theresienstadt found itself in the immediate war zone; German military and armed SS groups, which did not belong to the teams in the two Theresienstadt camps, prowled near the town and repeatedly crossed through it, although they did not penetrate the actual area of the camp but passed back and forth toward Prague or Leitmeritz [Litoměřice], remaining on the "bypass road." The self-administration published a warning that, due to fighting in the immediate neighborhood, walking the streets was permitted only for official business. Standing in doorways or by windows also was forbidden. Children were not allowed out. At the sound of weapons fire, people were to go to the cellars, and open flames were to be avoided. In the early morning hours, the western side of the hospital in E VI was shelled by the Germans. Around 7 P.M., a Russian grenade landed near the builder's yard of building Q 704, which was damaged. An elderly Austrian colonel was taken from the ruins dead, and a Dutch general was badly injured; he died several days later of his wounds. There was further shelling, and the last heavy German tanks fled in the direction of Prague. Around 9 P.M., the first Russian tank rolled through the town, greeted with cheers by the liberated. It did not stay but continued its journey to Prague, followed by many others. The Russians entered the camp itself in the early morning hours of May 9 (see 112a).

We run out to greet them; the Russians throw us cigarettes, tobacco, bread and sugar. English and French prisoners of war come to us in the camp. Brotherly love! Wilder than ever, and talking in every language at once, there is no more blackout, in the evening the town is brightly lit, fires burn everywhere, we sit around, laugh, drink, sing. We ride out on Russian tanks to the big road, on which the beaten German Wehrmacht trudges to prison camps. We confiscate supply vehicles, drink real bean coffee and eat chocolate. We buy directly from wholesalers, boots in a German leather factory.... We go to the small town that is only a few kilometers away [Leitmeritz (Litoměřice)], and ride back on bicycles or horses. But the world is so empty and the future before us bleak. I just want to sleep. Otherwise nothing else.

(256)

On May 10, Dunant transferred command of the camp to a Russian officer; the responsibilities of the self-administration passed to engineer Georg Vogel, a Prague Communist who had been in the camp since 1941 and had been a member of the first Council of Elders. On May 13, Major M. A. Kusmin, the Russian commander, held his first public muster. Vogel translated the address. All the functionaries, down to the room elders, who had put themselves at the service of the camp received salaries.

The liquidation continued into November, when the last men left the city, after finishing the cleanup work (see 261). Administratively, the dissolution lasted much longer (see 209d). Repatriation took months and proved to be difficult, especially for some German Jews. Before May 10, when the Czech repatriation commission began working in Theresienstadt, some 1,000 mainly Czech Jews left the town; between May 10 and May 14, some 3,000 people left, generally using privately obtained means of transport. On that day, because of the outbreak of typhoid fever that was beginning to spread to surrounding villages, the Russians imposed a strict quarantine. On May 14 there were 25,301 people in the camp (not including the former prisoners from the "Small Fortress"), including 1,897 children under fifteen years of age. On May 12 or 13 the Russians directed a health group to the camp; it achieved extraordinary results and pleasantly distinguished itself from many Czech aides in its goodwill toward the Theresienstadters. On May 24, the Czech repatriation commission was able to begin its work again, and, when the quarantine was relaxed on May 28, departures resumed. Some 300 people had run away in the two weeks of the strict quarantine. In addition to the Czech authorities, a French repatriation commission and the American Joint Distribution Committee from Budapest were active in Theresienstadt, while the Russians who had been sent to the camp were taken care of by the Red Army. On June 30 there still were 5,952 inmates in Theresienstadt. The Berliners had to wait the longest for transports home; their turn did not come until August 8. At the orders of the Czech authorities, repatriation had to end on August 17, 1945. Around 700 German and Austrian Jews wished to travel to their relatives abroad; they were taken on by the Americans in Pilsen [Plsen] and were brought to the interim camp Winzern, near Deggendorf in Lower Bavaria (see 46a, 52b, 271), where they were to await further travel documents. Some 500 Polish Jews who wanted to join their relatives in Palestine also were taken by the Americans in Pilsen [Plsen]. Approximately 1,000 lone children were sent to England, and in some cases to other countries, with the help of Jewish institutions (see 50a, 224c).

The liberation of Theresienstadt did not end the misery in that place. This was true not only for the former prisoners, whose suffering certainly was not finished with the recovery of outward freedom, but also for new prisoners, whose misery was just beginning. Germans from the country and Reich German refugees were brought to the "Small Fortress." Certainly, there were some among them who had done bad things during the years of occupation, but the majority, including many children and adolescents, were imprisoned only because they were German. Only because they were German ... ? The sentence is horribly familiar; one might simply have exchanged the word "Jew" for "German." The rags with which the Germans were wrapped were smeared with swastikas. The people were miserably fed and mistreated, and they had it no better than had been the norm in German concentration camps. The difference consisted solely in the fact that the heartless revenge at work here lacked the large-scale extermination system on which SS actions were based. The camp was under Czech administration, but this did not prevent the Russians from raping imprisoned women. To the credit of the Theresienstadt Jews, it should be said that none of the old prisoners assaulted these prisoners – who were sent to the town to sweep the streets and perform other dirty work as well as to care for typhoid patients – although the Russians and Czechs encouraged them to do so (see 69, 243e). The number of prisoners varied and probably never exceeded 3,000. Only a few were tried and convicted of crimes; many were killed or perished in the camp. Some were released after decent Czechs made the effort to intervene, and the courageous Czech humanitarian Přemysl Pitter was able to rescue many children (see 60a). Most of the prisoners were deported as part of the mass expulsion of Germans from Czechoslovakia to Germany. The camp was closed down probably toward the end of 1946 (see 321).

We have come to the end of the story. The town remained deserted for only a short time. Perhaps it should have been left so. How could people still live on these horrible sites of doom? Nothing should have stood there; the camp should have been left to the Nothing that had taken hold there. But that is not what happened. At first, in early fall 1945, the Czech military moved into a barracks, and a year later, the first civilians followed, former residents of the town. Vehicles no longer avoided the place by taking the "bypass road" but used the old road once again. The national Prague-Leitmeritz [Litoměřice] bus line soon stopped in front of a newly opened store. The texture of this meager little town, painfully violated by the coerced community, was transformed. Soon the courtyard walls that had been torn down stood again. In 1947, Theresienstadt was an inhabited town; the "ghetto" was gone, but its traces were far from being erased everywhere. Nor will they disappear very soon, but who will notice them, today or tomorrow? It is one more site of suffering for Jewish history to remember, a history that has so infinitely much to tell about the persecution of human beings by human beings. Although people neglected to erect a place to commemorate the "ghetto," or at least to keep one house in the condition it was in during the camp period, in 1956 a dignified memorial to the dead was placed on the cemetery grounds of the Bohušovice Kessel, with an inscription in Hebrew and Czech.

Approximately 155,000 Jews lived and suffered in Theresienstadt from November 24, 1941, until the day of liberation on May 8, 1945, in a coerced community of a type that no one ever before had been asked to endure.

PART II

SOCIOLOGY

As long as we do not also consider to be just the injustice that is happening to us and that presses from us the cooling burning tears, we still are trapped in thickest darkness without a glimmer of light.

Rahel Levin-Varnhagen (1799)

8

Administration

On August 10, 1944, the "Central Secretariat" published an "organizational plan" listing all administrative subdivisions by their official titles as of July 1, 1944. The lack of internal organization had been replaced by a flood of unprecedented, inflated bureaucracy. The plan set out in minute detail the camp's external structures, the development of which we already have analyzed. This "organizational plan" seems to be designed for an almost normal society, a powerful state, rather than for a concentration camp. Formalities compensated for the lack of structure; a giant mechanistic diagram took the place of the life that was lacking. The list was merely names and definitions without concrete reality, concealing an enormous nothingness.

The pathological energies that controlled the camp constructed a distorted image of a kind of order, the confusing structure of which was modeled on the gas chamber. Human beings and human structures seem doubtful and endangered today, even in normal countries, but there they were treated entirely impersonally. Institutions no longer were subject to the standards associated with healthy existence. In fact, they were torn nearly out of existence itself, while at the same time their function was inflated, as if to demonstrate the madness of a super-administration emptied of life, resembling a gigantic factory, created to deal with a "faceless mass" – to categorize it a hundred times over, record its statistics, nourish it with calories, and so on – but entirely removed from anything human. Humans were no longer human, and their business was no longer human business; there was nothing anywhere but a faceless mass. But human beings are incalculable and will avenge themselves against this process, because in reality they cannot be reduced to a mere faceless mass. In this way, the stage is set for the chaos that humans strive to escape. Outside the boundaries of such a camp they may partly succeed. Here, however, it led to self-destruction, to annihilation in gas chambers, to nothingness.

The "organizational plan" (278) is a monstrous document that delineates the administrative scheme of the camp, with all its offices, operations, departments, and so on. Its purpose was to clarify the hierarchy of all institutions, known as departments, that were subject to the authority of the central offices. Together, they formed a "self-administration" that resembled government:

182 *Sociology*

Leadership
Labor Central
Department of Internal Administration
Economics Department
Technical Department
Finance Department
Health Services and Welfare
Youth Welfare
Recreation

OVERVIEW OF THE ADMINISTRATIVE STRUCTURE

Leadership

The "leadership" was comparable to both a cabinet and a president's office. It was headed by a senior "Jewish Elder" and two "deputy Jewish Elders." Immediately subordinate to them were the following departments:

Community police
Detective Department
Fire brigade and air defense
Office of Economic Supervision
Central Registry
Jewish self-administration bank
Central Secretariat (the actual president's office)

The first four departments listed above formed the camp's security services.

Central Registry
The Central Registry was a complicated residency registration office that recorded important personal data, including the "transport numbers" of everyone ever "received into the ghetto." It kept lists of all arriving and departing transports (more about the activities of this office can be found in Chapters 9 and 10). The Central Registry was structured as follows:

Central index (a registry of inmates)
Family index (a registry of family relationships)
Transport registry (the "transport lists")
Statistics
Central Status Office (charged with creating a day-to-day record of the number of inmates)
External registry (a registry composed of four "district registries" and nine "building registries")
Registration Office (charged with maintaining an overview of transfers, deaths, etc.)
Research service (charged with providing information about inmates for offices and prisoners)

Administration 183

Jewish Self-Administration Bank
The Jewish self-administration bank served the SS as a propaganda showpiece. Its main task was to process all wage and payment lists submitted by the "departments" or house elders, as well as payment of the amounts due (see Chapters 5, 13, and 14). The Jewish self-administration was structured as follows:

Bank manager
Correspondence
Cashier
Accounting Office
Bank Advisory Board (!)
Board of Directors (!)

Central Secretariat
The Central Secretariat was the executive body of the Jewish Elders. All other "departments" as well as the remaining "subdepartments" of the "leadership" were subordinate to it; internally, however, they were independent and had their own leaders, who were answerable to the Jewish Elder. The Central Secretariat was structured as follows:

Office of the Central Secretariat
    Central Receiving Office
    Duplications Office
    Central Archive for Statistics
    Complaints Office
Personnel Office
Transport Department (which determined the deportees; see Chapter 9)
Tariff Commission
Department of Special Tasks
Family Research Department
Book Registration Group (Bucherfassungsgruppe; see Chapter 19)

The "Office of the Central Secretariat" was the camp's nerve center. All official requests to the Jewish Elder and the Council of Elders were addressed to the "Central Receiving Office." The "Duplications Office" took care of the "orders of the day" as well as "memoranda" and forms for all the "departments" (using a Gestetner process). The "Complaints Office" accepted verbal and written complaints; several complaint boxes were set up in the camp. This office was intended to serve as a "lightning rod" for the leadership; it was not of any serious importance.

While the "Central Secretariat" managed the camp, the "Personnel Office" was the main office for those holding systematized positions, known as "personnel" or "staff of the self-administration," in contrast to all other employees, known as "deployment" (*Einsatz*). A distinction was made between "regular workers," which included permanent employees of the various "departments," and "mobile groups," which were subdivided into "regular groups" (*Ständiger Einsatz*) (those employed in specific jobs) and "squadrons" (*Hundertschaften*) (workers with varying jobs). One could become a member of "personnel" only upon approval by the Personnel Office and a "regular worker" only upon approval by the Central Employment Office (see also Chapters 13 and 15).

The "Tariff Commission" determined the value of the "voucher" (*Bezugscheine*) (if I am informed correctly; see also Chapters 5 and 14.) The term "family research" referred to the administration of all circumcision registries; an official of the Reichsvereinigung who had already been in charge of this in Berlin continued this work in the camp.

Labor Central

The Central Labor Office was structured as follows:

Management
Registration of workers (or) labor index
Male deployment
Female deployment
Youth deployment
Labor supervision
Labor welfare
Productivity registry
Medical Supervision and Examination Office (doctors' offices; see Chapter 13)
Deployment offices

Management

The management of the "Central Labor Office" was in charge of the complicated structure of this extensive department and had to master the nearly impossible problem of finding and utilizing workers. It was structured as follows:

Administrative Office
Organization
Planning
Statistics
Personnel registry (for employees of the "Central Labor Office")
Auditing

Labor Index; Male, Female, and Youth Deployment; and Labor Supervision

The labor index kept a registry of everyone able to work. The Male Deployment and Female Deployment Departments (with divisions for "regular" and "mobile" deployment), as well as the Youth Deployment Department, directed the use of available workers. The Labor Supervision Office oversaw adherence to labor regulations (see Chapter 13); its "divisions" were as follows:

Operations control
Deployment control (control of the workers, roundups, etc.)
Business Inspection Office
Evaluation Office for Special Remuneration
Industrial accidents
Aptitude tests (psychological tests and graphology evaluations)

Administration 185

Labor Welfare
The Labor Welfare Office was the welfare office for all workers. It had its own experts on each "deployment sector." The "Labor Welfare Office" distributed the so-called *Dekaden*, food stamps provided on a continual basis to all employees. One could apply to this office for additional food stamps, certificates for "special vouchers," or "mending certificates" for clothes, undergarments, shoes, and so on; this office also provided applications for better accommodations. One could receive additional allowances for use of the "central laundry facilities" and tickets for the "Central Bath"; tickets or reservations for offerings from the office for "recreation" were also available. Workers who had fallen ill received "sick benefits" instead of *Dekaden*. The "Central Labor Office" had one "storehouse" for food supplies (see Chapter 12), which supplied the *Dekaden*, "sick benefits," and special allocations. The structure of the "Labor Welfare Office" was as follows:

Applications Office
Procurement and Allocations Office
   Nutrition
   Clothing and equipment
   Accommodations
   Hygiene (orders for the laundry facility and bath tickets)
   Recreation
   Welfare for sick workers
Workers' Advice and Complaints Office
Supply room

Productivity Registry
The productivity registry was structured as follows:

Productivity records (an overview of workers' performance)
Status reports (daily workers' attendance lists)
Wage calculation (for fictitious remuneration in "ghetto crowns")

Deployment Offices
The deployment offices (six for adults and one for youth) were satellite offices of the "Central Labor Office." They maintained contact with the workers and directed the workers in "mobile" units, particularly the "squadrons," each of which were subdivided into two "convoys" and ten "comradeships."

Department of Internal Administration

The Department of Internal Administration was comparable to a ministry of the interior. Its structure was as follows:

Leadership
Legal Department (see Chapter 15)
Space Management Office (see especially Chapter 11)
Building Management Office (see especially Chapter 11)
Registry Office and Funeral Department (see also Chapters 15 and 16)
Post office and Transport Management Department (see also Chapters 4, 5, and 18)

Leadership

The leadership was structured as follows:

Leadership Office
Intake Office
Personnel registry
Personnel files
Deployment files
Wage accounting

Legal Department

The Legal Department was structured as follows:

Criminal justice section
Criminal court (previously the "ghetto court," a trial court)
Criminal appeals court (an appeals court)
Labor court (a trial court)
Labor criminal court (an appeals court)
Disciplinary court (for "personnel")
VVV chamber ("court, chamber for supply [*versorgung*] violations")
Mediation offices (a substitute for the nonexistent civil court)
Probate court section
Inventory
External services
Probate administrator
Office of Custody Issues (guardianships)

Space Management Office

The Space Management Office was structured as follows:

Central Office
Accommodations offices
Mattress section

The "Central Office" of the "Space Management Office" was further subdivided as follows:

Administration
City settlement
Habitability of rooms
Section for storage and production sites (inventory issues)
Section for buildings located outside the city (such as the "clothing warehouse")
Section for preferential housing ("VIPs"; see Chapters 10 and 11)
Occupancy registry (an overview of housing occupants)
Statistical graphs
Index of occupancy status
Building catalogue (an overview of all buildings)
Inspection
Technical section (determining condition of housing)
Department of Resettlement (mass and individual resettlement)

The accommodations offices (*Ubikationskanzleien*) were subdivisions of the "Space Management Office." There were four "district accommodations offices" and twelve "accommodations offices" in buildings and barracks colonies. This included the "mattress section," which oversaw the Central Mattress Warehouse and mattress production (repairs)

Building Management Office

The building administration was both landlord of all buildings and accommodations and the disciplinary authority for all inmates. Prisoners therefore had to deal with this bureaucracy on a daily basis. It was structured as follows:

Central Office
  Complaints Office
Security and Order Service (SOD) (a subordinate police formation in charge of traffic regulation at the barracks gates, keeping order during food distribution, guarding "stores" [*Verschleißstellen*], etc.)
Cleaning service (*Reinigungsdienst* [RD])
  Seven RD subdivisions (divided into branches, which included "cleaning crews" for staircases, offices, etc., but generally not for the quarters)
Rationing service (*Menagedienst* [MD]) (see Chapter 12)
  Central Ration Card Office
  Twelve MD subdivisions (these offices monitored "ration cards" [*Essenkarten*] at food-distribution points)
Kitchens (in almost every building; see Chapter 12)
Aides for the sick and infirm (charged with supervision of food deliveries, etc.)
Kitchen complaints offices (see Chapter 12)
District organizations (branch offices of the "Building Management Office")
  Four district organizations (with one "district elder" each)
  Ten building elders (for eight barracks and two barracks colonies)
  One administrator (for the "clothing warehouse"– the "house elders" reported to the "group elders," who reported to the "district elders")
Room orderlies (servants for the quarters of high functionaries)
Laundry rooms (a few here and there; they were not important)

Registry Office and Funeral Department

Before a rabbinical office was established in December 1944, its function was fulfilled by the "Registry Office" (responsible for ritual weddings, "declarations of marriage," and a registry of births and deaths; for a limited period of time it was authorized to issue death certificates). Deaths were announced by public notice, except on the Sabbath, giving information such as the name, year of birth, and "transport number" of the deceased and the time of the ritual ceremony (usually at 9:00 A.M. and 9:30 A.M. for Jews and at 10:00 A.M. for Christians). This "subdivision" was structured as follows:

Central Office
  Funeral services
  Coroner's Office

Pallbearers (charged with transporting the deceased to the "Central Mortuary")
Funeral team (unofficial *Chevra kadisha*)
Central Mortuary
Funeral sites (crematoria and urn sites)
Registry Office
  Catalogue
  Registry

Post Office and Transport Management Department
The post office was structured as follows:

Central Office
Letters
  Mail registry (regarding the "writing rotation" and its utilization)
  Mail censorship (by Jewish "censors")
  Mail delivery
Packages
  Train station service (package pickup)
  Package administration (receipt of packages)
  Package delivery
  Collection point (storehouse)
  Mail authorizations (*Postvollmachten*)
  Research (charged with verifying addresses in the "Central Registry")
  Appeals Office

The "Transport Management Department" must not be confused with the "Transport Department" in the "Central Secretariat." Even though most of the work of the "Transport Management Department" related to transports, the "Transport Department" determined the victims of the transports. The "Transport Management Department" transported private possessions, whereas the "Shipping Department" (part of the "Economics Department") transported public goods inside the camp. The following list illustrates the "Transport Management Department's" areas of responsibility.

Central Office
Department of Special Tasks
Registry and inspection
Resettlement (including transports)
  Resettlement of individuals
  Mass resettlement
  Transport crew for decedents' property
  Central collection point for luggage (especially during transports)
Transport of luggage and other movable goods
  Four district branches
  Six branch offices
Transfer for disinfection procedures (transport to and from the disinfection site)
  Storage rooms (for storing luggage during "disinfection")

Economics Department

The Economics Department was structured as follows:

Management
Central Supply Office
Central materials and inventory administration
Manufacturing Department (Produktion)
Agriculture Department
Warehousing and Businesses Department
Shipping Department

Management
The management of the Economics Department was structured as follows:

Management Office
Personnel registry
Accounting and records
Supervisory group (plants inspection)
Security group (an internal police force and warehouse guards)

Central Supply Office
The Central Supply Office was structured as follows (see especially Chapter 12):

Office
Central apportionment (determination of rations, etc.)
Central allocation (allocation of food supplies to the kitchens, etc.)
Distribution
    Nine distribution points (called *Provianturen*; they supplied bread and other
       rations to the prisoners)
Delivery (delivery of food supplies and meals)
    Ration transport crews (delivery of prepared foods to buildings)
Potato section
    Seven potato-peeling stations
    Potato carrier crew
Production sites for the Central Supply Office
    Three bakeries (producing baked goods, meatloaves, etc.)
    Central butcher shop
    Roux (thickening agent) production (*Einbrennerzeugung*)
    Curd production (quark, which prisoners of course did not receive)
    Bone processing
Regular kitchens
    Six regular kitchens (to feed prisoners)
    Central children's kitchen (for young people up to sixteen years of age)
Kitchens for the sick and special kitchens (see Chapter 12)
    Three kitchens for the sick
    Infant kitchen
    Toddlers' kitchen (for small children)
Dining hall (*Speisehalle*)

Central Materials and Inventory Administration
The central materials and inventory administration was structured as follows:

Central materials administration ("materials" refers to supplies – such as laundry detergent, buckets, nails, etc. – needed for buildings and quarters)
　Seven materials administrations (branch offices and distribution points)
Central inventory administration ("inventory" refers to furnishings of rooms, etc.)
　Seven inventory administrations (together with "materials administrations")
Fuel section
　Seven fuel sections (distribution points for coal, etc.)
Salvage recycling section

Manufacturing Department
The Manufacturing Department, frequently also referred to as the "Economics Department – Manufacturing" (WAP), was almost a department in itself (see Chapter 14 as well as Chapter 13). Its structure was quite complex:

Secretariat
Administration
Production Management Department

The following subdivisions were part of the "secretariat" or were affiliated with it:

Management Office
Organization
Supervision
　Administration and works inspection
　Deadline supervision (for deliveries)
　Complaints (noncompliance with deadlines, deliveries, etc.)
Personnel registry (a registry of the employees in the "Manufacturing Department")
Writing Office
Archive and Records Office
Chemical-technical laboratory

The structure of the "administration" was extremely mechanized:

Accounting
　Payroll Department
　Business accounting
　　Advance calculation
　　Postcalculation
　　Cost accounting
　Statistics
　Accounting control
Administration
　Space
　Machinery

Plant equipment
Tools and fixtures
Raw materials
Additional materials and supplies
Finished goods
Orders
Orders registry
Deadline registry
Distribution site (charged with the allocation of orders to plants)
Acquisitions (charged with supplying the materials for "manufacturing")
Acquisition
Acquisitions registry
Storage
Two warehouses and one lumber warehouse
Shipping
Administration of factories and businesses
Builder's yard (*Bauhof*) administration (workshop complex H II)
Südbaracken administration ("manufacturing barracks")

Even more complicated was the "Production Management Department," which oversaw the actual manufacturing processes; it, too, was initially overburdened by a complex administrative apparatus, which included the following subdivisions:

Development and design
Efficiency and planning
Plant supervision
Metal processing
Wood processing
Paper processing plants
Garment factories
Soil and stone processing
Mending shops
Cleaning shops
Food plants
Collection
Other plants
Structure of "metal processing"
Administration of metal processing
Tool storehouse
Shipping
Tinsmithy
Smithy
Welding
Toolmaking and grinding
Machine fitting
Precision mechanics
Optics workshop
Watchmaker's workshop

Fountain pen repair
Sewing machine service
Typewriter service
Orthopedics workshop
Bandage (*Bandagisten*) workshop

There were several divisions charged with "wood processing":

Wood processing on Badhausgasse (Q 321, the "riding school")
   Administration of wood processing on Badhausgasse
   Machine carpentry I
     Shipping for machine carpentry
   Cabinetmaking I
   Manufacture of building materials (for the barracks)
   Wooden soles manufacture
   Tool grinding
   Wood desiccation plant
Wood processing at the builder's yard (H II)
   Administration of wood processing at the builder's yard
     Wood warehouse at the builder's yard
   Machine carpentry II
   Cabinetmaking II
   Barrel making
   Reimann assembly group
   Joinery
   Carpentry (carpentry work)
   Wood molding
Two youth carpentry divisions

The Production Management Department also oversaw many "paper processing plants":

Carton manufacturing workshop
   Administration of the carton manufacturing workshop
   Hand carton manufacturing workshop
   Machine carton manufacturing workshop
Fashion accessories manufacturing workshop
   Administration of the fashion accessories workshop

And it was responsible for "garment plants":

Administration
Workshop for uniform maintenance
Gunnysack mending

The "soil and stone processing" divisions included the following:

Mica splitting
Administration of mica splitting

There were many "mending plants" within the structure of the Production Management Department, including the following:

Central Garment Mending Workshop (ZBRW)
   Garment mending and alteration
      Administration of the ZBRW
         Incoming and outgoing undergarment warehouse
      Men's garment mending
      Women's garment mending
      Undergarment mending
      Stocking mending
      Glove mending
      Hat mending
      Boys' garment mending
      Girls' garment mending
      Men's alterations
      Women's alterations
      Laundry alterations
      Baby coat alterations
      Bandage production
   Repair and manufacture of footwear
      Footwear administration
         Incoming and outgoing footwear warehouse
      Shoe repair
      Manufacture of footwear (wooden sandals)
      Minor footwear repairs
   Transport crew
      Cleaning crew and orderlies
   Bag making (mending of rucksacks, etc.)
District mending rooms and home work crews
   Administration of the district mending rooms and of home work crews
      Four district mending rooms
      Four home work crews (responsible for knitting, work for the blind, stocking darning, and bandage making)
      Individual workshops
      Repair workshops I–V
      Shoe repair workshop VI

The department oversaw the following "cleaning plants":

Central Laundry (see Chapter 14)
   Administration of the Central Laundry
Central Bath (see Chapters 4 and 5)
   Bath Westgasse 3 (which was located in the "community house" as of summer 1944)

There were also quite a few "food plants":

Administration
Central Bakery (a bread bakery; see Chapters 5 and 12)
Noodle making (noodles and rubbed dough for kitchens)

The "collection points" under its direction included the following:

Central receiving and issuing point for laundry and mending
Administration of the central receiving and issuing point
Laundry transport crew

Finally, the Production Management Department oversaw several "other plants":

Room furnishings workshops
Administration of room furnishings workshops
Three workshops (ceramics for use and decoration, lampshades, etc.)
Ink powder bag filling
Laundry detergent production workshop

Agriculture Department
The following list illustrates the activities of the Agriculture Department, the profits of which were delivered to the SS:

Management

Storage
Materials and tools warehouse
Raw materials warehouse
Products warehouse

Crops
Vegetable cultivation
Grain and root vegetable cultivation
Lawn cultivation
Flower cultivation
Parks (maintenance of city parks)
Fruit cultivation

Animal production
Horses
Cattle
Pigs
Sheep and goats
Rabbits
Poultry
Silk worms
Beekeeping

Secondary agricultural industries
Smithy
Wainwright
Glazier
Saddlemaker
Basket weaving
Vegetable and fruit preservation

Administration

Warehousing and Businesses Department
The department responsible for storage and businesses (see also Chapter 14) was structured as follows:

Central Warehouse
 Office
 Warehouse index
 Machine registry
 Central Supply Warehouse
 Central Potato Warehouse
  Nine potato warehouses
 Central Materials Warehouse
 Central Medication Warehouse
Central Lumber Warehouse

Businesses
 Offices
 Stores (*Verschleißstellen*; see Chapters 5 and 14)
  Two men's clothing stores (L 413 and L 316)
  Two women's clothing stores (Q 309 and Q 507)
  Children's clothing store (Q 507)
  Two undergarments stores (L 312 and L 309)
  Two shoe stores (L 307 and L 309)
  Food store (L 411; see also Chapter 12)
  Suitcases and fashion accessories store (L 413)
  Hardware store (Q 317)
  Perfumery and paper store (L 307)
 Shaving and hairdressing parlors (see Chapter 13)
  Administration of hairdressing parlors
  Twelve barber shops
 Coffeehouse (see Chapters 5 and 19)
 Artificial ice production (for the butcher; ice cream was available in limited quantities during "beautification" at the "community house" and the "coffeehouse")

 Storage of necessities
  Central Garment and Equipment Warehouse
  Clothing warehouse (see especially Chapter 14)

Shipping Department
The Shipping Department was structured as follows:

Shipping by train (transport to and from the train)
City shipping (internal transport within the camp)
Permanent shipping crew
Weigh station (city scales)
Vehicle rental (see Chapter 13)
Workshop (wainwright)
Draft animals (this division was minimal; see Chapter 13)

Technical Department

The Technical Department consisted of nine subdivisions:

Management
Building Inspection Office (responsible for building inspection assignments)
Construction Department
Public Works Department
Public Enterprises Department
Central Building Maintenance Office
Surveying Department
Graphics and Reproduction Department
Mechanical Engineering Department

Management

The management of the Technical Department was subdivided as follows:

Management Office
Statistics
Personnel registry
Materials section
Materials and inventory administration
Accounting

Construction Department

The Construction Department generally conducted only minor remodeling projects yet still had a complex structure:

Office for Technical Issues
  Planning
  Construction
  Drafting room
  Statistics
  Archive
  Building supervision
Administration
  Correspondence
  Orders registry
  Wage payment
  Liaison service (responsible for interactions with other departments)
  Construction trade
    Estimates – procurement of materials
    Distribution of jobs – allocation
    Payment of jobs – registry
    Inventory and materials supervision
    Accounting
  Plant management – construction
    Construction
      Building engineers
      Foremen and team leaders
      Regular workers

Bricklayers
Cement workers
Space-clearing (*Assanierung*) workers
Assistant bricklayers
Roofers
Assigned workers
Temporary work crews
Transport crew
Storehouse for construction materials
Plant management – workshops
Workshops (these frequently shared space with the Economics Department)
Office
Wood processing
Carpentry
Joiner
Storehouse
Barracks component warehouse
Metal processing
Locksmith
Tinsmith
Small-parts warehouse
Warehouses
Component warehouse
Tools
Construction materials
Equipment

Public Works and Public Enterprises Departments

The Public Works Department included subdivisions responsible for "railway construction," "roadbuilding," and "water purification and laboratories"; the Public Enterprises Department included the following subdivisions:

Electricity section
Office
Plant Administrative Office
Workshops
Water section
Office
Operation of waterworks
Construction of waterworks
Sewage system
Installation and heating (cooking pots, etc.)
Garbage disposal
Street cleaning

Central Building Maintenance Office

The Central Building Maintenance Office (Gebäudeerhaltungszentrale [GEZ]) was responsible for the technical maintenance of all buildings. It was structured as follows:

Seven building maintenance offices (branches)
  Office
GEZ workshops
  Installation crew
  Apprentice training workshop
  Carpentry
  Spray painting crew
  Blackout crew
  Heating stove section
  Varnishing and painting workshop
  Glaziers' workshop
  Heating stove repair workshop
GEZ small parts warehouse
GEZ materials warehouse

Graphics and Reproduction Department

The following list illustrates the activities of the Graphics and Reproduction Department:

Drawing and crafts (tables and illustrations for reports)
Planographic printing (oscalide procedure)
Lithography

Mechanical Engineering Department

The Mechanical Engineering Department included the following subdivisions:

Medical technology workshop
Chemical technology workshop

Finance Department

The Finance Department was primarily an internal accounting department that worked for the "Economics Department," the "bank," and so on, and it was responsible for economic relationships with the world outside the camp, for which the SS acted as liaison. It was structured as follows:

Management
Central Accounting Department
  Consumption accounting
  Output accounting
    Output for outside sites
  Production accounting
    Branches of the Economics Department
    Branches of the Technical Department
Balance and Statistics Department
Pricing Office
Ration Card Office
Remittance Office
  Index

Administration

Wage consignment verification
Complaints
Accounting Department

Health Services and Welfare

The "Health Services Department" (see also Chapters 4 and 5) and the "Welfare Department" (see Chapter 17) were structured as follows:

Management
Administration
Care of the sick
Central Medical Supply Warehouse
Laboratories and support facilities
Sanitary facilities
Public health officer
Welfare Department

Management and Administration
The management and administration of the Health Services and Welfare Departments were structured as follows:

Scientific institutions
    Central Medical Library
    Medical lectures
    Training of care personnel
Management Office
    Graphic illustrations
Health registry
    Statistics
    Registry of sick persons
    Nutrition and treatment section
    Central Archive of Case Histories
Personnel registry
    Personnel deployment
    Personnel index
    Wage payment
Technical institutions
    Laundry and bed linen
    Beds
    Acquisitions section

Care of the Sick and the Central Medical Supply Warehouse
The division charged with care of the sick included the "health units" of the four districts (hospitals, outpatient clinics, etc.; see Chapter 16). It should be mentioned here that the hospitals, clinics, and so on, also had significant administrative apparatuses (see also Chapter 14), and that there were two "disinfection laundry facilities" and one "orderly crew." The Central Medical Supply Warehouse was structured as follows:

Equipment (medical inventory)
Medical glass and glassblower
Pharmacy
Production of pharmaceutical preparations

Laboratories and Support Facilities
The laboratories and support facilities were structured as follows:

Central Dentistry Department (inoperative)
Pathology Department at the crematorium (see Chapter 16)
Central Laundry Facility
  Procurement and delivery of laundry
  Laundry section
  Mending facility
Bed linen section
  Mattress administration and repairs

Sanitary Facilities
The division responsible for sanitary facilities was structured as follows:

Sanitary facilities specialists
Disinfections (see especially Chapter 5)
  Administration
  Technical facility
  Administration of technical materials
  Sanitary disinfections
  Disinfections (against vermin)
  Delousing baths
    Central Delousing Bath
    tub bath for nonambulatory patients with lice
Fly and rodent control
  Production and processing of disinfectants and support materials
AMSI (a hygiene inspection service working for the Public Health Office)
  Referral Office

Public Health Officer
The functions of the public health officer were as follows:

Public Health Office
  Health statistics
General hygiene
  Inoculations registry (an overview of mandatory inoculations)
  Preventive medicine
  Popular medicine (lectures, etc.)
Occupational hygiene
Food hygiene (meat inspections, etc.)
  Veterinary hygiene

Welfare Department
The following list illustrates the numerous activities of the Welfare Department:

Management of the Welfare Department
    Administrative Office
    Personnel registry
    Allocation and goods section (for the unemployed, instead of "workers' care")
    Infant care section
    Section for care of the elderly
    Section for care of the infirm
    Section for care of the sick
    Institutional care section
    Section for care of the blind
    Section for care of the deaf-mute and the hard-of-hearing
    Section for care of the physically handicapped
    Section for care of the war-disabled
    Section for prisoner care
Ten welfare offices (branch offices)

Youth Welfare

For more about the work of the Youth Welfare Office, see Chapter 17. The office was structured as follows:

Management
Educational Services Department (which included illegal education, among other things)
Social Services Department
Institutional care (for children living in "homes")

Management
The management of the Youth Welfare Office was structured as follows:

Management Office
    Administration
    Wages accounting
    Child registry
Technical section
    Planning and tasks
    Materials and inventory
Space planning and resettlement
Personnel registry
    Work performance reports
Organizational oversight
    Monitoring
    Parents' complaints

Educational Services Department
The Educational Services Department was structured as follows:

Educational Advisory Council
  Therapeutic pedagogy
Occupational education
  Youth gardens (gardening work)
    Work performance reports
    Work performance monitoring
    Services for youth gardeners
Youth training (courses for apprentices)
Daily activities
  Nursery schools
    Infant care
  Youth centers (an alternative to schools)
  Sports and playgrounds
Recreational services
  Events
  Music
  Library and reading halls (there was a library created especially for young readers)
  Children's library

Social Services Department
The Social Services Department was structured as follows:

Social administration (in place of "workers' social services")
Nutrition
  Allowances office
  Clothing and personal items
  Social institutions
    Children's hairdresser
  Care of single people (children)
  Block care (for children outside the "homes")
    Barracks
    Mother-and-child homes (*Kindermütterheime*)
    Infirmaries

Institutional Care
The department supervised several "homes," including the following:

Children's convalescent home (part of the "beautification" effort)
Three youth homes
Two homes for problem children
Youth work home (also the "home for apprentices")
Mother-and-child home
Infants' home
Girls' home
Boys' home

Recreation

The following list illustrates the overall activities of the Recreation Office (see Chapter 19) during the "beautification" period:

Management
Administration
  Secretariat
  Programming
  Financial management and admission tickets
Technical services
  Materials procurement
  Inventory administration
Theater
  Artistic Advisory Council
  German-language theater
  Czech-language theater
  Yiddish theater
  Cabaret
  Block events (in the houses)
Music
  Operas and vocal music
  Piano music
  Orchestral music
    City band
  Coffeehouse program
  Instruments administration
Lectures
  General lectures
  Jewish lectures
  Foreign-language lectures
  Hebraica
  Chess
  Women's lectures
Central Library
  Research and circulating library
  Public reading room
  New Hebrew library
  Youth library
    Children's library
Sporting events
  Soccer
  Volleyball
  Handball
  Basketball
  Table tennis

204   *Sociology*

Supervisory and field services
Administration of equipment and halls
   Community center
   Hall administration

DESCRIPTION AND DISCUSSION

This plan provides a hopelessly schematic cross section of the "paradise ghetto." Everything was anticipated, everything provided for – the only thing missing was life. The monstrosity and absurdity of this structure could hardly be surpassed, as responsibilities were hopelessly entangled and overlapping; a superstructure like this, in which each inmate and object was repeatedly registered and categorized, was ultimately unable to register anything. It was a deceptive ordering of chaos – a spectral order that was embellished with powerful-sounding terms but that in fact had no power over itself. It could not be cohesive and immediately would have dissolved into the nothingness that it really was had not a mixture of active insanity and passive obsession held it together under the pressure exerted by the SS. Incidentally, none of the leaders of the self-administration and certainly none of the SS men could have taken this ludicrous arrangement seriously; it was a depraved game, combining outrageous cynicism with an infernally childish naïveté. The centrifugal tendencies that constantly threatened to explode this structure from within contrasted starkly with the SS's power in the form of the transports they ordered, which destroyed large portions of this framework, tearing living members from the community and sending them to their deaths. For this reason, centripetal tendencies were also at work, as people clung to the camp's deceptive structure, secretly hoping to be saved, begging mercy from it, and trying to hide within it, although it did no good and rarely saved anyone. This tendency was again matched by the persistence of those who still thought themselves protected by traditional habits and who were unable to act any differently; yet only a fulfilled life within a true order – not a mimicking of traditional customs that long since had ceased to apply petrified into cramped mechanisms in which only an animalistic instinct allowed the continuation of the solemn bustle associated with a decaying way of life – could guarantee this kind of protection.

Almost the only result of this type of conduct by many people was that, despite all the damage it suffered, the structure continued to function mechanically even after May 8, 1945. Had more fulfilled people worked within this structure, such an overblown apparatus never could have become as "real" as it became here, not even on paper, even under such overwhelming pressure. If at least a certain number of insightful people had been part of this net, the camp would not have retreated so far into its illusory reality; for when a person who had preserved balance and dignity was drawn into this web, he formed an island of humanity, and a post could become a true office. Some of the sinister quality was immediately lost; a living person felt something, and there was sympathy. This was a rare occurrence, and it had to be. In a shadowy world where human lives were whirled about like dust, only a true sense of morality that required no morals could survive – and this kind of morality is rare. When a state makes it its business to encourage what is most evil, the consequences must inevitably be those that Theresienstadt yielded.

No individual could remove himself from the intricacies of the camp apparatus as long as he remained within the camp, except through death. Even those who participated in nothing, neither good nor bad – those who seemed merely to be victims – suffered inescapably and, before they knew it, were actively involved a hundred times over. Thus the camp was in fact a coerced community. Never before, perhaps not even in a strict concentration camp, had everything been so broadly immersed in a bottomless abyss of coercion as in Theresienstadt. There, freedom concretely meant death. Yet the kind of freedom that refused to die was forced into a kind of solitude that was almost not of this world, because the coercion in the camp did not allow any other form of freedom. But when there reigns a coercion that closes the door to any stirring of freedom, the unquenchable desire for such freedom takes revenge through an unrestrained caprice that may be tied down, but that breaks through nevertheless in places where the insufficient coercion fails to reach. Thus is generated a chaos that corresponds to nothingness. Chaos is the Something found in nothingness, for there is no such thing as nothingness, in an ultimate sense; there is only worthlessness (*Nichtswürdigkeit*), a devaluation of all that exists, which considers existence worthless and treats it as worthless.

This chaos was "dealt with." In a towering but comprehensible pyramid, the leadership reached from the senior Jewish Elder down to the last captive Jew. Formed and maintained by coercion, this pyramid affirmed itself and deemed itself a value; it recognized, in contrast to itself, a nonvalue, which it denied. This nonvalue, too, was represented as a pyramid, but only as a mirror image, and a mirror image must be worthless. This mirror-pyramid was "nothingness." At its head was the Führer; its base reached down to the SS functionaries who led the camp. But this pyramid, too, affirmed itself, deemed itself a value, and saw the Jewish camp, in a mirror-pyramid, as a nonvalue. The SS commandant, empowered by the "Führer" to construct his pyramid, made decisions for the camp, yet rarely by direct intervention. He generally called on the mirror-pyramid to carry out his orders. The mirror-pyramid had to obey him: if it did not, he would break the mirror, and then the pyramid and its people would no longer exist; the imprisoned people would become shadows; their system, a pyramid conjured up by a mirror, would become what it was – nothing. This mirror-pyramid, with the senior Jewish Elder at its head, was forced to recognize that the other pyramid – even if it was a nonvalue and a bewitched mirror – represented power; thus even though it was cursed, it remained real. And if the camp-pyramid wanted to continue to exist, the senior Jewish Elder and all his Jews had to obey. Only in their obedience were they entitled to a revocable existence. This is why, in this reflected shadow-empire, functions analogous to those that maintained the "Führer's" pyramid were echoed yet were strangely transformed and inverted. Power was reflected as authority, and violence as coercion; in this way, the *Führerprinzip* was perpetuated in the community of prisoners. The "Führer" was mirrored in the figure of the senior "Jewish Elder," whether they liked it or not, and every single captive Jew mirrored the roles of all non-Jews. The worthlessness assigned to the Jew in this system avenged itself on the non-Jews through this mirroring, for there is no such thing as nothingness. The worthlessness of those one would like to consider Nothing would become a Something that would in turn become the demise of he who wants to be Something.

It may be impossible to comprehend this schematically. Under these conditions, amalgamations occur in which, consciously or unconsciously, those who cause suffering themselves suffer, and, under the same laws, those who suffer cause suffering. Even if one disagrees with the scenario outlined here, it still remains true and verifiable that the persecutor comes to resemble his victim, while the victim comes to resemble his persecutor. The inside-the-camp pyramid that mirrored the pyramid in the outside world functioned as a tightly woven progression of authority, from the senior Jewish Elder at the top down to the base. It was only a short distance from the Jewish Elder to the house elder or room elder to the last, lowest Jew, and thus the improbable was achieved – this last Jew was "linked to the all-powerful Führer of the Grossdeutsches Reich." Through these connections, which are easily established, he who made himself into a God would know of him, the last Jew, who was now "oriented toward the Führer"! These conditions were hardly deliberate, but that did not make them less effective, and – for a short time – they did hold together a Reich and a "ghetto."

The Jewish leadership had an enormously difficult task. Not even the greatest integrity could have prevented the sum of its decisions, in an absolute sense, from being bad. No freedom but self-destruction would have remained to the leadership had it offered the kind of resistance that would have countered absolute evil with absolute good. But an infinite amount of good could have been done within the existing boundaries. The SS's special plans to preserve this camp might have been better used to the advantage of thousands of people. Here, apart from its purely tragic responsibility, begins the leadership's much more terrible guilt. They did not have to adopt so unhesitatingly the immoral standards of their environment. A much more determined battle was possible against dirt, corruption, theft, and the worst kind of protectionism, all of which were twice or ten times as criminal here. Almost nothing that could have improved these circumstances was done. The leadership was divided; suspicion, mistrust, and base characters took their ugly toll.

The rights that were tolerated, or to which the leadership was officially entitled, were extensive. Edelstein rejected too few of the privileges for the leading functionaries with which the SS tried to tempt him. And he did so for too short a time. All too soon, a privileged class emerged as the leading group, while Edelstein remained silent; and even he failed to remain entirely uninvolved. By the time his influence waned and he ultimately fell, corruption among the upper class had progressed to such a degree that it resembled a swamp. People stuck together in cliques and were able to cut down any energetic attacker. Leo Baeck, Robert Stricker, and Karl Loewenstein never tired of trying to counteract this, but they never achieved any significant success. Loewenstein broke down as a result of his daring. Those who led the field as of 1943 no longer were willing to introduce change. They joined in the general goings-on without hesitation.

And now one wrong followed on another: the vulnerability of the frail, whom the other prisoners harmed rather than treating according to the commandment "honor thy father and mother," and the inhumanity with which the leaders added to, or at least tolerated, the inhumanity of the camp, rather than lessening it. Despite all their talk, they permitted the theft of communal property and the robbery of newcomers' belongings, thefts and robberies that had the same effect as thousands of murders, although the leading functionaries had many unused means in their own spheres of influence that would have allowed them to create if not order then at least tolerable conditions. Safeguards and punishments such as writing bans, confiscation of packages, and removal from office would have worked miracles!

Young Czech Jews sang a song that criticized the top functionaries in a mixed German and Czech text:

> My father is a member of the Council of Elders,
> *Krade rád, krade rád, krade rád …*

Krade rád means "he likes to steal." It is true that we must take these kinds of accusations with a grain of salt, because, aside from the accusation, they also say something about the accuser, whose own behavior may not be so pure as to free him from the desire to steal; words like these also reveal powerlessness and envy. Nevertheless, they do illuminate the overall morality found within a community.

The senior Jewish Elder seemed the master of the "ghetto," with dictatorial powers. He was much more than a mayor or president: he was an absolute ruler, to the extent that he was not restricted by the SS. Almost everything within the "ghetto" was done in his name. In his name, justice was administered and pardons pronounced. He determined the policies of the community, and he alone was accountable to the SS for everything. Theoretically, he was not accountable to the camp; he did not have to answer to the prisoners for his actions. All functions performed in his name had legal status because they represented the authority of his position. Therefore every prisoner was directly accountable to him, as long as the SS did not intervene. In his name, the "Personnel Office" confirmed the most important employees of the self-administration or removed them from office. He was the only Jew with the right, although limited, to deal with the commander of the SS, whose orders he took and to whom he was allowed to present wishes and requests. Otherwise, according to the regulations, no other prisoner was permitted to talk to an SS officer except in cases of "imminent danger."

It is difficult to appreciate his position. Because he was powerless against even the lowliest SS man, his position had no gloss for those on the inside. The Jewish Elder was the leader, but his hands were tied. He could be envied, loved, feared, or hated – but he was powerless. His decisions and orders, good or bad, could determine destinies and could save a life or condemn it, but they had no weight. To an incomparably greater degree than in any normal society, his success – and thus much of the well-being of the community – depended on his personality. None of his personal merits necessarily had a beneficial impact on his underlings, but any mistake in his own conduct, any flaw in wisdom, foresight, demeanor, or courage – in short, in any aspect, even a mere error – would inevitably have a disastrous effect on the community.

The world of the "ghetto" was confined to such frighteningly narrow circles that any measure could mean immediate life or death. If one wished to study the laws of cause and effect, this would have offered a unique opportunity; rarely has there been a place in which chronological "history" has occurred in this short a time span. Events that otherwise would have stretched over centuries and years were reduced here to months, days, and hours. Thus the three and a half years of the "ghetto" are not just an episode but actual history. If one wishes to investigate the laws of historical development and effect – their dense network of guilt and fate and their flawed presence in human endeavors – he can take this coerced community as an example, if he has the courage to explore a tightly knit web of horror that includes in one tangle the sum of a misery that usually is diluted over wide areas and longer spans of time. In Chapter 20 we present a definition of history as irrational life, as it unfolds in and between people, including all the material values accessible to human beings and the immaterial values that can be grasped by their consciousness. Here we discuss the problem differently than we do in a later context. Even if individuals create history, history itself is not biography but a progressive process of the becoming, acting, and passing away of a community, a multitude of people affecting one another – people who cannot simply be considered an addable sum. If one were to do that, one would be operating with physical quantities, and by analogy with history-less masses of people, rather than with historical people capable of a history. History raises to a higher power the workings of any area of human affairs; this multiplication comes from the institutions, relationships, and activities of every single community and of all communities. Here we speak of community rather than society. Society is the condition of communities; community is a reciprocally acting multitude of individuals that becomes a unity through a certain shared and definable destiny. This explanation in itself articulates the fact that history never can be expressed or grasped through details alone.

It would be utterly wrong to say that, because there was much suffering in Theresienstadt, what the tightly packed community did first and foremost was suffer, and therefore it must be portrayed from that standpoint. No; like all history, this one, too, is made up of a cosmos of countless relationships in which every imaginable human tendency came into play and created its own institutions. The elements that, in the history of normal communities, come together as a result of rational actions as well as apparently irrational events – this ideational sum of a community's total existence that is recorded in a pragmatic writing of history – are represented here through the "organizational plan" (that is, rational actions) and the exercise of power by the SS (that is, apparently irrational events). Normal history grows; this one seems almost a random product. Nevertheless, no history can be created merely by experiment, because mercy and fate happen and never can be subject to experiment; incidentally, there existed no conscious will in Theresienstadt to engage in such an experiment, even if the mechanical planning might have made it appear otherwise.

To destroy the Jews it was not necessary to conduct historical experiments with them. To keep them alive for a period of time for certain reasons, confused and ever-changing plans were improvised. Even if the SS had wanted to experiment, it jeopardized any possible success with its negative attitude toward the potential subjects of such an attempt. One cannot conduct an experiment and hate the subject of the experiment, for experiment requires a renunciation of such passion and demands a positive attitude toward the values being researched. Values were not recognized, and therefore nonvalue became a characteristic trait of the history of the "ghetto." It was a result of super-rule within anarchy, deceptive order in a malevolently conjured-up chaos. The community of this history, as a "nonvalue" (*Unwert*), took revenge on its environment by being "there," by being "Something" (*Etwas*) and being unable to accept the nonvalue assigned to the community. Theresienstadt is a history of the self-assertion of Something within its own negation. There, the Something had to strive infinitely harder for its existence than it would have in a world of value. Therefore, this Something had to bestow on itself and acquire values to an extent not otherwise necessary. The more such values were negated, the more carefully they had to be sought. The community had to seek out areas where the negation did not reach and that were able to withstand it. These values were not found in those institutions that the negation still needed to provisionally maintain the community's "nonvalue." The opposite was true: the institutions were infused with nonvalue, and this had to lessen their potential value, if not render them entirely worthless.

There is only one area that negation cannot penetrate, no matter how much it may attempt to negate it: a personality that, in Kogon's words, resists its "grinding down of character." As soon as such a personality appears, negation can no longer prevail entirely, because it is thrown into question itself. This kind of personality *sets* values, which then remain active within a community even after a voluntary, sacrificial death. They propagate and live on in other personalities.

Theresienstadt did not lack for these kinds of people; they were rare, yet they always are rare. Also, it is not they alone who make history; however, they are the measure of history and are the ones to implement its purpose, which is fulfilled by these bearers of value. History, as we have seen, cannot be biography; rather, it is drama, as has often been recognized – drama in the contrast of creative personalities. This observation is equally true whether one sees the tragic conflicts in the interplay of power, or in morality, or in other forces that insist on action. The grandeur of history, or a historical epoch, depends on the grandeur of the personalities who emerge to take responsible positions within the community. In the case of a coerced community such as the one assembled in Theresienstadt, for the reasons developed previously, the personality in question could only be a morally outstanding one. As no man of this kind, among those mainly responsible for the task, was granted the opportunity to determine community policies in the "ghetto," a value judgment had in a certain sense already been made regarding this history: it was not a great history, but a history that by no means lacked greatness.

Certainly, none of the Jewish Elders, not even Edelstein, was a personality who could have resisted the "grinding down of character." At least Edelstein was able to come up with a concept; yet, when it lost its way in error, he lacked the strength, and probably the opportunity, to refashion it. For it was no longer possible to adjust it to the existing situation; the strength required of a Jewish Elder in Theresienstadt exceeded the extent of Edelstein's support and intellectual abilities. Edelstein's successors had no concept beyond their desire for self-preservation and thus were not safe from the SS and never gained true respect within the camp. Eppstein's attitude probably led to his own undoing. Murmelstein's sly intelligence may have saved him and may even have helped the camp at times, but, lacking love and compassion, he acted as a clever operator; moral greatness was as foreign to this man as it was to the weak Eppstein. Both men functioned as authorities only through the borrowed illusion of power. As essentially powerless men who were merely empowered, they were answerable in an almost unprecedented way to the power that had appointed them, just as they were not answerable to their community: they were not responsible to it externally – a state of affairs that corresponded to the *Führerprinzip* – nor were they responsible themselves for the community. When questioned, none of the Jewish Elders, and no one in the same boat as they, yielded to criticism of the measures they imposed; instead they barricaded themselves behind the real or pretended orders of the authorities. The favor of the Jewish Elder therefore had an unmistakable place to retreat, on which he frequently relied. Thus the Jewish Elders were responsible to the SS not for their community but merely for the feigned order.

Edelstein alone tended to be as responsible for the community as he was for himself, which is why as a speaker he liked to present himself as a representative of the people (*Volkstribun*). He strove at least to be an intermediary between the prisoners and the SS. As much as Eppstein also liked to hear himself speak – his speeches remained empty chatter – both of the later Jewish Elders lacked any pretense of responsibility, and thus the community was defenseless against the power that negated it.

No dictator can rule a state by himself; he listens to those who confirm and fulfill him. He is surrounded by advisors, officials, and swarms of women who influence him and help to extend his domain, and on whom he must delegate functions in his name. This entourage forms the ruling class in a disempowered community. At times a strong personality in such a circle gains enough influence that he approaches – or even surpasses – the position of the dictator. In Theresienstadt, the Jewish Elder was initially surrounded by his deputies and the Council of Elders, as well as some other top functionaries. The deputies represented the Jewish Elder to the SS in his absence and frequently accompanied him to these negotiations. Edelstein, at least, preferred this practice, whereas Eppstein liked to avoid it. Conditions in Theresienstadt were such that the people in this group could gain lasting influence on conditions only if, within the system of this mock order, they also occupied materially significant posts in the economy or administration of the camp, and if, in addition, they bent with the prevailing winds, even if those were repugnant to their personal opinions and aims. During the period when Edelstein was the Jewish Elder and Zucker his deputy, various factions already existed within the leadership, but these factions coordinated themselves and were coordinated by these men; in contrast, under the triumvirate of Eppstein, Murmelstein, and Edelstein – who later replaced Zucker – this coordination was maintained externally only through prevailing pressures, such as in the common goal of rejecting the outsider, Loewenstein. At the same time, each of them, and his respective camp, was fighting internally for the top position; harmonious cooperation with the Jewish Elder could not develop. This was what the SS had intended, as its spies kept it quite well informed about conditions within the leadership and in the camp itself.

The three Jewish Elders who had to cooperate had come from Prague, Berlin, and Vienna, together with their supporters. Edelstein's circle felt threatened by the new arrivals and became ever weaker in the course of time. The newcomers found people from Prague in every office. At that point, "directives" by the SS took effect, and all positions had to be shared among the groups. Intrigues that already had existed within the groups now intensified; a unified leadership was no longer imaginable. Endless quarrels took place between parties and personal interests. Edelstein was toppled in the fall of 1943, and his followers were significantly weakened. Barely a year later, the same happened to Eppstein and his circle. Murmelstein and his assistant, Prochnik, remained and stood their ground until the end. As significant as it was that Baeck was appointed Murmelstein's representative in December 1944, this had little effect on the general situation, as Murmelstein continued to occupy the main position and as the history of the camp was determined less and less from within during the final months.

The "cabinet" of the Jewish Elder was the Council of Elders. It had almost no "power" of its own, even if many of its functions were formally carried out in its name, rather than the name of the Jewish Elder. Moreover, after 1942, the power of the Council of Elders was increasingly reduced, as can be seen in the "orders of the day" and other documents. But many of its members, who simultaneously occupied most of the higher posts in the various administrative branches, were influential. Even

Administration   211

if it seemed as though the Council of Elders was directing fate, making decisions, and voting, it still was merely an advisory committee for the senior Jewish Elder, who served as its chairman. The senior Jewish Elders, together with the Council of Elders and several other functionaries, among them former members of the Council of Elders, made up the "government" and the "leading society" of the "ghetto"; they were entitled to many special privileges, some of which were granted by the SS and some of which were arranged internally. Each member of the Council of Elders had a right to his own room for himself and his family, and almost all furnished their quarters luxuriously. Most lived in B V and kept orderlies as personal servants. The Council of Elders was protected from deportation. Only persons who "transgressed" were shipped off, until the fall of 1944, when most were sent to their deaths by the SS, even if they had not been accused of "wrongdoing." Each person was permitted to draft a "protection list" of thirty people who would not be deported. The identity cards of the members of the Council of Elders bore the following description: "Jewish Self-Administration Theresienstadt – certification no. _____ (name) _____ identity no. _____ Residing at _____ is a member of the Council of Elders – The Jewish Elder: _____ Theresienstadt, Date _____." It entitled its holder to visit many otherwise off-limits locations, particularly the Schleuse. These men generally arrived with luggage and furnishings that were otherwise forbidden, and they were able to keep them in the camp. They more frequently enjoyed the right to write letters and also were permitted to send longer messages, and to receive packages more often. They reserved the right to receive regular, unscheduled allotments of food from community supplies, which enabled them to cook, bake, and maintain their own home economy. In this way they already were legally distinguishable from all other prisoners.

They stood out even more, however, through the patronage they enjoyed and were able to provide to their protégés (93). A single word from one of them often was enough to decide whether a human life would or would not exist. With their authority, which they used in various ways, they could do evil or good. When they helped someone, this often could be accomplished only by wittingly or unwittingly harming others, and thus their position always was clouded by a sense of doom. For this reason alone, they rarely had a beneficial effect on the community. By special arrangement they made their privileges available to a wider range of functionaries and other prisoners and accepted additional food supplies, for instance, not only for themselves but in the same amount also for their wives and children. They had access to all public goods and supplied themselves with furnishings, clothing, electric cookers, coal, and so on. They improved their material status many times over without ever having to act illegally, and few passed up the opportunity to enrich themselves.

The leading society initially emerged from the "staff," experts in technical and municipal fields who were chosen by Edelstein in Prague for the purpose of building up the "departments." The "staff" was granted special privileges that encompassed accommodations, luggage, luggage checks, protection from deportation, and, initially, even possession of money. Some of the "staff" soon disappeared from the leading society or chose not to be part of it. Later, references to the "staff" were no longer made, because the term had become meaningless. As of March 1942, after the arrival of the families of the Council of Elders, a social class gradually formed; it considered itself "distinguished" (vornehm).

Two incidents serve to illustrate this. On arrival, the wives of the leading men moved into B V, which until then had been a barracks for men. The ladies of the "staff" succeeded in being assigned a lockable latrine plus its key. One woman refused to accept this privilege and was called to order by another: "But madam, you wouldn't do this to us, such a distinguished set ... !" Another woman in this group was very particular about a civilized way of life and entirely forgot that she was in a camp. In Theresienstadt it was common to gather the young leaves of a weed called "lebeda" in Czech; it was prepared much like spinach. This woman was heard boasting at a social function, "I sent out my orderly to pick lebeda." This was what life was like in the "ghetto" as early as the spring of 1942.

Cliques, gossip, pleasure seeking, social events, and invitations to aesthetic and culinary enjoyments created a make-believe world; that is unacceptable in a camp but is, above all, pernicious. People competed to be or become socially accepted, and a kind of royal household formed, complete with toadies (*Schranzen*). They were not afraid to hold parties and dances in suites (*Herrschaftszimmer*) or fixed-up offices. There were even masked balls; one was held even on the eve of the departure of a transport! One had to be well-dressed for these occasions. Seating was a bit crowded but took place at real tables, and guests were even served something demonstratively "modest," as befitted such "sad" conditions. This company thought highly of themselves. They adorned themselves and their homes. The royal household made sure to spread the necessary glamor. People sought to outdo one another, for the social events were discussed and critiqued. Birthday celebrations were especially excessive. An apparent aspect of the perversity of National Socialism and its victims was that nothing was more celebrated than birthdays, when fake glamor illuminated the shadowed and shadowlike existences with fleeting memories and even more fleeting pomp. Followers and admirers and artists and subordinates prepared for such festivities, and communal property was even sometimes donated, along with significant private gifts designed to express "gratitude and reverence." Particularly memorable in this respect was a birthday celebration for the Jewish Elder, Eppstein. Artistic presentations were performed, poems composed, compositions dedicated, and wooden implements carved in "youth homes"; no one wanted to be left out. The "Central Provisions Office" donated thirty kilograms of food to be made into a birthday cake for the table of this important gentleman, in honor of the day. Reprehensible extravagance was the order of the day, and people in the camp knew it and spoke of it.

The three Jewish Elders were described in Chapter 5. What follows here are several facts about the members of the Council of Elders, which was formed on December 4, 1941, after the arrival of Edelstein:

- Dr. Leo Janowitz: Janowitz was the head of the "Central Secretariat," a Zionist, and a follower of Edelstein. (He was sent to Auschwitz in September 1943 "for disciplinary reasons"; he was later murdered there.)
- Otto Zucker: Zucker, an engineer, was the first deputy of the Jewish Elder until the first camp restructuring; after Janowitz he became head of the "Central Secretariat" and, after Edelstein's arrest, again became deputy to the Jewish Elder. He also held many other offices. (He was sent to his death in September 1944; his successor in the "Central Secretariat" was Murmelstein's assistant, Robert Prochnik.) Zucker was a Zionist and an eminent architect and bridge builder; he also held the highest war decorations and was

Administration 213

musically inclined – he was a fine violinist. In the camp he was a frequent antagonist of Edelstein. He was a man of many talents – intelligent, tough, with a stubborn nature – and he served as protector of many prisoners, particularly musicians and painters, whom he successfully promoted.

- Karl Schliesser: Schliesser, who was the head of the "Economics Department," was a capable official and yet was also capable of anything. Politically, he was an assimilated Czech with conservative (*bürgerlich*) views and was almost the most powerful man within the leadership (see also Chapter 14). (Schliesser died along with Zucker and was succeeded in office by Dr. Ludwig H. Merzbach, a German Jew.)
- Georg Vogel: Vogel, an engineer, was a Communist and the leading functionary of the "Technical Department." (He generally stayed out of the limelight and was inconspicuous and tough; after liberation he headed the self-administration that liquidated the camp.)
- Dr. Rudolf Bergmann: Bergmann, an assimilated Czech, was the head of the "Finance Department." (He was sent to his death in the fall of 1944.)
- Dr. Rudolf Freiberger: Freiberger, an engineer and a Zionist, was the head of the "Manufacturing Department" until the end of the war. A rather unscrupulous opportunist who always knew how to come out on top, he was one of the most hated men in the leadership (see also Chapter 14).
- Julius Grünberger: Grünberger, an engineer and a Zionist, was the head of the "Technical Department" until he was removed by Burger in the summer of 1943 (his successor was the engineer Max Sever) but remained a member of the Council of Elders (until he was sent to his death in the fall of 1944). He was a typical bureaucrat of moderate talents, essentially a harmless man whose tendency toward self-righteousness and self-indulgence made him unpopular; his social ambitions knew no bounds.
- Leo Hess: Hess, an engineer and an assimilated conservative, was the head of railway construction until he was sent to his death for punitive reasons in September 1942 (see Chapter 5).
- Dr. Erich Munk: Munk, a friend of Edelstein's, was the head of the "Health Services Department" and a talented and ambitious despot (see Chapter 16). (He was sent to his death in the fall of 1944; his successor was the well-known ophthalmologist and lecturer Dr. Stein).
- Dr. Erich Klapp: Klapp, a Zionist, was the head of the Internal Affairs Department of hospital E VI. Modest and businesslike, he was probably the most humane member of the first Council of Elders. (He was sent to his death in the fall of 1944.)
- Dr. Egon Popper: Popper, the leader of the camp before Edelstein's arrival, was the chairman of the "Department of Internal Administration." He was a weak character; as a Czech Jew, he was a rival of Edelstein's. (He was sent to his death in the fall of 1944.)
- Erwin Elbert: Elbert, an engineer, was the head of the "Building Management Office." (He was sent to his death in the fall of 1944.)

The members of the Council of Elders were, without exception, younger men.

On October 1, 1942, the Council of Elders was restructured, and Austrian and German Jewish representatives were admitted. In addition to the previous members –

Edelstein, Grünberger, Janowitz, Munk, Popper, Schliesser, and Zucker – the following members from Germany were included:

- Heinrich Stahl. Stahl became the deputy Jewish Elder but died in November 1942.
- Rabbi Dr. Leopold Neuhaus: Neuhaus came from Frankfurt. (He survived until liberation.)
- Karl Stahl: Stahl served as the head of the "Economics Department." (He was sent to his death in the fall of 1944.)
- Professor Dr. Hermann Strauss: Strauss was involved in the "Health Services Department." (He died several months before liberation.)

The council members from Austria included the following individuals:

- Dr. Desider Friedmann: Friedmann, who served as the head of the "bank," was a man of integrity; although somewhat insecure and fearful, he was one of the most pleasant men in the leadership. After Heinrich Stahl's death, Dr. Friedmann was appointed deputy Jewish Elder on November 24, 1942. (He was sent to his death in the fall of 1944.)
- Robert Stricker: Stricker, an engineer, was involved in the "Technical Department." An early Zionist champion, Stricker was an upstanding and decisive man with a dignified manner; he always listened to complaints and did his utmost to counteract the general depravity as well as the shortcomings within the leadership and to ameliorate the fate of the infirm. (He was sent to his death in autumn 1944.)
- Dr. Jakob Wölffing: Wölffing, a genteel elderly man from Aachen, was appointed to the Council of Elders after Heinrich Stahl's death. (He was almost sixty-eight when he was sent to his death in autumn 1944.)

On January 31, 1943, a new leadership was set up under Eppstein, Edelstein, and Murmelstein. The previously appointed members of the Council of Elders remained in office. Over time, the council grew to twenty-seven persons due to new appointments, in addition to several so-called "guests of the Council of Elders." All former members retained their privileges internally, although not in relation to the SS, and continued to be consulted during advisory meetings – they were referred to as the "expanded Council of Elders."

No one was ever excluded by the Jews. Until the fall of 1944, only Hess and Janowitz were deported. In 1943, the SS removed Dr. Friedmann from the Council of Elders because he had allowed smoking in his presence, but on January 16, 1944, he was reinstated, together with Freiberger. A committee of six was appointed the same day as an inner cabinet. Over time, the following people were appointed to the Council of Elders:

- Rabbi Dr. Max Friediger, representing the Danes, with whom he was liberated in April 1945
- German Jews, including Philipp Kozower, the deserving head of the post office (he was sent to his death in the fall of 1944), and Moritz Henschel, the head of the "Recreation Office" and later of the postal service, a weakling close to Eppstein (he survived until liberation)

- Czech Jews, including Dr. Erich Oesterreicher, a friend of Edelstein's, the clever head of the "Central Labor Office" (he was sent to his death in the fall of 1944, succeeded by his friend Dr. Weinberger)

In addition, two other men came to the camp from leading posts in the official Jewish Community (Jüdische Kultusgemeinde) in June 1943 and immediately joined the Council of Elders by order of the SS:

- Salo Krämer, who had performed dirty work for the SS in Ostrau [Ostrava] and Prague but did not get very far in Theresienstadt (he was sent to his death in the fall of 1944)
- Dr. Franz Weidmann, spokesman of the Czech Jews, a spineless weakling (see also Chapter 19; he was sent to his death in the fall of 1944)

They were joined in September 1944 by the chairman of Amsterdam's Joodsen Raad (Jewish Council), Dr. David Cohen, who survived until liberation.

The most memorable personality on the Council of Elders was Rabbi Dr. Leo Baeck of Berlin, who had the dubious honor of being appointed honorary chairman of this body. In the camp he dedicated himself especially to "public welfare"; he headed the department devoted to it starting in the fall of 1944. This, however, does not do justice to Baeck's work and accomplishments within the camp, where he played a special role starting from his arrival in late January 1943. Baeck had almost no enemies, or at least nobody dared identify himself as an enemy; he was generally well respected among prisoners from many countries, and this respect increased due to his willingness to help others. He never isolated himself from the camp, yet it did not seem to exist in his presence, which may be due to the fact that he was untouched by the general filth. Baeck was able to affirm the dignity of old age, which was so often violated, as evidenced by the frailty of so many of the old people at the camp; for this he was revered, as it spread an aura of peace. He could be gentle, but that was not the extent of his emotions; he could also show rage and scorn. He understood what was called for, and he was aware of the fateful failure to which this history subjected him and everyone else. It had bent him and thrown him into mourning, yet it did not break him, because he kept himself ready and open to fresh tasks in a spirit of tenacity and courage. He saw himself as a witness to the existence of another world beyond this fatal "ghetto." He was unerringly aware of the weakness and corruption of his environment, which he attempted to counteract as best he could, first and foremost through his honorable example. Baeck opposed Eppstein, whom he warned repeatedly and hoped to steer onto a better path; he took care to avoid Murmelstein. He frequently showed tactical skill but was nevertheless unable to prevent evil. Baeck embodied the conscience of the camp and was the focus of a moral resistance movement against the corruption and wretchedness of the Jewish leadership. He guarded the gates behind which even greater evils loomed, and no one could push him aside; but there were other gateways into the abyss that he was unable to guard. In a state of powerlessness, the only effective power is the power of personality, not the power of office. Baeck accomplished much through the power of office, but like everyone else, he was overwhelmed by the prevailing powers. Yet he did demonstrate that power: in a beacon of light and a sea of tears in the midst of a surge of despair (see 3d).

Following the fall catastrophe of 1944, the Council of Elders was essentially dissolved. Sixteen members were deported, and the others were relieved of office.

Murmelstein headed the administration with the help of several assistants. In December 1944, a new Council of Elders was appointed, with one representative from each of five countries.

Baeck presided, and he also became the deputy to the Jewish Elder. Other members – in addition to Baeck and Friediger, who represented the German and Danish Jews, respectively – included Dr. Heinrich Klang, who represented the Austrians and was the head of the "Legal Department," an important jurist, and yet an unfeeling person (see Chapter 15); Dr. Alfred Meissner, who represented the Czechs and was a former minister of state and a respectable man who wished to be Czech and not Jewish; and Professor Dr. Eduard Meijers, who represented the Dutch. At this point, the Council of Elders consisted only of old men, with the exception of Murmelstein, and they remained in office (even after Friediger's liberation) until the end of the war. After Murmelstein's removal, the council was responsible for the camp until the engineer Georg Vogel took over its liquidation.

Janowitz drafted "rules of procedure" for the Council of Elders. The draft was subjected to various changes before its adoption.

1. The head of the ghetto is the senior Jewish Elder.
2. Subordinate to him is the deputy Jewish Elder, who, together with the Jewish Elder, is in charge of all affairs pertaining to the ghetto.
3. The Council of Elders forms the leading organ of the ghetto and consists of the Jewish Elder, his deputy, and the leaders of Departments III through VII and their deputies, as well as the head of the Central Secretariat.
4. The Jewish Elder appoints the members of the Council of Elders. The Jewish Elder makes new appointments and reassignments after consulting with the Council of Elders.
5. The Council of Elders makes decisions about fundamental questions that influence the life of the ghetto. These include:
   a) Issues of concern to the entire ghetto, and that are placed before the supervising departments for decision. This refers to creation and dissolution of departments of the Council of Elders.
   b) Internal decisions that could lead to changes in the life of the ghetto, such as significant alterations in questions of nutrition, accommodation, work, etc.
   c) Issues that could influence harmony and peaceful coexistence among ghetto inmates.
6. For all other questions, the Jewish Elder or his deputy decides whether they should be placed on the agenda of the meeting of the Council of Elders.
7. The Jewish Elder and his deputy consider themselves bound by decisions of the Council of Elders in questions of fundamental significance. If however, the Council of Elders should arrive at a decision that, in the opinion of the Jewish Elder or his deputy, is not justifiable, they reserve the right to reject the decision on reasonable grounds.
8. The Council of Elders will convene:
   a. at least once a week for regular sessions,
   b. for extraordinary sessions when called by the Jewish Elder or his deputy,
   c. for extraordinary sessions if requested by at least 5 members of the Council of Elders.

Administration 217

9. The Council of Elders will be chaired by the Jewish Elder, and in his absence by the deputy Jewish Elder.

10. The Central Secretariat is obligated to announce every regular session of the Council of Elders to all its members in writing at least 24 hours in advance. This period need not be adhered to for extraordinary sessions. Important motions to be dealt with in regular sessions must be submitted to the Central Secretariat in writing, in 13 copies and with sufficient substantiation. The Central Secretariat will ensure that these copies are forwarded in timely fashion to the members of the Council of Elders.

11. All 13 members of the Council of Elders are eligible to vote. Decisions are made by simple majority. In case of a tie, the Chairman will decide.

12. The Council of Elders constitutes a quorum when at least 9 members are present, among them the Jewish Elder or his deputy. If a quorum cannot be achieved, the Jewish Elder will come to a decision in consultation with the present or reachable members of the Council of Elders, and will report to the Council of Elders during its next plenary session.

13. Should the necessity arise for the Jewish Elder or his deputy to come to an immediate decision when there is no opportunity to call the Council of Elders into session, the Jewish Elder or his deputy must call a session of the Council of Elders after the impediment has been removed and make a report on the decisions reached and explain their urgency.

14. The members of the Council of Elders have access to all offices and agencies of the Council of Elders and may be present during all sessions and at all commissions of all departments.

15. The members of the Council of Elders are bound by the decisions of the Council of Elders and are obligated not to discuss the content and progress of consultations. In their functions as department heads, they are subject to the directives of the Jewish Elder or the deputy Jewish Elder, and are answerable to the Jewish Elder or his deputy for their implementation in their departments.

By decision of the Council of Elders
June 2, 1942.

(300)

The sessions usually took place on Sunday mornings and lasted from two to three, sometimes four, hours. In most cases they were opened and closed by the Jewish Elder. Generally one or more reports were submitted; these then were discussed and put to a vote.

Other than the Jewish Elder, the only leader who worked directly with the SS was the head of the "Economics Department," who paid a daily visit to the SS at 8:00 A.M., except on Sundays and major holidays. Although economic issues, or at least their details, were discussed by the appointed German and Jewish functionaries, only the Jewish Elder appeared before the leader of the SS "office" or his deputy. During Burger's time, no SS functionary was allowed to speak privately with a Jew, a rule to which Burger himself always adhered. Seidl and Rahm frequently spoke with the Jewish Elder in private. The Jewish Elder had to note down the results of each visit in a "file notice." This practice, which long had been standard in Prague for dealings between the "Central Office" and the JKG, continued in Theresienstadt in dealings between the SS "office" and the "self-administration" and was followed without exception until the end of the war. Thus the authority of the ruling SS men was limited to the spoken word, which may well have been binding but did not actually obligate the rulers to do anything; this shifted responsibility onto the Jews who implemented their orders, while removing their own activity to a place of almost transcendental power. This unique relationship in the administration of a social organization shaped the character of the coerced community it controlled; it illustrates the camp's illusory, spectral existence. This state of affairs is evident in the language in these "file notices" and many other internal camp administrative documents influenced by them. The motivations for the indirect administration of the camp through "file notices" are as numerous as its results:

1. The autonomy of the Jews appeared to be maintained.
2. The SS dictatorship was absolute, yet disguised.
3. The SS delegated nothing and could hide, like an oracle, behind the Jewish executive authority.
4. The SS saved itself a great deal of work; its laziness should never be underestimated.
5. The groundwork for the Jewish self-annihilation desired by Heydrich was laid by this administrative enslavement.
6. This enslavement promoted Jewish adaptation to National Socialist doctrine, an adaptation that was most consistently achieved in the system of the SS.
7. The Jewish functionaries were reminded daily of their absolute powerlessness.
8. The resistance of the Jewish functionaries was weakened.
9. The fictitious authority of the Jewish functionaries was maintained, in the form of reflected power.

During his visits, the Jewish Elder had to present a daily "status report" (*Standmeldung*) and report on the implementation of orders. Other items included submission of sickness reports, letters to be forwarded (frequently to the JKG in Prague), announcements of planned events, receipt of orders, "directives" of all kinds, announcements of arriving or departing transports, submission of petitions, and suggestions. Purely economic concerns were addressed, as noted previously, only in cases of major importance or when fundamental issues were concerned. The "memoranda" drafted immediately after the meetings were forwarded in whole or in part to the various "departments" and were sent to all members of the Council of Elders. If the departments had concerns, the material was communicated not only verbally but also in written form to the Jewish Elder, to be submitted to the SS. What he would discuss was left largely to his discretion. One such "file notice" illustrates this form of communication:

File notice L 46
Meeting with Camp Commandant
SS Hauptsturmführer Dr. Seidl
on March 22, 1943, 8 o'clock

1. Status Report
   presented; further list of persons with Aryan acquaintances, after addition of dates of birth.
2. Report on Number of Sick Persons

presented; further, report on the special courier from Prague, with supplementary report for the 18th and 19th of this month, as well as birth announcement (Bandler); further evidence of infectious diseases; this will be forwarded after being signed by Camp Commandant Dr. Krönert [a German health official]. Weekly report on typhus cases as well as death certificates and birth announcements of the week are submitted to SS-HSCHF [Hauptscharführer] Baltrusch.

3. Construction of Beds

It is stated that if construction of beds is discontinued the supply of nails for coffin production will last only another ten days. The Camp Commandant has no reservations about discontinuing construction of beds and requesting Department IV to arrange for accelerated acquisition of nails.

4. Items Required to be Surrendered

A note regarding items to be surrendered from estates (RM 186.52 in pfennigs, other coins, 45 dentures as well as securities and savings books) is submitted and handed back signed. The items are delivered (via courier) to SS-OSCHF [Oberscharführer] Scholz.

5. Recreation

A survey of the events planned for the week from the 22nd to the 28th of this month is submitted.

6. Letter to Prague

is submitted to be forwarded.

7. Access to the Park

It is stated that on the 21st of this month the guard posted at the park received the directive that passage through the park between Q 6 and Q 7 was prohibited. The Camp Commandant refers to the directive and remarks that access to the streets leading through the park is permitted, however walking on green areas and lawns is prohibited. The next order of the day must mention this again, with the added clause that anyone walking on the lawns should expect measures to be taken.

8. Custody Rudolf BUNZL

A note is submitted requesting that Bunzl be made available for the reorganization of the Central Accounting Office as part of his work dealing with the introduction of a monetary economy. The Camp Commandant approves this request with the comment that it is very unlikely that Bunzl would again be considered for leadership of the Central Accounting Office.

9. Items to be Surrendered during House Searches

Additional receipt SKUTSCH is submitted, signed and handed back by the Camp Commandant.

Theresienstadt, March 22, 1943

Eppstein		Edelstein	
Dr. Baeck	Dr. Friedmann	Dr. Popper	Schliesser
Dr. Eppstein	Engineer Zucker	Dr. Neuhaus	Engineer Stahl
Edelstein	Dr. Janowitz	Engineer Elbert	Engineer Vogel
Dr. Murmelstein			
Dr. Bergmann	Engineer Grünberger	Dr. Munk	Dr. Loewenstein
Dr. Wölffing	Engineer Stricker	Dr. Strauss	Dr. Oesterreicher
Dr. Freiberger		Dr. Klapp	

The "Central Secretariat" issued "orders of the day," which were later referred to as the "announcements from the Jewish self-administration." In addition, the leadership and several individual departments regularly published "newsletters" (*Rundschreiben*) intended for officials, such as house elders, but generally not for the prisoners themselves. The leadership had to deliver monthly and yearly "activity reports," as well as oft-requested special reports to the SS (see 146b); these were based on the reports of the individual departments during the same time periods. The departments themselves required such reports from their subdivisions. In this way life, work, and all special occurrences in the "ghetto" were noted down repeatedly; thus the camp continued to write its own history – of course not in an objective or always truthful manner, but tendentiously, to prove its accomplishments and importance and, as far as possible, not to displease the SS. The reports written by the senior Jewish Elder for the SS were therefore political. It goes without saying that these writings, of which few have survived, contain invaluable material, but they provide an accurate image of the actual circumstances only if they are critically evaluated.

The overmechanized administration stood in glaring contrast to the constant interference, as systematic as it was senseless, that threatened the entire order and frequently invalidated it altogether. Behind the whirling busyness there existed nothing but an abyss of annihilationist intent and an infantile play instinct. No one who had to work within this bureaucracy believed in it as a trustworthy reality; its overblown nothingness was apparent, but fear of the reality of the next transport led the prisoners to cling to the apparatus. Thus they served it and led it to perform with ever more nervous activity, no matter how dazed and almost broken it was, like an exhausted boxer. Such an administration had to become tragically grotesque; it was difficult to maintain measure and dignity, or even reason, and the administration became sheer lunacy. Some people recognized this, but for many reasons they participated in it. At the same time, the lack of belief in such a damaged institution was pernicious – how could one seriously accomplish anything? Inwardly weak and often elderly people escaped into bureaucratic gesture, and because the apparatus reinforced this kind of behavior in them, they strove to rescue their violated illusions of power and order by means of perverse red tape. These people were then blinded and used their offices to create hell for themselves, and more frequently for others. Others sabotaged the enterprise but did not always do so in the right places, because clear-headedness was needed to distinguish between real and sham duties. Some who had lost their inner stability transferred this stability into insane regulations; they sought to hide in them and fought for the illusory existence of their offices. Few were able to stay true to themselves in this confusion, so that they could remain inwardly free of the entire business and try their best to stay out of its way. But in the end this activity caught up with every single prisoner, especially as even the most primitive needs could be satisfied only through bureaucratic formalities.

At first the administration was content with simple pieces of paper, but soon the apparatus swelled. Forms were replicated in the camp using the Gestetner or the chemical oscalide method; later it became possible to generate lithographs, and also to receive extravagant amounts of letter paper and forms from outside print shops. On the other hand, the extremely limited paper supply had to be conserved and frequently was unavailable for private use. People made do with small and extremely small formats. Letters were folded – there were no envelopes – and taken from one

Administration 221

department to the next by couriers, who always made certain to confirm receipt. Letterheads appeared more or less as follows:

Jewish Self-Administration Theresienstadt Central Secretariat
    To   _____   Reference   _____   Your   letter   _____
of _____ Your signature _____ Our signature _____ Date
_____ 1944.

Special form letters, which were at first simply duplicated and later mostly printed, existed for all imaginable purposes. Particularly important were the summons forms, which were designed according to the following pattern for all departments:

Summons   Name   _____   Transport   number   _____   Quarters
_____ Reference _____
    You are required to appear on   _____   at   _____o'clock in
_____ building, room number   _____   and report to date
_____ department _____

Anyone who did not have a personal identity card received identity papers, which read as follows:

Ghetto Theresienstadt The Council of Elders Transport Number   _____
residing in _____
    Identity Card First and Last Name _____ Date of Birth _____ In
_____ Nationality _____ Home community _____ Status
_____ Last place of residence _____ is listed in the Theresienstadt
register under the transport number _____ This identity card was issued based on the transport list, the family register and the sworn statement of the holder of the identity card. Theresienstadt, date _____ The Council of Elders [signature and stamp] Jewish Self-Administration Theresienstadt.

The reverse side contained a description of the person, space for a photograph (if available; no photographs ever were taken in the camp, not even by the SS), and the signature of the holder of the identity card. Later on, the identity cards were adjusted to civilian standards. The first page of the card read as follows:

Jewish Settlement Area Theresienstadt Personal Identity Card
    Last name of Holder: _____   (for women also their maiden name):
_____ First name of Holder: _____ Date of Birth: _____
Place of Birth: _____ Family Status: _____ Address: _____

The second page contained a detailed description of the person, his or her last place of residence prior to Theresienstadt, and the number of the identity card. The third page continued as follows:

Print of the right index finger _____ photograph _____ Signature of Holder _____ Theresienstadt, date _____ 1944. [space for stamp], The Jewish Elder: _____

The various "transit passes" were of particular importance. Until June 1942 they were issued by the SS at the request of the Jewish Elder, and later by the Jewish Elder, except for those that permitted leaving the "ghetto." What follows are two samples from the initial phase:

> This Day Pass T9984 authorizes Löbner Egon SK to leave the barracks between May 11 and June 10, 1942, even outside the city limits, for reconstruction work for the waterworks, as well as to have access to all women's and men's barracks. Theresienstadt, May 11, 1942 [stamp] Central Office for the Regulation of the Jewish Question in Bohemia and Moravia, regional office Theresienstadt [signature]: Bergel, Camp Inspector

> This Permanent Pass authorizes Klaber Josef 10/St BV, in his role as deputy head of the Security Service, to leave the barracks even after 9:00 P.M. as well as to go outside the city limits.

After the autumn of 1942, a pass was necessary within the camp only during the nighttime curfew. Later, mechanically duplicated or printed pieces of paper were used, with the following text:

> Theresienstadt Ghetto The Council of Elders [later, Jewish self-administration Theresienstadt], Pass No _____, in effect after 8 p.m., transport no. _____ quarters _____ reason _____ on/from _____ destination _____ The Jewish Elder [signature or stamp] Dr. Paul Israel Eppstein [stamp] (star of David) Theresienstadt Ghetto – The Jewish Elder

Passes for factories, particular buildings, kitchens, the Schleuse, and so on, were issued by the individual departments. One had to wait a long time to be issued a pass, even to attend a funeral.

> Department of Internal Administration
> Registry Office and Funeral Department
> Confirmation Last name and first name Klepetar Elsa, transport number Am 697 is attending the funeral of Klepetar Leop., on April 28, 1943 at 9 o'clock. Valid only for the route to and from the Central Mortuary – Theresienstadt, April 28, 1943
> (signature)

If one considers the effects of this administration, the condition of the camp becomes clear: it was a constant battle between abstract regulations (as legal theory) and daily life (as a practice that was mainly possible only illegally.) In Theresienstadt the function of the prohibitions was not to guide unlimited arbitrariness; the narrowly defined authorizations just barely allowed these people, who had been robbed of their freedom, to lead their lives in misery. Generally, anything that was not expressly permitted was prohibited. This is why the human being here continued to exist only illegally. He had no right to exist, so as long as he remained in the camp, and he continually had to commit illegal acts, thus constantly exposing himself to the "measures of the authorities in charge." This had a harmful effect on even the most unbroken of characters.

The legal directives were unrealizable and were violated in various ways. This happened from the outside at the hands of the SS men, who continued to disrupt and undermine the barely tolerated apparatus; from the inside, it happened as a result of the prisoners' will to live, as they strove to ease their almost unbearable existence. Between these fronts, the frail administration found itself with its back to the wall: hounded by the SS, pressured by the prisoners, ambivalent itself, and driven by its own desire for self-preservation. The results were chaotic, although the administration never succumbed to complete anarchy.

If people wish to survive – to live through – a dictatorship that denies their very existence, consistent anarchy is impossible; yet a social structure and institutions scraping by in this way become almost insanely unbearable and inhuman and will display anarchic traits. To assert himself, the individual strives to protect himself from the anarchic acts of his neighbors; he must also be careful not to commit serious anarchic acts himself. Thus these people formed a society despite everything – a society held together by *one* shared distress. It was continuously adversely affected by the despised and hated administrative bureaucracy, whose actions, supported by the power of the SS, appeared to be saturated with the aura of power but were merely the work of a powerless authority. Its dictates were obeyed, if reluctantly, and in some cases were even obeyed with disastrous consequences, because the aura of power spread a fear that was irresistible and stronger than the counteracting will to assert oneself.

When studying this kind of administrative apparatus, one can perceive the true nature of terror: it is a paralyzing horror, a fascination that hardly anyone in a society can avoid. Acknowledgement of power and belief in authority are extremely deeply rooted in most people; far less deeply rooted is their aversion to even the most reprehensible representatives of power. Healthy people want to be sheltered and affirmed by an existing power. In the apparently civil Theresienstadt, this belief was severely damaged but was not destroyed, as it often was in undisguised concentration camps. This is why, in Theresienstadt, contempt went hand in hand with recognition of the existing "order."

We do not wish to subscribe to problematic generalizations, but we believe there is in the Jewish character (*Volkscharakter*) an active skepticism of authority that has not disappeared even in the heavily assimilated Jews of Central Europe. This could be observed in Theresienstadt. Its deepest roots lie less in the objectively dubious nature of most authority than, subjectively, in the original views of the Jews, who considered power to be based solely in God, particularly because for more than sixty generations they had not been attached to an earthly power in a state of their own. Even when this traditional concept is no longer effective among Jews, their skepticism toward worldly powers generally remains. In the camp this skepticism was heightened; the administration was mocked, and its senseless ludicrousness was recognized – and yet it was accepted; it acted like a criminal court.

Thus the pale reflection of the prestige of all the positions in the administration was in itself conflicted – at its heart was a curse with a bitter comedic quality, yet it was surrounded by the fleeting aura of the kind of magic associated with the hierarchies of any power structure. There developed a whirl of activity that might under different circumstances have served as an object of satire, but that, in the camp, took on clearly demonic characteristics. The arrogance of many high functionaries was exposed to the envy of regular "ghetto inmates." Some positions appeared "lucrative" and "advantageous," and those who held them, and on whom family and friends relied, were courted. The functionary's entourage increased in direct proportion to the influence of his position. "Vitamin B and P," *Beziehungen* (connections), and *Protektion* (patronage) became important, and the administrative ladder also became the ladder of the social hierarchy that was forming. In general, it was assumed that higher functionaries were well informed about all questions regarding the good and ill of the community. Expressions such as "I have it straight from the Jewish Elder, it's definitely true" or "I have it from a member of the Council of Elders" were common. Those who had someone "upstairs" would pay him frequent visits in order to be assured of his favor. This is why influential persons frequently would isolate themselves, particularly during transports, when guards would block access to their offices and only passers-by with special permits were allowed entry. Signs designed to keep away uninvited visitors would be affixed to their apartment doors.

Although the positions of leading functionaries were in many respects opaque to the general public, their lives and work took place before everyone's eyes. No gossip newspaper could have matched the tales in the camp – rumors, self-important and false information, lies, anecdotes, sensational stories, fantasies, and wishful thoughts flooded the camp and were spread and gullibly believed; almost no one was disturbed by their flavor of stupidity. In no other society could official announcements and secret reports have been more confusingly contradictory than was the case here.

No position was truly permanent; nothing lasted more than a short time. Concepts such as fulfillment of a mission or deserved retirement did not apply, for one could not earn merit where the value of existence was denied. Thus one had to wait. But this was not sufficient: one had to persevere, one had to survive in order to again achieve merit – in any sense of the word – and one was not always choosy about one's methods. The SS carefully monitored high-ranking positions – woe to those who fell out of favor. Everything was uncertain. A position could be very useful and bring many advantages, but none of them brought what they would have in a normal society, namely, security, permanence, and satisfying respect. Lower-level posts may not have been watched as carefully by the SS, but each incumbent lived with the threat of the next transport. Thus every position was hopeless and became despicable. This administration was sick and monstrous, and as it became increasingly uncanny, it became one of the primary torments of this camp.

9

The Transports

Every year, Jews celebrate a holiday of wandering – Pesach, the feast of the Passover – in which a "transport," the exodus from Egypt, has been forever entered into Jewish history as an act of liberation. Elias Canetti speaks of inherent national symbols that unconsciously determine the fate, development, and behavior of a people (32d). For Jews, this symbol is the exodus from Egypt, a migration that will lead them to the Promised Land. In the history of the Jewish people and of its individual members, exodus has proven to be a distinguishing feature in all periods and from many exiles. At times, migration was a conscious choice; at other times, it was forced upon the Jews as a necessity or a fate. Other peoples, too, have viewed the Jews in this way and have turned them into restless wanderers – homeless, rootless Ahasueruses. For a Jew, the end of his wanderings in an unknown future becomes an eschatological goal, equivalent to his fulfillment and deliverance. This immanent, insatiable drive is important to the Jewish concept of messianism, although this may be difficult to understand and even uncanny to other peoples, especially those influenced by Christian doctrine. Any migration that does not bring the Jews to this ultimate goal either proves to be an act of violence – a forced "transport" – or represents an attempt to secularize the goal.

Moses, the actual founder of the nation, let the Jews wander; in any case, he made mobility a principle, as is apparent in the Pentateuch in the command to build a tabernacle rather than a stone temple. Whenever the Jews have no longer wished to recognize this principle, they have made an effort, spiritually and in practice, through settlement and assimilation, to transform the provisional nature of their overall situation and their actual residence into that of a permanent home. But such attempts fail; historically, there have always been other grounds that, sooner or later, denied their apparent success. Where it nevertheless succeeded, it involved not the nation as a whole but only individuals or small groups. This willingness to migrate – which, despite a willing acceptance of the provisional nature of their temporal social existence, on occasion allowed them to settle and sometimes even be secure in one country – was replaced with expulsion or violent "transport." Internal or external assimilation could thus be achieved only in exceptional cases. If larger groups wished to escape into assimilation and persisted in it, they were expelled or destroyed.

The wandering upon which a Jew decides to embark of his own free will may lead through the desert and bring privation, but the goal is a land of life and of promise. The wandering that Adolf Hitler and his SS imposed upon the Jews led to a land of extermination and the gas chambers. The great majority of modern Jews would like to escape wandering and prefer not to accept the forgotten – and therefore doubly difficult – task of Judaism. Two alternatives, only superficially contradictory, present themselves:

1. Equality of Jewish individuals with members of other nations, so that the Jews can free themselves from wandering
2. Equality of the Jewish collective with other nations through the completion of one last, "final" migration

In the first alternative, the Jewish aspect is denied and assimilated to members of other nations; in the second, the Jewish aspect is acknowledged, but conformity with other nations endangers Judaism – although unintentionally – to the point of surrendering its metahistorical uniqueness. The majority of the unthinking and uncaring move between these two alternatives; those who move beyond these alternatives, today, are lonely individuals who consciously accept Judaism and reject any sort of assimilation.

How did the Jews behave when National Socialism appeared? Voluntarily or involuntarily, they fulfilled their symbolic destiny. They fled in time or were expelled, fortunately for them; they chose the path of wandering. Others remained, because they could not or did not want to do otherwise, and National Socialism imposed migration on them through the "transports." Thus in every country under Hitler's heel, most Jews were forced to fulfill the fate presaged by their national symbol; in almost all of Europe the years of the Second World War were marked by "transports." In Theresienstadt, the problem was manifested in three ways:

1. Through the decreed transports to Theresienstadt and away from it
2. Through the wish to be able to "go home" or to a chosen destination after the war
3. Through the desire of some Zionists in the self-administration to turn their time in the "ghetto" into preparation for the "final" migration to Palestine, into a *hakhsharah*

Thus the transports became a central problem, whether one still was free or already in a camp. Subjectively, a transport could lose significance only if a Jew arrived in a very bad camp, was separated from his family, and was robbed of his last possessions, at which point he had lost all human dignity. But even then, transports remained important: they could lead to a "good" or "bad" camp or to bearable conditions or certain death. Only if one ended up in Auschwitz, for example, did the transports lose their paralyzing terror, their almost transcendental character, for there one was aware of the possibility or certainty of doom. In Theresienstadt, on the contrary, the horror of the unknown – hidden behind a far-from-merciful veil – was at its worst. There the transports were at all times the number-one problem, and all other concerns receded before them.

Administratively, the transports were dealt with by the "leadership" (*Leitung*) and its subsidiary departments, the "Transport Department," the "Central Secretariat," and the "Central Registry." The practical responsibilities were taken on mainly by the "Transport Management Department," a section of the "Department of Internal Administration." In "quieter" periods, the "Transport Management Department" had little to do, and many of its employees led a comfortable life, especially those who had enriched themselves in their terrible trade through corruption, fraud, theft, and robbery. This group's other responsibilities were internal resettlement within the camp and the transport of estates (see Chapters 11 and 15). Later the staff was reduced and assigned to other services during lulls in the transports, or permanently.

INCOMING TRANSPORTS

Chapter 3 described how transports to Theresienstadt were carried out. Here we will describe their reception in the camp. The transports arrived in passenger or cattle cars and, until June 1943, were brought to the train station in Bohušovice and then directly to the camp. Arrivals from the "Protectorate" wore their "transport numbers" on strings around their necks, hanging over their chests. Soon after the train's arrival they were unloaded, which took about two hours for 1,000 people. Those who could walk left the cars with their "hand luggage," if they were able to carry it themselves. The "accompanying luggage" (*Mitgepäck*) and other inventory assigned to the transport were in special freight cars and were unloaded by workers from the "Transport Squadron." Several SS men stood on the platform, generally with the camp commandant at their head, along with Czech gendarmes, Ghetto Guard (GW) men, staff of the "Transport Management Department," workers, and usually also the Jewish Elder and other members of the administration. Except for some members of the "transport assistance" (*Transporthilfe*), all were men. Those who could walk, including the elderly and mothers with children, were gathered into a column and were subjected to unending tirades by the SS, some gendarmes, and at times even some Jews. Occasionally the SS doled out slaps, blows, and kicks and threw stones. The much more harmless gendarmes seemed threatening, with their weapons and fixed bayonets.

The arrivals were exhausted, on edge, and fearful, and their mental clarity was often greatly impaired after a frequently long and difficult journey, and also due to bad weather. No one knew what lay ahead, and their imaginations magnified the expected dangers in proportion to their temperament. Few were calm, let alone reflective, although some – especially older people – seemed apathetic. Most worried about their luggage; others asked fearfully about conditions in the camp. The presence of the SS and the confusing, unfamiliar surroundings, filled with haste and noise, created insecurity and increased the general level of fear. The newcomers' psychological shock was determined by many traumas, which one can envision in detail only with a vivid imagination. These included the events that preceded arrival: deportation orders, the collection camps, loading onto trains, and the journey itself – all this brought a flood of agitation even to strong people. One witnessed the arrival of people whom one had known previously, and whose whole personality now seemed different and disturbed. The transports, especially for old people, resulted in a confusion that subsided rapidly or more slowly, accompanied by loss of memory, amnesia, and other disturbances. Many people fell into neurotic or manic and depressive states or suffered hysterical outbreaks or screaming and crying fits; more rarely, stupors were observed. Almost everyone who was subjected to a transport suffered an inextinguishable trauma, even if the recognizable disturbances dissipated.

Some never overcame the transport experience; others merely repressed it to a greater or lesser extent. The feelings of disgust that filled a new arrival, generally to the point of nausea, due to the hopeless situation and the degradations, usually continued to have an effect for a long time and generally persisted for the duration of his time in the camp. As a rule, this had a negative influence on moral character.

In one fell swoop, people were torn from their familiar surroundings. Everything that was near and dear to them – everything they had achieved, that had provided security and happiness – was lost, apparently irretrievably. I have compared arrival in the camp with birth. This is an accurate image, but it was a birth at which consciousness was active, as strained as it may have been. With tense expectation, the newborn thus entered into an unknown future, but one filled with ideas and fantasies. Those who expected to find relatives or friends in the camp, those who counted on useful relationships, placed their hopes in such connections. They would not have as hard a time as those who entered a totally alien, perhaps even hostile, environment.

The newcomers had to march in rows of four with their hand luggage. They covered the barely three kilometers in two to three hours, in the company of gendarmes and ghetto guards. The gendarmes usually were patient, did not rush people, and allowed many breaks. The SS did not take part in these terrible processions. The sick and the elderly were packed so closely on trucks and tractor trailers that they could neither sit nor stand. SS men steered the bouncing vehicles quickly and heedlessly. The destination was the Schleuse, which only a few of the privileged were spared. Anyone who met an acquaintance among the staff here or at the train station was asked for his "transport number." This could mean help during the difficult time in the Schleuse, and often the rescue of luggage.

The "transport lists" brought by the escort went to the "Central Secretariat" and the "Central Registry." There the lists were read out, and anyone able to gain entry could note the names and numbers of the newcomers. The "transport lists" were not made public; only in summer 1943 did an exception occur. Nevertheless, word of who had arrived got around quite quickly, although it sometimes took months before old residents and newcomers found out about each other. Both were interested in knowing about the presence of certain people and attempted to reach each other through inquiries, messages, and letters. As soon as people were released from the Schleuse, anyone could receive information on names and addresses from the "Central Registry."

Families were often deported together and remained together in the Schleuse, where they continued to walk around with "transport numbers" hanging about their necks. The procedures did not change much over the years; the only change was when the march from the train station ceased, in July 1943. The Schleuse changed; often it was housed in the worst areas. The main buildings used for the Schleuse were the following: in the first half of 1942, E VIII, E 1, and C III; in the second half of 1942, A II, B IV, B V, H V, A IV, I IV, L 124, L 313, and L 417; in 1943 and 1945, A II; and, in 1944, C III.

The first four transports in 1941 were spared the Schleuse. In the Schleuse, the newcomers were brought to numbered spots that, until 1943, were not set up for even a short stay; they were casemates, stalls, or attics. At first people lay on bare wood or stone floors, then wood shavings were strewn about, and later there were bedframes, but without pallets. In summer 1942, as transports streamed ceaselessly into the camp, there usually was a shortage of everything, even of the most Spartan rooms.

People were forced together in semidarkness, where they crowded together or squatted helplessly. They were not allowed to leave, and other prisoners could not enter the Schleuse. This was the strict order, but the reality was often milder if the SS did not happen to be on the lookout. However, entering the Schleuse was always dangerous for the "unauthorized," because they could be discovered at any time by an SS man or hostile gendarme. The GW and the Order Constabulary (OD), and sometimes also the gendarmes, kept watch. Aside from the Council of Elders and some functionaries and doctors, only members of the "Transport Management Department" and the "Transport Squadron" were allowed entry, all of whom had to be equipped with a "Schleuse pass."

The unloading of the sick and elderly was horrible. It had to be done quickly, in order to avoid exciting the rage of the SS drivers. A wooden crate was dragged to the truck – it looked like a conductor's or speaker's stand – and the helpless people attempted to climb out. Many did not succeed, and they were unloaded in a manner worse than that used for livestock. "Schleuse sickrooms" were set up; these differed little from the other rooms. In summer 1942 the school building L 124 became the "Schleuse hospital."

The newcomers took the "hand luggage" they had brought with them to the Schleuse; the "accompanying luggage" went to the storehouse (*Magazin*), and members of the "Transport Management Department" called out the number of each piece of luggage and handed it over to the owners. It was fortunate if this did not happen until after the luggage inspection by the gendarmes, who did not care about the things in the storerooms. At first the behavior of the Jewish staff was generally irreproachable and often even helpful. Unfortunately this soon changed, specifically after the arrival of many transports from Germany and Vienna, starting in June 1942. After that, it was scarcely ever the case that someone generously held on to luggage and forbidden objects and returned them after the search. Sham helpers disappeared with the goods they had elicited, never to be seen again. Cigarettes, food, and money were wheedled and extorted. Individuals and organized groups stole luggage in large quantities, and even robbery occurred. Starting on July 10, 1942, the "accompanying luggage" was confiscated by the SS, but "hand luggage" was plundered by the gendarmes and dishonest prisoners.

Arriving transports were processed according to the following procedure:

1) assignment of barracks for a new transport
2) cleaning [of the barracks]
3) making it possible to blackout [the barracks]
4) inspection of installations
5) heating
6) collection area [*Auffangsstelle*] [receiving the transport]
7) Schleuse barracks
8) refreshment [*Labedienst*]
9) separating men from women
10) assignment to residential barracks
11) registry – 11 a), statistics; 11 b), health inspection
12) assignment to quarters
13) registry in the provisioning index [*Verpflegstand*] – 13 a) issuance of ration cards
14) introduction to camp regulations

15) Central labor office [*Arbeitszentrale*] – 15 a) card – 15 b) section [occupation]
16) assignment to workplace

This information is taken from a descriptive chart, probably for a monthly report in 1942.

The period in the Schleuse went more or less like this, with some deviations: people remained for two to three days, or for one day, in the case of small transports. It often took a long time before a meal was distributed. People ate from their own stores, if they had anything. Finally they were given "ersatz" coffee, soup, or a "real" meal, which many at first detested and could not keep down, in exchange for punching a provisional "ration card." They did not receive bread or other rations, because they were entitled to these only after two or three days. If transports came in miserable condition and without stores of provisions, protracted negotiations were required to get the "Central Supply Office" to issue bread, which they preferred to save for other purposes.

During the first two years, the luggage was searched by Czech gendarmes, who were supposed to remove anything considered "contraband." The list of contraband items changed little over time:

> Medications, tools, instruments of all types, tobacco products, canned goods and non-perishable packaged food; electrical appliances such as cookers, heating pads, flashlights, batteries; candles, matches, lighters, money, jewelry and valuables of all types, chemicals, cosmetic articles, soaps, toothpaste, razorblades and all shaving implements, spirit lamps, hard liquor, rubber articles such as tubes, hot water bottles, irrigators, condoms, thermos bottles; spirits, cocoa, chocolate, tea, coffee, newspapers, at first also writing materials (especially paper), and toilet paper.

The majority of gendarmes behaved benevolently, but too many were more interested in taking advantage, and they plundered. Transports from the "Protectorate" usually were dealt with more leniently. Many gendarmes studiously overlooked forbidden items or seemed to take things away, while the items passed to the accompanying ghetto guards were immediately returned to their owners. They also often responded to pleas; only cigarettes and alcohol were always taken by the gendarmes. Sometimes half a transport was not searched. While the gendarmes were in a room it was strictly guarded, and no one was allowed in or out. Confiscated items were taken to their barracks by Ghetto Guard members, and later by the "Transport Squadron," under the supervision of the gendarmes; there, more was plundered, and then it was delivered to the SS. For a transport of 1,000 people, an average of five to six boxes of 100 kg each was confiscated. A worker on the "Transport Squadron" reported,

> Because every newcomer appreciated the work we did day and night, and the people saw that very little food was distributed here, and finally everyone was glad to get his suitcase and knapsack from out of the tens of thousands of pieces of luggage, the pleasant custom arose of rewarding us with food they had brought along, a bonus which was of course very welcome. Even more so because our squadron leader's efforts to get hold of more food for our difficult work were disregarded by the administration for a long time. (57)

The work was indeed very difficult and could last fifteen to twenty hours without pause, but it paid off! The permissible weight of 50 kg per person was exceeded once it became known in Prague that everything arrived safely. People then brought ten or

The Transports 231

twenty suitcases weighing 500–600 kg. The SS kept most of the luggage from an April 1942 transport. After that, people again adhered to the permissible amount. The report continues:

> On the way [to the gendarmes' barracks], more items often were pilfered from the confiscated goods by the gendarmes or the ghetto guards ... by agreement, which ultimately was not immoral, since this formerly Jewish property ... had become Nazi property, and by withholding it, the robbery by the Nazis was reduced. Aside from that, the gendarmes were then in a friendlier mood toward the Jews and did their jobs less harshly. Over time, almost every gendarme had business relations with a large number of ghetto guards – or later with members of the Transport Squadron, [which were used to] make the gendarmes compliant and sympathetic during smuggling ... from outside into the ghetto. (57)

The existence of this reprehensible practice becomes clear, and there is even an attempt to justify it ethically. This was bound to lead to ever greater corruption. It is true that the SS was deprived of part of its loot, but the SS men did not for long stand idly by while their privileges were reduced; as mentioned previously, they generally confiscated the "accompanying luggage," which went to the "clothing warehouse," where it was sorted under SS supervision. As the cited report ensures us, however, things were stolen there too, apparently with the participation – on the Jewish side – of the Ghetto Guard, the "Detective Department," the "Transport Squadron," the staff of the "clothing warehouse," members of the "Central Supply Office," and even members of the Council of Elders. According to the report, it was understood that the "rescue" of luggage was valued as a "big score" and was "rewarded." The thieves thus never missed out; they also appropriated the "hand luggage," which the elderly, in particular, did not themselves bring from the train to the Schleuse. In any case, the rightful owners could only hope for their "hand luggage," although even that seldom went without losses. It continued to be searched by the gendarmes, until, starting in 1944, the SS no longer let this business escape them.

In the early months, arriving transports were announced with stereotypical words, such as the following:

> Instructions for the transport arriving on 24 April 1942. This transport will be processed through [*durchschleust*] Kavalier 8 [E VII]. Processing will occur from 24–26 April 1942. Entering the Schleuse is completely forbidden, except to members of the Council of Elders and persons directly involved in transport work, from the 24th at 12 o'clock noon until the 25th at 2 P.M. From 25 April 2 P.M. to 26 April 12 noon, entering Kavalier 8 for official purposes is once again permitted; from 26 April 1942 12 noon until the transport is completely processed, complete lockdown [*Sperre*] is again in force.... Those possessing passes outside the city boundaries are further notified that entering the train station is permitted only to those persons involved in transport work. (daily report, April 23, 1942)

Later on, arrival was even bleaker than in the early months, when one could call out comforting or important words to the newcomers on the street as they marched in. After that point, all streets through which the transport was led had to be blocked off, and the windows had to remain closed. Thus one entered an apparently empty city and had no idea what might await. The following note was smuggled to a newcomer in the Schleuse in February 1942:

> Dear X, I am very sorry to have to welcome you here. Who would have known that we would come together again so soon. I hope you are here as a K. G. employee. I work as a draftsman in the technical department of the Magdeburg Kaserne, no. 100, and live in the Sudeten Kaserne. My address; F, K., 396/R, Sudeten Kaserne, Hall II/A. The bearer will help you with everything. If you need anything from headquarters [Stab] or the office, write me, that's all here in the Magdeburg Kaserne. Hopefully it is not too cold for you here, and you have brought stoves with you. I am in a great hurry, answer soon and let me know your final address. Sincerely, your F. – Monday morning.

Aside from the inspection of luggage, additional formalities were completed in the Schleuse. On detailed questionnaires all possible personal information was recorded for the "Central Registry" and "Central Labor Office." In order quickly to attain "secure" positions, people attempted to make connections and drew up applications with "curriculum vitae." Many camp functionaries put in an appearance in order to look for acquaintances, but also to preserve their own privileges. Their protégés were to be removed from the Schleuse as quickly as possible. The newcomers crowded around the functionaries, who were assailed with pleas, and people were unstinting with small gifts. At the end of their stay in the Schleuse, people were assigned quarters in the camp. They gathered up their luggage, if they had not given it over to the "Transport Management Department." Their exit brought more bitterness, especially at first, for at that point families were separated, and therefore they hardly felt their situation had improved as a result of "completed processing."

In the initial period, people were not examined very carefully for illness and vermin; this changed after the arrival of transports full of lice in summer 1942. But for a long time there was no possibility of proper disinfection and suitable accommodations. Even when conditions finally had improved technically, this operation nevertheless remained particularly thoughtless.

I take from one report a telling detail on how newcomers were accommodated. When the source of the report was released from the Schleuse, he went looking for his mother, who had arrived in the camp a few days earlier, and finally found her in an attic with no pallet, blanket, cushion, or luggage. The house elder explained that he had no room, but, once he received a few cigarettes, the man immediately discovered a place to sleep in a room, and even a pallet, for the old woman. Even if it is true that it was not possible to accommodate in any halfway proper manner the hordes of people who were thrown precipitously into the camp, there still was a lack of good will on the part of many of those involved.

It seems to be a rule that in difficult conditions people stand by one another the least when extraordinary suffering is added onto familiar, everyday, difficult conditions. In such cases an impatient and irritable mood emerges. All sorts of evil are aroused in otherwise perfectly agreeable people; they brutalize and spoil any forbearance and mildness in themselves. Given their own experiences, they should be eager to help in carrying out the work assigned to them, but instead it becomes a disgusting and untidy business devoid of all human feeling. There probably were laudable exceptions, but this was the rule. All respect for one's fellow man was lost. The human being overwhelmed with disgust became disgusting himself and was treated like something disgusting; the victim was hated as the object of a repulsive profession. The victims generally were helpless and reacted, in blind self-defense, with hate, which could have been dissolved only through overflowing compassion. The people who worked with the transports were likewise victims and downtrodden creatures;

The Transports 233

they felt sorry for themselves and thus hardened themselves against those who were even more unfortunate. Soon hardly any obstacles were left to their descent into meanness. Because they owned little, if they did not suffer from actual privation, their predatory instincts were aroused. Some of them hunted for others' benefit as well; they robbed from one what they gave to others. They were not always bereft of all goodness, but their goodness, too, went astray; they now lived only according to uncontrolled impulses and lost any sense of proportion. A large number of those involved in the transports were morally depraved and collected possessions that no individual in a desperate community (*Notgemeinschaft*) had a right to have for his or his family's use. Many major or minor functionaries, without any sting of conscience, fattened themselves on the remaining belongings of their own kin and possessed things that were valuable and difficult to come by during the war, not only in the camp but even in the outside world. The deportees had sacrificed all their savings to equip themselves for the journey to misery – now they often lost everything. The Jewish leadership was aware of these deplorable circumstances, but they rarely intervened and often were just as bad as the blackguards whose activities they tolerated and sometimes encouraged.

Several reports illustrate the experiences and impressions of newcomers. First, from Theresienstadt, a record of a transport in April 1942 reads:

> We arrived in Theresienstadt in the evening. One didn't arrive, one was delivered and handed over.... They had decreed, for we were no longer we; we were objects, numbers, ghettoized – a demoralized, ground down, crushed, crumpled mass of humanity that, formed into three rows on the ramp, was driven from Budweis to the ramparts and gates of Theresienstadt.... Dead tired and deathly ill, desperate for rest and sleep, we arrived in the cellars and dark holes of the Kavalier Kaserne. And again the mass was mixed, trampled, chopped up, besmirched, rolled and kneaded on the ground, until it became a shapeless pulp, a pile of refuse, which covered and contaminated everything and poisoned it with the taste of the stable. Acquaintances appeared ... the first hand of an acquaintance on my shoulder.... For five days we lived in the Schleuse like rats in a cellar and became fearful of light and fearful of people.... I knew nothing about my future in the ghetto. Whether I would manage to remain, to work, to live. Our transport melted together. Lightning transports [*Blitztransporte*] departed rapidly for the East, one after another. One did not register it at all, one understood even less, before friends and acquaintances already were gone, for a while, forever. There were fewer of us; the feeling of isolation, of helplessness, became stronger and stronger, and exposed in this way one was placed in an enormous hall in the Sudeten Kaserne among hundreds of strange people, on "makeshift bedding" [*Notbelag*], on a concrete floor. One was once again totally alone, and had only oneself. (64)

Second, another report describes the arrival of the first Slovakian transports from the Sered camp in December 1944. We can see how similar the initial experiences of the camp remained, whether in the early or in the final phases of the "ghetto."

> From the "window" of a cattle car one can see only straight ahead, not forward, not backwards. There are fields with deep furrows in which snow lies, hills far off on the horizon, there a scrubby pine tree and then another one, and the cold bites one's nose red. Then a small building with a large swastika flag, a few soldiers in front of it, next to it a barrier. A country road. Then a compact brick structure, "Central Mortuary," the first building with large notices on which a death's head rests peacefully on crossbones, "Danger, poison gas, deadly." Thus begins our new life. We have arrived at the model

234   *Sociology*

camp.... Finally they opened the cars, leave the luggage, one by one into a ground-level, long building with heavily barred windows [A 11]; at the door one had to give one's name and got a number. Then a long room, pleasantly heated. Don't undress, the registration is coming. Eat something, they will take away all your provisions, smoke your last cigarette, the last in this life. Water, please. Water! Water! They are not allowed to give us anything. We stand around, as crowded as in the train carriage; the sick writhe on the floor. The room is overheated. We have on everything we could possibly wear. Most of us feel nauseous. Other rooms? We may not leave the room. For hours. We don't take our clothes off, there's no room. There is nothing to drink. Just waiting. We open the window. "Close it immediately!" Sometimes a German comes. Distributes a few kicks, a few slaps. Then we wait some more. We left the train at nine o'clock in the morning. At six in the evening we form rows of ten. Whoever still can stand, whoever still can walk, whoever is not yet hysterical. The others already are too apathetic to move at all. Not even kicks help anymore. Another long corridor – names and number. Sign here.... Then another long corridor, Germans and prisoners behind a table. One surrenders whatever one has, a ring, a bit of money, the last cigarettes. Keep going. A long corridor, one has to wait there. Behind a door, a body search.... An angled corridor. A red arrow: doctor. One trundles in, arms full of clothes. "Do you have lice?" Mostly, yes.... "Are you ill?" "Water, please!" "There isn't any." We stand and wait our turn. We will certainly have a turn. The doctor barely touches us with two fingers. "How dirty you are. Your home must look lovely. I've never seen such a rabble." "Please, we've been in cattle cars for five days and six nights, without water to drink, how could we have washed ourselves?" ... "Illnesses?" rasps someone from behind a table. We list them. A finger, apparently permanently bent from this work, points to the right. Inoculation....

When new transports come, we are asked: "Say, what's it like in the camp?" The official version is: Well, we aren't exactly overworked, we don't exactly overeat. We while away the time, smuggle, and wait for the end of the war.... Another locomotive howls wistfully through the night. And since the prison camp, we no longer can stand this sound, it tears at the nerves, evokes the horrible deportation transports. How will we ever enjoy traveling again if trains whistle like that? ... Once again, only old people, the sick, women with small children came to our model camp. But they all bring greetings for us, packages. Now they find themselves in strict quarantine. But we already have acquaintances, connections, we borrow authorizations from the police authorities, the Rationing Service. Go to the quarantine during noon break. (256)

It always was customary to bring gift packages and greetings. Some newcomers gave generously of their provisions to acquaintances and friends, while others immediately lost their bearings and did not carry out the commissions they had undertaken. Old-timers, meanwhile, took improper advantage of the newcomers' good nature. It was said of a young man in a good position, and who could always be found in the Schleuse, that "a package came for him and brought his grandmother."

The author of a third report came to Theresienstadt at age thirteen:

On 18 September 1942, the first Jewish transport left Ostrau [Ostrava]. In our home, and perhaps everywhere, chaos reigned. Where could we hide our possessions? What do you think, will this woman give us back the things? Should we bring some money with us? For heaven's sake, I forgot to buy vitamins! What's the matter with me? Do you have more than 50 kg. of luggage? Where are my identification cards? Mom, Mr. Novotny has come for the icebox. Don't keep getting in my way, you darned scamp, how often do I have to tell you, go, go play marbles! The bag of food we'll take with us. Oh my goodness, look how you're packing the things; roll them up, they'll press against your

The Transports

back during the march. Mom, what should I wear for the trip? So, today we'll bathe in this apartment for the last time and lie down in our beds. Who knows what we'll be sleeping on tomorrow? The car is here! Please Mrs. Novak, if a message comes from our relatives, send it to us; here is a letter for the Red Cross. Let's hope we see each other again. But don't cry, the war will be over in three months, and everything will be all right. Yuda! Here I am, Mom. Do you have all the luggage? Just stay together!

So this is the collection camp. You know, Mom, when I was in summer camp, it looked like this. We also made coffee outside, in the open, and we stood in line with the ration bowl. It was great! I don't like it here, there's too much noise, and the people are yelling so much. Why is the woman crying, the one holding the children, a baby in her arms? Is it true that our school principal Eberson wanted to poison himself? Mom, now "all guards report for roll call," what's roll call? Why is the gentleman yelling and getting all excited, the one with the armband on his sleeve that says "Administration"? Ms. Rawitz, did you hear that we aren't even going to stop in Theresienstadt? We'll keep going to Poland. Do you know Mr. Edelstein, he's supposed to be the director there; if he wants to, he can get us out. I don't know him, but thousands know him, how can he help you? But papa, I know his son from the moshavah, the summer camp, and Ms. Mirjam Edelstein too, you'll see that they'll get us out. Don't talk nonsense, you'll never get to him, you won't even have time to talk to him. Hush!! Quiet! Damn it, will there be quiet here or not?! What's wrong? Did someone come? Are we going already? Everyone must board. We take the luggage that we can't carry and pass it on. The train is here already, get ready everyone! How long are we going to stand here? Shut up, don't you see that soldier, how he's looking over here?! They're going already! Brr, that's terrible, look at how they're pointing their guns at us. Faster, faster, you Jewish pig, you don't want to carry? Whack! I can't carry it anymore, I feel sick! You have to hold on, you see? There's the train station already! Ms. Prochazka, you see? What do you say to that? Look how he's sweating. Such a little child. Faster, faster! Finally: the train station. Don't push, everyone will have room.

The train starts to move. Whenever a German soldier comes, everyone stands up and takes off their head covering. What's going on here? What?? What's your name? Joachim Krummholz. Smack, smack. What? Joachim Israel Krummholz. What? You don't know? Whack! Stinking Jew Israel Krummholz, you get it? Yes sir, my name is Stinking Jew Israel Krummholz. We could suffocate here, open the window! Don't you dare open the window, get it? Do you have water? I can't stand it anymore. We traveled only 24 hours from Ostrau [Ostrava] to Theresienstadt, but to me it seemed horribly long before they finally switched us from one track to another, this time for the last time.

We were in Bohušsovice. A small train station, almost deserted, except that a train with cattle cars stood on the opposite track, and there was something very interesting and new that I observed as the train slowly pulled away in the opposite direction; that is, I saw an elderly gentleman who looked out of an opening in the cattle car, and then another head, and then the "Jew" star on a coat. So this must be a transport to Poland, of which we've heard so much.

After a short time our carriage was opened. It was Czechs and, as we heard right away, Jews from Theresienstadt who had been sent to help us. On the platform there were some Germans in uniform, Czech gendarmes and above all strange Jews in uniform with a sort of conductor's cap, but with yellow stripes, and on their chests they had metal numbers and GW. They told us to take only the necessities and leave the rest in the carriages, we would get everything. But only a few people believed that. We dragged as much as we could with us. The train station looked colorful; I had never in my life seen so many people leave a train, with so much colorful luggage, so nicely dressed, actually fully draped. Everything I had on was new, and in duplicate or triplicate, three pairs of socks, two shirts, sweater, jacket, winter coat, and special pockets everywhere in which I had all sorts of things. In one of them a pocket apothecary, vitamins, in another one a sewing kit, pencils, paper, sugar, paraffin, spoon, knife, a flashlight, an address book, a large number of handkerchiefs, a water bottle. I think nothing was missing. And everyone around me looked the same. The mood was depressed, full of expectation.

In half an hour I will know what was right and what wasn't, what we should have packed in our accompanying luggage and in our hand luggage, and what kind of money has value here, and whether cigarettes or flour are better for barter, and whether we will be searched. And whether we will be sent on, and whether the people who went to Theresienstadt a year ago and yesterday will be there. And whether we will stay together or be "torn apart," the men from the women, and what will happen with food, with letters. How everything will be. What a ghetto is. In half an hour we will be there. That's what the people with the yellow stripes say to us; they are supposedly police there – ghetto guards. The look like us, these people, the first people from the ghetto.

We go slowly. For the first time in my life I see streets, buildings, windows, nature that are different from Ostrau [Ostrava]. And so many people, our transport, now I am Bl 214. That is on the paper that I have around my neck. I am surprised at these surroundings; now I know it looks like a fortress, like barracks. Tractors drive past us back and forth, and we can see that the luggage on it is ours. The tractors drive there full and come back for more luggage. But who knows if we'll get the luggage? We went through a dead village or something like that, not a single civilian was in the streets, and only from closed windows here and there did someone occasionally look out. But people live here, because I saw stores with displays. We go on past strange trees that frighten us like the trees in the film "Snow White and the Seven Dwarfs." Gradually, we see roofs in the distance, a small barrier, a low building in front of it, it has a red roof and grass growing on it, and the walls were made of large geometric stones; at the edge there were always a large and a small stone. . . .

And near the low building, as we slowly approached, I saw a whole wall of wooden boxes. As I got even closer, I saw that they were long, low crates. Only when we passed by the large pile of crates did I notice tags with names and dates of birth on them, and then I knew they were coffins. We went on, arrived in a strange city, and at first no people could be seen, the windows of the buildings were closed, and all this made an oppressive impression.

Finally, we arrived at a large building with a giant gate, and we went through a corridor into a courtyard, and then another small passage, and we stopped. This was a large courtyard and around it lots of buildings, it was actually one single large building, and the adults called it a barracks. Men and women with small children had to separate. We thought that they would split us up, and so we quickly bade farewell to our mother and sister. I was tired, but nevertheless I looked around. A lot of traffic, lots of people, everyone looked at us from the building. The building had unusual windows or large arches like the balcony in a movie theater, and even above, on the roof, there were a lot of small windows, and at each of these windows were many heads. And suddenly I saw a pal and was happy that I wouldn't be alone.

Suddenly we were standing in front of a table – that is, streams of people went between a table and two gendarmes. People asked us whether we had prohibited items and searched us a bit. Then we were already going into the strange building; until now we had been in the courtyard. We went through a curious staircase to the attic; there it looked desperately bad, insufficient light, but nevertheless we saw layers of dust on the huge posts over which we crawled. Soon I figured it out and could find my way; there were tags there, Bl 1,000–1,500, with an arrow, and between two posts there were always numbers for 25 people. There were Jews in the attic and they filled out file cards with us. The people who lay on the ground like cattle seemed frightened. When my father went away for a while I cried, I was afraid of losing him in the terrible chaos. We literally sat on our luggage so it wouldn't be stolen. It seemed to me as if I was breathing

The Transports

nothing but dust, so I crawled onto a high post and looked out a window like the ones in large attics. It was drizzling outside, and you could see a street, roofs, a church tower and symmetrical banks that we would later call bastions. I was nauseous from everything, from the tiredness, I didn't want to do anything, I just wanted to be alone and have peace. After a while, we were reunited with Mom and my sister.

Then there suddenly appeared an uncle who had gone to Theresienstadt long before us, and whom we had been sure already was in Poland. My uncle had come with the first and had a good position, he was cantor in the Magdeburg Kaserne (that was what the building we were in was called), and so he didn't live in the attic, but in a large room with some 7–8 families. He told us right away that we shouldn't be afraid, he knew the Jewish Elder, and that we would not go to Poland, and that he would integrate us well [that is, find us good work], and that in addition we could live with him and then we would get into a *Kaserne*, where we would have a bed and not have to sleep in an attic on the floor, and that we would not be hungry; that's how he comforted us. We asked him about thousands of things. Now we knew what we were dealing with, what we should have brought with us, what had "value" here. Slowly, I calmed down. We moved to our uncle's, so that actually I didn't have to sleep even one night in the attic. We went up only to eat. That was called "catching food." (11)

The Jewish Elder usually was notified of the arrival of transports a while in advance. Sometimes, however, the "transport notification" did not arrive until the train already was in the station. The following is one example of a "transport notification":

Central registry 22 April. 7:40 A.M. To dispatch BV/138 Transport Notification
    The arrival of a 14-car transport is announced. Place of arrival: _____ Time of arrival: approx. 8 A.M. Number of persons: _____ Central Registry

Numerous reports had to be written; some went to the SS as "memoranda" via the Jewish Elder. Several such documents have survived from 1945.

Subject Area
Special Deployment   Th., 2 February 1945

Report
On receipt of the transport from ERFURT. The transport lists consist of four sections with

105	
44	
13	
9	
171	persons

Not included in the list:
    Grosch, nee Ullmann Else – 19 September 1864 –   1   person
    A II received   172   persons

This figure was also found upon counting during entry to A II.

The questionnaire, as well as the occupation index for work deployment, was carried out. This transport had not signed postal authorizations, and this has to happen later, until forms are delivered.

Following delousing, the persons were brought to their intended quarters.

Entry into the Schleuse was at 4:30 A.M. The work ended at 4 o'clock P.M.

We later received an arrest warrant from the Schleuse, under which the following listed persons from the Erfurt transport on 2 February 1945 were to be taken into labor

238 *Sociology*

custody] for possession and failure to surrender prohibited objects, and we request that the investigation group do what is necessary:

> Baruch Otto
> Salaman Louis
> Schönauer Sophie
> Dietsch Margarete
>
> SPECIAL DEPLOYMENT
> [signature unreadable]
>
> To the Administration,
> Secretariat,
> Labor Deployment,
> Central Registry,
> Investigation Group

The medical report on the last regular transport to arrive in Theresienstadt reads as follows:

Subject Area Health Service   Theresienstadt, 15 April 1945
Medical Examiner

Report   on the
transport that arrived in Theresienstadt today at 11:45 A.M. from

Amstetten

On the above-mentioned transport 77 persons arrived in the settlement area today.

The general condition of the transport members was impaired by the difficulties of the journey, but no serious acute illnesses are present, so that it may be assumed that the favorable conditions in the settlement shortly will have the commensurate effect.

None of the transport members showed any signs of acute infectious disease or phenomenon arousing suspicion of infection.

Clothing lice were found in 20 cases, head lice in one case, and clothing lice nits in an additional case.

Three male transport members were transferred to the infirmary due to heart ailment or fever. (Building Hauptstrasse 1 [B IV]).

Four people were excluded from inoculation against typhoid fever due to old age and one person due to epilepsy.

The high incidence of lice makes necessary the isolation of the entire transport and its placement under strict quarantine, which was ordered.

> [signed:] Dr. Weisz   Medical Examiner [signed:] Dr. Klaar

A newcomer's shock is betrayed in the following document:

Subject Area Health Service   Theresienstadt
Medical Examiner   12 February 1945

Medical Examiner's findings and report:

Upon arrival in the Schleuse, Zelinka Marta, AE III-177, showed symptoms of a high degree of nervous shock, tearful-excitable nature, profound trembling of the entire body and such feelings of weakness that she could not stand on her feet and had to be transported to her quarters on a stretcher. This condition creates an inability to work, but will in all likelihood subside in a short time, so that one may expect the above-named to be able to work in a few days.

> Medical Examiner
> Dr. Paul Israel Klaar

The Transports

The following provides a general view of the transports:

> The Jewish Settlement Area of Theresienstadt is occupied by a population that has neither grown and developed in a natural manner, nor arrived after a particular screening and in conformity with the economic circumstances existing here.
>
> In the course of the regulation of the Jewish question, Theresienstadt was designated to take in Jews chosen with respect to age, illness, war injury, war decorations, dissolved mixed marriages, and achievements in their careers.
>
> The persons ... picked to reside here arrived in collective transports, a circumstance which was decisive not only for the course of their integration, but also for their equipment and supplies, and thus for the further development of conditions in Theresienstadt. . . .
>
> The arrival and departure of transports at times decisively influenced life in Theresienstadt. Thus on 8 September 1942 alone, four transports with 1,995 people ... arrived, and one transport of 1,000 people ... departed. On 6 September 1943, 5,000 people left the settlement area in one day in two labor deployment transports.
>
> The organization of the Jewish self-administration therefore had to be prepared, on the one hand, for the absorption, accommodation, feeding and also, very often, for the medical care of a large number of people arriving at one time, and on the other hand for the orderly completion of the tasks assigned in connection with the processing of transports.
>
> It goes without saying that the transfer of the persons arriving in the transports and their integration into these unfamiliar conditions took some time. Investigations found that even in regard to health, in the initial period ... the rate of illness and mortality were far above the usual average. Only after a time did the newcomers become accustomed to the new conditions. In regard to health, developed immunity increased their ability to withstand infection.
>
> The transports that arrived in Theresienstadt brought tens of thousands of Jews of the most varied ages, habitats and professional circles, and who had to create their lives within the given framework. One of the most important tasks of the Jewish self-administration is to ease and promote this development. (274)

The substance and the style of these words are equally noteworthy. Certainly it was unusually difficult to adapt to the "unfamiliar conditions." Those to whom no helping hand was offered or who did not themselves have the strength to "create their lives within the given framework" were badly off. This was especially true of the old people, who often lived without assistance for months in the unadapted, stifling attics, where they had to feel their way over the beams and down steep stairs to reach the courtyards. There they spread out their meager things; they wanted to clean and organize them, but the awkward haste of their trembling hands only created even worse confusion. They wanted to wash themselves but had neither soap nor towels. They did not know where their things were, they had brought nothing with them, or they had lost everything. Thus the old people were burdens on themselves and others. Very old people in misery are the least suited to a coerced community. They were thrown pitilessly into the dirt – what could they have held on to? Therefore one should take care not to call Theresienstadt a "better" camp. Helplessly, these creatures tottered to the food distribution point and, instead of real containers, held out dented washbowls and even chamber pots, in order to receive miserable soup and spoiled potatoes. Most had no spoon and had to slurp the bowl of broth. Some of the most horrible scenes occurred among the people who had first received their "transport number" in Theresienstadt, when aides, equipped with pails of whitewash and brushes, were sent to paint the transport numbers of these new arrivals on the unstrapped leg prostheses of cripples. True, Theresienstadt was the salvation of some old people, for whom an extermination camp would have meant certain murder; but even in the "model camp" the terrible interplay between the SS's inhuman methods and the inhuman behavior of some Jews cost many people their lives. Often they faced a gruesome death. And when death came only after weeks, or even months, it was that much more unmerciful an end for those thus condemned.

OUTGOING TRANSPORTS

All the horrors described previously were exceeded by the transports to the East, in which the horror of the "paradise ghetto" was consummated. The terror of deportation never left the camp, from the first deportations in January 1942 until liberation. Subjectively and objectively, not everyone was equally affected, and the situation changed depending on internal circumstances and the course of the war, but no one was spared the fear of the transport, and there was no one, perhaps with the exception of the Danes, who did not have every reason to fear transports. This fear overtook everyone, healthy or sick, young or old, "protected" or "unprotected." Chapter 4 describes some grounds for exclusion from the transports, but no one was safe consistently or at all times. Thus, in the autumn of 1944, not even *Mischlinge* were automatically protected, although previously they had to get permission from the SS "office" to report voluntarily for a transport.

Of what were people afraid? They were afraid of the unknown *and* of being separated from the familiar conditions of Theresienstadt, to which they clung, as little as they liked them, as much as they hated them; but their fear of the unknown was stronger, fueled by the horror of unconfirmed rumors, doubtful information, and uncertain forebodings. Until the end, few people had detailed knowledge of the true terrors in the East. A very few who had themselves been in the East for a time had been brought to Theresienstadt for some reason; they had to keep silent. Some had heard this or that about the East before their deportation to Theresienstadt, but the information sounded too unbelievable. People knew of terrible conditions, severe hunger, and even pogroms, but systematic mass extermination was neither known nor believed. This was fine with the SS, who did not wish dissemination of the truth, but who preferred to calm and lull, for which reason they also chose euphemisms such as "delivery to a different maintenance camp" (*Versorgungslager*) and "labor deployment transport to the Reich territory."

Material and psychological elements make this lack of knowledge of the truth more comprehensible (see also 342). Even in the face of the chimneys that spewed flame almost continuously, there were people in Auschwitz who did not "know," or at least did not want to know, what was happening a few hundred meters away. Thus it was even more likely that such horrors would remain unknown and disbelieved in the masked Theresienstadt. A vital person in great danger is seldom so realistic or such a pessimist as to fully recognize the possibility of a fateful *and* incredible truth. For this, one must possess real strength of mind *and* a certain amount of knowledge. But in Theresienstadt there was no knowledge, just dull forebodings circulated among the prisoners; precisely for this reason, horror and fear prevailed, nourished constantly by lurking "measures" and malicious "directives" and by the threatening proximity of that which was not talked about but talked around, as it forced its way into the camp through, for example, the strange behavior of the scrupulously segregated Bialystok [Białystok] children. Those who had neither settled accounts with their lives nor knew or were convinced of the truth – how could they not go onto the transport with some hope, however great their anxiety? The worse the war seemed to be going for Germany, the more "paradisiacal" Theresienstadt became, and the more people doubted that deportation was as bad as it had been rumored to be. People thought that Germany needed workers, that the "voice of world public opinion" had been aroused, that the "Red Cross" would protect the Jews, and that the powers would prevent really bad treatment and respond with reprisals. With its "city beautification," the SS blinded the prisoners in Theresienstadt no less than the world, which watched the destruction of the Jews much more indecisively and inactively than was necessary.

The SS was clever at deceit. Had they announced real or fictional transport destinations, they would have done an even better job of achieving their goal. It was the Slovak Jews who first brought more exact news to the camp, in December 1944, but the full truth only got through shortly before liberation. Murmelstein, Eppstein, Zucker, Baeck (see Chapter 6), and some others knew with greater or lesser certainty what those who were sent away faced, but, for most, the fate of the departed remained a mystery as long as transports traveled eastward. In Theresienstadt, as in the transit camps in the West (Drancy and Westerbork), this had a dull reassuring effect that was almost impossible in Eastern Europe, given the greater level of distrust among Jews there.

The inmates of Theresienstadt preferred the known evil to the unknown evil. Only in the externally difficult months at the beginning, when the camp seemed especially unstable and no one yet felt "at home," were there people who were indifferent to being sent away; they thought that it could hardly be worse in Poland, where it might even be freer. Such things were no longer heard later on. The old-timers especially adapted quite well to the "ghetto." Many had a "pleasant" life, a "good" position, and real or apparent privileges that they had no desire to give up. No one could become accustomed to conditions in Theresienstadt without suffering harm, as much as one might adapt to the situation. People would become too psychologically attached to "safe" Theresienstadt and would be in high spirits when no transports were expected; however, once a transport threatened, people would fall alternately into despair or rebelliousness.

> Whenever we forgot for a few days that we were interned in a concentration camp, when it was said that transports were leaving, everything changed at once. People slunk anxiously through the streets; cowering, they waited for the lists to be delivered, again and again the same picture: fear, terror, "Are you on it?" "No, I'm not on it, I'm protected." "My mother is on it!" "Did you already complain?" "Yes, but there's no hope." Everywhere the same topic of conversation, the same haste, the same excitement. Packing is precipitous. Hardly has the list been delivered when one sees the oh, so common picture. Heavily loaded figures, number boards around their necks, move to the Schleuse, a barracks that gathered in the unfortunate victims who had to journey into uncertainty – that is, to a certain death. Hardly was everyone assembled there when the gates shut; they no longer belonged to us, they were foreign bodies to be ejected; they were now first segregated, demarcated, separated. Then they were entrained, the carriages sealed, and the transport is gone. And now the miracle occurs. Everyone breathes a sigh of relief; what's gone is gone. Perhaps here a girl cries after having to watch her parents leave, and there is a mother whose son has gone away. But life in Theresienstadt

goes on; this time it turned out all right. For God's sake, when is the next transport leaving? Ah, well, by then it could be "sof" (the end), and every day is life gained. (193a)

This is a good summary of the average behavior of the majority: despair combined with stupor. The feeling of unconditional helplessness did not allow one to be constantly depressed. One left that to the weak, who constantly worried and grieved themselves to death for the departed and for their own future. To revolt against fate seemed pointless. Strong people, anchored in themselves, to whose cheeks thoughtless levity would bring a blush, were rare, but they, too, could not lose themselves constantly to the sorrow of reality, and they protected themselves with intense labor, serious lectures, and study; they took on social duties and buried themselves in art, philosophy, and religion.

> Each yearned to learn something about his fate, attempting to repel the threatened danger through connections or in other ways. After days and nights of constant meetings, the lists finally were made up, and then at night, in fact essentially only at night [this is not quite true], the transport members were delivered notifications with their names and the information that they were leaving on a transport. Everyone waited tensely for the notifications, which were delivered in the barracks by the building elders, in the civilian houses by the house elders. On such nights, no one could think of sleeping. The slips of paper with the names of those who had been called up arrived continuously, and each person waited painfully to see whether the house elder would come to his room, and whom fate had chosen. To increase the tension, the call-up slips were not delivered at once, but in batches. Until the transport's departure, no one actually was sure he would not have to go with it, since individuals were removed from transports as a result of illness or on the basis of various connections, and until the transport departed the commission had to meet constantly in order, if necessary, to pick replacements. Thus fear and agitation prevailed until the last moment, and only subsided once the train had left. It is difficult to describe the feelings of a house elder whose duty it was to pass on the sad news of departure. When I entered a room with the slip in hand and turned on the light, everyone stared at me, and in each person's distraught eyes I read the question: am I on the list? And then the most difficult part began: telling the person involved that he was among those chosen for departure. Despair took hold, wailing and crying, particularly when, as often happened, families were torn apart, parents from children or siblings. But there was nothing to be done but to accept one's fate. Everyone got up and helped with packing. Sometimes one of the chosen tried to avoid fate through an intervention at the Magdeburg Kaserne, or went to the doctor to get confirmation that he was incapable of transport. They were rarely lucky. Nothing remained but to go to the examination, then to the train station, and then to the East. (16)

Most people were fixated on the "transport" as a complex. They chose the smartest and dumbest – the most bizarre and well considered – methods to save themselves. People sought "objective" grounds for protection, which led to false statements about war medals, "mixed" extraction, or "protective" citizenship. If the SS discovered something like this, one was arrested for "attempting to mislead the authorities" and was "transferred to a concentration camp." People tried to save themselves through a "position," falsely assuming that they could gain protection through diligence and by working in a "business important to the Germans." Some occupations, such as mica splitting, really did provide permanent or temporary protection. People strove for higher positions that seemed to be internally "protected," but what use was it once the position of the Jewish boss collapsed, or the

The Transports 243

SS intervened with a "directive"? People made efforts to be "permanently incapable of transport" through sickness. This could be achieved with sufficient connections and bribery, but ultimately this, too, failed. Help was sought through the patronage of the leadership and other influential persons, and if one had this, one was bound to one's protector for better or worse; if he fell or no longer was strong enough, one was lost. The more powerful the patron seemed, the more his patronage was sought. If one patron could protect thirty or more people, other patrons could protect some as well, and thus a consuming trade in souls began, as patrons considered whom to abandon and whom not to; many victims fell by the wayside.

One could buy one's freedom from the functionaries of the "Transport Management Department," and possibly also from those of the "Transport Department." This certainly was not easy, but it was attempted, and undoubtedly also achieved. Reports confirm that "changes" were made in the Schleuse through "exchange of money and good words" for members of the "transport reserve"; gold, hard currency, watches, tobacco, and food were the price. Some young women saved themselves through prostitution with members of the administration. Ransoms of this sort generally helped for only one transport and were no longer valid for the next one.

For single women, it was possible to register with the camp authorities a "cohabitation arrangement," or later a "marriage announcement," with a "protected" single man (see Chapter 15). This method was chosen for honorable as well as dishonorable reasons. If a woman's partner's grounds for protection lasted, she was saved; if they did not, she was delivered over to disaster.

One final method for avoiding being transported led directly to the SS. The last camp leader, Rahm, like Möhs, who often was present at the transports, could sometimes be appealed to. At the last minute, they might free sturdy boys and girls, even with their families. For such interventions it was best if one knew the SS man personally from work, or if someone else mediated. But sometimes it did not help, and it rarely helped repeatedly. One would then be slapped and kicked before being sent away.

The story of a transport or a series of transports within a short period went according to the following pattern. Eichmann gave orders to the SS "office" in Theresienstadt on the number of transports and persons, the date, general guidelines, and "special instructions." The camp leader, sometimes together with other SS officers, gave more specific orders to the Jewish Elder, who was told what age groups, countries of origin, and other categories of people to choose or to protect. Only on occasion was someone named individually: the "instructions" were issued in Berlin, Prague, or Theresienstadt itself, and Jewish interventions against them almost always were useless. The SS went no further in choosing the victims but left this entirely, or largely, to the Jews. Only for certain transports, described in earlier chapters, did the SS choose other methods. But it could happen that someone attracted unfavorable attention, as happened to a dystrophic dwarf during the "beautification" before the May transports of 1944; he was accosted by Rahm on the street with the words: "You, you're spoiling our whole beautification. Report immediately to the Jewish Elder for the next transport!"

When transports threatened, word went around like lightning. Rumors often began to circulate through the indiscretions of SS men long before the Jewish Elder knew of them officially. Disclaimers made no difference, for experience always confirmed the truth of such rumors. Sometimes the transports departed later than first intended, which fed confused hopes: "The Germans don't even have enough train cars for transports!"; "The trains are no longer operable!" But the train cars would come twenty-four or forty-eight hours later, and the trains never failed. In autumn 1944, it seems that – and, in April 1942, it is certain that – the final number of transports was larger than even the SS in Theresienstadt expected beforehand. During this period, the orders on the choice of victims often were changed only a few hours before departure, so that the transportees had to be hastily rearranged.

As soon as the Jewish Elder had been informed, the Council of Elders met to discuss the internal guidelines, but they did not compile a list. Feverish activity began in all the "departments." Everywhere the workers' lists of qualifications lay ready; workers were qualified according to four degrees: indispensable, relatively indispensable, relatively expendable, and expendable. It was the task of all the heads of "departments" and "subdepartments" to make such lists. Once a transport had left, the lists had to be updated immediately and kept by the department head.

The "Central Registry" separated out the names of everyone who could be considered for the transport; the names of members of exempt groups, such as Reich Germans or people over sixty-five, were removed. As far as was possible in the rush of preparation, all internal guidelines also were to be considered – for example, high functionaries, members of the Construction Kommando (AK) transports (for a long time), and families with children under four years old were exempted. In this way, the so-called preliminary lists came into being. They were brought to the "Transport Commission," also called the "Poland Commission" and for a short time the "Commission," which was made up of representatives of all "departments" and was furnished with the qualification lists and other orders. The "Commission" was an organ of the "Transport Department," which was part of the "Central Secretariat," and its agile head was named Wilhelm Cantor. The "preliminary lists" were read out, and the representatives of the "departments" raised their objections, which automatically also affected spouses and children under eighteen or sixteen years old, as deportations took place by family within these bounds. Then horse trading began, based on the number of available people, and on who was and was not to be sacrificed. The members of the Council of Elders, and the functionaries who were, internally, on the same level with them, had the agreed-upon right to a "personal protection list" of thirty persons, but some lists contained up to seventy names. Cantor maneuvered carefully and nimbly during the treacherous operations. Once the "Commission" had agreed, the "lists" – including a "reserve" list – were made final. The "reserve" was necessary because of the "appeals" after "delivery" of the "lists"; objective and subjective errors slipped in and sick people with "transport incapacity" and other circumstances had to be considered. As a result, some "appeals" were always granted. This was possible because the SS received only the final "list" and was not interested in who was on it, as long as the prescribed total was correct.

As long as the "Commission" was in session, a dangerously large crowd gathered on the staircase and in the corridors in front of the administration's offices in B V; it increased considerably after "delivery" of the "list," although the entrances were kept locked. Consecutively numbered lists were typed up, with many carbon copies on machines in the "Central Registry." After each number came the individual's previous "transport number," last and first name, date of birth, and address in the "ghetto." The pages were cut in such a way that each name was on a narrow strip.

The strips were sent by messenger in separate "batches" from B V to the building elders and house elders, who handed them out to the victims or had them delivered. Originally they were given out separately, and later they were pasted to "call-up slips." In the autumn of 1944, the notifications bore this text:

Call-up [*Einberufung*]
We must herewith inform you that you have been included in the transport. You are to appear for processing punctually, according to instructions from the building or house elder, at the collection point
Lange Strasse 5 (3) [C III]
Following receipt of this call-up, you must immediately prepare your luggage. Only small amounts of luggage appropriate for work may be brought along; that is, only hand luggage that can be carried personally, with work clothes, underwear, blankets, etc. Luggage must be brought by you personally into the Schleuse.
To avoid official sanction, it is absolutely necessary to appear punctually.

Last-minute "appeals" usually were permitted. People generally were "called up" a few days before departure of the transport. Theoretically, one could be brought to the SS "office" via the Jewish Elder to present objections. This probably rarely happened. Official internal "appeals" made sense only if there were objective protective grounds. Those who hoped to escape disaster through illness were not supposed to "appeal" but were supposed to go to the Schleuse or have themselves brought there. There a doctor could apply for "transport incapacity," which he was supposed to do only if the sick person had a high fever or dangerous infection, recently had had an operation, or was moribund. Patronage also worked differently. Sometimes a doctor or a commission was allowed into the quarters of potential transportees, to free sick people from "reporting to the Schleuse." Seriously ill patients in hospitals sought this protection from the chief physician. But it was the "Commission" that made the final decision on "removal"; in regard to this decision, the word of Reinisch, the medical examiner (*Vertrauensarzt*), was binding (see 246). This man, a sinister camp bigwig who had never completed his studies and wrongfully used the title of doctor, enjoyed the unreserved confidence of the SS; the masters let him treat them, showered him with favors, employed him as a prison doctor even for those imprisoned in the SS bunker, and had him issue and sign the death certificates of the slain, asserting natural causes of death. The appreciative SS sent Reinisch, who had to be honored as a "guest of the Council of Elders," to the gas chambers of Auschwitz with the last transport. Doctors frequently saved people from transports out of sympathy, and sometimes for less attractive reasons. A doctor and a nurse who had infected with typhoid fever people in danger of transport were hanged in July 1943 at the "Small Fortress" (see 162).

Many attempted to extricate themselves through their connections or their bosses, but some higher functionaries, such as the head of the health service, Dr. Munk, were unavailable to speak to their subordinates during transport periods. Others made efforts to help. Official "appeals" were presented in writing. The following form was used for the May transports in 1944:

Appeal   Trsp. No. _____
Name_____ First name _____ Quarters _____
FAMILY MEMBERS included in the same transport
Name _____ First name_____ Relationship _____ Trsp. No. _____
Quarters _____
[Five lines for information on relatives]

246   *Sociology*

Reason
    Each family may submit only one appeal (not separately for each family member).
Indicate only the persons included in the same transport.
    Accepted ____   Processed _____
    On _____ at _____ o'clock

Unless it had been favorably processed beforehand, which rarely happened, a "appeal" did not postpone the affected person's appearance at the Schleuse. If it was granted, one generally could not leave the "Schleuse" and return to one's quarters until after the transport's departure. Sometimes people were freed only at the last minute; people were even taken off the trains, so they could never be sure whether they would in fact be allowed to remain, if someone were trying to help them. It therefore could happen that luggage left while the owner did not, but sometimes the reverse was true. The "removed" (*Ausgereihten*) were informed in writing:

Lfd. No._____ Trsp. no. new _____ Trsp. no. old _____ Name _____ Quarters or Schleuse _____ was removed and need not report to the Schleuse or is to be released from the Schleuse. The Jewish Elder [stamp and signature] Jewish Self-Administration Theresienstadt Dr. Paul Israel Eppstein Theresienstadt, _____ 1943

Before July 1942, transports were especially difficult for the people involved because men and women could not communicate with each other. A "transport post" system was introduced for them; letters were marked with a large T and were brought from barracks to barracks by an authorized messenger. The "transport members" did not see one another before the Schleuse, or even before the loading of the train, during which families always were loaded together.

The procedures in the Schleuse were carried out in various ways. The transports in January 1942 were strictly isolated behind a hastily erected wooden fence. Sometimes the treatment was mild and visitors were tolerated, except before departure; those who already had "reported" were even allowed to leave. Ordinarily things were quite strict. The hour of "reporting" was supposed to be adhered to exactly but often was greatly exceeded, even by half a day. In April 1942, some transports marched to the train station without spending time in the Schleuse. Those who had been called up received instructions about the amount of luggage they could bring along; it generally was limited due to lack of storage space. A distinction was made between "hard" and "soft" luggage, and often only soft luggage was allowed; thus one could take along much less than one had brought to the camp. As a result, many transportees were in doubt about what they should pack. Few were matter-of-fact or skeptical enough to tell themselves that all probably was lost. People wanted to be smarter than on the trip to Theresienstadt, and so they carried whatever possible on their bodies: underwear and clothes, in duplicate and triplicate. Pockets were lined, and prohibited items were sewn in and carefully hidden. The transportees preferred to use easily manageable luggage, for example, homemade knapsacks, satchels, shoulder bags, sacks and pouches, along with a "bed roll" with blankets and cushions. Down blankets could not be brought along; often the number of blankets was limited.

Much was left behind, put aside, or given away. Roommates and friends often were helpful and even self-sacrificing. One did what one could, encouraged and comforted. Those who were helpless and living among the helpless generally were in bad shape, because the official "transport assistance" often failed in its duties, and many thought only of their own advantage. People took leave of one another soberly. Brave people who had to depart joked in front of their aged parents and cheered them up; conversely, the elderly, too, bore themselves with dignity. Volunteering to go with family members was not permitted for persons over sixty-five or sixty-seven. Sometimes entire families traveled voluntarily when one relative was affected and could not be saved. Besides examples of selfless behavior, people also were unkind or capable of only feigned love. There were quite influential people who did not even seriously attempt to rescue their relatives, and some people, after big speeches about how they would rather go along than be robbed of their father and mother, let their parents leave and easily got over the loss. Many also sensed that they should not drag people along with them and did not accept the sacrifice of a loved one's voluntary journey to destruction.

The sojourn in the Schleuse lasted from a few hours to several days. People were given the normal fare. They were supposed to hand in their "labor identification card," "ration card" – people got a special one for the Schleuse – and "ghetto crowns." They rarely did so. Therefore, after a transport had left, the "ration cards" of those who remained were always stamped by the "rationing service" (*Menagedienst*) to prevent misuse of the cards of the deported. On arrival in the Schleuse, people were received and assigned a place based on their "transport numbers." By the time they arrived at their quarters, the victims already had been given pieces of paper with these numbers on them, with which they marked their luggage and which they hung around their necks, as described in Chapter 3. Fellows with whitewash came to the Schleuse and painted the numbers wherever one wished. People had "hand luggage" with them; "accompanying luggage," if it was ever permitted, went to the storehouse. Life in the Schleuse was a diabolical chaos, but departure from Theresienstadt was different from arrival. Newcomers were intimidated and thereby prepared for the camp, whereas the departing were in despair and often were still attempting to escape their doom. Before departure there was little thought of sleep; those who did sleep did not undress, as it was hardly possible. The gendarmes never appeared, nor, generally, did the SS. If they did come, it was always unpleasant; they reprimanded, confiscated luggage, and hunted down prisoners who were in the Schleuse without authorization. The entrances originally were guarded by gendarmes, and later by the Ghetto Guard.

Before the people marched out, the SS men appeared; they were generally irritable, yelling and hitting. As long as boarding took place in Bohušovice, those who could walk had to run to the station in the same way they had come to the camp. Often they had primitive little wagons, or sleds in the winter, on which they loaded their possessions. The "Transport Management Department" was supposed to take care of the rest. On leaving the Schleuse, people displayed their numbers, and they were crossed off the list. It took several hours before a transport was loaded, with an average of seventy to eighty people per cattle car. Before autumn 1944, passenger cars generally were not used, but it was no less crowded in them. If larger pieces of luggage could be brought along, they were put into separate cars. Generally the storage space was insufficient, and most of the luggage stayed behind. A bucket was placed in every car for relieving oneself. Provisions generally consisted of 1,500 g of bread, a bit of margarine and sugar, 250 g of liverwurst or sausage, a pinch of salt, and sometimes some jam. Water was never provided. During the first transports in 1942, the same functionaries were appointed from the ranks of the deportees as in the

248 *Sociology*

transports from the "Protectorate" to Theresienstadt. The cars were closed and sealed. The escort, generally German police officers, had its own car. Often the train stood for many hours before finally departing.

THE SINISTER NATURE OF THE TRANSPORTS

How sinister the transports were can be illustrated by the deportations in April 1942. No one was sure if he was safe. Men and women, in separate barracks, could not see each other. The transport calendar between April 18 and April 30 makes the horror apparent. Up until April 18, 21,575 people had come to the camp, and some 5,075 were deported or otherwise removed. During the period under discussion, one transport arrived on the 18th, with 909 people, and two arrived on April 24 and 28, with 1,000 people each. By the end of April, 496 inmates had died. Thus some 18,900 people were available. Six thousand people were supposed to depart on six transports, on April 18, 23, 26, 27, 28, and 30. Protected persons included (1) persons over sixty-five years of age (at least 3,000 people), (2) members of the Construction Kommando (AK) transports and their closest relatives (at least 1,500 people), (3) those doing "outside work" and their closest relatives (approximately 3,000 people), (4) members of other protected groups (at least 700 people) – altogether, that is, at least 8,200 people. Thus the transportees had to be chosen from a pool of at most 10,700 people. Most had friends among higher- or lower-level members of the administration, and Edelstein still fought in his camp to rescue younger Czech Jews.

The nature of those dark days is evoked in the following series of orders of the day:

According to instructions from the camp commandant's office, the persons chosen for the transport to the East on 25 April 1942 will receive notification ... during the day today.

Choice of transport members is made, via instructions from the camp commandant, from all transports that have so far arrived in the ghetto, with the exception of Construction Kommando [AK] I and Construction Kommando [AK] II. In consequence of the necessity of dispatching the transport before the arrival of new transports, a number of persons who already have been put to work, and families with children, will be included in the transport. (orders of the day, April 23, 1942)

Transports to the East:
The Camp Commandant's Office has, as announced in the orders of the day ... of 24 April 1942, given orders that, aside from the already scheduled transports on the 18th, 23rd, 25th and 27th of the same, additional transports should be arranged for 28 and 30 April as well.

This directive places the ghetto in enormous difficulty. The danger existed that it no longer will be possible to prevent the breakup of families, for which reason everything must be done to provide the required number without breaking the closest family ties.

The Council of Elders attempted during the entire time not to include in the transports anyone on work deployment, specialists, qualified laborers, and office workers as well as their closest relatives. This was done in the interests of building up the ghetto.

The danger of family breakups leads to the imperative necessity of including families from these groups rather than letting it happen that the closest family ties are broken.

The Council of Elders is aware that a step is thus taken that most deeply affects the lives of all staff, but hopes they of all people will understand that this is a necessity that no longer can be avoided.

The parents of staff, administrative employees, specialists, qualified laborers, and other staff who have previously been removed, through appeal, from the transports to the East in cases deserving of consideration must now expect, beginning with the transports on the 28th of this month, to be included if necessary.

Staff members have the opportunity to submit appeal petitions in which they provide special grounds for the removal of their parents, but must at the same time indicate whether, in case of a negative decision on their petition, they will voluntarily agree to go along. (orders of the day, April 26, 1942)

Regarding: Transport to the East

Today at 12:30, the following order was issued:

All persons over 65 years of age are removed with immediate effect from the intended transports to the East. An exception is made for people 65–67 years of age, as long as they are found capable of transport by a doctor. The Camp Commandant's Office orders that the transport list for the 27th of this month [for the following day!] be changed in the course of this afternoon such that all old people be removed and replaced by younger people. Persons so far exempted from the transports to the East as a result of their deployment in industry, the economy, administration, etc., now also will be included in the transports. In line with this decree by the Camp Commandant's Office, all people over 67 should consider themselves removed from the transport. They will not be given written notification. All other transport members chosen for the transport to the East on the 27th of this month, with the exception of relatives of Transport Am, should expect their latest notification by this evening. Persons from Transport Am who have been removed due to urgent appeals will also receive their notification by this evening.

To assemble the transport for the 27th of this month, the necessity arises of including the following transports:

V, W, X, Y, Z, Ac, Ad, Ae, Af, Ah, Ai, Akb.

The members of these transports must expect to receive a notification by this evening on their inclusion in the transport to the East. The same is also true for persons who came with other transports but whose closest relatives were members of the above transports. They should thus be prepared and make sure that their luggage is within reach.

In addition to the elderly, those excluded from inclusion in the transport to the East include members of transports AK I and AK II, as well as relatives (spouses, minor children and parents of minors) of groups of workers employed in ... outside work.... In consideration of the shortness of time, an appeals procedure is not possible this time. (special orders of the day, April 26, 1942)

According to orders, ... a further transport to the East must be dispatched on 28 April 1942....

In consideration of this order and the shortness of time, no appeals procedure will be possible for this transport either.

Members of the following transports and their closest relatives ... are to ready themselves and their luggage immediately.

G, H, K, L, M, N, R, S, T, U, V, W, X.

The list of transport members will be compiled during the day today, and transport members will receive notification during the day. (special orders of the day, April 27, 1942)

Transports to the East 25 and 27 April 1942.

The transport to the East scheduled for the 25th of this month and postponed until the 26th of this month departed yesterday, Sunday, the 26th of this month from the

Theresienstadt Ghetto to the East with 1,000 persons. The transport to the East scheduled for today also left for the East with 1,000 persons.

Transports to the East, 28 April 1942.
In consideration of the fact that notifications for the transport leaving tomorrow morning cannot be issued until during the day today, it is absolutely necessary that the members of the transports listed in the special orders of the day for the 26th and 27th of this month ready all their luggage to be handed over.

In the various barracks ... work groups are available, these will help with packing if necessary.

Attention is called to the fact that transport members who do not ready their luggage in time risk being transported to the East without luggage if they are included. (orders of the day, April 27, 1942)

Because of this frantic pace, no Schleuse was set up. All the residents of the barracks were in confusion, especially the included and the removed, who were informed only a few hours before departure. The barracks were full of makeshift piles of luggage, which often had to be first laboriously dragged from the storehouse, where suitcases were stored at the time. The nights became days, the blackout rules were lifted, and strong floodlights – hurriedly mounted – illuminated with a bright yet pallid light the mad turbulence that swirled from the barracks into the courtyards. In summer and early fall 1942, the most frantic conditions prevailed. For months, transport personnel could barely leave the Schleusen, the storehouses, and the train stations, and nonstop shifts of thirty-six hours were not unusual. This furthered these people's moral decline. In July 1942, 25,111 people had to be received; there were only three days when no transports arrived. Moreover, 2,000 people were deported, and 26,429 had to be internally "resettled." A "memorandum from the Central Secretariat" on the "old people's transport" in October 1942 invokes once again the nightmarish fear of sinister horror. We should recall that, instead of five transports of 10,000 victims, in the end four transports of 7,866 victims left Theresienstadt.

Theresienstadt Ghetto   Theresienstadt, 12 October 1942
Council of Elders
To the District and House Elders
For announcement in all buildings, houses and rooms.
Regarding: Old People's Transport

The Council of Elders hereby announces that instructions have been received from the higher authorities that 10,000 persons, admitted here on transports from the Protectorate of Bohemia and Moravia, must be dispatched from here.

Composition of the transport will be based on registration with the commandant's office and the persons thereby allotted to the Council of Elders by the higher authorities.

The total number of elderly persons from the Protectorate is 7,500. Approximately 1,000–1,200 were marked as "T" cases by the Commandant's Office; that is, they must remain in the ghetto. Roughly 6,000 elderly persons may be considered for the transport.

The remaining 4,000 persons must be chosen from the remaining total pool of approximately 20,000 ghetto dwellers belonging to the Protectorate.

For the first transport, which will consist of 2,000 persons and is departing on the 15th of this month, voluntary inclusion is possible, so that the danger of family breakup seems to be eliminated.

For the second and probably also third transport, the aspect of age will be considered, or those people chosen by the Commandant's Office for the Old People's Transport.

The Transports 251

The choice of remaining transport members will take place in consideration of the needs of the ghetto.

The list of the 2,000 people for the first transport on the 15th of this month will be announced today, the 12th of the month, in the evening and tomorrow, the 13th of the month, in the early morning hours. A few days later, the list of the second transport will be released. In a short period of time, the approximate lists for the remaining transports will follow.

Central Secretariat
[signed] Dr. Janowitz

We should again recall that of the 6,000 people who journeyed to Treblinka, no one survived the transport.

10

Population

Population

On November 24, 1941 ... the first construction group arrived, consisting of 342 Jewish craftsmen and workers. By December 31 ... the Jewish population had grown to 7,350.

The figure temporarily reached 15,372 as of 1 April 1942, but had declined to 12,986 by the first of May. In June, the first transports arrived from the Old Reich [Altreich] and the Ostmark [the territory of pre-Anschluss Austria] and resulted in an increase to 14,300 on 1 June 1942, to 21,269 on 1 July, and to 43,403 on 1 August. Thus during the month of July, an increase of 22,134 could be noted – that is, the population doubled....

The mortality in September 1942 was 3,941; in October 1942 it was 3,096....

As of 1 November 1942, a population level of 45,312 was reached, which was sustained with certain minor fluctuations until 1 September 1943, when it was 45,635.

In the last quarter of 1943 ... there were approximately 40,000 persons.

A further reduction ensued ... so that on 1 January 1944, the population fell to 34,655, its lowest level since July 1942....

For classification ... according to sex ... it is significant that within the areas of origin from which transports were dispatched to Theresienstadt, a large number of men previously had emigrated in order to create conditions for their families to follow.

Therefore, men predominated ... only during the first few weeks.

As of March 1942, there was a slight preponderance of women, which had resulted by July 1942 in a surplus of 2,600 women.

The arrival of the transports from the areas of the Old Reich and the Ostmark, where the emigration of Jews already had reached particularly large proportions, brought yet another significant shift in terms of gender. On 1 August 1942, the surplus of women amounted to nearly 10,000. On October 1 it exceeded 12,000.

It is evident from this that the arriving transports, depending on the age group, were bringing either widows or single women....

The total numbers ... pertaining to 27 February 1944 were as follows:

Total entry   127,836
Total exit   90,922
Population level   36,914

Population

Age Distribution

The age composition of the ... transports reflects the general structure of the Jewish population in the Protectorate.... . Thus in addition to ... old and sick persons, they brought mainly laborers of working age, as well as craftsmen and specialists.

However, what affected the age structure of the population ... was not only the composition of the arriving transports, but also that of the departing transports.

Particular categories of persons (the very old, the sick, decorated war veterans, those injured in the war, those with Aryan relatives, and foreigners) had to remain in Theresienstadt, according to official regulations. Therefore, transports to be dispatched toward the East included for the most part those fit for work.

The percentage ... of people over 65 years of age, which in January 1942 amounted to approximately 6%, had risen to 27% ... by May. In June 1942 the first transports arrived from the Altreich and the Ostmark; the average age of their occupants was more than 70 years.... .

The very elderly portion of the population ... continued to grow until October 1942. At that point, the increased mortality rate as well as the departure of transports of the aged became apparent as a type of adjustment. This development was reinforced by the arrival of younger staff members of liquidated Jewish organizations in Berlin, Vienna and Prague.... .

Distribution by Countries of Origin

... Designed to hold Jews from the Protectorate ... , Theresienstadt was also destined to absorb Jews from the entire area of the Reich. They were selected according to official criteria (age, illness, war injuries and war decorations, dissolved mixed marriages, accomplishments).

Only Jews from the Protectorate came ... during the period from 24 November 1941 to 2 June 1942 ...

In June 1942 ... the first transports from the Altreich and the Ostmark began to arrive.... . They consisted almost entirely of persons ... over 60 years of age. There were two reasons for this fact:

1. 1 September 1939 was preceded in the Altreich as well as in the Ostmark by a lengthy period of emigration ...
2. Persons of working age from the Altreich as well as the Ostmark were immediately dispatched for deployment to the East.... .

The average age of members of the initial transports ... from the Altreich and the Ostmark was between 69 and 73 years.

Only after the migration transports ended and existing Jewish businesses were liquidated in Vienna (fall 1942) and Berlin (spring 1943) did ... persons of working age began to arrive; they were staff members of the Israelitische Kultusgemeinde [Jewish Community] in Vienna, the Reichsvereinigung der Juden in Deutschland [Reich Association of Jews in Germany], Berlin, as well as persons who were retained for work deployment for significant reasons.... .

In total, by 29 February 1944, 69,723 persons had arrived from the Protectorate ... 40,164 from the Altreich, 15,026 from the Ostmark.

... Members of the initial transports from the Old Reich and the Ostmark had to rely on the assistance of others; the people who later followed were able to help with work and building.

Intermittently, other transports from the Protectorate ... also carried inmates of old-age homes and hospitals. The liquidation of the Jüdische Kultusgemeinde [Prague Jewish Community] resulted in the relocation of its leading functionaries to Theresienstadt.

It became necessary to meld together in Theresienstadt the Jews from these various areas to help facilitate good relations among them, and to balance the resulting diversity.

In April 1943, the first group ... from Holland arrived; additional transports followed in January and February 1944, increasing the size of this group to a total of 2,259. In October 1943, the first Jews arrived from Denmark, and the total number of this group was 464. The age stratification of this group is ... entirely normal. Their numerical ratio in terms of the total population is such that their integration presents no difficulties whatsoever.

[274]

By September 1944, the Dutch group had increased to almost 4,900. Few people from other countries came during this time. Danes were no longer arriving. The May transports in 1944 reduced the "level" by 7,500 people, although the age distribution and sex ratio were barely altered. The fall catastrophe of 1944 spared the elderly and affected men and children more than it did women, whose majority significantly increased. Now only approximately 11,000 prisoners remained, which approached the "level" of February 8, 1942. Between the end of 1944 and mid-April 1945, the number of prisoners rose to approximately 17,500 people. They were Jews from "mixed marriages" from the "Protectorate" and Germany, as well as groups from Slovakia and Hungary – most of them fit to work. Women were in the majority.

The character of the "ghetto" was determined by Jews from Czechoslovakia, and, to some extent, by German and Austrian Jews, next to whom other groups played a minor role in every respect. Of lesser importance were smaller groups from Luxembourg (see 166b) and from Danzig, which can be classified as German. The family of the minister and mayor of Le Havre, Léon Meyer, was deported from France via Bergen-Belsen.

In this way, Theresienstadt differed from old ghettos in the East, which were forced labor camps run by the SS and which held mostly indigenous Jews; in those ghettos, expellees from the West remained foreign and were always in the minority. Only in the days before liberation did people arrive, in a confused mix, at Theresienstadt from many countries. Before this, only a small number of Jews there did not originate in the countries from which they were deported. With the exception of recent emigrants, they generally had adapted to a large extent to the languages and the way of life of the Jewish and non-Jewish communities of the countries to which they had immigrated. These "foreign" Jews came mostly from Poland, Hungary, and other eastern countries and, despite being in the minority, were a formative influence on the character of the camp; after all, the Jewish Elders Edelstein and Murmelstein came from Galicia. Among the Viennese were Jews from the East, primarily from Galicia; conditions in Leopoldstadt (Vienna's second municipal district) had allowed them to partially maintain traditional ways of life. Among the Czech Jews were people of Slovakian, Carpatho-Russian, and – particularly from the Ostrau (Moravian Ostrava) region – Polish descent. This group on occasion included refugees from Germany and Austria, who were positioned in the camp between Jews from their homelands and Jews from their place of refuge. There also were eastern Jews among the Dutch and Danes, although there were relatively few among the Reich Germans.

The Jews of Theresienstadt never constituted a homogeneous group. They shared only their fate within the enforced community, and the Jewish star affixed to them. Their appearance, origins, nationalities, languages, religions, customs and traditions,

Population

ways of life, social backgrounds, and interests were as varied as can be imagined among Europeans in general. If anything might have served as serious evidence to counter the views of Jew-haters and "antisemites" and their emotional or "scientific" theories, it would have been this "ghetto." The isolation of the Jews was a trick devised by Jew-haters, aimed at facilitating generalizations about them; the public was presented with sweeping accusations that were hard to examine or refute, while the Jews were debased in inhuman conditions that seemed to confirm all the accusations.

What did "the" Jews look like? Tall and short statures, individuals with lighter and darker skin color, those with a sturdy or slight appearance, and Ashkenazi and Sephardic types composed a multitude that was "Jewish" only through the "Jewish star." Many Czech Jews, particularly those from the countryside, very much resembled Czechs. Some German Jews seemed quite "German."

Even without noting their dialects, some were obviously "Bavarians" or "Rhinelanders." There were all kinds of hair and skin colors. There were "obvious" representatives of the Nordic, Dinaric, Alpine, Mediterranean, and other "races"; "specifically" Jewish types were in the minority. One could accomplish little in Theresienstadt using contemporary German "race theories," which promoted prejudice but completely missed the truth. What were referred to as "Jewish" noses, mouths, almond-shaped eyes, and so on, were not often found. Something more commonly noticed was the "Jewish look," an expression of suffering around the eyes more revealing of a destiny than of a "race."

Hunger and camp life did very little to emphasize Jewish traits in any noticeable way. As a result of severe emaciation, Jewish-seeming features tended instead to recede, while their expressions frequently became "more Jewish," as befits tormented creatures. Flat feet, which are cited maliciously as a typical Jewish trait, were the result of malnourishment, which also leads to other pathological alterations of the bone structure, as can be seen from the numerous cases of osteoporosis and osteomalacia in Theresienstadt. Loud manners and strong gesticulation, also frequently cited as Jewish characteristics, may have been frequently noted, yet, given the irritable atmosphere prevalent in all concentration camps, the Jews hardly outdid the "Aryans" in that respect. All the characteristic changes and degeneracies typical of life in prison appeared in Theresienstadt, as elsewhere. Changes in demeanor and character usually tend to intensify the appearance of phenotypical characteristics. Yet when exposed to the severe progression of biological degeneration, these exacerbated traits tend to dissolve to a great extent; the purely animalistic comes to the fore and blurs the characteristics of any strongly developed individuality, until it completely neutralizes them. Alterations in moral character tend to increase its weaknesses, which are sublimated in the course of normal life but now break through abruptly.

The percentage of people who, according to the "race laws," were not considered "full Jews" was much larger here than in any other Jewish camp. There were many "three-quarter Jews," "half Jews," and even some "quarter Jews" who had been sent to this "preferred camp," especially from Germany. There were prisoners there who had been barred from the Wehrmacht, after taking part in the invasion of Poland in 1939. In very rare cases, even non-Jews were admitted. I know of three such cases: two involved "error"; the other was the result of slander. Some thirty-one inmates were discharged from the camp – the official term was "deghettoization." These were people who were of partial Jewish decent, but who did not "count as Jews" under the laws.

In terms of nationality, the prisoners considered themselves as belonging to either the Jewish people, their country of origin, or their mother tongue. The nature and degree to which they felt a sense of belonging varied. The ambivalent attitude of the Central European Jews to the question of their national allegiance had grown increasingly critical in the previous decades and played itself out in many forms in the camp: indifferent and indecisive attitudes, amphibian-like views, national consciousness, and sometimes chauvinistic and occasionally even cosmopolitan viewpoints were represented here. Those not indifferent to questions of national allegiance rarely tolerated differing opinions. It is almost impossible to estimate the numerical distribution of national loyalties among the prisoners, because there is no documentation for this. The SS saw only Jews, and, at least formally, the Jewish leadership adopted the same view. Most of the heads of the self-administration were Zionists, whereas the minority was composed of assimilated Czechs or long-time members of national-liberal (*deutsch-liberal*) Jewry whose leanings had outlived themselves and who found no support in Theresienstadt. Baptized Jews or half Jews rarely held posts of authority in the camp. The distribution of prisoners according to their countries of origin affords few insights for our investigation. The following table presents the number of prisoners living in Theresienstadt by the end of the years indicated:

	Protectorate	Reich	Austria	Holland	Denmark	Slovenia	Hungary
1942	24,500+	17,000+	7,000+				
1943	15,000+	13,000+	5,500−	250+	400+		
1944	3,500−	4,000+	1,500−	1,700+	400	400+	
April 20, 1945	7,000	5,500−	1,250+	1,250+		1,400+	1,000+

The Jews from Bohemia-Moravia spoke either Czech or German. Only a small number spoke both languages equally well, but even fewer had no knowledge of the other language. German was the vernacular of those who came from areas that at the time were mainly German, and of some of those who came from the large cities. At the beginning of the war, Czech was the mother tongue of the majority, but the situation in Bohemia was different from that of Moravia-Silesia. Of the 117,180 persons from the old countries belonging to the Bohemian Crown and who had declared themselves to be of the Jewish faith in the census of 1930, 42,669 (36%) declared themselves Czech, 35,657 (30%) declared themselves German, and 36,778 (31%) declared themselves to be of Jewish nationality (*nationale Juden*); the Czechs were heavily represented in Bohemia, and the Jewish nationals the least so, whereas in Moravia-Silesia the Jewish nationalists (*Jüdischnationale*) were strongest, and the Czechs were underrepresented (see 185). In terms of their mother tongue, more than two-thirds of the Jewish nationalists probably were German.

Among the country's German speakers a progressive assimilation to the Czech language was evident, the development of which shall be briefly outlined here. The emancipation of Jews in the Austro-Hungarian monarchy began at the end of the eighteenth century under the rule of Joseph II and was closely linked to the adoption of German as the official language; for those coming to it from Yiddish, this language was easier to learn than any of the other national languages. Thus emancipation in Bohemia and Moravia took place via the German language and culture. In those days, Czech-language schools barely existed, which is why the Czech intelligentsia spoke German and, at least in writing, had a better command of German than of Czech. The linguistic and national rebirth of the Czechs was nascent and truly took root only in the first half of the nineteenth century. During the course of these changes, the Jews in the countryside and to some extent also in the larger cities began to use Czech more frequently. However, because Czech was not the native tongue of the Jews, it was for a long time unable to establish itself to the same extent as German, which in the beginning was not itself an indigenous language. Yet it was the language used in schools, especially because the universities and a large portion of the remaining schools would use German exclusively for decades to come. In the second half of the nineteenth century, a Czech assimilationist movement was gaining strength and gradually spreading; it became organized in 1876 and, through various inter-mediate stages, created a powerful body by the name of Svaz Čechů-židů v Československé Republice (Association of Czech Jews in Czechoslovakia) in 1919 (see 315). As usually is the case with the assimilated, these Jews aimed to be more Czech than the Czechs themselves. As early as the census of 1900, 54% of Jews in Bohemia and 23% of Jews in Moravia claimed to speak Czech as their mother tongue. It is interesting to observe that this percentage did not rise in the first census after the establishment of Czechoslovakia in 1921, because it was then possible, for the first time, to enter one's nationality as Jewish. In Bohemia, approximately 50% registered as Czechs; in Moravia, the percentage was close to 18%. In Moravia, slightly more than half registered their nationality as Jewish; in Bohemia this was true of only about 14%. In both lands, the community of Germans had lost significantly more members than the community of Czechs. The national language gained ground in the young republic; it grew slowly at first but increased steadily. After 1933 this process gained tremendous momentum, even in theretofore German-speaking areas, as a reaction to events in Germany. Following the catastrophes of 1938–39, many Jews, particularly younger ones, refused to continue speaking German. Yet this development had not brought many new followers to the Czech nationalist Jews since 1918; the rejection of things German mainly benefited the Zionists. Even before the years of deportation, as well as later in Theresienstadt, it became evident that young people frequently no longer knew German, while at the same time their parents often were not fluent in Czech. German was passionately rejected, and occasionally the language itself was equated with German nationalism and Nazism per se.

Within the camp, the majority of younger Jews from the "Protectorate" felt that their mother tongue was Czech, whereas the older generation tended to prefer it, for conversation, at least. At the same time, German was the official language of the camp, and all correspondence and other documents, even for internal use, had to be drafted in that language. This is why German, already familiar to most educated Czech Jews, played a greater role among them than otherwise would have been the case. Czech (and other non-German) assimilated Jews were able to inflame their passions with the values and the spirit of resistance that characterized their people of choice, and with whom they felt united in their feelings against "the" Germans. For

German-speaking or even self-consciously German Jews, the foundations of assimilation had been shaken. Few had the desire or the courage to hold fast to their old opinions. This was especially true of German Jews from Czechoslovakia. Rarely was this rejection of Germanness a well-thought-out and mature act, more often it was fueled by resentment, an understandable reaction to everything that had been endured, which pushed these people in the direction of Zionism or Czech nationalism. There was a natural inclination to feel a bond with the oppressed Czechs, although, going beyond these understandable sympathies, some cultivated a false nostalgia with regard to all things Czech, which was not quite dignified. On the other hand, for many Czech Jews, the process of both internal and external assimilation already had progressed to such a degree that their way of life and appearance were barely discernible from the Czechs. Not only the uneducated but even intellectuals, and especially semi-intellectuals, displayed impatience and spite toward German-speaking Czechs, as well as toward Jews from the German-speaking countries. They resented the Zionists equally and viewed them with undisguised suspicion. The hostility between Czechs and Zionists dominated the development of the camp from the first days and weeks of its existence; agreements were reached, but feuds within the leadership as well as among the workers flared up repeatedly. There were Czech Jews who claimed it to be an injustice that they were in the "ghetto" – because they were not Jews – and they maintained that only the "Germans" were to blame for everything; had the Jews in Czechoslovakia not insisted on speaking German and "Germanizing," Hitler would never have found an excuse to occupy the country, and all this misfortune never would have happened.

Occasionally, serious antagonism emerged between Jews who spoke Czech and Jews who spoke German. This would become evident when a German speaker turned out to be a Danish or Dutch Jew and immediately received an apology for the cold and impolite treatment he had received due to the fact that he had been mistaken for a German. Fortunately, others were agreeable and tolerant, but an underlying tension nearly always was present. Others appeared indifferent, sometimes speaking Czech and sometimes German, depending on the situation. Too many, however, lost sight of the judicious principle that language is primarily a means of communication and not a creed. The Zionists among the Czechoslovakian group in the camp included more young people than old people and may have amounted to about a fifth to a quarter of the entire group.

However diverse the Bohemian-Moravian Jews may have been within their own group, they did in fact appear homogeneous when compared to the other groups; as the first group within the camp and the one that long set the tone, they imparted to it some of its characteristic features.

German and Austrian Jews formed something of a unit only through language. Almost all the Austrians were from Vienna, and their eastern origin was occasionally revealed in their temperament. The German Jews were regionally varied in character and dialect – Saxons, Rhinelanders, Franconians, Swabians, Bavarians, people from Berlin and Hamburg, and Silesians could be recognized with some practice. The Viennese, like the Czech Jews, could be distinguished from German Jews by their practical approach to daily life. Yet the two groups were connected by their shared circumstances, which separated them from the Czechoslovaks.

Generally the German Jews did not understand what the camp was about. They were hopelessly at the mercy of the situation, without being able to understand it. Their advanced assimilation took bitter revenge on them. They were so used to obeying the authority of the state with blind faith that they had to feel Hitler's whip on their own bodies before they were able to acknowledge it. Even then, their judgment was frequently clouded, and they tended to blame conditions in the camp less on the SS than on misunderstandings or on the internal leadership. These people often still saw the Germany of 1942 as the Germany of 1900. They were frequently stubborn, pedantic, and, under the circumstances, tragicomically "correct," particularly in regard to trivial matters. With the exception of their religious traditions, they were even further removed from the Jewish character than the other groups, in spite of their Zionist sympathies. A considerable number were Jewish only according to the "race laws," in addition to the many who had been baptized or were "*Mischlinge.*" The Germans from the Reich were at a disadvantage due to the camp language, which was for the most part very difficult for them to understand, with its mixture of old Austrian military terms shot through with Czech expressions, Slavisms, Nazi German and Zionist terminology, and coinages particular to Theresienstadt and the Bohemian-Moravian dialect. It was easier for the Viennese. The prim manner of many German Jews often made them appear obtuse to others. They were not canny and were less able to assess a situation than the less sincere, but more shrewd and humorous, Czech Jews. The Germans from the Reich took almost everything much too seriously. They (along with many Hungarian and some Slovakian Jews) lacked the other European Jews' agile defensive stance and elasticity, which enabled them shrewdly to ward off danger, block and parry, and take the inevitable beating. Unbowed Czech and also Viennese Jews frequently behaved like Schwejk, sometimes flaunting stupidity, and sometimes equipped with superior cunning. They certainly did not equal the Eastern European Jews, with their passive and active courage uniquely mixed with feigned submission and apparent, or actual, cowardice; yet they were shrewder than most German Jews and quickly had a credible explanation or a white lie ready when confronted with danger. They had greater presence of mind and were colder than the German Jews, who, with their dogged and frequently no longer justifiable passion for the truth, broke down more easily – their graceless, "German" response became their undoing.

The majority of German Jews came from liberal milieus, such as the Centralverein deutscher Staatsbürger jüdischen Glaubens (Central Association of German Citizens of Jewish Faith). Now they suddenly found that they had lost the foundation for their bourgeois (*bürgerlich*) way of life, and many were either too old or too helpless to deal psychologically with this sort of loss. Because all of them did not become immediately impoverished, they were not entirely aware of the collapse of their world. A small number were entirely estranged from Judaism and sympathized, unshaken over time, with the spirit of German nationalism. If they were tactful, they kept quiet about it. Some of the baptized Jews and half Jews, however, who in this environment tragicomically represented themselves as Germans and wanted nothing to do with Jews, particularly Czech Jews, even went so far as to say that "everything that is happening is the fault of the Jews" or claim that "if the Führer knew about this, everything would be different; he just doesn't know; he would never tolerate it."

The Viennese Jews were not as deeply assimilated, nor did they make a particular point of being Austrians or Germans. They enjoyed a less tense relationship with the German and Czech Jews than these groups had with each other. Some of the German and Austrian Jews who came to Theresienstadt as emigrants from Prague helped to keep the balance.

Many of the Czech Jews had the advantage of being familiar with the conditions in the country; they still felt somewhat "at home" in the camp. Some of them had lived in Theresienstadt, in Leitmeritz [Litoměřice], or in another town close by; others, including Austrians, had served as officers and soldiers in the garrison of Theresienstadt.

The Dutch group contained many German, some Austrian, and occasional Czech refugees. They and the "real" Dutch Jews in many cases had been interned in the Westerbork camp for some time and for the most part only reluctantly integrated into the new camp, where they were not always given a friendly reception. Their willingness to work left much to be desired, and they generally were more cunning and inconsiderate, yet also more indolent, than the other groups. Whereas many of the Czech Jews foolishly felt themselves to be part of the camp elite and many Jews from Germany were too pedantic, these people no longer seemed to hold anything sacred. Everything, even the work necessary for the camp, seemed merely ridiculous to them and was sabotaged. Among themselves they were split into hostile subgroups; the tension between the native Dutch and the refugees was particularly distressing. A highly cultured minority, some of whom were among the finest people in Theresienstadt, distinguished themselves positively from the rest (see 49, 243a.).

In spite of its uneven composition, the small Danish group appeared outwardly unified. They had not been persecuted prior to their abrupt deportation to the camp. Perhaps for this reason, they generally displayed a stronger resilience, even though it was more difficult for them to make the physical adjustment. After overcoming the initial hardships, they attained an unusual position of privilege due to the knowledge that they were safe from deportation, and this influenced their demeanor. Their sense of community was, with some exceptions, compromised by shameful stinginess. Thanks to generous assistance from home, it was easy for them to be proud, assimilated Danes. They got along quite well with the other groups and were particularly popular with the Czechs. Their relative wealth was also the object of envy, which tempted some Danish Jews into arrogance and sexual corruption.

Jews from Slovakia and Hungary arrived only in the final months, so their characteristics barely affected the camp. The situation of the Slovaks was similar to that of the Dutch, in that their imprisonment in Sered was comparable in many ways to imprisonment in Westerbork (see 193c).

An open avowal of Judaism was essentially equivalent to Zionism. The Zionists claimed to be the backbone of the camp. The group around Edelstein flirted with the fantastical idea of transforming the "ghetto" into a Zionist model camp, where Jewish youth would be saved, reeducated, and prepared for emigration to Palestine. This expectation was shaken at the very beginning and essentially prevented, because some of Edelstein's closest associates as well as the core of the labor force were Czech nationalists. The politics of the SS, with its shortsighted and ill-planned deportations, and the flooding of the camp with elderly Jews also put an irrevocable end to these ambitious Zionist plans, although Zionist supporters often did not want to see or acknowledge this fact. Many did not understand that what was called for in the face of the existing misery were very different measures of preservation, rather than an inopportune model of national and political education; this reality brushed aside all of these efforts. It is all the more important, then, to stress the great merit that some old and young Zionists were able to earn in an atmosphere of refreshing freedom from constrictions and doctrinaire barriers.

The Communists constituted yet another special group; they were present in significant number only among the Czech Jews. After the Zionists, they were the most

Population 261

politically aware and active group, and it seems that the SS did not know much about them. During the first two years, and actually all the way up to the fall catastrophe of 1944, within the camp the Communists played a certain role that, after the war, was claimed to have been more significant than it actually was. In terms of leadership, the Communists were represented only by a member of the Council of Elders, the engineer Vogel. However, leftist Zionists such as Edelstein and, not without coquetry, Eppstein did maintain contact with this group. This became important insofar as, under a secret agreement, the leaders of the Zionists, Communists, and Czech conservative (*bürgerlich*) assimilationists were internally protected from the transports. Among these groups there was, one might say, a modus vivendi that was reluctantly expanded, due to the entry of foreigners, into the leading stratum of ghetto self-administration, but that also, in part through SS tactics, was gradually weakened and eventually all but destroyed. Yet as long as and to the extent that this internal and illegal coalition existed and functioned, one can indeed speak of an internal political history of the camp. Its influence on the ultimate fate of the camp should not be overestimated, yet at the same time one must not underestimate the fact that many of the essential characteristics of Theresienstadt's society and structure were the result of it. Here one could see embodied a certain resistance by the coerced community to the much more powerful SS, but also the fateful weight of internal conditions in which this internal coalition finally did become complicit, because it was merely a political coalition without moral grounding. Internally, between 1941 and 1944, it represented the possibility of power; attacks against corrupt elements therefore always also targeted the political leadership, which in turn could not help but cover for the guilty and eliminate the critics, or, as in the case of Dr. Loewenstein, at least incapacitate them. It is therefore understandable that the efforts of men such as Leo Baeck began to achieve significant and lasting successes only starting in the fall of 1944.

Nor was the camp homogeneous when it came to religion. No other "ghetto" had such an extensive Christian minority. The reason for this was to be found not only in the widespread inclination toward baptism among Central European Jews but, more important, in the "bureaucratic criteria" that determined the selection for Theresienstadt. In addition to Roman Catholics, there were members of many other churches and sects. Lack of religious affiliation was kept a secret by some, partly due to shame, and partly due to opportunism. However, we must not forget that when applying for positions within the camp, religion had to be indicated; this rule was strictly observed, particularly during the first two years. To the end, nonaffiliated Jews occupied high positions only in exceptional cases. The number of non-Jewish "Jews" increased with time, but there are no records at all before October 1943. At that time, the proportion of Christians was approximately 9% and the proportion of people with no religious affiliation amounted to about 6%. For later periods we have more detailed numbers.

	Mosaic groups		Non-Mosaic groups	
	Number	%	Number	%
December 1943	30,480	87.9	3,925	12.1
May 1944	23,529	84.2	4,193	15.8
December 1944	8,346	72.1	3,112	27.9
April 20, 1945	11,104	63.4	6,194	36.6

The non-Mosaic groups are divided as follows:

	Catholic	Lutheran	Member of a Sect	Nonaffiliated	Not specified
December 1943	1,321	830	207	1,567	250
May 1944	1,439	1,084	195	1,475	255
December 1944	943	1,198	139	832	110
April 20, 1945	2,014	1,808	368	2,004	117

This is a strange result of the SS's adopted (anti-)Jewish policies, which were aimed at the extermination of the "race" and in the end affected religious Jews the most, until this unusual ratio of non-Jewish "Jews" in a "Jewish settlement area" resulted.

Among the Jews were members of all denominations. The majority were not interested in religion or were what was known as "Jews on the three major holidays." Religious ties were much more common among German, and especially Viennese, Jews than among the Czechoslovaks. Few were traditionally Orthodox. There was a slightly larger number of neo-Orthodox Jews (Agudists), but the majority belonged to the various gradations of liberal-reform Jewry. Members of Sephardic communities, some of whom observed their rituals very strictly, came from Hamburg and later from Holland.

No serious conflicts arose between the faithful and the indifferent or nonreligious, or between the religions. Occasionally someone would say that Theresienstadt was a Jewish camp in which Christians had no rights. Many Christians, particularly among the Catholics, took their faith seriously yet were able to fit with dignity into the Jewish camp. Others lacked the necessary tact. In Theresienstadt, one never had the impression that religious life was a priority (see Chapter 19).

Linguistic differences corresponded mostly to the countries of origin, but as in other camps, German served here too as a general vehicle for communication. People wanted to live and if possible work with those who spoke the same language as they did. German was heard in a great variety of dialects, the particularities of which led to amusing as well as annoying misunderstandings. Czech and Viennese Jews sometimes grew irritated with Reich German pronunciation and unfamiliar expressions. Turns of phrase unique to the camp were universally adopted and gave distinctive color to spoken German and Czech. Three tendencies applied to Czech borrowings from the German: rejection, ridicule, and convenience. The adopted language was dealt with randomly using Czech grammar and syntax. Few adults attempted to learn any Czech, and, conversely, few expanded their command of German; but some foreign expressions and turns of phrase were used quite commonly. Children tended to absorb more of the foreign language, yet it will come as no surprise that the language in question was a quite corrupted German or Czech. Yiddish was barely known, but certain expressions from the colloquial language of Central European Jews became common usage even among those with no previous knowledge of it. The cultivation of New Hebrew was promoted by Zionists, but few of them had mastered the language. What children learned in the "homes" was limited mostly to the texts of songs and a few sentences.

Customs and ways of life were equally varied and depended on background, social origin, and personal views. Very little would have appeared "typically Jewish" to an unbiased observer. Members of the middle class were mixed in with exclusive circles, but the camp leveled previously defined social categories and created three new classes: "notables," workers, and beggars. They were not always strictly separated, and intermediate stages existed. Jewish individualism still was such a strong force that only highly assimilated people identified entirely with the new classes.

The occupations of the prisoner population reflected the social conditions of Central European Jewry between the two world wars: there were industrialists, bankers, manufacturers, lawyers, doctors, rabbis, scholars, university professors, teachers, artists, journalists, technicians, merchants, civil servants, craftsmen, farmers, and laborers of all kinds. Based on their former wealth, all social classes were represented, from the multimillionaire to the beggar. Most prisoners were from the middle classes, which had become largely impoverished even before deportation; now all were reduced to poverty. Concepts of rich and poor within the camp were in no way comparable to civilian conditions.

The experience of the camp teaches that collective trends opposed to the tendencies within the coerced community could neither survive nor prevail in any way. Value was assigned only to one's personality, not to any particular trend. The internal leadership made it easy to be deliberately Jewish. Out of spite or opposition, others played the offended assimilationist and "non-Jew." From time to time, some fell victim to certain phrases. This went so far that a member of the Council of Elders ended internal official letters, on the model of "with German greetings" (*mit deutschen Gruß*), with the words "with Jewish greetings" (*mit jüdischem Gruß*). The German assimilators had to keep silent, but the Czechs, no more dignified in their demeanor, ridiculed the "Jewish goings-on." Thus were formed cliques that plotted and schemed against one another. But there was no consensus among the groups themselves, and subgroups – whether of assimilationist or Zionist persuasion – formed that rarely feuded openly but fought all the more fiercely in secret. In addition, opportunists were on the prowl, working to take advantage of the situation. The weakness of assimilation, attempting to be Czech or German and a Jew, was pernicious and did nothing to promote true cosmopolitanism. The disastrous overall course of events ultimately led foolish minds to turn all opinions into schemes, which were no longer animated with the power of mind or heart.

It was almost impossible to recognize behind this social structure the system that would have emerged had the prisoners been classified according to their previous social positions. The large number of people who were unfit to work, and were stripped of all their means, itself distinguished the camp from any normal society. The leadership was composed of an unusual group of individuals: a large number of the most able and humanly superior of Jews had emigrated in time; those left behind, who now had to take on leading roles and responsibilities, were either too old or too idealistic and long had been worn down by the burden of their duties. They were joined by questionable characters who secured positions with the Jewish authorities for the sake of protection. Weak of principle from the very beginning, they inevitably went astray, under the control of the SS, gaining the trust of their masters and therefore influential positions. These compliant creatures were sent to Theresienstadt "as a reward" and there, with a wink and a nod, were given influential positions. Thus the level of the average high-ranking Jewish functionary was far below that of the average prisoner population. This disproportion could not be remedied through the influence of the more moral members of the leadership, especially after Edelstein's emotional breakdown.

The "notables" – a term introduced by the SS in the fall of 1942 – constituted a unique group. A distinction was made between two subgroups, A and B. "A-notables" were persons identified to the Jewish Elder by the SS. They were either people of international repute or highly decorated German and Austrian officers; in some cases, such as the notorious Mandler (see Chapter 3), they were henchmen of the SS executioners or odd quantities such as the widow of an SA-Obergruppenführer who had been shot on June 30, 1934. Later they were joined by Danes and the Dutch, including the head of the Dutch Red Cross and the vice-governor of Indonesia. The Council of Elders could itself suggest "notables" to the SS; if confirmed, they were called "B-notables." Among these were university professors, men involved in Jewish life, and sometimes even people hardly deserving of commendation. This "notability" also extended to family members. In 1944, 114 "notables" lived in the camp, with 85 family members. Internally, the term "notables" was further extended; this led to a large number of people being raised up from the mass of common prisoners to various intermediate stages. Privileges included better accommodations (if possible, an entire family in one room), protection from deportation (which the SS in some cases revoked), and freedom from the duty to work, which some foreswore. "A-notables" also enjoyed more frequent permission to write. When it was necessary to fool the Danish commission, the "notables'" quarters were fixed up especially well. The SS's propagandistic intentions with regard to the "notables" can be illustrated with an example: at the beginning of September 1942, the renowned geography professor Alfred Philippson of Bonn was summoned early in the day to the commandant's office, with no reason given. There, the seventy-eight-year-old was asked about his relationship to Sven Hedin and then given a letter from Hedin, which he was required to answer on the spot. Until that point, he had lived as miserably as the other old people from Germany. Now he was allotted his own room, with his wife and daughter, and after a short wish list was passed on, he received scholarly books from his confiscated library in Bonn (see 3b). In a letter to Hitler, Hedin apparently had made his attitude toward Germany dependent on Philippson's fate.

A group soon formed around some "notables" of superior nature; they created a social elite that, while seemingly out of place and anachronistic in their misery and materially worse off than the lowest kitchen help, nevertheless constituted a counterweight to the social set around the Jewish leadership that theretofore had set the tone.

The leading social circles in Theresienstadt emerged out of the highest levels of the self-administration, the "notables," holders of remunerative posts, and favored package receivers; these circles were, of course, far less uniform than would be the case in any normal social order, because conditions here and there were based on different characteristics. Material wealth, which always is an element in the origin and composition of a leading social class, is not otherwise subject, to such a great degree, either to the power of chance – present here through the circumstance of frequent receipt of packages (see Chapter 18) – or to regular and tacitly acknowledged illegal enrichment, as was common in Theresienstadt. This new society also was distinct from the still-perceptible reflection of the society to which the prisoners had belonged before their time in the camp.

Relationships existed among all the groups that have been listed, from various perspectives, in this chapter; naturally, they were closest based on country of origin, language, common outlooks and interests, and prior and newly developed social ties. Shared quarters and workplaces played a preeminent role as well. Some exclusive groups also formed – the "posh society" around the Council of Elders and among "notables," artists, and musicians. Interconnections occurred everywhere, and often created surprising friendships; among those who became close were people who otherwise probably would not have met and certainly never would have associated with one another. Many people had neither relatives nor old friends in the camp and sought contact with strangers if they did not want to give up the possibility of having a social life. If one saw the camp as a temporary arrangement, one saw its social circles and social life as an improvisation. Theresienstadt was jokingly called an involuntary summer resort, prolonged for an undetermined period. An inwardly free lifestyle, intelligence, and tact made it possible to maintain genuine friendships and pleasant comradeship, which made all the evil more bearable.

It remained difficult to spend time with one's own family and closest friends even after the barracks gates were opened to prisoners in July 1942, because everyone worked long hours in different places, sometimes not even at the same times. Even later on, most families did not live together; thus, people often found little time for undisturbed meetings with their relatives. Such meetings required so much effort that people could hardly maintain other acquaintanceships. In this regard, the old people who did not work were better off.

The many unsettling events, particularly in transport periods, and the question of space also made contact more difficult. Those who had their own "apartments" were in good shape, but in the mass quarters, everything was twice as difficult, and a social life of one's own choice was hardly possible. People had to be considerate of their roommates and did not know where to put visitors, except on their bedsteads, which often were not on ground level. There was no space for social gatherings, but offices and workplaces were sometimes used; it was forbidden, so the SS could not be permitted to find out about it.

People also were restricted by the early curfew of 8 P.M., which was extended for only a short time during the summer, until 9 and 10 P.M. At ten o'clock, everyone had to be silent, and lights had to be out. Passes that were valid at night were desirable, but they were only for official purposes. Nevertheless, they were misused for social activity; the leadership even tolerated their being issued for this reason, although a pretense of official business was necessary. It was dangerous to be on the streets after curfew, and people seldom risked doing so illegally. It was far more common to spend a night or, for a longer period, several nights outside one's own quarters and even to "live" in offices or workshops. This sometimes was tacitly tolerated, and then once again strictly forbidden.

One also could go for walks or sit around in alleys and courtyards. In 1944, a few parks and redoubts were opened, and they were sought out by thousands of people. In the early months, where one lived had a strong influence on one's social life: relationships were more likely to be formed among those who shared common quarters and a neighborhood in the same "residential unit." For old and young people in the "homes," this remained important, and at the beginning, despite all obstacles, good friendships developed in the barracks. These friendships proved valuable as long as contact with families was almost impossible and social distinctions were not yet sharply felt in the camp. The "normalized" circumstances brought nothing but terrible self-delusion and a caricature of civilization, which concealed the profound deterioration of more noble forms of society.

The "Central Registry" and its branches had to determine the daily number of inmates; this "status record" (*Standführung*) was the obligation of the prisoners, whereas the SS ordered only occasional "censuses" and only once carried one out themselves. Except for Sundays and high holidays, the Jewish Elder had to supply the SS with daily "status reports" (*Standmeldungen*) The information required can be seen in a surviving report (see 93).

8 August 1943

Status today		46,111
Status yesterday		46,127
A difference of		minus 16
Increase:		
Decrease: deaths	16	
on 7 August		
Yields above		minus 16
difference of		
Total arrivals in		123,362
ghetto		
Total deaths until	26,290	
today		
To Stapo etc.	83	
Transports to	50,878	
East		
		77,251
Yields above		46,111
status of		

Births until today	132	(status unchanged)
Outside work	165	(status unchanged)
In custody	160	(Departed 4, Fröhlich Otto, Beck Peter, Mandel Hersch, Stein Franz)
		Increase 4, (Stark Oskar, Wittler Paul, Mauksch Rudolf, Höveler Arnold)
Sick	5,132	

8 August 1943

When newcomers first received a "transport number" or "identification number" in Theresienstadt, they were informed by way of a form such as the following:

Central Registry – To _____, residing _____. You have been assigned identification number _____. This is the only identification number that you may use in Theresienstadt. Date _____ Central Registry.

A daily "tally report" had to be drafted for each building and submitted to the "Central Registry" by way of the "barracks leadership." All living areas were to be

Population 267

listed separately, with their own "tally." The following information had to be reported: the "tally" of the previous day, divided into the number of men, women, and children; then the number of people according to the members of the various "bread categories"; and then the increase and departure numbers with the same information. The "tally" of the day of the report was recorded in the same way, and in addition, persons who were "in custody" had to be counted. A "memorandum from the barracks leadership" on March 25, 1944, illustrates the meticulous precision with which the "tally reports" were kept:

> Keep exact tally lists. The responsible organs must be told repeatedly that the tally lists must be kept as exactly as possible in all details. It must not happen that tally changes are not immediately recorded or names or transport numbers are listed incorrectly. Negligence in this regard is unforgivable and will be disciplined.

Although the statistical material assembled by Prochnik in Theresienstadt after the war is not entirely reliable, his listing according to age groups comes close to the truth and imparts an impressive overview (see also 299, 299b, 299c). The figures quoted refer in each case to the end of the month; the figures for 1945 refer to the period immediately before arrival of the concentration camp transports and to the day of liberation:

		0–15	16–60	61–65	65+	Total
Men						
July	1942	1,376	6,537	1,067	7,935	16,915
December	1942	1,787	10,673	1,588	5,964	20,012
July	1943	?	?	?	?	9,009
December	1943	1,586	8,575	1,126	2,913	14,200
May	1944	1,430	8,015	939	1,686	12,070
October	1944	378	1,406	236	1,248	3,268
April	1945	815	4,284	497	1,243	6,839
May	1945	1,083	9,501	2,046		12,630
Women						
July	1942	1,311	8,735	2,466	13,976	26,488
December	1942	1,708	14,368	2,966	10,242	29,282
July	1943	?	?	?	?	27,123
December	1943	1,445	11,155	2,033	5,822	20,455
May	1944	1,302	10,039	1,301	3,265	15,907
October	1944	441	4,036	507	2,825	7,809
April	1945	796	6,922	541	2,417	10,676
May	1945	1,065	12,883	3,349		17,297
Both Men and Women						
July	1942	2,687	15,272	3,533	21,911	43,403
December	1942	3,495	25,041	4,554	16,206	49,296
July	1943	3,875	30,650		11,607	46,132
December	1943	3,031	19,730	3,159	8,735	34,655
May	1944	2,732	18,054	2,240	4,951	27,977
October	1944	819	5,442	743	4,073	11,077
April	1945	1,611	11,206	1,038	3,660	17,515
May	1945	2,148	22,384	5,395		29,927

Source: 216

On the same dates, the percentage of men and women was as follows:

	Men	Women
July 1942	39.1	60.9
December 1942	40.8	59.2
July 1943	41.07	58.93
December 1943	41.0	59.0
May 1944	43.1	56.9
October 1944	29.5	70.5
April 1945	39.0	61.0
May 1945	42.25	57.75

The average age of the prisoners was as follows:

	Men	Women	Total
December 1941	37.92	39.91	
July 1942	51.8	55.6	54.4
December 1942	48.91	52.83	51.3
July 1943	?	?	46.6
December 1943	44.74	50.11	48
May 1944	43.38	46.71	45.4
October 1944	50.2	51.1	50.9
April 1945	43	45.5	44.4
May 1945	37.8	40.1	39.2

Source: 216

Reliable information about the camp at the time of the "city beautification" (*Stadtverschönerung*) is provided by a chart, "Distribution of the Population According to Sex, Origin and Age on 22 May 1944":

	Men	Women	Total
Altreich	3,413	5,800	9,213
Ostmark	1,521	2,361	3,882
Protectorate	6,022	6,634	12,656
Holland	925	991	1,916
Denmark	225	198	423
TOTAL	12,106	15,984	28,090

	Altreich		Ostmark		Protectorate		Holland		Denmark	
Age	M	W	M	W	M	W	M	W	M	W
0–15	325	300	110	100	832	759	135	126	25	18
16–60	1,802	2,971	878	1,379	4,570	4,871	612	673	160	142
61–65	407	652	177	235	271	340	75	71	13	14
66+	879	1,877	356	647	349	664	103	121	27	24
TOTAL	3,413	5,800	1,521	2,361	6,022	6,634	925	991	225	198

Population 269

There were 230 births (other figures show 205–209) and 350 forced abortions (see Chapter 16). The figures of 273 suicides and 211 attempted suicides (Prochnik's figures are 270 and 210, respectively) seem relatively low and attest to the prisoners' will to live. It is psychologically interesting that the number of suicides and suicide attempts went down from year to year; aside from two attempts in 1941, the figures are 264 for 1942, 164 for 1943, and roughly 50 for 1944, whereas no cases were reported for 1945. It is equally remarkable that, until the end of 1943, fear of deportation was determined to be the motive in only 58 cases, and that generally only old people wanted to take their lives – the average age was 62! Up to the end of 1943, poison (often Veronal) was taken in 285 cases, 65 people cut themselves, 45 jumped out of windows, and 35 hanged themselves.

Escape from a camp was considered by the SS to be a major crime and was to be prevented at all costs; even attempted escape was punishable with the death penalty. Few people managed to escape Theresienstadt; from 1941 to 1944, 37 escaped, of whom 12 were brought back to the camp as prisoners. In April 1945, 4 fled; in May, before the final liberation, 723 people ran away. In the early months, when the camp still was only partially guarded, some succeeded – one escaped to Switzerland – and many succeeded at the end of the war, when well-meaning gendarmes looked the other way. At that point, one couple wanted to escape without the slightest caution, in broad daylight, but a good-humored gendarme told them, "Don't go now! You can hold out, go at night!"

Most escape attempts were undertaken by young Czech Jews. The fact that this happened relatively rarely can be explained not only by the considerable obstacles but also by concern for relatives inside and outside the "ghetto," as prisoners feared that their relatives might be punished for their escape. A captured escapee could expect nothing good; death was almost a certainty. A "memo" from the second-to-last day of the SS's power reads:

Regarding: Missing persons reports
Number of received missing persons reports on 4 May 1945 71
Total number in the period from 1 to 4 May 1945 87

Increasingly longer and more complicated rules about "reporting suspicion of escape" were repeatedly issued. Following is one version, not the longest by far, which was published in a "Memorandum from the Building Leadership" in May 1943:

Regulations on Reporting Escape Attempts:

1. Every room elder is obligated to determine the presence of all room occupants after lights-out. Room occupants who have night shift or cannot return to their quarters until later for other urgent reasons must inform the room elder, stating the reason, the location and the probable time of return. The room elder is to collect these reports and in turn report to the group elder or the building elder, who is to report to the block elder, that all occupants of his room or of the house were present or have explained their absence, so that no escape attempt and no reason for a missing persons report is present.
2. The block or group elders will then report the results, based on the reports received, which they will keep for up to a month, to the proper registry office through signature on one of the forms available at the proper registry office:

Registry _____
Group _____

I declare that, according to the reports received of the day's evening count of the registered occupants of my group's quarters, there is no reason for suspicion of escape or to make a missing persons report.

Group elders are to report to the registry office at 10 P.M.

3. If, during counting at one of the quarters, an unexplained absence is determined, the room or building elder must notify the block or group elder in writing. He will immediately notify the district or barracks elder, who will examine the case and have the missing person sought by the assigned Order Constabulary. The Central Registry will be informed immediately of the result of this search.

The group elder must at the same time report the unexplained absence to the registry office in a written report, including the name, transport number, quarters and a precise description of the missing person, as well as the exact circumstances of his absence. He will then note in the signature area of the registry's form: a missing persons report attached.

4. Barracks and district registry heads must obtain from the Central Registry Office in timely fashion the necessary forms for the number of group elders for the current month, and additionally for the subsequent month, before the beginning of the month. At the end of a month, the forms bearing the signatures of the group elders must be retained.

5. These regulations go into effect on the day following their announcement.

6. Violations of these rules regarding written reporting of absence will be punished by the appropriate district or barracks elders.

Residents who do not report absence on time and properly:

    a) in less serious cases not involving negligence or the like, 7 days' confinement to quarters.

    b) In other cases, 8–14 days imprisonment.

Form of Reports:

    I. Occupant's Report:

       House no. ___, Room no. _____, Name _____, Transp. No. _____. I report that I work from _____ to _____o'clock in _____ and will return around _____.
       Date _____

    II. Room Elder's Report:

       Block: _____ Room no.: _____ House: _____ Room elder: _____. According to inspection undertaken at _____o'clock, all room occupants are present or have given proper notification of their absence. There is no reason for suspicion of escape or missing persons report.
       Date _____ Room Elder (signature)

(262)

This not-at-all-extreme sample of bureaucratic nonsense – the dregs of the SS style that flooded the internal camp administration – demonstrates that the basis of society in this coerced community was an unremittingly controlling and limiting authority. The society did not develop its institutions and authorities; the authority was the only valid central institution, and it shaped society and regulated and molded its content. As regards people, one certainly cannot allegorically speak of a *zoon politikon* (political creature); here the beings were totally subjected to authority. Socialists and other reformers should be warned.

Population

The Jewish functionaries' far-reaching fear of suspicion of escape is evidenced by a letter, miserable in style and content, from the head of the "Central Registry" a few weeks before liberation:

Central Registry
Dr. O/P Theresienstadt, 23 March 1945
To the legal authorities
Att.: Administrative Judge

On 21 March 1945 at 9 o'clock in the morning, the Block Leader of Block G IV Kreuzer Hermann, 385-VIII/I, residence Postg. 8 appeared at the office of the Central Registry-Registration Section and reported that Gebauer Berta, 265-XVIII/7, Hauptstr. 23, has been missing since yesterday evening.

In line with existing regulations, the absence of the person involved should have been determined at the evening count on 20 March at 9 o'clock in the evening, and after this determination, a missing persons report should immediately have been filed at the Central Registry. The fact that this did not occur, or only after a delay of nearly 12 hours, is a gross violation of the effective regulations. It is, however, the purpose of these regulations (evening count, duty to report) to ensure a state of affairs in which the Central Registry is *immediately* apprised of any situation where suspicion of escape – which cannot be ruled out here – exists; only in this way is it possible for the Registry to do everything necessary, especially to notify the Jewish Elder. Only if the prescribed report is immediately submitted to the higher office can one defend oneself against the charge, the consequences of which can affect the entire public, of having abetted the person involved. In the instant case, the accused does not even claim that he knew where Gabauer Berta was located during the evening count and expressly states that this person is "missing." The purpose of the specified arrangement has been thwarted by the omission. All these elements must be considered in assessing the issue. We therefore request the conviction of the above, and all other persons at fault in the matter. As regards the sentence, we emphasize that it should be graduated and in proportion to the person's fault, which, as already said and explained in detail, is to be considered most grave, irrespective of the disciplinary procedure that may be initiated.

Central Registry
[signed] Dr. Weisz

A "memo" lists the people who fell victim to the Gestapo up to the summer of 1944, probably in most cases in the "Small Fortress":

To Stapo
Incl. 21/VI 1944 .... 204 persons

			Men	Women
Of these,	Protectorate	150	112	38
	Altreich	25	17	8
	Ostmark	29	10	19
	TOTAL	204	139	65

By the end of the war, the number had risen to 280.

11

Housing

Living Space

The Jewish settlement area ... has an area of 335,056 square meters at its disposal, of which 42 percent is built up, 16 percent of the space is in converted courtyards, and 42 percent is allotted to streets, public places, and public gardens.

Approximately 95,000 square meters are used as living space. Another portion must be reserved for storage and economic activities, for health institutions and workshops.

The division of living space is in accordance with the settlement plan established in agreement with the principles of the utilization of labor and care of the elderly. Able-bodied men are concentrated in two large housing units [at that time, B IV and A II] so that these groups can go to work in cohesive groups and so that workforces are always available for performing work as it arises. Similarly, able-bodied women live on Westgasse in five barracks that can be comfortably heated and are furnished with complete sanitary facilities. In the city center, on Hauptstrasse, a further five barracks, which originally were used as production shops, were likewise converted to house working women.

It is not possible to effect total separation of those fit for work from those with diminished working capacity and persons unfit for work because the elderly, invalids, and sick should have at their side those able to offer active assistance. For this reason, the population of two larger housing units [H V and E IIIa] was arranged differently, so that rows occupied by bed-ridden patients or being used as a home for the elderly are connected by corridors in whose rooms working women are housed.

In the vicinity of the hospital [E IV], the lodgings for the doctors, nursing staff, and those who transport the sick are adjacent to the rooms for the invalids.

The houses in the blocks, excluding certain exceptions due to special circumstances in individual cases, are for the accommodation of persons of both sexes who are no longer fully capable of active work duties, but who, nevertheless, are not in need of constant care. Invalids, those wounded in the war, adolescents and children are accommodated in buildings that are suitably furnished as homes.

For organizational and administrative reasons, care was taken to use neighboring houses for the same purposes. Hence, homes for the war-wounded [L 231, 233, and 235] and twelve buildings for invalids [G V] are concentrated in one block.

Five houses have been placed at the disposal of persons who are to be classified as notables or favored by reason of previous accomplishments. These live in individual rooms with their families. (274)

Housing

All rooms were administered by the "Space Management Office," which was part of the "Department of Internal Administration." Until his deportation in October 1944, this office was headed by the intelligent and witty Dr. Walter Löwinger, who was notorious for his corruption and gross mismanagement. The most difficult tasks of the "Space Management Office" were mass moves that were ordered suddenly, upon the arrival of large or numerous transports. In addition, the attempt to house certain groups together constantly presented this office with serious problems that never could be smoothly resolved. A "memorandum from the Central Secretariat" on January 13, 1944, illustrates the difficulties presented by a last-minute mass transfer of 3,200 women:

> According to instructions from the Office, the building at
> Langestrasse 5 [C III]
> must be completely cleared of inhabitants and possessions by tomorrow, January 14, 1944, at 7 P.M. at the latest, because at this hour work on delousing will commence. Therefore, all inmates must immediately pack their bags without waiting to receive a transfer order and prepare for removal. All luggage that they will not be taking with them for the transfer, but instead wish to entrust to the transport administration for forwarding, should be clearly labeled with name and transport number....
>
> Transfer orders will be issued continuously during the night.... In consideration of the shortness of time, no submissions of appeals against transfer orders will be allowed. After the evacuation has been completed, it will be possible ... to file an appeal against potential breakup of families or other hardship cases.
>
> All inmates are required to comply with the transfer order to the letter and *in a timely manner*. On January 14, 1944, at 8:00 P.M. they must be at their assigned places unconditionally, or face the danger of being reported to the office *as missing*. We expressly emphasize the serious consequences of such a report for those affected. The building and house elders have strict orders immediately to report as missing all persons who are not present on the 14th at 8:00 P.M. in their assigned quarters.
>
> Those persons to whom final quarters are assigned in the city barracks or another place that must first be prepared for habitation will receive a *provisional* transfer order and will be informed by the 17th of the month, at the latest at their provisional quarters, where they have been permanently assigned. The same strict regulations apply to provisional transfers as to permanent transfers.
>
> In case a transfer order does not expressly state that it is "provisional," it is a permanent transfer.
>
> In the course of the morning, the building and house elders shall receive from "Space Management" a consignment of those persons assigned to their buildings. Where the accommodations offices provide no special orders, assignment within the building is up to the building or house elders, who are directed to take special care in accommodating children, the sick, and other persons in need of help.
>
> On January 14, 1944, at 8:00 P.M., the building and house elders will check, using this list, whether all the persons assigned to them have arrived, and will report to the competent registry office those present as well as those persons missing. They are personally responsible for ensuring that no one who is not assigned to it stays in their building overnight under any circumstances.
>
> [Instructions follow concerning bread distribution, the kitchen, the health service, and materials administration.]
>
> Transferred persons will be subject to the offices responsible for their new living quarters with respect to work duties, registry, and accommodations....
>
> Those provisionally transferred will be settled in their permanent quarters on January 26, 1944.

274   Sociology

Execution of the transfer: In order to facilitate smooth ... implementation and avoid loss of luggage, the following is decreed:

Luggage designated for delivery by the transport administration should be packed and marked in accordance with regulations and ready by 8:00 A.M. It will be picked up room by room by the transport administration in exchange for a deposit receipt and delivered to the owners at their permanent quarters as quickly as possible. The order for luggage pick-up will be announced to the rooms by the building management.

In the Schleuse, the new arrivals were assigned their permanent quarters. Individual transfers could be privately requested from the "Space Management Office" or could be ordered by it. Regulations on relocations changed very little over time, but they were enforced sometimes more strictly and sometimes more leniently. By contrast, the regulations for moving patients to the hospitals, which also was the "Space Management Office's" responsibility, became more and more complicated. An "excerpt from the transfer regulations" of March 30, 1942, explains this practice:

Transfers are allowed only on the basis of a written transfer order issued by the competent office. Without written permission, no ghetto inmate may switch rooms or transfer from one barracks to another. Every transfer order must be complied with in timely fashion. The building elders, the floor and room elders, as well as the Ghetto Guard, the building registry manager, and the housing officers shall ensure that these regulations are strictly adhered to.

1. Transfer within a building.
    Transfer within a building shall be ordered by the building elder's housing officer. He delivers a copy of the transfer order to the receiving room elder as well as the releasing room elder. The receiving and releasing room elders shall ensure adherence to the transfer order and must report the completed transfer to the housing officer. . . .

2. Conveyance of sick patients to the sickrooms, or release from the same.
    Conveyance of the sick from their quarters to the sickroom or the reverse occurs only pursuant to an order issued by the senior medical officer or his deputy. . . .

3. Transfers from one building to another.
    . . . shall be ordered only by the Department of Internal Administration (Space Management Office). The Space Management Office delivers the transfer permit, which is valid for only one person, to the housing officer of the building being exited. The housing officer informs the person transferring . . . and simultaneously informs him of all regulations to be complied with. On the day of transfer, the housing officer of the building from which the person is departing hands over the transfer order to the person moving and supervises the move and compliance with all registration requirements. The departure to the new building takes place in groups . . . together, escorted by a person chosen by the transport administration. The escort transfers the group, along with the transfer permits, to the building records officer immediately upon entering the arrival building. He thereupon reports the group's arrival to the housing officer, who shall assign new rooms and supervise adherence to all registry regulations. [These regulations on escorting groups were dropped or amended in the summer of 1942, with the start of conditional freedom of movement within the camp.]   (260)

Housing

The wording of the "transfer permits" (*Übersiedlungsverfügungen*) varied according to whether they were drafted in the same building, in the same "district," or in another "district." Here is a form for a transfer within the same "district":

[Front of page] Space Management form A/1 Transfer Order No. _____ (within the district) Bread [category] _____ Name _____ Transport No. _____ Year of birth _____ must resettle on _____ by _____ o'clock from house _____ no. _____ to house _____ no. _____. Theresienstadt, date _____ [signature] Housing Office of the ___ District.
[Back of page] Sleeping quarters were surrendered and notification of departure given on _____. [Signature] The house elder of the exited building. Sleeping quarters assigned in room number _____ date _____. [Signature] District Registry Head Officer date _____ [Signature] District Housing Head Officer

The form for a "provisional transfer permit" for disinfections read as follows:

[Front of page] Space Management provisional form. Provisional transfer permit number: W_____ Name _____ Transport number _____ can resettle for _____ days starting on _____ from _____ to _____ and must move back at the latest by _____. Date _____ 1944. Room Management.
[Back of page] Transfer notification of departure. House Elder _____ registry _____ registry for notification of arrival _____ Housing office _____ House Elder _____ Transfer back to previous quarters [the same data as for the "transfer notification of departure"] Transfer to the registry. Name _____ Transport number _____ was admitted to the _____ quarters. Date _____, 1944 Registry transfer back to previous quarters [same data]

Special forms were used for transfer to the hospital, among them a directive to the "medical orderly squad" (*Krankenträgergruppe*):

Space management form To. On _____ 1944 [lists the hour], the medical orderly squad shall transport Name _____ year of birth _____ transport number _____ from building _____ to hospital _____ room number _____ section _____. Receipt of the transfer permit must be confirmed. I am responsible for ensuring notice of departure and arrival to the competent registry authorities. [Signature] House Elder of the building vacated. Date _____ 1944.

The patient's old living quarters, to which he was supposed to return after recovery, generally were reserved during these transfers. The baggage remained there for safe-keeping; bed frames, mattresses, or paillasses were not to be transferred, as they belonged to the registered inventory of the quarters.

To maintain an accurate overview of the assigned and available sleeping quarters, the "Space Management Office" kept a record of this information, listing each building and the total number of quarters, separated into men's and women's quarters: "Space management Form. By. House _____ regular occupancy Status on _____. In the accommodations _____. In garrets and expanded attic spaces _____. Signature _____." The "Space Management Office" repeatedly compiled directories of all available buildings, listing their intended use. One such directory from the early period of "beautification," at the end of 1943 and beginning of 1944, provides an overview of the living quarters and workrooms in which, in a total camp area of 334,600 m², this coerced community of approximately 35,000 souls had to live their lives.

The buildings are listed by their numbers, first L, then Q. This is followed by block identification and district (see map). Not named are: E 1 ("Berlin Office"),

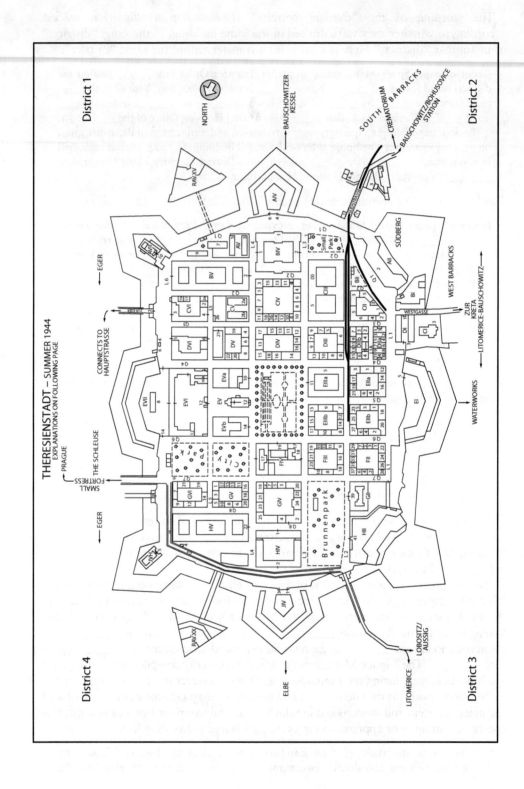

EXPLANATION OF CITY MAP (LEGEND)

———	Eisenbahn (railroad)
Q	Grünenlagen (parks)
L 1	Seestrasse
L 1a	Kurzstrasse
L 2	Bahnhofstrasse
L 3	Lange Strasse
L 4	Hauptstrasse
L 5	Parkstrasse
L 6	Wallstrasse
Q 1	Bäckergasse
Q 2	Jägergasse
Q 3	Badhausgasse
Q 4	Neue Gasse
Q 5	Turmgasse
Q 6	Rathausgasse
Q 7	Berggasse
Q 8	Postgasse
Q 9	Egergasse
Stadtmitte (City Center)	Marktplatz (marketplace)
Südstrasse 1	Kindererholungsheim (children's home, convalescent home)
Südstrasse 3	Zentralleichenhalle (Central Mortuary)
Südstrasse 5	Zeremonienhalle (ceremonial hall)
Südstrasse 4/6	Urnenhain (crematoria)
Westgasse 3	Sokolhalle (Sokol Hall)
Komplexe C I & D I, A VII & I VII, Rav. XV & XX for Zwecke der Landwirtschaft (complexes for agriculture purposes)	
A II	Jäger Kaserne (Männer) (Jäger Barracks [men])
A IV	Heeresbäckerei (Zentrallager) (main bakery [central camp])
C III	Hamburger Kaserne (Holländer) (Hamburg Barracks [Dutch])
B IV	Hannover Kaserne (Männer) (Hannover Barracks [men])
B V	Magdeburger Kaserne (Sitz der Selbstverwaltung) (Magdeburg Barracks [seat of the self-administration])
E I	Sudetenkaserne (Berliner Dienstelle) (Sudeten Barracks [Berlin Office])
E IIIa	Geniekaserne (Krankenhaus, Altersheim) (hospital, old-age home)
E VI	Hohenelber Kaserne (Zentralkrankenhaus) (Central Hospital or Infirmary)
E VII	Kavalier Kaserne (Altersheim) (Kavalier Barracks [old-age home])
G II	Offizierskasino (Gendarmerie) (officer's casino [gendarmes])
H II	Bauhof (Werkststätte) (garrison workshop)
H IV	Bodenbacher Kaserne und Zeughaus (Berliner Dienstelle) (Bodenbacher Barracks and Armory [Berlin Office])
H V	Dresdner Kaserne (alte Frauen) (Dresden Barracks [elderly women])
I IV	Aussiger Kaserne (Kleiderkammer) (Aussig Barracks [clothing warehouse])

Additional details in Ch. 11 and throughout text.

278 *Sociology*

the future "Community House" (the gymnasium), and the "West Barracks" and "Südbaracken" outside the city. Of the 207 buildings listed in the city or the fortifications, at present 7 are allotted as offices and apartments for the SS and the gendarmerie. Of the remaining 200, another 12 were not suitable for living quarters for the prisoners:

L 101, L 103 ("agriculture," silos and stalls, etc., basically for the SS)
L 201 (a small house with only one room, the city scales, used for the same purpose during the camp period)
L 301 (a small house, used for "silkworm breeding")
L 412 (the locked Roman Catholic Church. Its clock tower had to be kept in working order by one of the prisoners. Officially the camp was allowed to hear about the beginning and end of daylight saving time only from the SS, but they forgot to inform the Jewish Elder. Thus, more than once, the "ghetto" had the wrong time for an entire day, leading to confusion, as when the "Aryan" cart ordered for burials came an hour "too late.")
"Former post office barracks" (in Complex E VI, first the package distribution, then the dressing room of the "Central Bath")
Q 109 (barracks; repair center, then a "dining hall")
Q 108, Q 110 (for "agricultural" purposes)
Q 321 (military riding school, now machine shop)
Q 903 (I IV, "clothing warehouse")
Q 905 (a bastion, storehouse)

Of the remaining 188 buildings, 6 were only partially inhabited:

L 502 (fire house and quarters for the fire fighters)
L 506, L 605 (a combined complex, "brewery," now "delousing")
Hut across from Q 321 (Office of the "riding school," 1–2 residents)
A IV ("central bakery" and "central storehouse," few residents)
Q 619 (City Hall, offices, some inhabited garrets)
Q 701 (the "Bauhof" with its workshops, almost uninhabited)

The habitability of other buildings was limited: (a) as hospitals, (b) through factories, offices, storehouses, etc. 182 complexes served to house 35,000, though occasionally even 50,000 or more people. 61 complexes served the indicated residential purposes:

6 ("blockhouses" for "notables," relatively few inhabitants)
1 ("blockhouse" for others given preference)
3 ("blockhouses" as hospitals)
2 (barracks as hospitals, E VI, E IIIa, the second also a "home for the infirm")
2 (small buildings, Q 217/19, children's hospitals)
13 (houses, "homes for invalids," L 416, 418, 420, 501, 503, 504 [L 603], Q 320, 711, 713, 715, 717, 708)
3 (buildings partially used as "homes for invalids," Q 206, E VII, H V)
4 ("homes for wounded veterans," L 231, 233, 235, Q 806)
1 ("home for the blind," L 404 [= Q 319])
6 ("homes for mothers and children," L 315, 411, Q 311, 401, 504, 603)
3 ("nurseries for infants," L 514, Q 719, 721)
1 ("nurseries for toddlers," L607)
5 ("youth homes" as one complex, L216, 218, Q 609, 708, 710, adolescents)
3 ("homes for boys," L 414, 417, Q 712)

1 ("home for girls," L 410)
2 ("children's homes," L 318 [= Q 617], Q 702)
1 (house for "electricians," L 323)
3 ("houses for officials," L 403, 407, Q 712, for more senior officials)
1 (house, L 313, which for a long time served as the GW's living quarters)

The following chart provides information on the disposition of space on June 15, 1944, at the climax of the "beautification," during which period there were around 28,000 inmates. The surface area is given in square meters; the first figure is the total available space, the second is the amount of space in the barracks, and the third is the amount of space in the houses and barracks:

	Total available space (m²)	Barracks space (m²)	House and barracks space (m²)	Percent of total camp space
Habitable attics	18,550	7,778	10,772	8.7
Areas without attics	195,890	96,241	99,649	91.3
Passages (corridors)	28,267	15,565	12,702	13.2
Pure available space	167,623	80,676	86,947	78.1
Accommodations	96,568	41,052	55,516	45.0
Infirmaries	8,854	6,164	2,690	4.1
Living areas in sum	105,422	47,216	58,206	49.1
Uninhabitable areas	330		330	0.2
Outpatient clinics	2,133	1,606	527	1.0
Offices	9,720	7,252	2,468	4.5
Kitchens	2,651	1,781	970	1.2
Sheds (shacks)	1,632	762	870	0.8
Shops	1,088		1,088	0.5
Warehouses (storehouses)	19,067	12,273	6,794	8.9
Workshops	9,214	4,519	4,695	4.3
Toilets and latrines	3,400	1,809	1,591	1.6
Washrooms	3,685	1,548	2,137	1.7
Miscellaneous (including areas for "recreation")	9,281	2,010	7,271	4.3
TOTAL AREA	214,440	104,019	110,421	100

On March 15, 1943, these figures were significantly worse, both in an absolute sense and in terms of percentages, for an average inmate population of 45,000. In the summer and fall of 1942, the average living space per person was less than two square meters; for August 1942 the per-person space was estimated at 1.6 m², including attic space. It should not be forgotten that, even at that time, a considerable number of people claimed substantially more than the average living space. The presence of three- and two-story beds only appears to increase the average figures, because those tightly packed bedsteads severely limited the available space, where luggage also had to be stored. In the following table, the space available on March 15, 1943, is listed first in square meters, then by the increase or decrease in comparison with the table for June 15, 1944:

	Total available space (m²)		Percent of total camp space	
	March 15, 1943	Increase/decrease compared to June 15, 1944	March 15, 1943	Increase/decrease compared to June 15, 1944
Habitable flooring	16,464	− 2,086	6.9	− 1.8 (beautification!)
Areas without flooring	215,784	+ 16,984	93.1	+ 1.8
Passages	29,268	+ 1,001	12.6	− 0.6
Areas of available space	186,516	+ 18,893	80.5	+ 2.4
Accommodations	99,252	+ 2,684	43.1	− 1.9
Infirmaries	14,410	+ 5,556	6.2	+ 2.1 (convalescence!)
Living areas in sum	113,668	+ 8,246	49.3	+ 0.2
Uninhabitable areas	1,419	+ 1,089	0.6	+ 0.4
Outpatient clinics	3,697	+ 1,564	1.6	+ 0.6 (convalescence!)
Offices	9,433	− 287	4.1	− 0.4 (bureaucracy!)
Kitchens	2,887	+ 236	1.2	(no change!)
Sheds	2,425	+ 793	1.0	+ 0.2
Shops	720	− 268	0.3	− 0.2 (beautification!)
Warehouses	28,253	+ 9,186	12.1	+ 3.2 (unproductivity!)
Workshops	12,502	+ 3,288	5.4	+ 1.1 (unproductivity!)
Toilets and latrines	3,555	+ 155	1.6	(no change!)
Washrooms	2,834	− 851	1.2	− 0.5 (beautification!)
Miscellaneous	5,123	− 4,158	2.1	− 2.2 ("recreation")
TOTAL AREA	231,948	+ 17,492	100	

In mid-March 1943, the average living space per person, including hospitals and infirmaries, amounted to 2.05 m². "Beautification" became possible only after the deportation of 17,500 people, after which the average living space increased, pitifully enough, to a little more than 3.05 m² per person. In comparison, in the Łódź Ghetto each inmate at first had an average of 3.75 m².

A chart by the "Space Management Office" from November 1942 provides information on the number of people living in unfinished attic space:

Date	Number of attic occupants
September 1942	5,626
October 1942	6,034
November 1, 1942	5,457

By overcrowding other rooms, the number of people living under such conditions was reduced to 370 in November 1942.

The following table, based on a chart for the 1942 annual report, lists figures on monthly transfers; transfers from or to the Schleuse are not included.

Date	"Normal transfers"	People moved into and out of hospitals	Total
December 1941	80	18	98
January 1942	210	65	275
February 1942	337	93	430
March 1942	440	190	630
April 1942	770	220	990
May 1942	428	282	710
June 1942	908	402	1,310
July 1942	1,856	886	2,742
August 1942	5,525	1,258	6,783
September 1942	6,772	1,032	7,804
October 1942	7,653	2,625	10,278
November 1942	10,289	2,545	12,834
December 1942	7,952	3,508	11,460

Not included in the hospital transfers are transfers within buildings.

For the summer of 1943, the population density in Theresienstadt was calculated at 130,270 people per square kilometer (before World War II, the population density in Berlin was 4,571 and, in Prague, 5,820; in contrast, this figure was 130,880 in the Warsaw Ghetto in March 1941).

Prisoners were housed in several types of structures:

1. Barracks
2. Former apartment buildings ("blockhouses")
3. Wooden barracks
4. Unfinished attics ("emergency occupancy")
5. Finished attics (mansards and partitions)

It cannot be said that a certain type of quarters was better or worse, aside from the catastrophic attics. Before rooms were officially or privately furnished, most housing offered scarcely more than a roof over one's head. The number of inhabitants per room alone also tells us little about the conditions of the quarters.

Some barracks had more or less functional washrooms, and others as good as none. The water supply often failed in those not on the ground floor. The "blockhouses" had no washrooms at first, and in many houses they never were installed. The toilets in the barracks were insufficient, unsanitary, and could not be flushed. In the houses it was often much worse. In 1942, in some buildings there was only one toilet for several hundred people. Where there were flush toilets, they usually did not work. The wooden barracks were scarcely better than the other mass housing, because their wood construction made it impossible to prevent the presence of vermin. The lack of insulation made them unbearably hot in summer. Better washrooms and toilets did not offset these disadvantages. In these pest-ridden quarters, some people made their beds at night in the courtyards, on terraces, and on roofs during the summer. This was not allowed but was tacitly tolerated.

The barracks had some advantages. Because they generally had kitchens, the inhabitants received their food in the house. Many of the offices with which people constantly had to deal were located there: the "deployment offices" of the "Central

Labor Office," the "housing offices" of the "Space Management Office," the branch offices of the "Central Registry," the "Central Provisions Office," and the "materials administration." Later, well-run "warming kitchens" were located there. Barracks were better suited for mass housing than were houses, which were simply insufficient for the overcrowding imposed on them. The barracks were impersonal and were more in accord with a camp than were the houses, in which the disparity between camp operations and the civilian veneer was especially burdensome. It is true that, in the barracks, the building elder was the responsible "landlord," but he was not really perceived that way, because his powers were shared by a staff; however, the building elder dealt directly with the residents, and thus whether life was bearable or unbearable depended on his ability and goodwill. In general, things were better organized in the barracks than in the houses.

The differences in the conditions in the buildings were the result of differences in the state of the buildings, as well as in the number and average composition of their residents (old and young people and healthy and sick people). The barracks, with the exception of B V, were very crowded. An overcrowded barracks was more bearable than was a small house, because of its larger ancillary spaces – corridors, courtyards, and so on. Houses in good condition were preferable if they were not too full. All makeshift housing was grim; it did not matter if it was in barracks or houses, or stalls or attics.

Every house had a reputation. People said that it was good or very good; but what one generally heard, in fact, was bad or very bad. Within the buildings, too, there were considerable differences: there were better or worse rooms, rooms in better or worse locations, and rooms with varying degrees of overcrowding. The largest living areas were the halls (never before occupied) in E I, where more than 400 people lived. Rooms in the barracks housed from 30 to 60 people on average. On average, 20 to 30 persons were packed into medium-sized rooms in the houses. Even the smallest rooms and sheds were occupied by 8 to 10 people. No room, no matter how miserable, remained unused. Where space and height allowed, three-story or at least two-story bunk beds were set up. On every level, lying in one's bed felt like lying in a coffin; this was true even of many of the top bunks, if the room's ceiling was low. The space between the bunk levels was 80 cm. An advantage of the lowest "bed" was that one lay almost level with the ground, which was appreciated in the dark. Disadvantages were the darkness and the dust that swirled from above. The most unpleasant was the middle bunk. The top level had the most air and light, although one usually could not straighten up there either, only sit. A narrow board used as a seat and a ladder to reach the highest bunk were attached to the three-level bunk beds.

The "dwelling" of a normal inmate actually consisted only of a place to sleep. When it rained or in the winter, people had hardly any other place to go in their free time, and they also received guests in this space. Originally there were few mattresses and paillasses. Many had to make do with the floor and could count themselves fortunate if it was made of wood and not stone. The bed frames were approximately sixty-five centimeters wide, so one could lay two normal mattresses on them the long way. The two-level bedsteads were, of course, more comfortable than the three-story monstrosities, especially in the higher-ceilinged spaces. Bunk beds are not suitable for the infirm, but of course those often were assigned to them anyway. Single beds were also built; as with the bunk beds, they were nailed together from crude softwood slats of the same length and width. Aside from the more privileged dwellings, these beds were placed in infirmaries and "homes for invalids" and were positioned so close together that nurses had difficulty getting to their patients.

Two- and three-level bedsteads were arranged in such a way that luggage could be stored on their upper ends. Whatever did not fit there went under the bed. The single beds had an attachment at the head of the bed with a board across it to store items such as bowls and washing utensils. Although beds began to be built in 1941, only during 1943 were they installed in almost all the living areas. Many preferred empty rooms if they had only mattresses, and the women were especially good at making their sleeping areas more comfortable and personal. By day the mattresses and blankets were piled on top of each other and used as sofas; covered suitcases became low tables, and in the middle of the room a quite wide aisle was created. The women in particular often resisted having the bunks installed, as they left only very narrow middle and side aisles, often no more than 60 or even 40 cm, and prevented any personal decoration of the rooms. But their protests did no good, although little space was gained. Hygienically, neither type of sleeping arrangement was much good, because the rooms could not really be cleaned. In 1942, "raft beds" (*Schlauchbetten*) – that is, mass bedding – were set up in some houses; spots in the middle could only be reached with difficulty, through other people's spots. The normal two- and three-story beds were intended for four or six persons, respectively. In the course of "beautification," the *Schlauchbetten* disappeared, and the top levels of the three-story bunks were sawed off.

At first, senior functionaries secured better housing for themselves in B V, where soon only a few men shared a room. Later, each family generally occupied one room. Midlevel functionaries also received larger rooms in B V, for ten to twenty men each. Living conditions changed for those designated as "notables" in the fall of 1942; they were given better living quarters, and it then became possible for people with sharp elbows to obtain better and more private accommodations through legal – or, more commonly, illegal or semilegal – methods. The use of unsuitable attics as quarters expedited this development; they were divided into mansards using sheets of insulation, holes were made in the roofs to create windows, and stoves (*öfen*) were installed with exhaust pipes that went through grotesque convolutions to reach the open air. Ultimately, the heads of the self-administration and some privileged people possessed quarters with one to two rooms. To be privileged meant to live with one's family, or at most with three people, in one room or to occupy a space of more than 3.5 m².

Separation according to gender basically continued for people of working age. A family living together was always an exception; even during the "beautification," this privilege was enjoyed by scarcely more than 5% of the prisoners. Even though both men and women lived in the houses, they were separated into different rooms and thus did not live together. Women were not housed better than men.

An effort was made from the beginning to house children separately, but it could never be consistently implemented. Children up to twelve years old lived with their mothers, and older boys lived with their fathers. "Homes" were established for young people according to age group, first in the barracks and then in separate buildings, where at least half the children later lived (see Chapter 17).

In general, higher spirits and greater harmony were found among the men than the women. Much depended on the size of the rooms and the ages of the occupants. People did not even know by name many of the cohabitants in their room. Even in rooms with fifty men, it took a long time before people got to know their roommates a bit. Often people knew only their neighbors in the nearby spots. Things were different in rooms with up to thirty inmates. Those who did not work, naturally, knew their fellows better. Younger people preferred to spend their free time outside their living quarters, where a rather crude and loud tone usually dominated. People were seldom very considerate, except perhaps to those who were sick, yet they usually got along quite well and were obliging in minor matters. Serious fights were rare among the younger men, but some did not fit in well and were a nuisance to those around them. Things looked much friendlier among the women; they liked to lend a personal touch even to the mass housing, but quarrels were much more common there. Among the young people, agreeability and order depended most of all on the "home leaders."

House order in the various quarters was enforced partly through prescribed rules, but also partly through unwritten ones, which were followed more or less strictly. Every room had something like its own system. Those who did not work at night or did not have the day off arose between six and seven o'clock and tried to find a place at the window for a few minutes to air their bedding. After nine o'clock, as decreed by the SS, bedding was not to be seen in the courtyards and windows, unless, in exceptional cases, this had been explicitly ordered. Jewish inspectors dealt harshly with things belonging to the forgetful or dilatory, throwing them to the ground or "confiscating" them. One then had to figure out how to get possession of one's things again through the house elder and, on top of it, had to deal with incivility.

After getting up, people crowded into the inadequate washrooms, where often there was no water, and one had to wait in long lines. The washrooms were equipped with small showers over sluices. Those who could manage it got up early to find a spot to wash themselves properly, for the rush came later, and then one could wash only from the waist up. The "water service" ensured that water was used sparingly. A piece of inferior wartime soap was given out every six to seven weeks by the "materials administration" through the room elders. People did not receive shaving articles or other items of personal hygiene, which made these items valuable, especially as they were confiscated from newcomers. Those who needed shaving cream, blades, or a toothbrush could obtain them only with difficulty and sacrifice. Those who earlier had shaved daily managed to do so every second or third day. It therefore is astounding how well groomed at least the younger people were, and they exerted moral pressure on their unkempt roommates. It was worse in those houses that had no washrooms; because people were not permitted to wash at fountains or water pipes, they used small basins and had to haul water into the rooms, a process that was too arduous for the infirm. Therefore, through no fault of their own, their physical cleanliness often left something to be desired.

In the morning, a crowd gathered at the inadequate and usually dirty toilets, where the "toilet patrol" was supposed to ensure order and cleanliness. People had to stand in line, which was torture during the frequent diarrhea epidemics and for the infirm. Older people became irritable and fights broke out. Young men took pleasure in dramatically shouting out clever allusions to camp conditions or events in the war. Pornographic inscriptions were rarely seen, but in the men's barracks one could find juicy scribbles on the walls about prominent people in the camp.

Next one had to put one's sleeping area in order, which was a feat of acrobatics given the lack of space and all the dust and dirt. Nothing was allowed to lie on the bed; everything had to be stowed on the 40-cm-wide board behind the "bed," and bedding could not be left out. If a person was lucky, he possessed one or two pillows and two to three blankets, including a feather-stuffed quilt. Bedding was usually variegated and could be changed only every two to four months, because the laundry could not manage a larger workload, and people did not have the time or means to wash their bedding themselves.

Before or after cleaning up, those who wanted to could get themselves an ersatz coffee. Most workers left after breakfast, so the workers' rooms remained almost empty until the lunch break. Only the sick; the room elders, who often were not otherwise employed; and some people who were off duty stayed at home. At midday most people came for the food, often only for a few minutes. Eating utensils usually were cleaned in the washrooms – cold water was enough to remove the traces of food that contained no fat. When work was over, people returned to their quarters if they did not hurry to see their relatives; the men preferred to spend time in the women's quarters. Until the summer of 1942, the rooms filled up after work hours; later, they filled up only shortly before curfew at 8 P.M. Groups formed to talk, and board and card games were popular. Others hurried to the washroom, put their belongings in order, visited other rooms, or went to the offices in their houses. During the day, these offices delivered summonses that were placed on people's spots by the room elders. Otherwise, people lay down early and read or rested. Nonworkers were much more dependent on their rooms. The worse the inhabitants' physical condition, the worse their accommodations tended to be; the residents huddled in their places and thought dismal thoughts, which ensured that their emotional decay kept pace with their physical decline.

The mandatory lights-out began at 10 P.M. No lights were allowed except in places where emergency lighting was authorized. If the season permitted, the windows were opened, although they were inadequate given the overcrowding; this was prohibited when lights were on, because of the strictly enforced blackout rules.

The heavy, antiquated gates on most buildings were locked during curfew. The entrances to barracks were watched day and night, mainly by the OD guards and sometimes also by the GW; as early as 1942, the "gate guards" were discontinued in the other buildings. The courtyards of the barracks were large and filled with light; those of the houses were usually quite narrow, often bumpy or unpaved, and, if not always dirty, then at least usually neglected. In the course of the "renovation," walls between the courtyards were torn down and rough openings were chopped out, without creating unified, clearly arranged areas, as intended. It probably seemed quaintly medieval but heightened the sense of desolate decay. The "beautification" efforts then covered these crooked structures with a more attractive veneer. Here and there stood a few trees, including fruit trees, whose fruits were stolen before they were ripe; there also were carefully tended vegetable gardens. During the "beautification," people were encouraged to plant vegetables. At that time, small areas on the redoubts and in the moats were given to some functionaries and privileged people for private cultivation. Every available terrace was used to grow radishes or tomatoes. In the courtyards there were drains, which often clogged, and containers for garbage and carefully collected rubbish. Sometimes it was not possible to remove the waste, even in makeshift fashion; as a result, especially in 1942, an unbearable plague of flies arose, and rats and mice could not be exterminated.

All the buildings, most of all the "blockhouses," were covered on the sides facing the courtyards and inside with ugly inscriptions in black and red, next to which was a chaotic flood of placards. Everywhere were labels such as "Metals," "Woven Materials," "Textiles," "Paper," "Glass," "Trash," or "Only for Ashes"; directions to offices and rooms, for example, "Office of the House Elders 1st Floor No. 113," "Urinal," "Toilet," or "Latrine." There were many exhortations: "Cleanliness – Order – Fellowship," "Pay Attention to Cleanliness," "Danger of Typhoid – Never

Forget to Wash Hands Before Eating and After Every Toilet Use," "Water Drainage Prohibited Here," "Cleanliness Is the First Duty," or "Laying Out Bedding After 9 A.M. Prohibited." During disinfection to eliminate vermin, yellow notices were pasted about, printed with a skull and crossbones and the words. "Warning! Beware! Gassing with POISONOUS GAS! Danger of Death – Access Strictly Prohibited!" Similar notices advised: "Warning! Rat Bait Set Out Here! Dangerous to People and Pets!" (of course, no one had pets), or "Never Forget: Before Eating, After Every Use of the Toilet, Wash Hands! Protect Against Contagion – Typhoid – Infection." During the typhoid epidemic, washbasins with disinfectant liquid were placed in the latrines, and the "toilet guard" ensured that people dipped their hands into it. All these texts for orientation and instruction were supposed to create the appearance of order.

Here is a small selection of seven placards; similar ones were the norm everywhere:

> 1. Signposts
> Jewish Elder Dr. Paul Eppstein B V
> Deputy Jewish Elder Jak. Edelstein B V
> Deputy Jewish Elder Dr. Benj. Murmelstein B V
> District Elder Eng[ineer]. Polaczek C III
> Block Elder Eng. Alex. Witz E IIIa, Rm. 10
> Central Registry B V, Rm. 103
> District Registry E IIIa
> Internal Administration B V 107/108/109/113
> Fire Department Parkstrasse 2
> Ghetto Guard Langestrasse 13
>
> 2. House Elder: Filip Schwarzkopf, Rm. 17
> Deputy House Elder: Flora Herz, Rm. 14
> Assistant: Jenny Bier, Rm. 13
> Assistant: Emil Kohner, Rm. 02
>
> 3. Authorized Deployment Office – labor welfare located Langestrasse 5 (Hamburg Kaserne) Rm. 91
>
> 4. Food shall be served only in clean containers.
>
> 5. House Rationing Commission
> Alexandrowitz Isidor Rm. 02
> Geiringer Paula Rm. 08
> Schweizer Flora Rm 14

[As of August 14, 1942, these commissions were supposed to monitor fair distribution of the food that the "ration transport crews" brought on carts to the "blockhouse" courtyards.]

> 6. Block Chief Physician: Dr. Lamberg in C III (Chief Physician's Office)
> Office hours: 9–10 and 3–4
> Block Physician: Dr. Oskar Rothbaum
> Office hours: In the building daily
>
> 7. Regulations for toilet and sewer maintenance. [This placard was typed.]
>   1. Every latrine shall have a person on duty at all times. Cleanliness of the seats and the floor shall be checked immediately after the user

leaves. Soiling must be corrected by the person responsible (for sick people, by the nurse).

2. A container, bucket or something similar must stand in front of every latrine and is to be used by every user to rinse out the toilet after use. Entering the W.C. without a filled container is prohibited.

3. Three times a day (morning, noon, and evening), the seats and floors and the foyer of the latrines shall be cleaned by the toilet [service] or cleaning service, preferably with disinfectant, where this is available.

4. In the evening, powdered lime (or chlorinated lime) must always be put into every toilet.

5. In those buildings in which the sewage from the wells does not flow to the latrines, 20–30 buckets of water must be poured into each toilet by the building staff daily after the greatest usage, that is, always at 9 A.M. and 3 P.M.

6. In every latrine there must be a sturdy 1 to 1.5 meter long pole or equivalent and a brush available for cleaning the toilet.

7. In the courtyard, easily visible notices shall be posted with the inscription that only wastewater, but no paper, rubbish, or similar items, may be poured into any of the drains. Using hard paper or excelsior instead of toilet paper, or throwing in leftover food, bread, rags, etc., is strictly forbidden. The cleaning crew must supervise enforcement of these regulations.

Additional, generally interchangeable placards gave information about periods when lights had to be out during the day and night, the blackout, or who was on call for duty in the building. There were also "status tables" on the number of men, women, small children, and all residents of the building, as well as the "daily allocation," which listed the rations to be distributed on that day, for example, bread, margarine, sugar, sausage, jam, salt, soap, and washing powder. Toilet paper was distributed only once in many months, if at all, and the ration consisted of only a few sheets per person.

The rooms were assigned numbers; the first numeral (0, 1, or 2) indicated on which floor it was situated (the ground floor, first floor, or second floor). The house elders and their families lived in one room; next to it, often in a former kitchen, was the "office of the house elder," which usually also served as a "warming kitchen." Here one could warm up food or cook food from private stores. If they were not set aside for privileged people or improved upon by their occupants, rooms were furnished with the beds, as described previously; a small iron stove; and, in the barracks, perhaps – although rarely – a table and one or two benches. People stored their clothes in their luggage, if they did not hang them on nails that had been driven into the walls or bed frames. A birch broom, a primitive wooden dustpan, and a garbage can completed the furnishings. In each room, occupied or not, there had to be an "inventory list," and in occupied rooms a "room list," indicating the building, room, name of the room elder, and the last and first names of the occupants along with their "transport numbers," as well as the number of men, women, children, and the "total inventory."

Electric lights had been or would be installed everywhere; people had to use them very sparingly:

The Electricity Department announces:
    With immediate effect, lighting of ancillary rooms in the quarters, including

Latrines
Hallways
Stairwells

is authorized.

Lighting shall occur only to the extent most necessary. The authorization under no circumstances means that bulbs shall remain lit out of negligence in the authorized rooms if daylight sufficiently lights these rooms. Illumination or the level of light in these rooms may under no circumstances be equal to that in the quarters or places of work.

(memorandum from the Central Secretariat, December 5, 1943)

Living quarters were so badly illuminated that it would have been difficult to do less. The light bulbs often were checked to ensure they were not stronger than 15 or 25 candlepower at the most. Even in large rooms, often only one lamp was allowed to burn. Most of the rooms were gloomy in natural as well as in artificial light.

Much depended on the house elder, for example, to which room one came and to which spot one was assigned. The building elders, whose duties were outlined in Chapter 4, had a much higher position than the house elders, but the house elders' behavior had a much greater influence on the well-being of their residents, who, if they were wise, got along well with them. There were good people among them, but many were unpleasant and most of them corruptible. Their duties included the daily "status reports," maintaining order and cleanliness, delivering official summonses to the inmates, receipt and distribution of all "allocations" (*Fassungen*), and monitoring of all regulations. The house directors had authoritarian powers; everything that had to do with the building had to be submitted to them, if one followed official channels. Together with some assistants (who, in large buildings, were members of the administrative staff and, in the remaining buildings, were unemployed people, referred to as "house service") and with the room elders, they formed the administration of their "housing unit."

In addition, the room elders had some influence on their fellow prisoners' well-being, even though their position was relatively insignificant among those able to work. If they were not decent, they tried to reduce the rations they had to distribute. They could also bully the inmates or become annoying with dangerous arrogance, and yet many were good comrades. They allocated "room duty": one or two people had to sweep in the morning and empty the garbage cans. In the women's quarters, the room elders insisted that the rooms be scrubbed. The men rarely scrubbed their quarters; this task was performed by the women's "cleaning crews," who also cleaned the offices, sickrooms, hallways, and so on.

Inferior lignite and firewood were distributed in laughably small amounts. The normal quarters could be heated only if someone was able to procure a little fuel through connections or theft. In 1943, 6% of the coal delivered was used for the living quarters, including the hospitals. Thus, of the 17,026 tons of coal (of which 10,638 tons was lignite) consumed that year, some 1,020 tons were allotted to occupied rooms. Only the sickrooms and the "homes for invalids" and "young people's homes" were more or less well heated.

The majority dealt quite well with the wretched buildings. If things were not too terrible, people took everything with patience and humor. The better one had lived before Theresienstadt, the more easily one adapted. The biggest problem was the filth, and people fought it in vain. Two or three days after a major cleaning, everything was the same as it had been before. There were vermin in unimaginable quantities, and not even the best quarters ever were free of bugs and fleas. When an entire building finally had been disinfected, the scourge quickly settled in again. The vermin could not be driven from their breeding grounds in the wooden frames and dust-covered mattresses. People tried every possible, although ineffectual, means of self-help, sticking nut leaves under the blankets and dismantling the nailed-together frames, scorching them with candles, and plugging up the holes with stearin. It was most unbearable in the invalids' quarters. As soon as the lights were out, the poor people were assaulted and could not sleep, even if they killed a hundred bugs in the course of a night.

Some points from the "memoranda from the Department of Internal Administration – Building Management" from March 18 and 25, 1944, furnish evidence of the "style of living" in Theresienstadt at the beginning of the "beautification":

Burning garbage cans

Recently there has been an increase in cases of garbage cans being set on fire by smoldering ashes thrown into them. Accordingly, the building occupants shall be instructed that hot ashes may go into the garbage can only after the ashes have been extinguished, or that they should notify the house elder immediately if smoke is rising from one of the garbage cans.

Depositing dirt, trash, etc.

It is continuously observed that trash, ripped mattresses, bricks, stones, and the like have been deposited in various places in the ghetto. Attention is again drawn to the fact that it is strictly forbidden to dump certain objects anywhere other than at the deposit sites specified for incineration.…

Scrap materials

After the large-scale removal of scrap materials during the clean-up week, it is likely in the foreseeable future that there no longer will be an accumulation in the buildings and houses. Should, against expectation, large amounts of scrap material again be found in the attics, cellars, or similarly out-of-the-way places, they shall – if the available containers are not sufficient – be left where they are and reported to the crew at the next pick-up. Special pick-ups probably will not be possible in the near future.…

Combatting fleas

The cold weather is well suited to combating fleas, so as to stop their reproduction before the warm weather begins. This is done by thorough brushing of the beds and mattresses, blankets and pillows with a diluted Lysol solution.… In the coming weeks, this is to be carried out in all accommodations. Nurses shall assist the sick and those under nursing care. Lysol will be handed out by the department of disinfection in L 506, upon the order of the building or block elder, one liter for every 100 people.…

Urgent cases of delousing

The department of disinfection will determine ambulatory and non-ambulatory cases of clothing lice regularly for the next day in the delousing bath. An examining physician will give notice on a special form. In urgent cases, the delousing bath in L 605 stands in constant readiness, and in extremely urgent cases, the quarantine in Q 810 serves non-ambulatory lice-ridden people.

Air-raid precautions

During the next few days, the construction department shall supply sand to the buildings and blocks for the purpose of air-raid precautions.… The use of this sand for other purposes, as well as failure to follow this order, are punishable.…

Material from discarded beds

The building and house elders shall be notified that they are obliged to consign any materials removed from block or raft beds to the proper places and are not allowed to use them for their own purposes.

Changing rooms with regard to preferred accommodations

The Space Management Office shall give to all house elders an inventory in which all rooms considered preferred are listed. Notice of all changes in these preferred rooms and in all mansards shall be given to the accommodations office without fail.... .

Small children getting lost

It repeatedly has happened that small children have been lost in the city and could give no information concerning their parents or their quarters. In order to avoid this, the transport number shall be clearly sewn onto the inside of the clothing of all small children.

The following is a short letter from the spring of 1942: "To Doctor X. – Dear Doctor! Today I moved to Stable No. 43. Cordial greetings, [signature]." Another source describes billeting in December 1944:

> We are moving into apartments. Where once bustling life pulsed in brothels and dives, prisoners are now housed. They are real houses. Funny, very old buildings with the side rooms on the *Pavlatschen* [balconies serving as corridors on the inner side of the building] and with a faucet in the courtyard. There are large five- and multi-room apartments in which one can get lost. In large, old-fashioned rooms, there are bunk beds of raw wooden slats, and in the middle a wobbly table made of unfinished boards, in the corner a tiny iron stove, as if from a doll's house. So one lives in filth and disease, in cold and hunger, with all of one's possessions on one's back. The barracks don't hurt as much, nor do the *Kaserne*. One never has lived like this before, these are new experiences, that's just the way it is. But a real building with steps up to a proper apartment. Where one can recognize by the less worn patches of color to what point a carpet covered the painted floors, where the contours of furniture long since gone still are visible on the walls, where lighter patches indicate that pictures once adorned the walls. Where, during sleepless nights, one feels that people lived here, really free people with furniture, with desires, people who slept in wide beds on the floor, next to which there surely stood a nightstand, old-fashioned people in whose rooms surely stood ornate sideboards and chairs with high backs around a mahogany table. People who walked on Persian carpets, and whose windows were covered by curtains, curtains on brass curtain rods, because the holes are still in the walls where they were fastened on either side of the window. In its place, black paper now quite stubbornly resists all attempts at a complete blackout. Our slat beds are narrow and deep, with boards on either side so that one doesn't fall from the upper bunk. One lies down in it as if in a coffin. (256)

The following quotation illustrates how one built up and lived in a mansard, with the permission of the "Space Management Office" and other authorities:

> However, materials in general were not made available. So ... we obtained materials where we could get them. My friend P.D. (in civilian life, he was a dental technician – in Theresienstadt, however, rationing service) had connections to people in the lumber warehouse, and there on several consecutive days we got ourselves vast quantities of wood boards, planks, moldings, squared timbers, all types of ship's planks, and I saw to the planing of the materials, again through my connections in the carpenters workshop.

I . . . worked in the accounting office of the Financial Department-Production, in which function I had free access to all . . . factories and could establish many connections. Thus it was also possible for me to procure a great deal of material, such as locks, door hinges, glass, nails, screws, tools, and similar things, likewise also lime, cement, sand, plaster, etc. wood-fiber board panels were lying in the courtyard . . . piled up in large heaps.

. . . I then started to build with P.D. and a second colleague, A.M. (a fur tailor by profession – in T., a carpenter) and we received the help of some specialized craftsmen such as glass workers, window carpenters, wallpaperers, bricklayers, and metalworkers. We paid them for their work for weeks with our rations of bread, jam, canned food, sugar, ate almost nothing and worked during the in-between times when we were not busy at our assigned employment, so that our health suffered. Still, in a few weeks we broke through the roof, the window was finished, the frame of the 16-square-meter attic apartment was set up, and in the course of several weeks, everything was covered with wood-fiber board and lined with bricks, sealed, painted, and finished with 3 sofas, an armchair, a chest of drawers, and built-in cupboards, and we moved in. From this point on, we led a kind of private life with our friends and spouses. We also got ourselves an electric cooker, an immersion heater, electric pads, and an iron. Everything was done with electric current, and during free time my wife especially managed the attic just like at home, i.e. she cooked, ironed, washed, sewed, all of which made her very happy. Both the other women had good apartments elsewhere, so mainly my wife and I enjoyed the attic apartment. Many friends came to visit us and, most important, . . . my mother was our daily guest. Right at this time we also received more packages. . . . Some of our friends were in agriculture, others were employed in the bakery. P.D. was able to procure some food here and there from the rationing service, and so in this period we lived more happily to a certain extent and hoped to survive the terrible war more or less protected in Theresienstadt. [A description follows of the furniture brought into the camp from Jewish apartments in Prague.] I, too, obtained two wire inserts from there for our couches, a folding table, three upholstered chairs, a cabinet, and a beautiful, large mirror, all of which we could use in the mansard apartment. My wife was especially happy with the mirror. We put . . . all our nice clean clothes and undergarments into the new chest, since constantly opening and closing our suitcases was extremely inconvenient. (57)

Those who were similarly proficient could arrange things quite comfortably over time, while others starved in misery. The line between illegal but harmless behavior and behavior that was ethically objectionable is difficult to draw. The majority was scarcely aware of the difference between self-help that was harmless to the community and criminal selfishness. In the end, almost everything one did was illegal, if one judged by the camp regulations. The boundary marking what is wrong in a normal society, at least formally, is roughly delineated by the realm of what is illegal, but in the camp this boundary was blurred, and the principles of ethical and legal prohibitions lost the character of perceptible correspondence, without which there can be no healthy social order – and thus, in Theresienstadt, morality was first endangered and finally lost.

Usually people improved their accommodations in ways that probably could be justified: by obtaining scraps of boards and some nails to make brackets and shelves, on which they placed their eating and washing utensils; clothing hangers; simple footstools, so they didn't have to squat on beds and suitcases; small tables; and additions to the bed frames. Such items also were given as presents, bartered for bread, or "inherited" from the unlucky ones who were deported. With these items, which filled up all the space; with cords hung with colorful gewgaws; and with the suitcases that blocked the aisles, the mass accommodations gave the impression of large junk rooms. Light and air were missing in these housing cages – it was a terrible state of affairs, whether one lived in a completely altered room in which one almost got lost in the chasms between the three-level beds or, much more hauntingly and tragically, in mistreated people's bare quarters in former restaurants and stores, still with their old shop signs, dusty displays, and glass doors, now barricaded by two crosspieces, which never could conceal the naked, groaning misery behind them.

When the weather permitted, the prisoners dragged footstools and pillows to the courtyards and corridors, where they spent time together in somewhat fresher air. Theft of wood was vigorously prosecuted, but this did not prevent almost all the rooms from being crammed with objects made of "smuggled" wood. Curiously, as soon as such pieces were finished and placed in the quarters, no one, not even the SS, found fault with them. The women, whose appreciation of decoration and nice things never faded, were especially resourceful. They obtained colorful fabric and fastened a pole or a stand in a corner with the fabric as a curtain, to create a "closet." Even in the mass quarters, personal taste showed in wall decorations and other ornamentation that people made themselves, received as gifts, or acquired with saved-up food. Portraits in red chalk, copied from photographs, were popular, as were all kinds of sentimental little pictures, often decorated with motifs from Theresienstadt.

Often the electric current was tampered with. People screwed in stronger light bulbs; then came an inspection, and again people sat in the dim dusk. Some tapped into the wires and attached small lamps to their beds – woe to them if this were discovered! Great caution also was necessary with electrical devices, which always were used, despite inspections and confiscations. It was rare for fellow residents to betray someone; nor, in the rooms, were other illegal actions, such as smoking, often reported. The misuse of electrical current resulted in serious disruptions to the lighting, such that the electricity was often cut off without notice or as punishment. Fuel was pilfered from storehouses but most often was stolen while newly arrived supplies were being unloaded. Usually only small amounts were stolen; people carried it away in their clothes or pockets. Fellow residents who had not procured any fuel rarely were allowed to put a pot onto the stove's small iron plate.

The preferential quarters that were not established by order of the SS should be viewed more critically than these harmless or still excusable actions. Officials in leading positions received the first special rooms, which still housed many more occupants than a military squad room. Even the luxury rooms that came later were not spacious in their dimensions in absolute terms, and the mansards were cramped. The luxury was in the furnishings. Before preferential rooms or garrets for capable people became a general nuisance, some people arranged so-called villas for themselves, for example, in the halls of E I. These were ingeniously reconstructed upper levels of three-story bunk beds for two people. To pay for building materials and craftsmen, people not only relied on their own resources but also abused their official positions and misappropriated food and other things, which harmed not the SS but their fellow prisoners (see Chapter 12).

Some had a customary right to better quarters or a garret by virtue of their position. Few did without these or furnished them modestly. It should be emphasized that some, referring to their parents' wretched housing, waived their right to preferred quarters; nevertheless, many were immune to the shamefaced horror of the fact

Housing 293

that they themselves thoughtlessly enjoyed forbidden pleasures while their fathers and mothers lived in misery.

For the dwellings of the high-ranking people, almost anything could be obtained. First of all, they commissioned interior decorators, who drafted nice designs. Then they procured the best things. Anything not readily available was ordered from and expertly produced in the workshops. The walls were nicely painted, the doors were varnished, and soft rugs were laid on the floors. There was flawless, new lacquered furniture; comfortable sofas with elegantly upholstered cushions; flowered curtains hung in the windows; and, on the walls, the best paintings by camp artists, and there was no lack of vases, flower pots, and porcelain. In the cupboards one found everything a person could want. They lacked for nothing and felt no privation. That is how some lived, with words of pity and solidarity on their lips, and they had scarcely an inkling of what things were like a few meters away in the camp; nor did they need to tremble in fear of a transport – for a long time. The most pernicious aspect of this inequity was the example that these unscrupulous beneficiaries of their positions set for people such as cooks, butchers, bakers, and others of lesser eminence. What the former extracted from the camp supplies, as their presumed and supposed right, the minor opportunists obtained for themselves through the law of the jungle and corruption. There were exceptions, who cannot be praised enough, but unfortunately they were all too rare.

At the orders of the SS, accommodations for the "notables," the Danes, and many of the Dutch were also better. Many passively and modestly accepted what was offered to them; then the rooms looked as if they had been furnished by a junk dealer. How the "city beautification" changed these rooms is related in Chapter 6. The devastation of the camp by the fall transports of 1944 brought this improbable whirlwind of activity to a standstill.

12

Nutrition

FOOD RATIONS

It is difficult to treat the subject of nutrition in the concentration camps objectively, because official records often were falsified and unreliable, and private accounts often do not provide an accurate picture. And yet, after the fear of deportation, there was no topic that so dominated conversations and thoughts in Theresienstadt as did food. We begin by considering official documents, which must be evaluated with the greatest of care, because, both wittingly and unwittingly, they distort the truth.

Food Consumption

The ... amount of meat, cereal products and potatoes allocated to each resident corresponds to the standard food rations in the Protectorate ... ; flour and sugar rations are smaller in Theresienstadt.

Larger rations of bread (2,625 grams per head per week, instead of 1,700 grams) and margarine (187.5 grams instead of 110 grams) should make up for the discrepancies.

Heavy laborers ... shall not be granted any extra rations from outside; supplementary fare will ... be found by making internal adjustments.... The Jewish self-administration will reduce the margarine, sugar and bread rations of those not working, which will make it possible to provide heavy laborers with 2,141 calories daily.

With regard to bread, margarine and sugar rations, provisions shall be allocated to the consumer in their raw state; otherwise, they will be in the form of cooked food.

Rations of sugar and margarine are to be centrally apportioned. In 1943, 2,343,000 portions of margarine and 691,000 portions of sugar were packaged.

Fifteen kitchens with a 25,000-liter cooking pot capacity distribute the morning coffee at daybreak, then, throughout the day: a midday meal consisting of soup and potatoes or a simple flour-based food, accompanied on certain days by a small portion of meat; as well as supper, consisting alternately of coffee – sometimes accompanied by a small baked item – or a thick soup. As part of the usual allotment, food for the sick will be cooked in a way suited to their particular ailment (heart, kidney, diabetes). The same applies to small children and toddlers.

In 1943, a total of 15,733,840 portions were distributed, corresponding to an average of 45,107 portions per day.

The output of the kitchens is augmented by that of the kitchen bakeries, which produce the simple pastries (400,000 kg in 1943).

Nutrition

Purchases bring in additional food. Every resident ... possesses a ration card, and each is called upon to shop in a predetermined order. Various spreads, spices, sweeteners and types of tea are available in grocery stores in exchange for the prescribed number of points and upon payment of the price in ghetto crowns.

Bread

.... Since no trained bakers were available, semi-skilled personnel had to be brought in.

Recently, attempts are even being made to employ, with prospects of success, ... a number of women for certain types of work.... . Production is kept strictly separate from administration.

At the start of operations, output ... stood at 3,600 loaves daily... . In 1942, 1,226,910 loaves of bread and 91,882 baked goods were produced in 131,481 hours. Due to improvements ... the number of hours ... were doubled in 1943, and output was almost tripled. In 263,085 hours, 3,078,068 kilograms were baked. The current daily output is 11,000 kg and is to ... be increased ... to 15,000 kg.   (274)

In February 1942 there were around 10,000 prisoners at the beginning of the month and around 14,000 prisoners by the end of the month; the following record indicates the amount of food consumed during that month:

| | Total Amounts | | | Total Amounts |
Items	Kilograms	Liters	Items	Kilograms
Milk		37,050	Margarine	5,882.85
Meat	8,860		Fodder beets	11,660
Bread	121,099.25		Sauerkraut	10,913
Potatoes	142,754		Salt	3,352.50
Jam	5,080		Tomato paste	15
Coffee substitute	3,828.20		Artificial honey	13.10
Sugar	6,754.50		Celery	255
Flour	14,914.50		Tea	21.55

Source: Orders of the day, March 8, 1942

Another order of the day records the food consumption in late November 1941 through January 1942 with that of February 1942:

Table: Consumption of Food Items

| | Daily Rations | | | | | |
| | [November 24, 1941–January 31, 1942] | | February 1942 | | Plus or Minus | |
	Heller[*]	Amounts	Heller	Amounts	Heller	Amounts
Bread	90.39	347 g.	96.90	372 g.	6.51	25 g.
Meat and Sausages	32.46	15	50.45	31	17.99	16
Vegetables	12.42	10	14.77	8	2.35	2
Fodder Beets and Kohlrabi			3.62	36	3.62	36
Sauerkraut	3.86	16	7.91	35	4.05	19

(continued)

Sociology

(continued)

	Daily Rations					
	[November 24, 1941–January 31, 1942]		February 1942		Plus or Minus	
	Heller[*]	Amounts	Heller	Amounts	Heller	Amounts
Legumes and Cereal Products	11.71	24	2.32	4	9.39 x	20 x
Coffee Substitute and Chicory	7.31	10	8.81	12	1.50	2
Potatoes	30.06	396	33.74	444	3.68	48
Margarine and Fat	28	16	31.09	18	3.09	2
Flour	23.19	64	22.81	64	0.38 x	—
Jam	1.45	1	27.16	16	25.71	15
Skim Milk	7.08	71 ml.	11.98	119 ml.	4.90	48 ml.
Saccharine and Sugar	25.21 Saccharine	2 g.	14.20 Sugar	21 g.	11.01 x Saccharine	2 x g.
Other	25.66	—	3.43	—	22.32 x	—
TOTAL	298.80	—	329.19	—	30.39	—

Numbers marked with an "x" = minus
[* 100 heller = 1 crown]

Commentary: Total expenditures ... indicate ... an improvement in value of about 10% on average.

a) Improvements:
    Bread: ... increased ... which can be attributed to the fact that ... for a time, the daily ration consisted of only 250 g and was only later increased to 375 g. The discrepancy between the actual rations of 375 g and ... 372 g lies in the time-lag between the day of the arrival of the transport and the first day of rationing. Meat and meat products: ... The disproportionate increase is a result of the price of the meat allocated.
b) Setbacks:
    .... Saccharine and sugar: The reduction in quantities is relatively slight, but nevertheless perceptible because of the elimination of saccharine.
    Other: Here the elimination of various spices ... is to be noted. (orders of the day, March 12, 1942)

The figures for August 1942 are recorded in yet another source (see 276):

Arrival and distribution of foodstuffs

Type of product:	Arrival:	Distributed:
Bread	627,488.70 kg	650,901.20 kg
Potatoes	1,021,603	856,897
Sugar	68,476.30	47,400.20
Salt	16,632.75	18,592.60
Margarine	44,846.50	42,001.75

Nutrition 297

Type of product:	Arrival:	Distributed:
Jam	2,020.15	8,667.50
Coffee substitute	22,224.15	28,109
Flour	71,027.75	114,905.25
Rye bread flour	191,607.50	128,755
Wheat bread flour	42,100	30,545
Cereal products	15,974.80	12,028
Yeast	1,310	1,295
Vinegar	160 L	228.50 L
Dried vegetables	403.60 kg	829.90 kg
Ditto	138 packets	283 packets
Liver paste at ¼ kg	20.50 kg	23,437.50 kg
Ditto at ⅓ kg	1,788.35	0.35
Ditto at ½ kg	73	—
Artificial honey	81.50	229.70

The following was … used in caring for the ghetto's inhabitants:

Item	Amount used:	Consumption per head per day:	Allotted per head per day:
Potatoes	652,794.95 kg	398 g	428.57 g
Bread	602,937.48	367.64	375
Flour	106,634.42	65.02	71.43
Sugar	41,871.85	25.53	28.57
Meat, Sausage	24,507.70	26.40	28.57
[Liver] paste	18,789.25		
Margarine	30,354.70	18.50	21.43
Coffee substitute	18,202.10	11.09	12
Cereal products	17,892.85	10.86	21.43
Jam	10,031.80	6.11	14.28
Dried vegetables	784.05		
Ditto in packets	760 packets	4.87	14.28
Milk	158,663.25 L	94 mL	120 mL
Salt	16,190.05 kg	9.87 g	

In August 1942, total consumption … 4,793,617.60 crowns. The figure for daily rations distributed in August amounted to 1,462,565 as compared with 949,741 in July 1942 and 485,419 in June 1942, so that one daily ration approximates 3.2775 crowns.

The difference between allotted and actual consumption is considerable. The daily expenses per person, including quarters, light, heat, and so on, were set at a limit of 4.2979 crowns. A diagram entitled "Provisions for Ghetto Dwellers" lists, for various food types, the average weight and percentage of the total allotted to each person per day:

	Weight (g)	Percent of total
Potatoes	423.5	40.7
Bread	366.9	35.2
Milk	93.8	9.0
Flour	51.2	4.0
Meat and sausages	27.9	2.7
Sugar	22.1	2.4
Margarine	18.9	1.8
Coffee substitute	11.0	1.0
Salt	10.5	1.0
Cereal products	8.9	0.6
Jam, vegetables	6.7	

Even if viewed uncritically, this table offers proof of poor nutrition.

A food distribution table compiled around July 1, 1943, for internal use is noteworthy:

Individual categories of recipients:

12,500	Non-working
21,900	Working
5,200	Heavy laborers
3,200	Children
57	Council of Elders and persons enjoying its privileges
718	Cooks
78	Employees of Central Supply
38	Flour porters
181	Bakers and bakery employees
69	White bakers (employed in the kitchen bakery)
40	Butchers
177	Potato porters
228	Shipping

Each week, each person received the following amounts, before and after decreases (reduced rations in brackets):

	Non-worker	Worker	Heavy laborer
Meat	225	225	342
Flour	418	418	604
Margarine	142	187	218
Sugar	133	193	226
Cereal products	112	112	140
Potatoes	2,195 (1,738)	2,195 (1,738)	3,075 (2,436)
Bread	2,333	2,625	3,500

Nutrition

	Child	Council of Elders	Cook
Meat	243	465 (340)	675
Flour	543	1,568 (993)	1,918 (1,668)
Margarine	217	337 (262)	457 (427)
Sugar	228	393 (293)	463 (433)
Cereal products	156	112	412 (312)
Potatoes	2,628 (2,143)	4,695 (2,738)	9,445 (6,738)
Bread	2,625	3,500	2,625

	Central Supply Employee	Flour porter	Baker
Meat	225	342	342
Flour	418	768	604
Margarine	257 (207)	288 (238)	218
Sugar	263 (213)	296 (246)	226
Cereal products	112	140	140
Potatoes	2,195 (1,738)	3,075 (2,436)	3,075 (2,436)
Bread	6,500 (5,500)	6,500 (5,500)	9,625 (6,125)

	White Baker	Butcher	Potato porter, Shipping
Meat	342	842	342
Flour	2,556 (1,892)	604	604
Margarine	491 (400)	218	218
Sugar	226	226	226
Cereal products	140	140	140
Potatoes	3,075 (2,436)	3,075 (2,436)	4,825 (3,500)
Bread	2,625	2,500	3,500

After decreases, distribution per person per week was on average:

Meat	250 g
Flour	500
Margarine	187.5
Sugar	200
Cereal products	150
Potatoes	2,000
Bread	2,625

of which the percentage received by each person was:

	Meat	Flour	Marg.	Sugar	Cereals	Potato	Bread
Non-worker	90	83	76	67	74	87	89
Worker	90	83	100	96	74	87	100
Heavy laborer	137	120	116	113	93	122	133
Child	97	108	116	114	104	107	100
Council of Elders	136	198	140	146	74	137	133

(*continued*)

Sociology

(continued)

	Meat	Flour	Marg.	Sugar	Cereals	Potato	Bread
Cook	270	333	228	217	208	337	100
Central Supply Employee	90	83	110	106	74	87	209
Flour porter	137	153	127	123	93	122	209
Baker	137	120	116	113	93	122	133
White baker	137	380	213	190	93	122	133
Potato porter and Shipping	137	120	116	113	93	192	133

Current total food rations per week in kg:

Meat	10,050
Flour	20,100
Margarine	7,537
Sugar	8,040
Cereal products	6,030
Potatoes	100,500
Bread	105,525

of which the following was distributed for special purposes:

	Youth welfare	Health services
Meat	43.75 kg	
Flour	25	1,300 (900) kg
Margarine	70 (40)	165 (65)
Sugar	140	450 (380)
Cereal products	115	300
Potatoes	350	2,400 (1,000)

Of the weekly total allocation, the following received an additional amount in kg of:

	Meat	Flour	Marg.	Sugar	Potatoes	Bread
Heavy laborer	608.40	967.20	395.20	327.60	4,576 (3,625.60)	
Children		320	80	96	960	
Council of Elders	14.25 (7.125)	65.50 (32.75)	8.50 (4.275)	11.40 (5.70)	142.50 (57)	
Cooks	359	1,077 (897.50)	193.86 (172.32)	157.78 (129.94)	5,205.50 (3,590)	
Central Supply employee			5.46 (2.73)	5.46 (2.73)		214 (156)
Flour porter		13.30	2.66 (1.33)	2.66 (1.33)		114 (78)
Baker						986.125 (422.625)
White baker		133.30 (88.87)	18.85 (12.60)	25.75 (10.60)		

	Meat	Flour	Marg.	Sugar	Potatoes	Bread
Butcher	20					
Potato					309.75	
porter					(247.80)	
Shipping					399 (319)	

Additional amounts of cereal products were received by the following, in kg:

Heavy laborers	145.60
Children	128
Cooks	215.40 (143.60)

A table, also from summer 1943, compares the official weekly allocation in the "Protectorate" and in the "ghetto":

	Protectorate	Ghetto
Meat	250 g	250 g
Flour	562.50 g	500 g
Sugar	300 g	200 g
Margarine	110 g	187.50 g
Butter	35 g	
Lard	20 g	
Potatoes	2,500 g	2,500 g
Cereal products	150 g	150 g
Bread	1,700 g	2,625 g
Jam	175 g	100 g (when available)
Artificial honey	70 g	
Eggs	1 egg	
Vegetables	Distributed according to available supplies	

Another document from summer 1943 presents a series of tables on food distribution:

Regular workers, 1,630 calories daily, distributed weekly:

	Grams	Calories
Margarine	195	1,453
Sugar	200	780
Potato	1,900	1,403
Flour	460	1,403
Barley	120	384 (cereal product)
Meat	250	375
Bread	2,625	5,775
Milk	420	175 (skimmed)

Rations for regular workers are reduced by the following amounts in order to feed:

Heavy laborers	Approx. 7%
Kitchen employees	Approx. 2.5%

Non-workers, 1,487 calories daily, distributed weekly:

	Grams	Calories
Margarine	− 45	− 323
Sugar	− 60	− 234
Bread	− 295	− 438
Other values remain unchanged		

This is 143 calories less per day than for regular workers.

Heavy laborers receive 2,141 calories, distributed weekly:

	Grams	Calories
Margarine	+ 30	+ 229
Sugar	+ 35	+ 137
Potatoes	+ 700	+ 392
Flour	+ 200	+ 610
Barley	+ 30	+ 96
Meat	+ 125	+ 188
Bread	+ 875	+ 1,925
Milk portions unchanged.		

This is 511 calories more per day than a regular worker. A heavy laborer receives 1½ portions of the midday meal every day.

Children (except for infants) receive 1,759 calories daily, distributed weekly:

	Grams	Calories
Margarine	+ 25	+ 185
Sugar	+ 30	+ 117
Potatoes	+ 300	+ 168
Flour	+ 100	+ 305
Barley	+ 40	+ 128

This is 129 calories more per day than a regular worker receives. Nothing is deducted from children's rations for heavy laborers, so that their regular fare is approx. 7% better.

The average number of calories per day, each year, was calculated as follows:

1942 1,597
1943 1,848
1944 1,955

Inadequate kitchens made providing for the inhabitants difficult, especially during the first year. The following table illustrates the available cooking pot volume in 1941 and 1942:

Time period	Available cooking pot volume (L)	Cooking pot volume lacking (L)
November 1941	200	
January 1942	6,000	2,000
June 1942	12,000	8,000
Ultimately		40,000

The following is a valuated list of supplies from April 15, 1945:

Product	Amount	Weight in kg	Value in Crowns
Rye bread flour		219,471	528,700
Wheat bread flour		52,287	124,000
Wheat flour		294,221	678,200
Bread		30,140	84,400
Cereal products		56,852	199,000
Potatoes		1,425,219	1,111,700
Cream of wheat		164	600
Sugar		56,334	383,100
Margarine		68,652	1,146,500
Fat		58	1,000
Meat and Sausages		8,456	118,400
Tinned blood sausage	97,624 cans	24,406	468,650
Liver paste	63,681	15,920	445,800
Canned hash	17,281	17,281	528,300
Jam		16,806	139,500
Coffee substitute		22,116	168,800

There follow numerous items – often in very small amounts – some of which were used as ingredients in the kitchens and some of which were sold in the "grocery store" (spices, flavorings, etc.).

A delivery receipt testifies to the quality of the meat:

Municipal slaughterhouse Kralupy on the Vltava

Kralupy on the Vltava 7/14

G.Z. 152/44

We are sending you the following low-quality meat:

124 kg meat	at 10.— Crowns per kg	1240.—
10 kg head (and tongue)	at 4.— Crowns per kg	40.—
1 kg liver	at 6.— Crowns per kg	6.—
		1286.—
	Shipping and handling	70.—
	Total in Crowns	1356.—

The meat originates from the animal: cow   Property of: Karl Schuster, Wojkowitz District of Raudnitz [Roudnice nad Labem] on the Elbe and is standard inferior quality

Muni. slaughterhouse authority   Muni. veterinarian

14 July 1944
[signed] Nalina

304 *Sociology*

On November 17, 1944, the chemical-technical laboratory reported the following about the potatoes: "Although it is natural that the potatoes would have to be moved from the trains or the heaps into the storerooms as quickly as possible, tests have clearly shown that continual biological and chemical testing is necessary. Otherwise, it is to be feared that the manifestation of rot in the coming months will quickly cause high potato losses." The same office reported to the administration on December 4, 1944:

Fourteen storerooms have been examined. The results show that several storerooms contain damp potatoes. In some cases, there are even the beginnings of germination. Although usually dry on the surface, the mass of potatoes is damp on the bottom, and sometimes rot was observed. Of concern are diseases caused by mould (e.g., Fusarium), rot and bacteria.... In some cases, mites were also found.

Shortly thereafter, the "potato warehouse" reported:

Memo to Dr. Merzbach [Economics Department].
    In the peeleries, of late, we have been exclusively processing potatoes that were sorted out from the different warehouses. Without exception, these potatoes are of poor quality, some half-rotten and with portions cut out, some of poor consistency. The yield after peeling is therefore very low.
    On 16 December 44, we achieved the following yield at the peeleries:

Potatoes processed   2,670 kg
Net left after peeling   1,435 kg
Resulting in a loss of   1,235 kg, which equals 47%.

Since at the moment we find a loss of only 30% in yield after peeling in the kitchens, there is a resulting 17% difference.
    17 December 1944 [Seal] W Central Potato Warehouse [2 signatures].

Based on the documents presented, an impartial judge might believe that, despite the difficult situation and the inferior quality of the food, rations were just bearable, in terms of nutrition and caloric value, such that even a nonworker could manage, after a fashion. How can one then speak of enormous hunger and claim that many people died of starvation? The answer can be found in a petition, dated August 20, 1943, from a member of the "Detective Department," Dr. Vladimir Weiss, to the Jewish Elder Eppstein:

In the course of an inspection of a distribution point some 15 months ago, I discovered, among other things, that because of various sorts of dishonest manipulation (inflated food supply figures, inflated figures for consumption, higher quantities of food reported distributed to the kitchens than was actually delivered, etc.) at the time, the total rations for food allocated to the ghetto dwellers by the German authorities were not delivered. The same sorts of manipulation went on at the other distribution points.... Through this downgrading of rations, the amount of food served the ghetto dwellers was inadequate, and throughout the ghetto's existence, starvation has reigned.
    To be able to cause ... this damage over the long term, it had to be organized. There have always been three groups here ... whereby one group of Czech Jews occupied leadership positions in the ghetto's economy.... These people put self-interest above the common good. They were happy to be better fed at the expense of the rest of the ghetto dwellers, and they therefore said nothing about all the irregularities....
    The employees and favorites of the Economics Department enjoyed privileged status in the ghetto, and the Economics Department backed up any employee accused of wrongdoing against the community. I would thus like to conclude:

Nutrition

1. that, in the case of the atrocious mismanagement and the scandalous harm to the community by the distribution point at the Bodenbach Kaserne, although the director of distribution was dismissed, the matter was swept under the rug and hushed up.

2. that, during an inspection ... of the baking of filled sweet buns [*Buchteln*] at the "white bakery" ... large-scale cheating on raw materials was found at the distribution centers at the Sudeten Kaserne, the Hamburg Kaserne and the Hohenelber Kaserne ... through production of buns at a weight lower than that prescribed. In these cases, as well, the guilty went unpunished and nothing was done in defense of the community – neither against the guilty directors of distribution nor against those responsible at the bakery.

3. that, at the butcher's, meat was deceptively manipulated to the detriment of the community.

    a) In one case, I discovered that the community was cheated out of 200 kg of pure meat through double write-offs on the books.

    b) I discovered that innards were delivered and charged to the ghetto at a ratio of 2:1 to meat (i.e., 2 kg innards as 1 kg of meat ...), but that, for a little extra on the side, the butcher delivered innards instead of meat to the distribution centers so that, as a result, the community was illegally deprived of a large quantity of pure meat on a weekly basis.

    c) that, in a single delivery of meat to the Sudeten Kaserne distribution center of ... approx. 500 kg, 65 kg less was delivered than was supposed to be delivered.

4. I discovered and reported that in cooking potato or goulash soup in the main kitchens, two types of soup were distributed: Soup from the bottom of the cooking pot, containing the entire content of meat and potatoes, went to the cooks and those favored by them; and the thin broth, without any substance, went to the common people. Nothing happened to the guilty.

5. that, during the production of sweet buns, the main kitchens almost always saved an entire sack of flour at the expense of those to be fed, even though ... they reported to Central Supply that this flour had been used. The guilty were investigated only in cursory fashion and went completely unpunished.

6. that, based on the amount of potatoes received by and cooked in the kitchen at the Dresden Kaserne, 10–20 dkg more should have been distributed than were actually distributed. Although the kitchen head was removed, she was reinstated shortly thereafter.

7. that, for their midday meal, the old people in the L 504 home for the elderly received a thin soup and a portion of potatoes weighing an average of 12–14 dkg at a time when potato portions consisted of 35 dkg.

8. that, at every kitchen where I monitored meal preparation from the start of cooking through to the distribution of meals, carried out in accordance with the food rations allowed by the German authorities, the results achieved in terms of quality and amount stood in stark contrast to the food usually distributed.

I ... uncovered ... all these cases ... ; all my efforts were in vain. Being disadvantaged in this way ... meant that the inhabitants of the ghetto ... attempted to obtain food in any way possible. They bought from Aryans inside and outside the ghetto, smuggled letters out of the ghetto requesting that foodstuffs be sent, robbed incoming transports, and in the end, robbed their comrades ... of their last scraps of bread. It was thus this inadequate diet, brought about by dishonest manipulations, that was primarily responsible for the fact that 16 young people were delivered into the hands of the executioner, that hundreds of other people had to endure harsh punishments for violating camp rules, that thousands more young people were taught to become heartless robbers and thieves, that many thousands did not simply pass away here, but rather died a wretched death, and that ... tens of thousands lost their inner strength and were pushed to the edge of despair.

The Economics Department constituted ... an indivisible whole, which systematically shut itself off from the rest of the ghetto and ... which prevented ... an assessment ... of the prevailing conditions by an outsider.... The following bodies were able to carry out ... inspections and uncover the abuses:

1. the so-called Kitchen Inspection, which consisted of 3 members and was an organ of the Economics Department,
2. the Criminal Guard (Detective Department)
3. the Economic Control Office, an organ of the Security Service
4. the Zelenka Monitoring Group, an organ of the Economics Department

Until Dr. Loewenstein's accession to office and ... the establishment of the Economic Control Office, the only monitoring body that was seemingly independent of the Economics Department ... was the Criminal Guard. Afterwards, however, when the Criminal Guard ... was investigating malfeasance and I insisted on exposing offenses against the nutrition of the community, but my superiors ... tried to persuade me to refrain from further pursuing the Economics Department in order to avoid severe punishment myself, I discovered that even the Criminal Guard toed the line of the Economics Department and that its activities stopped short of anything that might have posed a threat to the Economics Department. Furthermore, many officials of the Criminal Guard had [family members, friends, etc.] in the Economics Department, be it in management, Central Supply, a bakery, a kitchen, a distribution point, the Materials Administration, or even the Rationing Service ... and therefore saw ... no reason ... to look into ... the abuses.... Moreover, the Criminal Guard did not pursue any investigation that would have proven unpleasant for even one member of the Council of Elders.

The Economics Department aimed to render the Economic Control Office, created by Dr. Loewenstein, a superfluous institution, and a separate auditing department ... was called into being within the Economics Department. This was the Zelenka Group. Since the Economics Department monitored itself through this monitoring group, but at the same time, nutritional conditions remained completely unchanged from what they had been previously, any commentary ... is superfluous.

The only consequence of this petition was that its author and his family disappeared on the next transport. Wherein lies the truth? Before we decide, a critical discussion – elucidating the technical issues involved in food preparation and distribution – of the available documents should help clarify matters.

Even if the rations of many food items in the camp were not substantially worse than in the "Protectorate," and even sometimes seemed better, the disadvantages concern the most valuable products, such as eggs, butter, and fat, which were never delivered to the camp. Bread and margarine could not compensate for them. A large part of the free populace received bread rations greater than the minimum allotment, and they could purchase bread and potatoes under the table at affordable prices. Unlike in Theresienstadt, additional allowances, for example, of meat, for a particular category of recipients did not lower the guaranteed minimum ration for those unable to work. Also, foodstuffs other than bread were easier and cheaper to obtain outside, where, in contrast to the "ghetto," items such as vegetables, fruit, cheese, and fish products, among others, were also allotted.

Nutrition

BREAD AND ALLOCATION OF UNPREPARED FOODSTUFFS

Different categories of recipients were not designated until May 1942, and it took approximately a year before the process was completed. The first additional allowances, which were mostly justified, already had been made some months earlier in the form of extra dispensations of bread and margarine in small amounts for night work and special tasks. On May 19, 1942, the "bread categories" S, N, and K were introduced, joined later by L. At first, bread rations came to 250 g. From December 17, 1941, they came to 350 g. Thus, workers (N) received 375 g, heavy laborers (S) 500 g, and nonworkers (K) 333 g, the same as "part-time workers" (*Kurzarbeiter*) (L). Beginning in the summer of 1944, the categories were limited to S, at 470 g for heavy laborers, and N, at 350 g for the rest of the prisoners. Toward the end of the war, bread rations had to be cut down to 700 g for four days.

At first, bread was brought in from outside; later, the "Central Bakery" baked most of the bread, and it surpassed the bread from outside in taste and quality. The dough was prepared from approximately four parts rye flour and one part wheat flour. The bread was digestible and usually reached the recipients in good condition. Only in the summer and fall of 1942 did it often get moldy even prior to distribution. The loaves never quite achieved the prescribed weight, supposedly due to evaporation. The rations, first distributed every two – and then every three – days, went via the "distribution points" to the room elders, who distributed them in the quarters, giving healthier people the proper portions, but too often giving the weaker ones incorrect portions, which was made possible by the fact that the portions had to be cut to size from the loaves.

Initially, margarine and sugar were distributed rarely and unevenly. Sometimes there was 20 g of margarine for dinner – distributed three times a week, as soon as operations were somewhat organized. Later on, members of groups S, N, and L received an additional allowance of 40, 50, and 60 g each week, respectively. Amounts were uniform for all members of these groups but changed over time. During the initial months, sugar, divided into portions of approximately 100 g, was available at irregular intervals, which were always many weeks apart. Once disbursements became regular, first 80 g and then 70 g were distributed per week, plus an additional allowance of 30 g for the S, N, and L groups. Sugar and margarine also were distributed from the distribution points via room or house elders. Margarine was cut and packed from 250 g cubes, a process that, even with the best of intentions, made exact portioning almost impossible, such that lower weights were unavoidable. But there were also deliberate reductions in weight. There were many problems with the sugar that house or room elders fetched in containers from the distribution points. There they received the total weight allotted to their house or room, which, because of imprecise scales and weights, was often inaccurate. Many house and room elders pilfered some of it; the sugar was distributed with spoons or in small containers. The infirm were the most shamefully deceived and often received not even a third of the allotted ration. In the infirmaries, rations were distributed by the nurses, who at times deprived their patients of sugar, bread, and cooked meals. As soon as Loewenstein enforced the distribution of sugar in sealed bags, the situation improved.

Initially, there was occasionally a low-quality root jam for dinner. It was distributed in the same manner as the sugar, and the prisoners were considerably deprived. A common trick was to water down the jam. In the summer of 1942, jam disappeared from the menu, but about a year later it was distributed again at intervals of many weeks, in the amount of 200 or 250 g. The quality was better. By that point people fetched their own portions at the distribution points, in containers they brought with them.

The camp received only small amounts of milk, at times so irregularly that general distribution was never instituted. Much of the milk was reserved for children and the sick. Officially, one was supposed to receive a quarter liter of skim milk each week. Distribution was conducted exactly as it had been originally for the jam. Thus, there was a great deal of cheating and watering down.

Early on, 50–60 g of a watery salami, produced in the camp, was distributed to everyone once a week or even less frequently. Slices were cut arbitrarily. Later on, it disappeared from the menu, except in a few cases, because a slice of about 30 g was distributed at the kitchen hatches (*Schalter*) as part of the midday meal. From May 1942 until around the middle of 1943, an additional allowance of 250 g for every four persons, that is, 62.5 g per consumer, of liver paste or blood sausage was distributed to groups S, N, and L.

Other basic food allocations included the following:

1. Salt: during the years 1942–43 there were occasional salt shortages; meals had to be prepared without salt for weeks on end.
2. Lettuce and unripe tomatoes: these were distributed, albeit very rarely, when the vegetables from the "Agriculture Department" were either close to spoiled or already half-rotten.
3. Root vegetables: the prisoners occasionally received a scrap of root beets (called "codfish").
4. Yeast: sometimes a small portion was available, beginning in 1943.
5. "Rabbit paste" (a spicy vegetable spread that was of poor quality and in fact harmful to health); defatted, bitter mustard; spices; and herb teas: these items were distributed on occasion, starting in 1944.

Beginning in September 1942, as a supplement to the usual fare, one could "shop" in a "grocery store" once every few months or weeks. The only items available were those not subject to economic controls in the "Protectorate"; that is, they had barely any nutritional value: low-quality spreads for bread, natural and synthetic spices, baking powder, soda powder, synthetic flavorings, and similar things, for the most part in tiny amounts. If one was very lucky, one might obtain some saccharine tablets, pickled tomatoes, or dried onions. The store was a farce, but its goods nevertheless helped to spice the bland dishes somewhat.

THE KITCHENS

Whereas the consumer could to some extent still inspect the basic food rations, the dishes coming from the kitchens evaded almost any sort of individual monitoring. Work in the kitchens was very arduous; only able-bodied young people were healthy enough to withstand it over the long term. But nothing can justify the extent of legal and especially illegal privileges enjoyed by the personnel in the kitchens and related facilities. At first, the kitchens differed considerably from one another. Later on, they became more standardized, with the same portions and quality and preferably the same fare. Nevertheless, the reputations of the kitchens differed – a lot depended on the decency of the chief cook. Over time, small special kitchens were set up for the

Nutrition

sick and children; then a central kitchen for the sick (*Krankenküche*) was opened up (in E VI), plus two additional ones (in Q 403 and E IIIa). They cooked the same quantities and used the same raw materials as the regular kitchens; the finished dishes tended to be even smaller, but the food was supposed to be more easily digestible. It complied with various regimens and could be received only with a prescription from a doctor. Some of the regimens provided included "light diets," semisolid foods diets, and diets for the heart, the kidneys, diabetes, enteritis, the gall bladder, ulcers, and jaundice; in addition, larger rations were given to those recovering from typhoid fever. A "central children's kitchen" cooked quite good meals and distributed richer dinners. For a short time, there was a small ritual (Kosher) kitchen, which fed a small number of people (see 195b).

Records of food consumption at the beginning compared with those of February 1942 could make it seem that nutrition soon improved, but the discrepancy between recorded amounts and what was actually distributed was particularly large until near the end of 1942. It is possible that much of what was on the books never made it into the prisoners' hands. We may never know the truth. Still, it seems plausible that, during the early months, wagonloads intended for the "ghetto" never arrived there but rather were embezzled for the benefit of some SS men. It is certain that, as soon as the goods were in the camp, sizeable amounts under the control of the "Economics Department" were stolen and embezzled. Likewise, many of the prepared dishes disappeared; as a result, consumers received only a fraction of the designated portions. Soups, porridge-like dishes (barley, millet, potato goulash, and noodles), sauces, and the so-called meat dishes (goulash and hash) were unscrupulously watered down. Those who could fetch their own food at the kitchen hatches were not as badly off as the old and the sick, who were dependent on nurses. These people were unrelentingly given only worthless nourishment, such as watery soups or dishes such as dumplings, which could not be reduced unobtrusively. Conditions improved only when, after a long and bitter internal conflict, the amounts distributed at the kitchen hatches were made public and were monitored as well as was possible by the recipients. The distributing nurses also were monitored. All this probably helped a little, but it could not protect consumers from being deprived of the portions that rightfully would have been theirs based on the total allotment made to the camp.

INDIVIDUAL MEALS (*SPEISEN*)

Meat

Initially, the prisoners occasionally received horsemeat; later on, the meat provided was nearly always beef, usually from animals that had been put down. Otherwise, on occasion, they ate tinned liver paste and blood sausage. They also occasionally had soup from the bones included with deliveries – it was little more than water. Contrary to official reports, during the early months there was almost no meat, often for more than a week at a time. Beginning in the summer of 1942, two meals per week included meat; even when the weight was prescribed, portions were no greater than 30 g. It was preferable when the portions were cooked separately, because then the prisoners could verify the weight, but this was the exception before 1943, and even afterward it was rare. Commonly, they were given a so-called hash or goulash sauce: a watery gravy, in which – not always – a few meat fibers floated. The serving size was 0.1 L, with hardly more than 10 g of pure meat. Beginning in 1943, meatloaf was

310   *Sociology*

prepared in the kitchen bakeries with an abundant admixture of bread. The portion size was 30 g, with certainly no more than 20 g of meat. For several months in 1943, instead of other meat dishes, there was liver paste cooked down into a thin broth; actual paste was also served. The average inmate certainly received no more (and probably less) than 50–60 g per week of meat at the kitchen hatches; before 1943, he hardly ever received more than 40 g, and unprotected individuals received barely half of that amount. For someone receiving no additional allowances, this was the only source of protein, aside from meager amounts of milk. This works out to, starting in 1943, an average daily portion of 8–9 g, at most, for healthy people who fetched their own food! In contrast to the official weekly ration of 250 g, therefore, the weekly legal ration was no more than 60 g for nonworkers, at most 120.5 g for regular workers, and at most 150.5 g for heavy laborers! Thus, most prisoners were never legally provided with the minimum amount of protein necessary to live.

Vegetables

Vegetables often were not available for months at a time. When available, the following vegetables were served:

1. Root vegetables (kohlrabi, here named "codfish"), with some potatoes mixed in, were cooked four to five times a week during the early months of 1942. They were of miserable quality: at first they were frozen, and later on, rotten; they were also sometimes raw. Later on, they were prepared only rarely, under the name "codfish cabbage."
2. Sauerkraut was occasionally cooked during the early months. Later on, it was rarely available, and sometimes was also raw. Often it was spoiled.
3. Other fresh vegetables were provided only rarely and in tiny amounts beginning in 1943 and included cooked spinach, lettuce, and half-rotten, unripe tomatoes, served raw.
4. Dried vegetables were used at first, and occasionally later on in 1944, for sauces and soups.

Cereal Products

1. Barley was rarely provided before mid-1943. From then on, it often was served for lunch, once or twice a week, in the form of a 0.4 L portion of a more or less thick porridge. From time to time (no more than twice a week), the prisoners received barley soup in the evenings. They sometimes received a mixture of barley and potatoes, which, because of the two different types of starches, often went sour before it was served. This mishmash and the barley itself were unpopular.
2. Millet was rare at first; between the fall of 1942 and the early summer of 1943, it was served once a week as porridge (in 0.4 L servings, with 14 g of sugar).
3. Peas were served for lunch very occasionally during the first year (0.4 L).
4. Coarsely ground potatoes (*Grieß*) were occasionally available in 1943, provided once or twice a week as a soup for supper (0.4 L).

5. Buckwheat was provided occasionally as a sweet porridge for children and the sick.
6. "Extracts" made from the scraps and pods of peas, lentils, and millet were provided as a soup, beginning in 1942–43, almost daily at midday (0.3 L), and three times a week or more in the evening (0.4 L, sometimes 0.5 L). The soup usually had a thin broth and was of minimal nutritional value. Because pea extract, which was comparatively better, was rare, the two other – barely edible – items were much more frequent. Although these soups were not supposed to be cooked for the evening, they had to suffice when barley or potatoes for better soups were lacking. These "extracts" were not included in the official cereal products allocations.

The legal weekly ration of cereal products, mainly barley, was 120 g for the average consumer, 150 g for a heavy laborer, and 160 g for children – in contrast to the official allocation of 150 g. An average midday portion of 0.4 L was prepared from 30 g. This, along with 0.3 L of a worthless soup, constituted, on average, the entire midday meal twice a week and clearly demonstrates what sorts of starvation rations the prisoners were served even during the better years of 1943–44. If such a meal were further adulterated with water and if, on top of this, the frail were not given their allotted portions, no further evidence is necessary that many must have died of starvation.

Coffee and Tea Substitutes

The coffee provided was not malt coffee but a low-grade plant derivative (from roots), out of which an infusion was made, 0.4 L of which was served – without sugar or milk – daily for breakfast, occasionally with a baked item at midday, and three times a week, or even more frequently, in the evenings. When the coffee substitute was not available, herbal tea was used.

Margarine

Margarine was the only fat used. The water content was high, and the fat content was low. Preserved with benzoic acid, it was tasteless when fresh and, later on, oily. Occasionally the kitchens served 10 or 5 g with unpeeled potatoes, or occasionally a spoonful of melted margarine (7–10 g) with dumplings or other dishes, but most things were prepared without fat. This is demonstrated by the fact that dishes could be effortlessly cleaned by rinsing them in cold water. Margarine was used for roux, to which red dye was added to prevent theft; porridge and soups made with roux were a lobster-red color. Margarine also came in the form of a sauce, 0.1 L of which was served with potatoes and dishes made of flour. When mixed with sugar and coffee substitute or jam, margarine also was used to make a popular crème served once a week (0.1 L) with sweet buns or dumplings. The least amount of margarine necessary was also used for baking the sweet buns and meatloaf. It is unlikely that, in the food provided by the kitchens, the average consumer received more than 50–60 g – or more than 75–80 g in the case of heavy laborers – of margarine per week. Because nonworkers received 60 g of margarine and workers, with their various bonuses, in effect received 140 g of margarine, the official ration of 187.5 g and the legal allocation of 150 g for nonworkers, 195 g for regular workers, and 225 g for heavy laborers (210 g for children) contrasts in practice with 110–120 g for nonworkers and an average of 190–200 g for regular workers, or 215–220 g for heavy laborers (children may have gotten as much as 200–210 g). Prior to the fall of 1942, amounts were nowhere near this, and even without any additional fraud, nonworkers, at least, always received significantly less than that to which they were entitled.

Sugar

Sugar was sometimes served by the kitchens, in portions of around 14 g, with dumplings or noodles, as an ingredient in the aforementioned crème, and sometimes also in sauces. The sweet bun dough also contained some sugar. In early 1942, coffee was sweetened, but this was an exception. Aside from when it was used in sauces, sugar was used in a meal only once or twice a week. The largest quantity of sugar ever used was certainly 40 g per week for those receiving the regular fare and 60 g for heavy laborers (and about the same amount for children); these numbers were not seen before the spring of 1943. Because nonworkers received 70 g of sugar in kind and workers, with their various bonuses, in effect received 140 g on average, the official ration of 200 g and the legal serving of 140 g for nonworkers, 200 g for regular workers, and 235 g for heavy laborers (230 g for children) contrasts in practice with 110 g for nonworkers and an average of 180 g for regular workers, or 200 g for heavy laborers (and about the same amount for children). Before 1943, however, nonworkers received barely more than a 70 g ration and regular workers barely more than 130–140 g in actuality.

Skim Milk

Skim milk was occasionally served in the amount of 0.25 L per person, although a regular serving once a week was achieved only occasionally. The small amount of milk available was needed for children and the sick. Some of it may also have been used in the dough for sweet rolls and for sauces. Certainly, the weekly 420 g allotment was never even approached.

Potatoes

Potatoes usually were of low quality, suffered from rot, and by the summer were virtually inedible. Freshly harvested potatoes were delivered late – in 1942, very late – and then were distributed in exceedingly small amounts. As has already been shown, the losses during peeling were extreme. This, plus theft from all sites involved and the variability in supply, forced constant changes in rationing; as a result, in general, serving the officially approved amounts was completely out of the question. At the "potato peeleries," work was done at first by hand and later on by machine. To avoid the large losses incurred due to both natural and dishonest means, there was a switch in the summer of 1943 to preparing mainly unpeeled potatoes. These were more popular than the unappetizing mashed potatoes, which previously had been the usual fare, even though the chances were higher of receiving rotten potatoes, which would not be replaced. On average, potatoes were served three to four times a week at midday. If none were available, then barley or dumplings were cooked. In 1943, unpeeled potatoes occasionally were served in the evenings, and by 1944 they were served regularly once a week. In addition, there was 0.4 L of potato soup twice a week, which was alternated with barley soup. There was often 0.4 L of potato goulash – a thicker, meatless soup – once a week at midday. In rare instances, 0.3 L of potato soup was also distributed at midday. The portions recorded fluctuated from 190 to 400 g; usually, they were between 270 and 360 g, and the most frequent amount was 310 g (or 220 g toward the end of the war). Assuming four midday meals and one evening meal of 310 grams each and two soups of 200 grams each, we arrive at a total of 1,950 g, on average, per week, which often was not achieved. Even according to official figures, only 1,738 g was designated at times for nonworkers and regular workers. What became of the 2,500 g of potatoes for at least 75% of the prisoners, which supposedly placed the ghetto on a par with the "Protectorate"? With the potatoes came the aforementioned meat dishes, as well as various spiced sauces (served in portions of 0.1 L and also, rarely, 0.2 L) made from flour or roux, margarine, milk, sugar, dried vegetables, vinegar, and other things.

Flour

Flour was used for several dishes in addition to bread and sometimes other baked goods:

1. Dumplings were served, once or twice a week on average; yeast was added after January 1942. They weighed 90 g at first, but later on, at Loewenstein's insistence, they were increased to 140 g. They were tasty when fresh, but their immediate satiation value was quite limited. Crème, sauces, sugar or jam, and margarine, as well as meat dishes on occasion, were served on the side.
2. Sweet buns were simple cakes made with the addition of a bit of sugar, yeast, and sometimes milk. Beginning in 1943, they were provided once a week at lunch, instead of dumplings, with some crème, coffee substitute, or nothing on the side. They were prepared in the kitchen bakeries and weighed 140 g.
3. Noodles, produced in the camp out of unsuitable flour, occasionally were served once a week with 14 g of sugar and some margarine; this was instead of other baked goods. Cooked portions were 210 or 220 g. This dish was unpopular, particularly because it was heavily watered-down.
4. Noodle dough sometimes replaced another baked good (0.4 L).
5. Beginning in 1943, the kitchen bakeries very occasionally produced rolls at 70–100 g apiece. They were distributed with dinner, as were the equally rare *Bosniaks*, rolls made of bread flour and weighing 100 g. These were produced in the bread bakery. With a doctor's prescription one could receive a white roll once or even twice without forfeiting one's regular bread rations. Small gingerbread cookies were considered a special bonus.
6. Finally, flour was also used for roux, sauces, and soups.

If we assume that flour was the basis of two meals per week, as well as an ingredient in other dishes, and if we take into account the fact that the weights listed refer to the prepared dishes, then nonworkers and regular workers received no more than 350–400 g instead of the authorized 460 g or the nominal 500 g, as compared with the ration of 562.5 g in the "Protectorate." Children and heavy laborers certainly also received no more than 550 g. Only when it came to bread was even the nonworker in a better position, with around 2,340 g a week, than the recipient of the minimum ration of 1,700 g in the "Protectorate."

ACTUAL AMOUNTS VERSUS RECORDED AMOUNTS

Thus, most prisoners' nourishment proves to have been much worse than official figures indicate, even in the period when conditions in the camp had normalized somewhat through improved allocations and a partly successful campaign against fraud and theft from within. Furthermore, after the spring of 1943, one certainly cannot assume more than 1,100 calories as the best average daily amount for nonworkers, or more than 1,300–1,400 for regular workers, not counting "food bonuses" (see 284). Previously – that is, during the early months – the figures were significantly lower, at around 800 or 1,000 calories, whereas now and then, at least, in 1944 and at the beginning of 1945, somewhat larger amounts can be estimated. Yet the significant food losses suffered by the infirm are also noteworthy. In 1942, these losses reached and even exceeded 50%–60% of the official rations. People were thus expected to live on 400–600 calories; it should be noted that these calories were not necessarily vital nutrients. Even later on, losses for some remained considerable. Man does not live by calories alone, and mechanically doling them out is inhuman. The most important substances – sugar, fat, and, above all, protein – were entirely insufficient even for an honest heavy laborer with his extra rations.

A typical menu might read as follows:

Breakfast
Coffee substitute, unsweetened and without milk, or herbal tea (0.4 L)

Lunch
Soup made from extracts or another watery soup; rarely (at most once a week) 0.3 L of potato soup, and sometimes no soup at all
Potatoes, three to four times a week: 270–360 g of unpeeled potatoes approximately three times a week and 0.4 L of goulash once a week
A sauce as a side dish, measuring 0.1 L (rarely 0.2 L)
Meat, not more than twice a week: either as a portion, as 30 g of meatloaf, or as 0.1 L of hash or goulash
Five or ten grams of margarine
Baked goods, twice a week: either dumplings (140 g) with side dishes, as above; crème (0.1 L); some margarine and sugar; or sweet buns with or without crème
Noodles, once in a while: either noodles with some margarine and sugar or 210–220 g of noodle dough
Barley, once or twice a week: either by itself (usually with nothing on the side) or mixed with 0.4 L (rarely, 0.5 L) of potatoes (or, in 1942–43, 0.4 L of millet).

Dinner
Coffee substitute or herbal tea (0.4 L), three or four times per week
A baked good made of bread flour (about 100 g), later on, sometimes once a week

Nutrition 315

Soups made of potatoes, barley, or semolina, three or four times per week, when available; otherwise, soups made of extracts (0.4 L)
Potatoes (300 g), once a week, although not regularly, beginning in 1943

Following is an actual menu from a regular kitchen from May 3–9, 1943:

Monday:	Lunch: lentil-extract soup, potatoes with sauce
	Dinner: coffee
Tuesday:	Lunch: lentil-extract soup, "codfish" [root vegetables] with potatoes
	Dinner: unpeeled potatoes
Wednesday:	Lunch: lentil-extract soup, goulash and potatoes
	Dinner: potato soup
Thursday:	Lunch: lentil-extract soup, barley
	Dinner: coffee
Friday:	Lunch: lentil-extract soup, noodles with 10 g of sugar
	Dinner: barley soup
Saturday:	Lunch: lentil-extract soup, barley
	Dinner: potato soup
Sunday:	Lunch: lentil-extract soup, potatoes with sauce
	Dinner: coffee

We can see that the food was much worse than in a regular prison, but it also was quite inferior to the fare most of the time in German concentration camps west of the Polish border. During the week referenced in the preceding menu, nonworkers in this kitchen district received no more than 10–15 g of meat! Efforts were made to prepare meals to be as tasty as possible, and, as a result, the flavor of the meals was better than in most concentration camps. Yet the fact that so many praised the food was only a result of their unspeakable hunger, and newcomers felt disgust for a long time before they, too, began praising the meals. Unique for a concentration camp were the baked goods, of which the sweet buns were quite good. Hygienic conditions in the kitchens were miserable, but they did improve slowly. Primitive containers, washing troughs, and barrels were used for serving, as were equally primitive ladles. The containers were barely cleaned; often the food inside them spoiled or turned sour. In the beginning, food was cold by the time it reached the consumer. Later on, food often reached the frail only once it had grown cold. Dumplings and noodles always were cold.

"SUPPLEMENTAL FARE" AND "FOOD BONUSES"

According to the table earlier in this chapter listing various categories of food recipients from the summer of 1943, of approximately 44,000 prisoners, 12,500 (30%) were nonworkers and were exposed to constant misery most of the time. Almost 50%, that is, just under half, were regular workers, who generally also had a bad time. A mere 8% were children, who, although badly fed, did not suffer such acute hunger, thanks to various supplements. Some 12% received heavy-laborer fare and other larger rations. The "supplemental fare" (*Zusatzkost*), introduced on June 25, 1942, originally consisted of a double portion at lunch, which was soon reduced to one and a half portions. Some of the hardest laborers, however, later received double portions. In addition, a set number of supplementary portions were given to individual groups, such as nurses, so that everyone received an additional allowance once or several times a week. Belonging to bread group S did not automatically mean that one received "supplemental fare," which was granted to more people than was "S bread." To the extent that an uneven allocation formula for distribution of food was justified, the majority of heavy laborers were rightly favored – which would have been all right if the minimum amounts to which the infirm were entitled had not been reduced. Members of administrative and other groups, who did not always deserve it, also were granted "supplemental fare," whereas some hardworking people were denied it.

There never was a serious attempt to ration food according to recipients' individual circumstances, which would have been fairly easy to determine. For example, some of those who worked for food-related services or who regularly received packages sold their ration cards. Cooks, butchers, bakers, members of the Council of Elders, and others – approximately 2.5%–3% of the prisoners – were the best off not only in reality but also by virtue of their official rations, which were out of proportion to their performance and to the food available. Of course, there were privileged people who shared their relative prosperity, but the majority improperly exploited their position and traded public goods in exchange for prostitution, cigarettes, apartments, clothes, and luxuries. For a long time, cooks were allowed to prepare better meals for themselves. Later on, they were entitled to 500 g of potatoes when coffee was served in the evening. Butchers could always cook special meals for themselves.

The "Central Supply Office" allowed the "Central Labor Office," "Youth Welfare Office," and "Health Services Department" to use some of the food. As already mentioned, the "Central Labor Office" determined the regular weekly "bonuses" (*Zubußen*) for all workers, who received small amounts of sugar, margarine, and sometimes paste, in various allowances. In our calculations of the average food distribution we already have factored in these extras, just as we did the "bonuses" that were divided into five "categories" and were at first distributed weekly and then every ten days as "*Dekaden*." Again, we are talking about a bit of margarine and sugar. When one got sick, these "*Dekaden*" would be replaced with "sick bonuses," determined by the "Labor Welfare Office." Quantities and types of bonuses were determined according to illness – they may be viewed as health benefits from unemployment insurance. Again, this involved sugar and margarine, to which barley, gingerbread cookies, jam, or whatever might be on hand could be added. After a serious illness, one applied for a one-time "special bonus." If the application was granted, then one received up to 3 kg of the kind of food mentioned previously. The "Central Labor Office" granted "danger allowance," for example, for nurses on infectious disease wards, and other special premiums, for example, for night work. In its capacity as a clemency board, the Council of Elders could be petitioned for "special bonuses." From time to time, in the early days, the cooks at the hatches distributed leftover food from the kitchens – "extra rations" (*Nachschub*); usually they were worthless soups. Later, the kitchens were expected to report their "extra rations" to the "deployment offices," which gave the workers vouchers (*Ausweisungsscheine*) according to a specific schedule. "Extra rations" were a rare and usually insignificant special handout, intended for workers who did not receive any "supplemental fare." This system usually did not work and was not always administered fairly.

The "Health Services Department" could prescribe "convalescent bonuses" (*Rekonvaleszentenzubusse*), known as *reko*, for short. These were recommended by physicians during or after illnesses and when a patient was underweight – the applicant had to be at least one third below normal weight for men and one quarter below for women. Applications had to be approved by the chief physician and the central office of the "Health Services Department." Usually granted for fourteen days, a "reko" consisted of an extra dinner, roughly equivalent to a regular lunch, but without meat. It was obtained from the kitchens for the sick. The *reko* was a boon, but even it was sometimes granted by way of illegitimate favoritism. Similarly, the "Health Services Department" could prescribe one to two white rolls or "milk bonuses" – usually fourteen quarter liters, spread out over four weeks – or sugar and liver for therapeutic purposes ("sugar bonuses" for enteritis and liver for anemia, as long as the patient's red blood cell count was below 3 million).

Following is an example of a petition to the "Labor Welfare Office":

[April 4, 1944]

[Name and Transport Number]
Bahnhofstrasse 11
Employment: Theresienstadt A. Construction, Mobile Crew of Building Workers, L 309

Petition to "Labor Welfare"

I am requesting the authorization of a convalescent or preventive bonus and justify my petition as follows:

For 7 weeks (from 2/28–3/31) I was sick and feverish. No clear diagnosis was given. In addition to general flu symptoms with occasional heavy diarrhea, heart problems (myocarditis) appeared over the course of several weeks. Doctors attributed my sickness and slow recovery (even now I still feel sickly) to my generally weakened state and malnourishment.

I have been in the ghetto for 26 months. I have lost approx. 18 kg. here. My current weight is 58–59 kg. and my height is 1.76 meters. By mistake, in February, the minimum angina bonus was applied for on my behalf and granted. I have never received a special bonus, even though my condition is almost catastrophic, since I have received almost no packages and those that I have received were of little value.

Other legal "bonuses" included orders from SS men to the Central Supply Office for personal services, for example, for doctors; gifts from Czech police for personal services (privileges of these two sorts were rare); the release of items confiscated by the SS, which then benefited young people, certain groups of workers, the sick, and, rarely, the elderly; and undeliverable packages, from which much was distributed to young people, but less to other needy individuals. Starting at the end of 1943, numerous sardine shipments, meant for individual recipients, reached the camp, a large number of which were undeliverable and were, again, given mostly to young people. In addition, beginning in the spring of 1944, parcels containing jam, sweetened condensed milk, and chocolate, among other things, arrived in the camp, donated by Relico, a relief arm of the World Jewish Congress, via the International Red Cross; this assistance was very welcome, although unfortunately too little and much too late. Gardening products were also distributed in 1944 to those who were allowed to cultivate small plots of land. Employees of the "Agriculture Department" were permitted to consume various things on the spot but seldom were permitted to take anything with them, although this nevertheless occurred often and at great risk. In this way, the SS, not the camp, was harmed.

The most important private source of aid was packages, sent by mail. A small number began arriving beginning in the late fall of 1942, and by 1944, they were arriving in considerable quantities. They contained all sorts of food: bread, potatoes, barley, semolina, oatmeal, flour, legumes, pasta, cakes, dried and fresh vegetables, onions, jam, dried fruit, apples, lemons, bouillon cubes, sugar, and margarine – and even bacon, meat, salami, fat, butter, cheese, eggs, chocolate and sweets, imported sardines, and almonds. Really valuable packages were rare, however. The best off were the Danes, who were looked after by the Danish and Swedish Red Cross. After them came inmates from the "Protectorate"; then, far behind, came the Austrians and Reich Germans, and the Dutch received very little. The packages gave rise to major social divisions and did a great deal of damage in addition to being a blessing. To make the situation more equitable, Baeck, Loewenstein, and Stricker tried to require those who received packages to give up part of what they received or to forgo some of the meals from the kitchens, depending on their personal circumstances. They also wanted to tax regular package recipients, but they never got very far. Package contents also were used for barter and bribery.

Few of those who were well supplied with packages were aware of their responsibilities. It is no wonder that jealousy and hatred arose. Throughout rooms and halls, people enjoyed delicious meals while, next to them, wizened old men and women rummaged in the garbage. There were no walls, so the surplus could not even be mercifully hidden from those in dire need. Misery drove some from room to room, begging for a bit of soup or bread. Some people had stocked so many provisions that they always cooked their own meals or used the camp food merely as the foundation for their own menus. Locked suitcases full of food stood next to the beds of the starving, who spooned up their "extract soup" and were pleased when a rich neighbor left them ration cards for worthless dishes that the more prosperous did not bother to pick up.

Some knew how to procure packages and food via the gendarmes or how otherwise to smuggle goods into the camp, always at great risk.

To a great extent, criminal or at least illegal "bonuses" resulted from theft and the embezzlement of communal property, whereas private property was misappropriated to a much smaller degree, at least once an inmate was housed and no longer was at the train station or the Schleuse – and once conditions at the post office had improved, beginning in the spring of 1943. As we have seen, the frail lost out the most, dependent as they were on go-betweens at the kitchen hatches and distribution points. "Comrade theft" – direct theft of private property – was relatively rare. Smaller offenses of various kinds must be clearly distinguished from unambiguous crime. Thus, for example, a couple of potatoes might have been snatched from the wagons as they passed by or were being unloaded. In such cases, individuals often were treated harshly amid high-sounding invocations of the "harm to the Jewish community," and without regard to social circumstances, while the true criminals were allowed to go free. For minor infractions committed out of dire need, individuals were ruined through formally "just" – but in reality inhumane – sentences, for usually the consequence of such infractions was "inclusion" in the next transport, which meant almost certain death. A poor wretch trying to procure a meal with a ration card he had found usually was caught right away. Such infractions – usually sincerely regretted – could have been effectively punished through internal measures, instead of with a farcical trial and sentencing before the "ghetto court," which only served the SS's amusement and delivered the offender over to the enemy who had evoked all this evil to begin with. If a major scandal was uncovered, everything was done to hush it up as much as possible, for no one wanted any part in making the SS aware of such "damage to the Jewish community." And yet the self-administration had at its disposal sufficient means forcefully to address such abuses internally. Yet nothing would happen, or people would be content with simply removing from office those so sullied. They soon would turn up again elsewhere, as "honorable men," to resume their crimes, perhaps with a bit more caution.

THE HOPELESS FIGHT FOR FAIR DISTRIBUTION OF FOOD

Tabulations of the food situation in the camp were – whether intentionally or unintentionally – nonsense. All the tables and statistics were window dressing that, at best, did the SS a favor. Much was written and calculated in order to hide the horror that lay beneath it all, a horror that no ink on paper could conjure up. Figures, diagrams, and formulas were meant to mechanically capture and preserve the life that was being heartlessly destroyed, in cooperation with the great exterminators – it was a wretched sort of insanity.

No one fought for the fair distribution of food in Theresienstadt with so much energy – if at times blindly and too recklessly – as did Loewenstein. It is therefore only fair to present documents from this struggle, documents that simultaneously also will give an unflinching and wholly truthful picture of the food supply in the camp. In a report shortly after liberation, Loewenstein explained:

> Before I assumed office, food, as well as weekly bonuses such as sugar, jam, etc., were distributed arbitrarily. The old, the frail, and even the sick were the most disadvantaged.
>
> My first concern was to provide correct weights and measurements and, in each kitchen, (1) to prescribe what amounts ... should be distributed, (2) to provide a sample of the food that should be served, (3) to set up a monitoring scale so that everyone had a chance to check the weight of his own food.
>
> Whereas previously there had been goulash sauce ... after much effort, I managed to have the meat and gravy served separately, and the meat served according to weight.... The first noticeable change was that the dumplings and sweet buns, which previously had weighed only 90 g, suddenly weighed 140 g. Instead of backing from the administration, obstacles were put in my way.... Naturally, kitchen and supply personnel were my biggest opponents.... Kitchen personnel [including their family members], for example, received 12 dumplings per head. For 2,500 people, this came to 30,000 dumplings. At that time, there were 45,000 people in the ghetto, so that the kitchen personnel alone ... consumed ... 2/3 of the total quantity of dumplings. After a long battle, I was able to bring the 12 dumplings down to 7 and to reduce the number of recipients. Nevertheless ... theft continued, or was at least attempted, and bribery did not stop....
>
> Since I was constantly told that the food situation could not be changed, I set up a kitchen ... in the barracks of the Ghetto Guard [L 313].... There was more food and it was better, because ... there was no theft. Instead of allowing other kitchens to follow ... this good example, ... my kitchen encountered opposition and was dismantled immediately after my ouster.... Furthermore, I collected the uneaten portions of lentil-extract soup and distributed it to 4,000 people daily. Instead of supporting me, the administration – which, at the time, consisted of Eppstein, Edelstein, Murmelstein, Zucker, and Janowitz – accused me of destroying worker morale.... The director of the Economics Department [Schliesser], together with his associates allied himself with the administration. They were afraid they would be driven from their comfortable

sinecures, especially once it became known that I was tracking meat deliveries.... . Weekly rations ... consisted of 250 g per head, but at most 100 g were distributed [this is still an overestimation, as we have demonstrated], so that for 40,000 people, 40,000 x 150 g, or 6,000 kg disappeared on a weekly basis. I was, therefore, a threat and had to disappear.

Nevertheless, some of Loewenstein's accomplishments remained in place, even after he had been sidelined. On February 1, 1943, he had the following announcement posted on every building's bulletin board:

Ghetto Dwellers

Everyone can rest assured that I am striving to maintain order and security in the ghetto.

I regard it as my most sacred duty and obligation to see that the goods with which we are supplied, in whatever form they may be, are used for their proper purposes.

No goods may be used for ulterior purposes, allowed to spoil due to carelessness, or fall into the wrong hands.

"Everyone must receive that to which he is entitled."

By myself, I am too weak to be everywhere. I need the cooperation of each and every one of you. Do not buy from dealers, because these are your goods. Maintain discipline. Bring me your complaints in confidence. Everyone will be heard. I regard no one who comes to me with a matter of concern as a nuisance.

I have been appointed to help.

Please help me in my fight against corruption.

It is a question of cleaning up the ghetto.

In early May of 1943, Loewenstein appealed to the heavy laborers:

Today, I am turning directly to you with a request, and I will be happy if you would respond favorably.

When I was officially present at autopsies, I discovered to my horror that our deceased old people are made of skin and bones.

You are all aware that the heavy laborer ration is possible only because of ... deductions from the food for other ghetto inhabitants. If once a week 3,000 people would forgo their heavy-laborer supplement, then 3,000 people could eat their fill one day every week. Wouldn't this be wonderful and worthy of all of you? Please consider that you yourselves have parents or had parents and that you too will grow old one day. How would you feel if you were to be thrown upon the scrap heap like something used up and useless, for which no one cares?

This appeal outraged the administration, and on May 8, 1943, Eppstein wrote Loewenstein:

I have informed you that by coincidence I learned of a letter that you ... sent to worker groups. I have expressed my regret that you neglected to inform me of your intentions ... particularly because this is an unusual case that far exceeds your authority and that is likely to endanger ghetto discipline. For you were aware that the administration and the Council of Elders already have dealt with the question of caring for the elderly and have decided to first obtain permission from the camp commandant for the measures under consideration.

In the interests of maintaining order and consistency in the collaboration between all divisions of the Council of Elders, but especially in view of the need immediately to thwart any interference with worker morale [*sic*], on behalf of the administration, I feel compelled to request that the SW [Security Service] refrain from ... all work in the area of care of the elderly. This directive does not affect the relief campaign that I have noted

Nutrition

undertaken by SW employees, in which half a heavy laborer's meal is made available for the elderly once a week. Additional relevant directives for care of the elderly will be issued by the administration.

... I look forward to the prompt transmission of the agreed upon written order of execution.

Loewenstein replied on May 9, 1943:

You remarked ... that my good will ... has an effect contrary to what I had intended. I countered that one might leave this up to the workers.... You told me that the Administration and the Council of Elders are dealing with the problem of caring for the elderly and asked me if I were willing to forgo my campaign for the good of the elderly. I answered, "Of course ... the main thing is that something be done for the elderly...."

... I have submitted proof that I told you: If 3,000 people were willing to forgo half a meal once a week, then 3,000 people could eat their fill once a week....

If you were not in agreement with this campaign you should have told me so immediately. You did not do this....

Further, you are dragging the camp commandant into this debate. On this point, I would like to say that I find it inappropriate to bring the camp commandant into a matter that concerns you and you alone. You write me that you would like to approach the camp commandant. This means you would like to put the responsibility on him. But you cannot put the responsibility on him; you and the administration are responsible.

In talking about ... members of the SW setting aside half a meal once a week, we are not talking about a campaign by the SW, but rather ... each individual member of the SW, for which neither your nor my permission is required....

I come now to the background of my campaign:

Some time ago, my associates reported to me that there was trepidation among the elderly Germans, ... because these people believed that they were to be deprived of food in favor of the workers. At the same time, the doctors pointed out to me that provisions for the elderly were below life-sustaining levels. I looked into this and discovered that our deceased elderly had simply starved to death. The skeletons consist merely of bones covered with skin. Go and take a look at these skeletons for yourself, and perhaps, in your horror, you will even go a step further than I have.

I considered how one could best assist the elderly without harming the workers. In order to (1) counteract the unease and, (2), give the elderly the feeling that they are being cared for, I turned to the Ghetto Guard and asked each individual member if he would be willing voluntarily to forgo ... half a meal. "Yes" was the unanimous answer.... Before starting this campaign, I had repeatedly proposed at the Council of Elders' meetings that a portion of undeliverable packages be diverted to the elderly. The response was that the elderly could not be helped; one should help the young people.... In the month of April, we had 1,527 undeliverable packages. If 1,000 packages had been allocated for Youth Welfare and around 500 for the elderly, do you realize what kind of a difference you could have made? I have explained that the young (1) arrive well-nourished, (2) have parents and relatives who take care of them, and (3) receive a better diet....

I am making five suggestions:

1. Distribute one third of all undeliverable packages to the elderly ... who have no relatives in the ghetto, who do not receive any packages.
2. Distribute extra supplies to the elderly.
3. Once a week, each heavy laborer forgoes a supplemental meal for the benefit of the elderly.

4. Serve to the elderly, on a rotating basis, soup that is not [otherwise] consumed.
5. Everyone who receives a package forgoes his midday meal the day after receiving the package.

It is in your hands to act beneficially.... I shall close with words I addressed ... to the heavy laborers: think about the fact that you too will grow old one day. How would you feel if you were to be thrown upon the scrap heap like something used up and useless?

These efforts were as decent and honest as they were naïve and hopeless, and they were buried in the general muck of the dominant society. There is documentary evidence, however, that such voluntary, internal relief actions were not only possible but also on the right track:

Sabine Lövinson
II/25–383, Qu 305/04
To the noble contributors at the Security Service!

Twice, we "old folks" had the singular good fortune of having been thought of by you in two ways: with an extra meal, which first of all allowed us to properly satisfy our chronic hunger, because we depend on what is given to us during food distribution; but even more because kindhearted, mostly young people even remembered the "old folks" – who are barely tolerated today – and showed them that there still exists something like sympathy for those who, after difficult lives filled for the most part with work and blessings, suddenly have not only lost their care and routine, but any claim to prestige, the right to exist and respect. We are accordingly deeply touched and very thankful. May Providence richly reward your goodness, your magnanimity and the idea that made us happy.

In the name of the "Old Folks"   [signed] Sabine Lövinson

Theresienstadt, 6 May 1943

THE METHOD OF DISTRIBUTION

We will now discuss the method of food distribution, insofar as it has not previously been clarified. Originally, all meals were to be picked up at the kitchen hatches; one could send a representative with one's ration card. All food for those in the infirmaries was picked up together. Soon, there were not enough distribution hatches for the number of people waiting on line, which is why food also was distributed in the courtyards. The OD (*Ordnungsdienst*) maintained order. Wooden shelters and walkways were built to protect from the weather those who were waiting. When the kitchens were modified, attention was paid to attaching enough large distribution areas. There were separate hatches for those receiving regular meals and for those receiving supplemental fare, as well as for the collection of many portions at once. Later, at least, the midday meal was picked up between 10:30 A.M. and 2 P.M. When the camp was particularly overcrowded, provisional distribution points were set up on street corners. In some houses, food for old people was distributed in the courtyards. In hospitals and similar institutions, the staff collected food by the barrelful.

Every month, the "Central Ration Card Office" distributed ration cards to everyone via the building management staffs and the room elders. To hinder abuse, over

Nutrition 323

time, four different reforms were introduced to create progressively more complicated printed ID cards, each of which received a stamped number. The cardholder's name, year of birth, "transport number," and room were all listed. Later, a symbolic stamp was added indicating the kitchen, called a "supply unit" (*Verpflegungseinheit*), from which one was supposed to obtain one's food, although some workers were permitted to use a kitchen closer to their place of work rather than the kitchen assigned them. Later, the cards also were marked with the current month and the person's house and block address; the date of birth was left off.

One had to sign a certificate that read as follows: "I confirm the receipt of a ration card. I have been advised that this card is to be filled out accurately. Further, I have been advised that lost ration cards will not be replaced. The card is to be kept in impeccable condition." A loss was to be reported to the "Central Ration Card Office." Food distribution for the lost card was stopped, and one had to fill out a form, as follows:

I _____ Trsp. Nr. ____ Accommodations ____ hereby declare under oath that I have lost my ration card Nr. ___ for the kitchen ____. I have so far received no replacement for this ration card. I am aware that misuse of a ration card shall result in my punishment. Theresienstadt, on _____

[Signature]

On completing this form, one received an "interim card," good for three days. It was renewed if the ration card was not found in the interim. Other cards that were introduced included the "heavy laborer supplement card," the "evening meal bonus card" for *rekos*, the "milk card," and so on (see 3b, docs. 102–07).

One, and later two, employees of the "rationing service" inspected the cards at the distribution points, used scissors to cut off the coupons that were due, and announced the number of portions to the cooks, who served these in twos and threes. Originally, amounts were measured arbitrarily and recipients did not know to how much they were entitled. In early 1942, every kitchen was assigned a three-person "rationing commission" for a three-month term to inspect the distributed raw materials and to deal with complaints from meal recipients. Added later were other agencies such as the Kitchen Guard (Küchenwache, referred to as "Küwa"), which was supposed to make sure that nothing was illegally removed from the kitchens. The menu with the prescribed quantities had to be written on boards, and in this way, one could be reasonably assured of receiving the designated portions at the serving hatches.

NUTRITION AS THE MAIN PROBLEM

Aside from fear of a looming transport, food, seen both objectively and subjectively, was the most important issue for most people. As great as hunger was, the mental state that accompanied it was of equal importance. Few spoke of food more than was absolutely necessary. One's behavior depended to a large extent on one's temperament and self-control; one forced one's thoughts in other directions, but suddenly one's stomach spoke up, and already one had succumbed to food fantasies – which might even pursue one into one's dreams – and began considering how to get hold of something. Food usually was devoured the moment it was received. Some took it away to warm it up or to prepare it further. Soups were improved from people's own stores, and potatoes were peeled, oiled, and fried – but many people ate them unpeeled. Inventive minds not only increased the value of a meal but also made it tastier. Dishes were prepared – magically, it seemed – from the most modest of ingredients. People's culinary imagination was inexhaustible. They saved up food items for weeks in order to have something special for a birthday and to surprise a loved one with a dish that, in normal life, no one would have touched. Hoarded sweet buns or bread were transformed into cakes with the help of some milk, coffee substitute, margarine, and sugar. Herbs served as spinach, and leaves from kohlrabi and red beets were regarded as the finest of vegetables. Many dishes were made of potatoes and a bit of flour. Bouillon cubes were precious and could be transformed into many things, such as a spread for bread, with the addition of potatoes, oatmeal, and mustard. A popular crème was manufactured out of a little semolina, water, sugar, and flavoring. Pudding mix was blended not only with milk or powdered milk but also with coffee substitute. Some allowed their small allotment of milk to go sour and made quark out of it. Dried onions and dried vegetables were used for sauces and soups. Sugar was burnt to create malt candies or mixed with margarine and oatmeal to make a brittle. Bread was toasted in very thin slices, because it was thought that rations could be stretched further this way. Other ways to save were sought as well, although some people devoured everything immediately in order just once to be satiated. Thus, all endeavored in different ways to master the difficult circumstances and yet were barely able to cope.

Each food item had a fixed price and exchange value. Bread and cigarettes were the common currency. There was hardly anyone who did not barter or "buy" something at least occasionally, but many did so regularly, and even professionally. Those who could not give up smoking were dependent on the black market. Some renounced tobacco voluntarily; few could afford more than one or two cigarettes a day. Often, one cigarette was smoked a little at a time or communally with others. Butts were carefully collected. The prices of food items, and even more so of cigarettes, were subject to great fluctuations. Food prices rose prior to transports, and cigarette prices rose when a black market center was uncovered. The cigarette brand Vlasta, a thin and paltry weed, cost 1 crown per cigarette with a voucher in the "Protectorate"; in the camp itself, the price climbed from 4.80–8.00 crowns in the early days, to 15–25 crowns later on, and finally to 70–80 and even 100–150 crowns. The average price for one kilogram of bread was 80–100 crowns, but later prices of up to 800 crowns sometimes were paid. A kilogram of margarine fetched 2,000 crowns, a kilogram of sugar sold for 1,000–1,500 crowns, and one sugar cube brought in up to 15 crowns. Saccharine also was in demand and was very expensive. A lemon cost up to 180 crowns, an apple up to 200, and an orange up to 250. Alcoholic beverages were almost unobtainable and reached unbelievably high prices. A primitive beer substitute was brewed and was not even that bad: cold coffee substitute was mildly sweetened, mixed with some yeast, and sealed in bottles. After a few days, the liquid became slightly alcoholic, and the "beer" was ready for consumption.

13

Labor

There is no greater evidence of the unbroken vitality of the Jews, from childhood to old age, than their desire to work and their accomplishments in Theresienstadt. Aside from the cultural tendencies in Theresienstadt, the work carried out there must be acknowledged as the most significant test of this coerced community, even taking into account the constant pressure to work. Nobody likes being forced to work, but the majority in the camp understood that they could remain alive only by working. Fear of the transports was not the only motivating force, even though, together with the hope of being "saved" by work, it tended to encourage performance; on the other hand, work was inhibited by the deportations, which made it clear that work was pointless there, both concretely and conceptually. In this way, work became tragic, regardless of the workers' intentions. Had the community acquitted itself even half as well in other matters as it did in regard to labor, the history of this unhappy "ghetto" – which then most likely would not have been quite so unhappy – could have served as an example of how a community ought to act in times of need. The fact that nearly all the products of this work were destroyed prematurely does not diminish this praise, for the community never became capable of enjoying the fruits or passing them on; in this it was innocent, or almost innocent. No community under the rule of the SS, whose ill will brought sickness and destruction to everything, could have held on to the fruits of its labor.

In Theresienstadt, the pressure to work did not place an SS man behind every prisoner, constantly driving and beating him. The self-administration functioned as a buffer that protected and reduced the pressure – although never reliably. It was no less possible to escape work in the short or long term than to work slowly, badly, or unscrupulously. This occurred as well, but less often than one might have expected. There were fewer sluggards than is sometimes the case in normal circumstances. If breaches of duty, carelessness, and laziness were seen more frequently there than in civilian life, this was because little can remain hidden in such a camp. Certainly the motivations for working were not always the best; frequently they were anything but. The reasons for this can be found, first of all, in the circumstances accompanying all work. The inner drive to work is rarely stronger than the desire for the goals it seems to make attainable. Its practical purpose can be identified as a means of preservation, its main aim the improvement of existence. The more orderly a society and the more worthwhile the ethical principle it acknowledges and to which it aspires, the more both its order and its ethics will act as correctives to selfish tendencies in the workers. In Theresienstadt this principle was devalued, because it was subverted by the power that had established the camp. Thus work could not even be the kind of boon that it would anyway only been to an imperfect degree had the leadership of the camp had been better.

The "Central Labor Office" was headed by Dr. Erich Oesterreicher, an energetic man from Edelstein's group. After his deportation, he was succeeded in the fall of 1944 by his colleague Dr. Robert (Vinczi) Weinberger. Many of the leading functionaries were capable, younger Bohemian Jews. In Chapter 8 we discussed the structure of this office; here we describe in greater detail how the prisoners were integrated into the labor process. Each able and healthy "ghetto inmate" between the ages of sixteen and sixty, male or female, was subject to unconditional work duty, and each inmate from fourteen to fifteen and from sixty-one to sixty five, to conditional work duty; but even older people were expected to work if possible, and no age limit was set. No moral pressure was exerted, but there were many, even among the very oldest, who enjoyed working voluntarily and sometimes occupied responsible positions.

People did this not only because of the advantages workers received but also in order to make use of their time, or because they thought it would not be right to remain idle in light of the great shortage of workers. Most of the leaders of the camp and those in high positions, however, were young – and sometimes very young – men who frequently prevented older people from attaining higher posts, even if they were healthy and very able. Disrespect for and rejection of old age, common for the time and for the camp, were unpleasantly apparent here and kept many vigorous older people from suitable positions or caused them to be ousted from such positions. All too often, the officials in charge were young people, who frequently were inexperienced and unqualified, while qualified older people were used as subalterns or unskilled workers. Aside from the physically unfit, only the "notables" were freed from the duty to work.

Everyone was required to work as soon as he emerged from the Schleuse, where the group responsible for "labor deployment" recorded his personal data. Each newcomer was expected to work initially in a "squadron" (*Hundertschaft*). In exceptional cases, generally as a result of connections, this step was skipped. Work in "squadrons" and in so-called regular groups (*ständige Gruppen*) was referred to as "mobile deployment." Those who did not aspire to, or never attained, permanent posts within a "department" remained in "mobile deployment" and were directly subordinate to the "Central Labor Office" or its "deployment offices." Yet only a minority were content with this. Being qualified for various posts and occupations, or having connections, was supposed to help people find permanent positions. Usually, people applied to the "departments" or the "receiving office" of the "Central Secretariat," with a "curriculum vitae" and references. Such applications frequently remained unanswered for months, or sometimes indefinitely, unless someone intervened. Only a few specialists sometimes had a chance to gain permanent positions even without connections, in the prescribed fashion, which required a "request" from the respective "department" to the "Central Labor Office." It could reject or "approve" this "request" – its decision, in turn, frequently was a matter of connections – at which point the person would be released from "mobile deployment" and

Labor

admitted into the "ranks" (*Stand*) of his "department." If the application was approved, one was included in "regular deployment." This approval was not enough to obtain senior positions, as well as some other positions; for those, one also would have to be "approved" by the "Personnel Office" of the "Central Secretariat." At this point the person was part of "personnel" and was on the "administration staff." As part of "regular deployment" or "personnel," he was under the direct charge of the "department" in which he was employed; as such, he generally no longer reported to the "Central Labor Office." Those in "mobile deployment" were responsible in practice – if not in disciplinary matters – to the "departments" to which they were assigned, for instance, when it came to the work required of them. The principles according to which the workers were divided into the four above-mentioned groups will become clear later on in a document issued by the "Central Labor Office" in June 1944: it is the focus of this chapter's analysis.

All labor was planned and carried out by the individual "departments"; workers were assigned, generally or by request, by the "Central Labor Office." For disciplinary purposes, the workers were subordinate to their foremen or party leaders and "squadron elders." In most cases the required number of workers exceeded the number of available workers. Therefore the "Central Labor Office" had to cut back its requirements regarding the number of people as well as the length of the period of work and often could send only weak people, young people, or women instead of the requested able-bodied men. Thus the "departments" were in constant conflict with the "Central Labor Office," which led to compromises after difficult negotiations. The "Central Labor Office" was even more interested in the speed of work than were the individual "departments"; this was ensured by its "Labor Supervision Office," which also had certain rights regarding people holding "approved" positions. The "Central Labor Office" could also, to a limited extent, make use of "approved" employees, who were utilized in urgent cases, working by the hour or for other periods of time, as "administrative squadrons" for physical labor.

Each worker had many connections to the "Central Labor Office"; its authority affected all those fit to work, both theoretically and, for those who did not occupy the highest offices, also practically. The "squadrons" were organized, as far as possible, in such a way that the workers were separated not only into groups of men, women, and young people, but also according to "work categories," representing degrees of fitness for physical labor. The strongest men and women were gathered together in "cadre squadrons."

The "Central Labor Office" was important because of its welfare activity, which was carried out by the "Labor Welfare Office." It awarded regular bonuses (*Zubussen*), at first weekly and later every ten days (*Dekaden*). It granted special bonuses, determined by an "appraisal office"; in addition to a "risk allowance," there were "bonuses" for night work and special tasks. The "Labor Welfare Office" had an "applications office" where people presented their cases and filed petitions. There generally was a great willingness to help, although use of connections was unavoidable. The "Labor Welfare Office" depended on close cooperation with other departments, and because the supply of clothes and other necessities, as well as opportunities for repairs, continued to be limited, other ways frequently had to be found.

The "Central Labor Office" had a medical supervision and examination facility; its task was to examine workers' fitness for labor, divide and regroup them into "work categories," confirm work accidents, and conduct screenings. A department of

328 *Sociology*

the "Labor Welfare Office" dealt with care of the sick. It issued "sick bonuses" (*Krankenzubussen*) in place of *Dekaden*; the bonus for typhoid and enteritis was considered advantageous, whereas that for angina and influenza was not – in any case, not much could be done. Hard laborers lost their "extra rations" when they became sick, and soon the "S bread" also was withdrawn; those who suffered a prolonged illness received only "K bread." This was taken care of by the "deployment offices" (*Einsatzstellen*), which maintained "bread indexes" for the workers. Thus, in Theresienstadt, as in most concentration camps, illness was punished. On returning to work, people did not automatically receive the larger bread ration but had to apply for it and wait a few days. They received the "extra rations" on their first day back at work.

The "deployment offices" – in 1944 there were seven, one of which was devoted to young people – possessed limited powers; the Central Office dealt with all relevant issues. The main tasks of the "deployment offices" were to administer the "squadrons," maintain card files, and serve as branch offices of the "Labor Welfare Office." The Central Office maintained an overview of all employees through the "labor index," in which were found personal data, including, inevitably, each individual's "transport number," location and type of occupation, civilian occupation, and what – if any – "retraining" he received for new jobs. The employment of more than one person from one family in the same "department" was strictly prohibited, particularly in higher positions, but this principle was not always observed.

The work performed was both real and imaginary. The "tally" of those really working, which every "department" had to report to the "Central Labor Office" on a daily basis, was often imprecise, and as a result, so were the figures calculated in the "monthly reports" and forwarded to the SS by the leadership. The falsifications were minor when compared with all figures regarding numbers of hours worked, which were particularly exaggerated for administrative offices. The hours had to be confirmed by supervisors, who tended to note down more time for major projects, because special allowances depended on it. This was almost the only way to reward diligence. Moreover, people wanted to claim many hours in order to display the high level of activity of a particular group and its leader. The "departments" recorded all relevant data – for the "squadrons," this was done by the "deployment offices" – and the lists were delivered each month to the "productivity registry" at the "Central Labor Office." There, imaginary wage calculations were carried out; the workers were paid in "ghetto crowns" by the "Jewish self-administration bank."

Work Deployment.

The establishment of the Jewish settlement in Theresienstadt necessitated the performance of significant work as early as November 1941. The buildings, which were to be occupied little by little, had to be cleaned and repaired. Skilled workers were needed for the technical facilities that had to be newly created. Among the members of the transports that first arrived here were a large number who were fit to work, and who were assigned to the various work projects as mobile deployment.

In February 1942 the daily average of workers already amounted to 2,875 men and 1,857 women; in May 1942 it was 3,812 men and 3,854 women. At the time, this stood against a figure of no more than 6,813 fully fit laborers, so that in order to make up for the deficiency, it became necessary to utilize less-fit people over sixty years of age, as well as young people who had not attained 16 years of age.

Labor

Around mid-1942 the arrival of transports of the elderly ... as well as the simultaneous processing of transports with people fit to work ... worsened the difficulties on the labor market. At this point, there were ... between the ages of 16 and 60, 3,393 men completely fit to work, with an actual daily deployment of 4,360 men. By the end of 1942, some 6,000 persons above the age of 60 or below the age of 16 ... had to be utilized, in order to ... free up those who were fully fit ... for the renovation of the blocks, construction of city barracks, the railroad, the crematorium, water pipes and road construction.

The number of non-workers reached its height in September 1942, at 38,912 persons. At the same time, there was for the first time a predominance of female workers. Care of the ... infirm seemed to necessitate an increase in the number of female nursing personnel. More and more women were employed in the newly established production workshops.

In 1943 work deployment began to be systematically organized ...; workers assigned to individual departments were now being recalled in order to deploy them on more pressing work projects.

This procedure was implemented for the first time during the construction of barracks on the Westgasse, and then in particular in the introduction of so-called box production, for which more than 1,000 workers from the administrative offices and other less important workshops were utilized; finally, the Südbaracken on the Bauschowitzer Kessel were constructed in the fall of 1943 using workers assembled in the same manner.

The total work deployment rose from 20,534 in January 1943 to 28,614 in August of the same year. After the departure of both work deployment transports in September 1943 ... a decrease in the number of workers was noticed, which in December 1943 amounted ... to 21,997. In January 1944, 20,697 persons were deployed, 4,000 of whom were under 16 or above 60 years of age. (274)

With the transports in May and in the fall of 1944 – 7,500 and 18,000 persons – the number of workers was extremely reduced, and the percentage of female, old, and young laborers increased greatly. This ratio later improved due to the influx of new workers in 1945.

Structure of Work Deployment

Every Jew in Theresienstadt up to the age of 60 is registered for work deployment. The health of every individual is assessed in a series of screenings. Workers are then ranked through placement in four categories.

The allocation of newly registered inmates usually is ... to a ... squadron. After completing a specific training period in the group, some workers are placed permanently according to their vocational abilities. Unless they are permanently assigned to a specific group as laborers, those who do not have particularly good vocational training remain in squadrons that are centrally steered by deployment offices, which are branches of the Central Labor Office. Men are usually taken from a squadron primarily for construction and excavation work; women are assigned to the ranks of cleaning staff. The individual types of work are the following:

1. Supply work:
    a) kitchens, bakeries, distribution points, butchers, warehouses, shipping.
    b) health care facilities such as hospitals and outpatient clinics, care of the infirm, geriatric care, nurseries, and disinfection.
    c) baths, laundries, garment and shoe repair, and other workshops, such as watchmakers and opticians.

330 *Sociology*

2. Public works:
   a) power plant, water works, sewers, street cleaning, garbage removal, plumbing and heating, construction planning and implementation, and building maintenance
   b) bank, finance department, post office, court, retail shops, registry, burials, library, coffeehouse, recreation
   c) security and order services, central registry, records
3. Work for outside contractors:
   a) road construction Leitmeritz [Litoměřice], excavation at the army reserve field hospital, gardening at the Small Fortress, raw feed collection point, road construction and sewage (Figlovsky Engineering Firm).
   b) Production of notions, boxes, rabbit shearing [*Kaninchenhaarschur*], filling of ink powder bags, mending jute bags, work in the clothing warehouse.
   c) agriculture.

To the extent they are able to work, people older than sixty or younger than sixteen are deployed in ways suited to their health. Inmates requiring care and others who are not fully able to work include the elderly, sick, frail and children; and part-time workers, those older than sixty and younger than sixteen – their productivity is extremely low – they are deployed only to make up shortfalls, for example in jobs such as house service, mending work, etc., employing people between the ages of sixteen and sixty [who are] not fully capable of work, primarily severely disabled veterans. . . .

The full registration of all available labor makes it possible to initiate and complete major projects. (274)

LABOR DEPLOYMENT STATISTICS I

The following figures are taken from a chart entitled "Work Deployment of Ghetto Inmates" for the 1942 annual report:

	Total number of workers at month's end		
	Men	Women	Total
January	2,869	1,589	4,458
February	3,050	2,303	5,353
March	3,896	2,633	6,529
April	3,856	3,150	7,006
May	3,751	3,751	7,502
June	4,614	4,155	8,769
July	5,334	5,312	10,646
August	6,826	7,176	14,002
September	8,124	8,529	16,653
October	8,810	8,804	17,614
November	8,623	8,966	17,589
December	9,551	9,744	19,295

Based on these figures, the total number of hours worked was more than 27.4 million, with more than 11.8 million of those carried out by women. These figures can be interpreted only with difficulty and great caution, particularly because – as already mentioned – all the groups tended to submit the highest number of hours

	Total number of hours worked		
	Men	Women	Total
January	338,220	157,860	496,080
February	496,853	283,070	779,655
March	775,745	389,995	1,165,740
April	898,507	592,886	1,491,645
May	898,507	685,104	1,583,611
June	1,043,003	642,425	1,685,428
July	1,379,325	967,955	2,347,280
August	1,672,137	1,223,353	2,695,490
September	1,777,761	1,481,400	3,259,161
October	2,062,930	1,774,280	3,387,210
November	2,071,328	1,647,697	3,919,025
December	2,125,347	1,937,109	4,062,456

possible. It is possible to calculate that, excluding days off, laborers worked an average of three hours and fifty minutes per day in January. In December, the figure was around six hours and fifty minutes, with men working an average of seven hours and ten minutes and women six hours and twenty-five minutes. In reality, however, the number of hours for normal workers was much higher. How can this be explained?

1. The number of workers varied daily, due to (a) the arrival and departure of transports and (b) numerous cases of illness.
2. The elderly and children also worked – these "part-time workers" (*Kurzarbeiter*) were required to put in four hours each day.

We come closer to the truth if we calculate differently. In December 1942, there were 24,000 people available to work, and 19,295 workers in December; of these, 6,000 were part-time workers. However, 15% of the workers were too ill to work daily (between the summer of 1942 and the winter of 1943 to 1944 the proportion was much higher):

$$19,295 \text{ full-time workers} \times 15\% = 2,895 \text{ (rounded to } 3,000) \text{ workers}$$

$$6,000 \text{ part-time workers} \times 15\% = 900 \text{ (rounded to } 1,000) \text{ workers}$$

Thus the actual number of full-time and part-time workers can be calculated as follows:

$$19,295 \text{ total} - 3,000 \text{ sick} - 6,000 \text{ part-time} = 10,295 \text{ full-time workers}$$

$$6,000 \text{ part-time} - 1,000 \text{ sick} = 5,000 \text{ part-time workers}$$

We can calculate the total number of working days as follows:

$$31 \text{ total days} - 4 \text{ free days} = 27 \text{ working days}$$

Based on the data from the preceding table, we can calculate the average number of hours per working day as follows:

$$4,062,456 \text{ total hours}/27 \text{ days} = 150,461 \text{ hours}$$

The 5,000 part-time workers worked four hours a day, so they were responsible for 20,000 of those hours. Thus the full-time workers were responsible for the remainder:

$$150,461 \text{ total hours} - 20,000 \text{ part-time hours} = 130,461 \text{ full-time hours}$$

And thus the healthy laborers were working an average of twelve hours and forty minutes each day:

$$130,461 \text{ hours}/10,295 \text{ workers} = 12.67 \text{ hours}$$

Regarding this breakdown, it must be said that before November 1944 the sick always were included in tables on "work deployment." Because the figures for individual groups are probably too high, we can take the average daily working hours for a healthy worker, starting in early 1942, to be 11.5; the average for men was about an hour more, and the average for women was somewhat less. Compared to a "normal" concentration camp, conditions in Theresienstadt – putting aside the conditions accompanying the work – were more favorable but nevertheless harsh and, given the allotted rations, were extremely unhealthy and hardly bearable for most people. The average workweek was sixty-nine hours long, with men working as much as seventy-five hours, rather than the official fifty-two hours for physical labor or fifty-seven hours in offices. There had been no significant change in working hours by autumn 1944. If anything, people worked longer, although living conditions also improved. When a seventy-hour workweek was introduced in November 1944, and a sixty-five-hour workweek in February 1945, those hours were without doubt considerably less than was actually worked. It also is certain that, at all times, some groups worked 100 hours or more during difficult weeks.

The annual report for 1942 provided an overview of the average number of workers each month and their distribution according to occupation.

Month	Number of workers deployed
January	2,756
February	4,732
March	6,220
April	7,485
May	7,526
June	6,050
July	9,704
August	12,615
September	15,396
October	17,265
November	17,823
December	20,000

The monthly averages and totals for workers vary due to constant arrivals and departures. If we were to calculate the hours worked using the figures in these tables, we would arrive mathematically at a lower result, but essentially nothing would change. Although the categorization by occupations provides a distorted picture,

Labor

Occupation	Percent distribution
Manufacturing	20.4
Kitchens, supplies, and storage	13.5
Doctors, nurses, and pharmacists	12.7
Cleaning and technical service	12.3
Housing, youth services, and Order Constabulary	10.0
Excavation and construction	4.9
Trades and home workshops	4.0
Shipping and transportation	3.95
Burials, delousing, and disinfection	2.7
Agriculture	2.25
Security	1.9

which we later correct in accordance with the June 1944 figures, the unusual ratio of production workers to medical personnel becomes clear.

Three specific charts prepared for monthly reports from the first half of 1943 indicate a further rise in the number of workers; this was not significantly exceeded until August 1943 and decreased from then on.

	Average daily deployments (1943)		
	February	March	May
Men	11,279	11,879	12,545
Women	13,627	14,038	15,212
TOTAL	24,906	25,917	27,757

A table similar to the one shown earlier provides a superficial reflection of the relationship between various occupations at the end of 1943:

Occupation	Number of workers (as of December 31, 1943)
Supplies	3,825
Contract work and assignments from the office	1,519
Agriculture	609
Construction and workshops	2,341
Health care	2,966
Security	964
Building management and cleaning	4,953
Various assistance services	2,195
Other administrative services	1,772
Total number of workers	21,144
Total number of inhabitants	34,655

On "labor deployment," Prochnik (214) and Lederer (166) have presented interesting figures that do not always agree with those found in other documents. The numbers always refer to the beginning of the month:

Month	Year	Men	Women	Number of workers deployed	Number of inhabitants
January	1942	2,869	1,252	4,121	7,348
July	1942	5,067	4,498	9,565	21,304
January	1943	10,202	10,323	20,525	49,296
July	1943	10,540	15,060	25,600	44,767
January	1944	9,462	10,976	20,438	34,641
July	1944	7,725	8,375	16,100	27,684
January	1945	1,693	4,071	5,764	11,465
May	1945	4,871	7,342	12,213	17,515 (old inmates)

Some 5,200 people over sixty years old were being deployed (according to Prochnik) on January 1, 1943; this figure decreased to 4,325 on January 1, 1944; 2,262 on July 1, 1944; and 1,301 on January 1, 1945. The following table presents the percentage of prisoners who were working on the first day of the month during various months in 1942–1945:

Month	Year	Percent of people working in shifts	Percent of men working	Percent of women working
January	1942	56.1		
July	1942	45.0	56.1	37.8
January	1943	41.6	50.9	34.7
July	1943	57.4	57.8	57.1
January	1944	59.0	66.75	53.5
July	1944	54.2	64.0	48.5
January	1945	52.1	52.0	52.1
May	1945	69.6	71.5	68.7

A population table for the years 1942–43 indicates monthly averages up to November 1943; the prisoners were divided into four age groups, and their numbers were recorded as a percent of the total. The ratios are unique in comparison with every concentration camp, and also with any free population.

	Percent rise or fall for 1942 (by age group)				Percent rise or fall for 1943 (by age group)			
	0–16	16–45	45–65	over 65	0–16	16–45	45–65	over 65
January	~ 9	56–46	30–36	7–10	~ 7	29–27	31–29	33–36
February	~ 9	46–43	36–34	10–13	~ 7	27–28	29–30	37–34
March	9–10	43–38	34–32	13–20	7–8	28–29	30–32	34–32
April	10–9	38–37	~ 32	20–21	~ 8	29–30	32–33	30–29
May	9–7	37–35	32–27	21–30	~ 8	~ 30	~ 33	29–28
June	7–6	35–30	27–24	30–39	~ 8	~ 31	~ 33	28–27
July	~ 5	30–21	24–23	39–51	~ 8	31–32	33–34	27–25
August	~ 5	21–20	~ 23	51–53	~ 8	~ 32	~ 34	~ 25
September	~ 5	20–23	23–27	53–44	~ 8	32–31	34–33	25–27
October	~ 6	23–25	27–29	44–39	~ 8	~ 31	~ 33	27–26
November	6–7	25–28	29–30	39–35	~ 8	~ 32	~ 33	~ 26
December	~ 7	28–29	30–31	35–33				

Note: Data presented in rounded numbers.

The following table juxtaposes the annual average number of nonworkers and workers.

	Nonworkers	Workers
1942	18,819	10,692
1943	17,472	25,827
1944	14,846	20,697

The most informative document is a list (259) prepared on June 30, 1944, by the Central Labor Office, indicating how many persons in each "department" and "subdepartment" were counted as "personnel" and "permanently deployed" in the previous month, and how many were in "permanent groups" and "squadrons" as "mobile deployment." It also showed who received which of five possible "ten-day bonuses" and who received "supplementary food" or "S bread." The excerpts from the lists make it possible to differentiate between "personnel" and those who were "continually deployed." The number of workers is in the first column; the second column contains the numbers of regular or occasional recipients of "supplementary food," and the third the number of recipients of "S bread."

	Personnel deployment			Permanent deployment		
	Workers	"Suppl. food" recipients	S bread recipients	Workers	"Suppl. food" recipients	S bread recipients
Management						
Central Secretariat	100	40	60			
Community Guard (GW)	200	200	176	1	1	
Detective Department	92	92	87			
Economic police and kitchen guards	166	164	138			
Fire department	51	51	51			
Bank	222	33	61			
Central Registry	93	16	10			
Finance Department	78	31	30			
Recreation Office	131	40	27	145	2	6
Central Labor Office	397	106	155	184	40	71
TOTAL	1,530	773	795	330	43	77
Department of Internal Administration						
Management	19	11	14			
Legal Department	44	13	14			
Space Management Office	100	18	24	9	4	1

(*continued*)

Sociology

(continued)

	Personnel deployment			Permanent deployment		
	Workers	"Suppl. food" recipients	S bread recipients	Workers	"Suppl. food" recipients	S bread recipients
Order Constabulary				134	16	96
Cleaning service				268	114	37
Rationing service	21	21		170		
Warming kitchens				105		
District and Building Management Offices	377	96	95	13		
Laundries				10	6	3
Aides for the sick				90		
Room orderlies				168		
Registry Index[a]	45	8	11	60	36	27
Postal service	187	85	73	1		
Transport Management Department	60	17	10	19	7	7
Complaints Office[b]	26	26				
TOTALS	879	295	242	1,047	195	171
Economics Department						
Management	59	41	20			
Zelenka Group[c]	16	15	2			
Supplies	69	23	21	44	2	2
Butcher	19	19	17	14	11	7
Pastry bakery	18	4		98	94	4
Ration transport columns				94		
Kitchens	187			246		
Central materials administration	27	17	12	6	5	2
Central Warehouse	5	2	1	3	3	3
Central Supply Warehouse	10	8	7	55	48	40
Potato storage	21	2	10	36	19	26
Central Materials Warehouse	23	19	17	19	18	13
Central Lumber Warehouse	6	5	4	23	22	19
Central Clothing Warehouse	54	34	17	52	33	3
Clothing storehouse	30	28	2	15	12	4

Labor

	Personnel deployment			Permanent deployment		
	Workers	"Suppl. food" recipients	S bread recipients	Workers	"Suppl. food" recipients	S bread recipients
Ghetto stores	67	15	4	3	2	
Coffeehouse	13	1	2	34		
Hairdressers	12			40		
Crafts workshops				2	2	1
Materials administration	45	14	15	20	15	4
Shipping Department	4	2	1	8	7	6
Security guards	1	1	1	39		
Agriculture Department	6	6	4	445	427	193
TOTAL	702	256	157	1,295	720	327
Manufacturing Department						
Management	118	36	15	7	3	2
Chemical-technical laboratory	4	1		5		1
Südbaracken administration	1	1		22	9	10
Metalworks	11	5	6	128	86	88
Cardboard packaging	21	7	10	148	138	98
Wood processing Bauhof	3	2	1	92	90	80
Wood processing Reitschule	1	1	1	77	24	4
Notion manufacturing	2	1	1	116	48	3
Cowhide manufacturing				9	9	1
Uniform manufacturing	4	1	1	40		
Repairs	27	8	9	669	129	36
Central Laundry	5	3	3	312	311	7
Central Bath				12	3	5
Collection point[d]	15	10	3	136	91	
Noodle manufacturing				17		
Room furnishing	5	5	1	42	29	3
Ink powder manufacturing	1			24	24	
Bag making	2	1	1	17	13	
Bandage workshop				4		

(*continued*)

Sociology

(continued)

	Personnel deployment			Permanent deployment		
	Workers	"Suppl. food" recipients	S bread recipients	Workers	"Suppl. food" recipients	S bread recipients
Orthopedics				6		
Central Bakery	8	1		144	139	
Mica splitting	2	1				
TOTAL	234	84	71	2,035	1,148	346
Technical Department						
Management	49	15	21	2		
Building	57	24	31	144	141	120
Railway management	3	3	3	4	4	4
Road construction	4	3	3	8	8	4
Water purification	5	3	5	1		
Electricity	14	4	5	97	96	86
Water Department	15	5	6	47	46	39
Telephone operators				4	4	3
Sewers	3	3	3	15	15	12
Plumbing	11	5	8	65	64	52
Garbage removal	1	1	1	6	6	4
Street cleaning	1	1	1	5		1
Building maintenance	67	14	25	173	159	139
Drafting, etc.	27	4	8	17	7	3
TOTALS	257	85	120	586	549	467
Health Services Department						
Management	57	31	17	5		
B IV clinic, etc.	45	18	6	45	10	5
B V clinic, etc.	22	4	5	16		
L 504 home for the infirm	24	15	5	116	85	14
Q 207/9 pediatrics clinic – infectious cases	6	5	2	31	27	5
A II clinic, etc.	14	2	4	7		
C III clinic, etc.	100	38	9			
C I veterinarian				1	1	
E IIIa block clinic, etc.	101	36	13	81	31	10
E IIIa hospital	55	34	18	182	117	29
L 124 hospital	5	3	1	2		1
L 317 hospital	16	10	7	63	40	12
Q 403 hospital	15	2	4	46	16	9
E VI block clinic, etc.	95	25	18	77	11	3

Labor

	Personnel deployment			Permanent deployment		
	Workers	"Suppl. food" recipients	S bread recipients	Workers	"Suppl. food" recipients	S bread recipients
E VI central hospital	93	58	45	289	139	103
E VII clinic, etc.	30	16	5	78	45	7
H V clinic, etc.	103	37	19	185	44	19
L 318 infirmary	6	2	2	12		1
L 410 infirmary	5	1	2	9		1
L 414 infirmary	4	1	1	10	1	1
L 417 infirmary	4	2	1	7	1	1
Q 710 infirmary	10	2	5	7		
Q 721 infants' home	23	10	6	90	37	12
G V block for the infirm	27	19	6	115	99	17
Pediatric dental clinic	9	2	1	5		
Central Medical Supply Warehouse	29	14	11	6	4	2
Central dental technology	18	2	3	6		
Pathology	4	2	2	7	6	5
Delousing	12	11		107	105	2
Central Laundry	3	1	2	16	1	1
Bedding section	3	1	2	37	34	4
Hygienic inspection	34	32	4	5		
Public health officer	32	19	2	2		
Welfare	190	9	3	55	17	
TOTALS	1,195	434	230	1,818	896	279
Youth Welfare Office						
Management	29	15	15	1		
Youth garden[e]	3			445	284	18
Home Südstr. 1[f]	10	1	3	1		
Home C III	10	3	3	5		
Home Q 702	18	3	2	3		
Home L 218	29	5	8	24	7	1
Home L 216	22	2	3	8		
Home Q 609	37	6	4	17	3	1
Home H V	6	1	1	1		
Home L 318	82	9	4	38	5	
Home L 410	53	10	5	21	1	1
Home L 414	54	9	6	33	3	3
Home L 417	31	5	3	21	2	

(continued)

Sociology

(continued)

	Personnel deployment			Permanent deployment		
	Workers	"Suppl. food" recipients	S bread recipients	Workers	"Suppl. food" recipients	S bread recipients
Welfare	24	6	5	18		
Nursery	16	1	2	9		
TOTALS	424	76	64	645	307	27

[a] Corpse movers and the crew at the crematorium are part of the registry office.
[b] This refers to the Complaints Office within the Building Management Department; it is not the same as the administration's Complaints Office.
[c] The *Zelenka* Group was the detective group in the "Economics Department" mentioned in Chapter 12.
[d] This was the collection point for laundry and mending.
[e] The youth garden was a garden in the "Agriculture Department" in which young people worked.
[f] Südstr. 1 home was the recuperation home for children with tuberculosis; it was set up as part of the "beautification."

The following table lists the number of people who were in "permanent groups" and "squadrons" as "mobile deployment." The source material does not make clear who was receiving supplementary food, although heavy laborers and people in the "squadrons" did receive it. Therefore, there are only two columns: the number of workers and the number of "S bread" recipients.

	Workers	S bread recipients
Mobile deployment: permanent groups		
Mechanics in the SS garage	6	6
Excavation, Small Fortress	20	18
Women, Small Fortress	13	
Turf group II	10	10
Stokers' unit E I, H IV[a]	15	14
Berlin Office, furnishings	11	11
Reserve clinic, barracks construction (for the military)	16	13
Suicide intervention squad (*Stoßtruppe*), 1st–4th district	4	1
Cleaning service C III district	169	1
Cleaning service E IIIa	36	
Cleaning service E VII	4	
Cleaning service H V	28	
Outside cleaning service	28	1
Cleaning service, paper gathering	6	
Cleaning service E IIIa district	16	1
Mattress section, Space Management Office	32	
Hand laundry L 506	15	2
Warming kitchen, services	5	5
Block services E IIIa	8	
Room elder B IV	29	
Building administration, B IV, various tasks	6	
Room elder C III	23	
Toilet attendants C III	18	
Room elder A II	12	

Labor

	Workers	S bread recipients
Floor monitor C III	24	
Room elder E VII	21	
Toilet attendants H V, exterior	3	
Room elder H V	43	
Toilet attendants, H V, interior	1	
Post service	11	9
Transport assistance	27	
Postal security	17	
Potato peelers C III	35	
Merchandise transport	12	
Potato group	22	20
Scrap materials, men	7	1
Scrap materials, women	4	
Coal group	11	11
Central Garment Warehouse	91	
Clothing warehouse I IV	22	
Clothing warehouse, transport work	12	1
Shipping, Economics Departments	160	158
Tree felling, agriculture	17	17
Land leveling	41	24
Seamstresses	31	
Knitting, home work	25	
Ink powder filling	13	
Knitting, home for the blind	20	
Laundry sorting C III	6	
Sock darning, home work	19	
Rail maintenance	10	10
Street paving	19	18
Pipe layers I–IV	36	29
Civil engineering group A II	34	29
Figlovsky Service Group (road construction, etc.)	17	16
Garbage removal, abattoir	24	17
Street cleaning	13	
Plumbers, fitters	6	4
Street cleaning B IV, miscellaneous	26	5
Südbaracken, road building	26	21
Technical Department, excavation	16	12
Pipe layers V	17	12
Technical service B IV	28	
Technical service C III	30	
Technical service A II	4	
Technical service E IIIa	14	
Technical service E VI	16	
Technical service H V	13	
Toilet attendants E IIIa	9	
Ration carriers E IIIa	6	
Home for the infirm E IIIa	4	
Medical service Q 403	4	
Janitorial orderlies	3	

(continued)

Sociology

(*continued*)

	Workers	S bread recipients
Bottle cleaners, pharmacy	3	
Pressers, infectious laundry	7	7
Nursery	9	
Delousing service	31	
Block for the infirm G V	39	
Hand laundry, Q 808	19	12
House service L 414	31	
House service L 417	11	5
Fire extinguishing pond, E I building (for the SS)	24	24
TOTALS	1,782	551
Mobile deployment: squadrons		
Youth, four groups	219	91
Adults, thirty-one groups	1,513	254
TOTALS	1,732	345

[a] The stokers worked for the "Berlin Office."

If we condense these figures into the nine "departments" of the self-administration, we obtain the following overview:

	Personnel deployment	Permanent deployment	Total
Management			
Actual administration	100		100
Security	499	1	500
Central Registry	222		222
Bank	93		93
Department total	924	1	925
Central Labor Office			
Department total	397	184	581
Internal Administration			
Legal Department	44		44
Space Management Office	100	9	109
Registry Office	45	60	105
Postal service	187	4 [1]	188
Order Constabulary		134	134
Other	503	843	1,346
Department total	879	1,047	1,926
Economics Department			
Warehouses	190	138	328
Supplies and rations	323	747	1,070
Stores, etc.	87	5	92
Shipping Department	4	8	12
Agriculture Department	6	445	451
Production for outside	10	266	276
Production for the camp	27	679	706
Production for the camp and outside	42	427	469

	Personnel deployment	Permanent deployment	Total
Laundry, bath	5	324	329
Administration	187 [181]	37	218
Other	61	254	315
Department total	936	3,330	4,266
Technical Department			
Construction	57	144	201
Town and communications	57	252	309
Building maintenance	67	173	240
Management and other	76	19	95
Department total	257	588	845
Finance Department			
Department total	78		78
Health Services Department			
Medicine	811	1,572	2,383
Businesses	137	186	323
Welfare	190	55	245
Management	57	5	62
Department total	1,195	1,818	3,013
Youth Welfare Office			
Homes	352	172	524
Management and welfare	69	18	97
Youth gardens	3	445	448
Department total	424	645	1,069
Recreation Department			
Department total	131	145	276
All departments			
Total (all nine departments)	5,221	7,758	12,979
Groups			
Work for the SS		115	115
Internal Department		592	592
Economics Department		550	550
Technical Department		349	349
Health Services Department		134	134
Youth Welfare Office		42	42
Groups total		1,782	1,782
Squadrons			
Total		1,732	1,732
Groups and Squadrons			
Total		3,514	3,514
All departments, groups, and squadrons			
Grand total	5,221	11,272	16,493
PERSONNEL		5,221	
PERMANENT DEPLOYMENT		7,758	
GROUPS AND SQUADRONS		3,514	
TOTAL (on June 30, 1944)		16,493	

The following table lists the number of people working in the departments in confirmed positions and groups:

Management	925
Central Labor Office (excluding groups and squadrons)	581
Internal administration	2,518
Economics Department	4,816
Technical Department	1,194
Finance Department	78
Health Services Department	3,047
Youth Welfare Office	1,111
Recreation Department	276
Work for the SS and squadrons (mostly for the Technical Department and Economics Department)	1,847
TOTAL	16,493

Caution is always called for when discussing statistical figures, especially in the case of Theresienstadt, because they abstractly schematize and often misrepresent conditions, but this material is worthy of some confidence, because the breakdown on which it is based served practical purposes, in particular the calculation of *Dekaden*. Each figure that specifies a type of occupation reflects neither the stratification nor the quality of the job. Analysis can provide only an approximate sense of the social structure of the camp. The numbers we have compiled and will assess are always to be taken as averages. The tasks of squadrons and other groups are not clearly set out; they correspond most closely to those of day laborers. Positions within the camp administration cannot easily be compared with those of civil servants, because the scope of activity of most of the employees covered more than one area.

The SS and the prisoners conceived of Theresienstadt as a provisional camp. The situation changed continually; what was important one day was worthless the next, and vice versa. Every job and every position was provisional. If a position remained relatively stable, it required constant adaptation. Administrative jobs were not the only ones to go beyond their formal purview; this was especially true for lower-level positions, and often the boundaries between administrative and technical and between physical and intellectual labor could not be drawn. In a normal society, the required work often would be performed by different people or groups; thus there were only a few occupations in the camp that corresponded exactly to civilian professions. It is no wonder that people's hearts were elsewhere, even when they conscientiously performed their day's work. Another reason for this lack of enthusiasm was that most were not practicing their original professions. Many already had been "retrained" in the difficult years before deportation. Bohemian Jews, in particular, had learned several trades and had succumbed to a veritable retraining fever. Others did not retrain until they got to the camp; their retraining took place without any guidance, because circumstances required that they be able to do something, even without formal training. Jobs of which Jews were said to be incapable or were said to avoid were performed in the camp with the most primitive tools. Adaptability, skill, industry, intelligence, and good will helped.

Only a few occupations were more clearly defined, and only a minority – physicians, for example – worked in their own fields. The large proportion of Jews in medicine proved a blessing here. There also were engineers, technicians, and craftsmen who worked in their professions, but many specialists hardly were used

Labor 345

and were more likely to be taken away on transports than less qualified but better-protected people.

Now we consider various figures from the material presented previously, organized in a different way, recalling that in the midst of constant change, the status on June 30, 1944, is fixed. First we summarize the percentages allotted to the nine "departments" and the "squadrons," without considering job type. From here on, we ascribe those in "mobile deployment" to the "departments" of which they were part because of their work.

	Personnel	Percent of the workforce
Management	925	~ 5.5
Central Labor Office	581	3.5
Internal administration	2,518	15.0
Economics Department	4,816	29.0
Technical Department	1,194	7.5
Finance Department	78	0.5
Health Services Department	4,147	19.0
Youth Welfare Office	1,111	6.5
Recreation Department	276	1.5
Squadrons	1,847	11.0

Occupations are not readily apparent from this list; thus the following tables compile the data differently. The first of these tables list the number of people in the administration:

	Personnel	Percent of the workforce
Management (excluding the fire department)		
Actual management	100	
Community Guard (GW)	201	
Detective Department	92	
Economic Supervision Office	166	
Central Registry	222	
Bank	93	
Department total	874	5.2
Department of Internal Administration		
Management	19	0.1
Legal Department	44	0.3
Space Management Office	109	0.7
Order Constabulary	134	0.8
Rationing service	191	1.2
District and Building Management Offices	390	2.35
Registry (personnel only)	60	0.4
Postal service	188	1.2
Transport Management Department (personnel only)	60	0.4
Complaints Office (ration commission)	26	0.15

(*continued*)

(continued)

	Personnel	Percent of the workforce
Economics Department		
Management of economics	59	0.4
Production management	135	0.8
Administration of the Südbarcken and *Bauhof* (workshop complex H II)	34	0.2
Security guards	40	0.2
Technical Department		
Management	51	0.3
Building maintenance (personnel only)	67	0.4
Draftsmen, etc.	44	0.3
Finance Department		
Department total	78	0.5
Central Labor Office		
Administrative personnel only	381	3.4
Health Services Department		
Management	62	0.4
Youth Welfare Office		
Management	30	0.2
Mobile deployment		
Room elders, building management	138	0.8
Attic guard C III	24	0.15
Post office assistance and postal guards	28	0.2
Administration		
TOTAL	3,441	∼ 21.0

It should be noted regarding these figures that engineers and support services fall under the administration but were not necessarily part of it. At the same time, it should be taken into account that offices not included in this table – enterprises run by the "Economics Department" and the "Manufacturing Department," hospitals and outpatient clinics, and the "Recreation Department" – also had their own administrative workers.

Some groups also could be aggregated using other criteria. Those employed in public safety included the following:

	Personnel	Percent of the workforce
Ghetto Guard (Community Guard)	201	1.2
Detective Department	92	0.55
Economic Control Office (Küwa)	166	1.0
Order Constabulary	134	0.8
Other security services	81	0.5
TOTAL	674	4.1

The "Legal Department" (that is, the court system) and the fire department can be added to the preceding list:

	Personnel	Percent of the workforce
Public safety personnel (from preceding table)	674	4.1
Legal Department	44	0.3
Fire department	51	0.3
Public security total	769	[≃] 4.65

If we highlight all the positions that involved administration of housing – in the "Space Management Office," the "Building Management Office" (including district, building, house, and room elders, to the extent that they are included in the statistics), and the "Building Maintenance Office," along with its support services – we arrive at the following numbers:

	Personnel	Percent of the workforce
Administration of housing	700	4.25

The "central registry" and "registry office" can be viewed as population offices:

	Personnel	Percent of the workforce
Population offices	267	1.6

The "Transport Management Department" and the postal service can be consolidated with a few other groups under transportation and traffic, but those figures are not included in our final table. As administration in the more narrow sense, we can add together the "Central Secretariat," the management of "the departments," and the entire "Central Labor Office":

	Personnel	Percent of the workforce
Central administrative offices	1,105	6.2

The "Finance Department" and the "bank" can be combined as follows:

	Personnel	Percent of the workforce
Financial management	171	1

CHARACTERIZATION OF ADMINISTRATIVE WORK

The following list provides a characterization of the work in the administrative fields.

1. *"Management" ("Central Secretariat")*: Positions in this department could be obtained only through personal connections, and its workers were reputed to be well protected from deportation. The

work was thankless and difficult. Overtime and night work – as in all main offices – were frequent due to constant special orders from the SS. The officials were said to be well informed on all issues and therefore were swamped, but not even the Jewish Elder could know what the next day might bring.

2. *"Ghetto Guard"*: This must not be confused with the frequently notorious institutions in the East that bore similar names; even its personnel composition was much better. From September 1942 until August 1943, the Ghetto Guard was combined with the "Detective Department," the "Economic Control Office," and the "fire department" to form the "security services." The work was strenuous but offered many advantages, and until August 1943 it also provided "transport protection." Later, members of this group were systematically deported.

3. *"Central Registry"*: Personnel in this department carried out difficult and important work that could continue day and night during deportations or the "census."

4. *"Bank"*: The monthly "payments" required a great deal of work. The cashiers' office was supposed to demonstrate Jewish civilian life to visitors from the outside. The usual business of banking was not carried out, but it too was simulated (see 243a).

5. *"Legal Department"*: Most of the staff in this department previously had worked in the judicial system.

6. *"Space Management Office"*: The work in this department was difficult and thankless (see Chapter 11).

7. *"Building Management Office"*: Hours often were virtually unlimited and the work was hard, particularly for people who took seriously their duties toward their charges. Higher-ranking officials had better accommodations; house elders and higher functionaries were internally assured of "transport protection."

8. *Order Constabulary (OD)*: The members of this group enjoyed no prestige. At first the OD was made up of only younger people, including women. Later, it was composed of a group of stewards made up of older people, mainly from Germany, who frequently made fools of themselves by taking their thankless jobs, which provided no protection, too seriously. At its height, the OD numbered 240 men and a group of women.

9. *Postal service*: The postal service employed only a few workers at first, when it was responsible only for distributing internal news and correspondence to the closed barracks. After September 1942, when parcels were allowed, the post office grew continually and ultimately employed 216 people, including assistants, or 1.3 percent of the workforce.

10. *"Rationing service," "Kitchen Complaint Department"*: The workers in this department had a good life to begin with, and with the exception of those in the "Central Ration Card Office," their work was not very hard.

11. *"Central Labor Office"*: The workers in this department made up nearly 3.4% of the workforce; this figure seems exaggeratedly high

Labor

but was necessary given the abnormally overcomplicated administrative apparatus. It was an evil common to all camps established by the SS, but probably nowhere was this problem as out of control as in this "ghetto."

DOCUMENTS PERTAINING TO THE WORK OF THE CENTRAL LABOR OFFICE

The text of the following forms sheds light on the position of the workers and the agenda of the "Central Labor Office" in characteristic detail. Explanations are provided only in places where the literal text is not self-explanatory. Nonessentials have been condensed.

Document 1. Printed Form from June 1943 (Two Pages and a Carbon Copy)

Central Labor Office

Structure of the
work deployment on _____1943   Place of deployment _____   Protectorate
                                                                    G. Reich

The following text is accompanied by eleven columns: four each for men and women, arranged according to age (under 60, 61–65, over 65, and all ages together); then one column for men and women together; and then two empty columns.

a) Outside work
b) Bakery – noodles
   Precision mechanics, optics, watches
   Notions workshops
   Mica splitting
   Clothing and laundry mending
   Metalworking
   Clog production
   Shoe repair
   Bag workshop
   Carpenter shop – Joinery – General
      Bed building
      Production of wooden soles
      Lumberyard [lumber storage]
      Machine carpentry
      Mass production [bed frames and wooden barracks components]
   Workshop "L" [handicrafts for the Lautsch family]
   Central bathhouse
   Central laundry – Collection area – Transport
c) Bandage makers – orthopedics
   Jewelry [production]
   Women's clothing [production]
   Hairdressers
   Gunnysack repair [production]
   Rabbit hair shears [production]

Cartons [production]
Clothing warehouse
Warehouse for "stores"
Shop personnel
Educational games and pastimes [production]
Mattress warehouse and repair
Sewing machine and typewriter – Service [internal]
Boots from cattle hide [production]
Uniform sewing [production]
Knitters
Ink powder bag fillers [production]

d) Painters – glaziers – interior painters
Concrete workers – roofers
Electricians
Plumbers and fitters
Sewers
Masons
Paperhangers – Blackout curtain makers
Wagon workshop
Waterworks
Other technical workshops
Building administration craftsmen

e) Agriculture and gardening

f) Small Fortress [Kleine Festung]
Reserve field hospital
Various jobs on outside commission

g) renovation – garbage removal
Street cleaning

h) Railroad building
Crematorium road [construction of an access road]
Leitmeritz [Litoměřice] [road building]
Bypass road

i) Pipelayers
Various construction and excavation work

Category I
Potato peeler
Coffeehouse
Kitchen work
Rationing
Goods transport
Central Provisions Warehouse

Category II
Doctors and dental technicians
Pharmacies and central medical supply warehouse
Male and female nurses
Welfare
Assistance and cleaning staff – health services
Infectious disease laundry
Delousing
Burial
Youth and child care

Labor

Category III
Order Constabulary
Order guard – Security Police [security services]
Lost and found, orientation service
Fire department
Group, building, and room elders
Administrative workers

Category IV
Luggage transport
Passenger transport

Category V
Clean-up and auxiliary work
General cleaning service
House service
Day workers, on-call

Category VI
Category I–VI together

Categories I–VI refer to the graduated *Dekaden*. The higher the value of a group's *Dekaden*, the fewer allowances (bread or "supplementary food") it was allotted – or at least that was how it should have been.

Document 2. Printed Form from 1944 (Double-Sided)

List of names
Place of work: _____   Date. _____   Page: _____
No.   Last and first name   Transport No.   Born   Remarks

Forty numbered lines are printed beneath these headings. These lists were for the "foreman" when a group began work. Other lists were read out when a group began work to check attendance and punctuality.

Document 3. Mimeographed Sheet from 1943 (One-Sided)

Confirmation of work   Date. _____
Place of deployment   Number _____
To _____
Men _____   Women _____   Foreman _____
Work site _____   Type of work _____

Work Hours

	Person	from	to		Hours
Morning					
Afternoon					
Full day					
Confirmed by the requester:			Confirmed by the foreman:		

352   *Sociology*

This form was used for groups or individuals who were sent to a "department" by the "Central Labor Office." Later, a two-page form was used with a carbon copy. The two forms were similar, although the latter one was overly mechanized, and both contained a list of names on the reverse side (see 3h, doc. 120).

Document 4. Mimeographed Form from 1942 (One-Sided)

Personnel questionnaire from the technical department

Last name _____	Transport _____	Quarters _____
First name _____	No. _____	Rm. No. _____
Birth date _____	Place of birth _____	Marital status _____
Nationality _____	Relig. _____	Classif. _____
Last resided at _____		

Family members in Theresienstadt _____

Last and First name   Transp. No.   Quarters   Relationship   Year of Birth
[three lines of space for relatives]

Schooling or apprenticeships _____

Experience as _____	at _____	duration _____
Skills _____	References _____	
Date _____		Signature _____

All the "departments" used similar questionnaires for job applicants. Classification relates to the assessment of the applicant's capability to do physical work. Such questionnaires were used by the "departments" as the basis for "requesting" workers from the "Central Labor Office" or the "Personnel Office." But, as we have seen, applicants themselves also could submit applications.

Document 5. Mimeographed Form from 1945 (Double-Sided)

Last name_____ First name _____
Residence _____ Work classif. ____ Year of birth ___ Ident. No. ___
Former primary profession _____ Specialization: _____
Trade schools and universities _____ Specialized training: _____
Experience in primary profession (duration, enterprise, function): _____
Former secondary profession _____ Specialization: _____
Practiced secondary profession (duration, company function): _____
Which of the listed professions have you practiced in Theresienstadt?
Date _____ Signature _____

Document 6. Printed Form from July 1943 (Double-Sided)

Theresienstadt Ghetto   To dept.: _____
    Council of Elders
Work assignment
This form is to be kept by the   Last and first name _____ Transp. _____ No _____
    department
                                  Year of Birth _____ Residence ____ Deployment ____

Is to be sent back to the
 Central
  Labor Office
As _____   Wage _____ Ration category _____
                                        Classif. No. _____
at the workplace _____   Assigned from: _____
A change in this assignment   To be included in the attendance list starting on this
 is   day
  allowed only with our
  permission!
                               On _____ 1943
File card   Squadron   Departmental confirmation: _____
 Ration card
Remarks by the room or   The certified person is to appear neither earlier nor
 house elder: _____   later than the day entered on the relevant attendance list
                                   or work report, which is listed in the relevant category on
                                   the front of this form. Should the start of work be delayed
                                   by a certified illness, this must be noted in the attendance
                                   list. The Central Labor Office must be informed
                                   immediately if the work is not done consistent with the
                                   assignment.

Document 7. Form Printed on Cardboard from March 1944 (One-Sided)

1) to the CLO-health office   2) on _____
3) to the Personnel Registry-Est Transport Number _____ Residence _____
Place of work   Summons _____
Disp. No.   Appear with this summons, the small health
Requested examination   card and worker' identification on _____
Type for work   at _____ o'clock at Hauptstr. 2, 1st Floor,
                                     Room A 15, for the purpose of a medical
                                     examination
Date. ___ Received ___   Date. _____ Registration No. _____
                                 Central Labor Office
                                 Public Health Office

These summonses were sent mainly to retrieve workers from factories for special
purposes, for example, barracks building, or to check their "work category."

Document 8. Mimeographed Identification Card from (May) 1942 (One-Sided)

Worker Identity Card
Trans. No. _____   Classif. _____   Year of Birth _____   Ident. No. _____
Last name: _____   Quarters: _____
Date _____   Employment _____   Confirmed _____

These identity cards had to be glued into one's identity document. Before May 8, 1942,
only handwritten identity cards on tiny pieces of paper or cardboard were used.

354   *Sociology*

Document 9. Mimeograph from April 1943: "Worker Identity Card" (Four-Sided)

This form included a four-sided insert, the "small health card" (see also 3b, doc. 119).

[Page 1]
Theresienstadt Ghetto
Worker Identity Card   Transport _____   No. _____
Last Name _____   First Name _____   Born on _____   Ration category _____
Quarters: _____
Date   lives at   Confirmed by the registry _____
[six lines of space for entries and records of changes of residence]
This worker identity card is to be inserted in the personal identity document.

[Page 2]
Classification of work:
Classification   Con[firmation] by Central Labor Office
[four lines for entries and amendments]
Employment:
Disposition No.   in _____ [department name]
from _____   to _____   as _____
Deployment site _____   Type of work _____
[space for two more employment entries, as above]

[Page 3]
[space for three more employment entries]
Remarks _____   Account No. _____ [for the "bank account"]

[Page 4]

Guidelines:

1. Every resident of the ghetto is required always to carry the workers identity card and to show it on request to authorized agents.
2. He is required to produce his worker identity card for official amendment: to the registry, in case of resettlement, to the deployment office, in case of changes in work detail, to the admissions office of the outpatient clinic, in case of illness, to the pharmacist, when various medications are taken, to the Central Labor Office, at reclassification [of one's "work category"].
3. In addition, he must ensure that his day off is entered in the worker identity card by the relevant department.
4. Failure to comply with the regulations listed above will be punished, as will changes made to the worker identity card by its bearer.

Issued on _____   194__   By _____
Certified by the Central Labor Office _____   Signature of the bearer _____

[A small health card, page 1]
        Name _____   Transp. _____   No. _____
        State of health
        Date   Clinic   Conclusion   Perm. to go out   Summoned
                                                                    Dr. at clinic
[fourteen spaces for entries]

[Page 2]

        [sixteen lines for entries]

Labor

[Page 3]
Drugs administered
Date   Administered   Pharmacist
[sixteen spaces for entries]

[Page 4]
Day off
on   from   to   o'clock   Personnel registry
[sixteen spaces in two columns for entries]

Beginning in April 1943, these identity cards replaced the one in document 8. Under "Conclusion" in the insert, doctors would enter "D," "C," "B," or "A." D stood for "bedridden," C stood for "ill and confined to quarters," B stood for "unfit for hard labor," and A stood for "healthy." "Going out" had to be approved by a doctor, who also determined when one could go out. If necessary, another insert was added.

Document 10. Printed Form from 1943 (One-Sided with Two Carbon Copies)

1   Central Labor Office Attendance List No _____ for the period from _____ to _____.   2   Employer: _____.   3.   Place of Work: _____.   4   Type of work: _____.   5   Number of workers M[en] W[omen] initially _____ newly arrived _____ departed _____ _____ at the end   6   [space] [For points 7 to 13, more than forty spaces follow, divided into numerous columns under the following entries:]   7   Consec. No.   8   Transport number   9   Last name   First name   Quarters   Account No.   10   Function   11   [Space is provided for entry of work hours during a *Dekade*; eleven columns are available, so as to include the thirty-first day of the third *Dekade* in odd months.]   12   Total hours Men Day Night Women Day Night   13   Remarks

The office responsible for a work group was required to submit these lists to the "Central Labor Office" at the end of the month. The entries were significant for determining "*Dekade* bonuses." The stubborn commitment to be fair to each worker, even though what each worker received was never enough, is what created this complicated system.

Document 11. Printed Form from 1943 (One-Sided with Two Carbon Copies)

Labor report for the Central Labor Office   1   Issuing department: _____   Sub-department: _____   Branch: _____   Building: _____   2   Number of workers _____ M _____ F _____ At the beginning of the work period _____ _____ _____ newly arrived _____ _____ _____ [with a line for the total] departed _____ _____ _____ at the end of the reporting period.   3   Department number _____   4   Month _____ 1943   5   Normal daily hours _____ Abbreviations I = 9½ hours, K = sick, U = on leave, O = unexcused [Sixteen lines of space follow in columns for points 6 through 15.]   6   Consec. No.   7   alphabetize!   Last name   First name   quarters   8   Personnel [= account number] No.   9   Trans. no.   10   Function   11   Wage (enter daytime hours in black, nighttime hours in red above.) [Space for thirty-one days follows, in which the number of hours or the symbol "K," and so on, are to be entered.]   13   Totals M F [In this way, the number of hours worked by men and women were listed in two separate columns.]   14   Amendments – Exact and complete entries must appear in column 14. For example: arrival (and departure) of a person must be entered: from where (to where) with the exact date!   15   Remarks [under these

columns] Brought forward [if more than one page is needed or] Total hours in all
M _____ F _____ 16 Processed by _____ 17 Signature of the department
head _____ 18 Signature of the Work Report Manager _____

These reports were used for "wage calculations" and statistical purposes.

Discussion

Nothingness (*Nichts*) cannot be organized, but in an attempt to create the semblance of something, a businesslike bustle developed, the psychological effects of which first numbed those in administrative positions and later spread to everyone, revealing a pathological character. An enormous amount of unproductive activity by numerous offices with overlapping powers placed great stress on the camp. When one considers the internal weaknesses and unwieldiness of this administration – with its constant new plans, new lists, perpetual monitoring and countermonitoring, mountains of paper filled with "memoranda," endless internal correspondence, records, reports, and statistics – it is surprising that anything at all was achieved. The fact that this small town of 30,000 residents had 16,500 workers who had to meet an extensive production schedule and an administration that, depending on the method of calculation, employed some 1,100 to 2,900 people had to have a crippling effect on working conditions. Everyone was in everyone else's way. There were plenty of decision makers, but no productive decision making. The normal prisoner did not understand this labyrinth, but even the functionaries understood it only vaguely. That is why, after the war, few were able to provide reliable information about the complex, interlocking apparatus. Without making any allusion to a particular metaphysical situation, one can almost make the comparison with the rationally incomprehensible authorities in Kafka's novels; and some really did call barracks B V – the headquarters of the "self-administration" – "the Castle." A simple prisoner who had to appear there was lost, and the officials were benumbed by the impression that they were working for a mysterious and strange enterprise, which led them to casually speak a coded language of a kind that no normal person could understand.

The administrative apparatus became an end in itself. Officials could not keep themselves from thinking according to the absurdities of a rigid structure and often took their positions extremely seriously, even if, as was the rule, they themselves did not perceive these positions as worthwhile. Efforts were made to hold the administration to civilian standards, the grotesque nonsense of which seemed alternatively demonic and tragicomic under the suzerainty of the SS. It was a fatal error to behave as if the world still was normal, rather than to defend against psychological infection and, in order to remain normal personally, to understand that this world was insane. Few managed to steer their sense of reality through these dangers unscathed. A delusional fascination was an enticement to bureaucratism, in which the memory of long-devalued norms was taken as proof that these norms still were intact and true. One wanted to command and to behave according to regulations, even though only common sense and practical reason could provide guidance. Thus the administration squandered its efforts; its hypertrophy was occasionally perceived, but all its reforms failed and usually created greater trouble. There were some reasonable people in the administration, but they were pressed into the system. Smart people, among them many intellectuals, were disgusted and preferred more healthy manual labor.

LABOR DEPLOYMENT STATISTICS II

We turn again to employment statistics. The share of inmates working in house services can be determined from the following groups:

	Personnel	Percent of the workforce
(Most of) building management	390	2.35
Warming kitchen staff	105	0.6
Cleaning service ("cleaning crews")	268	1.65
Assistants	90	0.55
Room orderlies	168	1.0
Groups for mobile deployment	520	3.15
House services total	1,541	9.3

The number of workers may have been lower, because the "building administration" (house elders, etc.) had a great deal of administrative work to deal with. Insofar as one can speak of "housekeeping," it almost always was taken care of privately and not by functionaries. The work of the "cleaning services" involved cleaning offices and workshops rather than quarters. The remaining house service workers were room orderlies, room elders, and the staff of the warming kitchens; together, these groups numbered 333 workers (2.1%). In the final statistics, we will assign the "warming kitchens" to welfare and care and leave room elders in administration. That leaves the room orderlies in their own group:

	Personnel	Percent of the workforce
Personal services	168	1

We will take the Economics Department as the next main group and divide it into consumer economy and production economy – that is, according to whether prisoners worked for the camp or for export. If a position served both purposes nearly equally, the numbers are entered into both subgroups. We count two-thirds of the "squadrons" as assigned to economics, and the last third are classified as public services.

	Personnel	Percent of the workforce
A. Consumer economy		
Economics Department		
Kitchen staff	433	2.6
Bakeries	258	1.6
Total nutrition occupations (including kitchen staff, bakeries, provisions, and others)	1,086	6.5
Stores, shops, etc.	314	1.9
Lumber warehouse (½)	14	0.1
Clothing warehouse (½)	22	0.1
Coffeehouse	47	0.3
Hairdressers	52	0.3
Collection point for laundry and mending	151	0.9

(continued)

(continued)

	Personnel	Percent of the workforce
Metalworking (½)	64	0.4
Wood processing (½)	132	0.8
Repairs (clothing, linens, shoes, etc.)	696	4.2
Central Laundry	317	1.9
Bag making (½)	9	0.05
Internal administration		
Mattress section of the Space Management Office	10	0.05
Mobile deployment		
Nutrition occupations	57	0.35
Warehouses, etc.	125	0.75
Clothing warehouse (½)	17	0.1
Tailors, darners, laundry sorting	58	0.35
Knitting home work (½)	23	0.1
Hand laundry	34	0.2
Squadrons (1/3)	577	3.5
All consumer economy groups		
TOTAL	3,804	~ 23.0
B. Production economy		
Economics Department		
Clothing warehouse (½)	23	0.1
Lumber warehouse (½)	15	0.1
Agriculture	451	2.7
Metalworking (½)	65	0.4
Wood processing (½)	132	0.8
Carton making	78	0.5
Cowhide and production of uniforms	53	0.3
Furnishings (handicrafts)	47	0.3
Ink powder bag filling	25	0.15
Mica splitting	2	
Youth Welfare Office		
Youth gardens (agriculture)	448	2.7
Mobile deployment		
Excavation work for the SS and other German offices	44	0.25
Various work for the SS and other Germans	101	0.6
Tree felling (agriculture)	17	0.1
Clothing warehouse (½)	17	0.1
Knitting home work (½)	22	0.1
Ink powder bag filling	13	0.1
Squadrons (1/3)	578	3.5
All production economy groups		
TOTAL	2,270	~ 13.0
All economy groups		
TOTAL	6,074	36.0

These figures emphasize how economically unproductive the camp was. Even though Theresienstadt was to be a "self-supporting ghetto" (*Versorgungsghetto*), it also was supposed to be productive. Tens of thousands of capable young people had been deported to the slaughterhouses in the East, while at the same time "production" was demanded of this camp; and it even managed to produce something, with scant personnel resources and the meager means of production at its disposal. On average, only one-eighth of the working prisoners were "earning" for the camp. These figures require some adjustment, however, because, at times, commissions such as "K production" and mica splitting achieved higher percentages. Occasionally other workers also accomplished productive feats, for example, those working in construction for the SS. On the other hand, working in the "clothing warehouse," where the theft of Jewish property was made economically useful to the SS, could not be described as production. Of course, it would be easy to isolate industries or enterprises from the rest of the economy, but, given conditions in the camp, that would not yield an accurate picture.

More than a fifth of the workers worked in production to meet daily needs. Most important were the nutrition occupations, which, taken together with their administrative offices – the "rationing service," "Kitchen Guard," and others – employed some 1,300 people, or about 8% of those working. The hairdressers were supposed to work without pay and solely cut hair, except for the elderly and the ill; hairdressing was not the lucrative job that it was in the concentration camps.

Work in actual productive enterprises was not nearly as profitable as jobs in the kitchens or storage areas, but it was easier than in stricter camps. The pace usually was fast but not murderous, and in general, there was no risk of physical or coarse verbal abuse. Strenuous work in the "Central Laundry" or "repair shops" offered advantages only when it was possible to take on "private" jobs. The "stores" were more profitable; there customers were given better goods for reciprocal services.

"Agricultural" jobs could involve either heavy or light work. Aside from the danger of being caught stealing or smuggling vegetables into the camp, there were considerable advantages. Workers enjoyed quite reliable protection from deportation, because the German head, who was not an SS member, behaved rather decently, successfully intervening repeatedly with the SS "office" on behalf of his people. It was considered a blessing to get outside the city walls and into the open air. Because the "agricultural" workers often needed help, a good arrangement was developed. Officially, there were no vacations, and often enough no days off. So it was made possible for workers in other departments to report for ten half days of agricultural work, which was known as "going on a *Dekade*." If one was lucky, one had the opportunity to bask in the sun and revive, but one might also be detailed to do hard labor within sight of the SS. The "youth gardens" were part of "agriculture" and offered young people an opportunity to work among the picturesque fortress moats. In all, 916 people, or 5.55% of the workforce, worked in "agriculture."

If we sum up the purely industrial enterprises – they were not factories but only workshops – we can see that, on any given day, there were only 700–800 people so engaged. Even though this number occasionally was exceeded by a considerable amount, it is clear how negligible "industry" was in the camp. A large share of production was for the benefit of the "ghetto," which somewhat mitigates the unusually disproportionate numerical relationship between administration and production. Only two workers were employed in manufacturing for each administrative worker.

Next we consider the public facilities and services:

	Personnel	Percent of the workforce
Management		
Fire department	51	0.3
Internal administration		
Cleaning service	268	1.6
Registry (deployment only = burial service)	60	0.55
Economics Department		
Chemical-technical laboratory	9	0.05
Central Bath	12	0.1
Technical Department		
Construction (engineers, electricians)	201	1.2
Road building	12	0.1
Water purification	6	0.05
Power (engineers, electricians)	111	0.7
Water Department (water supply)	62	0.4
Sewers	18	0.1
Plumbers, fitters (heating systems, etc.)	76	0.45
Garbage removal	7	0.05
Street cleaning	6	0.05
Building maintenance (skilled workers)	173	1.05
Mobile deployment		
Cleaning service, etc.	328	2.0
Paving and various excavation work	160	1.1
Street cleaning	39	0.2
Garbage removal, abattoir	24	0.15
Plumbers and fitters	6	0.05
Technical service (assistance to building maintenance)	122	0.7
Squadrons (1/3)	577	3.5
All public facilities and services		
TOTAL	2,348	~ 14.5

The preceding figures more or less correspond to those for normal towns with the same population. The number of people working for the "cleaning service" is striking, because they never succeeded in ridding the city of hopeless filth. Garbage removal, which had few workers and few vehicles, never could deal with all the trash that befouled the place. If one adds up the number of people employed to keep the town clean, one arrives at 821 people, or not quite 5% of all workers. The "cleaning crews" were composed of strong women, whereas "street cleaning" was the responsibility of elderly men.

The electricians were supervised by an "ethnic German," who behaved correctly. He and a Czech chimney sweep were the only civilians who came to the camp regularly. Besides the crematorium, the wooden barracks, and two wooden structures built for the "beautification," no new buildings were constructed. The shortage of skilled workers was severe, and the material supplied usually was substandard; therefore sound plans for new buildings and alterations never were satisfactorily carried out. The wooden barracks were built unprofessionally and would not have survived long, even had they not been destroyed at the end of the war.

The small number of personnel working at the baths should also be emphasized: there were 12 workers for 30,000 people, not considering those employed in the delousing bath.

The next group we will tabulate is transport and traffic:

	Personnel	Percent of the workforce
Internal administration		
Transport Management Department (deployment only)	19	0.1
Economics Department		
Shipping	12	0.1
Technical Department		
Railroads	7	0.05
Telephone operators	4	
Mobile deployment		
Transport service	27	0.15
Railroad maintenance	19	0.1
Shipping (for the Economics Department)	160	
All transport and traffic		
TOTAL	248	~ 1.5

This total could be augmented by adding several groups that we allocated differently. The postal service, the "Transport Management Department" ("personnel"), the "ration transport crew," and groups from "mobile deployment," a total of 387 workers, could have been included under traffic; the total then would be 639 people, or approximately 4%. Other transport work was dealt with by individual "departments." Squadrons, in particular, did a great deal of transportation work. During deportations, mass resettlements, and special assignments, the town resembled a disturbed anthill; sometimes at least a third of the inmates were required to help. Telephone operators worked in a central office in B V, which was connected to the SS and had several subdivisions in top internal offices and at the fire department. Private telephone calls were forbidden.

"Shipping" counted as a permanent transport group for public freight, and the driving crews from the "Transport Management Department" did the same for private freight. Shipping workers had great advantages because of their contact with the outside world and also because they had many opportunities for dishonest manipulation. The work was hard, had to be done rapidly, and frequently required large amounts of overtime. Initially, heavy loads were shipped on rented vehicles managed by outsiders; later, only SS tractors were used. Shipping groups did the loading. Carts, wheelbarrows, and hand trucks were used to transport freight internally, along with, especially, more than fifty decommissioned hearses, which gave the town its characteristic image. Due to the shortage of vehicles in the camp, the SS ordered that hearses from disbanded rural Jewish communities in the "Protectorate" be sent to Theresienstadt. After they arrived, the coaches, which were completely unsuited for the purposes they were expected to serve, deteriorated quickly and soon were in deplorable condition. Initially, they still had their tall riggings with pillars, corniced roofs, and impractical drivers' boxes. Later, the bodywork was removed and often sloppily sawed off, so that only stumps of the pillars remained. The decorative trim broke and fell off; the black-and-silver paintwork faded. Some coaches had been modified so that only the lower portion betrayed their earlier purpose. The vehicles were numbered with whitewash and assigned to individual departments, which often added additional lettering; thus one might see a vehicle marked "Central Bakery," "Central Supply," "Butcher," "Delousing," "Youth Welfare," or "Roofing Express." Because there were no horses, one or two people pulled the shaft, while four to eight others pushed the loaded carriage. Frequently, these groaning and swaying vehicles were operated by elderly men and women or by children. During the day, these vehicles pushed their way slowly and sluggishly through the overcrowded streets. Hearses in Theresienstadt were meant to be used by the living, whereas coffins carrying the dead (up to thirty at a time) were driven from the mortuary to the crematorium by a Czech coachman on an open, horse-drawn carriage (see 3b, pp. 188 and 209).

Another group was composed of those responsible for health and hygiene:

	Personnel	Percent of the workforce
Economics Department		
Bandages and orthopedic workshop	10	0.05
Health Services Department		
Hospitals, sickrooms, outpatient clinics, etc.	2,383	14.4
Central medications storage	35	0.2
Central dental technology	24	0.1
Public health officer, coroner, etc.	145	0.9
Delousing (disinfection)	119	0.7
Mobile deployment		
Various service workers	62	0.4
Delousing assistants	31	0.2
Ironing of infectious linens	7	0.05
Pharmaceutical-bottle washers	3	
All health and hygiene		
TOTAL	2,819	~ 17.0

It is unlikely that this ratio ever was achieved in any other community, whether a city or a camp. If we combine the figures for administration and health services – a total of 6,200 people – they exceed the number of people employed in productive enterprises – 6,106. For every 1,000 workers, 170 were dedicated to the sick, day in and day out, and there was nearly one "health service" worker for every ten inmates! Even if disinfection workers are left out, 2,500 doctors, nurses, and aides remain. Chapter 16 shows these workers had more than a little to do – they were overextended.

We include the following groups in the category of welfare and care:

Labor

	Personnel	Percent of the workforce
Internal administration		
Assistants	90	0.55
Warming kitchen workers	105	0.6
Health Services Department		
Welfare	245	1.5
Nurseries (*Kindergarten*)	25	0.15
Youth Welfare Office		
Homes and nurseries (child care workers, etc.)	549	3.35
Welfare	42	0.25
Mobile deployment		
Nurseries (*Säuglingskurs*)	9	0.05
Support personnel in homes	42	0.25
Warming kitchens, support	5	
All health and welfare		
TOTAL	1,087	~ 7.0

Care workers in the "Health Services Department" and "Youth Welfare Office" served the same role for nonworkers as "workers' welfare" (*Arbeiterbetreuung*) did for all workers, and their approximately fifty officials can be allotted to this group. But those charged with "welfare" (*Fürsorge*) had many more responsibilities than those who carried out "workers' welfare."

Because teaching was officially banned, it was provided illegally by teachers who were called "youth counselors" and "home leaders." Therefore, the system of education cannot be portrayed statistically, but the number of educators can be estimated at some 200 people – employees of the "Youth Welfare Office" and "Recreation Department" – or 1.2% of all workers.

We present figures for the members of the "Recreation" Department as follows:

	Personnel	Percent of the workforce
Independent professions	276	~ 1.7%

This group, which was unusual for a camp, grew to this size only during the "beautification." For a long time it was merely tolerated and had only part-time and volunteer workers. Members of the "town band" and library workers, as well as actors, musicians, lecturers, and others, can be included in this group. Support workers and civil service administrators must be subtracted, whereas some draftsman, the staff of the medical library, some "Youth Welfare Office" employees, and the rabbis who worked in the registry must be added.

Now we present a table that approximates the actual distribution of jobs in the summer of 1944:

	Personnel	Percent of the workforce[*]
Administration	3,441	21.0
Economics Department	6,106	36.0
Public facilities and services	2,348	14.5

(continued)

Sociology

(*continued*)

	Personnel	Percent of the workforce[*]
Transport and traffic (excluding the postal service)	248	1.5
Health and hygiene	2,819	17.0
Welfare and care	1,087	7.0
Independent professions	276	1.7
Personal services	168	1.0
Workforce total	16,493	100

[*] All figures in this column are approximate.

Some categories in normal occupational statistics do not appear here; trade, for example, which could be extrapolated imprecisely and misleadingly from groups under the "Economics Department" and liaison offices such as those for "workers' welfare" and "welfare." If only the stores are included, one would obtain a count of ninety people (0.55%). The number of craftspeople is another figure that is difficult to calculate. These workers are distributed between the "Economics Department" and the "Technical Department." Hospitality is omitted because the "coffeehouse," with its forty-seven employees (0.3%), and the kitchen serving stations cannot be classified in such a category. This pseudocommunist society also rendered the concept of free professions dubious; every position was assigned, and everyone was an employee of the "Jewish self-administration." Nor can the exact number of "workers" and "civil service administrators" be provided in the strict sense. Thus, almost all the professions and jobs found in a contemporary, normal society existed in Theresienstadt, although in modified form, or they were replaced by professions that, in a different social order, would have been impossible in this form, even in a slaveholding or socialist or communist society. The uniqueness of this "ghetto" was dictated by the fact that quasi-normal conditions were combined in an exceedingly complex fashion with the establishment of a concentration camp.

The social structure of the coerced community at the height of its development truly becomes clear in an overview of the general population. The following table provides an overview of the working and nonworking population of Theresienstadt on June 30, 1944:

	Prisoners	Percent of prisoner population
Workers	16,493	58.23
Nonworkers	11,309	41.77
Total	27,702	100.00

At that time, the Welfare Department looked after some 8,000 people, or around 30% of the inmates, but a small portion of this group was included in the work process. Among those being cared for were 1,638 disabled veterans (6.6% of all prisoners), including 881 people who were completely disabled (3.9%); 1,398 cripples (around 5.8%); and 333 people who were blind (1.2%). More than 4,450 people (more than 17%) were over sixty-five, and more than 2,650 (some 9.7%) were children under sixteen. Around 12,000 inmates (43%) were male and more than 15,700 (57%) were female.

Labor

Information about "work deployment" during the final days is provided by a document likely prepared for the monthly report on March 1, 1945. It also mentions the construction project at the ravelins – the planned gas chambers and mass execution sites:

Work deployment.
In its current state, Work Deployment includes:

4,040 men	6,558 women

Experience indicates that a sickness rate of 15% is to be expected, so that actual work deployment will be

3,434 men	5,574 women

The distribution of Work Deployment appears in the following table:

	Men	Women	Total
Outside Work[*]	20	–	20
Agriculture	82	415	497
Manufacturing	636	3,116	3,752
Public Facilities and Works	1,559	195	1,754
Internal Supply	435	558	993
Health Services	385	873	1,258
Security and Registration	85	121	206
Cleaning and Building Administration	266	627	893
House and Support Services	537	569	1,106
Administration	35	84	119
Total Deployment	4,040	6,558	10,598

[* After the Zossen barracks builders returned on February 10, 1945, "outside work" was done only by a small group who lived in the camp and worked during the day in the vicinity (most likely in Leitmeritz [Litoměřice]). No workers were sent on overnight assignments outside the camp until after March 10, 1945, when 102 wooden barracks builders left Theresienstadt and returned on April 20, 1945, from Regen and Schnarchenreuth bei Hof in Bavaria.]

In the "Public Works" group, the building groups should be particularly highlighted (wooden barracks building, *Südberg* and West Barracks, Ravelin XI, Ravelin XVIII, silk worm breeding, etc.). All the men from the final transports who are able to work, if they have no special skills, are included in this group. Of the women who arrived on the final transports, large cohesive groups are employed primarily in mica production, at the Central Laundry, in agriculture and in the clothing warehouse.

The number of personnel in Work Deployment [formerly called the "Central Labor Office"] currently consists of:

	16	men
	43	women
Special Deployment:	9	men

The 119 people listed under "Administration" are comprised of the staff of the Secretariat and of Work Deployment. Including the Secretariat and the Work Deployment, the actual administration consists of 652 persons. (258)

During this period, "production" experienced an upswing, and, after the collapse of autumn 1944, the size of the "administration" shrank. The preceding table, too, must be viewed with caution; it does not lend itself to in-depth analysis. The still-high percentage of workers in the "health services" (around 11.5%) and the reduced size of the "security services," which was down to only a few men, are noteworthy. In February 1945, the number of inmates increased from 12,714 to 15,681, which had to have an effect on "work deployment." At the end of the month, around 9,000 people were working, which was not quite 57.5% of the prisoners—proportionally, a ratio similar to that of summer 1944 but, in absolute figures, a much greater burden on the workers, because the same amount of work, and in some branches much more, had to be completed with 6,500 fewer people than before (see also 299a).

Work carried out by women was particularly important in Theresienstadt. They worked in nearly all areas and were not spared hard labor, for example, in "squadrons." Only women were used for mica splitting, and they also were heavily represented in agriculture. In contrast, only a few worked in the kitchens and in similar workplaces. In the final quarter of 1944 and in January 1945, nearly all the work was being done by women. But no women ever became members of the Council of Elders, nor did women hold leading positions in the administration. Insight into the issue is provided by lecture notes by a female staff member of the "Central Labor Office"; the conditions described are those that could be observed in January 1944.

Working Women in Theresienstadt

I. *General picture*
How many women are there?

Women in Theresienstadt:	tally on January 31, 1944	21,653
of whom	13,523	62.5% are from the German Reich
of which	8,130	37.5% are from the Protectorate

For the sake of simplicity, foreigners and stateless women have been included with women from the German Reich [including Austrian women]

The proportion of women of the whole	36,478
is therefore on average	60%
The proportion of women from the German Reich among all people from the German Reich is	64%
The proportion of women from the Protectorate among all people from the Protectorate is	52.6%

. . . .

II. *Age distribution (31 Dec. 1943)*

Are the women young or old?

(Protectorate women younger)

Age	G.R.	%	Prot.	%	Tot.	%	Vienna 1920
0–15	555	4.1	964	11.9	1,519	7.1	16.9
16–45	2,476	18.3	4,031	49.5	6,507	30.1	56.3
46–60	3,649	27.1	1,813	22.3	5,465	25.2	17.3
over 61	6,843	50.5	1,322	16.3	8,165	37.6	9.5
Totals	13,523	100	8,130	100	21,653	100	100

Explanation: ratio for German Reich according to type of internment.
ratio for the Protectorate is normal with fewer elderly due to deportation of the elderly and higher mortality rate.

Labor   367

Average age of women: 50½ years (31 January 1944)
            Vienna 1920:   33½ years

For orientation:
Deportation from home – Internment – Adaptation – development until today.

III.   *Women and Families*

Not general adjustment issues, but only additional issues specific to women.

1. Loss of own home
    Dissolution of family life
2. Attitude toward work
on 1)
    a) Disruption as a whole
    b) Separation of family (most serious)
Camp life: Complete separation of men and women (women's prison)
    Consequences: apathy, neglect, attacks of hysteria
    Relief: carrying suitcases
    Awakening of vanity
    Tightening of the family unit (insecurity)
    (as they say: There have never been so many good marriages.)
    Opening of the city – loosening
    Elderly living together in houses
    Differentiated living quarters
    Daily meeting of families. Streams of women pour into the men's barracks, an
        unfamiliar picture.
    Illusion of family life
    Simultaneously through living parallel rather than together:
    Loosening of the family unit
    Children's homes
    Separation from children
    Initial mistrust
    Today: total number of children up to 16 (December 31, 1943)   3,367
             in homes   1,969
             with their mothers   1,398

Mothers with children up to 18 years old (September 1943)

with children	7	6	5	4	3
	1	3	3	34	70

on 2)
Women in Work Deployment

Duty to work and regulations
Exemption from duty (temporary and permanent)
    a) mothers with children up to 3 years old
    b) medical cases
    c) welfare cases
Relief: (4-hour deployment)
    a) mothers with children from 4–6 years old
    b) medical cases
    c) welfare cases (war-wounded)
    d) aged, over 60

368 *Sociology*

Tally of current work deployment (monthly average January 1944)   10,981 women

Ratio of women's and men's deployment:

For every 1,000 working men there are

1,180	working	women	in Theresienstadt, January 1944
550	"	"	in Germany 1933/1934
460	"	"	in Poland 1921
275	"		Jewish women in Poland 1921

How did we get the first women to work?

1. For men, work always primary.
   Women as a rule in the home, only single women pursued careers, mainly in commerce (traditional prejudices)
2. Woman in the home – queen – dependent on no one.
   Now we demand discipline, work not for her, but for the community.
   Necessary: to awaken feelings of community in the women, at least within the barracks
3. Psychological Factor (problem in the ghetto: seeing the family).
   Cleaning- and potato crews in men's barracks.
   Deployment offices: mediation offices

Similar problem with later transports, but order and organization already exist:

Squadron – Convoy – Squadron of Cadres
For every 1,000 women present, on the dates below there were

January 1, 1942	270	in work deployment
July 1, 1942	310	
January 1, 1943	340	
July 1, 1943	490	
January 1, 1944	520	

For every 1,000 women of working age, 850 were actually deployed.

Explanation:
1. The duty to work alters previous, normal conditions (dissolution of the family; all work seen as obligatory).
2. The share of women in the entire population is far higher than usual.
   What work did the women do before?
   What are they doing today?
   Occupational groups within Theresienstadt (according to their own figures) (tendentiously – no saleswomen at all)
   Of all women working at the moment, only 40% gave an occupation, 60% had no profession or worked in own household.

Previous profession (training):

In,	1st	place, as office staff (employees of the Community)
	2nd	as craftsperson
	3rd	as nurse, caregiver
	4th	as independent professional (artist, teacher)
	5th	as laborer
	6th	as cook

The same women work today in the following jobs:

Labor   369

In 1st   place, 2,600 manual support workers (squadron, cadre, cleaning, transport)
    2nd   1,900 workers in workshops or facilities (laundries, manufacturing, etc.)
    3rd   1,540 nurses and care givers
    4th   1,520 house service
    5th   1,300 administrative
    6th   620 in economic facilities such as supply, kitchens, etc.
    7th   540 service workers (order [OD], ration service [MD], cleaning service [RD])
    8th   510 youth counselors
    9th   300 in agriculture
    10th   450 various (including 107 physicians, 63 saleswomen)

Chronological development of work:
  Each job is only valued according to its value to the community.

1. Large-scale household work (in economic facilities, kitchens, etc.)
2. Workshop jobs (for example tailors, glove crocheting, crafts)
3. Light men's work (staff shortages due to outside work, shipping, bed building, supply transport, etc.)
4. Agriculture – Pürglitz [forestry in spring 1942]
   1. Female Jewish workers for once in competition with the outside world
   Problem of tearing apart families – substitute: group of friends
   1. Transport put together by Central Labor Office and without Schleuse.
5. Increasing production: mica breaking, notions, carton making, ink powder bag filling, uniform spraying
   Possible work for the blind as well.
6. Importance of cleaning service increased after takeover of town.
7. Nurses (transport of the elderly)
   First as support service, hundreds of women day and night.
   Later: permanent staff of the Health Service

How do women work?

Performance.
Job satisfaction – work ethic.
Job satisfaction, if in proper deployment and in job corresponding to her nature and skills.
Initially: arbitrary deployment
Later: suitability tests
Proportion of trained people in the groups:

For example youth counsellors	246	
of whom	119	trained,
	98	retrained,
	47	untrained.

1. Performance of women in the ghetto in comparison with performance of women outside the ghetto.
   Compare productivity with enterprises outside the ghetto.
   Wage rate set 20% lower than outside. Reason: nutrition situation, living conditions.
2. Women's performance adequate compared to men's performance in the ghetto.
   Differences in wage: 30% for the same wage classification.
   Concept not very modern.

Alternative concept by Central Labor Office.
Same work – same productivity – unequal pay.
 Greater productivity of women.
 Additional burdens. Rations, accommodations, clothing.
 Recognition: taking on this increased productivity as a matter of course (202a)

WORKING CONDITIONS AND OVERALL PRODUCTION

Every job was officially assigned. The workers were employed by either the "Jewish self-administration," the Jewish Elder, or the Council of Elders. As employer, the Jewish Elder was represented by department heads and by the "Central Labor Office." Self-employment was banned, but during the initial period it occurred frequently and also happened later in occasional cases (see 146b). Obedience was demanded: "Each task must be quickly, dutifully, attentively and carefully executed." In reality, the pressure on subordinates was frequently no greater than in a normal society. Respect for superiors might even have been rarer in Theresienstadt than in a free society, but open disobedience was infrequent. Generally, directives were complied with to the extent that the work absolutely required it. Many workers relied on insight and instinct to avoid overexerting themselves and instead to do as much as necessary, which was, anyway, a great deal. This caused many to overwork and become ill. Many fled into sickness or simulated illness in order to gain a vacation. One could expect superiors and doctors to be understanding as long as one did not abuse this expedient. Sudden orders to do unexpected work during expected free time were unwelcome. The physician in charge – and, if necessary, the public health officer – decided who was fit for work. Unexcused absences and other violations of the regulations were dealt with using both disciplinary and penal measures (see Chapter 15).

The attitude toward work underwent major fluctuations. When people still believed the camp could be built up, or if there were longer pauses between transports, an optimistic and honest desire to work became evident. Gradually this disappeared almost entirely, but people assumed responsibility for the essentials. Some hoped to dull or overcome their worries through work; others were indifferent or negatively disposed. Among the Dutch and the new arrivals in 1945, one occasionally observed a virtually anarchic negativism. During transport periods, labor discipline suffered greatly, and, during the respites, people strove to prove to their superiors that they were "indispensable." Conscious sabotage was rare. People understood that it was pointless and that it could only harm the camp, especially as production for the war economy was negligible – a game that can be assessed as sabotage of Germany's war aims by the SS (but not by the Jews). Sometimes an overeager Jewish supervisor or official from the "Work Monitoring Department" would call an incomplete or sloppy job sabotage, but this could not be taken seriously.

Relations between superiors and subordinates usually were neither particularly good nor bad. Solidarity without consideration of position was rare, but it always came through immediately when confronted with the SS. At work there was much complaining and arguing, but people calmed down and made up quickly, because the irritability usually was caused by nothing more than general nervousness and exhaustion. Among hard laborers a coarse tone prevailed; off-color jokes were no less common than is the norm in all camps, among prisoners, and in the military. Strict masters rarely got their way with a squadron. Administrative employees were also servile; superiors' birthdays were marked by Byzantine affairs involving collective gifts, thank-you speeches, and poorly rhymed birthday wishes. Gossip spread in offices, and intrigues were common. The situation was much better among workers. The informal form of address (*Du-Ansprache*) was not generally used and was taken for granted only among young people and younger workers. Social differences, the wide variety of age groups, and the presence of men and women in the camp contributed to a preference for the formal form of address using *Sie*.

> Show up for work deployment at quarter to seven. Eighteen of us get the assignment "salvage." You walk through the whole town ..., present your pass at the barrier, say the number, get a foreman and a gendarme, and continue for a few minutes in complete darkness, crowd into a wooden hut and wait until it's light enough to see. Then you recognize the big dung heap, the public garbage dump, and the collection point ... there since the camp came into being. Suddenly a job from the Office: Sort empty cans. Sardine cans to the left, paste cans to the right. The sardine cans are to be melted down for zinc. Work decisive for victory in the war.... "Berta, look, what a good pot." "Leave it, it's junk." "But we don't have a container for water." A shrug. After not much more than a week we have the most wonderful household items. There's nothing you can't find in such a trash heap: a wash basin, pots, spoons, a salt cellar, a wonderful metal container, a pullover, even a curling iron. The tableware can be boiled.... There are bearable jobs, and some that are not.... We no longer notice how low we have actually sunk, how much any sense of proportion has been lost.... Then you get ordered to transport management and get the task of cleaning out empty garrets the residents of which long since have been deported. There's always something to find there, a shawl, a dress ... officially it's supposed to be brought to the collection point, where it is picked through again [*geschleust*] and officially sorted. Then it all goes to the laundry, where it's picked through, officially washed, then to the pressers, where it's picked through again, officially ironed, and sent on to welfare, where it's picked through again. Hardly anything ever gets allocated. You need to file a petition, but it's just ignored. Then you follow up. Then you're called in. And after all that, you don't end up getting anything anyway. Finally, an on-call day. That means no work assignment, so you can scrub, wash windows, and properly and thoroughly wash clothes and get your hands into a condition that's worthy of a human being. If some unforeseen work comes up ... then you get called.... Some phantom from Deployment comes by and says, for example, "Girls, one of you has to come along." And then we draw lots. (257)

Here we provide an overview of the entire infrastructure produced and maintained in the course of the camp's three and a half years. Twelve barracks and 162 civilian houses – in addition to factory buildings, houses for the SS, and numerous ancillary buildings and storehouses – were taken over and maintained. The crematorium; four wooden barracks complexes, with nineteen double-wall insulated and four single-wall wooden barracks; five additional wooden barracks; one pavilion for children; and one music pavilion were erected, in addition to numerous building modifications for the camp and for the ever-demanding SS. In addition, 2,850 meters of track were laid, including a coke-loading ramp and a provisional ramp. Roadwork included the "bypass road" (543 × 9 m), the crematorium access road (267.5 × 4 m), and an access road to the "Südbaracken" (South Barracks) (200 × 5 m). Several water-distribution systems were taken over; these included a well with a capacity of 3 liters per second, a water tower that could hold 337 m³, a water main 460 m in length, and a 5 km long water-distribution network to which the larger barracks and sixteen houses were connected. Three new wells were drilled, 860 m of new water mains were laid, the distribution network was expanded by 11.5 km, and 196 houses were connected to it. The sewer system was improved by the construction of 1.5 km of new pipe. A chlorination plant with a basin 135 x 4 m around and 1 m deep and a pumping station 8 x 6.4 m in size were built. The transfer station for electricity was expanded, three new transformers were built, and the power grid was expanded. Buildings for "agriculture" included concrete silos, six containers with a capacity of 59 m³, four fire-extinguishing ponds, one park, and 300 benches. All public facilities had to be maintained, adapted for enormous overuse, and repeatedly altered. The fire department; crematorium; heating plant, with its attached delousing bath, central bath, and laundry; and more all required so much work! Supply facilities – bakeries, large-scale kitchens, butcher shops, and so on – had to be expanded and maintained; manufacturing operations and workshops had to keep filling new orders and frequently had to change their entire production; hospitals, outpatient clinics, and sanitary facilities had to be built from scratch; accommodations, offices, and workshops had to be set up; the oversized administration had to be run; and so on – not to mention the work involved in carrying out the horrible transports.

Had the sum of the diligence and energy of tens of thousands of Jews not been applied in the shadow of doom and of a purposeful wish to exterminate them, this effort – the only point of which was the self-assertion of the prisoners by often mistaken means – would not have had to succumb to nothingness in its struggle for something. In Theresienstadt, however, perhaps not for all individuals but certainly for the whole group, work became not a blessing but a curse.

14

Economy

Movement of Goods

Each resident is basically ... entitled to the same lodging and provisions, as well as necessary clothing and personal items.

About 350 rail cars arrive each month ... to meet these requirements. Perishable foodstuffs equaling 85 rail carloads are brought in by truck from the surrounding area each month.

.... A special work group is responsible for unloading the goods. The Central Warehouse is responsible for recording, taking possession of and administering the arriving goods.

Bread, flour and foodstuffs are delivered to the Central Provision Warehouse while potatoes are secured in the large cellars of the individual buildings. Bread is supplied to individual bread storehouses according to priority lists and then distributed by the buildings organization. Sugar, margarine and also, when needed, salt are packed at the rationing station and immediately passed on to the distribution points.

The Central Provision Warehouse delivers to the kitchens and bakeries the necessary ingredients for the preparation of meals.

Meats are stored directly in the butcher shops, from which the individual kitchens take delivery.

Milk for small children and the sick is likewise delivered directly to the individual distribution points.

Fuel is stored in the cellars of individual buildings. Lignite intended for the central heating system is kept in the storeroom attached to the boiler works.

Factories that use construction materials take them directly from the Central Warehouse, or they are kept until needed in the storehouses of the construction department, the water works, or the plumbing department.

The quantities of wood for construction and production purposes are properly finished in the wood storehouse and then distributed to the workshops as needed. During the year 1943, 74% of the permitted use of wood went to manufacturing and external projects, while 26% was used for construction and other projects internally.

Equipment and other materials are moved from the Central Material Warehouse to the materials administration units ... and delivered to the buildings organization for distribution.

Materials issued during 1943 amounted to ... 240,000 pieces of tableware and other household items, 100,000 bars of soap [about two bars per person!], and 74,000 kilograms of laundry detergent and other chemical and technical supplies.

In 1943 ... some 33,000 inventoried items were distributed, including 5,809 beds, 7,479 chairs, 3,158 tables, 3,061 cabinets [averaging one table or cabinet for every twelve to fifteen persons, even in offices and factories!], and 1,961 chairs.

(274)

We consider three aspects of the economy:

1. The external economy: Economic relations between the camp and the outside world, importing and exporting through the SS office
2. The internal economy: The movement of goods that served not individuals but the entire camp community, as well as connections between the "departments" in which the procurement, maintenance, production, delivery, and consumption of goods occurred
3. Small enterprises: Connections between the inmates and the organs of self-administration whereby individuals obtained goods, as well as other business conducted among the prisoners

EXTERNAL ECONOMY

Internally, the "ghetto" was similar to a communist or quasi-communist society with collective means of production. Private property was severely restricted to clothing and a few other personal articles, rationed consumer goods, and – the sole legal loophole within the system – packages received through the mail. The system of graduated distribution of community goods to consumers was established by authoritarian decrees issued by the Jewish Elder, the unelected head of the community, or his organs. Internally, these decrees counted as law. Neither an individual nor an institution within the community had veto power; the most that was possible was to register an objection or request through a strictly controlled complaint process. No legal recourse existed to change authoritarian decisions. Contravention of their decisions brought the risk of punishment by the organs of the Jewish Elder, although in many cases violations were tolerated and sometimes tacitly approved.

The "ghetto" itself was able neither to maintain itself nor to receive or produce needed goods. The camp also was unable to barter for necessary supplies with the goods it produced itself. Originally, it was the intention of the camp leaders to produce an amount of barter goods sufficient to maintain the camp. Edelstein's ideas were worthy; however, they incorrectly took into account the greed of the SS, which in Theresienstadt was satisfied by exploiting the Jewish workforce for German wartime production only a little and very inefficiently. To the extent that enslaved Jews in all camps were engaged in this process, it was unsystematic and mindless, and in constant conflict with the primary tendency toward extermination, which was further obscured in Theresienstadt by the camp's propagandistic purposes, but which generally triumphed over rational purposes.

Insofar as one can speak of a partnership between two peoples, in the territory of the Reich this relationship generally no longer existed between Jews and Germans. This became especially true from the outbreak of the war and was completed with the internment of the Jews. By this point they were entirely separated from Germans and other ethnic groups, and there was nothing resembling any kind of normal personal or business relationship. The Germans created a "ghetto" for the Jews in Theresienstadt, which, aside from its name, had nothing in common with historical ghettos. It was a type of imprisonment, yet it was sociologically unlike any other prison. Jews were banished behind the closed gates of the concentration camp and were allowed a sort of constitution through the "self-administration." Thus the "ghetto" of Theresienstadt represented an unprecedented socioeconomic unit. The "ghettoized" prisoners were legally forbidden any business connections with the outside world, and, in practice, such connections were nearly impossible. Thus partnership was replaced by servitude, or barely disguised slavery – but in the "Protectorate" (among other places), this situation had been prepared before the creation of the "ghetto." The German rulers selected Jewish representatives from the Jews' autonomous bodies as their only permissible partners. Thus the SS coerced the Jews, even before their imprisonment, into an antecedent form of what would come, controlling them through functionaries who were authorized as partners but represented nothing more than the long arm of SS rule; they were robbed of any power of their own but empowered by those rulers. This displacement of power onto a partner nullified any genuine partnership, for helplessness and lack of rights can coexist with monstrous power only in a relationship of submission. The outcome is submissiveness or slavery – instead of partnership, orders and obedience, even if it is a reluctant, secretly sabotaged obedience. Consequently, the Jewish representatives were degraded into mere tools, but they did not need to be weak willed. The rulers were in fact convinced of their tools' unbroken will and therefore sought to tame or to break it. Measures used included threats, violence, deceit, persuasion, and bribery for short-term advantage. The Jewish representatives had few means at their disposal with which to enforce their will, but they bore an enormous responsibility. Their own personalities were all they had, and with almost superhuman engagement they used these to struggle with those in power. This fundamentally unequal struggle had some small expectation of success only if the responsible personality were filled with reliable moral principles, for the smallest misstep would deliver him inescapably into the hands of the ruler. The representative needed to be smart, quick-witted, and cunning, to be able at any moment to take advantage of his opponents' psychology, if he hoped, in his helplessness, to win some influence. We do not need to describe again the situation in Theresienstadt. The representatives became ever weaker and were completely defenseless against the SS.

Because no real partnership existed, economic relationships resembled those between master and servant. The Jewish Elder nominally saw to the camp economy. In the outside world, the elder's economic sector was known as "the commander of the Security Police and SD, Central Office for the Regulation of the Jewish Question in Bohemia and Moravia, Theresienstadt Office." In this way, the "ghetto" was only an annex of an office that, as buyer and seller of commodities, acted as a company that needed and disposed of consumer goods. In its relation to the "ghetto" as an economic unit, the SS "office" did not resemble a firm. It supplied nothing from its own stores but instead purchased goods for the community. In this sense the SS "office" acted primarily as an administrative office and middleman and could not be compared with agencies and trade institutions in a normal society. From the SS "office's" perspective, the "ghetto" was an economic enterprise with sections, and the working inmates were forced laborers. The SS "office" could also be seen as a representative authority safeguarding German interests in regard to the "ghetto," and, conversely, safeguarding the "ghetto's" interests vis-à-vis the outside world.

Organizationally, the SS "office" was divided into three parts, which largely corresponded to the social structure of the state within a state that the SS had created in the "Reich Security Main Office" (RSHA). The subjugated sectors of the Reich and, even more so, the conquered territories – all of which were as much concentration camps as the "Jewish settlement area" in Theresienstadt – had to be governed, which meant that they had to be (1) administered, (2) economically operated or secured, and (3) protected, in their desired state, against potential enemies from within or without. In the "ghetto," the administrative, economic, and security departments within the SS "office" were responsible for these tasks.

Beyond this general review, it is not necessary to study the sociology of the SS and its RSHA, or even just the SS command structure of the Jewish camps in Theresienstadt. But it is important to understand the legal institutions of the coerced community as correlates, and always as implementers, of the various social functions for which the SS "office" provided the paradigms, and which were unified, in authoritarian form, in both the office itself and the individual head of the SS office. This authority had only limited power, as it was dependent on superiors in Prague and Berlin, but this fact had little relevance to the ongoing operation of the self-administration and the everyday activities of the camp. The pseudoautonomous internal government of the "ghetto" was an administration of slaves imposed on a slave community; the leaders were appointed from the midst of this community, or were at least legalized, by the masters. This dependence, as it was reflected and perpetuated inwardly from the outside through institutional correlates, was expressed most perfectly in the economic sphere, because in this realm the relationships could be least impaired, psychologically or through their impulses of will, by the prisoners. This makes sense: the prisoners and the SS generally (although not always) had opposing concepts of camp security and different views of administration, which was decisive; but however differently one may see the economy, it operates primarily on the basis of practical considerations. Thus in this area, despite diametrically opposed intentions, practical cooperation emerged between the two sides; they depended on each other, like it or not. The SS's authority gave it tremendous strength, but that alone was not enough; at the same time, the Jewish functionaries, in this area even more than elsewhere, had to acknowledge the real situation if they hoped to at the very least ensure the continued existence of the camp.

Thus the economic departments of the "ghetto" and of the SS "office" had to cooperate closely. It is difficult to determine just how independently the SS "office" functionaries were allowed to operate. It is clear that most exploited their position for their own gain, but some occasionally showed understanding of the needs of the camp. The office director decided the most important issues if no higher functionaries interfered. The camp had no freedom in its economic relations with the outside world, and almost none internally; formally and nominally, everything was taken care of by the SS "office." Minor issues and the disposition of ongoing business transactions were assigned to the German and the Jewish "economics departments" so as not to burden relations between the Jewish Elder and the office director.

Karl Schliesser, who headed the camp's Economics Department from December 1941 until his deportation at the end of September 1944, was a wood industry

Economy 377

specialist and a shrewd businessman of above-average talent. All the threads of the economic activities in the "ghetto" came together in his hands. It cannot be denied that he was successful in obtaining essential necessities. Nevertheless, it is unfortunate that Edelstein picked this man, because Schliesser was neither particular about the means he chose nor guided in the least by ideals. He was among those primarily responsible for the corruption in the camp. He served his masters with skill and prudence, which helped secure many things for the camp; but this benefited not the wider community but a select group of minions. Schliesser was perhaps the most powerful man in the "ghetto" – at least behind the scenes. He had to appear at the SS "office" every day to report on the progress of SS orders, the running of operations, the supply situation, and production; to discuss economic and business correspondence; and to receive orders. All correspondence exchanged with outside firms, and also with authorities if the subject was related to business matters – inquiries, responses, orders, and so on – was prepared in the camp by Jewish officials by order of the SS "office" but always was signed and remitted by German officials. Thus the self-administration of the camp was, from an economic perspective, a dependent apparatus utilized by the SS, although to some extent in the interests of the prisoners.

The SS exploited the "ghetto's" goods, as well as the work, competence, and inventive talent of the Jews for partly and purely private purposes. German soldiers bled to death, allegedly for the fatherland; the civilian population was "deployed," allegedly to the last man, for the sake of the German war economy; and in Theresienstadt, the Jews completed important work for a war that was allegedly their fault. Meanwhile, the gentlemen of the SS lived well in the "ghetto," as in all the other camps. There was almost nothing that Jews were not required to take care of for them. For example, Burger, the greatest Jew-hater, had his horse ridden daily by a former Czech officer. Jews painted pictures and frescos for the apartments of the SS men, cooked the most delicious dishes, and designed and created decorations, such as hand-painted place cards and German oak leaves, for SS parties. Jewish women served at their feasts (but without the ugly yellow star). Jewish hands created toys for the children of the SS men, dressed them from head to toe, maintained their cars and Burger's limousine, and furnished SS rooms with new furniture and Jewish art. Jewish physicians had to treat the SS men and their relatives and carry out forbidden procedures when they got women pregnant. Seidl even selected Jews to draft and copy out almost an entire "scholarly" work, supposedly his dissertation, on a Jewish subject, and in addition had them beautifully paint and letter his Ur-Aryan family tree. To keep the SS men in good humor, Edelstein went so far as to have Jews prepare birthday presents for them, which were graciously accepted (see 146b). The following document reveals how the Jews were expected to provide for the private needs of their oppressors.

IV/3 MT/Pck 9 October 9, 1942
Memorandum to Mr. Schliesser

Reference: Outstanding orders for our workshops from the Camp Commandant.

Wood processing workshops:
No. 4093 from September 10
2 tables, 1 chest, 1 tabletop for the German post office have not yet been processed, as no production order or other official request has been submitted. We have already asked for these.

No. 4001 from September 7

1 bookcase for 200 books for Mr. Hantschke work was begun on October 5. The job cannot be completed until the delivery of the veneer is confirmed.

No. 4341 from September 10

Work was begun on September 21st on 1 conference table, 1 combination radio and telephone table, 1 flower stand and 1 table for the offices of the camp commandant. The job cannot be completed until the delivery of the veneer is confirmed.

No. 4871 from October 2

1 radio table and 1 liqueur table for Government Chief Inspector Wüstehoff is not yet being processed, as the necessary materials (oak that is stored in the brewery) have not yet been released.

No. 4357 from September 24

Work was begun on October 9 on 2 card tables, approval number W 50 for SS Unterscharführer Puhze. The work did not begin sooner because the client did not wish it to.

No. T 1 from October 5

Work was begun on October 6 on 1 table and 3 armchairs for SS Hauptsturmführer Clausen. These should be completed on October 17. It is anticipated that the work will be turned over to the technical section/upholsterers on that day.

No. T 17 from October 6

Work was begun on October 7 on 1 frame for Camp Commandant SS Obersturmführer Dr. Seidl. It is to be ready October 12.

No. T 25 from October 7

Sixteen beams for the jails in the Camp Commandant's Office were ordered on October 9 and will be completed on 10 October.

No. T 38 from October 9

Work was begun on October 9 on 1 therapy table [*Manipulationstisch*] for SS Unterscharführer Puhze, in the same format as the last delivery. It will be delivered on October 11.

Metal processing workshops:

No. 2840 from August 28

Work has been in progress since September 30 on platform gates for trailers for the SS garages. The delay is due to a late materials delivery, only part of which has arrived so far. The first set will be completed on October 15. The remaining material will be ordered in Prague on October 1, 1942 under Nos. 613 and 614. The material was ordered on September 23 in Raudnitz [Roudnice nad Labem].

No. 370 from August 30

Doors for the electrical plant are not yet being processed. Neither Raudnitz [Roudnice nad Labem] nor Prague has yet made available the ordered and urgently re-ordered material. . . .

No. 4345 from September 20

(Production Order 45)

Work was begun on September 22 on 1 children's automobile for Mr. Streschnak. It is to be delivered on October 10. Because certain difficulties arose during completion, delivery will only be possible in 5 to 7 days.

No. 4832 from October 1

For the Commandant's Office we have made 4 metal bins, which now are being varnished.

The connections between these Jews and Germans who were officially appointed as annihilators of the Jews had peculiar consequences for the camp. Although a number of commodities could not be bought by any German company or private citizen, such items still were available to the SS "office" of this all-powerful police authority, even during the period of need in 1944–45. The Jews only had to fill out orders and mark them as urgent, and high-quality raw materials were immediately delivered. These materials were seldom dedicated to really productive purposes and of course did not benefit the prisoners. Thus the corrupt SS, addicted to luxury, helped weaken the war economy and hasten Germany's defeat.

The SS established an intricately – but heedlessly – planned "labor and supply ghetto"; as a result of their economically senseless decision to use Theresienstadt for this purpose, in addition to the many other impossible conditions that were almost entirely created by the SS, the camp never could succeed in creating a functioning economy and production system by which the "ghetto" could have met its economic needs, even with minimal demands. With only slightly more clever policies, which, of course, also would have meant without the desired "Final Solution," the camp could have worked perfectly and been very profitable for its exploiters. But that never occurred to anyone. Whatever the SS skimmed off was a result of overexploitation and open theft. Thus the "ghetto" was never self-sustaining and never achieved a solid balance of trade.

Theresienstadt was also a "supply ghetto," and in this context debts seemed theoretically justified. It was not difficult for the SS to cover these liabilities. Through the famous "home purchase agreements" between preferentially treated Jews from the German Reich and the "Reich Association" (Reichsvereinigung) in Berlin, the Gestapo, with a few strokes of the pen, acquired great wealth (see Chapter 3). Through this arrangement, 109 million Reichsmark was transferred to the account of the "Jewish Emigration Funds for Bohemia and Moravia" at the Bohemian Union Bank, which, as asset manager for the Prague "Central Office," financed the "ghetto."

This fund also received the extorted and stolen Jewish assets from the "Protectorate" (see Chapter 3) as well as the property of dissolved Jewish corporations in Berlin and Vienna. Altogether, it received probably 120 million and 8 million Reichsmark from Germany and Austria, respectively. When Theresienstadt was expropriated on February 16, 1942, through a decree by the "Reichsprotektor," the fund obtained the resources needed to purchase the private property in the area, including 149 apartment buildings. Additionally, 10 buildings owned by the community were acquired, and the "emigration fund" leased the military's property, including 12 barracks and 3 buildings. Also acquired was 311.34 hectares of agricultural land, of which 35.04 hectares was leased to the "Small Fortress." Most of this land had to be managed by the Jewish "agriculture" work group for the benefit of the SS. The following table lists the size and type of land included:

	Size (in hectares)
Farmland	70.98
Gardens	15.22
Orchards	2.10
Fields	84.04
Grazing land	73.36
Basket-willow plantations	1.60
Forest	29.00
TOTAL	276.30

This area of production, which benefited only the economy of the Germans and was of no benefit at all to the Jews, included cattle breeding. Some of the animals were bought; the rest were brought to Theresienstadt from the destroyed town of Lidice. By the end of the war the prisoners were looking after the following types of livestock (figures taken from 261):

30 horses
64 cows and calves
66 sheep
83 pigs
210 chickens
108 geese
10 turkeys
1 bee colony
1 silkworm colony

The self-administration had no control over the amount of resources allocated for the maintenance of the camp; those decisions were made in Berlin and Prague. The allocations probably were not very large. If the bank transfers from Berlin and Vienna to the "emigration fund" in Prague amounted to RM 128 million, I doubt that the allocations exceeded RM 38 million, because the balance in the camp's bank account at the end of the war amounted to at least RM 90 million. As we later show, the camp was credited with RM 150,000 for wages in February 1945, and anticipated expenditures for the same month totaled RM 775,000, leaving an unmet amount of RM 625,000. Daily expenditures for one prisoner were limited to K 4.30 (RM 0.43). However, the average amount spent in 1942 was K 3.16, and in 1943 it was K 3.71. Only toward the end of the war was the limit exceeded, by K 0.16. If we estimate the average number of prisoners in February 1945 at 15,000, we get 420,000 daily expenditures times RM 0.45. That amounts to RM 189,000, or approximately RM 36,000 more than the earned wages. The discrepancy between expenditures for the prisoners and the presumed real expenditures amounts to RM 586,000! This deficit would have been greatly reduced by the profits made by the SS and other income for which files no longer exist. However, probably only a small amount of this was credited, one way or another. Thus a large deficit remains, presenting a puzzle that cannot be explained through the materials available to me. A few possibilities suggest themselves: (1) The expenditures were used to maintain not only the prisoners and the camp but also the SS and the Czech police. (2) Part of the deficit was covered by the allocations. (3) The deficit was reduced by other profits and credits. All of this may be true, and more; yet this still does not illuminate the real situation.

Likewise, I know nothing about the costs related to the expropriation of the property of the city. They could not have been too large, as Theresienstadt is small and poor, the population was impoverished, and it is known that compensation in such cases was modest. It was paid out by the "emigration fund" from confiscated assets of the Bohemian-Moravian Jews. The fact that government property in Theresienstadt was leased only for the duration of the war shows that it was considered only an interim solution, even if a victorious Germany had allowed some Jews to live. In the meantime, the Jews were kept barely alive through the output of their fellow prisoners and through small allocations from their own property, which had been obtained by extortion and fraud; but no one took exception when, in September

1942, 10,000 "wards" (*Versorgte*), who assumed they had an honest right to live in Theresienstadt, were killed in the area around Minsk.

The camp was financed from the following sources:

1. The "Jewish emigration fund," with Jewish property
2. The productive enterprises and individual work of the imprisoned Jews
3. Revenue from agriculture, horticulture, and cattle breeding
4. The leasing of Jewish manpower to outside companies and offices
5. The utilization of possessions confiscated from inmates

The "emigration fund" opened up three different bank accounts at the Bohemian Union Bank in Prague under the name "Jewish self-administration Theresienstadt." The balance on February 28, 1945, was as follows:

Account no. 22881	K 287,693,130.00
3-month withdrawal notice account	K 308,716,130.00
6-month withdrawal notice account	K 308,716,130.00
Total sum	K 905,125,390.00

The "autonomous" camp had no control over its bank accounts and was excluded from all dealings with money. As late as April 1945, half of the above assets were invested in Reich treasury bills, supposedly because they had higher interest rates. The camp's "Finance Department" and its Central Accounting Office were only administrators for the "Economics Department" and the SS "office."

"File memos" were kept on the visits of Schliesser – and, after his deportation, of Dr. Merzbach – to the SS "office." One such "file memo" – we quote only a few selected points from this document, which consists of six densely typewritten pages – illustrates the topics addressed during these meetings:

W/OO-SCH/W

File Memo No. W 732

Concerning the visit to SS-OSCHAF. Bartels, SS-HSCHAF. Ulbricht and Mr. Schade on 19 June 1944, attended by the Jewish Elder:

Submitted:

Original letter from the 17th of the month from the Prague engineering firm V. Klásek, regarding cartridge radiators

Shipment notice from the 17th of the month from Kaliwerke A.G. regarding twelve crates of Zyklon hydrogen cyanide

Delivery receipts No. 10080 and 10081 from the 13th of the month from the firm Josef Burda, Prague

Original letter from the16th of the month from printing firm Dr. Ed. Grégr and Sons, Prague, regarding the shipment of printed material

Original letter of 13 May 1944 from the Emigration Fund for Bohemia and Moravia, Prague, regarding payment for a desiccator

Authorization of the release certificate No. 20222 from the 13th of the month regarding 110 pairs of orthopedic shoes from the clothing warehouse at Egergasse 3 for use by disabled persons, through the shoe store.

Mr. Streschnak offered the following information:

3) Untergeorgsberger, Grafia: an order, with samples attached, for 600 numbered index cards, 5000 routing slips and 5000 medicine certificates should be submitted.

4) Gasser, Raudnitz [Roudnice nad Labem]: an order for 5 kg phosphoric acid, 5 kg sulfuric acid, 500 count tooth soap and toothpaste, 10 kg acetone, 500 kg Glauber's salt and 5 kg sodium sulfate should be submitted.

6) Maruška, Raudnitz [Roudnice nad Labem]: is able to supply only ordinary, not Kremser, mustard. If caraway is ordered, thyme must also be bought. Decision must be made.

7) Venclícek, Raudnitz [Roudnice nad Labem]: an order for sanitary napkins should be submitted. Three barrels must be sent to Strangmüller to be filled with Lysol. The firm Venclícek will be the supplier.

The following notations from the Central Supply are presented:

No. 6053 – rotten potatoes
No. 6054 – acetic acid mixture
No. 6064 – potato shipment of 17 June 1944
No. 6065 – meat confiscation

Listing of necessary foodstuffs for 4 weeks of the 64th rationing period for 33,000 people

Memo No. 5233 about production re: rabbit hair shears is presented, client no. 18

Submitted: The original letter from the 6th of this month from the Military Garment Office in Munich concerning invoices for materials

The original letter from the 13th of this month from the firm A.O. Kühl, Bad Pyrmont, regarding ink powder OK 3

Submitted: List of foodstuffs for the 107th Theresienstadt transport

Schliesser

An item from "file memo W 760," from July 29, 1944, provides yet another example of the procedure of these meetings: "SS-OSTF Synderhauf is informed about the wagon shipment from Switzerland and asked where it should be brought. SS-OSTF Synderhauf first gives instructions that the wagons should be brought to the Aussig Kaserne. Later, this disposition is changed by Mr. Bartels and instructions are given to have the boxes brought to the Office." This is how relations with the outside world were conducted. Every little thing in the camp was controlled, and relief consignments from Switzerland were first stored with the SS (see 229a). The use of goods stored in the "ghetto" for internal purposes also had to be authorized with a "certificate of release." The following is one of many forms that reveal the impersonal method of interaction between the self-administration and the SS "office":

Jewish Economics Department

Theresienstadt, (date _____)

Notice
to Department 11/2 of the Office
Re.: Complaint about Received Shipments.

1. Shipper: _____
   Sender: _____
2. Sent by _____ No. _____
   Weight (or Count): _____
   Content: _____

Delivery document: _____

3. Loading station: _____
   Departure station: _____

4. Request to arrange the following:
at _____ in _____
Record a factual protocol
Reweighing   Recount
Inquiry
5. Request to file a defect claim against shipper
6. Reasons: _____

Signature: _____

Non-relevant items to be deleted.

Germany was already collapsing, but the "Economics Department" kept writing letters, such as the following, to be forwarded to outside companies by the SS:

Theresienstadt, 14 April 1945

To the firm
Karl Gottfried
Regensburg 2.
Re.: Gb. No. VI/ 147 of 20 June 1944
With the above order, you order

15 gross of saw blades for wood and horn
80 gross of saw blades for metal
No. 00. 000. 0000 assorted

Since these items are urgently needed, and the order has not yet been entirely filled, we ask you to inform us if we can expect delivery in the near future.

As if nothing were happening and one firm were writing another at the height of peace, they carried on an eerie correspondence with the outside world. Mention of saw blades appeared in one of the memos signed by Schliesser, who, by that point, had long since been gassed; the topic appears again in this foolish and demonic enterprise, which played itself out until the very end. Confused minds believed that the hardworking Jews in Theresienstadt still desperately needed these goods, while a great Reich collapsed in ruins; its rulers, paralyzed upon completing their criminal work, and having lost their instincts, nevertheless had to proceed with their follies. The masters of evil and their cronies had devastated and destroyed human lives as well as goods; yet they did not recognize that their time had come. And then they wasted all their time in thinking of – saw blades.

The following list notes which goods the camp regularly needed:

A. Necessities

Fittings, installation material, technical supply articles
Construction by outsiders
Construction material (lime, cement, plaster, light construction panels, bricks, roofing board, glass, sand and gravel)
Fuel
Lumber
Iron (iron and metal ware)
Electric supplies (electrical material, electric bills)
Machinery and spare parts
Paints, drugs, chemical products
Fire protection and air raid protection supplies

384   *Sociology*

Notions
Glass and rubber goods, ceramics
Hemp and rope goods
Wood and basket products
Household appliances, kitchen equipment, eating utensils
Lighting and fuses
Paper goods, office supplies, printing supplies
Cleaning supplies (soap, detergent, brushes)
Repair kits (shoes, undergarments and clothes, clocks and optics)
Transportation and related supplies
Investment projects (water system, rail connections, barracks construction)
Other (chimney sweep, repair kits and accessories for musical instruments, tool
repair, packaging purchase and rental fees, telephone, pump rentals, instrument
grinding)

B. Hygienic Requirements

Medicines
Medical instruments
Bandages
Laboratory supplies
Pest extermination
Examinations
Dental support
Special supplies

C. Everyday Needs

Soap, tooth powder, powder, razor blades, shoe polish and leather grease [These
items, with the exception of some soap, never were distributed to the prisoners
and could, later on, once in a great while, be "purchased" at the stores.]

D. Agriculture

Animal husbandry, plant breeding, other

E. Foodstuff Requirements

Bread (outside bakers' wages and supplies)
Bread spreads, including tomato paste, etc.
Vinegar
Meat, meat products, preserved meats, intestines
Vegetables (fresh, pickled, sauerkraut)
Beverages [? *sic*!]
Spices
Yeast
Legumes [barley!]
Coffee substitute
Potatoes
Margarine
Marmalade
Flour
Milk
Processed foods
Salt
Mustard

Tea, tea essences
Soup powder, bouillon cubes and soup spices
Dried vegetables and dried onions
Sugar and sweeteners
Ingredients (cooking and baking powder)

An estimate of the money required was submitted on a monthly basis:

Expected Funding Requirements
for the Month of September 1944
(based on an assumed population of 28,000 inhabitants)

1. Food Supplies (September consumption plus reserves for an additional
    4 weeks)

Meat and meat products	K	530,000
Flour		277,000
Potatoes		542,000
Processed foods		112,000
Coffee substitute		66,000
Margarine		8,000
Bread and bread flour		1,060,000
Milk		53,000
Yeast		10,000
Dried vegetables		300,000
Vegetables		100,000
Dried soup [extracts]		593,000
Vinegar		8,000
Bread spreads		50,000
Marmalade		150,000
Tomato paste		50,000
Dried onions		20,000
Mustard		50,000
Miscellaneous		100,000
Spices, salt, etc.		50,000	**4,129,000**

2. Requisitions from the stores for the month of September, 1944

Bread spreads	50,000
Mustard	50,000
Tomato paste and catsup	50,000
Tea essence	150,000
Various flavorings	150,000
Vegetables in vinegar	100,000
Bouillon cubes	50,000
Saccharin, lemon extract, etc.	40,000
Cooking and baking powder, salt, spices, tea, etc.	80,000
Tooth powder	20,000
Razor blades	30,000
Eating utensils, etc.	100,000	**970,000**

3. Material Requirements

    a) Coal   600,000
    b) Lumber   1,000,000
    c) Construction materials

	Lime	10,000	
	Cement	40,000	
	Plaster	10,000	
	Light construction panels	300,000	
	Bricks	50,000	
	Roofing tiles	20,000	
	Roofing paper	40,000	
	Sand and gravel	100,000	
	Glass	20,000	
	Painting supplies	200,000	
	Iron goods	300,000	
d)	Cleaning and disinfection supplies	400,000	
e)	Medical goods (including hospital equipment)	800,000	
f)	Repair supplies (tailors and cobblers)	200,000	
	Leather wax and shoe polish	400,000	
g)	Machinery and technical equipment	400,000	
h)	Funds for electricity section	200,000	
i)	Funds for agriculture	50,000	
j)	Other	250,000	5,590,000
	Total requirements	K	10,689,000

This listing does not include funding requirements for services from outside the settlement (Pštross, Artesia, Figlovský) and the payment requirements for freight.

Most of the economic relationships with the outside world fell to the production facilities, which worked for outside accounts or supplied customers through the SS "office." The "Production Department" was a subbranch of the "Economics Department" and was headed from start to finish by Dr. Rudolf Freiberger. He was a competent and resolute man whose work proved so critical to the SS that he was never deported. From his subordinates he expected the utmost, setting a fast-paced tempo, sparing no one, and hardly lifting a finger to help his people during difficult times. Freiberger was in a difficult position and was unpopular among the workers, so it is not easy to do him justice. He was responsible for the issuing of "certificates"; one such "certificiate" read as follows: "K – with gratitude and recognition for excellent service in the raising of production "K" – Economics Department, Production, Theresienstadt, 19 June, 0001 hours 1943." It was inevitable that production be promoted and, in Edelstein's spirit, thereby keep as many inmates as possible in the camp by making them indispensable. Nevertheless, it was at best undignified to praise workers with such awards while Freiberger was not to speak to endangered colleagues before transports.

Production orders filled in the camp came from either German companies or government offices, for example, the Wehrmacht. The SS "office" had a strong interest in production because such activity convinced its supervisors and other authorities of the economic value of the camp, despite the fact that the camp's factories were insignificant and often even ridiculous. Some operated for only a certain period of time or were expected to fulfill only a short-term order. The following undated register, probably from early 1944, lists all tasks – regardless of

Economy 387

whether they were carried out by the "Production Department" – that were not merely for the internal economy:

List of Operations Designated for Special Tasks

1. SS Office
2. Comrades' Home
3. SS Garage
4. Small Fortress
5. German official post office
6. Reserve Field Hospital
7. Berlin SS Office
8. *Gendarmerie*
9. Reich genealogy research
10. Agriculture
11. Peat offloading
12. Sluice mills
13. Railroad construction, Engineer Figlovský
14. Railroad construction, own accounts
15. Firefighting ponds E I, H IV
16. Road construction, Leitmeritz [Litoměřice]
17. Road construction for account of Engineer Figlovský
18. Clock repair workshops
19. Central Office for the Regulation of the Jewish Question in Prague
20. Waterworks construction (T 423)
    a) Engineer Figlovský b) Artesia, Prague
    c) Engineer C. Pštross, Prague d) Other entries
21. Silage construction, Engineer Figlovský
    (Emergency Service, Engineer Figlovský)
22. Sewer system work (T 45)
23. Sewer system work for account of Engineer Figlovský
24. Silage pit construction, Engineer Figlovský
25. Quarry in Kamaik
26. Crematorium construction
27. Unskilled work and shooting range, Kamaik-Leitmeritz [Litoměřice]
28. Crete buildings and maintenance costs ["Kreta" – or Crete – was a newly built section of wooden buildings at the western edge of the bastion, separated from the rest of the ghetto.]
29. Chemical monitoring tasks
30. Dr. Weidmann Group [see Chapter 19]
31. Bookkeeping Group
32. Safety glasses fabrication
33. Uniforms
34. Leather galoshes
35. Central Bath (Aryan section)
36. Mica splitting
37. Rabbit fur shears
38. Ink powder sack filling
39. Electricity plant
40. Box fabrication
41. Educational games
42. Production of articles for military shops (previously notions)

388   *Sociology*

43. Uniform repair
44. Jute sack repairs
45. Jewelers
46. Street maintenance and street cleaning
47. Jungfern-Breschan Working Group
48. Project plan for central water control
49. National Socialist Flying Corps (NSFK) air strip
50. Slaughterhouse
51. Shooting gallery
52. Charcoal production

The camp's actual production lines included the following: fabrication of leather galoshes, safety glasses, uniforms, rabbit fur shears, educational games, notions, and jewelry; mica splitting; ink powder sack filling; cardboard box workshops; uniform repair; jute sack repair; and charcoal production. On occasion, prisoners were sent to work at other factory operations. "Glimmerspalterei G.m.b.H." in Tabor became the most important one. Women and young girls were put to work there, especially during the last months of the war, and were made to work at an ever-faster pace. Thin, flat panels of split mica were used as insulation for electronic equipment.

Except for "crate fabrication," most production enterprises considered "important to the war effort" never amounted to much. The remaining goods produced for outside orders were made for German firms. Among other things produced were leather bags, purses, wallets, tobacco and chest pouches, vellum goods, puzzles, envelopes, artificial flowers, powder dispensers, pendants, oil and watercolor paintings based on postcards and other models, wall motifs, bookmarks, statues, vases, pots and other ceramics, and cheap jewelry; the prisoners also provided bookbinding services.

Work hours were billed monthly:

Compilation of Hours of Work Performed for Groups Outside the Settlement in February 1945.

Serial No.	Invested Work	Ongoing Expenses
	Hours	
1. Office	2,403	2,178
2. SS Garage		1,929
3. Comrades' Home		738
4. Small Fortress		12
5. Reserve Field Hospital		5,619
6. Berlin Office	242	18,075
7. Police Headquarters		574
8. Reich Genealogy Research		561
9. Agriculture		
a) Direct Work		
Horticulture	42,519	
Orchard Work	1,725	
Livestock	25,630	
Field Work	13,075	

Economy

Serial No.			Invested Work	Ongoing Expenses
			Hours	
Maintenance		9,547		
Parks		2,615		
		95,111		
b) Indirect work	39	118	39	95,229
10. Peat Offloading				2,160
11. Sluice Mill				10
12. Road construction for account of Engineer Figlovsky			2,896.30	
13. Crete Buildings and their maintenance costs				60
14. Bookkeeping Group				725
15. Uniforms				27,312
16. Central Bath, Aryan section				96
17. Mica Splitting			120	323,177
18. Box Fabrication				5,855
19. Firing range			211	3,179
20. Charcoal Production				38
TOTAL			5,911.30	487,527

These figures add up to 493,438.30 hours, charged at various rates and totaling K 1,539,356.15, or an average hourly payment of K 3.12. The consideration offered the prisoners each day was worked off in 85 minutes! The only client for the "ghetto" was the SS "office," which kept all profits and also had to bear any losses. If we compare the sum of all hourly wages – approximately K 1,500,000, billed monthly – with the expected expenditures during the same month – K 7,750,000 – we find a deficit of K 6.25 million. This deficit is much reduced if we take into consideration the much greater amounts the SS received from purchasers; subtract expenditures for food reserves; and calculate the net profit obtained from revenues from "agriculture," theft from the "clothing storehouse," and other probable sources of income. The raw materials and semifinished products processed in the camp had to be provided by the customers. This should prove that the "ghetto," including the SS and the gendarmerie, could survive only through subsidies, while at least 75% of the actual expenditures on bare necessities for all the prisoners toward the end of the camp's existence – and probably also before – were covered by the wages charged for the prisoners' labor on behalf of the SS.

Those who wasted all values and goods nevertheless had all of the camp's refuse collected. These gentlemen had their own conceptions of thrifty economy. Thus, in 1944, they earned approximately 34,000 crowns by selling tens of thousands of kilos of rags, bones, bedsprings, cast and smelted iron, scrap metal, and zinc plates to a dealer in Bohušovice. Thus the SS acted like "proper businessmen":

The Commander of the Security Police and the SD,
Central Office for the Regulation of the Jewish Question
in Bohemia and Moravia,
Theresienstadt Office
Conditions of sale and delivery

390 *Sociology*

1. Offers: All offers are subject to confirmation and not binding on me.
2. Orders: Are considered accepted only following written confirmation....
   If there is a delay in the agreed-upon supply of material, machinery, tools,
   stock, etc., I have the right to extend the contracted date of delivery.
3. Prices: Prices are calculated ex-Theresienstadt, net cash, not including
   packing and loading charges, nor the costs of receivership and
   inspection....
4. Samples: .... Samples, drawings or models produced in Theresienstadt
   using our own patterns may not be released to other companies or
   persons without my written approval.
5. Shipment: ... the purchaser assumes the cost and risk....
6. Material: The purchaser will deliver to Theresienstadt, in a timely
   manner, the necessary material for fabrication in accordance with the
   sample. Should the purchaser be unable to meet the delivery schedule, he
   must bear all costs related to the lost time. The purchaser retains ownership of all materials he provides. I will look after such materials with the
   care of a proper businessman....
7. Liability: My liability extends only to subsequent work free of charge or
   replacement of incorrectly delivered goods. In such cases, the products or
   parts will be repaired or replaced free of charge.... Necessary materials
   must be provided for replacement goods.
8. Customer complaints: ... 8 days after arrival....
9. Delivery commitment: Delays caused by incidents of war, force majeure,
   especially lack of electricity, damage to machinery, etc., release me from
   the terms of delivery....
10. Payment: ... net without deductions, to be paid immediately upon receipt
    of the invoice to the Raudnitz [Roudnice nad Labem] municipal bank,
    local branch Bauschowitz [Bohušovice].

(266)

INTERNAL ECONOMY

Like the other "departments" – for example, the "Technical Department" or the
"Health Services Department" – the "Economics Department" supplied its own
offices with goods according to strictly regulated procedures. The "Central Warehouse" made deliveries to the "Central Supply Office" and to its branch offices and
workshops; to the "Central Medicine Warehouse," "wood warehouse," "fuel warehouse," and "Central Warehouse for Clothing and Equipment" (which was supplied
mainly by the "clothing storehouse"); and to the various "warehouses" of the
"Technical Department." Card files were kept in all of these warehouses.
A "release certificate" was needed for dispensation. The process is explained in a
document from January 31, 1943:

> Draft. Concerning setup and management of holdings card indexes for use by the L.K.T.
> [Theresienstadt Camp Commandant's Office]
> A means is sought ... to manage the holdings card indexes in the camp for material,
> wood, coal, and provisions for the L.K.T.
> Management therefore needs to ... proceed parallel to the registries for the Central
> Materiel Warehouse, Central Lumber Warehouse.
> The following will ... discuss only the Central Warehouse –C. W.

I. The ORDER FORM CARD INDEX is reserved for the L.K.T.

II. The MAIN PRODUCT CARD INDEX for the L.K.T. will be managed by Central Accounting.

III. The Central Warehouse is responsible for the correctness of the MOVEMENT REPORTS (entry and exit).

I. Order form card index.

Nothing can be changed in the procedures that have been followed to date. It is desirable that incoming invoices be entered in the Order Form Card Index ... of the C[entral] A[ccounting] Price Office, and further to the relevant Central Warehouse ... for the purpose of comparison with actual delivery of goods.

II. Main product card index.

1. For each C.W., the C.A. will keep a product card index in duplicate, of which one will be recorded in the morning and one in the afternoon. In the morning and at noon, the L.K.T. shall receive the index just recorded, so that the L.K.T. always has one recorded index at its disposal.

2. Every C.W. shall keep journals on its products' movements in carbon copy, of which one [goes to] the ... main product card index (MPCI), one ... [to] the L.K.T. Journal entries shall be based on records of actual movement of products, therefore according to arrival reports ... and outgoing shipment reports....

3. A ... MAIN PRODUCT CARD INDEX will be created as part of the C.A. It is incumbent upon the MPCI to maintain index cards ... on the movement and status of all goods brought into the ghetto or present there, on the basis of the journals it receives from the C.W. These are to be kept according to volume....

Internal instructions will be issued on cooperation between the MPCI and the other departments of the C.A., especially with the price office and with production and consumption accounting.

[A diagram explains the procedure: Orders are passed on to suppliers via the LKT, and that is where the invoices are sent. From there, they are submitted to the price office of the CA (Finance Department) and on to the central materials and inventory administration (Economics Department), which passes them on to the six central warehouses for medicine, provisions, potatoes, material, wood, and fuel. These central warehouses receive deliveries from outside and keep card indexes and journal pages on inventory as well as on the entry and exit of goods. The journal pages go into the six corresponding card indexes of the CA, which simultaneously makes entries in the card indexes according to the invoices, collates them with the journal pages of the Central Warehouse, and finally also makes entries for the LKT. It is the job of the Central Warehouse to record and report that the products ordered and delivered are in agreement, qualitatively and quantitatively. The central warehouses themselves deliver, by order, to various parts of the "ghetto" or to the outside world.]

One characteristic example shows how business was transacted. In Chapters 8 and 13, we portrayed the elaborate administrative apparatus that devoured vast amounts of paper. Every office and every prisoner seemed possessed by a writing fever. But the prevailing paper shortage limited the SS and the Jews they had infected: paper was tightly rationed. Once again, the guidelines for its permissible consumption were convoluted and long-winded:

392 *Sociology*

Instructions for materials administration (B V 140)

Beginning on 1 February 1944, paper will be distributed to individual departments only on the basis of RECEIPT SHEETS.

In the receipt sheets, the Central Secretariat notes the amounts approved for the department, separated according to the various types of paper, and the notes are confirmed a month in advance by the official in charge of distribution, Mr. Brod, so that the receipt of paper within the framework of the approved quotas is not subject to any additional approval procedure. Apart from the paper amount, two Receipt Days a week are set for each department. The Materials Administration is entitled to refuse to disburse on other than the receipt days.

The Materials Administration receives a carbon copy of the receipt sheets and is supposed to register every disbursement of paper on both the receipt sheets submitted and the copy accompanying them.

The Materials Administration has the receipt of paper confirmed by the recipient on the copy of the receipt sheet, and [the department] itself confirms the disbursement on the original.

Before disbursing the paper, the dispenser must examine whether the approved quota (noted at the top of each column on the receipt sheet) was reached or even exceeded. In case of a positive answer, he must refuse any additional disbursement.

These most complicated and ridiculous of regulations go on and on. This apparatus, which took itself so deadly seriously, did not realize to what tragically grotesque delusions it had succumbed. This society – without real order and lacking all kinds of goods, where everyone distrusted everyone else and reason was defeated by a schematic norm – tried to hide its misery; but all it had left was a barren profusion of damaged language in which people lost themselves in unending drivel. The quota of writing paper for all departments amounted to 134,940 sheets in March 1944. Nobody was satisfied, and there was a hail of petitions and complaints:

[Stamp:] Health unit HV
T/Sch Chief physician   Thst. 2 July 44.
To the materials administration, Hauptstr. 22, to be forwarded to the Central Secretariat

Re: Recalculation of the quota for typewriter paper Category I.

The health unit at Haupstraße 22, which is coupled with the Infirm Block G V and the Children's Dental Outpatient Department for purposes of Category I typewriter paper, is receiving 320 sheets monthly of the fixed lump sum for the three units, a reduced quantity that is not even sufficient for the most essential written agenda of health unit H V.

Therefore we are requesting today

1. that the linkage between the Infirm Block and the Children's Dental Outpatient Department be dissolved.
2. an increase in the allotment of Category I writing paper to us, and we provide the following reasons for our request:

The Health Unit H V has charge of approx. 8,000 persons and includes a Chief Physician's Office, an Admissions Office, a Patient Registry, 30 sickrooms, 8 outpatient clinics, x-raying, wards for physical therapy, kitchen for preparing hot meals for sickrooms, foot care, a bath for the physically handicapped and delousing. Fifty-six physicians work in the health unit, 180 nursing staff, 54 administrative. We cite these figures in order to make clear to you the size of the administrative apparatus, whose management and supervision requires a major portion of paper because of the necessary written

Economy

agenda. As an example, we require 40 sheets of paper alone every month for copies of the attendance lists and work reports. It is necessary to list other correspondence necessary for the management of the personnel matters of an apparatus like this. The sickrooms, which receive neither any kind of notebooks nor forms designed for this purpose, must keep the following records: laundry inventory, issue of clean linen to the patients with signature, dirty laundry drop-off, list of bed linens, receipts, disbursements, list of allotment of ration bonuses to individual patients with signature, request for ration bonuses such as white bread or sugar, material requests, etc.

We want to mention again that we have 30 such sickrooms with more than 450 beds.

The written agenda of the outpatient clinics is likewise substantial. It consists of almost daily reports to the leadership of the Health Dept., sometimes deficiency diseases, sometimes underweight patients, sardine campaign, then certain kinds of illnesses, infections etc., a great deal of paper is used every day. In addition, there are monthly reports of a statistical and medical-scientific nature; in other words, a great deal of paper is used every day.

Just the mass screenings on the x-ray ward, with the necessary lists, require 50–60 sheets of paper monthly; then there are stool examinations for the kitchen personnel, monthly reports from all the physicians, etc. etc. Thus there is no longer any paper available for managing the agenda of the chief physician's office in regard to personal data and care. At the same time, new reports containing pages and pages of records are required by the administration of the Health Dept., as can be seen specifically from a Health Dept. memorandum. It would be going too far to provide additional details. The examples cited certainly will suffice to prove that the health unit cannot get by with 320 sheets monthly....

On this occasion, we would like to draw attention to the fact that other writing materials, such as lead pencils, colored markers, etc., still are allotted to us in a completely insufficient manner, and we would be grateful if you would also undertake the necessary corrective measures in this regard. We request the quickest possible disposition of our petition and thank you in advance.

Copy to the administration of the Health Dept. [stamp and signature]

Where a community experiencing material distress drowns in the undergrowth of a bottomless administration and is constantly shaken and almost demolished by ever-new acts of terror, no economy can flourish; it will attempt pitifully to maintain itself through endless difficulties, from one catastrophe to the next:

Annual Report from the Central Materials Warehouse.

On 24 November 1941, 342 men from the future ghetto's first Construction Kommando marched through the gate of the Sudeten Kaserne. This construction team brings tools and equipment, chiefly cabinetmakers' and locksmiths' tools, as well as equipment for earthworks. This material is stored in a ground floor room and forms the basis for the ghetto's first Materials Warehouse.

The Materials Warehouse was constantly expanded with newly arriving goods. The camp commandant's office allocated raw materials and tools, and the transports that arrived at short intervals brought material of the most diverse kind.... On 14 December, the materials brought by Transport M were stored in a storage room with 138 square meters' floor space in the Aussig Kaserne. The CENTRAL WAREHOUSE is set up in this building....

A year has gone by since these modest beginnings. Tens of thousands ... arrived in the ghetto....

All the homes, workshops, factories were built through diligence and perseverance. The Central Warehouse provided the material for this.... Shortly before it was ordered to relocate to the Central Bakery ... three large warehouses and eleven garages with a total floor space of 4,900 square meters ... are available. ...

On 27 June 1942, in the evening, the command to relocate is issued. ... Barely an hour later, several hundred people have been sent for as an assistance crew and are busy dismantling shelves, packaging goods, shipping them on trucks and tractors, and unloading the goods at their destination. By the new day's dawn, the last fully loaded truck has left the building. ... Relocation is accomplished in one night.

While ... sufficient warehouse space was available in the Aussig building warehouse, proper storage ... is difficult in the new building, since the space ... is more than fifty percent smaller than in the old building. The lack of ground floor rooms makes itself especially felt, since large and heavy pieces can be brought up to the second floor only with effort by way of the stairway ramp, and no ground floor storage room with a large entrance ... is available. The situation is eased by the storage elsewhere of sewing machines, mattresses, and furniture, as well as by storing building materials in house L 407. In light of the constant deliveries ... the shortage of space ... is still great. Additional rooms were claimed by the bakery. This demand cannot be met without endangering the operation of the Central Materials Warehouse.

In order ... to give ... a brief numerical overview, it suffices to note that more than 2,000 material consignments, some of them quite extensive, have been received. The diversity of the warehouse, which must satisfy every conceivable demand from the production sites, factories, and a population of several tens of thousands of people, is best documented by the figure of 2,360 existing warehouse articles. Materials from more than a hundred transports that arrived in the ghetto were received and stored, and 42,000 people who left the ghetto in 33 transports to the East were provided with the prescribed material.

In mid-September ... the Department of Sales Sites was ... annexed. Some of the clothing and linen items, shoes, articles for daily use, notions, and dishes stored in Building I IV was ... made available.

Items produced in the ghetto ... were received, packed, and sent to customers. Over 2,800 such consignments have so far been dispatched. ...

Theresienstadt, 23 November 1942.

[279]

The following passages are taken from three annual reports from the lumber warehouse:

[1942]

The work must be performed under the most adverse conditions imaginable; in the winter there were temperatures of −20 degrees [Celsius], no warming-up room for the workers, no lighting in the warehouse yard. Removal from the train generally had to be undertaken abruptly at night after large quantities accumulated on the ramp in Bauschowitz [Bohušovice].

In ... August ... two major special jobs had to be done. In a single night that will remain unforgettable in the annals of the ghetto, the four remaining garage boxes, including adjoining rooms in the Aussig Kaserne, had to be cleared out. Mountains of boards of wildly jumbled types and dimensions were piled to the skies in the lumberyard. And only a few days later, night work almost as extensive had to be done again. Room had to be made ... for the bypass road. A large number ... of the very tallest piles had to be torn down ... and hauled away as far as the redoubts.

[1943]

Apart from coping with the normal work, a series of extraordinary jobs had to be undertaken. Thus we had ... to clear away the piles of wood ... to fence level ... after the bypass road went into operation. In addition, relocation of the road to the Aussig

Kaserne made the transfer of large quantities of wood necessary. But the biggest job was relocating the entire warehouse stock ... to the building near the Sokol House. This relocation took place for the most part at a forced tempo.... Unfortunately, the new yard already has proven ... to be too small.... The maneuver was made much more difficult for us by the lack of an unloading ramp. Major deliveries often take place sporadically, mainly by night, with the consequence that our yard sometimes offers a truly desolate picture. But we have always succeeded in establishing order in a short time.

[1944]
... The relocation of the warehouse behind the Dresden Kaserne to the Sokol House, and then from there to the Südbaracken, placed great demands on each of our colleagues.... Although for 3 months we have had to cope with all the work using only 7 men (average age: 64) [following the autumn transports in 1944], the lumberyard near the Südbaracken was straightened up.

[280]

Everything was managed with unending effort in the quickest time and by a few, often completely unqualified, workers. With no rest or repose, no good work was possible; all was patchwork and improvisation. No sooner was anything done, or even merely begun, than a new order arrived that rendered the work already done invalid. Thus, in the freezing cold February of 1942, in the courtyard of E I, a barracks was hastily erected overnight; no sooner was it finished than it had to be pulled down, before it had even been used. It was no different with other buildings, production orders, and jobs; orders that absurdly canceled each other out almost always kept the camp in suspense, even when there were no immediate threats of deportation. This confusion was caused by the SS, even when it did not always explicitly intend it. Therefore the prisoners could accomplish nothing solid. Everything was frayed and confused; helplessness and ruin beset everyone and inhibited every beginning. It is astonishing that, nevertheless, not all life was stifled, and that a daily routine could be mastered after all!

This economy, already so greatly hampered by the administration, was absurdly burdened by the infantile introduction of economically unnecessary "ghetto money." The supposed moral value of graduated "wages" had practically no significance, nor was it taken seriously by anybody. Internally, people held to a clumsy, quasi-communistic payment-in-kind economy, in spite of the "ghetto money," which procured very few goods or services; these could be provided just as well, if not better, without money, and that is what happened. The money added just one additional delusional feature to the strange, marginal existence the prisoners were forced to carve out. In embarrassment, an official report attempted to justify this "money economy":

The settlement area ... has its own currency, the ghetto crown, which is by nature a form of payment issued by the Jewish self-administration by way of its bank....

Every worker receives a monthly contribution applied according to six graduated wage categories. For non-working persons ... a monthly subsidy will be paid. After living expenses are deducted, the surplus is partly paid out in cash, partly credited to a blocked account....

Introducing a money economy should

1. facilitate the exchange of goods through the mediating function of the banknotes,

396　　　　　　　　　　　　　　　*Sociology*

2.　bring about an increase in labor output through the gradation of wage payments,
3.　regulate the additional procurement of foodstuffs and consumer goods by way of purchase. [274]

PETTY ECONOMY

The allocation of accommodations and food was explained in Chapters 11 and 12. These goods as well as medical services were available to everyone free of charge, but for those who were capable of labor, these resources were allocated according to the work they performed. Labor took the place of any other services and contributions for the public benefit. Although the quality of the labor performed was on average good – it was usually not inferior to, and sometimes certainly superior to, the average activity in a normal society – the pressure to work, as a rule, was not so strict that it required the individual to carry out his allotted task conscientiously, as is necessary in the competition of a free or even of a planned labor market based on making money. The self-administration could, to be sure, assign bad quarters and the smallest permissible rations, but it could not deprive anyone of shelter, bread, and a ration card. It seemed that the prisoners were guaranteed to receive a minimum amount of resources, for which nobody needed to apply, as with unemployment benefits. Even cultural enjoyment and amusements were offered without requiring anything in return (see Chapter 19). Therefore, for some people – especially typically poor earners, dreamy spirits whom one so readily calls "impractical," and also certain work-shy people – this type of economy had undeniable benefits and even sometimes led to carefree, even spirited behavior, of a kind not readily observed in many healthier societies. The camp's typical worries, especially deportations and the inferiority of the payment-in-kind services, acted as a counterweight against contentment with what was on offer.

Usually, one had to make do with only the clothing and personal items that one had saved. Acquisitions and repairs always were difficult and largely were left to personal ability. If one had enough resources, it was possible privately to acquire many things, even valuable ones, while the self-administration never was capable of satisfying even the most essential needs. The "ghetto" was never provided with new clothes, linens, or shoes; the prisoners obtained these and other items only from confiscated goods that were released and also, to a small extent, from the possessions of deceased prisoners. The only new things available were wooden clogs, in small quantities. Items for personal hygiene were much too scarce in the camp, and those allocated were of wretched quality. There always was a serious shortage of soap, laundry detergent, and shoe polish. And other items needed for daily use, such as spoons or pots, also were scarce.

Before the "shops" were opened, the aforementioned things, except for soap, were issued only from the "Distribution Office" on the basis of approved requisitions. But even then – just as was the case later on in the "stores" – it was difficult to obtain anything that might really have served the needs of the requestors. Applications often were processed only after several months and repeated urgent requests, and then patronage or bribery played a major role in receiving anything at all useful. The majority of prisoners wore pitiful, even tattered, but quite clean clothing. The most coveted items were work clothes and warm items. Older people from Germany, in particular, had brought with them skimpy and unsuitable outfits more appropriate for a summer resort than for a prison camp. Hats did nothing to protect against the cold; therefore, almost all the women wore headscarves, and the men, caps. Among the men a semimilitary fashion caught on, but this slowly disappeared after the summer of 1942. Even if they wore civilian clothes, underneath their jackets they secured a belt or a belt substitute, to which, usually over the buttocks, they attached an eating bowl. This getup was typical for work groups. The outfit was supplemented by a soup spoon, which most prisoners carried with them at all times. In an odd contrast to the workers, the unfortunate elderly went about in dilapidated clothing – either their own or, more often, from others – that had seen better days. Female workers used manganese to dye overalls and aprons that they had sewn themselves. Younger women liked wearing pants and pant-skirts. Sports clothing – especially clothes for winter sports and high boots – was popular among young people of both sexes; they loved tomboyish and flashy things. Adolescents and children had their special fashions, especially regarding head coverings. The more people succumbed to the influences of "beautification," the more they wanted to look civil and elegant. Many women wore makeup and practiced cosmetic arts as soon as major caution in the face of the SS was no longer warranted.

The following document reports on the activities of the "Distribution Office" in the period from September 15 through November 30, 1942:

The job of the Distribution Office is to distribute community property appropriately to the most needy ghetto inmates.

1. Applications will be introduced and dealt with separately according to the 4 groups: Workers, Welfare Cases, Youth, Offices.
2. For the Groups W and Y, neediness will be examined by the Central Labor Office and by Youth Deployment.
3. The application will be dealt with after a thorough examination by the officials in charge and the Delivery Order submitted to the camp after notation in the card index.
4. From September 15th to November 30th, 22,162 entries were made and 178,166 objects delivered.

Applications	Workers	8,964	
	Welfare cases	10,851	
	Youth	1,497	
	Self-administration	850	[departments for workers]
Objects	Laundry	106,322	
	Clothing items	21,653	
	Shoes	11,123	
	Notions	15,548	
	Bed linen	14,868	
	Miscellaneous	8,662	

When the "stores" were opened, "vouchers" were introduced, which were initially duplicated and then later printed in three colors: red for the two highest "pay brackets," green for the remaining workers, and blue for the nonworkers. The vouchers were distributed in sections based on four groups of goods: group A, for "food items" (120 points); B, for clothing, laundry, and shoes (600 points); C, for dishes, household goods, notions, and suitcases (80 points); and D, for paper goods and perfume (40 points). In each "sales rotation," which was of different length for each of the four groups but always lasted several weeks to months, goods were allocated in specific quantities, and a number of points were taken. Often goods were unavailable for weeks or months on end, and the unused points ultimately became invalid. We have already discussed the goods that were available in the "grocery store." People were glad to receive something useful – for example, a razor blade, a belt, or some shoe polish – in the other "stores" ; with luck, there might be linens, but clothing and shoes rarely were found in useable condition and the right size. Because not even the most urgent needs could be met in this manner, allocation remained tied to the Welfare Office's authorization procedure; men's and women's suits, summer and winter clothing, coats, sweaters, pullovers, shoes, and suitcases never could be "purchased" without "special vouchers" (see 3b, docs. 113–14).

In order to obtain an authorization – as with every step taken in this camp, the administration of which can only be characterized but never entirely depicted – a great deal of paper was used. One filled out a "special voucher application," which required numerous details and contained phrases such as "I urgently need ..." and "I own .. items of similar clothing in good condition; .. items in need of repair, .. items incapable of being repaired," as well as a disclaimer: "I hereby declare that the information I provide is true. False information will be subject to the withdrawal of the voucher and possible criminal punishment." After lengthy research and urgent requests, some people actually received their "special vouchers," with which they could immediately visit the "store." But there was almost never anything to be had, and after a while the hard-to-obtain slip of paper expired, unless its validity could be extended – which required a new procedure. Clothing, linens, and shoes were categorized as "quality I," "II," or "III"; the quality category corresponded to the three colors of the "vouchers." Quality I and II items could be obtained together, and quality III items were available in other "stores," but in practical terms there were almost no distinctions. All the same, anyone entitled to the better sort also was allowed to "buy" the inferior kind. Anyone could obtain the necessary "money," even if he had none and did not want to apply for "loan" from the "bank."

One was unlikely to get repairs done if one was not able to take care of them oneself or did not have the means to pay for them. Small workshops for repairing clothing and linens already had been established in the first few weeks, but materials and workers were scarce; thus one could, with great patience, have only small things mended. Gradually, the system for repairs was expanded, but it always was inadequate. Operations were combined in the "Central Clothing Repair Workshop," which was in charge of repairing clothes, linens, stockings, gloves, head coverings, and footwear.

Receiving and distribution sites mediated between the workshops and the public. They were later centralized and merged with the collection point of the "Central Laundry." Repairs also were linked to an authorization procedure by the responsible welfare offices. For instance, the "work supervisor" in the "Deployment Office" could authorize so-called trifling repairs on his own, but if one needed something else, permission was required from a central office, such as the "Work Supervision Office," and so it was better to bring one's application there directly rather than take it to a branch office. If the request were approved, one received an "order certificate"

Economy 399

with precise information about the repair; it was made out to one person only, identified by name; was not transferable; and, without it, the collection point was not allowed to accept anything. There were certificates for the most varied purposes: for example, for watch repairs – but only for workers in urgent cases – for repair of bags, for "footing up stockings," and for dropping off dirty laundry outside the "laundry rotation." Usually, repairs did not turn out well, and many months could go by before one got one's shoes back (some of which were repaired outside the camp by the firm Báta). Anything that was handed in had to be prepared according to the regulations – in particular, the items had to be cleaned and provided with names and "transport numbers." When the items were ready or the laundry washed, a note was delivered to the quarters, saying:

> Re: ... The object designated [on the] overleaf is ready to be picked up! Bring along certification, receipt, and this communication! To be done at the earliest opportunity! Should another person be entrusted with pickup, owner's ration card is to be presented. The Collection Point. [The other side listed the name, transport number, and address of the person informed, along with a work number.]

The "Central Laundry" began working at the beginning of 1942 and was well equipped but much too small ever to satisfy demand; there, too, mismanagement and patronage prevailed. One could drop off laundry only once in the course of a "laundry rotation," which lasted three or even four months. In addition, there was a limit on the weight allowed, which fluctuated between 2 and 5 kg. Certain work groups received special allocations from their "departments." If one wanted to drop off bedding, one could barely have anything else washed. The public had to mark every item in a specific place with marking ink. At drop-off, as with repairs, a detailed receipt certificate had to be made out. Laundry came back clean and well ironed, but for this, too, one often had to wait patiently for many weeks, because delays were frequent due to lack of detergent or equipment damage, or during transport periods. Therefore, one needed to decide whether to wash things oneself in cold water and with inadequate detergent; this later became somewhat easier due to occasional distribution of laundry powder. Out of necessity, people changed underwear and bedclothes far too seldom and often wore the same shirts for a week or even longer. It was especially difficult to clean clothes, because the necessary detergents were unavailable. One could have clothes ironed only privately. It testifies well to the prisoner's love of order that, in spite of everything, they generally looked clean, except for helpless, old, and sick people.

Nothing needs to be said here about private economic relations between the prisoners, because the references in other chapters suffice.

15

Legal Conditions

Nothing could appear more absurd than to speak of the rule of law in an SS prison camp for Jews. Nevertheless, the camp was organized, albeit in its own twisted way, in accordance with general social norms. Every society develops behavioral standards; they become binding – or, in other words, "legal." The totality of these standards is deemed law, and this was true in the "ghetto" as well. In a highly developed society, these standards are made permanent by their establishment in written form.

Any assessment of the law, or any definition that is intuitive or orients itself around an absolute ethical norm, must be omitted here, because they contradict the actual phenomenon; only in a hypothetical situation would this not be a contradiction. Many schools of jurisprudence postulate idealistic hypotheses that well may be, in and of themselves, admirable or desirable. However, they overlook or misinterpret the morphology of the social patterns and constructions (e.g., of modern states) in which a structure is developed, under the influence of various and complicated tendencies; this structure then functions within communities as actual law. Law is neither what any individual decides he would like it to be nor the sum of codified mores. It is a set of rules and regulations with which those in power within a society assert and promote certain modes of behavior and relationships. Society as a whole and its individual members – institutions and individuals – exist in accordance with the law or must conform to it. In this sense, the law becomes an abstraction of life, but not so much a "natural" life as one that is planned and determined. Because the legislator formulating the law presumes that actual, "natural" life will not fully conform to its law, it makes sure that breaking the law, under threat of punishment, appears dangerous. In order to protect and represent established law, the lawmaker delivers perpetrators to a judge. It is from this practice – namely, that of law enforcement – that the practical administration of law emerges.

In this way, anything that contradicts the law becomes wrongful. In order to define a specific act as illegal, the administration of law requires legal investigation. Investigative methods separate right from wrong. For the lawbreaker, the administration of justice provides punishment, through which law is pronounced and appears restored. In this sense, the wrongful act is "adjudicated" – that is, set right – by the law. Those holding power in a society transfer the law's administration to certain functionaries who uphold the law and are expected to ensure its continuity. Part of the definition of social community is that the society's constitution, whether it is handed down or borrowed from another source, is taken straightforwardly as law, ensuring that the community itself is law – that is, a community of laws (*Rechtsgemeinschaft*). This is no different if the society is regarded, whether metaphysically, theologically, or subjectively, as un-just – if it is perceived as repugnant to a "natural" sense of justice or civilization.

According to this line of thinking, the "Jewish settlement area" was indeed a legal community with its own "law." The differences between this camp and any normal community were necessarily reflected in its legal system. The "ghetto" was a coerced community to which no one came by choice. Certainly, the legally relevant act under which the "ghetto" was formed was formally unsound and contravened all normal legal systems among ethical, or even merely civilized, peoples. Nevertheless, the act was the direct consequence of the law of its creators. It goes without saying that deportations, concentration camps, and "ghettos" are incompatible with any untainted sentiments, but it must be recognized that, for the SS, they were legal. The horror lies solely in the fact that acts that contradict any other legal sensibility and that, from an ethical perspective, can be viewed only as premeditated, common crimes were transformed into "law" in a way that violated any noble sense of the concept. Therefore, individuals and the coerced community in Theresienstadt rejected this law as unjust, even if it had to be obeyed. The rejection sprang, however, not from scientifically defensible definitions but rather – happily – from *ethical* impulses.

In the camp, a concept that is – not only ideally but also practically – the common norm behind all laws was turned into its opposite. To a large extent, both theoretically and in practice, all moral foundations fell away before the principle of raw power. "The law is what serves the German people": this is how the principle was formulated in this insane system. Where arbitrariness and power in and of themselves serve as law, it is possible, as here, for criminal acts to become law, and vice versa.

The camp already had a special law bestowed on it when the "ghetto" was founded as a separate community within the bounds of the larger community that enclosed it. If this law had been only a disciplinary code, as is enacted for a prison or for prisoners of war, then it could not be called a special legal status or a law particular to the camp. But as soon as a self-administering apparatus – albeit only limited and fictitious – was provided for, a conditional, autonomous legal community also was created. It was brought forth primarily by the authority of the SS and, afterward, was maintained by it. Hence, the self-administration could not be seen as an authority unto itself, but it could of its own accord derive levels of authority and institutions.

In this way, two legal spheres developed, existing parallel to and permeating each other:

1. The law that those in power recognized as binding, to the extent that they abided by a law other than the force of their power: The "ghetto," including all its subjects, was subject in its entirety to this law.
2. The law that the "ghetto" provided for itself through its organs of self-administration, be it received or new, which had no power of its own except as bestowed by the SS.

The SS involved itself much more in the camp's prerogatives, even in trivialities, in the beginning than it did later on, and it explicitly reserved the right to carry out a number of procedures. All SS orders were *eo ipso* legally binding. Gradually, the self-administration was granted greater authority. Once it desired to cultivate an appearance of normalization, the then-as-ever all-powerful SS paraded the autonomy of the Jews and concealed itself in the background, while still reserving for itself any intrusions into law enforcement and court proceedings. It also could revoke or revise any court decision; in reality, to bring the farce full circle, every decision of the "ghetto court" had to be approved by the SS "office." The SS may have imagined that "independent court adjudication" would convince outside visitors that civil relations prevailed, and so the commissions were shown carefully selected and prepared court proceedings. All regulations by the self-administration required approval, and yet attention was paid to their form, so that they more and more resembled traditional legal statutes, as would be expected in the normal order of society, rather than mere disciplinary provisions.

The lawyers in the camp who were instructed to draft the rules were so dependent on "higher authorities" that they never succeeded in finding an approach that worked. They were in fact seasoned experts, and yet none seemed to have grasped what was going on. They were moored too deeply in the conception of a normal order of things and failed to adapt instinctively to the situation in either theory or practice. They were unable to free themselves from the rehearsed theorems that they applied to a concept of justice of a sort that would have met the standards of normal law outside a concentration camp. Because every conviction by the largely petty "ghetto court" had to be reported, conviction usually meant deportation with the next transport for the person convicted, and was therefore probably a death sentence. This was true even of infractions and minor offenses that could have been punished with more humane, and therefore effective, disciplinary action. So if a half-starved person was convicted of illegally obtaining a meal with a ration card he had found, he was sentenced to two days in prison and, often, soon after had to atone for this action with his own death. Even ignorance of the fate of the deportees should have warned the self-administration and the judges against practices that only played into the hands of the SS, placing the appearance of justice above the command to love thy neighbor and above natural solidarity. To attempt to counter a judicial power that was proving to be a threatening instrument, Loewenstein created the "police criminal code" (*Polizeistrafordnung*), which was announced later in the camp's history. However, because of the camp's inflexible bureaucracy and narrow-minded lawyers, it had limited success. In most cases, the court never tried true wrongdoers but dealt only with minor crimes or misdemeanors and infractions better punished with disciplinary measures. Nowhere more than here would it have been necessary to carefully weigh the defendants' motives in the evidentiary proceedings and the judgment. Nowhere would a court have needed more carefully to consider the sections of the criminal code to be applied. The general corruption and the constant struggle waged against the SS required judges and lawyers to proceed wisely. Even if they never could expose the corruption, they at least could have kept the trials to a bare minimum. Much misery would have been avoided.

The complete lack of understanding of the problems of adjudication in an SS camp is evident in a memorandum by the renowned Viennese jurist Dr. Heinrich Klang, the highest and most respected judge in Theresienstadt, who even in May 1945 was

Legal Conditions 403

unable to overcome his rigid, academic point of view. The document was drafted soon after the liberation of Theresienstadt; here we have cited just the portions that pertain to the practice that preceded liberation.

Memorandum concerning the exercise of jurisdiction in Theresienstadt.
The power to adjudicate in the courts of the Jewish self-administration ... was derived from authorization by the local office of the German security authorities [*sic*! that is, the SS]. It included jurisdiction over guardianship, probate and criminal matters.... The courts' jurisdiction in criminal matters originally coincided with the usual jurisdiction of a district court. For special cases, jurisdiction was broadened through a special authorization that ultimately included crimes and misdemeanors, the trial of which, like those of other offenses, was entrusted to an individual judge....

Criminality ... had a unique hue; in addition to a small number of claims for insult to public officials and minor bodily harm ... almost the only offenses were those involving property, caused by meager nourishment and consisting of either thefts from the communal stores or deception during food distributions. These offenses were problematic because of their large number and required disproportionately more severe punishment than was usual for sentences for such offenses outside Theresienstadt. These offenses continued to be committed and most likely will not cease. The competent district court most likely will not be in a position to concern itself with the trial of these things, which are considered minor under the general circumstances. But they must not go unpunished.

Organized by the German authorities, a displacement in the composition of the population was caused by the last deportations, which significantly worsened conditions with respect to crime. Transports have arrived from concentration camps containing not political prisoners, but rather common criminals [In fact, these were starving Jews, among whom an occasional criminal element had landed]. Moreover, it is difficult to accustom the remaining inmates of the concentration camps to maintaining law and order. (146)

The mentality of these judges, who even after the war neatly divided concentration camp prisoners into "political" and "common" criminals, permits merciless insight into the "justice system" in Theresienstadt, where an eerie yet dangerous arrogance held sway, unaffected in the slightest by the SS or the fact of imprisonment. This memorandum contrasts with an anonymous report, written soon after the end of the war, in which the sore spots of the coerced community were recognized much more accurately than in the judge's unemotional words. The remarkably rough and primitive yet well-informed document begins with an introduction (perhaps by another author):

For purposes of clarification, the following observations must be made:
Obviously this is a specific description and not a general one. According to certified statistics, the percentage of unreliable and dishonest workers in the so-called "nutritional" professions was 10 to 20%; a further 30% limited themselves to small enrichments for their own personal use. The moral problem was complicated by the fact that in many ration centers, they worked directly or indirectly with the Germans, and that thefts were counted as harming the Germans and not the Jews.

At various times, the ghetto administration contended with greater or lesser success against these people who harmed the general public, and one can say, consistent with psychological analyses, that criminality rises with hunger and falls with prosperity.

[The actual report:] After extensive deliberation and internal discussions, the various leaders and heads of the cook-shop, bakery, confectionery, butcher, in short, the nutritional professions ... decided to give to their personnel an ... unofficial-official ration of food.

The question remains whether this ... was seen as recognition for really extraordinarily strenuous physical labor or for the purpose of thwarting the terrible increase in "smuggling" [*Schleussens*].

In any case, this was a tribute in the truest sense of the word, by means of which the above superiors wanted to make plain ... the difference between raw material and the finished product of the "Economics Department." ...

"Smuggling" was thus no longer really necessary. With these rations, employees could cover their personal needs (parents, relatives, friends, etc.).

However, as is known, the cat can't stop catching mice. Unfortunately, some of the gangster types were not satisfied with the quantity apportioned to them. It is very enticing, after all, and very exciting to act on one's own or, in the jargon of the ghetto, "to go solo." Surely (once one could afford it) one might still permit oneself, and be allowed to buy, certain luxury items: cigarettes, clothes, shoes, women, etc.?

Thus, complete "smuggling gangs" and organizations were formed out of these elements who blatantly jeopardized the normal running of many operations.

With the establishment of the Economics Police, supervision of all "nutritional" operations by experts, posting of security personnel at the exits and entrances of enterprises and assigning them to "frisk" all ... persons, i.e. to conduct a physical search, the gangster smugglers faced a tough challenge. With time, however, those same parties realized, using some really ingenious ideas, how to preserve their questionable sources of income.

Thus, for example, it was not unusual that the person responsible for heating the kitchen would throw glowing cinders into the ash can on purpose ... and then dousing it with water, shouting that the ash can is on fire, and loading himself to the teeth with various foodstuffs would pant past the kitchen police until he got outside, in order to empty the goods into the waiting bags or knapsacks of his accomplices.

One day someone came to work with high-water boots. In spite of the incredible heat in the kitchen, he didn't take them off, only to be able to tell his friends the following day that he had hidden 8 kilograms of dough in them and that the characteristics of the fermenting dough had almost aroused the suspicion of the police officer on duty. So, as is evident, there also were people who regarded "smuggling" as a sport.

Boiled beef bones were taken out of the kitchen in large cartons that provided cover for large amounts of smuggled goods hidden underneath. The helpful kitchen police usually assisted in lifting these rather heavy cartons, which then were carried away by their confederates in the transport columns.

The Central Butcher and Smokehouse ... had their own police officers who were used as transport or cover-up teams for major or minor smuggling of meat and sausages, and were compensated accordingly.

The backs of two houses encircle the butcher shop's courtyard. The residents of the second floor ... often were surprised by juicy pieces of meat or sausage they found in the hallway in the morning. For purposes of clarification, it must be noted that this abundance of meat was in fact "smuggled goods" that had been forgotten or not retrieved, which a clever hurler had sent from the dangerous courtyard to the second floor ... whence they could be removed without risk.

Meat was primarily ... brought to safety in the more or less expansive folds of the clothing of female meat employees [!]. Sometimes, a woman's body that had been angular the day before could be seen bobbing off, plump and round.

Bread and bakery items usually were smuggled out of the bakery in hidden "smuggling pockets" in suits or dresses. One loaf of bread is fastened horizontally along the length of the spine, the coat over it as camouflage, and one can then stand the test of a cursory frisking.

Legal Conditions 405

The most stable "nutritional" operation purportedly was Central Supply.... . This undertaking had the fewest "smuggling exposures." ... There, only large-scale smuggling took place, in fact mainly on the open street. The vehicle is left in the street, shadowy figures take charge of the waiting packages or boxes and disappear into the next entryway.

Writing about "smuggling" in the ghetto could easily fill the pages of an average-length book. (257)

After this preview of the incongruity between the mentality of the administrators of justice and the alarming rate of criminality, we examine the law itself. As a result of the haste with which the "ghetto" was created, its regulations, which were prepared at the desks of the Jewish Community in Prague and by the "Central Office," were overwhelmed to a certain extent by the reality of the camp. At first, there was hardly any written legal foundation. This was supplied only gradually and was often amended. Initially, few lawyers were involved in its formulation – the "legislators" were the SS and the Council of Elders. Only later were more lawyers included, in order to codify the existing law and its legal foundations. Finally, at the behest of the Council of Elders, the law was compiled for internal use and was published in mimeographed form. The second edition of this work is titled "The Law of the Jewish Settlement Area Theresienstadt (First Edition: Ghetto Law in Theresienstadt) – Compiled as of 15 July 1944, and Briefly Explained by the Former *Oberlandesgerichtsrat* Dr. Jur. Ernst Rosenthal, Director of the Detective Department" (225). After some general observations and a commentary, the regulations were presented in the form of twenty annexes, which took the place of laws. The course of their development – from purely disciplinary to more civil regulations – is apparent in it.

Even after the collapse in the autumn of 1944 (Rosenthal, too, was sent to his death), curiously, the legal comedy had not yet reached the conclusion that is then contained in two "memoranda from the Secretariat" of March 10, 1945. The titles of these memoranda themselves betray the fact that these documents are unique in the history of all concentration camps and similar institutions:

Amendments concerning supplementation and standardization of the criminal law regulations.

Text ordinance concerning the establishment of the new wording of the regulations amended by the ordinance concerning the supplementation and standardization of criminal law regulations. (293, 305)

The following excerpts from Rosenthal's introduction and the texts of the regulations, which have been only negligibly condensed, provide the best overview of the law of Theresienstadt. The following abbreviations are used throughout the introductory portion; these are not in the original but have been added for the sake of brevity.

CE   Council of Elders
DD   Detective Department
DDD   director of the Detective Department
DLD   director of the Legal Department
JE   Jewish Elder
P   the Protectorate of Bohemia and Moravia
S   (Jewish) settlement area
S-A   (Jewish) self-administration
T   Theresienstadt

I. Introduction

In November 1941, S T was founded in P as a ghetto ... by means of a directive from the German authorities in pursuance of the National Socialist policy on Jews. It consists of a coerced community for which there is no historical model, because the ghettos of the Middle Ages were completely different in inception, development, and regulation. Because tens of thousands of Jews live in T, it was necessary, as in every human community, to regulate this communal life through norms and thus to establish a basis for law and order.

There were two ways to achieve this. First, the possibility of adopting applicable law from another source, or establishing a law of its own. In T, both these routes were taken. In principle ... the law of P ... applied.

Special regulations were required, however, for a range of legal relationships under public and private law, because local law was intended for a human community structured in a very different way....

II. Constitution

1. General Provisions
   No basic law for the community ... , no "constitution," has been issued by the German authorities; rather, life in the S is regulated in accordance with the respective regulations of the supervisory authorities....

2. The Jewish Elders
   Under the general provisions of the S-A (see above), the JE is the highest Jewish organ in T. Even without an express directive stating as much, he has the power to exercise authority, i.e. his position in the life of the Jewish community is regulated in accordance with the *Führer* principle. There is neither a general provision concerning the position of the JE, nor is there a charter of the S-A.
   ... The following powers of the JE should be highlighted:
   ... The CE, under the direction of the JE, is the highest Jewish organ.... The JE ... may consult with the SS Office, which is otherwise strictly prohibited. The JE also is the highest Jewish judge in T. Other members of the CE who are exempt from the jurisdiction of other Jewish organs are subject to his punitive power. Moreover, the JE ... is responsible for final decisions concerning appeals of punishments by the Detective Department.... . [There follows citation of many other rights of the JE emanating from the twenty ordinances.]

III. Administration

... The highest Jewish administrative organ is the CE under the direction of the JE.... He has 2 deputies who, with him, carry out the day-to-day "operation" of the S. No particular regulations on the authority of the CE have been published so far: it has an advisory role vis-à-vis the JE [see, however, the regulations governing the CE in Chapter 8, which were more or less followed, at least internally].

For internal administration as an intermediate level of authority, the S is divided into 4 districts, each headed by a district elder. The building elders are subject to their authority. District and building elders can issue orders, within the framework of the authority given to them by the JE.

The lowest-level administrative officials are the house elders, who utilize the room elders to carry out their responsibilities....

IV. Criminal Law

A. Substantive Criminal Law
   ... The buying and selling of objects for personal use and personal possessions or arranging for non-commercial, non-habitual exchange between owner and

acquirer ... is not ... a [forbidden] transaction. It is herewith made clear that the buying and selling of objects for personal use and personal possessions, naturally also in the form of barter, continues to be permitted. Also, in accordance with the actual situation in T, the non-commercial, non-habitual arrangement of such business dealings ... is permitted. Transactions with numerous middlemen and commercial enterprises, of course including usurious ones, are forbidden and punishable.

B. Formal Criminal Law

Where no special regulations exist ... criminal proceedings ... shall be conducted according to the provisions of the Austrian Code of Criminal Procedure of 23 May 1873.

    a) The SS Office at first reserved to itself the punishment of crime. In accordance with a directive of 4 October 1943, however, ... criminal jurisdiction in the S was henceforth also transferred to the criminal court for criminal acts.

    b) The criminal courts also shall have jurisdiction over misdemeanors and administrative infractions....

    e) Police Criminal Law

    ... According to a JE regulation of 2 June 1944, the Detective Department has the authority to punish minor property crimes when the case involves a heretofore blameless suspect, the deed is not aggravated, e.g., it does not involve breaking and entering or group theft, and only the following amounts ... are involved: no more than 3 kg of potatoes, 1 kg of bread, 0.06 kg margarine, 0.1 kg sugar, 3 kg firewood, 10 kg coal.

    [Later amended:] In accordance with an agreement ... approved by the JE on 16 August 1944, the limitations ... are suspended. All minor property crimes are therefore considered petty cases. In these cases, however, the Detective Department may not impose imprisonment of over 5 days.

V. Civil Law

The S is constituted as a social community of occupants. It is entitled to the ownership of all consumer goods, for which, as a rule, private property rights are not recognized. Private ownership is possible only for those inmate possessions ... that were left to inmates when they settled in T, following state confiscation of property at the point of deportation. Private property can additionally be acquired ... in shops ... or from the distribution point. [It is forgotten here that private property obtained through legally received packages, as well as through other internal allocations of goods, was allowed.] ... Property acquired in these ways is also subject to free disposition within legal limits (no profiteering).

To the extent ... that provisions of civil law are involved in specific relationships in T, the Austrian Civil Law Code ... shall be applicable.

A substantial number of transactions under civil law are possible in the area of obligations [*Schuldverhältnisse*]. It is the inmates' prerogative to exchange their possessions for others, or to sell them for ghetto money. They may lend out their possessions at no charge, or rent them for a fee (food items, ghetto currency). Gifts are also permissible. Nor are there reservations against loaning another person property or money. Thus sureties may also be given.

Similarly, service or work-for-hire contracts also can be concluded. The most common cases are the assumption of housework and cleaning tasks, repairs of items, clocks, mending and laundry, suits and the like.

... However, there is no place for complicated legal relationships.... Simple bank transactions, savings accounts in ghetto currency are possible ... that retain the character of savings bank transactions....

Property law is lapsing, as no real property ownership rights are recognized. . . .

It is a peculiarity of civil law in T that legal transactions rely solely on the mutual trust of the inmates. There is no civil jurisdiction through which civil claims could be enforced. However, the ghetto court and the Detective Department are helpful in the settlement of civil disputes.

1. General provisions of Jewish S-A (special camp regulations) as approved by the Camp Commandant SS Hauptsturmführer Dr. Seidl of 5 January 1943, as amended on 2 May 1943.

A. General Part

§ 1. Every ghetto dweller is obliged strictly to adhere to the rules and regulations. Violations will be punished.

§ 2. The highest Jewish organ is the CE under the direction of the JE.

§ 3. The ghetto is divided into four administrative districts. Each district is headed by a district elder; direction of the buildings is in the hands of the building elders.

§ 4. There is a house elder for every building; a group elder is appointed for every group of buildings or for every partial section. He is responsible for quiet, order and cleanliness in his section and also ensures implementation of the directives of the building and district elders and higher offices within his section.

§ 5. A room elder is appointed in every room. He is responsible for quiet, order, and cleanliness in his room. It is his duty to inform the occupants of his room of directives issued by higher offices. All occupants of his room must comply with his instructions.

§ 6. The cleaning crews are responsible for cleaning the courtyard, hallways, stairs, washrooms and toilets. Their superiors are responsible for thorough daily cleaning.

§ 7. Food must be picked up room by room in closed ranks under the direction of the room elders.

§ 8. Appointed doctors provide for the health of the residents. They will see sick patients at appointed times. Doctors will see seriously ill patients in their rooms. Doctors are responsible for transportation to sickrooms. They are also responsible for maintaining sanitary conditions in the rooms.

§ 9. The ghetto guards protect the safety of residents and their property. Their instructions must be followed.

§ 10. Deployment offices determine the division of labor. Anyone who has been assigned to work is obligated to carry out his assigned job in a timely manner to the best of his ability and will. Absenting oneself from the workplace without authorization shall be viewed as a refusal to work and punished in accordance with camp criminal regulations. Leaving the marching crews to and from work stations is not permitted. The instructions of the work crew's leader are to be followed without hesitation.

§ 11. Anyone who has been empowered by the appointed organs to issue orders is a supervisor.

§ 12. Supervisors may give directives and orders only within the scope of the authority granted them.

§ 13. Directives and orders shall be issued in a form comprehensible to everyone.

§ 14. In cases of infractions or disciplinary offenses against the rules set forth in §§ 3 and 4, the district or building elder may impose the following punishments, if they were committed, respectively, by a ghetto dweller from a building in his district or its courtyard, or within his building or courtyard.

I. Administrative penalties:
a) severe reprimand
b) work during free time, at most for 3 days for 4 hours

Legal Conditions

c) deprivation of one daily bread ration
d) deprivation of one hot meal
e) deprivation of daily hot food rations
f) fines to a maximum of 50 ghetto crowns

II. Disciplinary penalties:

a) Fines up to the amount of a monthly cash payment,
b) confinement after work with or without the application of I(d) and (e) for three days at most (confinement to quarters),
c) confinement for up to 8 days with or without the application of I(d) and (e).

Bread and hot rations may be withheld for only 24 hours. Once they enter into force, disciplinary penalties shall be recorded in the penalties log kept by the building and district elders.

Administrative penalties are not registered.

If the guilty party already was punished for his deed by the ghetto court or by the director of the Security Service [note: later renamed the Detective Department], the district and building elders have no authority to punish.

§ 15. Before a sentence is administered, the guilt of the accused must be established for the act of which he is accused.

§ 16. Criminal law shall apply when residents have received three disciplinary punishments.

§ 17. No right of appeal exists against administrative penalties (§ 14 I).

A complaint may be made to the appeals chamber of the ghetto court against the imposition of a disciplinary order (§ 14 II) within three days of its pronouncement or notification. It should be filed orally or in written form to the building or district elder who imposed the penalty.

In particular, the appeal may challenge lack of jurisdiction or deficiency of process and may address the guilty verdict and sentence.

The appeals chamber of the ghetto court shall issue a final decision in the case, following completion of court proceedings, for cases in which the building and district elders have allowed an appeal outside their own purview. In these proceedings, the function of the public prosecutor is taken on by a legal expert from the Department of Internal Administration.

The imposition of a heavier penalty by the appellate court is possible.

B. Special Part

§ 1. Ghetto dwellers shall greet every member of the camp command, the SS guard and government police officers by removing their hats. Women must bow. In addition, anyone wearing a uniform shall be greeted.*

§ 2. When spoken to, inmates shall immediately stand at attention.

§ 3. If not otherwise instructed, a distance of one meter shall be maintained in all cases.

§ 4. It is strictly forbidden for ghetto dwellers to speak unbidden to persons listed under § 1. An exception is made in cases of imminent danger.

§ 5. Visits to the camp head offices are strictly prohibited. An exception is made solely for the JE or his deputy.

§ 6. Ghetto dwellers shall immediately and unconditionally obey orders from members of the camp command, the SS guard, and the police.

§ 7. The same applies to orders by the Jewish organs.

§ 8. Ghetto dwellers are permitted to write once a month. Special provisions apply to members of the Council of Elders. Letters may be written between *Kaserne*. Smuggling letters is punishable by death. Attempts are treated identically to the act.

§ 9. Ghetto dwellers are strictly forbidden to use the telephone. Exceptions require the approval of the camp commandant.

§ 10. Leaving the ghetto without authorization shall be viewed as an escape attempt. During escape attempts, police are authorized to make immediate use of their weapons.

§ 11. Ghetto dwellers are strictly forbidden to enter restricted areas. Exceptions require the approval of the camp commandant.

§ 12. Noise-making is strictly forbidden.

§ 13. Hallways, courtyards and streets shall be kept spotless. If a ghetto dweller sees paper, straw, etc. lying around, he shall pick it up immediately, without being asked, and shall dispose of it in the proper container.

§ 14. Spitting is strictly prohibited.

§ 15. Male ghetto dwellers must wear their hair at a length of 3 mm, women in short male haircuts. Each inmate must visit the barber once every three weeks. Special provisions apply to members of the CE.**

§ 16. First-degree family members may attend burials and cremations.**

Camp Commandant
Dr. (h.c.) Seidl
SS Hauptsturmführer

* repealed: file note 1.348 of 4 March 1944, numeral 28
** no longer in force.

These "camp regulations" were first issued on February 9, 1942 (see 261a). In style and substance, they still evince elements consistent with a concentration camp, but, between the lines, something else had been interpolated and later paved the way for normalized conditions. Some things had long since lost their practical significance, some things were never entirely effective or had since been superseded, and the monthly letter allowance was never put into practice. It is noteworthy that people formally adhered to old regulations that were unknown to those deported to Theresienstadt later.

2. Rules of procedure for the ghetto criminal courts
(edition approved on 5 January 1943 by the Camp Commandant SS Hauptsturmführer Dr. Seidl)

§ 1. In the ghetto, criminal jurisdiction over offenses and misdemeanors is exercised ... by the ghetto criminal courts. At the lowest level, this is a court with one presiding judge and, in the intermediate and highest courts of appeal, cases are decided by a panel of three judges.

§ 2. In regard to substance, the courts are bound by existing criminal law as well as camp criminal regulations.

§ 3. Judges are obliged to consider the merits thoroughly and to reach a decision as rapidly as possible.

§ 4. The form of the proceedings is determined by the presiding judges within the parameters of this and any other rules of conduct.

§ 5. At every deliberation and proceeding a court reporter shall take notes, which shall be signed by all officials taking part.

§ 6. Decisions must be made in written form, short and objective in their findings and signed by all participating judges. The decision shall be provided to the defendant within 5 days of the pronouncement or proceedings.

§ 7. The judges and court reporters may be rejected for partiality. If judges are involved, the decision is made by the DLD; for court reporters, a judge or presiding judge decides.

§ 8. Judges and court reporters who ... are excused from duty because of proximity to the accused or his deed ... must recuse themselves from any proceedings and immediately report the matter to the DLD.

Legal Conditions 411

§ 9. An appeal may be filed ... against judgments from the court of first instance.... The mere declaration that a party wishes to file an appeal is sufficient. Appeals ... are not allowed where the sentence is no longer than one month.... If several defendants are sentenced for the same crime, but only one of them to more than 1 month's detention, all the guilty parties may submit an appeal if the defendant sentenced to more than 1 month of confinement ... has filed an appeal....

§ 10. The appeals court shall reach its decisions ... by majority vote.

The court also decides complaints ... against the imposition of preliminary detention by the first-instance judge and complaints against sentences imposed by the head ... of the security services and the district and building elders.

§ 11. Motions for new trial made by both the defendant and the public prosecutor may be made before the court of first instance.

§ 12. [Regulations follow concerning the admissibility of a motion for a new trial made by the public prosecutor.]

§ 13. The accused has the unrestricted right to file ... a motion requesting a new trial.

§ 14. The camp commandant is entitled to grant clemency.

§ 15. The public prosecutor is subordinate to the DLD and must adhere to his directives.

§ 16. Defense counsel are permitted to take part in the main trial and the appeal. They are also authorized to submit motions in the name of the accused. Juvenile defendants shall have defense counsel appointed for them by the court ... if they ... have not designated their own.

§ 17. The indictment and keeping the list of defense counsel are duties of the Legal Department.

§ 18. Execution of sentence occurs as a rule without delay as soon as the final judgment takes effect. The judgment of the first-instance court is final if ... neither side challenges the decision, the judgment of the court of appeals ... upon its pronouncement or publication.

§ 19. As long as a money economy ... has not been introduced, in place ... of fines, the penalties shall be public censure or deprivation of hot food rations for a period of 1 to 5 days; however, 48 hours of normal rations must come between two days without food.

§ 20. The Legal Department is responsible for supervising execution of sentences.

§ 21. Conditional sentencing is permissible.

§ 22. Each judge swears upon taking office ... "I swear that I will fulfill my duties as judge to the best of my knowledge and will, disinterestedly, fearlessly and with humility, and in true service to the community."

§ 23. Proceedings and decisions concerning cases of defamation of private persons, to the extent they are independent of other misdeeds, are, in principle, outside the jurisdiction of the ghetto courts. They are assigned to special organs.

The Camp Commandant
Dr. (h.c.) Seidl
SS Hauptsturmführer

Theresienstadt, 5 January 1943

According to instructions ... of May 2, 1943, the provisions of § 19 no longer apply.

As a result of the introduction of a money economy ... fines shall be imposed as provided for in the criminal code.

3. Regulations concerning supplemental penalties (RSPe).

The CE has decided to ... supplement existing criminal law with the following regulations concerning supplemental penalties:

§ 1. In cases where community interests are harmed willfully or through gross negligence, the following supplemental penalties may be imposed ... in addition to those provided for in the general law or ... regulations:
   a) Eviction from preferred dwellings,
   b) Loss of the ability to occupy senior positions in the S-A,
   c) Loss of employment in operations where the job description includes procurement of additional goods or is associated with other privileges.
§ 2. The imposition of supplemental penalties is effected simultaneously with the judgment and sentencing by the court, the labor court, the juvenile court, or the disciplinary tribunal, in the form of a supplemental decision. The defendant has the right to appeal the supplemental decision.
§ 3. The Detective Department and the Juvenile Commission may also ... impose ... supplemental penalties with the approval of the JE.
§ 4. ... Authorized authorities may impose supplemental penalties for a specified period of time or with no time limitation. The shortest period ... shall be 6 months.
§ 5. The authority ... to revoke the ability to occupy positions shall not be affected by the right to impose supplemental penalties.
§ 6. Supplemental penalties may be imposed singly or in conjunction with others.
§ 7. The JE shall issue ... implementing regulations.
§ 8. These regulations ... shall take effect ... on 4 May 1944.
   Theresienstadt, 26 April 1944.

4. Implementing regulations concerning supplemental penalties (IRSPe).
§ 1. A preferred dwelling shall be defined as: a family dwelling, dwellings in rooms with an especially low number of occupants, i.e. with more than 3½ sq. m space per person, or in rooms in which fewer than 4 people reside.
§ 2. Senior positions shall be defined as ... those in salary class IV or higher.
§ 3. The list of enterprises ... shall be compiled by the Personnel Office together with the Central Labor Office. It requires the approval of the JE.
§ 4. The imposition of supplemental penalties ... is effected by the Personnel Office and the Central Labor Office.

5. Ordinance against offenses concerning supplies (OOS)
   The CE of the S-A has issued ... the following regulations:
§ 1. Whoever violates regulations meant to ensure the procurement of food, essential goods or services for the inhabitants of T or intentionally by his actions or omissions hinders, disrupts or merely endangers the procurement measures of the S-A shall ... be punished in accordance with these regulations, if no ... more stringent punishment has been imposed.
§ 2. Whoever traffics with essential commodities or arranges such transactions shall ... be punished if no ... more stringent punishment has been imposed.
§ 3. The punishments under §§ 1 and 2 shall consist of detention of up to 3 months, in serious cases detention of up to 6 months.
§ 4. Existing criminal law provisions on attempt, complicity, participation or party to an offense shall apply; ... assistance following commission of a criminal act is punishable in all cases.
§ 5. Adjudication ... under §§ 1 and 2 shall take place in court, in the tribunal for offenses concerning supplies. The tribunal shall be composed of a presiding judge and two lay judges not belonging to the judiciary.
§ 6. The judgments ... take effect without the right of appeal.
§ 7. For juvenile defendants ... the provisions of the juvenile court code shall apply.
§ 8. The indictment ... shall be presented ... by a specially appointed public prosecutor.

Legal Conditions

§ 9. Implementing regulations ... shall be issued by the JE.

§ 10. These regulations ... take effect ... on 4 May 1944.

6. Implementing regulations for the ordinance on offenses concerning supplies (IOOS)

§ 1. [The tribunal is composed of a presiding judge from the court, appointed by the DLD with the approval of the JE, and associate judges in rotation from a list, determined by the JE and approved by the Legal Department.]

§ 2. [The associate judges are sworn in in same manner as judges.]

§ 3. The offices of the S-A conducting investigations shall initiate proceedings with the court on elements of crimes over which they believe the tribunal for offenses concerning supplies has jurisdiction. They shall also submit investigative reports to the court.

§ 4. The indictment ... shall be presented ... by a public prosecutor, appointed by the JE with approval of the DLD.

§ 5. Should there be a question of whether the tribunal ... or the single presiding judge has jurisdiction, the DLD shall make a determination without regard to the status of the proceedings.

§ 6. Should the presiding judge of the tribunal determine that a preliminary investigation is necessary, he shall either conduct it himself or assign it to ... another judge of the court.

§ 7. The term "supplies" includes delivery of goods up to the time they are distributed among consumers. Offenses against property ... after distribution ... shall no longer be considered offenses [under this ordinance]. . . .

§ 8. Buying and selling of goods for personal use and from one's personal property ... is not defined as trafficking.

7a. File note L 121 of 9 June 1943, point 15 b.

The camp commandant advises that the following cases involving sentence enforcement shall be transferred to the S-A:

The camp commandant instructed that in such cases, disciplinary orders shall be issued by the security services, countersigned by the JE, for violation of camp regulations, in particular the regulations concerning objects that must be surrendered. Therefore, the possession of cash, jewelry, diamonds, and other such items does not in itself constitute a crime. Only possession of tobacco products should be mentioned specifically. No reference shall be made in these disciplinary orders to instructions from the commandant's office. However, disciplinary orders shall adopt the term "by special permit." Thus ... punishments can be imposed that exceed the maximum of 4 weeks in the police criminal code. In principle, imprisonment with labor should be imposed. Work shall be chosen in accordance with the prisoners' physical abilities; hence ... prisoners over 70 years of age can be assigned cleaning duties.

7b. File note L 297 of 29 December 1943.

SS Obersturmführer Burger declared categorically that, in all cases in which violations of the order and discipline of the ghetto are to be punished – that is, that involve punishable acts against guards or other representatives of public order – the punishments pronounced by the ghetto court might be formally justifiable according to the letter of law, but they surely appear too lenient in contrast to the seriousness of these crimes in the ghetto. Therefore, in future, criminal acts of this sort shall be adjudicated through special permit, by way of Detective Department disciplinary orders, and hence without limitation of sentence to 30 days' detention, rather than through the ghetto court.

8. Regulations concerning defense counsel

§ 1. In criminal matters, defense counsel is a civil servant within the meaning of the "Internal Regulations for Administration Employees."

§ 2. Defense counsel has the duty to defend ... before all ghetto offices furnished with punitive powers.... No representation is permitted in matters other than criminal and disciplinary cases.

§ 3. Counsels for the defense are maintained as the "Defense Office" within the Legal Department.

§ 4. Defense duties are assigned ... on a rotating basis.

§ 5. [Technical details follow.]

§ 6. Ghetto dwellers seeking appointment of defense counsel can refuse the appointed counsel by stating grounds for refusal. [The decision is made by the director of the Office of Defense Counsel; it is possible to make an appeal to the DLD.]

§ 7. The Director of the Office of Defense Counsel may refuse to assign defense counsel if he considers the appointment clearly ... unwarranted in light of the facts and legal situation. This refusal may be opposed before the DLD.... . The decision of the DLD ... is binding on the Office of Defense Counsel.

§ 8. Civil servant counsels for the defense shall conduct the cases assigned to them to the best of their knowledge and beliefs in accordance with existing standards for defense counsels.... . [Appointment replaces the power of attorney.]

§ 9. These regulations ... become effective on 1 December 1943. On that day, the defense authority of all heretofore appointed part-time defense counsel will lapse.... [Transitional regulations follow.]

The above regulations ... were adopted by the CE of the S-A on 21 November 1943, and approved by the SS office with the proviso that they take effect on ... 1 January 1944.

9. Ordinance to ensure labor discipline (resolution of the CE on 21 March 1943.)

In order to guarantee the universal duty of labor in the service of the community and to ensure the comradeship and discipline of all workers, the CE in T adopts the following ordinance ... :

A. Scope:

1.) Willful or negligent acts and omissions that serve to harm the systematic performance of the work force are subject to the following regulations if

a.) the worker is at least eighteen years of age;

b.) they are not liable for more severe punishment under camp regulations ... or police criminal regulations.

2.) These acts and omissions include in particular

a.) violations of the labor registration rules,

b.) violations of working hours,

aa.) failure to appear at work,

bb.) lateness to work,

cc.) quitting work too early,

dd.) unauthorized breaks,

ee.) inexact or incorrect statements in reports and inquiries,

c.) unjustifiable sub-standard performance,

d.) violations of work discipline and comradeship,

e.) failure carefully to handle tools, materials and inventory before, during and after work.

3.) These regulations shall apply to all working persons, including employees of the administration.... .

B. Labor Court

4. a.) The Labor Court shall reach its decisions in the name of the Jewish Community of T,

b.) Organs of the Labor Court are:

Legal Conditions

a sole presiding judge (labor judge) at the first instance stage,
for appeals, the Labor Criminal Court, consisting of an expert presiding judge and two lay judges.

5.) The judge in the Labor Court, the presiding judge in the Labor Criminal Court, his deputies, and 30 lay judges shall be appointed by the CE; the Central Labor Office has the right to advise.

The designation of lay judges shall take place every 3 months.

6.) If possible, judges should:
   a.) be qualified for the office of judge,
   b.) have language abilities ... as well as ...
   c.) have been present for 6 months and
   d.) have worked in manual labor.

7.) If possible, lay judges should:
   a.) have been present for 6 months,
   b.) have worked in manual labor.

The appointment of lay judges should occur in a manner such that as many as possible of the branches of labor in the ghetto are taken into account.

8.) Upon taking office, every judge and lay judge shall swear the following oath of office in the presence of the JE: "I swear to fulfill my duties as judge to the best of my knowledge and conscience, impartially, fearlessly, and in faithful service to the community."

9.) The presiding judge for every proceeding shall choose the associate judges ... who shall be, where possible, from the same field of work as the accused.

10.) All ghetto administrative offices are required to give legal assistance to the Labor Court.

11.) The Labor Court determines ... whether one of the acts or omissions ... is present and the sentence to be imposed.

12.) Penalties are:
   a.) severe censure,
   b.) imposition of indemnification through additional work after normal working hours up to at most 4 hours and for at most 3 days,
   c.) deprivation of daily bread rations,
   d.) deprivation of bonuses in food stamps and money for 1–2 ten-day periods,
   e.) confinement to quarters ... for up to 14 days, if necessary with deprivation of food stamps
   f.) detention at the end of the work day for up to 8 days, if necessary with deprivation of food stamps
   g.) detention for up to 14 days, if necessary with deprivation of one daily bread ration.

C. Procedure:

13.) [The trial is to be held before the first-instance court within three days and before the appeals court within eight days, and judgment is to be rendered within a further forty-eight hours.]

14.) [The Labor Court determines its rules of procedure with the permission of the administration.]

16.) [Technical details follow.]

17.) [Where there is a risk of suppression of evidence, preventive detention is possible.]

18.) Proceedings ... shall be open to the public.

19.) Permitted ... counsel is ... any adult ghetto dweller of good character.

20.) to 23.) [Various technical provisions follow.]

24.) Decisions shall be set forth in writing, stating grounds. . . .

25.) Conditional judgments are permissible. Probation may last for up to 3 months.

26.) [Appeals against judgments from the court of original jurisdiction are allowed; a declaration is sufficient.]

27.) [This point discusses the decision concerning an appeal.]

28.) [This point discusses when decisions are final.]

29.) The Legal Department is entitled to supervise the implementation of sentences.

30.) Penalties shall ... be recorded in the penalties log kept by the Labor Court judge. Copies of the judgment shall ... be given to the Central Labor Office, the Personnel Department and the relevant department.

31.) These regulations take effect upon publication. . . .

Theresienstadt, 4 April 1943.

File note of

27 October 1943 concerning appeals in juvenile criminal cases (in accordance with an approved proposal of 19 September 1943.)

1. Appeals of Juvenile Court judgments are admissible before the juvenile appellate court division of the Ghetto Criminal Court. . . . [It consists of two judges and one lay judge.] . . .

2. The juvenile division's jurisdiction extends to decisions concerning appeals against findings of the Juvenile Commission, in so far as they do not concern findings ... against the ordinance to ensure workplace discipline.

3. [These appeals] are directed to the Labor Criminal Court ... expert presiding judge, an associate judge from the Labor Criminal Court and one from ... the Juvenile Court. . . .

10. Juvenile Court Code

CE resolution of 4 April 1943.

§ 1. Juvenile court judges shall have jurisdiction over juvenile criminal offenses and infractions.

§ 2. Juveniles are those ... 14–18 years of age.

§ 3. [Directives follow on Protectorate laws as part of ghetto regulations.]

§ 4. Youth Welfare shall be viewed as the Office of Youth Welfare provided for by law.

§ 5. [The court is composed of a juvenile court judge and two lay judges, appointed on the advice of the JE.] Upon taking office, each associate judge must swear the following oath to the JE: "I vow to carry out my office to the best of my knowledge and conscience and that I will keep strictly confidential the content of closed proceedings and court deliberations." Lay judges are required to participate in the main trial. They have the right to pose questions and shall be included by the Juvenile Court judge in the deliberations on a verdict. The Juvenile Court judge shall remain responsible for rendering the decision.

§ 6. Under its supervisory power over the implementations of sentences, the Legal Department shall take appropriate measures regarding the imprisonment of juveniles.

§ 7. Concerning crimes for which punishment falls to ... the security services, the district or building elders or the Labor Court, the Juvenile Commission ... shall hear and decide the case.

§ 8. [The court is composed of an expert presiding judge and two lay judges from the Youth Welfare Office, or one judge from the Central Labor Office.]

§§ 9. and 10.) [Technical regulations follow.]

Legal Conditions
417

§ 11. [This point discusses conditional release after partial serving of a sentence.]

§ 12. A juvenile may be brought before a judge by the police or administrative agencies; however, he should be released at the earliest opportunity, except if he appears to have committed a crime in the objective sense. Detention ... shall be reported without fail to Youth Welfare.

§ 13. With the approval of the camp commandant, the JE has the right to grant clemency regarding rulings by the Juvenile Commission.

Theresienstadt, 27 May 1943.

11. Conflict mediation in the ghetto

1. Hearings and decisions concerning defamation ... of private persons ... fall strictly within the jurisdiction of the mediation offices.

2. The mediation offices conduct hearings and reach decisions in panels consisting of 3 members (mediators) and one secretary....

3. Each *Kaserne* shall create a mediation office by appointing a permanent secretary and issuing a list of twenty mediators.

4. The list of mediators may include only persons of good character. Those possessing law degrees shall have priority.

5. The aggrieved party must deliver ... a short written complaint ... within 3 days of the defamation. He may name one of the mediators ... and may also exclude 2 mediators from the chairmanship. The secretary shall present a copy of the complaint to the opponent, who also has the right to choose ... a mediator and to exclude 2 mediators from the chairmanship. He may also file his own complaint against the original complainant on grounds of reciprocal defamation within 3 days after delivery of the complaint.

6. Should no particular mediators be named, they shall be appointed by the secretary.

7. Both appointed mediators shall choose a presiding mediator from the list of mediators, whereupon the hearing and decision shall proceed ... without delay.

8. If the mediators are unable to agree upon a presiding mediator ... the decision shall be made by lot....

9. Before the start of the proceedings, the presiding mediator and other mediators shall pledge, by handshake with the parties, to decide fairly.

10. Mediation proceedings shall be decided ... by majority vote....

11. The form of the proceedings shall be decided by the mediation panel.

12. The mediators' first priority is to attempt to reconcile the parties. If this is unsuccessful, they may, if the offending party is not acquitted, sentence him to the following penalties:
   1.) public censure,
   2.) deprivation of hot meals for 1–3 days ...
   The public censure shall be posted on the mediation office's notice board.

13. The secretary shall report any penalty immediately to the court.

14. Offenses ... committed together with other crimes, or defamation by perpetrators who have more than three previous convictions by mediation offices, shall be sentenced ... by the court if charges are pressed by the complainant.

Approved
Camp Commandant
Dr. (h.c.) Seidl
SS Obersturmführer

Theresienstadt, 9 February 1942.

Defamation occurred frequently but usually was settled in private where possible and seldom was sent to mediation. Insults to public officials were handled by the court.

12. Criminal Code of the Detective Department (formerly Police Criminal code).
This version in accordance with the instructions of the camp commandant of 22 May 1943, amended by ... directive of the JE of 22 September 1943 concerning abolition of the Security Service main division.
§ 1. The Director of the Detective Department is responsible for punishing those ghetto dwellers guilty of violations of existing precepts and prohibitions, to the extent that they do not concern crimes punishable by the camp commandant's office, the ghetto court or the district or building elders....
§ 2. Sentencing authority ... does not extend to members of the CE and those who enjoy the rights of the CE. They are subject to the punitive power of the JE....
§ 3. The ... penalties to be imposed are
    I. Administrative penalties,
       a) severe censure,
       b) work during free time, for 3 days at most and for 4 hours each,
       c) deprivation of a daily bread ration,
       d) deprivation of a hot meal,
       e) deprivation of meals for one day,
       f) fines of up to 50 crowns.
    II. Penalties by the Detective Department
       a) fines of up to one month's salary in cash,
       b) confinement with or without application of I.(d) and (e) for up to 30 days (confinement to barracks). Bread rations and hot meals may be withheld for only 24 hours.
§ 4. [The rules of procedure are the same as those used before the district elders.]
§ 5. The criminal court shall intervene in cases where occupants have been sentenced 3 times by the Detective Department (§ 3, II).
§ 6. [Appeal to the JE is permissible.]
§ 7. The JE or the appellate division of the ghetto court decide ... as courts of last resort in cases where the appeal has not been allowed by ... the Director of the Detective Department.

13. Regulations concerning lost items and decedents' estates in the ghetto.
§ 1. In light of existing conditions, ghetto dwellers' personal property, to the extent it is in the ghetto and does not consist of family or personal mementos, accrues to the community of ghetto dwellers.
§ 2. The court is the final arbiter of whether an item is a family or personal memento.
§ 3. Should there be ghetto dwellers who have a testamentary or legal right to inherit any such items, some of these items may be left to them upon request within 10 days of the death, if they are needed for their personal use. Decisions are made by the Social Assistance Office....
§ 4. Heirs may also have other inheritable items bequeathed to them even when they cannot use them personally, but have ... an urgent need ... for these other items....
§ 5. In every building, any death must be reported immediately by the room elder to the building elder. The building elder is required without fail to secure all of the deceased's belongings and immediately take them into safe-keeping. At the same time, the building elder shall report to the Legal Department ... that he has taken possession of such items. The ghetto court shall record and describe items of the estate in detail and shall have their common value estimated by a certified appraiser

as of 1 September 1939. The court shall entrust the estate items, after whatever family and personal mementos have been delivered, to the Social Assistance Office. . . .

§ 6. Lost personal property items found in the ghetto and not claimed by their owners within 6 weeks . . . shall also devolve to the community.

§ 7. Honest finders may be granted an appropriate portion . . . as a finder's reward if they have an urgent personal need for the items in question, which shall be determined by the Social Assistance Office.

§ 8. and § 9. [These sections discuss the rules of procedure for found objects.]

§ 10. Whoever receives items as an heir or as a finder's reward must confirm that he has taken them into possession and commits himself to passing on or providing a substitute for these items in the possible case of a more rightful claimant.

§ 11. Should the owner prove ownership of lost property that has . . . devolved to the community . . . within 1 year . . . , it shall be returned to him if still available. . . .

Theresienstadt, 21 January 1942   The Council of Elders.

Decedents' property did not always reach the court and almost never reached it untouched. Relatives, often with the help of those who had lived with the deceased, took valuable objects for themselves, and the less valuable remainder was turned over to the court. Not counting gold dental crowns, wedding rings made of precious metals were the only gold items that Jews were allowed to keep before their time in the camps and in Theresienstadt. Legally, the court was supposed to hand any of the deceased's illegal possessions over to the SS "office." Some people divided up their property themselves before dying or requested that their neighbors take certain things. Often much – or even all – of the estate was stolen, in particular when the deceased had been without family or friends. Sometimes belongings disappeared before the relatives were called. What was then passed on to the administrative functionaries was also pilfered, such that only items of little value arrived at the prescribed offices. How often did relatives search at the court in vain for objects that were rightfully theirs! The heirs seldom received anything, or the promised items could not be found. What happened on a large scale to the property of arriving and departing deportees was practiced in the camp on a smaller but no less reprehensible scale, and the large- and small-scale robbers were never punished by the camp legal system. Few authorities in the "ghetto" enjoyed a reputation worse than the estate administrators of the "ghetto court." Another of their duties was to appoint guardians for children who became orphans in the camp. More commonly, guardians needed to be found for children who arrived as orphans, for children whose parents had emigrated or had already been deported to the East, and finally for children of "mixed marriages," when the Jewish parent was deceased and the "Aryan" parent had remained at home.

It is almost impossible correctly to measure the finders' attitude in the camp. Trifles, documents, and purely personal items often were turned in, but even items that counted as valuable by camp standards found their way to the Lost Property Office. A considerable number of the found objects were never claimed, due to the death or deportation of their owners. More often, finders turned in worthless things robbed from the transports, for example, cases marked with names and "transport numbers." The Lost Property Office was attached to the "Detective Department" and was set up in such a way that, in addition to the "Central Lost Property Office," branches could be found in the barracks and in the various Schleusen.

420   *Sociology*

14. Regulations concerning marriage
    (approved by a resolution of the CE on 30 January 1944)

§ 1. Ghetto dwellers belonging to the Jewish religious community may conduct marriage services before the rabbinate according to the precepts of Jewish religious law.

§ 2. Ghetto dwellers who do not belong to the Jewish religious community or who do not wish to conduct marriage services before the rabbinate may marry in the presence of the JE or one of his deputies. In this way the partners give evidence that they intend to enter into a lasting partnership for life and that they shall carry out the legal formalities of marriage as soon as it becomes possible to do so.

Filing of a marriage announcement may occur only upon meeting those requirements that would permit conclusion of a marriage outside the area of T's S-A.

The announcement of marriage shall have the same effect in law as a religious marriage ceremony for all ... administrative agencies subordinate to the S-A.

§ 3. Special registers shall be kept by the registry office for religious marriage ceremonies and for filing of marriage announcements. The participants shall be thoroughly informed of the legal significance of their declaration. . . .

§ 4. The commitment made by ghetto dwellers through a marriage announcement may be dissolved within the area of the S-A only through special allowance granted by the JE or by an office authorized by him.

§ 5. The JE shall issue ... rules for implementation. He decides on applications for exemption.

15. Implementing rules governing regulations concerning marriage
    I. In the contracting of religious marriages, the following ... regulations shall be observed:
        a) A marriage may occur only upon meeting those requirements that ... would permit a marriage under national law.
        b) Notice of intent to marry shall be given before a religious marriage. Advance notice shall take place both through 10 – ten – days' public notice on the notice board of the Registry Office and Funeral Department, and oral announcements ... during the main worship service at Hauptstraße 2 on three consecutive Sabbaths and holidays. The rabbinical office shall keep a record book of all notices of intent to marry.
For good cause, the required length of time for the advance notice may be shortened or ... an exemption may be approved. . . .
        c) To the extent that ... certified documents are required to be presented but ... cannot be produced, exemption requests shall be filed with the rabbinate. . . .
        d) Parties intending to marry ... shall be instructed by the rabbinate ... about the significance of concluding marriage under civil law and public law. Such instruction shall be registered.
        e) The rabbinate ... shall give notice to the registrar of completed marriages so that the registrar can enter them in the special registry. Notification to the remaining offices of the S-A ... shall be made ... by the registrar.
        f) Through religious marriage, the wife attains the right to use a hyphenated last name in dealings with the S-A by appending her husband's last name to her erstwhile family name.
    II. The following shall apply to the filing of marriage announcements:

Legal Conditions   421

a) By filing a marriage announcement, the marital partners assume the duty to lead their lives in a partnership that may not be dissolved of their own volition. Accordingly, they mutually agree not to abandon each other, to stand by one another faithfully and devotedly in all situations of life, and, if one of the two parties is assigned to a certain place as a dwelling or temporary domicile, that they shall go to this place together. To the extent that the residence can be chosen freely, the wife shall follow the husband to the place of his choice. With the announcement of marriage, the participants solemnly vow to transform their union into a legally valid marriage as soon as the opportunity arises.

b) The petition for permission to file such an announcement . . . and to set a date for the marriage announcement ceremony shall be brought to the registrar of the S-A. . . .

c) The ability to file an announcement of marriage is assumed to exist on the part of those persons who have the capacity to marry under the laws of their own countries.

d) The filing must be preceded . . . by public notice . . . for 10 days . . . in the record book.

e) The JE has sole competence to grant an exemption from producing official documents, for circumstances that otherwise would hinder the ability to contract a marriage, or from providing advance notice. The petition for exemption . . . shall be filed with the registrar. . . . Evidence, to the extent it is available in T, shall be offered concerning the statements made therein. . . .

f) The marriage announcement should take place only when all required official documents have been presented and any obstacles have been . . . eliminated.

g) If no objections . . . are raised, then a date . . . may be set.

h) The registrar . . . shall be charged with . . . receiving [the announcement] . . . two witnesses. The registrar shall . . . instruct the partners about the meaning . . . of the marriage announcement. It shall be made known to the partners that the filing of a marriage announcement does not confer the status of marriage in the civil or public law sense. . . .

i) [The S-A shall treat the partners as married.]

k) [The wife may add her husband's last name to her own.]

l) [This point discusses recording the marriage in a special registry.] The parties shall receive a confirmation document only upon application. . . . The confirmation shall be countersigned by the JE and the registrar and stamped with the S-A seal.

III. The conclusion of religious marriages between persons not of the Jewish faith is not possible because there are no ordained clergy other than those of the Jewish faith within the jurisdiction of the S-A. . . . However, after filing a marriage announcement, [they remain free] to have their union blessed, by a representative of their faith, in the form possible here.

IV. Applications for dissolution of a marriage that resulted from the filing of a marriage announcement shall be submitted to the JE. An employee of the S-A shall be assigned by the JE . . . to carry out a preliminary examination. The employee shall possess qualifications for the senior civil service or . . . a judgeship.

Dissolution of religious marriages shall be carried out, under religious law, by the rabbinate. The rabbinate has the duty ... to examine each case first ... and to report to ... the JE. Divorce may be carried out only if it is confirmed, on the basis of this report, that ... there are no objections to it. A registry of divorces ... shall be kept by the registrar. ...

V. The following shall apply to entries into files:

    a) Religious marriages ... or marriage announcements ... shall be entered into the files of the S-A in T.

    b) The current practice of entering cohabitation arrangements [*Lebensgemeinschaften*] in the family index shall end.

    c) Entries heretofore made in the family index concerning cohabitation shall be expunged. Those affected shall first be informed of this ... and referred to the possibility of making a marriage announcement. If no application is made, the file shall be expunged ... within 10 – ten – days after notification has been sent out; otherwise the old information shall be expunged at the same time as the new entry on filing of a marriage announcement.

    d) The current practice of entering engagements in the family index shall end. With respect to expunging such information ... section c) above ... shall apply.

Directives concerning the waiver of objection of breaking up families.

I. Ghetto dwellers who are legally married to each other but whose marriage has broken down and who cannot obtain a divorce in T may make a declaration that they waive the objection of family breakup for transports or labor assignments.

II. The corresponding request must be signed by both spouses. The signatures shall be certified by the ghetto court, which shall inform the spouses of the legal significance of their declaration. The declaration shall then be presented to the Transport Division of the Central Secretariat for entry into ... the transport index.

III. Such registration ... has the effect that, when one of the spouses is conscripted for transport or labor assignments, the other spouse will not automatically be conscripted as well. ...

Instructions concerning the acknowledgement of partnerships of circumstance [*Schicksalgemeinschaften*].

I. In cases in which ghetto dwellers have formed close emotional relationships, but because of external circumstances neither a religious marriage ceremony nor a marriage announcement are viable options, a request can be made to be regarded as "partners of circumstance" in the index of the Transport Division.

II. Such registration has the effect ... that the other partner of circumstance shall be called up at the same time; however, the entry does not create a claim for protection for the partners of circumstance during transports. ...

III. Requests ... shall be filed with the Transport Division of the Central Secretariat. When presenting the request ... the parties should consider if one of the two partners of circumstance has protections and what they are, and for what reason the application for registration is ... being made.

VI. Such registration ... should be applied for only if the request appears justified from the perspective of the entire Jewish community of T. An essential criterion ... is the duration of the existing partnership. If the

Legal Conditions

partnership of circumstance has not been in existence for more than 3 months, the request should as a rule be refused.

V. No justification needs be given ... for refusal.

21 March 1944

Consequently, legal marriages and divorces were impossible. Before these regulations were issued, not even ritual weddings were recognized, or at least they were not formally recorded. People improvised by having "cohabitation arrangements" and "engagements" entered into the "family index." Some relationships were based on genuine affection; others were entered into out of pity or in hopes of "transport protection." Before the 1944 regulations there was no substitute for divorce. Saving a spouse from deportation first became possible in 1943; otherwise deportation automatically claimed both partners and their children up to around eighteen years of age. In 1942, 142 "cohabitations" were recorded; in 1943, 233 were recorded. In 1944, 97 religious marriages, 88 "marriage announcements," and 20 (or 9, according to other figures) "divorces" were concluded.

16. Internal regulations for employees of the administration.
(Council of Elders resolution of 21 March 1943.)
First section: staff regulations.

I. Scope

§ 1. a. A civil servant under these regulations is anyone who has been appointed by the Personnel Office in this capacity to work in the ghetto administration.

b. The provisions ... shall also be applicable to temporary or probationary employees. These persons may ... be terminated by order of the personnel office.

c. These internal regulations shall not be applied to members of the CE and persons having the rights of those in the CE.

d. For judges and judicial functionaries of the ghetto court, the provisions of special court regulations shall apply.

e. Special internal regulations shall apply ... to members of the Ghetto Guard and the Criminal Guard.

II. Official duties.

§ 2. The civil servant is responsible for the conscientious fulfillment of his official duties and shall prove himself ... worthy of trust through his behavior on and off duty.

§ 3. a. The civil servant shall not undertake any official action from which he himself, his relatives, or third persons could derive advantages.

b. Accepting gifts of any sort ... is strictly forbidden, even if only remotely connected to official duties.

§ 4. a. The civil servant shall follow the orders of his superiors unconditionally within the scope of the general regulations and the directives of supervisory authorities.

b. On instruction from his superior, the civil servant shall assume and carry out every activity that can be expected of him according to his abilities, and to work past normal working hours.

§ 5. Every civil servant shall keep confidential those matters that become known to him, in the course of his official duties, that must be kept secret by official directive or because of their sensitive nature. His superior's authorization is required for statements ... made to the court or another authority. This duty remains incumbent on him ... even after leaving office.

424 *Sociology*

§ 6. When taking office, the civil servant shall vow conscientiously to fulfill the incumbent and assigned duties of his official post.

III   Retirement.

§ 7. Employment ceases:
   1. with death,
   2. by a directive from the personnel office by reason of
       a. a final judgment by the Criminal or Disciplinary Tribunal . . .
       b. an official doctor's finding of long-term . . . disability or incapacity . . .
       c. a disability or incapacity . . . as decided by his superiors with respect to the fulfillment of his official responsibilities,
       d. facts antithetical to the civil servant's appointment . . . that become known to the personnel office after his appointment.
       Second section: Staff disciplinary rules.

IV.   Staff disciplinary penalties

§ 8. Staff disciplinary proceedings shall be conducted by the Personnel Office (V) or by the Disciplinary Tribunal (VI), independently of the procedures as provided in the Ordinance to Ensure Workplace Discipline. . . .

§ 9. Disciplinary penalties are:
   a. simple censure,
   b. severe censure,
   c. partial or total exclusion from the possibility of receiving work bonuses . . . for up to 3 months,
   d. removal from office, if necessary accompanied by . . . denial of the ability to be employed as a civil servant in the future in the ghetto T.

§ 10. [This section discusses the powers of the Personnel Office and the Disciplinary Tribunal.]

V.   Rules of procedure for the Personnel Office.

§ 11. a. Should facts become known that justify a suspicion of neglect of duty, . . . an investigation shall be ordered by the Personnel Office either of its own accord or at the request of the Division Director, and shall be carried out by the duly qualified specialists of the Personnel Office.
   b. When the Personnel Office . . . calls for an investigation, . . . it shall inform the proper head of department.
   c. The material outcome . . . shall be communicated to the suspected civil servant for a response. . . . The civil servant, the head of department, and head of the sub-department can propose supplements to the inquiry.

§ 12. Depending upon the findings . . . the Personnel Office may
   a. Suspend the proceedings,
   b. . . . order . . . disciplinary penalties or,
   c. Initiate proceedings before the Disciplinary Tribunal.

§ 13. [In the case of § 12c, they may suspend the civil servant.]

§ 14. [They have to do so at the request of the head of the department.]

§ 15. The suspended civil servant shall be transferred to the Central Labor Office for other services until a verdict is reached by the Disciplinary Tribunal. Employment shall occur in consultation with the Personnel Office. The ability to mount a defense . . . shall not be prejudiced.

VI.   Rules of procedure before Disciplinary Tribunal

Legal Conditions

§ 16. a. [The tribunal is composed of a presiding judge, two lay judges, and a secretary.] The presiding judge and his deputy shall be professional judges.

    b. The presiding judge, his deputy and a ... number of lay judges shall be appointed to permanent positions by the CE....

    c. A lay judge of the court chamber must be drawn from the administrative branch to which the accused belongs. This lay judge shall be chosen by the Personnel Office. The accused shall nominate the other lay judges from the ... list of lay judges on the Disciplinary Tribunal. If the accused ... does not choose, then the presiding judge of the Disciplinary Tribunal shall make the appointment.

§ 17. The Disciplinary Tribunal shall decide by majority vote....

§ 18. The Disciplinary Tribunal conducts proceedings and reaches verdicts in closed session, even in cases when the duly summoned accused party does not appear.

§ 19. ... the accused may employ the services of ... a defense counsel.

    VII. Right of appeal

§ 20. a. There is no right of appeal ... against disciplinary penalties.

    b. An objection may be filed with the Disciplinary Tribunal ... against a stern censure by the Personnel Office.

    VIII. Temporary provisions

    [Technical provisions follow.]

    Theresienstadt, 4 April 1943.

    17. Staff regulations for the DD [previously the Criminal Guard, abbreviated "Kripo."]

    1.) The DD is composed of male and female members, whose number shall be determined by the JE on the recommendation of the DDD.... The DDD. If there is a hindrance ... a ... chosen deputy.

    2.) Upon commencing their duties, the members ... shall swear an oath in the presence of the Director. The DDD shall apply ... disciplinary law with the approval of the JE.

    3.) and 4.) ...

    5.) The DD is responsible for:

        a. conducting investigations of offenses and making identifications on the instructions of superior authorities, ghetto authorities, and the ghetto court,

        b. administering the Jewish jails,

        c. presiding over the Lost Property Office and

        d. carrying out investigations for the Central Secretariat.

    6.) The DDD exercises punitive power at the behest of and in the name of the Jewish Elder ... under the Police Criminal Code.

    7.) Members of the DD are authorized to undertake all necessary measures to secure the perpetrator, especially arrest and search of his dwelling and person. They have no such rights with regard to members of the CE and those who enjoy of the same rights as the CE. In this case, they are authorized to report only to the JE by way of the DDD.

    8.) Members of the Detective Department enjoy heightened criminal law protection in accordance with § 68 of the criminal law.

426   *Sociology*

In accordance with the resolution of the CE of 14 March 1943, and the ordinance of the JE concerning the main department of the security services.

18. Staff regulations for the Community Guard [previously Ghetto Guard (GW)].

1.) The Community Guard is an organized guard unit with male and female members whose number is determined by the administration on the recommendation of the Community Guard, depending on how many posts need to be filled.

2.) Upon commencing their duties, members of the Community Guard shall take an oath of office to the JE. The chief of the Community Guard shall possess disciplinary authority.

3.) The Community Guard shall receive instructions solely from the JE or his deputies.

4.) The Community Guard shall be composed of:
   a. the chief of the Community Guard,
   b. the chief's deputy,
   c. the chief's adjutant,
   d. administrative personnel, 1 chief registrar, 1 office manager, 1 secretary, 3 other administrative employees, 2 orderlies.
   e. two guard groups, each led by 1 watch group leader, split into 4 district watches with 1 watch group deputy each, 1 watch each led by 1 duty officer and reserves each with 1 deputy duty officer,
   f. patrol supervisor.

5.) Arming and Uniform: on duty, service caps, service number, service belt (only for duty officers and their deputies), whistles, flashlights.

6.) Community Guard responsibilities: As an executive body for the administration, the Community Guard ensures not only adherence to directives of the authorities ... but also the law, order, and security of the lives and property of ghetto dwellers. Each member of the Community Guard has the duty to carry out unconditionally all commands of his superiors. He must take immediate action on any offenses he discovers on and off duty and shall report them through official channels. In cases of criminal violations, the perpetrator shall be taken into custody and delivered to the nearest District Guard unit.

7.) Each member of the Community Guard is responsible for carrying out his official duties, to use force if resistance is encountered so that his commands are obeyed, and to defend himself from attacks on his person by any means necessary.

8.) Members of the Community Guard are subject to general rules and regulations.

9.) Internal staff regulations and the general guard regulations of the Community Guard are supplemented to the service regulations of the Community Guard....

10.) Obligations:
   a. The chief of the Community Guard receives his orders from the ghetto administration; he is responsible for education, training, and order in the Community Guard and in the Community Guard Auxiliary. He applies for promotions and, if necessary, terminations....
   b. His deputy ... is obligated ... to act on his behalf ... in all aspects of duty. Beyond that, he stands ready to assist the chief, helps ...

with administrative duties, training the team, and supervising watch duty.

c. The adjutant to the chief ... is the link between the chief and ... the Community Guard. He is responsible ... for assigning daily duties, putting together reports, and supervising all ... commands....

d. The patrol supervisor assists the chief and checks in with sentries day and night.

e. The watch group leader and his deputy are responsible ... for training and discipline. They hold training sessions, announce the orders of the day, and are, in their official divisions, leaders on duty or commanders of the reserves. They assist the duty officers and their deputies in carrying out their official duties.

f. The leader on duty is responsible for:
    1. assigning guard duty,
    2. inspection of all watches and sentries. He is in charge of guard assignments and gives guards the exact time.... . At least once a day and twice during the night (once before and once after midnight), he inspects all watches and sentries. He shall remedy any problems on the part of watches and sentries immediately and shall report them to the chief of the Community Guard.
    3. immediate intervention in unforeseen incidents. He shall determine what is required at his own initiative and shall report it immediately to the chief of the Community Guard, if it involves an important matter, or for insignificant matters in the stipulated early report....
    4. Turning in the ... early report by 6:30 A.M. ...

g. The commandant of the reserves will always be present in the building at 13 Langestrasse [L 313, the longtime office and residence of the Community Guard]. In case of fire, he ... takes teams to cordon off the area. Under no circumstances ... is he to ... issue orders ... regarding extinguishing the fire.... . If crowds gather, among other things, he shall take similar action ... he shall simultaneously alarm all off-duty members of the Community Guard team.... . He shall sign the assigned early and noon reports on behalf of the team.

h. The duty officers and their deputies are responsible ... for carrying out all commands of the watch group leader. They are responsible ... for the correct disposition of sentries. The deputy duty officer represents the duty officer during guard duty from 1 A.M. to 6 A.M.... During the day, the deputy posts the sentries.

j. The team performs guard duty, security, and patrols. Should unusual incidents occur during off-duty hours ..., without waiting for orders, the off-duty team members shall go to the reserve post....

11.) Reports: Sentries' oral reports are included in the general guard regulations. Prescribed forms shall be used for written reports and morning and noon reports.

428   *Sociology*

12.) Arrests: These shall be carried out by guard officers on duty. If necessary, however, off-duty Community Guardsmen may be called upon. Arrests result from:

I.
    a. orders from superior authorities,
    b. orders from the Community Guard,
    c. orders from the Public Prosecutor.

II.
    a. finding of offenses and crimes,
    b. being caught in the act of insubordination,
    c. manifest danger of collusion and
    d. if it is in the public interest.

Arrest shall be made with the words: "I declare you under arrest." The person in custody shall immediately be taken to the next guard post, or to wherever ordered. Members of the CE may be arrested by the Community Guard only if the Community Guard can produce ... written orders from the JE or the administration. Otherwise, they have only the right to report them. Arrestees shall be taken immediately from the guard post to the DDD for interrogation. From that point on, decisions lie with the DDD.

13.) Official channels: Reports shall be made and forwarded through official channels. Petitions and complaints shall likewise be submitted ... through official channels.

14.) Criminal law: [The chief of the Community Guard can impose the following penalties: censure, severe censure, confinement to barracks, medium confinement for up to fourteen days, and strict confinement for up to seven days; only with the approval of the JE can he impose demotion in rank and exclusion from the Community Guard.] The watch group leader has the right to impose confinement to barracks for up to 3 days. All severe punishments are imposed by the ghetto administration.

15.) Admission: This occurs through physical examination. Only men of good character and of sound morals and body, 45 years old and over [before July 1943, guards could be up to forty-five years old] shall be admitted. Previous military service is a prerequisite.

16.) Duty to greet: ...
    a. by removing one's hat:
        1. all members of the SS office,
        2. anyone wearing the uniform of the German Reich,
        3. government gendarmes,
    b. by saluting:
        1. the JE or his deputies
        2. all superiors,
        3. each other,
        4. the DDD, the Economic Control Office, fire fighters and the head of the Security Police [OD] and their deputies,
        5. members of the Community Guard Auxiliary Service....

17.) Identification papers: Each member ... receives a ... certificate ... regarding his membership in the Community Guard; it shall be signed by the SS office. Such identification papers confer the right ... to enter any property, any place of work at any time of the day or night....

18.) [Regulations and technical details follow.]

19. Statute of the Office of Economic Supervision [also known as the Economic Control Office, abbreviated "Wipo"].

§ 1. The Office of Economic Supervision is the sole supervisory and auditing institution in questions of the economic practices of individuals and the CE's institutions. It was created by the management of the S-A in accordance with a resolution by the CE.

It is directly supervised by the JE or the management of the S-A.... The members of the Office of Economic Supervision shall swear an oath to the JE upon taking office.

§ 2. The Office of Economic Supervision shall attend to the supervision and auditing of economic practices ... in particular ... whether

a) goods meant for provisioning, equipping, accommodation and other maintenance of ghetto dwellers are or were delivered for their designated purpose,

b) this use and distribution to the ghetto dwellers is occurring or has occurred ... as ordered,

c) in those operations and institutions entrusted with the handling of these articles, measures necessary for preserving these goods are or were carried out in accordance with regulations,

d) as soon as the goods ... have been available for use or consumption by the public, that this use or consumption takes or took place in the most efficient way and that most useful to the general public, and whether any intentional or negligent misuse is being or was avoided.

e) the processing of provisions takes or took place in an efficient manner,

f) to the extent that the free trade in essential goods is permitted among ghetto dwellers, that this occurs without any unfair advantage or exploitation of the situation.

§ 3. The Office of Economic Supervision shall investigate especially ... where there exists suspicion of intentional or clearly negligent harm ... to the ghetto or ghetto dwellers.

It does not require a concrete report, but may initiate an investigation based on its own observations. During investigations related to the business financial practices of an entire department or sub-department, before the search is commenced, the head of the Office of Economic Supervision must obtain the approval of the JE or the administration.

In the same way, investigations involving members of the CE or persons enjoying the rights of those on the CE require the prior approval of the administration or the JE. If the Auditing Office intends to conduct examinations of the economic practices of audited persons, institutions or departments and these examinations fall within the authority of the Office of Economic Supervision, the Auditing Office must authorize determination of the facts by the Office of Economic Supervision, by way of the administration.

§ 4. In the course of their official duties, the properly authorized members of the Office of Economic Supervision shall have access to all areas, business premises and workplaces in the ghetto. They must have access to books, notes, statements of accounts and other official documents, and be given all information relating to the matter under investigation.

For inspection of the books, notes and other documents of the administration and the Central Secretariat ... the approval of the administration or, respectively, the Central Secretariat is required.

§ 5. Members of the Office of Economic Supervision are authorized to interrogate ghetto dwellers. Moreover, [they] have ... the same rights and duties as the members of the Detective Department, with the exception of the right to make arrests....

Sociology

§ 6. The head of the Office of Economic Supervision shall report ... to the administration on the outcome of the investigation ... along with possible suggestions on
measures to undertake.

In cases of acts punishable under criminal law ... simultaneous criminal charge
to the ghetto court. . . . .

Theresienstadt, 15 October 1943.

20. Prison rules

1.) To punish the crime, sentences must be enforced without inappropriate leniency. They also should serve to deter the perpetrator and
other persons from committing crimes.

2.) Any unauthorized communication with persons outside the prison is
prohibited.

3.) Wake-up call is at 6:30 A.M.; between 1 April and 30 September,
complete lights out begins at 9:00 P.M., between 1 October and 31
March, at 8:00 P.M.

4.) Prisoners may use only the bedding prescribed for the particular season.

5.) In their cells, prisoners may have 2 changes of clothes (one of them
for work), 1 coat or the like, a head covering, 2 pairs of shoes, 2 pairs
of underwear, eating utensils, washing implements and toiletries.
Bringing other personal property to prison is not allowed.

6.) Receiving any food other than what is found on the communal menu
is forbidden.

7.) The prisoners, separated into men and women, may spend 30 minutes
3 times a day, morning, noon and evening, in the yard for the
purpose of exercise, including use of washing facilities and the toilet.
Communication with strangers is strictly forbidden during this time.
Every two weeks prisoners shall be taken to bathe (or shower).

8.) Medical attention ... shall be available only from the prison doctor,
who is authorized to ... consult other doctors.

9.) Prisoners shall keep order in their cells and shall unconditionally
obey the cell elders chosen by the wardens.

10.) Prisoners are subject to the universal duty to work.

11.) Prisoners are allowed to receive visitors once every 14 days with the
approval of the DDD.

12.) Correspondence ... in accordance with the writing rotation requires
the approval of the DDD.

13.) For infractions of provisions and proscriptions of prison rules, the
prisoners are subject to the disciplinary authority of the DDD. Penalties are deprivation of food (fasting) or solitary confinement, possibly without light.

14.) To submit petitions and complaints, prisoners may also request that
they be brought before the JE. The decision is made by the DDD.

15.) Prisoners in investigative detention shall be kept separate from convicted prisoners whenever possible. The DDD may otherwise regulate their treatment differently from the prison rules.

16.) These prison regulations shall be effective immediately. They shall be
posted in every cell.

Theresienstadt, 2 October 1943.

In March 1945, the regulations were altered almost solely as a formality. The rules
on "mediation offices" and the "disciplinary regulations for the Detective

Department" were repealed. Building elders and other officials, now called "directors" (*Leiter*), retained only the right to issue warnings. The power to punish in these cases was transferred to the administrative judge in the "Jewish court." The greatest changes were made to the "staff regulations for employees of the self-administration," the first paragraph of which now read: "Employees of the self-administration are responsible for the conscientious fulfillment of their duties, and by their conduct on and off duty shall prove themselves worthy of the trust placed in them through their appointment. In their interactions with the parties, they shall maintain an appropriate tone (279)."

In the early months, when punitive procedure had serious consequences for those convicted, it generally involved "crimes" prosecuted by the SS, on whose orders most arrests took place at the time. Arrestees were held under harsh and miserable conditions in the custody of the gendarmes – men were held in E I, and women in H V – and were constantly exposed to abuse by SS men. On the orders of the SS, they were clubbed even by the Community Guard members, who were themselves beaten if they did not beat hard enough. People were released on the orders of the SS as soon as the arbitrary sentence was served, sometimes after Edelstein's successful intervention. Meanwhile, however, an internal camp prison already existed in B V. Later, all prisons were transferred to Jewish control; however, this did not include those imprisoned in the SS "bunker," who were thus, in any case, completely removed from the jurisdiction of the Jews. However, as circumstances developed, and as reflected in the regulations issued, more and more authority was transferred to the self-administration. A table for the 1942 annual report lists "criminality in the ghetto in 1942," according to the provisions of Czechoslovakian criminal law, as follows:

§ 134	Murder	none
§ 140	Manslaughter	none
§ 190	Robbery	none
§ 132	Serious bodily injury	none
§ 76	Public violence	none
§ 68	Insurrection	none
§ 125	Rape	none
§ 461	Misappropriation	8 cases
§ 460	Theft	156 cases
§ 462	Fraud	13 cases
§ 312	Insulting guards	62 cases
§ 411	Offenses against bodily security	14 cases

Since 24 November 1941, 109,193 people have arrived in Theresienstadt.

These figures are obviously wrong; moreover, they do not correspond to the figures provided in another table for the same period:

The following offenses were reported

January	78	These include :		
February	85	Thefts – losses	3, 798	72%
March	90	Estate matters	620	12%
April	136	Insults to guards & acts against the police	520	11%

April	136	Fraud & misappropriation	102	2%
May	164	Fighting	92	2%
June	381	Defamation	51	1%
July	700			
August	821			
September	728			
October	671			
November	613			
December	716			
TOTALS:	5,183		5,183	100%

Even if these statistics do not provide a reliable overview of criminality in Theresienstadt, they are nevertheless instructive, because they indicate, as early as the first five months of 1942, a decrease in the level of solidarity and, in June, the first month in which foreign elderly people arrived, rose by a full 130%, whereas the population increased by only approximately 33%. Thus they confirm the general moral decline starting in the summer of 1942, as described in Chapter 5. Serious crimes as defined by the criminal code were infrequent in the camp, but we have already shown that there often occurred conduct that cannot be described as anything other than serious crimes, because it harmed the victims repeatedly and severely and often was the cause of – or at least hastened – their deaths. Therefore, it is misleading to summarize the criminality in Theresienstadt, which has not been recorded statistically, by saying that neither murders nor other serious crimes – which, according to otherwise adequate definitions, always were rare among Jews in any case – occurred there. For example, in one case – which was known but kept quiet by the SS – an elderly woman was robbed, and the outcome for her was fatal. No serious sexual offenses are known of; however, sexual extortion – for example, in connection with impending deportation – did occur.

The following are judgments by the "ghetto court" in the form in which they were published in the orders of the day (men's names were given as N.N., and women's as M.M.; the following "transport number" was designated "A" for members of the Construction Kommando, "P" for other prisoners from the "Protectorate," and "D" for Germans and Austrians):

Judgment of the ghetto criminal court.

a.) N.N., A, residing in the Sudeten Kaserne, on 13 March 1942, incarceration for a period of 3 days, increased with deprivation of warm meals on the second day of the sentence. Crime: On 4 March 1942, he caused minor injury to a camp dweller.

b.) M.M., P, residing in the Hamburg Kaserne, on 18 March 1942, incarceration for a period of 3 days. As a result of conviction, the loss of the right to hold a position in the ghetto was imposed. Crime: In February 1942, she stole various items from a roommate. (daily report, March 24, 1942)

The following were sentenced by the ghetto criminal court in Theresienstadt:

N.N., A, residing in the Sudeten Kaserne, incarceration for a period of 2 days. Crime: On 6 March 1942, he committed an offense against an on-duty ghetto guard. (daily report, March 25, 1942)

The following were sentenced by the ghetto criminal court: N.N., A, residing in E I, incarceration for a period of 2 months, increased by deprivation of warm meals one day per week and solitary confinement for the last 3 days of the sentence. As a result of

Legal Conditions   433

conviction, loss of the right to hold a position in the ghetto was imposed. This punishment is unconditional.

Crime: The person convicted stole various items in I IV. [The theft took place in the "clothing warehouse"; hence it most likely harmed the SS and not the "ghetto."] (daily report, November 9, 1942)

N.N., D, detention for a period of 4 days. The person convicted procured food with a ration card he had found.

M.M., D, detention for a period of 48 hours, commuted to a fine of 100 crowns. The person convicted was guilty of verbally insulting an on-duty house elder. (daily report, January 10, 1944)

Sentences: N.N., A, was sentenced to 6 months' detention for violating the regulations concerning the surrender of items during processing into the ghetto and for possessing prohibited items (1 packet of tobacco products) [the person convicted was a member of the "Detective Department"], ... for stealing 20 dkg [200 g] of spinach, 3 days of detention. [Three names follow. These were thefts in the "agricultural sector," to the detriment of the SS.] (daily report, March 11, 1944)

The most frequently prosecuted offenses were violations of SS regulations, whereas objective criminals were, often enough, not called to account at all. Furthermore, misdemeanors and infractions often were punished with disproportionate severity compared with truly criminal acts, which, however, could not be formally classified as crimes; judges, with questionable leniency, liked to impose astonishingly low sentences for such criminal acts. The "ghetto court" held open sessions, but the SS sometimes monitored the audience, and those who were supposed to be working could not allow themselves to be caught. Imprisonment was mild in the Jewish prison; the difference between "freedom" and "confinement" in the camp was negligible and often barely perceptible. It was nearly impossible to isolate anyone, especially someone sentenced to labor. Later, when the Jewish prison was only in H V, there was no difference between it and the normal quarters of "free" inmates. The prisoners received normal camp rations in ample portions, as a result of a solidarity that, oddly enough, did function there, as well as out of pity; therefore, they starved less than many other "ghetto dwellers."

The "Detective Department" developed out of the Community Guard, and some of its functionaries were entrusted with special assignments. At first two, and later seven, "investigators" were employed. When the central "Security Office" was created in the summer of 1942, the "Criminal Guard" and later the "Detective Department" – with its "investigators" – were formed. In the fall of 1942, the personnel of the "Detective Department" consisted of two "investigative branches"; twenty-five male and fifteen female detectives; four prison wardens, called "provosts" (*Profose*); and some administrative employees. Later the group grew, and by the summer of 1944 it employed ninety-two persons. The "Detective Department" was assigned the following responsibilities: maintaining the lost property offices; accepting lost item reports; filling out reports and carrying out investigations in connection with crimes; determining infractions; performing house and body searches; inspecting buildings, kitchens, and other workplaces; carrying out police raids; guarding freight transports; investigating personnel; determining the identity of the dead; and running the prisons. The department did not enjoy an especially good reputation in the camp; too many foxes were guarding the hen

434 *Sociology*

house. The same soon became true of the "Office of Economic Supervision," founded by Loewenstein, which was supposed to combat the inextinguishable number-one evil in the camp. After its founder was eliminated, creeping corruption spread further and further there as well, such that all this organization achieved in the end was to increase the number of beneficiaries of the general mischief, to make it more difficult for individuals to partake of the ill-gotten gains, and decrease the average personal share of the booty. The "Office of Economic Supervision," to which the "kitchen guards" who were posted near every kitchen belonged, counted 166 members in the summer of 1944. A report from the "Detective Department" offers insights into their work:

> Detective Department   Theresienstadt, 31 January 1944
> B V/114.   Dr. Ro/K.
> To the Economics Department.
>
> The night shift from the 26 to the 31 of January 1944 reported the following:
> Kitchen at Langestrasse 13. Distribution window poorly locked. Laundry at Neue Gasse 10. Despite the break-in of a few days ago, the entrance door has not been locked with a padlock.
> Kitchen at Hauptstrasse 6/8. The side window skylights are left open for airing. Because these skylights do not have bars, there is a danger of someone climbing in.
> Diet Kitchen at Neue Gasse 3: the storehouse window (to the courtyard) poorly locked (already often criticized).
> Kitchen E VII. Distribution window unlocked. The cook was woken up at night to see to its locking.
> A IV – Rationing Office: people sleeping in the Rationing Office, therefore unlocked.
>   Detective Department
>   Director [signed] Dr. Rosenthal

The "Ghetto Guard" was described more fully in Chapter 5. At first attached to the "Department of Internal Administration," it was separated from it when the "Security Office" was created. After August 1943, it – along with all other decentralized police formations – was made subject to the authority of the Jewish Elder and the administration. By March 1942, the Ghetto Guard had already been reduced to a nominal 250 men; in actuality, there were only 220. When it was broken up in May 1942 and temporarily changed to the "Order Guard" (*Ordnerwache*), the staff was reduced to 50. The "opening of the ghetto" and the gendarmes' withdrawal from the city made it necessary to increase its size to 170 on July 6, 1942. In early 1943 it reached its largest size, at 420 men, including an additional reserve force. Loewenstein wanted to create a quasi-military body in order – he hoped – to lead the camp safely through the most difficult periods to liberation, as soon as the regime should collapse. But even before his fall, in July 1943, the Ghetto Guard had to be reduced to 150 and was transformed into a high-class veterans' club. Eventually, the force was again increased to 200 persons. In the fall of 1944, the Ghetto Guard was finally shattered for good and was allowed to maintain around 50 men approximately until the end of the war.

The scope of the responsibility of the "Security Office" at its most developed, around May and June of 1943, was described in an undated document, which said the following about the Ghetto Guard:

The Ghetto Guard is a guard body ... providing guard service in the ghetto. This guard service is assigned many special tasks. Of these, the most important are:

a.) The service of the Ghetto Guard as sentries; it prevents unauthorized exit from the ghetto and entrance into prohibited areas ... , it is the duty of the guard to prevent unauthorized persons from entering the ghetto.
b.) Barracks duty (maintaining law and order in the barracks as an assistance to the Security Division).
c.) Guarding the prisons and detainees.
d.) Assistance with arriving and departing transports.
e.) General guard duty, as part of which the Ghetto Guard shall ensure that the administrative rules of the superior authorities and the Council of Elders in the ghetto are observed.
f.) Identification of persons, arrest if necessary....
g.) General reserve duty....

... The team shall relieve those on duty every 24 hours.

As part of the Ghetto Guard, an auxiliary was created out of elderly people, tasked with providing camp inmates with information on the addresses of the authorities and bringing lost persons home. The auxiliary also regulates traffic in the shops.

The following "staff regulations of the Community Guard" are a slightly altered excerpt from Loewenstein's "internal and disciplinary regulations of the Ghetto Guard." Some portions of this passage show what was important to Loewenstein and what he demanded of the team:

The Order Guard [Ghetto Guard] is a guard body organized on military principles. German is the official language. The team's first responsibility is guard and security duty on the streets and also in the barracks.... . The members of the Ghetto Guard are required on and off-duty to dress in a clean and orderly fashion, behave in a respectable and polite manner toward other ghetto dwellers, and act in exemplary fashion in every respect. Fulfillment of these requirements is a particular obligation while on duty. Furthermore, the team on duty shall be quiet, discreet, comradely, and helpful, without lacking requisite energy. Only in an emergency shall they make use of the instruments of force at their disposal. Every single case of the use of the instruments of force shall be reported to the administration; it will be examined, and excessive uses of force shall be punished most severely.

All members of the Ghetto Guard shall be informed about the local situation, offices, functionaries, first aid, etc., in order to be able to give the public information. They shall receive a service notebook for this purpose. Daily assignments: 6:00 A.M. (in winter 7:00 A.M.) daytime watch, airing out the beds, 6:30 to 7:00 A.M., alternately, gymnastics, calisthenics, jiu-jitsu, shadow boxing, 7:00 to 8:30 A.M. washing, dressing, cleaning the rooms, breakfast, 8:30 to 10:00 A.M. activities: exercises and training in accordance with a defined program. Report. Issue of orders, mess assignments. Guard assignments, changing of the guards and reserves. Guard members returning after duty shall have the afternoon free.

The Ghetto Guard members had to take the following oath: "I swear by God the almighty that, to the best of my will and conscience, I shall serve the Jewish Elder unselfishly, fearlessly, and loyally, for the benefit and good of the Theresienstadt Ghetto."

On May 2, 1942, the camp took possession of the city's volunteer firefighters' equipment, including a motorized pump truck with a trailer, a truck with a trailer

436   *Sociology*

and a motorized spray, and a riot squad vehicle with a trailer. In the summer of 1942, fifty firefighters with their commanders moved into building L 502, which bordered the equipment building. In the fall of 1944, the entire team was deported. Only the commanders were retained; they then had to train a new team. In the first year, approximately 200 fires were extinguished, and, by liberation, the number had increased to about 800. Some dangerous fires had to be dealt with, but no major fires occurred. "Fire safety regulations" mandated that no open flames, for example, candles and cookers, could be used; of course, no one adhered to this regulation. Ovens were to be put out an hour before bedtime, two full buckets of water were to be present in all living quarters, hallways and attics were to be equipped with a sufficient amount of sand, and house elders and guard posts were to have access to extinguishing tools such as buckets and sand.

The undated document previously cited in regard to the "Security Service" also mentions the fire department's responsibilities (see also 110, 308):

> With the exception of duties that arise from the designation of this department ... air-defense duties must also be fulfilled; these consist mainly of observing the black-out rules. The broader scope of duties include: burning infected and vermin-infested straw mattresses, assistance at the train station with arriving and departing transports, working with the extension ladder for the telephone office, first aid, general assistance in various jobs where rapid response is needed, rescue work during floods, reserve units on the Eger, completion of various types of technical work, e.g., setting up tents for *K-Produktion*, various tasks related to sewer problem, e.g., flushing out sewers and other water works, etc. etc.
>
> Organization ...: It is headed by a director. Two reserve teams of up to 25 men have alternating duty every 24 hours. Every reserve team has a reserve team commander and two commanders in charge of equipment.

Air defense was limited to the same general measures used in less threatened areas. No planes were directed at Theresienstadt. To the prisoners' joy, air-raid alarms were sounded on occasion. This happened more often starting in 1944, at which point people began to look longingly at the high flying Allied squadrons. The prisoners hoped that these squadrons would help them achieve the rights (*Rechte*) that would fulfil l their wishes. But most confused law (*Recht*) with justice (*Gerechtigkeit*) and with the indomitable claim to freedom of shamefully mistreated creatures – as has been related throughout the history of humanity since time immemorial.

16

Health Conditions

The coerced community constituted a diseased society. The Jews were considered the scum of the earth; before the ability or desire to kill them all existed, many were taken to Theresienstadt, to an intermediate sphere between life and death. Thus, this place came to be an "infirmary" for the disenfranchised and the sick, during a sick and lawless time. In this enterprise everything was enfeebled and was condemned to plagues and infirmity; the spirit of the "Reich" and the "ghetto" was ill, as all was dominated by a decay that tainted the soul and plunged the people into an abyss. The chilling reports of past horrors appeared, in comparison, like the weathered fables of a long-forgotten nightmare. What could have prevented this complete breakdown; what could have sustained the health of body and soul? The dynamic of all known human passions – strangely transformed, exaggerated, and shrill – played itself out in this demonic twilight zone, in a constant struggle for salvation from dark forces. Most important was the struggle to preserve or to regain health; it found its expression in the institution of the "Health Services Department." This department attempted to cure countless ailments through sacrifice and precious remedies, but those close to recovery, although still weak on their feet, were categorized as "fit for transport" and might be deported to Auschwitz two days later, where a flick of the finger sent them to the gas chambers, to be burned to ashes in gigantic ovens, namelessly, a few hours later.

The "Health Services Department" was as good or as bad as other departments of the self-administration. It employed the best and most capable as well as the worst and least capable people. This department, too, was overmechanized and had grown into a monstrosity, like the rest of the administrative apparatus. The insanity of the camp – its "transport numbers" and "categories" – made people ill even outside the sickroom, and this illness accompanied the prisoners when they fell victim to organic diseases. The anxieties of camp life were not lessened; illness was simply added to them. But sometimes sickness so preoccupied one that a sense of euphoria temporarily neutralized other concerns. The sick were surrounded by doctors and nurses who demonstrated all sorts of behaviors toward their patients, from devotion to indifference, and from corruption to aversion. Yet the people attending the sick were sick themselves, harassed by similar needs and driven by similar desires; the all-encompassing inhumanity made it difficult for them to remain humane and to transmit the sense of security that a patient needs for rest and recovery. Everyone was ill – equipped with a greater or lesser strength of will to fight evil but hopelessly tired and sore. In this environment, physical well-being seemed almost an insult or a challenge, or perhaps as just a laboriously sustained mental state that imparted, through denial or playful thoughtlessness, an attitude reminiscent of health.

Naturally, disease in the medical sense was frequent. It virtually offered itself up and often was unavoidable. A psychological predisposition to illness was a given; illnesses and their symptoms were a clear, or sometimes more mysterious, response to a shattered existence and an emotional state that bore this existence, acknowledged it, and tried in many ways to process it emotionally. The reports and statistics subsequently made available represent only a small portion of the suffering that reaped its terrible harvest in Theresienstadt. No struggle against it, even with super-human effort, could have had satisfactory results. In external appearance alone, Theresienstadt itself soon resembled a hospital or an insane asylum.

The symptoms of disease were closely connected to the conditions of the camp. They frequently diverged significantly from familiar clinical patterns. Some diseases typically took less serious, sometimes even abortive, form; others were barely even noticed or were simply ignored. But this was less often the case than was its opposite, as diseases frequently took a turn worse than otherwise would have been the case. Complications were frequent, symptoms more confusing, the duration significantly longer, and the illnesses' resistance to therapy more stubborn, particularly because the prisoners' psychological disposition was so different from that of normal life. Mixed infections or linked illnesses appeared simultaneously or in succession. Physicians had no easy task when it came to patients and their "cases." They would have had to have been psychiatrists to be able to recognize the neurotic symptoms accompanying many of the ailments. The degree of self-administration that was allowed made possible an escape into disease that took place to a much larger extent and involved comparatively lesser risk than would have been the case in a stricter camp, where murder frequently put a quick end to all suffering. In this sense, disease did not represent a threat in Theresienstadt, although, following express orders, tuberculosis patients and the mentally ill on several occasions were deported in groups. Illness may have been detrimental, yet it was possible, with some skill or good luck, to make up for this with other benefits, such as more pleasant accommodations for a time through transfer to one of the better hospitals. One avoided work and was able to rest. One was able to escape – as happened in cases of tuberculosis and assumed or real encephalitis – into a *Magic Mountain* atmosphere, where one existed within a much more serious disease, the disease of the society itself.

As in other camps, illness was an everyday topic of conversation, even among children. The distance between a "normal" patient and a "normal" physician in a normal society had nearly disappeared, even if this distance may always have been less among Jews than among other peoples. Everybody knew everything. The colloquial language was interspersed with medical terminology or semimedical slang. Children conversed professionally about the diagnosis and prognosis of their ailments: "I just have a hilus." They knew their blood pressure and the names and doses of medications. Medical issues had become part of daily life. Simulated illness was not combated as firmly as it should have been, yet it did not occur excessively. The abundance of objective, rather than merely imaginary, illnesses remained overwhelming – a fact confirmed by the occurrence of epidemics and numerous ailments even in

Health Conditions

the "healthy" people's quarters. On the other hand, misuse of outpatient services took place even more frequently than for illnesses for which bed rest was indicated. People ran to the doctor for the most minor skin abrasion or faintest sign of indigestion, to be given a bandage or a powder. The general sense of suffering was transferred to any incident that interfered with physical well-being; people secretly hoped to receive from the doctor something altogether different from what they tried to make him, and themselves, believe. After such a visit, having been examined and prescribed iodine or an aspirin, the patient was often satisfied for a time; there would be occasion soon enough to consult the doctor about a different ailment. There also were permanent patients whose ailments refused to disappear, and who therefore constantly asked for things the doctor could not give, such as a simple piece of bread or a remedy against deportation, or innumerable other things. Of course, these creeping, latent, imaginary illnesses – diseases in an imaginary world – were accompanied by very real sensations of pain, such as difficulty walking (a slouching walk was typical of Theresienstadt), headaches, stomachaches, and heart ailments. This made it much harder to draw the line between illness and health than in a normal practice in which neurotic, hysterical, and hypochondriacal states overlap much more rarely with so-called objective diseases, and certainly in very different ways. Many of the countless outpatient visits were of course medically justifiable. This even held true for the fear of a potentially real illness. People observed themselves more closely than would have been the case in a different environment; they saw roommates who felt well and then suddenly fell severely ill, due to long-undiscovered illnesses – such as lung disease – that then progressed swiftly. People were aware of how even the smallest wound could initiate a protracted septic process, and how slowly a neglected abrasion would heal. Such worries often contrasted with carelessness about serious infectious diseases. People were surprised when they were advised of the dangers of contact with the typhoid or scarlet fever patients who had lain among their roommates before being transferred, whereas, before, those same people would have anxiously avoided these patients.

Initially, there was a disastrous shortage of medication and other therapeutic or clinical necessities. This situation slowly improved. Eventually, the available resources were comparable to those of clinics in major cities: there were X-ray machines, photography and radiation equipment, electrocardiograms, long- and shortwave diathermic devices, sunlamps, Sollux heat lamps, and so forth. All sorts of laboratory tests could be conducted, although bacteriology was restricted to bacterioscopy, because breeding and animal experiments were forbidden. The supply of medications also improved, although it frequently was necessary to resort to substitutes: iodine, for instance, was replaced by *jox* or *sepso* (a manganese combination); for a long time, there also was a shortage of much-needed sulfonamides, which were acquired in 1942 on the black market for 2,000 crowns, or more for a roll of tablets or a packet of injections; and alkaloids were essentially unattainable. Coloring agents such as Panflavin were rare or completely unavailable. Other special medications, some of them quite expensive, were available in surprisingly large amounts; in some cases they were used in place of much cheaper preparations that would have been equally effective. A strange kind of abuse of medications took place, almost as though people wanted to replace the lack of natural remedies, such as a healthy diet and plenty of rest, which frequently simply were not to be had, by these means, although their value often was questionable or would have made sense only in

440 *Sociology*

combination with natural means. In some cases the patients simply swallowed the contents of ampules of glucose!

Doctors and patients succumbed to a strange faith in the most varied of remedies. It should be kept in mind that the system in Theresienstadt differed from the system of practices accepting government insurance and private practices, just as it differed from the health system in, for example, the Łódź Ghetto or from ordinary concentration camps. Treatment and medications were free. The physician was not bound by any strict rules. Patients were not limited by the inhibitions that might have forced them to avoid expense or abuse. It was easy for doctors to order or for them to conduct clinical examinations that otherwise would occur only in serious cases or at large hospitals. Thus, they took puncture specimens and conducted unnecessary bloodwork, complicated urinary tests, sedimentation tests, and the like. Superfluous physical diagnostic procedures also were undertaken; something had to be done, after all. A report by Dr. Reiss, a prudent practitioner, presented to physicians in Theresienstadt on March 4, 1943, served as an introduction to these kinds of problems:

There is no sick pay, no pharmacy tax, no choice between cheap and expensive medications, etc. We frequently are forced to practice the exact opposite of economical prescription practice.... We can save money only if we prescribe medications when they are truly necessary to cure the patient.... In that case, the principle to be observed is to combat polypharmacy. Some examples: gargles for throat infections need not be prescribed at all, as ... it has been proven that they are useless, as they do not come into contact with the tonsils at all, and on the basis of experience indicating that a swollen organ should be left alone.... We know that illnesses of the nasal passages, especially colds, really cannot be influenced by nose drops. The same is true of throat painting for chronic throat ailments.... Because times are difficult, not only were many of our patients forced to go from being heavy smokers to non-smokers without suffering withdrawal symptoms, but also people who had to have their daily sleeping powder, Hoffmann's drops, baldrian drops, pyramidons, etc., suddenly were forced to do without these completely, without suffering harm to their health; in fact, the opposite was the case. The fight against the abuse of hypnotic drugs, narcotics, nervines, etc.... thus seems justified. It is polypharmacy, and harmful to the patient, to give him such medications by injection when they would have the same effect orally. This must be especially emphasized in the ghetto, because 1. few injections are available, 2. there is no alcohol, no tincture of iodine, no benzine to disinfect the skin, but only substitute preparations, 3. our patients' skin is not as clean and the tissues not as resistant to infection as is normally the case. I would like to offer as a glaring example of polypharmacy the fact that one of our skin doctors determined that hundreds of calcium injections had been unnecessarily administered for urticarial skin ailments that had been induced exogenously by insect bites, although it is common knowledge that in such cases these injections have no effect. Prominent phthisiologists have described calcium treatments for tuberculosis as ineffective and inappropriate. Nevertheless, they continue to be administered, even here in the ghetto, where they can have no effect, if only because the medication is given in inadequate doses. Dipron and related preparations were introduced as specifically effective medications for coccus infections. It was reported here that this preparation had little or no effect on *Streptococcus* infections, but had a positive effect on furuncles, carbuncles and phlegmons.... The head of the Internal Medicine Department even reported that, in a period in which no Dipron was to be had in the ghetto, erysipelas was treated without Dipron and, surprisingly, healed very well and very quickly. If we nevertheless take the position that it is a professional error today not

Health Conditions 441

to use Dipron for erysipelas, then we must always have Dipron for erysipelas.... But not only does the population of the ghetto see Dipron as a harmless all-around cure and take it for every illness; even our doctors have practiced a great deal of polypharmacy in this regard. The effect of Albucid on enteritis is not always impressive. We could see for ourselves that serious cases of enteritis deteriorated and could not be remedied by any medications, including Albucid. On the other hand, acute enteritis quickly disappears in young, strong people, even if no medications are prescribed at all. Thus, we give Albucid only in serious cases, but not for less-serious enteritis in young people. Scientific tests were undertaken here with sulfonamides, to see if ... they are effective, for example, for typhoid fever. I consider this process ... in which we often are forced by shortages to refrain from using them even where their positive effect already has been determined, for example for pneumonia, to be unacceptable. The administering of Dipron and similar preparations "prophylactically" to healthy people threatened with "angina" is even more deplorable. Much polypharmacy is being practiced with Ichthyol treatment for erysipelas, but also for other illnesses of the skin and subcutaneous layer. The results with Ichthyol never have been impressive. Yet it stops the skin from breathing.... Much bandage material has been used and a great deal of laundry dirtied. I myself have almost never used Ichthyol and yet have had good results. Given the existing shortages of bandages and soap, I consider its use to be contraindicated. It is a well-known rule that excoriations should not be painted with tincture of iodine and, if possible, should not be bandaged. We see that a harmless skin abrasion is painted with strong disinfectant solution and then, if possible, covered with a salve bandage. And if dermatitis then appears, it is again treated with salve and bandages. An excoriation that, without treatment or with simple washing and perhaps some application of grease to the skin, otherwise would have disappeared without a trace in a few days is thus treated for weeks with salve and bandages, with great effort and to the detriment of the patient. It always is a mistake to apply bandages or adhesive tape to fresh furuncles that are not open. Even more so in Theresienstadt.... Here only the application of warmth, especially through irradiation, is correct.... For surgical treatment of wounds, it must be ensured that even the type of incision creates favorable conditions for the draining of pus and the healing of the wound.... Finally, I would like to remark that administration in desperate cases or to the dying should be avoided, not only from an economic point of view, but also from a human and medical standpoint. There is no point in injecting the dying with all sorts of expensive preparations, although we are only too aware that no help is possible.... We come to the conclusion that even a conscientious doctor, as long as he was a self-employed entrepreneur, often had to practice polypharmacy even against his better judgment. He was, after all, dependent on the favor of the patient, and patients demand "modern" treatments with vitamins, hormones, sulfonamides, etc., because they have been influenced and trained by the powerful propaganda of the pharmaceutical industry.... And as detrimental as life in the ghetto has proved to be for us, in this regard it can be considered a plus that the doctor in the ghetto is not dependent upon the patient's favor.... However, we have the opportunity to examine thoroughly and conscientiously, and, even with the limited means at our disposal, much can be achieved.... We must work to ensure that the doctor is not just a prescription and medication machine.

Unfortunately, such insights did not have the desired results. Sulfonamides were used to an alarming extent, although serious medical experts in Theresienstadt claimed that their success in curing pneumonia was offset by a higher susceptibility to tuberculosis; the high relapse rate for pneumonia also was blamed on this treatment. Some doctors conducted examinations in an indifferent and superficial fashion, because they were overburdened or distracted by private worries. With greater care, errors could have been avoided. Some doctors had become numb, which made them indifferent, particularly toward elderly patients. Other doctors were tempted by experiments devoid of human or medical maturity. They saw only interesting cases rather than the suffering of fellow human beings.

Old, abandoned people sometimes chose to behave in a way best characterized as psychological suicide (in stricter camps this sometimes also was observed in younger people). Even in normal life, one sometimes meets patients who no longer want to live and who let themselves go in such a way that they succumb to illnesses that normally could be cured. All this became much more evident in Theresienstadt. People fell into disease, summoned it through their own behavior, and died. Everything worth living for seemed to slip away, but people were unwilling to actually hasten matters through mechanical intervention; so they sank into a form of psychological death that sent an appropriate disease to an already weakened body. And yet the camp itself had a deadly effect. The evil spirit that had created it seemed to burst forth from it, with the result that sudden attacks of illness progressed turbulently, with a lethal outcome for many people.

Many patients exhibited a striking infantilism, a condition prefigured by the infantilism of those who were still healthy. The need to escape horrifying events or the repulsive monotony of reality forced injured souls to regress into childhood and drove the patient, as it once did the coddled child, to someone who could help, to "Uncle Doctor." In addition, although they were not necessarily an aspect of the usual definition of infantilism, so-called childhood diseases – including not only diphtheria, scarlet fever, and measles but also even mumps and rubella – were a frequent occurrence. Older people survived these diseases in mild, entirely childlike forms. A man of eighty-six was cured of mumps, and rubella was found in people in their seventies.

People could not choose their own doctors. Instead they had to visit or call for the physicians assigned to their "health unit." Violations of this rule were frowned upon but happened nevertheless. There were attempts to socialize the health services, but conditions in the camp canceled out these good intentions. One could be transferred to a hospital or referred to a specialist. If several doctors specializing in one field were practicing in an outpatient unit, it was easier to choose a doctor, despite the fact that this generally was not permitted.

The overall quality of medical care was very high. The nursing staff, however, was not very good, because of either poor training or a lack of personal skills, although there were a remarkable number of exceptions. The worst cases were when incompetence was paired with a lack of feeling. Among the sorriest chapters in the camp's history was the neglect of elderly, helpless patients. Services were not provided, were performed negligently, or were made dependent on gifts. The sick were not cared for, fed, or washed. Often, their food was taken from them or denied them, and what they received frequently was inedible or cold, although, with a bit less heedlessness, a way to warm it could have been found! Many patients perished as a direct result of this deplorable state of affairs. One might ask why, in this of all fields, so many grudging helpers were found, as care of the sick never was considered easy work. The answer is that some of the women and girls did indeed find this work relatively less strenuous, sensed advantages, and erroneously hoped this occupation would provide "transport protection." Even capable physicians badly neglected their supervisory responsibilities. As a result, patients frequently were left to their own devices; thus they often came to one another's aid, handing one another their bowls, cutting bread, or feeding one another soup. It also happened that stronger patients, while feigning a desire to help, exploited and stole from their even weaker charges.

The leadership of the "Health Services Department," headed by Dr. Erich Munk, did not prove very successful. Under different circumstances Dr. Munk might have been able to utilize his considerable medical and organizational talents to build up a big-city medical service; in Theresienstadt, however, his stony coldness, nonconciliatory manner, dictatorial self-righteousness, and vanity proved fatal. He worked ceaselessly and discovered many mistakes; he was always full of plans, monitored everything, and was not afraid of hard physical labor – the only thing of which he was incapable was making order. What good were his intelligence, his lightening grasp of situations, his brilliant wit, and even his self-sacrifice – which nearly killed him even before he was sent to his death in the autumn of 1944 – if he was hardly capable of any normal human emotion! In the face of his overwhelmingly difficult responsibilities, this man seemed to have stifled all feeling. He was never available to talk to anybody; he worked through the night and terrorized both himself and his subordinates. This lent the organization an air of agitated confusion. How could this "health service" cure those in need? Munk was personally beyond reproach, but his integrity became a rigid mask to which corrupt elements flocked, and it was of little help that this obsessed man wrote on his office door, "I know friendship, but no patronage," and outside his living room, "Dr. Erich Munk lives but does not officiate here." He thus created an impressive departmental structure with the help of good and not-so-good colleagues but never was able to give it a soul. With this overwhelming task, Munk, like his friend Edelstein, was in over his head.

Building this structure out of nothing was possible only through consignments from Prague and the Reich; supplies arrived from the property of Jewish physicians, hospitals, and retirement homes, and much was also improvised in the camp. Thus, for example, a special glassblowing facility was set up to make laboratory equipment. Anything that was available in Prague or Roudnice was bought, and it was even possible to get the SS and the helpful German supervisory doctor, Dr. Krönert, to assist with the acquisition of medications and other supplies. Progress was thus made, despite many obstacles; but internally, the enterprise suffered from the usual terrible conditions in the camp, as described in a letter from Loewenstein to the Jewish Elder on December 13, 1942:

Dear Mr. Edelstein,
    As a result of our deliberations I have chosen several nurses to make certain that the patients in the hospitals receive what they are supposed to.
    The work of these nurses already has led to some beneficial results.
    Some time ago, the deputy head of the Health Services, Dr. Fleischmann, paid a visit to the chief of the Criminal Investigation Department, Dr. Wessely, and, because conditions at E I are intolerable, asked for the assignment of a female detective to act as a nurse in the sickrooms of E I in order to investigate the irregularities.
    Yesterday, Dr. Wessely introduced this lady to Dr. Fleischmann ... in the presence of Dr. Munk. After Dr. Munk had ... listened to the subject of this official conversation, he declared that he was strongly opposed to placing outside persons in infirmaries as observers. He disagreed with a system of spying. Dr. Munk persisted in this opinion and this decision, although Dr. Fleischmann explained to him ... that he himself had initiated it.

It is an insult to the police to have its activities referred to as "spying." ... I was under the impression that a member of the Council of Elders would very much want to eliminate the untenable conditions in particular in infirmaries, hospitals and isolation wards.

It seems that Dr. Munk, who himself never has attempted to bring order and cleanliness to his organization, is, out of pure contrariness, resisting my attempts to make order.... He seems to be insulted by the fact that attempts are being made to expose the unfortunate problems that have arisen in the Health Services....

How fearful the Health Services must be, that they should try to suppress forces helping to serve the common good.

Sincere greetings, [signed] Loewenstein.

The organizational plan discussed in Chapter 8 provides insight into the organization of the Health Services Department. The purely medical institutions were subsumed under the heading "care of the sick." They were made up of "health units." These units were either groups of people in charge of the outpatient clinic – including infirmaries within a particular district – or hospitals and special facilities not immediately accessible to the sick.

Classification of "health units" according to districts: first district: B IV (outpatient clinics and infirmaries), B V (outpatient clinics only, previously also infirmaries), "Home for the Infirm" L 504 (mostly the frail elderly), children's hospital Q 217/19 (scarlet fever); second district: A II (outpatient clinics), C III (outpatient clinics and infirmaries); third district: E IIIa (outpatient clinics, invalid section with urology and neurology wards, tuberculosis section with outpatient clinics for lung diseases, tuberculosis ward with central sputum lab, heart ward), hospital L 124, Q 710 (outpatient clinics and infirmaries for young people) and hospitals L 317 and Q 403 (particularly infectious diseases); fourth district: E VI (outpatient clinics, general hospital with internal, surgical, urological, ophthalmic, otolaryngologic, gynecological, isolation and dermatological departments, X-ray and cardiology wards, central laboratory), E VII (psychiatric unit, outpatient clinics and infirmaries), H V (outpatient clinics and infirmaries), Q 619 (outpatient clinics and infirmaries for children), L 410, L 414, L 417 (outpatient clinics and infirmaries in "Youth Homes"), "Small Children's Block" ("Baby and Infant Home"), "Block for the Infirm" G V and "Central Children's Outpatient Dental Facility" (Q 619). After the collapse in the autumn of 1944, only two centers remained: E VI and E IIIa.

In urgent cases, patients could visit outpatient clinics at any time; otherwise, one could visit only during fixed hours of operation. One had to make an appointment and, as of May 1943, present one's "patient card" (see Chapter 13). Demand was great, and the waiting rooms were inadequate, with insufficient seating. Patients became impatient and made the doctors' work more difficult. Discipline was difficult to achieve, although the authority of some physicians worked wonders. Several doctors often had to examine and treat their patients simultaneously in tiny rooms. Pharmacies were attached to the outpatient clinics; they administered the prescribed medications or substitutes, when available (frequently in containers brought by the patient). These medications were supplied by the "Central Medical Supply Warehouse" or the "pharmacy," which also prepared medications. In the outpatient clinics, "sick lists" were kept, and decisions on hospital admissions were made. Patients were subjected to a lengthy wait before being admitted, until a vacancy could be found and complicated formalities taken care of. Doctors also could prescribe periods of light work. Outpatient clinics maintained night shifts for urgent cases. When special examinations were called for, the patient would receive a referral from his primary physician to the X-ray ward, the laboratory, and so on. The results of the exam were to be revealed only to the primary physician and not to the patient, although the patient usually found out anyway.

If someone fell ill at home, he had to report this in the evening, or at least by the following morning, via the room elder. The report would then reach the respective "block" or "room" physician, who would visit the patient in the morning during his rounds – or sooner, in an emergency. In the case of minor illnesses, and sometimes even in severe cases, the patient would remain in his room. The prescribed medication then was picked up at the assigned pharmacy. For as long as the patient was "registered sick," he was visited once a day – or, if necessary, more frequently – by the doctor.

The doctor could request transfer to an infirmary or hospital. However, the decision had to be made at a higher level. Once someone was admitted, two members of the "orderly group" would come with a stretcher and carry the patient to the hospital; later, the stretchers were transported on a cart. The patient would take with him utensils and plates, toiletries, a towel, undergarments, and sometimes books; his other belongings remained in his quarters. Later on, the hospitals provided their own bed linens, and some rooms even had real beds, although they were placed so close to one another that it was difficult for nurses to get to their patients' beds. The scarcity of space made it necessary to discharge patients as quickly as possible. The operation of the hospitals, particularly the hospital in E VI, continued to improve and could, in some instances, actually be considered exemplary. In all hospitals except the infectious disease wards, patients could be visited during regular visiting hours, or even at other times, depending on the goodwill of the personnel. The sick frequently walked out into the corridors to chat with one another or with visitors.

Following a very primitive initial phase, the outpatient clinics and hospitals became increasingly specialized. At first, for example, dental equipment was nearly unavailable. E I had only one drill, and it was foot operated. Later on, doctors' offices were equipped with everything they needed. The dentists were not forced, as was the case in other camps, to perform unnecessary extractions, and they were able to treat people conservatively (including in the case of root canals). Fillings consisted of silver amalgam or cement. More extensive dental procedures, however, were difficult and rarely could be performed satisfactorily. All outpatient clinics suffered from a lack of water and frequent disruptions of electricity. Treatments then had to be interrupted and complicated surgeries performed by candlelight. Those who needed to wear glasses had the worst of it. The wait for usable glasses could last six months or longer. All glasses taken from the dead and from confiscated luggage were collected at the optical workshops. Obtaining orthopedic shoes, insoles, and bandages always was difficult.

Health Conditions
... Through comprehensive measures we have succeeded in containing the danger of epidemics.

What cannot be prevented are diseases of the respiratory system, circulatory organs and digestive tract, especially dangerous to older people.

A diet consisting of roughage and food containing a great deal of fluid leads to enteritis in older people, whose absorption is disrupted. In many cases, circulatory

446   *Sociology*

weakness leads to dehydration, with lethal consequences. In younger people, the progress of the disease sometimes leads to complications, yet rarely is fatal.

Nearly half of the available sickbeds are at the disposal of the Division for Internal Medicine, due to the frequency of cases.

... Quarantine is available on the infectious disease ward....

For ambulatory patients, illnesses of the eyes, ears and skin are most common. There are also a considerable number of dental cases.

In addition to the existing outpatient clinics, special facilities are available ... there also is a tumor ward.... The available equipment and instruments make possible an operational capacity that is entirely up to modern standards.

A special curative area is represented in the care of the infirm who need not be treated in clinics but for whom medical services must constantly be provided.

256 general practitioners, 225 specialists and 68 dentists work in Theresienstadt [in February 1944].

(274)

Various documents make clear the structure of the "Health Services Department," the type of work involved, and the difficulties its employees faced. The following is taken from a report on its activities from February 1942:

Infirmaries: in 6 residential units, the ghetto has more than 17 infirmaries with a total of 314 beds. In February, 488 persons were treated in the infirmaries in 4,394 days of care, in addition to 42 persons on the infectious disease ward in 1,715 days of care; this amounts to 530 patients and 6,109 days of care.

Outpatient clinics: The Health Services ... has 14 treatment rooms in 6 residential units. Their performance can be determined from the ... table below:

Division:	Number of Examinations:
General Medicine	10,665
Internal Medicine	633
Surgery	871
Neural Ailments	398
Skin Diseases	1,341
Urology	39
Gynecological Illnesses	603
Pediatric Illnesses	2,460
Eye Ailments	2,470
Ear and Nose Ailments	3,981
Dental	3,657
TOTAL:	27,118
Doctors' visits to quarters:	7,786
Work deployment examinations	341
Mass screenings for hygiene and infectious diseases	4,457
Total number of interventions by physicians:	39,702

It is the aim of the Health Services to provide all residents of the ghetto with the most expeditious and best medical attention.... Lately, particularly in the women's barracks, doctors have been summoned to patients' quarters unnecessarily, especially in cases where patients could have made the trip to the outpatient clinic themselves. Physicians have rightly complained that visits to the patient are requested after only a quarter hour ... and ... that once the doctor arrives ... the person who claimed to be sick is not in bed, or has no fever. . . .

In February 1942, 91 ... physicians were in service.
During this time, they conducted approximately

16,500	treatments
8,000	house calls
11,000	special treatments
In all, 35,500	medical interventions were performed ...

This figure ... shows that each ghetto resident has received medical attention nearly three times during the month of February. . . .

In addition, there is the infectious disease ward with ... approximately 120 beds and another internal medicine ward ... , which was opened today, providing another 30 beds.

The hospital also has ... a dental technician, a central laboratory and an X-ray ward. By the end of the month [March], a surgical ward ... is to be opened.

(activity report, March 13 and 15, 1942)

The following is from the monthly report for September 1942:

[In E VI, a typhus ward has been established.] Considering the large number of diarrhea cases, laundering the very soiled garments of the sick became a major problem. In the Health Services it was necessary to set up a special service that was in charge of collecting and sorting the very soiled clothing and transporting it to the central laundry. In spite of the lack of crates and transport difficulties, the project nevertheless succeeded. . . . Over 2,000 kilograms of clean laundry are delivered weekly ... to the various health units.

(276)

At the time there were 36 outpatient clinics; 438 infirmaries (47 with 1,081 beds in E VI and 162 with 979 beds in E IIIa); 4,660 beds; 379 "extra bed areas"; and also 16 isolation rooms with 70 beds, all of which totaled 5,109 sickbeds for approximately 52,000–58,000 prisoners. Even though, according to this calculation, there was one sickbed for every ten people, this ratio was completely inadequate for conditions at the time, because thousands of people were lying ill and helpless in rooms and attics. According to the report quoted previously, some of the "infirmaries" were located in attics or other inappropriate places where these lost ones, packed tightly together, were condemned to a living decay. Nothing was available: no bedpans, urine containers, or charcoal were to be had, and all was thick with filth and excrement. In late September 1942, the camp had 601 doctors, of whom 249 were over sixty-five years old, and only 363 were practicing in their area of expertise. Seventy-three doctors worked in infirmaries, 76 worked as "block" or "room" doctors, and 194 worked in outpatient clinics; the rest worked in laboratories or other wards (see also 246).

The following table illustrates the number of people treated in August and September 1942:

Treatment type	August 1942	September 1942
Outpatient services	53,794	37,976
At-home treatments	67,031	93,900
Special treatments	55,713	74,289
TOTAL	176,538	206,165

448   *Sociology*

The special treatments can be broken down as follows:

Treatment type	August 1942	September 1942
Eye treatments	15,134	22,165
Ear treatments	8,112	8,700
Dentistry	10,242	10,550
Gynecology	1,745	2,383
Dermatology	4,713	5,670
Internal medicine	3,609	4,579
Orthopedics	1,220	1,478
Pediatrics	5,378	6,891
Neurology	1,564	2,135
Surgery	1,644	6,203
Urology	2,992	3,535

This is what it was like in the "ghetto" in its worst period. The numbers speak for themselves, even if they may not be perfectly accurate. Six months earlier, each prisoner still was receiving three treatments per month, by September 1942 the number had risen to four.

> One practicing doctor treats approximately 570 patients per month. This average is exceeded by ophthalmologists in particular, who have been in great demand, due to the current conjunctivitis epidemic. As a result of the enteritis epidemic, this also applies to doctors carrying out housing block services or visits to quarters.
>
> [Regarding hospital E VI:] 29 physicians, 229 nurses and other personnel, or 391 people altogether, perform sanitary and administrative duties. To complete the tasks satisfactorily, 64,538 hours of work were necessary.
>
> [A kitchen for the sick was opened, with the capacity to serve 302 people.] Its effectiveness is limited ... due to small space and an inadequate stove. For the time being, not all of the inmates ... can be fed. Not until next month will the hospital kitchen be expanded to a maximum capacity of 1,000 people....
>
> The surgical division admitted 71 patients in September and discharged 58. Thirty of those died.... 76 major operations were performed.
>
> [The surgical "outpatient clinic" treated approximately 150 cases per day. The Internal Medicine Department admitted 75 patients and discharged 54 persons. The maternity ward performed nine deliveries (one Cesarean section) and fifteen major operations.] The psychiatric unit started the month with a total of 204 patients. Another 217 patients were admitted in September: 206 of them died; 48 were dispatched on transports to the East. Sixteen patients were considered cured and discharged. The majority of patients consists of very old people. The scarlet fever ward ... admitted ... 161 new patients. The average occupancy of the infectious disease ward always was around 300 patients. The X-ray division conducted 528 examinations. It already was possible to prepare X-ray photographs. The electrocardiography ward examined 251 patients. The central laboratory carried out ... 2,178 analyses. The bacteriology laboratory ... handled 430 examinations. Work in the pathology department was complicated by difficulties with the supply of corpses. Nevertheless, autopsies were conducted on 137 of 3,941 bodies. Of particular importance were autopsies for diarrhea-related illnesses, which were conducted in 48 out of 1,938 cases. The dental laboratory carried out 396 technical procedures, 15 of which involved new false teeth....

Health Conditions

[Activities of the public health officer:] Particular attention was paid to the manipulation of the most important food items, i.e. bread and potatoes.... . Attention was devoted and everything possible done to prevent bread from spoiling due to mold and potatoes from deteriorating prior to cooking.... . During the reporting month, 9 audits, 9 inspections, 12 inspections by commissions, 24 official acts and 6 meat inspections were conducted. As a result of this process ... the following were destroyed: 3,745 kilograms of moldy bread; 786 containers of spoiled liver paste ... 174 kilograms of beef spoiled due to cachexia and gelatinous infiltration of the entire musculature.

[Mass screenings for hygiene:] ... a total of 43,226 persons were examined. Head lice were found in 614 cases; lice were detected in clothing in 564 cases; and head lice and lice in clothing were detected in 191 cases. If we consider that ... only 546 cases of lice were found in August and 206 cases in July, the increase is alarming. This situation is the result of the catastrophic lack of space ... as well as the lack of undergarments and clothing, the lack of adequate quarantine ... the inadequate number of barbers and ... the impossibility of conducting larger-scale de-lousing measures. The danger will increase in the coming winter months, which brings the imminent threat of a typhus epidemic.

(276)

The following figures survive regarding visits to outpatient clinics in April and May 1943:

Treatment type	April 1943	May 1943
General medicine	19,309	17,064
Internal medicine	9,280	9,316
Surgery	10,716	10,396
Ear treatments	14,212	13,109
Dermatology	13,005	10,638
Neurology	3,176	3,618
Dentistry	16,730	17,033
Gynecology	2,158	1,999
Urology	3,083	2,353
Eye treatments	20,952	23,027
TOTAL	112,621	108,553

When we compare these figures with the special treatments in polyclinics during August and September 1942, an alarming increase in illnesses becomes evident, even though general conditions had stabilized somewhat and, in comparison with September 1942, the inmate population in April and May had fallen by approximately 10,000, to fewer than 44,000 persons.

Wolff-Eisner provides a statistic regarding the number of "consultations and treatments in outpatient clinics and in hospitals and quarters" for 1943. His data on the number of visits to outpatient clinics significantly exceed those quoted in the previous table for April and May (reliable, exact figures will never be available, as the various surviving tables were drawn up in different ways and served different purposes):

Month (1943)	Outpatient clinics	Hospitals, quarters, etc.
January	145,644	400,498
February	117,141	357,635
March	141,007	386,932
April	132,424	246,726
May	127,670	332,599
June	122,546	300,121
July	129,034	300,905
August	130,767	295,873
September	108,380	244,799
October	113,109	242,270
November	118,272	268,174
December	109,744	261,464
TOTAL	1,495,741	3,737,976

Source: 349, p. 23

Considering that around February 1, 1943, 7,000 people were deported to Auschwitz, and that another 5,000 people were deported at the beginning of September and again in December, and that the number of prisoners in the course of that year fell from 49,397 to 34,655, one can hardly speak of an improvement in health conditions.

In a program lasting from July 23 to July 25, 1943, the "Health Services Department" conducted a tour of its facilities for leading camp functionaries and physicians. On this occasion, invitations that contained interesting information were sent out:

Scientific Committee of the Health Services Department –
Manager: Privy Councilor Prof. Dr. Hermann Strauss
Lecture series starting 21 July 1943 [The lectures cited continued until August 5. They took place at 6:30 or 8:00 P.M., generally in the "coffeehouse" or in the attic space of L 203.]
"Dermatology lecture series," Lues I, Dr. Ernst Reiss.
"Personal hygiene," Dr. Karl Fleischmann, relief activities in the ghetto, challenges and solutions.
Physicians' meeting: 1) Prof. Dr. Przibram. The relationship between blood pressure, neural stimulation, organs and hormones; 2) Dr. Robert Pick: Pellagra.
Conference of neurologists.
"Dermatology lecture series," Lues II, Dr. Ernst Reiss.
"Dermatology lecture series," Pruritus, prurigo, urticaria, etc., Dr. Karl Huth.
"Dermatology lecture series," Lichens and lichen-like processes, Dr. Oskar Singer.
"Dermatology lecture series," Blister-forming processes, Dr. Karl Kovanic.
"Dermatology lecture series," Lupus, tuberculoid skin tumors, Dr. S. Habermann.
"Dermatology lecture series," Radiotherapy of skin diseases, Dr. P. Bachrich.
"Personal hygiene" for laymen, spread of disease by insects, Dr. Arthur Braunfeld.
Physicians' meeting – Dr. S. Teichner – Dr. Ervin Lang, general disease as a result of dentogenous focal infections, sweat cures, Dr. C. Wasserbrenner.

Central medical library, E VI, 1st floor:

Open 9 A.M.–12 P.M., 3 P.M.–5 P.M., Monday, Wednesday and Friday, as well as 8 P.M.–10 P.M. Saturday 2:30 P.M.–6 P.M.

Health Conditions

Visiting hours in hospitals and sickrooms:

Tuesday, Thursday and Saturday, from 3 P.M.–3:45 P.M. and from 6:30 P.M.–7:30 P.M.

[The actual program took place on two mornings and three afternoons and included visits to hospitals, outpatient clinics, infirmaries, "homes for the infirm," homes for the blind, infant wards, tuberculosis wards, the Central Pharmacy, the glassblowing facility, the dental technician, and the "disinfection" center; it concluded with a final meeting with lectures and an open discussion, titled: "What Pleased and Displeased – the Guests Have the Floor."]

The following figures may be of interest:

Number of inmates:

Largest number of inhabitants (18 September 1942)	58,491
Number in July 1943	46,395
Daily cases of illness	10,000
Outpatient cases	4,500
Bedridden patients	5,000
Number of sickbeds	5,200
Number of health units	23
Staff of health services	4,066
Physicians who died	240
Nursing personnel who died as of March 24, 1943	45
Number of patients receiving care (Welfare Department)	10,000
Number of practicing physicians	635
Number of nursing staff	1,432
Number of infirmaries	217
Number of infirmaries for the very ill	35
Number of outpatient clinics	50
Number of rooms for the infirm	45
In inpatient care	2,200

Nearly 9% of the camp inmates worked in the "Health Services Department." A year later, the number of health service employees had shrunk to 3,147 persons, but this then corresponded to 11–12% of the prisoners. Before the autumn catastrophe of 1944 there were 740 physicians in the camp; afterward, there were 76.

The following table presents the average number of patients in the indicated years:

Year	Bedridden patients	Outpatients	Total
1942	3,184	2,518	5,702
1943	6,243	4,154	10,397
1944	2,945	3,085	6,030

Even if these numbers are not exact, they still illustrate how ill the inmates of the camp were and, beyond that, how ill they felt. It is interesting from a psychological point of view that in 1942, which was without question internally more difficult and objectively less healthy than the later period, fewer people succumbed to disease or allowed themselves to fall ill than in 1943 and 1944, when nearly every fourth prisoner was treated daily for at least one ailment. More precisely, in 1942–1944, for every 1,000 inhabitants there were the following number of sick people:

1942   192
1943   240
1944   231

The largest number of sick persons was recorded on February 16, 1943:

	Number	Percent of total
Deaths	79	0.18
Sick persons	13,672	31.30
Healthy persons	29,932	68.52
Inmates (total)	43,683	100

The less credible it became that the camp would be a permanent structure, the more it was "beautified," and the more vulnerable the prisoners' bodies and souls became; illness is, among other things, a waiting period for those unable to master difficult situations. Thus, many people – motivated by the secret will of a barely recognized vitality – desired an ailment and then long maintained their illness or exchanged it for another. When resistance to an adverse existence becomes difficult, and often nearly impossible, the defenses of people who are violated every day manifest themselves as palpable illnesses, which necessarily take the place of more desirable behaviors. For the patients' fellow prisoners as well as the patients themselves, this transformation excused the absence of such desirable behaviors. This could have been different if most people had been able, continually and consistently, to be their own masters – this is surely an illustrious goal but is just as surely one that consciously could be achieved only by strong personalities. Hence, this escape into the lesser evil, as one might call it, should not be condemned. The fact that it was so readily achievable in Theresienstadt is likely unique among known social conditions. In a normal society, illness is less desirable; in stricter concentration camps, although it might not have been avoidable, vigorous prisoners nonetheless feared it and knew how to battle it and, frequently, to overcome it through sheer will. The conditions in Theresienstadt, tolerated by the SS and unchecked by prisoners' moral or financial considerations, remain extraordinary even if one considers the high average age of the camp inmates, and particularly of the patients.

The following table presents the average yearly resources available to this sick society:

	Practicing physicians	Persons per doctor	Nurses	Persons per nurse
1942	563	87.50	1,583	31.0
1943	556	62.25	1,306	26.6
1944	120	96.25	257	41.0

The significant reduction during the final year is a result of the autumn catastrophe. It is likely that, with the possible exception of a health spa, there never before has been a community with one practicing physician for fewer than 100 people.

Health Conditions

In contrast, bathing facilities, even during the period of the "beautified" camp, were limited. The Central Bath in E VI was supplied with 6,000 L of warm water per hour; in the shower facility, which held 68 showers, no more than 140 people were able to take showers per hour. The facilities, which were brought up to this capacity little by little, long functioned badly and, at times, did not function at all; they were rarely used for more than eight to ten hours per day. In addition to the showers, there also was a swimming pool holding 75 m³. It could be used only in exceptional cases by a fortunate few. There also was a bathroom with six tubs. Furthermore, the patients in hospital E VI had limited bathing opportunities. The disinfection bath in L 506 had four showers and nine tubs; eventually, up to 1,000 persons could be disinfected within twenty-four hours, once the facility, following a long period of complications, finally was brought into working order. To disinfect clothes and other items, two additional disinfection boilers and eight gas chambers were available. They operated with Zyklon, the murderous gas from Auschwitz; it also occasionally was used to disinfect individual living areas or entire buildings (see 356).

The burden imposed on medical facilities can be illustrated using the example of the central laboratory, which worked with other laboratories. Later on, some ten people worked there: the physician Dr. Gertrud Adler as chair, the hematologist Professor Dr. Hans Hirschfeld as consultant, a physician and a chemist as assistants, a bacteriologist, four laboratory assistants, and one general assistant. The annual report for 1942 illustrates the complicated structure of the laboratory; the report for 1943 includes just figures, ever-higher figures. . . .

1942 Annual Report

Since the history of the laboratory's development is connected to that of the clinic for internal medicine, it was a matter of only several weeks before it was thought necessary to consider assigning separate space ... to laboratory operations. . . . We found a separate ... space, which, however, initially lacked everything. There was no sink for the water pipes, so that at first the water ... had to be carried in by hand; the oven ... had to be newly constructed; blinds had to be installed; in short, the most basic things had to be done. . . . A hunt for furniture followed; a wooden table is found, which must at first suffice; then a real metal-covered lab table is discovered and secured after a struggle, and now we can begin to think about transferring the basic stock for medical chemistry work from the Sudeten Kaserne: the microscope, the polarimeter, a few reagents for qualitative urine analyses, several test tubes, a spirit lamp. . . . It began on 15 January: the beginning was modest – 10 urine analyses ... the next day a few blood counts – then a break in the monotony: Spirochaeta pallida, which was not actually discovered, but found and identified via the Giemsa staining method. . . . Little by little, other hand laboratory methods are introduced, in particular bacterioscopy ... sputa and feces are examined, spinal fluids and puncture specimens. Initially, mainly external services are provided to other barracks. By the end of the first month the total analyses conducted amount to 235. By February there have been 689. In the meantime, what joy to receive the first batch of sedimentation vials, making it possible to do 5–6 sedimentations simultaneously. And soon clinical operations will commence, when by the end of March we will have performed 966 analyses, including blood types. . . . By mid-April (1,055 analyses) we have succeeded in getting hold of several burettes, and now gastric juices are being titrated. During this period our laboratory celebrates a small triumph. Several cases of acute meningitis appear; the progress of the disease very much resembles an epidemic. Opinions vary but, from the first case on, the laboratory firmly and steadfastly sticks to one point of view: we are dealing with pneumomeningococcus,

454   *Sociology*

and there is no threat of epidemic. The pneumococcus is detected only via staining methods, as ... no culture could be taken. The materials sent to Prague confirm this diagnosis.... . Similarly, earlier mass cases of pneumonia ... were identified as pure pneumococcal pneumonia. In May (1,308 analyses), the laboratory has repeated night shifts, conducting frequent tests of spinal fluids (trepanation) or transfusions.... . New methods: bleeding time, coagulation counts, and counts of the thrombocytes. In June (1,433 analyses), calcium diagnosis is introduced, blood sugar levels initially (we have only 2 pipettes) taken twice weekly for each patient using the Hagedorn-Jensen method. Resistance of the erythrocytes, diastase in the urine. Mass screenings can begin; for X-rays, sedimentations are performed at the same time as lung tests.... . [In] July (number of analyses 1,368), new laboratories have been opened, yet the number here increases. In August, 1,704 analyses. Counts of reticulocytes were rather inexact at first, as the necessary dyes could not be obtained, but we have now developed our own method that needs only to be standardized.... . A small gratification – we are allocated an electric centrifuge, we work on two microscopes simultaneously. September, 2,205 analyses. The Internal Medicine Department makes ever greater demands ... often the mixers are hardly enough, since, although we do have a water-jet pump, but not enough water pressure to dry them quickly enough, we sometimes had to do up to 20 blood counts a day, especially towards the end of the month, when cases of typhus increased ... the number of analyses is often 100 or more per day, yet in September we have minimal staff. For lack of reagents, blood sugar is done colorimetrically, around 30 analyses per month. We have completed 10,958 analyses.... .

In 1943, 49,784 analyses were handled – the lowest number, 2,925, in March, the largest, 4,772, in November. Of the total, 26,366 involved urine, 14,218 blood, 5,348 stool, 1,840 gastric fluids, and 976 were miscellaneous.

In March 1944, 5,474 analyses, of which 1,625 were chemical and 1,020 microscopic urine analyses; 1,071 blood counts; 462 "blood sedimentation"; 118 blood sugar, thrombocytes, reticulocytes and resistance; 141 blood clotting and bleeding times; 55 group determinations; 29 blood calcium and protein; 373 bacterioscopy and sputa; 271 gastric and duodenal fluids; 102 feces; 227 puncture specimens, spinal fluid, diastase, chloride and sternal specimens.

TYPICAL DISEASES

Infections are the most interesting of the typical diseases found in Theresienstadt.

The increase in inhabitants in relation to available space and existing facilities ... makes it apparent that the struggle against infectious diseases is one of the most important tasks of the Jewish self-administration. The difficulties to be overcome in this area are increased by the constant fluctuations in population, when people who already had been immunized or who were immune because of past illness left the settlement area, while at the same time vulnerable human material arrived in new transports, sometimes bringing fresh diseases with them.

(274)

Enteritis and Colitis

Vitamin and protein deficiencies fostered the development and spread of the most common camp disease: infectious diarrhea, which usually manifested itself as enteritis, and less frequently as colitis. The progress of this disease was varied and

Health Conditions 455

frequently atypical, and the prognosis for elderly or weakened persons often was hopeless. Most cases probably involved mixed infections, and frequently dysentery, even though this was proven only in cases occurring after April 20, 1945 (see 62a). The SS leaders preferred a more harmless-sounding name, just as during the typhoid epidemic, when they repeatedly had demanded that the illness be called "flu." Wolff-Eisner claims that bacteria were merely the triggering factor, and that the illness was actually sprue. The enteritis epidemic was at its worst in midsummer 1942, quickly peaking at nearly 7,000 cases per month and dropping off at the end of 1942, without ever disappearing altogether. The inadequate amount and poor quality of the often spoiled food and the dismal sanitary situation were equally responsible for the catastrophic rate of disease. New arrivals were the most vulnerable. Gnawing hunger was deadly for those weak with illness; they devoured the indigestible food, relapsed, and were unable to recover. Bread was most valuable but was dangerous when fresh, and only those who could toast it were able to avoid negative consequences. Equally harmful, when not melted, was the generally old margarine.

> The progress of the disease varied greatly. Among the various combinations and transitional forms, two types could be identified: pure enteritis and pure colitis. Colitis – an inflammation of the large intestine – was the primary disease of mainly younger, resistant and otherwise healthy individuals. Its course ... was violently febrile and particularly aggravated due to typical tenesmus. The outcome of this form nearly always was benign, and few fatalities are known of. Enteritis – inflammation of the small intestine – was more common.... The disease sometimes appeared as the underlying illness, but more frequently as a complication in people with no resistance [and] who already were suffering from severe chronic diseases. This ... marantic form nearly always ran its course with no fever or pain, though the prognosis was very poor. As regards the etiology, ... it centered on infectious diseases, even though lowered resistance played a role. Using ... its course and the clinical and laboratory findings, cholera or cholera nostrus, typhoid fever, paratyphoid fever and other typhoid diseases can be ruled out, so that only ... dysentery remains.... . Effective therapy was almost impossible in an epidemic of these proportions. Treatment with the standard diarrhea medications, though it placed a heavy burden on the pharmacy, was insufficient. Although the pharmacy dispensed medications by the kilo, each patient received barely 0.5 grams of charcoal and albumin tannate per day. Treatment with sulfonamides seemed to be successful, but these could be administered only in rare cases. Dietary treatment was nearly impossible, and the only prophylactic measure that could be carried out was the removal of the feces. The patients completely lacked such cleansing opportunities. The number of cases of illness exceeded the high point during the first week of September [1942]. At this time, more than 5,000 patients were registered.

(276)

During the second half of 1942, 35,000 cases were registered; the total number was very likely closer to 50,000–60,000 cases. The disease was the cause of death in 4,912 cases (Prochnik: 5,271, Wolff-Eisner: 5,296) in 1942; 2,787 (2,722, 2,790) in 1943; and 671 in 1944. In September 1942 alone, 1,938 patients (Wolff-Eisner: 2,134) died of enteritis. Occasionally, the course of disease in adolescents – accompanied by serious toxic symptoms, with as many as fifty bowel movements per day – was so virulent that they could not be saved. Opiates were barely available. Other diarrhea medications were scarce, and, in addition, they were not very effective. Among the sulfonamides, Albucid proved most effective, but its beneficial effect ended in most cases as soon as the patient stopped taking it, at least in the case of

456   *Sociology*

elderly patients. Later on, younger patients in particular were treated with massive doses of sugar. All other food was withheld for two to three days, and sugar alone – 400–500 g – was administered without any other medication. Diarrhea frequently was a complication, particularly in older people – for instance, in cases of pneumonia – and, along with severe cachexia, accelerated the rate of decline. Bowel incontinence due to a weakened sphincter frequently occurred. Even otherwise healthy people occasionally suffered from incontinence, particularly following a lengthy stay at the camp. General exhaustion, lack of good-quality food, anxiety, and the aforementioned psychological regression into childhood were reasons for this, as well as for troublesome flatulence and widespread polyuria and pollakiuria (it was observed that some people urinated fifteen or more times per night) in cases of enuresis and *pavor nocturnus.* Solutions of table salt and calcium were injected intravenously to correct the polyuria, but with limited success. Here the alarmingly frequent occurrence of decubitus in older, and even in younger, patients should be noted; this was a result of insufficient care, filth, and all the other evils of the camp.

Typhoid Fever

There had been approximately 1,300 cases of typhoid fever by April 20, 1945. The epidemic peaked in February 1943.

> In 1942, typhoid cases ... for the first time. Typhoid fever always was endemic to Theresienstadt. However, it was proved beyond a doubt that a number of people on transports ... imported the disease, which they initially had contracted at their points of origin [Cologne and Vienna.] It is spread primarily through contact infection. The highest numbers of cases were reported in October 1942 and in February 1943. The course of the disease ... did not deviate appreciably from other observations. The mortality rate, at 13 out of 100 cases, remained below the general norm. The fight against the typhoid epidemic was effected through rapid isolation ... sweeping inoculation campaigns ... mass screenings of all people employed in food-related establishments for carriers of the bacteria – and separate accommodation of healthy people who were discharged.
>
> (274)

There were 536 cases in the second half of 1942 and 1,165 cases by July; 918 of these patients recovered, 153 died, and 94 still were ill when the data were recorded. One hundred twenty-seven new cases were reported in January 1943, 414 in February (a general inoculation campaign was conducted), 150 in March, 79 in April, 28 in May, and 7 in June. The first two cases appeared in February 1942, and the next in August 1942. By the summer of 1943, the danger had been contained. Prochnik and Lederer report other, less reliable figures: 356 cases (44 fatalities) in 1942, 839 (80 fatalities) in 1943, 31 (3 fatalities) in 1944, and 8 in 1945. More cases were reported after April 20, 1945, especially among long-term residents. The immunizations resulted in both imperceptible reactions and stronger ones involving fevers of up to 40 degrees (Celsius, or 104 degrees Fahrenheit). Wolff-Eisner correctly concludes "that under the conditions in Theresienstadt a considerable number of people fell victim to the prophylactic immunizations" (339, p. 14), which was true in particular of tuberculosis patients and in cases of calcification. Blood samples were taken from the sick – or those suspected of illness – for the Widal test, which was conducted by the Hygienic Institute of the German University in Prague. All samples were to be sent

Health Conditions

there for analysis, via the SS, as long as they could not be, or were not allowed to be, performed in the camp itself. Every known form of the disease appeared. Toxic secondary illnesses appeared in tuberculin patients, and included polyneuritis, arthritis, edemas, and activated nodes. Relapses occurred often and frequently manifested themselves as new diseases. Familiar heart complications became a common cause of death. Paratyphoid fevers of both strains were found but did not spread to any great extent (see 1c, 321b).

Scarlet Fever

The first 8 cases of scarlet fever appeared as early as December 1941; during the second half of 1942, 896 cases were counted. By July 1943, 1,601 cases had been reported, of which 23 ended in death. By April 20, 1945, approximately 1,900 cases had been recorded. Prochnik and Lederer's unreliable figures again differ: 1,247 cases (15 fatalities) in 1942, 48 (7 fatalities) in 1943, 68 in 1944, and 53 in 1945. The disease attacked a particularly large number of adults. The early cases usually were remarkably mild; later, complications and mixed infections appeared, even in children, and included measles, otitis, and diphtheria. Cardiac complications (myocarditis) were common. On the other hand, many cases went almost unnoticed and were discovered only when the infected person's skin started to peel.

> The scarlet fever epidemic ... is spreading [as of September 1942]. Each day new cases are reported, and after each transport carrying children and adolescents, the number of cases increases.... During the reporting month, 17 cases (as of today) have been imported.... During the month of this report, 161 cases have been recorded, 50% of whom are adults (over 16 years).... Toxic cases were brought in with the summer transports.... Nearly every sick adult is suffering from rheumatoid scarlet fever; regardless of age, inflammations of the lymph glands, inner ear infections, and in some cases nephritis have appeared.... At the present time ... more than 300 persons are bedridden.
>
> (276)

Encephalitis

> Encephalitis (inflammation of the brain) was first diagnosed ... in 1916–17.... In Theresienstadt ... isolated cases were treated in 1943. Encephalitis cases became frequent only following the appearance of poliomyelitis (infantile paralysis), and reached their peak in December 1943. In general, it can be said that these are brain inflammations the symptoms of which bear a certain resemblance to other descriptions of the epidemic, but that are distinguished by the remarkably benign and easy course of the disease, compared to all other previous descriptions of the illness. Symptoms include mainly low fever, headache, dizziness and double vision, caused by the slight paralysis of various ocular muscles. Cases of extreme hypersomnia are rare. The symptoms change rapidly, but do not disappear entirely for several weeks. In the majority of cases, the illness is mild and is not accompanied by any particular discomfort. The illness is transmitted by contact and attacks mainly younger females.
>
> (274)

Approximately 1,000 cases of encephalitis were identified by April 20, 1945; the disease peaked in December 1943. Prochnik quotes 410 cases in 1943 and 540 (27 fatalities) in 1944; Lederer quotes 401 cases in 1943, 544 (3 fatalities) in 1944,

458 *Sociology*

and 33 in 1945. Several experienced physicians questioned whether the majority of cases, or any of them at all, were even encephalitis. In any case, imaginary or real encephalitis was the fashionable disease in Theresienstadt in the years 1943–44, and for a long time it was a daily theme, next to enteritis, typhoid fever, tuberculosis, and scarlet fever. Patient hysteria (mainly among girls and young women) and some doctors' suggestive behavior may have influenced the diagnoses. The methods of examination, particularly by neurologists, caught the suspected patients by surprise. Once a patient was suspected of having encephalitis – this was also the case for typhoid fever and tuberculosis – the diagnosis was more or less unquestioned. The doctors allowed their suspicions to prejudice them. This was not only a Theresienstadt phenomenon; there, however, the frequent occurrence of particular illnesses caused panic, and the physicians, along with the patients, were drawn into a desire for disease. They paid special attention to particular symptoms and organs. In cases of suspected encephalitis, reflex tests for double vision typically were performed; with typhoid and epidemic hepatitis, doctors checked for tumors of the spleen. Each of the common diseases in the camp – encephalitis, tuberculosis, scarlet fever, and typhoid – generated its own particular atmosphere, which took hold of the sick, especially those in isolation. The children in the scarlet fever hospital in Q 217/19 let themselves go, appearing at the windows in their pajamas and involving passers-by on the street in their morbid activity. The most vexing were the encephalitis patients; the female patients, in particular, turned neurotic and acted out the most predominant disease, the one that is called Theresienstadt, by means of mischief, extravagant fantasy, and oppressive moods (see 55a, 157).

Diphtheria

Diphtheria appeared soon after the initial cases of scarlet fever.

> The course of the diphtheria wave ... was remarkably mild. The small number of sick children was striking.... The oldest healthy patient who was discharged was 86 years old. It is assumed that ... the inoculations administered to children in recent years ... have resulted in a certain level of immunity.
>
> (274)

By July 1943, 547 cases had been recorded, 31 of which ended in death. Shortly afterward the epidemic surged, peaking in August 1943. By April 20, 1945, approximately 1,100 cases had been reported. Prochnik and Lederer's figures are unreliable here as well: 142 cases (7 fatalities) in 1942, 708 (23 fatalities) in 1943, 177 (8 fatalities) in 1944, and 61 in 1945. The frequently mild course of the disease diverged little from the norm. Occasionally, a numbing of the soft palate and heart damage occurred. Cases of Vincent's angina (trench mouth) were frequent, as well as simple or suppurative anginas.

Epidemic Poliomyelitis

> During the late summer of 1943 the first cases of epidemic infantile paralysis ... appeared, in the course of which only a very small number of toddlers were affected. Most patients were ... between 15 and 20 years old. Altogether there were 25 cases ...

Health Conditions 459

for which both the time of appearance of the disease, its progress and its mortality rate [four cases] remained within normal limits.

(274)

No additional cases were reported (see 234b).

Tuberculosis

By April 20, 1945, about 2,100 new cases of tuberculosis had been contracted. Lederer speaks of 1,584 new infiltrates and 488 tuberculoid pleurisy cases, a total of 2,072 cases. For every 1,000 fatalities in the camp, 160 were caused by tuberculosis in 1943 and 325 in 1944; of the 686 fatalities in 1943, 7 were children less than fourteen years of age, 12 were between fifteen and twenty-four years of age, 303 were between twenty-five and sixty-four, and 364 were over sixty-five. Prochnik cites the following fatality figures: 1 in 1941, 189 in 1942, 589 in 1943, and 844 in 1944; Wolff-Eisner lists the figures as follows: 199 in 1942, 703 in 1943, and 431 in 1944 (January through April alone). Acute progression worsened, and calcified foci erupted again. Other organs in addition to the lungs were affected; tuberculosis of the intestines was the most frequent. Occasionally tubercular patients were deported on the "instructions" of the SS, among them desperate cases in the last stages of the disease. Adolescents contracted mild or severe cases, and everything was done to aid their recovery. The disease was a daily topic of conversation among children. Surprisingly enough, quite a few progressions were brought under control – and sometimes even cured – under these very unfavorable internal and external conditions. Frequently, progression followed inflammation of the lungs or the pleura or appeared in elderly people as a disease secondary to other ailments, accelerating the catastrophic decay. Mass screenings were performed to identify all cases and to prevent them from spreading. Even though the sick were given additional food, nutrition remained sparse – they received no butter or eggs, little milk, and almost no meat. In addition to physical intervention, one had to make do with rest cures, often in the tiny, unhygienic rooms of the so-called TB ward in E IIIa. In 1944, the sick were left to lie in the garden of the E VI hospital, where there prevailed a *Magic Mountain* atmosphere that was particularly uncanny under the circumstances (see 62a, 209g, 209h).

Erysipelas

Prochnik provides the following figures on cases of erysipelas: 233 cases (100 fatalities) in 1942, 851 (128 fatalities) in 1943, and 219 (9 fatalities) in 1944. The disease first appeared in the spring of 1942 and reached its peak at the beginning of 1943. The cases were protracted but later on rarely were severe.

Epidemic Hepatitis

The number of cases of infectious hepatitis has not been established but is estimated at a minimum of 2,000. The disease first appeared in September 1942; during the second half of 1942, some 600 cases were reported. Its occurrence increased in the late winter of 1942–43, reaching its peak in the fall of 1943; after that, the epidemic

460 *Sociology*

quickly subsided. Nutrition probably was one of the causes. The cases often were protracted, and sometimes even occurred without jaundice (*sine ictero*). The sick received sugar, and at times glucose injections. Some patients could not tolerate sugar and experienced revulsion toward sweets. The lack of butter proved particularly unfortunate. Even months later, patients frequently could not tolerate margarine, and this induced relapses.

"Childhood Diseases"

Measles occurred most frequently during the second half of 1942, in which period 831 cases were reported. The figures according to Prochnik are as follows: 891 cases in 1942, 236 (8 fatalities) in 1943, and 2 in 1944. The course of disease sometimes was severe, and the convalescence period lengthy. Small children often were afflicted, whereas adults rarely fell ill. Whooping cough usually was mild, yet protracted cases did occur. Prochnik's figures are as follows: 282 cases in 1942, 110 (1 fatality) in 1943, and 13 in 1944. Mumps was widespread, particularly in the fall of 1942, when approximately 70 cases were reported per month. Many adults were affected; the progress of the disease occasionally was lengthy and was complicated by orchitis or other glandular swellings. Prochnik's figures are as follows: 587 cases in 1942, 366 in 1943, and 25 in 1944. Rubella spread in 1942, particularly among adults, but cases were mild. The number of cases according to Prochnik is as follows: 110 cases in 1942, 92 in 1943, and 59 in 1944. Chickenpox occurred almost exclusively in children and progressed simply. Prochnik offers the following figures: 226 cases in 1942, 448 in 1943, and 172 in 1944.

Epidemic Conjunctivitis

Conjunctivitis was one of the most common infectious diseases; it frequently was lengthy in duration and affected the cornea, resulting in keratitis. Night blindness (nyctalopia), as well as keratomalacia and acute glaucoma, occasionally occurred. The number of cases can be estimated to be at least 9,000; in the second half of 1942 alone, before the epidemic reached its peak in the spring of 1943, 4,500 cases of "eye disease" were reported. The disease occurred less frequently after the summer of 1943.

> The most common cause of this infection is pneumococci, less frequently other cocci or bacilli. In 30–40% of the cases, complications ... of the cornea are observed; in addition to sensitivity to light and pain, they cause significantly impaired vision. 25% of these cases heal through scar formation. Isolated observations indicate that this very frequent complication of the cornea can be attributed to a lack of Vitamin A.
>
> (276)

This assumption was confirmed when vitamin A was prescribed and had beneficial effects; unfortunately, it could hardly be found in the camp. The illness started with a dust infection and often proved to be extremely persistent and resistant to therapy, with the result that cases easily could last several months, and patients were prone to relapse. Patients were anxious and irritable. Permanent damage sometimes resulted.

Epidemic Typhus

It almost seemed as though the camp would be spared typhus, in spite of the sometimes intense lice infestation. In 1944, a case that was brought in from Berlin had fatal consequences; further infection was prevented by quarantine. Not until the liquidation at the end of April 1945 was typhus reintroduced; it then took a terrible toll even among long-term residents, of whom approximately 200 were infected, mainly doctors and nurses. Fatalities continued to occur long after the war ended. Some 2,500 people fell ill, and 502 had died by the end of June 1945 (see 50, 62a, 108a, 207, 330c, 340a).

Various Infections

Staphylo- and Streptococcus infections existed in a variety of forms. From 1942 to 1944, approximately 900 people died from blood poisoning. Phlegmons, festering inflammations of the bones, furuncles, carbuncles, and so on, were frequent and, in most cases, of long duration. The prisoners' resistance was so low that great caution was necessary when administering intramuscular or subcutaneous injections, due to the threat of suppuration. Unfortunately this caution was not universally applied. Children and adults suffered from impetigo, which was slow to heal and frequently lasted for months. Pneumococcus and mixed infections were abundant. These included many of the large number of cases of pneumonia (pneumococcus pneumonia), several cases of meningitis, and finally the numerous cases of otitis. Scabies occurred sporadically. Colds and influenza always were present in the camp and often lasted much longer than normal. A constantly wet, runny nose was the norm in this camp, as in all others.

Deficiency Diseases

Deficiency diseases were extremely widespread. Many of the previously described illnesses, such as diarrhea, conjunctivitis, and colds, belong in this category to at least some extent. One could characterize these illnesses as vitamin deficiencies (mostly of vitamins A, B, and D) and as illnesses related to protein and hormone deficiency. The supply of vitamins A and D was virtually nil, while only about a quarter of the demand for vitamin B and half the demand for vitamin C were met. Disorders of the sense of touch as well as hypo- and hyperchromatic anemia occurred. Even the blood counts of healthy people often showed a certain "leftward shift." Accelerated blood sedimentation was common; the values exceeded the norm even in people who seemed unaffected. Hemoglobin levels frequently were below normal. People sought help from liver and iron supplements. Common inflammations of the nerves usually responded favorably to vitamin B. The frequent pellagra and pellagra-related cases also were the result of the shortage of vitamin B. Many older people – some 3,000 cases – suffered from hunger edemas. This was due to a lack of protein, which also is indicated by the poor results of yeast therapy. Vitamin C deficiency was evident in mild cases of scurvy, stomatitis, and various skin diseases. In early 1943, more than 40% of prisoners were more than 30% underweight, thereby confirming information regarding hunger in Theresienstadt. The most significant weight loss usually took place between the first and the sixth month of an individual's stay, whereas weight gain—due to water retention in the tissues—was frequent from the ninth to the twelfth month.

In late May 1944, an order to report actual deficiency diseases was issued. By June approximately 1,200 cases had been reported, 500 of which were labeled as D deficiencies. None of the patients were under thirty, and few of them were between thirty and fifty years of age; that is, almost all the cases occurred in older people, and longer stays in the camp increased one's susceptibility. In June 1944 the following cases were identified:

	Slight	Medium	Serious	Total
Spontaneous fractures	4	7	4	15
Indications of tetany	8	3	4	15
Bone deformities	74	39	21	134
Pelvic pain	154	196	64	414
Waddling gait	171	135	48	354
Flat-footedness	77	86	33	196

Patients frequently complained of osteoporosis and osteomalacia. Femoral fractures, sometimes repeatedly, and fractures of the proximal femur were not infrequent; sometimes merely using a stethoscope or adjusting the patient for an X-ray could fracture ribs. Also noteworthy was the high incidence of caries. To what extent significant bradycardia, and less often tachycardia and other pulse irregularities, belong in this category, or are instead neuropathic disorders, is an open question. One of the psychological effects to be noted is the alarming memory loss from which many suffered (see 5a, 97b, 185b, 208a, 209, 209h, 234c, 349).

Heart and Lung Diseases

Heart and lung disease were reported as the cause of death in nearly 4,000 cases in 1942, more than 4,000 cases in 1943, and 1,750 cases in 1944. Long-standing cardiac defects often worsened, although some cases improved due to weight loss and withdrawal from tobacco. New diseases were acquired (kidney complications, edemas, etc.). All known forms of lung infection were present in large numbers; they frequently were protracted and difficult and were accompanied by complications, exudate, and pleurisy. In older patients the outcome usually was fatal. If sulfonamides were available, either in ampules or in tablet form, this treatment was preferred above all others. These medications, which sometimes were all but unavailable, especially in 1942, were believed to be a cure-all.

Psychological Disorders

The layperson's notion that "this could drive a person crazy!" certainly was justified in the camp. But it should not be thought that real psychoses would have broken out simply as a result of circumstances, without a preexisting tendency in that direction; thus cases of acute psychosis were no more frequent in Theresienstadt than in any other environment. However, it is certain that the shock of arrival at the camp caused disturbances of all kinds, including confusion and neurotic and hysterical episodes. Escape from the present moment, regression into childhood, and a clouded sense of reality – all were symptoms of both slight and severe psychological damage. Manic and melancholic states of mind, severe irritability, and outbursts of rage that, however, did not reach the level of psychosis were well known. One should speak of prison psychoses only in terms of symptoms, rather than in terms of a specific, objective disease. In any case, camp psychosis, if one chooses to use this term, was something different. It is no exaggeration to assume that a majority of the prisoners were afflicted with neuropathic or psychopathic alterations. It speaks for the unusual vitality of the Jews in Theresienstadt that they did not deteriorate psychologically, in ways quite different from the disorders described in this volume, as a result of the debilitating situation. However, it is certain that these psychological changes went beyond the framework of a general medical or psychiatric discussion. Neither psychiatry nor psychology provides precise terms for these kinds of subtle processes; the specific problem area would need to be the subject of a separate study. The transformation undergone by one's moral "substance" and the reactive mechanism of one's mind is, I believe, located outside the realm of traditional research methods. Surely, anyone who was paying attention would have noticed these changes after living in Theresienstadt for a time, but they did not correspond to any clinical definition. To define them accurately, one would need a body of scientific character – or characterology that would encompass all aspects of daily life in such a camp. Some aspects of this are suggested in Chapter 20.

In the psychiatric unit, which was located in the casemates of the E VII barracks, the place least suited for this purpose, conditions were abominable and evoked deep horror even among the most hardened of Theresienstadt's inmates. A wooden fence partitioned off a small portion of the yard to be used by the sick. Those patients who were not occasionally allowed to go out there, or who could not get there, were condemned to huddle in the miserable dens behind barred windows in dimness or complete darkness; there, the wretchedness of the entire "ghetto" reached its nadir (see 70, 70a, 70b, 209f, 209h, 349a).

Conditions Requiring Surgical Medicine

Reflecting the age distribution is ... the fact that certain types of diseases, such as strangulated abdominal fractures, ileus, bone fractures ... occur in large numbers. The opportunity to conduct proper ... surgical procedures therefore is of the utmost importance. The general hospital has available (in February 1944) a surgical unit with 200 beds and 2 large operating rooms, one of which is designed for septic, the other for aseptic procedures. Adjacent to the septic room ... is a sterilization room, which is equipped with a modern electric high-pressure steam sterilizer, a facility to generate sterilized water, glassed-in instrument shelves and three warm-water sinks.... Operations are performed on state-of-the-art operating tables, while an ... electric-light ... makes it possible to perform first-rate procedures even at night. Septic and aseptic procedures are separated to such an extent that suppurative interventions are performed by doctors who deal only with these kinds of cases.... For this reason, sick persons with suppurating surgical wounds are accommodated ... in adjacent hospital barracks.... For throat, nose, and ear operations a small ... operating room is available, it also is used for eye operations. It should be stressed that ... in many cases the preferred method is to attempt manual restoration and re-set the fractures. The oldest fracture patient was 90 years of age.

464 *Sociology*

Operations have been performed almost without complications. In particular, no anesthesia-related complications were reported. In more than a thousand laparotomies, no post-operative thromboses or embolisms occurred. This phenomenon is most likely related to lifestyle and a low-fat, low-protein diet. Generally ... the preferred procedures are as simple as possible. Healing processes following septic operations are entirely satisfactory. The mortality rate is no higher than is otherwise customary in comparable age groups. Suppurating infections usually are treated with more or less extensive incisions. Amputations of the legs or arms have been necessary in only a small number of cases. Bloodless methods of treating fractures nearly always have led to a satisfactory completion of the healing process.

(274)

During one year, most likely 1943, the surgical department performed 689 operations, the ophthalmologic department, 343; the gynecological department, 302; the laryngological department, 254; and the urological department, 136. Altogether, approximately 250 hernia and ileus operations were performed, which works out to an average of 50 cases per year.

Amenorrhea

Menstrual complications were common in the camps. In Auschwitz, according to Lingens-Reiner, 80% of the women suffered from amenorrhea caused not only by hunger but also by the psychological shock that began with arrival in the camp. On December 19, 1943, Dr. Franz Baas reported:

It is likely that the massive incidence of amenorrhea in Theresienstadt is related to malnutrition in the camp, similar to cases of world-war amenorrhea and other comparable conditions.... To resolve these questions, data was collected indicating that approximately 54% of the women in Theresienstadt showed temporary symptoms of amenorrhea. The duration ... ranged from 3–17 months, during which time menstruation resumed in all but 6%. The remaining 6% continued to be amenorrheic in spite of all attempts at treatment. The incident curve ... reaches its peak during the first month and sinks back to almost zero during the third month. The resumption of menstruation occurs at a rate of about 8% per month from the 3rd to the 5th month. It may be inferred from these curves that the condition does not result ..., as expected, ... from malnutrition, but rather from an indefinable psychological shock manifest in the cessation of ovulation. Living in barracks might also play a role in the absence of menstruation. Cases are remarkably resistant to therapy. In some patients, involutions of the uterus and the ovaries occur.

(see also 12)

One also could classify these symptoms as infantile regression. Women filled out during amenorrhea and took on a radiant appearance. In this way, the absence of their period may have represented a natural self-defense. In general, women were more resistant to illnesses and to the hardships of camp life than were men. Disruptions of menstruation other than amenorrhea occurred in the form of altered or irregular cycles. Such disruptions did not necessarily affect libido, which was, however, generally weakened in both sexes. In contrast, this was not the case with most adolescents.

Some ailments, among them heart disease and diabetes, were on occasion positively affected by the situation. However, as a rule, people were more susceptible, the

Health Conditions 465

diseases were more serious, and the complications were greater; therefore, recovery also took much longer. Nevertheless, many people escaped illness.

BIRTHS

Figures on the number of births in Theresienstadt vary between 205 and 209, but the number may actually have reached 230 (see 302); the average weight of infants born alive was far below the norm, at 2,820 g. In some 350 cases, pregnancies were terminated (see 11c, 246). At first, the delivery of children not conceived in the "ghetto" was permitted. In July 1943, this, and especially the delivery of children conceived in the camp, was strictly forbidden. This order never was revoked, but exceptions later were made, and ultimately nobody paid much attention to the restrictions. The required procedures usually were performed during the third or fourth month, and sometimes much later. On August 21, 1943, the following memo had to be sent to all senior physicians "to be made known to all gynecologists":

> On the occasion of the two latest birth announcements, SS Obersturmführer Burger announced that, in future, all fathers of children conceived here, as well as mothers and children, shall be included in the transport and deported. We therefore request again that you report all pregnancies of which you are aware, if they have not yet been reported, since non-compliance with the duty to report in timely fashion makes the treating gynecologist an accessory and therefore a guilty party. The notice to pregnant women must be very clear that abortions must be performed by official order.
>
> The Head of the Health Services
[signed] Dr. Erich Munk

A "memo" from the "building administration," dated March 18, 1944, indicates how far-reaching the system of snooping for pregnancies had become:

Pregnancies
The regulations regarding pregnancies, [regulations] which already have been announced several times ... in the form of orders of the day, now must be reiterated to the female inmates in a very clear manner. All women born between 1928 and 1889 must confirm by signature that they have been informed of their duty to report to the respective women's outpatient unit for examination as soon as the first signs of pregnancy appear. This also must occur at the merest suspicion of pregnancy. In case of doubt, the physician will make the determination.

The room elders, and in succession those above them ... up to the building elders, are responsible for ensuring that each woman in the aforementioned age group living within their jurisdiction confirms in writing that she has been informed of this. This confirmation must be provided anew for every new arrival, regardless of whether this involves old or newly arrived transports.

In addition, room elders must urge women of whose pregnancies they become aware to observe the order for medical examination and, if need be, to ascertain in writing from the women's outpatient unit that such an examination has indeed taken place. If the patient refuses to submit to such an examination, this must immediately be reported to the head of building administration, so that the health services can initiate the necessary steps.

In future, should there arise cases in which pregnancies were kept secret, room elders will be held equally accountable in regard to compliance with the duty to report.

466   *Sociology*

A report of enforcement according to paragraph 1 must be submitted to the building administration by the district or building elders for each building and housing block by 25 March.

(see 246)

Behind the facade of self-administration, a person's most intimate details were "registered by the higher authorities." One's body and soul were equally administered. People were denied the freedom to determine their own lives, their births, or their deaths (as a result of the prisoners' duty to report suicide attempts).

With regard to births, the situation in the first few months was primitive: "The delivery was easy.... Now everything was all right. All right? She had given birth in a room at the barracks, on a borrowed iron bedstead, and three hours later she had to return to her quarters, as rooms were referred to there" (193a). The newborn immediately received a "transport number." The number following the highest number in the transport was added to the transport number of the parents or the mother.

MORTALITY AND DEATH

The average age of the deceased was 74.4 years in 1942 and 71.11 years in 1943. The highest average age ... was found in August 1942, at 76 years.... In 1943, the average age in January was 72.51 years, in June it was 70.14 years, in December approximately 69 years ... which has to do with the increased death rate amongst the most elderly population. Thus on 1 January 1943 ... there were 680 men and 694 women between the ages of 80 and 85; on 1 January 1944, only 105 men and 335 women were left in that age group. The number of persons ... above 85 years was 320 at the beginning of 1943 and 210 at the beginning of 1944....

The correlation between age group and mortality also can be seen in the classification ... according to countries of origin. In 1942, 15,891 persons died ... ; 12,618 of them were from the Altreich and the Ostmark, 3,273 from the Protectorate.... The corresponding figures for ... 1943, with 12,696 fatalities, list 10,438 of the dead as coming from the Altreich and the Ostmark and 2,258 from the Protectorate.... In December 1943, 83.6% of all residents ... over 65 came from the area of the Altreich and the Ostmark.

Among the 15,891 deaths in 1942, 9,859 were women and 6,032 were men, out of a population in that year of 29,622 persons, 17,386 of whom were women and 12,236 were men....

... In 1943, 7,572 of the 12,696 deaths were women, 5,124 were men, out of a population in that year of 43,181 persons, of whom 25,454 were women and 17,727 were men....

... Altogether, 29,113 persons died between 24 November 1941 and 31 January 1944. The leading causes of death were ... :

1.	Illnesses of the digestive tract	8,506
2.	Decline due to age	6,195
3.	Respiratory illness	5,515
4.	Illnesses of the circulatory system	4,285
5.	Infectious diseases	1,377

In 1943, the order was as follows:

1.	Illnesses of the digestive tract	2,950
2.	Respiratory illness	2,624

Health Conditions

467

3. Decline due to age	2,443
4. Illnesses of the circulatory system	2,059
5. Infectious diseases	429

(274)

The following table does not always accord with these reliable figures but is neverthe-less noteworthy:

	Number of deaths			Percent of population	Average age of deceased	Daily average death rate
	Men	Women	Total			
1941						
December	9	2	11	0.74	55.18	0.4
1942						
January	32	16	48	0.70	63.00	1.5
February	39	25	64	0.60	63.60	2.3
March	55	59	114	0.90	70.50	3.7
April	99	160	259	1.70	74.20	8.6
May	71	84	155	1.10	72.90	5.0
June	127	142	269	1.60	73.60	9.0
July	384	599	983	2.10	75.90	31.7
August	869	1,458	2,327	4.89	76.30	77.5
September	1,385	1,556	3,941	7.30	76.00	127.0
October	1,202	1,894	3,096	6.11	74.90	106.5
November	893	1,312	2,205	4.77	73.00	73.6
December	913	1,517	2,430	4.96	73.30	78.3
TOTAL	6,069	9,822	15,891			
1943						
January	941	1,532	2,473	5.20	68.80	79.8
February	896	1,314	2,210	5.10	72.40	78.9
March	747	1,163	1,910	4.40	71.40	61.6
April	538	747	1,285	2.90	71.30	42.8
May	429	548	977	2.20	72.20	31.5
June	309	457	766	1.70	70.60	25.5
July	236	392	628	1.36	70.70	20.2
August	235	324	559	1.24	70.10	18.0
September	173	257	430	1.06	69.80	14.3
October	209	297	506	1.25	70.70	16.3
November	190	237	427	1.06	70.50	14.2
December	223	307	530	1.43	70.50	17.2
TOTAL	5,126	7,575	12,701			
1944						
January	221	299	520	1.50	71.27	16.6
February	284	351	635	1.80	69.62	22.2
March	285	443	728	2.00	69.01	23.5
April	289	464	753	2.00	69.31	24.3
May	229	384	613	1.90	68.74	19.1
June	144	220	364	1.30	68.57	12.1
July	90	163	253	0.92	66.64	8.1

(*continued*)

468   *Sociology*

(*continued*)

	Number of deaths					
	Men	Women	Total	Percent of population	Average age of deceased	Daily average death rate
August	84	156	240	0.87		7.8
September	58	107	165	0.65	66.12	5.5
October	42	78	120	0.86		4.0
November	21	39	60	0.54		2.0
December	38	42	80	0.69		2.6
Total	1,785	2,746	4,531			
1945						
January	26	47	73	0.57	72.10	2.3
February	28	33	61	0.39	70.00	2.0
March	25	49	74	0.41	70.00	2.4
April			189	0.65		6.3
May			735	2.45		23.7

Source: 216

What stands out in this table is that conditions (1) worsened significantly with the arrival of the very old in the summer of 1942; (2) improved following the large-scale deaths in the following year; (3) improved again after June 1944 as a result of the "beautified camp"; (4) actually normalized at this average age between November 1944 and March 1945, due to improved nutrition for the previously unprotected victims; and (5) worsened again only toward the end of the war, with the arrival of the concentration camp prisoners.

If one wishes to take the trouble, one can compare the largely precise monthly figures in the preceding table with the normal average mortality rate in Central Europe before World War II: Approximately 3% of the population died annually, or 300 out of every 10,000 people – that is, 25 people per month. From January 1942, the death rate in Theresienstadt was several times – occasionally as much as thirty times – higher than the average. The following table also is sometimes inconsistent with the correct figures in 274:

Cause of death	1942	1943	1944	Total
Enteritis	3,271	2,722	671	8,664
Decline due to age	3,703	2,443	412	6,558
Pneumonia	2,529	2,489	1,242	6,260
Heart disease	1,420	1,558	495	3,473
Infections	355	836	892	2,083
Blood poisoning	256	550	92	898
Brain hemorrhage	329	330	90	749
Malignant tumors	250	214	91	555

Wolff-Eisner cites the following figures: decline due to age: 3,704 deaths in 1942 and 2,338 in 1943; pneumonia: 2,699 deaths in 1942 and 2,694 in 1943.

The statistician Gutfeld (see 93a) determined that, following an understandably high mortality rate among weakened persons during their first month in Theresienstadt, resistance to illness increased during one's second month. One's first year in the camp was the most critical; one's fifth month in the camp proved to be the most dangerous, although the twelfth month was no less dangerous. Yet another critical period was the second quarter of a prisoner's second year in the camp. Inmates from Germany were the most susceptible to illness, followed by those from Austria; the situation understandably was better for prisoners from the "Protectorate," and the Danes fared the best. Men were more at risk than women, with the exception of those between twenty and fifty years of age. Among the oldest people from Germany, the mortality rate reportedly was thirty times higher than the norm; among children, it was about two to three times higher. Infants were at greatest risk during their fourth, fifth, and eighth months. According to Gutfeld, infant mortality amounted to 25%; according to other figures, it was 30% in 1942, 14% in 1943, and 20% in 1944.

The highest mortality rate was reached in September 1942, at 3,941 people. It is true that the average age of the deceased was high; however, this only adds to the guilt of those responsible for the deportation of the aged, while not otherwise contradicting the situation described here, because quite a number of these elderly people had enjoyed undiminished, or at least decent, health before deportation, and it was only the "journey" and their stay at the camp that caused their rapid demise. We include the shortening of the life of the elderly in our definition of murder.

Younger people are resistant to difficult circumstances; for them, the conditions in Theresienstadt cannot be compared to those of a strict camp. Inside the "ghetto," the SS was only rarely directly responsible for the death of a prisoner. Living conditions always were above the threshold beneath which younger inmates might have given up their will to live, or at which physical weakness would have become dangerous enough to allow death to reap a rich harvest among them.

The strictest concentration camps confronted life with almost certain death, where Jewish prisoners were concerned. Theresienstadt placed disease in its stead and remained a place of opportunity that offered a middle ground, at least for people who were not too old. This is what lent the "ghetto" its eerie imprint and its afflictions. One said to oneself: Either you will be able to live or you will die, but here you are sick. The powers of life and death balance each other; sometimes death wins, but more frequently life does. This is an intermediate realm of perpetual twilight, and no one knows whether day or night will follow. As for the elderly ... yes, of course, it is bad that they were sent here to die, but they must die; but you, you are young, and here you can live. Yet, should you be deported – true, you don't know what awaits you – maybe you can survive even "there"; you will survive somewhere, but stay here, if you can. Then freedom will come, and you will have won.

Such thoughts, whether conscious or unconscious, occupied the majority of younger people. Births were forbidden, but even suicide – that is, death – had been prohibited, although not as publicly. People were confronted with the death of older, and sometimes even younger, people, because no one erected a protective barrier between life and death. Even children saw the carelessly wrapped, desiccated, and dirty corpses carried past them on stretchers or shoved by on carts, followed by the gravediggers, spectral in white, as they paced through the gray city – the pestilential city, as the young painter Peter Kien called it. A dying animal hides itself away, but a

470 *Sociology*

dying person is taken by his fellow humans into protective solitude, where he is supposed to be cared for before being given over to the unknown. But in Theresienstadt there was no protection that either nature or culture could have provided. The secret – the private – was torn from the substance of the prisoners' souls; it was prohibited. All that was warm and gentle within them was wounded or paralyzed; a clattering bustle had found its horrible way into everything, and one lay in wait for a pitiful residue. The weary, no longer moored to this world, sank into a peaceless proximity in the midst of all this to-do. The dying, although alone in their final solitude, and the dead were seen by their fellow prisoners, but their glances wandered past them, if they did not, in the end, turn away in shame. People warbled the bad Jewish tune "Bei mir bistu shayn"; they worked, distracted themselves, took refuge in illness, or were ambushed by it. But because they had the chance, they took it – I will get better; I will live. This was the dreary twilight in the coerced community of violated creatures, the world between life and death in Theresienstadt.

The following comparison is noteworthy: during the first half of 1944, 3,589 people died, 426 of whom were "able to work"; they made up approximately 12% of all deaths. Of these, 490 were from the "Protectorate" (238 men and 252 women; of those who were "able to work," 49 were men and 56 women, a total of 105, or more than 20%), and 3,099 came from Germany and Austria (1,206 men and 1,893 women; of those, 142 men and 179 women – a total of 321, or more than 10% – were "able to work"). A person who worked was in a better position; he was more inclined to hope, and he might be allowed to live.

[The first, initially rare, autopsies were performed in December 1941, in a basement room of E I; they always were ordered by the director of the health services.] When I began to assist them (1 June 1942), the autopsies were conducted under very primitive conditions. We had only one iron table and one wooden table ... and only one set of dissecting instruments. At first, we had no gloves at all.... During this time, 3–4 cases were dissected each day.... The corpses chosen for autopsies were chosen according to certain criteria (infectious diseases, sudden death, unnatural death, rare diseases, tumors, imprecise diagnosis and dissection of all adolescent individuals ...).... Around September 1942, regular autopsies were discontinued because the room that had served this purpose was to be converted into the aseptic operating room. Once again, only the most urgent cases were autopsied; this took place in the basement rooms of the Hohenelber [E VI] and the coal cellar of the Sudeten Kaserne [E I]. Sanitary conditions ... were extremely bad, since we were dealing primarily with infectious diseases, among them typhoid. Around February 1943, the autopsy room was moved into an annex of the crematorium, where the equipment was better.... At least one could perform histological work.... After the move ... to the crematorium, the corpses were transferred to the central mortuary, which was headed by the kabbalist Prof. Philipp Bock. Funerals were conducted as follows: at approximately 8:30 A.M., the Catholic and Protestant funeral ceremonies were held.... Several rabbis conducted Jewish funerals at 9 A.M. in another room. Eulogies were given in Czech and German; otherwise, the services were very sober and as brief as possible. After the coffins were loaded ... the corpses were brought to the crematorium.... Originally, the corpses were left wearing the clothes in which they had died; this means that some of the dead were brought in their bedclothes, others in civilian clothes and shoes. According to orders issued by the commandant's office, the dead later had to be undressed; the clothes were taken to the distribution point. At the time, shrouds were used. After some time, this too was prohibited, and the dead were simply covered with jute paper. Jute [paper] caps and stockings were sewn for the Orthodox dead. The shrouds were made into doctors' coats. The coffins were built at the riding school; initially there was a coffin for each corpse. They were made from thin, rough planks; how sturdy they were depended on the nails that were used. At times when longer nails were not available, so-called "paper-nails" were used, which led to embarrassing scenes at the crematorium when coffins would completely fall apart. To save material, the corpses were later cremated resting only on the coffin's cover. The coffins themselves then were disinfected with Lysol and sent back to the central mortuary to be reused. Infectious corpses and corpses from the Small Fortress, which was supplied with the same coffins, were cremated immediately.

The organization of the so-called pallbearers was very important, particularly in the summer of 1942.... The pallbearers were assigned specific districts, corresponding ... to the health units to which deaths were reported. They carried the corpses from the infirmaries and the living quarters to the morgues of the individual barracks. From there, they were transferred to the central morgue, located in the casemates of the fortifications at the Bohušovice Gate. During the period of very high mortality, several hundred corpses were kept there in extremely irreverent conditions. The corpses were piled on top of each other in several layers....

The crematorium, which was equipped with four electric ovens that ran on naphtha, went into operation during the summer months of 1942. During these months, the mortality rate was so high that the crematorium was not sufficient and some of the corpses had to be buried in the ground, although all four ovens were operating day and night, and each cremation lasted approximately 40 minutes. At first, the corpses were buried in individual graves, and later in mass graves. The space designated as the cemetery on either side of the crematorium ... was not suitable for a cemetery, because the earth was moist when dug to one meter, and upon further digging the graves would fill with water. Extremely embarrassing scenes resulted when corpses were to be buried in mass graves, when people who had been forcibly recruited to perform the burials balked at this kind of work. The corpses were tossed into these water-filled graves so that the water splashed in all directions. Chlorinated lime then was strewn into the graves.

Once death was confirmed by a physician and a coroner, a so-called toe tag was affixed to the corpse, and at the same time, the senior physician's office issued a death certificate, which was sent with the corpse to the morgue, the crematorium, the columbarium and the registry office.... . The ashes were separated ... and deposited in individual paper urns. A paper tag with the name of the corpse was thrown onto the ashes and the name of the corpse noted on the outside of the urn, along with the cremation number. Then the urns were transferred ... to the columbarium, which was located in the casemates of the fortifications, just opposite the central morgue....

The following two incidents took place: a nurse on the night shift believed that a particular female patient had already died and arranged for her to be brought to the mortuary of the Bodenbach Kaserne. The apparently dead woman woke from a lethargic sleep amidst several corpses. In another case, a doctor who had just confirmed a death happened not to have a toe tag available, and therefore wrote the name of the deceased on a piece of paper he had found on the floor. He did not notice that this piece of paper actually was the back of an envelope. The undertakers entered the corpse under the name noted on the envelope, which was different from the person who had actually died. The error was noticed only when the person, whose name it actually was, died.

One of the most characteristic and urgent issues in Theresienstadt was the question of gold. Very early on, anyone who came in contact with corpses was ordered to collect and turn over all precious metals.... . These valuables then were to be delivered to the commandant's office. Sometime later it was ordered that the ashes of the cremated be searched for precious metals.... . Under the supervision of Czech gendarmes, the ashes were sifted and inspected. When, after some time, no gold was found, the Germans undertook experiments to determine whether gold might be melting when exposed to the great heat, perhaps flowing off somewhere, and thus being lost. The experiment found that the gold was indeed melting and therefore no longer was retrievable. Wedding rings and other golden objects that were discovered were turned in. No gold ever was found among the ashes.

(147)

The passage of the dead was similar in all the camps; here, it was merely accompanied by the addition of a few meager civil ceremonies, which could barely disguise the SS's naked lust for extermination and its insatiable greed for gold. Two hundred and seventy-three suicides and 211 suicide attempts were reported in Theresienstadt. The actual number of attempts probably was higher, as these sometimes were not revealed in an attempt to evade the duty of disclosing them to the SS. Sixteen persons were executed; an unknown number perished at the hands of the SS men in secret executions, murder, or torture in the bunker or other rooms at the SS "office," if executions were not carried out in the Small Fortress or in other camps. Moreover, several incidents of negligent homicide occurred at the hands of the SS, particularly during transports. A number of people also died as a result of accidents; for example, some died from an unfortunate incident involving gas poisoning after the disinfection of a building with Zyklon, and one person died as a result of a fall from a scaffold.

PUBLIC HEALTH CARE, MEDICAL RESEARCH, AND MEDICAL EDUCATION

Public health care included periodic inspections of drinking water (which had an iron content of 4 mg/L and a hardness of 20°dH); disinfection of sewage with chlorinated lime; meat inspection; food examinations (carried out through chemical testing and inspections); hygiene monitoring in the kitchens and workshops; examinations for vermin; mass screenings for tuberculosis; obligatory immunizations (generally for typhoid and scarlet fever, and sometimes also for diphtheria and smallpox; typhus immunizations were initially planned but not carried out); installation of latrines and provision of nutritional allowances for convalescents; and so on.

Many physicians felt themselves forced into experimentation and scientific work. The SS did not exactly encourage this work but tolerated and sometimes even approved of it and required reports of the findings of such experiments. In September 1944, shortly before the deportations began, this research was largely discontinued. Experiments in treating phlegmons with curative vapors were conducted on German orders; the experiments were satisfactory (see 157a). Practical and theoretical work was conducted in nearly every medical field. This scholarly zeal was entirely under the influence of the camp, driven by it and primarily carried out for its benefit; but the enterprise itself, as much as it had to rely on improvisation, was far more reminiscent of a research institute or a university than of a camp controlled by the SS. The academic nature of this research was baffling, frequently impressive, and even superb. In the process, the conditions and particular issues of the coerced community became the chief object of its insights, just as sociologists, philosophers, psychologists, and legal scholars strove systematically to analyze Theresienstadt. We may look on these efforts with reverence, while at the same time recognizing with horror that any proper sense of proportion became blurred in these attempts, because one forgot all too easily that one also was part of the camp and was an object just like the other

Health Conditions 473

prisoners, and that one could not feel superior to the camp but had to remain a part of it, just as fate had mercilessly decreed for most of the others.

There was a quite respectable medical library, for which the SS even approved acquisitions. The untrained or poorly educated nurses required further training. Students and young doctors wished to continue their studies and add to their knowledge; numerous courses were set up, arranged by Professor Dr. Hermann Strauss, an internist from Berlin. He also organized physicians' meetings, lectures, and entire lecture series featuring work that was generated in Theresienstadt, much of which unfortunately has been lost. The nature of the camp was seductive and brought too much of a good thing, making it too easy to overlook the human beings who were first and foremost in need of human kindness. This is not to belittle the truly admirable accomplishments. In June 1942, a scientific council was established; to become a member, one had to be appointed by the head of the "Health Services Department." There were outstanding physicians from nearly all fields, including some scholars of great acclaim. Many of the most outstanding physicians did not survive the war; many of them died there, and many were sent to their deaths in the autumn of 1944. Men who gave their all for two and three years perished nameless and in misery. The disease to which they fell prey was stronger than the suffering they had fought, with varying degrees of success, in Theresienstadt.

17

Welfare

WELFARE FOR THE ELDERLY AND INFIRM

At first, only one welfare office within the "Department of Internal Administration" dealt with personal and material care. Then the "Economics Department" was made responsible for material welfare, whereas the personal care of workers was entrusted to the "Labor Welfare Office." Those who did not work were charges of the "welfare" subdepartment of the "Health Services Department," with which the "Youth Welfare Office" – operational since the camp was opened – was long associated. After the fall catastrophe of 1944, the "Welfare Department" and "Youth Welfare Office" were combined into one "group" (*Sachgebiet*). Dr. Karel Fleischmann, a physician who was also talented at drawing and poetry, directed the "Welfare Department" until he was sent to his death in fall 1944. Fleischmann was an interesting character – hardworking, ambitious, intelligent, resourceful, and good humored. He was always concerned with improving the grim situation, but he was no match for such a huge undertaking: too much stood in the way. His knowledge and good intentions arguably exceeded those of most of the high camp functionaries. But given the prevailing conditions and the authoritarian dependency of Munk, a friend of his, he was unable to lead with an iron hand, as would have been necessary to improve conditions. A speech by Fleischmann gets to the core of the problems:

To the blind of Q 319.

> We labor only to stuff the memory, and leave the conscience
> and the understanding unfurnished and void. (Montaigne)

A sighted person speaks to you. A person who has an advantage over you, but who also has a great disadvantage because the way to you is difficult and nearly impassable, since the way is blocked by a barrier on the border between light and eternal shadow....

I see you are sitting on benches of rough boards, not painted wood, made by someone who had never even studied carpentry. Someone, almost entirely on his own, not only set up the benches but turned the entire attic into an auditorium, a stage, so that poor Jews could forget their lives, their present destiny, for at least a few hours. Under these rafters ... a space laid out toward the top like cards rests on a floor covered with brick tiles; this space was once was divided by plank walls where onetime residents dried their laundry and stored their junk.

Welfare

... The transports arrived ... and the attics were cleared out, cleaned in a hurry, the plank walls removed. The attics were filled with people – the elderly, the frail, the sick and infirm.... Here I learned about misery, about pain and misfortune.... I saw filth, I saw dislocated, contorted limbs, emaciated bodies, I see the ghastly grimaces of the dying, I see the blank eyes, the open, rattling mouths.... I see the chimney walls with their crumbling mortar, the nails, laboriously pounded in, on which the wretched overcoats hang; I see exposed bodies stewing in the heat of summer, the colorfully striped mattresses and the matte red of the hard, cold stone tiles; I see dead-tired nurses and the sad, despairing physician....

I see still more. I see the entire town, I see it in its normal appearance, with stores, with offices, with movie theaters, where people lived the way people live in other towns, with wife and child, happiness and sorrow, work and time off. Then suddenly, I see the dead face of the town, the bloodless town, as the population disappeared overnight like ghosts and the houses and streets suddenly stand empty, and we encroach upon empty living rooms.... You didn't see all of that. You don't see the narrow, worn-down staircases. You don't see the narrow courtyards, the stores, the workshops whose bleeding, sad windows seem to be crying. You don't see the neglected gardens, in which the first fruits have begun to ripen. And you don't see the trucks filled with the sick and infirm.... You don't see the sad battalions of newcomers, expelled, bent, stooped figures, the blood-red sweaty faces, the horrified, appalled, hopeless eyes. You don't see the old mothers and old men dragging their shabby belongings behind them through the dust of the street. You didn't see the thirsty hands and didn't hear the hoarse throats crying for water. You didn't see the wavering figures in the hot attic, [near the] chimney, suddenly knocked down like pins from a stroke. You don't see the misery of the Schleusen. You don't see the aged women, how they rolled down the steep, vaulted passage of the outer barracks, moving like marionettes, like the dolls in a tragic child's game, ever faster in a creepy dance and fantastical rhythm, until they fell onto the cold stone floor with a cry, spreading their arms and throwing their bags and canes away, breaking their heads and coloring the floor red, before anyone was there to help.

And you don't see the miserable quarters in the blocks. You don't see the crammed rooms, the damp walls and pocked floors. You don't see all this sadness, all this misfortune, all this desperation. You don't see the infirmaries, the outpatient clinics with the endless rows of waiting patients, you don't see the pace of the grueling work and cannot measure what difficulties, what obstacles had to be overcome and how the primitive medical facilities slowly changed into actual treatment rooms....

... It takes a certain amount of mental and moral strength not to lose your bearings in such a fundamentally altered situation.... Now I'm closing my eyes and placing myself in your position. You were taken by the hand, loaded into train cars, yelled at, and after a while arrived someplace and were yelled at again, and were set down somewhere and badly cared for. The voices around you changed. The food changed, the beds changed and the quiet rhythm of your day changed.

... I ask you, those who cannot see, who have been protected from so much of the ugly, dirty, evil that we have to see through our eyes, and who because of that have more time to reflect on it, how and by what means have you tried to achieve the vast task of being human? How have you ... helped to form and achieve the idea of a higher humanity? ... Through your suffering, you are the ones who should show us the way to greater humanity.... Human happiness requires inner peace, harmony, being at one with yourself. You will rightfully object: that is all well and good, but if one is starving and freezing and unable to sleep because of a plague of insects, one would have to be a saint to follow this path.... It is a question of basic attitude ... we wish dutifully to take on the care of your bare existence and to achieve it honestly and fairly and conscientiously with the means and possibilities at hand. (63)

The aesthetic fumes of such a speech open our eyes to the way in which needy elderly Jews were welcomed to the "Reich Home for the Aged." But especially for the least fortunate ones, most of whom knew more and were wiser than the clever speaker in front of them, such well-meaning attempts at education were most inappropriate. Perhaps it would have been better to direct serious words to the director of the self-administration and the health care workers, but, above all, the most important task was to ensure necessary care through integrity in the camp. Only then would the leaders have earned the right to demand and encourage the psychological cooperation of the poorest. Nevertheless, it should be noted that Fleischmann was filled with true horror and compassion. Luckily, he found co-workers who selflessly struggled to help. Of the best of them, especially, few survived the war. By the time the "Welfare Department" did make noticeable changes, terrible wrongs already had been done to the helpless, and not until 1943–44 did conditions improve slightly, despite unceasing resistance. Tragically enough, conditions began to become healthier in the fall of 1944, when Baeck led the whole of the "Welfare Department" after the fall catastrophe.

In 1942, the situation looked grim:

> Another sad chapter was the treatment of the very old and the sick. [Their quarters are described.] Hundreds of people lay in these rooms, in the care of some retrained and some untrained personnel. The care of these poor people was extremely meager. Caregivers swiped food from their limited rations. Unfortunately ... the ghetto administration had little compassion for these poor people. Regrettably, some of the doctors and nurses also took this attitude. (16)

In the monthly report from July 1942, the "Welfare Office" in the "Department of Internal Administration" stated:

> The use of the Welfare Office has experienced a significant increase. This is attributable to the fact that, in this period, members of transports Am and Ao [whose luggage had largely been confiscated] participated. At the same time, the needs of those being sent to the East are increasing. ... There were 2,593 requests, and 1,527 had been addressed by the 25th of the month. The caretaker at the Hamburg Kaserne in the ward for infants and small children and the home for the infirm was responsible for 61 women and 16 children in three to five visits per day. During office hoursthere were 30 similar supplicants and interventions daily. Our specialists dealt with the following asocial cases as they appeared in all the men's and women's barracks: 42 asocial cases were handled daily in the various barracks and 75 received outpatient care. Some cases were dealt with by our staff in the inpatient psychiatric department also. Our interventions were required every night. (290)

The pressure on the staff, whose numbers grew too little and too slowly, made the work extraordinarily difficult.

In July 1943, the "Welfare Department" dealt with the following in- and outpatient cases:

	Outpatients	Inpatients
Infirm	1,550	2,350
Blind	275	290
War-injured	1,491	105
Physically handicapped (crippled)	1,563	558
Deaf-mute and hard-of-hearing	200	17
Infants	262	323

Of the 46,395 residents, 8,984 were in need of partial or total care – more than 19%. In addition, there were older children, cared for by the "Youth Welfare Office," and many sick people. A total of 3,623 people, more than 40% of the needy, were placed in "homes," which was not an advantage in every case (see also 299). The work of and plans for the "Welfare Department" in this period are described in the following document:

Health Services We are here for everyone
Welfare Department
                        Short report
                                        about
                                        Scope of duties
                                        Organization
                                        Activities
                                        Planning
                of the Welfare Department
                                Theresienstadt, October 1943

The Welfare Department
was established in October 1942.

Assignment:
Supervision and care of all physically and mentally disabled and disadvantaged people in the Jewish settlement of Theresienstadt.

Organizational scheme:
... in addition to the Central Administration, there are 9 special sections:

1. Care of the infirm
2. Care of the blind
3. Care of war-disabled
4. Care of the physically handicapped
5. Care of deaf-mutes
6. Care of unattached persons
7. Care of small children (never turned over to "Youth Welfare")
8. Care of the sick (the sick will receive psychological care)
9. Care of prisoners

Introduction to Activities:

A) In-patient care
in homes for the elderly (E IIIa, L 504, infirm blocks G V) and rooms for the elderly ... (H V, E VII, L 206, L 205, Q 215 and others), in the home for the blind Q 319, homes for the war-disabled L 231, 233, 235, deaf-mute home in E VII, homes for colostomy patients in the colostomy home H V and homes for the physically disabled in G V, infant and toddler homes in the children's block G VI.

B) Out-patient care
Care and supervision in the houses of the entire town. Close collaboration with the doctors on duty ... under the direction of the lead welfare worker. The houses are supervised by permanently-assigned people who live there, mostly former nurses, but welfare workers visit the houses (several times a day).

All welfare workers are organized into one uniform group.... They will be trained and instructed together so that each becomes a model caregiver who can perform all tasks....

The personnel	Total number	319
thereof		
Welfare workers		115
Caregivers		154
Administrators		26
Heads of section		9
Supervisory physicians		6
Support staff		9

Number of patients in the past month in

	Institutional Care	Open Care
Infirm	3,700	2,200
Blind	497	171
Physically Handicapped	2,181	542
War-disabled	1,826	155
Small Children	383	304
Unattached Persons	520	
Physical and Mental Care	2,008	
Prisoners	200	
TOTAL	11,315	3,372

The mode of operation and scope of work:

The majority of welfare work will be done according to feasibility, without unnecessary bureaucracy, on the spot. In the home for the infirm and other homes, branches will be set up with a head welfare worker as the director.... Only questions of principle and important matters will be dealt with by the central office.

Following registration, the patients will be housed in inpatient facilities. In the year of the report, 4,000 people were placed in Homes for the Infirm.

The actual caretaking, the day-to-day tasks, are done by the welfare workers. There are 115 people who care for nearly 12,000 patients. The welfare workers are an elite corps comprised mostly of professionally trained women with an unusually strong work ethic. They perform high-quality, efficient and dependable work with a commitment, honesty and enthusiasm that is rarely matched in this place. The administration of the whole system is carried out by only 26 people and nine section heads. This work as well as the contact with the public is done in inadequate rooms that are much too small, with two typewriter stations and hundreds of visitors daily. The Section for Care of the War-Disabled alone had a total of some 20,000 visitors in the year of the report. The Section for the Care of the Physically Handicapped alone reports 1,611 visits and 1,050 house calls in September of last year.

Type of care:

These range from subtle psychological work to minor and major substantive and social problems. They include the care of the infirm, sick, louse-ridden, physically handicapped, blind, etc., and the work of psychotherapists in their own clinics through talks and discussions in people's quarters, alone and in groups, in the Schleuse, at funerals, in attics and with all of the people who are registered with Central Welfare as attempted suicides.

Welfare 479

Range of care:

1. Procurement of repair orders for clothes, shoes, sheets, glasses, hearing aids and orthopedic equipment.
2. Shopping in stores for welfare cases.
3. Special approval for the purchase of clothes and shoes.
4. Postal services (writing letters, collection, arranging appointments).
5. Book loans.
6. Information to relatives and research at the central registry office.
7. Research on missing and misplaced property.
8. Recreation tickets.
9. Recreational activities in the homes and homes for the infirm for the blind and war-disabled.
10. Finding jobs for the blind, physically handicapped, war-disabled and deaf.
11. Procurement of new prostheses, orthopedic shoes, trusses, etc.
12. Repair of ambulances.
13. Registration and numbering of ambulances.
14. Registration and inspection of yellow armbands (for the blind).
15. Procurement of dressings for colostomy patients and amputees.
16. Procurement of soap for colostomy patients and amputees.
17. Baths (showers and baths).
18. Issuance of crutches and canes.
19. Issuance of chairs and arm chairs.
20. Issuance of mattresses.
21. Procurement of sick beds.
22. Advice of all kinds.
23. Procurement of accommodations.
24. Preferential status at mealtimes.
25. Preferential status for shopping.
26. Aid from the caregivers and block nurses.
27. Bringing the disabled outside from their attics in good weather.
28. Procurement of blankets, pillows and quilts.
29. Children's beds.
30. Strollers.
31. Fruit for sick children.
32. Knitting clothes and linens for infants.
33. Guardianship of infants.
34. Warming food.
35. Procurement of documents.
36. Repair of linens.
37. Caring for the suicidal.
38. Examination of borderline cases (psychopaths, epileptics, addicts, and the senile).
39. Speech and reading courses.
40. Hearing aids and batteries for hearing aids.
41. Distribution of food packets to prisoners.
42. Depot of nonperishable food for prisoners.
43. Interventions for prisoners.
44. Shaves, haircuts and baths for prisoners.
45. Transport to hospitals.
46. Finding jobs for prisoners.
47. Extra nutrition for the chronically ill and those on work assignments.

480   *Sociology*

Planning:
... Combination of welfare work ... into a single welfare department with the guarantee
of appropriate distribution and monitoring of assets and improvement and integration
of every aspect of welfare services.

> Dr. E. Munk
> Director of Health Services
> Delivered by:
> Dr. Karl Fleischmann
> Director of the Welfare Department (287)

These words sound rather better than the harsh reality. Almost everything was caught in a vicious circle. Even if it was not impossible to find a pair of glasses, a hearing aid, or a prosthesis, it was certainly a lengthy ordeal. When one finally obtained the sought-after object, it usually was no good, and one was no better off than before. A malaise became noticeable; it often turned into despair or lethargy. The responsibilities were too great, and despite much goodwill and the touching devotion of selfless helpers, everything remained in rudimentary condition. This is shown in examples from the monthly reports of the "Welfare Department" from March and June 1944, the period of the "beautified" camp.

The following passage is taken from the March 1944 report:

Overall: The organization of the implementation of practical welfare work is ... proceeding, but a dearth of individual supervision is evident. This can be attributed to:

a)   a shortage of welfare workers,
b)   the old age of the workers in this division (average age is over 55),
c)   bad health conditions (over 30% absenteeism),
d)   shortage of space in the branch [offices].

Director's Office and Personnel Office. The total number of workers [is] ... 286 people ... 56 caregivers for the Home for the Blind.... An average of 90 welfare workers were available for about 10,800 people receiving material aid and about 3,000 others receiving aid due to physical disabilities but working nonetheless – or 150 people per welfare worker!! ....

Section for Care of the Blind.... Of 445 blind people, 164 live in the Home for the Blind and 281 live in the blocks. Of 56 caregivers, 23 are over 60 years old ... 8 people work just 4 hours a day, so that here, too, we must refer impersonally to the inadequate quality of the caregiver personnel.

Section for Care of the Sick. It must be noted that two rooms in House L 207 have been occupied by asocial residents, so one could say a home for asocials has been established. There remain substantial difficulties in finding qualified supervisory personnel. Only when this difficulty is addressed can an expansion be considered, and the same is true for the grouping of bedwetters.

Institutional Care Section. The department and its comprehensive and extremely important scope are inhibited by unclear distribution of authority....

Section for Prisoner Care. In the month of the report, 125 people were released and 99 were admitted.... The efforts to create a separate youth prison have not been successful thus far.

Section for Care of the Elderly.... Approximately 2,500 baths were prescribed ... around 1,200 showers for men, ... around 5,025 ... for women.... It must be noted that, because of a coal shortage, bathing was not always possible.... By using the

Welfare 481

showers and bathtubs in the Disinfection Bathhouse and the showers in the Central Bathhouse, the people being cared for could bathe about three times every two months.

Storehouse L 506 (disinfection). Distribution was brisk to fulfill the requirements of arriving transports. In all, 2,000 pieces of underwear or clothing were lent out to patients and new arrivals.... . In 15 cases, some 1,000 pairs of underwear were delivered for people being de-loused, and were returned in dirty condition after being used.

Special Vouchers Agenda. In the month of the report, 588 applications were made and 524 approved.

Recreation. A total of 15,082 coffeehouse tickets and 2,192 theater and concert tickets were distributed. Here each week we succeeded in our efforts to have approved a special event in the form of a concert, from Recreation. That was only for those served by our department. The first three events already have taken place.

Activity Report of the Institutional Care Section.

... We are currently attempting to introduce into the Homes for the Infirm work whereby women from among the inmates who are qualified for simple sewing will mend the underwear and clothing of the men and women in the relevant inpatient units.... . This measure is at once appropriate as a sort of work therapy, while ... the deterioration of clothing would be controlled.

E VI: On 19 and 20 March, a transport departing from the Psychiatric Division was equipped with the essentials and prepared for travel. [On March 20, 1944, a transport of forty-five people left the camp, headed for Bergen-Belsen. I do not know whether all were mentally ill.]

E IIIa, TB Department: As part of the recreation program, activity programs were established in the so-called Children's Rooms (Youth). Lectures were held by inmates of the department.

E IIIa, Home for the Infirm: .... because of the extraordinary crowding, the following should be considered ... remove beds for the infirm from two or three of the badly-lit front rooms and set up a cloakroom for the rest of the infirm living there. Cleanliness and order in the rooms for the infirm could be greatly improved by removing clothes and luggage.

L 206: ... In general, it may be reported that overall hygienic conditions have improved, but the plague of vermin is agonizing.

Activity Report of the Section for Care of the Physically Handicapped.

We cannot provide an exact count of the number of people served this month because almost all of the workers, including the department head, are sick. An estimate ... is 2,050 people.

Prosthesis storehouse in L 410. We have determined that some 120 leg and arm prostheses are stored in an attic of building L 416, where the orthopedic workshops are. They are in a condition that makes them less and less usable.... More requests for repairs of prostheses come in daily, mostly from people who have been here for two years or longer and whose prostheses are in such bad shape that they must be exchanged if they cannot be repaired. It is urgent that the prostheses stored in the attic be transferred to a better storage area. At the same time, we have asked the Estates Division of the ghetto court not to let prostheses, crutches, etc. be delivered first to the central storehouse, but to send them directly to us ... as it has been determined that at delivery ... which often does not happen until months after a death, big pieces of the casings, which are made of leather, were cut out, and most recently, prostheses are being delivered with carrying straps cut off.

Repair Coupons.... Because of a number of discrepancies among the various administrations over the allocation of laundry coupons, meetings have been held in the Central Secretariat, from which precise suggestions were made to us. But this issue still has not been resolved. We believe that the best thing would be to cancel the supplemental laundry coupons and introduce laundry cards for all ghetto residents. In this way, all would drop off their laundry more frequently than they do now, when laundry can be turned in only every three to four months.

Activity Report of the Section for Care of the War-Disabled.

[On March 20, 1944, there were 1,835 people with war injuries; 921 with severe injuries (543 from Germany, 160 from Austria, and 218 from the "Protectorate"); and 914 with nonsevere injuries (615 from Germany, 118 from Austria, and 181 from the "Protectorate"). In three homes, there were 149 disabled men, housed with 97 women.] ... From July 1943 through 1 March 1944, 170 people with severe war injuries died, 17% of the total number in eight months. It should be noted that this high death rate cannot be attributed to natural causes, but is attributable to bad accommodations and undernourishment....

Activity Report of the Section for the Care of Small Children

... Three orphaned children, including an infant, arrived with the Berlin transport [of March 10, 1944].

The Purim festival could be celebrated only modestly. Child Welfare managed to distribute marmalade ... so that every child received 20 dkg (200 grams).... In ... March the children in the Children's Block received:

12	children received 25 grams of parsley each,
25	children received ¼ of an apple each
46	children received 25 grams of carrots each,
8	children received one portion of red cabbage each, and in addition,
2	stations in the infants' home received ½ head of red cabbage.

100 children from the blocks and barracks each received ¼ kilogram of soup seasoning.

Recreation was limited to two lectures ... :
Mrs. Dr. A. Feigl: Epidemic diseases and their prevention
Mrs. Dr. G. Bäumel: The upbringing of the young child

Activity Report on Recreation for the Welfare Department

...In the wards for the frail and infirm, the Dr. Leo Strauss group conducted 40 events, including two special events ... as opera aria nights.... Discussions about the expansion of recreational activities (reorganization of the lecture group and events) are taking place.

Activity Report for the Welfare Office of Block G V for the Infirm.

... There have been repeated complaints that residents cannot count on regular visits from the hairdresser, but must rely on nursing staff to look after their hair and beards, or on strangers in exchange for food. All such concerns lead to an unsatisfactory situation.

Activity Report for Q 319, Home for the Blind.

... Recently, the shortage of certain materials and inventory has become an issue. Besides mops and brooms, the most urgent need is for buckets and larger dishes to ensure hygiene and cleanliness during food service and dish washing. This bad situation must be taken especially seriously because of the increase in cases of enteritis.

Welfare 483

Activity Report of the Welfare Office L 310.

... We are happy to report that some bunk beds have been removed, which has improved living conditions. The residents feel freer and healthier. We already have received questions as to which quarters are still without beds, and hopefully we soon will be able to help these people by installing beds.

Activity Report for the Welfare Office E VII.

By hiring a new welfare worker after the recovery of both sick welfare workers, it was possible to give more personal and individual care to the patients. This was noted with appreciation (one of the women even had poems written to her out of sheer gratitude) and had an especially beneficial and calming effect on the many lone patients who otherwise have no one to care for them. (288)

From the June 1944 report:

Situation:

Reduction in the number of people being cared for, these reductions through transports [that is, the deportation of May 1944] and deaths, to around 8,000, a reduction of 20–25%. [This was still more than a quarter of the prisoners.] ...

Administration and Personnel Office: The department has 250 employees, an increase of approximately 11 percent. [According to job statistics for the same month, which we used in Chapter 13, the department employed only 190 people. The discrepancy can be explained by the fact that support staff were counted elsewhere in that case.] The shortage of trained welfare personnel continues....

Section for Care of the Infirm. There are 1,488 people in the homes for the infirm.... At present, there are still about 600 of the infirm in the blocks.

Section for Care of the Blind ... 333 people. 130 of them are living in the Home for the Blind.

Section for Care of the Physically Handicapped. There are 1,398 people, 924 of whom can be considered severely handicapped and 474 of whom have minor handicaps....

Section for Care of the War-Disabled. Severe war injuries 881, minor war injuries 757, total 1,638. Some 146 men with war injuries and 85 women live in the Homes for the War-Disabled.

Section for Care of Deaf-Mutes. About 40 deaf-mutes ... and 450 people who are hard of hearing.

Section for Care of Small Children. 425 children ... :

4-year-olds	84
3-year-olds	94
2-year-olds	123
1-year-olds	103
under 1	21

Section for Care of the Sick ... 181 people ... being cared for.

Recreation. 19,200 coffeehouse tickets and 3,224 theater tickets were distributed. The lecture series for inpatient welfare continues.

Section for Care of the Elderly. No advances in overall planning. The standard caregiving took place; in addition, some 3,000 tins of sardines were distributed. The old people continued to be bathed on schedule. In the Central Bath, 5,320 showers were given. Taking into consideration the baths and showers given by the Material Goods Section of the Disinfection Department, some 8,000 people were bathed [!]. Every person was bathed at least once.

Section for Care of Prisoners. The number of inmates fell to 29.

484 *Sociology*

Activity Report for the Personnel Office
[The Personnel Office had 250 employees: 66 administrators, 125 welfare workers, 21 block caregivers, 18 block nurses, and 20 support staff, plus an additional 8 people with floating assignments. This explains the discrepancy with the statistics in Chapter 13: that chapter refers only to the first two groups, a total of 191 people: 190 people counted as "welfare workers" and 1 counted as the "director."]

Activity Report for the Section for the Care of Small Children
... The children were given the usual portion of 1/3 of a loaf of white bread per week. Weak or sick children now receive two portions. 353 children each received 20 dkg of cookies. 258 small children received ¼ to ½ liter of milk daily, in rotation ... 100 children each received alternately 10 dkg. of curds (that is, "quark"). 130 heads of lettuce were given to 33 children.....

Activity Report for the Section for Care of the Elderly
... L 504 ... As in the other homes for the infirm, special attention was given to the heating of food, whereby it was determined that warm food was distributed only sporadically. Patients often were forced to give up their bread to ensure enough wood to heat the food. We have been unable to discuss the matter with the Section on Coal.

E VII. The residents of rooms 19–21 for the infirm were moved to L 206, which has been only partly and insufficiently disinfected with sulfur. This greatly eased crowding of rooms 32–38. Nevertheless, the overall impression has not changed much, because the insufficient lighting and sanitary conditions remain unchanged.

... The insect plague in E IIIa borders on the intolerable. Patients sleep mainly during the day, as they spend the nights sitting on their beds, to the extent they are able.

G V [Block for the Infirm] Here, too, some of the houses are hit with the insect plague.... There also are complaints about small food portions, as there are wherever food is delivered by shipment (G V, L 504, E IIIa in comparison to E VII). The reason is that less food is distributed, due to fears that the amount of food supplied will be insufficient. Leftovers are being served as extra rations, but this does not help everyone.

Activity Report of Storehouses L 506.
... To expand the storehouse, some 4,000 pieces of clothing were given to us by the Central Warehouse. Among these were 500 nightshirts and 500 pairs of women's underwear, which essentially are more of a burden than a help, because there is almost no demand for them. The quality of the remaining 3,000 items was quite bad. It is impossible to give out these items in this condition. The provisional new storage of clothing and shoes located in the basement has not had the desired results. These goods soon will be completely moldy and useless. Warehouse Management can take no responsibility for this, as they made every effort to prevent it.

Operations Report of the Material Goods Section
[A total of 4,680 order tickets for repairs were given out this month.] (291)

The elderly people who were relatively spry and had survived the dangerous initial period often withstood the camp fairly well, especially if family members helped them. The two oldest people to arrive on the transports were 100-year-olds, and they died there. Some old men over eighty and even ninety years old lived a long time in Theresienstadt, and even survived until liberation. Although they were not actually senile, they often did not quite comprehend what was happening to them (see 271), and this sometimes strengthened their resistance. They called the deportation a "trip," asked what newspapers they could read there, and considered the margarine and ersatz coffee to be butter and real coffee. Even if they once had been demanding, now they were satisfied with everything. They probably were hardly aware of the value of the food and other private aid they received through others' sacrifice, or of the difficulty involved in procuring these goods. Sometimes they did not even notice the crowded, miserable living quarters and considered Theresienstadt to be "quite good." When the war ended, an eighty-seven-year-old man who had been in the camp for a long time said that things were "quite fair" there. When the name "Hitler" was mentioned, he warned that people should speak quietly or not at all about such dangerous things. Such people were a small, fortunate minority who shut out the present and lived in their memories.

The majority felt abandoned and hardly could orient themselves at all, although often they understood the situation quite well. The general debilitation of age became more apparent. Emotional subtlety sometimes was lost; many lived like animals, waiting for bread and mealtimes. Such people were also inconsiderate and selfish. Others complained and became careless, lethargic, and dependent. Usually they died quickly, even when family members cared for them. Others were more energetic and went off in all sorts of attempts to acquire the necessities of life. Still others, as frail as they were, tried to comfort themselves through hope and introspection; they thought about anticipated reunions with their children in other countries, basked in fantasies about a happy future after the war, unearthed treasured memories from the past, or rejoiced that certain people already were long dead and did not have to live through all this. But few had the strength (or the weakness) to live completely in the present.

The old and the frail often were willing to undertake activities. They loved small tasks, lectures, and chess and other games, as well as the "recreational activities" that were offered in general or especially for them. If they were able, they went on visits or hung around the corridors and courtyards. Almost all were thankful for conversation; they would ask what it was like "outside" and whether the war was almost over. Even though the "coffeehouse" was an embarrassing farce, it was good for these people to have at least one chance to sit in decent chairs, and to be able to warm up during the winter. They were pleased with small attentions and favors, which they rewarded with affectionate loyalty. The sometimes envied those capable of working, whereas they considered the behavior of adults and young people, often justifiably, to be inconsiderate and brutal. If one of the elderly experienced real or perceived injustice, he bickered helplessly, screaming as he tried to fight back. Shamelessly taken advantage of, the elderly became skeptical of nearly everyone and suspected even real supporters of wanting to harm them. At the same time, with small gifts, they tried to buy favors that usually offered nothing more than that to which the recipients already were entitled.

Physical and psychological deterioration often balanced each other. Sometimes the bedridden infirm were surprisingly composed and lucid. The unwieldy bureaucracy often presented them with insoluble problems, and they could neither adapt nor orient themselves. If they were able to figure things out, they –particularly the German Jews – began to follow the rules more literally and rigidly than was beneficial. Many imagined a normal, bourgeois order, to which they wanted camp operations to conform. The more helpless an old person was, the more he was turned into an object of the coerced community; it brushed him aside and ground him down. One should never forget that, with the exception of the first six months, frail old people

486 *Sociology*

were the ones who primarily determined the character of this camp, and they were always its primary victims.

YOUTH WELFARE

Much attention was paid to the care and upbringing of children. The fact that this remained an unsolved and insoluble problem was a result of the despairing existence of children thrown off course and of the camp conditions, in which no child could thrive or be protected from significant harm. This was true despite the fact that children received the undivided compassion and attention of the rest of the prisoners, and especially of the administration, who saw this as one of their most important and even primary duties. Regardless of which path the administration had chosen, in the short or long run, they would inevitably have stumbled. There was no positive outcome. Even the right path – namely, the morally correct path – could only go tragically wrong. Thus it is not a criticism of the chosen path to say that, despite some partial successes, the work of the "Youth Welfare Office" was largely a failure. The "Youth Welfare Office," at first a division of the "Health Services Department," later became its own "department" and was responsible for children ages four to sixteen and, in some cases, youth up to ages eighteen and even twenty. The department was responsible for children in the "homes" as well as for children living with their families. It was their goal, supported by the self-administration, to put as many children as possible into the "homes" and to raise them according to comradely principles. Children from ages four to ten lived in "children's homes," children from ten to sixteen lived in "boys' and girls' homes," and boys from sixteen to twenty lived in "apprentice" and "young worker homes." It never was possible to place all of the youth into "homes," and the self-administration never strongly pressured or coerced parents in an effort to do so.

At the end of 1941 the administration already had begun to establish "homes" – which were, at first, special rooms – in the barracks. At this time, it was not possible to consider serious educational work. The new arrivals were not used to the ghetto. Most of them had been separated from at least one parent, which – in addition to the constant turnover caused by the deportations – made progress difficult. On top of that came the questionable politics of the internal leadership. Lacking vision, Edelstein's circle was obsessed with the thought of turning an SS camp into a preparatory school for life in Palestine, especially for young people. That did not succeed, and so they unilaterally chose immature youths – although they were idealistic people who often came from a Zionist-socialist youth movement – as the leaders and staff of the "Youth Welfare Office," regardless of whether or not they were cut out for the work, personally and substantively. Besides these young people, oddly enough, the office employed only several rather chauvinistic assimilated Czechs. Meanwhile, for a long time, experienced educators, of whom there were many in the camp, were passed over for appointment – and later they were employed mostly only as teachers and rarely as youth workers. Thus the "Youth Welfare Office" was set up almost as a Zionist youth association, and therefore it is not surprising that the youthful leaders had even less understanding of the true requirements of the coerced community than the leaders of the self-administration. It would have been necessary to recognize and instill a general human solidarity in everyone wearing the star, which did not have to mean surrendering Jewish and general humanitarian ideals but did mean renouncing political tendencies of any stripe. It cannot be denied that goodwill, effort, and dedication were shown by some members of the "Youth Welfare Office." But experience and insight were lacking, especially in the first year. Over time, some idealists became disheartened camp realists who lost their intellectual capacity and then their ethical sense in their attempt to function as educators. The head of the "Youth Welfare Office" was Egon Redlich, a young Zionist. He was ambitious and vain; his character pitted a strong ego against a weak will, so he was not well qualified for the job. Besides him, Fredy Hirsch played the greatest role. In the early months of the camp he had great influence in other areas as well, but soon his influence was restricted solely to the "Youth Welfare Office." As the sports instructor, a somewhat dictatorial hero to the young people, and a Zionist idealist, he was, at least at first, an inspiring example, especially for the younger children. He wanted only the best, but he, too, was obstinate, inexperienced, and unfortunately also imprudent; thus he never was in control of the situation and could not prevent the moral deterioration of the youth. In September 1943, he was sent to Auschwitz. His death there is reported on in Chapter 3. When Redlich and Hirsch finally were given the assistance of genuine educators, such as the professor Maximilian Adler and the distinguished Zionist Emil Nohel, as an "education advisory board," it was already too late. The aforementioned professors, Redlich, and most of his young co-workers went to their deaths in fall 1944.

A December 1942 petition against the leadership of the "Youth Welfare Office" provides information on conditions there. Some of the suggestions contained in this report were later implemented.

The Youth Problem in the Theresienstadt Ghetto
(with special consideration for the problems of the wayward)

 I) Introductory remarks. . . .

 II) Preamble
  The basis and goal of all education is the harmonious development of the personality and its orderly integration into the human community. This goal should not be abandoned even in difficult times or under adverse conditions. The extraordinary nature of the task should not give reason to neglect pedagogic duties. Youth workers must adjust and prove their skills especially in such special circumstances.

 III) A.) General Description
  Children through [the end of] their third year . . . are the responsibility of Health Services.

 1.) Infants and
 2.) Toddlers . . . .

Most of these children live with their mothers in the Infants and Toddlers Homes, as long as there is room. Around 250 children live there.
  Children and youth from ages 3 to 18 are subjects of Youth Welfare. . . .

 1. Pre-school children ages 3 to 6
 2. School-age children
  a. 6 to 10 years of age
  b. 10 to 14 years of age,
 3. Apprentice and youth workers
  a. 14 to 16 years of age
  b. 16 to 18 years of age.

Youth Welfare oversaw 3,541 children and young people as of 6 December 1942. Of these, some 2,000 are living in homes and some 1,400 with parents and relatives. The rest, approximately 150 children, were sick and in the hospitals. . . .

Those in hospitals, as well as the few mentally handicapped children, were entirely out of the hands of the Youth Welfare Office. . . .

The number of personnel . . . is at least 300, so that there is one adult for every 10 children.

III. B.)

a.) The administration

Three things may be noted about the administration:

1.) It is clear that they are unprepared for their role, as the program proposed by them has been carried out inadequately.

Evidence) Neither the physical nor mental care of the children has been adequately provided for. The Program or Culture section is essentially unstaffed, so that work is done without plan or system, and clear goals or a uniform will are nowhere in evidence. The administration makes little or no use of its rights of oversight.

2.) The administration has only an incomplete grasp of its responsibilities.

Evidence) The personnel are not chosen according to their qualifications, so that inappropriate . . . workers . . . can be working in every department. The administration creates complete confusion in filling positions, as its leaders obviously themselves lack the necessary training and experience. This is exacerbated by the fact that, in many cases, it appears that only ideological and political views are taken into consideration. In youth homes with Czech-speaking children, there are counselors who speak no Czech, so they are helpless in the face of even the most primitive kinds of educational work. . . . It must be pointed out that new approaches to Hebrew teaching are constantly being tried, while the children lack the most elementary knowledge of reading and writing in their mother tongue, as well as in mathematics.

3.) The administration's work is irresponsible . . . .

Evidence) The de-lousing of nearly 1,000 children. The miserable condition of the toilets, etc.

b.) The youth workers (counselors, home directors)

It is clear . . . that only a very small number of youth workers . . . have the essential qualifications in terms of morality and education. Therefore, it is understandable that the youth workers do not collaborate, but rather operate autonomously, each for himself. home directors have no contact with counselors working in the same room . . . which is a primary reason that our youth are running wild. We had an opportunity to observe situations in which some youth workers stand helpless before their noisy charges, unable to control them for good or for evil.

The few workers who were completely on top of things are at the end of their rope from overwork. . . .

c.) The teachers

The teachers' abilities are very mixed, but even the genuinely good ones in the instruction program suffer from the general lack of a system. Though the special difficulties should be strongly emphasized, the desired minimum standards are not attained because most children lack the most elementary knowledge.

d.) Supervisory bodies

are almost non-functional, which becomes clear by looking at most quarters or paying a late-night visit to the youth barracks. Filth, noise and disorder of every type are everywhere.

Welfare 489

e.) Other personnel

The support personnel (manual workers, menders, kitchen workers, etc.) generally do good work. The menders, for example, may be thanked for the fact that the children wear decent clothes. The work of the many nurses should also be lauded.

III. C.) The children

a.) Cleanliness and order

The physical cleanliness of the children is fairly good. Their clothing and other belongings are also in order . . . but the cleanliness of their rooms leaves something to be desired.

b.) Upbringing

The children suffer from the widespread lack of a program or system. They feel the absence of a hand to guide them. The counselors are merely maids who hand out their assignments. . . . The children have far too little to do . . . they doze without thoughts or purpose, because they lack stimulation and encouragement. The excessive free time itself is not the problem, but its lack of structure. . . . Therefore, most of the children completely lack collective spirit, as well as initiative; . . . when parents get involved, conditions appear even worse. . . .

c.) Discipline

There is no standard or uniformity at all in praise and strictness. The children respect almost nothing and fear nothing. They sense the provisional nature of their living conditions, which is unavoidable. It therefore is doubly deplorable that, behind the ephemeral nature of daily phenomena, no one offers something durable that could give them moral strength and support.

III. D.)

1.) Some children with severe mental illness are isolated in the psychiatric ward . . .

2.) Some cases of slight debility and enuresis are in the care of Dr. Bäumel (psychoanalyst).

3.) At the moment, the Health Services are in the process of determining sensory defects (such as deafness) among children.

4.) The problem of waywardness

. . . The actual youth problem . . . is the wayward child. A rough estimate reveals 8 to 10 percent . . . can be considered wayward, but early signs of waywardness are found more or less clearly in all of the children. . . . All the causes suggested in the relevant literature are present to a high degree. The destruction of the family, the miserable housing, light and nutrition, the bad sanitation, the disenchanting reality that tramples any ideals in the bud, the way children are forced to grow up quickly, the poor or inadequate education, misguided, unnatural activities; . . . the many bad examples . . . make it understandable that waywardness takes on a form that is not only dangerous for individuals, but also represents a very concrete danger to community life in the ghetto. Emotional impoverishment, wildness, brutality, false independence, an unhealthy haggling spirit, arrogance, unbridled selfishness, shiftiness, as well as hypocrisy, a proclivity toward occasional or even systematic cheating, theft and robbery, and maybe also shamelessness and sexual deviance are the obvious consequences. . . . [Several suggestions for reform follow.] (265)

Understandably, this waywardness never could be really controlled, as revealed in a report written during the camp's later period:

And then one meets so many small children outside, children who already have been in the camp for two or three years, children who do not have to work yet, whose parents are busy all day and often all night – and these small children have big pockets and collect pieces of coal. And then they brag to each other: I took this today, I took this, I took that. This makes one very sad. How will these children ever become decent people ... if we have to urge them to "oohleusen" – plunder, steal, rob. (256)

Life in a "youth home" is described by Yehuda Bacon:

We arrived at L 417, the Czech youth home, where young people from 10 to 16 years old lived. We reported downstairs. In the office, we were told to go to the "home," to room No. 10. The other rooms were full. In room No. 10 there was a former teacher of ours from Ostrau [Ostrava], *madrich* (director) and a certain Pick. There were many 11- to 13-year-old boys here, so we were the oldest. Having our heads shaved was the first thing that was unpleasant. It wasn't an order, but in L 417 it was necessary to shave everyone's head because of lice and the danger of typhoid. My first impression was that the house had a good atmosphere, we felt better here somehow. We were taken care of.

We had to air the bedclothes early in the morning. It was winter then and while we still were in pajamas we washed together down to the waist with horribly cold water. Then we went back up and made the beds nicely, because after breakfast was the morning roll-call. A "ration-carrier" always was chosen for a given period to bring the troughs of coffee, lunch or dinner that would be handed out in the homes. Jobs were distributed during roll-call: who had to sweep, who looked after the oven. Officially, we got some coal and wood. But it never was enough, and we always went out at night *"schleusen"* – stealing – after dark, to the other big barracks or to places with large piles of coal or wood. Our *madrichim* [guides/leaders] knew, and they had nothing against it; on the contrary, when someone returned with a full load (we went out with crates with slats nailed to the sides as handles) the director praised him. Our youth director and the house elder came to roll-call. They distributed points for order, such as how well the beds were made, how well it was swept, etc. It was a sort of contest. L 417 had a cleanliness pennant. Every Friday the cleanest home got it. . . .

The program, as we called the daily schedule, was as follows: After breakfast, we went to school. In general, the Germans prohibited education, but we learned anyway. Elementary school and the first to fourth grades of secondary school [*prima* to *quarta*], and later the fifth [*quinta*], were held in L 417. Every class was divided into a, b, c sections. For example, I went to *Tertia* a. We had classes in all of the rooms. A room in L 417 was big enough (L 417 once had been a school building). In one room there was an average of 5 to 6 bed nooks with six places, or half-nooks with three places. In addition, each room had two long tables and four benches. And these rooms looked different from those in the apprentice home, L 218; they were cleaner. We had more room, especially in comparison to the typical barracks or block rooms where there was frightfully little room and all of the stuff, suitcases, boxes ("box furniture") was on the beds. In the youth home there were rules – suitcases in the attic that you could go to every Friday, shelves for shoes, a special "closet" for coats – two poles with a solid bar on which everyone had his clothes hangar, and the whole thing covered with jute paper or with a colored sheet – so that everything made an orderly impression. Behind the bed everyone had a shelf that he made himself if he had stolen some wood and nails. And even there order was necessary, cleanliness, everything nice, it couldn't be too crowded and disturb the overall orderly image of the home.

The bunks were "stained": you painted them with a common manganese solution, which served as paint. Everyone attached little ornaments to his bunk, and the most important thing was that each person felt that "his" home was like home and his surroundings like brothers. In the morning we had school. We studied mathematics, geography, history, physics, grammar, nearly all the same subjects as in school. . . . We had the best teachers. A blackboard had been found in the attic. Pupils wrote on the wrapping paper of the packages they received; paper was scarce, and so were pencils. We sat around a table. If there wasn't enough space on the benches, we sat on the bunks. Two pupils always kept watch, one by the gate and another by the door. They signaled when an SS man went by. We knew how we were supposed to behave, we started talking about something specific right away, or someone started reading out of a book. We quickly hid all our papers.

Then came lunch. We had free time until 2 o'clock. You could visit your parents, or whatever. At 2 o'clock there were different possibilities. Sometimes we had lessons from 2 to 5, or we played soccer. Every home had its own team, with its own pennant and uniform. And we talked about soccer a lot. Or we played ping pong. We had a big courtyard where we organized all sorts of ball games, did gymnastics, and ran around. A favorite game was table soccer, a game with buttons. We played in competitions with different homes, and even the *madrichim* played. We called this game "schprtetz." We also had other kinds of competitions. We organized chess tournaments, cultural competitions between the home, etc. In the evenings we had free time from 6 to 8 o'clock and we went wherever we wanted. We had enough freedom. For instance, we could cut class and disappear from school, we could feign illness or go to the infirmary. Our youth home had its own little hospital with an infirmary and clinic. One always was supposed to go there in the mornings. Mostly the boys had blisters on their tongues or crusty eyes, sore throats, and furuncles that were called impetigo. All of these were vitamin deficiencies. If someone didn't feel well he stayed in bed and someone took care of him. The doctor made house calls in the morning.... In general, the boys didn't feign illness. In the evenings, for as long as we were with the younger boys, we sang and played, and the *madrich* read books to us or just told stories. Sometimes there were lectures and even children's operas in different "theaters" belonging to the Recreation Department. For instance, in the Magdeburg they put on "Brundibar." At the so-called "Bastei," they performed various plays, for example "David and Goliath." We also went to the "Hamburg" women's barracks, where we sang....

The cadre of boys from L 417 actually was established in the Sudeten Kaserne.... They were mostly children ages 11 to 13, mainly from orphanages in Brno. Each group of 15 to 20 boys was overseen by a *madrich*. When Theresienstadt finally was opened they came to L 417 and set up homes. The first homes were: No. 7, with Madrich Arno, who taught in the Czech spirit (excessively chauvinistic). The boys called themselves the "Beavers" (after a Czech Boy Scout book). Then there was home No. 5, with Madrich Arnošt Klauber, we called him Schmudla, he led us in the Zionist spirit.... One room was called Schkid, and its *madrich* was Prof. Eisinger, a teacher from a Jewish *gymnasium* in Brno. More homes were added later, some with younger children. But the three homes, No. 1, 5 and 7, were the model homes in L 417. That was also where the boys between ages 14 and 16 lived. Each of these three better homes had its own character, its own typical boys, its own typical "language" (meaning its own secret words, swear words and jokes).... The Beavers, for example, had their own soccer uniforms and flags.... They were good guys, they already knew each other from before and led a very comradely life. Those of us from the other homes didn't have much in common with them and we said they were children, squirts, embryos. But we all felt part of a whole, of L 417. "Schkid" published its own wall newspaper, which was quite sophisticated. The paper had editors, staff, cartoonists, and they were very proud of it. It was called "Vedem" ("We Lead"). There were a lot of intelligent and gifted boys in that home. Their *madrich*, Prof. Eisinger, whom they called Prtzek ("Squirt"), was very good at setting up and running a happy home. It had its own board of directors, adjutants, and various experts. It worked like a parliament. Every Friday there was a plenary session, preceded by singing in chorus (a Russian song). As in all the homes, the boys had it neat as a pin on Fridays, everything was clean, fresh laundry, the electric light was installed, the tables were set end to end. This all seemed very festive and we 14-year-olds thought it seemed very demagogic. In the plenary session, the newest issue of "Vedem" was read aloud and there was singing. It was more beautiful than anything described in any novel. For a while the boys there had great decorations. As a decoration above every bunk they had pictures of Prague. On every bunk there was a little sign with the nickname of every boy. For instance, there was "Bearded Child" (a 14-year-old who already shaved), "Billy Goat Sardanapal," "Schagrübu" (a combination of *Schammes* [synagogue caretaker], his real name Grünbaum, and the word bulldog), "Kakibus," "Bejtschek" (from the name Beck), etc. Above all, the *madrich* tried to make them cultivated; he cared less about book learning. Their symbol was a coat of arms containing a bucket, a broom (as a symbol of order), a feather, another symbol, and the word "Schkid." The boys were famous for their cabaret acts, which they performed in L 417 and elsewhere. In "school," which is what we called L 417, you could recognize them at first (when our heads were shaven) by their little colored wool caps (usually knitted by their girls). The caps had long wool tassels with a pom-pom at the end. The boy with the finest cap and the longest tassel and the nicest pom-pom was proud and admired....

The boys from No. 5, where I lived, were considered the best behaved. We were very fond of our Madrich Schmudla. For a time, he was like a god to us, but gradually that passed..... Schmudla put a lot of emphasis on upbringing; we were trained like soldiers. Our home was "democratic." We called ourselves "Dror" (Hebrew for swallow, the symbol of freedom), a word we also used in our insignia. There was a very clever boy among us, and he made our badges out of silver or some other metal. Only those who were recognized by the "Asefa" (our assembly) were permitted to wear our badge. I came to the home a little later. The Asefa was two weeks later, and someone told me that I already could get a badge. No one objected, so I received one. Our votes included the right to veto. Our room made a good impression when one entered it. On both sides one could see only the jute paper that we used to cover the bunks nicely. Across from the entrance were two emblems with the sign "Dror." To the right and left were the made-up beds that had paper glued to the front of the bed frames. There was a "small gazette" on the last bed frame, listing various announcements, Recreation Department events, our soccer matches, various competitions, and chess tournament results. Likewise, on the opposite bedframe was a graphic "Points Chart" listing all the names. When someone got a certain number of points he would receive a brightly colored sticker. Each color represented a certain number of points. We had various competitions, such as throwing a tennis ball at a target and foot races. Sometimes, after we already had gone to bed, the *madrich* told us to get dressed immediately, make the beds, and then we headed to the gym. Or we had to compose a poem on a given subject in a set amount of time. The results were noted on the Points Chart....

The home was not religiously observant. If an observant boy wanted to pray, of course no one disturbed him. Saturdays began with us being allowed to sleep in, and we had no lessons. By 10 or 11 o'clock, we had to have everything clean and tidy. Then we had roll call. We stood in a square and, when everything was ready, one boy went to get the *madrich*. The *madrich* came in and checked to see if everyone was present. Everyone had a number according to his bunk. The *madrich* called out the numbers, and we answered "Here!" There were 36 boys. At our roll call, like other roll calls, namely the roll call of the youth leaders on Friday afternoons, Schmudla inspected the bunks. Woe to any boy who had a sloppily-made bed, or if he found dirty dishes or dirty laundry (which happened frequently with us) that had been hastily hidden under the covers! If he discovered something like that, Schmudla could make a terrible "*Prûser*" (fuss). He might even throw the bedclothes out the window and into the courtyard. He would smash dirty dishes on the ground – even if they were stoneware – and rant. Then the boy responsible was restricted and was not permitted to leave the building. That was especially unpleasant on Saturdays, when we usually went to watch soccer matches and had the entire afternoon free. One was also restricted if there were complaints about brawling with younger boys from another home, etc. After the conclusion of Saturday morning roll call we formed two rows. The youngest boy took down the flag that was hung above the door and stood in front of the group. Then orders were given solemnly in Hebrew. We stood "at attention" and sang the anthem that a *chaver* (comrade) had written:

> We are thirty in the room;
> Each of us is different;
> Clever, good and honest,
> Bad and lazy.
> But in spite of that, we live together well,
> We must hope and have hope.
> The sun is rising in the distance,
> A brighter day will come,
> We will study and we will work,
> The past will be but a dream.
> Work, struggle, build our Fatherland,
> The past will be but a dream.

After singing our anthem, we would march to the big roll call that was held only on Saturdays. Each home entered in two neat rows, each with its own badge or flag. Then all of us stood in the staircase, and the director, the teacher, and the *madrichim* would all stand on the first floor and give speeches. First, they praised cleanliness and order. Then the criticism followed – because one home was disorderly, or had a clogged toilet, or because teachers had complained. . . . . This roll call lasted twenty minutes, and then all of us would go back to our rooms, where various debates would begin.

Mostly, we discussed scandals, rumors, and sensational events. For example, it was a scandal when ration cards disappeared in an unusually short time. We considered it theft when someone stole ration cards. If we discovered that someone had done that, he was lucky if we didn't kick him out of the home. But "*schleusen*" was not considered theft. Early in the morning, for example, we would go into our garden, which had pear trees and apple trees. One boy kept watch while another climbed a tree and shook it hard, and we would end up with a sack full of fruit. The fruit was supposed to be given to specific Jewish offices, but we got it first. We often went looking for potatoes. The Children's Mess Hall was in the neighboring building, Children's Home L 318. That's where the boys went down into the cellar to get potatoes. Once they were surprised by a cop. The boys punched him in the stomach and escaped. Shortly after that, "the wind blew our way," there was an investigation, and the case went before the Youth Court. The boys got a "final warning." ... During vacations, those who wanted to could work in the garden on the bastions; they were actually outside the ghetto. On the way back, a gendarme "frisked" us; it was obvious that each of us had things under his arms or in his pants: tomatoes and cucumbers, etc. It was worse when bread disappeared from the home. Everyone blamed each other, and everyone was happy when it stopped happening.

At night, when everyone was in bed and many of us already were asleep, Schmudla would come in and tell stories. Once, he came and explained various sexual issues. In our home, the boys born around 1928/29 already had been "enlightened." A few of them were a year or so younger, but they were at the same stage of physical and psychological development as we were. Schmudla told us that he knew who he was talking about, and the nightly visits to the beds of other boys had to stop. Schmudla said that this was almost a normal, and temporary, stage of puberty. But the boys involved might get accustomed to it, and it was better to find a girlfriend, of which there were plenty. He was talking about only three to five boys. The visits then stopped. Most of the boys had girlfriends, but in the youth home nothing happened between the young people. That was true for L 417. The older homes each had joint lessons with a girls' home in L 410. We invited the girls to our events, and were in turn invited by them. However, the girls in L 410 were older, 17–18 years old, and for the most part they sought company in the apprentices' home, and also had other acquaintances.

As the Youth Home for Czech boys, L 417 was actually the only one of its kind, and therefore the best. Young people also lived in Hanover [B IV], but they were all the same. Whoever got there stayed there. They did not have the same opportunities for cleanliness that we did. They lived with adults in one building, if not in the same rooms. That was very obvious. They didn't have many *madrichim*.... There was neither a daily program nor lessons that could be compared to L 417. The boys there really could do whatever they wanted. They also were certainly more disturbed by the arriving and departing transports, which we did not notice as much. The rest of the young people lived in the blocks among the adults. The only thing that distinguished them from other people was that they went to the Hamburg (C III) to get milk and sweet bun bonuses, and got other supplementary rations here and there.... They worked more, while we mostly learned.

Why did the Apprentice Homes have such a bad reputation? The fellows worked all day long in the youth squadron. After that, they usually were assigned to a lucrative post in the kitchen or the supply room or the bakery, etc. Or they worked in the locksmith shop, the engineering shop, the carpentry shop, or in the garden. And they didn't get any more education. The *madrich* of the room just made sure that there wasn't too much "bordello" (disorder) and that the fellows did not skip work for no reason. Some of the homes there had a really bad reputation – there were always complaints, mostly about malingering, clogged and filthy latrines, or brawling and theft. There was almost no such thing as friendship in those homes. Sometimes a professor went into a home like that and lectured until the fellows fell asleep on their beds.... On some evenings they had classes of a sort from various teachers. Generally, they were taught theory pertaining to the practical subjects in which they were apprenticing such as locksmithing, plumbing, etc. In L 218, there also was a little room where five or six fellows lived. That situation functioned pretty well, but there were few such model rooms. Religion was not taught as a subject. In general, there were no textbooks, at least not for each student. But there were a few that were lent out. The *madrich* explained everything, we took notes, and when necessary, he got us a book or an atlas. The rooms in the children's home, for children up to age 10, were very nice and clean, and had "children's furniture." The walls were covered with proper pictures. There were toys. The children already were being taught to be orderly. Someone always was on call and was responsible for cleaning up. Almost all of those in charge were young females. In the mornings, from our courtyard, we could see the children as they played under the supervision of their caretakers.

Officially one lived in the Youth Home only between ages 12 and 16. However, there was no age limit in the apprentice homes; even 22-year-olds lived there. We had nothing in common with the boys and girls in the German and Austrian children's home in L 414, except soccer. We called those children "*Piefke*" [a derogatory word for Germans]. We had children only from Czechoslovakia, and all of us spoke Czech. But in L 410, there were a few girls from Czechoslovakia who couldn't speak Czech and had to learn it.

Most of the children in the older homes did not collect razor blade wrappers, but the younger children did. Some boys collected all sorts of printed materials, tickets to recreational events, ghetto money (as collector's items, not as currency). But their greatest treasures were the pennants from the soccer tournaments. Camaraderie reigned

Welfare

among the boys – even very close camaraderie. For the most part, the young people were optimistic. But our *madrich* told us quite deliberately that, after the war, it would no longer be: "Good day, Mr. Industrialist." And when he told us about the German blitzkrieg, he also told us that it was possible that eventually they would take us away in trucks. He did this mainly so that we would not be too naïve. (11)

A girl describes a child's life in the "block" as follows:

My mother died when I was very small. My father lived in Hanover [B IV], and I lived with my grandmother and six other old women in the block. The old women stank awfully. In the mornings, I cleaned up, washed the dishes and did the laundry. Once in a while I got something, such as some soup, in exchange for cleaning up the block. We got food from the Hamburg [C III]. Later on, when the children's mess was in L 318, I used to go there. We got practically nothing from the Youth Welfare Office. Once they gave us a *Schmonzes* bonus [i.e., something worthless]. For a while, we had a program. You know how that was in Theresienstadt. If you wanted to, you showed up, but your presence would be recorded. We would come together in all different blocks and have educational programs. In one block they cleared out a hallway and set up benches and two tables. Madrichim from the homes taught the classes. As you know, most of us brought notebooks with us to Theresienstadt and so we had something to write in. We learned singing, Hebrew, history, and everything else they could teach. But we didn't have very regular classes, and then (after the September 1943 transports) the program was canceled. So then I really didn't do anything. Sometimes I borrowed a book or I took walks to see if I could find a bowl of soup, or went potato hunting. For a while I volunteered to work in the youth garden with the girls from L 410. Yes, L 410 was the best Czech youth home. That's where they were encouraged to collect points in various competitions. Most of the kids lived in the blocks because their parents wanted to have them nearby. As you know, some people had it good, the "notables." They received lots of packages and had beautiful mansards on their attics [see the attachment to 11].

These reports demonstrate that the children did not entirely comprehend their own situation and the general misery. They led a sad existence, closely watched and always nervous, squeezed by the hated machinery of the camp system, which encouraged fears, hatred, and contradictions and yet compelled an inescapable obedience. It was a terrible influence on the children to see their parents and all adults stripped of their rights, powerless and reduced to the status of children who had to bow before an empty, meaningless discipline. They deserved pity rather than the healthy respect of the children. Even the youth workers seldom had the children's real respect. Thus, the rule of the pack generally prevailed among the children, who were encouraged to think and function on their own, rather than putting their faith in role models and good examples, which characterizes youth socialization in normal society. Like the sick in relationship to the doctors and nurses, the children were in an awkward situation in relation to those in charge of them – prisoners of their own dire situation, a situation that they could not change and that they rarely could spiritually overcome. Although there was, undeniably, some goodwill on the part of the youth leaders, it benefited only a few children, and, as has become clear, it was too overloaded with doctrinaire intentions and wishful thinking adequately to take into account the immediate challenges of the moment. Even if the young people were, at that point, taken care of physically, they were mostly left to their own inner devices. They were a group who pursued their own ends, for whom any means seemed justified, and it is understandable that the means often were anarchic. The situation was a bit better among the smaller children and was the worst among the postpubescent and the pubescent youth, especially in the case of those individual boys and girls who possessed no special interests or seriousness – which normally would have been encouraged by their parents and other helpers – to counter the spiritual neglect that otherwise was recognized as a general characteristic of at least the older Theresienstadt children. Of course, in many cases there was considerable physical neglect as well, although genuine efforts were made to control it, with varying success. The threat of deportation, and the attempts to avoid it by all means, carved bitter and evil tracks in these young souls. Even though the better-cared-for children in the privileged homes were protected from the worst misery and hardship – unfortunately at the expense of their less fortunate comrades – this influence could not be completely suppressed, and it functioned as a baleful modulator of one's emotional constitution. The only norms of interest were belief in a distantly desired future; escape through small pleasures; and, most commonly, surviving the next difficult moment. There was nothing in between these competing interests, which also form the framework for the development of healthy young people in a normal society. No connection existed between the contradictions of the future, the present moment, and escape; there was barely anything even to bridge them, and thus the children could not grow and develop in an organic way. At most, individual compulsions sprouted forth like the pale shoots of a plant unaccustomed to the light.

It is therefore understandable that the children were simultaneously emotionally underdeveloped and too mature for their years, that they knew both too little and too much. But they hardly could be called dull. The majority of the children were extraordinarily bright. They had to figure out situations quickly and without help, and they understood what could be useful or harmful to them. Although they lacked things such as sufficient nutritious food, or small treats, or the proper toys that every child deserves but that were available here only to a limited degree, these sacrifices were too prevalent for each child to be vividly aware of them. For the most part, young people were thankfully spared the worst physical hardships, due to more and better food as well as regular and special extra rations, and it was very rare for anyone to take advantage of them; most people were glad to make sacrifices on their behalf. The young, especially the children in the "homes," were spared the misery of the elderly and the infirm. In fact, a more regretful circumstance was that the children were allowed to look on the suffering and hunger of the helpless without sympathy or understanding, and indeed that they learned to despise that misery. The majority of the "counselors" raised their charges in a rather selfish collective spirit. The caregivers themselves hardly understood the needs of the community and thus could not very well ask for understanding. As one would expect, the typical educational level was generally inadequate, because children often had not been permitted to attend school even before they arrived in the camp and rarely had received regular private lessons. Unless a child had an inborn desire to learn, one that compelled him to find a teacher, or unless parents themselves took this in hand, the level of school learning was sketchy and quite poor. Children under the age of ten were particularly neglected; many could hardly read or write. They often were surprisingly knowledgeable in a single subject that they liked, or that was taught by a particularly good teacher, and in other subjects they were completely at sea. The fact that classes were illegal did not make them

Welfare 497

attractive – in fact, it had a devastating effect. Later on there were wonderful teachers, but regular lessons remained impossible. Books and teaching supplies were lacking. Younger children had no idea what a house pet or a wildflower – or countless other objects that were part of normal life – looked like. In order to remedy such sad facts, people made lithographs or other copies of simple pictures. The most important accomplishment in this regard was an illustrated Czech reader in two volumes (see 297).

All prisoners in Theresienstadt had been subject to restrictions on their freedom of movement, often years before they got to the camp, so such restrictions did not appear to have a particularly negative effect on the children. Evening curfew did not particularly affect the children in the "homes," and often they hardly perceived it, due to their communal lifestyle. Children who lived with their mothers simply shared everyone's fate. Otherwise, young people generally were better off than most adults because their "homes" usually were roomier than typical quarters and often had large courtyards or even gardens. Things were especially bad for the children until the summer of 1942, however, because they were limited to the residential barracks; but that year they were permitted to use parts of the otherwise inaccessible green bastions and redoubts for games and sport at certain hours of the day. This was a benefit that adults were not allowed to enjoy until the "beautification" in 1944. The forced breakup of family life, which few children were spared, had a much more negative effect; fathers and mothers and children were split up among three or even more mass living quarters. It is no wonder that many children became estranged from their families and not only saw them infrequently but also ceased asking for or missing them and went their separate ways. It became a battered and disintegrated society, forced into new forms that attested to a sickly social structure in which different groups – the elderly, the infirm, the ill, men, women, and young people – confronted one another as separate units and developed specific class interests that distantly resembled the groups in a class society. These conditions always existed everywhere in Theresienstadt, but for young people they took on an even greater weight. Only for them did these forced, unnatural structures become a determining force in the social behavior of their own classlike group and in relation to the community. Although they were no more oppressed than anyone else, the youth believed that the older generation was largely responsible for the unjust situation. One had to pursue one's own interests. The powers of the others were to be feared, but one did not need to recognize ethical demands and social mores imported from the outside – they were suspect and considered hypocritical. This is the core of the tragedy of the Theresienstadt youth, although hardly anyone recognized it at the time.

These conditions had the most glaring effect on the age groups one would have counted among the most mature, and they had a greater effect on boys than on girls. Unless some special fate protected them, these older boys felt that the camp had cheated them out of their basic right to a late pubescent creative imagination, as well as the right to have bold adventures, for which a normal society would have provided outlets. Unfortunately, very little sympathy was shown in Theresienstadt for this age group, and any efforts to help them were misdirected. Thus it was not surprising that most boys aged sixteen and older were disagreeable. They worked hard and, as we know, generally worked in advantageous occupations but were not inculcated with a sense of responsibility toward the community. The fourth biblical commandment, already undervalued in modern Western society, was presented to this generation, almost with a certain enthusiastic pleasure, as superfluous or even nonexistent. The defiled essence of their own humanity knew no other escape than to seek revenge for the ignominy it had endured by indulging in uninhibited exploitation. The Youth Welfare Office generally was successful with the younger children but was powerless in the face of this situation. However, one must admit, in their defense, that the leaders simply did not have the means or the strength to intervene effectively. So these fellows, deprived of all virtue, acted out without restraint. The situation was especially bad when they were assigned work related to the mounting misfortune of their neighbors, for example, as "transport helpers." It was not pleasant to visit their quarters; one would be assaulted without provocation by boorish behavior. Theft and robbery could be dangerous, but these crimes did not appear to be forbidden by any recognized law, and they "snatched" (*schleuste*) for sport and for pleasure. The sexual wildness of many of this generation completed the picture of their utterly hopeless decline into deptravity.

The following gives an overview of the organization of the Youth Welfare Office and the dominant views of its leadership:

Youth Welfare, 1941–1945

Origins and Development

The Beginning
The first children arrived as early as December 1941. At first they were housed with their parents – that is, girls and boys up to 12 years of age stayed with their mothers, and older boys with their fathers. In all the men's barracks, special rooms were set up for boys up to age 16; later, rooms were set up for children of both sexes in the Bodenbach Kaserne [H IV].

The First Homes
The first Girls Home was established in the Hamburg and Dresden Kasernen in February 1942 [C III, H V].... These rooms evolved into the first youth homes, which were housed in their own buildings starting in the summer of 1942....

The staff was made up of volunteers ... ; there were few professionals among them. They were mainly young people. To the extent they had any experience at all, it came from summer camps and the youth movement. [The "Youth Welfare Office" generally rejected experienced volunteers on ideological grounds.]

Life in the Homes
Over time, there developed in the homes a certain lifestyle based on principles of collective child raising. The counselors lived together with the children in order to influence their entire lives.

Status of Children in the Ghetto
Only after the opening of the ghetto did it become possible for children freely to move about the redoubts, and to run and play. At this juncture, it must be noted that the Jewish self-administration was inclined to help the children as much as possible, even at the expense of the elderly. Enjoying the open air was an unattainable pleasure for older people. The areas designated for children [in the homes] were roughly twice as large as the areas designated for adults.... Nevertheless, an average of 20–30 children lived in rooms without beds or other furnishings [this changed after autumn 1942]....

Organization.
After the ghetto was opened, the organization developed.

Institutional Welfare
This concerned children from 4 to 18 years of age, in homes.

Nationality	Sex	Age	Bldg. former use	Bldg. current designation	Max/min. usage in Summer 1943
Czech.	Boys	10–14	School	L 417	350
Czech.	Girls	10–16	Military Admin.	L 410	450
German	Children	10–14	Military Comm.	L 414/II	350
Czech., Germ.	Children	4–10	Health Insurance	L 318	300
Czech., Germ., Dutch	Children	4–12	Rooms in Apprentice Home	C III	100
Czech, Germ.	Boys	14–18	Rooms in Apprentice Home	Q 706–10, 609, L 218	250

... A children's hospital with a tuberculosis department was also established. These children (about 100 children) were gassed in the fall of 1944.

A home for typhoid convalescents was established in 1943 in L 216, after the massive typhoid epidemic that claimed a great many children.

Internal Organization of the Homes
... In the summer of 1943, when there were roughly 5,000 children in Theresienstadt [certainly no more than 4,000 children under age fifteen], the Youth Welfare Office cared for approximately 2,500 children in institutional homes. In addition to the child-care staff (counselors, home directors), each one of these institutions had welfare staff who supervised the repair shops.... In addition, a social worker cared for weaker children, who received an additional evening meal.... Each home had an infirmary with a physician and medical staff.

Public Welfare
... The institutions were made up of: homes for mothers and children (these were quarters ... , occupied exclusively by mothers with children under 6 years old), with no staff; a Czech kindergarten with about 300 children, and one Hebrew kindergarten ... with about 70–100 children.... The public welfare system was administered by social workers who visited the children regularly, evaluated their health, and provided them with necessities, to the extent possible.

The Welfare Administration maintained the orphan registry and other customary matters (guardianship, etc.).

Education and Activity
... These were extremely difficult under these circumstances.... The results [of education] were good, considering that classes were irregular and illegal.

Kindergarten.
Children up to age 7 received the foundations of their education in the kindergartens.

Classes in the Homes.
Older children in the homes had 3–4 hours of regular academic lessons as part of their daily schedule, even though officially the schedule consisted of song, crafts and drawing.... The lack of professionals played a large role [this is incorrect: professionals were simply not accepted for political or other reasons], as did interruption of school-work due to external events (deportations, inspections, etc.).

Day Centers.
Children . . . , up to age 14, who lived with their parents attended day centers, where they received lessons under the circumstances described.

Youth above Age 14.
Older children were subject to the work requirement. Generally they were deployed as required ... in agriculture or military production. Some were incorporated into the ghetto workforce, and a small percentage were trained in the skilled trades. Special evening courses were arranged for them... . The Apprenticeship Commission was responsible for the young people learning skilled trades; these sat for apprenticeship examinations upon conclusion of their courses.

Public Education.
A children's library was established for children up to age 13, and a youth library was established for older children. In addition, regular lectures were held on a variety of subjects.

Educational Goals.
In addition to ethical and practical lessons and an education infused with a collective spirit, we strove to awaken the children's self-confidence. In consideration of their future lives and labor we wanted to distract them from the joylessness and hopelessness of their situation. [The self-confidence of the children did not suffer – rather, it was overemphasized. Instead of further awakening it, it would have been better to direct it into the right channels.]

Deportations.
A total of 15,000 children went through Theresienstadt. [This figure is too high; there were approximately 8,200 children up to fifteen years of age.] The main goal in the homes was to create an atmosphere free of the physical and moral deficiencies of their surroundings. This intent was repeatedly frustrated by departing transports. At first, it was possible to protect children under 12. But the age limit was constantly lowered, and by October 1944 even infants in diapers were deported.

Beautification project.
... In the course of this project, all of the homes were adapted.... Shortly before the arrival of the commission, 7,500 people were sent to Auschwitz. Included among them, by special order, were all orphaned children. The remaining orphans over the age of 5 were deported in October 1944 along with the administration and the majority of the staff.

Conclusion.
Of the 15,000 children ... 1,086 remained by the winter of 1944–45. [In fact, there were slightly more than 800 up to age fifteen.] At the end of the war, no more than 100 children over the age of 14 returned....

Situation in 1944–45.
Following the major deportations in October 1944, the Youth Welfare Office and Care of the Elderly were combined under the leadership of Chief Rabbi Dr. Baeck and Mrs. von Stengl. The situation in the homes was a disaster; the children had been demoralized by the horrific month of deportations. There was hardly any staff. Even before October 1944, almost all of the homes were forced to move to other locations, since the Germans confiscated the buildings for office space or living quarters.

Deportations to Theresienstadt.
In November 1944, a transport from the Celle concentration camp (Bergen-Belsen) arrived in terrible condition, with about 70 small children of Dutch origin (from 2 to 8 years of age), orphaned children, some of whom lacked even a name. [In fact, there were fifty-one children, and they arrived on November 20, 1944.] In mid-January [1945], a transport of Slovakian women and children arrived. Later, there arrived a transport containing Jews from mixed

Welfare

marriages in Bohemia and Moravia (mostly fathers and children). The homes filled up again, and there were new aides. When children arrived from Hungary later on, they could no longer even be housed in the homes. Some families had up to 12 children.

Commission of the IRC (April 1945).
All homes were renovated for the IRC Commission, and the Youth Welfare Office was assigned the former Grand Hotel [Q 403, which was a hospital until fall 1944] and the newly reopened Children's Convalescent Home. It was around the time that news of the terrible mass murder of children in Auschwitz was reaching foreign countries. Apparently, the Germans wanted to demonstrate that Jewish children were still alive. Perhaps that is why the order was given to deport children of mixed marriages above one year old to Theresienstadt.

Conclusion of the War.
Shortly before the conclusion of hostilities, ... prisoners from the concentration camps arrived, ... among them, approximately 600 young people ages 12 and older, but mainly between 14 and 16 years old. Of them, 450 were housed in the homes, where they physically recovered from the typhus epidemic. (45% of the children in Theresienstadt contracted typhus.) (298)

The Jewish leadership's attitude toward the youth issue is revealed to us by another staff member of the so-called Youth Welfare Office:

.... And there were some individuals among the ghetto leadership who understood the responsibility towards the children. Foremost among them was our own Jakob Edelstein, who participated in the weighty and critical debate in the Council of Elders concerning the principle of who should receive a ration of bread, and who should not. After a courageous and clear analysis, he contributed to a decision that favored the children, which was perhaps unusual and harsh in its treatment of the elderly. However, given the situation at the time, it was the sole correct conclusion: for the sake of a better future for the Jewish people.

In this book, we already have so thoroughly considered the problem of the helpless in Theresienstadt that we need not show again why this "sole correct conclusion" was wrong.

This depiction of the life of young people is rounded out by excerpts from a comprehensive internal report written on the first anniversary of "Youth Home L 417," in July 1943. The document had a number of authors, and in addition to reports concerning all areas of home activity, it also contains a series of programmatic essays.

From July until the end of 1942, we experienced a significant scarlet fever epidemic. In August and early autumn there was an epidemic of diarrhea, which was closely followed by infectious jaundice. Measles, mumps, rubella, chicken pox, and whooping cough caused us less worry, except for measles cases with complications, all of which took a turn for the worse, but fortunately all were cured (numerous lung and middle ear infections.)

The explosive emergence of abdominal typhus caused us much concern in late January 1943. 50 children fell ill within two months ... some quite seriously. Fortunately, all of them recovered; ... there were periods of time when 30–35% of the children lay ill.... It was a heavy burden for us, especially since the nursing staff, small enough as it was, often fell ill at the same time (influenza). Such flu waves also gave us many single or double pneumonias.

The Nescharim (Hawk) Home consisted of 41 children. The home had three *madri-chim*. The home kept going mainly thanks to the joint contribution of the whole community, for example through the preparation of a dramatic rendering of the 10 points of law of the young Jewish "Fatherland, Nation and Language," or through decoration of the rooms. The first self-administration was elected. A system of chores was established, which rotated weekly.... .

Daily Schedule

6:45 A.M.	Wake up, quarter hour morning exercises
7:15–8:45 A.M.	Personal hygiene, home hygiene, breakfast
8:45–9 A.M.	Morning roll call, cleanliness inspection
9–12 P.M.	Morning program
12–1 P.M.	Lunch
1–2 P.M.	Afternoon rest period
2–2:30 P.M.	Afternoon roll call, inspection
2:30–5 P.M.	Afternoon activities
5–6 P.M.	Evening meal
6–8 P.M.	Free time
8–10 P.M.	Evening program, washing
10 P.M.	Bed

... In addition to regular evenings to celebrate Erev Sabbath [Friday evenings], there were celebrations of holidays, educational and entertainment events, and gymnastic exhibitions. The following pieces and recitations were performed: "*Auf der Eisscholle*"; "Fatherland, Nation, Language"; "The Pied Piper of Hameln"; "*Der Vierfach Gehörnte*"; "The Prodigal Son"; "Schimke"; "Biblical Ballads"; "Nebuchadnezzar." A choir was established, originally made up only of boys from the home, and which later included children from other homes. The choir performed publicly. There was an attempt to work together with the parents in the form of a parent meeting, but it never happened because the parents had no time....

If we consider the young people ... if we imagine Jewish youth in the time before Theresienstadt, we must acknowledge that Theresienstadt caused certain changes for the better – in spite of all the negative influences and effects. One need only recall the boys from bourgeois families who took wealth for granted ... who were catered to ... and who thought about nothing but themselves.

And today: forty boys have grown into a unified whole, which is more important than any school groups, circles of friends, sports teams, scout troops and gymnastic clubs. Here came together a group of children, of different ages and social strata, children raised in institutions, children from large families and only children, athletic children and purely intellectual children, strong and weak, from big cities and from the countryside, children full of life and used to social interaction, and loners ... they all shared the same quarters. At first, they eyed each other cautiously. When, two months later, they bade farewell to comrades who were being deported to Poland, the quiet that ensued was not simply a formal silence, it was a cry of sorrow that seized everyone....

The work discipline is always good where adults know how to interact with youth. Complaints come exclusively from workshops where apprentices are treated "like civilians."

Overview of working youth on June 1, 1943:

Agriculture and gardening:	194 boys	366 Girls	560 Total
Tutoring:	328	207	536
Skilled trades:	281	120	401
Health care, education, professions:	52	124	176
Total	856	817	1,673

[From the essay:] "Our Mission – Our Journey"

.... What is the situation of the Jewish child with the Theresienstadt experience? ... The children lack a great deal, which particularly affects their physical development.

A number also have experienced separation from their parents, which adds a difficult psychological element. However, most children here experience a children's collective that is much better suited to their needs and their children's world than anything that came before [*sic*]. Those children who are still unable consciously to grapple with the causes of the Theresienstadt experience see no connection to their earlier lives.... They are most impressed here by the world of the adults.... in all its reactions, the world filled with corruption, the unbridled drive for self-preservation, unlimited selfishness, the hunger for power, etc.; reactions that generally can be ascribed to the impact that Theresienstadt has on adults.

[From the essay:] "Educational Problems in the Ghetto"

... On 1 June 1943, there were 1,620 boys and 1,548 girls between the ages of 0 and 14 years old among the 43,806 inhabitants. If the 10-year-old children here were taken into a home, they escaped the isolation that the urban Jewish child has felt in recent years, and entered a community where children became more self-sufficient, better able to survive and even cheerful [*sic*].... The highly gifted among them have absorbed the necessary knowledge even without regular lessons.... It is important to determine the level of knowledge of reading, writing and arithmetic. Furthermore, the number of illiterates and their exact age should be determined; age 7 can be equated with age 6....

[From an essay by Gideon Klein:] "On the So-Called Political Education of the Youth"

... Meanwhile, the first differences of opinion were developing concerning the issue of Jewish assimilation. A group of nationally conscious Jews, or Jews who developed a national consciousness under the pressure of prevailing circumstances, faced a group of assimilationist Jews, for whom the Jewish identity that had been thrust upon them is temporary and not authentically felt. The mission of the youth workers was ... to avert unproductive and often poisonous political debates.... The fact that the ghetto leadership was controlled by men whose political views arose from a national-Zionist consciousness necessarily carried over into "Youth Welfare," which was ... headed by Zionists. The leading men of the ghetto often emphasized the character of Jewish education, even though it was obvious that the assimilation of the earlier environment could not be extirpated even after such fundamental and deep, powerful social change.

The youth thus was supposed to be raised in a nationalist-Jewish spirit. To this end, it was necessary to have youth workers who were capable of educating in a Jewish spirit. This situation led to misunderstandings, which often turned into sharp disputes with ideological overtones. The majority of youth workers in Youth Welfare were unqualified individuals who were either inadequately trained or not trained at all. It should be emphasized that Youth Welfare appointed people without any concern for their way of thinking [Note: this is largely incorrect.] ... Since the directors themselves ... had been members of the Jewish youth movement, it goes without saying that they preferred youth workers who also had belonged to the youth movement.

... The educational apparatus grew to unforeseen dimensions. Political education slowly but surely became a major problem. Political education begins with the smallest children, of kindergarten age [*sic*]. Children whose mother tongue is Czech or German are taught Hebrew in the form of Hebrew folk songs and fairy tales. In elementary school, pupils study Hebrew, often without any inner connection to Judaism. But the actual conflict begins just prior to puberty....

... At least half of them originally came from non-Jewish environments. The sudden, often nonsensical teaching of Jewish subjects through catchwords and slogans, offered by laypeople, was bound to fail with young boys with very sensitive reactions. The directors of L 417 were well aware of this fact, and therefore they soon abandoned this superficial Jewish education. However, this realistic attitude was viewed with incomprehension. Although they insisted on consistent application of guidelines they had issued for the purposes of Jewish education, the leaders of the Youth Welfare Office were nonetheless unable to provide a conceptual foundation for Jewish education. This led to conflict between the leadership of the Youth Welfare Office and L 417, which ended with an agreement in favor of fundamentally apolitical education. However, this agreement appeared workable only from the outside. Within L 417, youth groups known as "homes" were formed. Each one had its own unique character, including a political dimension.... The boys were inculcated with a historical consciousness. The Jewish problem was illuminated from a societal perspective. Such political education is based on a much broader foundation and does not necessarily lead to assimilation. On the contrary, it can give Jewish consciousness a modern, genuinely progressive form. (281)

This essay and other examples show the effect of the inner resistance of people with a wounded sense of self-worth, people both emotionally and politically confused, who suffered so greatly because of the events of their time that they no longer could fully comprehend them. And then, these people – themselves still practically children, for their emotional development was stunted by severe shocks – were to dedicate themselves to the moral task of educating children in Theresienstadt. Obviously, this was far too much to ask. Thus the unavoidable failure is not the fault of the Jewish leadership; the fault lies with those who placed this burden on the Jewish people and its youth. One can measure how misdirected this generation must have been by examining the extent to which they were looked after or could be looked after at all. Amid the misfortune of loss, the poor fools who welcomed the "children's collective" and who believed in a "life-affirming and cheerful community" defended possible gains that in fact hardly existed and that, when the children tried to create them with their group leaders, were unable to flourish. Although this optimism was foolish, it nevertheless was a touching trait, as it was an attempt to gain insight into evils that, even if they had existed, had no relevance there. Threatened youth always tries to preserve its vitality, and so, even in Theresienstadt, the youth managed to create valuable foundations for collective formations, corresponding to its aforementioned classlike character. For that reason alone, it was an especially painful blow whenever a comrade was sacrificed to deportation, because the sense of value so painstakingly achieved was damaged and shattered. Moreover, an individual's survival instinct was damaged when he was faced with the bitter judgment that the fight for survival already was lost. No society could treat a child worse. Not even in ancient Mexico, where a "bad" child was threatened with exclusion from his family, were all young people threatened with such an arbitrary yet almost systematic terror of perdition as in Theresienstadt, where neither virtue nor vice had the slightest influence on whether a child could be sustained or saved.

These children were denied everything that every society owes to future generations, any sense of security that children should reliably be offered in the first ten to twenty years of life. All of this was stolen from these children at the most tender age, as soon as they began vaguely to perceive the situation that affected all members of this coerced community. Thus the children were denied the primary rights that everyone owes to children; the Theresienstadt youth workers were expected to provide a temporary and timeless substitute, and they had no idea where to begin. The values that once had meaning, and that one day would have meaning again, had been snatched from these people, and they may never have been aware of it in the first

Welfare 505

place. Therefore, as they fled from these values – which they believed to be suspended and which they did not really believe in – they had to search for other types of information with which they could fill the – younger and, especially, older – children's days in the camp. But because they were tragically interwoven into the monstrous ruin of this epoch, they saw only corollaries to the personalities from whom the misery of the Jews in Hitler's Germany has issued. They could recognize nothing that transcended, accompanied, or was free of that misfortune. In other words, they no longer understood the values of the past and no longer were part of them. So they nourished the children with a disastrous mixture of influences. Instead of simple humanity and an enduring Jewish identity, they could offer them only fragments that were born in the spirit of resentment and that were hard to digest and made up of clichéd thoughts and rhetorical guidelines, a patchwork of all sorts of Zionism, assimilatory chauvinism, and communism. Much of what was called "Jewish" was superficial. The children knew Hebrew songs and sayings but generally did not understand a word of it. As a result, the older children hardly could get their bearings, and although they could get excited by certain ideas, they soon realized how fragile and noncommittal were these offerings, which they seldom took seriously and often laughed at. The leaders couldn't even offer the children in this horrific environment the comfort of knowing that if they survived the horrors of Theresienstadt, as the harshest school of life, the lessons learned might someday be a blessing. The fact that this did not happen does not justify, in retrospect, any complaints against the young youth workers and teachers; it is simply lamentable.

It also should be reported that, as slow progress was made, more mature people came to the fore in the Youth Welfare Office, introduced positive characteristics, and, with humanity, even bridged the gap between children and the elderly. The collapse of autumn 1944 did not spare the youth and their caretakers or the volunteer group "Youth Helps." The first and last annual report they left behind is a moving document:

> In the spring of last year [1943], some colleagues in the Youth Welfare Office ... formed an aid effort called "Youth Helps." The group was formed out of the dual need to combat the increasing brutalization and waywardness and to aid ... the elderly and frail....
>
> It was a volunteer project. Every volunteer had to commit at least three hours each week of free time and could not, of course, receive pay for helping others.
>
> There were 300 young people, organized into groups by 30 counselors who gave them their assignments. Fulfillment of the assignments was very closely monitored. It was considered important that the young people themselves carry out the research into what they could do to help. All home visits were conducted by the youngsters themselves.... The young people were supposed to learn to keep their own eyes open, while it was hoped that the elderly would experience the joy of being cared for by volunteer helpers rather than the welfare bureaucracy.... The project did not include old-age homes or homes for the infirm, to avoid exposing the youth to infectious diseases. As they made their rounds through the ghetto, they found elderly people isolated in blocks and attics, completely intimidated and not even aware that they could take advantage of social welfare assistance.... Depending on the age of the youngsters, the work consisted of beating mattresses, making beds, cleaning, mending, getting food, errands of all kinds, helping with moving, recreational activities and birthday wishes. The last two tasks in particular, which could be carried out by even the youngest volunteers (12- to 13-year-olds), made people very happy. We organized game groups, and the best proof that we

provided a little light and joy was the repeated requests of the elderly that we soon return. At birthday parties, we gave out coffeehouse tickets, homemade board games and slippers made from scraps. Often the home visits resulted in so-called "patronages." This sort of assistance was particularly valuable because it created a kind of family relationship. So-called "major projects" also sometimes were accomplished, i.e., 20 to 30 young people would clean entire blocks and attics.

We also had special projects on holidays, after we once were once given 3,000 cushions to distribute, and another time some linens for the infirm.... In each case, a play group took over the festive distribution of the presents.

From the start, we had all kinds of difficulties ... : sometimes the incomprehension of the house elders or the understandable distrust of the elderly.... It is important that people thought of our youth group as: "Youth Helps. Oh yes, those are the youngsters who don't take anything...."

A few figures from our organization:

Average number of helpers:	550
Young people between the ages of 13 and 17:	1,734
Helpers among this group:	15%
Visited persons over age 65:	5,500
Average number of people over age 65:	10,000

... (282)

The Jewish leadership's idea to save the youth but damn the elderly – the choice of the supposed "lesser evil" – was unjustifiable, for two reasons: (1) the leadership had the duty and even the ability greatly to reduce the theft that caused such harm to the infirm, and (2) the leadership was proven wrong, because the transports affected the youth and the elderly to the same degree. In these already doomed circumstances, the leadership tried to play the role of destiny. The conclusion of the story shows how, in the end, all their endeavors were futile.

The insights presented in this chapter have given us an overview of the youth problem in Theresienstadt. Considered against the background of general camp conditions, this overview is accurate and, considering the proportions of those conditions, reasonable. Therefore, this overview accords with the point of view underlying this book. It is only fair to note that children who were raised in a Zionist manner and who considered themselves Jewish in this spirit, along with their equally youthful youth workers, had a completely different perspective. They experienced Theresienstadt and the world, with its coerced restraints, in a way totally different from almost all other inmates. The children already had been cheated out of their childhood happiness, and for their enthusiastic educators the Zionist ideal appeared to be the only dependable, promising, and valuable goal, for all other ideals had been shattered or appeared repulsively hypocritical. Thus, even in the questionable protection of the ghetto, a community itself paralyzed by terror, a kind of freedom existed for the younger generation of Jewish youth. They had not been able to enjoy such freedom in the areas under National Socialist control before they were imprisoned; in contrast, in the camp they could feel especially secure, because the internal leadership supported and approved of this feeling. Young people who do not feel secure cannot survive; they can only founder. They do not possess the knowledge and certainly not the ability to account for the truth and value of the foundations of the ideals according to which they live, so that they believe themselves to be safe in the unclouded splendor of those ideals. And youth must believe. That was generally

Welfare 507

true for the misdirected youth of the time and was especially true for the youth of Theresienstadt, who lived with the daily threat of murder and doom.

What assimilation brought the Jews, a scattered minority among the nations, was thus obviously proven "false" or tragic. One glance out the window of the "youth home" into the dirty city streets and the locked exits spoke volumes. There was nothing left but hope for a different kind of life someday in one's own country. To the extent possible, that dream was sought to be realized in the here and now in the communal solidarity of the homes, in which the youth lived according to their own social and psychological rules, which seemed to have little in common with the reality in the rest of the camp. In this manner, the children who were assigned to the young Zionist youth workers were given a world of their own in which there was no lack of subjective happiness. The achievements that were possible in the collective satisfied the vital needs of young people and could even calm turbulent spirits. The few young adults – boys and girls – who reached freedom after the horrific detour through Auschwitz understandably portrayed Theresienstadt after the war as a "good" and wholesome place. They felt only gratitude for everything that united them in the homes and encouraged communal activities. The period they spent there (two years on average) was easily distinguished from the anxieties of the time before Theresienstadt and the horrors thereafter. What some have called the pleasant illusion of this camp, the sultry and pernicious illusion under which the few more aware adults suffered, given the immeasurable misery of Theresienstadt – that illusion did not subjectively exist for the children within Theresienstadt's walls. There, if anywhere, the illusion was justified. It remained dangerous; otherwise it would not have been an illusion. But there was a genuine value in the initially comforting and blinding glow of that illusion. The small minority who benefited from this value and who immersed themselves with pure impulses in the Zionist youth movement of the camp were granted the support of this illusion, despite its illusory nature. Those of this group who survived the catastrophe had a collection of treasured experiences to draw on for a long time. One can only hope that the survivors became aware of the illusion later, so that they could understand the fate of their group against the background of the communal fate. This recognition is and remains an easily forgotten or under-appreciated legacy for later generations.

In conclusion, I attempt to provide an overview of the number of children under the age of fifteen in Theresienstadt. A report written shortly after the end of the war (298), which is still often cited in the literature (see 332a, in which it is particularly misleading) estimates the number at "approximately 15,000," which is far too high. By the time of the fall deportations of 1944, 130,955 people (excluding the Polish children) had arrived in the camp, among them 7,407 children (about 5.75%). By the end of the period of deportations from Theresienstadt, 86,936 people had been deported, among them 6,588 children (more than 7.5%). However, this last figure includes children who were born and died in the camp, although this addition does little to change the total number. At the end of October 1944, 819 children – not quite 7.5% of the inmates – remained in the camp. By April 20, 1945, 139,902 people had arrived in Theresienstadt, among them 8,821 children (less than 6.5%). This last figure also includes a small number of children born in Theresienstadt. We may assume that, including all of those born there (a total of no more than 230 children), approximately 9,000 children spent time in Theresienstadt, although, at liberation, only 1,633 children lived there. If we reckon that 1,000 of the 1,260 in the

Bialystok [Białystok] group were under the age of fifteen, we arrive at a figure of 10,000 children, of whom approximately 8,400 were murdered in the East. Hardly any children left the camp with the Swiss transport, and only a few left with the Danish transport. Documents concerning the number of children under the age of seventeen are not available. Including the Bialystokers [Białystokers], the number probably was less than 12,000. Among deported children over the age of fourteen, approximately 100 survived until liberation. Children who were under the age of fourteen when they were deported from Theresienstadt rarely escaped extermination.

18

Contact with the Outside World

Through the prisoners' agonizing isolation from the outside world, the SS pursued two aims: (1) wearing down the victims and (2) keeping others unaware of their fate. Both goals were largely achieved. This "ghetto" was in some respects more thoroughly closed off than some concentration camps, where correspondence and other communication were allowed on a broader scale. After several varying SS directives, uninterrupted postal service became possible only in September 1942, when the general ban on writing was lifted. Before then, private correspondence rarely made its way into or out of the camp legally. After permission to write was granted, it took several months – until around March 1943 – before order was brought to the postal service. The messages themselves always remained limited and were shaped by cumbersome regulations interpreted by overly fearful and pedantic Jewish postal censors. Initially, letters were limited to only thirty words, including the salutation and signature, written on one side of a card. Prisoners were required to adhere to a "writing rotation," which was published in the "orders of the day." During this period, each person could send one card. When the rotation, which might include a "repeat" (a second call), ended, those who had missed the opportunity lost their right to correspond for the rotation that had just expired. At first, this rotation lasted several months, and later, it was never shorter than many weeks. Nothing, of course, could be said about conditions in the camp. As a general rule, caution was necessary. It was at times forbidden, and never advisable, to mention people by name. One could point out that receiving packages was permitted, but one could not make specific requests. People dealt with this by disguising their wishes. More lenient regulations for correspondence applied to members of the Council of Elders, "notables," and Danes.

Receipt of news from outside was similarly restricted. A "memorandum on postal correspondence with Theresienstadt," issued by the Council of Elders of the Jews of Prague in August 1943, read:

> Postcards [from the "Protectorate"] to Theresienstadt may be sent only through the Council of Elders of the Jews of Prague or its branches. Postcards may contain 30 words in addition to the date, salutation and signature. Only cards written legibly in block letters in ink will be forwarded. Proper space must be placed between words. Letters

must be at least five millimeters high. Postcards may also be typed. If a card is written in ink, it must be signed in ink. Typed cards may be signed in pencil. Postcards may under no circumstances be written or even signed in color. It is not permitted ... to mention the position or department of the Council of Elders of the Jews in which the sender is employed. Only one card may be sent at a time from the same sender to the same recipient, not many cards at the same time. A sender must also avoid sending a large number of cards to multiple addressees. Mention of packages or authorization labels [see subsequently] is permitted. It is inadmissible to list the contents or weight of the package. Remarks about the extent of correspondence, such as "I will write daily" or "once a week" are not allowed. Descriptions such as "Aryan mother" or *Mischling* are also prohibited. Once every six months, a photograph may be sent in postcard format, but it may only be a picture of the sender.

Writing was conducted according to an established practice. People received blank postcards and wrote many drafts before setting down the final text. Writers devised farfetched ways of making their needs understood – for example, by sending greetings to the "Bread" or "Butcher" family. At some point the censor, a Jewish postal service employee, came by to inspect the cards, which were collected by the house elders. Usually, the censors were older men from Germany who read through the cards with difficulty. If they met all the regulations, the censors took them to be mailed; those that offended were marked, and the author received a replacement card. If this card, too, failed to follow the regulations, his right to correspond was forfeit during that rotation. The postcards were sent by the Jewish postal service via the local SS office and the central SS offices in Prague, Berlin, and Vienna to Jewish authorities in those cities. There, the postcards were stamped and sent off to addressees in the proper jurisdictions. Mail to Theresienstadt took a similar route, in reverse. Given these hindrances, it is surprising how much information could be passed on in disguised form, although awareness outside the camp of the situation inside necessarily remained very limited. Much of the mail meant for Theresienstadt failed to pass the censors or did not even reach them; thousands of cards went unsent, and others were lost or destroyed.

More important than written correspondence – and often its fulfillment – was parcel post. Although postcards from senders in the "ghetto" frequently took more than a month to reach recipients in Prague, and mail to Germany took even longer, parcels usually arrived not much later than they would have with the normal postal service. Packages could be sent from any post office. The first parcels from the "Protectorate" reached the camp in October 1942. Both parcels and postcards had to be addressed "Mr. X Y, Theresienstadt, Street No., Bauschowitz [Bohušovice] Post Office." From this post office, parcels were sent to the Jewish postal service in the camp. Then they were sorted, and a written "notification" was delivered to the recipient's quarters. This *aviso* then was used to pick up the package at the distribution point. In the first few months many parcels were either stolen or plundered there. A group of twenty-one gendarmes accounted for a considerable share of these thefts. Loewenstein managed to have only one gendarme designated as a monitor. Items classified as "contraband" were confiscated. A "memo" from the "Detective Department" on June 6, 1943, describes how this was done:

Re: Parcel Post Processing (Schleuse)
In view of the fact that ... I receive complaints daily about alleged and proven incidents that occur in the parcel post processing system, and further, in consideration of the fact

that the commandant of the so-called processing unit, Gendarmarie-Stabswachtmeister [Gendarme Police Sergeant] Škoda, is not prepared to change the composition of this group, I find it necessary to make the following proposal:

At the moment, processing of parcel post is handled in such a way that incoming mail bags are first unloaded in a separate room to which only the gendarme on duty and the 25 members of the processing unit have access. Here, parcels are opened and searched for contraband under the supervision of the gendarmes. Members of the unit are free to eat whatever they wish from the parcels (by permission of SS-Obersturmführer Otto). After being searched, parcels are resealed and passed through the connecting window to the Jewish postal service for further official processing. There, packages are numbered in sequence and shelved.

The public's main complaints are that those who work in the processing remove the most valuable items from the parcels, eat them, take them themselves or smuggle them in other ways (as we have already determined) in parcels of their own or for relatives, friends, etc. Although the officers I have been assigned subject people to constant searches, even when they temporarily leave the room, this monitoring has so far yielded negative results.

I therefore propose applying to the camp commandant's office and attempting to achieve a reorganization. I imagine the procedure as follows:

Incoming parcels would first be numbered sequentially, notifications of receipt would then be issued and parcels shelved in numerical order.

Recipients would turn in their notifications of receipt in exchange for the package in its original condition. They would then pass tables at which members of the parcel processing unit are seated. Supervised by the gendarme on duty, they would search the packages for contraband. Every member of the group would have a list of contraband items to prevent needless debate from interfering with official business.....

The proposal was accepted, and the result was less pilfering. Also, until February 1943, frequent theft of entire packages and withholding of parcels during deportation periods had been common; thereafter it occurred more seldom. Anything printed or written was removed from parcels, even sheets of old newspaper. Beginning in the autumn of 1943, prisoners receiving packages had to pay up to fifty "ghetto crowns," depending on the size of the parcel. In addition, recipients were given "confirmation-of-receipt cards" that could be sent outside the writing rotation periods. The cards read as follows: "Theresienstadt, on ... 1944, [space for the salutation] I gratefully confirm receipt of your package of ... 1944 [space for signature]." These cards reached their destinations in a few days and also were used for secret messages.

News of the opportunity to send parcels spread most quickly in the "Protectorate." In other countries, particularly in some parts of Germany, it took much longer. Except in the "Protectorate," and later in Denmark, no one really understood the importance of assiduous support through packages containing valuable and scarce foodstuffs. This probably was due to the fact that illegal information got through there to a greater extent than it did in other places, where people were less likely to understand hints and perhaps less able to contribute. But, as time went on, valuable parcels began to arrive from every country. The quantity of packages sent led the Czech postal ministry, at the behest of the SS, to issue the following directive on July 5, 1943:

Postal Service to Theresienstadt. Parcels and packages.
The Central Office for Regulation of the Jewish Question in Bohemia and Moravia supervises the mail for Jews living in the Theresienstadt Ghetto. In order to direct the

flow of packages and parcels, an authorization label will be introduced effective 10 July 1943.

The Camp Commandant's Office will issue a limited number of authorization labels to Jews in the ghetto, who can send them to their relatives residing in the Protectorate.

The authorization label for parcels must be affixed to the parcel. A date stamp must always be placed on the authorization label. Packages and parcels can be accepted only if they bear an authorization label. To Jews in the Theresienstadt Ghetto, packages and parcels originating outside the Protectorate remain unaffected by this regulation and need not bear an authorization label. (218)

Initially, this was a harsh blow, but its effects were not as adverse as they could have been, as is apparent in the following excerpt from the aforementioned August 1943 "memorandum" from the Prague Council of Elders:

Parcels and packages sent to Theresienstadt must bear an authorization label. These are non-transferable. A label may be used to send only one package to the recipient whose name is printed on the label. The Council of Elders for Jews in Prague does not issue authorization labels, but only distributes them on the basis of a list. An authorization label permits the shipment of a parcel weighing a maximum of 20 kilograms. It is forbidden to place smaller packages in the parcel for people other than the addressee listed on the parcel. Sending packages, parcels, letters and samples without an authorization label is forbidden. Parcels that arrive in Theresienstadt or the Bauschowitz [Bohušovice] Post Office without authorization labels will neither be forwarded to the addressee nor returned to the sender. We now emphasize that evading current regulations not only endangers the sender, but also, in the extreme, the entire postal service of Theresienstadt.

Many packages were filled to the allowed maximum capacity. During a cycle, every person in Theresienstadt was allowed to file an "application for granting of an authorization label" with the "Central Secretariat of the Transportation Department." Applications went to the Central Office, where approval was granted based on the supply of labels allocated to that office. The first rotation for approvals lasted nearly half a year; later it was shortened to as little as two months. In the camp, prisoners could purchase "applications" by promising to pay a third of the contents of the packages that they received once the application was accepted. The contents of the packages – almost exclusively foodstuffs – are addressed in detail in Chapter 12. It is surprising that the SS admitted, unchallenged, valuable items that could only have been bought on the "black" market. Parcels came not only from Bohemia and Moravia but also from Germany (see 294a), Austria, Denmark, and, on rare occasions, Holland, but otherwise not from countries occupied by Hitler or allied with him. The prisoners also received packages from the neutral countries Portugal, Sweden, Switzerland, and Turkey.

Once parcel post was allowed, postal authorizations were introduced. A prisoner deported from the camp could assign to another the right to receive all mail addressed to him. Recipients of such parcels were not allowed to send "confirmation-of-receipt cards." Some individuals served as proxy for many people, because they would shamelessly approach deportees and ask to be their proxy. This arrangement proved foolish and was abolished after the autumn transports in 1944. From then on, parcels for deportees were turned over to the welfare authorities.

Traffic in illegal mail also went on all the time, although the practice was punishable by death, even if "only" in the form of deportation. Such dealings could be

Contact with the Outside World

costly, because those involved usually demanded that they be paid handsomely. Likely couriers included civilians, particularly before the town was evacuated, as well as gendarmes, railway workers, or middlemen to whom prisoners with "transit passes" could gain access. At times, Christian relatives or friends would, at a venture, toss letters over the fence and into the camp from the "bypass route" around the camp. People sent and received messages and received packages and money.

The main features of relations with the SS are described in Chapters 8 and 14. With the exception of senior functionaries, relatively few people had much to do with them. People who worked for the SS had closer contact, although personal contact in these cases was rare. The gulf between individual prisoners and the SS men seemed infinite. But the SS occupied the imagination of many Jews, and it was the subject of many conversations. People felt the power of the SS usually without being able to assess it properly. Familiarity with the nature of the SS came from rumor rather than knowledge. People debated whether one SS man would be "better" and another one "worse." Particularly for those who did not work, the SS became more and more remote as time went on. They seemed like evil spirits who appeared on occasion, made mischief, and then disappeared. When high-ranking officials – the feared Eichmann, Günther, or Möhs – appeared in the camp, unease took hold. More often than not, it was justified. When Eichmann appeared, it was an almost certain sign of impending deportations; his adjutant Möhs also liked to be on hand for such occasions. Some people maintained varying relationships with lower-ranking functionaries, often on a business basis. Occasionally, an SS man would reward certain services with small gifts, even cigarettes. Spies kept the SS informed about important events in the camp, and often even about the most insignificant ones. With the exception of the arrival and departure of transports, public mistreatment was rare. Two cases became quite well-known:

> The elderly mother of Dr. Arthur Schlesinger of Proßnitz was crossing the street. At the same time, Poljak, an SS man, came racing down the street on a tractor, intentionally zigzagging wildly. The old woman stopped, terrified, in the middle of the street. Poljak ran her over with the tractor and drove on. The old woman was killed instantly. . . . An elderly man is making his way down the main street. Suddenly, he is hit on the head so hard that his hat flies off and lands far away. Czerba, an SS man, screamed at him, "Can't you salute, you cur!" The old man involuntarily raises his hand to protect himself and is instantly shot dead . . . for attacking an SS man. (242)

It was an open secret that the Poljak mentioned here had an intimate relationship with a Jewish woman in the camp. But the SS usually maintained a pointedly haughty distance from the prisoners. In fact, although Poljak wore the uniform, he did not belong to the SS but only worked in the camp headquarters as a driver.

Although the prisoners' interactions with the SS were mostly "legal," this was not the case with the Czech gendarmes. Of course, there were among them evil creatures who were hardly better than the SS men, but most were decent and some even willing to perform services, although often in return for considerable compensation. Officially, gendarmes were required to maintain the same distance from the prisoners as were the SS. The gendarmes were closely supervised and spied upon. Some paid for their altruistic or compensated services with harsh punishment, or even with their lives; thus there was every reason for caution. In October 1943, on the orders of K. H. Frank, fourteen gendarmes were executed at the "Small Fortress" for their connections to prisoners (see 232). Nevertheless, the gendarmes continued to risk even traveling for prisoners, and they carried messages, goods, and money. During transports and when escorting labor details, the gendarmes usually behaved irreproachably and in some cases were even friendly.

Relations with other non-Jews were rare and were reserved for only a few people once the civilians had left the city. Until then, illegal contacts with Czechs were frequent. Friends and relatives of prisoners came to Theresienstadt, and Czechs wearing the "Jewish star" even visited the barracks. Even after the town was cleared of civilians, this continued with the help of the gendarmes. To visit their relatives in the camp, *Mischlinge* would enter in a work detail and leave after a few hours (see 224b). Some visitors even were able to get into the "ghetto" at night. Prisoners and free people also conversed through the fence that ran alongside the bypass road, where relatives often would agree to meet. I know of at least one instance in which the reverse took place: in the early months, a prisoner removed the "Jewish star," went to Prague, and then returned to the "ghetto." Those working outside jobs in Kladno or other places had many connections in the area; they received visits and traveled to Prague and other cities. Later, illegal contact generally was possible only with a "pass to leave the ghetto." There are many accounts of the kindness of Czech railway workers. There were official (and private) contacts with the German heads of the "agriculture" and "electrical" sections. A Czech chimney sweep came into the camp on a regular basis. It also was advantageous to have contact with members of the German Wehrmacht, for whom a firing range was being built near Leitmeritz [Litoměřice] in 1943. The work detail was guarded only by soldiers (see 146b). Contact with other Germans (including work details in the "Small Fortress"; peat cutters; road workers; and workers at the airfield for the National Socialist Flying Corps [Nationalsozialistisches Fliegerkorps, or NSFK], at the Wehrmacht's reserve field hospital, and at the "Berlin SS office") usually was unpleasant and even marked by abuse.

Neither legal nor illegal contacts were sufficient to gain accurate information about what was going on in the world. Yet the hunger for "authentic" news hardly was less than the hunger for bread. People were mainly interested in the progress of the war. Newspapers and radio were banned in the camp. Small children were no less obsessed with news than old people on their deathbeds. For a few weeks at the end of 1942, the Prague daily newspaper *Nowy Dziennik* was posted in several places, but this stopped immediately when it became possible to read between the lines about the disaster at Stalingrad. Otherwise, only a small number of people had the opportunity to read newspapers regularly or even, if they served the gendarmes, to listen to the radio. Supposedly, there was an illegal radio receiver in the camp for a time. In any case, most prisoners were essentially cut off from any reliable source of information (see 191a).

Still, reports made their way into the camp in a variety of ways. A few newspapers were smuggled in almost every day. They were considered valuable even if they were many days old. They had to be hidden carefully and read in secret. The ultimate source of spoken news was mainly the gendarmes, whose accounts were based on permitted newspapers and broadcasts, foreign broadcasts, and rumors among the Czechs. News that infiltrated in this way was eagerly spread, rapidly noted, and passed on. Few people did not have, or purport to have, new information each day.

Only a tiny fraction of this information was accurate; although some of it contained a kernel of truth, most of it was pure fabrication.

From the time of arrival in the camp, almost everyone was absolutely certain that Germany would lose the war; how long it would take was the only subject of dispute. Few ever would have admitted that the war could last longer than a few months. When new transports arrived, prisoners threw themselves on the new arrivals, asking, "So, what's going on? Where are the Russians? Who's winning?" Nearly all the news from new arrivals was wrong, or at least optimistically colored, as if all these unfortunates had taken with them into an uncertain future the comforting thought of an impending end to all their troubles. Something as horrible as the "ghetto" could not last long. The signs that Germany soon would collapse were – always! – unmistakable. The slightest traces of supposed or actual weakness were vastly inflated. Just as the SS still was hoping for Hitler's miracle weapon at the end of the war, the prisoners clung to their belief in the opposite. Waves of the most fantastic rumors washed over the camp repeatedly. These orally transmitted messages noticeably changed as they moved from person to person, as each person, depending on his temperament, either passed on the report word for word or embellished it. Few had the strength of mind to resist joining in this frenzy of information or hoping that at least some of it was true. Accounts were reinforced by citation of "reliable" authorities, and people found the strongest words to cling to the "absolute truth." "The gendarme at the gate just told it to so-and-so." How often did word of mouth have it that the Turks or Swedes had declared war, or that the Russians were at least as far as Kharkov, if not at Smolensk, Minsk, or even the border of Upper Silesia and Tilsit! How often was the invasion already under way! Woe to those who dared to receive such reports with skepticism! A typical joke went as follows: A gendarme tells a Jew an unbelievable story. The Jew questions it, to which the gendarme responds: "The news is absolutely true. I heard it from a ghetto guard."

Sometimes, although rarely, a severe depression descended on the camp, specifically on deportation days. Then it became clear that the Germans could not be doing so badly if they still had enough trains for transports. The prisoners were unaware of the SS's absurd policies: up to the very last moment, they kept trains available to transfer prisoners from camp to camp and preferred to evacuate camp inmates rather than look out for their own betrayed people.

The rumor mill was an expression of the psychological neediness of the coerced community, which was aware that its salvation could come only through the collapse of Hitler's regime. Because this event remained distant, it had to be conjured through rumor. If one asked otherwise critical and rational people why they failed to question nonsensical pieces of news, they would say, "We don't really believe them, but it's so nice to enjoy them for a moment." By the next day, the news was already outdated and forgotten. People simply wanted their daily ration of consolation; then they became rational again, awaiting the next day's fresh dose. In this way, they hoped the time away: "One day these wonderful things have to come true!" Thus, there was little disappointment the next day about the previous day's lies, and the "ghetto" remained a hotbed of rumor. People obtained maps or drew their own and traced the front lines on them carefully, if often unreliably. Every supposed or actual achievement of the Allies or Russians was met with enormous jubilation. With eyes shining, prisoners whispered to one another in voices as loud as secrecy would allow, "Good news today!"

News of significant events, particularly those that boded ill for Hitler's Germany, spread through the camp with amazing speed. In such cases it usually was a gendarme who immediately passed the latest news broadcast about the fall of Mussolini or the invasion in the West to a ghetto guard. He then would continue spreading the news, until, even through the night, it made its way through the camp. Roommates woke one another to deliver good news. Reports that seemed more favorable to the Nazis spread much more slowly and were noted only by more discerning thinkers. Thus, for objective and subjective reasons, the number of people who were at least somewhat correctly informed was small. They soberly tried to clarify the situation by using German military reports and the places mentioned in them to glean a modicum of truth. A few elderly imperial German and Austrian officers proved most skillful at factual analysis.

The report of an illegal visit to Theresienstadt shall conclude this chapter:

[The author describes a secretly agreed-on visit by her mother to Theresienstadt. In it, she explains how her mother walked down the bypass road, from where she could see barracks H V through the fence. The daughter was waiting for her nearby in a ground-level room that had (always had) barred windows.]

I rushed to the window and gripped the bars. Two women are walking and conversing as they come through the fortress gate. They glance towards the windows unobtrusively. I clutch the bars until my knuckles are white.

As they approach I cry, "Mother!"

It seems to me that my voice is so terribly loud that they can hear me as far away as the Small Fortress. But in reality, I can barely hear myself. I am so excited I cannot even speak.

My mother instinctively looks around for the voice. She sees me in the window but does not recognize me.

My aunt says: "That's her!"

Both look towards where I am standing. I cannot stop the flood of tears that streams from my eyes. I see only a blurred image of two women, one paler than the other. That is my mother. I have not seen her for two years. She looks bad, miserable. I would like to say a few kind words, but I cannot get out more than, "How are you?" and "You're not hungry?" I understand barely a word of what they say to me because the blood pounding in my ears deafens me. Only towards the end do I hear, as if on the fly, "We'll come again in fourteen days."

"Be reasonable, they are coming back in fourteen days. Prepare ahead of time what you want to tell them so the words won't stick in your throat. You've held out for two years. You'll manage to get through the few months left until the end. Look, she came."

"Mother came," I whisper brokenly and sit down on the stool closest to the window.

And then, as if a bar of ice within me had cracked, I stand up and cry out:

"She is healthy, she is healthy – and she is alive!"

19

Cultural Life

Culture and this "ghetto" would seem incompatible, and yet, no matter how contrived its features, culture existed in Theresienstadt, and this culture's best achievements were valuable and worthy of respect. What did the term "culture" mean in this camp? It meant values that went beyond the mere physical survival of the community and were lived out and fulfilled as aspiration and creation, surpassing the minimal amount of vitally necessary achievement. The prisoners tried to express themselves intellectually whenever and wherever possible. Without this, for many of them life would not have seemed worth living. This tells us nothing about the nature or content of these intellectual efforts, or about their ethical quality. It does, however, show that life was conducted with serious expectations, and that it was not enough to be satisfied, even under the most difficult conditions, with the things that enabled one simply to scrape by. Even in the "ghetto," a minimum of culture had to be preserved and maintained. We do not examine what became of the spirit of Judaism in Central Europe prior to the period of the SS regime – or to what extent it recognized its responsibility to understand itself as Jewish or was justified in so doing. It is well known to what sort of assimilation this spirit succumbed, in the process turning its attention toward matters that by any definition hardly can be characterized as "Jewish." However, this does not alter the fact that this inquisitive spirit was at work, penetrating foreign cultures in order to comprehend them, do justice to them, prove itself within them, and accomplish something of its own.

The majority arrived in Theresienstadt with a stock of this kind of culture. As soon as they had arrived they attempted as much as possible not only to live off this reserve but also to cultivate and promote it through exchange with other prisoners; the cultural drive – it cannot be termed otherwise – had to be acted upon. Those who previously had been productive had no wish to give up; instead, they were eager to continue creating, either by making a conscious effort to adjust to their new environment or by defying and perhaps disengaging and closing themselves off from it, but nevertheless creating. This serious, indomitable will commands respect, although the outcome represented nothing more than the noble documentation of a remarkable self-assertion, and even the highest-quality creations hardly reflected the spirit of Judaism, because they were accomplished by people who were Jews only as defined by a mechanical classification, or even by the "race laws."

Cultural life was always alive in this camp, although in the early months it encountered extreme difficulties, later repeatedly experienced severe setbacks, and suffered serious crises during transport periods. When deportations jolted this small world, which was never free of fear, some prisoners' intellect and urge for pleasure at times asserted themselves in a questionable type of culture, whereas more sensitive natures abhorred these expressions because they did not conform to a culture of ethics. Transports arrested cultural life. However, not long after the deportees departed, not long after the paralyzing fear had subsided, people threw themselves with redoubled fervor into new activities and, even worse, into the often unhealthy tumult of available pleasures, as if nothing had happened. No matter how much there was from which to choose, it seemed never enough; people deceived themselves mindlessly, with shameless insatiability. But this raging drive, which found numerous outlets, no longer could be called culture.

Without necessarily being able to truly grasp or interpret it, anyone in possession of his senses was aware of the special quality of this camp and attempted to understand and process it. This could happen in many ways. For example, one might accept the Theresienstadt "episode" as a sustained misfortune that was unavoidable and might strive to resume the trajectory of one's previous ambitions and actions. Except for a movie theater, almost all the cultural institutions and forms of light entertainment that would exist in any major city were available in the camp, although they always were altered in a way that was unique and typical of this "ghetto." There was an abundance of theater performances, concerts, lectures, books, and lighter entertainments. All this was readily available and essentially free of charge. The people who unhesitatingly grasped for these things used them to nullify the conscious knowledge that they were living in a camp and remained as frivolous or snobbish as before. One might suddenly feel called to do cultural work, even if one was not talented, or only barely so. One could give lectures, perform in the theater, sing in a choir, try one's hand at drawing, keep a careful diary, philosophize, and, above all, write poetry, for which one was certain to be recognized and admired. Activities and interests about which one had not thought since one's youth, or that one had never considered at all, suddenly became important and crucial. The harsh reality drove many to fantasy and illusion – one might even consider this trait a regression into childhood (see Chapter 16). Many otherwise everyday tasks – such as cleaning, shopping, running a business, and carrying out one's professional life and social obligations, as well as excursions and travel – were entirely, or at least partially, eliminated, and family life had been destroyed; now, despite the prescribed, restrictive time schedule, people found sufficient leisure to begin a variety of endeavors. Nonworkers had far too much time on their hands, and they liked to devote it to writing. What this desire to write was all about was expressed by one of those men in the following, distressingly awkward way:

> Strange, so strange!
> More than 65 years
> I devoted myself to acquiring,
> Had no appreciation for rhyming.
> But nature is not lazy,
> It stirs one's resistance,
> Which we need, so that we can
> Impose our own will.

Cultural Life 519

[*Sonderbar, hödchst sonderbar!*
Über 65 Jahr
Gab ich dem Erwerb mich hin,
Hatt' für Dichten keinen Sinn.
Aber die Natur nicht träge,
Macht die Abwehrkräfte rege,
Die wir brauchen, um den Dingen
Unser Wollen aufzuzwingen.]

(180)

However, people could also devote themselves to culture without participating in the official program, with its countless events. They could strengthen their internal protest against the times and the camp. They could attempt to contribute to the intellectual leadership of their environment, and to demonstrate the immense difference between temporal and timeless questions. They could strive to shape the intellectual face of the camp through thought and artistic creation, whether for the moment or "for later."

Culture appears organic by nature, and yet it cannot be organized. Our era's belief – to which groups obsessed with pseudocollective plans pay particular homage – that culture can be "produced" and then "organized" is a widespread, and therefore especially disastrous, misconception. Thus it is no surprise that Hitler's Germany – one of the most inorganic nations in modern history – imagined it could manage this, too, with the aid of the numerous institutions it established. Previously, the Jews of Theresienstadt had been denied and forbidden "culture," but now the SS demanded it, for propaganda purposes; suddenly even this "ghetto" under SS control was forced to "organize" its culture. Germany had chosen the pompously inhibited term "strength through joy" (*Kraft durch Freude*), communism the machinelike word *proletkult*, Italy the simple term *dopolavoro*, and Czechs under Hitler the conciliatory-sounding "joy in life" (*Freude am Leben*). The amorphous little world forced on the Jews was assigned the painful misnomer "recreational activities" (*Freizeitgestaltung*).

One of the accomplishments of the office in charge of "recreational activities" was that it refrained almost entirely from organizing in the manner criticized previously and resembled more a center for popular education and amusement; it concentrated, and rightly so, on making possible public and, generously, private cultural life and providing it with technical support. It avoided promoting any specific ideology without also providing a forum for other voices. This was mainly owing to the men who were in charge of it starting in 1943; they were guided by the astute and serious Dr. Franz Kahn, one of the most able Zionists in the "ghetto" (he was sent to his death in the fall of 1944, even though he had lost an arm in World War I). The "Recreation Office" demonstrated a degree of sympathy with the prisoners that was otherwise rare in the self-administration and supported – or at least allowed – anything that the SS did not clearly make impossible. The SS had to be informed of the official program, but the office protected numerous more or less private events and made the necessary space available without interference. Certainly even the "Recreation Office" was not free of intrigue and other human weaknesses, but such complications were less frequent and less harmful than in other departments. Anyone who felt a need to speak, perform, or play music could be certain of finding support. If the head of the lecture department, Professor Emil Utitz, found a kernel of potential in a proposal, a way to make it happen almost always was found. This also was true of other officials; here we mention only the head of the Youth Education Department, Professor Maximilian Adler, an outstanding humanist and Philo expert and one of the most high-minded and honorable men to hold a position in Theresienstadt.

Much time passed, however, before things reached this point. Indeed, in the early weeks, all cultural activity was strictly prohibited. On December 28, 1941, "comradeship evenings" with mixed programs were permitted in the rooms or halls of the barracks. They were simple improvisations – honest, touching, and artless, reflecting the needs of those in hardship looking to comfort themselves. Ownership of musical instruments was forbidden; exceptions were made only for members of the "staff" and the GW. But, in secret, some people might have a harmonica, an accordion, or even a violin. When music was being played, someone had to stand guard. After December 1941, one could hear arias and songs, either unaccompanied or sung to an accordion. Performances soon were moved to uninhabited spaces, the office of a building elder, or a potato-peeling room. Soon people were rehearsing what they presented, be it lectures or cabaret. Rehearsals and performances could take place only during free time, usually in the early evening.

In 1942, the "Recreation Office" was established as part of the "Department of Internal Administration." For a long time it was merely tolerated and its existence often threatened, for its activities were stopped several times as punishment. The more the SS wanted to "normalize" the camp, the more recreational activities were allowed. When the "coffeehouse" was established in December 1942, not only were musical instruments permitted, but a band had to be assembled, and more and more instruments and sheet music were acquired from stolen Jewish property in the Protectorate. What did it matter that many of the instruments were of second-rate quality? The musicians made up for it. In the evacuated city someone had left behind a badly damaged grand piano that was thought to be useless – it had no legs and could hardly be played. The piano, on which serious music probably never had been played, was brought into the gymnasium of the old school L 417, placed on wooden blocks, and roughly repaired, and Professor Bernhard Kaff and Gideon Klein soon were performing works by Beethoven, Bach, and Brahms (see 3b, doc. 191).

The heyday of the "Recreation Office" coincided with the "beautification"; the SS hoped to submerge the horror of the camp in music, theater, and amusements. A "town band" had to perform each day in the "music pavilion." Starting in December 1942, uninhabitable rooms and attics gradually were made available for events, and frequently also as prayer rooms. Some were furnished in such a way that theater, too, could be performed there, and some of the attics made very good poor man's stages. On SS orders, the halls had to be amply refurbished to allow theatrical events, concerts, and lectures.

> Two former movie theaters were splendidly refurbished: the Sokol House for all purposes, and L 514 for concerts. In addition, there were six rooms that could serve as theaters, in the Kaserne B V, H V, C III, and attics in L 203, L 318, Q 619, as well as other rooms for lectures, etc. The conference room of the City Hall, Q 619, was used for concerts. For a time, there also was a larger stage in the GW building, L 313, but it had to be given up in 1943.

The "Recreation Office" now functioned as a separate department and employed a large staff of full- and part-time workers.

It was considered good form to participate in this life. The heads of the self-administration – Eppstein, Zucker, and Murmelstein – attached great importance to lecturing as part of the "recreational activities" program, whereas Edelstein, who also enjoyed lecturing, preferred to appear as an informal public speaker.

The "Recreation Office" also played an important role as an educational institution, partially compensating for and supplementing the absence of formal education. In the years 1943–44, the official weekly program was publicly posted; it included general and Jewish lectures in German, Czech, and other languages; theater performances in German, Czech, and Yiddish; readings (including readings in Hebrew and ancient languages); concerts; cabarets; and sporting events. The organizers often sent out private invitations. Events meant only for a specific house or room and private functions generally were arranged by word of mouth. The "Health Services," "Welfare," and "Youth Welfare" Departments gave various presentations, arranged by the "Recreation Office," in infirmaries and "homes." Finally, there were lectures, lecture series, workshops, and so on, organized by groups or individuals only for a particular audience or for invited guests. There were weekly group meetings dealing with Jewish concerns, science, history, politics, art, the sociology of Theresienstadt, and so on. The lectures usually were followed by discussions. Seminars – such as the one held by the Jewish Elder, Eppstein, dealing with national economy – also took place. Many religious communities held meetings: Practicing Catholics gave lectures about Christian philosophy, patristics, Thomism, and so on. Anthroposophists and theosophists held meetings. Finally, there were groups that excluded the public entirely; of these, the "Recreation Office" had no knowledge.

However, they hardly needed to meet illegally, because the SS concerned itself little with what was being discussed and done. Only a few minor precautions had to be observed. Thus a lecture could not be entitled "Jews in German Literature"; instead, it was called "Jews Writing in German in Literature." As of July 1944, the SS demanded more precise topic information and required that texts for readings and theater performances be submitted. Soon after, they forbade performances in Czech. Shortly before the end of the war, however, such performances were explicitly ordered.

The level of interest in most events was remarkably high. Aside from sports, which particularly fascinated the young, people especially loved theater and similar events, such as revues, cabaret, one-act scenes, readings of plays, and opera concerts. At times, it seemed as though the small world of the "ghetto" was about to dissolve into nothing but play and theater. Everything was tempting, from serious art to worthless honky-tonk acts. The small rooms necessitated frequent repetition of plays; some were performed serially, as in a big city. A ticket system had to be introduced, and, eventually, the charge for theater performances and some concerts was set at five ghetto crowns. To gain admission to the more desirable performances, one had to use other means, such as connections to people in the "Recreation Office," as acquiring tickets by reservation required more patience than was healthy. Thus it was necessary to turn to the "Recreation Office," to the "recreation officer" in the "Labor Welfare Office," or to other welfare organizations (see 3b, doc. 168).

Some young people with talent and even more enthusiasm performed serious theater in Czech, as well as in German, although despite more practice, the German performances were blander and poorer. The plays performed included, for example, Molière's *George Dandin*, Gogol's *The Wedding*, *Cyrano de Bergerac*, *Mary Stuart*, and the works of Shakespeare, among others. Also performed were works by modern authors such as Shaw, Hofmannsthal, Molnár, Herzl, and the Czech writers Wolker and Langer. The Yiddish plays performed included "In Mitt'n Weg," a fragment of *The Golden Chain*, by Peretz. A sequence was put together from Villon ballads, with accompaniment by Viktor Ullmann. The old Czech folk play *Esther* was presented, with musical accompaniment by Karel Reiner. These compositions originated in the camp, as did some of the plays presented, such as *The Dolls*, by Peter Kien; *The Success of Columbus*, by Otto Brod (a brother of Max Brod); and the Czech play *Comedy about a Trap*, by Zdeněk Jelínek.

Operas were even more popular than dramas and had to be repeated frequently. They were offered mainly as operatic concerts with piano accompaniment, but occasionally there were staged performances in costume, usually also with only piano accompaniment. *The Bartered Bride* was first presented, to great acclaim. Then there were rehearsals of *The Kiss* by Smetana, as well as *La Serva Padrone, Bastien and Bastienne, The Abduction from the Seraglio, The Magic Flute, Carmen, Aida, Tales of Hoffmann, La Bohème, Tosca, Die Fledermaus*, and others. A work such as *The Magic Flute* could not go well, and, as Viktor Ullmann advised in an internal critique for the "Recreation Office," a bit less ambition might have been in order. Also, the young conductors Raffael Schächter and F. E. Klein, as well as some singers and directors, allowed themselves to be carried away by a cult of celebrity. The accomplishment as a whole, however, remains admirable. The greatest success was the children's opera *Brundibár*, by Hans Krása, which was composed in Prague but performed for the first time in Theresienstadt; it was repeated at least thirty times under the direction of the composer. The work was based on a cheerful animal fable, and its simple construction was well suited to the camp. The children participated enthusiastically and gave excellent performances. (The composer and nearly all the children who were involved in this project are now dead; see also 93, 240a.)

The inmates even tackled oratorios, which they performed on the piano. The program included Haydn's *Creation* (*Schöpfung*), Mendelssohn's *Elias*, and, an unfortunate choice, Verdi's *Requiem*; Ullmann wrote about it as follows:

> ... Yesterday's performance was the nth repeat performance and nothing more should be said about the technical aspect. In this case, however, there may be reason to stress again that Raffael Schächter, to whom the musical world in Theresienstadt owes so many ideas and artistic accomplishments, achieved a performance of cosmopolitan standards. Reaching far beyond the merely technical, Schächter gives form ... to the spirit of the work, with frugal yet evocative gestures. The choir's singing was precice, but also dynamically flawless. The soloists support the conductor faithfully. (322)

A high standard was achieved in concerts by various instrumentalists, chamber musicians, singers, and ultimately even an orchestra. Works by nearly all the great masters since Bach were performed. The artists, who frequently had to make do with instruments in poor or second-rate condition, tackled serious and difficult programs, which were carefully rehearsed. Concerts, too, had to be repeated several times. The care taken with works created in Theresienstadt was noteworthy. The most significant artist among the productive musicians in the camp was the pianist and music educator Professor Bernhard Kaff, from Brünn [Brno]. Long before there was even a piano or before anyone imagined concerts, this unusual man lived in his beloved music. One cannot say of his playing that it was good despite the camp and the bad piano. No: it was good because he could not play otherwise. The spirit of the work he presented was continually brought to life. In this way, Kaff made it possible for his audience to have a deep experience that did not evaporate with the applause but continued to exert a beneficial effect long afterward. When he performed Beethoven's Sonata Opus 111 or the Händel variations by Brahms, these evenings became triumphs of pure morality over the adversity of an almost unbearable present. Kaff met his end in the fall of 1944, in Auschwitz, when most of the remaining artists also were sent to their deaths. Among them were other fine pianists such as Gideon Klein and Mrs. René Gärtner-Geiringer, and other excellent performers who had rendered great service. There also were some remarkable violinists, although none of these artists were of Kaff's stature. Also worth mention is Professor Egon Ledeč, who founded the first string quartet in Theresienstadt, in Dr. Erich Klapp's room. They came together as early as the beginning of 1942 and played works by Haydn, Beethoven, and Dvořák. Of the many other soloists who did not survive the war, we should mention at least the very young cellist Fredy Mark and the kind old oboist Professor Armin Tyroler, who presented works by Händel and rare compositions by baroque masters.

Chamber music ensembles were formed for occasional or permanent collaboration. There was a piano trio and several string quartets, and people came together to play in string quintets or sextets. One of the most valuable accomplishments in Theresienstadt in this area was the rendering of a Brahms sextet and a Schubert quintet. Singers gave concerts with excellent classical and modern programs, and artists such as the ladies Hilda Aronson-Lindt and Ada Schwarz and the gentlemen Walter Windholz and Karel Berman far exceeded the good-quality average. The Prague conductor Karel Ančerl (who survived the war) conducted many performances of two concerts with an orchestra consisting of members of the "Recreation Office" and volunteers. The first program offered a concerto grosso in F major by Händel; the violin concerto in E major by Bach, with the young violinist Fröhlich; and Mozart's *Kleine Nachtmusik*. The second concert was devoted to Czech music: Suk's *Meditation on an Old Chorale*, Dvořák's *Serenade*, and the world premiere of the *Study for String Orchestra*, composed in Theresienstadt by Pavel Haas. Ullmann lauded the conductor's work: "Karel Ančerl is a conductor of high caliber and significant talent; the fact that he welded together this body of sound in a heroic effort and made it be, is proof of his gifts, and of his superhuman patience" (322).

Choir concerts were rehearsed with much dedication and frequently presented excellent programs. Ullmann wrote the following about a children's choir:

> R. Freudenfeld and his choir, whose accomplishment with Krása's "Brundibár" has not been forgotten, this time offered us Czech and Hebrew folksongs in various interpretations (Gideon Klein, Adolf Schächtner, Otakar Sin, J.B. Förster and others). Freudenfeld is a true educator and good musician; we are grateful to him, not only for the mostly difficult choirs for 3–4 voices, which were cleanly rendered and boldly sung, and where young as well as older singers held their own, but also for his loving dedication to the children of Theresienstadt in general. (322)

The following report by a female singer offers insight into the history and problems of "recreational activities":

> When I arrived in Theresienstadt on 17 December 1941 ... we could not imagine that we would be able to sing or perform theater in this prison. We simply had prepared

ourselves for a life of factory work, etc., as had been intimated to us. But after two months ... the need emerged to add at least a bit of spiritual food to the bad nutrition, and one day, Fredy Hirsch and Rabbi Weiner [the first head of the "Recreation Office"] showed up ... and appointed me to create something, which was officially called Recreation. In short, I was to put together entertaining and instructive programs, language courses and lectures, and if possible, a library consisting of books ... that people had brought with them.... I organized a room, a hall, which happened to be unoccupied at the time, and I had benches brought in, or brought them in myself; I searched for an instrument, at the very least a harmonica, which had to be used in secret.... We held a so-called test of all the people who were involved in readings, singing and dance and I arranged the first mixed program. On 21 March 1942, the so-called staff and the Jewish Elder Edelstein came to see us at the women's barracks.... The first cultural evening was staged, though at 3 in the afternoon. I compiled a stylistically appropriate and high-quality program. I even participated as a singer; a group of young girls danced a Czech polka, the Adler sisters, daughters of the poet Friedrich Adler, gave a reading, and a former opera soubrette sang.... The entire thing was so successful that we not only had to repeat this program several times ... we were given permission ... to visit other barracks, men's barracks, where we presented this performance. And so we began to offer our art to the wrtched people, so that they could forget for a while the miserable conditions in which they found themselves. We also visited hospitals, giving readings and singing songs among the beds. Usually without any instrumental accompaniment.... We enjoyed doing that.... After a while ... more and more singers, musicians and composers came together ... and this is how it became possible for us to take on the rehearsal and performance of "The Bartered Bride," under the direction of the conductor Raphael Schächter, who died in a concentration camp. Schächter, who rehearsed with Jewish choirs ... in the evenings merely with the help of a tuning fork, had the idea of rehearsing the choir passages from "The Bartered Bride." I found girls in our barracks and he rehearsed with the men, and finally, when we had found acceptable soloists, it occurred to him that we could perform the entire opera, but concertante. Somewhere ... there was a half-broken piano without legs; he had in the meantime acquired a broken harmonium and had found a small room somewhere in a basement. And so we held our rehearsals in the bitter cold, wrapped up to our ears.... We were given access to the gym at the L 417 home for boys, and finally, we performed "The Bartered Bride" for the first time on 28 November 1942. It made an unforgettable impression.... "The Bartered Bride" was performed some 35 times.... The cultural and theatrical life was so rich in 1943–44 that a medium-sized city in peacetime would not have had as many performances as our ghetto.... It seems strange that the SS allowed the Jews ... music, art, lectures, etc.... but the gentlemen knew quite well what they were doing.... Because they expected a commission ... they ordered that the operas be performed with impeccable staging, with costumes and wigs; in short, that it should be real theater.... Arch. Zelenka, Prof. Lederer and other well-known artists worked unceasingly to fit out the various stages; in the end, all the lighting apparatus and light bulbs needed to operate a theater had to be delivered to Theresienstadt. On the square constructed was a pavilion in which the town band had to play; all were excellent musicians, each one a virtuoso. At the coffeehouse, a trio played and cabarets were presented (Hans Hofer), and in summer there were open-air performances in the court-yards. Thus Theresienstadt in the summer of 1944 actually seemed like an absolute Eldorado in Europe, with no air raids, far from the theater of war, with nothing but diversions; no danger seemed to threaten. And the worthy commission came and was obviously amazed.... Actors were ready in the theaters; the moment the commission arrived, they began performing in the middle of an opera or drama. The commission moved on five minutes later, and the play was stopped. People went home.

Cultural Life

The composers Haas, Krása, Ullmann and Gideon Klein were urged to compose operas and songs that were later performed. All of this on the orders of the SS. . . . Almost all the men – artists, actors, composers, singers, conductors, instrumentalists – perished. And of the entire ensemble, only seven women who had been forgotten remained in Theresienstadt. . . . When the last transport . . . was being dispatched . . . and the Jewish Elder Murmelstein was about to present to the camp leader Rahm those who had not marched past him . . . Murmelstein asked whether they [the seven women] were to be lined up to join the last transport. Rahm, smiling graciously, said in a Viennese dialect: "No no, let 'em stay. Let 'em sing and play again." But we had to immediately report for the mica splitting work . . . some three days after the departure of the last transport, I received orders to arrange a new concert program. So, in the evening we had to meet in the unheated auditorium of the gymnasium, quickly arrange a program and . . . sing again. Four months passed in this way, until 7 March 1945, when Mr. Rahm took us out of the mica plant and ordered us quickly to rehearse the [Czech] children's opera "Little Glowworm" and "Tales of Hoffmann," because yet another commission was expected. So we wrote down musical notes day and night, compiled orchestral material, rehearsed with the "Aryan-intermarried" (*arisch-versippt*) musicians who since had arrived [in addition to Dutch musicians with the conductor Leo Pappenheim], and thus we performed again in costume in the gymnasium, with its magnificently equipped stage. The commission indeed arrived and everything went well, and life again seemed . . . just as it had before the departure of many thousands of people. Around 20 April . . . the first transport of the so-called pajamas arrived . . . and this is when our eyes were opened. Now we recognized the reality, and from that day on all singing, playing and amusements ceased. We no longer felt like singing. . . . I can say that Theresienstadt was the longest and worst-paid engagement in my entire musical and theatrical career. (87)

This report reveals the social function of cultural life, the business of which frequently became unstable and dishonorable, blinding active and passive participants and often degenerating into an almost dangerous pleasure seeking. The cultural activities that initially had fulfilled a real need, with diligence and devotion, turned into a curse when they became a gift from and an order by the SS, and they lost all sense of proportion and reflection. The behavior of a large number of prisoners, particularly the more influential groups, created the conditions that fueled this curse's corrupting influence. Many young, still immature musicians and theater people lost all restraint, putting on airs and nearly forgetting about the camp and the SS. A gifted conductor thoughtlessly led the life of a star, a darling of the muses, celebrated by his audiences. People anesthetized themselves, denying the present, and, most disturbingly, fulfilling the wishes of the SS with naïve eagerness. The deliberate deception of strangers became the self-deception of the prisoners; they enjoyed performing on one of the most horrific stages in the entire country. Human dignity was hollowed out from within, without the victims even noticing. The world was in flames, the ghetto caught up in misery, but people still found the time for petty vanities and artistic intrigues. People continued to play when silence – or a more serious tone – was called for, but few artists or listeners understood what was appropriate. When, on the eve of the Day of Atonement in 1944, people were gathered in the Schleuse for deportation, Eppstein was shameless enough to send over a band to play dance music and happy tunes. When he was questioned, he rejected the criticism and cynically said: "Those are bourgeois prejudices; let the people have their fun!" Two days later, most of the deported had been gassed, and Eppstein had been shot.

Sociology

"Light entertainment," in particular, was frequently enjoyed under rather unfortunate conditions, which were for the most part avoided in performances of more serious art. Cabarets, revues, jazz band pieces, and operettas were specially composed and tailored to the camp, sometimes daring ribald foolishness. There were comics who fulfilled the expectations of large numbers of people by pronouncing helpless and cheap truths in the style of the Viennese couplet, or by performing on a higher level, in the mode of the more political and socially engaged Czech *Überbrettl*; but, frequently, the formats chosen were inappropriate, and a certain frivolity prevailed, a sometimes humorous, sometimes sentimental mindlessness. Such presentations amounted to nothing more than brief distractions, and afterward the audience, now doubly impoverished, returned again to the constant misery. Occasionally a performance was better than average, making use of bitter, sometimes self-deprecating humor:

> Our Aristophanes [Svenk] from Theresienstadt unfortunately showed up rarely, although he would have enough material and imagination to transform his annual contributions into monthly reviews. "Shake well before using" in this case does not refer to medicine, but to the patient, and after having laughed for an hour and a half it is quite impossible to raise any critical objections.... In significant scenes, Svenk unquestionably reaches the level of satire and thus true art, as for instance in the musically outstanding choir parodies, in the sound-film newsreels and in the parody of theatrical events in Theresienstadt. (322)

Conditions in the camp were sometimes harshly criticized, and daily worries were aptly depicted. In many instances, however, humor and sentimentality adapted to the conditions in a foolish way, not rising above them but identifying with them. Ensembles with pompous names were formed.

> I am informing you that I intend to appear in public with a jazz orchestra that will feature preponderantly Jewish music. The members are as follows: [there follow the names of seven musicians, along with a list of their instruments]. The orchestra will appear under the name The Ghetto Swingers. I would be grateful if your music officer would contact us so that I can inform you in detail of our intentions and desires.
>
> (letter to the "Recreation Office," January 8, 1943)

And thus it happened; the "ghetto" had its swingers, playing their music in the "coffeehouse." In this camp there was almost nothing that did not in some way imitate the institutions of a normal society. Whatever good or bad aspects the Central European Jews had adopted from their non-Jewish environment were reflected in Theresienstadt, along with whatever material the prisoners might consider to be "typically Jewish."

People came together for specific occasions to give artistic or entertaining performances. Everything else was in short supply, but not the enterprising spirit. Several hundred sheets of paper could be quickly organized, and soon afterward one might receive a carefully reproduced, illustrated invitation from the ladies of the "cleaning squad": "Mr. – Mrs. – Miss ... The cleaning service H V introduces itself and takes the liberty of inviting you to a cabaret evening on 1 January 1943 at 8 P.M. in the potato-peeling room of H V" (3b, doc. 171). Of course, only inmates of the barracks and people possessing a "night pass" were able to attend. The illustrations depicted a woman cleaning windows; a boy is handing her cleaning solution. Also depicted was a ballet of cleaning supplies and a poster displaying the following verse:

Cultural Life

Working is an utter joy,
Join the Cleaning Squad today.

[*Arbeiten ist eine Wonne,*
Tretet bei zur Putzkolonne.]

Folded programs used similar techniques, as in the following:

[Title page: A fashionable young girl is depicted, sporting a pant-skirt and a Ghetto Guard cap. The accompanying text reads:] The Klauber stage presents, under the patronage of the Head of the Ghetto Guard Mr. Kurt Frey – The GHETTO GIRL.

[Inside pages:] A contemporary opera by Kurt Klauber and Th. Otto Beer. Music: Th. Otto Beer [Three other names follow. There follows the names of those in charge of] dance and production – musical direction – stage design – technical direction [followed by the characters of the play, such as:] Erika Preiss, a revue star – Jiří Wolf, an AK I – Herbert Eichinger, a GW man – Margot Kortner, an emergency service nurse – a ghetto inmate – a ghetto boy. [After that, the people participating in the ballet are listed. At the end it says:] Musical interlude: My Golden Baby, from the operetta "Flowers of Haway" by P. Abraham.

And so this troupe produced a cloying, painfully comical self-portrait in the form of an operetta. This performance also included a "march of the Ghetto Guard," titled "Theresienstadt, the Most Beautiful City in the World."

The following program from the "Recreation Office" lists a wealth of stage performances (not counting opera), all of which took place in the space of one week:

Monday, November 1, 1943		
Hauptstr. 22/Attic	2:30 P.M., 5:15 P.M.	"Game in the Castle," directed by B. Spanier (tickets [T], money[M])
Langestr. 5/Attic	6:00 P.M.	Variety Group Smetana (T)
Tuesday, November 2, 1943		
Hauptstr. 22/Attic	3:00 P.M., 5:30 P.M.	One-act evening (Schnitzler, Herzl) Director: E. Österreicher (T, M)
Langestr. 5/Attic	7:30 P.M.	"Jewish motifs in Song and Verse." Irene Dodal (T, M)
Bahnhofstr. 3	6:00 P.M.	Strauss Ensemble (T)
Wednesday, November 3, 1943		
Hauptstr. 22/Attic	5:00 P.M.; 6:30 P.M.	Molière: "George Dandin" (Cz), Direction: Arch. Zelenka (T, M)
Bahnhofstr. 3	6:00 P.M.	Strauss Ensemble (T)
Saturday, November 6, 1943		
Hauptstr. 22/Attic	5:00 P.M.	Revue "A Day in H V," direction: S. Gruenfeld (T, M)
Hauptstr. 22/Attic	7:30 P.M.	Strauss Ensemble (T)
Langestr. 5/Attic	7:30 P.M.	"Beggars Ballad"; direction: Irene Dodal (T,M)
Sunday, November 7, 1943		
Hauptstr. 22/Attic	5:00 P.M.	"Game in the Castle," direction: B. Spanier (T,M)
Langestr. 5/Attic	6:00 P.M., 7:30 P.M.	Nora Fried "Radiowave" Children's Revue (T)
Bahnhofstr. 3	6:00 P.M.	John Cabaret (conf. Lindenbaum) (T)
Wallstr. 8/16	7:15 P.M.	Strauss Ensemble (T)

528   *Sociology*

Eighteen theatrical performances – plus ten other presentations, five of them serious, four of them light, and one for children – for 40,000 people took place in one week. Even in 1942, the abundance of offerings during work-free days was no less remarkable than in the previous example, as is evident in the following complete program for November 28, 1942:

B V	2:00 P.M.	Room 118: docent Dr. Stein: Conjunctivitis and Keratitis (for health services)
	4:45 P.M.	Room 100: Dr. H. G. von Weinberg: Elements of Matter
	8:30 P.M.	Room 118: Zdeněk Jelínek: "Comedy of the Trap," only for B V
B IV	6:15 P.M.	see above
E VII	3:30 P.M.	Room 32: John Cabaret for G IV–G VI
	6:30 P.M.	Room 32: Thorn: Three Kinds of Humor
Q 307	4:00 P.M.	"The Fool and Death" (premiere)
L 203	5:00 P.M.	Variety Hour
L 514	3:30 P.M.	Treu: Readings
L 316	6:15 P.M.	John Cabaret
B V	6:00 P.M.	Room 88: Variety Hour

The lectures held in Theresienstadt may be the most impressive example of its "recreational activities." This is a sample dating from the period when cultural life was most active:

General lectures – Program for the period from 10 July to 16 July 1944:

Monday, July 10, 1944		
Westg. 3/Terrace	7:00 P.M.	Reading hour
Badhausg. 19/Attic	7:00 P.M.	The Colors of Creatures. Dr. Elise Deiner
Langestr. 5/105	8:00 P.M.	Dr. Paul Blum: German Humor, French Esprit, Jewish Wit
Tuesday, July 11, 1944		
Wallstr. 8/16	7:00 P.M.	Dr. Fr. G. Weinberger: Economic Trends and Economic Crisis.
Bahnhofstr. 3/Attic	7:30 P.M.	Else Dormitzer: Encounters with Famous Contemporaries
Langestr. 11/Attic	7:30 P.M.	Prof. Dr. Arthur Stein: From the World of Papyrus. General introduction
Hauptstr. 2/144	8:15 P.M.	Prof. Dr. Blumenthal: Circular Relationships and Stereometric Projection.
Wednesday, July 12, 1944		
Hauptstr. 22/88	6:30 P.M.	Dr. Erna Sonneberger: Value and Meaning of Money.
Langestr. 11/Attic	7:30 P.M.	Dr. Rolf Grabower: Profession and Ethics.
Hauptstr. 14/11	7:45 P.M.	Prof. Dr. Erich Feldmann: Balance and Taxes.
Langestr. 5/105	8:00 P.M.	Docent Dr. Leo Pollak: Chemistry of Food and Nutrition.
Badhausg. 19/Attic	8:00 P.M.	Anna Aurednicek: Famous Actors.
Thursday, July 13, 1944		
Westg. 3/Terrace	4:00 P.M.	Reading hour

Cultural Life   529

Hauptstr. 22/82	6:30 P.M.	Dr. Wilhelm Mautner: Unknown Holland.
Langestr. 11/Attic	7:30 P.M.	Dr. Max Popper: On the Occasion of Dr. August Stein's 90th birthday (c).

Friday, July 14, 1944

Rathausg. 19/hall	6:30 P.M.	James Simon: Beethoven's Sonatas (with explanatory comments at the grand piano) III.

Saturday, July 15, 1944

Hauptstr. 22/82	6:30 P.M.	Dr. Georg Siegmann: The Berlin Aquarium.
Hauptstr. 22/82	7:00 P.M.	Dr. Hans Zweig: Psychiatry (modern medicine) V.
Langestr. 11/Attic	7:30 P.M.	Prof. Dr. Max Brahn: Nietzsche's "Zarathustra" (with excerpts and comments).
Parkstr. 14	8:00 P.M.	Memorial Service for Dr. Eduard Lederer-Leda. Speakers: Dr. A. Meissner, Dr. F. Weidmann. Also participating: Ančerl Sextet and Ledeč quartet (c). (tickets.)
Badhausg. 19/Attic	6:30 P.M.	Ernst Östreicher: Experiences of a Theater Professional.

Sunday, July 16, 1944

Hauptstr. 22/82	6:30 P.M.	Dr. Emil Meissner: Taxes and the Science of Finance (c).

During the same week, the following "Jewish lectures" were offered (the places and times have been omitted):

Monday – "Herzl Memorial"
Tuesday – Dr. Josef Pollak "Jewish Mysticism"
Wednesday – "Bialik Celebration" (in Hebrew)
Thursday – "Herzl Celebration." Speakers: Dr. Adolf Grünfeld, JUD. Karl
    Fleischmann. Accompanied by the Fischer Choir.
    Paul Kohn "Intellectual Trends in Judaism."
Friday – Eng. Otto Zucker, JUDr. Karl Fleischmann: "Herzl and Us"
    Dr. Jakob Jacobsohn: "Herzl and Hirsch, Two Opposite Poles"
Saturday – A. Schön: "Optimism in Judaism"
    Hebrew celebration hour: Egon Redlich: "Creative Youth"
Sunday – Fritz Baum: "Herzl as Poet"

This adds up to thirty-three official lectures, in addition to all the other presentations, in one week! A list of the "general lectures" during the week of August 14 to August 20, 1944, can serve as a comparison:

Monday:

Adolphe Hamburger recites from "Jaakob's Dream" by Beer-Hoffman.
    D. Wasserman sings Dutch folk songs, S. Duke: Sephardic songs,
    S. V. D. Bergh: piano.
Dr. Elise Deiner: Hiking Tours Through the Heights and Depths of Nature.
Dr. Max Popper: 19th-Century Prague (c).

Tuesday:

Alice Bloemendaal: The Child in Literature (French).

530   *Sociology*

Dr. Oscar Goetz: The Figure of Shylock.
Dr. Georg Siegmann: Helgoland.
Dr. E. Sonneberger: The Economic Significance of Money.
Prof. Dr. Otto Blumenthal: Integral Theorems of the Theory of Function.

Wednesday:

Rudolf Knapp: Visits to Painters' Studios (c).
Prof. Dr. Max Brahn: Nietzsche's "Zarathustra" (with excerpts and explanations) V.
Else Dormitzer: From My Memories.
Dr. Wilhelm Mautner: Unknown Holland II. (repeat).

Thursday:

Max Böhm – Franz Weil: Evolution of Modern Oil Painting.
Counselor Dr. Heinr. Klang: Legal Life in Theresienstadt (Scholarly Society).
Dr. Richard Bäumel: Cheerful Memories (c).
Alice Bloemendaal: André Gide (French).

Friday:

Dr. James Simon: Romantic Piano Music I: Felix Mendelssohn-Bartholdy (with
   examples performed at the piano).
Dr. Fritz Goldschmied: Basic Physics.
Dr. Walt. Stern: How Is Illness Inherited?
Engineer E. Pollak: The Engineer's Statistics.

Saturday:

Dr. Gerhard Knoche: From His Own Works (Animal Sketches and Poems).
Lecturer Dr. Ludwig Cohn: Remarks on the 2nd Part of Faust.
Docent Dr. Leopold Pollak: Food Chemistry and Nutrition.
Dr. Wilhelm Mautner: Petroleum: World Demand and Supply.

Sunday:

Dr. Erich Stern: Reading from the "Iliad" VI and the "Odyssey" IX in the original
   language (with explanations).

It is remarkable how often the presentations addressed topics that had become meaningless in the camp, such as money and taxes; topics concerning memories of a past existence, such as travel and other things far removed from the prisoners' immediate environment; or tragicomic topics such as food chemistry. The efforts of the presenters and the serious interest of the generally numerous listeners deserve the greatest respect and are honorable testimony to the seriousness and intellectual courage of a considerable minority of prisoners. Commemorations of important Jews and non-Jews became occasions for celebration; Zionists (see 33) and Czech-assimilated prisoners vied to honor their role models. Franz Kafka's sixtieth birthday was not forgotten; his sister Ottilie, other relatives, and two of the poet's classmates attended the celebration in his honor. The Jews, who were otherwise easily hypercritical, showed themselves grateful for anything that provided an intellectual counterweight to camp life, trying to overcome it and point a way out of it. This is still valuable, even though escape from reality was the rule, and delving deeper into reality – dealing with it, or even attempting to interpret it and give it meaning – remained the exception. The lectures themselves generally were quite good, and sometimes excellent, and were among the best of the intellectual offerings in Theresienstadt.

Cultural Life

The institution of lectures truly began in the summer of 1942 [actually, it began around New Year's Day of 1942] and ended in May 1945.... The demand for lectures was very strong. 40,000–50,000 ghetto inmates, among them thousands of intellectuals, insistently demanded intellectual stimulation. Young people, who had been without schooling for years, urgently demanded further education. The many professionals needed to share experiences, etc. The situation was greatly complicated by the fact that the authorities had prohibited any form of education or academic research. Thus the program announcements constantly had to resort to camouflage and the organizers of the event themselves had to take responsibility. Special gratitude is due to those, the majority of whom are now dead, in charge of the young people. With great selflessness, they assumed great risks again and again in order to impart to the youth at least a modicum of education.... Because publications of any kind were prohibited, the only venues to communicate the results of scientific or artistic production were lectures or readings. Therefore, the institution of lectures ... fulfilled a much more significant function than would have been the case under normal circumstances, and was therefore divided into the following categories:

1. Scholarly lectures: These centered on the various scholarly associations, for example the law association, the association for further education in medicine, the department of engineering, the academic circle, whose aim it was, in biweekly meetings, to study the problems of existence in Theresienstadt.
2. Language lectures: In addition to the German language, the only one officially permitted, we were able to hold numerous lectures in Czech as well as in English, American, French, Italian, [Dutch,] Hebrew and Yiddish.
3. Jewish lectures: Particular emphasis naturally was placed on discussing the Jewish problem in its entire range.
4. Readings: Some writings composed here, others already existing ...
5. Associations: Small groups of people with common interests – such as women as social educators, nature lovers, etc. – who held their meetings in the form of lectures, followed by discussions.
6. Entertaining lectures: Lighter in character, for relaxation and recreation.

Attendance, which was erratic at first, increased so much that in winter 1943–44 a lecture series dealing with difficult philosophical problems already had a regular audience of nearly 400, despite the bitter cold and an inhospitable room. In some weeks, approximately 100 lectures took place.

Despite all the obstacles, the constant threats to existence, and the wretched poverty of life, a strong desire for serious intellectual fare remained unbroken. It was moving, even elevating, when on the eve of catastrophic transports, organizers and audiences searched for consolation and composure and received it from presentations of true artistic or scientific quality. (325)

The strong cultural drive gained its power, of course, not so much despite but because of the difficulties. It had two main roots: (1) psychological need, which led the prisoners in part to seek an escape from reality and in part to strive to gain control over their circumstances, and (2) the paradoxical heedlessness of existence in the camp. Many of humanity's cares on the other side of the fortress walls no longer applied, and that left a certain cultural freedom as the only possible freedom. One felt or knew oneself to be on the brink of great danger, close to the destruction of life. One was relieved of a great many duties toward one's relatives and oneself. Outside, war was raging, and one could do nothing to influence it except through one's wishes. Were this war to devastate the world, people told themselves, at least it was being fought also for the sake of the prisoners, who were far too easily inclined to regard Theresienstadt as the center of world events. All intellectual forces were given a previously unimaginable forum and demanded active expression in order to justify their vigorous existence in this "interim period." About what else should worried thoughts concern themselves other than the fate of this "ghetto" – one's relatives and oneself. There were the transports, of course. Like violent death, they had taken many loved ones from the community. But did departure necessarily have to mean death? Couldn't one survive even in the "East"? Thus departure was still better than death. It was easier to be consoled by a lack of knowledge than by the certain knowledge of death. And those who had been deported to Theresienstadt alone could derive satisfaction from the notion that their loved ones probably were living in circumstances more pleasant than here, in England, in America.... For many people, remembering their relatives, if they believed them to be saved, was heartening.

These were circumstances that lent mental freedom to the best people in particular, making their lives more bearable and encouraging them to engage in lively cultural activity. This culture should not be judged by normal standards, for it had to share in and reflect the pathological aspects of the camp. The more deeply this culture penetrated, the more painful were the features it exhibited, for not even the most steadfast natures were ever allowed to stand entirely above it all. This was prevented by the endless pressure of life in the camp, which weighed heavy on everyone. It is one thing for a wise man to be aware of the inevitable proximity of death in the midst of life, and to be reminded that death is always a possibility, that – as the familiar story goes – a brick might fall from a nearby roof and end one's life; it is quite another for a man to be captured in a murderous enemy's trap, which could crush him to death literally at any minute. People may bear this pressure – they had to and did bear it – but it was engraved on their souls; thus even the most worthwhile cultural statements, to the extent that they were not limited to purely ethical topics, were suffused with these sufferings. One *was* in the camp, after all, and this had consequences always and everywhere. No one can live on intellect alone, and few can live almost exclusively on it, without ever, threatened and hungry, thinking about deportations or his next meal.

Private cultural life in the camp had a quality all its own; it frequently was limited to personal work or intimate exchange, but it often did reach the public. The elderly Philipp Manes from Berlin, whose enthusiasm and intellectual interests endeared him to everyone, deserves particular credit. His position as head of the "orientation service" (see Chapter 5), which was made up of elderly gentlemen, was not enough for him and left him sufficient time to organize more than 500 lectures and other presentations, which for a long time were held in his dark, angular office in B V (see 178c). Manes knew how to engage excellent lecturers and readers and added atmosphere to the evenings through his moving, informal introductory and concluding remarks. It was important to him to support the writings produced in Theresienstadt, particularly those of young talent. Because the room was small, people had to approach Manes for tickets, unless one was invited to attend in the form of a handwritten and decorated invitation. Manes, a patron in the camp, held poetry competitions, complete with prizes (see 3b, doc. 178); religious celebrations for the Jewish holidays; readings of classical pieces with assigned roles (e.g., an unabridged version of *Faust I*, split into two evening performances, and *Nathan the Wise*); and a recitation of the lyrical drama written in Theresienstadt, "Orpheus," by Georg Kafka, which was often repeated with great success. The following is one of Manes's monthly programs (dates are omitted):

Cultural Life

Orientation Service Lecture Series

B V, Room A 6, II. Courtyard
For the month of July 1943

Dr. Carl Castelin: "Early Assyrian History"
Councilor Professor Dr. Heinrich Klang: "From My Life"
Rabbi Dr. Neuhaus: 3rd lecture "Midrash"
Variety Hour
Oscar Quittner: "To India with the Bata Plane"
Prof. Dr. Maximilian Adler: "Aristotle"
Dr. David Schapira: "The Blind and Their World"
In memoriam Arthur Schnitzler: Introductory Remarks by Dr. Bacher,
   "Countess Mizzi"
Czech Poetry and Music
Prof. Dr. Maximilian Adler: "Socrates and the Sophists"
Dr. Rudolf Freiberger: "Preserved Music"
Siegmund Reis: "The Changing Figure of the Jew in German Dramatic Literature"
Dr. Rolf Grabower: "Fellowship – Community"
Variety Hour
Rabbi Dr. Schön: "From the Workshop of Ancient Jewish Story Tellers"
Prof. Dr. Emil Utitz: "Overcoming Expressionism"
Lessing's "Nathan the Wise"
Variety Hour
Rabbi Dr. Leo Baeck: "Spinoza"
Dr. Desider Friedman: "From My Life"

Lectures begin at 6 P.M.

Manes's invitation on the occasion of his 200th event read as follows: "Professor Dr. Emil Utiz discusses "Classical Man" – Friday, August 27 – Room A 6 – 6:45 P.M. Due to limited space we request speedy response [stamp] to the assistance service of the Ghetto Guard – lecture series [signed] Ph. Manes." Manes, too, was sent to his death in the fall of 1944 (see 178b).

The heads of the self-administration and their families also displayed cultural ambitions. They invited people to events in their offices and, even more frequently, in their rooms. The best-known events were evenings with the Council of Elders members Dr. Klapp, Zucker, Grünberger, and Dr. Eppstein. The style was simple at Dr. Klapp's events, where chamber music was performed every week in sight-readings; Klapp usually played the cello (see 3b, doc. 202). Anybody who wanted to could attend, as long as there was sufficient space. Zucker, one of the most musically gifted people in the leadership, acted as a patron of the artists and made it possible for painters and musicians to work undisturbed as much as possible. He himself was a good violinist; he had the finest private library in the camp and was the only one to own a gramophone, along with some precious records. He and Eppstein also had brought a piano into their rooms. Zucker hosted regular evenings featuring concerts, gramophone music, readings, lectures, and discussions. It was not easy to attend these events; the circle of those admitted resembled a small royal court but also represented a certain cultural elite. There were similar evenings hosted by the parochial, vain, yet harmless Grünberger, who attempted to compete with Zucker for the status of sponsor of the premier cultural center in the camp, but he did not possess

534   *Sociology*

Zucker's breeding or cultivation. The evenings at Grünberger's were sometimes characterized by unintentional comedy, but the artists came anyway; the painters depended on him because he was nominally their superior and controlled the drawing and painting equipment. Sometimes the evenings in his, Eppstein's, or Zucker's rooms consisted of advance performances of programs that would later be presented to the public; the following is an example of one such evening: "Invitation! – Tuesday, November 30, 1943 – punctually at 8:15 P.M. – B V – Mr. Julius Grünberger, engineer, and wife – room 250 – request your company for an evening of readings of selected Theresienstadt poetry – direction Dr. Felix Noskowski – cast: Steiner – Lerner – Perlsee – from the works of 10 Theresienstadt poets."

The intellectual activity among older people, in particular, is evident in a note written by Mrs. Else Dormitzer, who was in Theresienstadt from April 1943 until liberation:

> I had the following occupations in Theresienstadt: domestic service (toilet and washroom guard), supervision of bread deliveries, potato peeler, coal-cart pusher, librarian, [mail] censor, post office employee. As a member of "Recreation," I gave 275 lectures on 22 topics (literary, travel, Jewish); they were given unscripted, and all found a large and grateful audience. I spoke not only publicly, but also in many hospitals, infirmaries and old-age homes. It was deeply satisfying to me to be able to remove the listeners for an hour from the atmosphere of Theresienstadt; I always succeeded in doing that.

Where possible, people – especially young people – played sports. Soccer was the most popular and initially was played in the yard of H V. This location, much like another one at the "Südberg" later on, made possible only games with teams of seven players. There was established a "Theresienstadt soccer league," with prizes. The standings were publicly displayed. In addition to teams organized according to membership in former clubs and to countries of origin, players also were grouped by occupation: ghetto guards, electricians, gardeners, employees of the Youth Welfare Office, clothing warehouse workers, cooks, butchers, and so on (see 3b, doc. 172).

Books played a very prominent role in the camp. Almost everybody had brought with him a few volumes, usually quality works that one might wish to read again and again. Some people had thirty or more books in their luggage, which spoke to the high level of education among the prisoners. The prisoners had chosen books such as Bibles, literary and philosophical classics, books of poetry, and scholarly works – such as a mathematical treatise or a Chinese grammar – to console themselves during the deportation. During the period of closed barracks there were no libraries, but lending services were set up from private collections. During the late summer of 1942, a "bookstore" was to have been established, in addition to the other stores, but the inmates succeeded in preventing this and obtaining permission for a "central ghetto library." The library was prudently headed from its first day until the dissolution of the camp by Professor Emil Utitz. On the occasion of its one-year anniversary on November 17, 1943, the following "report" was prepared:

> Note concerning establishment of a library and study room [included in the "report"].
> Process: Commissioned by Camp Commandant SS-Obersturmführer Dr. Seidl.
>
> I.   Book Inventory:
>   At this time, the ghetto has a small stock of books at its disposal.

Cultural Life

a. A portion ... derives from communal property from previous transports and will be collected, organized and catalogued. A list ... will be given to the camp commandant for review.

b. A second portion derives from book supplies confiscated during the search of luggage from arriving transports. It is requested that these books be handed over to the Council of Elders.... .

This stock of books may well be significantly enlarged and improved if books from the homes of evacuated Jews ... are made available once they have been viewed and selected. [To some extent, this happened in Prague.]

The books currently available consist of light reading, but also of books with more serious content, didactic writing, etc.... and probably do not exceed ... a total of 4,000 books.... The only books that shall be circulated are those that were released ... by the Camp Commandant's Office after inspection of the lists ["undesirable" and valuable books were concealed from the SS].

II. The Space Issue

... the bookstore [Q 619] ... shall be used. This store is too small.... .

III. The Lending Library

Therefore the following is suggested ... :

1. Light reading ... , which might be appropriate on average for the very aged and the ill.

2. Books of more serious content ... , which might be appropriate for a narrower circle of readers.... .

It is assumed that the existent books will comprise about 3,000 of the former and about 1,000 of the latter category. From holdings ... of the first category ... small traveling libraries of about 30 volumes each could be established.... .

These traveling libraries will lend books to individual houses ... according to a schedule. The house elder will receive the box of books and ... distribute the books.... . In approximately 14 days, the house elder will return the box, after which ... it will become available to another house according to schedule...

As the inventory increases, the number of circulating book boxes will be increased.... .

Books in the second category ... can become available for loan ... at the lending libraries in the usual way.... .

To avoid too much growth in the number of readers, a user permit shall be issued to appropriate persons.... .

The holdings of small reference libraries containing specialized sections shall not be affected by this regulation.... .

Theresienstadt, October 29   1942 Council of Elders

Work began on the basis of this memorandum... , so that the orders of the day for November 22, 1942, announced:

Ghetto Library:

The ghetto library will ... open on November 25, 1942, in L 304 [a former store with adjacent rooms. There was not enough space. During "beautification" in the spring of 1944, it was moved to L 514, into adequate rooms.] It is equipped as a traveling library. Depending on the available inventory, book boxes will be loaned out .. to the building or house elders. Initially, however, only a small number of boxes can be circulated.

Individual borrowers can only be persons with a special interest. A special permit ... will be issued to these persons ... by the head of the library, Prof. Dr. Emil Utitz.... .

Activity report for the initial year:

1.) The "Theresienstadt Central Ghetto Library" ... today [November 17, 1943] owns 48,710 volumes.

2.) The stock of fiction volumes is very small. The available space is very cramped.... . They are being circulated as "traveling libraries." In this way a virtue is made of necessity, because a significant influence over the reading public can be exerted through Jewish fiction.

3.) The large inventory in other subject areas makes it possible to set up the library as a research library. It is available as a lending library to people who can prove scholarly, artistic or religious expertise.

4.) Each borrower is obliged to make a security deposit of 50 ghetto crowns. Generally, only one volume per party may be borrowed. To date, security deposits of 120,000 ghetto crowns [2,400 persons] have been made to the bank.

5.) In order to place each book where it will have optimal effect ... agreements have been made with the Health Services, Youth Welfare, the Central Medical Library and the library of the Young Hebraists.... .

6.) Infirmaries, contagious disease hospitals and homes for tuberculosis patients were supplied with reading material by giving them books that otherwise would have been destroyed, as well as duplicate newspapers.

7.) Prayer books were made available to the rabbinate [registry office] free of charge; they were also handed out to individuals; the sum of distributed prayer books is approximately 5,000 copies.

8.) The New-Hebraists, who ... established a library of their own, were supported through the handover of nearly all holdings in Yiddish and New-Hebrew.

9.) The reading room was opened in June of last year. It receives approximately 110 visitors per day.

10.) The general lack of viable reading materials, as well as the heavy demands on the library and the reading room, resulted in a number of restrictive measures.

[A frequency table reflects the constant rise in the number of individual borrowers: there were 115 borrowers in December 1942 and 3,775 in October 1943. A classification of holdings follows:]

Hebraica	10,810
Hebrew Magazines	270
Judaica [Zionist writings]	10,930
Jewish Magazines	1,900
Yiddish Literature	100
Philosophy (general and religious philosophy)	1,550
History (art and music history)	1,300
Ancient Languages	600
Modern Languages	500
Natural Sciences	600
Publications	2,100
Activity Reports	7,000
Fiction	5,300
Classics	3,000
Materials for Young Readers	250
Miscellaneous	2,500
Total	48,710

Cultural Life

[The number of employees rose from six to seventeen (later it rose even higher). An essay attached to the report and written by the librarian Hugo Friedmann, who was sent to his death in the fall of 1944, follows, in abbreviated form:]

The Ghetto Library of Theresienstadt ... most likely is the only public library of its rank in Europe that is unable to have any direct influence whatsoever on its holdings and its acquisitions. Because it is entirely dependent for its incoming materials on consignments from outside and on donations, its shape has emerged on its own and haphazardly. In spite of this, the library has gained a particular profile that is characteristic of the conditions of development of the Jewish settlement.

The Central Ghetto Library [Ghettozentralbücherei (GZB)] emerged from the holdings of Youth Welfare, donations from the authorities, the remnants of German-Jewish private libraries from Prague and Brünn [Brno], as well as, in large part, from the holdings of various *Hachsharot* libraries, the traveling library of the Association of Prussian District Communities, the Jewish *Kulturbund* in Germany and the Academy for the Study of Jewry in Berlin. . . .

We will evaluate the GZB according to two criteria:

as a library of entertaining fiction and
as a Jewish research library.

Given the number of people interested, the fiction holdings are not substantial. The influx of private donations is not very significant. Further, ... a large number of books in circulation were lost as a result of evacuations of quarters and work transports. . . . An attempt is made through collective reading (reading aloud) of individual books to make them accessible to the largest possible number of readers. . . . It is understandable . . . that this process ... does not fully satisfy the hunger for reading materials. The reader is forced to read the book slowly ... and to contemplate it. The skimming of texts, habitual from earlier newspaper reading, is made more difficult. . . .

The research library ... is a library of a special quality as a Jewish library. Its holdings of Zionist and Judaic literature represent the accessible specialized literature in nearly complete collections. Corresponding to origin ... the Bible-related literature (exegesis, homiletic, rhetoric, etc.) preponderates . . . ; it is followed by various specialized texts by Protestant and Catholic theologians, Bible translations in most languages and by the most important translators and commentators.

It is understandable that ... philosophy takes up a great deal of space. First of all, there is religious philosophy, with works by Christian and Jewish scholars, yet the philosophy of Islam is also well represented. The holdings in general philosophy may be modest, but most of the classics are available in good, if perhaps outdated, editions, ending with Hermann Cohen. Modern philosophy is unfortunately completely missing.

The opus of Latin and Greek writers is available almost in its entirety in the original languages. . . . Foreign-language literature is available, if only in small quantities, in most European languages.

Some fiction is available in the English language, as well as a great deal of Judaica from the USA, some aesthetic works in French and a history of Judaism; there also are books in Italian, Spanish and Norwegian, and a rich selection of Hungarian classics. Unfortunately, the available holdings in Czech are entirely insufficient and unable to satisfy ... even the most modest requirements. In accordance with the original character of the library, its holdings of Orientalistics are particularly large. There are works in Arabic, Persian and Turkish, as well as a rich selection of Assyrian texts. . . .

Naturally, Jewish history is documented almost completely. Many copies of both the older historians (Flavius, Jost, Ewald, Cassel, Herzfeld, Schürer, Bäck, Grätz) and the modern historians (Weinheimer, Brann, Stern, M. Philippson, Dubnow) are available. Jewish literary history is represented by Winter, Wünsche, Zunz, Karpeles, Bernfeld, and

538   *Sociology*

Klausner. Various important complete works of general world history are in stock, in addition to numerous historical publications from antiquity to most recent times. It goes without saying that a wealth of books are available on the history of religion, as well as Jewish local chronicles,

The holdings of technical, chemistry, physics and mathematics works are scarce Equally unsatisfactory is the number of works on natural science and geographic and ethnographic writings. The same is true of specialized books on law. However, the GZB has particularly ample holdings of works on agriculture, popular medicine, commercial specializations and cookbooks, which complete the collection of nonfiction books.

It is understandable ... that the existent travel and autobiographical literature ... is insufficient. One must consider that in the ghetto these areas ... are in particular demand. Sadly, the stock of works dealing with music history and literary history is small.... The situation is similar with art history ... even though numerous monographs on artists and other standard works are present. The available works, however, permit quite a clear overview of the "art history of the Jewish people."

Of the Jewish periodicals, most ... are available. The same is true of the publications of nearly all German-language Jewish scientific institutions, the annual reports of rabbinical seminaries in Germany, Austria and Hungary, and the activity reports of almost all Jewish associations in Germany....

The largest specialized area ... is the Hebrew section.... It includes the most important rabbinical literature, ancient Hebrew philology, as well as numerous Hebrew and Yiddish newspapers.

It may very well be one of the most extensive Hebrew libraries in Europe today.... In addition to other fields ... it includes ... prints dating from the 16th–18th centuries from the famous workshops, with artistically significant woodcuts and copper plates, frequently still in their beautiful contemporary bindings....

Maintaining very close connections with the GZB are the other ghetto libraries such as the Youth Library designed for young people and their counselors, ... the Central Medical Library ... , the specialized Technical Library of the WAP [Wirtschaftsabteilung Produktion (Economic Section for Production)], the New-Hebrew library and the private reading circle in C III begun by Miss Hanne Weil (1,500 volumes). The establishment of such private circles for the exchange of readings in the fields of national economy and sociological literature ... is being undertaken.

The extensive areas covered by the local libraries, the chance to pursue intellectual interests here, the expert advice available ... from library personnel have made the GZB one of the first and foremost cultural institutions in the ghetto. It doubtlessly occupies first place among the self-administered Jewish areas of settlement in Europe and, considering its holdings, is one of the greatest Jewish libraries in the world. (330)

With these strange words the essay ends, and with it this remarkable report. Books from Germany and Prague were brought in on boats from the river Elbe and in train carloads. The SS's intentions are not entirely clear in this case, because the library was not used for propaganda purposes nearly as often as was the "money economy" and the courts. Be that as it may, the prisoners in Theresienstadt benefited from this property stolen from Jewish institutions and private collections. Its size increased steadily, and during the "beautification" a "popular reading room," with a small library of its own, was established in the "community house."

> ... Let it be mentioned right from the start that, over the years, there had passed through the hands of the librarians far more than 200,000 volumes, of which only about half remain. The loss is due to wear and tear, transports, departures [at the end of the war] and infectious diseases. The [1944] fall transports, in particular, resulted in a

catastrophic decline in the holdings.... It should be gratefully acknowledged that we always succeeded in finding enthusiastic and selfless officials. Unfortunately, most of them, older, younger and very young people, are no longer alive.

Our organization was as follows:

1.) Traveling Library.... We were able to invest 50,000 volumes in this way.
2.) Specialized Libraries. All departments had these, particularly Youth Welfare with its numerous homes.... Between 20,000 and 25,000 volumes found their way to the public in this way.
3.) Social Libraries. These were established in all hospitals, homes for invalids and tuberculosis wards....
4.) Individual Lending Libraries.... The monthly patronage varied between 2,000 and 4,000 persons. Thus it was possible to utilize our large collection of scientific holdings.
5.) Popular Reading Room. A library comprising 6,000 volumes, which had been compiled according to educational criteria. This hall was constantly filled beyond capacity.
6.) Exhibits. In this way we attempted to familiarize the public with masterworks of Jewish culture.
7.) Hebrew Room. With 10,000 relevant works for specialized research.
8.) Prayer books.... Over time, 8,000 volumes were acquired.

In summary, it may be said that all legitimate reading requests were for the most part satisfied. In spite of severe obstacles, we succeeded in creating a center of cultural activity, and even in rescuing a number of prohibited works. (326)

The total assets consisted of 180,000 volumes, three-quarters of which were from Czechoslovakia and a quarter from Germany. In addition to these volumes, which were meant for the "Central Library," the SS also brought in approximately 60,000 works of Judaica, some of them extremely valuable and rare. These books were to be catalogued for Nazi purposes, according to the Prussian State Library system, by the "Book Registration Group" (see 191) under Murmelstein's guidance (see also 247). Most of its learned members were sent to their deaths in the fall of 1944. By the end of the war, approximately half the material had been catalogued. The SS also assigned other scientific and pseudoscientific tasks, among them a retranslation of several passages of the Talmud. For a long period, a Jewish group, headed by Dr. Weidmann, had to work in the "office," cutting out and collecting any texts in National Socialist periodicals relating to Jews and Jewry.

Religious life played a relatively minor role, and it also remained on the sidelines officially. The majority of the younger prisoners, especially Czechoslovaks, had only weak ties to religion and were not much interested in its public cultivation. The situation was different among German and Viennese Jews, among whom members of all Jewish denominations could be found. Camp activity paid little attention to the Jewish religious calendar. People cooked and ate what food was available, and not many fasted on the Day of Atonement. On Passover it was possible, by request, to obtain different food, as well as matzoh made in the camp in place of bread – but not many took advantage of this. Very few observed the ritual dietary laws; it would have been very difficult to do so, given the nature of camp food, without avoiding meat altogether. For a time, a small ritual kitchen was set up. The work assignments took little account of the Sabbath, even aside from the attitude of the SS. Religious life seldom gained greater depth in the camp, and it certainly took place only outside traditional practices; it was much more common to turn indifferently away from religion. Even though Edelstein and other leading men were attached to traditional religious practices, the prisoners rarely were influenced in this direction. Among the young people, too, more effort was made to impart national than religious education; even though importance was placed on observing the Sabbath and the holidays, this was done primarily for national reasons. All the youth homes had homemade menorahs, made of wood or tin, for Chanukah, and the youth homes, along with some of the adult quarters, celebrated Passover seders, in which they had to make do with nothing but substitutes. There were even lithographed depictions of seder plates for this purpose.

> Groups planning to hold seders on April 7 and 8 must report this to the district or building elder in charge by April 3 at the latest, including the number of people and the quarters in which the seder is to be held. If no one in the group is familiar with the seder rites, this is to be reported so that the rabbinical office can make the appropriate persons available.
> (memorandum from the Department of Internal Administration, March 25, 1944)

Booths were built in the barracks courtyards for Succoth, and the children were allowed to celebrate Purim.

The majority of prisoners witnessed Jewish religious rituals only during memorial services. The ritual washing of the dead and the customary prayers and songs were observed. Because mistakes had occurred during memorial speeches, Leo Baeck composed a simple address, which from that point on was read in German and Czech at all funerals. After the hearse with the coffins had departed, people came together for Kaddish. Services were tolerated from the beginning. During the "beautification," the SS even ordered that they be held. Religious objects from all the religious communities in the Protectorate were collected in Prague (see 332); from there, Torah scrolls and other ritual items needed for services were sent to the camp. Many transports from the Reich brought ritual items from German communities.

Rabbis from many different countries were present in the camp, most of them elderly gentlemen. Four rabbis, including Baeck, were part of the Council of Elders. Prayer rooms were set up in some of the rooms and attics, some of which were even referred to as "synagogues" or "temples," although at the same time they were considered part of the "Recreation Office." Services were held every Sabbath and on holidays. The smaller rooms could barely accommodate the constant visitors, such that the devout had to secure space beforehand. The members of several German congregations met regularly in order to listen to sermons by their rabbis. During the "beautification," a prayer room was set up in the Sokol House. In 1945, the prayer room in B V was renovated and decorated by a painter.

The proportion of Christians of different denominations, who had been brought to the camp as a result of the "race laws," rose to 36% of the prisoners by 1945. Although later they rarely faced any difficulties and were granted prayer rooms, as a minority, they still sought to justify their existence in this Jewish camp through a strict religious life. The Catholics were better organized than the various Protestant denominations. Among Catholics (see 10), the Viennese occupied the most prominent position; among Protestants (see 84, 101a), the Dutch held this position. The Catholics never had an ordained priest; the Protestants had a minister from Holland only after September 1944. Regular services and celebrations of the major church holidays were observed.

The relationship between Jews and Christians was outlined in Chapter 10. Baeck's quietly effective work promoted peace among the denominations, and it is worth mentioning that he, to whom the cultural life in Theresienstadt owed so much thanks to his personal efforts and invaluable advice, gave lectures to one of the Catholic groups at their own request.

It was odd that many Jews, accustomed to the main formal rituals of the Christian year, could not refrain even in the "ghetto" from celebrating Christmas. Many unbaptized Jews exchanged small presents, and fir branches were brought into their rooms without much protest.

The "coffeehouse," too, played a cultural as well as a social role. Admission was gained by way of tickets that were free of charge but not always easily attainable; they were much coveted by older people, whereas many younger people rarely frequented this place. One's turn came only once in the rotation; one appeared punctually at the appointed time and was seated by a waiter (in the appropriate costume) at a table with a marble surface. One would sit at the table almost like a student in a classroom, in the always overcrowded space, until one had to leave two hours later. After 2 P.M., there were performances in almost constant succession, and although the piano was in particularly poor shape, serious artists still often played an hour of good music, unless cabaret performances or light music were offered instead. It was the saddest coffeehouse in the world, but it gave the older people some better moments, which they accepted with gratitude; no loud words were spoken, and they listened in rapt silence (see 3b, doc. 196). The outdoor concerts in the summer of 1944 were less noted. They were rightfully considered a mockery, however good the music was.

Arts and crafts played an important role. In the quarters, the desire for personal ornaments and one's own decorations was especially widespread among younger people. People made rings, bracelets, brooches, necklaces, and pendants from various kinds of material, sometimes taking elaborate designs as models. The makers could count on an illegal, yet tolerated, additional income. In some of the rooms one could see objects made of wood or ceramics, often artistically designed. There were unusual handicrafts made of wire or engraved metal. These and other products made in Theresienstadt were given as presents and were much admired. From wire, a blind sculptor formed peacocks and other animal figures, which were mounted on wooden bases.

An odd material value was placed on cultural accomplishments. The "Recreation Office" remunerated special service providers or volunteer workers through the "workers' care," doing so with the usual "bonuses" of sugar, margarine, meat paste, or gingerbread. Thus for giving a lecture, performing in a concert, creating a stage design, or producing a new composition, one proudly collected a small paper bag of sugar or other treats. Popular artists almost always had materially influential benefactors. Some of the good, or even bad, painters and illustrators enjoyed the best conditions; for their works – which often replaced photographs or color lithographs that were not available – they received significant amounts of food and cigarettes. Certain painters, including Peter Kien and Dolfi Aussenberg, had painted their rooms with cheerful frescoes; then other people also ordered frescoes. Musicians, actors, and so on, also were materially supported by their sponsors.

Nevertheless, the material background of art and culture played a much smaller role in Theresienstadt than in a normal society. More important were indirect rewards, a generally respected position, a lucrative or comfortable job, better quarters, advantages for one's family, and most significantly – quite generous internal transport protection until the fall of 1944. Kien and some other artists unfailingly took care of newly arrived artists, so as to secure protection and acceptable living conditions for them.

In all fairness, significant accomplishments were made in Theresienstadt in art, medicine, science, and engineering. Even if much of this cultural life was meaningful only for the moment and for the small world of the coerced community, and if other parts of it were merely vain and superficial, the foundation itself was strong and resilient. In Theresienstadt the prisoners defied their inevitable doom until the last day and stood their ground. There came together people who once had played outstanding roles in academic, artistic, religious, political, economic, military, and social life. United in common suffering were former ministers, diplomats, parliamentarians, high state officials, university professors, scholars in all areas of learning, physicians, lawyers, engineers, artists, theater people, men of letters, teachers, industrialists, high-ranking officers, and aristocratic Jews – a colorful assortment from the wide world, among them European celebrities and parents, siblings, children, and heirs of people with famous names. After years of success, they were to spend their final days with "makeshift quarters," "ration cards," and "transport numbers," and with their "building elders." All were thrown together: people who had only just been elevated as a result of recent events; people from cities and villages; people who once had been rich or poor, respected or despised; Jews and non-Jews; the sensitive and the dull; noble-minded people who sacrificed themselves, along with common criminals; the sick and the tired; and unsheltered youths, from among whom the very talented would be found and protected. To mention even briefly the most remarkable of the people who lived in this camp for a time would go beyond the scope of this book. I can only make a small and necessarily subjective selection, through which I would like to commemorate some of the young artists to whom I was closer, or about whom I know more. Nor will I speak of those who survived the war, or of those whose lives were extinguished here or in the East but whose most significant accomplishments were achieved before the years of deportation. My intention is limited to commemorating a number of artists, most of whom reached maturity only in the camp, and who are in my opinion characteristic of the cultural life typical of Theresienstadt.

In no other art form could the camp be portrayed as immediately – without temporal remove – as in painting. Almost everything of significance was initially perceived through the eye, and themes were plentiful, even if they did not move the creative spirit or the painting hand to act. All great painters of horror possess an agitated temperament and perhaps had to seek the menacing and uncanny themselves. In Theresienstadt, agitation was a given; it was inescapable and overwhelming. To pass over the world of misery and the transports, and to see only the human face or the topographical motifs, one needed to be old and detached, such as the painter Stein from Prague or Mrs. Else Argutinsky from Berlin. This was not the case for younger talents. In addition to most of the children, who were encouraged to do so, hundreds of people painted and drew. The majority dabbled or worked (even commercially) with stencils, but they sometimes were gripped by a desire to depict the

Cultural Life

horror of the camp. Many of these efforts are interesting from a documentary perspective, but here I would like to focus on only five illustrators and painters.

Fritta (a contraction of Fritz Taussig), born in 1907, saw and recorded the evil most clearly and ruthlessly, and sometimes even pitilessly. He arrived from Prague with the first "Construction Kommando" and became head of the illustration room of the "Technical Department," which emerged as the center of fine arts. Together with Kien and other illustrators, as well as some calligraphers, he himself drew or supervised countless illustrations for reports to the SS; much like Kien, he never was able to hide what he thought of the "ghetto." If we compare his depiction of the same motif in an illustration for a report and in a drawing made of his own accord, we recognize a consistent point of view on two levels. Fritta never attempted to soften his harsh and bitter impression with a conciliatory note; he sought to expose the cruelty and inhumanity around him. As it was not possible to make etchings or wood engravings, he worked with pen and brush, mostly in ink. Inclined to harshness in his personality, he judged his environment unsparingly and took his subjects to dramatic extremes, depicting scenes such as departing transports and scenes from the Schleuse, attics with helplessly fumbling old people, emergency infirmaries, blind and crippled people in courtyards, dark casemates with knots of people, young people in their rooms, and theater and cabaret performances in building courtyards. He portrayed the diabolical quality of the "beautification" – a fashionable lady applying makeup to one side of the garishly illuminated face of an old man, while the other side reveals his unvarnished decay – and Theresienstadt as a Potemkin village, with some houses and several "shops" as a backdrop, and behind them skeletons and barbed wire. Other subjects included a withered, shivering woman, wrapped in blankets, fetching her watery soup; a haggard child on a cot in a cheerless courtyard; and abandoned pieces of luggage among walls and barbed wire (see 3b, 80, 81).

Fritta, Unger, and three other painters and their families were arrested for "atrocity propaganda" on July 17, 1944, and were taken to the "Small Fortress." Fritta died miserably in Auschwitz. The works of these painters were quickly hidden and buried. Some were retrieved after the war, but much is lost.

The physician Karel Fleischmann, from Budweis, was, in addition to his official role as director of the "Welfare Department" (see Chapter 17), a prolific painter and poet who approached his artistic accusations with the eyes of a doctor and welfare worker. His office gave him access to scenes less frequently witnessed by other painters. Because of his lack of time, he confined himself mainly to sketches in pencil, pen, or brush, drawn with a few strokes, yet fully realized works of his have also been preserved. Although he was inferior to Fritta as an artist, he surpassed him in maturity. Like Fritta, he softened nothing; but he sought to depict human misery more than pervasive horror. He immersed himself in the helpless existence of old women and exhausted cripples and explored the most hidden recesses of the town (see 3b). Fleischmann was sent to his death in the fall of 1944. His poems did not achieve the raw power of his drawings, yet they were among the best Czech-language literary achievements in the camp (see 63–68). What follows is a translation of the first stanza of his poem "Transport":

> There are walking numbers, once called humans
> Walking one after the other, a tangled band,

They are no longer walking, because they are writhing,
In the folded gut of alleys, disappearing.

[*Es gehen Ziffern, Menschen einst genannt,*
Und gehn einander nach, ein wirres Band,
Schon gehn sie nicht, da sie sich winden,
Im Faltenwanst der Gassen schön verschwinden.]

(67)

Otto Ungar, from Brünn [Brno] and born in 1897, was the true painter in the camp, whereas the others mainly drew. In early 1942, he lived in an overcrowded hall in E I and used every moment, even in the bitter cold, to paint watercolors of small scenes and faces. Ungar was a witty melancholic. His humor was expressed in his dealings with people; his melancholy, more in his works. He embodied the prisoners' yearnings; longingly, he observed the outlines of the nearby mountains, which often form the background of his street scenes. His depictions of horror in courtyards and of miserable quarters, his views of corners and courtyards wrenched from tranquility, are the accusations of an elegiac, and many can be considered still lifes of terror, as it were. If Fritta embodied reality itself and Fleischmann its analytic observation, Ungar was the personal perception of this reality. Ungar's journey to human fulfillment took a particularly tragic turn. His right hand was crippled in the "Small Fortress." From there he was sent to Auschwitz and Buchenwald, where he began to work again with his destroyed right hand. Deathly ill, he did survive until liberation but was not granted the chance to return home (see 3b, 323).

Peter Kien, born January 1, 1919, came from a small village in Moravia and arrived in Theresienstadt in 1941, at the age of twenty-two. There, several patrons spoiled this precocious artist so much that he sometimes lost a sense of proportion and self-criticism; nevertheless, he remained refreshingly naïve, elemental, and imaginative and at the same time was a selfless friend and helper to all the other artists. He strove for truth but not accusation; each object was to him first and foremost an object on which to prove his virtuosity. Although he had a strong and supple mind, he was not as intellectual as the artists previously discussed. He was interested in the individual and was intrigued no less by anonymous types than by the important people in the camp. The people he wanted to paint could not avoid him; they had to sit for him, became transparent before his searching gaze, and were almost devoured. His ability to capture character also benefited his excellent caricatures, which often were intentionally repulsive and at other times intentionally benign but always revealed something essential. Kien utilized all types of drawing techniques and also left behind some less successful oil paintings. He also tried his hand – with less luck but here too with talent – at writing dramas, fairy tales, and poems (see 3b, 141–143). In October 1944, Kien, the ever-faithful son, perished with his wife and parents in a gas chamber in Auschwitz.

Dolfi Aussenberg, from Prague, was a few years older than Kien. From early childhood on, he had been bedridden for long periods of time due to a congenital heart defect, and he frequently was ill in Theresienstadt. In this delicate person, who never overcame an artistic amateurishness, lived a touching love of everything beautiful, particularly painting. For him, the world resolved itself into moody reveries, which he tried to capture in the form of southern fantasy landscapes on the

Cultural Life

walls of children's homes and in rooms in the "ghetto." When his health no longer allowed this, he painted watercolors depicting similar themes or animals. Aussenberg was last seen in Auschwitz, where he still was painting. Hardly any of his works survived; so may these words preserve his amiable memory.

Poetry demands a certain internal distance in order to process experiences, and thus in Theresienstadt poets were at a disadvantage compared with painters. The painter can depict, and therefore is better able directly to reflect, the face of life in the camp. The poet needs superior understanding of his subjects, which requires maturity and great ability. Otherwise, he stays on the surface and offers only a report, an illustrative document, that does not even skillfully reproduce reality but instead usually lags objectively behind it and at the same time colors it with too much emotion. Thus poetry in Theresienstadt would have been possible only if it were unrelated to daily problems and external realities or in a superior vision that was achievable only by more mature artists, who could attain a higher reality. The young poets Georg Kafka and Hans Kolben, who are discussed later, were able to strive for artistic poetry only in a realm beyond actual events in the camp, or in opposition to them. The authors who dominated literary activity remained, more or less naturalistically, superficial. Yet their work did not necessarily lack a sense of personal agitation and emotional immediacy, although it could be unintentionally humorous, and the writers could not overcome some small vanities. The immense, mostly lost torrent of these writings consists largely of verses. They are generally clumsy, dreary rhymes, testimony to their aged authors' will to live and their boredom; there also were more sophisticated efforts, which sometimes were remarkable documents but hardly works of art, as their authors hoped. Far less prose was written, aside from many diaries and notes; even longer works – as well as dramas – were a rarity. Verses, and especially rhymes, as a form of lonely social entertainment for oneself, were the only appropriate expressions of the prisoners' will, which probably encouraged not so much actual creativity as preservation – protection in a probably unsuccessful form. However, once more or less achieved outwardly, such expressions granted the poor authors a certain sense of security; writing even an awkward meter promises greater protection and continuity than merely eking out a beaten and merciless existence (for references, see the "Sources and Literature" section).

The first two stanzas of a poem entitled "Dedicated to the Members of the Security Services" may serve as an example of the most commonly practiced flat rhyming:

> It rings like a march through the city's streets,
> No screaming, no shouting of orders,
> The gaze straight ahead, the steps are firm,
> They tell a story of discipline.
>
> Each person is happy to see the crowd,
> As it walks toward the guardhouse.
> The good citizen can rest without care,
> He need not strive for anything.
>
> [*Es hallt wie ein Marsch durch die Strassen der Stadt,*
> *Kein Schreien, kein Rufen von Befehlen,*
> *Grad aus die Blicke, mit festem Tritt,*
> *von Disziplin sie erzählen.*

546　　　　　　　　　　　　　　　　*Sociology*

Es macht jedem Freude, die Schar zu sehen,
Wenn sie auf die Wache gehen.
Der gute Bürger kann sorglos ruhn,
Er braucht sich für nichts zu bemühen.]

Thousands of such poems were written, in German and in all the other languages common in the camp, and they even found grateful admirers.

The literature designed for the public was composed in German and Czech couplets. Here, translated from the Czech, is the refrain of the "Theresienstadt March," by Karl Svenk:

Everyone goes, and those who know how,
Hold each other's hands and see,
To have humor in your hearts despite bad times
Each day, blow by blow
Always the vexation of moving,
And no more than 30 words per letter.
Hurray, life starts tomorrow, and with it comes the time,
When we pack out rucksacks and go home free.
Everyone goes, and those who know how,
Hold each other's hands and see,
We laugh our hearts out on the ruins of the ghetto.

[*Alles geht, wer's versteht,*
Fasst an Händen euch und seht,
Böser Zeit zum Trotz Humor im Herzen haben
Jeden Tag, Schlag auf Schlag,
Stets die Übersiedlungsplag,
Und nicht mehr als 30 Worte für den Brief.
Holla, morgen fängt das Leben an, mit ihm beginnt die Zeit,
Da wir unsre Ranzen packen und nachhause gehn befreit.
Alles geht, wer's versteht,
Faßt an Händen euch und seht.
Und auf Ghettotrümmern lachen wir uns schief.]

(255)

This kind of rousing and unthinking optimism was popular. In his poem "The Cow," Hans Hofer asks why the meat rations are so meager. It begins with the following couplets:

If I consider the present,
I always ask myself, what do people live on?
Because with the rations they give us here,
All one can do is die, not live.
Even though these days we do get hash,
But when I look at the little in my bowl,
I ask myself with a bad conscience,
For this ration an ox had to die.

[*Wenn ich mir betracht so die heutige Zeit,*
So frag ich mich stets, von was leben die Leut?
Denn von den Portionen, die sie uns hier geben,
Da kann man doch sterben, nur aber nicht leben.

Cultural Life   547

> *Zwar haben wir ziemlich oft jetzt Haschée,*
> *Doch wenn ich das Bißl im Eßschuß beseh,*
> *Da frag ich mich immer mit schlechtem Gewissen,*
> *Weg'n dieser Portion hat ein Ochs sterben müssen.]*

(104)

The basic themes of hunger and the transport come up over and over again. The final stanza of "Theresienstadt Dreams," by Rudolf Lederer, may serve as an example of a typical hunger poem:

> I had a nice dream:
> It was fantastic, barely possible.
> I dreamt that without decorations
> I suddenly was a great man.
> Courted by a great many friends,
> I had encounters with love;
> Everyone wanted to be related to me,
> Or at least know me intimately,
> There was no wish that was not granted,
> No desire that was not fulfilled,
> No hope that was crushed,
> I dreamt I was the boss of the kitchen!
>   But when I awoke
>   My proud dream was in shambles.
>
> *[Ich hatte einen schönen Traum:*
> *Der war fantastisch, möglich kaum.*
> *Ich träumt, ich wäre ohne Orden*
> *Mit eins ein großer Herr geworden.*
> *Umworben von der Freunde Menge,*
> *Mit Liebe kam ich ins Gedränge,*
> *Ein jeder wollt mit mir verwandt sein,*
> *Zum mindesten intim bekannt sein,*
> *Kein Wunsch, der sich mir nicht erfüllt,*
> *Kein Sehnen blieb mir ungestillt,*
> *Kein Hoffen ging mir in die Brüche,*
> *Ich träumt, ich wurde Chef der Küche!*
>   *Doch als ich dann erwacht war,*
>   *Mein stolzer Traum zerkracht war.]*

(165)

Here are four stanzas from the transport poem "Recognition," by Kurt Kapper:

> Dear ghetto inmate: let me tell you,
> That you stood proud,
> That you bore the heavy burden,
> Wood planks and boxes and many a load.
>
> You swept and scrubbed the hallways,
> You carefully peeled the potatoes,
> And, as labor deployment affirms,
> You worked yourself to the bone in the kitchen.

548   *Sociology*

You were needed as a mechanic,
And used as a shoemaker in the *Sudeten*
You never smoked in the ghetto
And never sent a letter home.

We thank you, you are a good Jew,
And tell you this straight out.
Now be so good as to pack your suitcase
Because it's your turn to go to Poland.

[*Lieber Ghettoinsasse: Lass dir sagen,
Daß Du Dich brav gehalten hast,
Daß Du die schwere Last getragen,
Bretter und Kisten von jeder Last.*

*Du hast die Gänge gekehrt und gescheuert,
Du hast genauest Kartoffeln geschält
Und, wie der Arbeitseinsatz beteuert,
Dich im Küchendienst abgequält.*

*Als Monteur hat man Dich gebraucht
Und als Shcuster in den Sudeten verwendet,
Niemals hast Du im Ghetto geraucht
Und niemals einen Brief gesendet.*

*Wir danken Dir. Du bist ein braver Jud,
Wir sagen es Dir unverhohlen.
Jetzt pack den Koffer, sei so gut,
Denn Du bist eingereiht nach Polen.*]

(134)

Poems such as the ones quoted previously can be considered the average product of the rhyming disease in Theresienstadt, but there was written a great deal that went deeper in insight and feeling yet remained amateurish as artistic creations. Two excerpts from poems by Ilse Weber serve as samples of this type. The author, who worked as a nurse in Theresienstadt for two and a half years, was asphyxiated with one of her children in 1944 in a gas chamber in Auschwitz.

Transport of the Elderly
A procession of tired old people moves through the city,
Figures bent and heavily burdened,
Toward the train station.
With eyes sightless from tears,
With feet that walk only with great pain,
This is how they walk.
Torn from children, once more expelled,
Robbed of their last possessions,
This is how they walk in silence.
In their hearts, worn down by dread,
In desperation echoes the name of the Almighty,
A plaintive WHY? ...

[*Altertransport
Durch die Stadt zieht ein Zug von müden Alten,
Schwer beladene, gebeugte Gestalten,*

Zur Bahnstation.
Mit Augen, die vor Tränen nichts sehen,
Mit Füßen, die nur mit Schmerzen gehen,
So gehn sie dahin.
Von den Kindern gerissen, aufs Neu vertrieben,
Des Letzten beraubt, was ihnen geblieben,
So schreiten sie stumm.
In ihrem Herzen, zermürbt vor Grauen,
Klingt verzweifelnd auf des Allmächtigen Namen,
Ein klagend WARUM? …]

The Sheep of Lidice
Fleecy, yellow-white sheep trot along the streets,
Two shepherdesses follow the herd; through the dusk one hears their singing.
It is an image full of peace and yet one stops and stands, deeply shaken,
As though one felt the dreadful breath of death passing by.
Fleecy, yellow-white sheep, so far from home,
Their stables are burnt, their masters killed.
Oh, all men of the village, they died the same death,
A small village in Bohemia, and so much misfortune and distress.

. . . .

They are the sheep of Lidice, befitting is their place here,
In the city of the homeless, the homeless creatures.
Surrounded by a wall, thrown together by cruel fate,
The most tormented people on earth, and the saddest herd in the world.

[*Die Schafe von Lidice*
Flockige, gelbweiße Schafe trotten durch die Straßen entlang,
Zwei Hirtinnen folgen der Herde, durch die Dämmerung tönt ihr Gesang.
Es ist ein Bild voller Frieden, und doch bleibt erschüttert man stehen,
Als fühlte des Todes Odem man grausig vorübergehen.
Flockige, gelbweiße Schafe, die sind der Heimat so fern,
Verbrannt sind ihre Ställe, getötet ihre Herren.
Ach, alle Männer des Dorfes, sie starben den gleichen Tod,
Ein kleines Dorf in Böhmen und so viel Unglück und Not.

. . . .

Das sind die Schafe von Lidice, und trefflich am Platze hier,
In der Stadt der Heimatlosen das heimatlose Getier.
Umschlossen von einer Mauer, durch grausamen Zufall gesellt,
Das gequälteste Volk der Erde und die traurgiste Herde der Welt.]

(334)

In this vexed, awkward way, shaken by dread, pity, fear, and despair, laymen and women and some writers attempted to grapple with the day-to-day issues in the camp and to console themselves by writing things down – to liberate themselves and their audiences temporarily through writing, from the ceaseless assault of adversity. Only if viewed in this way can even the best poems of this kind, in relative terms, endure and remain exempt from artistic judgment. I would like to refer to two young authors whose approach went beyond this kind of work.

Georg Kafka of Treplitz-Schönau, a distant relative of Franz Kafka, was twenty-one years old when he arrived, in the summer of 1942. When his mother was sent to

550   *Sociology*

Auschwitz in May 1944, he went with her voluntarily and was sent on to the Schwarzheide camp. Unable to cope mentally or physically with this harsh camp, the young poet died there wretchedly. Overly refined and gentle natured, he responded to the lurid stimuli with an exhausted yet extremely alert melancholy. His genuine talent never was able to mature artistically. His youthful – although not naïve – traits went hand in hand with an almost doddering pessimism that was softened by an often surprisingly detached and resigned nature. In Theresienstadt he was admired as the poet of the camp, and a circle of German- and Czech-language literati and poetry lovers flocked to him. Kafka wrote fairy tales, poems, translations of modern Czech poetry, a prose poem entitled "Alexander in Jerusalem," and a lyric play in sounding rhymed verses entitled "Orpheus" (see 128–130). His dreamlike poetry, which almost never refers to the camp or to issues of the period, can be seen as the accomplishment of a likeable young person who tried to free himself, through poetry, from the difficulties of an unbearable reality. No sample of his larger and better works can be offered, and so what follows is a poem that is a testimony to his pure and, at the same time, tragic disposition rather than a significant work of art:

> **Dedicated to Ph. Manes on the occasion of the 200th lecture organized by him.**
> Love, light and life are the magic lights
> Left to us from Master Herder.
> Oh, the land that we still love in secret,
> Germany is no longer the land of poets.
>
> The cathedral of our God lies in ruins,
> His altar celebrations, deserted, orphaned,
> Where neither priests nor disciples serve,
> Yet we always called this God a spirit,
>
> And you are entirely devoted to him.
> Build him, now, a chapel in the forest,
> A resting place for his last followers.
>
> And at the consecrated place
> The nine muses themselves sometimes visit,
> The altar of love, light and life.
>
> [*Herrn Ph. Manes zum 200. von ihm veranstalteten Vortrag.*
> *Liebe, Licht und Leben sind die Zauberlichter,*
> *Die von Meister Herder uns geblieben.*
> *Ach, das Land, das wir doch heimlich lieben,*
> *Deutschland ist nicht mehr das Reich der Dichter.*
>
> *Unsres Gottes Dom liegt in Ruinen,*
> *Öde feiert sein Altar, verwaist,*
> *Da ihm Priester nicht, noch Jünger dienen,*
> *Doch wir nannten diesen Gott stets Geist,*
>
> *Und du bist ihm gänzlich hingegeben.*
> *Bautest ihm nun eine Waldkapelle,*
> *Seinen letzten Jüngern heimatliche Rast.*
>
> *Und es sind an der geweihten Stelle*
> *Die neun Musen manchmal selbst zu Gast,*
> *An dem Altar Leibe, Licht und Leben.*]

Cultural Life

Insecure and disconnected from daily life in Theresienstadt, Hans Kolben of Prague, who came to the camp in early 1943 at the age of twenty-one, wrote despairing poems. In the fall of the following year his journey led him through Auschwitz to Kauffering, where he recited poems by Goethe and Rilke while at work. There he contracted epidemic typhus, and there he starved to death. Anyone who heard Kolben recite his own or another's verses in his brittle, almost boyish voice had no doubt that this ungainly young man with the huge hands and wonderful large eyes was a born poet. He wrote with difficulty and wrestled with every single verse, while struggling with Rilke and other models who still stood in the way of his own unique character. In Theresienstadt, he wrote a number of serious poems and one story, "The Traveler to the North Pole," in which he described a murder motivated by hunger (see 152, 153). Kolben's deep despair allowed him to absorb more of the horror in his environment than was possible for Georg Kafka, who fled from reality. Kolben's best verses sound like a different, sadder Eichendorff:

> **Premature Death**
> From the forest the huntsman's horn exults,
> Evening shadows are approaching,
> Out there the ripened grain is rustling,
> It rustles in wide yellow waves,
> Waiting for their death by sacrifice.
>
> Riders, moving through the open fields,
> Hooves tread on ripened life,
> They leave behind a trail
> Of the dead, who gave us nothing,
> Who were waiting for a better end.
>
> Why do you sound so sadly, horn,
> And mourn a few yellow sheaves;
> Soon, new grain will have grown once more
> From old and long forgotten scars,
> And all will be well again.
>
> From deepest dreams the horn is heard;
> You're wrong, never will be born again,
> What perished so uselessly and in violence,
> What was lost before the harvest
> Is gone forever, irreplaceable.
>
> [*Vorzeitiger Tod*
> *Vom Wald her jauchzt des Waidmann's Horn,*
> *Der Abendschatten kommt gezogen,*
> *Dort draußen rauscht das reife Korn,*
> *Es rauscht in weiten gelben Wogen,*
> *Die ihren Opfertod erwarten.*
>
> *Es ziehen Reiter durch die Flur,*
> *Die Hufe treten reifes Leben,*
> *Sie hinterlassen eine Spur*
> *Aus Toten, die uns nichts gegeben,*
> *Die eines bessren Endes harren.*

Was tönst du denn so traurig, Horn,
Und klagst um ein paar gelber Garben;
Bald steht von Neuem reifes Korn
Auf alten längst vergeßnen Narben,
Und alles, alles wird gesunden.

Aus tiefem Traum das Horn erschallt:
Du irrst, niemals wird neu geboren,
Was nutzlos umkam durch Gewalt,
Was vor der Ernte ward verloren,
Ist unersetzlich hingeschwunden.]

Whereas in Theresienstadt thematic reference to current events was fruitful for painters and dangerous for poets, in music, such reference is not possible almost by definition. In this sense, we cannot speak of music that was typical of the camp, even though composers took into account the available technical exigencies. Yet relatively high standards could be set, because there were enough artists who were able to perform difficult vocal and instrumental chamber music. Understandably, it was mainly professionals rather than amateurs who engaged in composition. Aside from Karel Reiner, who survived the war, five serious composers worked in Theresienstadt.

Viktor Ullmann, a student of Schönberg, was born in 1898 in Teschen but came from Vienna and later lived in Prague; from there, he was sent to Theresienstadt in the summer of 1942. He had shed Schönberg's influence and loved classical forms, which he cultivated in a unique and technically masterful manner. In Theresienstadt he produced many compositions: songs (including music set to lyrics composed there); theatrical music; the opera *The Emperor [Kaiser] of Atlantis*, set to lyrics written by Peter Kien; choral works (including works set to Hebrew texts); a lost symphony in D major; a string quartet in one movement; and two piano sonatas. At the end, he was planning a Jeanne d'Arc opera, for which he also had written the text. Ullmann was strongest as a vocal composer. He had the unusual gift of interpreting texts with powerful melodic strides, embedded in a fabric of harmonically rich accompaniment, full of thematic variation and counterpoint. He was particularly good at dramatic climax. His instrumental music sometimes is marred by a certain obstinacy, although he freed himself of this trait in exquisite slow movements.

Pavel Haas was born in 1899 and was a student of Janácek's. He arrived at the camp in early 1942 from Brünn [Brno]. He felt as far removed from Judaism as a Czech as Ullmann did as a German. Haas was a cheerful, carefree person who shared Janácek's love of spirited minstrelsy. Thus his work represented quite the opposite of Ullmann's metaphysical ponderings. Nothing could seriously threaten this Brünn [Brno] composer's cheerfulness, and thus even the works he created in the camp seemed unburdened and bright, testimonies to a mature and stylistically settled music, such as his study for string orchestra and many piano pieces.

Hans Krasa, born in Prague in 1895, was the most popular composer in the "ghetto" because of his children's opera *Brundibár*. He studied composition with Zemlinsky and later studied in Paris. Krasa was an imaginative musician with a great deal of humor; his style followed French rather than Central European music. I know only a few of his works from Theresienstadt, among them several choral pieces, including fresh movements to Yiddish folk songs. Ullmann, Haas, and Krasa were consumed by Auschwitz in October 1944.

Cultural Life 553

Siegfried Schul came from Kassel, lived as a refugee in Prague, and arrived in Theresienstadt at the end of 1941. He had begun his studies with Hindemith and completed them in Hába's circle. Schul had a melancholy temperament and was from the start no match for the camp, where he quickly lost an alarming amount of weight and suffered great psychological anguish. He died of consumption in the summer of 1943, at only twenty-seven years of age. In Theresienstadt he wrote short instrumental works, songs, and choral pieces in a ponderous and relentlessly harsh style. He loved to work in strict counterpoint, which he wove into his compositions without regard for harmony. This bitingly painful, cold music can perhaps most readily be considered the musical expression of the "ghetto." Schul, who had delved deeply into Jewish mysticism, underlaid his works with Kabbalistic-religious programs, which he only rarely revealed in his personal dealings. The tormented and morbid nature of this eminently talented man also was evident in some of his poems, which did not survive.

The character and activities of Gideon Klein, born in Prague in 1919, contrasted sharply with this kind of artistic experience in Theresienstadt. He had not yet completed his training when he came to the camp in 1941. According to Kaff, he was the best pianist there. If Schul was unable to offer internal resistance to the ghetto, Klein felt a calling to master it, and thus to serve as a model for others. Like Peter Kien, who was his friend, this extraordinarily handsome and adored young artist stood at the center of the leading social circle in the camp, where his morbid aestheticism was mistaken for true spirituality. This atmosphere was more dangerous to this irritable, talented musician than to the naïve Kien. Klein wrote his coolly mechanical, dynamic music with a natural sense of form. In Theresienstadt he composed a string quartet, piano music, and several impressive choral works. In October 1944, Klein, too, was deported to Auschwitz. In January 1945, while the camp was being evacuated, a gunshot ended his life.

PART III

PSYCHOLOGY

Their visage is blacker than coal; ... their skin is shriveled upon their bones; it is withered, it is become like a stick. Those that are slain by the sword are better than they that are slain with hunger.

Lamentations 4:8–9

Right wouldst Thou be, O Lord, were I to contend with Thee, yet will I reason with Thee.

Jeremiah 12:1

20

The Psychological Face of the Coerced Community

EXPERIMENTATION AND DESTINY IN HISTORY

In introducing his essay "Psychology of Life in Theresienstadt" (327), Emil Utitz remarks that the camp was an "experiment" like no other, and other prisoners, too, could not avoid the feeling that they had been the objects of a monstrous experiment (91, p. 8a). But this expression should be used only with great caution. Every experiment is premised on conscious preparation and implementation. Yet this hardly was the case in National Socialist Germany, and particularly not in Theresienstadt. The SS leaders were, to be sure, imbued with a fantastical play instinct; they could also be curious and sometimes developed a bizarre love of systematic processes, but in the strict sense, they certainly were not experimenters. One must not be misled by the fact that the reality of the "ghetto" was the result of tendencies that developed into a caricature of a planned economy and thus forced human beings into a network of instructions and prohibitions, to the point that their natural independence virtually vanished and they took on the character of objects of decreed measures. Nevertheless, aside from the obscured goals of the "Final Solution to the Jewish Question," no experiment was concealed behind the fog of blurred ideas that attempted to dictate the existence of the camp. As elsewhere, in Theresienstadt the SS leaders were satisfied to modify the original plans and make do with confused improvisations.

Thus there was no experiment, but analogies to this concept can be recognized. Whatever was supposed to happen was not only striven for and systematically pursued, but attempts were also made to command and enforce it. Hitler might have had an experiment in mind when he wrote:

> What excluded national Germany from any practical activity in shaping the German developments was the lack of a unified collaboration of brutal force with brilliant political will.... Firm belief in the right to apply even the most brutal weapons is always bound up with the existence of a fanatical faith in the necessity of the victory of a revolutionary new order on this earth. (102, p. 596f.)

What seems important here is the mechanical postulate of a historical process that is to be reduced to a "brutal," "fanatical," "brilliant" experiment. Yet we should not ignore the fact that it is only the coldness of the approach, but not the means that

Hitler enumerates, that corresponds to the objective endeavors of an experimenter; one soon realizes that anything experimental in this has been turned into coercion. What in the end might appear to be a problem solved – a lesson that could be learned – hardly was prepared for and certainly was not awaited. An experiment requires patience, but who was more impatient than the National Socialists? No, the aim was assumed; coercion *itself* was the result, however different the indeterminate result ultimately might have been. We already know that Theresienstadt harbored a coerced community; it was created through coercion and at the mercy of quasi-experimental interventions; as a community, it was subjected to as varied a range of destinies as is conceivable in any society. We must therefore regard the camp not as the subject of an experiment but as the scene of an exceptional history.

We are left with the following question: experiment or history? What is history? It can be, and is, experienced, but it certainly is more than an experiment that initiates, sets in motion, and observes events in a specific order. Our definition is as follows: history is irrational life, which develops within and among human beings and involves all the material values accessible to human beings and all the immaterial values comprehensible by human consciousness.

In this respect, history seems effectively without beginning and without end. Only if we accept boundaries – be they of a temporal, spatial, or phenomenological nature – is it possible to speak of history as an ideational abstraction. The special history in question exhibits an experimental character due to its easily surveyed duration (three and a half years) and its spatial limitation (a small town almost entirely cut off from the surrounding world – a superheated history in a test tube); nevertheless, this history proceeded in accordance with the suggested definition.

No history can exist on its own, in isolation, or can be treated with such scientific abstraction; therefore, confrontation and comparison with other histories is justified and even necessary. If we reconsider the history depicted in this book – that of a society that developed in an abnormal fashion – we certainly are tempted to see what is exceptional about it, and this then suggests parallels with experimentation. The almost mechanical origins of the camp – initiated in the offices of Eichmann, Günther, and the Prague JKG (Jüdische Kultusgemeinde) – and the technique of "processing people in and out" (*Ein- und Ausschleusung*) deprive this history of any organic norm and constitute its experimental component. If, however, we look more closely at the interventions into the course of events, which were not left to natural processes, we see that they, too, are effective as history, and that is how these interventions were perceived by the prisoners.

It is possible to describe the history of human beings controlled in captivity as the history of powerlessness. For every individual appearing in history, even if he is thought of as active, it is possible to demonstrate a factor of powerlessness in his life, because every creature's will is limited at the point where his power – that is, his ability to act – turns into powerlessness. We call this factor of powerlessness "destiny" in history, because it is given, allotted to the creature, so that he recognizes his limitations as a created, transitory individual. In normal society, in quieter times, this factor appears to be removed to a seemingly unfathomable distance, and where one does feel its impact, it is experienced sometimes as divine agency, and always as beyond the human.

This perspective hardly suggests itself in a "total" state, and certainly not in a concentration camp or in the Theresienstadt "ghetto," for destiny appears in the

The Psychological Face of the Coerced Community

form of human action, for example, in the guise of an order from Berlin. Thus destiny has come threateningly close and is alarmingly palpable in its omnipresence, yet it is anything but comprehensible or even avoidable. In other words, the coerced community is overwhelmed by destiny. Actions are increasingly reserved for the ruling class, while the ruled can only follow. Here the sentence "Leader, you order, we follow!" becomes meaningful. Thus we understand that the actions of the ruled toward the rulers become acts of powerlessness; they no longer have an effect and have turned into endured destiny. One's personality is shackled and eventually extinguished. What consequences result from this?

1. With respect to the experiment, in which a human being almost rises above his biophysical norm, seeking to play the master of history.
2. We realize that destiny may be superhuman but need not necessarily be above the human sphere, because human beings not only can become destiny but can impose it on themselves.

Institutions of power created and defined by other than human and human actions impose destiny on human beings. The more these institutions limit people's freedom within these inconsistently developed boundaries, the more formidable destiny inevitably becomes for them, and the more hopeless their powerlessness becomes. Through the modern concentration camp and its variations, recent Occidental history has achieved the most extreme limitation of freedom, along with the most powerful influence of destiny. The power and powerlessness of the inhabitants of a state were to be divided between two classes of human beings. Unlike other camps, Theresienstadt contained a distinctive feature, a "self-administration" possessing in some respects considerable internal independence and pseudofreedom. Nowhere did the adaptation to civilian norms go so far as there, where it was first ordered by the SS and then implemented by the prisoners themselves, even beyond what was demanded of them. Because this adaptation did not change or, in reality, even weaken the law of destiny at work in concentration camps, the paradoxical contradiction between powerlessness and pseudofreedom, on the one hand, and power and destiny, on the other, was shaped in a unique way.

If we single out the history of the Theresienstadt camp from the rest of history, the two histories must be seen in relation to each other. There are two main ways to do so:

1. We can view the history of the camp as an episode in a simultaneous overall history.
2. We can view the history of the camp as an episode in the overall history of the Jewish people.

THERESIENSTADT AS AN EPISODE IN SIMULTANEOUS HISTORY

Theresienstadt is part of the history of an empire, and thus part of the simultaneous history of the world. The subjects of the camp's history could not evade this interrelationship; the course of its history is first of all involved in and then largely determined by the surrounding history. This dependency would continue even if the camp acted in opposition and developed visible or invisible signs of resistance. Thus the history of the camp is defined by the surrounding history as the power that becomes destiny; in other words, one history is the object of another. This describes the state of defenseless powerlessness and the limits on possible freedom in this confined society. Where power encroaches, freedom can hardly exist; where it does not take hold, it is very difficult to maintain freedom. This power induces its intentions even where its direct intervention is no longer perceived, and as a result, the inner power of resistance is boundlessly endangered. Why did this have to happen? Because the intruding power was *bad*.

We must now prove, by portraying them, that the ruling class and their power were truly bad. The history of this power is marked by the deification of the state, which this power used to determine its own progress, most especially in all the concentration camps. The power of every state develops, through extremely complicated processes that cannot be examined here, into a consistently functioning, suprahuman agent; but it is represented by human beings, by subjects of history. In Hitler's state, this human power was purposely increased, brought to the fore, and placed in a position of leadership. The rulers deified themselves as "controllers of destiny"; Hitler claimed omnipotence, and it was granted to him by his paladins.

At the same time, this power distorted, denied, or annihilated every traditional or generally accepted human value. Above all, the value of life and its subjects was so twisted, in terms of all theretofore applicable norms, that it was tantamount to a repudiation of life. National Socialism unhesitatingly transformed the human being from a personality capable of and meant for autonomy into an acted-upon object. In this respect, the National Socialist ruling class adhered absolutely to the materialistic thinking and feeling of its era; even prior to and outside this sphere of power, the leaders had dared to speak of people and nations as "masses" in a pseudocollectivist sense. We must refrain from examining the phenomenon of "the masses" as an arbitrary number of people from a psychological perspective, but we must point out that the moment we begin to speak of people as "masses," human consciousness is disturbed, even if the current state of humanity allows it to be described and treated as a "mass"– whereas the same human beings would immediately protest against the far less insulting expression "cattle."

It becomes possible to speak of human beings as masses only if the concept of organic life is devalued and lost, such that we can perceive only an undefined, mechanical quantity of unknown variety and size. The definition of the masses as a materialized idea of a human group construct permits an attentive consciousness to read only generalized conclusions; the masses are beyond any benevolent recognition and feelings, but at the same time they become hazily indefinite, and objectively material. On a moral scale, they are not even unworthy, because they are simply worthless. The masses have no shape; their respective form is merely accidental. The masses can be shaped, but during undamaged cultural periods this was understood as merely the shaping of inorganic quantities and qualities, which would, in the process of shaping, become commodities in a materialistic culture. In this sense, "human masses" cannot be shaped; they can only be brought into formation. And thus we typically speak of the "party formations" of National Socialism, a concept derived from military jargon, which has always reduced human beings to objects. Yet human beings are not formed in society but are educated in it. An educated human being is a civilized human being; in him alone is there a solid relationship between spiritual and material culture, a culture that he can create and re-create in a given order (*Ordnung*) or even in subordination (*Unterordnung*). The human being as a mass appears only

The Psychological Face of the Coerced Community 561

when this order is violated or abandoned, when subordination neither bestows justice nor is protected by law, culture dissolves itself, and mechanical materialism prevails.

It may be surprising that National Socialism employed the humane word *Volksgemeinschaft* (people's community), but one can read how Hitler himself really meant it:

> The nationalization of the great masses can never take place by way of half measures, by a weak emphasis upon a so-called objective viewpoint, but by a ruthless and fanatically one-sided orientation as to the goal to be aimed at.... The great mass of a people consists neither of professors nor of diplomats. The small abstract knowledge it possesses directs its sentiments rather to the world of feeling. In this is rooted either its negative or positive attitude. It is open only to the expression of force in one of these directions, and never to a half measure swaying between them.... Their sentimental attitude, however, is caused by their exceeding stability. It is more difficult to undermine faith than knowledge, ... and at all times the driving force of the most important changes in this world has been found less in a scientific knowledge animating the masses, but rather in a fanaticism dominating them and in a hysteria which drove them forward. He who would win the great masses must know the key which opens the door to their hearts. Its name is not objectivity ... but willpower and strength. (102, p. 370f.)

We believe that most readers will understand what we mean by "mechanical materialism." It is a way of thinking that is devoid of ideas, colorless and coarsely sensual, and that exists in poor, rigidly rational forms that are unable to see or accept the potential of life. The few ideas still prevalent in such a society have been abstracted from life as such yet cannot be maintained in the world of pure ideas; they subside and become material ideas, as paradoxical as this may sound. In Hitler's concept, nothing that resembled a *Volksgemeinschaft* remained. Hitler saw only the "great masses" on one side, the Führer on the other. There was nothing in between. Hitler understood only material dualism, conceived as inorganic and detached from life, because anything located between the two poles he insecurely subsumed under what he considered the highly suspect notion of the "so-called objective point of view," which he classed with "half-measures" (*Halbheiten*). Thus Hitler could not even imagine the many supposed, or even actual, half-measures from which human history actually accrues. The abundance of life, which, as an organism, also contains numerous contradictions, was unknown to Hitler; it was cast out. What remained was the rigid framework within which the mechanical struggle of strength and will unfolded. We may recall that, in his speeches, Hitler reduced these contradictions to a succinct formula without "half-measures": "this way – or that way" (*so – oder so*). There was nothing else – and in particular nothing "objective," nothing ideally dominant in this de-deified (*entgöttlicht*) world – that would be able to stand above "this way – or that way." There is an obvious reason for this. "This way" is in fact the "Führer," and "that way" is his opponent. We maintain that Hitler could perceive only a "one-sided" – that is, mechanical – "attitude," which certainly did not recognize or acknowledge any higher order above it. The "destiny" sometimes invoked was never taken seriously; since destiny had appointed the "Führer," God was dead, and now "this way" – which was identical with Hitler – prevailed.

Hitler proved to be a poor judge of human nature, but apparently a good judge of the soulless "masses," in his conclusion that there was a mechanical, highly simplified duality not only in the realm of the rational but also in the world of emotion; for he stated that one's "positive or negative attitude" lies in emotion. Once again, this is "this way – or that way," which does not allow for any negotiation. According to this perspective, the *Volksgemeinschaft* had to be tormented; everything had to be extreme and, if possible, blindly fanatical and hysterical. For in the view of mechanical materialists, objectivity is weakness; they condemn knowledge but need the "driving force of the most important changes" in order to race through the soulless cosmos of power for the sake of the Führer.

So everything organic was mechanized to a previously unheard-of degree; the fullness of life, which ultimately proves itself through action, was transformed into an acted-upon substance. Power reduced life's rationally indescribable richness, the totality of which is history, to the object of an inorganic experiment in which all history was unconsciously negated and driven almost to dissolution. Power itself was conceived of in material terms, and every organic structure was captured using the tools of a technical-administrative apparatus. Thus life, the existence of which cannot be denied, became a "mass to be recorded," a subject for administration that is "deployed" and "supervised," and for which, in any case, "measures are taken." This certainly reflected the general Occidental crisis of culture, and the demise of Hitler's regime will by no means suffice to overcome this crisis. The consequence of turning every human being into a number denoting an "item" is obvious if life becomes a thing; this has become an almost uncontested practice in the administrations of modern states. Instead of serving to create order in life, administration imperiously becomes an end in itself, and life, as an administrative matter, is recognized only for administration's sake. Once overmechanization is taken seriously and all moral inhibitions fall away, National Socialist treatment of human beings is only a small step away. Thus Germany, and eventually almost all of Europe, became the object of a near-experimental procedure that took the place of history. It should come as no surprise that this antihistorical process would replace history and was even taken for history as it ran riot in manic plans, mechanical application of theories remote from life, and abstract ideas of biology and race, to the point of exterminating "life unworthy of living." In their mission, the rulers felt themselves so elevated above their "objects" that they came to believe in fictions such as the "thousand-year Reich," on the one hand, and a "historical moment" on the other. What could have happened only through history was anticipated in the postulate; what should only have been unmediated life would be anticipated as history.

The mechanical treatment of nonmechanical values that constantly were wrested from one's grasp stretched this kind of pathological materialism so tremendously that it required a counterbalance; this was provided by another pathological step – by regression to an apparent myth forever closed to rationality, although its rational core, in all its wretchedness, is easily revealed. This mythical function may be irrational and may develop an irrational effectiveness, but its construct is derived from more or less serious biological principles and scientifically harnessed racism.

To the extent that racism becomes a creed or even a pseudomyth, it makes sense only to interpret, but not to attack, its irrationality in this area. It makes more sense to point out its crude materialist roots. Racism is an ineffective attempt to interpret the richness of life on the basis of specific biological and purely material components. Uncovering its many mistakes and lies is not our task here and need not concern us in this context. We simply note that racism – as strongly as it became part of the

The Psychological Face of the Coerced Community

National Socialist myth – is based on mechanical materialist premises, in which the middle ground between extremes is arbitrarily rejected as too "objective," as "half-measures," as "swaying"; it turns out that the entire content of this myth already has been determined by Hitler's "this way – or that way."

In a world devoid of gods, a myth is artificially and amorphously created from the tip of a possible component of knowledge (*Erkenntniskomponente*) of the organic world and human history; this myth lacks the binding force of a natural, collective feeling for life but becomes its grotesque surrogate: an "ideology." That remnant of idealism – which, experience tells us, no consistent materialist view, regardless of its form, can avoid, if it is to move beyond a paper program into the reality of human communities –we say, is transformed into an ideology that is the final reflected splendor of a genuine worldview that has now become a "complex," that is, a psychomechanical correlate of the mechanized human "masses." What one might term the "schizophrenization" (*Schizophrenisierung*) of the Occidental human being – which occurred when the formation of his intellectual concepts was reduced to a choice between two unfortunate alternatives, either idealism or materialism, that were never unified into a real and lasting synthesis – ultimately produced National Socialism, through a painstaking combination and devaluation of elements. Any contradictions, as well as the dialectic of National Socialism, which impresses with its abysmal disingenuousness, can be explained by the chaotic, irreconcilable juxtaposition of rational materialism and irrational ideology.

In its dogma, National Socialism classified the human beings it dominated as material units in its system of values (*Werteinheiten*). Its ideology, as a schematic view of reality, was so inorganic that it contradicted the actual life of every nation – including, of course, the German nation – in the extreme. This ideology contained so many demands that contradicted any natural or developed feeling for life that its implementation necessarily met with extreme difficulties, even though many people, after generations of mechanization, were so emotionally deformed that they agreed in theory. In practice, most would have shrunk from some of its consequences. Who, of his own volition, would have decided to suffocate thousands of naked, defenseless people – women, children, old people, sick people – like vermin through the almost effortless operation of the Auschwitz gas killing mechanism? How many people could have stomached simply knowing about and approving of it? That would have required a state of mind that was barely conceivable, even in the age of the mechanization of human beings (*Menschenmechanik*).

Only the development of a terrible method made it possible to put such aims into practice. The method consisted of two combined and coordinated principles:

1. The potential for power was assigned to the "conspirators" in the party formations: namely, the SS.
2. The dominated peoples were made defenseless and were devalued to a "mass," which became a commodity before there was any need for institutionalized slavery, to the point of the exclusion of certain groups from the rest of society through shipment to human warehouses – the concentration camps.

This is not the place to discuss the second principle, but the first must be explained. There were two possibilities, applied in combination, for putting it into effective operation:

1. The worst human beings were recruited. Criminals with no moral inhibitions were called on to commit the most dreadful deeds envisioned by the ideology.
2. Those who, although not criminal by nature, had joined the so-called movement or had been forced into it were further entangled in the movement through guilt.

National Socialism, and the SS in particular, rightly saw itself as a conspiracy. To the "conspirators," the immoral acts they were ordered to commit became semi-"moral" commandments. In this system, the only thing left to them, aside from disobeying, which was tantamount to suicide, was obedience. Once they obeyed an order, they were enmeshed in the common guilt. The moment they became complicit, they were inseparably tied to the other conspirators. Thus, along with primarily inferior individuals, they joined the criminal collective – perhaps at first unwittingly, because at the beginning the things they were asked to do were often actually or apparently harmless. To the chieftains, the "conspirators" were considered "innocent," as long as they were willing to give further obedience. If they refused even once, they became "guilty" and could be punished.

To themselves – and to the world order – they are, in any case, guilty. This is obvious to them, at least subconsciously. Guilt that cannot be expiated before any accessible authority becomes so oppressive that it must be numbed. The chieftains left open two escape valves: corruption of every kind – which makes one's entanglement in guilt even more hopeless, for corruption remains illegal – and the intoxication of oblivion by any accessible means – which also increases the guilt.

The "guiltlessness" of many party functionaries, which they so often claimed after the collapse of their reign, is not, as Max Picard (206) believes, a sign of a nihilism that is no longer capable of remembering; it is a result of the morality of the conspirators: they had merely "obeyed orders." Nihilism itself is a result, not a premise, of National Socialism. In the beginning there was an ideological plan that was, in a mechanical way, to be translated into its material goals. In the process, there was great resistance and difficulty, such that all along this delusional road and at the end of it, *nothing* remained – the work of nihilism, with its terrible symptoms and visible symbols.

Nihilism is the only remaining escape from inexpiable guilt in empirical reality. If the guilty are those in power themselves, who – acting as the fate for good and ill over the subjugated peoples – pulled into a flood of complicity everyone who was or wished to be an active subject, then the result can be what National Socialist dominance taught. The events to which the "bearers of the idea" succumbed brought about nihilism. It was not a "revaluation of values" in the Nietzschean sense that led to the practical realization, but the "decay of values," as Hermann Broch called it (see 31). This decay can be heard in the words of "camp inspector" Bergel in the early days of the "ghetto": "Nobody knows what will happen with us today or tomorrow. Nobody knows. We don't know either."

The values themselves were devalued. When all values – including life itself – of an immaterial nature were transformed into material values, this was a devaluation. Because it was unnatural, the transformation could only seem to occur, or the next step had to be extermination. If life was a nonvalue (*Unwert*), it could be thrown away like a rotten thing, as happened in the gas chambers. Hair, human

The Psychological Face of the Coerced Community 565

fat, bone meal, and gold from teeth could be considered the "valuable" by-products.

Before this "liquidation" occurred (note the mercantile expression, which conceals a "mythic" function), the thing "human being" could be marketed as a slave – the people who had become individual numbers could be forced to work. The institution of the National Socialist (and some other) concentration camp can be classified as part of the system of slavery. The introduction of slavery was neither its first and proximate nor ever its admitted purpose, but this statement can be clearly proven. According to F. B. Steiner's clear definition (251), slavery is, briefly, the exploitation of man by man with no contractual relationship. A person excluded from society in this way cannot survive on his own, and, of late, has been affiliated with institutions. If he is not included in a household but is the property of a chief, this is the starting point of state slavery. In each case of slavery, a human being has power over a human being, without the relationship creating reciprocal legal obligations; the master can impose penalties on the slave, but not vice versa. Because the relationship is only one of ownership, what applies, in terms of Roman law, is *jus in rem*, not *in personam*. Thus the National Socialist concentration camp – and, although more cleverly camouflaged, the Theresienstadt "ghetto" – was a case of slavery: that is, state slavery or, more precisely, SS slavery, because the SS, with its Reich Security Main Office, was not actually the state but a secret order that dominated it to a virtually unlimited degree and enjoyed the privilege of arbitrariness, which was neither regulated nor supervised by any objective legal order. To be more precise, one would have to describe it as crypto-slavery, because in this case slavery was not a publicly recognized and legally based institution but a clandestinely tolerated and encouraged SS practice; it lacked official recognition, because the true meaning of the concentration camp was concealed from the world, and even from the members of the Nazi Party (see 3c, 202b).

This mechanical materialism statistically recorded its slaves' labor process. This is the root of the countless tabulations and calculations, of which neither this power nor – as this book teaches – its victims could get enough. In this system statistics played the role of mysticism: the graphs and figures that, even aside from falsifications and a lack of a desire for truth, provided no reasonable correlates of actual procedures but at the same time imparted information about mysterious functions.

Power played the role of fate. Powerlessness was humanity, degraded to a commodity, which was sorted, numbered, and, through the magic of statistics, turned into the object of a perverse mysticism. The treatment of the masses inevitably led to nihilism – objectively, in the scrapping of the "commodity" and, subjectively, in the attitude of those in power. The "ghetto" must also be understood from this perspective. Because the "masses" acted upon were in reality alive, they resisted their treatment so vigorously that those in power were forced, even against their ideology, to make occasional small concessions to devalued life. This was provided by instruments of power such as violence, corruption, temporary fake alliances, persuasion, and deception; these means were applied as appropriate to all the oppressed or those chosen from their ranks. Just as one makes an animal useful for certain purposes through training, here powerless human beings were trained and forced into certain types of behavior. Because, however, unlike animals, one man is not naturally superior to another, special ruses were necessary. Although most of the victims were treated as commodities (some SS men would have been accountants or salesmen if times had been different), some individuals were chosen to play the role of dogs in a herd of sheep. They were given no actual power but were granted authority and wide latitude for arbitrary action; thus a pseudohierarchy was created among the victims. Ideologically, it was denied, but, in practice, it was allowed to operate as a capitalist invests his money, which he can reinvest or call in at any time.

As long as this pseudohierarchy was permitted to exist and was left relatively undisturbed, it essentially developed according to the same laws as the hierarchy of power. Those occupying lower positions could at any time become numbers and things to those of higher rank, while the gap between the highest-level representatives among the prisoners and the lowest-ranking individuals among those in power remained theoretically unbridgeable. This was generally also true in practice, but for private or tactical reasons there could develop a sort of interaction that could even become intimate. The "masses," however, were no longer noticed, although they were available at any time as statistical quantities and qualities. There were seemingly inconsequential factors, such as the fact that prisoners were forced to greet SS men, but such factors were merely a degrading form of training; the fact that this commanded "mark of respect" was ignored makes clear how little value was attached to the "masses."

To be able to see human beings merely as "masses," it is necessary to segregate them from other human beings who, for whatever reasons, must still be accorded a certain value that is not purely material. In this case, enslavement became a side effect of massification. The average party member must have known that his fellow human beings, even as hated Jews, were still living beings and not merely "masses." Thus segregation in camps was a necessary step. Although the first concentration camps were built for different reasons, their increase in number and incredible expansion were the fulfillment of this principle. By the end of the war, things had developed almost to the point that the entire "mass," that is, the dominated class of human beings inside and outside the camps, was administered by a class of rulers that was quite small in number. In the end, power came close to transforming the entire country into a system of concentration camps (see 154): the Reich, a mechanism in the service of an ideology, statistically recorded as a powerless object of power – this was the final situation.

This completes the observations that sought to show that the power of the dominant class was *bad*. This power was bad because it devalued and nullified every vital order and sought to replace it with its perverse mechanism.

The relationships – better not to say laws – that apply to general history also had an imposed and accepted validity in the special history of the coerced community in Theresienstadt. Due to the special function intended for the "ghetto," much happened there in a different way; the general conditions that developed were more difficult to decipher, and the theories that Kogon (149, 150) and Kautsky (137) suggested for a camp of the Buchenwald type cannot be adopted without modification, because the individual personality was granted wider latitude in Theresienstadt. The prisoner "self-administration" in Buchenwald, with its internal battles between staunch opponents of the regime and criminals, on the one hand, and the Jewish "self-administration," on the other, operated very differently, despite certain convergences. The freedom to do evil, which was almost unlimited in Buchenwald, was restricted in Theresienstadt by moral standards that had not been degraded to the core; not even the most inferior men in the leadership could openly scorn them.

The Psychological Face of the Coerced Community   567

Things were also different from the ghetto-like camps in the East, where the SS did not make the same allowances.

Even though individuality was theoretically impossible, prisoners in all the camps made history. This happened illegally, through the unquenchable protests of people whose vitality contradicted total massification. The modest degree of freedom or pseudofreedom permitted the prisoners in Theresienstadt allowed them to perform historical activities within the legal framework of the rights bestowed on them. In some areas the SS permitted developments that feigned the illusion of autonomy, not only to the Danish commission but even to many inmates. We have seen how, through this SS behavior, the resistance and morale of the "ghetto inmates" were so damaged that they misjudged the seriousness of their situation. This is addressed later; here we note that the history of the "ghetto" is first of all an object of the history of the National Socialist state, which governed the camp with an experiment-like, matter-of-fact administration. The psychological treatment of the prisoners necessarily contradicted this, in order more easily to lead the victims to fulfill the true, yet concealed, goals of the camp. Thus the all-powerful character of the SS grew into destiny, which then became unfathomable providence.

The objective character of history was faced with a subjectivity within which the prisoners and their internal leadership attempted to act. They sought to avert disaster using good and bad means. The corruption of one's personality and the moral norms one is supposed to respect were connected with the devaluation of all values, which, from a psychological perspective, often results in a reversal of values. Sincerity and honesty became relative. Not only did these characteristics become disadvantageous from a selfish point of view, but, in some cases, they even became vices. Who could then judge what was moral and immoral? A subjective judgment, but no system of traditional and recognized values that are the essence of any culture. In this context nihilism threatened to overwhelm the prisoners as well, and a breakdown of morality that had merely been acquired superficially occurred, and that was publicly considered to be the recognized norm of behavior. Personal morality, which largely depends on moral standards, is lost if it is not secured by mature probing of the conscience, which does not need any further external supports.

This had a devastating effect on young people and those with weaker natures. It was almost impossible to teach a child that lying was not only necessary in the everyday life of the camp but also morally justified in the camp's morally devalued world, although, unconditionally speaking, it was reprehensible. The worst consequence of the regime was that it turned everything good into bad and everything bad into good. In the camp, unconditional morality was impossible from a purely vital standpoint. A justification of conditional morality can be achieved only through active probing of the conscience, in which one always sees a lie as a lie and can judge all its moral consequences. Only a small minority were capable of this, whereas the vast majority foundered in the thickets of double standards.

Because only the worst intentions existed in regard to the prisoners, the worst prisoners were chosen as accomplices, just as the worst individuals among the German people were selected to head the camps and "ghettos." Those who were not bad to start with inevitably were corrupted through entanglement in guilt. It was almost a miracle if an SS man did not become entirely bad. Among the functionaries from the ranks of the prisoners, those who resisted becoming bad, despite the great demands made on their steadfastness, are to be admired. Morality is always invoked to defy an adversary's immorality. In general, only bad fellows allow themselves to become accomplices of the bad, but even people who were not obviously bad succumbed sooner or later, once they got involved with the SS. Others who began with good or well-meaning intentions may have erred just once, through lack of wisdom or human weakness, and became caught in the clutches of guilt, with no chance of retreat. Yet there also were people with moral intentions who infiltrated the internal functions in order to protect the prisoners, or at least a small number of them, from the worst evils. But even these people could not always prevent the worst from happening, and often they, too, were caught, despite their best intentions, in the entanglements of guilt. These conditions applied first of all to the high-ranking internal functionaries, but they generally also applied to the anonymous classes of prisoners. Nevertheless, one always could find strong personalities who sought, with varying degrees of success, to resist any entanglement in guilt; but there was no camp, not even Theresienstadt, in which these people had a good chance of staying alive.

Probably nobody who ever took an active role in a camp remained free from entanglement in guilt. This is because every intervention in this history ended up yielding to destiny. Every intervention became a loan from the power that came from evil. If, for example, the kindest person in the internal administration intervened to save the best people from deportation to Auschwitz out of the purest of motives, this inevitably led to the destruction of another human being, and thus the person became tragically entangled in guilt.

The camp's entanglement in this mechanism became more and more complicated through induction from the influence on internal conditions of those in power. This was noticeable even when those in power had neither the will nor the interest to impose themselves on the camp or on individuals. That is why we speak of induction. General resistance against it would have been difficult, if not impossible. Such resistance did not happen, as we showed with regard to the treatment of the elderly and sick, and with regard to incidents in connection with the "beautification." Thus people internally made common cause with the source of all evil, although they detested it as the enemy, and very few offered real inner resistance.

It is not enough to reject an immoral adversary because of his opposing "ideology." Immorality itself must be rejected and combated along with *all* ideologies, which are complex elements of mechanical materialism. No personal ideology that happens to oppose a hostile ideology that makes one suffer can provide the protection and resistance necessary for the salvation and reconstruction of a humanity free of mechanical schematics and dogmas; this can be accomplished only by eliminating inhuman thinking and feelings in "targeted," rigid "complexes" and by shattering all ideologies, including one's own.

Humanity will be destroyed by massification if it is accepted without protest, and every ideology forms a mechanical substitute for the animated intellectual life of an educated human being. Through massification, human beings surrender to an ideology and become easily receptive to its predetermined normative ideas for an uncertain period of time, while the human being as an individual becomes merely a function in the mechanism of an inhuman apparatus. Then, going beyond inorganic abstraction and the dull motor skills of strength and will, he denies the autonomy of his moral personality, because he subsumes it beneath the dogmas of the ideology that dominates him. He does this just as he denies the autonomy of the initiating individuality with which he should have proven himself conscious and responsible in

The Psychological Face of the Coerced Community   569

his actions and reasoning. To preserve or create such superiority would have been a great triumph in the desperate plight of the "ghettos" and concentration camps; but, like their persecutors, many of the persecuted had succumbed to mechanical materialism even before their enslavement. Tormentors and tormented suffered from the same social disease; all had succumbed to an ideology, however different the symptoms of the evil may have been. We should not lose sight of the fact that it is part of the psychology of a humanity contaminated by mechanical materialism to recognize and value neither independent character nor moral behavior but only ideologies. Unbridled rationalism considers only schematic wreckages of thought, defined as automatic, barely changeable creeds: that is, ideologies that are believed to be absolute values, and whose tendencies are confused with morality. *Shortsightedly, people fail to recognize that no one ever has suffered from standing the test of morality*, whereas people inevitably suffer under dominant ideologies, especially if these ideologies exclusively determine the machinery of state. This is true, first of all, if one does not or cannot adopt such ideologies, as was the case for the Jews in this context. Ultimately, however, it is also true for the adherents of an ideology the moment the ideology comes into conflict with reality and is defeated by it, as in the case of Hitler's Germany.

Nevertheless, people never learn, and they persist in seeing only the immorality and intolerability of the ideology that happens to be their enemy; as the oppressed party, they are to a certain extent in the right in this regard (for each person gains a metaphysical rightness because of his suffering, even if he is not blameless and suffers from some guilt). This rightness is lost as soon as they are liberated from their persecutors and from suffering and are no longer acting morally but are merely acting according to the pattern of their own ideology. In this case, the oppressed people did not in the meantime consider whether, aside from the transient rightness of the sufferer, a more permanent rightness could have been acquired, one that would have been morally stronger than the rightness of the opponent. Then it turns out that the relatively higher degree of morality they might have retained in the "ghetto" was only compelled by necessity and was not actually present. In practice, this state of affairs might already have shown itself in the camps, in certain people's behavior toward fellow prisoners and the community. Thus they already had forfeited their rights as sufferers and had become entangled in the guilt of their oppressors.

Humaneness is the only party that can offer moral fulfillment in the face of immorality. With this in mind, any other concerns about where greater or lesser wrong, guilt, or wickedness is found are moot. It remains up to the individual in what way he stands the test of humaneness and what views he honors. There are many paths – but only *one* morality.

Let us continue with a corollary point: Dominant ideologies exercise an inductive force on ideologies that appear to be alien to them. In the camp, one could observe the extent to which the National Socialist mindset mushroomed not only in the prescribed institutions but throughout the prisoners' entire lives (see also 19). The prevailing ideology infiltrated the "ghetto" with totalitarian thinking, intolerance, a ludicrous bureaucracy, the insanity of statistics that covered everything and nothing, and the development of certain modes of behavior and everyday speech. The prevailing ideology made noxious inroads everywhere, even poisoning the protests that dared to contradict it. Other observers have recognized this as well; for example, Lingens-Reiner observed this process among the female prisoners in Auschwitz:

But the truly terrible thing was that women who had striven for integrity, who still took life and ethics seriously, proved in the end too small for their overwhelming destiny and never noticed when they acted according to principles that in reality corresponded to those of National Socialism. Without question, the most dangerous victory National Socialism ever achieved was that it took root in the spirit of its opponents. (174, p. 91)

And Kogon says, correctly, "The concentration camp squeezed the souls of its victims as if between millstones. Who could come out of this process whole? No one came out as he went in."

Kogon also says, "Whether one was able to process the camp psychologically was not primarily a matter of social origin or the position one previously had held in society; it depended almost entirely on strength of character and the presence or absence of religious, political, humanitarian objectives." Except for his assessment of political objectives, I agree with this. Political objectives may have lent steadfastness, but at bottom it was not political character but general human depth beyond politics that made it possible to deal psychologically with the camps; this was also the case for religious objectives. Political convictions alone remained mired in doctrinally abstract ideologies that had unfortunate consequences in all the camps, as Kogon confirms. With this correction, we recognize humanitarian objectives as the heart of Kogon's proposition. Here we can see what gave people meaning in this history, and only in this way was this history overcome – a history that allowed no meaning other than standing the test of humaneness.

Guilt is the sum of history in a country or a camp, a manifold guilt that no one has escaped, for humanity is a community of guilt (it is also a community of mercy, but this need not be pursued in this context). How should we describe this guilt? The guilt of humanity in the confused state it was in even before Hitler's rise to power; the guilt of inhumanity that, if one wishes, can also be considered godlessness; the guilt of an unkind era in which order is transformed into schematics, the organic into mechanics, life into masses, the human being into a commodity, the soul into complexes, and the mind into ideology; the guilt of the misconception or devaluation of values and the confusion of concepts that led to decay; the guilt of a dull species so blinded in this transformation by foolishness, hate, self-interest, and lies that it could not see the disaster that was conjured up and would inevitably follow, as mechanical materialism and its destructive, all-consuming outgrowth in the form of National Socialism overtook the world; and finally, the greatest guilt, which we call the inability to experience guilt, because humanity that has become "masses" can no longer conceive of or accept any kind of guilt.

Guilt was finally transformed into punishment, as all guilt eventually is. Punishment does not ask about the guiltiness of the individual, how he contributed to it and how he became complicit, or whether he remained free of it by human standards. Punishment has an effect, it is said, into the third and fourth generation and is augmented and prolonged through the denial of guilt. Thus the question of whether one may justifiably assert one's innocence becomes unnecessary – the punishment that has come to pass has already given the answer.

Only someone with a limited mindset could believe there is no community of guilt. The reality of the community of punishment taught otherwise. Certainly, this era, which fears and cannot bear fancy talk, after such language has so long been misused, would not want to hear of such an "unmodern" juxtaposition of guilt and

The Psychological Face of the Coerced Community

punishment; but anyone fearlessly seeking truthful investigation of recent history will discover this connection and the set of problems suggested.

THERESIENSTADT AS AN EPISODE IN JEWISH HISTORY

As long as members of the Jewish people have lived among the nations, they have claimed the attention of their surroundings. We need not solve this problem here; it will suffice to establish that the Jews have remained a mystery to their environment in all periods. Jews and non-Jews felt that there was about them "something very different" from other people. Out of the contact between Jews and non-Jews emerged phenomena that are otherwise unusual for the way nations live together. For the Jewish people, or a portion of them, these were represented by periods of tolerance, endurable pressure, harsh oppression, and national catastrophe. Throughout their eventful history, all the Jews' advantages and mistakes took on an exaggerated character that – although it did not become a "specifically Jewish character," as has been claimed by enemies and friends of this people – did lend a significance to their virtues and vices that is otherwise less pronounced or is ignored in the assessment and self-assessment of a people. Whatever Jews or non-Jews did, nothing caused this people to perish, and nothing solved the problem that the Jews remained to their surroundings and to themselves. It was primarily the German Jew-haters who, starting in the second half of the nineteenth century (see 3ax), made the Jews – or, to be precise, the supposed, as well as real, differences between Jews and non-Jews – the center or almost the sole content of a so-called worldview, through a schematically exaggerated antithesis; for them, in National Socialism, "the Jew" ultimately became the essential element of a "mythic" ideology, as the opponent of the Führer. An analysis will show that we have once again arrived at a mechanical dualism: "this way – or that way."

It is not surprising that a totalitarian power would seek the solution to a supposed or real problem that had proven insoluble in all previous historical constructions, as, for example, the history of the Church teaches. The "solution" could easily be postponed in epochs in which people felt that history was presided over by a noumenon, because they trusted in a transcendental order; however, the mechanical materialism of National Socialism did not permit this. Any possible otherworldly solution had to happen in this world; the afterlife was "abolished," because it had no place in the polarized domain of the cosmos of "this way – or that way." The entire core sentiment of Hitler, Alfred Rosenberg, and Julius Streicher consisted of the paired values "Aryan" and "Jewish." The space between these was limbo, a place of half-measures, the empty internal sphere in which mechanical war games could run riot – games that would transmit their impulses of strengh and will from the positive "this" of the "Aryan" and the negative "that" of the "Jew." Hitler and National Socialism, which mean the same thing here, could see themselves only as the positive "this," and thus the negative "that" necessarily fell to their supposed or actual opponent, who was subsumed under the concept and notion of the "Jews" in a bold generalization that was not, however, surprising for mechanical materialism.

Jewishness had already previously been perceived as the "other" per se; in the history of contradictorily motivated Jew-hatred, all of people's own inferiorities had been transferred onto the Jews a thousand times over, until no one doubted Jewish inferiority – the Jewish people's well-known position as scapegoats for all society's ills. Thus nothing was easier for the National Socialists than to adopt this popular conception and, in accordance with its totalitarian mania, to take it to the extreme. Whatever was not National Socialist, or affected by it, had to be "Jewish" or affected by it. Thus anything defined as evil was also "Jewish": for example, capitalism, plutocracy, democracy, socialism, Marxism, Bolshevism, Freemasonry, sexual lust and perversion, exploitation, usury, materialism, atheism, Catholicism and sometimes all of Christianity, the Jewish religion, Zionism, internationalism, pacifism, atrocity propaganda, warmongering, the Talmud, and the Bible and especially the Old Testament – in short, anything, depending on the need and the emotion of the moment. All of it together formed the irrational "world Jewish conspiracy." It was the most dangerous secret alliance the National Socialists could imagine; because it was so dangerous, they then appeared to be justified in themselves conspiring against "Jewry" and its "allies" and in establishing truly secret institutions, with the complicit apparatuses of the SS and the "secret" state police. Hitler and every devout National Socialist could, with sincerity, have said, "Anything I am not is 'Jewish.'"

Thus one could "bring into line" (*gleichschalten*) everything – but the Jews, Hitler most likely felt, remained "differently brought into line" (*andersgeschaltet*); they had to be brought into line with the negative "that way." Incidentally, one might also feel that the Jewish people have always consciously or unconsciously opposed all totalitarian claims that any earthly power has ever made, and the majority certainly were not suited to a mechanical process of bringing into line. In Hitler's thinking, a power based exclusively in mankind belonged to him. Power was transferred to the conspirators, starting from the Führer at the top, in such a way that it worked its way down the hierarchy, with the full fury of its original power, and in the process renounced all responsibility, so that the "masses," to whom no more power was conferred or permitted, could perceive the power only as fate. In the process, the lower functionaries pledged obedience to the higher ones and were deprived of any power; they were thus "powerless." Each level of function was a pathway to power, the character of which took on the sheen of a fiefdom at the Führer's pleasure. Hitler raised Mussolini's words "*il Duce ha sempre ragione*" – "The Leader is always right" – to absolute legal validity and lent unconditional obedience its apparent moral justification. Thus responsibility for every exercise of power was passed from the lowest to the higher functionaries, and finally to the "Führer." He was the source of law, he was the authority, and he bore all responsibility.

In this way, National Socialism showed itself to be "godless" rule. We have shown that this power was bad, as is best illustrated by one of the attributes used to describe the Führer: "mankind's greatest benefactor" (see also 351). Once power called itself "good," each of its participants had to be "good," for "good" power can join only with "good" people. It follows that anything less powerful was less "good." Someone who was powerless could only be "bad." Two of the most dangerous equations derived from Nietzsche's philosophy are significant:

$$Power = Good$$

$$Powerlessness = Bad$$

A conceptual confusion arose and was forced on humanity, which had been degraded to "masses." The metaphysical consequences of National Socialism, which saw in the Führer the *summum bonum* and in the "Jews" the *summum malum*, become clear.

The Psychological Face of the Coerced Community

The "greatest benefactor," who was always "right," had to combat the "others," the "evil ones," the "Jews," in order to complete a "work of liberation." The "Führer of the movement" presumed to take on the role of a redeemer.

It can be clearly proven that the extermination of the Jews really became a pseudoreligious doctrine of salvation. In World War II people sang a tune that praised the hoped-for destruction of the Jews with the words:

> The waves are beating down [*schlagen zu*]
> The world has peace.

But even after World War I (see also 186), the following verses expressed the same "messianic" expectation:

> Crush the skulls of the Jewish pack
> And the future will be won.
> The flag flies proudly in the wind
> When Jewish blood runs from the saber.

The mythical antithesis could be understood only in light of the battle against them. This also is how we should understand the assessment of heroes and the heroic that Hitler and others developed into a paranoid system of delusions. The National Socialist myth represented a serious social disease and could achieve political victory for a certain period only because the society already had succumbed to a different social disease: that is, massification. Mechanical materialism as an ideology was joined by mechanical myth. In an editorial in his *Stürmer*, Streicher employed what probably was the clearest, and certainly the most absurd, language:

> Who are the enemies of our state? We summarize them under the term reaction [!]. And this reaction is a tangle of manifold shadings. We see red flags. We see coal-black flags. We see black-red-yellow flags. We even see certain black-white-red flags. The Führer [!] of these reactionary armies, however, is the Jew! The Jew is the general who leads the whole army of reaction. Who is preparing the final battle [!] against Adolf Hitler and his movement. Who gives the signal for the battle for life and death.... While the German people still slept and did not want to know about a Jewish question, the "Stürmer" stormed. It stormed against Alljudas' most powerful bulwark. Stormed – and prevailed.... The SA man's ... eyes were opened. Now he recognized completely that no redemption [!] of the German people was possible without a solution to the Jewish problem. And the "Stürmer" reaches a hand to this honest SA man. Reaches a hand to him for the defensive battle [!] against Alljuda. The battle for the National Socialist state and its Führer, Adolf Hitler. (No. 25, 1935)

These samples substantiate our interpretation. Now the question arose of how one should recognize and define Jews. A spiritual formulation, for example, in the sense of the church, was not an option. The way out offered by the racists was too confused a description and thus proved to be too complicated and impractical. Thus the Jews were defined schematically, through the famous "racial laws" of 1935 and further through the yellow star of 1941 – and now the Jews were finally defined!

Totality triumphed as an omnipotence that missed nothing. No definition had ever before achieved this. Thus it came to pass that countless human beings who were not, or were no longer, Jews according to a less mechanistic definition – most of whom did not feel part of Jewry in any way – came together, as "racial Jews" or as people "counted as Jews" (*Geltungsjuden*), with the actual Jews to form a uniform "mass" that was brought into line at least among its members. The delusional dream of contrasting "God-Hitler" with the "Devil-Jews" had been accomplished in reality. It need merely be noted that the phonetic similarity between "Jew" and "Judas," and the emotional identification of Judas with Satan, helped to create the following equation:

$$Jew = Devil$$

That which is good – the National Socialist, who knows no god but Hitler, who is "always right" and "beneficent" – must wrestle with the Devil. The Jew was Hitler's affliction: "Destroy the Jew, and there will no longer be evil in the world!" This was an unconditional article of faith, which Streicher formulated thus: "Whoever fights the Jews fights the Devil! Whoever defeats the Devil conquers Heaven!"

The cosmology of National Socialism was unconsciously created on the model of Persian or Manichean dualism, denuded of its spirit, and, if one may say so, on a doctrine of redemption and eschatology (213, p. 56). The destruction of the "Devil-Jews" became the most meritorious work. When "Alljuda" was beaten, the Parousia, the "Reich," would be won. In Hitler's words, this meant that the "historical moment" had arrived, and materialistic eternity could exist, in the form of the "thousand-year Reich." The demonization of the Jews and the deification of the Führer were complete, and children were told to say the following prayer:

Fold your little hands, bow your little head
And think of Adolf Hitler!

Our confrontation between National Socialism and its concept of the Jew always views the term "Jewish" only in the sense of the National Socialist faith, which we have taken as our basis for the sake of the problem being investigated, in order to do it justice; and this is how one should understand the end of this analysis.

The final deed – made evident in the chosen catchphrase, "Final Solution" – was a pseudosacral sacrifice. The Jews were offered up as sacrifice through increasingly mechanized mass rituals, which were really called *Aktionen* (actions); this was how mass slaughter was conceptualized. It was ultimately done industrially, through gas and fire, and the official, pseudoritual designation chosen for it was "special treatment," whereas the more vulgar, and therefore somewhat more honest, expression used was a material, commercial one: "liquidation." Thus did Occidental civilization end up taking part in human sacrifice. And even if many of those who carried out the sacrifices must have perceived their misdeeds as common murders, the murderers believed they had done "good" work; the Führer had ordered it, and responsibility lay with him. The appointed murderers, however – SS men as minor clerks or subpriests of that macabre secret church, the "Reich Security Main Office" – became "innocent" cogs in the instrument of the "masses," without responsibility to themselves, their victims, or God. This confirms the terrible joke that Hitler would have had to invent the Jews if they hadn't existed, because, as an earthly "good" God, he had to have an earthly representative of the Devil. Thus we believe we have clarified the innermost core of National Socialism, which served as an unconscious precept for the "theoreticians of the movement."

The National Socialists had created a delusional image of their supposed – and, eventually, actual – adversaries, which they used as a model for the establishment of their own hegemony. The party – and within the party, again, the SS and its "Reich Security Main Office" – truly had established what men such as Hitler and Himmler

The Psychological Face of the Coerced Community

had imagined to be, as a paranoid bogeyman, the demonic apparatus of the enemy, in the anonymous power of either the "Elders of Zion" or a Freemason's lodge. Created out of insanity, the enemy who did not actually or substantively exist had to be represented by millions of unsuspecting creatures who were innocent of this demonizing slander. The "good" power had to destroy the visible representatives of the "Devil" using the "Devil's" supposed own weapons, even though the victims were objectively defenseless. The Jews of their imagining thus were embodied in the leading National Socialists themselves; the world "Jewish" conspiracy *was* the Nazi Party and the SS – except the lunatics themselves did not know this, at least not entirely (see 248). Heydrich, however, elevated this insanity to a pathological, metaphysical work of liberation. After his death, Himmler said of him:

> He was still wonderfully useful for something else, for the battle against Jewry. He had overcome the Jew in himself through pure intellect and had pivoted to the other side [!]. He was convinced that the Jewish part of his blood was damnable [!], he hated this blood that had dealt so badly with him. The Führer really could not have chosen a better [!] man in his fight against the Jews than Heydrich. Towards the Jews he knew no sympathy and no mercy. (139, p. 131)

Unlike Otto Weininger, who only vilified his people, Hitler's Reich offered Heydrich unlimited power to send to extermination the hated Jewish seed within himself – which probably was a Jewish great-grandparent – by murdering any Jews within reach. We can derive a sociology of this lunatic SS association first of all from its counterfunction to a hypothetical, hostile apparatus of power; this is best shown in the words of one of Himmler's followers:

> Furthermore, the Reichsführer applies what he recognizes in his adversaries as the system [!] and foundation of their power [!] consistently [!] for the establishment of the SS's position of power in the state. From this perspective, the SS is nothing other than a counter-lodge, although the Reichsführer doesn't want to see this, with the help of which, without much ado, he is striving to fill the leading positions in the state and the Party. (139, p. 30)

Why were non-Jews, too, locked in camps? Because they – as, for example, criminals or opponents of those in power – were "evil" and thus resembled or equaled the "Devil-Jews," but one could still "correct" them to some extent. Only the Jews could not be corrected and thus could not later be released from a camp. This explains why Jews always were treated worse when they were imprisoned with non-Jews. The harshest punishment for a non-Jew was to be equated with the Jews, to live in a "Jewish block," and to have to work with them. The ideology of the common corruptor was carried over, in all its sordidness, to the prisoners who considered themselves better; only a small minority behaved well toward the Jews. When they did, their actions rarely occurred without a caveat: "I'm behaving decently towards you, even though you're a Jew."

In his book *Devil and Damned*, Benedikt Kautsky says that Jewish prisoners as a rule accepted their martyrdom as a mere "fate," and that those who were "only" Jews – those had no specific religious or political ties – lacked the strength to resist. This is true if we also count general humanitarian ties, as defined by Eugen Kogon. The Jews suffered "only" a fate; they were nothing but "victims." When Hitler overcame to them, they were in no condition to play anything but the role of mere victims that the prevailing ideology ascribed to them: many "came [to the camps] only with something like the will to die," according to Ella Lingens-Reiner. Most of the assaulted Jews were not prepared for anything but the role of victim, in which they acquiesced as if under hypnosis. Just as Hitler was only motivated by ancient Jew-hatred, most Jews west of Poland had little in common with Jews of earlier times, about whom they really knew little. Only their old ability to suffer and their willingness to endure continued as a mute inheritance. Thus Kogon's general statement also applies to the Jews: "Most prisoners left the concentration camps with exactly the same convictions they had had before; at most, they were more sharply accentuated." The staunch assimilationists, Zionists, Communists, atheists, religious people, and humanists found their views confirmed as "right" by the events that took place and therefore did not need to change them.

What happened to the Jews as a result of this regime, the deep opposition of a theologically accentuated and truly mythic nature, was not recognized or even suspected. If they were contaminated by an ideology, the Jews interpreted events according to its formula. The rest only dully perceived the action of fate. Few looked for deeper complexities, and very few buried themselves in questions about the meaning and essence of Judaism and its connections with humanity. The majority had, along with their environment, succumbed to mechanical materialism and had not resisted the disintegration of values. Assimilation – against which orthodox conservativism still fought and against which Zionism, which externally rejected assimilation, already had fought – had gone much deeper than the Jews were aware even in the years after the catastrophe. They had, wittingly and unwittingly, taken on the mental constitution of their surroundings, which the most venerable traditions could not avert and dogmatic ideologies could not even comprehend. Thus the Jews were not forearmed and had lost their old feel for lurking dangers. Especially in Central and Western Europe, they had largely secularized the values that were historically considered a fundamental asset. However they had been defined, now they were too rigid to assert themselves against the Enlightenment. But the new values that some had adopted could offer no spiritual protection, if only because they were too dependent, too similar to the spirit of the surrounding world, to strengthen Jewry in a healthy opposition to a surrounding world lost in falsity.

It is no wonder that many Jews were blind and deaf to what was happening and did not take Hitler's threats seriously or at least underestimated the demonic impulse of his "myth." At first, people made fun of it, even though – honestly for once – Hitler had warned against that very response; then people also hoped, as the calamity struck, that it would not be so terrible. Many German Jews, in particular (as well as some Western European and Hungarian Jews), yielded to a hopeless foolishness, ascribing to Hitler's Jew-hatred merely demagogic or profit motives, and not sensing his abysmal depths. Those who had not escaped in time were almost unprepared for the ruin that overtook them. People of the most varied dispositions and characters suddenly became, with the stroke of a pen, nothing more than "Jews"; few accepted this identity, for good or for evil. They did not seek meaning in community; few strove for it. They in any case rejected the mechanical coercion of the identity and failed to consider whether, aside from superficialities, it might be correct. Such an attempt could have produced fruitful continuity with earlier phases of history and would have enabled them to envisage a way to determine Jewish history in the future. This definitely did not happen in Theresienstadt.

The Psychological Face of the Coerced Community

How could such an attempt have emerged, and what would the result have been? As a first step, one would have had to acknowledge shared identity among Jews; this proposition, although created out of extreme necessity, would not have required approval of the coercion. In reality, however, many rejected even shared external identity as victims, to say nothing of "Jews," and they accepted it only under extreme protest. The second step would have been to become aware of Jewry and its mission. What would people have learned in the process? An answer suggests itself in this train of thought: Judaism, with its great revelations, strives to achieve concrete salvation for all of humanity, together and indivisible; the road to this salvation cannot be reconciled with the recognition of any doctrine of salvation that has supposedly already been achieved historically or that could be achieved currently – such as doctrines that take salvation out of the empirical community and relegate it to a super-reality or a mystical reality of individual salvation, or that try in vain to force it on society through secular political action. In the spirit of this realization, the National Socialist "thousand-year Reich" can be seen as an extremely perverse attempt to achieve a "salvation" sought through violence, whereas the Jewish concept of salvation must be seen as exactly the opposite, because it was obvious that Hitler's "totality" represented the most brusque repudiation of the world's current inadequacy for a messianic totality.

Such ideas had difficulty developing in Theresienstadt, and therefore the prisoners hardly knew why they were suffering and what they should have been suffering. Instead of an awareness that would have given meaning and perhaps even form to this fate, there was only inadequate inner protest and various degrees of willingness to accept suffering. The mechanism of the Hitler state was not countered by any Jewish organism. Pious Jews most likely glimpsed in their fate a "punishment" for Jewry's sins, and Zionists believed that the errors of past generations were now coming home to roost, whereas assimilationists or those who had turned away from Judaism though the thoughts appropriate to them; but none of these views developed beyond mutual recriminations and apologetics into a fruitful position.

One's own guilt, the guilt that, as a Jew, one has to account for through Judaism, was not taken as a starting point to develop a creative principle. People did not realize that those who suffer the most are those who always blame others and believe themselves to be blameless. In the relatively bearable conditions of Theresienstadt people failed to realize that persecution presented an opportunity for a human catharsis and for the rediscovery of a Judaism that most knew only superficially. Hardly anyone found his way back to Judaism as a result of being in Theresienstadt, nor did being there cause those who already were followers of a "Jewish" ideology to find their way to a freer and deeper approach. People did not admit to themselves that the trends that dominated the world had dragged them along without resistance because they had not seen through the ideological façade. They took the dominant ideology itself to be the essence of the hostile calamity and were satisfied to distance themselves from it, because they had to, even if they did not want to. The essence behind the rejected ideology remained no less alien than their own essence, which was equally enshrouded in ideologies that were mistaken for the essence itself. Thus they did not suspect that their own essence had almost become identical with the alien one, that this identity already almost determined their own inclusion in the mechanism of the enemy's sphere of control. People spent too little time immersed in Jewish history and could not see beyond the external similarities between current and former martyrdoms to the common meaning of the community of suffering. Suffering always seemed to be simply a "misfortune" – the reasons for it were incomprehensible. Strange: previously one could – perhaps! – have escaped the suffering by doing this or that, by being baptized; now that many were willing to pay this price to escape, the possibility no longer existed. Being a devout Christian, a member of the nations, did not grant freedom. Were not the Jews historically always accorded external or internal characteristics that, in large part, made escape from the Jewish fate impossible? Times of particularly intense persecution have always pointed the Jews back to their own community, even despite their most extreme protest. Should it not have occurred to them that they were the "others," the Jews, and that as such they had to recognize their particular task, which had been expressed in the great monuments of antiquity and would be called to mind even if they betrayed or wished to forget it? Should they not have realized that the hostile negation of the Jews by other peoples always should be countered with their own position? Should they not have learned that the hardest blows always had fallen when the prescribed task was neglected?

Such obvious questions were rarely posed, and there was no insight to show that the doctrine passed on by a theocratic power throughout the ages irreconcilably opposed history's most unscrupulous secularization of power. People unconditionally accepted the idol of the day, mechanism, and disapproved only of its horrible apparatus. Only in this way was it possible for those in power, without decisive opposition from the victims, to overreach so far with their deification of the "Führer" and demonization of "the Jews." Judaism, however, which was chosen to make a crucial contribution to the realization of a different, true power, was turned into its opposite in a demonic collapse of values. The temporal power, which ultimately was consumed by powerlessness, was bad; it portrayed itself as "good" and described as "bad" those destined for a mission for good. The representatives of this mission did not become aware of it, despite such terrible challenges. They did contradict the damning judgment of the temporal power but did not know how to free themselves, at least internally, from the effects of its malice; at the same time, many prisoners persisted in their own baseness and even took strength from it. Someday we may point to this as the worst tragedy of the Jews in the history of this persecution.

The Jews of Theresienstadt have integrated themselves into the history of the Jewish people as a segment in its experience of suffering, in which the history of Theresienstadt forms a small but particularly curious part.

THE TYPOLOGY OF INDIVIDUAL BEHAVIOR

The age of mechanical materialism and the ideologies analogous to it prohibit the collective achievement of value. Never before had the concept of community been discussed as frequently as in Hitler's Germany, but such pseudocollectivism leads, in reality, only to masses and complexes. The community of the National Socialists proved to be merely a community of fate, and in the camps it took the form of a coerced community. Within this framework an individual could preserve his personality only in the parts of his life where even this power could not penetrate, at least until the moment of physical murder. Many possibilities, for both good and bad, remained open to a person in the camps. By "person" we mean an individual who recognizes only his own conscience or nonhuman entities as authorities for his acts

The Psychological Face of the Coerced Community

and omissions. Not for nothing did the herd leaders of the pseudocollective condemn individualism by recognizing the last bulwark of a position that opposed their demands. Only within the areas of one's life into which terror could not intrude did true humanity assert itself. Externally, people became numbers, because power had decided that it should be so; internally, people recognized this power by, for example, wearing their numbers as "jewelry," etched or cut into tin. The pressure that compelled massification was almost irresistible. Externally, one could not entirely escape it, but even internal resistance was limited. This is where the personal tragedy of National Socialism, which goes beyond the community tragedy, begins. The individual had to choose among two pairs of possible behaviors:

1. Participating or not participating
2. Observing or not observing

Participating and Not Observing

Those who participated in the camp could rarely observe it; they were engaged in its workings, without the will or opportunity to recognize what was unfolding. These people generally were entangled in guilt and did not know what game they were playing. They took their actions and behavior seriously, although their intelligence should have warned them against this. Because of the apparent importance of their role, they believed themselves important, or – and this was particularly fatal – they believed in their power. They mistook their role for reality. Many became deceived deceivers. These included influential functionaries and less important people, all the way down to the Order Constabulary members at the barracks gates, house service staff, and lavatory attendants. The behavior of such people in high positions, even house elders, had a disastrous effect; the behavior of those in lower positions often seemed unintentionally comic, but more often these people were the ones who made the difficult lives of those around them even less bearable. It was fortunate when the presence of a rational person could lighten the nasty, tormented mood with good nature and robust humor.

Some participants at first intended not to forget to observe, but they soon succumbed and took part with less and less reserve; even intelligent men became victims of their own participation, especially if they were unable to overcome weaknesses of character. The appearance of power, love affairs, vanity, developed selfishness, complacency, corruptibility, and an inability to resist acquiring forbidden indulgences were dangerous. Human error caused one to stumble much more quickly in the camp than in normal society, in which adherence to moral standards and relative prosperity, as well as personal advantages, would compensate for and mitigate many weaknesses. In the camp, even the tiniest violation of strict legalities had a disastrous effect; no step could be recalled, atonement was very difficult or impossible, and there was no escape other than to participate.

Because, in general, the work required was evil, people participated evilly. One could observe this descent in the workers in "nutritional professions" and in many other functionaries; it was also significant in the development of the "court life" surrounding the Jewish leadership. A harrowing letter from Edelstein, written in early December 1942 to Zionist friends in the "Central Labor Office," is located tragically at the crossroads of such behavior:

I would like to ... tell you, 12 months after the memorable 3 December 1941, how I see our decision and how I judge my attitude. On 2 December, I had a meeting with the chief [of the SS, Günther], who gave me information that deeply distressed me. At the time, I did not dare commit it to a written memorandum; I told only 2 or 3 people superficially what wind was actually supposed to be blowing in the Theresienstadt Ghetto. Now you will perhaps understand my farewell address [in Prague], which was in fact sad. Was it right to take his best friends with him, to drag them along into chaos and misfortune? Where did I find moral justification for my conduct? Today I can say it: our *chalutz* [Zionist-Socialist] worldview taught us always to be where the fate of the Jewish people is tragic, but is also being newly formed. ... I never understood or interpreted the term *chalutz* very narrowly. To be *chalutz* does not merely mean being a worker, but also being the bearer of fulfillment [*Verwirklichung*] [*sic*!; note the usage of this National Socialist–influenced term], finding the positive in the negative, and developing new bases of life for the community. ... The year in Theresienstadt has not passed any of us by without a trace. I sense it most strongly in myself. The consciousness of fulfilling a historical [!] function and the constant fear of not living up to the great task determined my attitude. I learned, to a greater degree than before, to be modest and to realize how little we have learned and how few creative and original abilities we possess. Under the pressure of these feelings, I became more nervous and uncertain, which was often interpreted by uninvolved observers as weakness and lack of courage in implementing items in the program [!]. ... When I survey the past year, I find that the things I really wanted ... became reality, slowly but surely. [Think of the "ghetto" in 1942, with its transport confusion and the starvation of old people!] However, this method affected my character so that I was somewhat less often open and direct, sometimes even towards my own friends. (51)

Here the tragedy of the era became apparent in Theresienstadt: the tragedy of ideological rigidity and the tragedy of the Jewish people, demonstrated by a man who believed himself to have the best of principles and who was deceived because he followed the "false alarm" (in the words of Kafka), and this could not be put right. This is the tragedy of the cooperator, who miscalculated in the confusion of his times and perished as a result, without being able to rescue his inner freedom. Often, this crossroads was a disastrous place to be, especially for people who did not consult their consciences as Edelstein did. Kogon's words applied to them: "The dominant prisoners formed the camp aristocracy. ... Some of them, just like the nobility in all eras and peoples, were a class of good-for-nothing parasites."

Participation could become ridiculous when it distorted people's sense of reality by recording a constantly simulated reality that no longer existed. First we consider a document, harmless in itself, which, in its claim to legality in a world of unconditional lawlessness, demonstrates the approach of participation without observation:

Declaration.

In the months of December 1942 to February 1943, Julian Glas, employee of the production accounting department of the Theresienstadt ghetto, created a carbon copy accounting process that is to our knowledge novel. Essentially, it involves ... .

The aforementioned system has been in use since January 1, 1943, in a mentioned system variant that was specially developed for our production accounting department.

Mr. Julian Glas has reserved all rights both in the ... described process and in the specially-applied process in our production accounting department, which we hereby confirm for the sake of order.

The Psychological Face of the Coerced Community 581

Theresienstadt, February 5, 1943.
For the Production Accounting Department of the Theresienstadt Ghetto
[two signatures]

This seriousness was a tragic aberration in a ruined world in which the inventor, along with his invention and all witnesses, probably was exterminated in the end. Nevertheless, this document makes sense; it is even "normal" and must seem so to anyone unaware of the reality of Theresienstadt. The prisoners used psychological justification to see the present as something provisional and in which one could preserve "rights" that might be real in the future. This almost healthy type of reaction was a rejection of the present. Much more dubious is the next example. The lapsed values of a bygone norm were adopted, in all seriousness, as substitutes in the present; through them, the existing reality was acknowledged as legitimate and, *via facti*, was stripped of its monstrous provisional nature:

> The most difficult day in the Ghetto Guard [G.W., *Ghettowache*] was the dissolution of the old G.W., which had a very depressing effect on me.
> The best day, on the other hand, was the moment that I, an enthusiastic soccer player, could fight for the honor of the G.W. in their uniform for the first time.
>
> Alfred Fischl
> G.W. 54

Thousands of the victims – including, of course, good people – were like this. Ignorance gave them temporary protection from the grim reality, but it destroyed these people because they succumbed psychologically to the will of their exterminators. They became a defenseless, administered "mass" that could be easily exterminated. The poor author of the preceding document sought "honor" and "fought" for it, as events determined the existence or nonexistence of nations, and as the gas chambers consumed millions of people and threatened this unfortunate "enthusiastic soccer player." These were the "devils" tracked down, in their innocent guilt, by Hitler's henchmen; these were the poor fools who, at the edge of the abyss, kicked their soccer balls not as a harmless distraction but as a significant action, until a transport dragged them away from the game and flung them into the vortex of extermination.

In summary, we can observe two types of behavior in those who participated and did not observe:

1. Negation of the existing reality (which they perceived as more or less perverse), connected with fixation on a past reality (also postulated for the future). Here the individual sense of reality was distorted to varying degrees.
2. Qualitative confusion of past and present reality, or a failure to take account of the change in the reality without fixating on a past reality, when the differences in reality are not verified by consciousness or not connected with such a fixation. Here the objective recognition of reality is distorted to varying degrees, with or without a disruption in one's individual sense of reality.

Both types of behavior are psychopathological phenomena. The source of these morbid aberrations is a trauma caused by changes in reality. The degree of the

582

Psychology

disturbance can progress through various stages and can increase from slight confusion to a serious clouding of consciousness. There usually is no awareness of illness. It would have been almost impossible to have any therapeutic effect on the psychological disorder within its sphere of activity – that is, the "ghetto." People exhibited a veritable wish for illness, a wish that was constantly nourished by events. When one suspected or recognized something abnormal in one's relationship to the environment, to reality, one did not believe it and refused to admit, even when confronted with it, that an individual illness was present; anything abnormal was doggedly blamed on and located in the external world. The only protection from such psychological disturbances was to preserve and cultivate the ability to observe.

Participating and Observing

Very few could keep up this role unflinchingly, for it required unusual self-discipline. It was particularly difficult for those in responsible positions, but nothing was as necessary as this to the camp's moral self-assertion. The best achievements in Theresienstadt were the result of participation and simultaneous observation. To accomplish anything within the self-administration in this way, discretion and much diplomatic luck were necessary. The attempt was more likely to succeed in less obvious places. Such efforts must be appreciated as evidence of active resistance; despite all the corruption of public life and all the setbacks suffered, these courageous actions occurred again and again. Evidence of this behavior in Theresienstadt was left behind by the composer Viktor Ullmann:

> Thus Goethe's maxim "Live in the moment, live in eternity" seemed to me entirely to reveal the mysterious meaning of art.... Theresienstadt was and is for me the school of form. In the past, when one did not feel the impact and burden of material life because it was displaced by comfort, this magic of civilization, it was easy to create beautiful forms. Here, where one must overcome material through form in everyday life, where anything artistic stands in complete contradiction to its environment – here is the true master craftsman's school, if, like Schiller, one sees the secret of artwork in the eradication of material through form, which probably is the mission of man in general, not only aesthetic but also ethical man. In Theresienstadt, I wrote quite a bit of new music, mostly to satisfy the needs and wishes of conductors, directors, pianists, and singers, and thus the needs of recreational activity in the ghetto. To list them would be as futile as to stress that one could not play piano in Theresienstadt as long as there were no instruments. The severe shortage of music paper will also be uninteresting for future generations. It simply should be stressed that in my musical work I was encouraged, and not limited, by Theresienstadt; that we did not merely sit lamenting at Babylon's rivers, and that our desire for culture was appropriate to our desire to live; and I am convinced that all who sought to wrest form from protesting material in life and art will agree with me. (322)

Observing and Not Participating

An actual observer was rare, and observing was not without risk. Vitality demanded participation; reflection demanded observation. The more the satisfaction of elementary needs required attention, the more reflection was prevented. Thus such behavior was accomplished less often in practice than in intention.

The Psychological Face of the Coerced Community   583

Those who did not understand this could easily be deported with the next transport. Members of this group recognized how tragically ridiculous the business was, and it filled them with disgust; they recognized the hopelessness of any intervention and the impossibility of radical improvement; they wanted to avoid dirtying themselves and to remain "innocent," but then their inactivity became harmful; it could result in selfishness and could accelerate their own demise. One could best comply with this attitude if one was alone in the camp and relatively independent; this was especially common among old people who no longer were required to work. Some observers who no longer wanted to participate beyond the vital minimum refused higher positions and worked in the "squadrons" (*Hundertschaften*).

Some people displayed humor, a cheerful or sarcastic way of seeing through the situation. This humor could, however, degenerate into cynicism, when, with higher intelligence, one's ability to observe was not lost, but one consciously and unrestrainedly participated in the events. An observer's harmless mockery, which is demonstrated in the following two documents, was something different. These documents evoke the conditions in a more lively fashion than does any other retrospective portrayal. In the first example – which concerns a harmless mystification – the author imitates the manner of internal regulations in a purposely exaggerated fashion and faithfully renders the usual style of such documents:

Theresienstadt, 6 June 1943
Ghetto Theresienstadt
The Council of Elders
Health Service
Memorandum to Room Elders
Re.: Reports of sickness

In order to guide the abuse of unnecessary reports of illness as far as possible, in all quarters in which workers live, reports of illness will be carried out only after prior vote. The following procedure is to be followed: In the evening, when the head count is complete, the room elder will ask who would like to report recumbent or ambulatory illness for the coming days. He will note the names and announce them to the room inmates loudly and clearly. This is followed by a vote of the room inmates on whether they agree to the report of sickness of those registered.

In order to be recognized for the report it is necessary that, in quarters with an occupancy of more than 10 persons, at least 5 persons, in those with more than 30 persons, at least 10, and in those with less than 10 inmates, at least half the occupancy announce their affirmative vote. It is up to the room elder whether to have the vote carried out orally or through ballots. The room elder is personally responsible for ensuring that no abuse of this procedure occurs. The room elder will note the sick people recognized by the room inmates in alphabetical order and will report the illness situation of his room in the usual fashion the next morning personally or through a trusted representative.

No vote is necessary in the following cases:

1.) if a recumbent sick person already has been acknowledged as such by the responsible physician and is bedridden and in treatment by the room physician.

2.) if an ambulatory sick person already is being treated by a physician in the responsible outpatient facility and has been summoned by him to

584 *Psychology*

undertake further treatment, about which the sick person must always be able to show identification on demand.

3.) for severe acute illnesses (high fever, vomiting, fainting), for which the results of a vote cannot first be awaited, and

4.) for accidents, especially in case of imminent danger.

This regulation seeks to raise the labor morale of the ghetto inmates by calling on each individual to stand by his neighbor. At the same time, this new regulation demonstrates trust in the ghetto inmates on the part of the leadership, so that each one can prove he possesses the necessary seriousness and sense of responsibility that the leadership of the ghetto, in the 19th month of its existence, may expect and also demand from everyone.

This new regulation takes effect from the beginning of the next *Dekade*, that is, beginning from 11 June 1943. The memorandum shall be read aloud to the occupants on three consecutive days and will be kept by the room elder.

The Head of the Health Service:
Dr. Erich Munk m.p.

The second example high-spiritedly spoofs the "commands and prohibitions" in a mixture that reveals all of the self-administration's absurdity in a wonderfully uncanny fashion:

> Lice, bugs and fleas to be avoided,
> Hands to be washed without cease,
> Where possible, typhus to be spread –
> These are the mottos of the ghetto inmates.

Memorandum from Building Elder B V

Attention: Complaints are increasing that memoranda, to the extent ghetto inmates by way of the building elder, even aside from the following day's visit, must wear Jewish stars firmly sewn on and every uniform-wearer through taking off caps to avoid long queues in the distribution of rations, smoking is prohibited inside and outside the quarters.

The Ghetto Guard will be responsible for ensuring that during soap distribution, neither the shoe repair workshops nor the building elders will be processed from 10 to 11 o'clock.

Cleanliness: It is once more noted that throwing paper scraps on the street is not permitted after 8 o'clock P.M. without an entry pass.

Recreation: All reserved tickets must be deloused in the office of the building elder every day except Saturday.

Rationing Officer: We call attention to the fact that in its function the rationing service should be viewed as an official and should not be spat a either on the street or in the quarters.

Blackout: Because the room elders are responsible for precise adherence to the blackout rules, they must wear their hair cut to 3 mm according to regulation.

Ventilation: It was recently announced that abandoned corpses cannot be laid out later than 9 o'clock in the morning.

The Building Elder

When people's humor somewhat distanced itself, it prevented unthinking participation. There also was another type of humor that felt like a worn-out dress from the bourgeois world: the official camp humor, with its thoughtless optimism, which remained absolutely mired in participation.

Not Observing and Not Participating

Such people had the most difficult status. They lacked the vitality to cooperate and the inner transcendence to observe. Only those who came to the camp broken, or became broken there, could belong to this group: the seriously ill and elderly people who had given up. Those who did this willingly can be described as psychological suicide cases. In contrast to more strict camps, in Theresienstadt this type rarely was found among younger people.

ON "REALITY"

The role of reality in the inmates' manner of behavior already has been touched upon; now it seems necessary to investigate its nature, as a phenomenon, from the point of view of the camp. One might naïvely share the view, in accordance with a superficial philosophy, that "reality" is a constant quantity throughout history. This is not the place to refute this philosophically, but it will be shown that this view is incorrect both factually and psychologically from the standpoint of human beings. Reality changes with the essence of the changeable and, in reality, changing circumstances, which are equivalent to empirical reality in their active and specifically construable totality. This is an objective criterion for practical reasons, and it is so seldom recognized because the process by which circumstances change flows smoothly, and the change does not impose itself as an abrupt act on the human being who judges reality. No other view of reality (which in truth cannot be viewed but only seen through a reflected abstraction) has any practical significance for human beings. The authority that renders judgment on reality is consciousness. Consciousness allows the recognition of tendencies that prevent the objective reception of reality at various, mutually contradictory levels. If these tendencies dull the power of judgment, one's consciousness postulates "realities" that are not real in other ways outside of consciousness except as objective correlates to these tendencies. To the extent that this is possible, existing (empirical) reality is then no longer recognized but is conceived of in modified form; it is reinterpreted and "changed," but only in the realm of consciousness.

Even in normal life, people undertake such changes countless times, and this process dulls the incorruptibility of their ability to achieve consciousness. When immense, violent changes take place, such as those that Hitler brought primarily to the Jews, consciousness is caught off guard. The human being cannot want such a reality, so he prefers not to accept it. He ignores it, not only when it is the right thing to do for moral reasons but also in judging his general situation. The more one misjudges this and fixates on an earlier reality, the more changes one will undertake – for example, in the moral sphere – in accordance with a law of compensation. One cannot completely ignore the objective changes, because one wants to continue to exist, but one does so to the extent that one believes one is not endangering one's physical existence. One "annuls" existing reality and retains the past reality or wishfully fixates on a future reality related to that which has vanished. This generally corresponds to the inclinations of these suffering people. Great uncertainty is the result.

Existing reality seeks revenge against those who ignore it and who attempt to change it using ineffective means; it does so by dulling their ability to discern. The majority of the prisoners suffered from this. The specific type of reality that had become valid brought about a particular complication. This "applied" reality was achieved in part by violent change and in part by a powerfully accomplished denial of the previous reality. The National Socialist agenda changed not only the nature of reality itself – although this too was intended – but the structuring of circumstances that can be exacted from people within a system of social power. The ideology applied guided the new structure's direction of change; the mechanism being practiced produced the change. Both components created the cosmos of the National Socialist state, with the way of the "Führer" at the top and the way of the "Jews" beneath it.

In order to at least temporarily enforce this reality, which contradicted any true order, preexisting real values had to be changed and denied. This was how the conceptual confusion of National Socialism was achieved; it constantly enforced a redefinition of values that never were entirely achievable in reality and at the same time had to hide those values through tactical caution. The Third Reich failed because of this unavoidable discrepancy; reality even avenged itself on National Socialism. It is true that National Socialism subjugated reality to such an extent that it temporarily became desperately different, but its power was not sufficient to develop and assert itself in all areas. It altered reality only to the extent that its power allowed. As soon as it had violated reality beyond a certain degree, its power and its reality shattered. Nevertheless, the power of the created reality became destiny to those who were overtaken by it.

For the prisoners in Theresienstadt, the reality of National Socialism existed de facto. It was sinister and contradicted any image of reality with which people are comfortable. Reality was dis-placed (*ver-rückt*, a play on the words *verrückt* [crazy] and *ver-rückt* [displaced]) in the truest sense. There was nothing in it that conformed to what was commonly seen as reality, or what it should have been according to original desires. It became improbable, eerie. Although it was real, it became unreal and was perceived as not real. Thus it was experienced as deceptive, bogus, a dream, the spawn of sick fantasies. Within the specific limits we have just described, this was not wrong.

If one connects the altered reality with the prisoners' relationship to it, one can perhaps imagine the conceptual confusion. It made Theresienstadt into a uniquely illusory world, where few could distinguish between reality and deception. Things were delusional in every camp in which people could live, but in Theresienstadt this was true to the highest degree, and this is one reason that life in a camp is so hard for "normal" people to understand, and why it is so hard to explain it to them if they did not experience it as an "observer."

Dr. Emil Utitz speaks, with good reason, of people's schizophrenization, but in addition it must be recognized that this psychosis did not just play out subjectively in people's consciousness, and that it was not a genuine clinical psychosis but an irritable condition that split consciousness in the area of inescapable psychological disorder, where the human being, confused and divided, had to behave in a schizoid manner, as it were, in order painfully to balance the elementary discords in his innate and learned worldview with the ceaseless flicker of irritating phenomena. It may seem bold but it better reflects the circumstances to say that the psychosis was established in the outside world, for reality itself was schizophrenically divided and decayed. Thus it was a "perverted" psychosis in the objective

The Psychological Face of the Coerced Community 587

world; the subjective degeneration was merely its reflection. For this reason, one may not simply claim that people felt and acted in a delusional manner. They often did so only to the extent that their reactions made it clear that reality was beyond their ability to grasp. Every value, every characteristic, and every trait had lost or changed its original meaning. This already was true of the world on the other side of the fortress walls, but it reached new heights in the "ghetto"; there, everything fell in on itself, only to rise anew and once again collapse, again and again. It is understandable that outside visitors were fooled; the reality could not be comprehensible to a brief visitor, because it remained incomprehensible to the prisoners who lived in the midst of the confusion. People were confused, were made confused, and even confused the confusion. This went so far that reality itself often was considered no longer to be present and degenerated into an impossibility, an unreality. This process, seen as a collective phenomenon, reached a level that is unique in written human history.

The world had been enlightened, in vain, at a no-longer-recoverable cost, by eliminating the uncanny, the unfathomable, and the apeiron; now this uncanniness had reappeared. It stood before people in the form of an SS man, but they also embodied it themselves and threw themselves into the curse of its epoch. One says of ghosts that they have the quality of being and not being at once. That is how it was in the camp. One was, and yet was not. One dreamed. People believed they were dreaming and did dream. They lived on the edge between Something and Nothing. Either reality was different from what one thought, or one was different from what reality wanted, or both were the case. One had turned into matter in such a way that matter itself became questionable. One almost could not be anything but an object. One waited and was dependent. One wanted to revolt, but it led to nothing. Fate decided otherwise. People went from one authority to another, all of which could only make the collective decision, which was that they were incapable of deciding anything. This was the "unreal" reality, which Camp Commandant Seidl called the "paradise ghetto": an existence on sharp edges, over unfamiliar chasms. People were violated by deceptions. These deceptions could pass by as dreams. But just when one wanted to see them as dreams, they became reality. And just when one wanted to take them for reality, one realized once again that they were deceptions. In the end, everything went in circles and produced ghostly turbulence. In the end it was a matter of fate – or, expressed religiously, grace – whether one took false steps in this dance and became ashes or whether one could one day say, with more unease than liberation: I survived; I am alive.

Thus the camp became a unique test. Existence and nonexistence had gotten mixed up. The last eschatological questions obtruded themselves, as they do wherever people find themselves faced with the outermost limits, with the apeiron.

THE PRACTICAL PSYCHOLOGY OF THE CAMP

We have developed the role of history, individual behaviors, and reality in the functioning of the camp. Now we must identify the individuals who were reluctantly pressed into this threefold framework. The previous chapters can serve, from the perspective now gained, as a collection of examples of the following ideas and words.

Changes in Character

The camp changed every character. Kogon says, "The new psychological disposition was formed in three stages of development: through the shock of arrival, the 'selection process' in the early months, and finally through the years of acclimation, which created the 'concentration camp' type." This was true in similar fashion, although less markedly, in Theresienstadt. However, this point seems to contradict Kogon's aforementioned words: "Most prisoners left the concentration camp with exactly the same convictions they had had before." One should not see this change in character as a change in views or a deterioration of established morality. Only outward civil behavior (better known as morality) was generally, sometimes as if overnight, dismantled as though it had never been. A self-contained personality could have had his equilibrium threatened or violated without suffering severely; he could have stabilized the basic state possessed in his previous life, usually rapidly, as soon as it was possible to examine his own concepts and values and protect them in relation to circumstances in Theresienstadt. The embodiment of the behavior we call character changed, if the vitality of a new arrival had not already been broken or collapsed as a result of the deportation. People rarely changed in such a way that previously operative traits were simply reversed; on the contrary, their inclinations did not fluctuate much and generally became much more marked. Every character trait became more sensitive than in a normal environment and inevitably was affected by the extreme world of the camp.

There were two ways in which one's character could change, with gradual transitions and mixed forms: cultivation of good or of bad characteristics. People much more frequently became worse – as a response to the badness of the world. Under these conditions, that was the "normal" reaction; there is no sense in denying this now, in order to make heroes of the pitiable victims. It was not the rule that one's character became very much worse, but that also happened, unpleasantly. If good traits made their mark, their effects contrasted particularly strongly with the bad surroundings. Every good deed, even every good word, was incomparably more valuable than in a normal society, often because the sacrifice connected with it was immense; in this morass, the names of those who committed acts of silent heroism were ennobled and were associated with devotion and self-denial.

Almost all changes occurred at the moment one suddenly was pushed into this world. Everyone, strong or weak, felt the shock of arrival, which we have compared with birth. How one's individual fate would be fashioned depended largely on how quickly one adjusted to the camp. A child must first orient himself in the world, and this also was true for new arrivals in the "ghetto." Some succeeded at it quickly, others slowly, and still others hardly at all. Robust health and personal connections to old, experienced camp inmates operated in one's favor.

Life in Theresienstadt was determined by fear of deportation, which joined – or even replaced – the normal fear of death. Reactions and behaviors in the "ghetto" must be understood to a great degree from this point of view. Fear of transports was seldom compensated for; it was difficult to truly overcome, but it was often disguised in every conceivable way, including, as described previously, by taking one's occupation in the camp seriously and participating in cultural life or entertainment. The better one adjusted and the longer one spent in Theresienstadt, the greater became the fear of the transport, which can be compared with the increased fear of death among

The Psychological Face of the Coerced Community 589

adults and older people, in contrast to the heedlessness of young people and children. But this fear, along with the efforts to numb it, increased the longer this camp existed.

As in a strict camp, the old "concentrationers" were found to some extent, especially among the younger Czech Jews; members of the first transports, and especially AK members, would have liked to think of themselves as a self-contained community and camp aristocracy, and a situation similar to that in Buchenwald was prevented only by the fact that the SS appointed high Jewish functionaries from Berlin and Vienna to crucial camp positions. The SS's influence on the appointment of the leading camp functionaries and "notables" distinguished the foundation of the social structure in the "ghetto" from that of other camps. The rudiments of many communities developed side by side, which lent the "ghetto" its complicated social structure. Members of earlier transports often felt superior to those of the more recent transports, and sometimes people resented the fact that the newcomers did not know certain things or had not experienced them directly. Then they would say, "You have no idea ... ," and, "You haven't experienced anything ..."

Characters According to Types

Despite some reservations about schematic classifications, the following sections emphasize certain main types of people. These types are independent of origin, social history, or position taken in the camp. We distinguish fourteen groups: the broken, the fearful, the numb, the heedless, pessimists, realists, optimists, illusionists, active people, brutal people, opportunists, strong-willed people, helpers, and kindhearted people.

Broken People

Broken people were found almost exclusively among the elderly and sick. Generally they neglected their appearance more than their helpless situation already necessitated. They were self-pitying in regard to fate. Their vitality had been extinguished or was limited to animalistic urges. They were desperate and had more or less finished with life. They simply let go. The tiniest problem ensured their rapid death. Generally, they were dully acquiescent; sometimes they still rebelled but then quickly sank back into lethargy. Nothing made them happy anymore; they could not be diverted. Their demise was certain; they were "the" victims per se. Robbery of their property, lice infestations, and other sufferings in the camp accelerated their collapse.

Fearful People

Fearful people were most common among the elderly. They lived in constant fear and were pursued by delusions. They were plagued by endless premonitions about the next deportation, which they believed would take them away. Every little thing upset them. They were restless. They resembled the broken people but differed from them in that they still were afraid. They succumbed to every panic and every evil rumor and sensed an "unavoidable" catastrophe, only too often with reason. Some resembled the illusionists, but the tiniest incidents, even unjustified ones, destroyed their illusions.

Numb People

There were two subtypes of numb people: (1) Some resembled the broken prisoners, from whom they soon could not be distinguished, if they did not recover. They usually were found among newcomers who had not yet adjusted. (2) Some were weaklings who could easily be knocked down by any adverse incident. They succumbed to every influence and had no opinions of their own. One minute they were pessimistic, and the next minute optimistic, they lacked judgment. They were found much more rarely among young people than among the elderly.

Unthinking People

Unthinking people were not as unselfconscious as the numb, whom they resembled in some respects. "What happens, happens," they said. They avoided effort and longed to swim to the top of the camp hierarchy. If they were sufficiently vital, they easily could become unscrupulous, wanting to snatch small advantages, and they were not choosy about the means they used. They generally sought pleasure. Sometimes they made fun of their surroundings and were cynical. They believed they had discovered that all considerations and efforts were pointless. They tended towards pessimism, without necessarily being fatalistic. "Times are much too difficult for me to worry unnecessarily," they told themselves. They fancied themselves natural and uncomplicated. Psychological stress was studiously avoided. This type occurred in all age groups, but more frequently among young people.

Pessimists

Pessimists were present in every age group. Generally they were weak personalities; strong people seldom fell victim to this trait. At every (all too frequent) opportunity, they confirmed how right their pessimism was: "That's what I've always said!" They were bitter, embittered, and generally humorless. "The food will get worse – the war will be endless – Hitler will kill us all." They rarely resembled the broken ones in manner. They felt hope more often than they would admit to those around them or to themselves. Sometimes their pessimism was caution, to avoid succumbing to unjustified optimism, or even to illusions. Such people could become temporarily optimistic if they had a "reason" to be. Then the incorrigible optimists and illusionists would say, "Well, if even he believes it, then ..." Pessimists generally were not well-liked; their defeatism distinguished them from the realists. They knew about all the bad things in advance, but as soon as such events occurred, they could become disappointed, fearful, and despondent.

Realists

Realists were found in all age groups, but not often. There was a coarser, more robust subtype of realists whose character approached that of the heedless and who took things as they came. Much less common was a deep type of realist; unlike the illusionists, such people held a balance between optimism and pessimism. The realists, especially the second subtype, were smart, critical, and self-critical. They confronted the facts openly and strove for the correct insights that were so difficult here. They were superior and often characterized by restraint. They rarely succumbed to general panic and were excellently suited to the role of observer, although, depending on their respective attitudes, they liked to be a part of things, for good or evil. The best of them were cautious, reliable advisers and thus resembled the helpful and kindhearted. They alerted others to trouble and helped the despairing. They attempted to diminish the influence of the illusionists and the overly jolly optimists.

Optimists

Optimists represented the most numerous group. Their behavior could appear in combination with any of the types that did not conflict with optimism. By nature they were less common among older people, but even in that group they were surprisingly frequent. They believed any agreeable information uncritically, even if they were smart. "The war will be over in six weeks – it can't be lost – the Germans have other worries now besides the Jews in Theresienstadt – there are no more trains to carry out transports – We're protected by the Red Cross – the Nazis won't dare do anything else to us because they're afraid of America." The optimists were the born voluntary participants. When their errors became clear, they always had ways to console themselves. They sometimes temporarily became pessimistic, but it was not their way to turn realistically sober. They thoroughly dominated the mood of the camp and became involuntary allies of the SS, whose game they failed to understand. The smartest of this group, those who had not lost all sense of proportion, could resemble the realists. They attempted to find the best in the situation and nourished hopes that did not appear too improbable. This semirealism, however, rarely succeeded, because the reasons that sparked their optimism were contrary to true realism. Most of them brooked no opposition and did not heed warnings. If one disagreed with the optimists' claims, they were insulted and could become unpleasant. As a majority in the living quarters, they silenced all skeptics, and anyone who did not agree was considered a hopeless pessimist.

Illusionists

Illusionists were more common among older than among younger people and were more dangerous to the camp than the optimists. They simply turned the truth on its head. The imaginings of the average optimist were not rosy enough for them. They lost all self-control and spun themselves into their own, or into a borrowed, web of lies that they took for unvarnished truth. If anyone were to destroy their illusions, they would have become broken people, from whom they were separated only by their lively vitality. They did not listen to pessimists or realists. They could not observe and had to unconditionally cooperate with the tactics of the SS, without ever realizing it. They rejected the present; the future and the past were their spheres. From the present they borrowed only optimistic ideals. Their intellect was necessarily clouded. In extreme cases, they suffered from pseudologia phantastica (pathological lying). They fell victim to events almost as easily as the broken people. This type was quite common, but pronounced cases were rarer, because camp life constantly unsettled their behavior.

Active People

Naturally, active people were found more frequently among the young. They tended to take part, to save themselves through involvement; they used this approach to overcome all difficulties. The restlessness of the camp most often swept them along and turned them into blind participants. They could resemble the heedless. If they lacked kindness, they could become ruthless. The better-natured of this type tried to step in everywhere and in this way sometimes resembled the helper type.

Brutal People

Brutal people represented an exaggerated form of the active type. They lacked inhibitions or consideration; they were aggressive and corrupt and harmful to the community to the point of criminality. They unscrupulously sent people on transports and robbed individuals as well as the community. They were heartless to the elderly and the sick. They were realists in their own way, with a shot of optimism; pessimism was rare in them. They dominated the top layer of camp operations and occupied profitable professions in which something could be "earned." Although found in all age groups, they were much more numerous among the young and youngest age groups. Many operated on a more or less illegal basis, although they often were clever enough to behave correctly. They were more rarely loners than members of cliques of like-minded people. In higher positions, they often were schemers or calculating diplomats and sometimes were quite ambitious. When their brutality occasionally turned into maudlin sentimentality, their behavior toward individuals could be kindly and even altruistic.

Opportunists

The opportunists often resembled the brutal people, from whom they differed in their lesser strength. What they lacked in robust vigor they had to make up in craftiness and servility. Sometimes they still had some scruples. They always had many connections and were jacks of all trades, forming the royal court of the camp bigwigs, whose orders and wishes they often fulfilled meticulously. They were insincere and jealously guarded their interests; they easily forgave themselves and blamed their bad behavior on the pressures of the prevailing situation. Many were a more vital variety of the fearful. They often wanted to be better than they "had" to be. They changed ideological colors, sometimes playing the good Jew, Zionist, or Czech – whichever role fit the circumstances. They generally were aware of their badness and sometimes privately strove to put right the wrongs they had done officially. They represented the most deplorable type in the camp.

Strong-Willed People

The strong willed were people with firm intentions; they never could be brought down. They were more purposeful and level-headed than the "active" and more responsible than the brutal ones. Nevertheless, the means they chose were not always harmless; however, they avoided pronounced badness. The more their will was aimed at maintaining their personal power to resist, the more pleasant this type could become. In their relations with their environment they resembled, depending on their principles, those who were brutal or the helpful and kindhearted. By nature, this type, which was always equipped with some optimistic realism, was found more often among the young than among the old.

Helpers

Helpers were found in all age groups. They were realistic or optimistic and usually also active and strong willed. They grasped every situation, often had a sense of humor, and knew how to get their own way sufficiently. Where necessary, they took a hand in things and knew how to make something more or less out of nothing. They were good comrades, but not all of them were free of calculation, and thus some of them did not mind being compensated a little for their help; but they were basically agreeable and good natured. Many were invested with freshness and naïveté, whereas some seemed rough. They were versatile and pliant by nature, and their company made daily life more bearable. They were more frequently found among the

The Psychological Face of the Coerced Community

low-level unknowns than among the leading figures in the camp. They were relatively common among assimilated people who did not feel Jewish; on the other hand, the relatively numerous brutal people among the assimilated is also noteworthy.

Kindhearted People

The kindhearted were, as is the case everywhere in the world, the rarest and were found among all ages and groups: the Jews and the baptized, the Zionists and the assimilated. They generally acted in silence, came without being called, and sacrificed themselves. They did what is in the nature of the kindhearted, which no outside circumstances can change and which has but one characteristic: kindness.

The Ethos in the Camp

When a world is turned upside down, traditional standards break down. The following three reports once again reveal to us the face of the coerced community:

> Sometimes I asked myself, will all of us meet in sanatoria in order to recover from kleptomania? Or, how many of us never will be outside when we are outside, but will have to end our lives in correctional facilities and prisons? I never would have thought that I would be capable of taking something that was not mine. Maybe there is in all of us the seeds of criminality? And I am sad about myself, that I can do that, simply take, otherwise somebody else will just take it. And I need these things. I wish I couldn't do it, couldn't be that way, would rather freeze even more, starve even more, and despite everything not be corrupted. But it's not true. That is what the Germans have done to us – they have made us into criminals, they have forced us to steal, to rob, to plunder. No, they do not teach us to work in these camps. I always worked, here it's not about that, I already could work before the Germans said, "Sordid rabble, we'll show you how to work! Naturally nothing but freeloading, exploiting others and living off their work. Get going, work!" But I never would have – now it's part of the daily routine. First come, first served, I've already been here this long, you haven't, I need this or that, I can get it only by taking it away from you. More new people will come, then you can take what you need. And one always needs everything, because one has nothing at all. (256)

> Here, living in fear and misery was established an artificial, sick community in which people whom one always had seen as respectable figures decayed morally. Conditioned by an actual prison psychosis, by deprivation, hunger, etc., the majority, especially the young people, reached a moral nadir. The difference between "mine" and "yours" often was completely erased, but mainly people offended against community property: kitchens, supply centers, food and other storehouses were the main fields of activity. Unfortunately, even people who were employed in caring for children and old people, the sick and the insane, exploited the helplessness of the people entrusted to them and stole from them. Later, when conditions in the ghetto had improved, "*Schleusen*" (stealing) no longer occurred out of need, but for enrichment and even as sport. There were individuals who came to Theresienstadt dirt poor and after awhile had enriched themselves at the expense of the community, that is, had stolen or fraudulently obtained a considerable fortune. Because of living conditions in general, relations between the sexes were to an extent very relaxed, and to an extent, of necessity, very public. Because of all these conditions, the morality of children and young people suffered greatly. (242)

> This positive attitude toward living in the moment – with the knowledge, or better put, with the suspicion that all this activity could at any moment come to a terrible, abrupt end – creates an atmosphere that is completely different from normal conditions. Aside

594   *Psychology*

from the poverty, the misery, the imprisonment ... it might be expected that, permeated with the senselessness of all activity, a general apathy, lethargy and depression would take hold. When the opposite occurs, ... an atmosphere arises that – independent of the normal driving forces of human behavior – contains a certain lightness and also greatness. Through the disengagement from the temporal ... every act attains an absolute quality, since it has no future, or only a very short one.... Being removed from time ... gives actions a timeless quality. Also a feeling of being, a feeling of love and friendship, gregariousness – but also an ephemeral quality. Of course there also are other reactions; hunger forces all sorts of skulking and dishonesty. The struggle for any improvement in living conditions, fear of the constant transports to Poland, and the struggle to remain in Theresienstadt ... lead to scheming, power struggles, the hunt for positions in which one is indispensable. The enormous overpopulation within too little space ... one can never be alone, there are almost no acts one can perform alone, even the most intimate. And this state of being forced together magnifies. One can see into others as if through a magnifying glass; one gets to know people as never before; need reveals the character of the oh-so-comfortable, veiled social forms.... Death loses its importance. One's dearest people are continually torn away through transports to the East, through death. Women and men seldom live together; the man's social function as head of the family and provider disappears. Women become independent. Relationships create almost no obligations. And in this atmosphere love flourishes as in a greenhouse, like colorful orchids on rotting stems, as an escape into life, as an attempt to banish the future to this lost present, into the endlessness of lust. It is admittedly not as hopeless as all that. People are up to date on the war news. More than up to date. The hope for a miracle, for sudden redemption, is alive in many people.... Rumors precede events by weeks. The optimists revel in good news; the clear-sighted sense that none of this will make a difference to us, that we are lost, whether the war ends in two months or two years.... On the other hand, the organization of this misery, this "Three Penny Opera" atmosphere of exaggerated tragedy, also has a comedic side.... The thousands of formerly bourgeois women and girls who now work as cleaning women with buckets and brooms, as nurses in nurses' uniforms and caps, as gardeners in overalls with rakes and baskets, as kitchen or laundry girls, or who march by in columns, give a theatrical impression – the more so because everything scrolls by in masses, in columns. One has the impression of a film in which everything is in costume, unreal. Just as life on the streets in general, against the backdrop of the mighty baroque barracks and small houses with their grotesque overpopulation, seems film-like. The individual vanishes; everything is a mass scene.... The juxtaposition of the often ruthless vitality of the young, and the helpless, weak elderly abandoned to the greatest misery results in a difficult situation. (13)

These reports once again demonstrate the entirety of the misery of the camp. The first one shows what happened to people, although it did not absolutely have to happen; the immorality of the accused Germans cannot excuse the immorality of the imprisoned Jews. Even if they held out physically, people fell almost irretrievably into a struggle of all against all, in which only people with a deeply anchored morality could keep from sacrificing their souls. Usually people made questionable compromises, and ultimately they were no longer compromises; people let themselves fall into the moral abyss. The intended physical extermination of the Jews was preceded by their moral extermination. Not only had Hitler described them as the paragon of all evil, but he had really plunged them into the Reich of Evil. This does not free the abused victims from their own guilt, but it increases Hitler's and that of his fellows immeasurably; they degenerated the world into one single evil.

The Psychological Face of the Coerced Community

Those who refused to allow themselves to be internally "brought into line" had not submitted to their enemy and were able to hold their own. Otherwise, they risked – even more than the splitting – the disintegration of their personality. As a general consequence of the prevailing ideology, in Theresienstadt massification seized even those who seemed untouched by it, for the SS had set out to extinguish the individuality of their victims; this was initiated in Theresienstadt and was completed in stricter camps. With the disappearance of a bourgeois order, many whose sense of self was derived from their position, their property, and the other external circumstances of a normal society found the rug pulled out from under them. As soon as they felt themselves separated from their protective environment, disintegration took place. The difference between culture and civilization became clear. Most civilizing pleasures were removed, but the possibility of culture remained. Although a culture can flourish fruitfully only if it can take shape in a concrete world, its foundation lies merely in the personality that is able to form and perceive it. The cultured human being (*Kulturmensch*) who achieves something that raises him above his animalistic abilities may be protected and encouraged by the values of civilization and an existing culture, but he is not himself created by them. He has first of all realized culture within himself and continues to work on it. Such a person could hold his own in Theresienstadt.

Arrival required an adjustment. The newcomer had to get his bearings. Soon thereafter, he achieved the disposition and form that he would maintain for the duration of his stay. In the process he had salvaged or given up his assertiveness (if he had ever possessed it), and the disintegration had occurred. If he did not have sufficient strength to assert himself and did not recognize the disintegration in himself, he summoned illusions and said, "Right now I am not whom I want to be, but I was something, and I will be something.... ." This was the escape from the present.

The Escape from the Present

For older people, it was more common to flee into the past, and the young tended to escape into the future, but normally both happened at the same time. One imagined a "reality" for oneself and one's immediate environment; one embellished it with more or less fantasy according to one's temperament and love of truth. People managed to argue about who had paid more taxes in the past. People lied through their teeth, saying they once had been rich, respected, and powerful; people dreamt of former pleasures – of food, clothing, homes, marvelous trips, wonderful friendships, and incalculable treasures. Or they transferred similar illusions into the future. Anything was better than the present. Strangely, even people who could see through all this bragging liked to listen to the recitation of such illusions. People sought intoxication even more passionately in Theresienstadt than in normal life, and illusions replaced unattainable narcotics.

Social Relations

One main source of thoughts and conversations, aside from illusions, was practical, everyday issues, often admixed with illusions. The prisoners talked constantly about topics such as food, accommodation, transports, clothing, possible pleasures, war and war's end, mail and packages, relatives near and far, and health, in addition to spreading gossip; but when the transports happened, they overshadowed everything else. Otherwise, food and accommodation, along with the plague of vermin and lack of heat, were generally the focus. More than anything else, one had to control oneself so as not to wallow in fantasies of food.

Friendships and enmities seemed heavily accentuated. Usually, all passions were exaggerated, although sometimes they were also weakened; normal standards did not restrain them. One often had to pull oneself out of a strange, creeping apathy. It was interrupted sporadically by fits of temper, which broke out fiercely but quickly ebbed.

There was little in the way of family life. Some relationships became looser, whereas others became firmer as a result of the conditions. People said cynically that there had never been as many good marriages as in Theresienstadt. Sexual morality was largely relaxed, especially among the leading functionaries, those who owned more, the brutal, and the young. Some situations can only be described as a brothel economy. Nevertheless, brutalization certainly was not the norm; aside from often apathetic behavior, much refined reserve was also practiced. Orgies probably happened on occasion but were magnified greatly through rumor. Homosexual relations apparently were rare among young people and were even rarer than previously. Discussions on sexual subjects were not everyday occurrences in Theresienstadt, and vulgar language was infrequent.

Most prisoners lacked the opportunity to keep a pet to serve as an object of their affection. Once, a leading functionary had a cat, and another was even permitted a wolfhound for a time. If a stray dog turned up in the camp, it was gazed at in wonder.

The fact that one never could be alone did not prevent inner loneliness, but it was this that made the camp into a seething brew of emotion, and therefore almost everyone was "nervous." It is astonishing that, under the conditions described, life was not even less bearable, and the vigorous essence of these tormented people surpassed all belief. It is a mistake to speak of the Jews' lack of vitality, or even decadence, just because it was true of individual cases; the history of the "ghetto" provided indisputable proof of the physical resistance of the Jewish prisoners. If reports from stricter concentration and extermination camps seem to contradict this, there remains the question of how members of any other people would have behaved in the same or a similar camp. Because there is no suitable basis for comparison – with the exception of the Gypsies, who yielded like the Jews to the most extreme state of ruin – nothing definite can be said about the Jewish people's and other people's degrees of vigorous resistance.

The extent to which the age groups were alienated from one another was painful. The children suffered most from this, because their parents' generation itself counted for little, and that of the elderly counted for nothing at all. The intention of many educators to lead "homes" and summer camps for a youth movement was an attempt to find a solution; this would have had a healthy function in normal life as a change of pace, but it could not continue in the camps as a permanent situation. Despite all the advantages offered the children, they lacked a home, care, and education. Age was abused physically, and youth morally. Attempts were made to bring together the age groups and various classes in conciliatory fashion, but only in ineffectual ways; even with the best of intentions, the problem would have remained insoluble. A coerced community of this sort can initiate only conglomerations and cannot achieve any real bonds, and it collapses as soon as the coercion ends. Values that are found in it can be recognized as part of the resistance against its history, and they flourish only as magnificent protest. They are attempts to carry on humanity in the Empire of Inhumanity and keep it from perishing, in order to overcome the coerced community and defend a humanitarian solidarity against the asocial.

People in the camp sought to influence their environment in various ways. We have seen how, disastrously, such efforts accommodated the SS's intentions, specifically through the "beautification." Of a different sort were tendencies in the manner of certain ideologies, among which Zionist propaganda took on the largest role, although its influence should not be overestimated. In addition, there was an undefined, nebulous tendency to characterize "Jewish" in general as a value and to speak constantly of "Jewish community," and yet to see Jewry as merely as a vague countervalue to anything that proved to be not Jewry or simply hostile. Among the Czech-assimilated prisoners, national propaganda had an influence. Greatly magnified since the beginning of the war, there was in these circles the beginnings of a political resistance movement that worked with communists and Zionists. Even the Jewish Elder Eppstein was said to have unproven connections to such a group. Certainly, none of these efforts had a noticeable effect on the history of the camp, as they did in Eastern European ghettos and other camps. More private attempts to influence the environment – to warn, advise, calm, encourage, support inner powers of resistance, and prevent or combat panic – took place in the moral and ethical sphere.

Judaism in the "Ghetto"

People rarely used genuinely Jewish ways of thinking to contemplate the problem of general humanity. Despite the influence of Leo Baeck and some others, it appeared that few people had any use for a Judaism that was not combined with the cheap tools of an ideology – that is, something fundamentally alien to Judaism. The humanitarian values that were fostered were more or less unconnected with Judaism or were sometimes explicitly outside Judaism. A simple humanity that came from the depths of a primal emotion and that did not rely on any particular theoretical tools occasionally broke through strongly.

However the prisoners might judge their fate, they rarely drew any revolutionary consequences from it. Previously acquired views were proved to be "correct," and adjustments generally were not undertaken, except for those that more firmly established existing opinions. Thus Judaism had difficulty gaining true adherents in the camps. Those who previously had wished to escape Judaism now desired this even more resolutely. Those who previously had, in whatever form, looked upon it favorably hardly found it necessary to change their relationship in any significant way.

This result would be psychologically incomprehensible were not one able to see it in connection with the analysis offered. The state of a world that denies and enslaves human beings, in which there are supposed to be only "masses" and "complexes," finds itself in irreconcilable conflict with life, as it presents itself in Judaism in particular and in humanity in general. The worlds of life and of the mechanical are unconnected; they may be homologous, but never homogeneous. Humanity cannot be internally affected by mechanics, but neither can it awaken any life in the mechanism. Therefore, humanity generally was unable to pry from the now-mechanical victims anything that might have come in handy as a contribution to humanity. Humanity and the mechanics of massification remained roughly the same throughout this history. The world's psychological situation retained the same oppression at the moment the National Socialist state collapsed as at the moment it began. We must admit that everything remained, and remains, as if "nothing" had happened. This history, a would-be experiment, has indeed caused the desolation and destruction of the outside world, but it did not change it inside. It simply illuminated more clearly the contradictions that exist between man and mass, between organon and mechanics, between life and complexes. Those who previously had tended toward, or succumbed to, mechanical massification were not cured; generally they only entangled themselves more hopelessly and clung even more tightly to "their" ideology.

Therefore it is no wonder that Judaism itself, too, showed little benefit. Among the Jews who came to Theresienstadt, even those whose beliefs remained useful the longest, who were truly religious and upheld a certain way of life, often found that Judaism became fossilized, rudimentary, and ultimately alien. When it was effective, however, it generally no longer was the original Judaism, but a diluted and – worse yet – mechanized extract with dangerous admixtures from the mischief of a world in whose construction Jews had participated. As an ideology, Judaism could offer itself only to those who remained in a spiritual state that was ready for it. Regardless of the vast differences among ideologies and the stages of their values, this ideologically devalued "Judaism" had become fundamentally the same as every other form of reality in the Occident outside the Jewish people.

If a Jew felt human, he would not allow himself to be impressed or captured by ideologies. The great majority, because they neither knew nor understood Judaism as an organism, saw in what they thought of as Judaism, and what they were offered as such, only a venerable relic or even an ideology like the ones they were trying to avoid; this inspired fear and disgust. Thus people in the "ghetto" – who were Jews according to the decreed "Reich laws" – seldom drew closer to Judaism, in any sense beyond devalued gestures and ideological masks, and they attempted to live their lives independently and "free" of it, or within the framework of ideas other than Jewish ones. For decades, the Jewish youth of Central Europe generally had suffered from an extreme lack of education. Moreover, many Jews had foolishly renounced and abdicated those immortal values that nourish one's spirit and heart and that had, for centuries, armed a small people against all attacks and persecutions and filled it with values, and whose acceptance and sanctification would have been a blessing to any people and any human being. This lack of education and renunciation, we say, could only cause disaster, for now the center – the home of one's heart, which never fails to give comfort and dignity in distress to the entire people and every one of its limbs – was missing. The results of history's refutation of Jewish assimilation did not stop the flight from Judaism, in that people saw, unknowingly and despondently, only those things that could be considered undignified about Jews – although not about Judaism. Such people may have rejected the new and dangerous assimilation to ideologies, but they still remained trapped in the shell of a form of assimilation that had frozen into a bygone ideal.

Once more, the Jewish tragedy was accomplished, in that not only the less valuable members but also some of the best descendants of their stock could be great in regard to all of the word's possible values and could prove their humanity but knew nothing

The Psychological Face of the Coerced Community   599

or wanted to know nothing about Judaism. Judaism was absent, and in these years it rarely appeared new to anyone. If it broke through in someone, it already had guided him in earlier times. Such a person lived in an extreme loneliness in which he grew aware of the extreme loneliness of Judaism, which seldom was situated amid but always above this people.

CONCLUSION

It often has been said that history is a book from which we never learn. However, we point out that pessimistic as well as optimistic words of such a general sort are never entirely wrong but in the same way certainly are never entirely correct; they reveal something of the truth, which is hard to reveal completely. For subjects such as we, the objective can be only a goal and a wish. The claim that we have learned nothing from history stands, as a sad realization, for the fact that we do not learn enough; but everything that mankind has ever learned it owes exclusively to history. One might say that it has learned only from history, for all learning is history; only from learning can the new and creative things grow that become history. Now, at the end of this particular history, we can ask whether it is worth preserving it and researching it in such detail, whether we can learn something from it that would be more than mere knowledge, more than chronicles and annals, more than a retrospective commemoration. The author has no doubt that the answer is positive.

We have explored a world – a small and joyless world, but an entire world – and because we lingered at various points, we also presumed to judge it. One might call this rash were we not also willing to realize that nothing justifies excluding ourselves from this world. We stand in the midst of this world, especially as contemporaries, but even in the near future this will not change much. Paradigmatically, and in rare concentration, the developments, experiences, and crimes at the camp in Theresienstadt contained the sum of all suffering and evil that could and actually do otherwise, with a wider dispersion and less visibly, operate in other communities. The unique aspect of the camp we have considered is that everything skewed, dangerous, foolish, and mean that proliferates in humans and human institutions, often in secret and ornamented with aesthetic conventions, emerged in Theresienstadt so uncannily and in such unmerciful nakedness that no one who did not turn his eyes away in fearful flight was spared insight into the prevailing situation. In other contexts, the calamities of persecution, exploitation, or, as it is rightly termed, crying injustice carelessly prevail, but one need not see or hear them; there remains the possibility of an aesthetic, mystical, intoxicating, and freedom-coveting rejection. But in Theresienstadt there was no evasion, at least not for the courageous. One could protest that the dark side of life is truly not all there is, and that wallowing in sadness, suffering, and misery, when all this is over, is not worthwhile, for we should pay more attention to all the good and noble things and, seeing as we have referred to history, all the luminous role models and impressive examples. This is probably true – one should not sink into endless grief – but, if one is honest and hopes to avoid lying to oneself, this can succeed only if, in the grace of the sublime, one also recognizes oneself in the curse of guilt, if one grasps and understands the evil, and if one knows that one is entwined in its mechanisms as both perpetrator and witness. Through this process, it became possible to prepare a way for freedom by means of which to oppose evil through ethical behavior, and to employ one's conscience to play a part, and not an entirely bad one at that, but above all with a conscience that is so easily defeated by what might be called an aesthetic delirium, and that, if still named as such, too easily becomes regarded as a good conscience, which cannot actually come into being before the millennium. For a conscience in fact serves to remind us of the imperfection of the temporal and must be good, because it is given to us, but must be bad, because we are not perfect. We are not perfect, and neither is our environment. The amount of imperfection in the world appears in us as a bad conscience for the sake of the greatest perfection, which must constantly be striven for, so that we do not die of too bad a conscience or try to rip it from our hearts.

Understood in this way, Theresienstadt becomes a useful study, and anyone who wants to can learn lessons there, which certainly may also be learned elsewhere. But those who have faithfully followed us until now may recognize the example here. They will agree with us – whether or not they are Jewish, whether or not they were in a camp, and whether they seem to be enmeshed in this history more closely or only in the broader sense – that Theresienstadt was a place in this world that belongs to all of us, that a history that can, and to some extent does, belong to all of us took place there. Theresienstadt is, admittedly, merely a name that may sound to many like a distant legend. But the legend belongs to all of us. The calamity that drove this history to its end did not reach its end, for the Jews or for the other peoples. There and in other camps, in Germany and in other countries, the survivors were released from their prisons, but other camps exist where our fellow men are enslaved, and camps threaten people in many countries. And when people were released, abased and bruised, they often were not really free, for they already were imprisoned in other prisons. Mechanical materialism, with its ideological antics, continues to proliferate. Theresienstadt is still possible. It can be imposed on a massive scale, and, in the future, the Jews – who in mankind's overall history of suffering so often have had to serve as harbingers and as those most especially at others' mercy – might not be the only victims. Theresienstadt stands not as an experiment but as the writing on the wall, and it is more alluring than our disgust at the horror is yet willing to admit. The ignorant might still today consider the institutions and conditions created there to be fantastical and fanciful, but it is important to consider that they were able to become real, and to consider why this happened. Here we see before us the demonic character of an administration that is generally possible, perhaps even real; even in a situation without deportations and threatened destruction, such an administration would even more likely result in a degrading existence in pseudocollective massification, in obedience or slavery. But what can reliably protect us and prevent the evil from breaking out in even worse form as a result of the delusion of phantom ideologies, and from mistreating myriad people and then destroying the "worthless" mass? Have we not heard the prophecies of doom? Are any of us free of blame? Was the word "humanity" spoken into the wind?

Let us go back to Theresienstadt once more. Stressed to the utmost, overstressed, constantly ripped from psychological equilibrium, their lives keenly and palpably threatened every day – only a scant minority of the prisoners could pass this almost superhuman test of the heart. The theory that suffering purifies human beings must be rejected if the suffering is excessive. Much may be demanded, but too much destroys. Then suffering no longer purifies, and the human being strays, loses himself, and commits disastrous acts, if he does not die. Anyone who survived this desert of the soul without great damage achieved the utmost. Only very strong people who

The Psychological Face of the Coerced Community

never succumbed to blind participation in the mechanism – who looked around, collected themselves, and tried to bring the eternal into the tormented present; whose views, acquired before the camp, allowed them to maneuver through the persistent corruption; and whose moral principles held fast – were able to gain true profit from the experience of the coerced community. But even one who had not too badly failed the test could not, as an active human being, pass through the camp free of any implication in guilt; this was even impossible for an inactive person who tried to avoid any guilt, because he was lost before he had passed the test, which demanded that every prisoner accept the community of guilt.

Humanity and Judaism, as a basic form of humanity, are values that stand above this history. They did not fail it, but they have nothing in common with it.

The human being is everything in his history. That is certain. But he must also know what presides over him and over all history. The human being becomes the herald of a higher mission, and he continues to form the history that forms him. At the limits of his ability to act, spurred on by his task, he also hopes to abide. In the words of a mother sent to Theresienstadt to her distant children, this tendency is recognized and is transformed into an effective message:

ONE MUST BE CAREFUL NOT TO ATTACH TOO MUCH IMPORTANCE TO ONESELF. ALL OF US ARE MORE OR LESS ON THE FRONT LINES AND TEND TOO MUCH TO CONSIDER OURSELVES AS THE CENTRE OF ATTENTION.

Chronological Summary

The following abbreviations are used throughout this chronology:

J   Jew(s)
Jw   Jewish
M   men
P   "Protectorate"
Pr   prisoners
T   Theresienstadt
Tr   transport(s)
W   women

Entries that do not refer directly to the Jw camp in T are *italicized*.

1930   Number of inhabitants in T: 7,181, approximately half of whom are with the military and living in the barracks (eleven total)
1935   Number of houses in T: 219, including those outside the fort

1939

Jan. 24	*The establishment of the "Central Office for Jw Emigration" is mandated. It is ordered that the Jw question must be solved by "emigration or evacuation"*
Jan. 30	*In the Reichstag, Hitler presages extermination of the Jews*
Mar. 15	*The "Protectorate of Bohemia and Moravia" is established*
July 4	*Germany's J are placed under the jurisdiction of the "Reich Association"*
July 26	*The "Central Bureau" (later named the "Central Office") opens in Prague (its establishment had been ordered by von Neurath on July 15)*
Sept. 1	*Germany invades Poland*
Sept. 27	*Reich Security Main Office (RSHA) is founded*
Oct. 8	*Himmler announces that he would like to deport the J from the P to Poland*
Oct. 17–26	*Moravian J are sent to Poland to be "reeducated"*
Nov. 23	*The "Jewish star" is mandated in Poland*

1940

Jan. 30   *Heydrich assembles a conference on the resettlement of J and ethnic Germans*

Feb. 16   *All of the P is placed under the authority of the Prague "Central Bureau"*

Feb. 22   *First deportation of Central European J to the East*

Mar. 15   *All Jw communities in the P are placed under the authority of the Prague community*

Mar. 23   *Göring halts deportations*

April   *Moravian Jews return from Poland*

June 14   *Auschwitz established as a concentration camp. The "Small Fortress" in the T concentration camp officially becomes a "police prison"; until the beginning of May 1945 approximately 35,000 registered inmates*

Sept. 2   *Last illegal transport from the P to Palestine*

Oct. 22   *Southwest German J are deported to southern France*

Oct. 25   *Prague J are not permitted to leave the city or relocate without prior authorization*

1941

February   *Viennese J are deported to Poland*

May 10   *The Prague Palestine Office is liquidated*

June 30   *There are 88,868 J in the P*

July 31   *Göring orders that the "Complete Solution to the Jewish Question" be drafted*

Sept. 15   *First experiments with gassing in Auschwitz*

Sept. 19   *The "Jewish star" mandated in "Greater Germany". J are forbidden freedom of movement*

Sept. 27   *Heydrich becomes the executive "Reichsprotecktor"*

Oct. 1   *Jw emigration is officially halted. There are 163,696 J in the Old Reich*

Oct. 9   *The first known document concerning Jw camps in the P*

Oct. 10   Heydrich designates T as a "ghetto"

Oct. 16   *Start of systematic deportations from Central Europe to Poland, the Baltic, and Belorussia. First Tr from the P to the East*

Oct. 25   *First known document to suggest the possibility of gassing J who are unable to work*

Nov. 2   *The assets of J in the P are frozen*

Nov. 11   *Hitler's final order for the collective annihilation of the J; Himmler informed*

Nov. 24   First Tr from the P to T. Number of Pr in T: 340

Nov. 26   First warm meal. Cooking pot capacity: 300 L

Dec. 1   Size of the camp: 7,400 m²; residential density: 181,500 people per square kilometer. Number of beds (*Bettplaetze*): 70 (5.21 beds per 100 Pr)

Dec. 2   Ban on all postal traffic

Dec. 4   Number of Pr in T: 4,365, housed in one barrack

Edelstein arrives with thirty-two employees ("staff")

Edelstein designated the chief Jewish Elder, and Zucker designated deputy elder

The Council of Elders formed

Dec. 5	First written notice issued by the Jw administration
Dec. 6	M and W are kept strictly segregated in separate barracks
	The "Ghetto Guard" is established
Dec. 8	*Chelmno starts functioning as an extermination camp (from Apr. 7, 1943, until January 1945 it is used only occasionally)*
Dec. 10	Those caught participating in illegal postal traffic are threatened with capital punishment
Dec. 14	"Central Warehouse" established
Dec. 15	The first "order of the day" issued. A daily diet of 1,640 calories allotted
Dec. 16	"Compulsory greeting" of all those "wearing a uniform" decreed
Dec. 17	The daily bread ration is set at 350 g (previously set at 250 g)
	The "ghetto court" is established
Dec. 18	Opening of the shower rooms
Dec. 19	Due to water shortages, washroom hours are restricted
Dec. 23	Start of the construction of sleeping pallets
Dec. 24	First orders issued requiring that illegal assets be relinquished
Dec. 25	First so-called census "Squadrons" are established
Dec. 28	"Comradeship evenings" approved, out of which develops the "Recreation Office"
Dec. 31	Average age: 38 years
December	26 L of water allotted per Pr per day
1941	7,365 Pr deported to T
	Eleven deaths

1942

Jan. 1	Number of Pr in T: 7,350 (4,045 M, 3,294 W, and 11 children)
	Number of ill Pr: 338 (4.5%)
	Size of the camp: 25,800 m²; residential density: 285,000 people per square kilometer
	Number of beds: 844 (11.46 beds per 100 Pr)
	Available living space, excluding sickrooms: 23,383 m²
	Cooking pot capacity (per person): 0.78 L
	The "Space Management Office" begins operations
Jan. 4	Open letters between barracks are permitted. Due to a water shortage, bathing is discontinued
Jan. 8	The opening of an isolation ward in E VI initiates the founding of a hospital
Jan. 9	The first Tr out of T: Tr of 1,000 people to Riga, 102 known survivors
Jan. 10	Nine executions
Jan. 15	Tr of 1,000 people to Riga, 15 survivors
Jan. 19	Eichmann visits T to evaluate its suitability as a privileged camp
Jan. 20	Conference on the "Final Solution to the Jewish Question" in Wannsee; T's role is defined. Pr over the age of sixty are not required to live in gender-segregated barracks
Jan. 21	Regulations concerning estates and found property
Jan. 23	Limited postcard traffic to the P is permitted; it doesn't function, however

Chronological Summary

Jan. 27	Control of the Central Laundry is assumed; the services are always unsatisfactory
January	6% of Pr are over the age of sixty-five 77% of all men are fit for work. Cooking pot capacity. 6,000 L
Feb. 1	Number of Pr in T: 9,903, of whom 2,751 are in H V, 2,716 are in C III, 2,536 are in E I, 741 are in E VI, 663 are in B V, 472 are in H IV, and 24 are in I IV
Feb. 3	Pr are allotted one small piece of soap substitute per Pr once every six weeks
Feb. 9	The "arbitration system" for affairs of honor is introduced
Feb. 10	The SS issues "special camp regulations"
Feb. 16	Prague orders the township of T be dissolved Children may spend two hours with their parents on Sundays
Feb. 21	The "Ghetto Guard" is sworn in by the Council of Elders
Feb. 22	There are 2,185 beds on sleeping pallets in fifty-eight rooms An "outside kommando" leaves T for the first time
Feb. 25	Hotplates are banned for the first time
Feb. 26	Seven executions
Feb. 28	There are 91 doctors employed, 14 outpatient clinics, 17 sickrooms with 314 beds, and an isolation ward with 120 beds
February	10% of Pr are over the age of sixty-five Number of medical encounters: 114,904, including in outpatient clinics Average number of workers daily: 4,732 (2,875 M, 1,857 W) Living space: 25,052 m² (58% of the total camp area for 12,000–15,000 Pr)
Mar. 1	A "rationing commission" is created as part of the kitchen inspection
Mar. 11	Tr of 1,001 people to Izbica, 6 survivors
Mar. 15	An internal medicine ward is established in the hospital in E VI
Mar. 17	Tr of 1,000 people to Izbica, 3 survivors
Mar. 17	*The Bełżec extermination camp opens (until mid-Dec. 1942)*
March	Control of waterworks is assumed
March	*Birkenau (Auschwitz II) opens*
Apr. 1	Number of Pr in T: 15,372 Tr of 1,000 people to Piaski, 4 survivors
Apr. 14	A psychiatric ward is established in E VII
Apr. 18	Tr of 1,000 people to Rejowiec, 2 survivors
Apr. 23	Tr of 1,000 people to Piaski, 1 survivor
Apr. 26	Tr of 1,000 people to Warsaw, 8 survivors
Apr. 27	Tr of 1,000 people to Izbica, 1 survivor
Apr. 28	Tr of 1,000 people to Zamość, 5 survivors
Apr. 30	Tr of 1,000 people to Zamość, 19 survivors A surgical ward is established in E VI
April	Luggage that had been placed in storage is searched; much is confiscated The civilian population begins evacuating from T
May 1	Number of Pr in T: 12,987 (6,276 M, 6,654 W, and 57 infants) Number of Pr in worker groups working outside the camp: 1,454 (an all-time high)

Chronological Summary

May 2	Pr are allotted one small piece of soap substitute per Pr once every seven weeks
	Control of city fire department is assumed
May 3	Start of the construction of the crematorium
May 7 or 8	*Sobibór extermination camp is opened (until Nov. 1943)*
May 8	"Worker identity cards" are instituted
May 9	Tr of 1,000 people to Ossow, near Sobibór(?), no survivors
	Control of army bakery (A IV) is assumed
May 14	The "Ghetto Guard" is dissolved as punishment and is replaced with the "Order Guard"
	Postal traffic with the external world is prohibited anew
May 15	A ten-day grace period for the handover of all illegal possessions announced
May 17	Tr of 1,000 people to Zulia, near Lublin(?), no survivors
May 18	The S, N, and K "bread categories" – corresponding to 500 g, 375 g, and 333 g in rations, respectively – are instituted; bread bonuses are given for additional work
	Extra food ("food bonuses") for workers is instituted
	Limited bathing hours resume
May 25	Tr 1,000 people to Lublin, 1 survivor
May 29	"Administrative squadrons" are instituted
May	27% of Pr are over the age of sixty-five
	Average number of workers daily: 7,666 (3,812 M, 3,854 W)
June 1	Number of Pr in T: 14,300
June 2	First transport from Germany to T
	Bylaws for the Council of Elders are approved
June 10	A burial crew of thirty men is ordered to go to Lidice
June 12	Tr of 1,000 people to Trawniki(?), no survivors
June 13	Tr of 1,000 people to an unknown destination, no survivors
June 17	A "manhunt campaign" in response to the assassination of Heydrich and a "census" in the courtyards
June 21	First transport from Austria to T
June 25	"Supplementary rations" (a larger lunch for those who perform heavy labor) instituted
June 26	Permission granted for loitering in courtyards until 9:30 P.M.
June 27	Transfer of the evacuated city to the "ghetto"
	The "Central Warehouse" is moved from I IV to A IV in one night
June 28	The official workweek is set at fifty-two hours with Saturday afternoon off for plant workers and fifty-seven hours with Saturdays off for office workers
June 29	Applicants for the position of "house elder" are sought
June 30	Number of workers: 8,769 (4,614 M, 4,155 F)
	Cooking pot capacity (per person): 0.66 L
June	More than 30% of Pr are over the age of sixty-five (until April 1943)
	Approximately 200 doctors and 1,000 caregivers are employed
	There are thirty-four sickrooms in locations other than E VI
	51% of men are fit to work

Chronological Summary

	Out of the 4,213 German J, 242 are of working age, but only 178 are fit to work. Cooking pot capacity: 12,000 L
July 1	Number of Pr in T: 21,269
	There are 2,600 more W than M in T
	Housing blocks and barracks are given names using letters and numbers; civilian names are abolished
	Area of camp already being used: 65,000 m²; residential density: 321,000 people per square kilometer
	Number of beds: 14,155 (67.9 beds per 100 Pr)
July 3	Streets are given names using the letters L or Q and numbers; civilian names are abolished
July 6	The city is opened to inmates; M and W are permitted to visit each other; kissing is no longer life endangering
	The police headquarters is moved from the barrack gates; the station is moved to camp exits
	The curfew moved back from 8:00 P.M. to 9:00 P.M.
	The "Order Guard" is equipped as was the "Ghetto Guard" previously
	40,000 new inmates are anticipated
July 10	From now on, all "accompanying luggage" of arriving Tr is confiscated
July 14	Tr of 1,000 people to Trostinetz, near Minsk [Maly Trostenets], 2 survivors
July 27	Leaving the house or lingering at the window during the arrival and departure of Tr is forbidden
July 28	Tr of 1,000 people to an unknown destination, no survivors
July 31	39.1% of Pr are M, and 60.9% are W
	Average age: 54.4 years
	Number of workers: 14,002 (6,827 M, 7,126 W) [sic]
July	Arrival of 25,111 Pr in fifty-eight Tr
July	*Treblinka extermination camp opens (until fall of 1943)*
Aug. 1	Number of Pr in T: 43,303. There are 10,000 more W than M in T
Aug. 4	Tr of 1,000 people to Trostinetz [Maly Trostenets], 2 survivors
Aug. 10	The "information service" is founded
Aug. 14	"House-management commissions" are instituted
Aug. 20	Tr of 1,000 people to an unknown destination, no survivors
Aug. 24	Construction of a train line from T to Bohušovice
Aug. 25	Tr of 1,000 people to Trostinetz [Maly Trostenets], 1 survivor
Aug. 27	*The "Central Bureau for Jw Emigration" from now on is called the "Central Office for the Regulation of the Jw Question in Bohemia and Moravia"*
Aug. 31	Number of Pr in T: 51,552
August	Arrival of 13,469 Pr in thirty-six Tr
	55%–56% of Pr are over the age of sixty-five
	176,538 medical procedures in outpatient clinics
	400 cases of scarlet fever
	Average number of workers daily: 12,615
	More than 6,000 Pr living in unfinished attics
	Average living space per person: 1.6 m²
	Cooking pot capacity (per person): 0.34 L

Summer	The workweek is set at 80–110 hours for kitchen and Shipping Department workers, 75–85 hours plus 20 night shift hours for caregivers, 65–75 hours plus 10 night shift hours for craftsmen, and 78 hours plus 16 nightshift hours for public sector workers
	There is one "block doctor" for every 1,500–1,600 Pr
Sept. 1	Tr of 1,000 people to Raasika, 45 survivors (women)
Sept. 4	During the day, people usually are permitted to move freely about the camp from 6:00 A.M. to 8:00 P.M., subject to certain restrictions
Sept. 7	The crematorium begins operations
Sept. 8	Arrival of 1,995 Pr in four Tr
	Tr of 1,000 people to Trostinetz [Maly Trostenets], 4 survivors
Sept. 14	The "stores" open
Sept. 15	Number of Pr in T: 56,717
	Number of patients in sickrooms: 3,462
	Available living space, excluding sickrooms: 115,004 m²
Sept. 16	Limited postcard and package traffic into T is permitted; it takes seven months for service to become regular
Sept. 18	Number of Pr in T: 58,491 (an all-time high)
	156 deaths (an all-time high)
Sept. 19	Tr of 2,000 people to Trostinetz [Maly Trostenets](?), no survivors
Sept. 21	Tr of 2,000 people to Trostinetz [Maly Trostenets](?), no survivors
Sept. 22	Tr of 1,000 people to the Minsk region, 1 survivor (he saved himself by jumping from the moving train)
	First case in which a member of the Council of Elders is shipped off on a transport as punishment
Sept. 23	Tr of 1,980 people to Trostinetz [Maly Trostenets](?), no survivors
	The central "Security Service" is established; Loewenstein is chosen as the head
Sept. 26	Tr of 2,004 people to Trostinetz [Maly Trostenets](?), no survivors
Sept. 29	Tr of 2,000 people to Trostinetz [Maly Trostenets](?), no survivors
Sept. 30	Number of Pr in T: 53,264
	45% of Pr are over the age of sixty-five
	Number of workers: 16,653 (8,124 M, 8,529 W)
September	Arrival of 18,467 Pr in thirty-eight Tr
	Departure of 13,004 Pr, 50 survivors
	3,941 deaths, of which 1,938 are from enteritis
	Between 106 and 156 deaths daily
	Number of "old, sick, and infirm": more than 30,000
	Number of cripples: more than 4,000, of whom approximately 1,000 are blind
	363 doctors are employed
	206,165 outpatient medical procedures
	161 new cases of scarlet fever
	Number of sickrooms: 454 (with 5,109 beds and 4,530 bed pallets)
	Number of nonworkers: 38,912 (an all-time high)
	Average number of workers daily: 15,396 (7,648 M, 7,748 W)
	5,626 Pr are living in unfinished attics
	Pr are allotted 19.5 L of water per Pr per day

Oct. 1	There are 12,000 more W than M in T
	The curfew is moved up to 8:00 P.M.
	The Council of Elders is reorganized
Oct. 4	*The J in German concentration camps are to be sent to Auschwitz*
Oct. 5	Tr of 1,000 people to Treblinka(?), no survivors
Oct. 8	Tr of 1,000 people to Treblinka, 2 survivors (they fled)
Oct. 9	"Welfare offices for severely disabled veterans and the physically handicapped" are instituted
Oct. 15	Tr of 1,998 people to Treblinka, no survivors
Oct. 19	Tr of 1,984 people to Treblinka, no survivors
Oct. 22	Tr of 2,018 people to Treblinka, no survivors
Oct. 26	Tr of 1,866 people to Auschwitz (from now on, the sole destination), 28 survivors
	The deported are permitted to issue "mail authorizations"
Oct. 27	A curfew and lights-out period is imposed from 6:00 P.M. onward, and "recreation" is banned; this is rescinded on Nov. 2
Oct. 29	A "census" is conducted in the quarters, because since the last Tr it is unclear how many Pr there are
Oct. 31	Number of workers: 17,614 (8,810 M, 8,804 W)
October	Arrival of 5,004 Pr
	Departure of 9,866 Pr, 30 survivors
	3,096 deaths (up to 127 daily)
	Up to 6,034 Pr are living in unfinished attics
	The "Welfare Department" is established
	Continuous graduated food bonuses for workers are instituted
	The "Order Guard" is once again called the "Ghetto Guard"
Nov. 1	Number of Pr in T: 45,312
	5,457 Pr are living in unfinished attics
Nov. 5	A II becomes a quarantine for those with lice
Nov. 13	3,000 Pr are living in unfinished attics
Nov. 17	The "Central Ghetto Library" founded; it opens on Nov. 25
Nov. 24	Approximately 26,000 Pr are housed in former civilian homes, and approximately 22,800 in wooden barracks
Nov. 26	*Jw armament workers in the Reich are to be replaced with Poles*
Nov. 30	An emergency room unit is set up in E VI
November	Arrival of 4,579 Pr
	Number of toilets: 988 for 46,000 Pr (one toilet per 48 Pr)
	Introduction of the "lending system"
Dec. 6	Number of children between the ages of three and eighteen: 3,541, of whom approximately 2,000 are in "homes"
Dec. 8	The "coffeehouse" opens. Making music is permitted
Dec. 24	Number of Pr in T: 50,006
Dec. 31	Number of Pr in T: 49,397 (approximately 24,500 from the P, 17,000 from Germany, and 7,000 from Austria)
	33% of Pr are over the age of sixty-five
	Number of M: 20,012 (40.8%); number of W: 29,385 (59.2%)
	Average age: 51.3 years
	Number of patients in sickrooms: 3,139
	There is one "block doctor" for every 500–600 Pr

Chronological Summary   611

	Number of workers: 19,295 (9,951 M, 9,744 W)
	Living space, excluding sickrooms: 104,801 m²
	Cooking pot capacity: 20,560 L
December	Arrival of 4,821 Pr
Second half year	Disease incidence: 35,000 cases (4,912 deaths) of enteritis, 4,500 of conjunctivitis, 896 of scarlet fever, 831 of measles, 600 of infectious hepatitis, and 536 of typhus
1942	Approximately 101,761 Pr are transported to T
	Tr of 43,871 Pr out of T
	15,891 deaths
	Average proportion of Pr who took ill yearly: 30%
	Average number of sick Pr daily: 5,702 (19.2%), of whom 3,148 are nonambulatory
	563 doctors are employed (one doctor for every 87.5 persons)
	Average number of nonworkers yearly: 18,819; average number of workers yearly: 10,692
	264 suicides and suicide attempts
	A daily diet of 1,597 calories is allotted

1943

Jan. 1	1,374 Pr are over the age of eighty, of whom 320 are over the age of eighty-five
	Size of the camp: 383,800 m²; residential density: 128,000 people per square kilometer
	Number of beds: 30,493 (62 beds per 100 Pr)
	The "Ghetto Guard" swears allegiance to the Jewish Elder
Jan. 5	The "special camp regulations" are amended
Jan. 9	The appellate court for the "ghetto court" and the "police criminal code" are created
Jan. 20	Tr of 2,000 people, 2 survivors
Jan. 23	Tr of 2,000 people, 3 survivors
Jan. 26	Tr of 1,000 people, 39 survivors
Jan. 28	Leo Baeck is in T
Jan. 29	Tr of 1,000 people, 23 survivors
Jan. 31	Eppstein becomes a council elder and forms a triumvirate with Edelstein and Murmelstein
January	Average number of workers daily: 20,534
Feb. 1	Number of Pr in T: 44,672
	Tr of 1,001 people, 29 survivors
Feb. 15	Arrests at the "ghetto post office" for theft
Feb. 16	Number of Pr in T: 43,683
	13,672 Pr (31.30%) are ill (an all-time high), and 29,932 Pr (68.52%) are healthy; seventy-nine (0.18%) deaths
Feb. 27	*Jw armament workers in Berlin are being rounded up and deported to Auschwitz or T*
February	Height of the typhus epidemic: 414 new cases
	Average number of workers daily: 24,746
Mar. 15	Living space per person: 2.05 m²

Mar. 18	The "bypass road" opens; isolation of the camp from the outside world is complete
Mar. 31	*There are 11,267 J in the P*
March	Average number of workers daily: 25,917 (11,879 M, 14,038 W)
Apr. 1	An outpatient clinic for those suffering from lung disease opens in E IIIa
Apr. 4	The "order to ensure work discipline" and "rules and regulations for employees of the self-administration" are instituted
Apr. 9	A general curfew and lights-out period is imposed and "recreation" is disbanded as punishment for escape attempts
Apr. 12	The "bread category" L – 333 g daily – for "light laborers" is instituted; bread bonuses for "extra work" are discontinued (retroactive to Apr. 1)
Apr. 15	Training seminars for new nurses
Apr. 19	*Warsaw Ghetto uprising (until May 16)*
Apr. 21	The "bank" receives 53 million "ghetto crowns"
Apr. 22	First Tr from Holland to T
April	New "worker identity cards" with "small health care cards" are distributed
	112,621 medical encounters at outpatient clinics
	The district heating plant is put into operation
May 2	The "special camp regulations" are revised again in light of the "money economy"
May 8	*The Minsk Ghetto is liquidated*
May 10	The general curfew is lifted, and "recreation" is reinstated
May 12	The first payout by the "bank" initiates the "money economy"
May 20	The "labor court" and "disciplinary tribunal" are instituted
May 22	The general lights-out order is rescinded
	"Monetary fines" are instituted
	The "police criminal code" is amended (renamed the "criminal code of the Detective Department" on Sept. 22)
May 24	New mail regulations: one postcard once every three months
May 27	The "juvenile court code" is instituted
May	Through Oct. 1944, never less than 25% of the Pr are over the age of sixty-five
	108,533 medical encounters in outpatient clinics
	Average number of workers daily: 27,757 (12,545 M, 15,212 W)
	Representatives from the German press tour T
Spring	More than 40% of Pr are at least 30% underweight
June 1	Number of Pr in T: 43,806, of whom 3,168 are children under the age of fourteen
	Construction of a rail line into the camp is completed; the railway begins operations
	"Crate production" begins
	The "juvenile court" opens
June 8	The "ghetto court" is permitted to impose only conditional penalties
June 9	A fourteen-day grace period for the handover of illegal possessions without penalty is announced
June 27	A delegation of the German Red Cross is in T for two days
June 30	Number of Pr in T: 44,621
	Number of patients in sickrooms: 3,561

Chronological Summary

	The daily bread rations are set at 375 g for approximately 26,000 Pr, 333 g for approximately 12,000 Pr, and 500 g for approximately 5,560 Pr; approximately 300 Pr receive a larger bread ration
	Daily, approximately 34,500 Pr receive a normal midday meal, 6,770 receive a larger midday meal, and 3,200 children receive specified additional food
	Living space, excluding sickrooms: 102,913 m²
July 1	Size of the camp: 374,800 m²; residential density: 118,000 people per square kilometer
	Number of beds: 38,485 (96.9 beds per 100 Pr)
July 7	All pregnancies must be reported, and coerced abortions are instituted (as of Oct. 1944 they are no longer enforced)
July 10	Authorization stamps are required for packages sent from the P to T
Mid-July	Number of Pr in T: 46,395
July 20	Privately owned tools must be turned in for camp use
July 24	Two barracks have to be evacuated within twenty-four hours; 6,422 Pr are affected
July 28	Civilian street names are introduced, effective as of Aug. 1
July 31	41.07% of Pr are M, and 58.93% are W. Average age: 46.6 years
July	Number of ill daily: 10,000, of whom 5,000 are nonambulatory
	Number of Pr requiring care: 8,984 (2,200 in quarantine care), of whom 2,421 are cripples, 1,596 are injured war veterans, and 565 are blind people
	635 doctors and 1,432 caregivers are employed
	4,066 Pr are working in the "Health Services Department"
	Number of sickrooms: 252 (with 5,200 beds)
Aug. 1	Fifty "ghetto crowns" is deducted from monthly wages for "recreation"; tickets to some events are provided only against payment
Aug. 8	Number of Pr in T: 46,127, of whom 5,132 are ill and nonambulatory
Aug. 16	Loewenstein is removed from office; the "Security Service" is dissolved
Aug. 21	*The Bialystok [Białystok] Ghetto is liquidated (until Sept. 15)*
Aug. 24	Tr of children from Bialystok [Białystok] to T
August	Number of Pr fit for work: 29,603 (an all-time high)Average number of workers daily: 28,614
Summer	Among a total of approximately 45,000 Pr, 12,500 nonworkers receive a daily diet of 1,487 calories, 21,900 workers receive 1,630 calories, 5,200 workers who perform heavy labor receive 2,141 calories, children up to the age of sixteen receive 1,759 calories, and 1,586 Pr receive a diet better than that of those who perform heavy labor
Sept. 1	Number of Pr in T: 45,635
Sept. 6	From now on every deportation is referred to as a "work deployment" Tr of 5,007 people (285 children fourteen years and younger, 3,925 fifteen- to sixty-year-olds, and 797 people over the age of sixty-one), 37 survivors
Oct. 2	The "prison code" is instituted
Oct. 4	Criminal law enforcement (to date, only violations and misdemeanors) is transferred to the self-administration

Oct. 5	Tr of 1,260 Bialystok [Białystok] children with 53 attendants, no survivors
	First Tr from Denmark to T
October	Number of welfare recipients: 14,687, of whom 2,723 are crippled, 1,981 are injured war veterans, and 668 are blind
	There are 115 welfare workers caring for 12,000 Pr in need of care
Nov. 3	*The Riga Ghetto is liquidated. Massacre of 18,000 J in the Lublin concentration camp (Majdanek)*
Nov. 9	Edelstein is arrested; Zucker is named his successor (confirmed on Jan. 16, 1944)
Nov. 11	An all-day "census" outdoors outside the city
Nov. 19	A second "census" conducted in alphabetical order and lasting until Nov. 24
	"Crate production" ends
Nov. 30	Number of Pr in T: 40,145
November	427 deaths
Dec. 14	Number of Pr in T: 39,957
Dec. 15	Tr of 2,504 people, 262 survivors
Dec. 18	Tr of 2,503 people, 443 survivors; composition of both Tr: 471 children fourteen years and younger, 2,758 fifteen- to sixty-year-olds, and 1,778 people over the age of sixty-one
Dec. 31	Number of Pr in T: 34,665 (approximately 15,000 from the P, 13,000 from Germany, 5,500 from Austria, 250 from Holland, and 460 from Denmark)
	Number of M: 14,200 (41%); number of W: 20,455 (59%)
	Average age: 48 years
	Number of children: 3,367, of whom 1,969 are in "homes"
	Number of patients in sickrooms: 2,446
	Number of sickrooms: 173 (with 2,163 beds)
	Living space, excluding sickrooms: 95,696 m^2
	Cooking pot capacity: 26,870 L
	Cooking pot capacity (per person): 0.77 L
	There are 650 wash troughs in the washrooms
December	Number of nonambulatory ill daily: approximately 5,000
	Number of blind individuals: approximately 600
	Number of outpatient medical encounters daily: approximately 5,000
	Number of sickbeds: 2,200 (in five hospitals)
	Average number of workers daily: 21,997
	12.1% of Pr are not Mosaic
	An order is issued for "city beautification"
1943	Approximately 16,388 Pr are deported to T
	Tr of 18,328 Pr out of T
	12,696 deaths
	31,495 Pr are admitted to the hospitals and sickrooms; 25,656 are discharged from them
	35,628 nonambulatory patients are treated in their quarters
	Average number of sick daily: 10,397 (24%), of whom 6,243 are nonambulatory
	Average number of doctors working daily: 556 (one for every 62.25 persons)

Chronological Summary 615

Average number of caregivers working daily: 1,306 (one for every 26.6 persons)
Average number of nonworkers yearly: 17,472; average number of workers yearly: 25,825
164 suicides and suicide attempts
A daily diet of 1,848 calories is allotted

1944

Jan. 1	Number of Pr in T: 34,655, of whom 21,144 are fit for work
	Number of Pr over the age of eighty: 445, of whom 210 are over eighty-five years of age
	Size of the camp: 334,600 m²; residential density: 103,400 people per square kilometer
	Number of beds: 38,836 (112 beds per 100 Pr)
	A "statute for defense lawyers" is implemented
Jan. 14	One barrack must be evacuated within forty-eight hours; 3,200 W are affected
Jan. 31	Number of Pr in T: 36,478, of whom 21,653 are W
January	Average number of workers daily: 20,697
	Number of W fit for work: 10,981
Feb. 27	Number of Pr in T: 36,912
Feb. 29	Size of the camp: 335,056 m², of which 42% has been developed, 16% consists of converted courtyards, and 42% consists of streets, squares, and gardens; size of the living space: 95,000 m²
February	Number of doctors working: 549, of whom 225 are specialists and 68 are dentists
	"City beautification," until summer 1944, transforms T into a place as "civilized" as possible
Mar. 2	The Zossen work detail, composed of 200 people, leaves T
Mar. 4	The "compulsory greeting" is abolished, announced on Mar. 6
Mar. 20	Tr of forty-five mentally ill individuals to Bergen-Belsen (and, presumably, from there to Auschwitz), no survivors
March	There are 2,050 cripples and 1,835 injured war veterans (921 severely)
April	*Start of the diversion of work-capable J from Auschwitz to German concentration camps*
May 4	Decrees are issued concerning "additional penalties" and "supply violations"
May 14	Number of Pr in T: 35,733
	Number of severely injured war veterans, as recognized by the SS: 915 (plus 800 family members)
	1,612 Pr are highly decorated war veterans (at the least EK I [Iron Cross, 1st Class]), with 1,418 family members
	Number of "mixed-marriage" (*Mischehe*) partners: 1,954 (plus 38 family members)
	Number of "people of mixed blood" (*Mischlinge*): 1,624 (plus 950 family members)
	Number of "notables" as recognized by the SS: 114 (plus 85 family members)

Chronological Summary

May 15	Tr of 2,503 people, 119 survivors
May 16	Tr of 2,500 people, 5 survivors
May 18	Tr of 2,500 people – composition of these transports: 511 children up to the age of fourteen, 3,601 fifteen- to sixty-year-olds, and 3,391 people over the age of sixty; 3,125 people from Germany, 2,543 from the P, 1,276 from Austria, and 559 from Holland, 261 survivors; going forward, it must be assumed that there are more survivors who are not from the P; total number: approximately 500
May 22	Number of Pr in T: 28,090 (12,106 M, 15,984 W)
May 23	Eppstein and five Zionists write an official letter to the "Jewish Rescue Committee" in Budapest
May 31	43.1% of Pr are M, and 56.9% are W. Average age: 45.4 years
May	15.8% of Pr are not Mosaic
June 15	Size of the camp: 335,056 m²; living space: 96,568 m² Living space per person: 3.05 m²
June 18	The "bread categories" are changed; only S and N – 470 g and 350 g daily, respectively – remain
June 20	*Edelstein is executed in Auschwitz*
June 21	Since Nov. 24, 1941, 204 Pr have been handed over to the Gestapo
June 23	A commission of two Danes and one Swiss visit T
June 30	Number of Pr in T: 27,702 Number of patients in sickrooms: 1,591 16,493 Pr are actually working; approximately 7,000 receive a larger midday meal, and 4,269 receive larger bread rations (S) 3,147 Pr are working in the "Health Services Department" Number of Pr receiving care: approximately 8,000, of whom 1,638 are injured war veterans (881 severely injured), 1,398 are cripples, and 333 are blind people
July 1	Size of the camp: 350,000 m²; residential density: 79,400 people per square kilometer Number of beds: 36,000 (129.7 beds per 100 Pr) The "community house" opens
July 12	*The Theresienstadt "family camp" in Auschwitz is liquidated*
July 17	Five painters are arrested for "atrocity propaganda" and transferred to the "Small Fortress" along with their families
July 31	Number of Pr in T: 27,475 (11,899 M, 15,676 W)
July 31	Number of children under the age of sixteen: 2,658 Number of Pr over the age of sixty-five: 4,452
Aug. 16	15,000 m of film is shot by Sept. 11
Aug. 21	*The Łódź Ghetto is liquidated (until Sept. 15)*
Sept. 1	*There are 14,574 J in Germany (Altreich)*
Sept. 23	Tr of 5,000 "full-fledged workers" is announced
Sept. 27	Eppstein is arrested and executed at the "Small Fortress" Murmelstein is the sole Jewish Elder (confirmed on Dec. 13)
Sept. 28	Number of Pr in T: 29,841, of whom 710 are doctors Zucker is deported and "liquidated" in Auschwitz Tr of 2,500 people, 371 survivors (P)
Sept. 29	Tr of 1,500 people, 76 survivors (P)

Chronological Summary

Oct. 1	Tr of 1,501 people, 293 survivors (P)
Oct. 2	An end to Tr is declared; it is rescinded two hours later
Oct. 4	Tr of 1,500 people, 127 survivors (P)
Oct. 6	Tr of 1,550 people, 76 survivors (P)
Oct. 9	Tr of 1,600 people, 22 survivors (P)
Oct. 12	Tr of 1,500 people, 74 survivors (P)
Oct. 16	Tr of 1,500 people, 110 survivors (P)
Oct. 19	Tr of 1,500 people, 51 survivors (P)
Oct. 22	The SS declares that 12,000 Pr may remain in T
Oct. 23	Tr of 1,715 people, 159 survivors (P)
Oct. 28	Tr of 2,038 people, 37 survivors (P)
	Conclusion of liquidation transports to Auschwitz
	Number of Pr in T: 11,077
Oct. 31	Number of Pr in T: 11,068 (819 children, 1,642 M, 4,543 W, and 4,064 elderly M and W)
	29.5% of Pr are M, and 70.5% are W
	Average age: 50.9 years
Nov. 2	*Gassing in Auschwitz ceases*
Nov. 9	The official workweek is set at seventy hours without any days off
Nov. 26	*Destruction of the Auschwitz gas chambers is ordered*
Dec. 13	A new Council of Elders and a new self-administration are formed
	Baeck is named deputy Jewish Elder
December	27.9% of Pr are not Mosaic
1944	7,439 Pr are deported to T
	Tr of 25,997 Pr out of T
	4,540 deaths
	13,252 Pr are admitted to hospitals and sickrooms; 12,923 are discharged from them
	Average number of patients lying in their quarters daily: 1,500–1,600 (as of October, approximately 500–600)
	Average number of ill persons daily: 6,030 (23%), of whom 2,945 are nonambulatory
	Average number of doctors working: 120 (one for every 96.25 persons)
	Average number of caregivers working: 257 (one for every 41 persons)
	Average number of nonworkers yearly: 14,846; average number of workers yearly: 20,697
	Approximately fifty suicides and suicide attempts. A daily diet of 1,953 calories is allotted

1945

Jan. 1	Number of Pr in T: 11,465 (approximately 3,500 from the P, 4,000 from Germany, 1,500 from Austria, 1,700 from Holland, 400 from Denmark, and 400 from Slovakia)
	Number of workers: 6,034 (1,963 M, 4,071 W)
	Size of the camp: 348,000 m²; residential density: 33,200 people per square kilometer
	Number of beds: 24,000 beds (204 beds per 100 Pr)

618 · *Chronological Summary*

Jan. 15	A curfew starting at 8:00 P.M. is renewed
Jan. 31	J from existing "mixed marriages" are deported to T
Feb. 5	1,200 Pr are released to Switzerland
Feb. 9	The official workweek is set at sixty-five hours with one afternoon off
Feb. 10	The Zossen work detail returns
Feb. 28	Number of Pr in T: 15,681
	Number of workers: 10,598 (4,040 M, 6,558 W)
	Number of Pr actually working: 9,008 (3,434 M, 5,574 W)
February	Gas chambers are to be built in T
Mar. 5	A new "city beautification" is ordered
Mar. 8	Hungarian J are transported to T
Mar. 28	Picture inspection (*Bilderkontrolle*) [SS effort to discover any visual images of the atrocities –Ed.]
Mar. 31	208 deaths since Jan. 1, 1945
Apr. 6	The commission from the IRC tours T
Apr. 15	Danish Jews are released to Sweden. Last "normal" Tr to T
Apr. 16	Kasztner of the "Jewish Rescue Committee" tours T
	Himmler's order to surrender the camp is delivered to the SS in T
Apr. 17	Commotion in the evening: "We are free!"
Apr. 19	Fictitious Tr to Switzerland announced
	Since Jan. 1, 1945, 7,984 Pr have been transported to T
Apr. 20	Number of Pr in T: 17,539 (approximately 7,000 from the P, 5,500 from Germany, 1,250 from Austria, 1,250 from Holland, 1,400 from Slovakia, and 1,000 from Hungary)
	36.6% of the Pr are not Mosaic
	Tr from concentration camps arrive; by May 5, there are approximately 13,500–15,000 inmates
	Himmler negotiates with Norbert Masur, a Swedish Jew, about T, among other things
Apr. 21	A representative from the IRC promises he will protect the camp
Apr. 24	A spotted fever epidemic is identified
Apr. 25	The group responsible for constructing the wooden barracks is to leave T
Apr. 30	Of the long-time residents, 39% are M, and 61% are W
	Average age of the long-time residents: 44.4 years
May 1	There are 17,515 Pr in T who are long-time residents
	Number of workers: 12,213 (4,871 M, 7,342 W)
May 2	An IRC representative takes over protection of the camp
May 3	E I is approved for inmates of the "Small Fortress"
May 4	The Czech Red Cross, including doctors, is admitted to T
May 5	There are more than 30,000 Pr in T
	The SS leaves T
	Murmelstein resigns
	The camp gains autonomy
May 5	*There are 2,803 J in the P*
May 8	Battles near T; shots are fired into the camp
	T is definitively freed at 9 P.M.
May 10	The Russians take over command of T from the IRC
	Official start of repatriation

May 12	Russian medical unit arrives in T
May 14	There are 25,301 former Pr in T
	A strict quarantine imposed for fourteen days
	Repatriation is suspended
May 28	Repatriation resumes
May	Height of the spotted fever epidemic
June 30	There are 5,952 former Pr in T
Aug. 17	Repatriation ends
November	The last of the former Pr leave T

1941–1945

7,000 J from the P are deported directly to the East, 265 survivors

Dimensions of T: 1,200 x 920 m (the entire fortress); 700 x 500 m (within the fortress)

In its later days the camp includes eight barracks used as residences and hospitals, an additional barrack, approximately 158 houses, and up to forty-three wooden barracks

Daily amount allotted per Pr for consumption (food, lodging, light, heat, health, public charges, etc.): 4.30 crowns (3.16 crowns in 1942, 3.71 crowns in 1943, and 4.46 crowns toward the end of the war)

Number of Pr transported to T until Apr. 20, 1945: approximately 141,000, of whom 10,000 are children under the age of sixteen and up to 62,000 (estimated) are persons are over the age of sixty-one

Number of Pr transported to T until the end: approximately 153,500–155,000

Deaths in T by Apr. 20, 1945: 33,521; by June 6, 1945: 35,088

Number of Pr transported from T: 88,196, approximately 3,500 survivors

Approximately 23,000 of those inmates who arrived in T prior to Apr. 20, 1945, survived

273 suicides and 211 reported suicide attempts

205–230 births and approximately 350 coerced abortions

Disease incidence: 50,000–60,000 cases of enteritis, 9,000 of epidemic conjunctivitis, 3,000 of hunger edema, 2,500 of spotted fever, 2,100 (new) of tuberculosis, 2,000 of epidemic jaundice, 1,900 of scarlet fever, 1,300 of typhus, 1,100 of erysipelas, 1,100 of diphtheria, 1,100 of measles, 1,000 of encephalitis, 900 of phlegmon, and 25 of spinal polio

Sources and Literature

ACRONYMS AND ABBREVIATIONS

319	works published by *Věstník* in Prague
DA	"documentation campaign"
HIŻ	Żydowski Instytut Historyczny (Jewish Historical Institute, Warsaw)
IfZ	Institut für Zeitgeschichte, Munich
RvO	Rijksinstituut voor Oorlogsdocumentatie, Amsterdam
T	Theresienstadt (spelled out in full in book and article titles)
WL	Wiener Library, London
YIVO	works known through the YIVO Institute for Jewish Research, New York
YV	Yad Vashem, Jerusalem
*	cross-references to other sources

PREFACE

I was in T for thirty-two months, and my experiences are the initial source for this book. I did not mix personal and overly subjective viewpoints in the portrayal. I wanted to delineate the face of the coerced community truthfully, to recognize and illuminate not just its external features but its essence; yet as a participant in the story, I was aware that I could not achieve unconditional objectivity.

When Bohemia was occupied in 1939, I lived in Prague. From mid-August to mid-December 1941, I was in the Jewish work camp Velká Losenice-Sázava. Then I was forced to work in a group dissolving the Jüdische Kultusgemeinde (JKG) until my deportation. I arrived in T with my wife and relatives on February 8, 1942. My wife, a physician and chemist, headed the Central Medical Laboratory until our deportation from T on October 12, 1944. I occupied only the lowliest positions: squadron member, room orderly, office assistant, barracks construction worker, "mobile construction squad" member, bricklayer, and assistant librarian. In addition, I gave lectures for the "Recreation Department" and to private groups. I knew many people in high and low positions, as well as those without positions, and was never at the center of events in the camp.

On October 14, 1944, I arrived in Auschwitz with my wife and her mother. The two, of blessed memory, were murdered by gas the same day. I went through *Lagerfelder* E (the "Gypsy camp"), A, and D before I was transported to the Buchenwald satellite camp Niederorschel on October 28. It was considered "good," but on February 16, 1945, I was sent to a "bad" camp: Langenstein-Zwieberge, also part of Buchenwald. On April 9 I avoided the evacuation of the camp, and on April 13 I was free.

On June 22 I returned to Prague and soon visited T, where Leo Baeck returned to me a bag of collected documents and my private notes. From July to December 1945, as a childcare worker and teacher, I helped the noble philanthropist Premysl Pitter, who took rescued Jewish children into hurriedly created homes immediately after the war ended, and soon after rescued German children from Czech camps (see 60a). From October 1945 to February 1947, I worked at the Prague Jewish Museum, where I devoted myself to building an archive of the persecutions and the camp in T.

The foundation was formed using objects from the "documentation campaign" by the Jewish Agency in Prague. Mr. Y. Z. Shek, its head at the time, communicates the following:

1. The decision to collect material was made at a meeting of the Merkaz Hechalutz in late fall 1942 in the Theresienstadt Ghetto. The direction was above all to record the traces of cultural and educational work that were accomplished illegally in the ghetto by the Hechalutz and its youth movement. Collection of documents about the ghetto administration in general ... was only secondary.... I myself was one of the three members of the commission formed at this meeting. At the time, I worked ... [unofficially] for the head of the Zofim-(Scout) movement ... (some 900 young people ages 12–16, divided into three large and some 100 small groups). I used this position in order to collect the material through trusted helpers, mainly the heads of the groups. Work plans, minutes of discussions, instructions etc. were automatically passed on to the commission.

2. In October 1944, when ... I myself was sent to Auschwitz, I bequeathed all the material to Miss Lisa Ehrmann. To a much smaller extent, the collecting continued. When the situation ... worsened in early 1945 ... Miss Ehrmann decided to bury the material in a trench and ensured that the outside world would find out about the hiding place in case the ghetto were destroyed.

3. I was the only member of the ... commission who returned to Prague from the concentration camp. At the end of May 1945, the documentation campaign was begun by the Czech Hechalutz. The Jewish Agency – EZRA committee – financed it with one clear goal: to get the material to Palestine. I became the head of this campaign.

4. We gave ourselves a single task: collecting. We had to do it quickly, before the material could be destroyed.... We had no scholarly ambitions and no plans to disseminate the materials.

The members of the "documentation campaign" worked with great idealism, but unfortunately for too short a time, with insufficient funds and untrained staff. The endeavor suffered from a general lack of comprehension and was dissolved some months later, after Shek had moved to Palestine in February 1946. The collection –

in large part, to the extent that it was related to the activities of the Zionist "Hechalutz," and, in smaller part, where it involved general camp documents (including, according to Shek, "certain extensive annual reports and other material that contained many illustrations and graphic depictions") – went not to the Jewish Museum, either as originals or reproductions, but only to Jerusalem. The material found only in Israel has not yet been studied and unfortunately is not even accessible, but there is hope that it will be made available in the foreseeable future and even published in part. The copies at the Jewish Museum, in the case of transcriptions, are unfortunately not always entirely reliable in wording, as I often found after publication of the first edition of this book, but I have not yet found any errors that would shake the substantive credibility of these documents; the cases found usually were a matter of minor carelessness.

The "documentation campaign" also recorded a number of protocols of unequal value. To the extent that they seemed significant to me, they have been listed here under the author's name and have been marked "DA."

I rescued the main body of the museum collection from the dissolution of the already assembled T materials; in addition, objects were left or lent to the museum. Altogether, there are tens of thousands of archival documents, and also other things that I viewed piece by piece. This remnant of a vast store of destroyed materials is enough to document the social structure and, to a large extent, also the history of the camp. Over the years, I have discovered many other primary and secondary sources, especially since this book was first published. Nevertheless, there undoubtedly is still in private and public hands much important material that was not available to me; it would enrich our knowledge, and sometimes also correct it, without changing the overall result.

This source and literature directory takes into account both original documents and published and unpublished writings. These include the following:

1. Materials from and about T. Of the many hundreds of documents used, only more extensive ones or some particularly important ones are cited separately. A total listing is impossible here. The hoped-for documentary volume that clarifies the role of T within the framework of the "Final Solution of the Jewish Question" is now available (*3b).
2. Reports, and so on, that were written after the war, in some cases in T.
3. Works on T or with important references to T.
4. Novelistic treatments of T, if published or if documentarily fruitful.
5. Poems with camp themes from T, if typical, as well as published verse and the most important works available to me by young authors who perished.
6. Several works on the Small Fortress (Kleine Festung) near T.
7. Documents on the Prague history of T.
8. Documentary material from the "Protectorate," mainly from the Prague JKG or the "Central Office," and material that concerns the persecution of the Jews and especially their deportation.
9. Writings in connection with the situation of the Jews in Czechoslovakia under German rule, specifically in the "Protectorate."
10. Informative works and unpublished material on the situation of the Jews under Hitler in Germany, Holland (Westerbork), Denmark, and Hungary.
11. Published and unpublished materials that illuminate the fate of Central European Jews in the East, and especially those deported from T – that is, material relating to

624   *Sources and Literature*

Poland (Auschwitz, various extermination camps, Lublin area, Łódź ghetto, Nisko, and also Bialystok [Białystok]) and Latvia (Riga).

12. English, American, and Swiss wartime publications and documents providing information on the fate of Jews in Central Europe, including T, and in Poland.
13. Standard works on the Jewish tragedy in World War II.
14. Some works of theoretical significance that were important substantively or to my view of the problems.
15. Magazines and newspapers. The number of essays on T that have appeared in the press, especially between 1945 and 1947, is enormous. Therefore, I have limited myself to references that I found correct or informative. Basically, it can be said that the majority of newspaper articles offer little that is accurate and often do more harm than good to the search for truth.

Works by unnamed authors are listed by key words among the authored writings.

I am always grateful for information about available sources and for supplements to the bibliography.

Works published by *Věstník* in Prague are marked bibliographically as 319 (information about this newspaper can be found under that number). Material from the Wiener Library, London, is marked as WL; from the Rijksinstituut voor Oorlogsdocumentatie, Amsterdam, as RvO; from the Institut für Zeitgeschichte, Munich, as IfZ; from Yad Vashem, Jerusalem, as YV; and from the Żydowski Instytut Historyczny (Jewish Historical Institute, Warsaw), as HIŻ. Cross-references to other sources in this list are marked with *. Works known to me only through YIVO, New York, were given the addition YIVO. See the list of acronyms and abbreviations at the beginning of this section.

LIST OF SOURCES AND LITERATURE

1. Abrahamsohn, A.: "Der Untergang der jüdischen Gemeinde Stettin." MS, WL, London, 1955.

An account of the first mass deportation from Germany (*185a).

1a. A. M.: "Theresienstadt – ein Propagandaschwindel!" In *Wie wäre es uns ergangen?* Olten, no year [ca. 1945], pp. 7–17.

An unreliable general report.

1b. Adelsberger, L.: *Auschwitz: Ein Tatsachenbericht*. Berlin, 1956.

The experiences of a Berlin Jewish doctor. The author, a woman, mentions (p. 31) that in early 1943, "for the only time, a Jewish transport was sent to Theresienstadt [from Berlin] in Belgian second-class carriages. The carriages were officially photographed and the photos were shown in the UFA's newsreel, entitled 'This is how the Jews travel.' A second picture followed, the well-known packed freight cars, with the title: 'And this is how they claim to travel.'"

1c. Adler, G.: "Das weisse Typhusblutbild während einer Epidemie." In *Medizinische Klinik*. Vol. 48. Munich, November 30, 1956, p. 2044.

The author was the head of the "Central Laboratory" in E VI from February 1942 until she was deported to her death, in October 1944. The text is a synopsis of a contribution to a discussion at a doctors' meeting on December 24, 1942, in T.

Sources and Literature 625

2. Adler, H. G.: "Danish Jewry under German Occupation." In *Wiener Library Bulletin*. London, January–April 1955.

2a. Adler, H. G.: *Der Kampf gegen die "Endlösung der Judenfrage."* Series from Bundeszentrale für Heimatdienst. Bonn, 1958.

The first attempt at a systematic overview of efforts to prevent the mass murder of Jews. The text contains references to the role of T and attempts to liberate or rescue its inmates.

3. Adler, H. G.: "Die Geschichte des Prager Jüdischen Museums." MS, London, 1947.

A lecture, at the London Leo Baeck Lodge of B'nai B'rith, on museum collection activities and work under SS control.

3ax. Adler, H. G.: *Die Juden in Deutschland – Von der Aufklärung bis zum Nationalsozialismus*. Munich, 1960.

This text treats, among other things, the nineteenth-century emergence of German "antisemitism," which was consistent with National Socialist Jew-hatred.

3a. Adler, H. G.: "Die Rolle Theresienstadts in der 'Endlösung der Judenfrage.' Aus 'Politik und Zeitgeschichte.'" B XXII/55. Supplement to weekly newspaper *Das Parliament*. Bonn, June 1, 1955.

3b. Adler, H. G.: *Die verheimlichte Wahrheit: Theresienstädter Dokumente*. Tübingen, 1958.

Two hundred and forty-one annotated documents and pictures from and about T, most published here for the first time. These documents form a long-planned supplement to this book, the problems of which often are illuminated in additional contexts. The text reveals the role of T from the viewpoint of the RSHA and the Reich authorities. The technology of deportation to the camp and its financial exploitation, specifically through "home purchase agreements," which are illuminated here for the first time, are studied. It also discusses transports from T and presents views of the city in photos and drawings and documentary insights into the camp's history and daily life, as well as its propagandistic significance as the "miniature Jewish state." Many of the documents are mentioned in this bibliography; others are not.

3c. Adler, H. G.: "Ideas Towards a Sociology of the Concentration Camp." In *The American Journal of Sociology*. Chicago, March 1958, pp. 513–22.

A seminal work on the sociology of concentration camps, especially in totalitarian states. It compares the National Socialist and Soviet systems.

3d. Adler, H. G.: "Leo Baeck in Theresienstadt." In Reichmann, E. G. (ed.), *Worte des Gedenkens für Leo Baeck*. Heidelberg, 1959, pp. 61–64.

The same general theme as *3b, with nine illustrations: two photos of scenes after liberation; two drawings by Fritta (nos. 194 and 195 in *3b); an image of the building of the crematorium, after a gouache by Ungar; a view of overcrowded quarters (drawing by Haas); the program "Colorful Music Hour" on the occasion of the IRC visit on April 6, 1945; the masthead of the "Announcements from the Jewish Self-Administration"; and a "personal identification card."

626 *Sources and Literature*

4. Adler, H. G.: "Zatímní návrh musea terezínského ghetta" [Preliminary Concept for a Museum of the Theresienstadt Ghetto]. MS, Prague, 1946.

A memorandum on the creation of a Prague Jewish Museum department in which life in T could be illustrated through objects, pictures, documents, and changing exhibits.

4a. [Adler, H. G.]: "Concentration Camps to Be Investigated by Social Science." In *Wiener Library Bulletin*. London, March–May 1947.

Principles for sociological study of the concentration camps.

5. Adler-Rudel, S.: "Alexandra Kollontay and the Jews of Theresienstadt." In *Jewish Frontier*. New York, September 1952, pp. 17–19.

As a functionary of the Jewish Agency, the author was able to gain access to the Soviet diplomat Alexandra Mikharlovna Kollontay (Kollontai) in Stockholm and to interest her in T, in order to achieve the quickest possible liberation during Red Army advances.

5a. [Anemia] "Long Essay on Anemia in T." MS, YV. T. o. J.

An unsigned work from the estate of Dr. Fritz Salus.

6. Andreas-Friedrich, R.: *Der Schattenmann*. Berlin, 1947.

Diary excerpts, including illumination of the fate of the Jews in Berlin and the transports.

7. Apenszlak, J. (ed.): *The Black Book of Polish Jewry*. New York: American Federation for Polish Jews, 1943.

Accurate information with astonishingly rich material (including illustrations) on ghettos, extermination camps, and so on, up to early 1943. However, nothing is reported on deportees from the West.

8. Arendt, H.: "Die wahren Gründe für Theresienstadt." In *Aufbau*. New York, September 3, 1943.

The author does not believe, for theoretical reasons, that T was planned as an "alibi" (in contrast to Fischer, *61a).

8a. Arendt, H.: *Elemente und Ursprünge totaler Herrschaft*. Frankfurt am Main, 1955.

Most important for our problems are the investigations in connection with ideologies. For example, see page 13: "The ideological susceptibility of the modern masses grows in proportion to the degree that common sense ... apparently is no longer able to understand the public world of politics and what happens in it." See also page 611: "The outstanding negative quality of the totalitarian elite is that it never stops to think about the world as it really is and never compares the lies with reality. Its most cherished virtue, correspondingly, is loyalty to the Leader, who, like a talisman, assures the ultimate victory of lie and fiction over truth and reality." We agree with the author: "The police are ... the highest institution in the apparatus of totalitarian rule" (p. 623). But we part ways with her when she continues, "In the concentration camps, moreover, the [police] have at their command a laboratory, fully equipped in every respect, in which the claims of totalitarian rule can be experimentally verified." In this sense, the camp is not an experiment; (1) practically, it has a political

Sources and Literature

and economic significance, and (2) theoretically, it has an ideological and – at least in National Socialism – a metaphysical, eschatological significance.

9. Arendt, H.: "Social Science Techniques and the Study of Concentration Camps." In *Jewish Social Studies*. New York, January 1950, p. 49ff.

The author recognizes that the extermination factories were more important to the Nazis than gains in the war; the crimes were committed because of their ideology. The author would have gotten a step closer if she had recognized the pseudoreligious and pseudomessianic roots of this ideology.

10. Auředníčková, A.: *Tři léta v Terezíně* [Three Years in Theresienstadt]. Prague, 1946.

Personal recollections. The author, in T from August 3, 1942, gave 348 lectures there. The source provides information on the Catholic community: the founding by Dr. Donath and Gerson, an engineer, on October 15, 1942, and the first service (in an attic) on November 29, 1942. There were 15 participants at first, 30–90 in 1943, 200 on Christmas 1942, and 300 on Easter 1943. New Year's 1944 was celebrated with a mass by Schubert.

10a. Asaria, Z.: *Die Juden in Köln*. Cologne, 1959.

This work contains two chapters on the Nazi period (pp. 320–400): "1933–1938 – Die Agonie einer Religionsgemeinschaft" by W. Unger and "Die Vernichtung" by Asaria.

This source can be used to compare the measures in the "Protectorate" (1. K.). The German sensibility of many Jews is noteworthy, as it continued to operate in T. At deportation, 25 kg of luggage was permitted; it was forbidden to take knives and forks. "The community administration had to prepare the list of people to be deported and to inform those on the list." The fairgrounds served as a collection point, and the Gestapo and Kripo searched luggage. Trains left from the Cologne-Deutz-Tief track. The first transport to T in cattle cars is said to have traveled for three days and nights. On the people from Cologne in T, see pages 388 and 393–96 (including a poem by W. Lindenbaum). In Cologne, 40–50 Jews survived the war illegally. On the Cologne residents' return home from T with Adenauer's help, see page 407. Pages 390 et seq. contain a list of the Cologne transports, which is "both unclear and incomplete." We compare her figures (left) with the best-established figures (*306a):

*10a		*306a	
Date	Number deported	Date	Number Deported
Late May 1942	1,000	June 16, 1942[a]	963
July 22, 1942	1,000	July 28, 1942[b]	1,165
July 27, 1942	?	(Date inaccurate or identical to previous one)	?
(Date not given)	?	September 5, 1942	50
(Date not given)	?	September 12, 1942	50

(continued)

628   *Sources and Literature*

(continued)

	*10a		*306a	
Date	Number deported	Date	Number Deported
(Date not given)	?	September 19, 1942	50
(Date not given)	?	September 26, 1942	50
(Date not given)	?	October 3, 1942	42
January 15, 1943	?	(Date inaccurate)	?
April 1943	?	(Date inaccurate)	?
June 1943	?	June 19, 1943	35
July 1943	?	August 1, 1943	45
November 1943	?	October 30, 1943	20
(Date not given)	?	1944	2
(Date not given)	?	March 14, 1945	45
TOTAL	2,000	TOTAL	2,517

[a] The first transport from Cologne
[b] Cologne-Koblenz

Of this total, which includes people from Bonn, Koblenz, Trier and other places, 194 survived the war in T.

A transport was reported on October 1, 1944: "300 men who were beaten to death with clubs after arriving in the 'small fortress' of Theresienstadt. 280 women." The figure is significantly exaggerated. (*162).

10b. [Auschwitz] *Hefte vom Auschwitz*. Vols. 1–3. Published by Państwowe museum w Oświęcimiu [State Museum in Auschwitz]. Auschwitz, 1959.

Documents and scholarly works. This exemplary series, which helps to lay the groundwork for a sober and nontendentious study of the entire complex of questions around the Auschwitz concentration camp, is to have an additional volume added each year. There is mention of T in volume 3, pages 98 and 108.

10c. [Auschwitz] [Materials on transports from T]. MS, State Museum Auschwitz, 1942–44.

Aside from some fragments of name lists, the museum has few documents related to prisoners from T.

The first transport of 1,866 people from T arrived in Auschwitz on October 28, 1942. Of these, 1,619 received "special treatment" (were gassed), and 247 (215 men and 32 women) entered the camp. On October 26, 740 men and 1,126 women left T (including 105 children under fourteen, 667 people aged fifteen to forty-five, 538 people aged forty-six to sixty, and 556 people over sixty-one). Thus it no longer really was a "transport of the elderly"; at that point, such a transport could not have been put together out of Bohemian and Moravian Jews.

From an illegal Polish organization, "Help for Concentration Camp Prisoners" (Pomoc Więźniom Obozów Koncentracyjnich), which received regular reports from Auschwitz, there have survived two documents that mention the Czech family camp. The first, dated March 26, 1944, says, in the original Polish:

> In Bohemia there is a special city, Theresienstadt, where the Czech Jews have been concentrated. They have their own self-administration, their own money, etc. and are

protected by the IRC. Using the promise of work in the Generalgouvernement under good conditions, the Gestapo was able to remove some 6,000 people from there. What kind of spell allowed the people to believe the Gestapo people's hypocritical tales, we really can't understand. [Some words about the family camp follow.] On March 15 [*sic*] some 4,000 people, most of them healthy (men [more than 2,000], women [1,800] and children) were forced into the gas chambers ... a group of chosen SS men and kapos [prisoner functionaries] inhumanly abused those sentenced to death for several hours. Approximately 60 people were beaten to death with clubs and rifle barrels. The entire action was carried out at night, with the greatest care, so that the Jews of Theresienstadt who stayed in the camp would not suspect anything. In order to fool the remaining Jews in Theresienstadt and the IRC, the unfortunate ones were ordered to write letters to their relatives in Bohemia four days before their gassing. All were ordered to date these letters March 25, 1944. The political department kept these letters and will send them only after March 25. In this way, the Gestapo hopes to prove that no one is gassed in Auschwitz, and at the same time seeks to entice new victims from Theresienstadt.

The second document on the period from March 1 to April 10, 1944, reports that some of those from T who remained in the family camp after the gassing of the first transport would be used for work, and others would be gassed (including old people, most of the women, and children).

Reports of the Birkenau work deployment for the period May 3–17, 1944, show that 210 boys under fourteen and 1,250 "adults" were listed as not capable of work on the first of these days, and 1,230 people were listed as such on the last day. In two weeks, therefore, 20 people died, which indicates the favorable conditions in Family Camp B IIb for Auschwitz (or any concentration camp).

10d. [Auschwitz] "Obóz koncentracyjny Oświęcim" [Concentration Camp Auschwitz]. Warsaw, 1955.

Fifty-eight informative pictures, no text.

11. Bacon, J.: "Můj život v Terezíně" [My Life in Theresienstadt]. MS, Jerusalem, 1947.

Bacon came from Ostrau [Ostrava] in late September 1942, at the age of thirteen, and was deported to Auschwitz in December 1943. The text contains descriptions of the journey to T and life in a "youth home." Parts of this valuable report are presented in Chapters 9 and 17.

11a. Bacon, J.: "Eyewitness Report." MS, YV, Jerusalem, 1959.

A report on experiences in Ostrau [Ostrava], T, Auschwitz, Mauthausen, and Gunskirchen.

This text contains information on Edelstein's death; Bacon was friendly with his son Aryeh. Probably on June 14, 1944, a car full of SS men came to get Mrs. Edelstein, her mother (Mrs. Ollendorf), and Aryeh from Family Camp B IIb. Mrs. Edelstein was in bed with the measles. "The doctor said they couldn't take her in this condition," which, however, did not help. Two of Bacon's acquaintances, of which one, Srulek Zuckermann, worked as a stoker in Crematorium 3 and the other, Kalmin Fuhrmann, also worked in the Sonderkommando, later reported that Edelstein (who had been brought out of Auschwitz I) met his family at the crematorium. Fuhrmann, who, during shootings, had to "hold [the victims] (generally by the ears) if they didn't stand quietly, saw Edelstein and his family in the last moments before death. He told me they were all very quiet, and that they were shot one after the other." Zuckermann had to burn the corpses (*238).

Fredy Hirsch was able to house small children in block 29, under the supervision of some mothers, and children between eight and sixteen in block 31, which became a youth home almost in the style of T. The inmates were collected in groups, each under a leader (madrich), who told his wards stories, taught them songs, or gave them schooling. The roll call was held in the block. Sports were performed outdoors with Hirsch in the morning, and he also supervised bodily hygiene. Adults gave lectures; the children rehearsed all sorts of performances, even theater. The SS was interested in this activity, especially SS Dr. Klein, who acted "almost like an uncle." Hirsch had good contacts with the SS man Pestek, who later escaped with a Jew but was captured and executed in Auschwitz. Hirsch was even able to set up a small library and managed to distribute packets, admittedly robbed of their most valuable contents, that had been addressed to non-Jewish prisoners who had since died. This continued until March 7, 1944; that evening, they celebrated the anniversary of a children's home in T. The next morning, the September 1943 transport members who were to be murdered had to leave (Bacon was part of the December 1943 transport). Only doctors, the sick, and twins remained behind. The youth home, in which Mrs. Edelstein had also worked, existed until the dissolution of B IIb.

Dissolution of B IIb: The critical day for the planned extermination of those who had arrived in December 1943 was June 20, 1944, but nothing happened on that day. Several days later, Dr. Mengele held a selection, of which he said, "The women with children will go to a special home, there would be white walls, white-painted buildings ... where they would have peace. He was naturally thinking of the crematorium, where everything was white." Those capable of working were selected: men and childless women from ages sixteen to forty-five. Women who were willing to be separated from their children could also have been selected, but they declined this favor. Bacon's mother and older sister were selected; his father and he himself (he was fourteen and a half at the time) remained behind. One week later, the preventive custody camp leader SS-OSTBF Schwarzhuber again selected the young people and removed some ninety of them; a few days later, Dr. Mengele repeated this procedure. It resulted in tragedies:

> To report or not to report, to go with one's parents or not. Some people said to their parents the first time, yes we will go wherever you go, and the second time they decided to go with the selection. The parents also sometimes tried to influence the children to go with them; in other cases, they said to the children: "You can still live, I'm going to die anyway."

On July 6, some ninety young people, including Bacon, were brought to Camp E (the Gypsy camp). Those who remained in B IIb died in the gas chambers on the night of July 10 (*237).

At the dissolution of Auschwitz, Bacon was evacuated, on January 18, 1945. The march, during which the weak were shot, led the prisoners to Blechhammer in thirty-six hours. There things were chaotic. Some people hid until liberation by the Russians; others were found and shot. Bacon rode in a transport (the young people rode in two closed cars, and the others in open lorries) via Katowitz (where there were deaths from air raids on arrival), Ostrau [Ostrava] (where they were fed bread and coffee by Czech aid organizations), Prague, and Budweis to Mauthausen, where they arrived on January 30. The young people did not have to work much or at all but were subjected to the worst privations and were tormented and mistreated by criminal German prisoner functionaries. They were quartered first in constructed blocks and then in a "tent camp." Air raids became more and more frequent. There was less and less food, and drinking water was scarce. In March, they picked grass and cooked it with some water. So many died that the crematoria could not keep up, and masses of bodies lay around. Some prisoners ate pieces of bodies. One comrade from T told Bacon openly, "You know, I was in the sick block, and in the chaos a person who had just died wasn't well protected. So we quickly took some pieces of flesh – imagine what happiness! I cut myself a piece of thigh." When Scharführer (SCHF) Buntrock, formerly of Birkenau, "found anyone cooking or eating human flesh, he shot him on the spot."

On April 15, or somewhat later, Bacon was evacuated on foot with the young people and many adults; the reason for this death march was unclear. The goal was the Gunskirchen camp, the horrors of which outdid even Mauthausen. There was no room and hardly any drinking water, and people ate tree bark and grass. The overcrowding became unbearable due to constant new transports. There Bacon experienced liberation in the first days of May.

Baeck, L.: *28.

11b. Baehr, H.: "So lebten wir in Theresienstadt." In *Aufbau*. New York, November 21, 1947.

A reproduction of an iconographic, misleading drawing of the quarters (L 306) with an equally misleading description.

11c. Barker, A.: "Affidavit," MS, WL, Berlin, 1958.

The author arrived in T in 1941, where she survived diphtheria, scarlet fever, and jaundice. When Burger ordered the implementation of artificial abortion methods in July 1943, 350 women are said to have reported immediately. For the author, this required a serious operation that caused lasting health damage. She was transported to Auschwitz on October 28, 1944, and from there to Bergen-Belsen; there, she faced endless torments, hunger, misery, and horror – but no work. After several months, she was deported to Raguhn (near Dessau) for factory work. On the several-kilometer road to the factory and back to the camp, children threw stones at the prisoners. An SS man injured the author's back with a blow from a gun barrel; it turned into tuberculosis of the spine. After the war, the author was therefore bedridden for nearly five years. In Raguhn, she also fell ill with serious diarrhea and vomiting, such that an overseer sent her to the typhoid barracks, but friends got her out. Seriously ill, with a high fever, she was dragged by friends to an evacuation train, which arrived in T after weeks of travel, with dead bodies and living skeletons, in the last third of April 1945 (*20a).

12. Bass, F.: "Amenorrhea at the Concentration Camp of Theresienstadt." In *Gynaecologia*. Basel, April 1947. YIVO.

13. Bass, F.: "Theresienstadt." MS, Prague, 1946.

An intelligent account of experiences.

632   *Sources and Literature*

14. Bednarz, W.: *Obóz straceń w Chełmnie nad Nerem* [The Extermination Camp Chełmno (Kulmhof)]. Warsaw, 1946.

Information on the history and technology of the camp.

15. Behrend, R.: *Verfemt und verfolgt: Erlebnisse einer Jüdin in Nazideutschland 1933–1944.* Zurich, 1945.

Berger, G.: *268.

16. Berger, M.: "Zpráva o ghetu v Terezíně" [Report on the Ghetto in Theresienstadt]. MS, DA, Ostrau [Ostrava], 1945.

The author was in T from the end of September 1942 to autumn 1944. The description is often substantively unreliable, but the conditions and character of the camp are accurately recorded. See the sample in *3b, doc. 100.

17. Bergh, S. van den: *Deportaties: Westerbork, Theresienstadt, Auschwitz, Gleiwitz.* Bussum, no year [1945].

A record of camp experiences. This text provides insight into conditions in Westerbork. The author was in T for a time until autumn 1944. The information is generally accurate.

17a. [Berlin] *Die letzten Tage des deutschen Judentums: Tatsachenbericht eines Augenzeugen.* Tel Aviv, 1943.

The author describes Jewish life in Berlin – with all its oppressions – and the deportations objectively, conscientiously, and accurately. The author treats the period from the start of the war until October 27, 1942, when she, along with other "exchange women," was brought to the Turkish border via Vienna by the Gestapo and found her way to Palestine. The sending of older people to T is mentioned: "I heard before my departure that the Reichsvereinigung in Berlin had received from Theresienstadt 50 letters that were supposed to be distributed to the recipients. . . . Some people were said to have reported that they were doing quite well."

17b. Berliner, A.: "Jüdische Jahreskalender." YV, T, 1943.

This calendar is decorated with drawings. I had access to various calendars, from private collections, produced lithographically in T for 1944 and 1945, as well as for the Jewish year 5705 (1944–45). YV also has calendars.

18. Bernadotte, F. (Count of Wisborg): *The Curtain Falls.* New York, 1945.

This text has no direct relationship to T but is a contribution to understanding the final phase. On the author's behavior, see *139.

18a. Best, W.: Affidavit under oath. Steengracht Document Book, no. 111, 29, reproduced. Nuremberg, Case XI, 1948.

Best claims to have hinted since September 8, 1943, at the impending action against the Jews. He says that once he knew the date, he gave it to Duckwitz to pass on to the Danes (*41, 42, 42a, 50b, 234).

19. Bettelheim, B.: "Individual and Mass Behavior in Extreme Situations." In Newcomb, Theodore M., and Eugene L. Hartley (eds.), *Readings in Social Psychology.* New York, 1948, pp. 637ff.

Sources and Literature

Bettelheim deals, among other things, with the prisoners' psychological adaptation to the functionaries in the camp hierarchy, who – in the unfortunate terminology of psychoanalytic jargon – were recognized as "the all-powerful father-imago."

20. Biermann, H.: "Der 'Dank' ihres Vaterlandes: Kriegsbeschädigte in Theresienstadt." In *Aufbau*. New York, August 22, 1947.

The author states that some 2,000 people with serious war injuries came to T; of these, approximately 600 were deported to Auschwitz in fall 1944, and there were only 175 survivors in T. These figures may be correct. In the previous issue of *Aufbau* (August 15, 1947), E. Marcus describes the fate of war-blinded Dr. Fritz Simon, and his wife, and his child, born in T.

20a. Birnbaum, S.: *Une Française Juive est revenue*. Paris, 1945.

The author went from Drancy to Auschwitz in January 1944, and to Bergen-Belsen on November 1, 1944. After a three-day trip on February 20, 1945, she arrived in Raguhn, which was called a "very good" camp, but the treatment soon worsened and terrible hunger prevailed, such that 78 of some 500 women died before the evacuation on April 13. They worked twelve hours a day in three airplane factories. After a one-week trip – first in motor vehicles and then on a train – the 428 women arrived in T. The reception was good, and the nurses were highly praised. The text contains some mistaken information on T. Starting on June 2, the French were taken to Pilsen [Plsen] in American vehicles and from there were brought by plane to Bron, near Lyon, on June 5 (*11c).

21. Blau, B.: *Das Ausnahmerecht für die Juden in den europäischen Länder 1933–1945, I Teil, Deutschland*. New York, 1952.

A solid compilation. Important things are in the original, and the rest is presented in excerpts, as well as samples of court practice.

22. Blau, B.: "The Jewish Population of Germany." In *Jewish Social Studies*. New York, April 1950.

Valuable demographic information.

22a. Blau, B.: "The Last Days of German Jewry in the Third Reich." In *YIVO Annual of Jewish Social Science*. Vol. VIII. New York, 1953, pp. 197–204.

Some information on T. The amount extorted through "home purchase agreements" is given as RM 125 million, and RM 110 million was paid by mid-July 1944. The text contains a description of the Musy Aktion and an erroneous claim that the prisoners in T refused to board the trains in Switzerland. Page 202 et seq.:

> On June 16, 1943, 200 patients in the Jewish Hospital in Berlin were deported to Theresienstadt [probably on transport I/96, which arrived on June 17 with 428 people]. Many were taken out on stretchers and mattresses. Shortly after, on November 22, 1943, all the mentally ill who had been brought to Berlin were deported to Theresienstadt [this must mean transport I/104, with 23 victims, whose members, like all the mentally ill, were all excluded from release to Switzerland (*249c)].

23. Blau, B.: "Vierzehn Jahre Not und Schrecken." MS, WL, New York, ca. 1947.

634 *Sources and Literature*

An account of experiences. The text contains important references to the latter period of the Reichsvereinigung, 1943–45, and the situation of the few nondeported Jews, of whom there were approximately 200 Jews with non-Jewish relatives in Berlin at war's end, mainly confined in the Jewish hospital or a collection camp. There are references to T.

24. Bloom, S. F.: "Dictator of the Lodz Ghetto." In *Commentary*. New York, 1949, pp. 111–22.

Information on camp conditions and the character of the Jewish Elders. Of the 19,980 people deported to Łódź from Central Europe in autumn 1941, 10,527 were sent to the extermination camp (Chełmno) within six months; 6,247 died in the ghetto, and only 3,206 were still alive at the end of the war.

25. Bloom, S. F.: "Toward the Ghetto Dictator." In *Jewish Social Studies*. New York, January 1950, p. 73 et seq.

A characterization of the position of Jewish camp leaders, who were neither heroes nor criminals. The Jewish police chief Genz in Vilna said,

> I stand and count at the gate, and do you know how difficult that is? The people ask me where they are being taken. I don't tell them, because I know where they are being taken. But I want to save at least some of them, and among them, as far as possible, the better ones, the more valuable ones, so they can renew our people.

The Jewish Elder of Łódź, Rumkowski, liked to say, "They call me a dictator. That is not true. My ambition is to rescue a remnant, and future Jewry will be beholden to me. Only history will be able to judge my work; looking back, it will be seen as a blessing."

26. Blumental, N.: *Obozy* [Camp]. *Vol. I of* Dokumenty i materialy do dziejów okupacji niemieckiej w Polsce [Documents and Materials on the History of the German Occupation in Poland]. Łódź, 1946.

Information on living and working conditions in camps such as Auschwitz, Majdanek, Treblinka, Sobibór, Bełżec, Chełmno, and so on, page 115 et seq. The text contains documents on the transports in January 1943 from T to Auschwitz; of these, one is reproduced on page 4 of the appendix.

26a. Blumenthal-Weiss, I.: *Mahnmal: Gedichte aus dem KZ.* Hamburg, 1957.

The author arrived from Westerbork on September 6, 1944, and remained in T until liberation. The poems were written years after liberation.

27. Boder, D.: *I Did Not Interview the Dead.* Urbana, IL, 1949.

This text is important for understanding the mentality of former camp inmates.

28. Boehm, E. H. (ed.): *We Survived: The Stories of Fourteen of the Hidden and the Hunted of Nazi Germany.* New Haven, CT, 1949.

The text contains two accounts of T: (1) Baeck, L.: "A People Stands Before Its God" (pp. 284–98) and (2) Liebrecht, H.: "Therefore Will I Deliver Him" (pp. 214–51).

Baeck relates experiences from the war years in Berlin, his deportation, and his sojourn in T starting in late January 1943.

Sources and Literature 635

Liebrecht, a Catholic, arrived in T in autumn 1942 and – as holder of Iron Cross First Class – was sent to Auschwitz in autumn 1944. The information on camp history is wrong, but what Liebrecht himself experienced is clear and accurate. The text is informative on his activity in the squadron, in the burial crew, in a street construction group, as a potato carrier, and in food transport. It also provides insight into the religious life of the Catholics.

28a. [Bohemia and Moravia] "Geschichte der Juden in Böhmen und Mähren." MS, University Library, Jerusalem. No details [Prague, 1943].

This work, on 287 typewritten pages, was certainly completed by a knowledgeable JKG functionary (or several of them) at the behest of the "Central Office" before summer 1943. The events of March 1939 to March 1943 are described on pages 273–87. T is mentioned, but its role is barely known or concealed: "In regular transports of up to 1,000 people, the Jews left their previous homes and in the ghetto formed a self-administered community with all the attributes of such, which fulfilled all their needs in the ghetto and itself took care of all necessary work."

29. Bondy, J.: "Malý zážitek v terezínském ghetu" [Brief Experience in the Ghetto Theresienstadt]. MS, DA, Prague, 1945.

Bondy describes how Rahm, Haindl, and a third SS man tested a bloodhound on him.

30. Borwicz, M., N. Rost, and J. Wulf: *Dokumenty zbrodni i męczeństwa* [Documents of Crime and Martyrdom]. Cracow, 1945.

A protocol providing direct insight into the tragedy of the Polish Jews. The text contains a description of "actions" such as those suffered by people deported from T in spring 1942. It cites harrowing statements by surviving children; one talks about the gassing in Auschwitz (p. 185): "They did it most often with transports of people who came from freedom or from Theresienstadt; they didn't know where they were going or what was going to happen to them."

30a. Brechner, S.: "Sosnowiec." MS, HIŻ, Poland, 1946.

On May 11, 1942, 1,500 Jews from Sosnowiec were sent on a transport for which T was the promised destination. But it went to Auschwitz.

30b. Breslauer, K.: "Erinnerungen an Theresienstadt." MS, WL. No details.

The author arrived in September 1942 from Berlin and soberly describes the conditions. At work – plucking excelsior for straw mattresses – "the Czech Jewish women at first viewed us as enemies like the Germans, for they claimed we had voted for Hitler."

31. Broch, H.: "Der Zerfall der Werte" [interpolated essay in vol. III of the novel *The Sleepwalkers*]. One-volume edition, Zurich, 1952.

This work's goal is to understand the decay of values that National Socialism made possible. It was written ca. 1930.

32. Brod, M.: "Helden." In *Aufbau*. New York, July 12, 1946.

A wrongly informed depiction with a hymn of praise to Edelstein. His arrest is explained through a fable, according to which escaped English prisoners of war were hidden in T in September 1943.

32a. Brod, M.: "Hotel in Haifa, 1943." In *Eckart*. Witten Berlin, October–December 1958, p. 323.

A poem with memories of the author's brother in T.

32b. Buchheim, H.: "Das Reichssippenamt." In *Gutachten des Instituts für Zeitgeschichte*. Munich, 1958, p. 281 et seq.

Among the tasks of the Reichssippenamt (Racial Purity Office) was the evaluation of the Jewish personal status registry, and thus all the lineage forms, showing one or more Jewish grandparents, that had been submitted to the census of May 1939. For this job, approximately a dozen Jewish experts were employed as assistants.

At least one of them was still working in T at war's end.

32c. Burešová, L.: [Four drawings from T]. In *Židovská ročenka* [Jewish Yearbook]. Prague, 1954–55.

The drawings are titled *Transport* (p. 99), *Courtyard* (p. 105), *Schleuse* (p. 115), and *Old Women in the Quarters* (p. 134).

YV has eight watercolors and charcoal drawings of T from 1943 by the young artist, who perished.

32d. Canetti, E.: *Masse und Macht*. Hamburg, 1960.

On the "mass symbols of the nations," see page 191 et seq.; on the Jews specifically, see page 201 et seq.

32e. Caro, Kl.: "Der Untergang der Synagogengemeinde Köln." In *Frau und Politik*. Bonn, March 1960, pp. 13–15.

Information on Cologne in the deportation period and people from Cologne in T.

32f. Caro, Kl.: "Die Persönlichkeit Jakob Edelsteins." In *Allgemeine Wochenzeitung*. Düsseldorf, February 13, 1959.

An appreciative description, with factual errors.

33. Caro, Kl.: "Stärker als das Schwert." MS, WL, 1946.

The author was in T from June 16, 1942, and was liberated by the transport to Switzerland. The text is a general report with errors but is informative on Zionist cultural life in the camp, in which the author took a leading role. "We had a card file of approx. 6,000 Zionists under the heading 'People Interested in Jewish Lectures.'" It contains references to religious life, youth welfare, and Zionist work. The Zionists in the leadership are lionized.

Mrs. Caro also told me in a letter that Edelstein never trusted Freiberger and Schliesser and "might even have feared them, even in regard to our Zionist work, but Schliesser never took action against it." On the activities of the Zionist women's group WIZO (Women's International Zionist Organization), she says: "We began secretly in a small meeting place with 15 people" in summer 1942; later, they met publicly in a large room in B V with 100 and more participants, and they sponsored

Sources and Literature 637

weekly Zionist and general Jewish lectures (history, biblical studies, philosophy, literature, etc.). Franz Kahn protected them through the "Recreation Office." The activity ended with the start of the fall transports in 1944. In addition, a leadership group for Zionist work, Hanhala, formed in T, with approximately fifteen personalities from Germany, Bohemia-Moravia, Austria, and later Holland. The members included, among others, Eppstein, Kahn, Fleischmann, Hanna Steiner, and Mrs. Caro. They met in E IIIa and discussed the program, lectures, courses, the future in Palestine, and so on.

34. Cholewa, S.: "Dansk skoleundervisning i Theresienstadt" [Danish schooling in Theresienstadt]. In Nordentoft, I. M., and A. Svendstorp (eds.), *Og hverdagen skiftede*. Copenhagen, 1946, pp. 139–50. YIVO.

35. Cholewa, S.: "The Danish Jews in Theresienstadt." In *YIVO Bleter*. Vol. 30, no. 2. New York, 1947, pp. 310–17. YIVO.

A translation from Danish into Yiddish.

Cohen, D.: *115.

36. Cohen, E. A.: *Het duitse concentratiecamp: Een medische en psychologische studie*. Amsterdam, 1952.

A psychoanalytical, sometimes skewed treatment of the problem.

37. Cohn, L.: "Potemkin in Theresienstadt." In *Aufbau*. New York, February 22 and March 1, 1946.

The author, the well-known Breslau blind reader, was in T from January 27, 1944 (from Westerbork) and describes the "beautification," not always accurately.

38. Cooper, R. W.: *The Nuremberg Trial*. London, 1947.

A brief summary of the most important prosecutions.

39. Christian, P., and H. Schmerling: *Gesetzliche Bestimmungen über die Versendung von Geschenks-, Umzugs-, Heirats- und Auswanderergut. Status.* Prague, no year [September 15, 1940].

The practical application of the complicated rules that were to be scrupulously obeyed. The text contains forms such as the "questionnaire for Jewish emigrants."

40. Čurda-Liptovský, B.: *Terezínské katakomby* [Theresienstadt Catacombs]. Prague, 1946.

An emotional report on the "Kleine Festung."

40a. Cytron, T.: "Zeznanie" [Protocol]. MS, HIŻ, Poland, 1946.

A report on the Bialystok [Białystok] (B) ghetto. The author mentions the children's transports that left B on August 20, 1943, and a rumor in B according to which the children were supposed to go to Switzerland via T. The issue was a planned exchange – two Jewish children for each German.
    See documents NG-1794 and NG-5049.

40b. Czarnoczapka, J.: [Protocol]. [Polish], MS, HIŻ, Poland, undated.

The author's life took him from Łódź to Izbica, Posen [Poznan], Birkenau, Jaworzno (evacuated on January 17, 1945), Blechhammer, Gross-Rosen, and Leitmeritz [Litoměřice], where he arrived on February 14, 1945. There he performed heavy double-shift labor, at twelve hours per shift, in the underground Elsabe munitions factory. On May 1 he was evacuated to T; he praises his reception there (*163, 181a).

41. [Denmark] "Bilag til beretning til folketinget" [Supplement to a Report to the Folketing]. XI (document 18) and XIII/3 (documents 735–745 and 759). Copenhagen, 1951 and 1954.

XIII/3 documents 727–734 also concern the Danish Jews, but only the documents from 735 on are connected with deportations and T.

Document 734: On April 19, 1943, Ribbentrop asks Best, the Reich plenipotentiary in Copenhagen, "whether one could, without causing serious difficulties for the Scavenius government, present certain demands to the Danish government regarding the Jewish question."

Document 735: On September 8, 1943, Best informs Ribbentrop:

> For consistent implementation of the new course in Denmark, in my opinion, a solution to the Jewish question must now ... also be taken under advisement. The measures necessary for this must be taken during the current state of emergency, because at a later stage they would bring about in the country a reaction that would lead to a renewed imposition of a state of emergency under probably less beneficial conditions than today. In particular, as I know from numerous sources, a more or less existing constitutional government would step down, and the king and Reichstag would cease their continued cooperation with the government of the country. In addition, we probably would have to expect a general strike, because as a result of these measures the unions would cease their activities, and therefore their moderating influence on the workers. If the measures were to be taken during the current state of emergency, however, the possibility exists that a constitutional government could no longer be formed, so that an administrative committee under my leadership would have to be formed and lawmaking practiced by me through decrees. In order to ... abruptly arrest and deport some 6,000 Jews, the police forces I asked for on September 1, 1943, would be necessary.... Additional forces would have to be made available by the commander of the German troops in Denmark. For the deportations, ships would probably be the main option.

Document 736: On September 18, 1943, Ribbentrop informs Best: "The Führer has decreed that the deportation of the Jews from Denmark should be implemented."

Document 737: On the same day, Best informs the Foreign Office that he needs fifty Sipo officers for three expected police companies and requires a ship with room for at least 5,000 people for Zealand, and trains for Fyn and Jutland. "Politically, the deportation of the Jews will undoubtedly greatly worsen the situation in Denmark." Best fears unrest and a general strike and therefore wishes to keep the requested police available "after the operation."

Document 738: In a telegram to the Oberkommando der Wehrmacht (OKW), the German envoy in Copenhagen, Barandon, states on September 20, 1943, that it is doubtful whether the police are sufficient for the deportation. He continues:

> Troops would be most heavily burdened with implementation and, especially since mainly younger recruits will have to be deployed in Copenhagen and on Fyn, they will be unable to take firm action.

Sources and Literature 639

Consequences of the deportation seem problematic to me. Cooperation of Danish official and police apparatus cannot be expected later on. Supply of food placed very much in doubt.

Willingness of armaments industry to supply will be impaired. Major unrest requiring use of troops is to be expected.

Document 739: On September 21, 1943, Barandon informs envoy V. Grundherr in the Foreign Office by telephone that Dr. Mildner, the new Sipo and SD commander, is against the deportations and has appealed to Himmler, on Best's authority.

Document 740: On September 22, 1943, Jodl writes to the military commandant in Denmark that Hitler has ordered the deportations through Himmler, who has transferred two police battalions to Denmark for this purpose.

Document 741: On September 29, 1943, Best telegraphs the Foreign Office on an intervention by the collaborating director of the Danish RC, Helger Rosting.

Finally, Rosting made another proposal that is typical of the view of National Socialists in Denmark: we should ... release the Danish soldiers and imprison all the Jews of Denmark in the camps freed up in this way.... . But we should not deport all the imprisoned Jews out of Denmark immediately and at one time, but should announce that for every act of sabotage, 50 or 100 Jews will be deported.

Document 742: Best writes to the Foreign Office on October 18, 1943: "So far, no cases of Jewish espionage or sabotage have been found in Denmark through police investigation and court cases.... . When it was announced here on Oct. 2, 1943, to justify the deportation of the Jews, that the Jews morally and materially supported sabotage in Denmark, this was done to achieve the purpose, without any concrete evidence."

Document 743: On November 19, 1943, Best writes to the Foreign Office:

Rosting informed me that the Danish RC has asked the Presidium of the German RC to clarify whether representatives of the Danish RC may visit the place where the Jews and communists deported from Denmark are held.... . The Danish foreign ministry also has asked me whether Section Chief Hvas[s] might be permitted ... such a visit. Carrying through such visits would have a very calming effect in Denmark. (*227)

Document 744: Deputy State Secretary Hencke notes that the Danish envoy Mohr had asked during a meeting on December 6, 1943, about the return of erroneously deported persons who did not count as Jews under the regulations. "Further, the lists of deported Jews, requested by the Danish government, have not yet been made available."

Document 759: Regarding Mohr's visit on January 5, 1943, Hencke notes, as point 3:

Return of people of mixed race with Danish citizenship erroneously deported to Germany.

I informed Mr. Mohr, based on the notes of Inl II on January 4, that the Schulz siblings and the half-Jews Groten, Baumann and Jensen would be returned to Denmark in the coming weeks. We have been unable to complete investigation of the other cases initiated by the Danes due to the destruction of large parts of the files.

At a corresponding remark by the envoy, I explained to him further that the documents on the deported Jews had been destroyed in the air raids. Reconstruction of the lists desired by him would be extraordinarily difficult and require a great deal of time.

640   *Sources and Literature*

Therefore, he could not expect the lists for the present. [With good will, he could have had them within days.]

We could not permit sending packages to the interned Jews. The Danish Jews in Theresienstadt received the same provisions as the German population, so there was no need. In addition, for disciplinary reasons, privileging the Danish Jews over the rest of the internees was not possible.

In point 4, Mohr notes that no news from Jews to their relatives in Denmark had yet arrived. It was therefore to be assumed that the mail that the Danes had been permitted to write at their reception into T had not been delivered (see Chapter 6 and 3b, doc. 225). Point 5 is an intervention to allow camp visits for Hvass and others.

Document 745: On May 12, 1944, Hencke notes:

The head of the Political Department of the Danish Foreign Ministry [Hvass], who visited me today in the company of the Danish chargé d'affaires, spoke of the ... permission to visit the interned Jews of Danish citizenship in Theresienstadt that he has long since applied for. Mr. Hvass remarked accurately that the prospect of a visitation permit for Theresienstadt had been held out for the second half of May. I replied to Mr. Hvass that the matter is still being considered. The visit might be able to occur around May 20. The final decision would be announced in the coming days.

XI, document 18: For the Commission of the Folketings, Hvass writes on July 18, 1949, about his visit to T with Henningsen (*98, 108):

At the time of the visit, approximately 40,000 Jews were living in Theresienstadt. Of these, 425 had been deported from Denmark. Czech gendarmes stood guard around the city. According to our investigations, there were 15 German Aryans. They were responsible for supervising the city and its ties to the outside world. Otherwise, the city was under Jewish self-administration. Chief physician Juel Henningsen and I were obviously aware that a great number of events that we saw in T were organized because of our visit. However, we devoted our attention during the visit not to the events but to the health, clothing and living conditions of the Danish Jews. We found that their health was better than expected, which for many can be ascribed to the fact that it had been possible from early on to send food to the Danish Jews. Their clothing seemed quite sufficient, and their living conditions in Theresienstadt, while they could be described as harsh, in no way compared with those under which their coreligionists in the actual concentration camps lived. They lived under extraordinarily strong psychological pressure. That the large majority of them nevertheless had survived their stay can be ascribed mainly, aside from the abovementioned food shipments, to the extraordinary efforts of the Jews, who made it possible within the framework of the self-administration to create such *relatively* good outward conditions for their coreligionists in Theresienstadt, and gave them the courage and strength to continue to live in hopes of a better future.

42. [Denmark] "Der Duckwitz kehrt zurück." In *Der Spiegel*. Hamburg, January 19, 1955, p. 12 et seq.

A portrayal of the wartime role of the German naval attaché Georg Ferdinand Duckwitz. "Duckwitz first secured respect in September 1943, when he informed [the Danish resistance] in a back room of the Social Democratic 'Folkets Hus' ... that the German occupation authorities were going to arrest all of Denmark's Jewish citizens on the night of October 1" (*234).

Sources and Literature

42a. [Denmark] Affidavit of Rudolf Mildner PS-2375 and -2377 on June 22, 1945. Mimeographed, Nuremberg.

In 2375, Mildner praises his and Best's behavior during the events surrounding the deportation of Danish Jews; The main responsibility was ascribed to Ribbentrop. According to 2377, Mildner later promised officials in the Danish Foreign Ministry that he would obtain permission from the RSHA for functionaries of this ministry, the president of the RC, and Danish journalists to visit T. In April 1944, when he was no longer working in Copenhagen, Mildner was again asked by Hvass to intervene, as a result of which Müller approved the visit. Eichmann or Rolf Günther was sent to T to see whether the city could be shown. At Müller's order, Mildner inspected T around June 13. "The city was overcrowded." He reported to Müller and was of the opinion that the camp could be visited (*121).

43. Daniel, J.: "Das Lied von Theresienstadt." In *Der Weg*. No. 4. Berlin, 1947.

The story of an eighty-year-old from Aachen who died in T.

44. "Danish Jews in Theresienstadt." In *Aufbau*. New York, February 4, 1944.

"The German authorities gave two representatives of the Danish Foreign Ministry permission to visit the Czech ghetto Theresienstadt, where 1,600 Danish Jews are imprisoned, along with other Jews deported from Germany, Austria, and Bohemia." It is noteworthy that *after* the visit, nothing was published either in *Aufbau* or, to my knowledge, anywhere else in the well-known Jewish or major international and German press, although reports were distributed by a Danish office in Stockholm (*288a) and by the deputy press chief of the Reich government (*254b, text in 3b, doc. 226).

45. Datner, Sz.: *Walka I zaglada Białostockiego ghetta* [Battle and Destruction of the Bialystok (Białystok) Ghetto]. Łódź, 1946.

The source contains no mention of the children sent to T (*40a).

46. Deeg, P.: *Die Judengesetze Grossdeutschlands*. Nuremberg, 1939.

An annotated status from May 10, 1939, published by J. Streicher.

46ax. [Deportations] Daluege's deportation order of November 24, 1941. PS-3921. Mimeographed.

It is obvious that the deportation orders were triggered by Hitler and were given expression by Himmler and the RSHA, we do not yet have documents proving this. In contrast, two of Daluege's orders have survived; they relate to the first two deportation waves. Addressed to a number of the commanders of the Order Police, the second one states:

> 1) In the period from November 1–December 4, 1941, the Sipo deported 50,000 Jews from the Altreich, the Ostmark, and the Protectorate to the East, in the region around Riga and Minsk. The resettlements took place in Reichsbahn transport trains holding 1,000 persons each. The transport trains were assembled in Berlin, Hamburg, Hanover, Dortmund, Münster, Düsseldorf, Cologne, Frankfurt on Main, Kassel, Stuttgart, Nuremberg, Munich, Vienna, Breslau, Prague and Brünn [Brno].

642 *Sources and Literature*

2). On the basis of the agreement with the Chief of the Security Police and the SD, the Order Police took over the guarding of the transport trains through provision of escort kommandos at a strength of 1/12. Details are to be discussed with the responsible office of the SD.

The task of the escort kommandos is completed with the proper transfer of the transports to the responsible office of the Sipo at the destination. They then will return immediately to their home offices.

3) The costs arising from the provision of the escort kommandos will be borne by the chief of the Sipo. The police authority's statement of costs is to be submitted to the chief of the Sipo after the completion of the transport.

46a. *Deggendorf Center Revue*. 12 vols. and a special edition by the camp leadership. Deggendorf, beginning of November 1945 to May 18, 1946.

The newspaper, published by former prisoners from T, appeared for a little longer. First, some 400 people traveled on July 11, 1945, from T to Deggendorf, where, of some 1,200 inmates, some 700 came from T. At the start, the food was meager, only 1,300–1,400 calories a day. It is interesting how the development of its "Jewish self-administration" was modeled substantively and linguistically on T. It was led by a "Jewish committee" (secretariat, canteen, coffeehouse); the departments were named as follows: the Central Labor Office; the Space Management, Culture (including the editorial staff), Emigration, Schools (primary and secondary school, language courses, retraining courses, and kindergarten), Legal (courts), Religious Affairs (*Kultus*) (registry office), Police, and Economics (kitchen and provisioning) Departments; the bank; the Welfare Department; the Clothing Department; the Information Office (group advisor, post office, registration, and ration card office); the Technical Department; the Health Service Department (an old-age home, a hospital, outpatient clinics, an infants' home, and massages); and the Supply Department. Only a few pieces deal with T. Number 3 contains "Theresienstadt Prayer" (a poem) by M. Mendelsohn, and number 6 presents an essay entitled "Theresienstadt Poetry" (with three poems) by Karrass.

46b. [Deportations] "Notes from a Discussion on October 10, 1941, on the Solution of the Jewish Question." MS, Prague, 1941.

This document, today in the possession of the Czechoslovak state, was shown in 1958 in an exhibit at the Prague Castle (see Kraus, F. R.: "Výstava archivních dokumentů na Pražském hradě." In 319, no. 7, 1958). The text says:

The following took part in the discussion:

SS-Obergruppenführer *Heydrich*
SS-Gruppenführer *Frank*
SS-Obersturmbannführer *Böhme*
SS-Obersturmbannführer *Maurer*
SS-Obersturmbannführer *v. Gregory*
SS-Sturmbannführer *Eichmann*
SS-Hauptsturmführer *Günther*
SS-Hauptsturmführer *Wolfram*

The discussion was called to discuss measures that were necessary, first for the solution of the Jewish question in the Protectorate and in part in the Altreich, and in

Sources and Literature 643

order to establish the explanation to be given to the press in the Protectorate for publication in the coming days. (For the press reception on October 10, not only the theme of the Jewish question, but also that of the resistance movements in the Protectorate should be dealt with in summary).

At present, *some 88,000 Jews* live in the entire Protectorate; 48,000 of them are in Prague. The focus is also on Brünn [Brno], with 10,000, and Moravian Ostrau [Ostrava], with 10,000. The remaining Jews are divided among the Upper County Commissioner.

Difficulties arose because of the evacuation. It was planned to begin on around October 15, in order to allow the transports to depart piece by piece until November 15, up to some 5,000 Jews – just from Prague.

For now, there must be great deference to the Litzmannstadt [Łódź] authorities.

The most troublesome Jews are to be sought out. Minsk and Riga are to get 50,000.

In the Altreich, the choice of Jews must be examined to determine whether one or another Jew is among those who are protected by high Reich offices, so as not to get too great a number of letters because of such Jews.

No consideration should be had for Jews with war medals. If a Jew in the Altreich has a medal, the restrictions that are currently being negotiated with the OKW apply to him. Under no circumstances should approximately all the Jews be kept in the Reich, for example, but on the contrary should be evacuated in appropriate proportion.

In the coming weeks, the 5,000 Jews from Prague are to be evacuated.

SS-Brif. Nebe and Rasch could take Jews *into the camp for Communist prisoners in the operational area*. This already has been initiated, according to SS-Stubaf. Eichmann.

On the Possibility of Ghettoization in the Protectorate

The only possibilities are a rather remote suburb (never a part of a city center, that has not worked), or a small village or small city with as little industry as possible.

The consolidation begins in the three largest cities [*sic*]; the Jews who live scattered about the country will be forcibly included.

Because it is more efficient due to oversight and supply with food etc., only two ghettos should be set up: *one ghetto in Bohemia, one in Moravia*, which will be divided into a "work" and a "supply" camp.

The Jews can be well *supplied with labor opportunities* (in the camp through production of small objects without use of machines, such as wooden shoes, straw mesh for the Wehrmacht in the north, etc.). The "Council of Elders" must collect these objects and in return gets the smallest amount of food with the calculated minimum of vitamins etc. (under the supervision of the security police). Small kommandos can also work outside the ghetto under guard; this is especially true for the necessary specialized workers.

In Moravia it is quite possible to *expand* an already existing *Jewish village into a ghetto for Moravia*; this would cause little major difficulty.

In Bohemia the options are: possibly the old Hussite burg *Alt-Ratibor*, but the best would be *taking over Theresienstadt by way of the Central Office* for Jewish Emigration. After evacuation from this temporary collection camp (whereby the Jews are already heavily decimated) to the eastern regions, the entire area could be developed into a model German settlement. The financial means to buy the entire area etc. are available and would be well invested, as the soil is excellently suited for vegetable cultivation. Proposal to Reichsführer-SS on this.

In discussions with the new military commander in the Protectorate, *Toussaint*, it should be discussed and implemented (by C. personally) that the elements of the Wehrmacht found in Theresienstadt (there are only small units) should be deployed to other garrisons.

In this way, the Czech population – which relied almost exclusively on work for the Wehrmacht elements in this old fortress city – will be forced to find employment elsewhere.

644   *Sources and Literature*

It should be considered whether the departure of the Czech population from Theresienstadt could not be encouraged by partial *assumption of moving costs*. Ample money for this could be raised at any time by selling the Jews' unneeded household effects. If the Czech population leaves Theresienstadt voluntarily, the necessary new homes, of the size that the families had in Theresienstadt, could be made available through Jewish homes that become free. These concessions must be made because of the mentality of the Czechs in the Protectorate – as opposed to the Gouvernement.

Families not willing to move could possibly be left there, but on condition that they conform to the needs of the ghetto.

Implementation of Ghettoization

Shortly before the transport a raid will be carried out on clothing, etc., a regular "*textile collection*," as the Prague Jews, especially, were impeccably clothed.

The Czech population should be warned in time not to accept any presents from Jews in the form of clothing, money, property, etc. or to purchase these things, since, according to the regulations, such goods would immediately be confiscated.

If a German who is married to a Jew is willing to separate voluntarily from her husband, she is to submit the proper statement; otherwise she must also go to the ghetto. This rule does not apply to Czechs.

The transport to the ghetto will not take much time; 2–3 trains could go to Theresienstadt every day, with 1,000 persons each. The resettlement proceeds according to the principles of the evacuation.

Using proven methods, the Jew can take up to 50 kg non-bulky luggage and – in the interests of making things easier for us – food for 14 days to 4 weeks. Straw will be distributed in the empty homes, as too much space would be taken by setting up beds.

The available larger homes in good buildings are available only to the "Branch Office of the Central Office in the Ghetto," the Council of Elders, the Food Office, and last but not least, the guard personnel.

The Jews are to make homes down in the ground [*haben sich wohnungen in die Erde hinab zu schaffen*].

The mills found in Theresienstadt should as far as possible continue operations, as the flour for the ghetto inmates can be milled here and thus deliveries from the Protectorate can be kept to a minimum.

Precautions should be taken to prevent epidemics in the ghetto from endangering the surrounding area. Particular attention should be paid to the sewer system, so that the Sudetenland is not endangered by sewage into the Eger.

The Jews may on no account be buried; instead, cremation should occur locally in a crematorium of the smallest type in the ghetto, not accessible to the public.

Guard duty can be carried out by the Protectorate police, that is, Czechs, under the supervision of the security police. *Some 600 men* will be needed *per ghetto* for three changes of the guard.

Jewish physicians must also be provided.

The *Gypsies* to be evacuated could be taken to Riga to Stahlecker, whose camp has been constructed according to the Sachsenhausen model.

As the Führer wants as many Jews as possible to be removed from the German area by the end of the year, the pending questions must be resolved immediately. The transport question should not cause any problems.

This document is the oldest one in which T is mentioned as a planned camp, and, in addition, it is an important predecessor to the "Wannsee Protocol," four days before Daluege's first general deportation order. Thus, at this time, the transports not only to Łódź but also to Minsk and Riga were already planned, and Hitler had already ordered the complete expulsion of the Jews "from the German area" by the end of 1941. Transport difficulties would not and could not exist; one can appreciate how the circumstances causing delays were abhorrent to the highest levels of Nazi leadership. The death sentence for these Jews is already addressed openly. At the time, Eichmann was not only in the process of preparing the construction of extermination camps such as Auschwitz in the hinterland (*106d) but was also negotiating with SS-Brigadeführer (later Gruppenführer) Arther Nebe and Brigadeführer Otto Rasch, the commanders of the murderous Einsatzgruppen B and C in Russia. But even for the Bohemian collection camp, that is, T, it already was planned that the Jews would be "heavily decimated" before they were sent to the "Eastern territories." The groups of people intended for deportation are more extensive than those Jews who were actually affected by early 1945, as Jewish husbands of German and certainly of Czech women were not to be spared, nor even the women themselves. Nor were those who had received war medals to be protected from transport, even though certain medals (probably those that later entitled one to preferential transport to T) promised protection – although only in the Altreich – under an agreement with the Wehrmacht High Command.

In light of these documents, the "file notes" (and so on) of the JKG in autumn 1941 and many measures in the "Protectorate" (among other places), as well as during the initial period in T, gain both a background and an explanation. Heydrich and his associates painted residence in T as far more unbearable than it actually was in the initial months. To have prevented the worst is Edelstein's greatest achievement.

46c. [Deportations] [Würzburg Gestapo papers]. MS, IfZ and RvO.

A stack of files from the local and Nuremberg Gestapo, the RSHA Iv B 4, and so on, distributed between the Nuremberg documents PS-1063 and PS-4072, in which the techniques of deportations from the Altreich to T and to the East are evident in detail (see samples in *3b, docs. 2, 4–9, 11, 15d, 16, 28, 29, 30, 31, 32, 33).

In the meantime, I am grateful to Mr. I. E. Wahler, New York, for clearly legible photos (now property of the IfZ) of the entire Würzburg Gestapo deportation file found by him. I will evaluate this material in a future book. The material makes possible some corrections in 3b of barely legible points – especially personal names – in the master document used there, which are not contained in the last three document pages of number 4. They are reproduced here (as a supplement to p. 19 in *3b):

Crim. Secr. *Klenk* is preparing the proper division of the rooms on Johannisstr. and the use of the staff. In addition, to maintain order, a guard kommando consisting of 4 SS enlisted men and 1 watch commander is to be assigned. Order in the rooms or temporary accommodations is also to be prepared by evacuation numbers. Jewish order personnel [*Ordner*] are to be made responsible for the various stories and hallways. In the interests of protecting the space, chalk markings may be made only on the floors. *Evacuations from Johannisstr.* to the freight station will be regulated as follows:

a) luggage	Pol. Secr. *Böhm*
b) the Jews	Senior Crim. Ass. *Unger*
At the freight station, transfer to	Senior Crim. Ass. *Fluhrer*.

The transfer [*Überholung*] of the Jews at *Wielandstr.* 6 (Ev. Gr. I) will take place under the command of Crim. Secr. *Bedacht*. He will be assigned:

646   *Sources and Literature*

2 Stapo officers,
3 SS men,
2 cleaning women,
1 bailiff.

The transfer [*Überholung*] of the Jews at *Knauerstr.* 27 (Ev. Gr. II) will take place under the command of Senior Crim. Ass. *Schneiderbanger*. He will be assigned:

6 officials,
6 SS men,
4 cleaning women,
1 bailiff.

Crim. Secr. *Fichtner* has *command of the deportation of the Jews at Knauerstr.* 27 and guarantee of their punctual arrival at the freight station, to which 4 SS men will be assigned. In addition, 2 SS men will be set as guards. In the deportation of bedridden Jews, special attention should be paid to attempts to smuggle hard currency.

Crim. Comm. a. Pr. *Kainz* is designated to take charge; during the period from 8–10 September 1942 he is assigned clerk *Hager* as secretary, as well as Senior Pol. Secr. *Mayer*, who is responsible at Johannisstr. for supervising the response to the intake orders [*Einholweisungen*] as well as keeping track of the card files and lists. He will have his office as of September 8, 1942, at Johannisstr. 17, *tel. number: 23669*.

Tel. no. of Ev. Gr. I, Wielandstr. 6, is: 23763
Tel no. of Ev. Gr. II, Knauerstr. 27, is: 63027
Tel. no. of the excrement shipping office is:
Tel. no. of the Stapo office (Section II B 4) is: 2951, branch office 3481,
my tel. no. is: 2951, branch office 330.

Dr. Rudersdorf will take responsibility for the punctual submission of property declarations as well as provision of the bailiff at Knauerstr. and Johannisstr., as well as Wielandstr., on September 10, 1942, and the procurement of the relevant forms as well as briefings for Würzburg and Bamberg.

For the three days, 2 passenger cars are to be ordered, of which one will be at the ready at Johannisstr. It should be ensured that the command of the regular police [*Schutzpolizei*] is informed in a timely manner for the purpose of setting up an *escort kommando* of ... police and 6 SS men. Bamberg and Würzburg are ready to assign 1 escort, including a responsible officer, per wagon to Nuremberg to secure the transport. After transfer of their individual transport to the overall transport in Nuremberg, those involved will automatically return to their stations.

Special instructions will be issued through Dr. Rudersdorf for the *property seized* in Nuremberg and Bamberg.

Expenses that arise (for auxiliary guards, etc.) can be immediately anticipated through corresponding offsets. No monies will be transferred from Nuremberg for these offices. Special instructions will be issued for Nuremberg.

Instructions will also be issued via Dr. Rudersdorf regarding transfer of the seized homes to the regional finance office in Nuremberg.

Given that there will be no summary by camp in the implementation of this operation, there can be *no board provided* for the officers used. The following will be assigned as secretaries and telephone operators at Johannisstr.:

Clerk Hager,
Clerk Barth,
Clerk Martius,

Sources and Literature

At Knauerstr:

> Clerk Wierer,
> Clerk Eichmüller,

At Wielandstr.:

> Clerk Pelloth.

Beginning September 8, 1942, the evacuation office is located at Johannisstr. 17, tel. no. 23669.

Crim. Secr. *Wetzel* is responsible for administrative matters, confiscated money, confiscated objects. Headquarters at the evacuation office at Johannisstr.

I will be responsible for overall direction of the Jewish evacuation on September 10, 1942.

> Nuremberg, August 19, 1942.
> Secret State Police
> State Police Office Nuremberg-Fürth
> on the instructions of Dr. Grafenberger.

> > Hag.

47. [Germany] *Den Unvergessenen*. Heidelberg, 1952.

Stories of German Jews up to their deportation to T and other camps.

48. [Germany] [Numbers of deportees and survivors]. In *Der Weg*. Nos. 41, 43, and 44. Berlin, 1946.

According to one list, 50,535 (recalculated to 50,175) people were deported from Berlin, 14,797 of these to T. This list was used by Sellenthin (*239b).

A second list to T counted 15,136 persons, of whom 1,574 survived in T. The difference from the first list can be explained by the fact that some people were transported from Berlin but did not come from there. According to *302, there were 571 surviving Berliners in T. This covers transport group I (corresponding to the Gestapo section).

Using data on the remaining transport groups from Germany (including "Sudetengau"), we juxtapose the number of people deported to T according to sources *48, *166, and *302, as well as the numbers of people who survived in T according to sources *48 and *302:

Transport group	Deportees			Survivors	
	*48	*166	*302	*48	*302
II (Bavaria)	3,678	3,094	3,096	289	297
III (Rhineland)	2,650	2,517	2,517	197	194
V (Saxony)	500	492	495	94	107
VI (Hamburg, etc.)	2,595	2,489	2,487	507	459
VII (Düsseldorf)	2,090	2,008	2,002	112	114
VIII (Hanover)	1,265	1,039	1,039	297	308
IX (Breslau)	2,920	2,818	2,817	160	159
X (Dortmund)	1,160	1,126	1,129	117	118
XI (Westphalia)	1,050	1,035	1,038	110	114
XII (Frankfurt)	4,475	4,223	4,226	762	784

(continued)

(continued)

Transport group	Deportees			Survivors	
	*48	*166	*302	*48	*302
XIII (Württemberg-Baden)	1,530	1,388	1,385	290	290
XIV (Königsberg)	860	809	803	51	54
XV (Kassel, etc.)	1,000	845	848	53	55
XVI (Leipzig)	1,367	1,217	1,219	348	358
XVII (Darmstadt)	1,295	1,351	1,351	61	63
XVIII (Upper Silesia)	300	293	294	50	51
XX (Magdeburg)	250	235	235	17	16
XXIII (Danzig)	120	117	117	12	11
Plus I (Berlin)	15,136	15,122	15,122	1,574	1,571
Total	44,241	42,218	42,220	5,101	5,131
Plus XIX, XXI, and XXII (Sudeten)	636	611	611	198	242
GRAND TOTAL	44,877	42,829	42,831	5,299	5,373

For Germany alone, a number of persons from Luxemburg (group X) would have to be subtracted. Members of group II originated from Munich, Nuremberg, Augsburg, Regensburg, and Würzburg; group III, Cologne, Bonn, Koblenz, Ludwigshafen, and Trier; group V, Dresden, and elsewhere; group VI, Hamburg, Bremen, Kiel, Lübeck, and elsewhere; group VII, Düsseldorf, Aachen, Duisburg, Krefeld, and elsewhere; group VIII, Hanover, Bremen, Göttingen, Hildesheim, and elsewhere; group IX, Breslau, and elsewhere, but also Osnabrück; group X, Dortmund, Bochum, and Hagen, as well as Luxemburg; group XI, Münster, Bielefeld, and Gelsenkirchen; group XII, Frankfurt, Wiesbaden, and elsewhere; group XV, Kassel, Chemnitz, Plauen, and elsewhere; group XVI, Leipzig and Thuringia; group XVII, Darmstadt, Mainz, Worms, and elsewhere; group XVIII, Upper Silesia; and group XX, Magdeburg.

Noteworthy in this listing in *48 is the fact that only there is a transport of fifty persons from Budapest listed among the groups from the Sudeten area, under XXII/5; elsewhere, this transport is labeled only as "Sudeten." The difference in the information in *48 and *166 or *302 can be explained by the deaths in the collection camps and during the journey, as well as the SS's redisposition and the generally unachieved precision of the documents. Compare also the Arolsen lists (*83).

49. Dormitzer, E.: [Three reports on T]. MS, WL, London, 1945/46/55.

The author, who was in T from April 22, 1943, describes the conditions. She came on the first transport from Holland. On April 20, 1943, a number of "worthy" Jews, generally Reich Germans but also Dutch and Czechoslovak Jews, were summoned to an SS barracks, where Eichmann's plenipotentiary for Holland, SS-Sturmbahnführer (STBF) aus der Fünten, presented the transport to T to the assembled persons as a special privilege. They were told that anyone who did not join it could no longer reckon with consideration. The conditions in the camp were described as ideal: complete freedom, SS rations, a movie theater, and so on. Because of the beautiful surroundings, aus der Fünten advised, "The ladies should bring sturdy shoes, because you can go on excursions." The next day they traveled in passenger cars, with only four people per compartment. During the approximately twenty-eight-hour journey, the escorts distributed postcards that were to be written to relatives.

Ms. Dormitzer became a postal worker in October 1944. At the time, there were twenty-six clerks (sixteen women), of whom thirteen were from Germany, and only one was from the "Protectorate." There were up to 168 "packet advisories" per day. At that time, an SS man also worked in the "package Schleuse."

Toward the end of the war, concentration camp prisoners broke into the apothecary and devoured everything edible, even the contents of Vaseline containers.

Some of the Dutch, including the emigrants from Germany – a total of 1,650 persons – were transported from T on June 7, 1945, in motor vehicles and, after two stops in Bohemia, arrived in Bamberg on June 18. A few days later, they continued in cattle cars that were locked at night and unlit. No provision was made for defecation. On June 21 they arrived in Maastricht and entered a quarantine camp (in Sittard, at the Eynbroek monastery), where the Dutch were released; the emigrants remained in detention under Dutch military guard and were not released until July, after English intervention. Immediately after liberation, the Dutch Jews in T began to be hostile to the emigrants, whom they held responsible for their own misfortune. Even the leading Dutch functionaries in the self-administration were guilty of this behavior (*243a).

50. Dormitzer, E.: *Theresienstädter Bilder*. Hilversum, 1945.

Poems on camp themes, 1943–45, written in T.

50a. Dow, J., and M. Brown: *Evacuation to Westmorland, from Home and Europe, 1939–1945*. Kendal, 1946.

The Jewish Refugee Committee in London took in 1,000 orphaned and homeless young people and children aged three to twenty from T. Three hundred came in August 1945 by airplane (*224c) and were brought to Windermere, near Carlisle. They were found to have nutritional deficiencies and edema, as well as harm from spotted fever, tuberculosis, injuries, and overwork. Some had had no education for six years. They were very eager to learn, especially English. Sleeplessness, bad dreams, and nervousness were frequent. Except for the youngest, they were mainly concentration camp children. The volume contains reports of experiences by one adult and four children. On January 7, 1946, housing was found elsewhere for the last five children from Windermere. A dentist's report (87% of the children had tooth damage) found the following:

> After their terrible experiences, it is probably not surprising that they anticipated their first visit to the dental clinic with great worry, the more so as "gas" was to be used. Gas had only one meaning for them, and some asked where the gas chambers were. Finally, one boy, who had been adopted for a time by American soldiers, declared himself willing to be the first to be treated. When he returned looking quite satisfied, everything was all right and the examinations continued without further disturbing fears. (p. 61)

50b. Duckwitz, G. F.: Affidavit. Steengracht Document Book, no. IV a, 85. Mimeographed, Nuremberg, Case XI, 1948.

Duckwitz speaks favorably about Steengracht because of his efforts on behalf of the Danish Jews.

650   *Sources and Literature*

51. Edelstein, J.: "To the Central Labor Office." MS, T, December 6, 1942.

A letter from the Jewish Elder to a Zionist colleague.

52. Edelstein, J.: "Speech, Held on the Occasion of the Swearing-In of the Ghetto Guard on January 1, 1943." MS, T.

52a. [Edelstein, J.]: [Unpublished documents in Holland]. RvO.

To judge Edelstein's tragic, problematic career it is important to gain insight into his position as a Zionist and – in spirit, or at least in intention – as resistor between the Jewish organizations at the mercy of the SS, on the one hand, and Eichmann and his retinue, on the other. In 1939/40, Edelstein already had decided, against the advice and will of other Zionists in Prague, such as Dr. Franz Kahn, on the fateful path of cooperation with the "Central Office" – although he recognized in its representatives the potential merciless murderers of his own people – for he nevertheless believed he could in this way manage a rescue effort, at least in part.

According to information in connection with the dossier of the trial of the Joodsen Raad in Amsterdam, Edelstein spent several months in Holland with Dr. Franz Friedmann (*78a), supposedly as early as late summer 1940, but in any case at the beginning of 1941 (Professor David Cohen claims that Edelstein was there for six weeks, starting in March or April). According to the witness Siegfried Willheim, they came to Amsterdam in an SD car – probably with Günther and Rahm – and stayed with the Prague emigrant Professor Dr. Starkenstein. They were charged with assisting leading Jewish personalities in Holland in establishing a "Jewish instrument" similar to the one in Prague. It became clear in the process that the "Jewish Council" in Prague (that is, the JKG) served to discriminate against the Jews there through all sorts of administrative measures. At the time, Friedmann said in Czech to Willheim that he was convinced that all Jews would be murdered. Cohen, who was prosecuted in 1948, mentioned in a memoir, *Collaboration*, that Edelstein had explained to him at the time that he had himself taken over organization of the Jewish "work deployment" so as not to let it fall into the hands of the Germans. Cohen said that he, in contrast, had left this to the Dutch. He said he was writing this only for his personal defense and did not wish to accuse Edelstein with this or with the statement that Edelstein later composed the transport lists in T, whereas he, Cohen, did not do the same in the Netherlands (*78a, 312c). Professor Cohen informed me in a letter, "Edelstein achieved the difficult task with great tact, so that even those who disapproved of his task and his work had the greatest respect for his character and the advice he offered us in other matters as well.... . Friedmann supported him with courage and devotion."

An Amsterdam letter to Cohen on April 7, 1941, reveals how Edelstein functioned, whether or not he chose to, as a tool of the "Central Office":

Esteemed Professor,

At the behest of Herr SS Haupsturmführer Günther, I must inform you that you are to rent several rooms for the purpose of setting up the branch. The apartment should be very close to the new emigration office on van Eeghenstraat (either next door or across the street).

Respectfully,
Edelstein

52b. Ehrlich, R. A.: "Aufzeichnungen aus Theresienstadt." MS, T, 1943/45.

On December 27, 1942, the war-wounded author and his wife were picked up in Berlin by two community aides. They had to pack in two hours and could bring one suitcase, knapsack, and "bedroll" each. They traveled by light rail and foot to the collection camp at Grosse Hamburgerstrasse (formerly the old-age home). The conditions were tolerable, but he complains about the Jewish camp leadership. On January 7, 1943, some 100 persons moved to Gerlachstrasse, where those bound for T assembled at the time. Conditions were worse there; the Jewish camp leadership threatened them with the Gestapo at the slightest excuse, or even none at all. On January 12, he was woken at 2 A.M. and was marched off at 4 A.M. The transportees traveled by streetcar to Anhalter Station and were placed into passenger cars in a normal train, with all their luggage, accompanied by the taunts of the public. They departed at 6 A.M., arrived in Bauschowitz [Bohušovice] after 8 P.M., and spent three days in Schleuse I IV.

He describes conditions in his chronicle, which was begun in November 1943 and later continued in short notes. After a brief time working in the "clothing warehouse," Mrs. Ehrlich became an "orderly" in house L 237, where the author, who did not have to work because of his "seriously war-wounded identity document," helped her (see the sample in *3b, doc. 101). A May 3, 1945, note that proves how separately many prisoners lived from the SS is noteworthy: "We saw Mr. Dunant from the Red Cross and also – for the first time – Camp Commandant Rahm."

On July 14, 1945, the Ehrlichs went to Deggendorf (*46a, 271). First they took a train to Pilsen [Plsen] and, days later, continued in twenty-three military cars with bad brakes. "Shortly before Deggendorf this problem turned fateful ... the first 16 cars successfully passed a dangerous part of the woods. The car in which we were sitting also ... stopped unharmed. But the car behind us drove into us, the third car tipped over, the fourth overturned and fell down the bank." More than fifty injured people had to be taken to the hospital. The uninjured finally arrived at the United Nations Relief and Rehabilitation Administration (UNRRA) camp in Winzern, where conditions were miserable. Starting July 24 in Deggendorf, it was at first even worse, if possible, under hostile camp leaders. "We were treated like prisoners, harassed with curfews, cleaning work, etc., and received insufficient and miserable food."

52c. Ehrlich, R. A.: "Eine 'Volkszählung.'" In *Friede über Israel*. Munich, March 1959.

Text excerpts from *52b on November 11, 1943, in T.

52d. Ehrlich, R. A.: "Erste Eindrücke in Theresienstadt." In *Friede über Israel*. Ansbach, March 1960.

Text excerpts from *52b.

53. Eisenbach, A.: *Getto Łódźkie* [Łódź Ghetto]. Vol. III of *Dokumenty i materialy*. Warsaw, 1946.

An important source work with annotated documents. Page 203 et seq. offer an official "experience report" on the arrival of those deported from Central Europe to Łódź (Litzmannstadt) in fall 1941.

652   *Sources and Literature*

54. Eisenbach, A.: *Hitlerowa polityka eksterminacji zidów w latach 1939–1945* [Hitler's Policy of Extermination of the Jews in the Years 1939–1945]. Warsaw, 1953.

A thorough, heavily documented study on the subject, including history from 1919; the various phases are clearly developed. Events in Poland are the focus. Aside from bows to "Marxism" and fundamental hostility to the "imperialist" powers, it is substantively reliable.

    Almost nothing said about T (there is no reference to the children from Bialystok [Białystok]). On page 341, a letter from Kaltenbrunner to Himmler in early February 1943 is mentioned (*256a), which is printed in *3b, doc. 218.

55. Ems, H.: "Letter on July 16, 1947, from Berlin." [Report on T]. MS, WL.

A description of life in Berlin and T, where the writer arrived on October 28, 1942, and remained until August 1945. It portrays elderly German Jews suffering from the chauvinism of younger Czech Jews (*30b).

55a. [Encephalitis] "Report on the Encephalitis Epidemic." MS, YV, T, no year.

A short, unsigned report from the papers of Dr. Fritz Salus.

55b. [Eppstein, P.]: "Geschichtliche Tragik: Zuschriften und Würdigungen." In *Jüdische Sozialarbeit*. No. 5/6. Frankfurt a. M., 1959.

Short pieces as an echo of *243e. It contains some genuine letters from K. Bachrach-Baker, Kl. Caro (who was the only one of the contributors who was in T), H. Grüber, and W. Rosenstock, and some quotes from S. Adler-Rudel (from a book review of *3b), E. Simon (a paragraph from *243c), F. Schwarzschild, and H. Strauss. All judged Eppstein positively, but except for Adler-Rudel, Caro, and Simon, they speak only of Eppstein's activities in Berlin. Ms. Caro incidentally wrote me on May 3, 1959: "In contrast to the vain, arrogant, Prussian Eppstein ... he [Edelstein] really had the best interests of the community unselfishly at heart." The editors did not use a letter from Dr. Karl Löwenstein, which is why it will be presented here in part:

> Unfortunately Dr. Baeck is no longer alive; his criticism [of Eppstein] exceeded mine....
>   As head of the Security Service in Theresienstadt, I worked with Eppstein and can therefore swear at any time that Eppstein was guilty of the death of thousands.
>   Among others: two young people, named Bergmann and Kahn, had looted 10 kg of bread during a break-in at a bread storehouse. The two ate the bread immediately out of hunger.... Privy Councilor Dr. Klang punished the two youngsters with eight months in prison.
>   At the behest of Dr. Rosenthal, the poor boys then were handed over to the SS by Dr. Eppstein, brought to the Kleine Festung in October 1943, and beaten to death there. A case that is unique in the Jewish history of Theresienstadt....
>   Wouldn't it have been better to have kept quiet?

55c. [Diet] "Unser Eiweißbedarf und seine Deckung." MS, YV, T, no year.

A brief, unsigned report from the papers of Dr. Fritz Salus.

56. Eucken-Erdsiek, E.: *Größe und Wahn*. Tübingen, 1950.

This text contains an excellent essay on Hitler; it is important for understanding National Socialism. In the spirit of our observations, it says, about Alfred Schuler:

Sources and Literature 653

> He is the one who … contributed to the horrible work of elevating antisemitism to a cosmic, a metaphysical matter and providing it with the gruesome mythology that "reveals" the Jewish God Yahweh as the deadly enemy of all true life. As long as antisemitism was determined only by politics or religion, it was by and large satisfied with driving Jews from their positions. A metaphysical antisemitism, however, soon would reach the frenzied fury of the witch-hunts and … provide the excuse for exterminating millions of people as if they were vermin. (p. 160)

57. [Fabera, H.?]: "Entstehung des Ghettos Theresienstadt und die Lebensverhältnisse in demselben vom Dezember 1941, seinem Beginn, bis zum Oktober 1944, dem Anfang seiner Liquidation." MS, DA, Buchenwald, May 5, 1945.

A depiction of not-always-reliable but informative details on the mentality of younger prisoners from the "Protectorate."

58. Fabian, H. E.: "Die letzte Etappe." In *Festschrift für Leo Baeck*. London, 1953, pp. 85–97.

A piece on "Die 'Reichsvereinigung der Juden in Deutschland'" and "Theresienstadt." The author, a staff member of the Reichsvereinigung, was sent to T and was brought back to Berlin by the RSHA in order to continue certain written work as a partial prisoner in the "collection camp" (*23). Fabian cautiously describes the activities of the Reichsvereinigung; he says little about T.

59. Feder, G.: *Die Juden*. Munich, 1933.

An official National Socialist Party publication.

60. Feder, R.: *Židovská tragedie – Dějství poslední* [Jewish Tragedy – Last Act]. Kolin, 1947.

A book by the Kolin rabbi, who was in T from early 1942 to liberation. Generally well-informed, it describes life in the "Protectorate" and in T.

60a. Fierz, O.: *Über dem Erdenstreit: Erinnerungen aus bewegten Zeiten in Prag*. Basel, 1956.

Přemysl Pitter's rescue work for Jewish and German children after the war is portrayed by his Swiss assistant. On May 22, 1945, the first forty Jewish children were taken from T; on July 26, the first thirty German children were rescued from Czech imprisonment and were housed in Pitter's home. Many German children also were brought out of the "Kleine Festung." Five illustrations.

60b. Fink, V.: "Diary." MS, WL. T and Křivoklát, 1942.

The author, in T from December 14, 1941, to liberation, was assigned to forest work in Křivoklát in early 1942 (*307a). The notes encompass the period from March 28 to June 5, 1942. The WL owns a manuscript by the same author, "Von Theresienstadt bis London," which describes her experiences from the creation of the "Protectorate" to her emigration at the end of 1948. The information on T is unreliable, and its temporal sequence is confused.

61. Fischer, A. J.: "Er bewahrte viele vor dem Tod." In *Allgemeine Wochenzeitung der Juden*. Düsseldorf, September 24, 1954.

Information on Duckwitz's service to the Jews of Denmark.

61a. Fischer, A. J.: "Theresienstadt: A German Alibi?" In *Free Europe*. London, June 18, 1943.

654 Sources and Literature

In this work, T is separated from the "Protectorate" and is integrated into the Reich. It describes old Jewish inmates who received sufficient food and medical care to stay alive. A self-help committee under German control cared for 40,000 people, housed in "Reich or Protectorate houses for aged Jews." Workers, who lived in barracks, received twenty crowns daily, with six crowns deducted for care for the elderly. A "coffeehouse" is also depicted. "Eminent Jewish personalities [Eppstein, Edelstein, Stricker, etc.] charged with administration of the self-help." This information may trace back to Nazi propaganda, perhaps to news from German press representatives who had visited T in May 1943 (although, as far as I can see, this visit never was described in the German press). Fischer attempts to explain this phenomenon: "Theresienstadt was opened as a conscious refutation of the terror in the ghettos in the East, where Himmler is the boss." On August 27, 1943, *Aufbau* in New York published excerpts from this article and pointed out in an introduction that "a war-wounded Jew who is sent to Theresienstadt is told that he can thank his war wound for it." Fischer's article, or the same information source, served as the basis for a series of other press articles (*8).

62. Fischer, A. J.: "The Twelve Hundred of Terezín." In *The Central European Observer*. London, April 14, 1945. YIVO.

62a. [Epidemic typhus] Typhus at Terezín. PS-385. Mimeographed, Nuremberg, 1945.

The author, a Czech doctor (probably Dr. Raska; *166, 221, 321a), says he came to T on May 2, 1945, although it is probable that functionaries from the Czech RC and doctors were not admitted into the camp until May 4. The author wrongly claims that he found many "genuine" criminals among the concentration camp transports. He records the start of the typhus epidemic in the "Kleine Festung" already at the beginning of April; of its 5,300 inmates (Lederer speaks of 4,500), at least 2,200 got sick. On May 6, a transport also mentioned by Lederer and Dunant (*228) arrived after thirty days of wandering, during which the transportees went without food for twelve days. It contained 2,000 people, including 87 dead men and children. The difficult situation, he says, arose when the commandant of the Leitmeritz [Litoměřice] concentration camp tried to send 3,200 prisoners to T.

> On May 8, at 8 A.M., when the war in Europe officially was over, Mr. Dunant of the IRC left Theresienstadt and requested that I take over the entire health service. It was clear that a great catastrophe could be prevented only if I received help rapidly. But there was the fighting in Prague. The Gestapo SS men, who fought near the road, would not let RC automobiles through. Only the Russian army could help. And so on the morning of May 8th I rode with Mr. Dunant in his car to see the Russian army doctor. We drove some 75 km north, deep into Saxony. But we were caught in mine fields and had to turn back. When we returned to Theresienstadt, we saw that the first Russian tank columns were in the process of encircling the city. We went to the Russians to demand help and received a tank that we rode to Prague, where we immediately took up contact with the Czech doctors and surgeons of the Red Army.

This somewhat muddled portrayal (Dunant unfortunately said nothing about these events) is impossible to untangle. On May 13, the camp received medical assistance from the Russians, who deloused more than 20,000 people and set up six infirmaries, where more than 4,000 patients were treated. A total of 52 Russian doctors, 75 nurses, and 214 aides worked under the direction of two lieutenant colonels. In the "ghetto," the epidemic peaked on May 15; on May 25 another increase was noted. The "ghetto hospital" had another 2,700 patients, as well as outpatients. In addition to the typhus patients, there were 3,000 patients with tuberculosis and dysentery (especially Flexner dysentery, and some cases of Schmitz and Newcastle dysentery). In July 1945, when the report probably was being written, there were 4,000 more people in T. Some thirty-five photos are attached to the document, depicting scenes of horror, mainly sick people and corpses (the large hall in E I with patients); one photo shows Himmler during a visit to the "Kleine Festung" (he probably was never in the "ghetto").

63. Fleischmann, K.: "An die Blinden von Q 319." MS, T, autumn 1942.

64. Fleischmann, K.: "Dr. Erich Munk." MS, T, 1943/44.

A document expressing appreciation of the person and achievements of the head of the health service in T.

65. Fleischmann, K.: "Držet!" [Persevere!]. MS, T, May 1944.

Five poems.

66. Fleischmann, K.: "Terezínské panoptikum" [Theresienstadt Waxworks]. MS, T, March 1944.

Sixteen poems of a slightly ironic character on well-known figures or typical characters in the camp.

67. Fleischmann, K.: [Cycle of twenty-four Czech poems]. MS, T, 1942/44.

Poems on camp themes. The YV has a number of additional poems.

68. [Fleischmann, K.]: *Katalog posmrtné výstavy [malíře a básníka] Dr. K[arla] Fleischmanna* [Catalogue of the Memorial Exhibit to Dr. K. Fleischmann]. Prague, 1947.

An exhibit of drawings created in T at the Prague Jewish Museum. The work contains introductory observations. One illustration is included in *3b, doc. 198.

69. Frankenhuis, M.: "Dagboek. Deel IV, Theresienstadt." MS, T, 1944/45.

This immensely detailed diary by the author, who came to T from Westerbork on September 6, 1944, provides abundant insight into daily life in the camp during its period of deterioration. Frankenhuis had money and thirty-one diamonds smuggled out of the Schleuse in exchange for an agreed-upon reward. He got the money back, but not the diamonds. The person to whom he consigned them, a member of the "transport administration" and an AK man, threatened to turn him in if he demanded them back and reminded him of his power. Even after the war, he managed to avoid returning them. Things were strict in the Schleuse, and the "Kleine Festung" was used as a threat. SS men seated at tables took away all money (in Westerbork one had been allowed to take along 300 guilders); precious metals, fountain pens, and cigarettes were collected in boxes. People had to undress, and their clothes and bodies were searched carefully for hidden objects. Then the newcomers were registered by camp functionaries, "labor categories" were determined, and ration cards were distributed. This was followed by a disinfection bath in L 506. Their hand luggage was returned two weeks later, along with the larger luggage,

656   *Sources and Literature*

considerably lighter. At the time, German and Czech Jews considered deportation from T to be "impossible."

September 9: Eppstein gives a speech to the Dutch Jews; Frankenhuis records it in key words.

> You will be disappointed. Regret the reception. Not good. Had only four hours' time. In despair, as no bread etc. This only transition period. You soon will settle in. Then speak differently. Every nationality or religion here together. Do what you can to stay here. Conditions in Westerbork, no longer possible to stay. Now main thing stay here. Here many difficulties. You must help us. We live here in a very tight space. 30,000 Jews. It was not possible to get barracks from Westerbork. No nervousness, not leave here. You will gain a degree of peace. Everyone can give his work, make himself useful, limited food, frugal.... We will make the best of everything. Surroundings here beautiful. Better than Westerbork. [But Frankenhuis finds Westerbork ideal in comparison with T.] Watch diet, cleanliness. Few infectious diseases here.... . Good to exterminate fleas. Difficult. Do everything to exterminate them. No foolishness, talking, etc. Life in a community, if a coerced community.

September 18: Transport rumors emerge, and three days later Möhs comes to T. Frankenhuis notes that many women spend the night illegally with their husbands. A "Dutch woman" acts as "maid" to the "Czechs," may take lunch and bread from there, and gets "presents" of ration cards.

October 2: "Many Jews are no longer called individually [to the transports], but 'en bloc.' Lists of entire categories are put together." Women receive postcards from their husbands on the first transport. People of "mixed race" are called up; the war-wounded follow the next day.

October 6: Use of others' ration cards is punished with fourteen days to three months' imprisonment.

October 7: Women with small children and infants must leave.

October 8: The food worsens because of the transports.

October 10: There is talk of deporting the entire camp. General Denekamp predicts another ten months of war.

October 13: A man, asked by Möhs why he had himself baptized and answering "out of conviction," is released as a Ruhr fighter [one who struggled against the 1923–25 French and Belgian occupation of the Ruhr].

October 17: "Hear that the transport was sent to Birkenau. The women were of course sent elsewhere.... Anna says they are sending the women to a ... better camp, in order to give the Red Cross the impression that they treat the Jews well." Around that time, General van Praag was summoned to the commandant and was allowed to write to the RC in the Hague that the baptized people and Barnevelder (a small minority of hundreds of "notable" Dutch Jews) are well (he did not mention the others) and could receive packages.

October 18: Children, single people, sick people, and invalids are sent on a transport.

October 19: Room elders, bedridden patients, and the personnel of the health service are called up. Half rations of bread must suffice for four days. The prisoners receive 1,800 g of bread weekly.

October 20:

> I go to the doctor at the "outpatient clinic" for treatment. I have just entered; the doctor is busy with me when suddenly someone comes in excitedly. The entire staff must go to

the commandant. All patients standing outside in line must be sent away and are, like me, half-dazed. "Finished, finished! Must come again on Sunday! Always closed on Saturday!"

October 27: Frankenhuis is a patient in the infectious disease barracks E VII, where food is the only topic of conversation. He learns that "recreation" is starting again. This is what it looked like in T a day *before* the end of the deportations!

October 30: A census is taken in which lists with the most impossible questions are filled out. The prisoners' diet is described as "pretty good."

November 7: Children from eight years old on (according to other sources, from age ten) are required to work. There are reports of the destruction of the urns with the ashes of the dead; this probably occurred shortly before.

November 8: Through roll call [*Appell*], it is forbidden to speak of transports on pain of being sent to the "Kleine Festung," nor may rumors be spread.

November 19: Elderly people up to eighty years old help to shovel potatoes that have arrived, and they are rewarded with up to two shovelsful.

November 20: A transport of Dutch children arrives with two women from Bergen-Belsen after a three-day journey; all of them are sick, badly clothed, and without luggage and must immediately go to disinfection.

November 23: One card may be written per month; the word "transport" is prohibited.

November 26: Someone is caught spending the night with his wife and is punished by deprivation of one midday meal, of one other opportunity to grab some food (*Fassung*), and of three days' worth of bread rations.

November 30: Dutch people receive fifty "ghetto crowns" "as reimbursement for the suitcases they did not receive."

December 1: Payment of two "ghetto crowns" for a bath is introduced.

December 23: A Slovak transport in eight cattle cars arrives after five days' journey. Many have frozen hands; nine children died on the trip [this is a rumor believed only by Frankenhuis].

January 14, 1945: A daughter of Frankenhuis works in the kitchen. "She is the queen and we feel like high authorities." Every acquaintance asks when and at which window she is distributing food. "Everyone in our family, friends and acquaintances want to profit from it."

February 23: An old man of eighty-three years works in the potato storehouse H V. A transport of spouses from mixed marriages and half Jews arrives from Frankfurt (February 18) after a five-day journey. "'Our Gestapo was very good,' a man tells me." There are rumors that an underground bunker is being constructed for 20,000 Jews. "I heard from some people that they would be needed to gas [the Jews]. According to others, it was a 'false rumor' it is not pleasant to hear that."

February 25: Rumors about gassing, especially of 5,000 nonworkers, gain strength. Some of the recently arrived "related" (*versippt*) women "are real Nazis." Among the newcomers there are said to be many spies.

March 1: On the mixed-marriage partners: "Most know nothing about Judaism, and some themselves cry 'Heil Hitler'!" Haindl is supposed to have set fire in nine places.

March 4: Rumors spread of an impending international commission. Someone says that children are being rehearsed in what they should say to the commission;

658   *Sources and Literature*

when they get sardines they are to say, "Ugh, sardines again," and then, "Uncle Rahm, when will you play with us again?" The rehearser answers: "Children, I don't have any time right now." This was the most stubborn, but inaccurate, rumor from T, which was passed on otherwise as an incident during an international visit on June 23, 1944, and which also found its way into Lederer's book. Even reviewers of this book's first edition mentioned it, as if they had read the episode here.

March 7: "The children of Dr. H are 8 and 9 years old and illiterate, they cannot read or write a single word."

March 11: The very neglected Hungarian transports arrive (March 8); many are without shoes and have gone three days without food. The new "beautification" becomes clear.

March 18: There appears a poster for "city beautification" with the city coat of arms and the inscription "Beauty on a Small Scale – Beauty on a Large Scale." Murmelstein commands the fire department during a fire in C III.

April 13: It becomes known that all significant documents up to January 1, 1945, are to be destroyed.

April 15: Rumors spread of the dissolution of the camp (encouraged by the deportation of the Danes). Bread rations are extended from three to four days.

April 20: A transport from Bergen-Belsen, which was shot at on the way, arrives after a fourteen-day journey. Another arrives with 1,600 people in terrible condition, most of them almost naked, unable to speak, and begging for food. Many cars have corpses in them. All are brought to the hospital. Bread is thrown to the people, which is dangerous for them; thus Dr. Springer cries: "This is rebellion!" There are always people (old inmates) around the potato wagons, asking for "two potatoes" or "a small hole" – that is, they want those responsible to make a hole in the wagon so that they can take some.

April 21: Additional transports arrive, for which H V is emptied. The members of one transport had to walk from Leipzig.

April 22: New transports arrive, the worst one from Buchenwald. C III is emptied. Up to 20,000 Jews are expected. Professor Meijers (a Dutch Council of Elders member) explains that T was not taken over by the RC because this was "not legally possible."

April 23: H V is occupied, and C III is being occupied.

April 25: Frankenhuis asks women in H V whether the gassing is true. "I asked other women who lay there in bed. 'Don't talk about it with him, he doesn't believe it!' they told the others, and they would not answer the questions I asked." One old inmate said that it would be better for the SS to be here than not, in case German troops should come.

April 26: "I ask a girl of 12 ... where her father and mother are. She answers 'That is a Heaven question [*Himmelfrage*].' I don't understand, or don't want to understand, and ask again, and she says, 'People don't ask us things like that.'" One inmate decides, "The Polish Jews brought all the misfortune upon us."

May 1: Typhus is found. The men are allocated three cigarettes each.

May 2: "There is now a total of 5,200 Jews in the Dresden [H V]. All receive double portions and still cannot be sated." Thirty to forty people from the most recent transports die each day. There is talk of the impending departure of a transport of notables who are to be held as hostages. There are rumors about the departed Danes: "They were shot at on the way and 20 were killed" (*184b).

May 3: "In the Hamburg Kaserne [C III] a disorderly band; they are completely brutalized. They open everything and even take the doors from their hinges." People speak of the departure of the SS and, at the fence, watch soldiers going toward Prague. Rahm approaches and asks what is so interesting to see. Then he leaves.

May 4: Three thousand people from the "Kleine Festung," including 300 Jews, are brought to E 1. Fifty Prague nurses have arrived. Dunant walks around T unescorted. Three cigarettes per person are distributed each day, for which one can exchange two loaves of bread. At night, the uniform barracks burn down; no more work is going on in the mica barracks.

May 5: The next day, peace is to be declared. Gendarmes shake hands with the Jews and congratulate them. Christian spouses are in the camp. German inscriptions are covered up. Czech flags are raised on the post office and by the gendarmes. There are rumors that the Americans are nearby; Rahm and Haindl are imprisoned.

May 8:

One still hears shooting in the neighborhood; by the partisans. They shoot at the Germans and the Germans shoot back. Suddenly a massive boom. The Germans are shooting at us in the camp from the Aryan street. Anyone they see is shot at; a small cannon on the street as well. Two Jews who were curious and sat on the hill [?] are ... shot. They are also shooting at the windowpanes of the Dresdener when they see a face at the window. There are several wounded.

Much shooting is still heard in the evening.

May 9: Bombs are still falling in the neighborhood. Russians, French and English people are walking around the camp. No light and no water.

May 10: Polish and Hungarian Jews (liberated prisoners) take everything from German prisoners of war; they must go on barefoot. The inmates of C III have broken out and steal whatever they can find.

May 11: Sixty gendarmes arrive to keep order.

May 12: People are saying that 500 prisoners of war will work in the camp.

May 14: The Russian commandant orders the same rations for his soldiers and the liberated prisoners.

May 17: The condition of the typhus patients in the West Barracks is said to be indescribable; they are lying in their own filth and get no water, despite terrible thirst, because they would wet the beds.

May 20: The inmates of C III get clothing, take off their rags in public and dress themselves.

May 25: German prisoners from the "Kleine Festung," in striped concentration camp outfits, smeared with swastikas and with shaven heads, are beaten with clubs by Jewish overseers and shouted at: "Faster, faster! We worked for you for five years!" A Polish woman yells, "Where are our children? Where are our fathers and mothers?" Others cry, "Pigs, pigs!" and others, "Died of hunger!" "Gassed!" "Crematorium!" A Pole takes a club and beats a German, with many cries: "Gas, crematorium, Auschwitz!" The same is yelled from windows. Generally, people are satisfied with insults and incitement, but most say that one should have no sympathy with the Germans.

May 27: Germans continue to work in the camp, but under better conditions. A Polish Jewish woman, asked for water, says, "I won't give you any, you gassed my husband and child."

May 28: People have stopped cursing the Germans. People say, "What good is it, our people aren't coming back." Many claim that these Germans are not the worst; others believe the opposite. It is generally said that only the Polish Jews beat them.

May 29: The former GW makes sure that Polish Jews do not steal the German prisoners' shoes. People no longer pay attention to the prisoners. Cars bearing the words "Welcome to the Homeland" pick up the Jews from Jena and Weimar.

May 30: The German prisoners are no longer required to perform hard labor.

June 3: The Polish and Hungarian Jews in C III still look bad and are very thin. They continue to steal what they can and are kept in line by gendarmes with clubs.

June 6: The Dutch are taken to Pilsen [Plsen] by car.

June 16: The Dutch continue on by car to Bamberg, where the rumor arises that Murmelstein has been condemned to death.

June 18–21: The Dutch travel by train from Bamberg to Holland.

69a. Frankenhuis, M.: *Westerbork and an Interview with Its Commander Gemmecke in 1948*. The Hague, 1948. [See also the Dutch edition.]

This text also contains camp photos. The commandant's correct name is Gemmecker.

70. Frankl, V.: *Ein Psycholog erlebt das Konzentrationslager*. Vienna, 1947.

A Viennese doctor, in T for two years until October 1944, provides an intelligent psychological report that refers to a concentration camp (not T) and investigates adaption by former prisoners to normal conditions.

70a. Frankl, V.: "Psychohygiene im Notstand; Psychotherapeutische Erfahrungen im Konzentrationslager." In *Hygiene*. Vol. 5/6. Vienna, October 1952, pp. 177–86.

Information on experiences in T, Auschwitz, and Dachau. The typology of characteristic behavior patterns – reception shock, character change during longer stays, and the release phase – does apply, according to Frankl, but it is also possible to retain one's humanity without "regression." He provides examples from psychotherapeutic practice in T.

70b. Frankl, V.: "Psychohygienische Erfahrungen im Konzentrationslager." In Frankl, V., et al. (eds.), *Handbuch der Neurosenlehre und Psychotherapie*. Vol. IV. Munich and Berlin, 1959, pp. 736–47.

Information based on experiences in Auschwitz, Dachau, and T.

71. Frenkl, J.: "Marcina pisen" [Song of a Mother]. In 319, no. 1, 1946.

A poem written in T in 1943.

71a. Freud, A., in collaboration with Dann, S.: "An Experiment in Group Upbringing." In *The Psychoanalytic Study of the Child*. Vol. VI. London, 1951, pp. 127–68

This concerns a group of orphaned two- to three-year-old children, some of whom had been imprisoned from infancy and (after an interim stay with Pitter, *60a) were brought to England in 1945.

72. Fried, J.: "Protokoll." MS, DA, 1945.

The author was arrested as a hostage at the beginning of the war and was brought to Buchenwald, where he remained until the end of the war. The text discusses the life of the Jews in this camp.

Sources and Literature   661

73. Friediger, M.: *Theresienstadt.* [Danish], Copenhagen, 1946.

A description of the experiences of the chief rabbi of Copenhagen, in T from October 1943 to April 1945. The information is not always reliable.

74. Friedländer, O.: "Protokol o 'Baukommando Zossen.'" [Czech], MS, DA, Prague, 1945.

A depiction of conditions in this small subsidiary camp, to which 200 young men from T went on March 2, 1944. In September 1944 it grew to around 260 men. In autumn, 45 prisoners were sent to Sachsenhausen and to the "Kleine Festung" as punishment (there were around 10 survivors). Zossen was evacuated on February 2, 1945; the inmates, who had received no bread for a week, received food for three days, but the journey to T via Berlin, Halle, Würzburg, Nuremburg, and Prague took eight days. Another "building kommando," approximately 20 men, left T on March 13, 1945, and went to Schnarchenreuth, near Hof. Documents from the "Central Registry" indicate that three small transports of 61 men left T between March 11 and 22, 1945, for the purpose of "barracks building," and that another transport with 41 men left on April 10. The former went to Schnarchenreuth, near Hof, and the latter to Regen, in the Bavarian woods, where they remained for only four days. All 102 men were back in T on April 20. The march back from Schnarchenreuth was said to have taken eight days (*86).

75. Friedman, F.: *This was Oswiecim.* London, 1946.

This work is informative but not always reliable, for example, regarding the information on the transports from T in September 1943 (the SS's intentions are not correctly understood here).

75a. Friedmann, Ph.: "Aspects of the Jewish Communal Crisis in the Period of the Nazi Regime in Germany, Austria and Czechoslovakia." In *Essays on Jewish Life and Thought.* New York, 1959, pp. 199–230.

The author deals especially with conditions in Prague and T. The work is, unfortunately, substantively deficient.

76. Friedman, Ph.: *Auschwitz.* [Spanish translation of the Yiddish original from 1948.] Buenos Aires, 1952.

Expanded in comparison with *75, this source corresponds to the author's part in *78, with which the information on the Theresienstadters (p. 129 et seq.) agrees.

76a. Friedman, Ph. (ed.): *Martyrs and Fighters: The Epic of the Warsaw Ghetto.* New York, 1954.

An excellent anthology, composed of documents on and eyewitness accounts of life and death in the Warsaw Ghetto (there are sociological parallels with T) and its heroic demise.

77. Friedman, Ph.: "Research and Literature of the Recent Jewish Catastrophe." [In *Jewish Social Studies.* Vol. 12]. New York, 1950, [pp. 17–26].

Thirty-five publications on T known to the author but not listed by name.

77a. Friedman, Ph.: "The Lublin Reservation and the Madagascar Plan." In *YIVO Annual of Jewish Social Science.* Vol. VIII. New York, 1953, pp. 151–77.

A valuable study with many source citations. The claim that 10,000–20,000 Czech Jews were sent in autumn 1939 to the Lublin "settlement area" is described by the

662   *Sources and Literature*

author himself as greatly exaggerated, but such transports, which are expressly distinguished from the transports to Nisko, did not take place at all. In contrast, in the "Protectorate," Jews of Polish nationality were arrested soon after the war began, and most probably were deported to Poland. I do not know their number, but it most likely was not more than 1,000 people. Also, probably only Jews of Polish nationality or origin were deported from Vienna at the time.

78. Friedman, F., and T. Hołuj: *Oświęcim* [Auschwitz]. Warsaw, 1946.

More precisely and in greater detail than in *75, Friedman here describes documents that also are available in *26, page 115 et seq. The story of the Theresienstadters' special camp and its demise corresponds to the information in *242. The information on other transports from T is not entirely correct. Hołuj provides important documents.

Friedman-van der Heide, R.: *344.

78a. Friedmann, C.: "Protokoll." MS, DA, Prague, 1945.

A report, by his widow, on Richard Israel Friedmann, born in Vienna in 1911 (he bore the forced name "Israel" proudly and did not wish to change it). This young, enthusiastic Zionist was transferred from the IKG Vienna, where he had helped many Jews through his untiring work, to the JKG Prague as an advisor to the emigration operation.

In October 1939, Friedmann and Edelstein went to Nisko (*77a, 94, 175b, 194, 350, 350a).

> The background to this operation was never entirely clear. From their talks with ... Eichmann, Friedmann and Edelstein gathered the following: he assumed that the territories in Poland between the Bug and the San ... were depopulated, and since that was exactly where the border between the Germans and the Soviet Union was located, he wanted to settle the Jews in that area as a "buffer." He sent men fit for work to build barracks there, to which additional Jews would follow. On the trip to Nisko, Friedmann was physically abused almost the entire time by the SS man Dresel. The initial days and nights in Nisko were filled with the most difficult hardships; they lived in the open forest, and the friendship between Friedmann and Edelstein developed during these ice-cold nights.... In a short time, a healthy collective spirit prevailed; a few barracks were built, and through their work with the surrounding peasants, the doctors ... acquired food.... Friedmann was able to prevail upon an SS guard [to take him to the Gestapo in Lublin]. There he attempted to convince the SS leadership that the operation had been undertaken on the wrong premises, that the area was not depopulated, and that, on the contrary, the native population was rebelling ... against the influx. From documents later found in Vienna ... it is clear that the Lublin Gestapo office was negotiating with Berlin, and we can assume that the continuation of this operation was stopped on the basis of these negotiations.... Edelstein was the first to return, after a few weeks.... In December 1939, Friedmann also came back.

Regarding Friedmann's principles in the JKG: They were to be a buffer. He "was strict about not letting the Gestapo in general know who had carried out various tasks, ... aside from Friedmann, Edelstein and Weidmann, no one was to know." Because Friedmann had no need to worry about relatives, he risked an attitude that, stereotypically, responded to SS threats literally more or less as follows: "You can no longer frighten me with your concentration camps. That has been my occupational hazard since I have been dealing with you." He concerned himself with social welfare, schools, and the JKG health service.

> In March 1941, Friedmann and Edelstein were charged with going to Holland to ... help the Joodschen Rat set up the "Central Office." ... The two months that Friedmann spent in Holland he himself called his "first vacation" in 5 years.... The Central Office was not established during Friedmann's first stay with Edelstein, or during Friedmann's second stay in May 1941, but only much later [?]. Friedmann returned from Holland in a particularly optimistic mood. It was the only time that he was politically unrealistic. People in Holland were expecting an invasion and an early end to the war.

This report is the only source that mentions R. I. Friedmann's trips to Holland, as *52a and *312c talk about Dr. Franz Friedmann. This emerges especially from *52a, which reports on a Czech discussion with Friedmann; R. I. Friedmann was not fluent in Czech. I have not yet been able to determine whether both Franz and R. I. Friedmann traveled.

Regarding the deportation period: Friedmann felt the beginning of the transports to be the "collapse of his years of work."

> He knew nothing of the highly-organized killing machinery in Poland; he imagined it to be a not so systematic but certain extermination of the majority of the population.
>
> This fundamental change in the situation also brought with it a fundamental change in his view of the entire task. He saw ... that the time for "negotiating and even for the lesser evil" was over. The rescue of one person essentially had to be bought with the life of another. He said in so many words that, from this day on, one was no longer in any way a negotiating partner; from now on, the Gestapo needed only executive organs....
>
> The transports in Prague were put together as follows. The Central Office had a card file on the Jews, and the SS men now took file cards completely at random. The KG had the right to prepare a so-called protection list containing the names of its staff. When each transport had 1,000 members, the Gestapo [Central Office] generally gave out 1,200 to 1,300 file cards from which the protected staff were to be removed. Essentially, the Gestapo decided the fate of individuals in this way; the Community had, so to speak, a limited right of reclamation, and this privilege of course became the focus of protection possibilities. It is self-evident that ... ideal conditions did not prevail. It would require a community full of superhuman idealists who ..., in a situation of life and death, would not have fought for the possibility of making their friends and relatives ... members of the community authority. The Community of the Jews was no worse, but also no better, than [those] in the outside world.

Friedmann fundamentally refused to "declare one person better or more valuable and to decide about his life," but he helped some of his friends' families with small children. "Still, he accepted a general political standpoint and helped people who were considered important by and for a community [group]." He refused to assist in carrying out "this devilish work."

> Mandler, a nasty type known in Prague ... was brought in and took over the implementation of the transports.... Friedmann was of course still responsible for the operations of the KG, which now had to be oriented in large part towards the transports ...
>
> He always found it uncanny that all these ... people ... obeyed the mass expulsion with such calm and discipline, without any resistance. He asked himself ... whether the administrative assistance from the KG eased this process or even made it fundamentally possible.... Each Jew personally had the opportunity to escape and go underground. In

the period of 3–5 days between being informed and the departure of the transport, one even had time to prepare everything for going underground ... and had time ... to disappear. No Jew who did not appear for the transport was seriously or consistently sought by the Gestapo in Prague. The Gestapo had agreed that the KG would inform the Czech police of such non-appearance and that [they] were to find the people involved. It need not be explained in detail that ... it was considered sufficient to visit the person's apartment once and declare that he was gone, and report the case as ["]unable to be found.["]

When T was established, Friedmann concentrated "on supplying the camp" through department "G," which aided him with daring illegal missions.

There was fundamental authorization from the Central Office to ... supply the ghetto with the "most necessary" things from Prague, in part through purchases the oversight of which was reserved for the Central Office, in part through KG stocks. Under the umbrella of ... "necessities," ... whatever was attainable by legal, and mainly illegal, means was bought and taken out in maximum quantities.

One can imagine what things would have been like, given the disastrous situation [*Notstand*] in T, if the camp had been supplied only through strictly legal means, or even exclusively by the SS. Friedmann eked out money from the "emigration fund" "by constantly falsifying the budget proposal."

None of this would have been possible, however, if the KG had not been supported by the assistance of SS man Bartels. He was the only SS man in all the years who provided illegal aid. [Friedmann did not give a motive for his behavior, and it is therefore unknown.] The Gestapo received a complaint from a pharmaceutical company ... against Bartels that he was authorizing disproportionate amounts of medication for Jewish purposes. At the Gestapo (Bartels was the official in charge of economic matters and ... was responsible for supplying Theresienstadt from the Gestapo side.) Bartels turned to Friedmann rather helplessly.... Friedmann drafted for him a letter to the pharmaceutical firm; in it he declared that he was willing at any moment to ... transfer the responsibility for the supply of medication to the ghetto ... to the firm itself, if it would give him written assurance that it was accepting responsibility for preventing epidemics, which recognized no racial differences.... The matter was settled in this way.

... The following ... is also connected with SS man Bartels.... A few months after the deportations began, inclinations emerged in the economic group around Bertsch [the economic representative of the "Reich Protectorate"] toward ending the deportations of the Jews and ... using them as part of general labor deployment. The considerations leading to this cessation certainly were not those of humanity; either they did not want to lose ... the far too cheap labor ... for their internal market, or there was fundamental opposition in regard to the Gestapo....

... The Bertsch economic group needed material to prove the "unprofitability" of the extermination of the Jews.... Bartels had connections to this group ... and Friedmann provided the statistical and other materials as a basis for the negotiations, which were repeated at regular intervals, two or three times. The stress that Friedmann ... experienced (he was kept informed by Bartels) can hardly be described. The Gestapo always won out.

Friedmann described his relations with the SS as "correct enmity" and indicated "that his aim was ultimately that of victory." This was relatively safe only as long as Germany was winning.

[Friedmann] was incautious enough to telephone directly to T, generally at night from his home, but in urgent cases even from his office.... One day, in December 1942, Friedmann was summoned to Günther[;] ... of course, he denied everything. A few days later, when Friedmann could hardly move his legs, ... he admitted to his closest friends that he was forced to do 140 knee bends at this interrogation. What else happened there, none of us ever found out.... On January 28, 1943, there was an unexpected incident. At the tenth anniversary celebrations of the founding of the "Third Reich," the Führer was presented with the "liquidated Jewish Question" as a present. The KGs of Berlin, Vienna and Prague were officially dissolved, the leading functionaries sent to the ghetto, and the remaining office in Berlin [in fact, there was no office there], Vienna, and Prague subordinated to a "Council of Elders." A few days earlier, those at the Central Office had a sense that something was in the works. The night before January 28, 1943, those most involved heard that Dr. Weidmann ... had received the assignment of ... preparing himself for T.

Friedmann prepared to flee, but his arrest and that of Dr. Franz Kahn on the afternoon of January 28 at the Central Office preempted this. From there, they were immediately taken to T. Their relatives and luggage were sent a few days later.

Following is a description of T, seen through Friedmann's eyes:

[The administration failed,] so that the common saying was correct that "Theresienstadt is a concentration camp made worse by self-administration." ... The majority of people involved in administration were recruited from the Jewish petty bourgeois. Through the grotesque miniature model of a state that Theresienstadt ... represented, these people gained positions they had never before held in their lives. In the grind of daily life, they lost ... the connection to larger events and used their positions of power in the most unpleasant way for the community. [To this was added their relative protection from deportation, such that each tended to] accommodate his family and friends in the administrative apparatus, and thus there emerged ... a veritable jungle of administration, corruption and cliquishness. The deepest roots of this ... evil were ... that ... the Jews themselves were entirely responsible for putting together the transport lists. It need not be described more closely what an apparatus of power the so-called transport department constituted. Friedmann understood all this [immediately], and when we reached Theresienstadt the next day, Friedmann was distraught and unsettled ... for the first time in all these years. In this sector, he was especially appalled ... that Edelstein, whose moral strength and purity he did not want to and could not doubt, had not been strong enough to prevent all this. [Friedmann] never understood that, in contrast to the practice in Prague, they had taken it upon themselves to decide on the life or death of individual members of the community....

Those who had arrived first later acted like some type of pioneers; it was the aristocracy ... who looked down with a degree of contempt on those who came later....

[Friedmann was officially a "notable" but – especially because he did not want a privileged position owed to the SS – refused the benefits associated with it, such as food bonuses, although he did accept a private room (because of the conspiratorial possibilities). He immediately entered a squadron and then took a low position in the Economics Department] but could not accept the conditions and ultimately no longer took part in its work. [Eppstein then accused him of sabotage and told him] that the "superior authorities" wanted him employed according to his abilities. Friedmann refused ... and entered ... an agricultural group as a worker. Shortly before his deportation, the Gestapo pressure was renewed in full measure, conveyed by Dr. Eppstein. Friedmann was told he had to ... take on a function in the Central Labor Office. [There he] had to deal with pettiness and vanity, and these things ... sometimes wore him down more than the perilous battle with the Gestapo.

[Friedmann assessed Eppstein as] not very original, not very brave.... He had given way to the enormous pressure of the Gestapo and had since been their willing tool in all

Sources and Literature

things.... [Cooperation between Eppstein and Edelstein], although it would have been extremely important for the good of the collective, was absolutely impossible....

While for [Edelstein and his group] falsification and sabotage were the highest goals, Eppstein was an absolutely proper, devoted servant. While the former consciously and consistently concentrated the Gestapo's entire pressure on themselves and never passed it along [more correctly: desired to pass it along], Eppstein was a tyrant towards his colleagues and constantly strove to keep the entire apparatus under pressure.

In order not to appear unobjective, I will add that friends who knew his life story attempted to excuse his attitude as follows. It was ... his Prussian correctness that had so entered his flesh and blood that he could not behave towards the Gestapo other than "correctly." This may explain some things, but does not excuse them.... It is immaterial to judge in this context to what extent Eppstein was responsible ... for Edelstein's and Friedmann's deaths. His guilt is more a negative, and consists in the fact that, as one of the few who were already well informed at the time, he went along with the Gestapo's comedy and did not once even hint at the danger. How great is his guilt in regard to the entire collective, and what must it have looked like inside a person who knew for years that people and friends around him were going to death by gas and could keep as silent as the grave....

... The night before the departure of the last [May] transport [1944], Friedmann was called to Eppstein and given the task of preparing for the transport. Dr. Eppstein explained ... that he did not know the motive for the sudden deportation, but at the commandant's office it had been suggested that this transport was not going to Poland, but to a new work camp, near Dresden, the establishment of which was assigned to Friedmann.

But the SS distrusted Friedmann's "credulity" and took him to the bunker and, from there, under guard, to the Schleuse. He boarded a normal train car but in Bauschowitz [Bohušovice] was taken out by Haindl and was brought to the special carriage in which Haindl himself and three Schupos (state policemen) were traveling. In Birkenau, Friedmann was taken to the "family camp" but was separated from others there; two days later, on May 21, he was taken to the punishment block of the men's camp. The next morning, while working, he was taken by an SS man a few steps past the permitted boundary and was shot from behind "while trying to escape."

79. Friedmann, F.: "Rechtsstellung der Juden im Protektorat Böhmen und Mähren." Prag, I – Stand am 31.7.1942, II – Stand am 31.3.1943.

A document written for the internal use of the JKG.

79a. Friedmann, H.: "Kunstführung durch Theresienstadt." MS, YV, T, 1943.

The author worked in T as a librarian from autumn 1942 to autumn 1944 and organized art tours through the city for the "Recreation Office"; their text is preserved here. See the sample in *3b, doc. 169.

79b. Frischauer, W.: *Himmler: The Evil Spirit of the Third Reich*. London, 1953.

A biography of Himmler and a history of the SS that draws on much information and many documents, which do not, however, convey a convincing or complete picture. It features contradictory statements about Eichmann. Kersten (*139–40) is assessed unfavorably.

80. [Fritta] *Terezín. Výstava malíře Bedřicha Fritty* [Exhibit of the Painter Friedrich Fritta]. Prague, November 1945.

An exhibition catalogue.

81. [Fritta] *Terezín Concentration Camp: Ink and Wash Drawings by Bedřich Fritta*. London, 1948.

An exhibition catalogue about forty-eight works by Fritta. It contains two reproductions and short statements about the artist and T. Nineteen works by Fritta, as well as two official sheets, are reproduced in *3b (docs. 86, 135, 180–97, 238).

81a. Frýd, N.: *Krabice živých* [The Box of the Living]. Prague, 1957. German translation: *Die Kartei der Lebenden*. Berlin, 1959.

The author was in T for a long time, and from there traveled via Auschwitz to Kauffering 3, where his novel takes place. The work contains reminiscences of T and the fate of the people deported from there to Kauffering (called "Gigling" here).

81b. Gabel, A.: "Kamp Westerbork in Schlagzeilen." MS, RvO, Holland, no year.

Detailed tables on the history of the camp, from its founding in spring 1939 to liberation on April 12, 1945. It is an important but not entirely reliable resource. When, in February 1943, the leaders put together the "list" (*Stammliste*) of prisoners who were to remain permanently in Westerbork, the parents of those protected in this way were "reset" for T.

81c. Gerron, K.: "Filmreportage Theresienstadt 1944." MSS, T, 1944.

Gerron was an author, the first director, and – among the prisoners – the one most responsible for the great propaganda film. A number of important documents were preserved in his estate.

1. "Die Jüdische Selbstverwaltung in Theresienstadt: Entwurf zu einer Filmreportage." This is the actual script that was largely followed, although not in every detail.
2. Film reports. A series of recordings in which the creation of the film and what was really filmed can be seen.
3. "Versuch eines Vorschlages für den Schnitt des Filmes 'Theresienstadt.'" According to this, the film consists of 1,148 sequences. Whether Gerron's suggestions were followed precisely or merely generally is not clear.
4. "Film Theresienstadt: Entwurf für einen Begleittext."
5. Internal letters and "memoranda" (fifty-one documents).

See the text samples in *3b, docs. 228–34.

82. Gerzonova, B.: "Protocol." [Czech], MS, DA, Prague, 1945.

The reporter left T with orphan children on October 23, 1944. Their "trip" and arrival in Auschwitz are described in detail.

82a. [Laws] *Ausnahne-Gesetze gegen Juden in den von Nazi-Deutschland besetzten Gebietes Europas* [Emergency Law Against Jews in the Areas of Europe Occupied by Nazi Germany]. London, 1956.

A brief, good summary, published by the WL.

83. "Gestapo Transport Lists." MS, 1942/45. [In the possession of the International Tracing Service in Arolsen].

The Tracing Service possesses a large number of transport lists, many of them involving deportations to T. The complete lists are those from Gestapo areas I (Berlin), IV (Vienna), V (Dresden), VI (Hamburg), VII (Düsseldorf-Aachen), and IX (Breslau). The lists from VIII (Hanover) are incomplete (they contain only VIII/1+5). The lists from the other areas are missing (the lists from the "Protectorate" are located with the Jewish authorities in Prague and were put together by the JKG, not the Gestapo). We provide the numbers from the Gestapo lists next to the information from *166 (Table V), *302, and 48.

	Gestapo lists	*166	*302	*48
I	14,877	15,122	15,122	14,797 (15,136)[a]
IV	16,177	16,404	16,402	
IV (Hungary only)	1,076	1,073	1,074	
V	492	492	492	500
VI	2,490	2,489	2,489	2,517
VII	2,009	2,008	2,007	2,090
IX	2,822	2,818	2,818	2,920

[a] The latter is another list in *48.

For the first transport of VIII, the Gestapo lists mention one victim more than do *166 and *302.

83a. Gilbert, [R.]: "Zulassungsmarke Theresienstadt." In *Der Deutschland-Sammler*. Munich, June 1, 1957, p. 94 et seq.

83b. Ginz, P.: "Gedichte und Zeichnungen." MS, T, 1944.

A collection of drawings and fifty-nine poems, in the possession of YV.

83c. Gobits, B.: "'Hitler gaf de Joden een stad!' Theresienstadt – zoals het werkelijk was ..." In *De Telegraf*. Amsterdam, May 4, 1955, p. 9 et seq.

The author, in T from September 6, 1944, until liberation, gives an account that is not at all free of error. The text provides a more detailed description of the period after liberation and repatriation, as well as an illustration of "ghetto money" (*3b, doc. 109), a postcard of the city hall, and a drawing (E VI, L 506).

84. Goldschmidt, A.: *Geschichte der evang. Gemeinde Theresienstadt 1942–1945*. Tübingen, 1948.

A documentation of the religious life of Protestants and Catholics in T.

85. Gollancz, V.: "*Let My People Go*." London, 1943.

The author knew that T had been established in 1941 and in summer 1942 was an "old-age home" camp with 40,000 inmates, of whom 10,000 were from Bohemia and Moravia.

85a. Göring, F.: Affidavit. Schellenberg Document Book, no. II, 40. Mimeographed, Nuremberg, fall XI, 1948.

SS-Obersturmführer Franz Göring (no relation to Hermann Göring) was charged by Schellenberg on January 22, 1945, with bringing Jewish transports from concentration camps to Switzerland via Constance for the Musy mission (*2a). The only transport that came about was one from T on February 5, 1945, which Göring took control of and accompanied to the border. His description of the events is in *3b, doc. 50. When news of this release reached Hitler through Kaltenbrunner, the operation, for which 1,800 prisoners from Bergen-Belsen originally were intended, had to be ended. Göring further reports a confusing story that "despite strict prohibition of release, numerous Jews still were released through clever manipulation by ... Schellenberg." Göring lists many names; the survivor lists in *302 provide evidence that only one was a prisoner from T. This was a woman of whose release there is documentary proof in the camp papers (letters in the collection *95c); it was the only release in the month of April (April 12). Göring says he could not have brought the freed prisoners to Switzerland, "since a connection between Berlin and Theresienstadt had been cut." This must have referred to a date after April 16, the day of the visit by Kasztner, coming from Berlin. Murmelstein mentions (in *192) the visit of an unknown Swiss person in the morning but is probably wrong by four days, for Göring and Benoit Musy speak of their visit to T (*192c), which probably took place on the twelfth: Benoit Musy traveled on April 9, after Göring, from Constance to Buchenwald, where he met with Göring and continued on to Berlin. As both were undoubtedly in Berlin again before the path to T was cut off, and as the releases on the 12th were connected to this visit, we can establish that the visit took place on this date. Göring said of this: "In the course of locating the families named [previously by Göring], Mr. Musy junior had the chance to view the Theresienstadt camp thoroughly with me and to speak personally with individuals." Whom Göring means is unclear, especially as

> before this viewing ... Möhs stated that all of families in question were present. In contrast, ... Günther declared ... after repeated questioning by Mr. Musy jun. that the Cilzer family was not in the camp at all, the Berger-Tottenberg family would have been [sic] transferred to Auschwitz at the beginning of 1945, and that the men in the Donnebaum family had been delivered to a satellite camp whose name was not known.

The web of lies woven by the men from Eichmann's office was in any case thick. Göring explained the Möhs-Günther contradiction as meaning that the persons involved "came from Auschwitz in January 1945 and were witness to incidents that were not to be made public. Because Kaltenbrunner" had ordered that such people should not be released, Günther declared that they could not be located. In the first half of April, around 100 vehicles from the Swedish RC gathered all the Scandinavian prisoners and brought them to Neuengamme, which Bernadotte was operating with Schellenberg's support. Only the Danish Jews were still in T, "against whose transport to Neuengamme Kaltenbrunner strongly protested, making reference to Hitler." The credit for their liberation belongs exclusively to Schellenberg.

86. Görner, W.: "K. Z.-Ghetto Theresienstadt." MS, Berlin, 1949.

The author came to T from Berlin on March 18, 1943, and experienced the end of the war there. He worked as a GW instructor. It is a factual account but is not always precise, and the dates and figures are often unreliable.

Görner's account of the "outside work group Wulkow" (Zossen, *74), where he started on April 26, 1944, is valuable. There were 235 workers, including some engineers. The SS personnel included OSTF Franz Stuczka (or Stuschka), three

Oberscharführer, and a guard detail of ten SS men with one commander. German experts did the work but were not always present. In the summer, twenty-five women came from T to take care of the men's quarters, clothing, and laundry. At first an internal camp guard was formed, composed of six men led by Georg Einstein, supposedly Albert Einstein's grandson. On April 26, 1944, six GW men, with the author at their head, came as a guard unit; Görner became camp head. He later was removed for being too lenient and then guarded a new construction site. His successor was a man named Raffaelsohn, who helped Stuschka with his mistreatments and was tried and hanged for this in Prague in 1947 (*209d). Provisions came from T, from which a wagon of food came every fourteen days. Provisioning was supposed to be 10% better than there, but which Stuschka reduced or completely stopped. "The young pods from the acacia trees were then the miserable nourishment for the workers." Every second Sunday was supposed to be a day off, but Stuschka tormented the prisoners for hours with roll calls and by forcing them to carry around tree trunks and stones for no purpose.

> One October Sunday, Stuczka allowed himself a special depravity. It had rained very heavily on the previous days, which made the ground completely soggy and allowed a large pool to form in front of the women's barracks.... He chose his particular favorites from among the women and ordered them to sit on the ground and, with their backsides, to shove the mud to a ... particular place. The women had to raise their dresses, so they were covered only by their underwear. The men also had to [remove] their outer clothing down to the shirt and watch the women working. [Two women] had to bathe in the puddle, first laying the fronts of their bodies completely in the puddle and then the back sides. Stuczka then stepped on their upper and lower bodies.... After five hours, this roll call ended.

In the summer the prisoners worked from 6 A.M. to 10 P.M., and in winter, from 7 A.M. until dark, with a one-hour lunch break.

> The work groups built 110 structures in the forest of Wulkow. These consisted of living, working and kitchen barracks, as well as document bunkers, fire extinguisher pools, car garages and coal sheds. A sewage system and a system of wells with modern automatic pump facilities were built ... for this small barracks town. This camp was the overflow area for the Gestapo headquarters in Berlin and was partially occupied in autumn 1944, heavily monitored by an SS guard group. [At the beginning of August] 1944, a building site [the Z site] was begun.... . This was built as a private office for the Führer. It consisted of living, work and kitchen barracks; it also included a document bunker, a fire extinguisher pool, a car garage and a coal shed. In addition, the construction of an information bunker, completely of concrete, was begun. A modern well system with sewers also was part of this.

Twelve members of the Berlin police with a chief constable were in charge of the Z construction site work group starting on October 1, 1944, and lived with them "in amicable accord." The humane behavior of an SS-Oberscharführer named Hanke was also praised; he "ensured very good provisioning of workers who were beaten by Stuczka and placed in bunker arrest."

86a. Grab, H.: "Der Hausball." In *Hochzeit in Brooklyn*. Vienna, 1958, p. 78 et seq.

A story beginning with a characteristic motif from T.

87. Grabova, H.: "Protocol." [Czech], MS, DA, Prague, 1945.

An account of a singer who was in the camp from December 17 to the end. The focus is musical life in T.

88. Grätz, P.: "Erlebnisse und Erfahrungen." MS, WL, London, 1955.

This report tells of H. M., the former owner of a mill in Bartenstein, East Prussia, who also worked as a consultant: "This continued even when he was deported to Theresienstadt [from Berlin], and it is no exaggeration ... that he still advised the directors of the mill from there. He was allowed to go to East Prussia from the camp. Even from Auschwitz, to which he was further deported, he was taken to Bartenstein.... Nevertheless, H. M. was killed in an Auschwitz gas chamber."

89. Graumann, S.: *Deportiert! Ein Wiener Jude berichtet.* Vienna, 1947.

The author was in Buchenwald from early 1939 and was transferred to Auschwitz and Monowitz in 1942; at the evacuation in 1945, he was sent to Buchenwald again and went from there to T at the end of the war, which he discusses on pages 156–60.

90. Gringauz, S.: "Some Methodological Problems in the Study of the Ghetto." In *Jewish Social Studies*. New York, January 1950, p. 65 et seq.

Fundamental thoughts on the sociology of the "ghetto."

91. Gringauz, S.: "The Ghetto as an Experiment of Jewish Social Organization (Three Years of Kovno Ghetto)." In *Jewish Social Studies*. New York, 1949, p. 3 et seq.

Like Utitz, Gringauz also sees in the "ghetto" "a unique social experiment.... It was not, however, a creative experiment, where the conditions were not set in the interests of research, but determined by the politics of persecution, defamation and extermination. Nevertheless, the 'ghetto' was a Jewish community that was created by artificial conditions, and thus it fulfilled [in the author's opinion] the requirements of an experiment."

91a. Grňová, J.: "Svatobořický tábor" [The Svatobořice Camp]. In Habrina, R. (ed.): *Žalm Moravy* [Moravian Psalm]. Brno, 1948, pp. 91–99.

The internment camp Svatobořice, near Göding, was opened on September 17, 1942. Its inmates were the family members, from fifteen to seventy years of age, of prominent emigrants and resistance fighters, including Jews, who were separated from the Christians. Its official name was "Internment Camp of the Non-Uniformed Police in the Protectorate of Bohemia and Moravia." It was guarded by Czech gendarmes under the Nazistic First Lieutenant Kaiser and the Gestapo functionary Tunz. The Gestapo often came to the camp. Concentration camp conditions prevailed. Kaiser was a terrible slave driver. More than 2,000 people were interned at the same time. Many Jews were beaten; later all of them were sent to Auschwitz. Forced labor was performed. As of Christmas 1942, receipt of packages was permitted. At times, children from five years of age also were interned. After the Slovak rebellion, Slovak Jews also were brought in. In December 1943, Kaiser was replaced as commandant by the German first lieutenant Schuster, who behaved much more humanely. When the Brno Gestapo evacuated the camp on April 13, 1945, some 800 people were released and nearly 200 were transferred to the Planá camp on the Luschnitz in Bohemia. The volume also contains seven pictures of the camp.

672   *Sources and Literature*

91b. Grossmann, K. R.: "What Happened to the German Jews? A Balance Sheet." In *Ten Years: American Federation of Jews from Central Europe, Inc.* New York, 1952, pp. 41–49.

Information on the number of Jews in Germany before and after the catastrophe. The following table presents the data in rounded numbers:

1925		564,000
1933	January	525,000
1933	June	499,000
1939	September	215,000
1940	November	160,000
1942	May	80,000
1943	April	32,000
1945	May 8	15,000

92. Grossmann, W.: *Die Hölle von Treblinka.* London, 1945.

Information on the technology of the extermination camp.

93. Gutfeld, A.: "Bemerkungen zum Theresienstadt-Buch." MS, Berlin, 1957.

These remarks were kindly written by Dr. Gutfeld, who was in T as of March 18, 1943, for the first edition of this book. Some things that, according to him, could not otherwise be included are reported here.

Regarding page 97, Chapter 5: "Eppstein was a curious mixture of real goodness and decency, snobbishness, vanity, courage and fear, cynicism and all sorts of other things. As with all weak people, the negative qualities overcame the better ones in the camp." Gutfeld knew Eppstein well through his work in the Reichsvereinigung in Berlin (*243e).

Regarding page 144, Chapter 6: "My stepdaughter, a particularly pretty little girl, was exhibited in the children's pavilion. Rahm gave each child a doll – for two hours."

Regarding page 155, Chapter 7: Eppstein said, as Gutfeld remembered it: "The ship must still fight, but our friends already stand at the dock. That was interpreted by us to mean: the war will soon be over, and then we will be free again" (*243e).

Regarding page 211, Chapter 8: Gutfeld reports that one did not have to refer to one's protector if the conditions were known. In contrast, a protégé of Eppstein was told the day after his arrest, "So, now your friend Eppstein is gone, now you need to come [to work] a little more on time."

Regarding page 266, Chapter 10:

> The statistics from the Central Registry also provided a breakdown by *Landsmannschaft*, sex and age group every night, as of midnight – that is, night shift to incorporate the last death notices, arrivals and departures on transports, etc. Age groups were not calculated by year of birth, but according to *date* of birth, with a margin of three days; this means that the figures on our basic table had to be corrected every three days by updating in each separate age group. Every night two people had to be present until around 2 in the morning to establish the reported status at midnight, to be reported at 7 o'clock in the morning. Because we were debilitated, we needed three or four people in the office, where otherwise one would have sufficed. In addition there was bureaucratic idling and red tape. Perhaps a quarter of the staff was always sick.

Sources and Literature

Regarding page 521–522, Chapter 19: Kästner's *Emil and the Detectives* was performed as a children's opera with the German-speaking children. "Of the children who performed in it, only one survived Theresienstadt."

93a. Gutfeld, [A.]: "Die Sterblichkeit in Theresienstadt in ihrer Beziehung zur Dauer des Aufenthaltes." In *Allg. Statistisches Archiv*. Vol. 35, no. 1. Munich, 1951, pp. 45 et seq.

94. Guttmann, T. (ed.): *Dokumentenwerk über die jüdische Geschichte in der Zeit des Nazismus*. Vol. I. Jerusalem, 1943.

Information on conditions in Nisko (*77a, 78a, 175b, 194, 350, 350a).

95. H. B.: "Noch einmal davongekommen … Leipziger Juden im Getto Theresienstadt." In *Leipziger Zeitung*. May 11, 1947.

This otherwise trivial report reveals that the Leipziger Jews were taken from the "Jewish buildings" on September 18, 1942, to a gymnasium as a collection camp. "The next morning, they marched to Engelsdorf, where the group waited in a POW tent for the train from Thuringia.... It arrived around 11 o'clock at night, filled with fellow sufferers." They arrived in T on September 20, 1942. An illustration by Ernst Kaufmann shows "food distribution in the ghetto" (Kitchen L 408).

95a. H. G.: "Protocol." MS, WL, London, 1955.

An account by an elderly woman from Berlin; she was in T from June 1942. The account is confused and full of rumors.

95b. Haarburger, A., and T. Haarburger: "Bericht über den Auftenthalt im Ghetto Theresienstadt." MS, WL, Melbourne, 1955.

The account of a married couple – the man was 80% war-disabled – who came to T in August 1942 on a transport from Württemberg-Baden. At liberation, of the transport's 1,079 members, only 32 were still in the camp. The wife was a house nurse, and the husband voluntarily carried out domestic chores; he lost an eye in an accident. Their daughter arrived from Cologne a month later as a nurse and transport escort and later was sent to Auschwitz but was rescued in Bergen-Belsen at the end of the war. The couple was protected by Rahm in autumn 1944, because both worked. They did not know about the gas chambers: "People believed that the SS honored the principle of sending the younger people to labor service and allowing the older people to die off."

95c. Haber, P.: "Statistik des Grauens." MS, YV, Vienna, 1952.

The author, who was in T from September 25, 1942, worked in the "Central Registry" and compiled statistical material for the entire duration of the camp's existence, but the information is not very reliable and is in part verifiably wrong. Most valuable is some original material, which unfortunately refers only to the months of April and May 1945. The author gives the overall number of people deported to T (not counting the concentration camp transports) as 149,168 – a figure that is much too high – and the number of concentration camp prisoners until May 8 as 12,777 (including 3 births and 77 who arrived dead). On May 9, the 16,832 liberated longtime camp inmates were distributed as follows among six countries of origin:

Protectorate	6,235
Germany	5,475
Austria	1,293
Holland	1,285
Slovakia	1,407
Hungary	1,138

95d. Hagen [Höttl.], W.: *Die geheime Front: Organisation, Personen und Aktionen des deutschen Geheimdienstes.* Linz and Vienna, no year [1950].

One must be cautious when using this as a source; however, the author has intimate knowledge of people and events surrounding the RSHA. The character portraits of Reinhard Heydrich and Heinrich Müller are important (*106d). Heydrich is described as the offspring of a Jewish grandmother on his father's side. Because of such claims, he instigated three libel trials before 1937, by questionable means. In 1931 he joined the Hamburg SS, where he set up a "security service." In March 1933, Himmler appointed him to the political department of the Munich police presidium. In April 1934 he became head of the Prussian Gestapo, as Himmler's representative. This put him firmly in control. He compiled the murder list for the infamous June 30 killings. His goal, according to the author, was to work his way up to minister of the interior (and to "Reichsprotektor" in Prague as the preliminary step) and to Reich chancellor, while Hitler and Himmler would remain representative figures as "Führer" and Reichsführer-SS. Heydrich, in the author's view, was always the intellect and driving force behind Himmler. He believed in an international Christian conspiracy against Germany, led by the Vatican and the Jesuits, and his hatred of Jews was also very deep. Otherwise, even compared with Himmler, he was free of delusions and ideological ballast. He created the "Central Office," through which he hoped to get all the Jews out of Germany by the end of 1941 (*46b). The author also attributes the Madagascar plan (*77a) to him, before he became the implementer of the "Final Solution," at Hitler's wish, in which "a main principle of his organization consisted in having Jews killed by Jews" (p. 38).

> It is typical not of Heydrich's generosity, but of his cynicism, as he had only inner contempt for ideologies, that in choosing his closest associates he placed far less value on National Socialist attitudes than on compliant devotion and absolute obedience. The later head of the entire Secret State Police, Heinrich Müller, for example, was an avowed opponent of National Socialism before 1933. Through Heydrich, he soon obtained a high SS position, but the party kept refusing to admit him because of his oppositional past.   (p. 15)

His admission did not occur until shortly before the beginning of the war. He is described as being as evil as Heydrich, but not of his caliber; ideology did not matter to him (p. 72 et seq.).

> It was Müller who brought to completion Heydrich's surveillance system, which was based on the principle of moral incrimination.... Müller envisioned creating, over time, a central registry in which every German would be filed, of course primarily with their "black marks."... The principles by which he judged people hardly corresponded with those of the NSDAP.... Müller knew no law but the omnipotence of the state.... Anyone suspected of being refractory or who might become so was for him a foe whom he pursued with all the brutality and cruelty of his character.

Sources and Literature 675

Kaltenbrunner, with whom the author apparently had a close relationship, is assessed as a weakling in thrall to Hitler, but not too unfavorably, and Best is described as a National Socialist "idealist." He therefore parted ways with Heydrich, who went after him until his death – that is, before Best went to Copenhagen. Kersten (*139, 140) is judged negatively, almost spitefully, but no reasons are given for this treatment.

96. Hartmann, K.: "Terezínská epopej" [Theresienstadt Epopee]. MS, T, 1942/44.

The author is a grandson of the poet who wrote *Chalice and Sword*, Moritz Hartmann, who is known from Heinrich Heine's biography. The author was in T for a long time, until autumn 1944, and died in Auschwitz. The work, a rhyming portrayal of the camp and its history, is factually correct. The contents lists the following subsections: "This Is the Ghetto," "Recreation," "Poland Transport," "Administration," "Ghetto Guard," "Graves," "The 'Bank,'" "Executions," "Census," "Beautification," "Sports," and "Film."

97. Havlíček, M.: *V terezínské pevnosti* [In the Theresienstadt Fortress]. Ostrau [Ostrava], 1945.

A work of fiction, only about the "Kleine Festung."

97a. Heimann, K.: "Die Postverhältnisse in der Judenstadt Theresienstadt." In *Der Deutschland-Sammler*. Munich, March 1, April 1, and June 1, 1957, pp. 47–48, 60–63, and 93–94.

97b. Helweg-Larsen, P. [and six other authors]: *Famine Disease in German Concentration Camps*. Copenhagen, 1952.

Observations of Danish prisoners, but not of prisoners in T (their number is given as 474). In contrast to the experience in T, the work does not emphasize the incidence of avitaminosis and infectious enteritis, but it does portray similar psychopathic symptoms (*185b).

98. Henningsen, J.: "Rejse til Theresienstadt, Juni 1944." MS, Copenhagen, 1944.

An official report by the Danish member of the delegation from the Health Office and the RC, based on personal impressions and information from Eppstein, the Jewish chief surgeon Dr. Springer (who is, probably due to a comprehension error, here called Dr. Stieler), and the SS. "Full of admiration for the Jewish achievements," Henningsen summarized,

> If one evaluates what we saw here and coordinates these impressions with the information from Eppstein and the German authorities, one gains the impression that the organizational conditions have improved specifically in the last half year. Health-wise, the overpopulation poses the greatest danger. There can be no doubt today that the Jewish administration is combating the health dangers as best it can under the prevailing conditions.　　(*188a)

98a. Herbenová, O.: "Kresby židovských dětí z Terezína" [Drawings by Jewish Children from Theresienstadt]. In 319, no. 5, 1959.

A report on the collection in the Prague Jewish Museum.

98b. Hershkovitch, B.: *The Ghetto in Litzmannstadt* (Łódź). In *YIVO Annual of Jewish Social Science*. Vol. V. New York, 1950, pp. 85–122.

676   *Sources and Literature*

Information on the living conditions, administration, and economy of the camp; it is also important as a comparison with conditions in T. In Łódź there was a workshop for the production of "winter toolboxes." The ghetto carpentry shops supplied the unfinished boxes, and the Germans supplied the tools needed for auto repairs in winter. The author does not say if this was a military contract, like "K-production" in T.

99. Herzberg, A. J.: *Kroniek der Joodenvervolging*. Partial printing of *Onderdrukking en Verzer*. No information [The Hague, 1951].

This thorough book gives the number of people deported from Holland to T (direct and via Bergen-Belsen) as 4,969, or 72 more than in the arrival lists at T. The short report on T is not without error.

100. Hirsch, C.: "Von Theresienstadt in die Schweiz." In *Der neue Weg*. No. 15/16. Vienna, 1946.

An accurate account by a member of the transport of February 1945.

101. Hirsch, G.: "Der Galgen von Theresienstadt." In *Das freie Wort*. Düsseldorf, January 12, 1952.

An account of the executions on January 10, 1942.

101a. Hirschberg, H. W.: "Christen im Ghetto." MS, Berlin, 1945.

The author was in T from February 10, 1944, until liberation and was active in Protestant community life. Services were led by Dr. Arthur Goldschmidt (*84), who painted an altarpiece used by both Christian denominations, and Dr. Otto Stargardt, who was in charge of the church music. At the beginning of September 1944, they were joined by the Dutch pastor Max Enker. In each of Stargardt's services, an intercession was recited for Martin Niemöller. Emphasis is placed on the good relationship between Protestants and Catholics, whose funeral services were taken over by the Protestants in autumn 1944, as the spokesmen for the Catholic Church had been deported. The author describes his fervent "missionary" activities in the camp.

102. Hitler, A.: *Mein Kampf*. 449th–453rd printings. Munich, 1939.

103. [Hitler] *Der Grossdeutsche Freiheitskampf: Reden Adolf Hitlers I–II*. 1 vol. Munich, 1943.

104. Hofer, H.: "Die Kuh. Die Theaterkarte." MS, T, ca. 1943.

Two popular camp couplets.

105. Hoffmann, C. [Camill]: "Sein letztes Gedicht." In *Aufbau*. New York, November 30, 1945.

The author, a well-known writer and translator from Kolin in Bohemia, was in T for almost three years and died in Auschwitz in autumn 1944.

106. [Holland] *Dagboek fragmenten 1940–1945*. The Hague, 1954.

A publication by the RvO that contains anonymous diary fragments about the persecution of the Jews in Holland, including reports on Barneveld, Westerbork, and Bergen-Belsen. Pages 389 et seq. and page 426 are fragments of a T diary in autumn 1944. The RvO has a considerable collection of other diaries from T and other camps.

106a. [Holland] "Dokumentbuch Albert Konrad Genmeker" (process-verbaal no. 414). [Dutch], mimeographed, Holland, 1948.

An important source on Westerbork, compiled from files from the trial of its commandant. The following table reports the number of people deported from Westerbork:

Time period	Transports	Destination	Transportees
July 15, 1942–September 3, 1944	83	Auschwitz, Sobibór	91,594
April 20, 1943–September 4, 1944	7	T	4,770
January 11, 1944–September 13, 1944	8	Bergen-Belsen	3,724
		Various camps	352
TOTAL			100,440

The difference between the number of Westerborkers in T given here and the number of prisoners who really arrived there from Holland arises from the fact that 297 people arrived in T without an intermediate stop in Westerbork, whereas others came to T from Westerbork via Bergen-Belsen. According to the Dutch RC, 4,350 deportees survived; according to other sources, up to 6,000 survived. The "Central Office" in the Hague was responsible for delivery to the camp. After the end of the deportations, 400 people remained in Westerbork; at liberation there were 1,000 inmates. The "holds" that originally provided protection from deportation were divided among ten lists:

1. The Puttkammer list (hidden Jews who were found and who bought their freedom from the punishment barracks for 10,000–30,000 guilders)
2. The Kallmeijer list (unresolved Mischling cases)
3. Protestants (members must have been baptized before May 10, 1940; Catholics were not similarly privileged)
4. The Palestine list (those possessing immigration certificates; they were to go to Palestine via Bergen-Belsen, which to some extent actually happened [*160c])
5. The Portuguese group (Sephardic Jews)
6. The Barneveld group (some 700 Dutch Jews, principally those with meritorious service to the country in the arts, sciences, etc.; they owed their protection to Frederik, the secretaris-generaal in the Departement voor Binnenlandse Zaken, who advocated for them with the Germans)
7. The T group (Jews from "Greater Germany" to whom the policies of the RSHA on deportation to T applied – that is, people with higher-level war medals, people seriously wounded in the war, notables, etc.)
8. Standing lists (internal camp functionaries whom Gemmeker considered indispensable)
9. The Diamond or Asscher family list (relatives of the deputy head of the Joodsen Raad and diamond workers)
10. The Cohen family list (relatives of the head of the Joodsen Raad)

Members of groups 3, 5–8, and 10 went to T (3, 6, and 10 remained completely protected from further deportation); groups 4 and 9 went to Bergen-Belsen (*114a).

678   *Sources and Literature*

106b. [Holland] [Transport lists and materials for deportations to T, etc.]. MSS, RvO, Holland, 1943/44.

See the samples in *3b, docs. 12–14.

106c. [Holland] *Joods Historisch Museum. Summary.* Amsterdam, no year.

A description of the Amsterdam Jewish Museum, with its collection of wartime documents, including a letter from the Gestapo to Seiss-Inquart on the Jews deported on February 25, 1944, from Westerbork to T (display case VI, no. 334).

106d. Höss, R.: "Die 'Endlösung der Judenfrage' im K. L. Auschwitz" [and other writings]. MS, WL, Cracow, 1946/47.

Notes by the first commandant of Auschwitz, written before his execution in Polish custody. In summer 1941 (the exact date is forgotten), Höss was summoned to Himmler, who assigned to him the mass murder of the Jews, on Hitler's orders. Himmler explained, "The Jews are the eternal enemy of the German people. All Jews we can get are to be exterminated now without exception during the war.... You will be given more details by Stubaf. Eichmann from the RSHA, who will come to you in the near future." Eichmann visited Höss soon after at Auschwitz and drafted the country-by-country extermination plan that was later formulated similarly in the Wannsee Protocol (see Chapter 2). As the means of murder the two chose gas, but Eichmann rejected gas wagons and the coal gas used for the murder of the mentally ill. He

> wanted to inquire about a gas that would be easy to obtain and required no special facilities....
>
> At the end of November [1941] there was a meeting of the entire ["]Jewish["] section in Eichmann's office in Berlin, to which I too was invited. Eichmann's representatives in the various countries reported on the status of the campaigns and on the difficulties ... such as accommodating prisoners, allocation of transport trains, scheduling conferences, etc. I could not yet find out the start of the campaigns. Nor had Eichmann yet gotten hold of suitable gas.

This gas was discovered by the preventive detention camp commander of Auschwitz, Hauptsurmführer (HSTF) Karl Fritsch, at approximately the same time. It was the disinfectant Zyklon B, which Fritsch tried out on Russian prisoners. Höss told Eichmann about this during his next visit, and they decided "to use this gas for the future mass extermination." The murders began "probably in December 1941, but perhaps not until January 1942." Himmler viewed the entire extermination process in summer 1942. "He found nothing about which to complain, but also did not talk about it." Himmler explained,

> The security police campaigns ordered by me may not be stopped on any account, least of all due to the shortage of accommodations etc. presented to me. Eichmann's program continues and will be increased from month to month. Make sure that you go forward with the construction of Birkenau.... Be just as ruthless in the extermination of Jews unable to work. In the near future, the work camps in the armaments industry will take on the first large contingents of Jews fit for work, and then you will get some breathing room.

Höss provides some remarkable character portraits. We learn that Eichmann was friendly with Kaltenbrunner and that he went to the SD after the occupation of

Sources and Literature

Austria and soon after to the Gestapo, until he ultimately took his final position with the RSHA. He had been an authority on the Jewish question "since his youth" and had visited Palestine in order to "get to know the Zionists and the nascent Jewish state on the spot." Because of "this knowledge, he became head of the Jewish section." Höss first came into contact with him during Eichmann's first visit to Auschwitz.

> Eichmann was a lively, always active man in his 30s, full of energy. He always had new plans and was always seeking innovations and improvements. He never rested. He was obsessed with the Jewish question and the ordered "Final Solution"! He constantly had to report directly and orally to the RF-SS about the preparations and implementation of the various campaigns.... He kept almost everything in his memory. His files were a couple of notes, with marks unintelligible to others, which he always carried with him. Even his permanent deputy in Berlin, Günther, could not always give thorough information. Eichmann was constantly on business trips; only rarely could one find him in Berlin at his office.... [His] staff had to have the transport trains ready and determine the schedules at the Reich Transport Ministry.... He acted with great certainty and concreteness, and was nevertheless very amiable and obliging, and was popular everywhere; people were glad to see him.... Eichmann was firmly convinced that, if Jewry in the East was successfully destroyed by complete extermination, Jewry would not be able to recover from the blow.... Eichmann was completely steeped in his task and also convinced that these extermination campaigns were necessary to, in the future, protect the German people from the Jews' wish to exterminate [them].... [He was a] determined opponent of the selection of Jews fit to work. He saw this as a constant threat to his "Final Solution" plans through mass escapes or other possible incidents. It was his view that all the campaigns ... should be implemented ... as rapidly as possible, since one never knew how the war would end. In 1943 he was already doubtful of a complete German victory and expected an inconclusive outcome.

On Müller, Höss says: "Müller remained fundamentally in the background; he did not like to be linked with any sorts of incidents or campaigns. And yet he was the one who organized and led all the important, major security police campaigns." After Heydrich's death, according to Höss, Müller took the lead, and Kaltenbrunner mainly dealt with the SD. Müller always acted in Himmler's name, although everyone in the know was aware that Müller made the decisions regarding prisoner questions; however, his personal view remained unknown. He seldom visited concentration camps, and he was never in Auschwitz. "I know from Eichmann and Günther that he [Müller] led even the most important aspects of the Jewish campaigns, although he gave Eichmann quite a free hand." Höss describes Müller as a tenacious worker, "very proper, but obliging and comradely; he never flaunted superiority or rank, but one could find no personal contact."

The texts on the "Final Solution" and Himmler are published in Broszat, M. (ed.): *Kommandant in Auschwitz*. IfZ, Stuttgart, 1958.

106e. Höss, R.: "Meine Psyche: Werden, Leben und Erleben." MS, WL, Cracow, 1947.

As in the writings mentioned in *106d, here, too, important clues are found on those in the SS mainly responsible for the "Final Solution."

> The RF-SS sent various high party and SS leaders to Auschwitz to watch the extermination of the Jews. All were very impressed. Some who had previously pontificated fervently about the necessity for this extermination went very quiet

upon seeing the "Final Solution of the Jewish Question" and kept silent. I was always asked how I, how my men, could constantly watch this procedure, how we could stand it?

I always answered that all human feelings had to be stilled – of the iron consistency with which we had to carry out the Führer's orders. Each of the gentlemen stated that he would not like to have this task.

Even Mildner [*42a, 121] and Eichmann, who were certainly "hard boiled," had no desire to switch with me. No one envied me *this* task.

I spoke many times with Eichmann about everything connected with the Final Solution of the Jewish Question, without ever confessing my inner difficulties. I attempted to get out of Eichmann his deepest, truest conviction about the "Final Solution." By all means. But even in the most advanced relaxed alcoholic state – just between us – he advocated, almost obsessively, the complete extermination of all Jews. Without mercy, ice cold, we had to carry out the extermination as quickly as possible. Any consideration, even the smallest amount, would come back to haunt us.

Höss tells of the two main attitudes in the SS toward the eradication policy.

The Jewish section – Eichmann/Günther – was unmistakably clear. According to the RF-SS order of summer 1941, all Jews were to be exterminated. The RSHA raised the most serious reservations when the RF-SS – at Pohl's suggestion – ordered the selection of those fit to work. The RSHA was always for the complete elimination of all Jews, and saw in every new work camp, in every new thousand of those fit to work, the danger of their liberation, their remaining alive, through some circumstance.

Pohl wanted to gain as many slave laborers as possible from every extermination transport, which Himmler applauded.

On the other hand, however, the RF-SS also wanted to exterminate as many Jews as possible. . . .

Because Pohl allowed himself to be misled by the RF-SS's ever-higher deployment demands, he unintentionally abetted the desires of the RSHA, since as a result of his pressure to fulfill what was demanded, countless thousands of prisoners died from work deployment, because pretty much all the living conditions absolutely necessary for such masses of prisoners were lacking.

The text is published in the IfZ publication Broszat, M. (ed.): *Kommandant in Auschwitz*. Stuttgart, 1958.

107. Hronek, J.: *Černá kniha Heydrichova režimu* [Black Book of the Heydrich Regime]. London, 1942.

Information on Heydrich's leadership from September 1941 to January 1942, portrayed in broadcasts on Prague radio.

108. Hvass, F.: "Besøg i Theresienstadt den 23. Juni 1944." MS, Copenhagen, 1944.

An official report by the Danish member of the delegation from the Foreign Ministry, based on personal impressions and information from Eppstein and the SS. The report ended as follows:

To conclude this report, I cannot fail to express my admiration that one must have for the Jews, who have made it possible, through their unique efforts, to create relatively good outward conditions for their coreligionists within the framework of the self-administration and to instill in them courage and strength to continue their lives.

Whether they will succeed in preserving this courage will – as we found confirmed during our stay in the city – probably depend to a not-inconsequential degree on the population's belief that their stay in Theresienstadt is of only a temporary character.

(188a)

108a. Ikle: "Sanitäre Verhältnisse im ehemaligen Ghetto Theresienstadt." MS, St. Gallen, June 15, 1945.

Three portions of this source are noteworthy:

1. The Russians working in T – 52 doctors and 340 nurses in five emergency infirmaries since May 13 – record 3,500 patients hospitalized and 15,000 people deloused in two weeks. The typhus epidemic was contained in three and a half weeks. At first there were 100–200 new illnesses at most per day; this figure soon dropped to 10–15. They could not determine the beginning of the epidemic, but there probably were no cases by April 20.
2. The Czechs emphasize the Russian contributions as well as the value of food and medications from the IRC.
3. Docent Stein, head of the Health Services Department, confirms the Russian figures and praises their achievements. "On the activity of the Czech aid organizations, Dr. Stein was more reserved." The number of sick people, including spotted fever cases, is given as up to 3,500. The main problem is described as the internal difficulties, the lack of desire to work among most of the long-term inmates, and the unstable condition of the former concentration camp prisoners (*62a, 340a).

109. Iltis, [R.]: "Bilance roku 1941" [Balance of the Year 1941]. In 319, no. 51/52, 1951.

Excerpts (translated) from the JKG 1941 annual report for the "Central Office." Following are some samples (retranslated):

The following special campaigns were carried out: On September 17, 1941, 248,000 Jewish stars were distributed, on October 1 the registration of the Jews was begun and a total of 88,105 people registered; these also were informed of the prohibition on disposing of their property; on October 25, 1941, 1,928 typewriters were confiscated and 3,317 bicycles, on December 20, 1941, 16,971 sets of ski equipment were confiscated from the Jews, 1,415 phonographs and 30,063 phonograph records. At the same time, 7,893 sewing machines were registered. On December 26, 1941, 4,893 musical instruments were confiscated, 2,411 cameras with accessories, and 531 technical meters....

The work necessary for the ghetto was dealt with in Prague by the liaison office [of the JKG], whose main function is to obtain raw materials and objects that are needed by the ghetto administration [in T].

110. I[ltis], [R.]: "Hasičský abor v terezínském ghetto" [The Fire Department in the Theresienstadt Ghetto]. In 319, no. 2, 1947.

Haindl committed arson in the camp in 1945 (as Görner also claims in *86), including the final fire on May 4, when he set the shoe repair workshop in the Südbaracken on fire.

On February 28, 1945 he set 12 fires at different ends of the city, almost simultaneously, while not allowing the fire department to be alerted. Only when [the fires] took on

682   *Sources and Literature*

greater dimensions did he give permission to call them. Finally, when the firemen were busy extinguishing the fire, he set a fire in the cellar of the fire department headquarters.

But see *308. The author reports implausible things about illegal work by the fire department: it was supposedly an information center for reports that were listened to on a radio in the cellar of the youth home L 417. It was also claimed to possess a "secret weapons storehouse" with ammunition and medicines.

111. Iltis, [R.]: "Jak došlo k založení terezínského ghetta" [How the Theresienstadt Ghetto Came to Be Established]. In 319, no. 48, 1948.

A description based on the documents in Chapter 2 on the Prague history of the camp.

112. Iltis, R.: "My, děti, žalujeme!" [We Children Accuse!]. In 319, no. 22, 1950.

The essay contains "Strach" (Fear), a poem by twelve-year-old Eva Picková, written in T. The child died in Auschwitz.

112a. Iltis, R.: "Osvobození terezinského ghetta" [The Liberation of the Theresienstadt Ghetto]. In 319, no. 5, 1955.

The author was in T from February 11, 1945. A Czech flag raised on May 5 was removed at Dunant's orders. The text provides a chronology of May 8: At 9 A.M. there is shooting at the west wing of E VI. At 10 A.M. there is renewed shooting. During the day, German tanks drive back and forth through T, sometimes toward the north, and sometimes toward the south (probably on the bypass road). At 6 P.M. a house near the railway station is damaged by grenades, resulting in dead (*sic*) and wounded; ten minutes later, there is renewed shooting, and the heaviest German tanks drive south. At 7 P.M., a Russian tank spearheads nearby; at 9 P.M., the first Russian tanks drive through T, and others follow.

113. Iltis, [R.]: "SS-Hauptsturmführer Seidel 'konal svou povinnost'" [... "has done his duty"]. In 319, no. 12, 1946.

An unrewarding description of the trial before the Vienna People's Court from September 26 to October 3, 1946.

114. Iltis, [R.]: "Statečný zachránce důležitých listin" [A brave rescuer of important documents]. In 319, no. 18, 1947.

A report on the rich collection of Josef Polák (an official in the "Central Registry"), on which Lederer's book (*166) is based.

114a. Israels, S.: "Het leven en verblijf in de joodse kampen Barneveld, Westerbork en Theresienstadt gevolgd door internering in Zwitserland" [Life and Sojourn in the Jewish Camps Barneveld, Westerbork, and Theresienstadt and the Subsequent Internment in Switzerland]. MS, Holland, no year.

A factual, impersonal description. The information on Barneveld is connected here with fortunate communications from Mr. M. Poppers. The general secretary of the Dutch Ministry of the Interior, Frederiks, used his connections to General Commissar Schmidt from the German civil administration to protect several Jewish friends. At first he limited himself to the children of his native city of Middelburg. Later, their families were added, and, additionally, they added officers in ministries and people

Sources and Literature 683

whom the general secretary of the Education Ministry, J. van Dam, had placed on a list: professors, doctors, lawyers, teachers, artists, journalists, generals, and so on, always with their families. Money did not decisively qualify one to be on the list; connections to Frederiks or van Dam were the only guaranteed method. In order not to subject the protected people, who had received identification cards, from the risk of Gestapo "infringements," starting on December 16, 1942, they were brought, in their own interests – that is, not forcibly – to a rundown palace in Barneveld with an estate. The count rose from 400 to 700 people. The camp was under Dutch command and was closed on September 29, 1943, by the SS, who brought all the inmates – except for 15 escapees – to Westerbork. Conditions in Barneveld were favorable; the personnel were exemplary; the food was decent, if not entirely sufficient; and receipt of packages and free exchange of letters were permitted. At first even vacations were possible. Cultural events had to be authorized by the camp leader. Every morning, people listened to British radio. Aside from the Barnevelders, who were not brought via T to the East, the Dutch Reformed who had been baptized (before the cutoff date of May 10, 1940) were also privileged in this way. These included Zionists and other self-conscious Jews who had gotten themselves baptismal certificates. In addition, there was a small camp, Doetinchen, in which Jews were interned at the personal recommendation of the Dutch Nazi leader Mussert. These included Jo Spier, who knew Mussert but was, Popper assures us, not a Nazi. Aside from Spier, all Jews from the Doetinchen camp were murdered, despite Mussert's protection.

Israels's portrayal of conditions in Westerbork and T is accurate. The trip to T, where he arrived with the Barnevelders on September 6, 1944, took thirty-five hours (the train, with 2,081 deportees, was switched from Bauschowitz [Bohušovice] in parts). Train personnel unhesitatingly provided the information, in bad German, that camp conditions had been bad before but had improved in the last few months and were now decent.

Those summoned for the Swiss transport had to go to C 1, where their personal information was recorded only if they wished to travel. Those who were willing were called to the courtyard of B V and were summoned to the office, where academics and businessmen were selected out. Those allowed to travel received a stamp in their identification cards. They were to dress well and make themselves ready. Ample food was distributed: bread, rolls, cakes, margarine, sausage, sugar, milk powder, and vitamin pills. During the trip, marmalade, jam, and a large jar of Ovaltine were given out. They left T on February 5, 1945, at 4 P.M.; the Swiss military took over the transport on the border soon after midnight on February 6. From the border town of Kreuzlingen, where there was a magnificent reception, the liberated people arrived on the evening of February 7 in St. Gallen (for more on this transport, see *3b, docs. 50–51).

114b. [Izbica] "Letter from the Jewish Council of Izbica on May 4, 1942 to the Jewish Council of Lublin." MS, HIŻ.

Regarding Transport from Theresienstadt on April 30, 1942.
On the aforementioned day, a transport from the Protectorate arrived here; it consisted of some 600 persons and, according to their own information, approximately 400 work-capable men, whose family members are now here, remained in Lublin. Should this information be based in truth, we ask that you provide the addresses of these workers or inform us to whom the family members here can write through your mediation.

684   *Sources and Literature*

The transport in question was one of 1,000 people (453 men and 547 women: 92 children up to fourteen years old, 412 people aged fifteen to forty-five, 324 people aged forty-six to sixty, and 172 people over sixty), which left T on April 27, 1942. Only one person survived the war.

115. Jacobson, J.: *Terezín: The Daily Life, 1943–1945*. Appendix: Cohen, D.: "The Russians in Terezín." London, 1946.

Jacobson's report is not always accurate; anything referring to the first two camp years is largely wrong. Cohen's short report is accurate.

115a. Jacobson, J.: "The Theresienstadt Ghetto." In *AJR Information*. London, April 1959.

A positive appraisal of Eppstein, which is gently critical of my portrayal. What Jacobson, like many others, fails to recognize is the fact that I do not attack the tragic failure of Eppstein and other leading or more minor functionaries, or even the tragic failure of every person acting in the camp (see Chapter 20), or their forced cooperation in things that in *any* case would be their undoing; rather, I attack the very personal failure that became guilt, independent of and beyond any collective individual tragedy due to function. I can only refer my critics again and again – and this is true of Eppstein as of others – to the incidents described and documented in my books. See the German translation, entitled "Gerechtigkeit für Paul Eppstein," in 243c.

116. Jacoby, G.: *Racial State: The German Nationalities Policy in the Protectorate of Bohemia-Moravia*. New York, 1944.

A thorough portrayal, based on sources, of the general and Jewish situation in the "Protectorate" until around spring 1944. Little is known about T (pp. 241–44) that is true; however, its propaganda role is suspected. The number of deportees from T is greatly overestimated at more than 400,000. The text features a valuable bibliography.

117. [Jewish tragedy] *Das "Wannsee-Protokoll" zur Endlösung der Judenfrage*. Düsseldorf, 1952.

The text of the notorious document, including later supplementary protocols.

118. [Jewish tragedy] *Extermination of Polish Jews: Album of Pictures* [Polish title: Zaglada żydostwa polskiego]. Łódź, 1945.

This picture book, mainly composed of captured German photos, reveals the Jewish tragedy in Poland, which was shared by everyone from the West and the deportees from T.

119. [Jewish tragedy] *Hitler's Ten-Year War on the Jews*. New York, 1943.

The situation of Central European Jews until around the end of 1942 is quite correctly presented. Its references to T are surprisingly precise. It is noteworthy that here, as in other wartime publications, it is emphasized how little is known abroad about internal camp conditions in T, whereas many precise details about the tragedy in the East had gotten through to the outside.

120. [Jewish tragedy] *Jews in Nazi Europe: February 1933 to November 1941*. Baltimore, MD, 1941.

Sources and Literature 685

This text is correct regarding Germany and excellently informed about the "Protectorate" up to October 1, 1941.

121. [Jewish tragedy] *Nazi Germany's War against the Jews.* New York, 1947.

A documentary report about the extermination of the Jews, based on the main Nuremberg Trial and its evidentiary material. The German documents are translated. Mildner's protocol 2375-PS is most easily accessible here. Mildner came to Copenhagen on September 15, 1943, as Sipo head and soon after was assigned the campaign against the Danish Jews (see *41 and Chapters 3 and 6). He claims to have opposed the order vis-à-vis his superiors for his own reasons; Eichmann then forced its implementation, and it was carried out by his henchmen. This may be true, but Mildner is also trying to exonerate himself with his statements, and they deserve little credit, because before his appointment in Denmark he was Gestapo chief in Kattowitz and repeatedly visited Auschwitz (*42a, 106e).

122. [Jewish tragedy] *The Black Book: The Nazi Crime against the Jewish People.* New York, 1946.

A first attempt at a summary. The text is unreliable and completely outdated. Only the reproductions of some documents are useful. Its information on Central Europe, and especially on T, is misguided and generally wrong. Three texts refer to T: (1) Klaus Mann describes the situation of the divorced wife of Heinrich Mann, who was liberated in T; (2) a journalist visited T, and the *New York Times* published his report – a model of the kind of unprincipled, sensational scribbling in the early postwar period that became for a long time a serious obstacle to sincere reporting and scholarly research into the problems posed; (3) a letter from a woman released in Switzerland in February 1945 is reproduced – it contains incorrect, sometimes bizarre statements about T (pp. 292–97). Original documents, too, such as the "ghetto money" in T, are interpreted wrongly or fancifully.

123. [Jewish tragedy] *Trial of the Major War Criminals.* Nuremberg, 1946/9.

Volume XXVI, pages 266 et seq., 710-PS: Göring's letter to Heydrich in July 1941, cited in Chapter 2.

Volume XXVII, pages 251 et seq., 1472-PS: Müller's letter to Himmler on December 16, 1942, on 10,000 Jews from T, cited in Chapter 3.

Volume XXVIII, pages 499–540, 1816-PS: A protocol of a discussion of principles on the Jewish question, in Göring's office, on November 12, 1938.

Volume XXX, pages 290 et seq. 2376-PS: Dr. Mildner's protocol on the originators of the deportation orders, cited in Chapter 3.

Volume XXXI, pages 1 et seq., 2605-PS: A protocol by Dr. R. Kas[z]tner that briefly repeats the facts contained in his report (*135).

Volume XXXI, pages 85 et seq., 2378-PS: A protocol of Dr. Höttl on a meeting with Eichmann at the end of August 1944, stating that 4 million Jews had been killed in extermination camps and 2 million Jews (mainly in the USSR) had been killed in other ways. Because Höttl's statements were those of an SS officer, it becomes clear that the German authorities estimated the number of people murdered to be quite high. Even if the actual number was lower, as we would hope, we can see how pathetic it is that certain Germans lowered this figure by millions, entirely aside from the fact that in a mass murder of such gigantic proportions, reducing the number of victims does not reduce the guilt.

686   *Sources and Literature*

Volume XXXVIII, pages 60 et seq., 219-L: A RSHA organizational plan as of September 1943. We cite the key to this plan in Chapter 1; in earlier days, Eichmann's office had the number IV A 4.

124. [Jewish tragedy] *Trials of War Criminals before the Nuremberg Military Tribunals.* Washington, D.C., 1952.

Volume V, pages 810 et seq., contains Wisliceny's statement, which indicates that in autumn 1942 Eichmann informed many of his subordinates, including H. Günther and two T commandants, Seidl and Burger, of the meaning of the "Final Solution." Wisliceny was a voluble and often unreliable witness. Eichmann's assistants certainly were aware much earlier (*3b, doc. 1; see also 2a, 106d, 175b), but the information is interesting and illuminates the special role of T, as well as the purpose of the letters sent by the deportees. In August 1942, Eichmann informed Wisliceny

> of a number of measures which he [Eichmann] had taken in order to keep these things absolutely secret. He mentioned that he was maintaining Theresienstadt for this reason in order to be able to take commissions of the International Red Cross or foreign diplomats into the Theresienstadt camp, to make it appear as though the standard at Theresienstadt was the normal standard of accommodation for the Jews. Besides, he had thought out a special system of postcards and letters, whereby he believed he could mislead the public. The Jews brought to Auschwitz or to other extermination camps were forced, prior to being murdered, to write post cards. These post cards – there were always several for each person – were then mailed at long intervals, in order to make it appear as though these persons were still alive."

Volume XIV, page 513, deals with the campaign to help Jewish children; this effort's significance for the history of T is touched upon in Chapters 3 and 6.

The way in which the extermination of the Jews was known beyond the RSHA (which was at least in part developed out of offices in the Ministry of the Interior) is important. At the trial of Wilhelm Stuckart, state secretary in the Ministry of the Interior, Ministerial Counsel Globke gave evidence: "I knew that the Jews were being killed in large numbers, and I was always of the opinion that there were Jews who were still living in Germany, or in Theresienstadt, or elsewhere in a sort of ghetto" (p. 642). Defense counsel then asked, "You thought that there were executions but no systematic extermination?" Globke answered, "I am of the opinion, and I knew this at the time, that the extermination of the Jews was carried on systematically, but I did not know that it was supposed to apply to all Jews."

125. [Jewish tragedy] *Decrees, Directives, Notifications.* Published by the Party Chancellery. Munich, no year.

Volume 3 of this seven-volume work, which was only for internal party use, contains an announcement – on pages 131 et seq., under the heading "V. L 66/881 on 10/9/ 1942" – that to my knowledge has been published only in translation (as document 3244-PS of the main Nuremberg Trial in *121 and elsewhere) and never in the original. Because it is a unique acknowledgement of the "Final Solution of the Jewish Question" after the Wannsee Conference (*117) and of the rumors and voices of conscience then arising in Germany against the mass murder, the text is supplied here in its entirety:

Sources and Literature

Preparatory Measures for the Final Solution of the European Jewish Question – Rumors on the Situation of the Jews in the East

In the course of work on the Final Solution of the Jewish Question, there have recently been discussions among the population in various parts of the Reich territory about "very harsh measures" against the Jews, especially in the Eastern territories. It has been found that such remarks have been passed on – generally in distorted or exaggerated form – by people on leave from the various organizations operating in the East, and who themselves have had the opportunity to observe such measures.

It is conceivable that not all fellow Germans will have sufficient understanding of the necessity of such measures, especially not those parts of the population who have not had the opportunity to gain a sense of the Bolshevik horror through their own experience.

In order to confront any formation of rumors in this context, which often are of a consciously tendentious character, the following remarks are conveyed for briefing on the current state of affairs.

For some 2,000 years, a heretofore fruitless battle has been fought against the Jews. Only since 1933 have we set to work finding ways and means of making possible a complete separation of Jewry from the body of the German nation. The solutions implemented so far may be categorized essentially as follows:

1. Forcing the Jews out of various areas of the life of the German people.

Here the foundation is laid by the laws passed by the legislature; these guarantee that future generations will be protected from being overwhelmed by the enemy.

2. The effort to force the enemy completely out of the Reich territory.

In consideration of the narrowly limited living space [*Lebensraum*] available to the German people, we hoped to solve this problem essentially by accelerating emigration of the Jews.

Since the beginning of the war in 1939, these emigration opportunities have decreased to a growing extent; on the other hand, in addition to the German people's living space, its economic space has also consistently increased, so that today, in consideration of the large number of Jews living in these territories, no complete elimination is possible through emigration.

Because our next generation already will no longer see this question as so essential and, based on their experiences, will no longer see it as clearly, and the matter that has already been started calls for resolution, the entire problem must be solved by the current generation.

Thus the complete expulsion or elimination of the millions of Jews located in the European economic area is an urgent necessity in the battle to ensure the existence of the German people.

Beginning with the Reich territory and transitioning to the other European countries included in the Final Solution, the Jews will be transported routinely to the East to camps, some of which already exist, some of which will be built, from which they will either be used for work or brought still farther east. The old Jews, as well as Jews with distinguished war decorations (Iron Cross First Class, Gold Medal for Bravery, etc.) will be routinely resettled to the city of Theresienstadt, located in the Protectorate of Bohemia and Moravia.

It is in the nature of the matter that these sometimes very difficult problems can be solved only through ruthless harshness, in the interests of ensuring the ultimate safety of our people.

The text, read carefully, requires no comment. It should only be noted that at the same time as this notification, 10,000 "old Jews" from the "city" of T had been "brought" "still farther east" to White Russia, and 6,000 "old Jews" had vanished into Treblinka.

126. Juratolt, S.: *Předpisy o židovském majetku a další předpisy Židů se týkající* [Regulations on Jewish Property and Other Regulations Relating to Jews]. Prague, 1942.

A thoroughly annotated resource on the most important property-law conditions arising from expropriation, especially through deportation, as of September 1942.

127. Juřašek, S.: *Ansprüche der Gläubiger bei der Abwicklung des jüdischen Vermögens und bei der Beschlagnahme des Vermögens.* Prague, 1942.

A source similar to *126, as of June 1942.

128. Kafka, G.: "Alexander in Jerusalem." MS, T, 1943.

A drama whose theme alludes to the present and places its hopes in a good end. On the author, see Chapter 19.

129. Kafka, G.: "Der Tod des Orpheus" [staged poem]. MS, T, 1943.

The best-regarded poem in T; it was written there. It does not make any allusions to T or the period.

129a. Kafka, G.: "Poems." MS, T, 1942/43.

Four poems found so far. Other known works by the author, including a puppet show, *Golem* (1944), have not surfaced. A short autobiographical sketch has been preserved (1943).

130. Kafka, G.: "Märchen vom Regen und dem goldenen Kipferl." MS, T, 1943.

A prose poem without any allusions to T or the period.

131. Kalwo, O.: "Wir fahren aus Theresienstadt." MS, DA, Prague, 1945.

This text describes transport to Auschwitz and reception there.

132. Kantorowicz, Gertrud: *Verse aus Theresienstadt.* No information. [Printed privately in the United States, 1948].

The author arrived in T on August 6, 1942, and died there on April 19, 1945. The camp as a subject shimmers through the skillful verses.

133. Kantorowicz, N.: "Excerpts of Letters from the Protectorate and Slovakia." In *Facts and Documents.* World Jewish Congress, New York, June 1943.

This work is mentioned in the bibliography of *116.

134. Kapper, K.: "Gedichte." MS, T, 1942/44.

Seven poems on camp themes.

Karrass: *46a.

135. Kasztner, R.: *Der Bericht des jüdischen Rettungskomitees aus Budapest 1942 bis 1945.* No information. [Geneva, 1946].

The activities of the committee and Kasztner play a role in the history of T through an aid mission in May 1944 and in the final months of the war. The author was assailed by Hungarian Jews (*170), but his achievements may be interpreted as an extremely clever attempt by a Jew to gain what he could from the RSHA, in the interests of endangered Jews, through personal negotiations. The report, unfortunately only privately copied and difficult to access, is an impressive, directly absorbing work that has been too little noted by historians and has not yet been used for information on the internal situation of Central European Jewry in the Hitler period and on the mentality of Eichmann and his assistants. Of fundamental importance is the clearly recognized psychology of the responsible Jewish leaders – who became, like it or not, executors for the SS – along with the ethical consequences that arose from this.

In 1956, a book by A. Weissberg appeared in Cologne. *Die Geschichte von Joel Brand* used Kasztner's book extensively, but more as a source for rumormongering and without considering the deeper problems; it describes the adventures of this assistant of Kasztner's and his achievements. The work does not substitute for publication of Kasztner's work, which should be made generally available as soon as possible as a memorial to this man's controversial activities, after the trials held against him and his murder by three Jewish fanatics in Israel in 1957 (for additional details on Kasztner's activities, see *2a).

136. Kaufmann, M.: *Churbn Lettland: Die Vernichtung der Juden Lettlands*. Munich, 1947. [Reprinted in German- and English-language editions, Konstanz, 2010].

A thorough description of the Riga ghetto, and so on. An evacuation transport to T at the end of the war is mentioned (*223c, 345a, 348).

137. Kautsky, B.: *Teufel und Verdammte*. Zurich, 1946.

Important information on the mentality of Jewish prisoners who do not know why they are suffering.

138. Kermisz, J.: *Akcje I wysiedlienia* ["Actions" and Resettlements]. Vol. II of *Dokumenty I materiały*. Warsaw, 1946.

Annotated documents. On page 32 et seq. there is mention of the transports from T to Izbica in March 1942, and on page 49, of the transport on April 8, 1942, to Rejowiece.

138a. Kersten, F.: "Memorandum über meine Hilfstätigkeit in den Jahren 1940–45." MS, RvO, Stockholm, June 1945.

Kersten's first notation of his humanitarian activities as Himmler's doctor; in subsequent books he describes this more thoroughly but not always with exactly the same details. He helped to prepare the Musy mission (*2a, 85a, 192b, 192c) in the following way: On August 2, 1944, an elderly patient, Ms. Immfeld of St. Gallen, asked "me for support for a mission that the IRC and a number of well-known Swiss industrialists had been planning for some time. It involved the release of approx. 20,000 Jews from various concentration camps ... and their conveyance through Switzerland to southern France, where they would remain interned until the end of the war." Kersten asked Himmler to receive Swiss representatives, including Musy. On November 28, 1944, Ms. Immfeld came again and reported on negotiations by some Germans in Zurich (Kersten did not know that this involved Himmler's envoy Standartenführer [STDF] Becher, accompanied by Kasztner [*2a]) on the release of ordinary Jews in exchange for a ransom of fifty Swiss francs and of prominent Jews for five hundred Swiss francs, which they were prepared to do, despite indignation. Himmler told Kersten that he had spoken with Musy; the money would make it easier to get Hitler's agreement to the operation and could be used to buy trucks and tractors. Later, Himmler refused the money.

139. Kersten, F.: *Totenkopf und Treue: Heinrich Himmler ohne Uniform*. Hamburg, no year [1952].

140. [Kersten, F.] *The Memoirs of Doctor Felix Kersten*. New York, 1947.

Although Hitler's idiosyncrasies are already clear from many publications (e.g., *56, or Bullock's major study and the "table talk"), there is still a lack of serious accounts or scholarly studies that seek to understand the other leading Jew exterminators in National Socialism. Here, important works now are available for an understanding of Himmler. The basic paranoid characteristics of mechanical materialism of the Nazi type become convincingly clear in these reports. Important spotlights also fall on Heydrich and other men, as well as on the formation of the SS. Eichmann is hardly mentioned, for which reason I asked the author by mail for information. Kersten barely knew Eichmann, but he told me that, even in leading SS circles, he was not well regarded. Kersten wrote, "Later I once asked Himmler about Eichmann, as I wanted some clarity about the man. Himmler answered evasively that I shouldn't ask him about him, that was an unpleasant story, but Hitler needed people like that too – we should talk about something more pleasant." The task remains to explore the characters of Heydrich (*95d), Kaltenbrunner, Heinrich Müller (*95d, 106d), and Eichmann (*106d, 106e). For us, the important thing is Kersten's intervention in T's history, and the extent to which Himmler proved to be receptive to Kersten's positive influence. He was the middleman for the campaign that led to the transport to Switzerland on February 5, 1945, and for an extensive rescue operation benefiting numerous groups who were liberated in cooperation with the Swedish foreign minister Günther by the Swedish RC. With the help of the Dane Hvass, this led, in T, to the liberation of the Danish Jews on April 15, 1945. Count Folke Bernadotte was to be the implementer of this work of liberation, but (see two articles on Kersten by Trevor-Roper in *The Atlantic Monthly* of February and April 1953) he badly endangered Kersten's work through anti-Jewish remarks to Himmler. Ultimately this unconscionable and unauthorized act by the count could only be smoothed over in Kersten's last discussion with Himmler, when a noteworthy conference took place on the night of April 20, 1945 between Himmler and Masur. Kersten's description of this discussion, which he brokered, is consistent with that of Masur (*182).

141. Kien, P.: "Der König von Atlantis, oder Der Tod dank tab. Legende in vier Bildern." [Music by Victor Ullmann]. MS, T, ca. 1943.

This text features a few allusions to T. The music has been preserved (like other of Ullmann's compositions from T deserving of notice).

142. Kien, P.: "Die grossen Fünf. Ein Märchen." MS, T, ca. 1943.

Dramatic poetry.

142a. Kien, P.: "Gedichte." MS, T, 1943.

Twenty-five poems. See samples and further details in *3b, doc. 179. Six official and three private drawings by Kien are also reproduced there (*45, 82, 95, 103, 104, 202–04).

Sources and Literature

143. Kien, P.: "Sabbatai Zwi." MS, T, 1943.

A drama.

143a. [Children's drawings] *Exhibition of Paintings by Children of the Theresienstadt Ghetto 1941–1945*. Jerusalem, no year [1959].

An exhibition catalogue for 201 of the approximately 4,000 children's drawings from the collection of the Prague Jewish Museum. The text contains eight reproductions and three children's poems in the Czech original and in English and Hebrew translation. Similar exhibits have been and are being mounted in many countries.

144. Klaber, J.: "Ein Jahr Theresienstadt." MS, T, 1942.

The text of a speech by Klaber on November 24, 1942, on the work of the "Security Service."

145. Klaber, J.: [Theresienstadt]. MS, Prague, ca. 1945/46.

A book fragment by the first head of the "Ghetto Guard," with important information on the early period in the camp. The account does not go beyond 1942.

146. Klang, H.: "Denkschrift über die Ausübung der Gerichtsbarkeit in Theresienstadt." MS, T, May 1945.

146a. Klang, H.: "'Rechtsordnung' in Theresienstadt." In *Der Bund*. Bern, August 6, 1946.

An essay on the courts, criminal law, family law, and inheritance law.

146b. Klein, F.: "Anmerkungen." MS, Buenos Aires, 1956.

I thank Mr. Klein, who was in T from January 18, 1942, to autumn of 1944, for these notes, written for the first edition of this book. Some of what could otherwise not be included is provided here.

Regarding page 100, Chapter 5: "The crematorium plans were already begun in January 1942; at the instructions of the commandant, the original small facility (*46b) was increasingly enlarged. Given the inhabitants of the camp at the time, the capacity seemed too large – proof of the SS's intentions, which were already set at the time."

Regarding page 127-128, Chapter 6:

> I read an illegal letter from Birkenau in which the sender reported quite clearly in early 1944 about the theft and the general conditions (child murder), only about the gas chambers he did not dare to write. He mentioned sulfur pits and exhaust gas and hinted at high death rates. Therefore, I thought at my own deportation that there were sulfur pits in Auschwitz, where the working conditions led to high death rates.

Regarding page 135, Chapter 6: The "signposts," the poster "Mr. Cvok," and some other things were designed by Peter Kien, whereas Fritta, the head artist in the camp, strictly refused to help with the "beautification." The music pavilion was decorated with carved friezes (designed by Kien or Spier).

Regarding page 155-156, Chapter 7: After the departure of the men's transports, Ms. Zucker made a speech in C III "in which she is said to have declared that she herself would be the first to volunteer, in order to follow her husband and build a new ghetto. She supposedly called upon wives and mothers to follow her example."

692   *Sources and Literature*

There seems no doubt that this speech was made, although it is surprising, for Zucker himself was well-informed, smart, and skeptical; he distrusted the SS's intentions extremely. Most judges consider it unlikely that he believed in the destination of the transport given by the SS and his task in it. Why he went on the transport without any resistance, without warning the youth or even his wife, is inexplicable and probably never will be explained. He has been reproached for not inciting a revolt, but he knew quite well that any such attempt would have been drowned in blood. According to Lederer's testimony, Murmelstein took leave of Zucker in tears, because the SS insisted that he and Schliesser ride in a special car, against which Zucker protested (*166, page 152). Klein mentions that of the thirty-four women in his mother's living room, thirty-two volunteered for the transport, which was typical of the mood at the time.

Regarding page 219, Chapter 8: At Edelstein's orders, the

> statistical information meant for Eichmann had to be illustrated, often in a way that Germans could view as "atrocity propaganda." The illustrators were Fritta and Kien. . . .
>
> Edelstein placed great importance on these illustrations and hoped they would be appreciated by the SS! Under Eppstein, the illustrations were once again left out. Edelstein attempted to use the SS's love of statistics by making the most ridiculous attempts to put the SS in a good mood. Example: graphically decorated "status reports" to Bergel and Seidl in the commandant's office. The reports to Seidl consisted of six large boards, each one approx. 1 m by 60 cm, corresponding to the [at the time] six main departments in the administration. The data gave information on the daily status of workers and the sick in all departments, the situation in the hospitals, etc. The number boards were changeable and were revised each day by a prisoner, which could take up to an hour. For his own pleasure, Bergel had a death curve on the wall. One day he complained to Edelstein that there were few deaths. At that, the system was changed: the daily number of deaths was no longer entered, as it fluctuated, since deaths did not always increase; instead, the data were used cumulatively, that is, the curve had to rise, mainly steeply. Bergel was enthusiastic about this curve, and in June 1942, as space had been planned only till the end of 1942, he indignantly demanded that it be lengthened. The SS gloated to visitors about this statistical data.

Regarding page 370, Chapter 13: In early 1944, "it was tacitly tolerated, probably on 'higher' orders, that one remained absent from his normal work all day and worked in his 'beautification' kitchen garden."

Regarding page 377-378, Chapter 14:

> One day Bergel gave the assignment that a stamp album be made for him by the next day. Based on data in the central registry, philatelists were mustered during the night and, without the help of catalogues, really completed an album, which was presented in the morning, bound. Seidl, in his turn, demanded a family tree be drawn, as he had supposedly found two ancestors from the 13th generation. When it was pointed out in a memo that, for 8,000 elements, the table would be 8 meters long, with only 1 mm per name, Seidl demanded a "pocket-sized format." The problem was solved by dividing everything into large squares, as in geographic maps, and folding the paper.

Regarding page 514, Chapter 18: The group that built the firing range

> was treated by the Wehrmacht members decently, in fact well, almost without exception. Typical of the psychology of the prisoners was that, during the march through Leitmeritz [Litoměřice], they counted the women in mourning ("today we met x widows, the Nazis

Sources and Literature 693

must be doing badly"). In addition, it was graphically demonstrated on the way that all of Germany was one large camp; one saw Russian prisoners of war, Poles marked as Eastern workers, and felt that one might have been on the lowest level, but there were others suffering a comparable fate. On the march, one read the headlines of the newspapers displayed in Leitmeritz [Litoměřice]. Sometimes it was even organized in such a way that individuals each read certain lines or newspapers, since the speed did not allow for actual reading. We sought cigarette butts on the road in the middle of the city. The Wehrmacht members seemed to be completely uninformed about the situation in the ghetto. I took a piece of paper and a pencil and, during the long midday pause, placidly wrote an illegal letter. I asked a soldier for a – hard to obtain – envelope, as well as a stamp, with the excuse that I had forgotten them. I myself threw a letter into the mailbox while getting water in town; another time I asked a soldier to do it; he helped without question. A corporal from Leipzig, a teacher, told me, while we were working in a group of five apart from the others, that he knew everything, we were suffering a terrible injustice, we would get everything back someday. The psychological effect of such incidents was unbelievable. Another told me that his ideal was imprisonment by the English until the end of the war.

A telegraph from Himmler, important to the history of this work group, is published in *3b, doc. 218.

147. Klein, R.: "Protocol." [Czech], MS, DA, Prague, 1945.

The author, who was in T from May 1942 to autumn 1944, worked in the pathology department. The text contains a description of funeral services and the crematorium.

148. Kočka, V.: *Lidice: Dějiny a poslední dnové vsi* [Lidice: History and Last Days of a Village]. Aussig [Ústí nad Laben], 1946.

On page 83, there is a protocol by Bohumil Smolka, who belonged to the burial kommando from T in Lidice.

149. Kogon, E.: *Der SS-Staat: Das System der deutschen Konzentrationslager.* 2nd ed. Berlin, 1947.

To this day, this text is the foundational and unsurpassed work on the subject. It is important for understanding the sociology of both the SS and the prisoners.

150. Kogon, E.: *Der SS-Staat.* Dusseldorf, 1946.

The first edition of *149. It is important because of some parts that were later shortened.

151. Kolár, E.: *Daleká cesta* [The Long Way]. [Script of the film of the same name, filmed in Prague and T in 1948 and premiered in 1949].

A scenario produced by E. Kolár, M. Drvota, and the film's director, A. Radok. Only the outdoor scenes were filmed in T; the rest was filmed in the studio. Life in T is shown toward the end of the war (Kolár arrived in the camp only on March 15, 1945), connected with a kitschy plot. In *319, number 40/41 (1948), three photos of the film are reproduced, and Radok's statement is quoted: "The external truth is deformed here, in order better to capture the inner truth." The main actors never were inmates of T.

151a. Kolb, B.: "Anmerkungen." MS, Vineland, NJ, 1956.

694   *Sources and Literature*

I thank Mr. Kolb, who was in T from June 18, 1943, to liberation, for these observations, written for the first edition of this book. Some of what could not be included elsewhere is provided here.

Regarding page 52, Chapter 3: Purchase price for T was calculated such that RM 150 was to be paid per person per month until one turned eighty-five. If the value of one's confiscated possessions exceeded the sum calculated in this way for the support of a person or a married couple, a tax of 25% of the remaining property had to be paid, and the rest still had to be paid "voluntarily." At the first Nuremberg transport, more than RM 5,000,000 was raised in this way from 533 people (including individual payments of more than RM 500,000); these revenues were paid into Account H at the banking house of Heinz Tecklenburg & Co., Berlin. For further details on "home purchase agreements," see *3b, docs. 22–25.

Regarding page 124, Chapter 6: "Because many people did not use the coffee-house tickets allotted to them, it occurred to smart alecks to take advantage of these. The entrance fee of two ghetto crowns did not matter, but one could trade the sugar for bread."

Regarding page 220, Chapter 8: The "Duplication Office of the Central Secretariat" produced "orders of the day" in runs of 300–400 and 50–100 copies of "file notes," as well as many forms. Each month, 200,000–300,000 sheets of paper were used. Lithographs were mainly done for the needs of the SS (song texts, place cards, etc.). "Until autumn 1944, each day a prisoner came to 'Duplicatio'; he had learned the official German communiqués by heart, I don't know where. We duplicated the report and passed it on to trustworthy acquaintances."

151b. Kolb, B.: "Briefbericht." MS, Vineland, NJ, 1956.

The author was the secretary of the JKG Nuremberg from 1923 to 1943 and the liaison to the Gestapo beginning in 1933. The work is an important contribution to understanding how an unimpeachable Jewish functionary could unsuspectingly become an instrument of Jewish self-annihilation (*95d). In July 1941, the local NSDAP wanted to confine all of Nuremberg's Jews in the area; this plan was thwarted by the RSHA in Berlin through Kolb's mechanation – it already had other plans. On November 29, 1941, the deportations from Nuremberg and vicinity began, during which everything had to be financed by the Jews and carried out by Kolb (*151c). In March 1943, the responsible community functionaries from Munich, Würzburg, and Bamberg were arrested because they had issued a list of the deportees to a Christian welfare organization, whereas in Nuremberg the same office had designated only orally the homes of those to be transported. The arrestees remained in prison until they were sent to T on June 17, 1943.

151c. Kolb, B.: "Die Juden in Nürnberg." MS, Nuremberg, 1946.

A history of the community, especially during the persecutions. At the time the deportations in Nuremberg began, 1,835 Jews were sent away along with those from Bamberg, Bayreuth, Fürth, and Würzburg. Barracks on the grounds of the Reich Party congress were designated as a collection camp. Kitchens and fuel were made available by the Gestapo. On November 29, 1941, the first transport left for Riga (Jungfernhof) with 512 victims, after they had been filmed for days. "Along the road stood SS guards with leering faces, while film equipment captured for posterity the 'departure of the Jews.'" The trip took three days and nights, with ten people in one compartment of a passenger car. Of the 16 survivors, some ended up in T, via Buchenwald, at the end of the war. Four hundred and twenty-six other Nurembergers went to Izbica on March 25, 1942. For each deportee, RM 60 was to be paid to the Gestapo; RM 10 of this was for "transport costs." RM 50 was to be paid out at the final destination in local currency. They got neither the money nor their luggage (see a letter from Izbica in *3b, doc. 28). The deportees wrote about their plight to Kolb, who consequently went to the Nuremberg Gestapo. He was shown the original receipts from the commandant of Izbica – a simple deception. No one survived from this transport nor from a third one, with 23 Nurembergers, which went to Krasniczyn (Lublin district).

Kolb became aware of the deportations to T in mid-July 1942. After an aerial bombardment of Nuremberg on August 28, all transport victims not housed in homes were to leave their apartments within a few hours and gather in an old-age home. There, 350 people had to be taken care of for ten days; a makeshift kitchen was set up outdoors. "Home purchase agreements" were concluded; their total proceeds in the Reich were estimated by Kolb to be RM 300–400 million. The transport departed on September 10, 1942; the victims were brought to the train from the homes. They generally were old, sick, and in some cases war-wounded people; one woman was ninety-four years old. The sick people were camped on mattresses in freight cars. The accompanying Schupo commandant stated that leaving the trains or opening the windows was forbidden on pain of death. Toward mid-December, some news arrived from T, "from which it was easy to infer the sad situation of the deportees." Sending bread and other provisions was "made especially difficult by the fact that according to a decree by the Reich Association [Reichsvereinigung], only one package (1 kg) could be sent per month." In mid-June 1943, only 175 people were still alive, and, by the end of the war, there were only 27. On June 10, 1943, the Gestapo announced the "closure of the Reichsvereinigung." On June 18, 1943, 16 Jews were deported to Auschwitz (no survivors) and 14 to T (4 survivors). On January 17, 1944, another 10 people were sent to T (5 survivors). Ninety-seven Nurembergers ended up in the deportation machinery in other ways (20 survivors). Of the 1,631 deportation victims, 71 survived the war.

152. Kolben, H.: "Die Nordpolfahrer." MS, T, 1944.

Tales.

153. Kolben, H.: "Gedichte." MS, T, 1943/44.

Twenty poems written in the camp.

154. [Concentration camps] *Catalogue of Camps and Prisons in Germany and German-Occupied Countries*. Vols. I–II and Supplement. Arolsen, 1949/51.

An extensive and yet incomplete list of numerous camps and subsidiary camps, especially in Germany, where many groups worked in factories and other businesses.

155. [Concentration camps] *Catalogue of Records Held by the International Tracing Service of the Allied High Commission for Germany at Arolsen*. Vols. I–IV. Arolsen, 1954.

Materials related to T are found only in volume I. These include deportation lists, lists of transports to Switzerland, lists of Danes transported to Sweden, and thirty-six pages of "Red Cross correspondence" (including *227) (pp. 186 et seq.); Gestapo deportation lists from Germany and Vienna (*83) (pp. 193 et seq.); and a four-page "report on the ghetto of Theresienstadt" (p. 235). However, these pages are not a report but copies of Czech press reports from June 6 to September 2, 1945, generally on the "Kleine Festung"; they also draw on *286 and *299 of this list.

156. Kopecký, J. (ed.): *Nevyúčtován zůstává život* [Life Remains Unaccounted For]. Prague, 1948.

A work of fiction from T by G. Schorsch, who made a name for himself as a director at the Czech theater here. The text also contains commemorations by his friends.

156a. Korherr, R.: "Die Endlösung der europäischen Judenfrage." MS, Berlin, 1943.

The so-called long Korherr report, Nuremberg document NO-5194. On Himmler's orders, somewhat later, the "short Korherr report," NO-5193, was produced on the basis of the long report; it was shortened but was supplemented by an additional quarter year of figures. It was first published by Poliakov-Wulf (*213a, p. 243 et seq.). Himmler had obliged the respected statistician Korherr to assume the position of "inspector of statistics to the Reichsführer-SS" and in January 1943 demanded a report on the state of the Jewish population as of December 31, 1942. The assignment was as follows:

> I assign you to assemble the statistics for the Final Solution to the European Jewish Question.
>
> The Reich Security Main Office will make available to you any documents necessary or desired for these statistics.
>
> Other than the statistical work to be undertaken by the Inspector of Statistics in this area, the Reich Security Main Office is to do no other statistical work.
>
> (Himmler Files, folder 62)

Korherr based his compilation on figures in the works of Jewish and non-Jewish scholars and on figures from the Reich Statistics Office but above all on the material supplied by Dr. Simon, a statistician in the Reichsvereinigung, and by the RSHA. In the process, the phrase "special treatment [*Sonderbehandlung*] of the Jews" in the RSHA documents wound up in Korherr's report. Himmler let Korherr know that these words had to be replaced with "transporting of the Jews" (*213a, p. 241). Later he wrote to Kaltenbrunner, "I consider this report quite good as possible material for later periods, for the purpose of camouflage. At the moment, it may be neither published nor distributed" (*213a, p. 240). Both of Korherr's reports were first used by Reitlinger (*223), although he quoted and interpreted them incorrectly. I used his figures, which were the only ones available to me at the time, on page 53 of the first edition of this book; through this use a particularly unfortunate assessment of Korherr arose. I now have enough documentation of his position in the National Socialist state and especially during the war, which leads me here to express my regret to Mr. Korherr – who personally and repeatedly risked a great deal for persecuted Jews – for the fact that he suffered insult through me, although unintentionally. On the other hand, however, Korherr's weakness is unfortunate, as it led him – as a great deal of correspondence with him in file 91 of the Himmler file shows – to write a letter to Himmler on April 28, 1943, in which, "on the occasion of my studies of Jewry," probably not falsifying the truth but certainly falsifying the developments, he poured oil on the fire: "The number of Jews in the [Russian Communist Party] was thus already two and a half times as high as their percentage of the population as early as 1927. In the heartland of the Soviet Union even almost four times as high."

From the reports, we learn that – according to the Reichsvereinigung – up to December 31, 1942, 100,516 people were deported from the "Altreich with Sudetengau and Danzig," 47,555 from the "Ostmark," and 69,677 from the "Protectorate"; at the time, another 51,327, 8,102, and 5,550 Jews, respectively, were still living in these regions. The numbers on April 1, 1943, cannot be determined from this short report, as another "evacuation" of 113,015 Jews included the "new Eastern territories" and the "Bialystok [Białystok] district," but the number of Jews in the "Altreich" sank to 31,910, of whom 16,668 were part of "mixed marriages." We learn further that – according to RSHA figures – 87,193 Jews had been taken to T by December 31, 1942. This is 21,933 fewer people than we have calculated, and more or less all other sources agree. It is inexplicable how these pedantically precise statistics, which had to be supplied to the RSHA by the Reichsvereinigung in Berlin, the IKG in Vienna, and the IKG in Prague, could arrive at such a fundamentally incorrect figure. Thus scholars will have to use great caution with the information from Korherr, which is based on RSHA figures. Recently, Korherr has commendably rendered his long report in such a way that the sources are always apparent (copies are in the WL and IfZ). The figures follow the RSHA's information on evacuation and the number of Jews in ghettos, camps, and other involuntary locations, as well as figures on Jewish "labor deployment." If we compare Korherr's breakdown of figures of deportees to T with those in Chapter 3, the following picture emerges (the figures for Sudetengau, Danzig, and Luxemburg are included under the "Reich"):

	Korherr	Adler (Ch. 3)
Reich territory	47,471	47,478
Austria	14,222	13,922
Germany	33,249	33,556
Protectorate	39,722	61,637
Gestapo		11
TOTAL	87,193	109,126

The figure for January 1, 1943, is provided correctly by Korherr as 49,392. He says, verbatim from the RSHA: "The reduction arose primarily through deaths. Aside from Theresienstadt, in the Reich territory there are a number of Jewish homes for the elderly and infirm with small capacity, which however are not seen as either ghettos or evacuation sites." Thus the further deportations to T, through which, by that point, 43,871 people had vanished from the camp, were concealed from Korherr; at the same time, he was expected to believe that the loss of 37,801 people happened in a horrifyingly short time "primarily through deaths." In fact, by that time, 15,902 people had died. According to the short report, in the first quarter of 1943, another 8,025 Jews were taken to T, which is more or less correct.

157. Kral, A.: "Epidemic of Encephalitis in the Concentration Camp Terezín (Theresienstadt) during Winter 1943-1944." In *Journal of Nervous and Mental Diseases.* Vol. 105. Chicago, April 1947, pp. 403-13. YIVO.

698 *Sources and Literature*

The author, a Prague lecturer in neurology, worked in his field for a long time in T.

157a. [Medical histories]. MS, YV, T, c. 1942/44.

An extensive collection of detailed medical histories with laboratory findings, and so on, as well as a number of thorough scientific autopsy reports from the hospital L 317, whose chief physician was Dr. Fritz Salus (sent to his death in autumn 1944).

158. Kraus, F.: *Plyn, plyn, pak oheň* [Gas, gas, then fire]. Havlíčkův Brod, 1946.

Stories of a young Czech Jew from his deportation from T in autumn 1944. This text is factually unreliable.

159. Kraus, F. R.: "Himmlerova finanční transakce s Terezínem" [Himmler's Financial Transaction with Theresienstadt]. In 319, no. 47, 1948.

A report based – although it does not provide sources (according to *Der neue Weg*, no. 3, Vienna, 1949, the source was an article in the New York *Staatszeitung und Herold*; further description of this article is not provided) – on a publication by the former German consul general in New York, Dr. Schwarz, on the Musy mission (especially *2a; see also *3b, 85a, 138a, 177a, 192b, 192c). Kraus relates a fable: Musy is said to have spoken with Himmler in Breslau in 1944, and Himmler is supposed to have said: "You bring me 5 million Swiss francs, and I will give you your favorites." Musy refused to have them march, as Himmler demanded; and Himmler ultimately relented: "We will send small transports by train to Switzerland."

160. Kraus, F. R.: "K 4, říjnu" [On October 4]. In 319, no. 38, 1949.

The author claims, without providing sources, that on October 4, 1941, at a Reichs Chancellery meeting attended by Hitler, Himmler, Heydrich, Bormann, Daluege, and others, T was decided upon as a ghetto at Rosenberg's suggestion.

Kraus, F. R.: See also *336.

160a. Kraus, O., and Kulka: *Továrna na smrt* [The Death Factory]. Prague, 1956.

An important book on Auschwitz. On pages 129–41 there is a report on the Jews from T, from which the first transport is said to have arrived on October 10, 1942. This is certainly an error; no people in T were transferred to Auschwitz before the transport of October 26, 1942. "Work camp Birkenau near Neu-Berun" is given as the address of the "family camp" in 1943/44. This address also appeared, as I could ascertain, beginning in 1942 on letters to Holland and Switzerland (unlike for the Hungarian Jews in 1944; see *164a). In the "family camp," up to 1,000 packages are said to have arrived daily. Camp elder Arno Böhm, also mentioned elsewhere, who was pegged to the Gestapo, was replaced by another German, Willy Brachmann. In contrast, the authors say nothing about the preparations for a rebellion before the murder of the Jews who came from T in September 1943; this story is related in Chapter 3, according to *243. The camp commandant, Höss, admitted during his trial in Cracow that the transport designation "SB with six months' quarantine" was a deceptive maneuver. On closure of the "family camp" on July 10 and 12, 1944, 6,000 Theresienstadters were exterminated, 80 young people between fourteen and sixteen years of age were left alive, 1,000 people were sent to Schwarzheide (approximately 200 survivors), 2,000 people were sent to Stutthof and Hamburg, and

500 people went to other German camps. Of the victims transported from T in autumn 1944, the proportion protected from the selection is estimated probably more or less correctly as 10%. The book contains two poems (pp. 162 et seq.) written by Theresienstadters before they were gassed on March 8, 1944: "My mrtví žalujem" (We Dead Accuse) and "Cizí hrob" (Foreign Grave). A farewell letter, before the gassing, is published in translation in *3b, doc. 49.

160b. Krausnick, H.: "Himmler on His Visit to Mussolini on 11–14 October 1942." In *Vierteljahrshefte für Zeitgeschichte*. Stuttgart, October 1956, pp. 423–26.

Among other things, Himmler described what he told Mussolini about the "Final Solution":

> The Jews would be taken from throughout Germany, the Generalgouvernement and all the countries occupied by us, as everywhere they are responsible for sabotage, espionage and resistance, as well as forming gangs. In Russia, we had to shoot a not inconsiderable number of Jews, including men and women, because there even women and adolescent children were couriers for the partisans. The Duce stressed on his own that this was the only possible solution. I told the Duce that we sent Jews who were politically tainted to concentration camps, that we used other Jews for road-building in the East, where the death toll was however very high, since the Jews had never worked in their lives. The oldest Jews were sent to old-age homes in Berlin, Munich and Vienna. Other old Jews were housed in the town of Theresienstadt as an old-age ghetto for the Jews; there they continued to receive their pensions and stipends and could lead their lives entirely as they liked; however, there they fought among themselves in most lively fashion. We had tried to drive other Jews to the Russians through gaps in the front in the East; however, the Russians had often shot these bunches of Jews and obviously didn't like them either.

160c. Kruskal, H. N.: *Two Years behind Barbed Wire*. Mimeographed, Jerusalem, 1945.

An excellent report on Westerbork and Bergen-Belsen, written in July 1944, immediately after the author's liberation. As a certificate holder, he was on a Geneva list for whose members Switzerland took diplomatic steps vis-à-vis the Reich. Kruskal was in Westerbork with his family from September 16, 1942, to April 5, 1944; the corruption around the deportations outdid anything familiar from T. For the transports that departed on Tuesdays, the commandant (Gemmeker) was interested only in "material" that was sent not according to a particular number but according to available loading space. Anyone on the Geneva lists (the "Palestine list"; see *106a) or anyone who had a Latin American passport (*2a) or a disputed "Aryan certificate" went to Bergen-Belsen. Ninety "genuine foreigners" (that is, anyone who possessed undisputed, genuine papers from a Western state, rather than merely "courtesy passes") went on March 9, 1944, to the RC camp Vittel in France. The transports to the East, on which entire families were always sent, were considered "work deployment" that included children and the elderly. A 102-year-old woman was freed because the commandant decided on "work deployment up to 100 years." The author mentions (pp. 18 et seq.) speaking with a gentleman who had to decide either for T or for Bergen-Belsen, because he had both a Palestine certificate and a distinguished decoration – he had been a German captain in World War I. "I advised him to go to T, as the camp was under Jewish administration and – according to reports – known for tolerable conditions. We were still completely in the dark about conditions in Bergen-Belsen." It turned out that they were those of a "normal" concentration camp;

Westerbork was considered paradise there. Those who had to work were not privileged regarding the miserable food, which was said to add up to 1,000–1,200 calories daily (daily, they received 325 g of bread, "coffee," and 1 L watery soup; twice weekly, they were given watery porridge, 75 g of margarine, one spoonful of cheese, and one spoonful of jam; children up to nine months received 1 cup of skim milk daily). There was little treatment of patients. Punishments included one day of fasting, standing for hours, and detention; people were also beaten, although it was forbidden. A heavily religious life predominated; German and Dutch schooling was provided for children. The camp elder was Isza Albalan, an evil Jew from Saloniki, who boasted of deporting 50,000 Greek Jews. On June 29, 1944, the Kruskal family, along with other fortunates, left the camp in first- and second-class express train cars and were brought to Istanbul via Vienna, where they stayed for a time, and then by ship and train through Syria to Palestine.

161. Kulišová, T.: *Terezín: Národní hřbitov. (Ghetto Terezín zavazuje)* [Theresienstadt: The National Cemetery. (The Theresienstadt Ghetto Obliges)]. Prague, 1952.

This work is tinged with political propaganda and is not very informative on the "Kleine Festung" and the "ghetto," about which it offers only what is generally known. It is hardly worth bibliographically listing the many editions of this booklet, which have insignificant variations and not always identical photos. It can be stated that there is one version that has been available, probably since 1953, in Czech, German, English, French, and Russian. The German title is *Kleine Festung Theresienstadt-Ghetto*. The ghetto is discussed on a few pages, with little factual care. Figures are based on the summary tables in *302. The "Kleine Festung" and the national cemetery, built after the war, are featured in twenty-six photos. A shorter version, in two variations (1953 and 1955), is available only in Czech and does not cover the "ghetto": *Malá pevnost Terezín (Kleine Festung T)*. A photo shows the Red Army's arrival on the bypass road, along with building H V. More important is the author's part in the book cited in *312a.

162. Kypr, P. (ed.): *Malá pevnost Terezín* [Kleine Festung Theresienstadt]. Prague, 1950.

A well-documented history of the camp; however, the role and share of non-Communist prisoners is distorted or concealed. The text describes three incidents reported previously in the present work: (1) the execution of a doctor and a nurse for injecting typhus as "transport protection," (2) the rerouting of a transport from Cologne to the "Kleine Festung" instead of to the "ghetto," and (3) the execution of Eppstein.

162a. Lamm, H.: "Über die innere und äussere Entwicklung des deutschen Judentums im Dritten Reich." Dissertation. Mimeographed, Erlangen, 1951.

163. Lang, P.: "Protocol" [Czech]. MS, DA, Prague, 1945.

Lang, who was in T for more than two years, tells of his deportation to Auschwitz and then to Kauffering 3 in autumn 1944. When a transport went from there to the Leitmeritz concentration camp (hardly more than three kilometers from T) on January 5, 1945, many "Theresienstadters" volunteered for it, and some 200 went with it. At the time, there were 5,000 prisoners in Leitmeritz; in April 1945 there were 9,000. When the Jews were evacuated to T on April 24 at the camp's closure, only

Sources and Literature

three "Theresienstadters" were still alive. The text contains a description of conditions in the Leitmeritz concentration camp (*40b, 181a).

164. Lanik, J.: *Oswiecim* [Auschwitz]. [Slovakian], Kaschau, 1945.

A factual and quite well informed source.

Laš, V.: *173.

164a. Laszlo, C.: *Ferien am Waldsee: Erinnerungen eines Überlebenden.* Basel, 1956.

The impressions of a Hungarian Jew who came to Auschwitz in 1944. He calls it "Waldsee" in the title because this and not "Birkenau" was the deportation destination given in Hungary; it also had to be provided as the return address on letters. Later he describes their evacuation to Sachsenhausen, to an unnamed work camp in Thuringia, and their evacuation through Buchenwald, where they were loaded up and after a – supposedly, although not correctly – six-week journey in open cars were "crowded into a liberated camp on the German-Czech border." Thus Laszlo came to T, which he does not call by name. He claims, "Our SS people were immediately killed by the reasonably sturdy prisoners." This and other information in this odd booklet are not true.

165. Lederer, R.: "Gedichte." MS, T, 1942/44.

Eight poems on camp themes.

166. Lederer, Z.: *Ghetto Theresienstadt.* [English], London, 1953.

The author was in T from November 30, 1941, to autumn 1944. This instructive text is the most thorough work so far on the subject, despite some errors. The statistical information does not always accord with Prochnik (*216). Both sets of figures sometimes contradict (although never significantly) other reliable sources and original documents, which, however, have the disadvantage (as far as they are available to me) of not providing a complete overview until liberation in some areas. In addition, many original documents similarly disagree (although rarely significantly) with one another. For this reason alone, many documents must be judged critically and can seldom be taken as unconditionally correct. I am grateful to Lederer's and Prochnik's figures for many things, but I have used them only when they roughly agree with other sources or when original documents were unavailable. Lederer's figures on the fate of those deported from T remain commendable. The Czech original of this book, more comprehensive than the English version, was never published in Prague due to the communist putsch in 1948.

On those deported to T, Lederer published figures that always include the 1,260 Polish children. In Table I (pp. 247 et seq.) he arrives at a total of 139,654 people. Table II (p. 249) compiles the data according to country of origin:

Bohemia/Moravia	73,608
Germany	42,832
Austria	15,254
Holland	4,897
Denmark	466
Slovakia	1,447
TOTAL	138,504

Lederer did not calculate the total. One can make the following chart from his Tables IV and V (pp. 252–62):

Protectorate	73,608
Germany (including Danzig, Sudetengau, and Luxemburg)	42,829
Austria	15,254
Holland	4,897
Denmark	466
Slovakia	1,447
Hungary	1,150
TOTAL	139,651

166a. Lehner, O.: "Theresienstadt: Besucht am 6. April 1945, durch Dr. Lehner und Dunant." MS, May 18, 1945. [In addition, a letter from Lehner to the IRC from Prague on April 7, 1945].

The text is an astonishing document; carefully chosen parts of this work form the basis for the portrayal in *228. See detailed samples and explanations in *3b, docs. 239–40.

166b. Lehrmann, Ch., and G. Lehrmann: *La Communauté juive du Luxembourg*. Luxemburg, 1953.

A history of the Jews of the country; it also deals with the period of persecution. Between October 1940 and January 1941, 648 people were deported to France, and 49 to Belgium. From October 16, 1941, to April 6, 1943, 733 Jews were deported to Poland and T (approximately 35 survivors). Of these people, 309 are believed to have gone to T, with 1 added in 1944 (according to *302).

167. Lengyel, C.: *Five Chimneys: The Story of Auschwitz*. Chicago, 1947.

The author provides a clear picture of the camp.

167a. Leschnitzer, A.: *Saul und David: Die Problematik der deutsch-jüdischen Lebensgemeinschaft*. Heidelberg, 1954.

A valuable contribution, among other things, to the history of German-Jewish assimilation and modern German Jew-hatred.

168. Lesný, B.: "Terezín – město odsouzenců" [Theresienstadt – City of the Condemned]. In 319, no. 1, 1946.

A secretly drawn up chart by an employee of the "Central Registry" on the number of deportees to T:

Protectorate	73,651
Germany	42,253
Austria (including Hungary)	16,336
Holland	4,904
Slovakia	1,102
Sudetengau	607
Denmark	474
Danzig	117
TOTAL	139,444

169. Lestschinsky, J.: *Crisis, Catastrophe and Survival*. New York, 1948.

Information on the situation and number of European Jews before, during, and after the Second World War.

170. Levai, E.: *Black Book on the Martyrdom of Hungarian Jewry*. Zurich-Vienna, 1948.

A comprehensively documented and illustrated account, probably unlike any done for any other country; however, it is almost entirely limited to events in Hungary and provides almost nothing on the fate of the deportees. There are no references to T. Levai judges Kasztner's activities (*135) somewhat unfavorably.

171. Levi, P.: *Se questo è un uomo* [If This Is a Man]. Turin, 1947.

A reflective book on Monowitz (Auschwitz III) and the Buna factory. It is valuable for its deep insights into the psychology of the prisoners in an extermination camp.

172. Levin, M.: *In Search: An Autobiography*. Paris, 1950.

The author came to Germany with the American army and visited T on May 10, 1945 (pp. 268–73). He also wrote a report in the New York *Forward* on May 31, 1945: "Twenty-Three Thousand Jews in Theresienstadt: One of Four Persons Sick" (YIVO).

172a. Levy, A.: "Bericht." MS, WL, Idar-Oberstein, no year.

The author arrived in T from Bonn with her husband and parents on the second Cologne transport; there they lost almost all their luggage. Her father died there. She was sent to Auschwitz on October 28, where her husband immediately died. The author ended up in Bergen-Belsen in early November and in Salzwedel around February 1945 with 300 women; with twelve hours of work per day, living conditions there were no better than in Bergen-Belsen. On April 14, the Americans liberated the camp. In July, she was reunited with her mother, who had remained in T.

172b. Lewin, H.: "Erlebnisse 1933–1945." MS, WL, Offenbach, 1955.

This text is mainly about Łódź, where the author arrived from Cologne in October 1941. Starting on April 19, 1945, the author was part of a hunger march from Schwarzheide through the battle of Bautzen to Warnsdorf; they ended up in a factory there from April 26 to May 5, almost without food. The starving people ate grass. They were then loaded into open coal cars and brought to Leitmeritz in the pouring rain. Shots were fired during the trip, and there were deaths. They arrived in T on May 8. There partners in German-Jewish marriages asked the Russian commandant for preferential repatriation. He asked, "What do you call mixed marriage?" When this was explained, he refused: "What? When dogs and cats together, that is mixed marriage!"

173. [Lidice] "Vzpomíná na den 10. června 1942" [We Commemorate June 10, 1942]. In 319, no. 24, 1951.

A report by V. Laš, who belonged to the Lidice burial kommando (thirty people) from T. The text also contains a report by R. Mautner, who had to level the mass grave in Lidice on June 13, 1942, with ten other men from T.

Liebrecht, H.: *28.

704 *Sources and Literature*

173a. Liepman, A. J.: "Westerbork en Theresienstadt" [Westerbork and Theresienstadt]. Bextel, Holland, 1945.

I have not seen this work (thirty-one pages).

Lindenbaum, W.: *10a.

174. Lingens-Reiner, E.: *Prisoners of Fear.* London, 1948.

A serious and dignified book of experiences by a (non-Jewish) Viennese doctor imprisoned in Auschwitz; it provides deep insights into the nature of the prisoners and the SS. So far it is probably the most ethically mature and – aside from Kogon's works (*149, 150) – the most important camp book; it is significant also for understanding the role and psychology of Jewish prisoners.

175. [Łódź] Note in 319, no. 13, 1948.

Up to August 7, 1944, 983 Czech Jews died in Łódź.

175a. Loeb, I.: "Briefbericht." MS, WL, Amsterdam, soon after the war.

The author was arrested in Amsterdam with her parents on November 8, 1942, and was brought to Westerbork, where she was a nurse. After her father's death in autumn 1943, mother and daughter came to T on February 26, 1944. The author was also a nurse there and around May was chosen for a new ward where twenty patients were treated with healing gas. "It consisted of Peruvian balsam, glycerin, hypermagnesium, quinine, chinosol, sodium iodate, ammonium chloride, and hexamethylentetramin. This mixture was heated to 300 degrees and the resulting gas directed at the suppurating wound. The resulting condensate was used with good success for serious stomatitides and [Sor]. The results of the treatment were very good in some cases." Three doctors and three nurses worked there.

On October 12, 1944, the two women had to go to Auschwitz; after two weeks they were sent from there to Lenzing, near Linz, a Mauthausen subsidiary camp. Sometimes the women were put to work in three shifts without gas masks in the sulfuric acid fumes of a rayon factory, and sometimes they performed the hardest excavation work. The author was the chief nurse for around 560 women who lived in the most horrible conditions. After January 1945 there was almost no food; they ate nettles, dandelions, potato skins, and snails. On May 5, the Americans liberated the camp.

175b. [Löwenherz, J.]: "Kultusgemeinde Wien 1938–1942." MS, Vienna, 1945.

An account by the author, who headed the IKG or the Jewish "Council of Elders" in Vienna during the Nazi period. On October 20, 1939, 912 men were brought to Nisko. Three days earlier, the "Central Office" demanded that the at least 5,000 men be transported to Poland within two weeks. On October 29, Eichmann explained "that in the spirit of the solution of the Jewish question planned by the Reich government," many Jews in the settlement areas

> would be resettled to Poland. The operation will be carried out in the most humane way; the Jews will be able to move freely there, to settle and make a life.... The Jews are first

Eichmann invited Löwenherz and "gentlemen from foreign organizations to go to Poland and ... satisfy yourselves as to the advantages of resettlement." These transports did not happen; on November 8, the postponement of the operation until February 1, 1940, was announced. Anyone who had not emigrated by then "should be sent to the East." On December 2, 1939, Eichmann authorized Löwenherz "to inform the Joint that the Poland transports would be postponed if the Joint continues to be willing to provide hard currency to the IKG until the end of 1940, and the IKG agrees ... to get Jews to emigrate, so that the liquidation of emigration can happen at the end of October 1940." After a trip to Amsterdam, Löwenherz informed Eichmann in Berlin on December 19, 1939, of the Joint's general agreement; Eichmann had shortly before taken over leadership of the "Central Office." On April 6, 1940, the return of 152 people from Nisko was announced.

At the beginning of 1941, Löwenherz negotiated with the Joint in Lisbon again about financing emigration from all of Germany, and he received assurances. Deportation rumors in Vienna led him on January 23, 1941, to warn Rolf Günther that "any such measures would preclude any further support from the Joint." Although Günther claimed to "know nothing of a resettlement plan to Poland," Government Counsel Dr. Ebner (a member of the Gestapo) announced the deportation of 10,000 Vienna Jews in the presence of Brunner (a member of the "Central Office"). The victims were determined by the "Central Office," which, for further action, submitted the list for each transport to the IKG three to four days before its departure. The IKG thus had to carry out most of the practical measures, while at the same time further pursuing emigration abroad. The deportation techniques that later were common throughout the Reich (*3b, docs. 1–40) – theft of property, document submission, and so on – were developed and tested at that time (in contrast, the reception of the deportees at the destination was systematically prepared by the RSHA only in winter 1941–42). Only five transports took place – a total of 5,004 victims were brought to Opole (twice), Kielce, Modliborzyce, and Łagów – from February 15 to March 12, 1941. On July 1, 1941, 53,208 "Jews by race" lived in Vienna, of whom 44,308 were "Jews by faith."

In response to questions from Löwenherz, Eichmann explained on September 8, 1941, that he knew of no impending deportations. "On September 30, 1941, Brunner ... informed me that, in consideration of the accommodation elsewhere of the Aryan population made necessary by the air raids, some of the Jews ... should be brought to Litzmannstadt (Łódź)." Five transports with 5,002 victims went there from October 15 to November 2, 1941. "Already, people are being collected and placed into ... collection camps; the IKG must take care of their provisioning." Normal emigration would be ended "with very few exceptions" starting on November 10, 1941. In addition to 3,000 first-time transportees, roughly 200 illegal returnees from the Poland transports in early 1941 had to go with the three transports (November 25 to December 3, 1941) to Riga and Minsk. In 1942, 32,700 Jews were deported; in 1943–44, 1,645; and, from the beginning of the war to December 31, 1944, a total of 49,000. The total number of people who emigrated with the help of the IKG is around 137,000.

The following table provides an overview of the deportations from Vienna:

Destination	Number
1941	
Opole, etc.	5,004
Łódź	5,002
Riga, Minsk	3,000
TOTAL	13,006
1942	
Riga	3,222
Minsk	8,550
Izbica, etc.	6,000
T	14,926
TOTAL	32,698
1943–44	
Auschwitz	308
T	1,645
TOTAL	1,953
1941–44	
East	31,086
T	16,751
TOTAL	47,837

To this total approximately 1,300 additional victims – expelled Polish Jews sent on individual deportations – should be added. J. Löwenherz gives the number of those deported to T as 2,831 higher than our, and roughly all other, calculations that are based on accessible documents from T. Only in 168 is the difference reduced to around 1,800 people, after subtracting 1,150 Hungarians. The inconsistencies cannot be resolved. In general, it seems that the figures from the sending offices, including the Gestapo (*83) and except those in the "Protectorate," tended to be higher than the figures from the reception office in T. The only reasons that can be given are transfers to other transports and deaths in the collection camps, where, especially in the case of Vienna, the deportees often spent many weeks.

As early as February 19, 1942, in Berlin, Eichmann revealed to the main responsible Jewish representatives in Berlin, Vienna, and Prague the systematic overall deportation of the Jews from "Greater Germany," including the groups destined for the East or T. The information, in Löwenherz's words, can be found in *3b, doc. 1. Before this explanation by Eichmann, the situation had dramatically worsened. Eichmann had the Jewish representatives summoned to him – six came from Berlin, two each from Vienna and Prague – and obliged them to stand against a wall for six hours. He then let them know that, in connection with a sabotage on the exhibit "Soviet Paradise" in Berlin, in which 5 Jews were actively involved, 500 Jews had been arrested in Berlin. Of these, 250 were immediately shot, and the others were transferred to a concentration camp. If any other act of sabotage should take place with Jewish participation, other measures of this type could be expected. Certainly, the as-yet-unexplained case was well timed for Eichmann. Through Löwenherz's information on the timing of these events we also know that the main functional players in and witnesses to the tragedy – of whom, aside from Löwenherz, only

Murmelstein survived the war – had already been let in on the disaster, one month minus a day after the "Wannsee Conference" (see Chapter 2), to the extent that Eichmann thought necessary; they had at least learned half the truth, the continued effect of which weighed on them tragically, guiltily, or both at once. This date may also be seen as that after which knowledge of the "Final Solution" was revealed to all the RSHA functionaries working on it, and especially those in Department IV B 4; this conceptualization rebuts Wisliceny's statement (*124).

In late summer 1942, the IKG had to give back the subsidy granted it by the "Central Office" – which was, in reality, nothing but money taken from Jewish emigrants or institutions – and had to deposit it into a "special account for Jewish resettlement" at the state bank. On November 1, 1942, the IKG was changed to a "council of elders for the Jews in Vienna," a "registered association" to which all remaining Jews had to belong. "Every Jews must also subscribe to and pay for the *Jewish News.* . . . Dr. Löwenherz takes this opportunity to urge the payment of the RM 738,000 of delinquent reimbursement for the costs of the resettlement transports" (RM 1,023,700 had already been paid). The property of the IKG Vienna would go to the Prague "emigration fund," supposedly to maintain the Vienna Jews in T; at the same time, these funds were supposed to cover possible deficits for the "Council of Elders" in Vienna.

Some parts of this report can be found in *2a and *3b, doc. 1. Doc. 76 in *3b indicates that, at the end of January 1943, it was intended that Löwenherz would be a leading man in T, in addition to Eppstein and Edelstein. But Eichmann left Löwenherz in Vienna until the end, and Murmelstein took his place.

The text dealt with here comes from the deputy head of the KG Vienna during the war, W. Bienenfeld, and was provided as a supplement to his testimony in the trial of von Schirach by a Viennese court. Bienenfeld used as a source the memoranda that had to be written by the IKG (undoubtedly by Löwenherz himself) and "submitted to the Gestapo for approval." Bienenfeld expanded on them from memory. The written version was available to the main Nuremberg tribunal as PS-3934.

176. Loewenstein, K.: "Minsk: Im Lager der deutschen Juden." In "Aus Politik und Zeitgeschichte" B XXXXV/56. Supplement to the weekly *Das Parlament*. Bonn, November 7, 1956.

A valuable report on experiences in the period from November 1941 to May 1942. The work is the beginning of an unpublished book in which the author deals with T, and specifically his own activities as head of the "Security Service" as well as his personal experiences. The author generously made available to me the rich documentary material on which the book is based.

177. [Loewenstein, K.]: "Internal Ghetto Guard Regulations." MS, T, 1942/43.

177a. Löwenstein, L.: "K. C. in Theresienstadt." In K. C. – Kartell Convent, *Association of Refugee Old University Students in Great Britain*. Circular no. 51. London, 1950, pp. 4–6.

When the author arrived in T on July 1, 1943, he found more than sixty members of the Kartell Convent of German Students of Jewish Faith (KC), including Dr. Ernst Rosenthal, executive director since 1933 of the "Reich Union of Jewish Front-Line Soldiers" and head of the Detective Department in T. The KC men expected there to be a Jewish community in Germany after the war, for which most wanted the rights

708   *Sources and Literature*

of a minority. High positions were held by Dr. Metz, Munk's deputy in the Health Service (who survived Auschwitz), and Hans Weinberg, a judge. Only four KC members survived the war in T; the others died there or in Auschwitz.

177b. Ludwig, C.: *Die Flüchtlingspolitik der Schweiz in den Jahren 1933 bis 1955.* Bern, 1957.

This important work, written for the Bundesrat, shows, among other things, what was known in Switzerland during the war about the Jewish tragedy. The author mentions the Musy mission (*2a; 3b, doc. 60):

> Without advance notice, 1,200 Jewish refugees [*sic*] ... from the concentration camp Theresienstadt arrived at the border on February 8 [actually, it was February 7], 1945, almost all of them old people, frequently in need of special care. They were housed in various places in Switzerland. Later it was possible, in consultation with federal authorities, to purchase and maintain for the Jewish refugees a house in Vevey, which became a real home for those "Theresienstadters" who did not emigrate.   (p. 300)

177c. Lustig, A.: *Noc a naděje* [Night and Hope]. Prague, 1958.

Seven stories that take place in T. The author experienced the camp as an adolescent and accurately describes his peers' wayward behavior in the young workers' home Q 710 (see Chapter 17), especially in the story "Morlání výchova" (Moral Education) and in places in "Modravé plameny" (Bluish Flame). On the other hand, he distorts other conditions more or less crudely, both historically and in the details (*336).

178. [Luxembourg] "Die Vertreibung der Juden aus Luxemburg." In *Aufbau.* New York, June 30, 1944.

Near the beginning of the war, on May 10, 1940, there were 4,800 Jews in the country. 1,800–2,000 fled to France or were set up by the SS in camps in unoccupied France. The figures on the deportations after October 1941 are outdated (*166b).

178a. [Majdanek] *Die Todesfabrik Maidanek*. Vienna, 1946.

178b. Manes, Ph.: "Letzte Berliner Tage" [Last Days in Berlin]. MS, T, 1943.

178c. Manes, Ph.: "Factual Report." MS, T, 1944.

The manuscript "Last Days in Berlin" was written in April 1943, and the almost 1,000 pages of this "factual report" span from February to October 1944; the report does not offer history but instead provides a cross section of life in the camp, detailed information on the author's official and cultural activities, and news about many interesting personalities in T.

   Manes arrived in T on July 29, 1942, and, although he was around seventy years old, was sent to his death on the last transport to the East on October 28, 1944.

   From August 1, 1942, he led the "orientation service," which he had founded; it was called the "aid service of the Ghetto Guard" after July 1, 1943. He began with a staff of twelve and in 1943 reached a peak of forty-five men and ten women. Almost all the staff were over sixty years old. On February 1, 1944, the service was dissolved, and most of the members were taken on by the OD.

The author's cultural activities, acknowledged in Chapter 19, began with a speech on September 21, 1942, and ended with the beginning of the autumn transports in 1944, in late September. These activities were officially named the "Orientation Service Lecture Series"; later the series was dissolved (at which point it nominally belonged to the "Recreation Department"), was renamed the "Manes Group Lecture Series," and was granted three assistants. On August 6, 1944, the series hosted its 500th event – a lecture by Leo Baeck on "age." Up to then, Manes had organized 367 lectures, 116 dramatic readings, and 17 special performances. Twice he announced poetry contests; both times, around 200 poems were submitted.

Manes, a man of strict fairness, optimistic spirit, and subtle powers of observation, did not succumb, like most of the inmates, to senseless political rumor; however, his outlook nevertheless confirms the tragic attitude of all too many elderly Jews from Germany toward the SS, whose abysmal villainy he did not suspect until the bitter end. Because people often do not believe in the presence of this attitude – this naïveté, which we have repeatedly described – in the camps, we present some evidence from the "factual report":

> The German authorities are imperceptible to us, they communicate only with a few members of the Council of Elders. We see the gentlemen only when they appear in Magdeburg [B V] for a visitation or meeting. Otherwise we see nothing of their supervisory activities.
>
> Now we have another present – the ghetto is allowed to write to the Birkenau ghetto in Upper Silesia. That is an expansion [easing] of our isolation that can hardly be sufficiently praised [angeschlagen]. We are able to give our friends, with whom we lived and worked in the ghetto for over a year, a sign of life and to receive one from them.
>
> [Admiration and acknowledgement of the "German authorities" during the "beautification" follows.] One may say in conclusion that a children's paradise has been created here, for which we must all be very grateful.
>
> [On the May transports, 1944:] Everything is done to make the journey to resettlement easy for the evacuees. The German authorities [the SS!], too, have shown great humanity and intervened only to assist; even their boss [Rahm!] permitted himself no rest in order to oversee everything and ensure the smooth progress of the transports.
>
> [Regarding preparations for the transport on October 12, 1944:] Bedrolls once again were permitted, a few kilos didn't matter. When I saw what most people dragged with them, I became fully aware of how generous the German authorities acted, despite warnings, and how tolerantly they overlooked the extra amounts.... Some hoped to be freed through an interview with Dr. Murmelstein or a member of the Council of Elders. Vain efforts. Only the Office was able to do this, and I know that every justified reclamation was given a sympathetic hearing. Nothing was rejected outright. Before boarding the wagons, one can be brought to the head of the Office and call for a decision. One is not at all defenseless, but the reason must be convincing.

Publication of particularly impressive passages from this valuable work as a book is planned.

Mann, K.: *122.

179. Mannheimer, M. E.: Theresienstadt and from Theresienstadt to Auschwitz. London, 1945.

The author came to T from Westerbork and was sent to Auschwitz on September 28, 1944. The text provides smart and generally correct information on T. It is

710   *Sources and Literature*

emphasized that the relationships among the prisoners in T were better than in Westerbork. At his arrival in Auschwitz, the author had no idea as to the reason for the selection.

Marcus E.: *Ein Schicksal dieser Zeit: Der Kriegsblinde aus Theresienstadt und sein Kind.* *99.

180. Marcuse, B.: *Erlebnisse in K. Z. Theresienstadt.* Ulm, no year [1945].

A short, essentially correct depiction. The author arrived in T in June 1944 and remained there until liberation. The main part consists of camp verses typical of the rhymes common in T.

181. Mark, B.: *Ruch oporu w getcie Białostockim* [Resistance Movement in the Białystok Ghetto]. Warsaw, 1952.

The text contains no mention of the children deported to T (*40a).

181a. Markiewicz, W.: "Moje preżycia z okupacji" [My Experiences during the Occupation]. MS, HIŻ, Poland, no year.

The author finally arrived at the Leitmeritz camp from the Lemberg Ghetto in April 1945, after varied experiences (*40b, 103). The prisoners were no longer required to work, conditions were terrible, and people ate grass. One day, all the Jews were ordered to the Appellplatz. They were told that they would be evacuated to Dachau, but people feared "liquidation." Finally, they were marched through the city of Leitmeritz to T. "The inmates surrounded us and accompanied us silently, while distributing sugar cubes and baked potatoes. That was my happiest moment since the outbreak of war." Later the author saw "that it was not rosy here either." People starved as in the concentration camps but were free of kapos and block elders. Typhus and diarrhea led to mass death. The good conditions were over when disinfectors came to the barracks and said, "These are pigs, not people." There were fights over soup and thefts of bread. "People took us for criminals."

182. Masur, N.: *En Jude talar med Himmler.* Stockholm, 1945.

A report on a discussion on the night of April 20, 1945, at which T was touched on (*139). The document is also available mimeographed in German.

Mautner, R.: *173.

183. Mazor, M.: *La Cité engloutie (Souvenirs du ghetto de Varsovie).* Paris, 1955.

The author, who was able to escape from a deportation train to Treblinka on September 4, 1942, attempts a "phenomenology" of the Warsaw Ghetto, for a sociology is impossible because of the lack of documents. This valuable study is therefore mainly based on his own recollections and describes social work in particular. The psychological phenomena, especially the optimism nourished by fantastical rumors, often were similar to those in T. The fundamental studies of the role of the Jewish Council are important. Mazor rejects any psychological, historical, or sociological explanation of National Socialist crimes; any causal justification goes astray (p. 175): "In addition, any explanation would contain an element of rationalization, and thus a certain justification of these incomprehensible events; it would integrate it

Sources and Literature 711

into the process of human history while this barbarism, the explosion of infernal forces, must remain outside the annals of all the peoples of earth."

183a. Mazor, M.: "La 'folie' Hitlerienne." In *Le monde juif*. Paris, January, p. 6 et seq.

A document on the "home purchase agreements" (Chapter 3) of December 14, 1942.

183b. Meijers, E. M.: [Statement on T]. In *Enquetecommissie Regeringsbeleid 1940–1945*. Vol. 60. The Hague, 1952, pp. 1011–16.

A somewhat confused report for the parliamentary investigative commission.

183c. Meiners, F.: "Deportation jüdischer Ehepartner nach Theresienstadt." MS, WL, Oldenburg, 1958.

The author, whose husband was a German (Christian) soldier in the East and who had a six-year-old child to care for, was summoned to the Gestapo in Oldenburg at the beginning of February 1945. She was told that she would be "taken with a transport to a work detail in T" on February 13. That day, she was taken to Bremen with two companions under Gestapo supervision and was loaded onto cattle cars the same day. The train also had cars from Kiel and Hamburg. The trip to T took ten days. The transport consisted of 294 people (*195a, 223b).

184. Meisterova, H.: "Ville de la morte lente." In *Droit et liberté*. Paris, January 9, 1946. YIVO.

184a. Menasche, A.: *Birkenau*. [English], New York, 1947.

Information on the tragedy of the Greek Jews. At the beginning of May 1943 there were only 900 of the original 50,000 Jews in Saloniki. Pages 15 et seq. are noteworthy:

> Finally it was announced on May 30 that the [collection] camp was to be reduced to 100 persons; the rest were forced to leave Saloniki the next day. These 800 were promised privileges.... They were not to go to Poland, but to a special camp, to Theresen-Stad [*sic*]. What remained of our property had previously been exchanged for so-called checks in Polish zloty. On the eve of June 1 there was much activity. The zlotys were changed to marks. Around 4 o'clock A.M., roll call.... Driven with whips and pistol shots, we were crowded into cattle cars, 60 at a time. The journey took eight days.

Their journey ended in Auschwitz. On pages 81–85, the author describes, largely incorrectly, the tragedy of the "family camp" from "Theresen-Stad," along with other topics (*188b).

Mendelsohn, M.: *46a.

184b. Meyer, C., and S. Meyer: "Onze belevenissen tijdens de Jodenvervolgingen in den Tweeden Wereldoorlog" [Our Experiences during the Persecution of the Jews in the Second World War]. MS, RvO, Copenhagen, 1945.

The Meyers, a married couple, were Danish citizens and lived in Holland with two small boys (born 1939 and 1940). On April 23, 1943, they were forcibly repatriated to Denmark, accompanied by a Gestapo man in civilian clothes. When the arrest of the Jews was imminent at the end of September, they prepared an escape to Sweden, the cost of which is given as 2,000–3,000 Danish kroner for a family of four. During the escape attempt, which they undertook after the roundup, the Gestapo captured the family and sent them to Copenhagen to the German section of the "Vestre Faengsel" (Western Prison). The Wehrmacht guards were friendly and brought children's beds, flowers, and so on. On October 1 they were transferred in prison transport trucks to Horserød, where there were two camps. One was filled with Danes who had been arrested at the proclamation of martial law on August 29, and the other was filled with Jews. It consisted of a men's, women's, and hospital barracks. Several hundred people were sent there in a period of four days. People in mixed marriages and half Jews were released, but not the Meyer family, although she was Christian and he was half-Jewish. On November 23, nineteen people, including a Czech Jew, were brought at 9 P.M. with their searched luggage to a second-class carriage in an express train. The transport was accompanied by an SS man and "green" police. After Copenhagen, some people escaped from the moving train. They changed trains in Warnemünde, and T was given as the destination. But that is not what happened. Ten women and children had to disembark suddenly, whereas the six men left the train at a later station.

On November 24, at 5 A.M., the men arrived in Sachsenhausen, along with thirty Danes from Odense. After the usual reception procedures, they were housed in quarantine block 14, but in a week they were issued some of their own clothing, and Meyer found out where his wife and children were: Ravensbrück. Along with other Jews, he was assigned to dock work, but one Jew was sent to the strictly segregated counterfeiting workshop. When the quarantine ended in two weeks, his comrades had to move to the Jewish barracks, whereas Meyer remained in the old block and worked as a translator of Danish, Norwegian, and Dutch. At the same time, he was allowed to write to Denmark for money and food. The luggage for his wife and children had arrived in Sachsenhausen with them; after many appeals, Meyer was allowed to send things to his family after New Year's of 1944. On January 10, Meyer was "released" with three others; the other two had to stay. At that point he discovered that nothing had been sent to Ravensbrück, but an SS man promised that Meyer would soon be reunited with his family. Meyer did not believe it, because it had been said a few days earlier that he would be going to Lublin – he knew about the gas chambers. After the usual signing of documents at release – in which one was sworn to silence about Sachsenhausen – the four Jews were taken away by an SS man in civilian clothing and were taken to a closed truck, which contained four Jewish widows of "Aryans" (the quarry of an *Aktion* that had just been carried out; see *88). The trip ended in the collection camp Grosse Hamburgerstraße, Berlin. Meyer was used to break rocks and to move archives from bombed-out houses until he fell ill with scarlet fever and was brought to a single room in the Jewish hospital on Iranischer Straße. He was treated by the chief physician, Dr. Cohen, and the department doctor, Dr. Elkan. The food was quite good, but not ample.

> Doctors, nurses, and also the patients were nice to me, and I was spoiled by everyone. In a week I had a visit from the director, Mr. Neumann, who however stood cautiously by the door. He asked me if my father was rich. I thought this was a strange question, but because I didn't know what he was after, I told him that he was not doing badly. Clearly satisfied with this answer, he let me know that the other patients were paying for their stays in the hospital, but I was not. He now wanted to write my father and ask whether he could pay 3–400 marks for my stay in the hospital

Meyer found this was a bit much but was glad that, in this way, his relatives would receive news of him. During this period his three comrades arrived in T. Heavy bombings destroyed a wing of the hospital, and the collection camp moved to a tract belonging to the hospital on Schulstraße. On April 13, Meyer was awakened by a nurse, who told him to pack. One hour later, a Jewish orderly brought him to Schulstraße, where the situation was miserable. On April 19, the transport left for T.

The women and children were brought to Ravensbrück after getting out of the prison transport trucks and, after the reception, were housed by two female SS officers in two prison cells, five to a cell. Two days later, they were moved to the "notables section," where the group was left to itself and was removed from the usual horror of the camp. On January 12, 1944, the group was picked up by three SS men in civilian clothing (a woman with a sick child had to remain behind and followed a quarter of a year later). The journey proceeded by train to Oranienburg, where the women hoped to be reunited with the men. They took the light rail to Anhalter Station. The transport leader said, "We have to hurry if we don't want to miss the connection." The train arrived five minutes before its scheduled departure; it was overcrowded. Nevertheless, the transport leader managed to get an entire second-class carriage by producing SS marks and saying "transport." Following difficult early experiences in T, Mrs. Meyer and her boys moved into the "infants home," L 607. This room, which had a view of the Aryan street, housed ten women with sixteen children. Finally, the family was reunited, and on June 22 they moved into their own room, in recognition of the Danish commission. What happened during the move can be read in *3b, doc. 223. The care of the Danes was excellent. They could expect four packages from the Danish RC per month, as well as packages from the Swedish and Swiss RC and deliveries of sardines from Portugal. Once, eight boxes of apples came from Denmark; the SS kept one box, and the rest were distributed, so that each Dane got six to seven apples. A library with 1,000 volumes was also sent to them from the homeland. Each month they were sent RM 10, the receipt of which had to be confirmed. But they did not get the money. Instead, the amount was added to their account at the "bank" as "frozen deposits," at an exchange rate of RM 1 for every GK 50. At the autumn transport in 1944, the freedom of the Danes from Sachsenhausen had to be fought for, because they had been registered under German transport numbers.

On April 13, 1945, a diplomatic car with a Danish flag appeared at the SS "office." Two hours later, the lists of Danish transports were demanded, and around 3 P.M., Friediger announced their transport to Sweden. The transportees were expected to be in the Schleuse, A II, that evening. Their suitcases were released, and they could take as many as they wanted. Rahm did not want to release the people from Sachsenhausen, but Friediger "fought like a lion" until Rahm gave in. Toward midnight before April 15, a convoy of Swedish cars arrived. The Czech personnel, probably staff of the "transport leadership," announced that chocolate and a packet of cigarettes had been placed on every soft seat, and plenty of food and hot chocolate was available. Once they heard this, the Meyer family gave their provisions to the Czechs. It turned out that the cars were equipped with wooden benches; nothing else they said was true. The Czechs had said it only to get the Jewish provisions. "Some of us thought the joke crude, but we younger people were amused nevertheless and had to admit that it was 1:0 for the Czechs." The convoy left at 10 A.M. on the 15th. It consisted of thirty transport carriages, a car that headed the transport, a kitchen car and an ambulance, and two motorcycles. Soon after T, it was stopped. An SS officer said that a responsible soldier would be placed in each carriage, and in larger cities, the blackout curtains were to be drawn. Provocations were to be avoided, especially when traveling through Denmark; the Jewish star was to be removed. Generally they drove very fast; only through Dresden did they go slower, because of the destruction. People devoured the bread and margarine and liver paste that they had received in T. The Swedish escorts were friendly. At 10 P.M., they stopped to rest for the night in a forest near Potsdam. On the 16th they left at 6 A.M. and continued through burning Potsdam; they finally reached Lübeck, where a hot meal was served and they were informed that they had passed the danger zone. They arrived in Denmark at 6 A.M. on the 17th. They got a bath and good food; small Danish flags were distributed, and cards were written to relatives. By the time the journey continued, Hadersleben was covered in flags. Flowers, chocolate, and cigarettes were thrown into the cars. In contrast, there were angry looks from SS men, which ensured that no welcome would take place in the later towns; people only waved from the windows. In the evening they were housed by the Danish RC in a mission hotel in Odense and were well fed. On April 18, they started out very early. At noon they reached the free port of Copenhagen and crossed to Malmö on the Swedish ferry. The new arrivals were either brought to Tyllesand, near Halmstad, or, like the Meyer family, were taken to Strängnäs and kept in quarantine for two weeks. The food in Strängnäs was bad. On May 15, the Danish Jews were freed.

185. Meyer, P., B. Weinryb, E. Duschinsky, and N. Sylvain: *The Jews in the Soviet Satellites*. Syracuse, NY, 1953.

Meyer, P.: "Czechoslovakia" (pp. 47–204).

An important work on the Bohemian-Moravian (and Slovakian) Jews, from the years before World War I to the fifth year of communist rule. Unfortunately, the statistical material on T is not always correct and is sometimes wrong, from a purely mathematical perspective. The work provides a clear overview of the combined anti-German and anti-Jewish attitudes of the Czech authorities after the war, as they deprived the survivors of T and other "ghettos" – especially those whose mother tongue was German and who had attended German schools – of their rights.

185a. Meyring, E.: "Erinnerungen." MS, WL, Stockholm, no year.

The author was deported on February 12, 1940, from Stettin to Lublin, where she headed a Jewish Council advice office for deportees. The German Jews were divided among the towns of Piaski, Bełżyce, and Głusk. This valuable report describes the conditions in Stettin and Lublin, with a subtle understanding of the mentality of the Polish and German Jews. Meyring presents views that the present work also advocates:

> No situation was more horrible and terrible than when, after all the formalities were fulfilled, all stakes pulled up, the rules of the country [of immigration] suddenly changed and the barriers closed....
>
> The Jews truly felt very little of the world's conscience. It must remain the subject of a special study by those familiar with it to show how this lack of understanding in all countries contributed to the fact that the evil that had befallen the Jews could take on such dimensions.

Mrs. Meyring was the only female German Jew allowed to leave Lublin. On June 26, 1940, she journeyed to Berlin and two days later to Stockholm (*1). See *Lebenszeichen aus Piaski*, page 144.

185b. Michael, M. (ed.): *Gesundheitschäden durch Verfolgung und Gefangenschaft und ihre Spätfolgen*. Frankfurt a. M., 1955.

A collection, with contributions by many authors, on camp illnesses during and after imprisonment. The studies do not involve T (except in one case, which addresses the "Kleine Festung") but provide comparative material. Whereas the doctors in T ascribed great importance to avitaminosis, in this work its role is judged to be much smaller in other camps (*97b).

186. Michel, W.: *Verrat am Deutschtum, eine Streitschrift zur Judenfrage*. Hanover, 1922.

This work clearly recognizes the pseudoreligious component of German "antisemitism."

187. Miklík, J.: *Vzpomínky z Terezína* [Recollections of Theresienstadt]. Prague, 1945.

The author, a Catholic priest, was arrested for communication with Jews and was taken to the "Kleine Festung," which is all he describes. A chapter is devoted to the life of Jewish prisoners there. There are thirteen pictures from the "Kleine Festung."

187a. Mirel, J.: [Transcript]. [Polish], MS, HIŻ, Poland, no year.

The author was in the Warsaw Ghetto; during the uprising there in late April 1943, the SS pulled him and sixty-two comrades from a bunker. He was transported to the airport in Lublin via vehicles packed with 200 people each. More than 100 people jumped off during the trip. They arrived in Majdanek on May 2, 1943. At the selection of the arrivals, all women and children were sent to the gas chambers. Mirel remained in Majdanek until the end of July 1943 and, after another selection, went to the Skarżysko Kamienna camp, where the conditions were terrible and people worked for the HASAG ammunition factory. In August 1944 the camp was closed, and Mirel went to Buchenwald and then to Schlieben, where 6,000 Jews had to work fourteen hours a day producing portable antitank weapons. More than 100 prisoners were killed in an air raid. Mirel was evacuated to T, where he arrived after a fourteen-day train trip (*234a).

188. [Mixed marriages] Document 3366-PS from the Nuremberg Trial. MS [Photocopy in WL].

The document consists of a decree by the RSHA IV B 4a of December 18, 1943, and an undated implementation report. The decree, signed by Gestapo chief Müller, reads:

> The Reichsführer-SS has ordered, on recommendation, that Jewish spouses from no-longer-existing German-Jewish mixed marriages [and] who are exempt from the identification requirement [Jewish star] be included in the measures for Jewish change of residence to Theresienstadt. Exceptions for now are Jewish spouses
>
> a) whose sons have fallen in war
> b) where, in consideration of existing children, a certain disturbance could be created.

716   Sources and Literature

What is necessary on the basis of the guidelines for technical implementation of the Jewish change of residence to Theresienstadt of February 20, 1943 – IV B 4a 2537/42, which remain unchanged except for the mentioned extension of the group involved, is to be implemented in the period from January 5 to January 10, 1944. Please take care, in the abrupt change of residence for these Jews, that they are given no opportunity to go into hiding.

In case of doubt regarding a possible postponement because of existing children, a decision is to be obtained from the Reich Security Main Office.

188a. Mohr, O. C.: Answers to a questionnaire. Steengracht Document Book, no. III, 22. Mimeographed, Nuremberg, Case XI, 1948.

The text of the statement by the former Danish envoy in Berlin in *3b, doc. 241.

188b. Molho, M.: *In memorium: Hommage aux victims juives en Grèce*. Vol. 1. Saloniki, 1948.

The standard work on the tragedy of the Greek Jews (*184a). Page 94 is noteworthy:

> On June 1 [1943], 820 people [from Saloniki] departed on a train that, according to SS assurances, would go to the ideal Jewish republic, the miracle of miracles, the new Israel, Theresienstadt. These were the privileged people who were admitted: members of the [Jewish] Council and of the various community commissions who had helped organize the forced exodus. Also, the teachers, community functionaries, and all those belonging to the elite of the Jewish population were allowed to go along. It was said that this was the reward reserved by the Commission [of the RSHA IV B 4] for all those who helped with its task. What a grotesque farce. The train was sent without a stop to the crematoria at Birkenau.

189. Morgenstern, R.: "Transcript." [Czech], MS, DA, Prague, 1945.

An account by the author, who left T on September 1, 1942, and went to Raasika (Estonia).

190. Moskowitz, M.: "The Jewish Situation in the Protectorate of Bohemia-Moravia." In *Jewish Social Studies*. New York, January 1942, pp. 17–44.

A documented status report up to early 1941.

190a. Mosse, M.: "'Umsiedlung' der Berliner Juden." MS, WL, Berlin, 1958.

Dr. Martha Mosse was employed by the KG Berlin starting in autumn 1934. She reports in depth on its housing advice office, which dealt with Jews robbed of their homes under a law of May 1, 1939. We quote at length from the section "Jewish Community and Deportation":

> a) It was in 1941 – as far as I remember, on October 1 or 2 – that two members of the executive board, Mr. Henschel and Mr. Kozower, and I, as head of the housing advice office, were summoned by telephone to the Gestapo on Burgstraße. There Criminal Secretary Prüfer disclosed to us that we would be transferred to a concentration camp immediately were we to speak to third parties about what he had to tell us (a later question from Mr. Henschel about whether he could inform the chief executive of the Reichsvereinigung der Juden was answered in the affirmative). Mr. Prüfer then informed us that the "resettlement" of the Berlin Jews was beginning, and that the JKG had to cooperate, otherwise it would be carried out by the SA and SS, "and you know what that would mean." First, several thousand Jews, would be summoned to the KG, using the

Sources and Literature

JKG's real estate registry, from whom the KG functionaries were to take questionnaires that would be supplied by the Gestapo. The completed questionnaires were to be submitted to the Gestapo. (I believe the deadline was 2 or 3 weeks). The whole thing was to be portrayed to the Jewish population as an apartment-clearance action. Based on the completed questionnaires, the Gestapo would then put together a transport for which approximately a thousand people would be considered and which would go to Łódź. The JKG should make sure the transport participants were well dressed; they should procure food and proper facilities for the train cars that the Gestapo would provide. As we were leaving, Mr. Prüfer said, "Yes, it's not nice that I have to tell you this on the Day of Atonement." The same evening, a meeting was held between the executive boards of the Reichsvereinigung ... and the JKG at which I was also present. Despite considerable reservations, it was decided in the end to comply with the Gestapo's requirement that we cooperate in the resettlement, as it was hoped in this way to do as much good as possible in the interests of those affected.

b) Of course, after the departure of the first transport, it was no longer possible to keep secret the purpose for which the questionnaires were filled out by summoned members of the JKG.

Within the housing advice office, there was created an office, headed by Ms. Mendelsohn, that was required to gradually summon the Jewish residents of Berlin based on the real estate registry ... and to fill out the questionnaires. Based on the experience in one case, when, before the completion of the first transport, the Gestapo, at my request, temporarily deferred a family because of a child's illness, members sought in collecting the questionnaires to note anything that could ... make a deferral possible. These were, for example, illness, old age, very small children, Aryan relatives, winding up of economic enterprises, etc.

One or two weeks before each transport, the Gestapo required that the KG send over ... the completed questionnaires (3–4,000 at a time). From these questionnaires, the Gestapo then chose the people who would take part in the next transport. These people's questionnaires were furnished with consecutive numbers. The numbered questionnaires were returned to the JKG, which now had the task of, in writing, calling on those affected to appear at a certain time with baggage ... at the former transit camp in the synagogue on Levetzovstraße. At the beginning, deferral requests were accommodatingly granted by the Gestapo, since enough Jewish residents of Berlin were available to ... reach the required number. As most of us hoped and believed that each transport would be the last one, we intervened in the expectation that those who were deferred would be rescued for good. But this was the case only for those who then immediately fled and went into hiding. Most were then included in later transports after all. Some Jews who had special connections to highly-placed ... persons were deferred once and for all. These persons were named to the JKG by telephone, with instructions to make sure that they did not on any account end up on some transport by accident. As a result of these orders, the JKG kept a list of [these] persons (so-called R List). However, even most of these were deported over the years.

c) The community's initial practice of summoning the people chosen for the next transport to the transit camp with the date of resettlement (the letter was required and approved by the Gestapo) was ended by the Gestapo after a few months, since too many people fled after receiving the letter. From then on, those involved were picked up from their homes by Gestapo officers and brought to the transit camp.

Because the Gestapo never provided anything written, some of the people who were picked up at the beginning ... had been temporarily deferred. To avoid such mistakes, the JKG was ... allowed to ... inform those involved of their deferral [in writing]. Only Mr. Kozower and I were entitled to sign [for this]. ...

d) By what standards the Gestapo put together the transports we did not know. [Aside from people already recorded in questionnaires], people [who had not yet been registered with the KG] also were chosen for deportation. The KG did not learn the reasons. Special assignments also were given. Thus, for example, the head of the Jewish hospital, Dr. Lustig, was ordered to register a certain number of sick people for each transport. The executive board of the JKG was constantly pressured by the Gestapo to reduce the number of its staff. But it was known that anyone who was dismissed (unless he belonged to one of the protected groups, such as privileged mixed marriages), would wind up on the next transport. This situation was especially difficult for the executive board, because of course among the large number of employees there were people whose work ... was not very valuable. Because the executive board of the KG did not respond to the Gestapo pressure to the extent desired, one day ... [Rolf] Günther of the RSHA showed up at the KG and had the staff ... report; he then chose some 500 for dismissal and inclusion in the next transport. This action took place in early November 1942. Günther warned [these] ... functionaries not to flee and pointed out that in place of every escapee, one leading functionary of the KG would be shot and the family of the escapee and the replacement would be taken to a transport to the East. Despite this warning, 20 of the affected disappeared; of them, two reported voluntarily in a few days. For the missing 18, 8 leading employees of the KG were ... shot. Ten more were assigned to the next transport and were immediately finished off in the concentration camp.

e) In autumn [in fact, this took place in June] ... the Theresienstadt camp was designated for Jews over 65 years of age, Jews injured or decorated in the war, and persons for whom non-Jewish authorities had put in a word. ... [Aside from minor exceptions, the Jews and the KG administration did not know what lay ahead of the deportees.]

f) In early summer 1942, the Gestapo department that implemented the transports of Jews was largely sidelined, and the Austrian SS took its place. The rumor circulated that the Berlin Gestapo was not harsh enough and that the Austrians wanted to show them how to deal with Jews. The leader was ... Brunner from Vienna, who brought his staff with him. The ... practice introduced was completely changed. The JKG office on Oranienburger Straße, which was supposed to carry out the work above, was eliminated. Brunner and his staff went to the former old-age home on Gr. Hamburgerstraße, which hitherto had served as a transit camp for transports to Theresienstadt. He ordered that within 24 hours ... all furniture (bedsteads, cabinets, chairs, tables, etc.) be removed, so that only the bare floors remained in the rooms. For nighttime, mattresses without sheets or blankets could be laid out on the floor. The doors to the toilets had to be torn out and replaced with curtains. Because the rooms could not be vacated properly in such a short time, the KG functionaries threw furniture out the window into the courtyard or onto the street. Then all the male JKG functionaries were ordered to assemble and were told by Dr. Eppstein, at the behest of Brunner: they were all from now on to accompany the Gestapo officers as so-called stewards [*Ordner*] to pick up the Jews and to help ... with packing. Anyone who evaded this task without valid grounds, warned Jews, or helped them to escape would be shot and his family members deported to the East.

His staff then went out onto the streets of Berlin, accompanied by some Jewish stewards wearing red armbands with the corresponding letters, without first finding out where exactly the homes of Jews were. The streets were closed off one by one, and the officers, accompanied by stewards, went from house to house to pick up Jews or catch them on the street. This method soon proved unfeasible in Berlin, especially as various mistakes were made and gave rise to furious representations by non-Jews.

Following this fiasco, they then had the JKG tell them which streets had Jewish homes. These were then picked up without warning and housed in the office on Gr. Hamburgerstraße until deportation.

Sources and Literature

g) In January 1943, the Berlin Gestapo once again went into action. Brunner and his people disappeared. But some of Brunner's practices remained.... Insofar as I recall, the transports also no longer were put together ... on the basis of questionnaires, but by street. In February 1943 came the sudden operation by the Leibstandarte [personal guard] Adolf Hitler. It was especially targeted at Jewish workers in the armaments industry. In one week ... some 7,000 people were registered, placed in some 5 transit camps, and then deported to the East. These transit camps (in factories or recreation halls ...) were ... not at all suited for such large numbers.... The action started when trucks driven by members of the Leibstandarte pulled up in front of the factories.... The Jews were ... loaded onto the trucks in their work clothes and transported to the transit camps. In addition, many Jews, especially old people and children, were picked up in homes without being given time to pack their things, dress properly, or even determine where their families were. Members of the Berlin Gestapo then tried, with the help of the JKG, to ... reunite the torn-apart families. The KG had registered 45 children who had been separated from their parents and were taken into custody. Otherwise, too, the collection was carried out very brutally. Thus it happened that older people who could not get into the trucks fast enough were literally thrown onto the trucks. This resulted in serious fractures. Of course, the postponements authorized by the Gestapo were ignored. Since the Gestapo, like the KG ... could not determine who was ... registered, it was possible only in a very few cases to intervene in the interests of the person involved. Thus, for example, it was not possible to segregate out old people or war veterans who were actually supposed to go to Theresienstadt. I know of only one case in which it was possible to protect a 76-year-old doctor from transport to the East and to transfer him to the Theresienstadt transit camp. Of the special action against Jewish partners in mixed marriages, who were quartered by the Leibstandarte in a JKG building on Rosenstraße, I know only that deportation of this group was prevented by the intervention of their Aryan partners and that the transit camp had to be vacated again.

After this action, neither the JKG nor the Gestapo knew which of the Jews was still in Berlin. The Gestapo therefore ordered re-registration by the KG. After its completion, it turned out that, aside from partners in mixed marriages, only a remnant remained in Berlin.

190b. Muhr, F.: "Theresienstadt." MS, Montreux, February 1945.

A rhyming description of the camp in almost 500 verses, from the deportation from Cologne in summer 1942 to liberation in Switzerland, February 1945.

191. Muneles, O.: "Report on the 'Book Registration' [*Bucherfassung*] Work." MS, T, 1945.

191a. Münzer, A.: "Letter Account." MS, Pacific Grove, CA, 1956.

The author came to T from Ratibor on April 21, 1943, and remained until liberation. In Ratibor, where she lived with her brother, life was bearable, because there were "loyal people." "A schoolmate of my brother's, who was in the Gestapo, secretly let us know. One day he said, Carl, in ten days you'll have to leave. Thus the sad chapter began." The text is a simple account of camp conditions.

191b. Murmelstein, B.: "Letter to Dunant." MS, T, May 5, 1945. Text in *3b, doc. 79.

192. Murmelstein, B.: "Historical Overview." MS, WL, T, 1945.

This work was written after the war by the last Jewish Elder in T. It is especially illuminating on the camp's later history.

192a. [Murmelstein, B.]: "Speech Given by the Jewish Elder Dr. Murmelstein to Welcome the Representative of the International Red Cross to Theresienstadt on April 6, 1945." MS.

192b. Musy, B.: Sworn affidavit. Schellenberg Document Book, no. 11, 51. Mimeographed, Nuremberg, Case XI, 1948.

This account by the younger Musy is similar to that of his father (*192c; see also 2a), with whom he went to Berlin in October 1944, where he remained while his father traveled with Schellenberg to meet Himmler in Vienna. The Musys's second trip in January 1945 also started in Berlin, before they traveled, this time together, to see Himmler in Wildbad in the Black Forest. Himmler negotiated privately with the elder Musy for two hours.

> Himmler had issued a prohibition on carrying off concentration camp prisoners; but I myself saw [in early April, accompanied by F. Göring; see *85a] in the Buchenwald camp that the commandant there was not ... adhering to the prohibition. I immediately went from Buchenwald to Schellenberg in Berlin, and he immediately intervened with Himmler for compliance with the ... abduction prohibition.

Kaltenbrunner sabotaged this and "wanted to carry off concentration camp prisoners, in order to get as many people as possible as security. I had meanwhile also been in Theresienstadt concentration camp [with Göring] ... ; 61 illegal Jews were liberated from this camp and brought to Switzerland." Unfortunately, we do not learn what the "illegality" of these Jews consisted of. The release, which cannot otherwise be proven through documents and did not take place, is not mentioned explicitly anywhere but by the two Musys. In connection with this intervention, a woman was liberated in T, but it is possible that Möhs and Günther were talking about other releases.

192c. Musy, J. M.: Sworn affidavit. Schellenberg Document Book, no. 11, 50. Mimeographed, Nuremberg, Case XI, 1948.

Musy describes in considerable detail the interesting mission he undertook in autumn 1944, through personal negotiations with Himmler, to free Jews in German hands. Through middlemen, who included Kersten (*138a) and Schellenberg (*235b, 235c), a meeting was arranged with Himmler in Vienna in October 1944. He negotiated with him on, among other things, the release of the Jews in the camps to Switzerland, with which Himmler declared himself essentially in agreement. "I recall that Himmler gave a figure of 500,000 Jews who could be considered for this action." Musy believed he had succeeded in having Himmler stop the continuation of transports to the East. In return he demanded "trucks and cars," as he had almost half a year earlier from Brand in Budapest through Eichmann (*135), but he was convinced by Musy to accept payment in hard currency. The Swiss succeeded in getting McClelland, representative of Roosevelt's War Refugee Board, to allow a deposit of SF 5,000,000 from the "Union of Orthodox Rabbis in the United States and Canada" into a Swiss bank. On January 12, 1945, Musy had another meeting with Himmler in Wildbad (Black Forest), in which he promised to release Jews from the camps and assigned the implementation of this task to OSTF Göring (*85a). Thus the Swiss transport in T came about on February 5, 1945. Hitler was informed of this by Kaltenbrunner, and a continuation of foreign transports was forbidden. The SF 5,000,000 then was not paid to Himmler but was returned to the Americans (*2a).

Sources and Literature 721

192d. Nabel, H.: "Izbica 1939–1943." MS, HIŻ, Poland, no year.

The author describes the ghetto up to early 1942. Before the internment of foreign Jews, the SS commanded all the Jews of Izbica to come to the Ringplatz at 4 A.M. on February 15, 1942, for "resettlement." Those who did not hide appeared with the most necessary luggage. These people were left for two days and, on the third, were forced on pain of death to surrender their money and valuables. This was followed by the deportation of approximately 2,500 people and the plundering of the ghetto. Soon after, Czech Jews "with elegant, rich luggage" arrived (2,001 Jews left T on March 11 and 17, 1942, with Izbica as the destination [9 survivors]); of them, 150 young men were turned into a "militia," with the help of which the SS caught 700 local Jews. The author worked as a woodchopper for a Czech Jew who lived in his home. The district administrator promised no punishment for those who hid from the "deportations," in exchange for a fine of 5,000 zloty and work in the armaments industry. Those who then reported were taken into custody and were transported to camps. Here the account ends.

193. [Nágl, Mořic]: "Výstava obrazů z terezínského ghetta" [Photo Exhibition from the Theresienstadt Ghetto]. In 319, no. 5, 1951.

In October 1950, 254 watercolors on camp themes were found by chance in an attic in T. The painter had been in T from May 22, 1942, to October 28, 1944, and died in Auschwitz. The work includes one reproduction: a courtyard scene. Twenty pictures of Nágl's are in the possession of YV.

193a. [Nasch, E.]: "Ich habe es gesehen." MS, DA, 1945.

The author, a doctor from Brünn [Brno], describes his life under German occupation, the fear of transport, and his time in T – he arrived on April 4, 1942, and his son was born five days later – until the journey to Auschwitz on October 19, 1944. His wife and child died there.

193b. Neumann, E.: "Transcript." MS, WL, London, 1955.

The author arrived in T from Vienna with an aunt (who was a nurse) in September 1942 as a fourteen-year-old and lived in the "German children's home," probably L 414. A Czech Jew and four friends directed the home, which consisted of five to six rooms with twenty girls each, in an excellent fashion as a "kibbutz." In December 1943, Neumann was deported to Auschwitz. This is a valuable account, from a human perspective, on T and later camps.

193c. Neumann, J. O.: *Im Schatten des Todes: Ein Tatschenbericht vom Schicksalskampf des slowakischen Judentums.* Tel Aviv, 1956.

A source work on the tragedy of the Slovak Jews, the activities of the "Jewish Central Office," and Jewish resistance. The overly wordy account suffers from a lack of chronological order but offers a wealth of important information. The Zionist-led resistance movement cultivated connections to Edelstein and Dr. Kahn until their deportation to T, to which packets were sent, "some of which had to be smuggled over the Protectorate borders." Later, lists of names for packet shipments from the "World Jewish Congress" were sent to Geneva. Page 174 is noteworthy: "The attempt to establish direct, personal contacts with Theresienstadt through envoys

722   *Sources and Literature*

failed because of its walls." Through the "Jewish Central Office," which it later controlled completely, the resistance succeeded in achieving a cessation of deportations in summer 1942, through negotiation with and bribery of Slovak authorities and Eichmann's representative in Pressburg, HSTF Wisliceny, after 55,000 Jews already had been deported and 25,000 remained in the country. However, a large number of those who remained behind had to go to work camps, including Sered, where conditions were bearable and even relatively good. At the outbreak of the Slovak rebellions in summer 1944, all were released. After the rebellions were suppressed, HSTF Brunner, Eichmann's feared assistant, took over the "solution to the Jewish question." Under his leadership, Sered was turned into a concentration camp; all interned Jews – including most of the functionaries of the "Jewish Central Office" and the resistance – were sent there. Starting on September 30, five transports went from there to Auschwitz. After the gassing ceased, transports were directed from there to Auschwitz, Ravensbrück, Mauthausen, and Sachsenhausen, and one with "partners in mixed marriages" went to Bergen-Belsen.

Before Christmas 1944, Brunner announced that the remaining women and children from Sered would be sent to T due to "danger of bombing," and the men would follow later. In this way, the first three transports to T were carried out; from the second on, some men also went along. On March 30, 1945, Brunner ordered the evacuation of Sered and announced, after the escape of two Jews, "I know you all have family in Theresienstadt! I call your attention to the fact that for everyone who runs away from a transport, ten people in Theresienstadt will pay. In one week I will be there!" The machines in the camp's workshops were disassembled and loaded, with all the goods and supplies, onto the transport trains, which left on March 31; even the kitchen and its provisions were taken along, so that there was cooking on the trip and warm meals were distributed. When the train stopped at Trentschin for two days, Jews were even able to shop in the town. At departure, only twelve people were missing; others, with Brunner's threat in mind, followed voluntarily on normal passenger trains. They arrived in T on April 7. During the "delousing," the men were examined, shaved, and treated by women. The "transport leadership" stole the newcomers' food, which admittedly was especially tempting and had been brought in large quantities. Otherwise, too, the reception was bad: "The Jewish order guards [GW] ... behaved badly toward the 'transport leadership,' which consisted mainly of assimilated Czech Jews ... in addition, this transport had arrived as 'privileged'! So they had to be 'collaborators' ... and a great witch-hunt ... began against the 'Slovaks'" (p. 286). Brunner soon appeared,

> inspected and viewed the machines, and then called together the Sered workers, with whom he spoke regarding the creation of their own workshops.... This fact, like the fact that he "recommended" [them] as good skilled workers in the presence of ... the Jewish Elder, annoyed the Therezin [*sic*] Czech chauvinists. Brunner then appeared a second time to settle the bill with the provisioner and was never seen again.

Murmelstein is judged unfavorably:

> The first discussion with this ... man, who had taken on all the manners and also the crude barracks language of his Nazi bosses, greatly depressed them [the leading Slovak Jews]. In his extremely pronounced egotism, he barely ... allowed the friends to speak... . In the process he made some "generous" gestures ... and proposed their inclusion in

Sources and Literature

the Jewish Council, although in the same sentence he emphasized that he cared nothing for the entire Jewish Council [Council of Elders]. (p. 287 et seq.)

The author, who had come from the resistance movement and through this had become head of the "Jewish Central Office," the Slovak equivalent of the Reichsvereinigung," founded a Zionist committee and made contact with the Czech Jews in order to defuse accusations of collaboration against the Slovak Jews. His description of Kasztner's visit to T is consistent with that of Kasztner (see Chapter 7).

193d. Neusüss-Hunkel, E.: *Die SS.* Hanover and Frankfurt a. M., 1956.

An overview of the history and sociological structure of the SS, with all its institutions, including the RSHA, and so on.

194. [Nisko]: "Nisko nad Sanem, první koncentrační tábor židovský" [Nisko on the San, the first Jewish concentration camp]. In 319, no. 1, 1947. (B.-Sp.)

Eichmann was present during the deportation from Ostrau [Ostrava] on October 17, 1939, and the arrival in Nisko on October 19. On October 21, only 400 people were in the camp; the others had been driven across the Russian border, in the course of which many perished. At the end of October, transports came from Vienna, Teschen, Bielitz [Bielsko], and Kattowitz, along with another 290 deportees from Ostrau [Ostrava]. Once again, the majority were driven away; 1,000 Viennese and Ostrauers remained. When another 500 were driven over the border on November 20, there were 320 Ostrauers and 180 Viennese there until the camp was dissolved on April 13, 1940. These are estimates, because, in fact, 460 people returned to Moravia. Of the 900 Moravian Jews in Russia, some were "directed" to Old Russia on June 29, 1940; others were sent to work camps in central Russia – the Urals, near Archangelsk – and to Siberia on June 29, 1940. "Only especially strong, powerful men lived until January 1942, when entry into the Czechoslovakian army ... was made possible for them through their release from the Russian work camps." Some 350 were permitted to remain in eastern Galicia; most of them died in summer 1941, but some succeeded in returning illegally to Ostrau [Ostrava].

195. Noack-Mosse, E.: "Tagebuch einer Überlebenden." In *Frankfurter Hefte.* March 1952, p. 163.

A short, largely correct overview of T.

195a. Noack-Mosse, E.: "Theresienstädter Tagebuch." MS, Oberstdorf (Allgäu), 1945/46.

A description of conditions according to notes from T; errors occur in this text when older events are related. The Gestapo's order in Augsburg regarding partners in "mixed marriages" – which preceded the transport and which Mrs. Noack-Mosse received on January 25, 1945 – stated:

> You are hereby required to report for use in urgent labor deployment in the Organization Todt on _____ by 10 o'clock at the latest to the Secret State Police – State Police Office – Augsburg, Prinzregentenstraße 11 (courtyard area). You are to bring provisions sufficient for 3 days, as well as sturdy work clothes and shoes, 1–2 wool blankets, and any available tools, such as saws, axes, spades, hoes, and the like.

Sources and Literature

This order immediately suspends any contractual relationship with your employer. You are to submit the order to your manager for inspection. Objections and the like are inadmissible. Salary you are owed from your current employment is to be paid to you.

Your current manager is to close out your labor book with the notation "On _____ required for special deployment by the State Police," and to sign you out of your health insurance as "furloughed."

Failure to follow this order will result in the most serious state police measures. You are obliged to observe the abovementioned deadline under any circumstances.

The transport left Augsburg on February 20 and arrived in T on the 23rd. Klaus Mann visited T on May 19, but his aunt, Mrs. Mimi Mann, had already had gone to Prague (*122). The same day, the first Berliner visited the camp, after bicycling there in ten days. The author embarked on her journey home on July 1 (*183c, 223b).

195b. Nothmann, H.: "Wie es war." In *Brüderlichkeit: Mitteilungen der Ges. F. chr.-jüd. Zusammenarbeit.* Nuremberg-Fürth, September 1954, March and July 1955, March 1956, March 1957, March 1958, and February 1959.

In letters following liberation (from Deggendorf), the author describes experiences and impressions from Baden, Berlin, and T, where he stayed from October 4, 1942, until liberation. The text discusses the life of Orthodox Jews in the camp. Because of insufficient nourishment, the Orthodox rabbinate recommended eating non-kosher meat, but some twenty people still refused to eat it.

196. Nyiszli, M.: "SS-Obersturmführer Docteur Mengele." In *Les Temps Modernes.* Paris, March and April 1951, p. 1654 et seq. and p. 1855 et seq.

The unmerciful truth about Auschwitz extermination methods. The figures on the transport from T in autumn 1944 are not correct.

197. O. K.: "Der Befreier von Theresienstadt." In *Aufbau.* New York, May 2, 1952.

Under this misleading title, the work presents an obituary of Musy (*192c), whose complex character (Nazi sympathies) is described.

198. Oppenhejm, R.: *Der skulde saa vaere: Marianne Petits dagbok fra Theresienstadt* [It Was Supposed to Be This Way: Marianne Petits's diary from Theresienstadt]. Copenhagen, 1945.

Cloaked as a novel, this work describes the capture of the Jews in Copenhagen, their transport, and life in T, generally accurately, from the Danish-nationalist standpoint.

199. Oppenhejm, R.: *The Door of Death.* London, 1948.

A translation of *198.

200. Ornstein, S.: "So war es ... Tagebuchblätter, i KZ geschrieben." In *Der neue Weg.* Nos. 1/2–37/38. Vienna, 1946.

The author admits in number 39/40 that she wrote the text from memory. She came to T as a Viennese emigrant on November 30 (not, as she claims, on October 30), 1941, and from there, in October 1944, she was sent via Auschwitz to Wilischtal and, at the end of April 1945, back to T. It is an inexact and unreliable account of conditions.

201. Ornsteinová, E.: "Iluse Terezín" [Illusion Theresienstadt]. MS, DA, Prague, 1945.

Sources and Literature

The author, who was close to Edelstein, describes the plans of the first Jewish Elders and the reality of the camp.

202. Ornsteinová, E.: "Vzpomínka na Jakuba Edelsteina" [Remembering Jakob Edelstein]. In 319, no. 3, 1945.

A work similar to *201.

202a. [Ornsteinová, E.]: "Die arbeitende Frau in Theresienstadt." MS, T, January 1944.

202b. [Panenské Březany] "Telegram from K. H. Franks to Himmler." MS, IfZ, Prague, August 28, 1943.

In Panenské Březany (Jungfern-Breschan), Heydrich's estate near Prague, where his widow later resided, 64 Jews were used for agricultural work; they were then sent to T on a transport on September 15, 1942, but were immediately brought back for "outside work." In spring of 1943, the group was increased to 110 men. When the last workers from the other outside groups in the "Protectorate" were sent back to T at the end of August 1943, Frank appealed to Himmler (NO-3027):

> In July 1942, with your permission, Reichsführer, a Jewish labor kommando 80-men-strong [not from T but from Prague] was sent to the estate of Jungfern-Breschan belonging to the wife of the deceased Obergruppenführer Heydrich from the Theresienstadt ghetto, and it is still there. The labor kommando is under special guard and is housed in isolation.
>
> The commander of the Security Police now has to send or return all Jewish labor kommandos to the Theresienstadt ghetto by September 1, 1943 at the latest, at the behest of the Reich Security Main Office. The labor kommando in Jungfern-Breschan would still be needed for various urgent tasks until the beginning of winter. I request a decision on whether this labor kommando can be left beyond September 1, 1943.

In the Himmler files (microfilm in IfZ) there is additional correspondence on Panenské Březany that illuminates the mentality and the slave business of leading SS officers. In response to Frank's telegram, Himmler wanted to know what tasks were meant. Frank answered: garden work, maintenance, and repairs. Himmler approved an extension until September 30, 1943, and asked if other groups from T were working externally. Frank answered that there were no more such groups. At Mrs. Heydrich's, however, the work continued; not until February 11, 1944, did the last thirty men from the group return to T. That day, fifteen Jehovah's Witnesses arrived at Lina Heydrich's from Flossenbürg. Pohl estimated the daily costs to her at RM 6 for skilled workers and only RM 4 for unskilled laborers. Himmler decided, "The costs of the prisoners … will be reimbursed from special account 'H'"; the money, he said, would be requested from the "coffers of the personal staff [of the Reichsführer-SS]." Later, Mrs. Heyrich was to pay by herself. The expenses were thus paid with Jewish money, as "special account 'H'" was composed of property extorted from the German Jews for T when they concluded the "home purchase agreements" and was intended to maintain the camp.

Lina Heydrich apparently was not told that she would have to pay for her slaves, and she sent a "claim" for June 1944 for RM 900 ("the assessment of the prisoners was made based on the usual daily rate of RM 3 for employment in agriculture"; Rpf 60 was deducted from this amount because Mrs. Heydrich took care of their board) to Flossenbürg, in the belief that "the administration had made an error." Pohl asked Himmler's personal assistant Brandt what to do and was told to get Mrs. Heydrich to pay, because, as Brandt explained, "the supply of prisoners for labor has its costs." Pohl then wrote a long, "tactful" letter to Mrs. Heydrich on August 26, 1944; it provides evidence that the leased concentration camp prisoners were state or SS slaves:

> I also believe that the office in charge did not tell you before making the prisoners available that the Reich (to whom the prisoners after all belong) expects payment for the supply of each worker. As a result of this omission, you must have believed in error that your obligation was fulfilled by accommodating the prisoners, that is, housing and feeding them. Unfortunately, as I have already indicated, this is not the case.

As a concession, however, Pohl did not demand payment until September 1, 1944:

> Here I find myself in agreement with the Reichsführer SS – both of us are bound by Reich regulations, which we do not make. Each of us, for example even the Reichsführer-SS, must pay a wage set by the Reich for each prisoner supplied to his household, in addition to housing and feeding. Thus we cannot get around it.

This was not true, as the lease of prisoners was a matter for the SS-Wirtschafts- und Verwaltungshauptamt, which Pohl headed, and he soon proved that he could "get around it." First he reported to Brandt that he could cover the costs by the end of August "from some fund or other." Brandt answered that Himmler was "of the opinion that one would have to subtract 10 prisoners from Jungfern-Breschan." This was not necessary, because Lina Heydrich was well able to defend herself, as another letter to her from Pohl on September 4, 1944, shows. In it, he said that he now understood "what was at the root of this property and how much work and costs you personally have expended for its production and must continue to expend." Through the fault of the prior owners, of which the Reich was one, the property had been in bad condition when it was taken over: "In this context, I can absolutely in good conscience refrain from calculating the prisoner costs at all in this situation, and will also advocate this officially." Pohl also let Brandt know: "I have now waived any payment by Mrs. Heydrich." Himmler finally agreed. When Himmler wanted to make himself presentable to the West, on January 14, 1945, he wrote to Kalten-brunner and Pohl about the matter again:

> As part of the campaign to give Jehovah's Witnesses their unconditional freedom as small colonies in isolation on separate properties, in order to achieve the best political effect abroad, I would like the Jehovah's Witnesses who are with Mrs. Heydrich to ... also ... be freed with restrictions and released from custody. The two Czech Jehovah's Witnesses should not be released ... they must leave there. There will then be 13, or perhaps only 12. All guards can also be eliminated. The release must occur in the usual formal way.

The letter contained an addition for Pohl: "I later heard that Mrs. Heydrich had a long correspondence with you about the workers, but I must say that the idea of starting a Jehovah's Witnesses colony here came from me and not from her. So as a tried-and-true philosopher, don't be angry at her."

202c. Patak, E.: "The Strickers in Theresienstadt." In Fraenkel, J. (ed.): *Robert Stricker*. London, 1950, pp. 51–53.

Sources and Literature

In addition to the information in this short memorial pamphlet, we make a few more brief remarks about T. Robert Stricker (1879–1944) of Brünn [Brno] joined Herzl as early as 1896. He was immediately arrested at Vienna's occupation, was soon released, was arrested again, and was sent to Dachau and then to Buchenwald along with other high Jewish functionaries from Vienna, including Desider Friedmann. With his health permanently damaged by abuse, he was released with Friedmann in 1939, but both were refused permission to emigrate. In September they were sent with their wives to T, where Stricker was the only leading Zionist of the old guard.

203. Peter, T.: Poems. In *Der Weg*. Nos. 13/14, 18, 49 (1948), and 11 (1949). Berlin, 1948–49.

The author, who was in T from June 1944, wrote the following poems in T: "In der Glimmerspalterei" (IA/113-14795), "Die Strasse Zurück," and "Strassenfegerlied."

204. Pfister, M.: "Aus einem schweizerischen Desinfektionslager für Flüchtlinge, Februar 1945." In *Eckart*. Witten-Berlin, January–March 1955, p. 122 et seq.

A substantively erroneous account of the intake of the transports from T.

205. Philipp, B.: *Die Todgeweihten*. Hamburg, 1949.

In this novel about T, the author distorts conditions in an unacceptable fashion.

205a. [Piaski] "Letter from the JSS Delegatory Piaski of April 26, 1942, to JSS Presidium in Cracow." MS, HIŻ.

Five thousand foreign Jews – including 1,000 who came from the "Protectorate" on April 25 – were "settled" in Piaski. This was the transport that left T on April 23. Only one of them survived the war. A letter from the Jewish Self-Help (JSS) Piaski (MS, HIŻ) on April 14, 1942, estimates the Jews sent from Germany and T at "around 4,200" and calls them needy.

206. Picard, M.: *Hitler in uns selbst* [Hitler in Ourselves]. Zurich-Erlenbach, 1946.

This text is important for understanding the psychological readiness for "massification," which made National Socialist and other attitudes possible.

207. Pick, J., R. Polák, and J. Pacovský: *Terezín očima hygienika: Zpráva ź terezínského koncentračního tábora o boji proti hmyzu a skvrnitému tyfu* [Theresienstadt Seen by a Hygienist: Report from the Theresienstadt Concentration Camp on the Fight against Vermin and Typhus]. Prague, 1948.

A scientific account by the camp's leading hygienist and pest controller (Pacovský was the head of "delousing").

208. Pick, J., R. Polák, and J. Pacovský: *Theresienstadt mit den Augen des Hygienikers gesehen*. Prague, [1948 or somewhat later]. YIVO.

A translation of *207.

208a. Pick, A., and F. Salus: "Klinik und Pathogenese der Theresienstädter Anämie." MS, YV, T, no year.

209. Pick, A., and F. Salus: "Clinical Aspects and Pathogenesis of So-Called Theresienstadt Anemia." In *Acta Med. Scandinav*. Vol. 129. Copenhagen-Oslo, 1947, pp. 389–410.

728   *Sources and Literature*

An English version of *208a.

209a. Pinkhof, M.: "Reschith hamachteret hachaluzith beholland" [The Beginning of the Chalutz Underground in Holland]. In *Jediot Beit Lohamei Haghetaot*. No. 13. Israel, January 1, 1956, p. 19.

During his visit to Holland, Edelstein visited the group to which Pinkhof belonged and assessed the Jewish situation in Europe as extremely inauspicious, if the war did not end soon – "and there is no chance at all of this."

209b. Pintus, E.: "Die Befreiung" [Liberation]. MS, RvO, O. O., 1947.

The author, a German emigrant, came to T on September 6, 1944, from Westerbork. This is a valuable account of the camp in the period from liberation until the return to Holland. The fear of gassing on the part of the concentration camp prisoners in T is typical: the people had to

> fall in two by two with a piece of soap and a bath towel at our bathhouse. The door ... was open, but no one moved from the spot. Everyone stood as still as a stone. Slowly they began to move, they screamed, they clamored, they begged, they threw themselves to their knees – let us live. A few thousand Hungarians who had come from Bergen-Belsen, emaciated bodies, none of them yet 30 years old – "let us live," they cried, even as the first ones were dragged inside.

209c. Plaček, M.: [528 caricatures of camp inmates]. YV, T, 1943.

209d. Pleyer, W.: *Aber wir grüssen den Morgen: Erlebnisse 1945–1947*. Starnberg-Wels, 1953.

A book by a German-Bohemian writer who, after the fall of the "Third Reich," extended the great hatred he harbored, especially for the Czechs, to the Nazis as well. At the collapse he fled to Bavaria but was deported to Czechoslovakia at the country's request. His experiences in Czech imprisonment only allowed his hatred to flare up more strongly. As fate would have it, it was this man, along with other thrown-together German prisoners, who had to deal with the sad detritus of the assets [*Liquidationsmasse*] of the T "Ghetto" – a terrible and grotesque epilogue to the tragedy. But before Pleyer was landed with this eerie inventory, still in Germany, he speaks of the war-blinded Dr. Norbert Stern, who was in T from July 1942 (*352b). Pleyer tells the story as follows:

> But in 1944 the fools of the Third Reich already had brought him to Theresienstadt. He wrote a book on his experiences there, with the righteousness of a God-fearing person. His description shows that it was to a disgusting extent Jews, those of the Jewish self-administration, especially camp police, who made the ghetto into the hell of Theresienstadt. The Americans opposed its publication, because this portrayal did not suit their intentions.   (p. 54)

In Prague, Pleyer found himself in investigative detention in the Pankrác prison, which rented out the prisoners – they had learned this practice from the SS – for various types of work. One of the jobs for political prisoners – including Gestapo members, Czech "collaborators," and so on – was the "Theresienstadt kommando, which sifted and organized all the movable property from the Theresienstadt camp, that is, Jewish property, and prepared it for return or for sale to benefit those who had been harmed" (p. 231). Those who had been harmed got little or nothing from it. The "Theresienstadt kommando" was housed in two cells in Pankrác. Pleyer also mentions Raffaelsohn, sent from Neuengamme, who had been known for bad behavior in Zossen: "As a kapo, he probably abused or denounced Jews or did both. For some reason or other he considered it advisable not to be a Jew" (*86, p. 264). Finally, Pleyer himself ended up [participating] in the liquidation[-of-assets] operation:

> Now I have been assigned to the Theresienstadt kommando, which is engaged in storing and shipping objects from the camp.... Clothing and linens are kept in an abandoned factory belonging to the Mehlschmidt firm; medical equipment and health care articles, as well as washing tables, sewing machines, and ovens are stored in part of a building belonging to the Karolinum. [Pleyer worked both in these storehouses, which had been squeezed into venerable parts of the university, and in the factory.] I stick to this work in order to outfit myself; I find myself a hat and a cap, a turn-down collar and necktie, handkerchiefs, socks, pants. These are parts of old stocks that now are considered only raw material, for the shredder.... When we load up outside, many of the idle stop near us, as well as the needy. They see that things that still are useful have ended up among the rags; they complain, they ask us if they can have something. We free up a few of the better things and throw them to the people. Then someone recognizes the highly political situation: Czechs allowing Germans to share with them, and things that don't even belong to the Germans! A menacing voice is heard, so we drive off.   (p. 283 et seq.)

209e. Pohl, O.: Testimony on May 19, 1947. Mimeographed, Nuremberg, Case IV.

Pohl testifies that there were 600,000 concentration camp prisoners at the end of 1944, of whom 230,000–250,000 were engaged in private industry, approximately 170,000 were under the control of the Ministry for War Production and Armaments for "underground transfer," and 10,000–12,000 were working to build the Führer's headquarters in Thuringia.

209f. Pokorná, L.: "Das Röntgenbild der Osteoporose im Konzentrationslager Theresienstadt." In *Radiologia clinica*. Basel-New York, November 1949, pp. 360–70.

209g. Pokorná, L.: "Die Lungentuberkulose im Konzentrationslager Theresienstadt im Vergleich mit der bei Häftlingen in anderen deutschen Konzentrationslagern." In *Der Tuberkulosearzt*. Marburg, July 1950, pp. 406–14

Of the 25,996 lung examinations performed in the X-ray ward E VI, there were 2,300 positive results, of which 2,072 were tuberculin illnesses, including pleuritis (this figure, as cited in Chapter 16, is also reported by Lederer but, erroneously, for all of T). This corresponds to a percentage of almost 8% of all those examined. In addition, at the end of the war, 416 concentration camp prisoners were examined, of whom 201 (48%) showed a positive result. One must agree with Dr. Segall – who worked as a specialist in E IIIa, where X-rays were taken later as well – that the overall number of cases had to be much higher. According to her figures, sent in a letter, tuberculosis was found with unusual frequency during autopsies. This was especially true, in the final months of the war, for prisoners from Slovakia and Hungary, most of whom, however, had become ill before their arrival in T.

209h. Pokorná, L.: "Eine Ärztin erlebt das 'Musterlager' Theresienstadt." MS, IfZ, Sao Paulo, 1948.

The author was in T from January 30, 1942, to August 3, 1945, where she was the chief radiologist. This comprehensive work, based on diary entries from the camp, offers a description, one that is not free of error, of the conditions and provides valuable information on the health system, particularly on her own activities, as well as things she herself experienced.

Regarding radiology: The practice was opened on March 15, 1942, and was at first extremely primitive; often the electricity failed, and at first only regular X-rays were possible, which could not be carried out in a lying position. They began with six examinations per day; in 1943, the daily high was 101 patients, and, in 1944, 203.

> The frequency increased ... and reached its peak in June 1942 with 1,950 examinations! At that time, besides me there was no radiologist in the camp. Later, x-ray examinations were undertaken in ten other places. But, even in this period, x-ray images could be made only in the hospital (E VI) and in ... the engineers' barracks [*Geniekaserne*] (E IIIa). When the health system was fully developed, and ten radiologists worked constantly, the frequency figures in most departments sank to 1,000 examinations per month. Thus it was that, when I left the camp on August 3, 1945, the outpatient records of the radiology department E VI ... showed 40,800 patients. Some of the x-rays consisted of screenings. The first ... involved labor deployment. For men ... between 16 and 55 years old, heart and lungs were x-rayed. At the time, there were also simultaneous screenings of children up to 14 years old and young people between 14 and 16 of both sexes.
>
> Later the screenings were extended to all occupations and every age. It affected primarily those ... who would have endangered the camp if the lung results had been positive, specifically cooks, bakers, provisioning staff, etc. The more x-ray wards ... the camp got, the more frequently other wards undertook screenings, in order to relieve the x-ray institute ... [E VI], which had been intended especially for bedridden patients. After the camp was partially evacuated, and other x-ray departments no longer existed (October 1944), I once again took over all screenings.

Some special observations: The average age of all X-ray patients with broken bones was sixty-seven and a half. "In the winter months, with ice and the very frequent blackouts ... we would sometimes see five femoral fractures in one day." Infiltrates after the frequent pneumonias starting in spring were at first thought to be a result of sulfonamide treatments but turned out to be tuberculosis, "generally localized on the basis of the pneumonia they had experienced. Curiously, the illness was in almost all cases localized in the middle lobe line." Concentration camp prisoners, many of whom had survived typhus, were also examined at the end of the war. Of these, 48% had serious tuberculosis of the lungs, in most cases on both sides. Caverns the size of oranges were found. In contrast, in 25,996 pneumonia cases among normal inmates, 7.8% proved to be tuberculosis. In T, the early belief that Jews had a particular disposition toward "malignant growths" proved false. Of the 40,800 examined patients, fewer than 20 were diagnosed with stomach cancer. However, benign stomach tumors of "unimaginable size" were discovered. Bowel obstructions (ileuses) were frequent. "The surgeon and I observed, working together, nearly a hundred of these otherwise very rare cases. Were the diagnosis made in time, it was possible in a large percentage of cases to save these people, who otherwise would be doomed." Regarding the discovery of cases of osteoporosis (loss of bone mass), which was frequent in T, she says: "The illness generally appeared in late autumn and winter, reaching its high point in spring and falling off in summer. The longer we were imprisoned, the more frequently this disease appeared." The poor quality of the bread and margarine was held responsible for the frequency of gallbladder conditions. "Those with diabetes and people suffering from high blood pressure had it ... relatively good in this regard. Blood pressure dropped due to undernourishment, and 80 mm of mercury blood pressure" was not rare.

Regarding psychiatric cases: A small Berlin transport – men, women, and even a four-year-old child – were housed together in a room in the psychiatric ward. The internment lasted fourteen months. Because several people fell victim to tuberculosis during this period, the commandant's office finally began radiological examinations of the group.

> The child was mentally somewhat underdeveloped, but not at all in need of institutionalization. I was understandably interested in what the ... internees lacked. Aside from a noticeable sadness that was sufficiently explained by the manner of their housing, they showed nothing obvious at all. From the answers to my ... questions, they were Berliners whom the SS wanted to dispose of in some way.

These unfortunates were deported as part of the extensive deportation of the mentally ill.

Regarding the German monitoring physician Dr. Krönert: "I heard many good things about him in the camp. He was also in charge of medical matters at the Kleine Festung, and he very often sent from there to the Grosse Festung [ghetto] patients who inevitably would have died there, but who were cured in our hospital." At times he had diphtheria patients transferred to the infectious disease ward in the "ghetto." "By the end, the SS distrusted him and did not leave him unattended for a moment when he spoke with the head of the health system."

Regarding vermin infestations: "Doctors no longer dared apply a cincture [*cingulum*], let alone a plaster cast. When removing such a cast, one found hundreds of lice. The area under the dressing formed a teeming brown mass." The author cites a saying from T: "You go to bed without bites and wake up with a thousand bites."

210. Poláček, O.: "Výročí hrdinství českých žen" [Anniversary of the Heroism of Czech Women]. In 319, no. 28/29, 1948.

At the closure of the Auschwitz "family camp" in July 1944, 600 women from T went voluntarily to the gas chamber with their children, even though they could have been included in labor kommandos without the children.

211. [Poland] *Biuletyn głownej: Badania zbrodni niemieckich w Polsce* [Main Bulletin: Research on German Crimes in Poland]. Vols. III and IV. Posen [Poznan], 1947/48.

Volume III offers important and factual pieces on Bełzec, Sobibór, the Treblinka labor camp, and police in Poland.

Volume IV contains a thorough factual account of Majdanek (the Lublin concentration camp). Jewish transports did not come to Majdanek, which, like Auschwitz, was never exclusively an extermination camp, until April–May 1942; the first transports came from Slovakia and the "Protectorate." From there they went via T (which the author did not know about) and transit camps near Lublin. In Majdanek there were 9,000, or perhaps somewhat more, Czech and Slovak Jews. Unfortunately the work does not provide figures separately, but the Czech group was certainly in the minority. It contains a death list for the period from June 1 to September 28, 1942; 90% of 7,026 names were Czechoslovakian. According to witness testimony, at the

732   *Sources and Literature*

beginning of 1943, only a few hundred members of this group were still alive. When 18,000 Jewish prisoners were shot on November 3, 1943, after being forced to undress, the last survivors from Czechoslovakia also died. A Budweis document in connection with the transport of April 18, 1942, from there to T indicates that the Majdanek victims included "Theresienstadters." The owner of the document undoubtedly ended up in the wave of transports from T toward the end of April 1942 and then, consistently with the information in this work, arrived in Majdanek in May.

212. [Poland] *German Crimes in Poland*. Vols. I–II. Warsaw, 1946/47.

This work discusses Chelmno [Chełmno], Bełżec, Auschwitz, Sobibór, Treblinka, and so on. It provides an overview for those who cannot read the comprehensive Polish original.

213. Poliakov, L.: *Bréviaire de la haine (Le IIIe Reich et les juifs)*. Paris, 1951.

The first and to date most successful attempt at a scholarly overview of the Jewish tragedy. Poliakov sees the "Manichean" components in National Socialism; in this system, the Jew is viewed as the archenemy and symbol of the devil. Jew-hatred, and even the "race laws," gains sacred significance. The assessment of the pseudomythical ideology as a religion seems to me not particularly felicitous: religion and ideology are mutually exclusive, but they can fulfill socially analogous functions. The brief reference to T is correct.

213a. Poliakov, L., and J. Wulf: *Das Dritte Reich und die Juden: Dokumente und Aufsätze* [The Third Reich and the Jews: Documents and Essays]. Berlin 1955.

The first representative documentary work on the subject in the German language. The work references T in the report by Wisliceny (XXXVIII-67, pp. 87 et seq.), the "Wannsee Protocol" (NG-2596, pp. 119 et seq.; see *117), and the so-called short Korherr report (NO-5192/3, pp. 239 et seq.; see *156a).

213b. Poliakov, L., and J. Wulf: *Das Dritte Reich und seine Diener* [The Third Reich and Its Servants]. Berlin, 1956.

Documents from the Foreign Office and the Wehrmacht on the Jewish question as well as the legal deprivation of the Jews' rights.

213c. Poper, M.: "Po deseti letech: Několik vzpomínek na Terezín" [Ten Years Later: Some Recollections of Theresienstadt]. In 319, no. 6, 1955.

An account of, among other things, an unusually courageous speech by Leo Baeck.

214. [Prague] "Classification Protocol from June 15, 1943." Mimeographed, MS, Prague.

This protocol, on pages 1,085–95, shows the work of the Jewish asset liquidation kommando that, for the SS, made preparations for the theft of the deportees' abandoned property. On that day, thirty-three apartments were visited, some of which were still inhabited – by Jews and non-Jews. A small old-age home was empty – the seventeen inmates had been deported – and it was said that "the furniture [beds and wardrobes] was sent to Theresienstadt."

215. [Prague] "Status Report for Sept. 21, 1943." Mimeographed, MS, Prague.

A camp list of the objects stolen from the homes of deported Prague Jews and stored in some thirty-six warehouses. There were, for example, 4,877 bathroom furnishings, 31,517 normal and 1,460 valuable pictures, 695,627 books, 2,116 cameras, 6,060 gas masks, 16,525 gramophone records, 6,965 lamps, 1,802 musical instruments, 8,122 eyeglasses, 2,455 rugs, 10,189 pots, 2,598 clocks, and 88,074 living room furnishings. Some items from these stocks went to T in the years 1943–44, although these items were generally only junk.

216. Prochnik, R.: "Juden in Theresienstadt: Ein statistischer Bericht" [Jews in Theresienstadt: A Statistical Report]. MS, WL, T, July 14, 1945.

The last secretary of the administration offers valuable, although not often reliable, material, in some cases with annoying typographical errors in the statistical figures. Nevertheless, what is presented is an indispensable source (*166). Prochnik's overview of those deported to T cites the following figures:

Protectorate	73,468
Germany	42,921
Austria	15,244
Holland	4,897
Denmark	466
Slovakia	1,447
Hungary	1,074
Total	139,517

216a. [Notables] "Intervention des Aufsichtsratsvorsitzenden der I.G. Farben, Dr. Krauch, bei SS-Obergruppenführer Wolff gegen die Deportation von Geheimrat Dr. Arthur von Weinberg." NI-13578. Mimeographed, Berlin, June 2, 1942.

This is a letter from Krauch, including an attachment. This text indicates that Weinberg

> received a directive from the Secret State Police, Munich office, yesterday that announced the confiscation of his property and at the same time ordered him to prepare himself for deportation from the territory of the Reich. As we also hear, von Weinberg already has been brought to Munich, from which his further deportation probably will take place the day after tomorrow.

Referring to Weinberg's many merits, Krauch wished to "allow [himself] to suggest checking whether it might not be possible for you to intervene in this special case and effectuate a change in the decision by the Secret State Police, as long as no police necessities stand in the way."

We learn that Weinberg was eighty-two years old at the time and that his two "Aryan" adopted daughters were married to men from the highest ranks of the nobility. Weinberg had been engaged in the entire First World War as a major and was highly decorated. Together with his brother Carl, he was a founder and for many years director of I. G. Farben. Although Krauch listed many other reasons, important even in the "Third Reich," for protecting Weinberg, he was sent to T on the first Munich transport on June 4, 1942 (his only piece of luggage was a briefcase), where he became a "notable" in September 1942 and died in early 1943.

734   *Sources and Literature*

217. ["Protectorate"] "Die jüdische Auswanderung aus dem Protektorate Böhmen und Mähren." MS, Prague, 1943.

A report by the JKG for the "Central Office" on Jewish emigration from 1922 to July 15, 1943. A total of 19,016 Jews emigrated in 1939 (from March 15), 6,176 in 1940, 535 in 1941, 273 in 1942, and 93 in 1943 (until July 15).

218. ["Protectorate"] "Erlässe betreffend Juden" [Decrees Regarding Jews]. Mimeographed, MS, Prague, 1939–44.

An omnibus volume with all known official decisions applying to Jews in the territory of the "Protectorate," compiled for internal use by the JKG in Prague. Its contents include 58 edicts and implementation decrees from the Reichsproteckor (or the Berlin Reich authorities), 2 oral directives from the Prague Gestapo, 23 documents in connection with the "Central Office" (2 directives remain unpublished), 122 edicts and decrees from the "Protectorate" government and ministries, 35 edicts from the Prague and Brünn [Brno] police directorate, and, in addition, directives from autonomous organs.

219. ["Protectorate"] [Various documents from the war years].

Most are forms from the Prague JKG or the "Central Office" related to the persecution of the Jews, especially their deportation. This material was in the Prague Jewish Museum in 1947 and permits extensive reconstruction of the bureaucratic apparatus to which the deportees had to submit (see Chapter 3). The documents used are described in the text.

219a. Radzyner, I.: "Łódź, Auschwitz, Stutthof, Drezno [Dresden], Theresienstadt." MS, HIŻ, Poland, 1947.

The author ultimately ended up in a camp of around 400 people in (or near) Dresden, where work was performed in a factory. One group was temporarily placed in Pirna. The bombardment of Dresden claimed no victims in the camp. They were evacuated through a thirteen-day march with detours to T. During the march there was almost nothing to eat; some died. In T, where no one else died, the soup seemed "better than anything in a long time" (*335a).

220. Rajewski, L.: *Oświęcim w systemie RSHA* [Auschwitz in the RSHA system]. Warsaw, 1946.

A clear outline of the camp structure.

220a. Randt, A.: "Die Schleuse: 3 Jahre Theresienstadt." MS, YV, Hanover, ca. 1946.

A very detailed portrayal by the author, who was in T from July 24, 1942, until liberation.

221. Raška, K.: "Concentration Camps of Terezín." In *Medical Press*. Vol. 219. New York, June 2, 1948, pp. 481–84.

A brief report on the "Kleine Festung" and the "ghetto." The author came to T as a physician with the Czech Red Cross in the early days of May 1945. On Raška's unfortunate role, see Lederer (*166), pages 192 et seq. See also *321a.

222. Reder, R.: *Bełżec*. Cracow, 1946.

Sources and Literature

An account of experiences in the extermination camp. An introduction by N. Rost explains the history and technology of the camp and provides important documents.

222a. Reichmann, E. G.: *Flucht in den Haß*. Frankfurt a.M., no year [1956].

A dignified, objective account of the problems, based on comprehensive knowledge and an assessment of the relevant sources. The work, supplemented by a valuable foreword, is the German version of the English original: *Hostages of Civilisation: The Social Sources of National Socialist Anti-Semitism*. London, 1950.

223. Reitlinger, G.: *Die Endlösung: Hitlers Versuch der Ausrottung der Juden Europas 1939–1945*. Berlin, 1956.

An improved version of the English original (*The Final Solution*. London, 1953). It is an attempt at a comprehensive account of the Jewish tragedy in all the countries occupied by Hitler. Following Poliakov's as-yet-unsurpassed outline (*213), and simultaneously with Eisenbach (*54), the main periods in the Jewish policies of Hitler's Germany are described for the first time. The major materials processed here provide essential clues for further research, but many mistakes and misunderstandings slipped in; they are reduced but far from eliminated in the German version. Unfortunately, even in the section about T there are many mistakes, for which I am not responsible, because Reitlinger prematurely ended cooperation with my revisions; thus I hardly deserve the thanks for reading it through that is given in the preliminary remarks. On the author's misunderstandings, see the Korherr reports (*156a).

223a. Reitlinger, G.: *The SS: Alibi of a Nation*. London, 1956.

This source contains a few spotlights on T.

223b. Rich, E.: "Verfolgung eines Tschechen im deutschen 'Protektortat' wegen 'Misch-Ehe.'" MS, WL, London, 1959.

The author was supposed to go to the forced labor camp Byštřice (Bistritz, near Beneschau), designated for "Aryan" spouses and *Mischlinge* from the "Protectorate," in July 1944 but was able to avoid this due to illness (there was another such camp in Postelberg, "Sudetengau"). On September 25, 1944, Mrs. Rich arrived at the forced labor camp Hagibor in Prague, from which she was sent to T on February 1, 1945 (*183c, 195a).

223c. [Riga] "Affidavit and Letters." MS, WL, Prague, 1948.

The following text was compiled from information from M. Bunzl, E. Klein, M. Reinigerová, M. Rothová, V. Schwarz, and B. Süß.

The first transport from T, which departed January 9, 1942, arrived in Riga-Schirotowa (or Skirotava) on the 12th, and the second, which departed January 15, on the 19th (or 20th). The first marched into the Riga ghetto. During the second transport, 924 people, including all the women and children, were loaded onto trucks, supposedly also to travel to Riga. They were never seen again and were killed right away. The rest, 76 men up to forty-five years of age, went on January 20 to the Salaspils camp, some eighteen miles from Riga.

Regarding Riga: Before the arrival of the Central European transports in November 1941, some 44,000 Latvian Jews lived in the Riga ghetto. On November 27,

736 *Sources and Literature*

40,000 were killed; some 4,000 remained. Like all camps in Latvia, the ghetto, under Commandant SS-OSTF Krause (1941–42), answered to the commander of the Sipo and SD in Latvia, SS-STBF Dr. Hans Lange. When the Jews arrived from Germany, Vienna, and, later, T, the camp was divided into a "Latvian" and a "German" ghetto. In early 1942, some 15,000 people lived in both ghettos; at the dissolution of the camp in November 1943, only around 6,000 remained. Most of the deceased did not die a natural death.

When the transport arrived from T, the people were chased from the train by German and Latvian SS men, and their possessions were taken from them. The elderly and sick were killed right away at the train station (even in the train cars). Bunzl, a witness, reports that he was appointed "car commandant" by the accompanying Schupo on the trip from T. He says,

> A woman already died on the transport. . . . When I reported to [OSTF] Krause that I had in the car old and sick people who were unable to walk, he said I should hang them. The situation was not yet clear to all of us. Krause then went into the cars himself and I counted six shots. . . .
>
> The transport was supposed to walk to the Riga ghetto from Schirotawa, and when the mass of people slowly began to move . . . an old woman, supported by her daughter, could not go on; Krause shot both of them from behind. . . . On the bridge in Schirotawa he beat a professor so hard on the head with a club that he died soon after.

The day after their arrival, a roll call was held with the Jews from T. One hundred and fifty men were sent to Salaspils; few of them were still alive when the inmates of that camp were brought back to the Riga ghetto. The women from T were used for "cleanup work" in the "Latvian" ghetto, during which a number were killed for petty infractions. Reinigerová reports,

> During the work, Willy Tuchel [of the SS] came to our group [of sixteen women] and checked whether we had textiles on us. He found a ball of darning wool and one stocking on one woman. We were then stood with our faces to the wall. The command to shoot was given, at which 4 women – the first, the fourth, the eighth and the twelfth – were shot from behind. I was the 13th in the row, while three other women were placed to one side and had to watch the procedure.

Some of the transports from "Greater Germany" (such as the second one from T) never even arrived in the ghetto but were murdered in "Hochwald," near Riga.

In autumn 1943, the SS came into the ghetto with whips and pistols early one day at the beginning of work and, at the gate, pulled Latvian Jews – identifiable because of the unlabeled yellow stars on their chests and backs – out of the column marching to work. Some 300 were executed before everyone's eyes as hostages, because the night before some Latvian Jews, including some camp policemen, had fled.

The dissolution of the ghetto was ordered in late summer 1943. Inmates in work details were billeted near their work units. Many were sent to the Riga concentration camp. According to one source, on November 3, 1943, some 2,800 old or sick people and children were murdered in "Hochwald"; another source reports that, on November 22, women and children were deported, supposedly to Auschwitz. The remainder in the ghetto first ended up in the Riga concentration camp or in the central prison. All the survivors still had a long way to go before liberation. For example, Süß was sent to the Riga concentration camp on September 4, 1943; to the military uniform camp 701 in Riga on September 18, 1944; to Libau on October 8, 1944; to the "SD

Sources and Literature 737

police prison" at Fuhlsbüttel, near Hamburg, in February 1945; and to a "work education camp" at Kiel-Hassel in April 1945. There he was ransomed on May 1 by the Swedish RC and was brought to Sweden (*136, 348).

Regarding Salaspils: This camp for young men capable of working existed from December 1941 to August 1942 and took some 2,000 people (probably all Central European Jews from Riga). Some 800 survived and reached the Riga ghetto; 1,200 died of cold, hunger, infectious diseases, murder, or execution (around 150). The person generally responsible for executions was STBF Dr. Lange, who often visited Salaspils and rampaged there. Living conditions were horrible. When the Jews from T arrived in mid-January, there already were Jews there from Germany, but at the time – in the depths of winter – no barracks had been completed. At first there was nothing to eat; later, the prisoners received a half liter of watery soup per day and one loaf of bread (2 kg) for every twelve, and sometimes twenty, people. If the bread was unavailable, people received three to four potatoes. For months, there was no water in which to wash. Klein says,

> We had ... four-story bunks, so that those at the top had to crawl down a ladder. Those who were sick and weak from hunger [could not use the ladders]. Every morning ... lay near me many dead people who had died of hunger or [cold]. . . .
>
> I was sick, had a fever of 39 degrees, but still went to work, since I knew that I would be murdered as a sick person. In the morning, before going to work, I was warming myself a bit in the sun, when suddenly [SS-Unterscharführer (USCHF)] Tekemeier fell upon me and beat me so badly that I lost my senses. I would certainly have been executed, as we were forbidden to be outdoors for no reason, if the head of my work detail had not hurriedly lined me up in a different group.

After the escape of someone from Brünn [Brno], STBF Lange threatened to shoot ten prisoners if the escapee was not found in three days. The deadline passed, and Lange had people line up in front of the gallows. In Bunzl's words,

> One prisoner was being hanged, and Lange asked who was from Brünn [Brno]. Of those who raised their hands, he chose 10, and they had to kneel under the gallows. The first was forced to pull down his pants, and Lange first had him receive 25 blows of a club. Each blow was so hard that his buttocks were black and blue. . . . Lange had the hanged person taken down from the gallows; the man who had been beaten had his hands tied behind his back, and then [he was] hanged. Lange ... screamed [at the hangman]: "Noose to his ears." The others were not hanged. However, because they had all been undressed the entire time in the great cold, all died in the next two or three days.

Süß says, "The actual extermination of the prisoners in Salaspils was undertaken by fellow Jewish prisoners who received orders from the SS [especially from Lange]."

Regarding Kaiserwald: After the dissolution of the Riga ghetto, a number of its Jews ended up in this concentration camp, including Klein, who reports, among other things, that SS-Oberscharführer (OSCHF) (or Hauptscharführer [HSCHF]) Hans Brunner sought out prisoners at morning roll call

> for the work detail "Stützpunkt" [base]. They had to dig up dead bodies from graves in order to burn them, and after doing this, they themselves were shot. This was repeated twice a week. At roll call, too, he looked for children, telling them they would be housed in clean houses and would be well fed. [They were murdered in a forest.] These children's clothes were loaded on a car in the woods by our people and brought back to the concentration camp. On New Year's 1943–44, SS men with kapos came to the

738   *Sources and Literature*

camp drunk. We were all driven from the barracks with clubs and whips; many of us jumped half-naked from the windows so as not to be beaten. Everyone was forced to stand for roll call. They [the SS and the criminal German kapos] chose their victims and threw them, alive, into a large latrine. Then they screamed at us: "Save your comrades!" Anyone who had the courage to pull someone out was thrown in himself by the German kapos. In this way, many of our comrades . . . died.

224. Ripka, H.: *We Think of You: A Message to the Jews of Czechoslovakia.* London, 1941.

This work correctly recognizes the persecution of the Jews in the "Protectorate" before the deportation period.

224a. Robinson, N. (ed.): *European Jewry Ten Years after the War.* New York, 1956.

A demographic and social overview of the Jews in the European countries (excluding Russia) affected by National Socialism.

224b. Roessler, K. G.: "Letter Account." MS, Ludwigshafen, 1956.

In February 1943, the half-Jewish author's grandmother, who was eighty-three years old and infirm, was deported from Plauen to T. He was able to visit her in prison beforehand: "It was one of the most harrowing moments of my life when, in a dark cell, near prostitutes, I saw my old and exceedingly dignified grandmother lying on a damp seaweed mattress on the floor. She did not complain; that had always been her way." Roessler promised to visit her in T if possible, which he attempted to do on April 8 or 9, 1943, without knowing that his grandmother had died shortly before. He went from Bauschowitz [Bohušovice] and actually made it to the commandant's office.

> I asked the guard how to get to the commandant's office. He answered, "Down the street to the market!" Without showing an identification card, I simply went through the barrier. . . . On the way I met a group of Jews and spoke to them. But they acted very frightened and said they were not allowed to speak to "Aryans." I explained to them that I was of Jewish descent myself and was on the way to the commandant's office to see my grandmother. The people I spoke to threw up their hands, cried "Oh my God," and quickly went on their way.

Roessler was able to get all the way to Seidl. He

> at first said nothing at all. The he suddenly screamed at me, how could I be so impudent and how had I gotten in. I answered calmly but firmly that I had not entered by illegal means. . . . I knew that, as commandant, he of course had the ability to prohibit me from speaking with her. In that case, I asked him to give me a pass to leave the camp. He blew up again and screamed that I should get out of the house, make myself scarce, I wasn't going to get a pass, he didn't care about anything else.

He managed to escape from T. Later, Roessler's mother was deported to T; he picked her up from there at the end of May 1945 on a motorcycle.

224c. [Rosenblatt, S.]: "Account of a Polish Jew." MS, WL, London, no year [1955?].

Rosenblatt fought in the Polish Army and was released after three months as a war prisoner of the Germans, "because they wanted to avoid the international rules, which were too good." Following many experiences, the author finally arrived, late in the war, via Buchenwald, at a Saxon satellite camp, from which he arrived in T on an evacuation transport.

> Many arrived as corpses. We came under the internal Jewish administration. The Jews saved their meager rations in order to give them to us. Many of our people died in Theresienstadt. The people were so weakened that they were placed in quarantine. Several thousand were placed in one barracks. There were so many dead that the mortuary was overcrowded. The stench was so horrible that one simply couldn't walk through it. Wherever one went, there were corpses. . . .
>
> I had begun during the quarantine to organize a children's home, with the permission of the Youth Welfare department of the Jewish administration. Many weak, sick young people came on the last transport to arrive in Theresienstadt, and in a short time we had taken the children out of the barracks and housed them in a provisional house, in a children's home in quarantine. But even many of them died of typhus. I was the head of the children's home. Some of the supervisors were infected as well. The Russians took very good care of us. There were better rations, milk, fruit, bread, medical care, and better clothing. The children began to get proper sleep. They were given clean bedding. Youth Welfare did very good work. Then UNRRA approached the English government and we received permission to bring 300 children to England.   (*50a)

225. Rosenthal, E. (compiler): "Das Recht des Jüdischen Siedlungsgebietes Theresienstadt." Mimeographed, MS, T, 1944.

See Chapter 15.

Rost, N.: *222.

225a. Rossel, M.: "Ghetto Theresienstadt." [French], MS, Berlin, June 1944.

A confidential IRC delegation report on its visit to T on June 23, 1944. This secret document (there are only a few hints of it in *230a) frequently overlaps with the reports by Hvass and Henningsen (*98, 108) but places the situation in a much more favorable light. This impression is strengthened by the fact that Rossel largely passes on the rehearsed, misleading statements by Eppstein as his own observations or findings, and, in addition, that he does not seem to notice how the camp had been prepared for the visit. For details on and discussion of this report, see *3b, doc. 224. Rossel was no match for this comedy and did not make nearly as much effort as the Danes, whose human involvement was very different. In Geneva, the IRC had received a letter dated November 30, 1943, with Eppstein's and Murmelstein's signatures, containing the following, which was rightly considered quite surprising:

> We confirm most sincerely the receipt of the medication delivery announced in a letter of September 30, 1943. We allow ourselves to remind you repeatedly that the supply of medications for the Jews in our care is so adequate that it is asked that you refrain from further deliveries; the health condition of the Jews entrusted to our custody can still be described as quite favorable.

During their visit the delegates could, to their surprise, see for themselves the abundance of medication in the camp. They provided a photostat of Eppstein's letter; he confirmed the information again verbally and signed the photostat. Now everything was proven! Aside from this attachment, thirty-eight photos by Rossel (photos

740   *Sources and Literature*

can also lie), a package confirmation card and block of four package-allowance stamps, and a 100 ghetto crown note were attached.

226. [Red Cross] "Memos by Gerhard Riegner of the World Jewish Congress on Negotiations with IRC Functionaries." MS, Geneva, 1942/43

Five discussions in this source are noteworthy:

1. A discussion with Professor Burckhardt on November 17, 1942. See the text in *3b, doc. 215.
2. A discussion with Andre de Pilar on February 2, 1943, in which he reported that nothing more was decided by the German RC, "from which convoluted letters are received"; decisions were made "in the Führer headquarters, by Himmler, the SS or the Gestapo." Relief shipments to T had been impossible thus far due to a lack of knowledge of the requirements, but they would soon happen. Pilar explained his view that the IRC could be concerned with the Jews in the occupied areas only if it received "an official mandate from the Americans, English or possibly other Allied governments." However, receipt of such a mandate was doubtful, as the Geneva Convention contained no such provision.
3. A discussion with several gentlemen on July 6, 1943. They mentioned a plan for America to recognize all captured Jews as enemy civilian internees, in order to "include them in the RC aid operation."
4. A discussion with de Pilar on July 7, 1943. The most important text, regarding the German RC's visit to T ten days earlier, is found in *3b, doc. 220.
5. A discussion with Dr. Feinstein on July 8, 1943, regarding delivery of medications and nutritional supplements to T.

226a. [Red Cross] "Aus der Tätigkeit der Hijefs" [Union of Orthodox Rabbis of the United States and Canada]. In *Israelitisches Wochenblatt*. No. 10. Zurich, March 9, 1945.

A photostat of a letter to the IRC on the letterhead of the T self-administration on November 15, 1944, signed by Murmelstein and a Dr. R. Levi:

> We received your gift package consisting of 100 crates of sugar cubes and 200 crates of spaghetti, at a total weight of 10,000 kg. We are convinced that we are acting in your interests if we distribute the gift package, with which we were favored, among the people in our care, and permit ourselves to express our sincerest thanks in the name of those cared for, as well as in our own name, for the aid placed at our disposal. Respectfully yours, Jewish Self-Administration Theresienstadt

The IRC informed Hijef on March 1, 1945, that the letter from T was forwarded from Berlin on January 8 and "reached us only in these past days." This is a characteristic example of the tempo of the RSHA.

227. [Red Cross] "Letter from the German RC on November 8, 1943 to the Danish RC." MS. [In the possession of the International Tracing Service in Arolsen].

The Danish offices' energetic intervention on behalf of the Jews is especially clear (*41):

> In response to the letter of October 15, the German Red Cross conveys the following after discussions with the relevant German offices:
> The Jews sent from Denmark to Germany have been transferred to Theresienstadt. The possibility of giving representatives of the Danish Red Cross permission to visit the

Sources and Literature 741

Danish Jews in Theresienstadt has not been entirely rejected. However, implementation must be postponed to a somewhat later date.

The German Red Cross can further inform the Danish Red Cross that it has managed to provide for correspondence opportunities for the Danish Jews taken into Theresienstadt, and that, in addition, it was given assurances that they would remain in Theresienstadt. There they are under the direct oversight of the Jewish Council of Elders.

The content of this letter should be seen as probably the first indication of the impending "beautification," as Eichmann received a copy: "sent for your information with reference to the meeting on November 4."

228. [Red Cross] Comité international de la Croix-Rouge: *Documents sur l'activité du Comité international de la Croix-Rouge en faveur des civils détenus dans les camps de concentration en Allemagne (1939–1945).* 3rd ed. Geneva, 1947.

This work contains excerpts of documents concerning T from 1945, but – like all the other publications of the IRC – no reference is made to the visit by Dr. Rossel on June 23, 1944 (*230a).

Here should be mentioned some other unpublished documents connected with the IRC's activities regarding T. On December 7, 1942, the IRC gave Riegner a "definitive denial" of the possibility of visiting T. On June 21, 1943, it was known in Geneva that Hartmann and Niehaus would visit T on June 27. The Berlin IRC delegation reported to Geneva on this visit on July 20, 1943. A shipment of prunes, dried vegetables, and condensed milk had reached T "and, as indicated, was used"; a confirmation receipt was promised.

Since the nutritional situation, as indicated, is normal and rations are commensurate with those in the Protectorate, the offices in charge [meaning the Jewish camp leadership in T!] have asked that we refrain from sending food and limit our shipments to medication, restoratives for the sick, and special dietary supplements [*Diätküchenpräparate*]. The undersigned was informed by the head of the pharmacy that all medications were available in sufficient quantity, and special aid was not desired.... Correspondence from T is not hindered in any way. Letters can be sent both domestically and to both neutral and hostile countries abroad. Letters for neutral countries are sent immediately following inspection by the defense office, while forms meant for hostile countries go through the German RC presidium and are forwarded in the same way used for other form communications.

From March to June 1943, 1,899 such forms were said to have arrived in T, and 379 were said to have been sent. A visit "to the Theresienstadt concentration camp by an IRC delegate [is] desired, but this visit should take place before the start of cold weather." On July 26, 1943, the Berlin IRC delegation reported to Geneva the probability of a visit to T, which would be undertaken by the German RC. But visits to other Jewish camps were out of the question. Months later, the German RC reported that the visit that the Danish RC had asked for had been approved but could not take place before early 1944. On February 21, 1944, the Stockholm IRC delegation reported to Geneva:

Baron Stjernstedt showed me a Swedish diplomatic report dealing with the Jews in T. It spoke of a meeting between a Swedish diplomat and a German legation councilor [probably Thadden], who had visited T personally. According to the German diplomat, conditions in T were "relatively good."... Mr. X [German diplomat] told us that a

742   *Sources and Literature*

suggestion in this regard [on a visit to T by the IRC] had been put forward, [but was not implemented]. He said that he however personally considered it probable that, if the IRC applied for permission for a visit by a commission, this application would be approved. The German diplomat then stated that ... as far as he knew, the IRC had never made such a petition. Baron Stjernstedt requested that I encourage an initiative in Geneva to visit T. Prince Carl, who happened to appear at the baron's office as well, expressed the same view.

On March 6, 1944, the IRC delegation in Berlin reported to Geneva that Niehaus, from the German RC, was discussing with the Gestapo a visit to T. "It seems that everything is on the right track, but the act still must be reviewed by Mr. Himmler. The visit is planned for May, so that the camp can be seen at the nicest time, when everything is in bloom." In Geneva, as an answering letter on March 22, 1944, to Berlin confirms, it was considered that "the intervention of the police [Gestapo] in this matter [is] a bad sign."

Some details on Dunant's actions in 1945 remain to be added. In his report on May 22, he stated (this is not yet published elsewhere): "On May 4, I found them [prisoner transports] at neighboring train stations and guided them to T. Three trains arrived there on the 6th. They traveled in a circle for ... several weeks. On the journey there were around 2,500 men and 600 children; we took in 1,800 men and 180 children." Many typhus patients were dead in the carriages. One barracks housed 600 healthy prisoners of war – Frenchmen, Belgians, Englishmen, and Canadians. On June 8, Dunant reported, on his most recent visit to T, that Murmelstein wanted to be evacuated, but the communists wouldn't let him go. Later the IRC was informed that, at the beginning of August 1945, 1,485 people still were in T: 875 Germans, 50 Austrians, 150 Poles, 50 Russians, and 360 people of various origins.

229. [Red Cross] *Het Nederlandsche Roode Kruis: Auschwitz*. Vols. I [and] VI. The Hague, 1947–52.

Volume I deals with all the transports from Holland. The number of victims of the transport in April 1943 was given as 98 rather than 297 (probably a misprint). Volume VI contains the figures for survivors of all transports from T to Auschwitz starting in May 1944. But these are estimates that are incorrect. Much effort was made to follow the deportees from Auschwitz up to the evacuation transports, some of which went back to T.

229a. [Red Cross] Joint Relief Commission of the International Red Cross: *Activities of the Joint Relief Commission of the IRC on Behalf of the Jews*. Geneva, August 1944.

On T, this source notes:

The shipments to this city in 1943 had a weight of 5,410 kg and a value of 13,600 Swiss F.; they included condensed milk, dried vegetables and prunes. Having been informed that medications were especially needed, the Joint Relief Commission sent 86 cases, weighing 3,232 kg, of pharmaceutical products and the largest possible amount of strengthening nutrients. The value of the shipment was 38,914 Swiss F. On July 26, 1944, a new shipment of 518 kg of pharmaceutical products was shipped.

The efforts of Jewish organizations – the World Jewish Congress, the Joint Relief Commission, Hijef – to provide material support to T began with the IRC in autumn 1942. Shipments to individual recipients were possible relatively soon

Sources and Literature

after that. The busiest and most successful organization was the World Jewish Congress, whose Geneva staffers, above all Riegner, achieved extraordinary results. The first collective shipment to T (100 cases of condensed milk [1,920 kg net], 1,000 kg of prunes, and 2,000 kg of powdered soup), addressed to Edelstein, could not leave Switzerland until May 1, 1943. Letters regarding these shipments, including confirmations by leading functionaries in T, have survived. It remains unclear how many of these shipments ended up in the hands of the camp community, as the SS stored them and had carte blanche in dispensing them. In 1943, most of the prisoners had not yet received anything. In 1944, this slowly improved. In addition to foodstuffs and supplements, medications were sent. Furthermore, the IRC sent packages to individual recipients; the money for these shipments, as for the collective shipments, was raised by the World Jewish Congress. On March 29, 1944, T confirmed receipt of 6,194 packages for the period from November 1, 1943, to March 28, 1944, and on September 20, 1944, the camp confirmed receipt of 13,444 packages during an unspecified period. The sardine shipments (500 g) from Lisbon were also brought about by the World Jewish Congress through its organization Relico.

230. [Red Cross] "Mitteilungen nach Theresienstadt – Red Cross übernimmt Briefbeförderung." In *Aufbau*. New York, March 3 and April 7, 1944.

Instructions on how to write and address letters.

230a. [Red Cross] "Note sur l'activité du Comité International de la Croix-Rouge au camp de Theresienstadt." Mimeographed, Geneva, June 1945.

A summary of IRC documents concerning T, specifically on the visits in 1944–45. These are the only IRC-published documents in which Rossel's visit is mentioned at all (*225a); they even quote from his report. There was every reason to suppress passages in his and Lehner's reports, whereas Dunant's reports were subject to no such caution. The IRC was constantly given to understand that the camps were the Germans' concern.

The International Committee frequently received answers to the effect that a visit to Theresienstadt had essentially been approved and only the date remained to be determined, but unfortunately the German authorities always found excuses to delay the visit. Finally it was set for June 26 [*sic*], 1944.

At that time, a member of the delegation from the International Committee in Berlin managed to enter the city of Theresienstadt; he had to assure the SS commandant beforehand that he would reveal to no one his conclusions about the camp. This restriction unfortunately prevented the International Commission from later publicizing the contents of the report received from its delegate. Contrary to expectations, the report was satisfactory, all in all, and in no way confirmed the information received from various sources on the treatment of those interned in Theresienstadt. The delegate ... , who had visited Theresienstadt accompanied by a representative of the SS and the Jewish Elder Dr. Eppstein, stated that according to his observations [*sic*!] and Dr. Eppstein's explanations, the 35,000 inhabitants ... lived in an independently organized community and under the control of an extraordinarily small German guard, under conditions that had nothing in common with those to which prisoners in actual concentration camps were subjected.

The inhabitants confined in the city were completely cut off from the outside world, but had been able to create an organization with a communist character in the city, which was in itself sufficient for all needs.

Sources and Literature

Aside from the observations that the delegate ... made, he could only doubt the value of Dr. Eppstein's explanations [unfortunately, Rossel did not manifest doubt], as he had no opportunity to speak without witnesses. In connection with this visit, the delegate ... reported that any desired individual inquiries could be handled in Theresienstadt and were to be addressed to Dr. Eppstein. It must be said here that none of the subsequent inquiries was ever answered, and that later interventions by the International Committee in Germany ... went nowhere.

In the course of 1944, the International Committee received numerous messages from Jewish organizations and private persons, all of which conveyed that they had heard that the Theresienstadt camp had been closed down or was in the process of closing down, afer the Jews had been sent to other camps, which it was assumed were extermination camps. At the same time, the International Committee received reports from people repatriated from Theresienstadt [meaning those released to Switzerland in February 1945] that spoke of the visit ... in June 1944 and claimed that the delegate's observations ... did not conform to reality, as a farce had been staged in the whole city for this occasion.

This is an admission of the failure of the self-confident Dr. Rossel. The events of April and May 1945 are further reported. Dunant spent May 2 to 10 in T and in this period also concerned himself with the "Kleine Festung." It is the beginning of the time period documented here that is important for an assessment of his activity (*321a). The IRC stated, "It is impossible to summarize Dunant's activities in this period, with all his interventions that were spread among the most varied areas."

231. Rothgießer, F.: *Das also war Theresienstadt*. MS [two versions], RvO, Amsterdam, 1945.

The author was in T from August 2, 1944, to liberation. The text contains a history of the camp (including the town since its founding) and a description of conditions. Despite some errors, it is mainly correct.

231a. Rothgießer, F.: "Gefilmte Lügen: Was die Nazis der Welt über Theresienstadt erzählen wollten." In *Aufbau*. New York, September 21, 1945.

An essentially correct description of conditions.

232. Roubal, J.: *Terezín zůstane věčným svědectvím* [Theresienstadt Remains an Eternal Testimony]. Prague, 1947.

An emotional account of life in the "Kleine Festung." The author makes reference to the execution of Czech gendarmes from the "ghetto." The work is an indictment against the commandant of the "Kleine Festung," Jöckel, from whom emerged the intent of destroying the "ghetto" in the final days of the war.

233. Roznitschko, J., and C. Goldberg: *Theresienstadt*. [Hebrew], Tel Aviv, 1947.

A camp description from the point of view of the Bohemian Zionists. The important people from these groups in the camp and the leading functionaries of the "Youth Welfare Office" are celebrated as heroes.

233a. [Radios] Letter from Best to Goebbels on September 16, 1939. PS-2161. Mimeographed.

Best refers to a telephone call with the officers of the Propaganda Ministry and writes:

Without being informed in detail about the intended regulations on confiscation of radios from Jews, the Reichsführer-SS and Chief of the German Police ... has ordered,

Sources and Literature

745

with the Führer's permission, that confiscation of radios in the possession of Jews should be undertaken by the Secret State Police, without anything being published about it. The Führer also does not want an order from the Ministerial Council. The confiscation will henceforth ... be carried out as a police measure.

234. Sabille, J.: *Lueurs dans la tourmente*. Paris, 1956.

This book, based on earlier essays by the author, describes in Chapter 2 the events leading to the escape of the Danish Jews to Sweden and the deportation of the remainder to T. Sweden took in 5,919 Jews, 1,301 half Jews, and 686 people married to Jews; the Gestapo captured only 477 Jews. The Danish visit to T is also dealt with. The fourth chapter is devoted to the rescue operation arranged by Kersten before the end of the war; it led to Masur's negotiations with Himmler (*2a, 139, 140, 182).

234a. Salcberg, Sz.: "Skarżysko, Schlieben, Teresina." MS, HIŻ, Poland, no year.

The author was sent from Kielce on May 14, 1943, to the Skarżysko Kamienna camp, and from there (in August 1944) to Buchenwald. Ten days later, 1,370 prisoners went to Schlieben, where the workers were supposed to produce 5,000 bombs (*Panzerfäuste* [rocket-propelled anti-tank grenades]) each day for HASAG; however, only 1,500 were actually produced. One hundred and twenty prisoners were killed in an air raid on the factory during the night shift. From then on, conditions worsened; daily work norms were raised to 10,000 bombs. The dissolution of the camp began in March 1945. After a fourteen-day journey, a transport of 800 prisoners arrived in T; they lauded their reception in T as good (*187a).

234b. Salus, F.: "Bericht über den Verlauf der Poliomyelitis-Epidemie." MS, YV, T, 1943.

234c. Salus, F.: "Osteoporose und Tetanie." MS, YV, T, no year.

234d. Salus, G.: "Eine Frau erzählt: Aus Politik und Zeitgeschichte." B XXXXII. Beilage zur Wochenzeitung *Das Parlament*. Bonn, October 30, 1957.

The author, who was in T for a long time, was sent to Auschwitz with her husband, Dr. Fritz Salus, the chief physician of hospital L 317, on October 23, 1944. Her husband was killed immediately; Mrs. Salus was shipped a few days later, with 200 others, to the Öderan camp, where there were 300 Jewish women, mainly from Hungary and Poland. They worked in a cartridge factory that was a few steps away from the camp. A twenty-two-year-old SS supervisor was the head of the camp; she was helped by thirty young guards, mainly workers in the Öderan factories attracted by the good living conditions in the SS. Among the prisoners, the supervisor kept a maid, four tailors, and a "whole group of weavers who had to make shoes and rugs for her." On April 14, 1945, the prisoners were loaded onto open coal cars, each of which also had a guard. The planned destination was Mauthausen. The train stopped for two days in Aussig [Ústí nad Laben], where it escaped a strafing with little damage. The train stopped for three days at Leitmeritz and then shuttled repeatedly between there and Aussig [Ústí nad Laben]. Instead of being evacuated, as planned, to Dachau or Flossenbürg, they were disembarked on April 21 in Leitmeritz, and the women were taken to T. This detailed report, in manuscript form better titled "At the Behest of One Hand" and somewhat shortened and edited here, is characterized by clarity, precision (for example, she details arrival formalities in Auschwitz!), and critical observation. The details on T are accurate: "Too many rumors.... . These whispering campaigns, in a good and bad sense, made the atmosphere impenetrable and enmeshed people so inextricably that they believed what they wanted to believe." She testifies to their ignorance of Auschwitz:

> People everywhere already knew [in October 1944] about the extermination camp Auschwitz-Birkenau; only we, in our warm swamp Theresienstadt, knew nothing. Our best boys even went cheerfully: "Aha, they need us to work" was what was said, and they already felt the morning air ... but not for them, since few survived Auschwitz. Then their wives even followed them, voluntarily, and experienced the same fate. That's how well trained we were, and how little effort we caused our tormentors.

235. Scheck, Z.: "Deti" [Children]. MS, DA, Prague, 1946.

A report on the children in T.

235a. Scheinowitz, A.: [Transcript]. [Polish], MS, HIŻ, Poland, no year.

We combine the information in this account with that of a second transcript at the HIŻ by M. Grunbaum (1946). The authors left the Płaszów ghetto near Cracow on October 9, 1944, with a transport of 402 prisoners and went to Schachwitz, 13 km from Dresden. Their hunger was terrible, but the work for the MIAG (Mühlenbau-Industrie A.A.) was bearable. Typhoid broke out, and air raids caused casualties. Finally, there began an ordeal that took them through Passau, Mauthausen, Flossen-bürg, and Leitmeritz to T.

235b. Schellenberg, W.: *The Schellenberg Memoirs*. London, 1956.

Heydrich told Schellenberg in the summer of 1941 (p. 207), "It is pure insanity to have created this Jewish question." No similar remark by Heydrich has been reported anywhere else. Schellenberg describes his interventions for the Jews toward the end of the war (pp. 428–45); his description generally is in accord with his Nuremberg Trial files. Credit for the freeing of the Danish Jews is given to Bernadotte; Himmler promised him that he would transfer the unevacuated camps to the Allies in good shape (p. 438), "especially Bergen-Belsen, Buchenwald, Theresienstadt and the camps in southern Germany." Himmler agreed, with serious misgivings, to a conference with a Jewish representative from Sweden once it was certain that Kaltenbrunner – and, through him, Hitler – would not find out about it. Himmler, according to Masur's information, wanted to postpone the talks with him; Masur refused to become involved in a long discussion and demanded practical measures (*182).

235c. [Schellenberg, W.]: Interrogation of Schellenberg by his lawyer, Dr. Mintzel. Mimeo-graphed. In minutes of meeting, May 12, 1948. Nuremberg, Case XI, p. 532 et seq.

Schellenberg gives himself credit for the Musy and Bernadotte campaigns, and for his mediating role with Himmler (and for Masur as well). Musy turned to Schellenberg in the late summer of 1944 to get all the Jews from the concentration camps to Switzerland. During talks in October with Musy, Himmler was difficult but compli-ant; no final agreement was reached. Schellenberg was to continue to maintain contacts with Musy and to attend to the release of the Jews mentioned on a long list of Musy's. This was achieved in some cases, despite Müller's resistance. On January

12, 1945, at Musy's second meeting, Himmler agreed to the release to Switzerland of 1,200 Jews every fourteen days. Through Swiss press reports on the first transport from T, the news reached Hitler via Ribbentrop, and the action was stopped immediately. Musy and Schellenberg then continued their efforts in other ways, for all prisoners, until the end of the war (*85a, 192b, 192c).

235d. Schnieper, A.: "Notre séjour á Theresienstadt du 2 avril 1945." MS, Geneva, April 1945.

Schnieper traveled to T from Geneva with four IRC trucks filled with food. Among other things, he was supposed to (1) ascertain the powers of the SS "office," (2) determine whether there were instructions from Berlin to release a number of prisoners, whom he would immediately take to Switzerland, (3) ask about the need for food and medications in T, and (4), if releases were refused, create a favorable atmosphere for further steps in that direction. Schnieper was not allowed into the camp and was permitted to meet with Murmelstein only in the presence of Rahm. Murmelstein did not speak freely and confirmed the delivery, which was unloaded in the presence of the bearer. Rahm telephoned Berlin regarding releases and then refused them. Schnieper then asked whether he could not decide himself, especially as Burckhardt already had received certain assurances from close associates of Himmler. Rahm answered, "This is an international matter that must be the subject of an international agreement. You are much too 'small' to discuss such a matter, and so am I. I will not permit any discussion of this matter." Schnieper was an outstanding observer and understood the situation in T well. His remarks on Rahm, Baltrusch, the SS, and the "comrades' home" (*Kameradschaftsheim*), where he spent the night, are excellent. It is only to be regretted that Rossel and Lehner, rather than men like Schnieper, were the ones to visit the camp.

236. Schommer, G. (ed.): *Persecution of Jews* (*Condition in Occupied Territories*, no. 6). London, December 18, 1942.

This official publication of the Inter-Allied Information Committee offers, among other things, one of the earliest, yet relatively well-founded and detailed, reports on T (p. 6):

> Shortly after Himmler's visit to Prague, Heydrich sent several hundred Jews, aged between 18 and 45, to T.... The Christian residents of the city ... were ordered to prepare for resettlement to various other districts by the end of May 1942. But at the end of April [1942], the Nazis changed their plans. They decided to create a "Jewish, Reich Old-Age Home" in Theresienstadt. By the end of July 1942, there were 40,000 men and women aged 65 to 80 in the Theresienstadt ghetto; 10,000 were of Czechoslovak origin, the rest largely from Germany and Holland. No one can leave the ghetto, and any such attempt is punished by death. Until the end of September 1942, no contact with the outside world was allowed. In October, however, one card a month with 15 words could be sent to relatives.... Nevertheless, there has trickled out some information, that shows the desperate situation – lack of hygiene, proper housing and food, as well as a barbaric Gestapo regime.... Representatives of the IRC were not allowed to visit Theresienstadt. Small packages of food sent from Switzerland through the IRC were returned.

237. Schön, A.: "Co byl Birkenau" [What Birkenau Was]. MS, DA, 1945.

A well-informed, generally reliable account. One section is devoted to the Czech "family camp" occupied by Theresienstadters in September 1943. Everyone had to

748   *Sources and Literature*

write at least one card but could write up to five, with the return address "Labor Camp Birkenau by Neu Berun, Eastern Upper Silesia" (when Jews in Auschwitz I and II were otherwise permitted to write, they had to provide the same address and could use only civilian postcards, never the usual concentration camp forms. Hungarian Jews had to write "Labor Camp Waldsee"). Children and pregnant women received butter and white bread. The children were taught in Czech and performed theater. In the evening there were concerts and theater performances, which were attended by the SS. In December, additional Theresienstadters joined them. The Jewish doctors were addressed by the SS doctors as "colleagues," and children were given special attention. On March 5, 1944, the September group was informed that they were to be brought to a new "Heydebreck family camp." Then they were isolated from the December group and were sent from a different part of the camp to extermination. Many weeks later, members of the December group still did not believe in the death of their comrades and were aided in their self-deception by the arrival of correspondence that referred to a date much later than the date of the mass murder. The May transport in 1944 also ultimately went to the "family camp." The December and May groups were "selected" in early July in the usual Auschwitz manner; the elderly, sick, and women with children were gassed on July 12, 1944, and the "family camp" was thus closed (*11a).

238. Schön, A.: "Transcript." [Czech], MS, DA, 1945.

A report on Edelstein's fate in Auschwitz. He and his comrades were arrested at the same time; they were brought not to the "family camp" but to the "bunker" in Auschwitz I. There he was interrogated frequently and accused of helping with a number of escapes in T. In February 1944, Eichmann visited the "family camp," where he had Fredy Hirsch and Janowitz report on camp conditions and summoned Mrs. Edelstein. He asked whether she had any requests and if she knew anything about her husband. She asked to be allowed to see him. Eichmann promised this for later and told her to write her husband a letter, which Eichmann promised to deliver, saying Edelstein was somewhere in Germany. On June 20, 1944, Edelstein was taken from the "bunker" and was told that he was going to his family. He was taken to Crematorium III. Afterward, Edelstein's family was taken there in the same car, and all of them were shot and the bodies burned (*11a).

Schorsch, J.: *156.

239. Schwalenberg, F. W.: *In den Händen der Gestapo* [In the Hands of the Gestapo]. Schönbeck/Elbe, 1945. YIVO.

239a. Sohn, J.: *Konzentrationslager Oświęcim-Brzezinka* [Auschwitz-Birkenau]. Warsaw, 1957.

A good account, based on sources and evidence, but it does not provide a history of the camp.

239b. Sellenthin, H. G.: *Geschichte der Juden in Berlin* [History of Jews in Berlin]. Berlin, 1959.

This text also describes the period of persecution and its aftermath. In June 1933, 160,564 Jews lived in Berlin; on May 17, 1939, 82,457 were registered as Jews; and on April 1, 1945, there were around 5,100 (there were 7,274 in November 1946). In the interim, 10,351 Jews died, and (according to the list, corrected with recalculations, on p. 84 et seq.) 50,175 were deported. The overview of transports to T, calculated according to lists prepared in Berlin, does not precisely match in either data or numbers the figures in *166 and *302, which are identical to each other and were compiled according to people who actually arrived in T.

	Sellenthin	*166 and *302
Number of transports	122	123
First transport	June 6, 1942	June 2, 1942
Last transport	March 27, 1945	March 28, 1945
Overall number of victims	14,797	15,122
Survivors in T (figures in *302)		1,571

Sellenthin presents the following figures on those sent directly to the East:

Destination	Dates	Number of transports	Number of persons
Łódź	October 18 (?)–November 1, 1941	4	4,079
Minsk-Kovno-Riga	November 14–27, 1941	3	3,175
Riga	January 13–August 15, 1942	4	3,395
Travniki	March 28–April 14, 1942	4	2,414
East (or unknown)	June 13–October 26, 1942	6	4,299
Auschwitz	July 11, 1942–January 5, 1945	40	17,961
		61	35,323

On January 5, 1945, fifty-five more people were sent to or intended for Bergen-Belsen, Sachsenhausen, and Ravensbrück (*48).

240. Semecká, I.: *Terezínské torso* [Theresienstadt Torso]. Prague, 1945.

Stories and sketches written in T by a *Geltungsjude* (person considered a Jew) with a Czech mother. Few themes relate directly to the camp.

240a. Shek, Z.: "Zum 10. Jahrestag der Befreiung von Theresienstadt." In *MB Mitteilungsblatt*. Tel Aviv, May 20, 1955.

In Givat Chaim, a former Zionist youth from T held a memorial ceremony at which *Brundibár* and other pieces from T were performed and a memorial grove was planted.

Siegel, E.: *321.

240b. Siegel, T.: [Recording]. MS, WL, Frankfurt a. M., 1955.

The author, born October 19, 1940, was taken from her mother in Frankfurt and was brought to T on November 10, 1943. What Siegel knows about the camp is based not on recollections but on later tales. Nevertheless, she was first placed in a

750   *Sources and Literature*

Czech children's home and was then "adopted" by a married couple. When the adoptive parents were deported, the woman's mother took the child; she was a Viennese woman who twice had protected Siegel from deportation. She then hid her and secretly fed and cared for her. After the war, the child returned to her mother

241. Silberschein, A. (ed.): *Augenzeugenberichte* [Eyewitness Accounts]. I–III. Geneva, July 1944.

Page 20 et seq. contain a description of the 1942 "action" in the Lublin area. The report on Posen – but not the report on T – is by Dr. Edith Kramer. She did come to T, however, and left on the Swiss transport.

242. Silberschein, A. (ed.): *Die Judenausrottung in deutschen Lagern* [Extermination of the Jews in German Camps]. Geneva, June 1945.

Pages 42–80 contain an account by a Berlin Jewish female doctor who was first active in the Jewish labor camp in Posen [Poznan] (which held inmates from the Łódź ghetto, including Czech Jews) and in July 1943 was brought to T via Berlin. The intelligent and highly humane description of this camp is unfortunately substantively erroneous and in part completely wrong.

243. Silberschein, A. (ed.): *Die Judenausrottung in Polen*. Geneva, August 1944.

Page 77 et seq. contain a report by two Slovak Jews who were in Auschwitz II from August 1942 and were able to escape on April 7. The text also provides a testimony regarding the T "family camp" and the tragedy of March 1944. According to *Noc a mlha* (Night and Fog) by O. Kraus and E. Kulka (Prague, 1958, pp. 382/4), the escapees were named Rudolf Vrba and Alfred Wetzler. They reached Slovakia on April 21. People did not believe their stories and thought they were liars. At the beginning of May they received counterfeit papers and money, but not until a five-hour meeting in June were they able to give the papal nuncio their reports, with plans of the camp, the gas chambers, and the trains. In this way, he says, news reached the Swiss press. In any case, the report went directly to the Jewish organizations in Switzerland and thus to the War Refugee Board in Washington, where it was supposed to be published in November 1944. It was submitted as document NG-2061 in the trial against Weizsäcker and his consorts at Nuremberg.

243a. Silten, F.: "Letter to Fritz Rathenau." MS, Amsterdam, 1946.

Critical remarks on an unpublished (and unknown to me) letter on T from Walter Rathenau's cousin (who was in T from April 22, 1943). Silten arrived in T from Westerbork on January 20, 1944, as a German émigré; there he worked as a pharmacist in the "Economic Oversight Office" [Wirtschaftsüberwachungsstelle] and then until liberation as the head of the "Central Medicine Storehouse" [Zentralheilmittellager]. The text provides insights into internal corruption in the camp; for example, the soda water intended for hospitals was drunk almost entirely by Eppstein and other high functionaries: "I gave my report, naming all names, to the head of my department, only to be asked by my colleagues whether I was eager to go on a transport."

A remark on the "bank" shows how people were able to succumb in T to the illusion of a normal social order as "officers of the self-administration":

Every year, a proper balance sheet had to be drawn up, and every month dozens of accountants sat to close the accounts of individual residents of Th. accurately. The gentlemen of the bank were so used to their work that they no longer felt its fictional nature, and I remember the agitation of one accountant when, despite all his efforts, an error of some 5 ghetto crowns was found in one account.

On the relationship of Dutch Jews to émigrés from Holland, Silten notes:

Dr. Eppstein told me personally that he had received an anonymous request that the stateless people from the Holland transport should be prohibited from wearing the "Jood" star and instead should wear the star with the German word "Jude." ... A small group of Dutch had suggested to Prof. Meijer that the stateless not be brought back to Holland. (*49)

243b. Simon, Erich: "Theresienstadt als autarkes Stadtwesen." [Transcript of a lecture held on April 13, 1946 in Berlin]. MS.

Simon worked in Berlin as a statistician in the Reichsvereinigung, where the statistician Korherr (*156a), compulsorily recruited by Himmler, vainly hoped to save him from deportation. Simon came to T in June 1943 and worked there, too, as a statistician. "I myself, when I was already in Theresienstadt, had in my hands files in which the chief finance officer of Berlin wrote to the Jewish Elders because some formality [in the "home purchase agreements"] had not been fulfilled." This work is a substantively intelligent – but not error-free – and humorless description of the camp; as a result, the picture that emerges is distorted and overly favorable. In autumn, Simon escaped deportation because he was able to utilize Korherr's intervention (probably with Möhs) to save himself.

243c. Simon, Ernst: *Aufbau im Untergang*. Tübingen, 1959.

This book on "Jewish adult education in National Socialist Germany as intellectual resistance" deals with T in its final chapter, in which the author also criticizes my portrayal. He gains no "reliable impression" from my "value judgements" on the "leading people" and notes Eppstein's part in particular, "without wishing to enter into a discussion of the facts reported by Adler," which however does not prevent Simon from concluding: "From a long acquaintanceship with him, I would like to assume that in the case of Paul Eppstein, even where he erred, there was more historical tragedy than personal guilt." This acquaintanceship existed only in prewar days. But what difference does all that make, if one "would like to assume"? One enters no "discussion" of "facts" but maintains without proof, in fact, without any desire to prove, that "thus Adler's misjudgment in this single case makes his other judgments of people and leading personalities problematic to a certain degree." Professor Simon retracted this sentence, which I felt to be an attack on my scholarly integrity (see "Erklärung." In *Bulletin für die Mitglieder der Gesellschaft der Freunde des Leo Baeck Instituts*. Jerusalem, April 1960, p. 70).

243d. Simonow, K.: *Das Vernichtungslager*. Moscow, 1944.

A substantive but not error-free report on Majdanek (concentration camp Lublin), which was the first large concentration camp and extermination camp to fall into enemy hands (quite undamaged). The work contains illustrations.

243e. Simonsohn, B.: "Seine Andenken wird weiterleben." In *Jüdische Sozialarbeit*. No. 3/4. Frankfurt a.M., 1959.

This work was first written in 1945, with the title "In Memoriam Dr. Paul Eppstein," and is published here, together with a translation of *115a, as "Memorial Pages for Dr. Paul Eppstein." In the following overview we quote from the manuscript. This is a brief biography of Eppstein, whose activities before and in T are recognized with almost complete approval. Eppstein already was associated with Chalutz Zionism before 1933 and was active in Jewish youth work, as, among other things, the founder of the "Reich Committee of Jewish Youth Associations" (Reichsausschuss der jüdischen Jugendverbände). In 1933 he moved to Berlin, where he became a functionary of the "Reichsvertretung" and later took over negotiations with the RSHA's Jewish Department (Judenreferat) (probably Eichmann's office). He wanted to maintain the autonomy (*selbstständigkeit*) of the Jewish administration as long as possible and, according to the manuscript, never was a traitor, although Eichmann tried, among other things, to win him over through bribery. "Eppstein spent four months in police custody on Alexanderplatz, with the inane excuse that he had sabotaged illegal emigration to Palestine." He then always carried cyanide with him (at his last arrest in T, he happened not to have it with him). He hid the continued illegal existence of the Hechalutz and, otherwise a solitary character, confided only in his young friends. When the deportations began,

> the most important thing was to save what could be saved, to try to maintain a core, and above all to protect ... the old people ... from the East. One may argue about whether a different policy might have been right at the time, a refusal to cooperate whatever the personal consequences, whether official advice to resist and hide could have saved more lives. With an elderly Jewry demoralized by years of harassment ... this would have been a mere demonstration, which ... absolutely did not suit Eppstein, although in many situations he showed personal courage and had long since seen his own life as lost.

In the creation of T, he saw "a possibility of saving people over time." Therefore, although we do not wish in any way to compare Eppstein with ghetto figures such as Rumkowski in Łódź or Genz in Vilna, we see him here going in directions that lead to the same catastrophe as there. It is typical that, according to Simonsohn, Eppstein could believe that he could achieve the deportation of "privileged groups" (within the meaning of the "Wannsee Protocol"; see Chapter 2) to T instead of to Auschwitz. In this view, Edelstein in Prague and Eppstein in Berlin had worked for chances or tried to "influence" the SS, who actually had long since decided. It probably was unknown to Simonsohn that the role of T had been determined in January 1942 at the latest, for reasons that were not affected in the slightest by the concerns of Jewish functionaries. He also had little idea what Eppstein, along with other Jewish representatives, had learned from Eichmann on February 19, 1942, about the deportations and specifically also about T (*3b, doc. 1; 175b). In any case, Eppstein (like Edelstein fourteen months previously) was deceived and tricked when he had to "resettle" to T "with the promise that he would continue to be head of the Reichsvereinigung in Berlin and would be able to travel to Berlin for important meetings."

Simonsohn's description of Eppstein's activities in T contradicts the portrayal in the present book; here his version is given a chance to be heard (my views are in *italics*). The goal of the deportations from T were "known" to Eppstein, "if not, at

Sources and Literature

first, to their full extent." He saw "disinclination to work, corruption, lack of responsibility towards the community and community property, neglect of the elderly. Eppstein took up the fight.... . He began ... with the disguised slogan: 'To improve productivity and fair distribution.'" He faced distrust and resistance but also found support in the struggle. "His tactic was, here too, to keep as many people as possible in Theresienstadt. This meant, however, ... maintaining the Gestapo's interest in its showcase and, through productivity, on the one hand raising the living standards in general – which gradually succeeded – and on the other hand tying young people to Theresienstadt through work in the war industry." *Simonsohn here sees achievements by Eppstein that were verifiably Edelstein's since the formation of the camp, or that were not carried out by either of the two, as, since Eppstein's arrival, nothing in the overall situation had changed that could have determined the camp's destiny through the initiative of its internal leadership. In particular, Eppstein's intervention had no effect on corruption and other morally questionable phenomena. He was unable to get rid of the previously strengthened corrupt groups, nor did he support efforts in this direction by other functionaries, if he did not actually hinder them and himself take on aspects of the corrupt lifestyle. Eppstein neither could nor wanted to maintain Edelstein's problematic but still unified administration.* In T, Eppstein again placed himself at the service of young people. "He always had contact especially with people from the Hechalutz, but in addition with all the young people who had a positive Jewish or socially progressive goal." He gained "the respect of the great majority of all classes." On the dangers for T after the invasion, he succumbed to no illusions. He had been informed some time before the catastrophe "through informants and through Möhs' public threats." Only he knew "that they intended to deport all men capable of bearing arms," and he is said to have explained: "I know that the moment must come when I can no longer say yes, when I will want to stand my ground before my conscience and the Jewish community." *If this is true, Eppstein's behavior in the critical period (during which, however, he was not alone in his knowledge and forebodings) is not easily understandable, for he would have had to confide in colleagues such as Zucker and not be satisfied with cynicism. Certainly, he wished for the rescue and not the destruction of the prisoners, but, by the time of his surprising arrest –that catastrophic day when he did not have his poison, a mistake the president of the Warsaw Council of Elders, Adam Czerniakow, did not make when he found himself in a similar situation – the moment to say "no" had long since passed, had passed years ago; the best of the camp already had been assembled for transport when Eppstein was arrested. Whatever the reasons, he was not arrested for saying "no."*

In a September 19, 1944, speech, which perhaps led to Eppstein's arrest, he said (according to Simonsohn): "We resemble a ship that already sees from afar the desired harbor, we already think we can see friends on the shore, but we still must steer through unknown rocks, and premature waving and greeting should not deceive us about the dangers that still must be overcome." Simonsohn believes, however, that it might have been attempts to prevent the extermination of the prisoners or at least to escape responsibility for it that led to his arrest. "Perhaps statements by him that announced intent to resist were denounced," or the Gestapo counted on his disagreement. After his arrest, which supposedly would last only during the transport period, food was sent to him daily until October 28, when Eppstein's wife was sent to her death at Auschwitz on the last transport (*55b).

754   *Sources and Literature*

243f. Singer, J.: *Erinnerungen aus Wien und Theresienstadt*. MS, WL, London, 1955.

A valuable account of experiences. In Vienna, as part of the IKG, Murmelstein and his adjutant Prochnik led the preparation and implementation of the deportations and were the liaisons to the "Central Office" (Zentralstelle). The "Jupo" contained the "evacuators" (*Ausheber*) – along with the SS, they raided homes and took the victims of the deportations – and the "Kripo," which found hidden Jews. The author arrived in T on September 25, 1942, after a nineteen-hour trip (her travel provisions consisted of two rolls, some sausage, and cheese). There her husband soon fell ill with typhus; it was kept secret, and Mrs. Singer nursed him back to health in the normal quarters with private medical help and medications she had brought. Both worked in the notions workshop from late 1942; the workday was ten and a half hours long, and sometimes they were given a free weekday. They produced imitation leather suitcases, eyeglass and cigarette cases, and leather bags for soldiers on behalf of a Viennese manufacturer; the Jewish workshop head had worked in the past in its Prague branch. The manufacturer visited the workshop, at first accompanied by a gendarme, and once brought food and tobacco for the Singers, whom he knew from Vienna; later he was allowed to enter only the SS "office" (*349b). In May 1944, the author's sister (the widow of a decorated Austrian officer who died in T) was to be deported. She entered the Schleuse wearing a folding chair around her neck; the hot-tempered Haindl wrenched the chair so violently that she fell to the ground dead. He then kicked Mrs. Singer, who had bent over the victim. Otherwise he had some sympathy for the Viennese, or at least for the blackguards who brought him information; his hatred was aimed at the Czech Jews, whom he called "the Wenzels." Mr. Singer was operated on for cancer in June 1944, soon relapsed, and, because he was considered to be dying, was sent with the last eastern transport; the author's volunteering was not taken into consideration. In April 1945, the notions workshop had to produce 8,000 knapsacks for the SS, and shortly before liberation, Freiberger and other major camp figures had large numbers of silk shirts altered there. After the war, the author helped with the dissolution of T until October 5, 1945; in the end, only twelve women and some men remained. They also came into contact with imprisoned Germans from the "Kleine Festung," including the intimate friend of an old camp inmate whom he had supported throughout the war and a younger half Jew whose mother had been deported from T. The author and some others were able, with the help of the Prague JKG, to ensure his release by the Czech authorities.

243g. Skarabis, R.: "Judicial testimony" [*richterliche Aussage*]. MS, Frankfurt, 1960.

Skarabis acted as provisional commandant of T at the creation of the camp. He testified about this: "[I was] posted to Prague for some 8 weeks and worked in Theresienstadt and Prague. I reported to ... Dr. Seidl and my activities consisted essentially of maintaining negotiations with the Wehrmacht on the transfer of military buildings [in T]." As can be seen in document NO-5412, Skarabis worked in the Guard Department (Referat Bewachung) of the Łódź Resettlement Office (Umwandererzentrale), headed by Krumey. The fact that he was temporarily posted to Prague and T is evidence of the close institutional and personal relationships among the various SS offices. The Resettlement Office's letterhead itself shows that it was affiliated with the chief of staff of the Security Police and SD in Łódź. In addition, it answered to the Higher SS- and Police Leader of the Reichstatthalter in Posen

[Poznan], in his capacity as representative of the Reich Commissar for the consolidation of German nationality (*Reichkommissar für die Festigung deutschen Volkstums*) (see NO-5348). This Reich commissar was none other than the Reichsführer-SS and Chief of the German Police, Himmler. Once Skarabis was employed at T, his boss Krumey could be assigned as an expert on "resettlement issues" to Eichmann's special kommando for Jewish deportation in Hungary. It should also be mentioned that OSTF Otto, who went to T "as a guest from Łódź," is probably identical to Krumey's subordinate with the same name in the Administrative Department.

244. [Slovakia] *Tragedia slovenských Židov* [The Tragedy of the Slovak Jews]. Bratislava, 1949.

A not-entirely-successful photomontage. It does not make reference to T.

Smolka, B.: *148.

244a. [Sobibór] *Sobibor*. Published by Afwikkelingsbureau Concentratiekampen. The Hague, 1946.

A brochure on the extermination camp and its victims from Holland. In 1947, the Dutch RC published an improved new edition.

244b. [Special treatment] Nuremberg Documents PS-1944, L-58, NG-4509, NO-246. Texts accessible, among other places, IfZ. Unpublished. 1939–48.

Little is known on the development of the concept of using the term "special treatment" (*Sonderbehandlung* [SB]) to mean "execution" – murder or killing by the police apparatus of the SS (RSHA) – and nothing has been published, for which reason the question will be dealt with briefly here.

So far, the earliest known evidence for "special treatment" as a euphemism for execution is found in an order from Heydrich to the Gestapo on September 20, 1939 (PS-1944); the phrase may have gained this meaning at this time – soon after the start of the war. At first, it dealt only with individual cases, as it read:

> For the cases under Number 1 [that is, "any attempt to subvert the German people's unity and will to fight"], a distinction must be made between those who can be dealt with in the heretofore usual way and those who must be subjected to special treatment. The latter case involves fact situations that, because of their reprehensibility or their propaganda effect, are suited for eradication without respect of persons through ruthless action (that is, through execution). Such cases are, for example, sabotage attempts, sedition or subversion of military members or a broad segment of the population, hoarding on a large scale, active communist or Marxist activity, etc.

This did not yet involve mass killing, and, in every case, protective custody had to be imposed and reported to Berlin, and the authorities had to await "further instructions" from there. This changed probably only with the start of the war with Russia and the activities of the Einsatzkommandos. On July 17, 1941, the RSHA IV (Gestapo) ordered that "special treatment" of prisoners of war, to the extent possible, should not be carried out in or near the Stalags but should take place only after return to Russian territory (L-58). On January 22, 1948, the former STBF and Kriminaldirektor Kurt Lindow in the RSHA declared in a sworn statement (NG-4509):

I can no longer remember exactly if the cover name "special treatment" for execution was introduced on the basis of a decree, and I also do not remember where and when I first became familiar with this code word. If I recall correctly, I first read it in the reports that arrived from the Einsatzgruppen. These reports contained … summaries of the number of … people shot.

On May 1, 1942, Greiser, as Reichstatthalter of Wartheland, asked Himmler (NO-246) for permission "to exterminate" some 35,000 Poles sick with infectious tuberculosis "with the available and experienced special kommando," after the "special treatment action approved by Heydrich of some 100,000 Jews in my Gau territory" (this involved, among other things, "resettlement" from the Łódź ghetto to the Chełmno extermination camp). This shows that, in the extermination camps, and thus also in Auschwitz, the mass murders of Jews, requiring no individual "authorization" by Himmler or other authorities, already were called "special treatment" in early 1942 and also were known under this name among the initiated.

244c. Spanier, J.: "Das Israelitische Schwestern- und Krankenheim." In Lamm, H. (ed.), *Von Juden in München*. Munich, 1958, pp. 80–83.

A report on this home, which had to be evacuated at Himmler's orders (published in *3b, doc. 3):

> "Evacuation" of the hospital of the IKG Munich to Theresienstadt. On June 4, 1942, the first transport … left. Some fifty sick people, seriously ill, even dying, with three nurses, headed by the chief physician, were loaded onto a furniture van on stretchers, the entire "freight" then was left at the South Train Station.… During the deportation, Hermann Schmid Strasse was … closed off; only a Wehrmacht major was allowed to … pass.… When he … was informed truthfully, he cried out loudly in horror and despite the presence of the Gestapo and SS: "What? Sick and dying people? I'm ashamed to be German!" And this first transport was followed in short order by two others.… Of the … "evacuees" from the entire building, only the former chief physician and his wife returned in 1945; of the nurses, only two survived. The matron and the head nurse were gassed in autumn 1944.

These three transports arrived in T on June 4, 5, and 6, 1942; of the 150 people in the transports, there were 5 survivors at war's end.

244d. Speijer, E. A. M.: "Entomologisch werk in den Nazikampen" [Entomological Work in the Nazi Camps]. In *Tijdschrift voor Entomologie*. Vol. 88. [Holland], 1945 (1947), pp. 358–74.

A work report by the author, who continued his scientific work in Barneveld, Westerbork, and T starting on September 6, 1944. In the last two camps he also was involved as a hygienist in fighting parasite-based epidemics and, at the end of the war, epidemic typhus, which he himself contracted.

244e. Spier, J.: [Sketches for the film *Theresienstadt 1944*.] Photocopies in the RvO, T, 1944.

Approximately 330 small drawings illustrating Gerron's *Draft of a Film Reportage*, the actual script (*81c). See the samples in *3b, doc. 237.

245. Spies, G.: "Aus Erinnerung – die Güte der Wissenden." In *Süddeutsche Tageszeitung*. Munich, September 13, 1947.

The author was in T from July 23, 1942, until liberation. The work contains camp recollections in poetic form.

245a. Spies, G.: "Erinnerungen an Elsa Bernstein." In Lamm, H. (ed.), *Von Juden in München*. Munich, 1958, pp. 292–94.

The recollections of a poet once known under the pseudonym Ernst Rosmer, who was blind when she lived in T. She was a granddaughter of Franz Liszt. One of her daughters was married to Gerhart Hauptmann's son Claus. Mrs. Bernstein liked to say about life in T: "If Gerhart only knew!"

245b. Spies, G.: "Heimweh: Erinnerungen an Theresienstadt." In *Süddeutsche Tageszeitung*. Munich, February 22, 1947.

245c. Speis, G.: "Hunger: Eine Erinnerung an Theresienstadt." In *Süddeutsche Tageszeitung*. Munich, September 11, 1948.

245d. Spies, G.: "In Memoriam Dr. Julius Spanier." MS, WL, Munich, 1959.

A memorial address for a Munich physician (*244b) who arrived in T on the first transport from Munich and did beneficent work there until after liberation.

245e. Speis, G.: "Rosenmann." In *Jüdische Rundschau*. Vol. 3, no. 17/18. Marburg-Giessen, no year [1948], pp. 46 et seq.

A remembrance of a kind person in T who died in Auschwitz in autumn 1944.

245f. Spies, G.: "Diary" [Fragment]. MS, T, September 16–27, 1944.

Insights into everyday life and mica production. See the samples in *3b, doc. 163.

245g. Speis, G.: *Theresienstadt: Gedichte* [Poems]. Munich, no year.

There are two editions of this work, which addresses camp themes up to and after liberation.

245h. Spies, G.: "Vom Abend bis zum Morgen: Auschnitt aus dem Theresienstädter Dasein." In *Jüdische Rundschau*. Vol. 3, no. 14/15. Marburg-Giessen, no year [1948], pp. 36f.

A description of a transport night in autumn 1944. Three illustrations by O. Nückel are iconographically not entirely correct.

245i. Spies, G.: "Wie ich es überlebte." In *Hochland*. Munich, April 1958, pp. 350–60.

Recollections of T. Artistic life – including the "Recreation Office" and the camp experiences that inspired the author to write her own poems – is at the core of this work. The text is an extract from a personal essay, "Ein Stück des Weges."

246. Springer, E.: "Zdravotnictví v terezínském ghettě" [Health Service in the Theresienstadt Ghetto]. In 319, no. 37, 1950.

A partial printing of a longer piece of the same name, written in German. The author was in T from December 4, 1941, and became chief physician of the camp and in autumn 1944 director of hospital E VI. He reports primarily on the organization of the health service and the E VI hospital. It was opened in January 1942 with an infectious disease ward, to which a surgical ward with forty beds was added in April.

758   *Sources and Literature*

Ultimately, there were 1,000 available beds, including a septic infection barrack (without the psychiatric ward in E VII): the infectious diseases division had around 480 beds, surgery had 212, gynecology had 70, urology had 65, optometry/ophthalmology had 50, laryngology had 50, dermatology had 45, and neurology had 30; in addition, there were some beds for psychiatry. According to Springer's estimates, E VI had served as a military hospital for 160–200 patients; during the war, some 900 patients and 100 doctors, nurses, and support staff lived there. Fifty-four doctors (twelve surgeons) were fully active; in addition, respected older doctors were consulted. At the opening of E VI, "there were only two trained nurses in T. There were only four toilets on each floor and a total of four bathtubs and one shower." Bearing children conceived in T was "allowed only with the authorization of the commandant's office."

> So in every case ... in which a woman wanted a child, a request had to be submitted to the commandant's office ... but the report went through the self-administration, and since it had received clear orders only to pass the request to the commandant's office in exceptional cases, almost all reports remained with the leadership of the self-government.

The author estimates the number of abortions at "many hundreds, perhaps thousands," which is certainly too high. "Once the order even came to examine all women of childbearing age, and several thousand women were in fact examined; only then was it possible to convince the Commandant's Office that such a mass examination was useless, and the examination was ended."

Three-person doctors' commissions examined people for "unsuitability for transport"; the SS installed the "doctor" Reinisch in June 1942 as the deciding authority.

247. Starr, J.: "Jewish Cultural Property under Nazi Control." In *Jewish Social Studies*. New York, January 1950, p. 27 et seq.

The RSHA Department VII collected a library of more than 2,000,000 objects in the Berlin Masonic temple: books, newspapers, manuscripts, and the like. In addition to Jewish works, which also came from Poland and other countries, Marxist and Masonic literature was collected. At the end of 1941, the Reichsvereinigung was charged with providing ten Jewish scholars. The head was Dr. E. Grumach, who succeeded in raising the number to twenty-five. The group remained in Berlin until the end of the war but was imprisoned except when working. The SS hardly used the collection. In August 1943, some of it was moved to Bohemian castles and to T. A large part of the Berlin stock was destroyed by bombs on the night of November 22, 1943.

247a. [*Steengracht v. Moyland*] Interrogation of Steengracht on June 24, 1948, and Interrogation Summary 2574 (June 23, 1947). Mimeographed, Nuremberg, Case XI.

Information on the Danish Jews and T. See the samples in *3b, doc. 241.

248. Stein, A.: *Adolf Hitler, Schüler der "Weisen von Zion."* Karlsbad, 1936.

Stein shows to what extent Hitler and other leading Nazis depended on the famous "protocols" and trained themselves according to the principles they thought were "Jewish." This is also significant for understanding Nazi "metaphysics," as I have developed it through the juxtaposition "this way or that way" in Chapter 20.

Sources and Literature

249. Stein, R.: "Terezín: Zdravotnický úkol" [The Sanitary Task]. MS, no information.

A brief report by one of the most capable doctors working in T. Stein was Munk's successor as head of the "Health Services Department." I do not know the piece that Lederer (*166) quotes.

250. Šteindler, S.: "Rodinný tábor B IIb" [Family Camp B IIb]. In 319, no. 8, 1950.

Information on the life of Theresienstadters in Auschwitz. The Jewish hangman at the executions of 1942 became a kapo and is said to have acted like a Gestapo man. He escaped gassing but died as the victim of medical experiments. According to Bacon (*11a), he was basically good natured and died in Mauthausen after the evacuation.

251. Steiner, F. B.: "A Comparative Study of the Forms of Slavery." MS, Oxford, 1949.

A basic account.

252. Steiner, Z., and J. Steiner: "Transcript." [Czech], MS, DA, 1945.

An account by twin brothers (born in 1929) who arrived in Auschwitz from T in September 1943. As experimental subjects of SS doctor Mengele, they survived the extermination of their group in March 1944 and remained in Auschwitz until liberation. The work is a description of their experiences.

252a. Sterling, E.: "Er ist wie du: Aus der Frühgeschichte des Antisemitismus." In *Deutschland (1815–1850)*. Munich, 1956.

An important work on the history of the Jewish tragedy; almost all of the basic themes of this tragedy were foreshadowed a hundred years earlier.

Stern, N.: *352b.

253. Sternberg, H.: "Gedichte." In *De Profundis: Deutsche Lyrik in dieser Zeit*. Munich, 1946, pp. 391–93.

Three poems written in T on the misery in the camp.

254. Stier, R., and H. Schmidt: *Die Ausschaltung der Juden aus der Wirtschaft des Protektorats Böhmen und Mähren*. Prague, no year [1941].

Information on the conditions as of March 15, 1941.

254a. Strauß, L.: "Also ob: Gedicht." Printed in *234a.

Leo Strauß, son of the operetta composer Oskar Strauß, arrived in T in 1942; there he was one of the best-known cabaret performers, along with Hans Hofer and Karel Švenk. In autumn 1944 he was sent to his death. "Als ob" was the most popular couplet in T. It begins,

> I know a little town, a really tip-top town
> I won't call it by name, I'll call it "as if."

A Czech translation, "Jako by," can be found in 319, number 2, 1957.

254b. Sündermann, H.: *Alter Feind – was nun? Widerbegegnung mit England und Engländern*. Leoni, 1953.

760 · *Sources and Literature*

In his book, the former deputy press chief of the Reich government deals with his statement at a Berlin press conference on October 7, 1943, soon after the capture of the Danish Jews (p. 196 et seq.). He does not mention his similar statement on July 19, 1944 (NG-5798), where he also alluded to a visit to T by the IRC. Both texts are available in *3b, doc. 226.

255. Švenk, K.: "Terezínský pochod" [Theresienstadt March]. In 319, no. 2, 1957.

An English and German translation of this poem is provided in Chapter 19.

256. Szana, T.: *Ehe auf Raten*. MS, ca. 1946.

Clothed in novel form, this work describes life in the Sered camp, the transport to T, and conditions there since late 1944. It contains some accurate insights or impressions that prove that, to a large extent, especially for newcomers, the face of the coerced community had not changed significantly from 1942–43 to the end of the war.

256a. Szternfeld, L.: [Transcript]. [Polish], MS, HIŻ, Poland, 1946.

The author's journey took him from the Cracow ghetto to the Płaszów camp and in May 1944 to Gross-Rosen; four days later, he was sent with 250 men to the Wüstegiersdorf satellite camp, where people worked for the Organisation Todt under tolerable conditions. On February 16, 1945, the camp was evacuated; after a four-day march with one loaf of bread, they traveled four days by train to Flossenbürg, with 120 men to a carriage, without food or drink. There were deaths on the trip. In Flossenbürg, the prisoners were not forced to work, and treatment was inhuman. Two weeks later they were sent to a satellite camp called Grawinkiel, where, under terrible conditions, they built underground depots for the Hermann Göring Works. On March 30 they survived heavy bombardment; on April 3 they were marched to Buchenwald, under fire and with other hardships. Four days later, a twelve-day train trip began to T in open trucks. "The hunger was so bad that people ate the bodies of those who died of exhaustion. I myself saw them cut off and devour flesh." They arrived in T on April 21.

256b. [T] "Abbeförderung von Juden aus Theresienstadt: Briefwechsel zwischen Kaltenbrunner (IV B 4a) und Himmler." MS, RvO, February 1943.

See the text in *3b, doc. 216.

257. [T] [Anonymous untitled transcript]. MS, DA, Prague, 1945.

Information on smuggling (*Schleusen*) in all the food services in T.

258. [T] "Arbeitseinsatz." MS, T, March 1, 1945.

An account of workers.

259. [T] [Aufstellung über den Arbeitseinsatz zum 30 Juni 1944]. MS, T.

See the analysis in Chapter 13.

260. [T] "Auszug aus der Übersiedlungsordnung." Mimeographed, MS, T, March 30, 1942.

261. [T] "Bericht über den Status des ehemaligen Konzentrationslagers Theresienstadt." MS, WL, T, June 18, 1945.

An analysis of the self-administration's property and assets, including administered goods and investments. It mentions agricultural and municipal properties, including new construction; investments related to new construction or the expansion of railroads, roads, streets, sewers, the electricity supply (T was connected to a land-based power station and had a main receiving station), and agricultural facilities; agricultural enterprises (nurseries, cattle breeding, and operating materials); public facilities and companies (the fire department, crematorium, district heating plant, Central Laundry, hospital laundry, etc.); provisioning businesses (a large-scale bakery, three other bakeries, a butcher shop, four steam kitchens, and twelve other kitchens); crafts businesses (sixteen workshops); health and sanitary facilities (two hospitals, outpatient clinics, homes for the infirm, disinfection stations, the Central Bath, etc.); inventory (vehicles, machines, furniture – e.g., some 5,000 beds and 20,000 bunk bed spaces – office machines – e.g., 300 typewriters – medical apparatuses, etc.); various materials and supplies (e.g., 10,000 kg of medications and 20,000 kg of mica, of which half was already split); cultural materials (most of it, at first, ended up in the Prague Jewish Museum); and archives (registry materials were taken over by the Prague Jewish authorities; the usual material – the blueprint archive, reports, tables, graphic portrayals, papers, and pictures – was not dealt with very carefully, but a considerable portion found its way into the Prague Jewish Museum).

261a. [T] "Besondere Lagerordnung." Mimeographed, T, February 9, 1942.

The text largely corresponds to the "general order" offered in Chapter 15 but contains additional regulations regarding the strict segregation of the sexes and the prohibition on visits.

262. [T] "Bestimmungen über Fluchtverdacht-Meldungen." Mimeographed, MS, T, May 1943.

263. [T] "Bestimmungen über Fluchtverdachtmeldungen." Mimeographed, MS, T, January 20, 1945.

264. [T] *Bilder aus Theresienstadt.* No year [T, 1944].

Eighteen hand-colored lithographs by Jo Spier on subjects from the "beautification" of T. This sorry piece of technically expert workmanship served as propaganda for the SS. A contest was even set up for the artists, titled "Views from Theresienstadt." They were told that a "brochure" had to be issued, one in which the camp character could not be obvious. The twenty-four best designs were framed and exhibited in a corridor of B V. One picture was titled "View of Theresienstadt from the Prague-Dresden Express Train."

264a. [T] [Letters from leading functionaries in T to friends in the World Jewish Congress in Geneva] MS, T, 1942 and 1944.

One letter each from Edelstein (text in *3b, doc. 211), Zucker, Stricker, and Friedmann (text in *2a), in 1942, and one from Munk, in 1944. Conditions are described in an exaggeratedly rosy light, in which – this was in October 1942! – construction was particularly praised. It would be difficult to read anything unfavorable between the lines, except perhaps by noting the artificial tone. A point in Munk's letter of March 12, 1944, is noteworthy: "In recent days I received news from Leo [Janowitz], who was very happy about your card. Jakob [Edelstein] reports that he is well and in good spirits." Janowitz was gassed the day this letter was written; Edelstein was in bunker detention in Auschwitz.

264b. [T] [Danish Jews] [Eleven short articles]. In *Jodisk Samfund*. Vol. 26, no. 3. Copenhagen, March 1955, pp. 3–10.

Reminiscences by Danish Jews on the occasion of the tenth anniversary of their liberation, by L. Bornstein, J. Brandt, A. Friediger, J. Grün, S. and B. Korzen, A. A. Margolinsky, A. and C. Metz, and anonymous authors. On T, it provides general information that is, in part, erroneous. It contains a reproduction of an April 13, 1945, travel announcement that was similar to a deportation announcement, but it was politely phrased: "You are therefore asked to reliably appear along with your luggage in the building Bäckergasse 2." On the cover of the text is a picture of the Copenhagen Jewish cemetery memorial for the 53 Danish Jews who died in T. According to this source, there were 476 Danish Jews in T.

265. [T] "Das Jugendproblem im Ghetto Theresienstadt: Mit besonderer Berücksichtigung des Verwahrlostenproblems." MS, T, December 1942.

265a. [T] "Denkschrift über Arbeiten zur Ausbesserung und Erneuerung von Gehwegen und Fahrbahnen des Straßennetzes in Theresienstadt und dessen Ausfallstraßen." ms. RvO, T, March 13, 1942.

A detailed plan for improvement of the bad roads. Weaker and older people were proposed as workers.

266. [T] "Der Befehlshaber der Sicherheitspolizei und des SD, Zentralamt für die Regelung der Judenfrage in Böhmen und Mähren, Dienststelle Theresienstadt: Verkaufs- und Lieferungsbedingungen." Mimeographed, T.

267. [T] "Dichtungen aus Theresienstadt." MSS, T, 1942/45.

Unpublished poems are introduced in this listing only if they involved texts with camp themes of some interest. The poems in this list are classed by the author's name. Furthermore, the surviving works known to me by Georg Kafka, Peter Kien, and Hans Kolben are mentioned. Essentially anything printed was included.

268. [T] "Die Wahrheit über Theresienstadt." In *Aufbau*. New York, June 8, 1945.

A description of conditions in a May 12, 1945, letter by a woman from Aachen, G. Berger, written from T, where she had been since July 25, 1942.

269. [T] "Dreieinhalb Jahre hinter Ghetto-Mauern: Theresienstädter Insassen berichten ausführlich." In *Aufbau*, New York, May 25, 1945.

A largely correct report.

270. [T] [An article on Jews in T]. In *Einigkeit*. Moscow, September 27, 1945. YIVO.

Probably the only Soviet publication on T.

271. [T] "Erlebnisse einer deutschen Jüdin in Berlin, Theresienstadt und Deggendorf." MS, WL, London, 1955.

A highly humane account by an elderly woman who arrived in T on December 16, 1942. To help her starving, sick husband, she exchanged their wedding rings, among other things, for bread; she received one loaf for each. She also gave pedicures and, as a rule, received one or two slices of bread for a treatment lasting three-quarters of an hour.

As a caregiver (*Fürsorgerin*) in the "block for the infirm," the author also brought her charges "ghetto money" from the "bank." The confusion experienced by some of the elderly can be seen in a conversation in which one old lady asked the writer, "Do you know why we are getting this money?" "No." "I'll tell you. The war will soon be over, and we (she meant the Germans) will lose it. Then we will have to pay reparations." The elderly lady really thought they would force the old German Jews to pay reparations, and therefore she saved her "ghetto money."

After the war, camp inmates who wished to emigrate and not be repatriated were sent on three transports from T to a waiting camp in Deggendorf under (American) UNRRA administration. It was in a neglected barracks that had to be cleaned up by the new arrivals. The camp was surrounded by barbed wire and could not be left without a pass. Only after the prisoners protested were they given freedom of movement, three days later. When the author emigrated to England on June 7, 1947, there still were former Theresienstadters in Deggendorf (*46a, 52b).

272. [T] "Erlebnisse in fünf Lagern." MS, WL, Amsterdam, 1946.

The author was taken from his home in Amsterdam on the night of July 15, 1943, along with his wife, and was brought to the collection point Schouwburg, and two days later to Westerbork. On September 14, 1943, they continued on a "Theresienstadt transport" of German war veterans and their families. They traveled in cattle cars with all their luggage, attached to a "normal" transport to the East, to Bergen-Belsen, where Seidl, who had been in T earlier, took in the newcomers. They were housed in a barracks with Greek Jews. Provisions were at first sufficient but got progressively worse. The RM 250 that they had brought along was taken away but could be used in the canteen for food and cigarettes. They worked twelve hours a day (with a half-hour lunch break), seven days a week, taking apart old shoes. One day Möhs decided that, except for a few people, everyone was to go to T. In mid-January 1944, more Westerborkers arrived and were treated worse; people seventy-five years old were made to clear wood and to perform similar work.

The first transport from Westerbork left for T on January 25, 1944, in cattle cars with no water; they arrived forty-eight hours later. The text provides an accurate, but not flawless, description of the camp. The author joined the GW, which on June 23, the day the IRC visited, had to "remove from the streets by force any cripples or people who looked particularly ill." The author went to Auschwitz on September 28, 1944, and on arrival gave his age as

> 51 – any other age would have been credible in the darkness – businessman as my profession, and to the questions about my state of health ... war invalid ... assuming that this ... might ease my situation. I was asked about the type of wound, answered briefly ... in response the brief remark, "Ach, nonsense," and was sent to the left with a wave of the hand ... to the camp.... One person ... ahead of me, a gigantic guy who gave a dozen different illnesses, was also sent to the left; he came back and showed his ... injured hand with the remark that he couldn't work with it; he was ... then sent the other way.

764   *Sources and Literature*

One can hardly give better evidence of the naïveté in T!

On October 28, they were transported to Meuselwitz, where some 300 male and 2,000 female prisoners lived separately in primitive conditions on the HASAG work site and worked in twelve-hour day and night shifts on Panzerfausts. Production continued haltingly and ended in January–February 1945 with air raids. Forty women were killed in a raid, and the men had to undress them with their bare hands. The camp was evacuated on April 12.

They traveled for forty-eight hours, in open coal cars with 100 prisoners in each, to Graslitz, where they camped in the cars in an open field, with one slice of bread a day. An English air raid resulted in deaths and injuries; some Czech Jews fled. Around April 19, they began to march on foot; in the evening, the author ran away with three comrades. After wandering for three days, they were picked up by a member of the Volkssturm and handed over to the police, who brought them back to Graslitz, where some 120 helpless prisoners still lay in the train. The author soon ran away again and was taken into the Graslitz hospital and operated on. "I was hungry to read and ... asked some of the nurses to ... lend me the Bible. No one dared fulfill my wish, even shortly before liberation ... because they said borrowing the Bible was forbidden." The Americans came on May 7. When the author was able to travel, he was sent to Falkenau, where he met Dutch people from T, including his wife. They were brought to Pilsen [Plsen] and from there traveled by plane to Holland.

273. [T] "Falsche Zehlen über Theresienstadt" [False Statistics on Theresienstadt]. In *Aufbau.* New York, March 10, 1944.

There were not 240,000 but at most 40,000 people in T, 700 of them Danish.

274. [T] [February report 1944]. MS, T.

This report, written by a leading member of the self-administration by order of the SS, is not one of the monthly activity reports but an overview of the history and construction of the camp. This is an important source.

274a. [T] Finanzierung der Massnahmen zur Lösung der Judenfrage: Memorandum des Reichsfinanzministeriums, Abt. I, Gruppe: Haushalt- und Kassenwesen. NG-4583. MS [mimeographed as a Nuremberg document], Berlin, December 14, 1942.

The text of a document in *3b, doc. 40, that provides important information on T and the "home purchase agreements."

275. [T] [Tour of Theresienstadt by the foreign commission on June 23, 1944]. MS.

A list of the places viewed, with precise time indicators.

275a. [T] [Rumors in Germany]. Affidavit *Werner v. Richter* NID-11446, September 24, 1947. Mimeographed, Nuremberg.

"In the final years of the war, rumors frequently circulated in the [Dresdner] Bank, under the leading gentlemen, that Jewish people in the Theresienstadt and Auschwitz concentration camps were dying violent deaths." It was believed that they were "liquidated" there.

276. [T] "Ghetto Theresienstadt." Activity report. Submitted to the Camp Commandant's Office, Theresienstadt, MS, September 1–September 30, 1942.

See the sample in 3b, doc. 134.

277. [T] "Ghetto Theresienstadt." Activity report. Submitted to the Camp Commandant's Office, Theresienstadt, MS, RvO, August 1–August 31, 1942.

See the samples in 3b, docs. 46, 84–85, 98, 130, 131, and 135.

278. [T] "Organizational Plan." Mimeographed, MS, no date [T, 1944].

Information on the camp administrative scheme (see Chapter 8).

279. [T] "Jahresbericht des Zentralmateriallagers" [Annual Report of the Central Materials Storehouse]. MS, T, November 1942.

280. [T] "Jahresberichte des Zentral-Holzlagers 1942/43/44" [Annual Reports of the Central Lumber Storehouse, 1942–43–44]. MS, T.

281. [T] "Jahresbericht [interner] des Jugendheimes L 417" [Annual Report (Internal) of the Youth Home L 417]. MS, T, July 1943.

This comprehensive document is partly German and partly Czech. Among the more than thirty authors are leaders in the self-administration and in the Youth Welfare Office and educators (*Erzieher*). Each one says something about his area of expertise or gives his views.

282. [T] "Jahresbericht 'Jugend hilft'" [Annual Report "Youth Helps"]. MS, T, 1943/44.

283. [T] "K terezínským sňatkům" [On Marriages in Theresienstadt]. Note in 319, no. 11, 1947.

In accordance with a decision by the Prague civil district court, ritual weddings in T were recognized as legal marriages under Czechoslovakian law.

284. [T] "Karel Rahm před svými soudci" [Karl Rahm Faces His Judges]. In 319, nos. 10–14, 16–19, 23, 25–26 (1947), and 18 (1948), 1947–48.

A report on the trial of Rahm by the People's Court in Leitmeritz.
Murmelstein's testimony on the "beautification":

> The first one to lead the beautification was the commandant at the time, Burger, and he did it badly, because he had no idea how. He was therefore replaced by Rahm, who, as a craftsman, better understood technical things and led the campaign with real energy....
>
> Almost every day, SS men came from Berlin or Prague for inspection, including K. H. Frank, accompanied by Moravec....
>
> According to Eppstein, Danes and a member of the Swedish Red Cross were on the commission.

The following Germans were described as present: the Günther brothers, Möhs, Rahm, and Günel.

Regarding the autumn transports in 1944, Murmelstein said that in his view they were ordered for political reasons, in connection with the invasion and the Slovak rebellion, in order to weaken the Czech element in the camp. With little credibility, he testified:

766 — Sources and Literature

In October 1944 we had no idea that the transports were going to the East. Only when the cars came back to Theresienstadt did the clean-up women discover the inscription "Birkenau." When Günther asked me what people were saying in the ghetto about the destination of the transports, I answered: "Birkenau." He made no response. We knew nothing of the fate that awaited the transports there. We learned from Slovak Jews in December 1944 that Birkenau was a code name for Auschwitz.

The witness Erich Kohn, an engineer and a member of the "staff" who was close to the leadership and well informed, had, however, testified earlier that people in T had known of the gas chambers since February 1943 through news from the East.

Rahm's testimony on Eppstein's end:

Eppstein was supposed to speak on the radio to the world public about how the bombardments had damaged a city [in central Germany] in which there were Jews, although the Allies protected Jews. . . .

Right at the beginning [September 1944], when Möhs was talking about a transport to central Germany, Eppstein was chosen as announcer for the radio. When I saw Eppstein on a bicycle outside the ghetto, I reported it to Möhs, and therefore Eppstein was subjected to detention.

Murmelstein described the ambiguous incident dramatically:

On September 28, I was summoned to the SS "office." Rahm called me into his office. Suddenly the doors opened; Möhs came through one, and at almost the same time, Eppstein came from the other side. Rahm then told Eppstein that he had seen him at the Dresden Kaserne [H V] arguing with a gendarme, whom he had told that he had permission from Rahm to leave the ghetto at any time. Möhs also accused him, with the words: "I will have you locked up until the transport leaves! That can be viewed as escape!" Eppstein was told to give me the briefcase, then Haindl came and took Eppstein away. Rahm also left: I had to wait around half an hour, then Rahm came back and ordered me to tell the Council of Elders that Eppstein had been arrested for attempting to escape.

On this, Rahm testified: "Eppstein was transferred to the Kleine Festung at Möhs' orders. Eppstein had the right to issue passes to leave the ghetto, but he did not have the right to give himself that permission."

Docent Dr. Richard Stein, head of the "Health Services Department" after Munk, testified:

The allocation was never more than around 1,000 calories, 1,200 at most, per person per day. . . . For people unable to work, the number of calories fell below 800. . . . There was almost no animal protein, and the digestive organs, especially among older people, could not digest the food. . . . German doctors exhibited [*sich vorführen*] avitaminosis, pellagra, night blindness and drying of the conjunctiva.

In May 1944, some 1,200 tuberculosis patients were deported to Auschwitz.

According to the testimony of SS functionary Scholz from the Economics Department of the "office," valuables and gold teeth confiscated in the Schleuse were sent to Prague (the "emigration fund"); at the end of the war, 16,000–18,000 "notables" were to be evacuated to Austria, and the rest were to remain in T.

285. [T] "Konfidentenbericht für die Dienststelle der SS" [Informer Report for the SS Office]. MS, T, end of April 1945.

Sources and Literature

286. [T] "Konzentrationslager Theresienstadt: Komitee ehemaliger politischer Gefangener." MS, Hamburg, February 7, 1946. [In the possession of the International Tracing Service in Arolsen].

An overview of figures that matches the list in *168; the final number of those sent to T is listed as 139,482 (139,444 in *168), plus roughly 13,900 evacuation transports. The number of deaths in T up to May 10, 1945, is listed as 33,341, which is close to better-supported figures. The number of those deported from T is a few thousand too low, at 81,939. The figures for the deported and survivors from transport groups I and VI (Berlin and Hamburg) are different here than in *48, *83, *166, and *302:

Transport group	Number deported	Survivors
I	15,105	1,643
VI	2,377	529

287. [T] "Kurzbericht: Gesundheitswesen. Abteilung Fürsorge." MS, T, October 1943.

288. [T] "März-Bericht [1944]: Gesundheitswesen und Fürsorge. Abteilung Fürsorge." MS, T.

[T] Mitteilungen der jüdischen Selbstverwaltung: *301.

288a. [T] "Meldungen des Dansk Presstjänst." Mimeographed, Stockholm, 1944/45.

Six reports by the Swedish-published "Danish Press Service" mention T.

February 28, 1944: There are 240,000 Jews of all nationalities in T. Approximately 500 of these are Danes, of whom 18 have died; most of them were diabetics who died due to lack of insulin. There is a disclaimer in *273.

June 26, 1944: "The fate of the Danish Jews deported to T is followed very closely by Danes at home. Illegal newspapers pass on the rumor that the Germans plan to send Jews capable of work to work camps, and emphasize that the Danish authorities must lodge a strong protest with the Germans." They should, it says, demand transfer to the Frøslev camp on Danish soil.

> The Danish freedom movement has let the German authorities ... know that anyone involved in the deportation of the Danish Jews is equally responsible for their later fate, and all those involved shall be treated as war criminals. Even inaction is a crime, the letter says, ending with a demand to Dr. Best that he do his utmost to make up for the misdeeds committed.

July 13, 1944: "Two Danish representatives, a doctor and a diplomat in the Foreign Ministry, have returned from a trip to T in Germany, where the deported Danish Jews are located. Conditions are described as relatively good and the rumors that a number of Jews are to be sent to forced labor were denied." This is, to my knowledge, the only press report to reach the free world about the Danish visit to T (without mention of the IRC); apparently, however, according to information from Mag. Ruge, it was noticed only by the *News Digest* of July 14 and 21, 1944, and the *Daily Digest of World Broadcasts* of July 19, 1944. Otherwise, it was not taken up by either the Jewish or the international press.

768   Sources and Literature

July 15, 1944: There is no prospect of transfer of Danish Jews from T to Frøslev.
July 17, 1944: The Danish underground press issues a warning about a Swedish
spy in the service of the Germans, who approaches Danes with Jewish relatives in T.
February 5, 1945: T is only mentioned.

289. [T] "Mitteilungen der Leitung." MS, T, December 5, 1941.

290. [T] "Monatsbericht der Abteilung für innere Verwaltung, Fürsorgestelle." MS, T, July 1942.

291. [T] "Monatsbericht June 1944. Gesundheitswesen und Fürsorge. Abteilung Fürsorge." MS, T.

292. [T] "Naar Theresienstadt." In *Nederland in Oorlogstijd*. Amsterdam, January 25, 1947,
p. 88.

A reproduction of a letter from the Hague on August 19, 1943, from SS-Brigadeführer Harster, in the office of the Higher-SS and Police Leader, to Reich Commissar
Seyss-Inquart:

> Attached are two lists of names regarding Jews, sent with the request to authorize the
> resettlement of those named in the list. These include
>
> 1) Jews who were decorated during the 1914–18 world war ,
> 2) Jews who can show peacetime service for Germany and some Jews who already have
>   relatives living in Theresienstadt.
>
> The list of Jews was made according to guidelines issued by the Reich Security Main
> Office, Berlin, on resettlements to Theresienstadt.

Seyss-Inquart's initials, in his handwriting, are on the letter, along with the word
"yes." On August 25, the letter was returned to the police office [*Polizeistelle*] with
the note, "As you can see from the note by the Reich Commissar, he is in agreement
with the transfer of the Jews to Theresienstadt." The text accompanying the reproduction claims – without an explanation – that, as a result of this letter, 305 people
were sent from Westerbork to Bergen-Belsen on September 14, 1944, with T as the
final destination (see *3b, docs. 12–14).

293. [T] "Novelle betreffend Ergänzung und Vereinheitlichung der strafrechtlichen Vorschriften."
Mimeographed, MS, T, March 10, 1945.

The text fills the secretariat's newsletter number 211.

294. [T] [Photographs, 1945–46].

Camp photographs after liberation and photos of paintings and drawings from T (by
Fritta, Ungar, Kien, etc.). Most of the negatives were in the Prague Jewish Museum in
1947. Some of these photos are reproduced in *3b.

294a. [T] "Correspondence with Theresienstadt Residents." Mimeographed, Berlin, July 1943.

The text of these guidelines is in *3b, doc. 158.

294b. [T] [Minutes of conferences between the Council of Elders and Dunant on May 3, 4, 5,
and 6, 1945]. [French], MS, T.

May 3: Dunant, who officiates at the city hall, describes his first duty as avoiding
avoidable incidents. Baeck states that the function of the Jewish Elders ends as soon

as the German authorities leave T but thanks Murmelstein for his activities until now and hopes for his further cooperation. Dunant reports on his visit to the "Kleine Festung," where there are 5,000 people. K. H. Frank and Weinmann had promised to release everyone accused of minor violations. Those who could not be released would be brought to E 1 and guarded there, whereas the sick would be brought to T's hospitals. He announces that a Czech physician's group in Prague will help these sick people. Dunant reproaches Murmelstein for answering negatively on April 6 when asked about the presence of South Americans (that is, prisoners with South American passports). Murmelstein explains that he was forced to answer according to instructions.

May 4: Dunant determines the following regarding the "Kleine Festung": all healthy women will be released after medical examination; healthy men will go to E 1, under the administration and guard of Czech gendarmes, and the sick shall go to the Südbaracken under separate administration. Murmelstein requests that Dunant tell the workers that it is necessary to preserve discipline. Dunant refuses.

May 5: Dunant is the official camp commandant.

May 6: Dunant is told that Rahm had asked Murmelstein to look for some small things he had left behind in his office (in the city hall, called the "office" until then). Dunant states that this is permissible only with RC passes.

294c. [T] "Rapport Theresienstadt." [Dutch], MS, Equipe de secours aux déportés Néerlandais en Europe centrale, Geneva, March 1945.

Information based on reports by Dutch Jews who came to Switzerland in February 1945. It provides a not-always-correct description of the camp.

294d. [T] [Legal situation] [Materials from T in photocopies]. Preserved in the Staatsarchiv Hamburg.

I was not allowed to study these documents, which probably mainly concern the labor courts.

294e. [T] "Collection Transports." MS, T, early May 1945.

A listing of prisoners who arrived in T between April 20 and May 5 – 12,863 people in all, of whom 88 were dead on arrival and 221 died shortly thereafter.

295. [T] *Schuld und Verantwortung: 10 Jahre nach der Kristallnacht 9 November 1938.* Hanover, 1948.

On page 31 there is a poem that a mother addressed to her child born in T.

296. [T] [Swiss transport]. In *Israelitisches Wochenblatt.* Zurich, 1945.

Number 6, February 9: The official report of arrival reads,

> Today [February 6] the first train of 1,200 civilians from Theresienstadt arrived in Kreuzlingen; it was released thanks to the efforts of former federal councilor Musy, the European Executive Council of the Union of Orthodox Rabbis of the United States of America in Montreux, and Agudas Yisroel World Organization in Germany. Following should be further transports that will continue from Switzerland to other countries, as soon as transport opportunities are available. The German government has been very forthcoming to former federal councilor Musy and sympathetically took up the question of the departure of Jews.

770   *Sources and Literature*

Numbers 7–8, February 16 and 23: "The transport from Theresienstadt." Arrivals provide contradictory but in part quite correct reports on the camp. A sentence on the autumn transports of 1944 is noteworthy: "A few months ago, deportations took place; it can be assumed that they involved labor in armaments factories."

Number 9, March 2: The "List of Arrivals from Theresienstadt" contains 1,200 names and birth dates. The information on countries of origin does not entirely agree with the lists from T (Chapter 3): 660 people from Germany (including Austria), 436 from Holland, 103 from Czechoslovakia, and 1 stateless person.

Number 15, April 13: In an article "Liberation of the Survivors" it is stated: "After that, Musy said that Himmler had never been in agreement with the extermination policy against the Jews, as demanded by Hitler, and there was no agreement between Hitler and Himmler on this question."

296a. [T] [Swiss transport]. "Bericht über den Transport vom 5. February 1945" [Report on the transport of February 5, 1945]. [Compiled by] Sekretariat. Annex 71 in *Enquetecommissie regeringsbeleid 1940–1945*. Vol. 6 B. The Hague, 1952.

The main portion of the report in *3b, doc. 50. It is striking that all the sources separate the 1,200 differently by country of origin. Here it says that 96 people came from the "Protectorate," 518 from Germany, 155 from Austria, and 433 from Holland.

297. [T] *Sluníčko* [The Sun]. I–II. Duplicated, T, 1943.

An elementary reader in two booklets, produced lithographically for illegal teaching in Czech-language youth homes. The illustrations show animals and other things that a child in T could not see. There are copies in Israel and the Prague Jewish Museum.

297a. [T] "So war es in Theresienstadt!" In *Basler Nationalzeitung*. August 28, 1945.

Some impressions with few errors.

298. [T] "Sociální péče o mládež: 1941–1944, 1944–1945" [Youth Welfare]. MS, DA, Prague, 1945.

A history of youth welfare in T.

299. [T] "Stand am 23. Juni 1943." MS. [In the possession of the International Tracing Service in Arolsen].

Whether this list is an original or a copy is difficult to tell. The figures are probably accurate.

Age	Men	Women	Total
Up to 15 years	1,849	1,763	3,612
16–55	9,106	11,453	20,559
56–60	1,418	2,253	3,671
61–65	1,531	2,768	4,299
66–86	4,153	7,767	11,920
87–90	18	88	106
91–100	11	18	29
	18,086	26,110	44,196

Including:

5,500	sick people	597	severely disabled	1,005	decorated veterans
1,565	people incapable of transport	580	blind		

Because, from then on, people over sixty-seven were rarely deported, a comparison of the high age brackets in this table with the information in *3b, doc. 96, and with the figures we provide in *302 is advisable, in order to establish the high mortality of the elderly in T, even when conditions had already significantly improved.

299a. [T] "Standmeldung des jüdischen Siedlungsgebietes Theresienstadt vom 21." April 1945, MS.

In April 1945, there were 17,539 people (6,851 men and 10,688 women) in T, including 97 children under two years of age. Of these, 1,610 were up to fifteen years of age, 11,214 were sixteen to sixty, and 4,715 were over sixty-one. There were 2,599 bedridden patients (almost 15%). Following is a breakdown of work deployment:

Type of work	Men	Women	Total
Outside work	22	0	22
Agriculture	105	432	537
Manufacturing	791	3,183	3,974
Public works and labor	1,913	269	2,182
Internal supply	437	569	1,006
Health services	472	1,048	1,520
Security and registration	129	110	239
Cleaning and building maintenance	326	959	1,285
House and support services	630	682	1,312
Administration	46	90	136
Total deployment (all)	4,871	7,342	12,213
Total deployment (ages 61+)	726	794	1,520

In addition, there were seven group transports in the camp of 8,256 persons each. The list of the number of workers can be compared with an identically structured table for February 1945 in Chapter 13; despite a small increase in the number of workers, the percentage relationships shifted only insignificantly.

299b. [T] "Statistical information." [Compiled for the IRC]. MS, T, April 1945.

On April 6, there were 17,556 people in T (6,800 men and 10,756 women).

Country of origin	Number	%
Protectorate	6,919	39.41
Germany	5,510	31.39
Austria	1,300	7.41
Holland	1,290	7.35
Slovakia	1,060	6.04
Hungary	1,065	6.05

Age	Number	%
0–15	1,595	9.09
16–60	11,184	63.68
61–65	1,051	6.05
66+	3,716	21.18

299c. "Statistisches aus Theresienstadt." MS, T, 1945.

A compilation of figures by an unknown person, found in T by Dr. Gutfeld. The following table, based on these figures, provides an overview of arrivals:

Protectorate	73,651
Germany	42,263
Austria	16,336
Sudeten	607
Danzig	117
Holland	4,904
Denmark	474
Slovakia	1,454
Total	139,806
Concentration camps	13,194
Grand total	153,000

The following table, in contrast, provides an overview of departures:

Transports	86,962
Other departures	311
Deceased	33,768
Departures to Switzerland	1,200
TOTAL	122,241

Following is a listing according to country of origin, excluding the concentration camp prisoners, as of May 10, 1945:

Protectorate	7,664
Germany	5,357
Austria	1,570
Sudeten	197
Danzig	12
Holland	1,300
Denmark	2
Slovakia	1,463

A listing by age on October 12, 1943, can be found in *3b, doc. 96.

300. [T] "Statut des Ältestenrates." MS, T, June 2, 1942.

301. [T] [Orders of the day from December 15, 1941, to April 12, 1944]. 432 issues. [Announcements under the title "Mitteilungen der jüdischen Selbstverwaltung" from April 15, 1944, to early May 1945]. Some 75 issues. [Similar announcements by the leadership even after liberation]. Mimeographed, T.

Sources and Literature 773

One of the main sources of camp history, especially for 1942. A complete collection was not available to me, but there are several in Israel and Prague.

301a. [T] "Telegrams to London from Gerhart Riegner, World Jewish Congress, Geneva." MS, Geneva, 1942/45.

1. Beginning of November 1942: The receipt of mail from Edelstein and others, as well as the general opening of correspondence, is announced. "Building the ghetto community seems completed for now. Whether deportees remain there, undetermined." It is possible to receive packages only from Portugal; test packages to T have been started. The JKG Prague "Department of Registration and Transports Administration refuses to provide information."

2. Around November 1942: The IRC (Commission mixte de Secours) is prepared to send monthly provisions valued from SF 50,000 to 70,000 to T and camps in Poland. Money is requested from the World Jewish Congress in New York (which had been promised a release of $12,000 per month by the government of the United States for this purpose), from the Czech government in exile, and from English Jewish organizations. The money would be sent to Switzerland to finance shipments by the IRC and packages from Lisbon.

3. December 21, 1942: The Jewish Department of the IRC is discussed (see the text in *3b, doc. 215).

4. January 29, 1943:

> Situation in Prague much worsened. Hanna Steiner [see *3b, doc. 17] reports on the heaviest work deployment, including women, until 8:30 in the evening. All demand food both from T and for Prague. Encrypted letter from T reports we are starving and freezing. . . .
>
> Prague Jews ask for requests through Edelstein [to T] and our recommendations to him, as the Jewish Council apparently decides on the selection for further deportation.

5. February 12, 1943: An attempt is made to include Czech Jews in exchange operations through the IRC.

6. March 10, 1943:

> You must understand at last that aid shipments are not procured by the IRC itself, which only carries out the basic diplomatic negotiations. Implementation of the shipments lies in the hands of the . . . Commission mixte de la Croix-Rouge Internationale, which is composed of representatives of the IRC and the League of National Red Cross Societies. This Commission mixte is the technical apparatus and the purchase and shipping office for all Red Cross aid shipments. All funds are paid to it.

There are reports of large-scale arrests in Berlin at the end of February and of Baeck's deportation to T. The extermination campaign against the Jews had reached its peak. "London radio must repeat daily warnings in the German language against collaboration with the extermination campaign."

7. March 26, 1943: Aid shipments to T are discussed (see the text in *3b, doc. 217).

8. June 11, 1943: Eppstein's and Murmelstein's activities in T are mentioned; Edelstein seems to be in his old position, after obstacles. Five thousand pieces of mail

are said to leave T monthly. "Mail contact still extremely difficult, responses only received months later in the rarest cases." Mortality is said to have increased "extremely steeply." Many men have suffered weight loss of up to 37 kg. There are approximately 50,000 Jews in the camp, including 20,000 from Czechoslovakia. Shipments to Prague are used for forwarding to T. Two thousand Jews are still working in the Prague JKG, "mainly in the Krämer operation [see *3b, docs. 34–38]. This is tasked with clearing out the homes of the deportees, repairing the furniture, cleaning clothes and linens, and passing them on to the authorities, who reserve them for Germans arriving from the Reich." News arrived in Prague and Slovakia from Poland (Lublin district) and Upper Silesia (Birkenau, Monowitz, and Jawischowitz), with requests for aid shipments.

9. July 2, 1943: A report is made on conditions in the Upper Silesian work camps, but nothing is said about Birkenau and its chimneys.

10. July 13, 1943: Funds are requested for additional shipments by the IRC.

11. July 13, 1943: A report is made on the visit to T by the German RC (see *3b, doc. 220).

12. July 13, 1943: The Joint will get in touch with Riegner to discuss the $12,000 authorized monthly for packages to Czechoslovakia.

13. July 26, 1943, to New York: Financial details are discussed.

14. August 12, 1943: Representatives from T confirm receipt of individual and group shipments to T.

15. September 29, 1943: Receipt of package receipt/confirmation cards is reported. Money transfers to T are rejected.

16. October 6, 1943: A large shipment of restoratives and medications from the IRC left for T on October 2. Munk "strongly urges further shipments."

17. October 7, 1943: A report is made on the "family camp" in Birkenau (see the text in *3b, doc. 221).

18. November 5, 1943: An "eyewitness" reports that a large barracks camp has been erected in front of T. There are said to be guard towers with machine guns and emaciated Jews working in the fields. The area is brightly lit at night by a spherical reflector because of attempted escapes. From July 15 to September 30, 6,800 people were deported from T to Birkenau "facing machine guns at the ready." The only truth in these reports was the construction of the barracks camp – the Südbaracken – and the deportation, although the number of deportees was 5,000. The presumption of 6,800 emerged because 1,800 were reported in telegram 17, and they seem to have been counted together with the 5,000 actual deportees.

19. June 20, 1944: A report is made on the significance of "SB transports" according to Auschwitz escapees (this is simultaneously the source for *243). "Fact, the first group [of September 1943] completely exterminated, danger of extermination of the second group [December 1943] extremely serious. Please arrange without delay for very stern warning to German murderers who lead the slaughter in Upper Silesia." This warning did not prevent the mass murder of July 12, 1944, at the dissolution of the Birkenau "family camp."

20. July 21, 1944: It is now possible to send packages of old clothes to T. A complaint is made regarding the lack of cooperation from Swiss Joint representative Saly Mayer on support services for T. Eppstein is the "leader of the self-administration, as Edelstein has been working in the East for months [sic]. His wife

Sources and Literature   775

Mirjam and son Arieh write on March 25, 1944 from Birkenau and beg for help and exchange certificates, confirming in this letter that Jacob is no longer with them." Edelstein and his family had already been shot a month before this telegram was sent! This is followed by lists according to Rossel's report on T (*225a), which Riegner, however, had not read.

21. July 25, 1944: Riegner does not believe Rossel's report and calls for a rescue operation for T (see the text in *3b, doc. 227).

302. _Terezín Ghetto_. [Published by the Repatriations Office of the Czechoslovakian Social Welfare Ministry]. Prague, September 1945.

The cover of this text features a drawing by Fritta. It is bilingual – written in both Czech (Slovak) and English and contains a short historical report on G. (or Jiři) Vogel, the Jew who oversaw the dissolution of the camp. The summary tables do not take into account the second Hungarian transport of April 15, 1945 (seventy-seven people). The summary on p. xxiv lists the following figures:

Czechoslovakia	75,695
Germany	42,103
Austria	15,254
Holland	4,897
Denmark	466
Poland (Danzig)	117
TOTAL	139,606 [_sic_; 138,532][*]

[*] This differs from 139,606 by the 1,074 from Hungary shown in the next three tables. – Ed. note.

If we calculate the figures according to the tables on pp. xvi–xxii, we come up with the following remarkable table:

Country of origin	Prisoners in T	Survivors (excluding deportees)
Protectorate	73,625	6,863
Germany	42,103	5,120
Austria	15,254	1,283
Holland	4,897	1,273
Sudetengau	611	242
Danzig	117	11
Denmark	466	411
Slovakia	1,447	1,406
Hungary	1,074	1,039
TOTAL (excluding the last transport)	139,594	17,648

Of these, the following table lists the prisoners who arrived before the last deportations from T:

Country of origin	Prisoners in T	Survivors
Protectorate	69,920	3,180
Germany	40,081	3,129
Austria	15,232	1,261
Holland	4,846	1,222
Sudetengau	451	83
Danzig	117	11
Denmark	466	411
TOTAL	131,113	9,297

The following table lists the prisoners who arrived after the last deportations from T:

Country of origin	Prisoners in T	Survivors
Protectorate	3,705	3,683
Germany	2,022	1,991
Austria	22	22
Holland	51	51
Sudetengau	160	159
Slovakia	1,447	1,406
Hungary	1,074	1,039
TOTAL	8,481	8,351

The main portion of the book contains lists of the names of survivors ("Theresienstadters" and concentration camp prisoners are listed separately) with their dates of birth and, if necessary, transport information. Additionally, it lists the people who died after January 1, 1945, giving the date of death. The released Danes and members of the transport to Switzerland are included and identified. From this not-entirely-error-free material (it also contains typographical errors), we can gain statistically significant information that comes closer to the truth than the previous lists (in which, however, I may have made minor errors in numbers and distribution by sex).

The following table provides a breakdown by age, as of December 31, 1945, of the actual camp inmates (that is, excluding concentration camp prisoners) who left T in 1945:

Age	Men	Women	Total
0–15	809	824	1,633
16–45	2,301	4,239	6,540
46–60	2,245	3,043	5,288
61–65	498	601	1,099
66+	1,488	2,842	4,330
No information	1	5	6
TOTAL	7,342	11,554	18,896

The heavy predominance of women can be explained only among the higher age groups by their higher average age and greater resistance in the camp, and otherwise by the deportation policies in autumn 1944. Nor could the ratio be equalized by the increases after autumn 1944. Only in the extremely small number of children are the numbers balanced. The number of people born in 1910 and after is particularly small: there are only 3,251 people (1,065 men and 2,286 women) in the 1910–1929 age group (16–35 years), and, among the 1915–1929 age group (16–30 years), there are only 2,153 people (732 men and 421 women). The lowest figures are found in the age group of those born in 1916–20 (15–19 years): 568 people (177 men and 391 women; in 1917, there were 30 men and 63 women). Children up to six years old are also very weakly represented: 465 children (240 boys and 225 girls). Also striking is the situation among the older age groups, a result of the deportation rules:

Birth year	Men	Women	Total
1873	105	211	316
1874	119	223	342
1875	172	304	476[a]
1876	155	258	413
1877	161	272	433
1878	137	276	413
1879	143	123	266[b]
1880	89	106	195
1881	88	121	209
1882	100	115	215

[a] This is the largest age group in T.
[b] The people in this age group were sixty-five years old in 1944!

The following table provides data on the number of elderly survivors in various age groups as of the end of 1945:

	70+	75+	80+	85+	90+
Men	892	323	86	14	5
Women	1,913	844	233	30	0
Total	2,805	1,167	319	44	5

The oldest survivor was ninety-six years old.

We also can gather from the list of names that twenty-five children born in T (eight of whom were conceived in the camp) survived the war:

Birth year	Number
1942	2
1943	3
1944	10
1945	10

Country of origin	Number
Protectorate	10
Germany	2
Holland	3
Sudetengau	2
Denmark	3
Slovakia	4
Hungary	1

The fact that there were Dutch, Danish, Slovak, and Hungarian children born in T comes only from this source. According to these figures, it can be assumed that the number of births was slightly higher than the official figures. One may therefore assume – during the camp's later period, after autumn 1944 – some 20 more births in addition to the 209 children born in T.

A preface to the list of names states: "A number of people were deported from Theresienstadt by the Gestapo on February 20, 1945." According to the list, these were thirty-seven mainly young people (thirty-one men and six women). These people, of which no other source speaks, are listed in the publication as survivors.

303. "Terezín – kalvarie českého národa" [Theresienstadt – The Golgotha of the Czech People]. Theresienstadt, 1948.

An advertisement with photographs for the national cemetery in T. The "ghetto" is merely mentioned.

304. "Thersienstadt." In *Israelitisches Wochenblatt*. Nos. 15 and 37. Zurich, April 13 and September 14, 1945.

A general report on T; it is, in part, incorrect.

305. [T] "Textverordnung betreffend die Feststellung des neuen Wortlautes der durch die Verordnung über die Ergänzung und Vereinheitlichung strafrechtlicher Vorschriften abgeänderten Vorschriften." Mimeographed, MS, T, March 10, 1945.

The text fills the secretariat's newsletter number 212.

306. [T] "The Prison Fortress of Terezín." In *Manchester Guardian*. September 17, 1942.

After a declaration on "Theresienstadt" by the Czech government-in-exile, published on September 4, 1942, in the *Berner Tagwacht*, this is probably the first report on T in the international press. T is described as a ghetto for elderly people from the "Protectorate," Germany, France, and Holland; the place was cleared of civilians in the second half of 1941.

> On August 15 [1942], 40,000 Jews aged 65 to 85 were crowded into newly-erected barracks or the old prison. In addition, Theresienstadt holds 7,000 younger people, all of them Jews, who perform forced labor. They receive 12 crowns per day, half of which – as the Germans say – is deducted to maintain the older inmates.... Before they came to Theresienstadt, all the unfortunate inhabitants were robbed of their personal belongings; they were evacuated from their homes and forced to leave behind their furniture, bedclothes, clothing and money, which were confiscated by the Germans.

Sources and Literature

779

306a. [T] "Vedem" [We Lead]. Mimeographed, YV, T, 1943.

Several editions of a youth newspaper.

306b. [T] [Transport overview up to October 12, 1944]. MS, T.

So far the best and most thorough primary source on transports and other movements, but it does not list births and deaths. See the samples in *3b, doc. 43. The table also makes possible an overview of the groups doing outside work. On February 26, 1942, 100 men went into the pits of Kladno. The all-time highest number of people employed there was 300; the last 3 members of the group returned to T on June 22, 1943. One hundred men (an all-time high) went into the mines of Oslavany on April 4, 1942; the last man returned on August 30, 1943. On April 10, 1942, 1,002 women and girls (an all-time high) traveled to Křivoklát for forest work; the last 918 returned on June 6, 1942 (2 appear not to have returned to T). On April 13, 1942, 60 men (an all-time high) went to Budweis for road building; when 39 returned to T on September 25, 1942, only 1 was still absent, and he was not brought back to T until June 23, 1943. On September 15, 1942, 48 men (the all-time high was 110) went to Panenské Břežany for agricultural work (*202b); the last 30 returned to T on February 11, 1944. On March 2, 1944, 200 men (the all-time high was 281) went to Zossen (Wulkow) to build barracks; the last returned on February 10, 1945. On March 11, 1945, 6 men went to Schnarchenreuth, again to build barracks; the all-time high, together with a group in Regen, was 102, all of whom returned on April 20, 1945.

307. [T] [Various documents]. 1941–45. Unpublished.

Most of these documents are in the Prague Jewish Museum or in other collections; some are in privately held collections. They include forms; mimeographed, typewritten, and handwritten originals, copies, or reproductions; handwritten or reproduced statistical material; plans; graphic works; and paintings and drawings (or reproductions of them). Together with the comprehensive surviving documents, this material makes possible a reconstruction of social processes in the T "Ghetto." Information on the documents used in the present book is found throughout the text.

307a. [T] "List of Transports Arriving in T between Jan. 1, 1945 and April 10, 1945." MS, T, April 11, 1945.

Fifty transports – including "individual travelers" – are listed; these transports brought 7,906 people, including 5,178 people as "parts of mixed marriages," to T.

307b. [T] [List of arrived and departed transports]. Mimeographed, T, ca. mid-April 1945.

This information is identical to the lists in *302, pages xvi–xxii and xxvf., and probably is their source.

308. [T] W.: "Preliceni s Rudolfem Haindlem" [Negotiations with R. Haindl]. In 319, no. 40/41, 1948.

A report on the trial before the People's Court in Leitmeritz. Haindl was acquitted of the charge of arson (*110).

308a. [T] "Wir fahren aus Theresienstadt." In Niemals vergessen: Gedenkschrift. Stuttgart 1946, pp. 15–17.

780   *Sources and Literature*

Information on the journey to Auschwitz.

308b. [T] *Yad Vashem Exhibitions. January–March 1960.* Jerusalem, 1960.

An exhibition catalogue. The catalogue contains some objects from T, specifically paintings and drawings by Friedrich Bloch, L. Buresova, Fritta, the fifteen-year-old Peter Ginz (one reproduction), Lev Haas, Karlinsky, P. Müller, Moritz Nagel (Nágl), and Ungar; all are from the collection of the YV. The text includes biographical notes. The same painters were represented, in some cases more extensively, in an exhibition catalogue in 1959; here, in addition to the work by Ginz, one drawing by Haas, too, is reproduced.

309. [T] "Zpráva evidenčního oddělení RŽNO" [Report by the Evidence Department of the JKG Council]. 111, IV. In 319, nos. 23–24, 1947.

Among those deported to Auschwitz, 28,551 people were from the "Protectorate"; among those who died in T, 6,180; among the survivors, 6,850 (3,233 of them had arrived before 1945). The number of survivors is slightly different from our estimate according to *302, as well as *299b and *299c. Several of the figures in the report differ from those in the present book: The report notes that 12,783 people emigrated from the "Protectorate" to European countries (total emigration: 26,111). The number deported to T "from our countries" (i.e., the "Protectorate") – in contrast to our breakdown as well as the information in (and according to) *166 and *302 – is listed as 73,635 people, and the total number of deportees to T is listed as 139,624 (not counting the Polish children). The number of deaths until May 1945 in T is listed as 34,266, in agreement with the detailed table in Chapter 16, but not with the final totals in Chapter 3. The number of survivors sent from T before the Auschwitz transports is listed as 225 (compared with 224 in our breakdown in Chapter 3).

310. [T] "Zur Vorgeschichte des Lagers" [On the Prehistory of the Camp]. MSS, Prague, October to early December 1941.

Twenty-six documents, mainly "file memos," regarding the segregation of the Bohemian- Moravian Jews and the creation of the camp in T.

311. [T] "Collection of Documentary Material on Theresienstadt." MS, WL, T, 1945.

Some (inexact) breakdowns of the number of prisoners, illnesses, and so on. It includes excerpts from "file memos" from 1945 and newsletters or memoranda from the self-administration from March 16, 1944.

312. Tenenbaum, J.: *Auschwitz in Retrospect: The Self-Portrait of Rudolf Hoess, Commander of Auschwitz.* New York, 1953.

An excellently documented and annotated appraisal of the memoirs written by the Auschwitz commandant in prison in Cracow in 1946 (*106d/e). The psychoanalytical character analysis, on the other hand, seems to me to miss the mark and does not explain anything significant.

312a. Tenenbaum, J.: *Race and Reich: The Story of an Epoch.* New York, 1956.

One of the most important attempts at a summary portrayal of the Jewish catastrophe.

312b. [Thadden, E. v.]: Interrogation of Thadden on March 13 and June 11, 1946, and Interrogation Summaries 2447 and 2512. Mimeographed, Nuremberg, Case XI. In addition, "Interrogations ... on December 5, 1947, ... by K.W. Swart," by order of the RvO. Mimeographed, Amsterdam, 1947.

From April 1943 until the end of the war, Thadden was legation counselor in "Inland II" of the Foreign Office and dealt with the Jewish question. He received interventions by foreign diplomats on behalf of foreign Jews and answered them after discussion with Eichmann, with whom he claims to have met no more than six times a year at meetings of the RSHA. Only when written petitions were unsuccessful did the legation counselor call on Eichmann or his representatives, with whom Thadden preferred to negotiate, as Rolf Günther, for example, was "more reliable." Thadden claims to have heard from Eichmann the usual veiled description of the Jewish work camp in the Lublin area, in which Jews unable to work were taken care of in the same way as in T. "Originally the weak and sick went to special camps, but when it was noticed that productivity suffered because of separation of the families, they were reunited." According to Eichmann, healthy people were sent to work in the big armaments factory in Auschwitz and to other regions. Bergen-Belsen was portrayed as an especially privileged camp; it "was considered purely a transit camp and not a pure concentration camp." Leaving there required the permission of the RSHA. Leaving T required permission from Himmler.

Thadden visited T, which Eichmann showed to him as "an example of a Jewish camp," three times: (1) in summer 1943, with a delegation from the German RC; (2) in June 1944, with the IRC representative Rossel and the Danish gentlemen (representatives of the Swedish RC and Foreign Ministry had canceled); and (3) on April 6, 1945, with Lehner from the IRC "and a representative of the protecting power [*Schutzmacht*] department of the Swiss mission" (Sweden had once again canceled). About the second visit, Thadden stated: "The Jewish Elder Epstein [*sic*] told me that the Jewish ghetto police, who maintained protection inside the camp, were particularly unpopular because of their harshness. What was noticeable to both myself and the foreign visitors was that in the entire place, filled with 35,000 Jews, only twelve male SS members and eight support personnel were employed." Otherwise, the description corresponds quite closely to the account by Hvass (Chapter 6). On the question of Dutch Jews, Thadden mentioned "a very talented painter," Spier, who "readily gave us information. He led us to the kitchen, we received a food sample, and he showed us a series of paintings that he had painted."

312c. Tijn, G. van: Contribution towards the "History of the Jews in Holland from May 10th 1940 to June 1944." Mimeographed, no information. YIVO.

A description of Edelstein's mission in Holland (*52a, 209a). Pages 34 et seq. are noteworthy:

In March 1941, we received a visit from two Jews from Prague – Edelstein and Friedmann – who told us they had been tasked to visit us by the "Central Office for Jewish Emigration" in Prague.... They told us that a similar SS office had been set up in Amsterdam, the emigration forms to be used in Holland would correspond to those in Czechoslovakia, and it was their job to familiarize us with both the content of these questionnaires and the general procedure.... Any feelings of distrust that I might have had at first towards Edelstein and Friedmann – towards Jews who visited us at the behest

782   *Sources and Literature*

of the Gestapo – were soon replaced by feelings of esteem, especially for Edelstein. I do not know how Czechoslovak Jewry assessed him and his activities, but I can only say that he taught me, in introducing me to my new job, above all how to cause difficulties and to delay.... While my negotiations with Edelstein and Friedmann concerned future Jewish emigration, they held many discussions with Prof. Cohen in his capacity as president of the "Joodsen Raads," and warned him about the task that lay before him.... . Edelstein appeared to have indulged in no illusions about this. I believe it was he who told Prof. Cohen that he probably would be made the bringer of such horrible news to the Jews that his own people would hate and despise him. This was said at a time, it must be remembered, when the deportations had not yet begun.

312d. [Means of transport] *Die deutsche Industrie im Kriege 1939-1945*. Berlin, 1954.

A study written before the end of the war by the "German Institute for Economic Research" and now published by this institute "with critical scientific review" (according to Professor F. Friedensburg in a foreword). Nevertheless, we learn nothing in connection with the "work deployment" (pp. 45 et seq., 88 et seq., and 123) or about the work of the concentration camp prisoners; the study provides only some cursory hints about forced laborers (p. 123).

The tables recognize only "foreigners and prisoners of war." The number of workers thus described increased from 300,000 at the end of May 1939 to 7,500,000 at the end of September 1944 (p. 139). Incidentally, an interesting book by L. P. Lochner, *Tycoons and Tyrants: German Industry from Hitler to Adenauer* (Chicago, 1954), also offers little information on the theme of forced labor and prisoner labor.

Important to us is the section "Decay of the Transport Apparatus" (pp. 93 et seq.). From July 1944, the condition of the trains worsened constantly. In that month, the Reichsbahn could provide 136,000 train cars per day; in contrast, in March 1945, the number was only 15,000. In addition, more and more freight trains were found on the tracks (due to backups). In that month, the number of cars was no longer enough "to ensure even the supply of service coal for the railroad itself in every case." The folly of deportation and resettlement transports of prisoners was more important until the end of the war.

312e. [Treblinka] *Das Menschenschlachthaus Treblinka* [The Human Slaughterhouse Treblinka]. Vienna, 1946.

313. Treitel, H.: "Letter to Her Brother in Tel Aviv." MS, WL, T, June 4, 1945.

The writer, who had been in T since June 12, 1942, describes the conditions there.

314. [Trostinetz (Maly Trostenets)] "Zwölf Blieben am Leben." In *Aufbau*. New York, July 21, 1944.

A report on the camps Minsk and Trostinetz [Maly Trostenets]. Trostinetz [Maly Trostenets], eight miles from Minsk, was a "death camp for Czech, German and Austrian Jews," to which 39,000 victims were deported in 1942. Only around 500 specialists escaped immediate extermination; some were employed in sorting groups for the luggage and clothing of the murder victims, and some were employed during the day in Minsk workshops. The mass murders in and around Minsk are described openly by the general commissar for White Ruthenia, Kube, in a letter on

Sources and Literature 783

July 31, 1942, to the Reich commissar for the Ostland, Hinrich Lohse, in Riga: "In Minsk city, some 10,000 Jews were liquidated on July 28 and 29, 6,500 of them Russian Jews – mainly old people, women and children – the rest consisted of Jews incapable of working, who were sent mainly from Vienna, Brünn [Brno], Bremen and Berlin to Minsk in November of this year, at the Führer's orders" (3428-PS).

315. [Czechoslovakia] "Dějiny českožidovského hnutí" [History of the Czech-Jewish Movement]. Prague, no year [1932].

An official brochure about Czech-assimilated (*tschechischen Assimilation*) Jews.

316. [Czechoslovakia] *Four Fighting Years*. Published by the Czech Foreign Ministry in exile. London, 1943.

Information on T and the situation of Jews in the "Protectorate" is scanty and relatively imprecise. It discusses events until the end of 1942. It is mentioned that representatives of the IRC had been denied access to T.

317. [Czechoslovakia] "Statistika židovského obyvatelstva v Československu" [Statistics on the Jewish Population in Czechoslovakia]. MS, Prague, December 17, 1946.

An overview from 1930 to 1946, drawn up by the council of the JKG in Bohemia and Moravia. The information on returnees from the camps proved, in reports over the next few years, to be slightly too low (in this book we have always used the optimal figures).

318. [Czechoslovakia] *Two Years of German Oppression in Czechoslovakia*. Published by the Czech Foreign Ministry in exile. London 1941.

Quite correct information on the persecution of the Jews until April 1940.

319. [Czechoslovakia] *Věstník židovské náboženské obce v Praze* [Bulletin of the JKG in Prague]. Prague, from September 19, 1945.

The most important contributions on our theme are presented alphabetically according to authors or key words in this bibliography and are identified with the number "319."

320. Tůma, M.: *Ghetto našich dnů* [The Ghetto of Our Days]. Prague, 1946.

The author was in T from November 30, 1941, until liberation and describes it from a Czech nationalist standpoint; the information is not always substantively reliable. The work features illustrations by the artist Lev Haas, who worked in T.

321. Turnwald, W. K. (ed.): *Dokumente zur Austreibung der Sudetendeutschen* [Documents on the Expulsion of the Sudeten Germans]. Munich, 1951.

Document 38 is an objective report by the doctor E. Siegel, who describes conditions in the "Kleine Festung" as a concentration camp for Germans from May 1945 to October 1946. Conditions under the first commandant, Průša, who was allowed to rampage until summer 1945, in particular, are comparable only to the brutality of the SS. Many were slain by him and his helpers as soon as they arrived. The work references the connections between the camp and the former "ghetto." The prisoners, most of whom were from Prague, were of both sexes and all ages, from infants to people ninety-two years of age. Some guards lent the women to Russian soldiers in

784   Sources and Literature

exchange for tobacco and alcohol, but Russians as well as Czechs, to whom the
prisoners were rented in accordance with unfortunate models, helped many of them
and even made escape possible. In the camp there also were a number of Jewish
prisoners, six of whom are mentioned by name, one died in the camp after six months
as a result of abuse and undernourishment. The hatred of Jews among the Czech
team was considerable; they often were heard to say that Hitler did his work badly,
as too many Jews were still alive.

321a. Tyl, O., and T. Kulišová: Terezín: Malá pevnost [Small Fortress] – Ghetto. Prague,
1955.

This heavily propagandistic book, with 127 prints and many pictures (including
12 uncharacteristic paintings from the "ghetto" after liberation), lacks scholarly
treatment but is based on some compelling material and represents the official view
of the two camps in T in Czechoslovakia ten years after liberation.

Tyl's account: The plans for the fortress were drafted according to the model of
the Meusier fortress in France by general of artillery Count Pellegrini. The site
consists of two octagons, 1,200 x 920 and 920 x 430 m, which are connected by
underground corridors. The cornerstone was laid by Joseph II on October 10, 1780;
its proclamation as a closed city dates to September 1784, and its identification as a
royal free city and its naming dates to December 9, 1787. The "Kleine Festung"
always served to hold prisoners (for example, Alexander Ypsilanti in 1823); there
were 700 prisoners in 1914. In the First World War, a prison camp was set up for
17,000 people. In interwar Czechoslovakia, too, there were prisoners. The Prague
Gestapo chief Geschke designated the "Kleine Festung" on April 10, 1940, for its
new purpose and appointed Jöckel as its commandant; four days later, the first
prisoners arrived. The camp was first set up for 1,200 and then for 3,500 prisoners
but was always overcrowded. At the end of the war, 6,000 people are said to have
been there. According to Jöckel's estimates, a total of around 90,000 prisoners went
to the "Kleine Festung." At the end of October 1943, on the order of K. H. Frank,
fourteen gendarmes from the "ghetto" were executed. In January 1945, 387 prisoners
came from Auschwitz (80% Jews), of whom only 30 were still alive at the end of the
war (*337a). Executions still were being carried out in the "Kleine Festung" on April
28, 1945, and on May 2, fifty-six people were shot. The Leitmeritz concentration
camp was opened approximately in early 1944. The town had 1,203 inhabitants in
1830, 2,990 in 1900, 4,000 in 1930, and 3,700 in 1940 (without soldiers) in 219
houses. On the "ghetto," the account reports mainly things already known; the
Jewish leadership is accused of collaboration. The crematorium, with a daily cremation capacity of 190 corpses, was also used by the "Kleine Festung" and the
Leitmeritz concentration camp. Harsh attacks are made on the IRC and Dunant;
he "works on the Nazi line" (p. 52). In the "Protectorate" on March 15, 1939, there
were 118,310 Jews; 26,111 emigrated, 7,479 died before the deportation, 73,608
went to T, 8,309 went directly to the East, 3,236 went to other concentration camps,
and 2,949 were not deported. The total number of victims was 79,310, and the
number of all returnees was 6,850; after the war, there were 17,113 Jews in Bohemia
and Moravia. This part of the book contains crude falsifications of history that do
not even have anything to do with T.

Kulišová's account: This account provides a precise description of the "Kleine
Festung." The prisoners did not enjoy the "self-administration," which was

Sources and Literature 785

otherwise usual in the concentration camps. Jewish prisoners could not be treated for illness; this was also true in the concentration camp Leitmeritz "Richard," where they were not accepted into the sick quarters. The author does not describe the "ghetto," but its fate intersects tragically with the "Kleine Festung." Aside from the incidents already reported by Kypr (*162), she tells of the brutal killing of a doctor and a nurse in August and the stoning of several people in autumn 1943. On April 27, 1945, Kaltenbrunner is said to have been in the "Kleine Festung." From late 1944 on, the Prague Gestapo and its head, Dr. Goerke, Geschke's successor, is reported to have been in T with extermination plans for both camps. After discussion and rejection of various methods (pp. 117 et seq.),

> a commission then came to T to discuss the extermination of the camp. Kriminalrat Schulze from the Prague Gestapo, Ghetto Commandant Rahm and two officers from the SS correspondents' school in Leitmeritz took part in the discussion. The discussion ended with the decision to drive all the prisoners into Courtyard IV, where they would be killed with machine guns, missiles and other explosives. This liquidation would be carried out by a guard battalion of the Waffen-SS in T. The Jews living in the ghetto would be similarly eliminated in a moat towards Bohušovice, next to the Eger, where a wall had been built for this purpose so that no prisoners could succeed in escaping.

Extremely harsh accusations were made against Dunant (pp. 93 et seq.). These accusations are concentrated in a declaration cited by the Czech delegate to the 18th Congress of the International Committee of the IRC in August 1952 in Toronto:

> In 1945, the IRC delegation was in Theresienstadt again. According to a professor in the medical department of Charles University, Dr. Karel Raška, who came to T on May 2, 1945 at the head of Czech epidemiologists, the IRC delegate Paul Dunant had been in T since April. This Mr. Dunant surrounded himself with Gestapo people and said nothing about the fact that 56 patriots were shot in the concentration camp on May 2, 1945, although he could have prevented this by his own intervention. That is not all; after liberation by the Red Army, this Paul Dunant hid fifteen Gestapo members and leading Nazi figures – murderers of Czechs – in the offices of the IRC in Prague III, Thungasse 18. He was not ashamed to address to Professor Karel Raška a request that this doctor advocate for the release from prison of a number of Gestapo members. In exchange he offered medicines and other material aid for liberated political prisoners in T, [aid] valued at several million in foreign currency.
> To Prof. Raška's question why the IRC was not concerned with conditions in the Kleine Festung, this representative explained that it was not his business to concern himself with Czech "rebels."

Such a harsh attack, made more than seven years after the fact, does not seem very credible but appears functional, in accordance with Russia's and its dependent states' genuine or feigned suspicion not only of the West in general but of international humanitarian institutions in the West. This policy of suspicion reached its height in the period from the conflict in Korea until Stalin's death; the protest in Toronto corresponds to this tactic. First of all, Dunant was not constantly in T since April but only since May 2, and he took leadership of the "ghetto" the next day; therefore, he could hardly have visited the "Kleine Festung" *before* the last executions (*294b). Only on May 5 – the day Rahm gave up his power entirely – did he officially become camp commandant. In the spirit of his agreement with Kaltenbrunner, on March 29 Burckhardt authorized the Berlin IRC delegation from Geneva to visit T,

786   *Sources and Literature*

accompanied by Rossell, and Dunant was to remain until the dissolution of the camp. Several days later, Dunant traveled on an official Swiss passport from the Confederation Political (Foreign Affairs) Department to Berlin, where on April 2 he received his written "mission mandate," signed by Lehner from the IRC delegation there. When the two men visited on April 6, Dunant was not permitted – contrary to Kaltenbrunner's promise – to remain in T, so he settled in Prague. From there, he informed Geneva on April 19 that K. H. Frank had given him no definitive residence permit for T. Before entering T on May 2, he was able to visit the "ghetto" only briefly on April 21 and 30 and could not visit the "Kleine Festung," for which he had no authorization at all from the IRC. Even though he made efforts to help there, this probably was a moral duty, not an intended mandate. This must have made it even easier for Jöckel and his Prague superiors to commit crimes in the "Kleine Festung" without Dunant's knowledge and behind his back on May 2, but – and this is decisive – no later. Dunant himself determined (*228, p. 132) that the commandants of the two camps in T had surrendered their power to him on May 2. Raška (and perhaps also one of his physicians) provided a description (*62a) of events on May 8. It proves that a quite friendly relationship existed between him and Dunant at the time, and that Dunant let no danger keep him from helping. In 1945, Czechoslovakia had no reservations about presenting this report at Nuremberg as an official document (PS-385). In addition, a letter to Raška from Dunant on May 8, dated and addressed Terezín, has survived; this letter proves that the relationship between the two men cannot have been bad, which would have been unthinkable if the accusations were justified. The letter reads as follows:

Doctor,

    The mandate with which Professor Carl J. BURCKHARDT, president of the IRC, has entrusted me ends with the cessation of hostilities.

    In your capacity as representative of the legal government of the Czech Republic, you will now ensure the security of the residents of Terezín and some fifteen thousand former prisoners and deportees who have found refuge in this city in the last two weeks.

    In your capacity as a physician, you have made it possible in particular to evacuate prisoners in the citadel to secure accommodations in the city.

    Your health organization was worthy of the immense task that you undertook for the welfare of all these unfortunates, despite the current epidemic.

    Please convey to your colleagues the expression of my deepest admiration for their service in the cause of humanity, and receive yourself, Doctor, the expression of my esteem.

A thank-you note from Baeck to Dunant in the name of the Jewish self-administration originated on the same day. It says:

The members of the council have the honor of expressing their deep thanks for the words that you addressed to them.

    Your appreciation of our work honors us extremely. But we want to make a point of saying that we have been fortunate to enjoy the privilege of working with you, and of being at your service.

    We hope that the important support of the past weeks and days will not cease. A period of heavy responsibility and hard work lies before us, and we will be grateful to you from the bottom of our hearts if you would maintain your unchanging support.

Sources and Literature 787

> The members of the council, as well as the entire population of Theresienstadt, will never forget what you did for us.

Dunant himself, in a report on May 22, 1945, described his activities as of April 30. Some of this is not published in *228, especially this important part:

> On May 3, evacuation of the Kleine Festung began, with 5,000 Polish prisoners entrusted to a Czech physicians association, led by Dr. Raška, and part of the responsibility of the IRC.... Everything happened without incident. At any moment, I would have to intervene between the patriotic Czech physicians and the SS. All the prisoners were evacuated on the 8th. At this time, on the day that hostilities ended, I ended the "tutelage" of the IRC (see my letter of this date to Dr. Raška). On May 10, I learned in Prague that Theresienstadt had been freed by the Czech patriots (that is a general custom in all countries that "liberated themselves.").

On June 8, 1945, Dunant wrote a final report on T, which he visited on June 3. He saw with surprise that the Czechs and Russians knew nothing about his activities from the Nazi period. In T, Raška had been replaced by Professor Patočka. Dunant found that he was as little desired in T as in Prague; the Russians viewed contacts with the IRC mistrustfully. Here we already can recognize the beginnings of the later enmity, which, as the documents prove, is objectively unjustified regarding Dunant's activity in T. Whatever Rossel and especially Lehner may be accused of, it does not apply to Dunant, who may not always have carried out his extremely difficult tasks with grace, but always acted with courage and prudence.

321b. [Typhus] "Der Typhus im Ghetto" [Typhus in the Ghetto]. MS, YV, T, no year.

A brief, unsigned work from the estate of Dr. Fritz Salus.

322. Ullmann, V.: "Kritiken musikalischer Veranstaltungen der 'Freizeitgestaltung'" [Reviews of Musical Events of the "Recreation Office"]. MS, T, 1944.

Twenty-seven reviews.

323. [Ungar, O.]: "Katalog posmrtné výstavy O. Ungara" [Catalogue of the Memorial Exhibit O. Ungar]. Prague, 1946.

An exhibition of paintings and drawings, done in T, in the Prague Jewish Museum, with an introduction by H. A. (H. G. Adler).

Unger, W.: *10a.

324. Utermöhle, W., and H. Schmerling: "Die Rechtstellung der Juden im Protektorat Böhmen und Mähren" [The Legal Status of the Jews in the Protectorate of Bohemia and Moravia]. Prague, no year [1940].

Information on conditions as of August 15, 1940.

325. Utitz, E.: "Das Vortragswesen in Theresienstadt" [The Lecture Office in Theresienstadt]. MS, T, 1945.

A short report on the activities of the head of the "Lecture Office."

326. Utitz, E.: "Das Zentralbücherei Theresienstadt: November 17, 1942–July 31, 1945." MS, T, 1945.

788   *Sources and Literature*

A brief report by the library director.

327. Utitz, E.: *Psychologie des Lebens im Konzentrationslager Theresienstadt* [Psychology of Life in the Theresienstadt Concentration Camp]. Vienna, 1948.

A calm, personal description of everyday events, especially cultural life. The author was in T from summer 1942.

328. Utitz, E.: *Psychologie života v terezínském koncentračním táboře*. Prague, 1947.

A Czech version of *327.

328a. Utitz, E.: "Terezínské transporty" [Theresienstadt Transports]. In 319, no. 6, 1955.

329. Utitz, E.: "Ústřední knihovna koncentračního tábora Terezín" [Central Library of the Concentration Camp Theresienstadt]. In 319, no. 47, 1950.

330. Utitz, E., and H. Friedmann: "Ghettozentralbücherei Theresienstaft: Rechenschaftsbericht vom 17. November 1942 bis 17. November 1943." MS, T.

330a. Valentin, H.: "Rescue and Relief Activities on Behalf of Jewish Victims of Nazism in Scandinavia." In *YIVO Annual of Jewish Social Science*. Vol. VIII. New York, 1953, pp. 224–51.

An account of, among other things, the situation in Denmark. Duckwitz informed the Swedish government of the planned action against the Jews. Sweden warned Germany on October 1, 1943, and offered to take in all Jews from Denmark. Germany did not respond to the offer. In Copenhagen, almost all Jews were warned on September 29. A total of 7,460 people were smuggled to Sweden.

330b. Vaňouček, O.: *Analyse psychologique des dessins des enfants juifs en captivité a Terezín*. No information [Prague, 1956?].

An edited version of a Czech study of children's drawings from T, in the possession of the Prague Jewish Museum. This text was published on behalf of the museum for a selection of drawings exhibited in Paris in 1956, along with a second publication: *Le martyre et le rêve des enfants de Terezín*.

330c. Vedder, A.: *Vlektyphus en vlektyphusbestrijding* [Epidemic Typhus and Combatting It]. Amsterdam, 1946.

The author, who was in T from September 6, 1944, describes the typhus epidemic there in an appendix (pp. 68–76). He was brought into the leadership of the Czech aid operation by Raška on May 8, 1945, and at Raška's request was also provided with unlimited authority. In the same way, Raška also assigned him to the area surrounding T. On the arrival of the first concentration camp transports – 5,500 and 3,500 persons – the SS had the prisoners brought without examination or delousing to two barracks, in which forty adults or sixty young people were placed in rooms of 50 m². There were no mattresses or blankets, nor any hygienic arrangements. There were fifteen toilets for 1,500 people, and dysentery ran rampant. Individual prisoners were brought into the general quarters by relatives or friends and were hospitalized in E VI after they became ill; there the author first made the diagnosis of epidemic typhus. On May 2, he was assigned by the Council of Elders and Dunant to combat

Sources and Literature 789

the epidemic, and the Czech doctors had him take care of the "Kleine Festung." Because everything was lacking and chaos prevailed, this was at first a nearly impossible task. However, it was possible to do a great deal before the arrival of the Russian aides, with whom the author also worked. A total of 2,500 people came down with typhus, and 500 of them died. This includes only the diagnosed cases; some 1,600 people arrived moribund in T, where they died without diagnosis and were not autopsied. Hundreds of them probably had typhus. A total of 2,264 people were hospitalized with typhus, as many as 1,700 at one time. These figures are for June 9, when 447 victims were claimed. Of the long-term camp inmates, almost the only ones to fall ill were the aides who worked for the typhus patients – a total of approximately 200 people, of whom 50 died, among them 10 doctors (*50, 62a, 108a, 207, 340a).

331. Vinohradský, H.: "Děti žalují" [Children Accuse]. In *Ústřední deník* 1. Československého sboru. February 21, 25, and 28, and March 3 and 9, 1945.

An account of three Jewish children from Czechoslovakia rescued in the East, including an eleven-year-old boy who arrived in Auschwitz from T along with his twin sister in May 1944.

332. Volavková, H.: *The Jewish Museum of Prague*. Prague 1948.

An English version of the simultaneously published Czech original, with illustrations. In the introduction, the author describes how, at the end of 1941, at the beginning of the deportations, some Jews got the "Central Office" to build a central Jewish museum, on which work began the following year. It contained the museum, which already had existed long before; ritual objects from all the synagogues in the "Protectorate"; and numerous objects of Judaistic interest from the private collections of deportees (pictures, books, religious objects, art objects, etc.). When eighteen Jews from Prague who had done significant work to close down the community for the SS were sent to their deaths in Auschwitz in October 1944, the senior staff of the museum was included. The SS knew how to reward.

332a. Volavková, H. (ed.): *Kinderzeichnungen und Gedichte: Theresienstadt 1942–1944.* Prague, 1959.

Reproductions of forty-seven works (plus one on the cover) or excerpts of works (one-color and multicolored drawings, watercolors, and collages) by thirty-nine children from 1943–44; it also features twenty-two poems or parts of poems and one prose fragment, all translated from the Czech. In addition, the book was published in the Czech original version as well as in English and French translation. Using these and other children's drawings, M. Bernat, in cooperation with H. Volavková and J. Weil, produced a film called *There Are No Butterflies Here* (Czech), in which films from T and – unnecessarily falsifying the documentary character – from the Kleine Festung were included. The first press showing was in January 1959.

332b. [Volavková, H., et al.]: *Pinkasova škola: Památník minulosti a našich dnů* [The Pinkas Synagogue: A Memorial to the Past and Our Time]. Prague, 1954.

The Pinkas Synagogue in Prague, today one of the oldest synagogues in Central Europe, has also served, since its restoration as a museum, as a memorial to the Jews of Bohemia and Moravia who died between 1938 and 1945; their number is given as 77,297.

333. Vosolsobě, J.: *Terezínská mučírna v obrazech* [The Theresienstadt Torture Chamber in Pictures]. Prague, 1945.

A brief text and twenty-six good photographs from the "Kleine Festung" and the "ghetto," taken during liberation in May 1945.

333a. Wachtel, B.: "Kaváraenský dvůr" [Coffeehouse Courtyard]. In *Hlas revoluce*. No. 25. Prague, December 25, 1948.

A painting reproduction with a brief accompanying text. Another painting by Wachtel was reproduced in *Aufbau*, New York, September 8, 1950. Wachtel painted approximately 100 small oil paintings on boards in T; 50 of these – most are now in Sydney – survived. The themes are city paintings with figures, generally courtyards. The paintings served as a model for the sets of the films by Kolar (*151). Three paintings appear in the catalogue *Exhibition of Paintings of Jewish Artists*, Sydney, 1951. One painting is reproduced in *3b, doc. 99.

333b. Wahl, K.: "*... it is the German Heart.*" Augsburg, 1954.

A justificatory book by the "Gauleiter" of Augsburg. If we believe his subjective sincerity, the following passage illustrates the innocent-guilty ignorance of this high party functionary outside the SS:

> I neither knew nor assumed that the sending of Jews to Theresienstadt was the beginning of a crime. I enquired repeatedly where the Jews were going and what they would do there. The answer was that they were going to a large, prepared camp in Theresienstadt and would have to perform work important to the war. I am not a bandit, that I would think of possible crimes against humanity. (pp. 178 et seq.)

334. Weber, I.: "Poems." MS, T, 1942–44.

Seven poems on camp themes. The YV possesses fifty-nine poems by the author. A Czech translation of the "Sheep of Lidice" is available in *336.

334a. Weber, I.: "Toto zde cesta je k Terezínu" [This Is the Way to Theresienstadt]. In 319, no. 12, 1959.

A Czech translation of a poem.

334b. Weglein, R.: "Theresienstadt: Erinnerungen einer Krankenschwester" [Theresienstadt: Memoirs of a Nurse]. MS, WL, Ulm, 1946.

The author came to T with her husband, a badly injured war veteran, from Ulm via Stuttgart on a transport of 1,079 people (only 32 survivors at liberation) on August 23, 1942, and was a nurse there the entire time. This activity is described in detail. On her arrival: "Because most of the old people could not get out by themselves, they were lifted from the train and ... simply laid on the ground." They were loaded onto "two very bad trucks." The sick had to "stand on it, regardless of whether they were able to or not. At reckless speed, these trucks drove to Theresienstadt.... One of these lovely vehicles was immediately wrecked; it was said that the bottom gave way, resulting in several dead and many injured." Nine hundred to a thousand people had to march. "Many collapsed on the way, but the [Czech] gendarmes beat the poor people unmercifully with their riding crops or set their large shepherd dogs loose on them." In the Schleuse, the plundering by gendarmes and Jews was followed by an embarrassing body search, in which the victim was completely undressed.

On her work as a night nurse in autumn 1942, she writes:

> I had to go from bed to bed with a lantern, and 5–6 people died on every night shift. After every death we had to ... call the doctor on duty.... On his right toe the dead person got a tag with his name, and then the stretcher bearers were alerted.... Because the toilets were on the opposite side of the barracks [H V], we had to go in wind and rain ... through the courtyard ... with the lantern ... empty and clean the pail – and what was often very bad, help to remove the dead who, from hunger and weakness, had died on the toilet.

Regarding the delousing ward, winter 1942–43:

> The people were ... brought in and had to go through a terrible treatment. Because many very ill people ... came to the bath, the mortality was very high. On one winter evening we had seven old people sent to us; of these, four died that night, and the other three the next day. All of them had gotten pneumonia because of the horrible procedure – a hot shower, then hours sitting in a cold room in a light towel until their clothing was deloused. I reported these cases, which were not rare, to the Health Service and said that such treatment was cold-blooded murder. I said we were human beings, after all, and not the SS, and it was our damned duty and obligation to help, as long as it was in our power.

The issue was investigated. Then "infirmaries were built and mortality fell somewhat." It was distressing that the stretcher bearers, themselves undernourished, carried the sick people "through the cold winter air" and "often had to place them on the cold earth" on the way.

Following liberation, too many Czech Jews left their posts; in protest, many from Germany went on strike. On June 10, Dr. Merzbach gave a reassuring speech. "We nurses did not strike.... Unfortunately, however, many Czech nurses ... left us in the lurch ... in the early days after liberation. It was so bad that a complete exit stoppage was imposed on the entire Health Service; only a few doctors and nurses were able to leave the camp illegally."

The 120 survivors from Württemberg were picked up from T in three buses that left T on June 20 and 21 and arrived in Stuttgart 24 to 50 hours later.

335. Weidmann, F. [Two speeches] (a) "Památce dr. Eduarda Lederera-Ledy" [In Memory of Dr. E. Lederer-Leda] (b) [Memorial speech for Dr. Jindřich Kohn]. In 319, nos. 12 (1946) and 7 (1947), 1946–47.

Before speech (a) is an article by F. Fuchs on Weidmann's work as director of the JKG, Prague, and later in T. Speech (a) was delivered in June 1944, and speech (b) in 1943 in T in honor of two of the most brilliant members of the Czech-assimilated community. These were national demonstrations.

335a. Węgrodski, Sz.: "Łódź, Auschwitz, Stuffhof, Drezno [Dresden], Theresienstadt." MS, HIŻ, Poland, 1946.

The author arrived in a camp in (or near) Dresden from Stutthof in November 1944. There were approximately 500 male and female prisoners, who lived in a factory. They were later evacuated to T (*219a).

792   *Sources and Literature*

336. Weil, J.: "An der Haltestelle zum Tode." In *Tschechoslowakische Gewerkschaften.* No. 9. Prague, 1958.

An essay on T and especially on the children, with four reproductions of children's drawings.

336a. Weil, J.: "Film Scenario." MS, Prague, 1943.

According to Erich Kulka, from Prague, and newspaper reports, two versions of a scenario for a documentary film about T – probably written in 1943 – were discovered at the beginning of 1960. The scenario included the arrival of a transport in T, its reception, life in T, and so on. Additionally, the film itself (or parts of it) is said to have been found. It was filmed supposedly in autumn 1943. This may be the film that was made, without the active cooperation of the prisoners, on January 20, 1944, at the arrival of the first transport from Westerbork to T. It has little to do with the film about the "beautified" T.

336b. Weil, J.: "Literární činnost v Terezíně" [Literary Activity in Theresienstadt]. In *Židovská ročenka* [Jewish Yearbook]. Prague, 1955–1956, pp. 93–100.

A report on literary documents in the Prague Jewish Museum: poems, notes, prose, scholarly essays, lectures, and reviews, as well as poems and style exercises by children in the Czech and German languages. The report contains works by Pavel Friedman (1921–44), Petr Fischl (1929–45 – a fictional diary interspersed with verses), Georg Kafka, Ilse Weber (1903–44), and Karel Fleischmann, among others. A prose work by Fleischmann, "Terezínský den" (Theresienstadt Day), mentions a "fairy tale" that children tell themselves: "Once there was a king, and he was hungry. He went to the hatch and said, 'Two!' That is the whole fairy tale, that is the whole of Theresienstadt. The children's fantasy of a double portion." Several children's poems by Miroslav Kosek and Alena, a ten-year-old girl, are reprinted here. Issue number 3 of a newspaper, *Sešit* (Notebook), from August 20, 1944, also survived. It contains mainly translations – Büchner and Kafka – and essays. Weil does not mention the publisher, Zdeněk Lederer. A children's play, *Esther*, was written in 1942; another, *Broučci* (Firefly), was rehearsed in 1943 and was performed thirty-eight times.

The same yearbook contains a story with T themes by F. R. Kraus, "Na schodech k Staronové synagoze" (pp. 148–52); "Růžova ulice," a factually deceptive story about T by A. Lustig, also included in *177b (pp. 120–33); and a translation of Ilse Weber's poem "The Sheep of Lidice."

336c. Weil, J.: *Žalozpěv za 77,297 obětí* [Elegy for 77,297 Victims]. Prague, 1958.

A literary montage about the fate of the Bohemian-Moravian Jews, including those in T.

336d. Weil, J.: *Život s hvězdou* [Life with the Star]. Prague, 1949.

A novel about the life of Jews in the "Protectorate." The hero experiences the transport period in hiding.

337. Weinberg, G. L., et al. (eds.): *Guide to Captured German Documents.* [Maxwell Air Force Base], Alabama, 1952.

An attempt at a bibliography of important National Socialist documents that are published in books or magazines or preserved in archives.

Sources and Literature

337a. Weinberg, H.: "Monowice, Gliwice, Mała Twierdza w Teresinie" [Monowitz, Gleiwitz, Kleine Festung Theresienstadt]. MS, HIŻ, Poland, no year.

The author came to Auschwitz-Monowitz from Łódź and marched to Gleiwitz at evacuation on January 14, 1945. Those who could not walk fast enough were shot on the way. This was followed by a hellish train trip. After eight days, Weinberg jumped off in Bohemia with a comrade. They hid in the snowy woods; Czechs gave them food but allowed them no refuge. On the third day, a Czech gendarme caught them; they were sent to a prison in Pilsen [Plsen], where the treatment and food were good. Two weeks later, they were taken to the Kleine Festung, where existence was most terrible for Jews. Of the 450 people imprisoned there, only 18 experienced liberation (*321a). They lay on damp concrete; it snowed through the roof. A Czech Jew carried out selections. The food rations were meager: on Sunday they received saltwater soup; on Tuesday, 250 g of bread and "coffee"; on Thursday, watery soup; on Friday, bread again; and nothing else. After the "mealtimes" some died of stomach illness. The raw flesh of bodies was also consumed. Suicides were carried out by hanging. Typhus, erysipelas, and phlegmons were common. "People died peacefully; in the evening they were still conversing, in the morning they no longer woke up." Attacks on prisoners were common, day and night. After transfer to T, at the beginning of May, Weinberg survived typhus and spent six weeks there and then another four months in other Bohemian hospitals, before returning to Poland.

338. Weinreich, M.: *Hitler's Professors: The Part of Scholarship in Germany's Crime against the Jewish People.* New York, 1946.

A seminal work on the mixing of scholarship and hatred of Jews in National Socialism.

339. Weinstock, R.: *Das wahre Gesicht Hitlerdeutschlands* [The True Face of Hitler's Germany]. Singen, 1946.

An account of a southwest German Jew who is deported to the south of France and from there to Auschwitz.

340. Weisenborn, G.: *Der lautlose Aufstand: Bericht über die Widerstandsbewegung des deutschen Volkes 1933-1945.* [The Silent Rebellion: Report on the Resistance Movement of the German People 1933–1945]. Hamburg, 1953.

Some documents on provision of aid or advocacy for Jews. It includes information on the fates of German Jews.

340a. Weiss, A.: *Le typhus exanthématique pendant la deuxieme guerre mondiale en particulier dans les camps de concentration.* Geneva, 1954.

The author was deported from Hungary via Auschwitz and Buchenwald to Gleina-Rehmsdorf; from there, after a hunger march, he arrived in T with his father soon after April 20, 1945. The father worked as a physician in C III, which had been emptied to accommodate prisoners; the son assisted him until he fell ill with spotted fever. On pages 45–68 this dissertation deals with typhus in T, epidemiologically and clinically.

For fear that the camp would be eliminated as a "protective measure," the self-administration did not tell the SS about the outbreak of the epidemic and therefore was able to do hardly anything against its spread. Not even an effective quarantine

794   *Sources and Literature*

was implemented. On May 13, the Russian medical train arrived. At that time 340 people, including 53 doctors, worked in the medical service. The patients were disinfected and hospitalized with so little consideration for their condition that many undoubtedly died just because of this. Treatment and care in the actual quarantine barracks were good. Once the fever subsided, the patients remained for another eight to ten days before returning to the camp. According to Russian figures, 1,958 cases (1,169 in the second ten days in May and 67 after June 1) were recorded; the author estimates the number at around 3,000, with a mortality rate of around 10–15% (which is certainly too low by at least 8%). At the beginning of June, the Russians left T and left the health service to the Czechs. Like Weiss, Lederer (*166) estimates cases of sickness between May 6 and 19 alone at 2,950; in his book, unknown to Weiss, the epidemic is described in detail (*330c).

341. Weiss, G. (ed.): *Einige Dokumente zur Rechtsstellung der Juden und zur Entziehung ihres Vermögens*. Schriftenreihe zum Berliner Rückerstattungsrecht. VII. No information.

The main portion of this collection includes documents, generally from the Reich Finance Ministry or other central authorities, on the material exploitation of deportations from "Greater Germany" from the end of 1941 to the beginning of 1943, which prove the authorities' shared responsibility for the RSHA's work of extermination. A decree labeled "immediate" by the district administrator in Fulda on August 31, 1942, "to all mayors in the Kassel government district" refers directly to T. The text of the decree reads as follows:

Re.: Evacuation of Jews to Theresienstadt.

On September 7, 1942, according to information from the Secret Police – Kassel State Police Office – in Kassel, the remaining Jews from the Kassel government district will be deported to Theresienstadt. Preparation and implementation of this deportation, after consultation with the office involved, are again exclusively in the hands of the Kassel State Police Office.

All Jews will be concentrated in a collection camp in Kassel before their transport to Theresienstadt. The secondary schools on Schillerstrasse, corner of Wörthstrasse in Kassel, are designated for this purpose.

The transport of the Jews designated for evacuation for the purpose of prior concentration in Kassel will occur in passenger trains, in cooperation with the Reichsbahn directorate. The departure times for the trains appropriate for the county of Fulda have been established.

The gendarmes with local authority hereby receive the mandate to bring the designated Jews to the trains and duly transfer them to the transport leader. Before transport to Kassel, the identity cards of the designated Jews must be checked by you for accuracy, especially their personal information, and stamped as "verified." No permit from the Reichsbahn or to leave one's place of residence is needed, as the transport is accompanied by police officers.

At deregistration of the Jews at the registry offices, the destination or the notation "evacuated to Theresienstadt" is not to be given, but only "moved, address unknown" or "emigrated."

As luggage, the Jews may bring a suitcase or knapsack with equipment, specifically

    a)   complete clothing (proper shoes),
    b)   bedclothes with blankets,
    c)   eating utensils (plate or pot) with spoon,
    d)   provisions for 3 days.

Sources and Literature

There are no reservations to the Jews carrying their provisions with them in a handbag or briefcase or in a net bag. Aside from this one piece of luggage, they may additionally bring serviceable objects (tools, mattresses, pails, pots, cleaning articles, etc.).

The Jews must take hand luggage (suitcase or knapsack) with them on the trains. The transport of the Jews' additional equipment will occur through freight shipments, which must be posted immediately by the Jews at the appropriate dispatch offices. These freight shipments must, however, be posted in time for them to arrive by September 2, 1942 at the latest at the Kassel Main Railroad Station (customs shed). The dispatch offices in question, including there, will be informed by the Reichsbahn directorate of the shipping of the Jews' additional equipment to Kassel.

The shipping costs are to be assumed by each Jew himself. The equipment will be sent to the address: "Secret State Police Office Kassel, Destination station: Kassel-Main Railroad Station (customs shed)."

Jews must label all luggage with a name tag to be fastened to it (name and address of owner). The suitcase key is also to be labeled with a name tag and fastened to the suitcase with wire or string. Luggage may not be daubed with paint.

In Kassel, the Jews will be received on the platforms at which the trains arrive by officers of the Secret State Police and the uniformed police. The Jews will then be assembled and sorted and then brought to the collection camp by officers assigned. The Jews are to carry their own luggage.

The State Police Office in Kassel will take responsibility if necessary for transport of this luggage from the railroad station in Kassel to the collection camp and from the collection camp to the evacuation train.

Jews are to bring along all money. They will be given 50 RM per person. The total amount will be supplied by the Jews in advance and collected by the Jewish Community in Kassel. The remaining cash will be taken from the Jews only in the collection camp.

The property left behind in the homes of the evacuated Jews will be confiscated after their deportation. To gain an overview of it, the Jews will be issued property declarations by the State Police Office in Kassel, which they are to submit to their Jewish representative at the State Police Office in Kassel.

The Jews are to label the remaining inventory with name tags in such a way that the former owner can immediately be determined. The Jews must give to you the keys to the abandoned homes, rooms and containers, also labeled with name tags. I request that the keys then be collected in envelopes with the appropriate label of the former owner and then sent to the Finance Office in Fulda. The rooms in question are to be reconditioned, at least through spot-checks, and then sealed.

The live inventory is also to be confiscated and is to be surrendered by the Jews to the responsible local agricultural leader, whom you are to inform if necessary. He is to keep a list and ensure its maintenance. The Jews are to make a report on this at the Kassel collection camp.

Easily perishable things are to be made available to the proper NSV office, without payment, in exchange for a receipt. I ask that submission of these things be arranged on your own responsibility in consultation with the NSV office. The term "easily perishable" should not be interpreted broadly, as potatoes and preserves, for example, will undoubtedly keep until they are taken by the Fulda Finance Office.

Any taking of property or giving or sale of objects to citizens of German blood is most emphatically to be prevented. Such objects are to be secured. Should difficulties in implementation arise before or during the evacuation, I request that you take care of them yourself in accordance with existing guidelines. Only if there are difficulties that are truly unbridgeable on site should my decision be requested immediately by telephone.

I expect your prompt report on implementation of the evacuation operation.

(pp. 93 et seq.)

796   *Sources and Literature*

The transport from Kassel arrived in T on September 8, 1942.

341a. Weiss, J., and P. Arons: "Bergen-Belsen." MS, WL, Tröbitz, 1945.

In early March 1945, Möhs came to the camp to initiate the transport of 7,000 persons to T. It was explained to him that 85% of them were sick and there was danger of contagion for the Germans. Möhs finally agreed to postpone the transport for four weeks. From this and other reports, it can be seen that approximately the intended number left Bergen-Belsen between the 5th and 9th of April in three transports. Only one arrived in T – on April 21 (1,712 people). Another (some 2,500 people) was liberated by the Americans on April 13 near Farsleben, not far from Magdeburg; the last (2,400–2,700 people) was liberated by the Russians on the 23rd, near Tröbitz, not far from Torgau.

342. Wellers, G.: *De Drancy à Auschwitz*. Paris, 1946.

An illuminating, serious work on the conditions and mentality in the transit camp Drancy. This work is instructive on the self-deception of the Jews and the parallels to T and Westerbork.

343. Weltlinger, S.: *Hast Du es schon vergessen?* Berlin, 1954.

Information on the author's experiences and the persecution of Jews in Germany in 1933–45. It lists figures for Germany and Berlin. The author worked for the Jewish Community in Berlin or the Reichsvereinigung, starting in 1938. "I was a leader in implementing the emigration, resettlement, and finally the Theresienstadt levies (home purchase agreements)." The work provides a description of the deportations from Berlin. The author lived in hiding starting in February 1943.

344. Wielek, H.: *De Orloog die Hitler won*. Amsterdam, 1947.

This comprehensive, well-documented work shows how similarly the phases of persecution of Jews in Holland and the "Protectorate" proceeded (incidentally, a similar process also took place in Belgium, France, etc.). For the "transport call-up," the Amsterdam "Central Office" used forms very similar to those used in the "Protectorate." Neither this work nor the better-known Dutch literature mentions that the future Jewish Elder Edelstein was officially sent from Prague to Amsterdam for several weeks (see *52a, 209a, 312a). R. Friedmann-van der Heide describes T (pp. 383–403), generally accurately. The work contains a reproduction of some original documents.

344a. [Vienna] "Die Juden in Wien." In *Israelitisches Wochenblatt*. No. 18. Zurich, 1946.

Of the 206,000 Viennese Jews, 136,000 emigrated, 15,000 died, 6,000 (those in mixed marriages) remained in Vienna, 47,000 were deported, and 13,000 of these came back. The number of returnees is greatly overestimated (*175b).

344b. Wiener, M.: [Transcript]. [Polish], MS, HIŻ, Poland, no year.

The author came from Poland via Auschwitz and Bergen-Belsen to Raguhn, near Dessau, where he performed difficult labor in a munitions factory. He was evacuated to T in a fourteen-day trip by motor vehicles.

345. Wiernik, Y.: *A Year in Treblinka*. New York, 1945.

Sources and Literature   797

An account of the extermination camp.

345a. Winter, A.: Sworn affidavit. Nuremberg Document NO-5448. Mimeographed, IfZ, Nuremberg, 1947.

The author came to Riga from Düsseldorf on December 14, 1941, with 1,000 Jews. With 500 young people from Hanover, Kassel, and Düsseldorf, he was taken to build the concentration camp Salaspils, 19 km from Riga. "There, 500 young Jews from southern Germany already waited; they had been brought somewhat earlier from the Jungfernhof camp [5 km from Riga]." They were given 200 g of bread and 1 L of watery soup daily. The text describes the brutal, murderous regime.

> On January 16, 1942, 80 people were loaded into a vehicle, supposedly to be brought to the ghetto. Some ... had their shoes and coats taken, although the temperature was at least 30 degrees below 0. ...
> The first mass shooting was on May 15, 1942. ... A Latvian Jew was raised on a gallows and then brought down again. Dr. Lange asked him how he liked it up there. He was then raised again, and 15 Jews had to take off their coats and were shot by firing squad.

These included a fourteen-year-old boy.

> On January 13, 1942, 70 Jews arrived [in Salaspils] from Czechoslovakia. ...
> Three days later, we had to unload three train cars of luggage and clothing. These were recognized by the Czech Jews as clothing from the transport members. One car was filled with shoes and clothing that were thrown around haphazardly ... and in some cases dirty. ...
> Most of the shootings ... took place ... from February 20, 1942 to the end of July 1942 in the Bickernick forest.

It seems that all of the members of the transports in September and October 1942 from Frankfurt a.M., Königsberg, and Berlin were shot in the woods near Salaspils. The author later went via Riga, Libau, Stutthof (arrived in July 1944 and spent seven weeks there), and Buchenwald (ten weeks) to Tröglitz, near Zeitz. The camp was evacuated on April 12, 1945. "On the way, on April 16, 1945, 1,200 Jews were shot by the SS after an air raid." They arrived in T on April 23.

346. Wolf, E.: "Transcript." MS, DA, Prague, 1945.

A report by a Zionist who remained, legally, in Prague until the end of the war about package mailings to T and other camps.

347. Wolfenstein, H.: "Poems." MS, T, 1942–45.

Eleven poems with camp themes, mainly about the sick. The author was the head nurse in T for around three years and died of typhus after liberation.

348. Wolff, J.: *Sadismus oder Wahnsinn* [Sadism or Insanity]. Greiz, no year [1946].

Information on the fate of a German Jewish woman, deported to Riga on January 20, 1942. Her experiences were also typical for those deported from T to Riga (*136, 223c).

349. Wolff-Eisner, A.: *Über Mangelerkrankungen auf Grund von Beobatchtungen im Konzentrationslager Theresienstadt*. Würzburg, 1947.

The aged author, a well-known clinician, arrived in the camp in 1943 and became a medical consultant in the Internal Medicine Department in E VI. The general information here is mostly accurate. The book offers good insights into hygienic and medical conditions. The monthly mortality figures are to some extent too low.

349a. Wolffheim, N.: "Kinder aus Konzentrationslagern: Mitteilungen über die Nachwirkungen des KZ-Auftenthaltes auf Kinder und Jugendliche." In *Praxis der Kinderpsychologie und Kinderpsychiatrie*. Vols. 11–12 (1958) and 1 and 2 (1959). Göttingen, 1958–1959, pp. 302–312 (vol. 1) and 20–27, 59–71 (vol. 2).

A study on children from T and other camps.

349b. Wolffheim, N.: "Leiden eines nicht-jüdischen Ehemannes." MS, WL, Vienna, 1958.

A description of the fate of Oskar and Margit Perschke in the war. At my request, Mr. Perschke gave me supplemental information, for which I thank him here. The couple lived in Troppau at the time of the occupation and moved to Prague in 1939. There Perschke ran a cardboard packaging factory and bookbindery, where he employed his Jewish wife's relatives. When his mother-in-law and his brother-in-law's family had to go to T in February 1942, Perschke promised to help them. Two weeks later, he traveled to T and approached the chief government inspector, Dr. Wüstehoff, who at the time headed the Economics Department of the commandant's office. Perschke did not mention the family relationship and explained that the deportation of his manager and various employees had made it almost impossible to run his firm in Prague. He said it would also be good to employ Jews in T. Wüstehoff liked this; he wanted to turn T into a small industrial city, and asked for Perschke's cooperation. Perschke suggested production of crafts items and paintings, for which he would supply the raw materials if he was given space for workshops and an office. Wüstehoff asked Perschke to bring product samples, aids, and materials to T to carry out tests. A week later, Perschke drove up to the commandant's office with a furniture truck and set up a two-story factory. When "Wüstehoff came to look towards evening . . . he was quite surprised." Wüstehoff and Seidl, to whom Perschke was introduced, had not imagined such an extensive operation but were ultimately satisfied; presents to Seidl may have contributed to this.

Thus the Lautsch firm began operations in T in early March 1942. It produced, among other things, paper and bookbinding products, such as painted bookmarks, congratulations cards, coloring books, toys, and puzzles; hand-painted lampshades and boxes; notions made from leather scraps and feathers; jigsaw work from synthetics and metal; handwoven cloth; and oil paintings, etchings, and drawings. The products were easily marketable, but the expenses were hardly covered. Perschke was able to have his brother-in-law made factory manager and his other relatives employed. The other workers, a total of several hundred, were both requisitioned by Perschke and assigned by the commandant's office and the Council of Elders. The company did not sign a contract with the commandant's office, but there was continuous correspondence. Seidl was cooperative. Wüstehoff was ambitious but "too soft for the desired course," for which reason he did not last long. The main connection to the camp leadership went through the contract employees Baumruck and Hantschke, who oversaw the factory and proved very accommodating. Hantschke was particularly decent; he knew Perschke's family relationships and warned him and his relatives in T about Burger when that man succeeded Seidl. Seidl and other SS men ordered portraits and also monitored the business. Along with the gendarmes, they inspected shipments of goods and occasionally carried out body searches. Perschke was often able to move freely in the factory but was hampered little even when accompanied. When Seidl eventually found out about Perschke's family relationships, Perschke was permitted to speak to his department heads only at the commandant's office in the presence of SS functionaries. This did not prevent him, however, from giving his people, in front of Seidl, sample goods in which letters were hidden. Meanwhile, Perschke's devoted Czech foreman Svoboda, during weekly visits to T, smuggled into the workshop, food, medicines, and other goods that the boss had previously obtained.

After one of the prisoners had a heart attack, Perschke approached the physician Dr. Zwilling in E VI, who asked him for medicines and medical instruments. Perschke obtained these through the JKG and brought them in double-bottomed boxes in his transports of goods to T. After the outbreak of the typhus epidemic, he supplied disinfectants to the commandant's office, saying that as factory manager he felt an obligation to do so, because otherwise the civilian population would be endangered by his transports of goods. When his workers were threatened with deportation, he intervened with Freiberger and Schliesser, Baumruck, and Hantschke, and in some cases with the SS. When Perschke's efforts to this end were not entirely successful during the September transports in 1943, he was denounced to Burger, who was told that he was employing relatives. His sister-in-law was able to warn him by letter not to bring anything prohibited. When Perschke reported as required at his next visit, Burger accused him of employing relatives and smuggling. He did not deny employing them but denied smuggling. Burger's search turned up nothing. He prohibited him from visiting T and had him escorted to Prague by an SS man. The facility was dismantled, and the employees were imprisoned for three days, but all the machines and other materials were sent to Perschke's Prague factory, which continued to operate undisturbed. Thus an unusual aid operation ended after eighteen months.

Ms. Perschke's mother died in Auschwitz; her sister, deathly ill, experienced liberation in Bergen-Belsen, whereas her sister's husband died in T, and her only son returned to T via Sachsenhausen toward the end of the war. Soon after, he fell ill with typhus in Prague and, in delirium, fell down an air shaft in the hospital one night and died.

Perschke was for the time being left alone in Prague. Only when "Aryan" spouses were drafted was he conscripted into the Organisation Todt; however, in 1944 he was taken to the Gestapo instead of being sent to a labor camp, because of his activities in T. They accused him of making false statements to authorities and sent him to prison. A month later he was taken to the Kleine Festung; earlier he had been advised to obtain a divorce in order to avoid that fate. In April 1945 he was sent to Flossenbürg. After the evacuation of the camp, he experienced liberation in May, during an infamous death march, near Cham in Bavaria.

A few days after Perschke's arrest, the Gestapo picked up his wife, also imprisoned her, and a week later sent her to the Kleine Festung. She was transferred to T before the end of the war, which preempted further deportation. In Prague, she found out that her husband was in a hospital in Cham, traveled there, and returned with him to Prague in July. "But there the Czechs gave them nothing and despite their honest disposition, their suffering and the loss of all their earthly possessions, treated them not much better than the Germans. In 1947 they then returned to their home [Vienna], but there too, no one took notice of them, sick, old, without property."

800   *Sources and Literature*

349c. Zadek, P.: "Report on the Experiences of Abraham D. in Poland and Germany." MS, WL, London, 1955.

Abraham, who was from Hrubieszów, was ten years old in 1940. He lost his family and went from one camp to another. These included the Sokal Ghetto, which was "liquidated" toward the end of 1942; the "Jewish camp" Budzin (early 1943), which was turned into a concentration camp; Majdanek (mid-1943); Auschwitz and a neighboring satellite camp; Mauthausen and a satellite camp; a camp near Leipzig; Leitmeritz; and, at the end of the war, T. There Abraham was surprised to see elderly Jews still alive. He reports what happened to him there in quarantine – C III – as he understood it:

> The newcomers were locked by their fellow Jews in a room in one of these blocks in groups of ten, and not let out, so that they would not spread any sicknesses. This is how they were held until May 8, the day of liberation, incarcerated. Although the other Jews still attempted to keep them locked up, Abraham's block broke out, by knocking down the Jewish police and killing all the Germans they found.

350. Zehngut, J.: "Nisko." In 319, nos. 7–10, 13, and 26–27, 1949.

A description of the first Ostrau [Ostrava] transport and camp life in Nisko. The camp, established by Eichmann, was officially named the "Central Office for Jewish Resettlement in Nisko on the San" and, as it was planned in 1939–40, was to serve as a transfer point for the "resettlement rayon" for transports from the West.

> The unfamiliar conditions were supposed to be studied by Jewish representatives, to which Edelstein and Murmelstein ... belonged. They were accompanied by additional escorts from the Protectorate and Austria. These representatives appeared early in the morning and gave the camp command a report on the results of their investigations. After a short period, further investigations were ended and the Jewish representatives returned home over the San.

350a. Zehngut, J.: "Transport." In 319, no. 10, 1959.

Additional information on Nisko (*350).

351. Zeller, E.: *Geist der Freiheit: Der zwanzigste Juli 1944.* 2nd ed. Munich, 1954.

This thorough, excellent work presents Dietrich Bonhoeffer's important thoughts on the problem of ethics under National Socialism (from *Widerstand und Ergebung*, Munich 1951). Among other things, he states,

> The great masquerade of evil has played havoc with all our ethical concepts. For evil to appear disguised as light, charity, historical necessity, or social justice is quite bewildering to anyone brought up on our traditional ethical concepts....
>
> Evil approaches him in so many respectable and seductive disguises that his conscience becomes nervous and vacillating, till at last he contents himself with a salved instead of a clear conscience ... the responsibility for [the command] rests on the commander, not on the person commanded.   (pp. 119 et seq.)

The only questionable topic is Zeller's (cautious) advocacy for Weizsäcker, whose behavior as a member of the resistance must still be proven with documentary evidence. Weizsäcker, who was appointed SS-Oberführer in April 1938, signed – as state secretary in the Foreign Office – too many documents that could reveal him as a dangerous player in the extermination of the Jews. His shaky

Sources and Literature 801

collaboration, which had him hesitating with worry and occasionally approaching men in the resistance, does not undo his misdeeds (see, on Weizsäcker, the excellent study by P. Seabury: *The Wilhelmstrasse*. Berkeley and Los Angeles, 1954).

352. [Central Office] [Note]. In 319, no. 12, 1946, p. 123.

A testimony by arrested SS officer Günel, one of Günther's representatives from the "Central Office." Günther escaped from Prague in a car on May 5, 1945. It was attacked by civilians some 10 km southeast of Prague, near Zadní Třebáň. Günther sank to the ground, shot, and fell into the hands of his attackers. In a long statement in possession of the Frankfurt am Main district court, his subordinate Fidler, who escaped with him and Günel, gave a detailed account of Günther's end.

352a. [Zentralstelle, Prague] "Document Fascicle from March 1, 1941." MS, RvO.

These documents, taken by Günther (or one of the Jews who accompanied him, Edelstein, and Friedmann) to Holland to erect the "Central Office" or "Jewish Council" there, supply a good overview of construction in the period before the deportations. At the time, sixty-six people were employed, including forty-two in the Prague Central Office, seven in the Brünn [Brno] branch, three in the "reeducation camp" Lipa, and fourteen in the "emigration funds."

352b. Zerres, G.: "Theresienstadt: Bericht aus einem Ghetto. Nach Aufzeichnungen von Dr. Norbert Stern." Cologne, 1955.

The text of a radio program. Based on an extensive diary kept by a war-blinded Munich man who was in T beginning on July 24, 1942, the montage uses paragraphs from this book. The diary, which unfortunately is not yet accessible, is written with great precision and is a valuable source.

353. Zucker, O.: [Instructions for the "census" on the night of November 10, 1943, and plans for a deployment the next morning]. Mimeographed, MS.

354. [Zucker, O.]: "Geschichte des Ghettos Theresienstadt zum 31.12.1943." MS, T, 1944.

One of the main documents on camp history.

355. Zygielbojm, S.: "Stop Them Now. London." No year [1942].

One of the earliest correct reports published on the Jewish tragedy in the East. It is particularly instructive on Chełmno.

356. [Zyklon B, delivery to T] NI-11901/04/06. Mimeographed, Nuremberg, no year.

Three letters from 1944 from the "Kaliwerke A.G.," Kolin, to the commander of the Sipo and SD in T on deliveries of Zyklon B. The Auschwitz killing gas was used in T for disinfection. The amounts ordered seem sizeable. Representatives of the potash plant wrote on February 28, 1944: "We ... have taken note of the fact that you are satisfied with 75 kg of Zyklon B per week. We will deliver this amount to you weekly, starting on March 1 of this year, until cancellation, and hope you are in agreement that for shipping reasons we will be sending the monthly amount of 300 kg all together." They announced, on May 27, 1944, the delivery of ten boxes, with no indication of weight, and, on October 4, 1944, the delivery of twenty boxes with twenty cans of 1,500 g each.

Afterword

Jeremy Adler

Translated by Jeremiah Riemer

In the language of Israel, faith, truth, and belief are one and the same word.
Leo Baeck

H. G. Adler's monograph on Theresienstadt was published in 1955 and came out five years later in a second, revised edition, which is fully reprinted here in translation. The wealth of detail in the book, the richness of its documentation, and its unbiased analysis aroused international interest from the moment it appeared in print. At that time there still were relatively few scholarly monographs on the world of the camps, even if a few notable works did exist. Eugen Kogon's seminal *Der SS-Staat* (1946; English version: *The Theory and Practice of Hell*, 1950) and Primo Levi's *Si questo è un uomo?* (1947; later published in the U.K. and U.S. versions as *If This Is a Man* and *Survival in Auschwitz*) come to mind. Numerous publications told about the camps, shed light on National Socialist crimes, and revealed the suffering of the victims. What distinguished Adler's work was the way he, like Kogon, presented a scholarly analysis while simultaneously giving his observations literary form, as did Primo Levi. This rare combination helped *Theresienstadt 1941–1945* achieve the status of a classic, regarded today as a seminal work of Holocaust research.

No other book demonstrated the truth about the camps so clearly, so soberly, and so penetratingly by shedding light on the "ghetto" of Theresienstadt down to the smallest detail – its founding, history, structure, daily routine, and dissolution – from every conceivable angle. In so doing, it used the case of Theresienstadt to show the historical link between German ideology and politics – between law, administration, and persecution – and to clarify the historical line leading logically from the crazed political program of a small party of outsiders to the violent acts of a totalitarian state, from the seemingly spontaneous murders on the Eastern Front to the calculating deliberations at the Wannsee Conference and ultimately to industrialized murder. At the same time, Adler does away with the stereotypical characterization of perpetrators and victims.

Perhaps the closest literary parallel might be found in an even larger project, Solzhenitsyn's *The Gulag Archipelago*, which pursues a related goal based on an entire system of camps. H. G. Adler deliberately limits himself, however, to one isolated case, although not as a case study but, rather, as the book's subtitle makes

803

804 *Afterword*

clear, as a paradigm for a modern social system. The vivid language and the documents (on the one hand) and his sympathy with the victims (on the other) convey to the reader a feeling of seeing the camp right in front of him, of experiencing the worst at firsthand. At the same time, however, the author analyzes what happened at an intellectual level, in that he provides categories for understanding it and conducts a logical disection in order to explain the causes behind this example of monstrosity. The neologism *Zwangsgemeinschaft* (coerced community) that Adler introduces demonstrates how radical this undertaking is. The author accepts neither the vocabulary of the Nazis nor the traditional concepts of social science. He wants to rethink modernity. Even today, *Theresienstadt 1941–1945* remains the definitive single case study of a "coerced community" – whether it is a prison, a "ghetto," or a camp – and has itself now become a topic for scholarly research.[1]

The author does not appear in his work; he appears only in the book's account of sources used. He wants to present this history factually and objectively, even if – as it occurred to him much later – his voice is ever present. An early essay renders an account of how it came to this testimony, yet this does not really amount to a personal story:

> It was as early as in Theresienstadt itself, to which I had been deported at the beginning of February 1942 with my wife and parents-in-law, that I first made up my mind to write my book. This is how it came about: in the first few days and weeks I spent in the camp, in that early period of the so-called "ghetto," when the prisoners were housed in a few dirty barracks, cordoned off from the outside world and even from their fellow prisoners, on miserable chutes of wood shavings or just on a wooden or concrete floor – it was in those weeks, then, since I often wasn't allowed to see the members of my family for days on end and succumbed to a terrible stupefaction in which I was incapable of thinking, much less accomplishing, anything proper, that I seized on a resolve, should the miracle of being allowed to survive this world of the camps ever befall me, to depict this world at length and comprehensively.[2]

He accepted his task as a mission, an assignment, to bear witness to the truth. This meant bearing witness not to God's truth but to the reality of hell, and not as a victim but as a witness to the martyrdom of his people as a whole. It was essential to portray this catastrophe.

His thinking matured in the other camps to which he was deported, including Auschwitz – that is, in places that exposed him to much greater dangers than in Theresienstadt. It was, above all, during his two weeks in Auschwitz that he pushed his thinking about God and the state to the very roots of human experience.

---

[1] Testimonials to the work include Willehad P. Eckart and Wilhelm Unger (eds.), *H. G. Adler, Buch der Freunde* (Cologne: Wienand, 1975), 62ff.; Franz Hocheneder, "H. G. Adler – Werk und Nachlaß, Eine bio-bibliographische Studie" (Phil. diss., 2 vols., Vienna, 1997); on the history of the book's impact, see Marcel Atze (ed.), *"Ortlose Botschaft": Der Freundeskreis H. G. Adler, Elias Canetti und Franz Baermann Steiner im englischen Exil*, Marbacher Magazin 84 (Marbach am Neckar: Deutsche Schiller-gesellschaft, 1998); Franz Hocheneder, "Akribische Dokumentation und sprachliches Kunstwerk. H. G. Adlers Pionierwerk 'Theresienstadt 1941–1945,'" *Literatur und Kritik* 375/376 (July 2003): 35–40; and (without reference to the book) on Adler's place in Holocaust historiography, see Nicolas Berg, *Der Holocaust und die westdeutschen Historiker: Erforschung und Erinnerung*, 3rd rev. ed. (Göttingen: Wallstein, 2004).

[2] H. G. Adler, "Warum habe ich mein Buch *Theresienstadt 1941–1945* geschrieben?," in Jeremy Adler (ed.), *Der Wahrheit verpflichtet: Interviews, Gedichte, Essays* (Gerlingen: Bleicher, 1998), 111ff.

Afterword

What had a lasting effect on his political views was experiencing firsthand how terribly the authority of the state can go astray, how seriously it can assault the person. This insight accompanied him his entire life. He always remained skeptical toward politics and the state. Shortly after the end of the war, he drew up his anarchistic reflections in an essay entitled "Against the State – Sharply Worded Ideas," in which he wrote: "Whatever man does that is good, the state grabs it and spoils it."[3] Even in the last year of his life he was defending his principles: "Whatever happens in the state by way of political action . . . is always, even where it takes place in a legally proper way and is applied with all due leniency, an act of coercion imposed from the outside on human beings."[4] By his subtle process of reflection, the prisoner became an observer, the observer a theorist, the theorist a witness, and the witness an admonisher. As soon as he had opted for this approach, he drew consolation from his decision. In the aforementioned testimonial essay, he goes on to write:

> Curiously, this resolve [to write a book] lent me a healing power. Admittedly, it took several more months until I had more or less regained my mental equilibrium, but this plan, still so undefined, to produce a book intended to become a memorial to our time beneficently changed my miserable existence. I taught myself to see things in cool contemplation. Cool – yes, when I think about it, that is the right word – but this coolness needed to be constantly won anew; [I] had to let the fire, the blaze, the glow of repeatedly and abruptly inrushing events wash over me so that they could be tested, hardened, and ultimately, when Theresienstadt had been exchanged for much more dreadful places, so unerringly safeguarded that I could bear the will to recognize the whole truth.[5]

In Adler's thinking one constantly encounters the search for truth. The difficulty of bearing true witness to the world of the camps was something he portrayed in his novel *Die unsichtbare Wand* (*The Wall*, 2014), in which he depicted the traumas of the survivors as well as the tribulations that fate exacted from him, because he aspired to convey his message to an indifferent world: "I want to endure the truth, sacrifice myself to it, and if I may carry out yet one more task, I want to bear witness to it as mercilessly as the truth itself."[6] This truth pertained both to the transgressions of the perpetrators and to the aberrations of the victims for which the perpetrators' offenses were to blame. Bearing this kind of difficult witness admittedly required a method all its own. Even before the war, through his friendship with the Prague poet and anthropologist Franz Baermann Steiner, Adler had been acquainted with the theories of Bronisław Malinowski, who had founded modern Anglo-Saxon social anthropology with his technique of participant observation. According to this method the researcher lives in an alien society. Yet he maintains a distance to arrive at a balanced and rounded understanding of the culture's societal forms.[7] Malinowski's method of participant observation supplied Adler with the means to interpret the

---

[3] "Gegen den Staat – Geharrnischte Einfälle," April 7, 1949, 3 pages, typescript, Nachlaß H. G. Adler [H. G. Adler papers], Schiller-Nationalmuseum, Deutsches Literaturarchiv, Marbach am Neckar (DLA Marbach).

[4] H. G. Adler, *Vorschule für eine Experimentaltheologie: Betrachtungen über Wirklichkeit und Sein* (Stuttgart: F. Steiner Verlag Wiesbaden, 1987), 30.

[5] Adler, *Der Wahrheit verpflichtet*, 112.

[6] H. G. Adler, *Die unsichtbare Wand* (Vienna, Darmstadt: Zsolnay, 1989), 323.

[7] On Malinowski's role in the development of anthropology, cf. Adam Kuper, *Anthropology and Anthropologists: The Modern British School*, 3rd rev. and enl. ed. (London, New York: Routledge, 1996).

806   *Afterword*

world of the camps as a social institution while simultaneously giving him that inner distance that (along with his healthy temperament and an ample portion of luck) made it possible for him to survive. In his essay he goes on to write:

> This will was something that needed to mature. I also looked around for a model and found it in the field research of the anthropologists. That is why I constantly had to tell myself: You need to view life in this society as impartially and soberly as a scholar who wants to investigate a little-known tribe, and in the process you dare not cut yourself off from anything in the prevailing order; you need to remain a participant in everything that happens here. In my situation this meant especially that, while I could certainly raise myself up, I could never put myself above, never crave not to belong to the community of sufferers as a fellow sufferer. So in the camp I lived simultaneously as a watching observer and yet as an ordinary prisoner, which I certainly remained as an anonymous inmate of Theresienstadt.[8]

This dual perspective characterizes Adler's point of view, not least of all in the final version of *Theresienstadt 1941–1945*. He depicts the "ghetto" objectively while simultaneously accepting the role of a person in the midst of the events themselves. He thus offers neither a report from personal experience nor an external account but, rather, what Thomas Nagel calls "the view from nowhere,"[9] a view that simultaneously comes from the "inside" and the "outside." In the novel *Die unsichtbare Wand*, this is reflected in the concept of the "placeless message."

After his deportation Adler began to formulate his experiences, in both a scholarly and an artistic manner. In a 1986 interview for ZDF, German Television's Second Channel, he recalled:

> When it came to the deportations, I said to myself: I won't survive this. But if I do survive this, then I want to depict it, in fact in two ways: I want to investigate it in a scholarly way, detaching myself completely (in this particular configuration) from myself as an individual, and I also want to depict it as a writer in some fashion.[10]

After the war he continued with this two-track procedure. The surge of his literary works, lyric poems, stories, and novels did not abate, nor did his scholarly effort to finish the major monographs end. To be sure, only a few readers, including Heinrich Böll and Hermann Langbein, were in a position to understand these separate activities as a unified whole. If scholarship strives for objectivity, literary composition wants to fix its gaze on the subjective. Only a combination of the two yields an overall picture.

Although Adler's monograph frequently is called a "documentary work," this is applicable only to a degree. This designation fails to recognize the subtlety of his method as well as the author's accompanying voice. In his foreword to the book, Leo Baeck highlighted Adler's achievement, and Walter Jens also discussed his method:

> I have often asked myself in what manner H. G. Adler succeeded – the only one to do so! – in illustrating not only the facticity, but also the atmosphere . . . the "how it is" of Jewish existence under the sign of National Socialism. Why is it that when Adler writes

---

[8] Adler, *Der Wahrheit verpflichtet*, 112.
[9] Thomas Nagel, *The View from Nowhere* (New York, Oxford: Oxford University Press, 1986), 6.
[10] Adler, *Der Wahrheit verpflichtet*, 44.

Afterword

history, the stones speak, and passports, administrative regulations, lists of clothing, and referral orders turn eloquent, whereas with other historians they remain silent?[11]

Jens cites examples of several features of Adler's work as a way of honing in on his question: (1) the dialectic of the general and the specific, of the "planetary view" and the close-up view; (2) the clarity with which every actor emerges; and (3) the fact that the author, "in everything he writes, is simultaneously chronicler and witness, historian and fellow participant, who . . . vouches for the truth of what is being described."[12] Jens gets to the core of the matter. But there are also other techniques, such as the interweaving of documentation and analysis as well as the integration of statistics into the narrative flow and the interdisciplinary intellectual orientation. Additional features were spotlighted by Zdeněk Vašiček, who sees *Theresienstadt 1941–1945* as a pioneering work that introduced several modern methods, including the book's interdisciplinary orientation and its focus on oral history, microhistory, and the history of "*mentalité.*"[13] Jens put more emphasis on the literary aspects, and Vašiček more on the historiographical innovations. Finally, Hermann Levin Goldschmidt draws attention to the religious aspect. For him, the book is a prophetic "indictment";[14] Adler was pronouncing a biblical warning. One thus finds in *Theresienstadt 1941–1945* a complex voice, a subtle methodology, and several techniques of analysis that were rooted in the prewar years, developed in the camps, and finally came to fruition in the postwar period, when the book was written.

H. G. Adler, along with his wife, Gertrud Klepetar, and her family, was deported on February 6–7, 1942, to Theresienstadt, where he worked as a prisoner until he was transported to Auschwitz on October 12, 1944.[15] As a physician, Gertrud was initially spared a worse fate, and that is also what rescued Adler himself from being deported to the East. He repeatedly emphasized that he owed his survival to her. This is also evinced by the dedication to this book. His letters to Gertrud, which begin with lengthy, philosophical observations before the war and end with poems and covert messages, present an unsettling picture. They lived together only for a short time and were separated through almost all their time in Theresienstadt. On November 27, 1941, shortly before their wedding, he wrote a letter to Gertrud from the work camp Velká Losenice-Sázava, where he was on a forced labor railroad construction crew, describing the hopelessness of the situation at that time: "Demonic destinies of Kafkaesque sorrowfulness enshroud us, against which our much vaunted free will can do nothing." The name of the beloved Prague author accompanied his spiritual descendent like a totem through the turmoil. But in his letters he also constantly conjured up love in the age of hate, as in this card from October 30,

---

[11] Walter Jens, "H.G. Adler zum 75. Geburtstag," *europäische ideen* 60 (1985): 5.   [12] Ibid.

[13] Zdeněk Vašiček, "Zrcadlo, obraz a stěna," in H. G. Adler, *Svoboda a bezmoc* (Prague: Prostor, 1998), 207.

[14] Hermann Levin Goldschmidt, *Das Vermächtnis des deutschen Judentums*, 2nd ed. (Frankfurt am Main: Europäische Verlagsanstalt, 1957), 137. The German expression used by Goldschmidt – "prophetische 'Zeiung'" – uses an archaic word – "Zeiung" – for "accusation" ("indictment," "inculpation," "imputation") in what may also be a pun on the last two syllables of "Prophezeiung," the German word for "prophecy."

[15] Cf. Atze, "*Ortlose Botschaft*," 179.

1942: "3 full years bind us – and we chose freely! Let it remain that way! I live in relation to you."[16]

In Theresienstadt Gertrud oversaw the central medical laboratory and worked tirelessly as a physician. H. G. Adler himself might have found a relatively comfortable office job, but he avoided any kind of official activity that might have bound him to the self-administration of the camp, and in this way he preserved his independence. In spite of his awkwardness, he became (among other things) a mason. For reading matter he carried around a copy of Pope's translation of Homer. When other prisoners, including Rabbi Leo Baeck, wanted to amuse themselves, they sought out his construction site and watched him. In addition to the preliminary work for *Theresienstadt 1941–1945*, he dedicated his free time to his poems and stories, as well as to his theoretical work. He wrote the first version of a novel, some stories, and many poems.[17] On one occasion he presented these works in a reading and held some lectures, and on July 3, 1943, he organized a memorial celebration commemorating the sixtieth birthday of Franz Kafka, which was also attended by Kafka's sister Ottla. He kept up his friendship with some of his friends from the Prague circle of artists, including the composer Viktor Ullmann, for whom he wrote the cycle "Der Mensch und sein Tag" ("Man and His Day[s]"),[18] and he attended to younger people, such as the sixteen year-old Tomáš Mandl, whom he introduced to the history of philosophy in a series of long conversations. Berta Gross, whose salon he had frequented before he war, and who was the mother of his second wife (that is, of Bettina, my mother) was also part of his circle. Her words stand at the conclusion of this book. Dedication and conclusion frame the catastrophe of Theresienstadt like memorial and hope with recollections of his loved ones.

Adler's most important intellectual and spiritual friendship in Theresienstadt was probably with Rabbi Leo Baeck. It was a rare stroke of luck for the young, assimilated Prague Jew to encounter the leading personality of German Jewry in the Bohemian "ghetto."[19] Internationally renowned as a rabbi and theologian, Baeck represented the highest moral authority in Theresienstadt. In 1933 he had been elected president of the organization renamed Reichsvertretung der Juden in Deutschland (Reich Representation of Jews in Germany) in the mid-1930s. He stood up for his people until the very end, and refused to abandon them when there was nothing left to be saved. In this way Baeck arrived as a "notable" in the "paradise camp," where he spent his seventieth birthday and continued his work in the Council of Elders. Baeck's theology certainly would have given his young friend substantial impulses, because it formulated the ideas that helped H. G. Adler survive both the forced labor camp and the evil years. To what extent his faith was inspired – or confirmed or broadened – by Baeck is something I am not able to assess, yet we can hardly be too far off the mark in assuming that Baeck helped to form the Jewish character of his thought and thus helped him draw closer to Judaism. In their faith, therefore, we catch sight of their friendship's spiritual center.

---

[16] Both quotes are from the correspondence of H. G. Adler / Gertrud Adler-Klepetar, Nachlaß H. G. Adler [H. G. Adler papers], DLA Marbach. The German line translated here as "I live regarding you" is "Ich lebe Dir zu" – which could also be rendered as "I live mindful of you" or "I live toward you."

[17] Cf. Adler, *Der Wahrheit verpflichtet*, 63ff.

[18] Cf. the autobiographical novel by (Herbert) T[h]omas Mandl, *Durst, Musik, Geheime Dienste* (Munich: Boer, 1995). In Mandl's book, Adler appears as a salesman.

[19] On Leo Baeck's life and personality, cf. the biography by Albert Friedländer, *Leo Baeck: Leben und Lehre* (Stuttgart: Deutsche Verlags-Anstalt, 1973), a translation of *Leo Baeck – Teacher of Theresienstadt* (London: Routledge & Kegan Paul, 1973).

Afterword 809

Here is the confession Baeck formulated in 1905 in his book *The Essence of Judaism*: "The optimism of Judaism is *belief in the good*, i.e., belief in God and consequently *belief in man*: in God who acts as guarantor for the truly good, and in man, for whose sake the truly good is there."[20] As many a testimony has shown, belief in the unshakeable existence of the good allowed countless victims to maintain their dignity even under the most horrific circumstances. In this crucible of suffering Adler transformed Baeck's mild credo into a combative watchword, for now we find his poems asserting "the power of good in the maw of evil."

Baeck also proved a reliable pillar of support in a practical regard. When H. G. Adler was deported to Auschwitz, he left behind his papers, including the materials that constituted the beginnings of his documents on Theresienstadt, in a briefcase with Baeck. He returned them in 1945 following the liberation. Later, during the writing of his book in England, Adler discussed the problem extensively with Baeck at numerous meetings. Above all, the moral verdicts he reaches were ones that he (as Adler emphasized in the preface to the second edition) conveyed to his older friend, who (and this is something critics have not really noticed before) explicitly approved each judgment. The severe criticisms H. G. Adler makes concerning the elders of the "ghetto" were not some personal views; they were accepted by the highest authority on Theresienstadt and its ills.

In addition to engaging with Jewish thought during his imprisonment, Adler was also preoccupied with philosophy in general, especially with Nietzsche. Even in his early letters to Gertrud, abstraction offered him the means to rise above his situation. Two projects adumbrated his worldview: a utopia for the future and a dystopia for which he found a model in the intellectual and spiritual origins of the Nazi persecutions. The former was his *Experimentaltheologie*, which he started in 1938 under the sign of the coming storm, and the latter was the theory of mechanical materialism he presented after the war in two lectures written to be held at the University of Cologne and in the concluding chapter to *Theresienstadt 1941–1945*. Like the main cultural critics of modernity, he sees the cause of contemporary social disintegration and of the specific form assumed by the coerced community in the philosophical separation of mind and body that began with Plato and Descartes: he held modern thought, which first facilitated the technical mastery of nature, responsible for that destruction of human values that culminated in the camps. In his first letter to Hermann Broch he explained how Broch's *Sleepwalkers* stimulated this train of thought:

> Canetti . . . was the first to tell me about you in 1937. Reading *Sleepwalkers* divulged to me, as it were, the necessary prehistory of the cultural and general social disintegration that was bound to follow, and whose immediate witness I became in its symbolic culmination in Auschwitz. I speak with good reason here about *Sleepwalkers* not as a work of art and great novelistic composition, but only as an achievement in the history of philosophy to which (in addition to Spengler's work) I probably . . . owe the most when it comes to understanding this time and my own thoughts. It was, above all, the "disintegration of values" that, at that time, and perhaps even more so today, frankly

---

[20] Leo Baeck, *Das Wesen des Judentums* (Berlin: Nathansen & Lamm, 1905), 60. In a revised English-language translation, *The Essence of Judaism* (New York: Schocken, 1948), a similar passage reads: "The optimism of Judaism consists of the belief in God, and consequently also a belief in man, who is able to realize in himself the good which first finds its reality in God. From the optimism all the ideas of Judaism can be derived" (p. 80).

810   *Afterword*

struck me as the key to understanding National Socialism and the cultural crisis of the Occident in general.[21]

After the war he elaborated on this theory and depicted it in detail in *The Wall*. There, reverting to a suggestion made in Thomas Mann's *The Magic Mountain*, he has his hero work on a sociology of the oppressed man: the intense sociological interest that always accompanied the genre of the novel thus becomes the subject and an endeavor to achieve something positive by means of sociology. In this fictional extension of Broch's theory of the degeneration of values we discern the premise for *Theresienstadt 1941–1945*:

> The dignity of man is a material and immaterial conferment of value that is accorded and guaranteed him by society. The complete fulfillment of this dignity corresponds to the optimum of freedom from any kind of oppression. An oppressed human being is one whose internal and external values are denied or withdrawn. The stronger or more effective this withdrawal is, the more unfree the man.[22]

It is easy to imagine how H. G. Adler tested his theory on a daily basis by observing the fundamental unfreedom all around him as well as the scale of the withdrawal of values, ranging from persecution through arrest, imprisonment, and all the way to annihilation. This knowledge decisively shaped his method. Hermann Broch, whose own mother died in Theresienstadt, must have been especially affected by Adler's book. He was among the first to recognize Adler's achievement, and in a testimonial he praised *Theresienstadt 1941–1945* as "doubtlessly a standard work."

It has often been remarked that H. G. Adler's approach does not follow the usual norms of exposition. In contrast to the concept of a value-free social science, as advocated by Max Weber, Adler saw value judgments as an inherent part of the method. This apparent methodological incongruity needs to be understood as a reaction to a social and political order that strayed into such perfidious constructs as the notion of *unwertes Leben* (worthless life). In the face of such an aberration, Adler answers with a critical sensorium that demonstrates the disintegration of values step by step. In this special case, at least, the only way proper scholarship *can* proceed is by making judgments. As he says in an early draft, though, he was concerned not with setting up scholarship as a "judge of good and evil" but merely with laying "building blocks" for a sociology and psychology of the camp.[23] As surprising as that method may seem, it certainly was not naïve. The attentive reader will be reminded here and there of Max Weber, as when Adler dissects bureaucracy, or in his critique of depersonalized rationality.

After liberation on April 12, 1945, from the underground factory Langenstein-Zwieberge, a satellite camp of Buchenwald, H. G. Adler returned to Prague in June. Eighteen of his closest relatives lost their lives in the camps, including his parents, his in-laws, and his wife. Two days after his return to Prague, on June 24, 1945, he reported to Franz Steiner:

---

[21] Ronald Speirs and John White (eds.), *Zwei Schriftsteller im Exil: Briefwechsel / H.G. Adler und Hermann Broch* (Göttingen: Wallstein, 2004), 8.

[22] Adler, *Die unsichtbare Wand*, 307.

[23] "Über die Soziologie der Ghetti und Konzentrationslager," March 4, 1947, 2 Blatt, DLA Marbach.

Afterword 811

As the only member of my family and of my wife's family to do so, I survived this most horrible of dreams, to which alas my wife also fell victim. The day before yesterday I returned from G[er]many, where I went through different conc[entration] camps. I haven't changed, my principles remain the same, only more firm, more intense, and perhaps more mature. I have experienced some terrible things, but since I experienced them, it is not something I regret, and I would not do without them. Only a few remain, and of these even fewer have remained true to themselves. Ruin upon ruin. When possible I worked during those years, worked a lot. It was always at the edge, always at the extreme. I have certainly been affected to some extent, but I survived it reasonably enough, and there is no serious damage to my health.[24]

Here, already, something of H. G. Adler's nature and career is heralded. The unbroken vitality that he demonstrated in spite of his experiences and his weakness (downplayed here) alienated some of his friends, such as Steiner and Canetti, who, if they had even anticipated his survival, were expecting a broken victim in need of sympathy. The combination of grief and optimism lent his personality and his writings a special tension. It is equally hard to fathom the absence of any kind of condemnation directed against the perpetrators, especially because one encounters in its stead a complaint about a general decline. Finally there is the formulation "I would not do without it." This testifies to an inner strength, a sense of superiority toward all those who want to look away, forget, repress, or even deny – a quality that in later years turned the lonely witness into an uncomfortable contemporary. Being on sentry duty "at the edge" would always remain Adler's vantage point.

After the war H. G. Adler worked for a while as an employee in Prague's Jewish Museum, where he brought to safety thousands of documents from Theresienstadt and thereby made a major contribution to Czech historiography on the camp. He also expanded his own collection of documents, which he had started compiling in the camp and later bequeathed to Amsterdam's Instituut voor Oorlogsdocumentatie, today called the Nederlands Instituut voor Oorlogsdocumentatie. Starting in February 1947, after fleeing Czechoslovakia in anticipation of the communist seizure of power, he resumed his studies in England. By that point he was researching above all at the Wiener Library and using material from widely dispersed sources. (For the second edition he even added secret documents from the Red Cross that only later became more generally accessible.) And, thanks to an enormous workload (he sat at his desk up to eighteen hours a day), he was able to finish the first edition of his book early in 1948, barely three years after the end of the war.[25]

That early draft, written soon after his emigration to England, sheds light on the book's genesis. Adler declares that there had previously been three sorts of literature on the camps: (1) descriptions of persecution, (2) writings in which the victims were

---

[24] Correspondence H. G. Adler / Franz Baermann Steiner, Nachlaß H. G. Adler [H. G. Adler papers], DLA Marbach.

[25] On the basis of Franz Hocheneder's research, we can distinguish among four main versions of *Theresienstadt 1941–1945*: (1) the original sketch, 1947 (679 pages); (2) the first version, 1947–48 (919 pages); (3) the second version, 1955 (830 pages), published with modifications as the first edition; and (4) the second edition, 1960, for which there is a manuscript with supplemental material (180 pages) as well as a corrected makeup of the first edition. The first edition was around 770 printed pages long; this grew to around 890 pages in the second edition. Cf. Hocheneder, "H. G. Adler – Werk und Nachlaß," 453–60.

idealized and heroized, and (3) literary depictions or records taken from memory. He wants to dissociate himself from all of these:

> This is what is necessary: The internal structure, say of a ghetto, should be explained, so that an important contribution to sociology can be made. . . . The particular social system, daily life in the camp, its concrete manifestation need to be noted and explored. The question needs to be asked over and over again: what follows from, and happens by virtue of, orders and proscriptions? How does the community, and how does the individual, deal with the predicament at hand? . . . What needs to be pursued is a consideration of *how* individual events are set in motion. This is more important than just recording and ascertaining *what* happened.[26]

Adler emphasizes the wish, furthermore, not only to publish documents about the camps but also to "interpret" them and study them through a "sociology and psychology" of the camp world. A letter to Wolfgang Burghart from October 17, 1947, provides additional information:

> I am at work writing a very comprehensive book (history, sociology, psychology) on Theresienstadt, the outline of which is almost finished. Nobody has yet written a book like this on a camp. I have tackled it in a strictly sholarly way, based on the really immense trove of documents I collected. At the same time, it is readable, lively, a Kafka novel with the terms reversed, transcribed according to reality. Whoever takes the trouble to read through the roughly 1000 printed pages will really have been in the camp himself.[27]

If the atmosphere in *Theresienstadt 1941–1945* recalls *The Trial*, the structure of Adler's book is not at all like Kafka's way of writing. One is reminded more of an experimental novel of the kind Joyce produced with *Ulysses*. Adler's great success lay in meticulously covering an entire world as well as in his aesthetic interweaving of the assembled documents, all the while maintaining a cool and distanced narrative attitude. This is more reminiscent of Joyce, whom H. G. Adler was reading at that time, than of the magus of Prague. Admittedly, one should not push these parallels too far. H. G. Adler's novel-like design serves one aim exclusively – the precise depiction of historical reality.

If there was a conscious paradigm for H. G. Adler's book, it would have to be sought in Malinowski's work. Beginning with his *Argonauts of the Western Pacific* (1922), Malinowski used his (always literary) monographs to produce a differentiated picture of the Trobriand Islanders, a picture that clarified every aspect of their social life (language, economy, culture, rituals, sex life, magic, etc.) and interpreted every sphere as part of a meaningful social system. Every institution had its specific function, and every seemingly irrational belief could be interpreted according to its meaning. This functionalist outlook inspired a new school of social anthropology, which flourished in England and America well into the 1940s and was finally supplanted by an early version of structuralism around the time H. G. Adler arrived in London. Much like Malinowski, Adler achieved his insights as an exercise in ethnology and then presented his results in the tradition of social science. Because

---

[26] "Über die Soziologie der Ghetti . . . ," DLA Marbach.
[27] Correspondence H. G. Adler / Wolfgang Burghart, Nachlaß H. G. Adler [H. G. Adler papers], DLA Marbach. Reprinted in Atze, *"Ortlose Botschaft,"* 84.

history itself had been shaken to the foundations, some other form, different from anything historical scholarship might offer, was needed in order to do justice to the historical rupture. At that time "contemporary history" (*Zeitgeschichte*) had only just started to emerge as a scholarly discipline.

Although he respected Weber and Malinowski, Adler felt particularly drawn to Georg Simmel. At the time of writing, Simmel's *Sociology* met with enormous resonance in England, especially among social anthropologists. In the last year before his death, Franz Steiner gave a lecture series[28] in Oxford in which he presented the great sociologist as a German-Jewish outsider to whom he felt an elective affinity. That outsider's role was one into which H. G. Adler increasingly felt himself pushed as he worked on his book and struggled to get it published. Some aspects of Simmel sharpened Adler's vision. Various insights in Simmel's *Sociology* – such as the idea of the polarization of the masses under the influence of a ruler who demands "a definite 'Yes or No'" – were probably important for him.[29] This prefigures Hitler's tactic as mass leader, a tactic that, as demonstrated theoretically by Simmel and empirically by Adler,[30] leads to ever-greater radicalism, to an ever-faster tempo in the "development of interests" as expressed in the "Final Solution." Above all, Simmel's sociological insight into the structure of diverse interests will have enriched Adler's way of looking at things. When Adler sought to capture complicated and widely ramified actions across space and time that had led to the "Final Solution," Adler, as a historian, needed new concepts to illuminate the most troubling of all phenomena. In order to capture the hidden interplay between persons, offices, and actions in a modern totalitarian state, to apprehend a crime committed by so many people at such different locations – whether at a desk or in a concentration camp – neither a chronology nor historical scholarship proved entirely adequate to the task. The process really demanded sociological clarification. The entire manner in which a forensic line of argument is employed in *Theresienstadt 1941–1945* – to guide the reader effortlessly, as it were, from documentation to analysis, from statistics to their interpretation, and from main text to commentary – betrays a perspective that, although seeking to come to terms with a historical cataclysm, manages to remain cool, aloof, and sociological.[31]

---

[28] Reprinted in Franz Baermann Steiner, *Selected Writings. Vol. 2, Orientpolitik, Value and Civilisation* (Oxford, New York: Berghahn, 1999). There is a German version in F. B. Steiner, *Zivilisation und Gefahr, Wissenschaftliche Schriften*, ed. Jeremy Adler and Richard Fardon (Göttingen: Wallstein Verlag, 2008).

[29] Georg Simmel, *Soziologie*, 3rd ed. (Munich and Leipzig: Duncker & Humblot, 1923), 74. English translation: Georg Simmel, *Sociology: Inquiries into the Construction of Social Forms*, trans. and ed. Anthony J. Blasi, Anton K. Jacobs, and Mathew Kanjirathinkal (Leiden, Boston: Brill, 2009), Vol. 1, 99.

[30] Cf. also H. G. Adler, "Hitler als Persönlichkeit," in Gert Buchheit (ed.), *Der Führer ins Nichts* (Rastatt, Baden: Grote, 1960), 79.

[31] Wolfgang Sofsky has picked up on this sociological way of viewing things. Cf. *Die Ordnung des Terrors: Das Konzentrationslager* (Frankfurt a.M.: S. Fischer, 1993). This outlook remains fruitful even in the most recent attempt to understand the interplay of forces at work in implementing the "Final Solution" as a network; see Wolfgang Siebel and Jörg Raab, "Verfolgungsnetzwerke," *Kölner Zeitschrift für Soziologie und Sozialpsychologie* 55 (2003): 197–228. Especially prominent is the echo reverberating from the theses of Zygmunt Bauman, who literally repeats the central argument of *Theresienstadt 1941–1945*, beginning with the basic idea that the lessons of the catastrophe should be absorbed into sociology and continuing through to the conclusion that the "Final Solution" should

Adler's adoption of the sociological method coincided in some ways with the efforts of Hermann Broch, who devoted himself during the war to the study of the theory of mass hysteria, as well as with the interests of his friends Canetti and Steiner, who had taken up the study of the masses and of slavery. Their work constitutes the intellectual context of Adler's ideas in the years immediately following the war. For a short, fruitful period between 1947 and 1952, these three formed a group[32] that, because of the nature of the times, refrained from the pursuit of literary ambitions and instead turned to investigation of the Jewish tragedy. The projects undertaken by the three friends were to a certain extent complementary and often reflected one another's ideas, as can be seen in Adler's synopsis for his publisher. Out of the public view, working in complete isolation, barely noticed by the literary establishment and therefore by prior researchers, this troika was among the most interesting groups in midcentury German literature. Although his two friends were able to work in freedom, it was, surprisingly, the former prisoner who was the first to finish his work, and also the first to be published and reviewed. This must have posed a challenge to the others. The interconnectedness of their thinking can be gauged from Steiner's original definition of a slave, based on Simmel's: a person living outside the social unit, cut off from his relatives, who is not himself able to take advantage of the rights that are wielded against him.

This definition reflects Adler's own experience and is, in turn, transformed by Canetti (though without listing the source) into the metaphorical language used in his *Crowds and Power*.[33] Yet each of the friends remained a loner; the differences are apparent. Whereas for Canetti, the masses – as a human, even biological, constant – expanded to become an ever more universal phenomenon, for H. G. Adler they remained a modern evil, the material correlate to ideology, which it was important to defeat. The provocative title of Adler's 1958 lecture, which takes up the central ideas from *Theresienstadt 1941–1945*, illustrates this point of view.[34] Whereas some émigrés, like Canetti, felt themselves forced to abandon certain of their values in light of the catastrophe, it was in fact the former camp prisoner who, precisely because of his sufferings, held fast to the humanism of the Jewish enlightenment. Thus the works that emerged from this group were all very different, each taking its own approach.

The way that H. G. Adler structured his book in 1947, dividing it into *history*, *sociology*, and *psychology*, is fundamental to his method. After the book was published, he described his decision as follows:

---

be conceived as a distinguishing feature of modernity, especially of modern administration; cf. *Modernity and the Holocaust* (Ithaca, NY: Cornell University Press, 1989), passim.

[32] On Franz Baermann Steiner and Elias Canetti, cf. Jeremy Adler, "Die Freundschaft zwischen Franz Baermann Steiner und Elias Canetti," *Akzente* 3 (June 1995): 228–31; on H. G. Adler and Canetti, see Helmut Göbel, "Eine lange und schwierige Freundschaft. H. G. Adler und Elias Canetti," in *H. G. Adler, text + kritik* (Sonderband, 2004), 71–85. On the group, see Atze, *"Ortlose Botschaft"*; Sven Hanuschek, *Elias Canetti: Biographie* (Munich: C. Hanser, 2005), 398; and finally Helmut Göbel, *Elias Canetti* (Reinbek: Rowohlt, 2005), 107ff.

[33] Canetti's definition of the slave pushes Steiner's structural definition into the realm of the mystical. This opens up an interesting perspective on Canetti's dependence on Steiner and the latter's early anthropology. Cf. Elias Canetti, *Masse und Macht* (Hamburg: Claassen, 1960), 440ff.

[34] Cf. H. G. Adler, "Mensch oder Masse?," in *Die Freiheit des Menschen: Aufsätze zur Soziologie und Geschichte* (Tübingen: Mohr, 1976), 1–85.

Afterword

> The arrangement of my writings informally suggested a division of the book into a historical, sociological, and psychological section. The more I became engaged with my papers and read the burgeoning literature on the camps and other important writings, while also becoming acquainted with other supplemental or otherwise important material, the more I realized that merely witnessing what happened or producing a personal account, no matter how much it might be reinforced by documentation, would not do justice to my subject. In lengthy reflections, I was driven to study a constantly expanding set of concerns. . . .[35]

This triad divides reality into three parts and presents three topics for discussion: the diachronic sequence, the synchronic structure, and the decisive *mentalité*. What Adler has in mind in terms of psychology is not so much psychoanalysis as the German anthropological tradition, in that his concept captures both elements of individual psychology and causes connected to intellectual history that led into the abyss. The intention to treat *three* levels of reality simultaneously is a way of sorting out the aporia expressed by the contradiction between the individual and history, as Tolstoy had attempted in *War and Peace*. Where are guilt and responsibility to be found: in the individual or in the system? On the one hand, Adler the sociologist recognizes the power of functional aspects,[36] such as the absurd bureaucracy of Theresienstadt. On the other hand, he reveals the psychological drive behind each individual decision: hence the forensic analysis of the character, convictions, and exact motivations of the participants. Differentiating between the structure of an institution, such as an administration that follows its own laws, and the operative ideology or psychology of the actors makes it possible to draw a basic distinction between the process, which proceeds almost independently, and the perpetrator. It is therefore in a person's deeds, no matter how heavily entangled that person might be in the web of the apparatus, that one recognizes either responsibility, just behavior, or guilt. Adler's masterful way of capturing individual figures, starting with Hitler himself, as well as his skillful grasp of "mechanical materialism" in general, exposes the mechanisms of power and rule in the National Socialist state, a historically unique state founded on the will of the people and its leader yet utterly criminal. The worse the offenses it committed, the greater the legitimacy it gained among its adherents. This, then, was the antireligion of annihilation disguised as politics. By exposing the conflict between humanism and technology, between human rights and totalitarianism, the author's discussion of the particular case of Theresienstadt also went to the heart of the multifaceted sociopolitical discussion that took place in West Germany in the 1950s – starting in 1949 with President Theodor Heuss's reflections on the role of memory in the Federal Republic and culminating in 1962 with Jürgen Habermas's critique of West Germany's political legitimacy. Thus, when his book came out, the lonely witness and author in exile suddenly found himself at the center of an explosive and highly topical debate.

The path from the first version to publication took seven years. Anyone who is interested in this story can look it up in *Die unsichtbare Wand*, in which H. G. Adler

---

[35] Adler, *Der Wahrheit verpflichtet*, 113ff.

[36] Hans Mommsen recognized the extent to which H. G. Adler anticipated the functionalist construction of the "Final Solution," although he refuted the notion of a wholly unplanned, cumulative radicalization of events, which is why he probably did not insist any further on this antecedence. Cf. Berg, *Der Holocaust und die westdeutschen Historiker*, 627, n44.

satirically recounts the difficulties of conveying his message. It is hard to imagine this problem today, given the international interest in the Shoah; yet at the time, no backers with sufficient influence could be found in either England or America, where Adler initially hoped to publish *Theresienstadt 1941–1945* in English. In the United States, initial attempts by Hermann Broch and Hannah Arendt to find a publisher failed, although it was thought that Einstein himself might be mobilized for the cause; even in the early 1950s, Franz Kobler was unable to make any headway there. In England, too, nobody apart from a few friends and public figures really took an interest in a serious, comprehensive publication. England's most important Jewish historian at the time, Cecil Roth, made disparaging remarks about the idea of writing a hefty book on Theresienstadt, because the camp had only a "tiny" place in the history of the Jews.[37]

Time passed, and the author, by then completely dissatisfied with the latest version of his book, took up the manuscript once more, beginning a rewritten version in early 1954. Two months later, he found a publisher in Germany with the courage to take the risk. On May 2, 1954, H. G. Adler sent his outline to Hans-Georg Siebeck, of the publishing house J. C. B. Mohr (Paul Siebeck). Before the war, this publisher had represented mostly Jewish authors; it shrunk considerably when its director Oskar Siebeck took his life in 1936, probably following unsuccessful negotiations with the Reichsschriftumskammer (the Nazi-era Reich Chamber of Literature).[38] In the 1950s, his son reestablished its list, with the help of influential friends such as Theodor Heuss, a student of Max Weber. Siebeck showed interest in Adler's book as early as June 6, although he noted that Kogon's *Der SS-Staat* (later published in English as *The Theory of Practice of Hell*) had already reached a broad reading public, with circulation in the five figures, which might have impaired the prospects for a second book about the camps. Adler answered promptly on June 10, giving advance notice of his manuscript and a list of revisions. The letter captures Adler's agenda at the time:

(1) Th. is different from all the coerced camps of the SS period, as it is from all other systems of oppression. Here, by order of the SS, the pretense of a quasi-"normal" community was maintained, which lent the camp – object-ively in its institutions and subjectively in the behavior of the inmates – certain (otherwise strange and heretofore never described) fantastically eerie features that are more reminiscent of a world based on Kafka's fantasies than on any actual social system. Thus, ipso facto, history and sociology acquire features from Th. that are novelistic and gripping, such as nobody describing any other camps could possibly offer.

(2) No book, not even a Polish one, offers so much documentary material from the internal operation of a camp. Thus the reader shares in the experience of everyday life in the camp and its history. The kind of life lived here and its consequences are interpreted and categorized as part of an overall

---

[37] How little sympathy Cecil Roth was able to summon up for the most recent sorrows of his people is revealed by his view that death by hunger or poison gas in Auschwitz constituted a "happy release" from even greater suffering. Cf. Cecil Roth, *A History of the Jews* (New York: Schocken, 1970), 399.

[38] For details on the book's publication history I am grateful to the publisher, Georg Siebeck. Cf. Ernst Klett, "'Einen der würdigsten Verlage, die wir haben . . . ,' zum Tod von Dr. h.c. Hans-Georg Siebeck" ["One of the Worthiest Publishing Houses We Have . . ." on the Death of Dr. h.c. Hans-Georg Siebeck], *Börsenblatt* 7 (January 25, 1991).

Afterword

understanding of human sociality such that a contribution to a general social anthropology smoothly emerges.

(3) The ms is, so far as I am able to assess this, the first attempt at a pan-synoptic depiction of a camp that paradigmatically describes the condition of humankind in the era of "mass" society. Thus, the book is not just important for researchers of National Socialism, the coerced camps, and antisemitism, but also more generally for the humanities in almost all fields, as in e.g. history, sociology, psychology, jurisprudence, medicine (including psychiatry), pedagogy, and even linguistics, and for anthropologists as well.

(4) The ms exposes for the first time the function of the Th. camp in the SS plan for the extermination of the Jews; in the process, this plan, including its history, becomes evident.

(5) There is no complete depiction of the Th. camp in any language; not even its history has been dealt with in German.

(6) For the first time to my knowledge, the ms contains a comprehensive glossary of camp language, with approx. 650 entries explained.

(7) The ms is the first camp book to offer a comprehensive bibliography of sources and literature (approx. 235 entries) with explanatory notes. The sources used in the work itself are never adopted blindly, but are critically researched, carefully evaluated, and examined for credibility.[39]

His objective is clear – even such details as medical findings were confirmed by subsequent research, and only the index of words (a constant source of pride to Adler) never entirely achieved the impact for which he had hoped. Siebeck replied on June 30, before he had even finished reading the manuscript, offering some concrete suggestions: "[My] first impression is already such that I no longer wish to have you wait any longer for a reply. I would be pleased to have the opportunity to supervise publication of your work."[40]

Rarely has such an ambitious work been accepted so quickly. One can imagine how happy the author was, even if he may have stumbled over the word "supervise" (*betreuen*), one of the Nazi terms he pilloried in his glossary. Siebeck immediately addressed questions of cost, price, percentages, and the allowance needed for printing costs. Adler, the outsider, had been taken on by the publisher of Max Weber, a publisher that shared the author's theological orientation. There remained only the question of a subsidy. Here Adler had a determined advocate in Theodor W. Adorno. They had already been corresponding for several years, because Adler had coincidentally reviewed the original German edition of Adorno's *Philosophy of New Music*, also published by Siebeck, for the BBC; although the two had not become more closely acquainted, Adler believed he could use the philosopher as a reference. This was confirmed on April 25, 1955, when Adorno gave the project his "enthusiastic" endorsement.[41] Adorno probably referred to an earlier edition of the text, which can be found today as a sketch in Adler's collected works. This secured him a huge subsidy of 8,500 Deutsche marks from the Bundeszentrale für Heimatdienst in

---

[39] Correspondence H. G. Adler / Hans-Georg Siebeck, Nachlaß H. G. Adler [H. G. Adler papers], DLA Marbach.

[40] Ibid.

[41] Correspondence H. G. Adler / Th. W. Adorno, Nachlaß H. G. Adler [H. G. Adler papers], DLA Marbach.

818   *Afterword*

Bonn and thus guaranteed publication. Adorno's short, moving appreciation is among the best testimonies we have to H. G. Adler himself.[42] Subsequently, though, the relationship became polarized.[43] Here is a quote from Adorno's sensitive appreciation.

> What impresses me most about Adler is the strength with which he wrought his work about Theresienstadt from conditions that seemed to make it absolutely impossible. It is beyond imagination that a tender and sensitive human being could remain in command of himself intellectually and be capable of objectivity in this organized hell whose stated purpose was the destruction of the self, even before physical extermination. Such strength is extremely different from the crudely vital kind, from the coarse will to survive. Maybe it even presupposes tenderness, which it is superficially believed is most likely to succumb – a sensorium that finds brutality and injustice so unbearable that it senses a duty, even in extremis where nothing more can be changed, at least to preserve memory, to speak the unspeakable, and thus to keep faith with the victims. But something in Adler might also have turned that Jewish-fraternal spirit of contradiction into a form of reaction that refuses to accept the inevitable, and that draws from this refusal the ability not merely to evade, but also to testify to that which, absent such a spirit of contradiction, would totally triumph. For Adler, the constellation of the tender and the resistant became a moral agent, a Kantian "categorical imperative," and for this we owe him not only the gratitude of these for whom he has written by proxy, but also the unspoiled admiration of those who cannot match him therein.

H. G. Adler and Adorno made an effort to establish a friendship, but these attempts ultimately foundered – like Adler's relationship with Canetti – due to the conflict between a thinker who had experienced Auschwitz himself and one who attempted to follow and reflect on the experience of the extermination camp from a distance.

The printing of *Theresienstadt 1941–1945* was completed on October 28, and on November 8, 1955, the author received the first copy in London. The public impact was astonishing. There was a flood of reviews in Germany, Austria, Switzerland, France, England, and the United States. Numerous public figures approached H. G. Adler personally to continue the conversation in private. In Germany, President Heuss wrote to the publisher[44] and received the author as a guest,[45] and in Israel Martin Buber and Gershom Scholem read the book and sought out Adler in London. Historians such as Karl Dietrich Bracher, sociologists such as René König, and writers such as Heinrich Böll and Heimito von Doderer[46] were among his earliest readers. The highest accolades came from an historian who praised the book as "the

[42] Theodor W. Adorno, *Gesammelte Schriften,* ed. Rolf Tiedemann, vol. 20.2, *Vermischte Schriften* II (Frankfurt a. M.: Suhrkamp, 1986), 495.

[43] Cf. Jeremy Adler, "'Die Macht des Guten im Rachen des Bösen.' H. G. Adler, Theodor Adorno und die Darstellung der Schoah," *Merkur* **614** (2000): 475–86.

[44] Heuss welcomed the book, which would prove "uncomfortable" for many Germans preferring to "look away." Cf. Theodor Heuss, letter to H.-G. Siebeck, November 15, 1955, archive, Mohr Siebeck, Tübingen.

[45] Theodor Heuss, *Tagebuchbriefe* (Tübingen: R. Wunderlich, 1970), 161 ff.

[46] Correspondence H. G. Adler / Heimito von Doderer, DLA Marbach. The main topic of the personal conversations between Doderer and Adler during the initial years of their acquaintanceship was not literature but, rather, problems of history writing.

most important personal achievement in the historiography of the Second World War."[47] One can gauge the political impact from an opinion by Germany's Constitutional Court. While reviewing West Germany's laws on reparations, restitution, and indemnification, the judges read Adler's work. Although a book cannot be used as evidence in court, the judges recognized *Theresienstadt 1941–1945* as proof that the "Final Solution" had in fact taken place. Based on this finding, it became possible to pass the laws on compensation[48] – from which, ironically, Adler himself, as a former resident of Prague, never benefited. The most bizarre testimony to the veracity of his book came from a perpetrator. While Adolf Eichmann was in jail in Israel, he received a copy of *Theresienstadt 1941–1945* from the authorities and read it before the trial in order to recollect details from his past.[49]

The foundation on which *Theresienstadt 1941–1945* rests, and without which both Adler's interpretation and his sociological analysis would not have achieved their characteristic ethical objectivity, is composed of facts and documents, data and statistics, the number and exact representation of which ensured the book's role as a reference work from the moment it appeared in print. Every historical detail available to the author, every twist and turn and contingency, every decision and order, along with the character of each actor, appears in coherent sequence. Yet a glance at the table of contents is enough to make clear the extent to which an encyclopedic order underlies all of this data; this order is necessary to lend the miniature universe of the ghetto and the confusing events of the period a meaningful shape that does justice to history. It is the facts that permit a truthful presentation of the entire story, and it is the coherence of their presentation that renders the empirical facts conclusive. Thus it comes as no surprise that *Theresienstadt 1941–1945* has found a place in the bibliographies of the published memoirs of some camp inmates,[50] or that the editors of these memoirs have used the book to fill the gaps in former prisoners' memories.[51] The data and statistics serve as evidence for individual case studies and broader overviews, whether the text is approached with deference or critically;[52] often Adler's own formulations have attained the status of objective fact.

The author's objective tone, however, consistently metamorphoses into figurative images: the ghetto presented a "ghastly carnival"; in the same place, a "sea of guilt" emerged; and only rarely was the situation there recognized in a "lightning moment of truth." In this way, the historical setting of the ghetto was reflected in language of a kind that Karl Kraus would understand – ethically harsh and truthful, yet also artistic. That H. G. Adler was inspired by an ethos along the lines of Karl Kraus's

---

[47] Louis de Jong to H. G. Adler, August 20, 1963, in Eckart and Unger, *H. G. Adler, Buch der Freunde*, 64ff.

[48] This was what one Constitutional Court judge communicated to H. G. Adler.

[49] Cf. Atze, "Ortlose Botschaft," 149.

[50] Cf., e.g., Ruth Herskovits-Gutmann, *Auswanderung vorläufig nicht möglich: Die Geschichte der Familie Herskovits aus Hannover* (Göttingen: Wallstein-Verlag, 2002).

[51] Cf. Norbert Troller, *Theresienstadt: Hitler's Gift to the Jews*, trans. Susan E. Cernyak-Spatz, ed. Joel Shatzky (Chapel Hill & London: University of North Carolina Press, 1991), xxiiiff., 161, 164, 165, 167, 169, 170, 171ff.

[52] Cf., e.g., George E. Berkley, *Hitler's Gift: The Story of Theresienstadt* (Boston: Branden Books, 1993). In spite of the objections Berkley pulls out of thin air in his afterword, in the main body of the book he frequently relies quite literally on Adler and does not even shy away from implicitly adopting Adler's data and views.

820   *Afterword*

critique of language is, as it happens, illustrated by the opening sentences of the 1955 introduction.

An aspect of H. G. Adler's objectivity is, not least, his lack of partisanship. All his life, he kept his distance from any political group or sense of nationalism; he liked to say that he was affiliated only with the "party of humanity." A letter to his friend Franz Kobler on September 22, 1955 (that is, shortly before the book was published) reveals that he clearly understood the difficulties of his position: "[My] book will be damned hard to swallow in many respects for Germans as well as for Jews and other readers."[53]

Although the National Socialists treated the Jews as a single "mass," the Jews by no means formed a homogenous group. An ancient author like Josephus might attempt, in his history of the Jewish Wars, to do justice to "both sides," Jews as well as Romans. Yet as a modern researcher, H. G. Adler was dealing with a much more complex society, precisely because it was modern; indeed, it possessed a wealth of contending identities that were, among other things, what made this ghetto distinctive. He therefore refused to separate this coherent yet internally segmented coerced community into two groups – victims and perpetrators, Jews and Germans. He never subordinated himself to an ideology or advocated the standpoint of a particular interest group, be it a religion, a party, or a nation – not even his own. For the members of these groups, this was not always easy to accept, especially because no party or institution escapes criticism in *Theresienstadt 1941–1945*. No group seems to have sacrificed itself completely for the community; none seems to have done enough for the common good. The Council of Elders, the self-administration, Jews, Zionists, Communists, Czechs, Germans – every institution, every party, every nationality saddled itself with guilt in various ways as time went on, and thus these very diverse, overlapping groups ultimately formed one big "community of guilt." It is understandable that the deeply distressing findings leading to this conclusion created a stir and some indignation when the book was first published. Fifty years later, even after the Auschwitz trial, its truth has lost none of its harshness. It goes without saying, however, that Adler's assessments do not erase the differences between victims and perpetrators, as happened in some places in the reception of his work and which, unfortunately, has been all too common in Germany more recently. What he describes is the failure of humanity, of goodness, of simple decency. In analyzing the Shoah, many have blamed the collapse of Enlightenment values or have even seen, in the rise of the Third Reich, proof of the failure of the Enlightenment and of humanism itself. But the problem, as framed by Adler, is much simpler. It has to do with the Ten Commandments, with ethics, with the simple norms of human existence that were so massively violated. This nuanced understanding of groups requires a similar treatment of individuals, and here, too, his moral judgments are strict. This anti-heroizing attitude, as it can perhaps be called, is warranted in service to the truth, because it is only through the admittedly painful exposure of human frailties and the tragic failures of real people under the pressure of a merciless apparatus of power that one can comprehend the full extent of the Jewish tragedy in the Third Reich.

[53] Correspondence H. G. Adler / Franz Kobler, Nachlaß H. G. Adler [H. G. Adler papers], DLA Marbach. Reprinted in Atze, *"Ortlose Botschaft,"* 140.

Afterword

Some of the controversies that were aroused after the publication of *Theresienstadt 1941–1945* have lost little of their virulence among specialists. Although the book does offer a complete overview, one should not expect any account to be exhaustive. On its own, Theresienstadt's diverse cultural life provides enough material for monographs – for example, on music in the camps, of which we already have an example.[54] A complete overview would mention, among other things, the great Czech writer and journalist Karel Poláček, and would also point out how the French surrealist Robert Desnos spent his final days in Theresienstadt. One would also have to reconstruct the contents of the Theresienstadt lectures, which have recently been cataloged.[55] There are also more recent findings that could not yet be evaluated in this book, in particular works like the diary of Egon Redlich[56] or other private documents such as those of Martha Glass.[57] Additional individual treatments – monographs that use illuminating cases to illustrate aspects of life in the ghetto – are also emerging today.[58] Yet even single case studies like these can barely exhaust or tap all the material. Yet, we should guard against becoming overwhelmed by the flood of facts. In the preface to the second edition, H. G. Adler foresaw that other sources would become available, but he warned about their one-sidedness. He had already been able to view much of the material that would become more generally available only much later – for example, the files of the International Red Cross – before writing the second edition.

Apart from these kinds of topics and details, including facts generally subject to verification, it was above all Adler's value judgments that gave rise to discussion. As far as I am able to judge, criticism has been directed against three main points: his assessment of certain individuals, his depiction of specific institutions such as the camp's self-administration, and his treatment of some groups. The reason lies partly in his aforementioned method of calling to account both Germans and Jews, perpetrators and victims. *Theresienstadt 1941–1945* strives for a nuanced depiction of moral failure, so as to disclose the devastating consequences of individual errors, whatever they might be, for the community as a whole. Various researchers have tried, always without indicating their actual interest in the matter, to refute some of Adler's views – sometimes soberly and sometimes by quite grotesquely distorting his

---

[54] Joza Karas, *Music in Terezín 1941–1945* (New York: Beaufort Books, 1985).

[55] Elena Makarova, Sergei Makarov, and Victor Kuperman (eds.), *University over the Abyss: The Story Behind 489 Lecturers and 2309 Lectures in KZ Thesesienstadt 1942–1944* (Munich: Saur, 2000; 2nd ed., Jerusalem: Verba, 2004).

[56] Czech [and German]: Egon Redlikh, *Zítra jedeme, synu, pojedeme transportem: deník Egona Redlicha z Terezína, 1.1.1942–22.10.1944* [Egon Redlich, "*Morgen, mein Sohn, fahren wir mit dem Transport.*" *Das Tagebuch von Egon Redlich aus Theresienstadt 1.1.1942–22.10.1944*], ed. Miroslav Kryl (Brno: Ústav pro soudobé dějiny AV ČR, Doplněk [Institute of Contemporary History at the Academy of Sciences, Supplement], 1995). English: Egon Redlich, *The Terezín Diary of Gonda Redlich*, ed. Saul S. Friedman, trans. Laurence Kutler, foreword by Nora Levin (Lexington: University Press of Kentucky, 1992).

[57] Martha Glass, "*Jeder Tag in Theresin ist ein Geschenk.*" *Die Theresienstädter Tagebücher einer Hamburger Jüdin 1943–1945*, ed. Barbara Müller-Wesemann [Landeszentrale für politische Bildung] (Hamburg: Ergebnisse, 1996).

[58] Cf., e.g., Miriam Intrator, "The Theresienstadt Ghetto Central Library, Books and Reading: Intellectual Resistance and Escape during the Holocaust," *Leo Baeck Institute Yearbook* 50, no. 1 (2005): 3–28; Miriam Intrator, "Storytelling and Lecturing during the Holocaust: The Nature and Role of Oral Exchanges in Theresienstadt, 1941–1945," *Leo Baeck Institute Yearbook* 50, no. 1 (2006): 209–233.

position and indulging in personal attacks. This is not the place to go into this criticism in detail, but what should be mentioned is the extent to which the preface to the second edition – usually neglected in the debates about Adler's book – strove to respond to these kinds of charges.

Here I should like to introduce two points from the preface. The first concerns the criticism H. G. Adler levels against individuals:

> By the time the first inmates arrived in Theresienstadt it was clear that this tragedy was already unfolding and could no longer be averted; it was inescapable. I never, however, assailed our martyred heroes – who were robbed of almost any free will – for their doomed fate. *I only critiqued those at the head of this inmate community for acts that exceeded the orders they were forced to carry out.* [emphasis added – J.A.].

What Adler criticizes rests within the narrow confines of whatever free will still existed in this coerced situation and is not aimed at the totality of the individual.

The second point applies to the disclosure of unpleasant truths: "Keeping guilt hidden exacerbates it and has a corroding effect, but revealing and investigating guilt has a cleansing effect and promotes the inscrutable mysterious workings of grace, which stir up the healing powers of the conscience and which cleanse the conscience of guilt." A sober depiction of what happened is meant to break the chain of guilt, to lead to purification. Adler is thinking here of a religious process; as in ancient tragedy, this is about catharsis.

After 1989 it was to be expected that intellectual horizons would broaden, since nothing now stood in the way of international cooperation in researching the ghettos located on former Communist territory. Yet, in the interim, a large number of new studies have appeared, and more material is constantly becoming accessible, the book itself continues to be regarded, even among its critics, as the point of departure for any consideration of Theresienstadt.[59]

H. G. Adler's book had a decisive impact on the development of scholarly research about the Shoah. This can be briefly substantiated on the basis of two examples. For one thing, the book has influenced the way monographs analyzed individual camps: Isaiah Trunk's authoritative study *Lodzsher geto*[60] mentions Adler's monograph as an example in the first sentence, and Trunk then follows Adler in the systematic composition of his own book, his citation of sources, his use of statistics, and more. *Theresienstadt 1941–1945* thus provides a model for individual studies in the future. For another thing, however, H. G. Adler's book created the decisive model for the manner in which one should explore the Final Solution as a phenomenon. For this, it is above all Raul Hilberg's *The Destruction of the European Jews*[61] that serves as an example. Hilberg's book is justifiably appraised as a turning point in the historiog-

---

[59] Miroslav Kárný, "Ergebnisse und Aufgaben der Theresienstädter Historiographie," in Miroslav Kárný, Vojtěch Blodig, and Margita Kárná (eds.), *Theresienstadt in der "Endlösung der Judenfrage,"* Edition Theresienstädter Initiative (Prague: Panorama, 1992), 150–55, 26. The revisions that Kárný explicitly proposes amount to a rehabilitation of individual persons or to a retrieval of honor for certain groups; cf. 26–27.

[60] Isaiah Trunk, *Lodzsher geto* (New York, Jerusalem: YIVO, 1962). English translation: *Łódź Ghetto: A History*, trans. and ed. Robert Moses Shapiro (Bloomington: Indiana University Press in association with the United States Holocaust Memorial Museum, 2006).

[61] Raul Hilberg, *The Destruction of the European Jews* (Chicago: Quadrangle, 1961).

Afterword

raphy of the persecution of the Jews.[62] But this should not obscure the extent to which many of Hilberg's putative achievements actually go back to H. G. Adler: the evidence about the connection between propaganda and politics, about the systematic murder of the Jews, about the function of administration ("bureaucracy," for Hilberg), and especially about the role of the Jewish Elders in the policy of extermination and, by implication, the problematic position of some Jews entangled in the tragic events. Here we see a direct line running from *Theresienstadt 1941–1945*, by way of Hilberg's *The Destruction of the European Jews*, to the controversial theses of Hannah Arendt. Hence, both the method and the point of view that H. G. Adler develops in *Theresienstadt 1941–1945* had an impact reaching far beyond the specialized literature on the Theresienstadt ghetto, in that they contributed to the establishment of a new field, the melancholy scholarship of the Shoah.

Considering how the book was generally received in the scholarly debate, one notices, in addition to the laudatory appreciations, a tendency that runs counter to the partisan critiques. This tendency – the tendency to oversimplify or even misconstrue uncomfortable truths – skews Adler's insights into something negative. Here the controversy surrounding Hannah Arendt's *Eichmann in Jerusalem* (1960) may serve as an example. After Eichmann's arrest, the Israeli government brought in H. G. Adler as an expert. He provided the prosecution with information proving Eichmann's role in the "Final Solution" and listed questions that should be posed in the interrogation or trial. The consultations remained secret, and Adler did not appear at the trial. His request for permission to interview Eichmann personally to clarify certain details that did not further incriminate Eichmann – about the structure of particular SS offices and command procedures that only Eichmann himself could have explained – was refused without explanation. When Arendt's reportage appeared, it banalized the nuanced analysis in *Theresienstadt 1941–1945* in order to corroborate her view that no essential difference existed between the guilt of the German perpetrators and the entanglements of their Jewish victims. Without knowing about Adler's participation or even about the legal situation, she went on to claim, wrongly, that, in order to conceal this, Adler's book had been suppressed at the trial. Adler preferred not to contradict her publicly, especially because he did not wish to intervene against an American publication; but he worked energetically behind the scenes, supplying Jacob Robinson with material for his thorough refutation of Arendt's theses.[63] But once Arendt's book was translated into German, and when Gershom Scholem referred to Adler's book in an open letter to Arendt in order to refute her,[64] H. G. Adler finally spoke out.[65] His message had acquired a life of its own that had nothing in common with his convictions. Even in more recent literature, this message – sometimes accurately captured and sometimes

---

[62] Tom Lawson, review of *The Destruction of the European Jews* (review no. 394), http://www.history .ac.uk/reviews/review/394.

[63] Jacob Robinson, *And the Crooked Shall Be Made Straight* (New York: Macmillan, 1965). Even today, Robinson's book is worthy of attention in the debate about Arendt.

[64] Gershom Scholem, *Neue Zürcher Zeitung*, October 20, 1963. Reprinted in Gershom Scholem, *Briefe*, 2 vols. (Munich: C. H. Beck, 1994–95), Vol. 2, 95–100.

[65] H. G. Adler, "Was weiß Hannah Arendt von der 'Endlösung'?," *Allgemeine Wochenzeitung der Juden*, November 20, 1964.

misunderstood – has found significant expression.[66] Peter Weiss, for example, tacitly adopted some of Adler's central insights in *The Investigation* and turned them into the focal point of his theses, by simplifying and sensationalizing Adler's nuanced analysis and subjecting it to a Marxist interpretation. In the play, the famous passage in which everyone involved is part of the "system" would not have been possible without *Theresienstadt 1941–1945*, as many verbal similarities make clear. Günter Kunert, by contrast, paid homage to Adler's book as a model for the end of the world. In the case of W. G. Sebald's novel *Austerlitz*, however, H. G. Adler is personally stylized into a mythic cult figure who provides the key to the persecution of the Jews.

Theresienstadt 1941–1945 constitutes the focal point of Adler's work, around which the rest of his oeuvre is grouped like a crystal. *Die verheimlichte Wahrheit: Theresienstadter Dokumente* (*The Hidden Truth: Theresienstadt Documents*; 1958) was conceived as part two of the book; *Der verwaltete Mensch: Studien zur Deportation der Juden aus Deutschland* (*Administrated Man: Studies on the Deportation of the Jews from Germany*; 1974) broadened the portrayal to include the perpetrators, in order to depict the entire process of deportation; *Die Freiheit des Menschen: Aufsatze zur Soziologie and Geschichte* (*On Human Freedom: Sociological and Historical Essays*; 1976) interprets such key categories of his analysis as society, freedom, and the masses. The novels, by contrast, trace a personal pathway and provide a private, interior view: *Eine Reise* (1962) depicts deportation, Theresienstadt, Auschwitz, and liberation, with the death camps experienced from Gertrud's perspective, and *Panorama* (1968) describes the work camp, Auschwitz, and exile, whereas *Die unsichtbare Wand* (1989) looks back in freedom at the catastrophe. Only through the totality of his forms of expression, the literary as well as the scholarly, could H. G. Adler perform his task as witness.

He could not escape the memory of the camps. From a practical point of view, it was not the writer's ambition but the far-reaching success of *Theresienstadt 1941–1945* that would shape Adler's future career. At first he hoped to publish an abridged popular version of the book, but J. C. B. Mohr, as a scholarly publisher, was not well suited for this plan, so what remained was the second, corrected 1960 edition, which brought the author greater prestige but no popular success. He was also unable to consolidate his position as a German professor might have – he did not seize the opportunity to apply for a professorship in Germany, because he did not want to live there, or in any country that Hitler had ruled. Yet as a private scholar in London, he participated in the creation of a new field of scholarship, the study of the Shoah. His Theresienstadt book was soon reviewed by colleagues such as Harry Pross and Eugen Kogon, Robert Weltsch and Hans-Joachim Schoepps; soon after,

---

[66] Starting with Franz Steiner's lyrical meditation on Jewish destiny, "Gebet im Garten" ("Prayer in the Garden"; 1947), Adler posed a challenge to poets and writers: echoes and quotes may be found in dramas such as Fritz Hochwälder's *Holokaust* (1960) and Peter Weiss's *Die Ermittlung* (*The Investigation*; 1966), in novels such as Robert Schindel's *Gebürtig* (1992; English translation: *Born Where*, 1995) and W. G. Sebald's *Austerlitz* (2003), and in short prose works and lyric poetry such as the verse of Günter Kunert (1972) and Heimrad Becker (1993). Cf. Marcel Atze, "'Wie Adler berichtet': Das Werk H. G. Adlers als Gedächtnisspeicher für die Literatur," *Text+Kritik* 163 (2004): 17–30; Judith Beniston, "Fritz Hochwälders *Holokaust*: A Choice of Evils," *Austrian Studies* II (2003): 65–84; Günter Kunert, *Tagträume in Berlin und andernorts: Kleine Prosa, Erzählungen, Aufsätze* (Munich: C. Hanser, 1972), 187ff.

Afterword

the next generation (Gerald Reitlinger and Raul Hilberg come to mind) began to adopt his theses. He developed an especially productive relationship with Hermann Langbein, the Auschwitz resistance fighter, who became one of the most important historians of Auschwitz in the 1960s. In 1962, one year before the Auschwitz trial, H. G. Adler joined with Hermann Langbein and Ella Lingens-Reiner to publish the book *Auschwitz Zeugnisse und Berichte*, which set new standards for the historiography of the extermination camp. Anyone familiar with Adler's convictions will also recognize his humanism reflected in Langbein's *Menschen in Auschwitz* (1972; English translation: *People in Auschwitz*, 2004), a humanism to which Langbein deliberately drew closer during his painful estrangement from the ideals of global communism in the Stalinist era. Adler thus became an international expert, collaborating with colleagues around the world and cultivating contacts with institutions dedicated to the memory of those evil years, especially with the Auschwitz Museum in Poland, but also with Yad Vashem in Israel, the Rijksinstituut voor Oorlogsdocumentatie in the Netherlands, and later the Imperial War Museum in London. As a result, the influence of his book intersected with his impact as a scholar and consultant.

Around the time of the second edition, the Munich Institut für Zeitgeschichte (Institute of Contemporary History), owing to its high regard for *Theresienstadt 1941–1945*, entrusted Adler with the task of writing a similar monograph on the Gestapo in Würzburg. The Würzburg Gestapo files had survived almost completely, and it was believed that they would enable the author to produce a detailed account of a relatively self-contained region. This is the origin of his second monograph, *Der verwaltete Mensch*. The view of the persecutions from the "inside" in *Theresienstadt 1941–1945* was now supplemented by one from the "outside" – that is, the depiction of the victims would now be followed by a portrait of the perpetrators. But because, as a result of the opening of the Würzburg archives, H. G. Adler became the first to gain insight into the mechanisms of the SS state in planning and carrying out the transports, the project became more extensive the more he worked on it, until it came to encompass (as the first such book in the field) the history and the entire process of the deportations. Adler systematically applied the methods and insights in *Theresienstadt 1941–1945* to the technology of extermination. Here, too, we find a precise depiction of all discoverable facts, careful appraisal of complex issues, meticulous examination of the documents, empathetic descriptions of human stories, and an overarching analysis of the entire situation in the form of a new theory. Adler attempts to approach the enormous question of the Shoah – "How was it possible?" – by answering a specific question: "How were human beings administered to death?" Step by step, he investigates the attitudes and actions that led to the "Final Solution," from the Evian conference and the "Night of Broken Glass" through the Madagascar Plan, the atrocities of the Einsatzgruppen in Eastern Europe, the Wannsee Conference, and finally Theresienstadt, Lublin, and Auschwitz.

Thus the book illuminates the interplay of politics and propaganda, orders and administration, and in the process addresses frequently controversial topics such as the connivance and complicity of the general population; this, however, is something Adler never investigates from a general perspective but always looks at individually, depending on each person's profession, function in the system, and, if possible, character. In the process, we see the extent to which all German administrative offices, especially the tax and revenue offices, were involved in the persecution of the Jews, from the Reichssicherheitshauptamt (the Reich Security Main Office, the highest SS and police office in the Third Reich) down to the local council heads and municipal police. In fact, the book contains sufficient material for several works. After dealing with the basic historical questions – those involving the "technology of deportation" and the "financial and material appraisal of the deportations" – it provides (in a distressing section entitled "Destinies from the Documents") portraits of forty-nine victims, reconstructed from the perspective of the deskbound killers. The concluding section, by contrast, is devoted to Adler's theory of the state or of administration. The continuity between modernity and the world of the camps, as explained in *Theresienstadt 1941–1945* using the theory of mechanical materialism, is something *Der verwaltete Mensch* locates concretely in the theory and practice of administration. This theory was borrowed by Zygmunt Baumann in his book *Modernity and the Holocaust*,[67] as Baumann has since tacitly acknowledged. With this approach, playing on the widespread confusion between "government" and "administration" (especially as evidenced by American usage), H. G. Adler turns deliberately toward the future. According to his new theory, only possessions may be *administered*; human beings, by contrast, can only be *governed*: "Human beings may not be administered, something reserved only for things. For man, the applicable law is jus in personam, which is vested only in the authority of power, in other words of government and enforcement; administration has no disposition over jus in personam, but only over jus in rem." Because the distinction had not yet been found in Montesquieu, H. G. Adler proposes amending the classical theory of the state: the separation of powers should also recognize administration as a form of power and should strictly separate it from the other powers. If we fail to do this, catastrophes like the extermination of the Jews are theoretically possible in every modern state, in the West as well as the East. Whereas the practical effects of this theory remain to be seen, the historical section of the work fit almost seamlessly alongside *Theresienstadt 1941–1945* and gave new impetus to the general dissemination of his documentary method. One sees traces of Adler's impact in Israel, for example, in the research of David Bankier; in America, where Christopher R. Browning took up the subject of deportations; and among the most recent generation of historians in Germany – be it in the formulation of the questions, in the methods, in the facts he brought to light, or in the views he held.

Writing his book *Der verwaltete Mensch* liberated H. G. Adler from his literary and scholarly involvement with the Shoah, but *Theresienstadt 1941–1945* remained the starting point and focus of his entire oeuvre. Here, where he writes both as witness and historian, poet and sociologist, the different strands of his work come together. The later books can easily be grouped around this earlier magnum opus, meeting and overlapping in many places, not least in the thoughts that reach their climax in his observations on *nothingness* in *Theresienstadt 1941–1945*.

The later books group easily around the earlier magnum opus, meeting and overlapping there at several points, not least of all in the thoughts that reach their climax in his observations on *nothingness* in *Theresienstadt 1941–1945*. These are thoughts that, though they deal historically with the end of Theresienstadt as a camp, also ethically sum up the full extent of the extermination in Auschwitz. In passages

---

[67] Zygmunt Baumann, *Modernity and the Holocaust* (Cambridge: Polity Press, 1989).

Afterword 827

such as this, one recognizes the author as a witness who takes on the task of sacrificing himself for the truth:

> It was the end: the end as doom, as Armageddon – as _nothing_. And there was no more substance. If one did not experience this annihilation oneself, one cannot know, will never know, what it was like. One must be silent. One must listen and examine one's role for oneself and as a human being in the world. But anyone who went through this final despair, this night of nights, this nameless doom – who survived it and attained new life, who once again _is_ and has regained his name, which was stolen from him – he should raise his voice and say what it was really like. He should proclaim the reality, beyond the aura of genuine but offended (and therefore not entirely genuine) heroism, beyond the sharp antagonism between the white innocence of the victims and the black guilt of the persecutor, and beyond all the theatrical horror of living decay and dead mountains of bones, which reveal none of the inner truth, for they are merely stigmas, not the truth itself. No, it is necessary to name the reality that a living soul can put up with in such a probing eradication (_Zernichtung_) – separated from any loneliness and any community – the reality of _nothingness_, which is neither imaginable nor comprehensible, for not thinking and not feeling is nothingness. That which has not been created will suffer in the final guilt of the world, where plain _nothingness_ figures as the meaning of life in the deepest dungeon of consciousness, in which all form, as the writer of Ecclesiastes understood, becomes a mere conceit. He, the crushed one (_Zerstossene_), has contemplated this reality, the reality of vanity, in which no value, no being still exists, in which nevertheless an unknown, mysterious force continues to act deep in the unconscious stream of life and tries to assert itself, although it is still capable only of acquiescence, which seeks to wrest the substance of Something from the improbable Nothing.

This is not the place for a discussion of these lofty reflections, behind which we recognize the prisoner's voice. But it is perhaps appropriate to note the way in which they point us to the intellectual and spiritual heart of H. G. Adler's message. It is necessary to set boundaries, honor the dead, and search one's soul. After a certain point, what happened eludes all understanding, all explanation. Not coincidentally, this statement overlaps with insights from poems Adler wrote shortly after the end of the war that speak of a barely comprehensible bleakness, as well as with reflections from _Die unsichtbare Wand_ and poignant images from _Eine Reise_. This literature of destruction uses almost incomprehensible means and devices to reach into a sphere that the intellect cannot understand and that feeling alone can perhaps attempt to grasp. Every earlier catastrophe left something positive behind. The Flood was a punishment, and Noah emerged from it; after the destruction of the Temple, the Jews escaped and entered the Diaspora. But here, nothing remained. And yet the author finds meaning in this catastrophe and overcomes the conquerors in the name of their victims, in order to escape the abyss. He turns his gaze from external events and directs it inwardly – toward suffering, the psyche, ethics. Whatever traces this commitment may have left behind among his contemporaries, as a warning to the future it remains a truthful testimony to dark times.

A NOTE ON THE TEXT

This translation is based on the definitive text: H. G. Adler, _Theresienstadt 1941–1945: Das Antlitz einer Zwangsgemeinschaft_ (1955; second, revised, and expanded edition, Tübingen: J. C. B. Mohr [Paul Siebeck], 1960). The text is here reproduced exactly, except for the German glossary, which does not lend itself to translation. A few minor errors have been silently emended. In addition, following a list of corrections found among the author's papers, first printed in 2005, a number of other slips have been put right. The afterword is an expanded version of that contained in the reprint: H. G. Adler, *Theresienstadt 1941–1945: Das Antlitz einer Zwangsgemeinschaft* (second edition, 1960; Göttingen: Wallstein Verlag, 2005).

Index

abortions, 465
  artificial methods, 631
  forced, 465, 613
    demographics, 269, 619
  punishment for, 121
Abraham, P., 527
abuse, 100, 114, 306
  deportation, 60, 102
  elder, 596
  illness reporting, 583
  medical, 440
  medication, 439
  ration card, 322
  SS, 117, 431, 629
  youth, 596
accommodation, 596
active people, 591
activity reports, 220
adjudication (memorandum, May 1945),
    402–3
Adler, Friedrich, 524
Adler, Gertrud, 453
Adler, H. G., 803–8, 810–27
  Adorno and, 818
  Arendt and, 823–4
  Baeck and, 808–9
  Broch and, 809, 814
  Canetti and, 814
  intent for *Theresienstadt* 1941–1945,
    811–12
  Nietzsche and, 809
  personal experiences in camps, 621–2
  Simmel and, 813
  Steiner and, 814

Adler, Maximilian, 487, 520, 533
administration (department), 182–4
  internal regulations for, 423–4
administrative squadrons, 607
Adorno, Theodor W., 817, 820
Africa, 6
Agudah, 162
Agudas Jisroel World Organization, 769
air defense, 436
Aktualita (Prague weekly newsreel), 148
Albalan, Isza, 700
Alexander in Jerusalem (Kafka), 550
alienation, age group, 596
amenorrhea, 464–5
American Joint Distribution Committee, 176
Amstetten, 238
Ančerl, Karel, 523
antisemitism, 653
apothecary, 144
appeals, 411
  chamber, 409
  rights to, 425
arbitration system, 606
Arendt, Hannah, 816, 823
Argonauts of the Western Pacific
    (Malinowski), 812
Argutinsky-Dolgorukow, Elsbeth, 542
armbands (OD, September 22, 1942), 117
army workshops (*Bauhof*), 80, 111
Aronson-Lindt, Heda, 523
arrests, 53, 70, 73, 129, 157, 431, 662
  bunker, 670
  causes for, 16, 242, 427
  house, 492

829

830   *Index*

arrests *(cont.)*
  justifying, 11
  post office staff (OD, February 16, 1943), 106
  procedures for, 428
arts, 541
Aryan Street, 87
Asia, 6
Association of Czech Jews in Czechoslovakia (Svaz Čechů-židů v Československé republice), 257
Auditing Office (Revisionsstelle), 429
Auschwirz: Zeugnisse und Berichte (*Auschwitz: Testimonies and Reports*, Adler, Langbein, Lingens-Reiner), 825
Auschwitz main concentration camp, 14, 17, 19, 161, 622, 746
  Birkenau and, 108
  established, 604
  gassing suspended (November 2, 1944), 617
  Jews to be sent to, 610
  medical experiments on children at, 48, 759
  section B IIb (family camp), 49, 629, 731
    dissolution of, 616, 630
Auschwitz Museum (Poland), 825
Aussenberg, Dolfi, 541, 544
Aussig, 23, 168, 382, 393
Australia, 6
Austria, 159, 512, 614, 616–18
Austrian Civil Law Code, 407
autopsies, 470

Baas, Franz, 464
Bachrich, P., 450
Bacon, Jehuda, 490
Baeck, Leo, 159, 174, 206, 210, 215–16, 261, 318, 533, 611, 617, 622, 806
  Adler and, 808–9
  Chelmno gas vans and, 127
  Eppstein and, 155, 215
  funeral address of, 540
  Judaism and, 597
  personality of, 215
  Welfare Department and, 476, 500
bank, 124, 136, 144
Barneveld camp for privileged Jews, 153, 157, 682
Bartels, Rolf L. A., 381–2, 664
barter, 324, 374
baths, 171, 453, 480, 483, 605, 607
  delousing (*Desinfektionsbad*), 200, 361

Baum, Fritz, 529
Bäumel, G., 482, 489
Bäumel, Richard, 530
Bauschowitz (Bohušovice), 23–4, 69
  train station, 110, 227, 235
Bautzen, battle of, 703
Bavaria, 167, 176
beautification (*Verschönerung*), 125–47, 152, 157, 280, 285, 614–15, 618, 741, 765
  recreation and, 520
  second, 163–6
Becher, Kurt, 150, 162, 165
beds, 290
Beer, Th. Otto, 527
behavior (individual)
  cooperative, 581
  typology of, 585
Bełżec extermination camp, 45, 606
Bełżyce, 714
Bergel, Karl, 20, 66, 71–3, 81, 109, 117, 120, 130, 135, 141, 168, 564
Bergen-Belsen main concentration camp, 134, 144, 165–6, 481, 676, 699, 749, 763
  as a convalescent, transit, and exchange camp, 49
  as privileged camp, 781
Bergh, S. V. D., 529
Bergmann, Rudolf, 213
Berman, Karel, 523
Bernadotte, Folke, 163, 746
Beruschky, 117
Bialystok [Białystok] Ghetto, 241
Birkenau (Auschwitz) main concentration/ extermination camp, 45, 108, 127, 146, 691
  as code name for Auschwitz, 766
  deceptions around, 108
  established, 606
  as family camp, 698
  work deployment, 629
births
  birthday celebrations, 212, 371, 377
  contraception, 144
  demographics, 34, 144, 269, 465, 619, 673
  forbidden, 469
black market, 324
blocked accounts, 7
Bloemendaal, Alice, 529
blood, mixed (*Mischlinge*), 18, 153, 156, 240, 259, 615, 639, 657
  Kallmeijer list, 677

Index

Blumenthal, Otto, 530
Bock, Philipp, 470
Bohemia, 512
Böhm, Arno, 48, 698
Böhm, Max, 530
Böll, Heinrich, 806, 818
Bonn, 264
Bonn, Hanuš, 16
bonuses
  food, 315–19, 607, 610, 612
  labor, 99, 143, 311, 314, 607
  regular (*Zubussen* and *Dekaden*),
    327, 393
  sardines, 160
  sick (*Krankenzubussen*), 328
  useless (*Schmonzes*), 495
Book Registration Group
  (Bucherfassungsgruppe), 539
books, 534–9
  prayer, 536, 539
boys' home, 144
Bracher, Karl Dietrich, 818
Brachmann, Willy, 698
Brahn, Max, 530
Brandt, Rudolf, 150, 163
Braunfeld, Arthur, 450
bread (categories), 607, 612, 616
Breslau, 637, 698
Broch, Hermann, 564, 809, 816
broken people, 589
Browning, Christopher R., 826
Brundibár (Krása), 552
Brünn, 11
brutal people, 591
Buber, Israel Martin, 818
Buchenwald main concentration camp, 11,
  166, 173, 566, 589, 622, 720, 810
Buchmüller, Werner, 164
Budapest Rescue Committee, 162
Budweis, 78, 233, 732
Bühler, Josef, 19
building administration, 187
building elder, 68, 77, 288, 406
buildings, uses, 275
Bürckel Operation (October 1940), 14
Burckhardt, Karl, 163, 786
Burger, Anton, 107, 114, 120, 130, 133, 148,
  377, 413, 465, 686, 765
  Edelstein and, 129
  Günther and, 134
burials, 410, 471, 644
butcher, 144

camp tally, 126
Canetti, Elias, 225, 811
cannibalism, 631, 760, 793
cards
  clothing, 9
  file, 4
  identity, 66, 100, 131, 221, 323, 353, 683
    citizen's (*Bürgerlegitimation*), 57, 59
    Council of Elders, 211
    verified, 794
    worker, 247, 354, 607, 612
  index
    logistical, 390–1
    main product (MPCI), 391
  laundry, 482
  patient (*Kleine Krankenkarte*), 444
  post, 42, 50, 76, 106, 108, 174, 605, 609,
    612, 649, 657, 748
    from Auschwitz, 686
    restrictions on, 509
    writing rotation (*Schreibturnus*) for, 509
  ration (*Bezugsscheine*), 10, 29, 57, 69, 105,
    187, 295, 655–6
    military (*Lebensmittelstammkarte*), 57
    OD (September 13, 1942), 105
    provisional, 230
    special, 185
  ration card (*Essenkarte*), 247, 322–3
  savings, 103
  small health care, 612
  soap, 57
care of the sick (*Krankenbetreuung*), 199,
  471
Castelin, Carl, 533
cattle cars, 233, 235, 247, 624, 627, 649,
  711, 763
censorship, 510
censuses, 77, 266, 614
  1941 (December 25), 605
  1943
    November 11, 129–33
    November 19, 131
    November 24, 131
    OD (October 28, 1942), 118
    OD (November 10, 1943), 130
Central America, 6
Central Association of German Citizens of
  Jewish Faith (Centralverein deutscher
  Staatsbürger jüdischen Glaubens), 259
Central Bakery, 110, 307
Central Bath, 110, 137, 144
  OD (May 18, 1942), 81

832   *Index*

Central Building Maintenance Office (GEZ),
    197
Central Bureau for Jewish Emigration, 603,
    608
Central Butcher and Smokehouse (*Selcherei*),
    404
Central Labor Office, 184–5, 316, 326–7,
    348
    documents pertaining to, 349–57
Central Laboratory, 453
Central Laundry, 110, 359, 399
Central Lost Property Office, 92, 419
Central Materials and Inventory
    Administration, 190
Central Medical Supply Warehouse
    (Zentralheilmittellager), 200, 444
Central Mortuary, 91, 233, 470
Central Office (Zentralamt), 4, 7, 603
    Protectorate and, 5
    RSHA IV B 4 and, 5
Central Office (Zentralstelle), 7, 754
Central Office for Jewish Emigration in
    Bohemia and Moravia, 4, 781
Central Office for the Regulation of the
    Jewish Question in Bohemia and
    Moravia, 5, 608
Central Ration Card Office (zentrale
    Essenskartenstelle), 322
Central Receiving Office, 183
Central Reception Office (OD, January 28,
    1942), 78
Central Registry (Zentralevidenz), 31, 182,
    244, 266, 348
Central Secretariat, 28, 181, 183, 347
Central Supply Office (Zentralproviantur),
    189, 230, 316, 390, 405
Central Warehouse (Zentrallager), 373, 390,
    484
certificate of release, 382
chalutz (Zionist-Socialist) worldview, 580
chamber music, 523
change of residence, 52
Channukah, 540
character
    changing, 581–9
    Jewish, 223, 571
    types, 589–93
Chelmno extermination camp, 15, 17
    established, 605
    gas vans, 127
children, 126
    effects of camp on, 495–8

effects of camp on, 507
exchange, 637
life in the block, 495
OD (February 16, 1942), 82
working, 502
children's homes, 144
children's pavilion, 135, 140, 144
chlorination, 100
choice, individual, 585
Christianity, 540
Claussen, Heinrich, 378
cleaning service, 360
clinics, outpatient (*Ambulanzen*), 64, 68–9,
    199, 392, 612
    1942, 447, 606
    1943, 449
    E IIIa (lung disease), 612
    health units and, 444
    services to, 445
    visiting, 445
    written agenda of, 393
clothing
    Central Clothes Mending Workshop, 109
    warehouse (*Kleiderkammer*), 68, 92–3,
        155, 231, 389
        theft from, 231, 359, 432
    winter (OD, October 20, 1942), 94
coerced community (*Zwangsgemeinschaft*),
    205, 558, 576, 804
coffee house, 106, 124, 485, 520, 541, 610
    OD (December 6, 1942), 106
coffins, 471
cohabitation arrangement, 243
Cohen, David, 215, 650
Cohen, Hermann, 537
Cohn, Ludwig, 530
collectivism, pseudo-, 578
Community Guard (previously, Ghetto
    Guard, GW), 425–8, 434
    responsibilities, 426
community house (*Gemeinschaftshaus*), 137,
    140, 538, 616
Complaints Office, 183
Complete Solution to the Jewish Question,
    604
comradeship evenings
    (*Kameradschaftsabende*, OD,
    December 28, 1941), 75, 605
concerts, 520, 522–3, 541
concessions, 167
confusion (*Bewusstseinstruebung*), 463
connections (*Beziehungen*), 223

consciousness, 585
construction, 10, 47
  Bauschowitz rail line, 110, 608
  beds, 219, 605
  Birkenau, 678
  box, 329
  camp, 78
    barracks, 81, 107, 111, 329
    wells, 100
  chlorination facility, 100, 372
  crematorium, 607
  Department, 196
  gas chambers, 163, 365
  group (*Barackenbaugruppe*), 167, 252
  road, 78, 330
  staff (*Aufbau-Stab*), 154
Construction Kommando
    (Aufbaukommando, AK), 26–7, 64,
    244, 248, 393, 432
contraband, 83, 160
  deadline for surrendering (OD, June 9,
    1943), 120
  extending grace period for (OD, May 15,
    1942), 84
  list of items considered, 230
  OD (December 24, 1941), 84
  OD (January 18, 1942), 83
cooperation (OD, November 24, 1942), 122
cooperators, 591
corruption, 231, 564, 567, 665
  Baeck and, 215
  butcher, 305
  deportation, 699
  distribution point, 304–5
  Economics Department, 304, 309
  Edelstein functionaries, 63, 206, 750
  Eppstein and, 753
  kitchen, 305, 319
  leadership, 304
  Lowenstein and, 114
  Löwinger and, 273
  nutritional professionals, 405
  Office of Economic Supervision and, 433
  rations, 316
  Schliesser and, 377
  SS, 13, 379, 402, 568
    food, 309
  Transport Management Department and,
    227
  Westerbork, 134
Council of Elders, 22, 25, 28, 406, 408, 604
  March 14, 1943, resolution, 425

expanded, 214
power of, 210
privileges of, 211
reforming
  OD (October 3, 1942), 96
  OD (January 31, 1943), 96
reorganization of
  October 1, 1942, 213
  MdS (December 13, 1944), 159–60
theft and, 207
coupons, shop (*Bezugsscheine*), 397
courts
  ghetto, 121
    criminal judgments, 433
    judgments, 432
    procedures for, 410–11
  juvenile, 121, 417
  labor, 121, 414–16
Cow, The (Hofer), 546
crafts, 541
crate fabrication (*Kisten-Produktion*), 388
cremations, 76, 163, 410, 644
crematoria, 81, 471, 609, 691
  Birkenau, 716
  Mauthausen, 631
criminal code of the Detective Department, 612
Criminal Guard (Kriminalwache, Kripo),
    433, 754
criminality, in Theresienstadt (1942), 432
Croatia, 76
Crowds and Power (Canetti), 814
cultural life, 12
  Council of Elders and, 534
  informal, 519
  organized, 519
  roots of, 531
curfews, 140, 144, 160, 222, 265, 285, 497,
    608, 610, 612, 618
  barracks, 77
  census, 118, 130
  extending
    OD (June 26, 1942), 83
    OD (October 4, 1942), 87
  prewar, 8
  violations, armed response to (OD, August
    29, 1942), 117
Czechoslovakia, 50, 89
  emigration from, 51
  Germans expelled from, 177
  Munich agreement and, 3
Czerba, Franz, 513
Czerniakow, Adam, 753

834 Index

Daluege, Kurt, 15
day centers (*Tagesheime*), 500
death notifications, 91
decision making authority (*Weisungsrecht*), 10
Dedicated to the Members of the Security Services (poem), 545
defamation (*Beleidigung*), 411, 417–18
  reciprocal (*gegenseitige Beleidigung*), 417
defense counsels, 413–14
Deggendorf, 176, 763
deghettoization, 255
Deiner, Elise, 529
delousing, 93, 109, 127
Denmark, 159, 512, 614, 617
  sabotage in, 639
dental equipment, 445
Department IV (Investigating and Combating Opponents), 5
Department of Health and Social Welfare, 29
Department of Internal Administration, 28, 185–8, 335, 474
deployment offices, 185, 408
deportation/transport, 6–7, 10, 13–20, 52
  Aachen, 648
  after 1939, 13
  aid service, 57
  Altreich (Old Reich Germany), 89, 697
  Amsterdam, 53, 107
  arriving, 227–40
  asset identification, 58
  assistance (*Transporthilfe*), 227
  Augsburg, 648, 723
  Auschwitz, 44, 49, 53, 128, 130, 134, 450, 500, 610–11, 628, 633, 695, 703, 722, 780
    concluded, 617
  Austria, 37, 607
  average ages during, 92
  Bamberg, 694
  Bayreuth, 694
  Belgium, 702
  Belorussia, 44
  Bergen-Belsen, 37, 41, 45, 53, 147, 162, 615, 631, 657–8, 722, 768, 796
  Berlin, 15, 32, 52, 89, 92, 641, 647, 668
  Bialystok [Białystok] Ghetto, 35, 48, 613–14, 697
  Bielefeld, 648
  Bielitz, 723
  Birkenau (Auschwitz), 42, 50, 108, 656, 774

Blechhammer, 630
Bochum, 648
Bonn, 648
Bremen, 648
Breslau, 641, 648, 668
Brünn, 15, 17, 65, 641
Buchenwald, 37, 658, 701
Budapest, 648
call up (*Einberufung*), 245–8
Celle, 41, 500
Central Europe, 14, 604
Chelmno, 634
Chemnitz, 648
Cologne, 15, 89, 91–2, 157, 456, 627, 641, 648, 700, 703, 719
Construction Kommando (AK), 244, 248, 432
Czechoslovakia, 37
Danzig, 37, 697
Darmstadt, 648
deceptions around, 90
Denmark, 37, 132, 614, 638–40, 740
departing, 240–8
Department (Prague JKG), 16, 31
Dortmund, 641, 648
Dresden, 52, 668, 677
Duisburg, 648
Düsseldorf, 15, 641, 648
Düsseldorf-Aachen, 668
the East, 250–1, 641
  exemptions from, 249
  first (February 22, 1940), 604
  OD (January 5, 1942), 76
  OD (September 11, 1942), 121
  OD (April 24, 1943), 248
  OD (April 26, 1943), 248–9
  OD (April 27, 1943), 249
exemptions, 253, 260
Flößberg, 37
Flossenbürg, 37
France, 604, 702, 708
France and, 14
Frankfurt, 15, 648, 657
Frankfurt on Main, 641
Fürth, 694
Gelsenkirchen, 648
Germany, 12, 17, 32, 37, 92, 607, 628, 647
  first, 624
Gleina-Rehmsdorf, 37
Göring and, 14
Göttingen, 648

Index

Greater Germany, 736
Gröditz, 37
group (*Sammeltransporte*), 31, 40
Hagen, 648
halted (March 23, 1940), 604
Hamburg, 15, 641, 648, 668, 699
Hanover, 641, 648, 790
Helmbrechts, 37
Hildesheim, 648
Himmler and, 13
Holland, 37, 612, 676, 742
individual travelers (*Einzelzuwachs*), 32, 40
Isbica/Izbica, 42–3, 606
Jewish community and, 716–19
Jungfernhof, 694
Kassel, 641, 648
Kattowitz, 723
Kauffering, 700
Kessel, 794–6
Kiel, 648
Koblenz, 648
Kovno, 15
Krefeld, 648
Kreuzlingen, 769
Leipzig, 648
Leitmeritz, 37, 654, 700, 703
lightning (*Blitztransporte*), 233
Lípa, 53
lists, 31, 54
   Terezín Ghetto (Czech publication), 33
Łódź, 15, 17, 634, 645, 705
Lübeck, 648
Lublin, 42, 607, 714–15
Ludwigshafen, 648
Luxembourg, 15, 37, 648
Magdeburg, 648
Mainz, 648
Majdanek, 44
Mauthausen, 722
memorandum (March 17, 1942), 43
memorandum (February 3, 1945), 162
Meuselwitz, 37
Minsk, 15, 17, 609, 645, 705
Munich, 32, 89, 92, 641, 648
  IKG hospital evacuation, 756
Münster, 641, 648
number (*Transportnummer*), 31–2
Nuremberg, 641, 648, 694–5
OD (April 23 and 24, 1942), 248
OD (January 10, 1943), 46
Öderan, 37

of the elderly (*Alterstransport*), 41, 104, 250
official summons, 55–60
orders, 15
Osnabrück, 648
Ossow, 43, 607
Östmark, 89, 697
Ostrau, 234–5, 723, 800
overview, 32, 38
Palestine, 700
  illegal, 604
Penig, 37
Piaski, 42, 606
planning for, 644
Plauen, 648, 738
Poland, 13–15, 603–4, 702, 704–7
Prague, 14–15, 53–4, 65, 89, 641
property declaration, 56
protection from, 133
Protectorate, 604, 668, 683, 697
punishment, 50
Raasika, 44, 609
Raguhn, 37, 631
Ravensbrück, 53, 722
real estate, 56
reasons for exemption from, 101
Regen, 661
Regensburg, 648
registration as prelude to, 11
Reich territory, 42
Rejowiece (Reowitz), 43, 606
responsibilities for, 226
return, 174
Riesa, 42
Riga, 15, 41–2, 605, 645, 694
  705
Sachsenhausen, 37, 701, 722
Saloniki Ghetto, 53, 716
Scharfenstein, 37
Schlieben, 37
Schnarchenreuth bei Hof, 661
Schwarzheide, 37, 698
separating Jews for, 43
Sered, 233, 722
settlement area, 26
sinister nature of, 248
Slovakia, 657
Sobibór, 44
Stettin, 714
Stuttgart, 641
Stutthof, 698
Sudetengau, 52, 697

Index

deportation/transport (cont.)
Svatobořice, 53
Sweden, 40–1, 161, 165, 713, 742, 745
Switzerland, 40–1, 49, 161–2, 167, 618, 695
technology and procedures for, 51–60
Teschen, 723
Theresienstadt, 27, 38–51, 78, 152–7, 162, 168, 171–2, 174, 239, 244, 248, 280, 500, 605, 608–9, 611, 614, 616–18, 654, 673, 678, 683, 695, 711, 735–6, 742, 749, 763, 765, 767–8
official records, 160
Thuringia, 648
Trawniki, 43, 607
Treblinka, 42, 44
Trier, 648
Tröglitz, 37
Trostinetz, 44, 608–9
Ulm, 790
Upper Silesia, 648
versus transport, 26
via
Buchenwald, 695
Budweis, 630
Constance, 669
Katowitz, 630
Ostrau, 630
Prague, 630
Stuttgart, 790
Vienna, 12, 14–15, 32, 52, 89, 91–2, 456, 641–705, 723
Vittel, 699
Warsaw, 42, 606
Westerbork, 53, 677–8, 768
Wiesbaden, 648
Wilischtal, 37
work deployment, 41, 107, 123, 132, 136, 613
OD (September 8, 1943), 123
Worms, 648
Württemberg-Baden, 673
Würzburg, 648, 694
Zamość, 43, 606
Zossen, 146
Zschopau, 37
Zulia, 607
Zwodau, 37
Der neue Tag (Prague daily newspaper), 4, 7, 107
Desnos, Robert, 821
destiny, 557–60, 567

Destruction of the European Jews, The (Hilberg), 822
Detective Department (DD, formerly police criminal law), 418, 425
1944 report, 434
responsibilities of, 433
Devil and Damned (Kautsky), 575
diagnostic procedures, superfluous, 440–2
directives (Weisungen), 82, 154, 222
Disciplinary Tribunal, 424–5
discipline, 72
diseases and epidemics, 21, 438, 445, 644, 664
cancer, 730
chickenpox, 460
colitis, 454–6
conjunctivitis, 448, 460, 611, 619
deficiency, 461–2
diarrhea, 284, 501
dysentery, 655
encephalitis, 457–8, 652, 697
enteritis, 93, 113, 454–6, 609, 611
erysipelas, 459, 793
heart, 462
hepatitis, 459, 611
imaginary, 439
infantile paralysis, 458
infectious, 26, 448
jaundice, 113, 501, 619
lung, 462
measles, 113, 460, 611
meningitis, 453
mumps, 460
phlegmons, 793
pneumococcal pneumonia, 454, 730
pneumomeningococcus, 453
poliomyelitis, 458
psychological predisposition to, 438
psychological suicide, 442
rubella, 460
scarlet fever, 70, 113, 457, 501, 609, 611
spotted fever, 618–19
symptoms connected to camp, 438
tuberculosis, 459, 655, 729–30
typhoid, 163, 172–3, 176–7, 286, 455–7, 499, 746
typhus, 113, 449, 461, 501, 611, 654–5, 659, 681, 730, 789, 793, 799
whooping cough, 460
disinfection facility, 109, 127, 199, 232, 289, 655

Index

distribution
  clothes, 470
  food, 68, 70, 99, 239, 298
    bread, 307, 656
    margarine, 80
    milk (OD, January 1, 1942), 80
  of imported goods, 373–4
  Loewenstein and, 115, 307
  mail, 106
  package, 136
  points (*Provianturen*), 189
Distribution Office, 94, 104, 397
district elder (*Bezirksaeltester*), 406, 408
documents, atrocity, 160–1
Doderer, Heimito von, 818
Doetinchen intern camp, 683
Dormitzer, Else, 530, 534
Draft Structure of the Ghetto Administration, 28
  organizational plan and, 28
Drancy transit camp for Jews, 151, 241
dualism, material, 561–2
Duckwitz, Georg Ferdined, 53, 640
Duke, S., 529
Dunant, Paul, 37, 164, 167–70, 173–6
  785–7
duty to salute (*Grußpflicht*), 428, 605, 615
  OD (December 21, 1941), 72
  OD (March 6, 1944), 140
  OD (June 18, 1944), 140

Economic Control Office
    (Wirtschaftspruefstelle, Wipo), 306,
    428–9
Economics Department, 29, 195–6, 357–9,
    474
Economics Police (Wirtschaftspolize), 404
economy
  brothel, 596
  essential needs, 396
  external, 374–90
  internal, 374, 390–6
  petty, 396–9
  small enterprise, 374
Edelstein, Jakob, 4, 14, 17, 20, 27, 64, 66,
    124, 209–10, 235, 319, 579, 604,
    611, 614, 645, 652, 782
  children and, 501
  elderly and, 501
  Eppstein and, 96
  executed, 616, 629, 748
  Loewenstein and, 116

personality of, 96, 209
  work group plan, 78
  Zionism and, 260, 650
Edelstein, Mirjam, 235
education, 10, 488–9, 495–6, 499–500
  advisory board (*Erziehungsbeirat*), 487
  political, 503–4
  school (L 417), 490
Educational Services Department, 202
Ehrmann, Lisa, 622
Eichinger, Herbert, 527
Eichmann, Adolf, 151, 163, 513, 645, 678–9,
    706, 748, 819
  beautification and, 137
  Central Office and, 4
  children's exchange and, 49
  deportation/transport and, 51
  extermination and, 680, 686
  personality of, 679
  RSHA IV B 4 and, 5
  Theresienstadt and, 17, 20, 123
  transport orders and, 243
Eichmann in Jerusalem (Arendt), 823
Elbert, Erwin, 213
elderly, 442, 486, 498
  health of, 445
  treatment of, 397, 476, 506
electrical devices, 291–2
  OD (October 3, 1942), 118
electricity usage (OD, February 25, 1941), 77
Elsabe munitions factory, 638
emigration (*aliyah*), 3–6, 18–19, 705
  after 1939, 5–6
  before Munich agreement, 3
  British Empire and, 5
  Cuba and, 6
  demographics of, 1939, 4
  destinations, 6
  halted (October 1, 1941), 604
  Holland/Belgium occupations and, 6
  illegal (through Poland and Slovakia), 4
  Italy and, 6
  Japan and, 6
  legal, 6
  Lisbon and, 6
  Palestine and, 6, 139
  Palestine Office and, 4
  quotas (Czechoslovakia, Germany,
    Austria), 5
  Russia and, 6
  Shanghai and, 6
  Spain and, 6

838   *Index*

emigration (*aliyah*) (*cont.*)
  Sweden and, 6
  United States and, 5
  versus SS regulation, 5
Emigration Fund for Bohemia and Moravia,
    7, 10, 30, 52, 381
  confiscated property and, 7
employees
  categorizing, 183
  deployment (*Einsatz*), 183
England, 49
Enker, Max, 676
Eppstein, Paul, 96, 138, 152, 165, 210
    319–20, 533, 611, 616, 652, 743
    753, 766
  arrest and fate of, 154, 614
  Edelstein and, 98
  escape attempt, 766
  inspection deceptions of, 141–3
  Loewenstein and, 116
  personality of, 97, 209–10, 672
  visitors and, 141, 148
Erfurt, 237
escape
  attempts, 119, 147, 410, 712
    OD (February 15, 1944), 147
    reporting (memorandum, May 1943),
      269–70
  successful, 129, 737, 750
Essence of Judaism, The (Baeck), 809
ethnic cleansing (Pilsen), 15
ethos, camp, 593–5
European Executive Council of the Union of
    Orthodox Rabbis of the United States
    of America, 769
evacuation, 37, 112, 643
  civilian polulation of Theresienstadt, 86
  to the East, 18
  Kessel, 794–6
  memorandum (January 13, 1944), 273
  Sered, 722
  Small Fortress (Kleine Festung), 787
  synomyns for, 52
  transfer and, 19
Evian Conference, 825
eviction, 412
exchange operations, 49, 163, 689, 773
  children, 49, 128
  Palestine, 6, 128
  Polish, 128
  Switzerland, 128
executions, 119, 605–6

deterrent, 82
Edelstein and, 75
Edelstein's, 130
machinery of, 19
public, 11
secret (*Sonderbehandlung*), 48
staffing and procedures for, 73, 411
expenditures
  camp maintenance, 380
  prisoner, 380
Experimentaltheologie (Adler), 809
experiments
  animal, 439
  historical, 208
  medical, 48, 442, 472
  melted gold, 472
extermination, 101, 685
  Eichmann and, 162, 678–80
  as Final Solution to the Jewish Question,
    13, 51, 679
  Globke and, 686
  Günther and, 680
  Hitler's final orders for collective
    (November 11, 1941), 604
  Hitler's targets for, 14, 603
  isolation as preliminary stage of, 21
  mass, 240
  moral and physical, 594, 818
  of life unworthy of living (*lebensunwerten
    Lebens*), 562, 564
  National Socialism and, 13
  as pseudoreligious salvation, 573, 653, 679
  RF-SS and, 680
  SS and, 154, 177, 262
  Subgroup IV B 4 and, 5
  through community leaders, 16
  toward war's end, 151
  unfit prisoners and, 46
  unprofitability of, 664

family breakup, 422
family research (circumcision registries), 184
farm guards (*Flurenwärter*), 117
fearful people, 589
Feigl, A., 482
fellowship evenings (*Kameradschaftsabende*),
  520
fever thermometers (OD, February 16, 1942),
  81
Fidler, Johannes (Hans Fiedler), 59
file notes (petitions from JKG to Central
  Office), 20

Index

ordering Edelstein to direct Theresienstadt work, 27
Final Solution (extermination), 13, 566 574–5, 686–8
  Heydrich and, 18, 674
  Himmler and, 18
  Himmler and Mussolini and, 699
  Hitler and, 13
    November 11, 1941, call for, 18
Finance Department, 29, 198–9
fire department, 436
fire station, 144
Fischl, Alfred, 581
fleas, 289
Fleischmann, Karel, 443, 450, 474–6, 480, 529, 543, 792
Flossenbürg main concentration camp, 167, 760
food, 9, 595
  bonuses, 315–19
  consumption, 294
    barley, 310
    bread, 294, 296, 455
    buckwheat, 311
    cereals, 310
    coffee, 294
    coffee substitute, 311
    dried vegetables, 310
    dumplings, 313
    extracts, 311
    flour, 313
    hash, 309
    individual meals (*Speisen*), 309–15
    laborers, 294, 307
    lettuce, 308
    margarine, 294, 307, 311, 455
    meat, 294, 296, 309–10
    milk, 308, 312
    millet, 310
    noodles, 313
    OD (March 12, 1942), 296
    peas, 310
    potatoes, 294, 304, 312
    prisoner (OD, March 8, 1942), 295
    rabbit paste, 308
    root vegetables, 308, 310
    salami, 308
    salt, 308
    sauerkraut, 310
    semolina, 310
    September 1944, 385
    soup, 294

    sugar, 294, 296, 307, 312
    sweet buns, 313
    tea (herbal), 311
    tomatoes, 308
    turnip jam (*Rübe*), 307
    typical menus, 314–15
  distribution, 319–23
  nutrition, 323–4
    1941, 605
    1942, 297, 308
    unreliable records on, 294
  packages, 317–18, 321
  perishable, 373
  prison, 430
  requirements, 384–5
  requisitions from stores, 385
food stamps (*Dekaden*), 185, 316
Förster, J. B., 523
France, 14
Frank, Karl Hermann, 14, 37, 140, 167–8, 174, 513, 725–6, 765, 769, 786
Frankenhuis, Maurice, 159
Frdek-Mistek, 13
Freiberger, Rudolf, 213, 386, 533
Freiheit des Menschen, Die: Aufsatze zur Soziologie und Geschichte (On Human Freedom: Sociological and Historical Essays, Adler), 824
Freudenfeld, R., 523
Frey, Kurt, 527
Frick, Hans, 4
Friediger, Max, 141, 214
Friedmann, Desider, 96, 214, 533
  resignation (OD, April 5, 1943), 119
Friedmann, Franz, 138, 650
Friedmann, Hugo, 537
Friedmann, Richard Israel, 662–6
  Edelstein and, 662–3
  Eppstein and, 665–6
  perceptions of Theresienstadt, 665
Friedrich II, Emperor, 24
Fritsch, Karl, 678
funding (Theresienstadt), 379
funerals, 76, 470
furniture, 125

Gärtner-Geiringer, Hilde, 523
gas chambers, 48, 109, 124, 126, 135, 149, 171, 173, 453, 564, 649, 712
  Auschwitz, 108, 127, 240, 437, 563, 604, 629–30, 635, 659, 731, 748, 801
  ordered to be destroyed, 617

840 *Index*

gas chambers *(cont.)*
  suspended (November 2, 1944), 151
  Bełżec, 43
  Birkenau, 691, 766
  Majdanek, 715
  Sobibór, 43
  Theresienstadt, 618, 657–8, 728
gas trucks (*Duschegubky*, devourers of
    souls), 44
Gebauer, Berta, 271
gendarmerie, 64, 66, 86, 229
    513–14
Geneva
  Convention, 169–71, 740
  lists, 699
Germany, 159, 512, 614, 616–17
Gerron, Kurt, 148
Gestapo, 7
  districts, 32
  JKG and, 11
  RSHA and, 5
  victims (memorandum), 271
  Würzburg, 825
ghetto court, 106, 605, 612
  convictions by, 402
Ghetto Guard (Ghettowache, GW), 28
    64, 69, 130, 229, 348, 408, 515, 581,
    605–6, 610–11
  dissolved, 607
  responsibilities of, 434–5
ghettoization, 645
Ghetto Law in Theresienstadt, 405
ghettos
  administration of, 28
  admittance segregation, 26
  Bialystok [Białystok], 126, 508, 613, 637
  defined, 28
  labor and supply, 379
  Łódź, 17, 151, 280, 616
  maintenance (*Versorgungsghetto*), 101
  Minsk, 17, 612
  old-age, 18–19
  Piaski, 43, 727
  residents, 28
  Riga, 614, 736
  Saloniki, 711
  self-supporting (*Versorgungsghetto*), 359
  Sokal, 800
  transit, 18–19
  Warsaw, xv, 281
    uprising at (1943), 612
  Zamość, 43, 606

Givat Chaim, 749
Glas, Julian, 580
Glass, Martha, 821
Glimmerspalterei G.m.b.H., 388
Glücks, Richard, 51, 151
Głusk, 714
Goetz, Oscar, 530
gold, 471
  SS and, 472
Goldschmidt, Arthur, 676
Goldschmidt, Hermann Levin, 807
Goldschmied, Fritz, 530
goods
  agricultural, 384
  camp maintenance, 383–4
  free trade in essential, 429
  hygienic, 384
  material, 385
  personal, 384
Göring, Hermann, 14, 604
  Reich Central Office for Jewish Emigration
    and, 4
Grabower, Rolf, 533
Graslitz concentration subcamp, 764
graves
  individual, 471
  mass, 42, 85, 91, 100, 163, 471
  winter, 77
Grawinkiel concentration subcamp, 760
Greiser, Arthur, 756
Gross, Berta, 808
Gross, Bettina, 808
Grosse Hamburgerstraße collection camp,
    651, 712, 718
Gross-Rosen main concentration camp, 152
group elder, 77, 408
Grünberger, Julius, 213, 533
Grünfeld, Adolf, 529
guilt, 564
  corruption and, 564
  covert, 822
  defined, 570
  establishing, 409
  historical, 207
  leadership, 206
guiltlessness, 564
Gulag Archipelago, The (Solzhenitzen), 803
Günel, Gerhard, 141
Gunskirchen concentration camp, 631
Günther, Hans Friedrich Karl, 4, 15, 21, 27,
    63, 134, 138, 141, 151, 162–4, 166,
    513, 686, 766, 801

Index

841

Günther, Rolf, 141, 705, 718
Gurs internment camp, 14
Gutfeld, Alexander, 469
gymnasium, 137
Gypsies, 596, 644

Haas, Pavel, 523, 552
Habermann, S., 450
Habermas, Jürgen, 815
Haindl (Heindl), Rudolf, 117, 133, 148
haircuts, 72, 410
hakhsharah, 226
Hamburg Kaserne, 476
Hamburger, Adolphe, 529
Hanhala (Zionist leadership group), 637
Hantschke (officer in T), 378, 798
Hartmann, Walter, 121
head counts, 71, 77
healing gas, 704
health and hygiene, 362
health conditions, 445–54
Health Services Department, 199–200, 338,
   362, 437
   challenges, 113, 126
   lecture series (1943), 450
   responsibilities of, regarding children,
      487
   treatment statistics for, 446
health units, 442, 444
Hechalutz, 622
Hedin, Sven, 264
heedless people, 590
Heinz Tecklenburg & Co. (banking house),
   52
helpers, 592
helplessness, 242
Henningsen, Juel, 141, 144–5, 640
Henschel, Moritz, 214
Hess, Leo, 213
Heuss, Theodor, 815–16, 818
Heydebreck family camp, 748
Heydrich, Heinrich, 50, 84, 559, 604, 607,
   645, 725–6, 746, 756
   Himmler and, 674
   personality of, 674
   Theresienstadt and, 17
Heydrich, Lina, 725–6
Heydrich, Reinhard
   Central Office and, 4
   as Reichsprotektor, 11
   RSHA and, 5
Hilberg, Raul, 822, 825

Himmler, Heinrich, 150, 161, 166, 575, 696,
   747
   Auschwitz and, 46
   Central Office and, 4
   deportation/transport orders and, 51
   Eichmann and, 690
   Masur and, 618
   Theresienstadt and, 17
Hirsch, Fredy, 48, 487, 524, 748
Hirschfeld, Hans, 453
history, 599
   community and, 208
   contemporary (*Zeitgeschichte*), 813
   as irrational life, 207, 558
   Jewish
      Theresienstadt and, 571–8
   simultaneous, 559–71
Hitler, Adolf, 13, 557, 571
Hitler Youth, 11
Hochwald (near Riga), 736
Hofer, Hans, 524, 546
Höfle, Hans, 43
Holland, 159, 254, 512, 614, 616–18
   Edelstein's mission in, 781
home purchase agreements
      (*Heimeinkaufverträge*), 52, 91, 379,
      633, 695
homes
   apprentice, 486, 494
   boys' and girls', 486
   children's, 486, 493, 497
      daily schedule for, 502
   girls', 494, 498
   infants' and toddlers', 487
   young worker (*Jugendarbeiterheimen*), 486
   youth, 498
      Czech (description of life in), 495
homes for the infirm, 126
   L 504, 136, 144
Horn, Martin, 17
Horserød police prison camp, 712
hospitals, 125, 199
   barracks as, 278
   bathing facilities, 453
   E IIIa, 278, 444
      radiology, 730
      TB ward, 459
   E VI, 175, 278, 444–5, 605–6, 610, 788
      garden, 459
      history of, 757
      personnel, 448
      radiology, 730

842   *Index*

hospitals *(cont.)*
 E VII, 463, 606
 ghetto, 655
 Jewish (Berlin), 699
 L 124, 144, 229, 444
 L 317 (infectious diseases), 444
 L 504 (frail elderly), 444
 movement to and within, 274, 445
 outpatient clinics (*Ambulanzen*), 608
 Q 217/19 (children), 278, 444
 Q 403 (particularly infectious diseases),
   444, 501
 Q 710, 444
 Sokol Hall infectious disease, 128
 surgical unit of general, 463
 visiting hours, 451
Höss, Rudolf, 678, 698
house aides (*Hausgehilfen*), 144
house elders (*Hausälteste*), 406, 408, 579
house guards, 88
house of the Jewish self-administration, 141
house servants (*Hausdienst*), 579
house services, 99
housing, 98, 134, 265, 275–93
 attic, 93, 98, 101, 113, 124, 236, 239,
   279–80, 283, 447, 475, 608, 610
 bedding, 284
 beds, 282–3
   tunnel (*Schlauchbetten*), 283
 blockhouses, 126, 278, 281
 children's, 498
 garrets (*Mansarden*), 281
 gender-integrated (OD, January 20, 1942),
   67
 gender segregation, 283
 heating, 288
 houses, 282
 Kaserne, 77
   advantages of, 281
   Aussiger, 73
   Bodenbach, 68, 305
   Dresden, 67, 69, 115, 170, 305, 498
   entrances to, 285
   gender segregated, 67
   Hamburg, 82, 305, 498
   Hohenelber, 68, 82, 305
   home for the infirm (*Siechenheim*), 67
   Kavalier, 67, 82, 233
   Magdeburg, 67, 237
   organization, 68–70
   punishment for visiting restricted (OD,
     December 21, 1941), 72

 Sudeten, 20, 69, 73, 85, 233, 305
 Theresienstadt, 64
 whitewashing (OD, February 11, 1942),
   64
 kitchens, 282, 287
 lights, 287
 living space, 22, 98
   1942, 279, 605–6, 609, 611
   1943, 280, 611, 613–14
   1944, 615–16
   arrangement of, 272
 memo on proper quartering, 20
 preferential quarters, 292
 prisoner (OD, November 30, 1942), 93
 sanitary facilities, 281
   regulations for, 286
 sheds, 282
Hungary, 76, 618
Huth, Karl, 450
Hvass, Frants, 141, 145
hydrogen cyanide, 109
hygiene inspection service (AMSI), 200

identity
 controllers, 100
 identification numbers, 139, 227, 266
 Jewish, 503, 505
   versus Aryan, 9
 papers, 221
 personal identification documents, 10
illusionists, 591
Imperial War Museum (London), 825
implementation plan (settlement), 22
index, vocational (*Arbeitseinsatz*), 237
infantilism, 442
infants' home, 164
infections, 461, 464
information from the self-administration
     (*Mitteilungen der Selbstverwaltung*,
     MdS)
 1944
   June 24 (announcing general holiday),
     139
   July 11 (announcing Herzl sporting
     event), 139
   August 31 (referencing transfers), 139
infractions, warning (OD, May 2, 1942), 83
insects, 484
inspections
 food, 472
 kitchen, 306, 449, 606
 luggage, 229, 232

Index

843

OD (January 19, 1942), 20
picture, 618
public health, 472
results of distribution point, 304
room, 117
street, 72
watch and sentry, 427
Institut für Zeitgeschichte (Institute of Contemporary History, Munich), 624, 825
Instituut voor Oorlogsdocumentatie (Amsterdam), 811
Investigation, The (Weiss), 824
Isbica/Izbica, 695
Israelitische Kultusgemeinde (IKG), 52, 253, 707
Istanbul, 138

Jacobsohn, Jakob, 529
Janeček, Theodor, 71
Janowitz, Leo, 107, 127, 212, 216, 319, 748
Jens, Walter, 806
Jerusalem, 623
Jewish (yellow) star (*Judenstern*), 8, 11, 14, 72, 74, 133, 162, 175, 377, 514, 573, 603–4, 681, 714–15
Jewish Agency, 622
Jewish City (memo), 21
Jewish Community in Prague (Jüdische Kultusgemeinde, JKG), 6–7, 11, 15, 51
Department G, 17, 21
Jewish conspiracy, 572
Jewish councils (choices confronting), 16
Jewish Cultural Association, *See* Israelitische Kultusgemeinde (IKG)
Jewish Cultural Union (Jüdischer Kulturbund), 12
Jewish Elder, 406, 408
senior, 207
Jewish Historical Institute, Warsaw, 624
Jewish Museum (Prague), 622, 789, 811
Jewish New Year (OD, September 29, 1943), 128
Jewish question
October 10, 1941, discussion on, 645
Becher and, 150
Brandt and, 150
Eichmann and, 164, 704
emigration/evacuation and, 603
Final Solution to, 18–19, 557
Heydrich and, 746

Himmler and, 150
Hitler and, 150
National Socialist solution to, 13, 573
Schellenberg and, 150
total solution (*Gesamtlösung*) to, 14
Wannsee conference and, 18
Jewish Refugee Committee, 649
Jewish Rescue Committee, 137, 151
Jewish *Samopomoc Spoleczna* (self-help, JSS), 43
Jewish self-administration bank, 103, 183, 348
Jewish World Organization, 151
Jews
Alsace-Lorraine, 14
Altreich, 253
appearance of, 255
as archenemies and symbols of the devil, 732
Ashkenasi, 255
Austrian, 259
Protectorate and, 3
Baden, 14
Bavarian, 255
Bielitz, 14
Bohemian, 17, 20, 24, 101, 784
Bohemian-Moravian, 258
Brünn, 21
Carpatho-Russian, 254
Central European, 737
Communist, 260
concentrating, 21
concessions, 151
Czech, 15, 45, 50, 102, 176, 254, 661, 722, 731, 747
Danish, 53, 132–3, 142, 153, 157, 165, 169, 240, 254, 260, 293, 618, 669, 714, 740, 745–6, 768, 788
Danzig, 254
demonization of, 574
disoriented (OD, August 10, 1942), 92
Dresden, 658
Dutch, 49, 133, 142, 157–8, 167, 254, 260, 293, 649, 660, 747, 751
Barneveld list, 677
Eastern, 254
evil and, 572
by faith (*Glaubensuden*), 3, 705
Galician, 254
German, 102, 134, 141, 254, 258, 603, 714, 747
Protectorate and, 3

844   *Index*

Jews *(cont.)*
  regional character and dialects of, 258
  German/Czech, 258
  ghettoization of, in the Protectorate
    (memo), 25
  Greek, 700, 711, 716
  half (*Geltungsjuden*), 52
  hidden (Puttkammer list), 677
  Hungarian, 49, 53, 159, 162, 254, 260,
    660, 748
  Katowice, 14
  Latvian, 736
  Leipzig, 673
  Luxembourg, 254
  Moravian, 17, 20, 603, 723, 784
  mythic ideology and, 571
  neo-Orthodox (*Agudists*), 262
  non-Mosaic, 10
  Nuremberg, 694–5
  old, 687
  Orthodox, 724
  Ostmark, 253
  Ostrau, 21
  as the *other*, 571, 578
  Polish, 170, 176, 254, 660, 662, 706
  Prague, 21, 24, 136, 604
  Protectorate, 142, 253
  racial or legal (*Geltungsjuden*), 3, 50, 573,
    705
  Rheinlander, 255
  Russian, 783
  Schneidemühl, 14
  as scum of the earth, 437
  Sephardic, 255, 262, 677
  Slovakian, 53, 254, 260, 721–2, 731
  sorting, 44, 46
  Stettin, 14
  Viennese, 14, 53, 95, 253, 259, 604, 796
  as wanderers (*Ahasvers*), 225
  Western Pomerania, 14
  worthy, 648
  Zionist, 258, 260
Joint Relief Commission, 742
Joseph II, Emperor, 24, 257
Joyce, James, 812
Judaism, 517, 578
  optimism of, 809
  in the Theresienstadt Ghetto, 597–9
Jungfernhof police camp for Jews, 797
justice (*Justiz*), 402
juvenile court, 612
  code, 612

Kaddish, 540
Kaff, Bernhard, 520, 522, 553
Kafka, Emil, 16
Kafka, Franz, 530, 812
Kafka, Georg, 545, 549–50
Kafka, Ottilie, 128
Kahn, Franz, 138, 165, 519, 637, 650, 665
Kaiserwald main concentration camp, 719
Kaltenbrunner, Ernst, 49, 51, 151, 163
  Central Office and, 4
  RSHA and, 5
Kamaik, 387
  -Leitmeritz, 387
Kapper, Karl, 547
Kasztner, Reszö, 16, 162, 165, 618
Kauffering concentration subcamp, 551, 667
Kautsky, Benedikt, 566
Kersten, Felix, 151, 161, 163
Kielce, 705
Kiel-Hassel work education camp, 737
Kien, Peter, 103, 135, 147, 469, 541, 543–4,
  552, 691
kindhearted people, 593
King of Atlantis, The (Ullmann), 552
Kitchen Guard (*Küchenwache*), 323, 359
kitchens
  bakeries (*Küchenbäckerei*), 294
  Central Children's, 110
  dietary, 110
  for the sick (*Krankenküche*, E VI, Q 403,
    E III a), 309
  kosher, 309
  Loewenstein's Ghetto Guard (L 313), 319
  ritual, 539
  steam, 144
Klaber, Josef (imprisonment, OD, June 19,
  1943), 119
Kladno forced labor camp for Jews, 74, 78,
  514
Klang, Heinrich, 165, 216, 402, 530, 533
Klapp, Erich, 213, 523, 533
Klattau, 11
Klauber, Arnošt (Schmudla), 491–3
Klauber, Kurt, 527
Klein, F. E., 522
Klein, Gideon, 503, 520, 523, 553
Klepetar, Gertrud, 807
Knapp, Rudolf, 530
Knoche, Gerhard, 530
Kobler, Franz, 816, 820
Kogon, Eugen, 209, 566, 570, 575, 580, 588,
  704, 803, 824

Index

Kohn, Erich, 766
Kolb, Bernhard, 695
Kolben, Hans, 545, 551–2
Kolin, 676
König, Georg, 72
König, René, 818
Königstein concentration subcamp, 154
Korherr reports (long and short), 696
Korherr, R., 697
Kortner, Margot, 527
Kovanic, Karl, 450
Kozower, Philipp, 214
Krämer, Salo, 215
Krása, Hans, 523, 552
Kraus, Karl, 819
Krause (OSTF), 736
Kreta, 24
Kreuzer, Hermann, 271
Křivoklát, 78
Krönert, Benno, 443, 731
Krumey, Hermann, 137, 165
Kube, Wilhelm, 114
Kulmhof extermination camp, 45
Kunert, Günter, 824
Kusmin, M. A., 176

labor, 8, 18, 99
    agricultural, 359
    aptitude screening for, 111
    civil servants (*Beamten*), 364
    court (OD, May 12, 1943), 121
    deployment
        mobile, 326, 340
        regular, 327
    deployment offices, 328
    firefighter appreciation (OD, August 21, 1942), 109
    forced, 778
    Heydrich and, 19
    impetus to, 325–6
    index, 184, 328
    integrating into the work force, 326–8
    Jewish, 21
    job applications (OD, January 20, 1942), 78
    job distribution, 363–6
    monitoring, 100
    office, 8, 10
    outside, 388, 779
    overview of accomplishments, 371–2
    paradox of, 377
    pay, 124

skilled craftspeople (*Handwerker*), 364
slave, 46–7
squadrons, 361
    OD (December 25, 1941), 605
    structure of, 370
    types of, 329–30
wage
    lists, 104
    system, 103
women's, 366–71
work deployment, 328–49, 680, 771
    1942 annual report, 332
    1943, 333
    1944, 335
    offices (*Einsatzstellen*), 329
    structure of, 329–49
work duty, 326
workforce (*Belegschaft*), 139, 328–9. 606–8
working hours (OD, June 28, 1942), 78
work on Bauschowitz rail (OD, June 8, 1943), 110
workweek, 158, 607, 609, 617–18
laboratories and support facilities, 200
Labor Supervision Office, 327
Labor Tribunal, 415
Labor Welfare Office, 185, 327, 474
Łagów, 705
Landsberg concentration subcamp, 163
Lang, Ervin, 450
Langbein, Hermann, 806, 825
Lange, Hans, 737
Langenstein-Zwieberge concentration subcamp, 622, 810
language, 262
    conflicts, 258
    informal form of address (*Du-Ansprache*), 371
Lautsch firm, 111, 798
law
    as abstraction of life, 400
    as binding behavioral standards, 400
    civil, 407–30
    community of (*Rechtsgemeinschaft*), 401
    criminal, 406–7
    serving German people, 401
    two spheres of, 401
Law of the Jewish Settlement Area Theresienstadt, 405
leadership
    Jewish, difficulties of, 206–24
    rights of, 206

846   *Index*

lectures, 521, 530–4
  categories of, 531
Ledeč, Egon, 523
Lederer, Rudolf, 347
Lederer, Zdeněk, 38, 42, 127, 456–7, 459, 524
legacies (mail authorizations left by deportees), 158
Legal Department, 186
Lehner, Otto, 165–9
Leitmeritz concentration subcamp, 22–4, 175, 260, 330, 514, 638, 692, 784, 800
Lenzing bai Linz concentration subcamp, 704
Les Milles internment camp, 14
Lesný, B., 33
letters, 409
Levi, Primo, 803
libraries
  Central Ghetto (Ghettozentralbücherei, GZB), 137, 534, 610
    holdings, 536–9
    as a Jewish research library, 537–8
    OD (November 22, 1942), 535
  Central Medical, 538
  lending, 535, 539
  medical, 473
  popular reading room (Volkslesehalle), 538
  reading room, 536
  social, 539
  traveling, 535, 539
  use, 9
  youth, 538–9
lice, 91, 98, 232, 238, 289, 449, 461
Lidice, 84–5, 380, 607
lighting (memorandum, December 5, 1943), 288
lights-out, 285
  OD (May 22, 1943), 120
lime, 76, 85
  chlorinated, 287, 471–2
Linden Retraining Camp (Lipa), 10
Lingens-Reiner, Ella, 464, 569, 576, 825
Lipa reeducation camp (Umschulungslager), 31
Lisbon, 138
lists
  preliminary, 244
  protection, 244, 663
  standing, 677
living conditions, pre-beautification (memoranda, March 18 and 25, 1944), 289

living space (Lebensraum), 687
Łódź, xv, 49
Lodzsher geţo (Trunk), 822
Loewenstein, Karl, 114–16, 120, 129, 206, 210, 261, 306, 318, 402, 443, 613
  Edelstein and, 114
  Eppstein and, 114
  food distribution and, 319–22
  personality of, 114
loneliness, 596
Lublin, 774
  ghetto work/concentration camp, 781
  settlement district, 44
luggage
  accompanying (Mitgepäck), 91, 227, 229, 608, 794–5
  hand, 91, 229, 245, 655
  hard and soft, 246
  OD (August 3, 1942), 92
  OD (December 19, 1942), 94
  theft, 229, 231
Luther, Martin, 133
Luxembourg, 76

machine carpenter's shop (Maschinentischlerei), 144
Madagascar Plan (Heydrich), 674, 825
Magic Mountain (Mann), 810
mail
  ban, 20, 27, 604
  revoking ban on (OD, September 16, 1942), 105
  service, See postal service
Majdanek main concentration/extermination camp, 43–4, 161, 614, 708
Malinowski, Bronisław, 805, 812
management
  Central Labor Office, 184
  Economics Department, 189
  Health Services and Welfare Departments, 199
  Technical Department, 196
Mandler, Robert, 59, 130, 264
Manes, Philipp, 532, 709
Mann, Klaus, 685
Mann, Thomas, 810
Manufacturing Department/Economics Department – Manufacturing (WAP), 190, 337
Maria Theresa, Empress, 24
marriages
  childless, 18

cohabitation arrangements
(*Lebensgemeinschaften*), 422–3
dispensations, 421
dissolutions, 421
divorces, 421
mixed (*Versippte*), 31, 76, 78, 153–4, 254,
615, 618, 644, 657, 697, 703, 715,
722–3
non-Jewish, 421
regulations concerning, 420–3
martial law, 11
massification, 568, 595, 598
mass murder, 686, 748, 797
Auschwitz, 756
authorizing, 756
Birkenau, 774
Minsk, 782
Masur, Norbert, 17, 618
materialism, mechanical, 561, 569, 571, 573,
578, 600, 815
defined, 569
racism and, 563
materials administration units
(*Materialverwaltung*), 373, 392
Mauthausen main concentration camp, 16, 630
Mautner, Wilhelm, 530
Mechanical Engineering Department, 214
mechanism, 578
mediation, 417–18
medical equipment, 439
medical examiner (*Vertrauensarzt*), 245
medical services, 9
medications, 439, 739, 741–2
substitutes for, 439–40
Meijers, Eduard, 216
Meissner, Alfred, 170, 216
melancholy, 463
memoranda, 183
from the building elder (*Rundschreiben*),
72
file (*Aktenvermerk*), 217–21, 381
results of, 218
from the Jewish self-administration, 220
miscellaneous administrative issues, 584
miscellaneous economic issues, 381–2
memorial services, 540
Mendl, Tomáš, 808
Mengele, Josef, 630
Menschen in Auschwitz (*People in
Auschwitz*, Langbein), 825
Mensch und sein Tag, Der ("Man and His
Day[s]," Adler), 808

Merzbachl, Ludwig H., 213, 304, 381
Meuselwitz concentration subcamp, 764
Meusier fortress (France), 784
Meyer, Alfred, 19
Meyer, Léon, 254
mica
production (*Glimmerproduktion*), 365
splitting (*Glimmerspalten*), 242, 366
migration, 52
Mildner, Rudolf, 51, 133, 136, 685
missing persons reports (memorandum, May
1943), 269
Modliborzyce, 705
Mohr, J. C. B., 145, 824
Möhs, Ernst, 116, 120, 130, 140–1, 151,
156, 164, 243, 513, 766, 796
money, 103–4
economy, 103–4, 124, 395
ghetto crowns (GK), 103, 139, 295, 395,
407, 657
Theresienstadt kronen (Th-Kr), 139, 143
memorandum (July 9, 1944), 139
Monowitz (Auschwitz III) main
concentration camp, 793
morality, 567, 569, 609
Moravec, Emanuel, 140
Moravia, 512
mortality, 126, 464, 466–73, 609
age correlation with, 466
causes of, 466
country of origin correlation with, 466,
469
daily, 93, 98, 144
gender statistics for, 466
war-disabled, 482
mortuary, 137
Moses, 225
movement
of goods, 373–99
restricting (OD, July 27, 1942), 88
movie theaters, 520
Mühlenbau-Industrie A.A. (MAIG), 746
Müller, Heinrich, 133, 151, 679
Auschwitz and, 46
deportation/transport and, 51
Heydrich and, 674
personality of, 674
RSHA/Gestapo and, 5
Munich agreement (1939), 3
Munk, Erich, 138, 213, 245, 465, 474,
480
personality of, 443–4

murder
industrialized, 803
list (Heydrich), 674
mass, 738
Auschwitz, 123, 501
Bełżec extermination camp, 43
Birkenau, 108
children, 501
erasing signs of, 162
extermination camp, 15
Himmler and, 678
Höss and, 678
Minsk, 381
organized, 165
Wannsee Conference and, 43
Murmelstein, Benjamin, 14, 96, 129, 135,
155, 159, 163, 165, 174, 210, 319,
525, 539, 611, 616, 618, 692, 754
personality of, 97, 722
music, 10, 12, 107, 552–3
musical instruments
forbidden, 520
permitted, 520
Musy, Benoit, 165, 669
Musy, Jean-Marie, 161
Musy mission, 669, 720, 746

Nagel, Thomas, 806
nationality, Jewish (nationale Juden), 256–7
National Socialism, 570, 574
camp consequences of mindset, 569
as a conspiracy, 564–5
dualism and, 574
ethics and, 800
ideology of, 563
Manichean components of, 732
reduction of humans in (party formations),
560
roots of, 563
as salvation through violence, 577
Nebe, Arther, 645
negligence, 412
Neuengamme main concentration camp, 165,
669
Neuhaus, Leopold, 214, 533
New Year's Thoughts 7505 (Eppstein), 155
news, 515
-letters, 220
-papers, 10, 106, 174, 514
Niederorschel satellite camp, 622
Niehaus, Heinrich, 121
Niemöller, Martin, 676

Night of Broken Glass, 825
nihilism
guilt and, 564
National Socialism and, 564
powerlessness and, 565
Nisko on the San concentration camp, 13,
723, 800
Nohel, Emil, 487
nonvalue (Unwert), 208
North America, 6
Noskowski, Felix, 534
notables (Prominente), 94, 109, 124, 133,
148, 157, 170, 272, 615, 665, 677
A and B, 264
accommodations, 293
exemption from work duty, 326
privileges of, 264, 283, 495, 509
nothingness, 826
Notice from the Discussion on October 10,
1941, on the Solution of Jewish
Questions, 17
Notice from the Leadership (December 5,
1941), 65
Nowak, Franz, 51
Nowy Dziennik (Prague daily newspaper),
514
numb people, 589
Nuremberg, 646
-Fürth, 647
Nuremberg Laws, 3, 705
Nuremberg Trial, 17, 685–6, 746
Protocol 2376-PS, 51

Öderan concentration subcamp, 745
Oesterreicher, Erich, 215, 326
office (SS, Dienststelle), 32, 51, 103, 154,
243, 374–5, 386, 406, 419, 472
divisions of, 376
Office of Economic Supervision
(Wirtschaftsüberwachungsstelle), 428–9
offices, accommodations
(Ubikationskanzleien), 187
opera, 522
Opole, 705
opportunists, 592
optimists, 591
Oranienburg, 46
oratories, 522
Order by the Reichsprotektor in Bohemia and
Moravia Regarding Measures to
Accommodate the Jews in Closed
Settlements of February 16, 1942, 30

Order Constabulary (Ordnungsdienst, OD), 64, 77, 229, 270, 348, 579, 642
Order Guard (Ordnerwache, OW), 84, 86, 434–5, 608
  renamed, 610
  replaces Ghetto Guard, 607
orders, 408
  disciplinary (*Strafverfügungen*), 413
  of possession, 7
  SS (legally binding), 402
orders of the day (*Tagesbefehlen*), 71, 183, 210, 509, 605, 694, 772
  information from the self-administration (*Mitteilungen der Selbstverwaltung*, MdS), 139
  watch group leader and, 427
ordinances
  juvenile court, 417
  labor, 414
Organisation Todt, 760, 799
organizational plan (settlement), 22, 181–204
  centrifugal tendencies of, 204
  Draft Structure of the Ghetto Administration and, 28
  as mirror pyramid, 205
organs of the Jewish settlement, 25
orientation service, 117, 532
Orpheus (Kafka), 550
Oslavany forced labor camp for Jews, 78
Österreicher, Erich, 138
Ostrau (Moravian Ostrava), 13
Ostrowo work camp, 41, 101
Otto (OSTF), 117, 511, 755
outside work group Wulkow, 669

packages, 374, 407, 509–10, 713
  authorization stickers for, 512
painting, 542–5
Palestine, 49, 486
  list, 677, 699
  Office, 6
pallbearers, 471
Panenské Břežany (Jungfern-Breschan), 31, 725
Panorama (Adler), 824
Pappenheim, Adolf, 525
passes
  entry (*Durchlaßschein*), 137, 221–2
  Schleuse entry, 229
  transit, 66, 68, 82, 86
    individual, 66

OD (September 4, 1942), 87
  work, 78
patronage (*Protektion*), 223, 243, 245
penalties
  administrative, 408
  disciplinary (*Dienststrafen*), 409, 424
  supplementary (RSPe, *Nebenstrafen*), 411–12
pensions, 8
people's community (*Volksgemeinschaft*), Hitler and, 561
Perschke, Margit, 799
Perschke, Oskar, 799
Personnel Office, 183, 424
Pesach (holiday of wandering), 225
pessimists, 590
pharmacy, 444
Philippsohn, Alfred, 264
Philosophy of New Music (Adorno), 817
Piaski, 714
Picard, Max, 564
Pick, Robert, 450
Pilsen, 11
Pitter, Premysl, 177, 622, 653
placards (blockhouse), 285–7
play, SS's malicious instinct for, 152
Pohl, Oswald, 46, 51, 151, 680
Poláček, Karel, 821
Poland, 76, 147
Poland Commission, 244
police
  criminal
    code (*Polizeistrafordnung*), 402
    code (renamed), 612
    law, 407
    provisions (*Polizeistrafordnung*), 425
  Decree on the Identification of the Jews (1941), 8
  deportation and, 638–9, 642
  Jewish (*Judenpolizei*, Jupo), 53, 96, 143, 754
  Protectorate (Czech), 644
  regular (*Schutzpolizei*), 646
  Security (Sicherheitspolizei, Sipo), 5
Poljak (officer in T), 513
Pollak, E., 530
Pollak, Josef, 529
Pollak, Leopold, 530
polypragmasy, 440–1
Popper, Egon, 27, 213
Popper, Max, 529
population
  1930–35, 603

Index

population *(cont.)*
 1941, 604
  July 31, 608
  August 1, 600
  August 31, 608
  September, 609
  September 15, 609
  October 1, 610
  October 31, 610
  December 31, 610
 1942
  January 1, 605
  April 1, 606
  May 1, 606
  June 1, 607
  July 1, 608
  September 30, 609
 1942–44, 252
 1943
  February 1, 611
  February 16, 611
  March 31, 612
  June 1, 612
  July 31, 613
  August 8, 613
  November 30, 614
 1944
  January 1, 615
  January 31, 615
  May 14, 615
  May 22, 616
  June 30, 364
  July 31, 616
 1945
  January 1, 617
  February 28, 618
  April, 771
  April 20, 618
  May 1, 618
  May 5, 618
 Altreich (Old Reich Germany), 604, 616
 civilian, evacuated, 606
 demographics, 252
  age, 253, 605–18, 672, 776
  children, 507
  countries of origin, 253–61, 614,
   616–18, 648, 673, 675, 701–2, 733,
   770, 772
  employment analysis (1943), 298, 315
  escapes, 269
  language, 256–8, 262
  missing persons, 269

 religion, 261–2
 social structures, 262–6
 women, 366–7
 health statistics, 451
 medical professionals (1942–44), 452
 Protectorate (1941), 604
Portugal, 512, 773
Posen, 41
Posen work camp, 17
postal service, 76, 105–6, 174, 348, 509
 authorization stickers, 512
 mail authorizations (*Postvollmächte*), 512
 memorandum (June 1943), 510
 memorandum (August 1943), 509, 512
 revising
  OD (September 24, 1942), 106
  OD (May 24, 1943), 106
post office, 9, 136, 144
potatoes
 chemical-technical reports, 304
 memorandum (December 1944), 304
power, 568
 good and, 572
powerlessness, 558, 560, 565, 572
powers of attorney (predeportation, OD,
  October 16, 1942), 106
Prague, 8
 exhibition palace (*Messepalast*), 59
 influence on Theresienstadt, 3
 -Leitmeritz road, 87, 177
 trade fair hall (*Mustermesse*), 59
prayer room, 540
precious metals, 471
pregnancies, 465–6, 613
 memorandum (August 21, 1943), 465
 memorandum (March 18, 1944), 465
Preiss, Erika, 527
Premature Death (Kolben), 551
Princip, Gavilo, 25
prison code, 613
prisoners
 negotiating release of, 115
 rules for, 429–30
Prochnik, Robert, 33, 38, 155, 159, 210,
  212, 456–7, 459–60, 754
production (*Produktion*), 386
 bed, 93
  OD (December 23, 1941, February
   5 and 22, 1942), 78
 bedding pad, 93
 box (*Kisten*), 111
 coffin, 93

factories, 111
mica, 111
paper goods, 111
plants, 81
women's clothing, 111
productivity
registry (*Evidenz der Arbeitsleistung*), 328
workshop (memorandum, 1942), 377–8
Professional Assembly, 28
professions, 138, 344, 352, 447
freelance, 364
independent, 363
Jews excluded from, 8
nourishing, 579
nutritional, 403
women and, 368, 478
profiteering, 407
property
abandoned, 8
confiscating, 5, 11, 795
decedents', 419
declarations, 11
personal
deportee, 7
emigration fund and, 10
liquidating, 7
order banning disposal of (1931), 7
Pross, Harry, 824
prostheses, 481
prostitution, 243
protection, 242, 245, 248, 263, 442
lists, 133, 211
Protectorate of Bohemia and Moravia, 3,
159, 603
demographics of, 3
Protestants, 153
provisioning, 26, 80, 98, 297
centers (*Proviantur*), 115
margarine ration (OD, May 26, 1942), 80
plans, 100
replenishment ration (OD, April 15, 1942),
80
soap ration (OD, May 2, 1942), 81
soup (OD, December 22, 1941), 79
Průša (Czech officer), 783
pseudologia phantastica, 591
Psychiatric Department, 144
psychiatry, 732
psychological disorders, 462–3
psychology, practical camp, 561–87
Psychology of Life in Theresienstadt (Utitz),
557

psychosis, camp, 463
Public Enterprises Department, 214
public facilities and services, 360–1
public health care, 472
Public Health Office, 200
public reading room, 137
Public Works Department, 197
Puhze, Edgar, 378
punishment, 577
collective, 82, 118
OD (October 27, 1942), 106
corporal, 114
for escape attempts (OD, April 9, 1943),
119
guilt and, 570
recinding (OD, May 10, 1943), 120
Pürglitz forced labor camp for Jews, 355
Purim, 540

quarantines, 47, 49, 174, 176, 234, 238, 446,
461, 619
A II, 68, 94, 610
block 14, 712
C III, 800
deceptive, 698
KZ-ers, 170
L 605, 289
lice, 109, 610
OD (November 5, 1942), 93
Quittner, Oscar, 533

R List, 717
race laws, 255, 259, 573
race theory, 255
racism (defined), 562
radio, 514
Raguhn concentration subcamp, 633, 796
Rahm, Karl, 16, 132, 140–1, 146, 151, 156,
162–3, 169, 174, 243, 525, 765–6
Eppstein and, 155
personality of, 134
Rasch, Otto, 645
Raska, Karel, 654
Ratibor, 719
rationing commission, 80, 606
rationing service, 323, 348, 359
rations, 170, 741
bread, 307–8, 605, 613
convalescent bonuses
(*Rekonvaleszentenzubusse, reko*), 317
extra (*Nachschub*), 316
ration cards, 322–3

Index

rations *(cont.)*
  supplementary *(Zusatzkost)*, 158, 319, 607
  unprepared foodstuffs, 307–8
Raudnitz, 23, 390
Ravensbrück concentration camp, 712–13, 749
Real Assets Section *(Sachgüterreferates)*, 484
realists, 590
reality, 581, 585–7
  Adler and three levels of, 814–15
  applied, 586
  changing, 585
  confusion of past and present, 581, 585
  displaced, 586, 595
  historical, 812
  National Socialism and, 586
  negating present, 581, 585
reclamation, 76
Recognition *(Kapper)*, 547
recreation *(Freizeitgestaltung)*, 140, 204, 363,
    481, 491, 502
  activities, 519
  Office, 106
  sample programs, 530
Red Cross, 167, 169, 241
  Czech, 174, 618
  Danish, 133, 318, 740–1
  German, 120, 134, 612, 740–1
  International (IRC), 37, 145, 151, 161,
    163, 165, 168–9, 174–5, 317, 618,
    656, 686, 740, 821
    commission of, 501
    Theresienstadt visit, 695–740, 744, 785
  League of National Societies, 773
  Swedish, 151, 161, 165–6, 169, 318
  Swiss, 170
Redlich, Egon, 487, 529, 821
refugees, 6, 133
  Austrian, 254
  German, 177, 254
  Protectorate, 3
  Theresienstadt, 708
Refugee-Welfare Institute of the
    Czechoslovak Ministry of Social
    Welfare, 4
Regen, 365, 779
registration, 11, 54
Registry Office and Funeral Department, 187
regression, infantile, 464
Reich Association of Jews in Germany
    (Reichsvereinigung der Juden in
    Deutschland), 6, 52, 95, 253, 603,
    695–6

Reich Central Office for Jewish Emigration, 4
Reich Chamber of Literature
    (Reichsschriftumskammer), 816
Reich Citizenship Law, 13
Reich Home for the Aged, 476
Reich laws, 598
Reich Representation of Jews in Germany
    (Reichsvertretung der Juden in
    Deutschland), 808
Reich Security Main Office
    (Reichssicherheitshauptamt, RSHA),
    5, 112, 376, 574, 603, 826
Reichsprotektor, 7, 11, 30
Reichssippenamt, 636
Reiner, Karel, 552
Reinisch, Otto, 245
Reis, Siegmund, 533
Reise, Eine (The Journey, Adler), 824
Reiss, Ernst, 440, 450
Reitlinger, Gerhard, 825
release (deghettoized, *entghettoisiert*), 40
Relico (relief arm of World Jewish Congress),
    317
religious life, 539–41
religious observation
  memorandum (March 25, 1944), 540
  restricting attendance (OD, December 23,
    1941), 75
religious services, 10
rent, 8
Reowitz Delegation, 43
repair shops, 359
  OD (December 23, 1941), 79
repatriations, 163, 176, 618
  to Denmark, 711
resettlement, 747, 752, 800
  from Berlin, 716
  from Izbica, 721
  from Theresienstadt
    Aryan civilian population, 86
residence, change of permanent, 8
resistance, internal, 7
restricted areas, 410
restrictions (on Jews), 8–10
retraining courses, 10
retrials, 411
Ribbentrop, Joachim von, 17, 641
Riegner, Gerhart, 145
Riesa, 154
Riga main concentration camp, 644, 736, 797
rights
  Christian, 262

Council of Elders, 423, 429
human, 82
leadership, 327
preferential (labor deployment), 158
previous ownership, 7
private property, 407–8
Rijksinstituut voor Oorlogsdocumentatie
(Amsterdam), 624, 825
ritual dietary laws, 539
Rivesaltes internment camp, 14
Robinson, Jacob, 823
roll call, 71, 73–4, 131
room elder, 68, 288, 408
Rosenberg, Alfred, 135, 571
Rosenthal, Ernst, 405, 707
Rossel, Maurice, 141, 145
Rosting, Helger, 639
Roth, Cecil, 816
Roudnice, 11, 30
rules of procedure (Council of Elders),
216–22
Rumania, 76
rumors, 515
Russia, 14, 699

sabotage, 370, 706
Sachsenhausen main concentration camp,
644, 712–13, 749
Salaspils work education/police prison camp,
670, 797
sanitary facilities, 200
Santo Domingo (Dominican Republic)
settlement project, 6
Schächter, Raffael, 522, 524
Schächtner, Adolf, 523
Schachwitz bei Dresden concentration
subcamp, 746
Schapira, David, 533
Schellenberg, Walter, 150
Schlesinger, Arthur, 513
Schleuse, 90, 102, 132, 228, 241, 246–7,
274
locations of (1942–44), 228
procedures in, 246
Schlieben concentration subcamp, 715, 745
Schliesser, Karl, 21, 115, 153–4, 213, 319,
376–7, 381
Schnarchenreuth bei Hof, 365
Schoeps, Hans-Joachim, 824
Scholem, Gershom, 818
Schön, A., 533
Schul, Siegfried, 553

Schuler, Alfred, 652
Schwarz, Ada, 523
Schwarzheide concentration subcamp, 550
hunger march from, 703
search operation (OD, June 16, 1942), 85
Sebald, W. G., 824
secretariat and economic planning and
oversight departments, 29
Security and Order Service (SOD), 187
Security Office, 433–4
Security Police (Sicherheitspolizei, Sipo), 5
Security Service (Sicherheitsdienst, SD), 5,
114–16, 121
security services (*Sicherheitswesen*), 348, 413,
609, 674
abolition of main division (*Hauptabteilung
Sicherheitswesen*), 418
dissolved, 613
seders, 540
segregation
arrival, 26
Bialstok children and, 241
gender, 67, 605
infectious, 128
Seidl, Siegfried, 20, 26, 64, 66, 73–4, 85, 97,
114–15, 118–20, 129, 135, 217,
377–8, 408, 410, 587, 686, 763
Edelstein and, 123, 129
sentencing, conditional, 411
Sered transit camp for Jews, 158, 233, 260,
722
settlement plan (Theresienstadt), 94
Sever, Max, 21, 213
sewage, 472, 644
Sheep of Lidice, The (Weber), 549
Shek, Y. Z., 622
shipping groups, 361
shopping hours, 9
shrouds, 470
*Si questo è un uomo? (If This a Man/Survival
in Auschwitz*, Levi), 803
sickbeds, 144
sickness
as protection from transport, 243, 245
reporting (memorandum, June 6, 1943),
583–4
Siebeck, Hans-Georg, 816–17
Siebeck, Oscar, 816
Siegmann, Georg, 530
Simmel, Georg, 813
Simon, James, 530
Sin, Otakar, 523

854   *Index*

Singer, Oskar, 450
singing/whistling (OD, October 9, 1942), 118
Sittard-Eynbroek quarantine camp, 649
Skarabis, Richard, 66
Skarżysko Kamienna concentration camp,
    715
slavery, 375, 565, 680, 725–6
  defined, 565
  massification (*Vermassung*) and, 566
  SS, 565
Sleepwalkers (Broch), 809
Slovakia, 76, 617–18
Small Fortress (Kleine Festung), 23, 40, 147,
    157, 174, 654–5, 769, 785, 793
  as a police prison, 604, 655, 659
smoking, 9, 83, 119, 133, 165, 170, 324
  OD (February 26, 1943), 119
smuggling (*Schleussens*), 404
  nutritional professionals, 405
soap, 284, 606–7
Sobibór extermination camp, 45, 134, 607
social events, 212
social relations, 595–7
Social Services Department, 202
society (as condition of communities), 208
Solzhenitsyn, Aleksandr, 803
Sonneberger, E., 530
Soubenitz, 22
source documentation, 622–4
South America, 6
Soviet Paradise (Berlin exhibit), 706
Space Management Office, 186, 273
Special Account H, 52
special camp regulations, 606, 611–12
special deployment, 365
special treatment (*Sonderbehandlung*, SB,
    extermination), 45, 48, 447, 574, 628,
    696, 755–6
Spier, Joe, 138, 148–9, 683
spitting (OD, February 16 and 17, 1943),
  118
sports, 521, 534
Springer, Erich, 144
squadron elders, 327
squadrons (OD, December 25, 1941), 77
SS (Schutzstaffel), 563, 618
  deceit, 241
  goals at Theresienstadt, 509
  power of, 513
*SS-Staat, Der (The Theory and Practice of
    Hell, Kogon)*, 803, 816
staff, privileges of, 211

Stahl, Heinrich, 96, 214
Stahl, Karl, 214
Stahlecker, Franz, 4
Stahlecker concentration camp, 644
Stargardt, Otto, 676
starvation, reasons for, 304–6
state, deification of, 560
status
  lists (memorandum, March 25, 1944), 267
  record (*Standführung*), 266–9
Stein, Otto, 542
Steiner, Franz Baermann, 565, 805–6,
    810–11, 813
sterilization, 18
Stern, Erich, 530
Stern, Norbert, 728
Stern, Walt., 530
storage and businesses, 195
stores (*Verschleißstellen*), 104–5
Strängnäs, 714
Strauss, Hermann, 214, 450, 473
Strauss, Leo, 482
Streicher, Julius, 571, 574
Stricker, Robert, 206, 214, 318
strong-willed people, 592
Stuckart, Wilhelm, 686
Stuczka (Stuschka), Franz, 669
Stutthof main concentration camp, 151, 791
Succoth, 540
Sudetengau, 3
suicides, 469, 472
  demographics, 269
sulfur pits (Birkemau), 691
summons forms, 221
supervision of homes (Youth Welfare Office),
  214
surgical medicine, 463–4
Susiec, 43
Svatobořice internment camp, 11, 671
Svenk, Karl, 526, 546
Sweden, 53, 512, 711, 788
Switzerland, 512
synchronization, 595

Tabor, 15
tariff commission, 184
Taussig, Fritz (Fritta), 543, 691
Technical Department, 29, 196–8, 338
Teicher, S., 450
telephones, 8
Teschen, 552
theater, 137, 521–2

Index

theft (*Schleusen*), 206, 318, 593
  comrade, 318
  from deportees, 233, 733
  fuel, 490
  package, 510–11
  ration card, 493
  SS, 379
Theresienstadt 1941–1945 (Adler), 809, 816
  Arendt and, 823
  author intent, 811–12
  Broch and, 810
  forensic argument in, 813
  Hilberg and, 823
  interdisciplinary orientation of, 807
  Kunert and, 824
  mechanical materialism and, 826
  moral failure and, 820–2
  premise for, 810
  as proof of Final Solution, 819
  publication of, 815–18
  reaction to, and impact of, 818–27
  uniqueness of, 803–4
  as view from nowhere, 806
Theresienstadt Dreams (Lederer), 547
Theresienstadt ghetto/police prison camp, 5
  administrative departments, 69
    Department of Internal Administration, 69
    Economics Department, 69
    Finance Department, 69
    Health Services Department, 69
    Technical Department, 69
  as an archival put-aside site (*Ausweiche*), 112
  children's home, 68
  civilizing (*Zivilisierung*), 82
  as a collection camp, 3, 17
  criteria for deportation to, 239
  demographics of (1930), 22
  designated a ghetto, 604
  districts, 94
  file notes establishing, 20–30
  film propaganda, 147–9, 163
  financing sources, 381
  gender segregation, 71
  as a historical experiment, 558, 627
  history of, 24–5
  housing, 66–8
  initial hours of, 27
  inspections, 165–6
  intercamp hostility, 89
  as a Jewish settlement, 123, 139

legal establishment of, 29
liberation of, 158–75, 618
life in, 207–24
liquidation trust (*Liquidationsmasse*), 623
lithograph of, 138
as an old-age ghetto, 18
as a new Israel, 716
original intent of, 718, 747, 778
overcrowding at, 136
overview (1941–45), 619
as a paradise settlement, 123, 132, 146, 148, 172, 204, 240, 587
as a period in Jewish history, 571–8
population
  after 1944 deportations, 157, 165
  between 1941 (November 24) and 1945 (May 8), 177
  at liberation, 176
property and assets of, 761
Protectorate and, 3
as a provisional camp, 344
provisioning, 69–70
Red Cross visit to, 695–740
second anniversary of (OD, November 24, 1943), 128
as self-supporting, 359
simultaneous history and, 559–71
site description, 24–5
South Barracks (Südbaracken), as a children's camp, 49
as a spa, 90
SS and, 13
surrender ordered, 618
unique role of, 17–18, 20
as a Zionist model camp, 260
Theresienstadt March (Svenk), 546
Theresienstadt soccer league, 534
time, 278
tobacco, 413, 433
toilet guard, 286
Tolstoy, Fedor, 815
total solution (*Gesamtlösung*)
  Göring and, 14
  Heydrich and, 14
town band, 520
trafficking, 413
transfer orders, provisional and permanent, 273, 275
transfer regulations, March 30, 1942, excerpt from, 274
transport and traffic, 361–2
Transport Management Department, 188

856   *Index*

Transport of the Elderly (Weber), 548
Traveler to the North Pole, The (Kolben), 551
Trawniki concentration subcamp/forced
    labor camp for Jews, 43, 607
Treblinka extermination camp, 45, 251, 610,
    688
  established, 608
trespass, authorizing armed response to (OD,
    August 28, 1942), 117
Trial, The (Kafka), 812
Trostinetz extermination camp, 782
Trunk, Isaiah, 822
Tuchel, Willy, 736
Turkey, 512
Türmitz, 23
Tyrol, 167

Ullmann, Viktor, 522–3, 552, 582, 808
Ulysses (Joyce), 812
Ungar, Otto, 543–4
uniform repair workshop, 111
Union of Orthodox Rabbis in the United
    States and Canada, 162, 720
Union of Soviet Socialist Republics (USSR),
    76
unsichtbare Wand, Der (*The Invisible Wall*,
    Adler), 805–6, 815, 824
Utitz, Emil, 148, 519, 533–5, 557, 586

Vašiček, Zdeněk, 807
Vedder, Aaron, 175
Vedem (*We Lead*, Schkid newspaper), 491
Velká Losenice-Sázava work camp,
    621, 807
verheimlichte Wahrheit, Die:
    Theresienstadter Dokumente (*The*
    Hidden Truth: Theresienstadt
    Documents, Adler), 824
vermin, 93, 109, 113, 232, 288, 481, 596,
    731
verwaltete Mensch, Der: Studien zur
    Deportation der Juden aus
    Deutschland (*Administrated Man:*
    Studies on the Deportation of Jews out
    of Germany, Adler), 824–6
Věstník (Prague newspaper), 624
Vevey, 708
Vienna, 138
Vilna, xv
Vlajka (Czech Nazi group), 11
Vogel, Georg, 176, 216, 261
Volhynian Germans, 14

Völkischer Beobachter (Nazi newspaper), 13
von Luckwald, Erich, 164
von Moyland, Steengracht, 145
von Neurath, Konstentin, 1, 603
von Stengel, Elisabeth, 500
von Thadden, Eberhard, 49, 120, 141, 164
Vrba, Rudolf, 750

Wahler, I. E., 645
Waldsee labor camp, 701, 748
wandering, 225–6
  National Socialism and, 226
Wannsee
  Conference (January 20, 1942), 5, 17–18,
    20, 43, 52, 133, 605, 686, 707, 803,
    825
  Protocol, 18–19, 154, 644, 678, 752
War and Peace (Tolstoy), 815
War Refugee Board, 720, 750
washroom usage (OD, December 19, 1941),
    77
Wasserbrenner, C., 450
Wasserman, D., 529
water
  ration, 605
  scarcity of, 81, 100, 605
  service, 77, 284
  supply, 80
  works, 109
waywardness, 489
Weber, Ilse, 548
Weber, Max, 810
Weidmann, František, 21, 539
Weidmann, Franz, 215
Weil, Franz, 530
Weil, Hanne, 538
Weinberger, Hans, 708
Weinberger, Robert (Vinczi), 326
Weiner, Erich, 524
Weininger, Otto, 575
Weinmann, Rudolf, 141, 145, 164
Weiss, Peter, 824
Weiss, Vladimir, 304
Weizsäcker, Ernst, 800
welfare and care, 362–3
Welfare Department, 199–200
  activity reports (1944), 484
  caseload (June 1943), 480
  challenges, 484
  personnel, 478, 483–4
  report on work and plans (October 1943),
    480

responsibilities, 477
type and range of care, 479
Weltsch, Robert, 824
Westerbork transit camp for Jews, 32, 133, 151, 158, 241, 260, 656, 683, 700, 710
Wetzler, Alfred, 750
white bakery, 144
White Russia, 688
Wiener Library (London), 624
Willheim, Siegfried, 650
Windecker, Adolf, 49
Windermere, 649
Windholz, Walter, 523
Winzern internment camp, 176, 651
wishes for Jewish New Year (OD, September 11, 1942), 121
Wisliceny, Dieter, 162
Wolff-Eisner, A., 449, 455–6, 459, 468
Wölffing, Jakob, 214
women
    pregnant (OD, July 7, 1943), 121
    working, 366–71
Women's International Zionist Organization (WIZO), 636
Worf, Jiří, 527
work deployment, 328, 365
workers' welfare (*Arbeiterbetreuung*), 363
World Jewish Congress, 743, 773
Wulkow, 779
Wüstegiersdorf concentration subcamp, 760

Wüstehoff (government senior inspector), 378, 798

Yad Vashem (Israel), 624, 825
Youth Helps, 505–6
youth homes, 136
Youth Welfare Office, 201–2, 339, 363, 416, 486–508
    challenges of, 487–98
    organizational evolution of (origins and development), 498–507
    personnel, 488
        failures of, 488
    public welfare (*offene Fürsorge*), 499
    responsibilities of, 486–7
    Zionism and, 486–7, 503–4

Zeitz, 797
Zelenka, František, 148, 524
Zelenka Group, 306
Zionism, 138, 146, 212–13, 226, 256–8, 262, 636
    Youth Welfare Office and, 486–7, 503–4
Zossen concentration subcamp, 153, 156–7, 162
Zossen work detail group, 615, 618
Zucker, Otto, 27, 66, 130, 132, 138, 153–4, 210, 212, 319, 529, 533, 604, 614, 616
Zwickau, 37
Zyklon/Zyklon B hydrogen cyanide, 381, 453, 678
    as a disinfectant, 801

CPSIA information can be obtained
at www.ICGtesting.com
Printed in the USA
LVHW061602270322
714519LV00005B/135